DIFFERENTIAL DIAGNOSIS
AND TREATMENT IN
SOCIAL WORK

DIFFERENTIAL DIAGNOSIS AND TREATMENT IN SOCIAL WORK

Fourth Edition

Edited by
Francis J. Turner

With a Foreword by
Florence Hollis

THE FREE PRESS

New York   London   Toronto   Sydney   Tokyo   Singapore

The Free Press
A Division of Simon & Schuster Inc.
1230 Avenue of the Americas
New York, N.Y. 10020

Printed in the United States of America

printing number
1   2   3   4   5   6   7   8   9   10

Library of Congress Cataloging-in-Publication Data

Differential diagnosis and treatment in social work / edited by Francis J. Turner; with a
    foreword by Florence Hollis. —4th ed.
        p.   cm.
    Includes bibliographical references and index.
    ISBN 0–02–874007–6
    1. Social case work.   2. Psychiatric social work.   3. Medical social work.
    I. Turner, Francis J. (Francis Joseph)
    HV43.D56   1995
    361.3—dc20   95–16212
                                                                      CIP

To Bert, brother and colleague,
June 17, 1935–June 22, 1957

CONTENTS

PART IV. PERSONAL ISSUES   561

FOREWORD

How strange it is that not until a half century after the publication of *Social Diagnosis* does a book appear in the social work field addressing itself specifically to the relationship between differential diagnosis and treatment! Over fifty years ago—in 1917—Mary Richmond wrote *Social Diagnosis,* a book dedicated to the then new idea that the social worker, like the physician, must think diagnostically, endeavoring to understand the nature of the disorder with which he is dealing in order to know how to alleviate it. This book so impressed practitioners that for many years it was a text, as if the subject of diagnosis were now understood and social casework could move on to concentrate on problems of treatment methodology. Even in the thirties, when psychoanalytic knowledge was permeating social casework, attention was directed not to diagnostic groupings, but rather to general principles of treatment on the one hand and the specifics of individualization of treatment on the other. It was not until the mid-forties that attention again turned to diagnosis, and the work started by Miss Richmond moved forward with concentration on the psychological component of diagnosis, often designated the "clinical diagnosis." Diagnosis had not been lost sight of during these intervening years, but the principles of social study and diagnosis presented by Miss Richmond seemed to provide sufficient guidelines for the type of diagnostic thinking upon which treatment was based until the mid-forties. This was a highly individualized approach with emphasis on idiosyncratic life happenings that could account for the problem under treatment.

With the emergence of the clinical diagnosis, attention began to turn to elements in personality which characterize some people to a greater extent than others, thus distinguishing a group of individuals who might respond in common ways to certain forms of treatment. It began to be recognized that knowledge of such groupings—of types of disorders, that is—could increase the ability of workers to fashion treatment more appropriately to the differentiated need of the individual. Furthermore, once such commonness was seen, knowledge could become cumulative and what was learned from the treatment of one individual could be put to the service of another suffering from a similar disability.

Dr. Turner's compilation is the first book to bring the results of this development to general attention and to provide the social worker a key to the diagnostically oriented articles of the past ten years. Not only is his selection of articles excellent, but the fact that he read virtually everything available in our English literature before making his selection means that this collection provides a reliable guide to the state of our current knowledge of work with differing diagnostic entities. Inevitably any other author would have made a somewhat different selection. I will leave it to the reviewers to comment on the merits of this and that inclusion or exclusion; Dr. Turner's choices seem excellent to me. His organization of the selections into the stages of human development, psychosocial pathology, physical handicaps, and sociocultural factors is logical and should enable the reader to locate easily material that will throw light on the difficulty about which he is seeking information. If no article is included which deals with the specific subject of concern, much may be learned from an article covering treatment of a related disorder.

In addition to Dr. Turner's contribution in making this material available, his Preface and the introductions to all of the major sections add greatly to the value of the book. I am strongly tempted to underscore some of his excellent points about diagnosis and about the education of the profession, but will content myself with urging you to read the Preface and the Part introductions with care. They contain many astute observations.

In the Part introductions Dr. Turner orients the reader to the writings in the area under consideration, briefly brings out important commonalities, and points to uncovered, or scantily covered, diagnostic areas. In the main, however, he allows the selections to speak for themselves. The coverage of the book is not meant to be exhaustive. The bibliographies within the individual selections will lead the reader to further references.

It is an important sign of the times that this book is addressed to group workers as well as to caseworkers and that in many categories material on group treatment is available. The extent to which these two social work methods supplement each other in treatment and the growing tendency for many workers to want to acquire some competence in both methods is one of the very interesting developments of the sixties. This book should contribute to the common knowledge of the two specialties.

A final contribution of the book upon which I should like to comment is its usefulness as a guide to further compilation of knowledge and to publication. As Dr. Turner notes, there is valuable information dealing with many diagnostic categories in agency records and reports which could be brought to light and published. This book can serve as a guide to prospective writers and to editors as to the gaps in our diagnostic literature. It can also provide points of comparison against which the practitioner reader's experiences can be studied. Articles based on either similar or different experiences should be written. While controlled experimentation and replication is the ultimate task of knowledge building, practical replication occurs constantly in our day-by-day work. Small groups of similar cases can be studied and reported upon, thus providing cumulative information about different diagnostic groupings.

It is altogether appropriate that *Differential Diagnosis and Treatment in Social Work* should appear so soon after the fiftieth anniversary year of *Social Diagnosis*. Dr. Turner is indeed making a substantial contribution to the teaching and practice of social work.

FLORENCE HOLLIS
School of Social Work
Columbia University, New York

PREFACE TO THE FOURTH EDITION

I have been aware for some time that a fourth edition of *Differential Diagnosis and Treatment in Social Work* was needed and am pleased that the task is now complete. As I reread the Preface to the third edition I found that I wanted to reemphasize the need for precision in diagnostic terminology, for a multiaxial approach to diagnosis, and for a better understanding of the significance of psychosocial stressors. As before the richness of our practice-based writing has continued to flourish, the number of our journals has expanded and the specific types and gravity of situations we meet in practice has increased.

Diversity appears to be the operational descriptor of current social work practice, diversity in setting, in theory, in method, and in presenting situations. With diversity comes the need for even more stress on the importance of accurate diagnosis. Hence skill in differential diagnosis remains the key to precision, as practice experience continues to reinforce awareness that our interventions can be powerfully helpful, when appropriately used, but, as well, dangerously harmful when misused.

However, for a variety of sociopolitical reasons, in North America at least, the term "diagnosis" is temporarily very much out of favour. Political correctness calls for it to be substituted with the much less precise term "assessment." It is not the purpose of this volume to address this terminological controversy. Rather, as in earlier editions, it is to bring together for the profession the increasingly rich range of authoritative articles addressing situations met with in practice that require specificity of understanding by the practitioner to ensure sensitive, appropriate, and effective response.

Whatever the future of this dialogue around the term "diagnosis," the conceptual foundation stone of this volume is unchanged from that stated in the third edition, that "diagnosis remains the heart of practice." Mary Richmond taught us this over sixty years ago, and Dr. Florence Hollis reinforced this idea in her introduction to the third edition. The challenge for this volume is to ensure that we keep this conceptual commitment contemporary by tapping the ever-expanding, complex, multiculturally based worldwide clinical practice of social work.

Even more than in earlier editions, the grouping and organizing of the articles continue to be the most challenging aspect of this work. At times the temptation to merely list the articles alphabetically by topic was strong. However, to do so would be a denial of the commitment of the book to the search for accuracy and precision, not only in how we practice but in how we describe and categorize this practice. I was not fully satisfied with the grouping of the articles in the third edition and hence spent considerable effort on the planning of this edition. What has emerged is an eightfold schema, an increase of three from the last edition. In addition I have changed the titles of the sections, with the major change being in expanding the use of the term "problem" as a substitute for the less desirable word "disorder." As well I have tried to develop a conceptual framework to unite the divisions and to more accurately reflect the growing spectrum of issues faced in contemporary practice. For example, an entire section has been given to the newly expanded and recognized role of the profession in providing immediate and follow-up service in disaster situations, a topic that was covered by a single article in the last edition and was included under the general heading of "Presenting Problems."

Hopefully, the final outline is a step forward, but undoubtedly not the final word. Hopefully, many of my theory-building colleagues will challenge my final scheme. I did in developing it, and changed it several times as I attempted to organize the rich range of precise topic-based articles that emerged from a review of the last ten years of social work practice-based literature. Even more, practitioners will dispute the placing of some articles in one section rather than another. For example, the distinction between personal problems, psychological problems, and interpersonal problems is not always a clear one. However, the concept is a precise one, with the understanding of the tremendous amount of overlap, and interconnection, both between the divisions, and the topics placed in each division. Practice as we know is not as precise as some of the topics might suggest. All of us have met situations where the client or family might well have to be considered from all eight of the subdivisions in this volume. This is the excitement and the challenge of our multisystemed practice.

Choosing the articles for this volume was of course a daunting challenge. Several hundred were considered in the process of selection. There were many more we would liked to have included, but the need to keep the volume to a manageable and useful size was ever-present. I do hope that my colleagues whose articles we might well have chosen will understand. The criterion we used was the article's precision of focus on both diagnosis and intervention. As before we have tried to cover the entire gamut of social work literature, with the understanding that, apart from some journals that publish in both French and English, the material reflects the literature of the profession published in English. We are aware that there are many quality journals in our profession published in other languages, and in subsequent editions of this work I hope that it will be possible to tap into this richness as well.

As the outline for this volume emerged I remained very conscious of, and hopefully fully responsive to, other works that have greatly assisted in the ongoing development of the profession's practice-based literature. Hence the tremendous assistance of the various editions of the *Diagnostic and Statistical Manual of Mental Disorders* to the profession needs to be recognized. As well I have viewed with considerable interest and respect the work that is going on to build on the above work from a more social work perspective. The role of Dr. Bob Barker's *Social Work Dictionary*, as well as *The Clinical Thesaurus* by Dr. Edward Zuckerman, is also to be noted.

One final theme that has increasingly influenced me in the preparation of this volume is the growing awareness that our profession is indeed worldwide, and that colleagues in all parts of the globe are meeting the same challenges as have we in this part of the world, albeit in different circumstances and in different cultures. However, as the complexity and universality of our practice increases so too does an awareness that there is a common, rich, and rapidly expanding core of knowledge on how to differentially respond to the complex biopsychosocial needs of the human family through the process of accurate diagnosis of person and situations. It is understood that this drive to precision will never end, but it is this very drive that will ensure that we will expand our ability to respond effectively to persons in need striving to achieve their rightful optimum human potential.

FRANCIS J. TURNER
Kitchener, Ontario
April 1995

PREFACE TO THE THIRD EDITION

It scarcely seems possible that it is already time to write a preface to the third edition to this book; it is only a short time since the work for the second edition was completed. Yet it was necessary that the book be reedited. In the six years since the last edition much new material has appeared in social work literature. This material is important not just because it is new but because it reflects the dramatic expansion that is taking place in the professional literature in social work; an expansion not just in quantity but in quality, precision, and diversity. New journals have appeared, applications of the wide range of practice theories have been made to various diagnostic categories, new problems have been addressed, and new applications of methodologies have been developed.

The goals of the book remain the same as before. The first is to provide a resource to practitioners that will permit them to obtain some immediate information on the understanding and management of a wide spectrum of presenting situations and conditions met in today's practice. In addition it gives students an entrée to a comprehensive look at the dimensions of current practice.

The organizing concept of the book is that diagnosis remains the heart of practice. Diagnosis is built on knowledge of individual cases, classes of cases, and classes of components of the complexity of the biopsychosocial reality of our clients and the range of problems they bring to us for help.

If one uses the literature of a profession as a reliable reflector of the reality of the practice of that profession, then we can conclude that as our practice is becoming more complex the role of diagnosis is also becoming more important. As we continue to appreciate the necessity and the utility of precision in diagnosis, we are also learning that it is a highly complex process, much more complex than we have ever appreciated.

The long-standing criticism of a too structured approach to diagnosis that relied heavily on efforts to classify clients is rapidly lessening. We are all aware of the potential misuse of uni-category diagnoses but equally aware that one cannot responsibly practice without well-developed and well-tested systems of classification.

An important development in the use and standardization of classifications as an aid to practice is exemplified in the recently published *Diagnostic and Statistical Manual of Mental Disorders: Third Edition.** This book helps bring into focus a component of

---

* *Diagnostic and Statistical Manual of Mental Disorders: Third Edition* (Washington, D.C.: American Psychiatric Association, 1980).

practice long a part of social work tradition, that is, the need for precision in diagnostic terminology, the need for a multi-axial approach to diagnosis, and the role of psychosocial stressors in understanding persons-in-situations. To what extent this approach to diagnosis will become standardized across professional lines is unclear. Whatever happens in this regard, the goal of that book is very close to the goal of this one.

As before, selection of articles was a difficult problem. In the original review of the literature for this edition several hundred articles were selected for possible inclusion. Narrowing this down to a manageable number was indeed difficult. Because of the richness and diversity of available material a subsequent edition of this book may have to consider the possibility of a separate volume for each of the five major headings.

Keeping the present edition to an acceptable size was a problem. There were so many excellent articles to be included and so many from the first volume that I wanted to retain. Finally the newer articles held preference over the older and diversity of topic over several articles on one topic. In the final selection 26 articles from the second edition were retained and 48 new articles included.

We were pleased to observe that there are many more articles being written from a group intervention perspective that deal with specific aspects of the diagnostic perspective. We were able to include some of these.

The same fivefold classification system has been maintained. The second edition added the category "Presenting Problems," which is included again with an expanded number of topics. As before, further work is needed in developing a classification scheme for presenting problems. Undoubtedly an important component of our assessment needs to be not only who the client is but what his reality is and how we make use of our knowledge of client as a person to deal with the aspect of reality for which help is wanted or indicated.

Few of the articles as yet are built on the formal analysis of data gathered to test hypotheses or to test our approach to treatment. For the most part they remain articles written from a practice wisdom basis, that is, built on the organized disciplined analysis of practice. Although there is a tendency to disparage these types of data, they are still essential to the building of a practice base that will permit us to develop and test the components of practice theory to which we aspire. Hence, even in the practice wisdom articles there is observed a strengthening analytic approach to practice and a disciplined commitment to knowledge building, rather than the arguments from authority that marked earlier articles.

Our writing continues to be uneven, in that some topics become fashionable at various points in time and get special attention. Deliberate effort was made not to reflect trends in the articles selected but to give as broad a basis to the selections as possible. Even in doing this it was necessary to omit some topics that are a part of practice. As will be noted in the Part introductions, we now have social-work-written articles on several topics which before we had scarcely addressed in the literature even though they were an important part of our practice.

Ours is a dynamic and growing profession, one that is facing with our colleagues in other professions the humbling awareness of the deficiencies in our knowledge and the limits of our interventions. But this very awareness draws us on to increase the precision of our understanding of those persons we serve, an understanding that will ensure that, as effectively as possible, we make available to them the range of knowledge, skills, resources, and services that make up our armamentarium of practice.

FRANCIS J. TURNER
Sudbury, Ontario
March 21, 1982

PREFACE TO THE SECOND EDITION

It is an interesting experience to write a preface for a new edition of a book, almost ten years after the work on the first edition was carried out. The task appears to divide itself into two components: first, there is the need to explain why the book is being republished, that is, why it is still seen as being a useful contribution to the profession at this time; second, if the book is viewed as still being useful there is the need to explain why it has been altered in the new edition. In the original edition of the book there were 62 articles and in this new one 71, of which 41 are new.

Why the re-edition? I am just as convinced today as before that this type of book provides a necessary aid to the clinical social worker committed to providing efficient and responsible services to clients. Because of the structure of our present delivery system most social workers carry a highly diverse caseload. We have not as yet committed ourselves to a highly structured specialty system. At the same time our periodical literature in clinical practice remains a principal source of new practice ideas and trends. But the periodical literature contained in the better known journals is not easily available to many of our colleagues. Further, with the emergence of several new journals in North America and Europe within the last decade, the question of accessibility becomes even more difficult. Hence the necessity to extract from the literature a series of articles around a common theme. Clearly the question of the utility of collections of articles as compared to independent authorship cannot be ignored. In several of the reviews of the first edition, this question was raised and the emergence of still another collection was decried. In my own view this is not an either/or situation. The present state of practice requires both kinds of books; the collection can present a broad spectrum of current practice issues from a variety of viewpoints, while the single-authorship book presents a longer range, more focused presentation. Both are needed in today's practice.

As before, the underlying unifying concept for the book is the diagnostic component of practice. I am no less convinced of its importance in today's practice even though my perception of its form and content has altered slightly.

Between the time the first edition appeared and the present, we have passed through a period where the whole existence of clinical practice was under attack. As a part of this storm of criticism questions of labeling, classification, and treatment based on diagnosis were severely criticized. Now that this phenomenon appears to be waning, once again we can turn to further efforts at making our work more precise and effective.

I mentioned that my perception of the form and content of the diagnostic component of practice has altered. Let me comment on this. I appreciate more than before that the concept of diagnosis is a much more complex process and activity than has been acknowledged by our field. Although we have often said diagnosis should never, and was never intended to be uni-dimensional, I think we have nevertheless projected a view that it was a more easily manageable phenomenon with rather clear boundaries than in fact it is.

I began to appreciate this misperception about five years ago. At that time, I observed that a common theme was emerging from students I met in many schools and at many levels. In talking with them it was clear that, although professional schools had done a good job in developing the concept of diagnosis and helping them identify with it, what we had not done was to teach them precisely what to do with the concept, that is, the content of a particular diagnosis. It was then that I became less sure that we are as comfortable about the "how" of diagnosis as our literature implied. Thus, I have become convinced there is still much more conceptualizing and experimentation to be done before we can begin to reach some common ground on the operational components of diagnosis in social work intervention.

In no way does this imply that I am less convinced of the need for greater specificity and precision in our practice. As long as we are committed to the value that what we do for, with, and to clients is somehow related to our knowledge about them, we must continue to connect our perceptions of persons and our professional actions with them.

Clearly, the expanding number of thought systems that are influencing current practice and the thrust to a multi-method form of practice have made our search for more precise diagnostic efforts more difficult. When these two developments are taken into account, in conjunction with the already wide array of significant factors in a client's inner and outer life affecting his functioning, the diversity of services we have to offer, and the wide range of clients' requests and expectations, the search for more precise diagnoses appears almost futile.

There is one other way in which I have modified my perception of diagnosis; this concerns its ever changing nature. I think we have always been aware that diagnosis is a fluid concept but nevertheless have somehow conveyed through the literature and to each other that there was a fixed quality to the fact of diagnosis. That is, we have always said we had to alter it as the case developed, but usually I think we meant that any such alterations would be minimal. I am increasingly persuaded by the spiral concept of diagnosis as portrayed by Gordon Hearn in his writings on social systems.*

Nevertheless, difficult as it is, humbly we must continue the search for unifying concepts that will help to bring order to the complexity. But, at the same time, in our search for unifying concepts we must not overlook the knowledge to be gained by focusing on the specifics of our clients and their situations. Thus, for example, there is still much to be learned about how to deal with the suicidal component of some clients. We can all benefit by improving our techniques in dealing with the psychotic aspects of other clients with whom we work even if our overall focus with them is not related to their symptoms. We know we can be more sensitive and responsive to an addicted client when we have the accumulated knowledge, experience and perceptions of our colleagues with similar situations and behaviors.

Thus, in this second edition, as before, I have sought out, from the literature of the

* *Social Work Treatment,* Ed. F. J. Turner (New York: Free Press, 1974), p. 350.

last ten years, articles that combined a focus on the understanding of a particular facet of human behavior, healthy or ill, and included related practice-based suggestions aimed at bringing about changes in the identified symptom or problem. Many have found this kind of information helpful in their practice.

As before, I utilized the periodical journals as the principal source of material. In so doing I am aware that there is much unpublished material that exists, although access to it is limited. Again, I found selection difficult. Certainly there was much more material from which to choose. My overall opinion is that the quality of solid clinical articles is improving. One of the new problems in selecting articles this time was the fact that some of our articles are becoming too precise for the goal of this kind of book. Thus, one article might deal with the interconnection between two concepts interrelated in a particular kind of case. Such articles were judged to be beyond the objectives I have for this book and thus, for the most part, were not used.

Once again, I observed that our writings have been uneven with some topics receiving much attention and others very little. I will comment more on this in the introduction to each section. As before, I had hoped to include more articles written from a group focus. A lack of such articles had been one of the criticisms of the first edition. Unfortunately, with the addition of more topics and a new section, I was not able to use all the excellent articles which I located. Some articles written from a one-to-one treatment focus were chosen because the diagnostic component was judged to be stronger, not because of a preference for this modality over groups. Several times, throughout the literature search, I wondered if it might be better to begin to prepare a companion volume that dealt only with group intervention with the same categories of client phenomena, rather than try and mix the two types of treatment.

Family treatment articles presented a different problem. A vast amount of family therapy literature exists, as we all know. Interestingly, much of it dealt with particular aspects of family treatment or very precise components of family functioning too specific for the kinds of general diagnostic clusters I had selected. Thus, there are few specific family therapy articles included.

As before, I retained the same fourfold division of articles with the addition of a fifth section entitled "Presenting Problems." I had resisted including such a section in the first edition, but have since decided it gives a fuller profile of the significant components of diagnosis. Thus in practice, in addition to considering the stage and maturation of the person, his psychological makeup and functioning, his physical health, and his socio-cultural milieu, we are also interested in the kind of situation he or she presents to us. Again, this could not include full coverage but, rather, an overview of some of the prevalent presenting situations we meet in our current practice.

One of the difficulties in deciding about including new articles was the concomitant one of deciding which ones to exclude from the original group. This was difficult. I did not want to assume that more recent articles were better than older ones. Yet it was apparent that in some categories more recent articles did give a richer perspective of interventions and expanded diagnostic thinking. This was not always the case and at times the original older article was retained, even with the availability of many more recent ones.

There was much less difficulty about authorship. In the first edition I apologized for using social work authorship as a criterion of selection. This was not necessary this time; almost invariably the social-work-written articles were the preferred ones from the viewpoint of quality and the book's objectives. Not only has the content of social work clinical writing improved, but so has the format of the articles. For the most part, the new articles have richer footnotes and bibliographies than the earlier articles. These should provide an additional resource to the reader.

Inevitably, our professional writing goes through repeating series of fads and, hence, some topics are very well covered in the literature while others are scarcely mentioned. At times the decision was which article was to be selected from ten or more and in other situations it was difficult to find a single article.

One of the criticisms of the first edition was the extent to which it reflected an ego psychology orientation. Although this did reflect my own primary orientation this is only a partial explanation. This is where the literature was in 1966. But this too has changed. I was pleased to note that the specific diagnostic articles that make up this book are to an increasing extent trying to reflect a multitheory base. This, of course, is good for the profession, but difficult for planning a book such as this, as it introduces a new variable and a new challenge for choice.

As before, my hope is that we are still actively committed to a search for making the diagnostic component of practice more rigorous, our diagnostic categories more precise, the therapeutic implications from them more interdependent, and outcomes more effective and predictable.

FRANCIS J. TURNER
Wilfrid Laurier University
Faculty of Social Work

PREFACE TO THE FIRST EDITION

The primary goal of this book is to help social work practitioners provide more effective treatment to their clients. Obviously such a goal cannot be attained in a total manner; it requires that one segment of the therapeutic process be selected as a substructure. I have chosen to utilize the diagnostic process as a focal point. This segment was chosen because, on the one hand, it is so crucial to effective treatment and, on the other, it has been a weak point in our practice. The method I have chosen is to bring together in four parts a series of articles from the professional literature, each of which deals with a specific diagnostic variable and the resultant treatment implications.

To say that we are living in an age where quantities of available knowledge are rapidly expanding is already a cliché. Such knowledge expansion, with the accompanying proliferation of writings, creates serious problems for practitioners in all disciplines. Social workers in agencies are well aware that much has been written and is being written of import to their day-to-day practice activities. They are also most aware of the difficulty in maintaining anything more than a fleeting contact or haphazard sampling of what is available. Such sampling is often more anxiety provoking than satisfying, as the little reading and formal studying that is possible clearly alerts them to the quantities of material which perforce are left untouched. Concomitant with the awareness of quantity is the realization that all that is written is not necessarily gold; much valuable time can be wasted in locating and reading material which in fact is not as useful as some other might have been.

Someday in the not too distant future, an agency social worker wishing to know quickly and succinctly what has been written about the treatment of a particular kind of client will turn to the agency data-retrieval unit. This in turn will be electronically connected with a national centralized programed library. In a few minutes he will receive a "print-out" of the requested data. As yet such resources, while theoretically possible, are beyond the scope, structure, and resources of our agencies. For the present, agency practitioners wishing to obtain such data must turn to the literature. This is not an easy task. Rarely is there time available to undertake the required search, presuming there are library resources upon which to call. In the meantime books such as this are required.

Most social practitioners are well acquainted with the major textbooks in individual and group treatment. These have tended to be treatises on treatment in general rather than the specific. Discussions of treatment of specific kinds of problems or diagnostic entities have largely been carried out in individual articles scattered through some 20 to

25 journals and going back 30 to 35 years. Thus, at best, a practitioner can only have a superficial knowledge of the precise type of practice-oriented literature available to him. Because of this, the tendency has been to teach and practice from general rather than specific knowledge and understanding about people and how to treat them. This has been effective, and I believe the majority of our clients have been helped to achieve improved psychosocial functioning as a result of the treatment they have received. When practitioners tend to operate from an intuitive and an *ad hoc* framework, it is clear that diagnosis in anything more than a diffuse manner is unnecessary. Effective as is such a general treatment style, a higher level of competence can be achieved when treatment is consciously and selectively based on a detailed diagnosis of the client. It is my conviction that many social workers would greatly improve the quality of their treatment if experience-based observations and discussions of the treatment implications of diagnostic entities found in the literature of the last few years were readily available to them.

The danger of bringing together articles dealing with specific diagnostic entities or variables is that this collection could be misused. There is the possibility of its being seen as a shortcut, as a "How to do it" book. The prospect of having a resource which will lay out a formula of therapy or a prescription of technique for each diagnostic entity is an attractive one. Unfortunately this is not such a book; anyone who tried to use it in this way would only be disappointed. What it does aspire to achieve is to give therapists some anchoring concepts, some experience-based benchmarks, some specific analyses of points of theory which will give direction and basic structure to the treatment of clients. The test of the therapist's skill is a dual one: first, to understand how much his client is like other clients of the same type and thus utilize what the profession has said about them; second, to understand how he is different from all other clients thus necessitating a peculiar combination of therapeutic skills most appropriate to him in his individuality. To follow slavishly a prescribed formulation of treatment because the literature suggests it makes the therapist a technician (and a poor one at that) rather than a professional. Whether this latter is a more serious detriment to treatment than working from no diagnosis is a moot point.

The book is designed to serve as a resource to be used in combination with the "practice wisdom" of the practitioner. It is primarily seen as important for the person in the multifunctioned agency who is called upon to serve a wide range of presenting problems and client types; the practitioner in the small agency and the private practitioner, who does not have a well-endowed agency library and readily available colleague consultation; the student and the teacher. It perhaps won't be as useful to persons in more specialized settings. It is presumed that in such settings there would be a concentration of literature appropriate to the field, for example, the treatment of marital problems. The articles chosen for the book on this former topic or on any topic can only be seen as an overview or a viewpoint rather than an exhaustive treatment or the final word. To aid in a broader coverage than one or two articles could give, bibliographies, wherever present, have been included. Thus a person interested in searching for additional information on a particular syndrome or diagnostic variable is given some leads for further reading.

This book contains a predominance of articles on individual treatment. Originally I had hoped to locate an article dealing with the individual treatment of each topic and another dealing with group treatment. This was not always possible. In the literature there have been more individual treatment-based articles than group-based articles. It is hoped that in the future, there will be more written accounts of appropriate group treatment with other client-types. In seeking group articles for each topic there is a presumed implication that every diagnostic variable lends itself to some form of group treatment. This may be incorrect.

Throughout the articles there can be seen a recurring theme. The social work practitioner of today must be a multiskilled person, comfortable in individual, joint, and group treatment, as well as a person skilled in educative and collaborative activities. This does not imply a generic method in the profession, but the necessity of multiskills, and these at a high degree of competence. Truly, this is a formidable challenge.

One of the unfortunate results of the gap between the professional literature and the mainstream of practice has been a tendency to devalue traditional knowledge. It seems fashionable in some segments of current thinking to suggest that much of our traditional theoretical orientation be scrapped and replaced by newer concepts and practice approaches. It is said that our psychodynamic approaches have failed and are unnecessary in understanding clients. Such presumptive thinking is only as valid as the evidence upon which it is based, and laudatory tributes to new approaches do not establish their validity. If the newer approaches to therapy are more effective than those presently used, then we must adopt them. Responsible professional behavior demands this. To make this comparison requires a full understanding and utilization of the old and the new. I raise this point because of a conviction that much of the disappointment in the results of treatment stems not from a fault in our theory and its applications but from a failure to utilize fully the rich amounts of data, knowledge, and skill accumulated over the years. One of the causes of this failure to tap effectively the rich resources of accumulated professional expertise in our profession has been our reliance on oral tradition and the reluctance to set out in an organized useful way what we know, what we do not know, what has been effective, and what has not.

A further purpose in planning this collection was to highlight the necessity of improved diagnostic habits among practitioners. Is not urging the importance of diagnosis to practitioners but a further example of preaching to the converted? In school and agency recent generations of social workers have been assailed with the triad of study, diagnosis, and treatment. Now every student learns early in his professional training that the unity of the therapeutic process is made up of these three elements. Why then emphasize diagnosis? It is because of a growing awareness of the divergence between our value commitment to the importance of diagnosis and the reality of our practice. Time and time again, records of social workers are examined without being able to locate within them a place where a diagnosis was formulated and set out, which the social worker then used to formulate treatment objectives and goals. That some form of diagnosis is made is indisputable; otherwise there could be no way to account for the large numbers of clients whose psychosocial functioning is markedly improved as the result of the therapist's activities and skills. The process of diagnosis evidently is operating, but the fact of diagnosis is lacking. Why should this be of concern? It is because without the availability of a concrete diagnosis there is no way to assess the effectiveness of our treatment except in a globular way. There is no way of correlating the various forms of social work intervention in relation to particular presenting diagnostic variables and assessing their outcome. There is no way of planfully and carefully improving our effectiveness with our clients. Until we can be more precise in declaring how we assess people and what therefore we choose to do with them and for them, our practice efficiency will remain static.

Why this divergence between fact and process? The answers to this are elusive and uncertain. It is easy to utilize the accustomed mutual recriminatory reflex and attribute this omission to a lack of desired professional behavior. This is too simple and obviously incorrect.

Part of the reason seems to be tied up in our strong commitment to the necessity of individualizing the client and maintaining nonjudgmental attitudes toward him. The process of working toward and from a precise, although flexible and evolving, diagnosis seems to evoke in some an emotional response that in some way the client is depersonalized through categorization and judged through opinion. There is also a fear that diagnosis somehow excludes the client. The thinking is as follows: Treatment in social work requires full involvement of the client; diagnosis is a professional assessment made by us not the client; therefore if we emphasize diagnosis we overlook the client. Obviously this is a misunderstanding of the process.

A lack of experience or perhaps of training also seems to be involved in this underemphasis of diagnosis. If there is a value-based reluctance to diagnose among practitioners, then it is to be expected that this is a skill which will not be given first-order priority. It is clear that if this skill is not acquired early in a professional career, it is increasingly difficult later to reorient oneself to it. I want to avoid overgeneralizing here; evidently many practitioners are highly skilled diagnosticians. The selections presented here demonstrate this.

Perhaps the most important explanation of this apparent gap in social work practice stems from the complex conceptual base from which we operate. The number of variables requiring assessment and the multitude of frameworks in which these can be assessed presents a formidable and, at times, seemingly overwhelming task for the practitioner.

Because there is not a single theory of psychosocial behavior which can serve as a unifying principle of practice, it is clear that the process of diagnosis must of necessity be a multifaceted one. Since in the diagnostic phase of treatment the therapist is bringing his professional judgment to bear on the information he has about the client, it is presumed that he has a framework in which he can order the data he has about the client and norms against which he can compare his client. In the complexity of our efforts to study our client in a biopsychosocial context, the process of synthesizing, interrelating, and then formulating a professional judgment about the client is indeed a monumental one. This should not deter us from attempting to do so even though we will never reach a point of complete satisfaction with our assessment of the situations with which we are confronted.

It has been implied at times that there is a danger in forming detailed diagnoses and then operating from them. Such a process, it is said, serves to make treatment too rigid by forming a "mind-set" toward the client. It is therefore better to keep our diagnosis flexible and open and permit the utilization of new understanding and perception of clients. It is true that a diagnosis must not become "locked in" so that we operate from it in an inflexible manner. To do this, of course, is a misuse of the diagnostic concept.

Obviously, we are going to shift and clarify and make more precise and enrich our understanding of clients; this in turn will affect the goals and methods of treatment we set for and with them. In no way should this deter us from constantly striving to set out clearly our assessments of them. More treatment efforts are ineffective and more client and therapist time is used uneconomically when a diagnosis is not made than there are gains resulting from nondiagnosing in order to remain, "flexible and open."

No doubt part of the reluctance to diagnose has resulted from misuse to which nominal diagnoses have been put. I am referring especially to the unidimensional type in which a one-word or a one-expression classification is used. Such terms are used to explain the entire client and by implication dictate the format of treatment. For example, Miss R is a defective, Mr. J is schizophrenic, the B's are a multiproblem family.

On the one hand, if a diagnosis consists of only such labels it deserves to be discredited; on the other, these labels or classifications have their place in spite of the current tendency to disparage them. It is one of the principal assumptions of this collection of articles that we have not used them sufficiently, nor appreciated the extent to which they could help us consciously and deliberately to plan our treatment of clients. That they must be used in concert with many other classifications or labels is also a prior assumption. For effective treatment it is essential to understand the significance of the individual variables designated by the "labels" as well as the peculiar and unique combination of them as presented in the life and person of each client.

Classification in any professional activity must not become an end in itself. Whatever other purposes are served, the process should and must be a pragmatic conceptual tool to assist us in applying the rich and extensive body of knowledge accumulated over the years. Viewing classificatory thinking about clients as a useful tool rather than an absolute helps us achieve some perspective about the classification systems presently available to us. It is clear that we do not have the last word in typologies of clients and the significant variables which must be assessed for effective treatment. Similarly, systems we presently use are far from perfect and complete. It is inevitable that most of them will be replaced as better understanding is achieved and as we become more skilled in integrating the multiple bodies of knowledge from which we draw our understanding of clients.

Our profession does not have a closed body of knowledge. Hence the concepts from which we operate are in constant flux. Theory is formulated in order to be replaced by better theory, better in the sense of helping us more effectively to achieve the treatment goals deemed desirable by the values of the profession. True as this is, we are not thereby excused from utilizing today what we already know.

A further reason for preparing this collection stemmed from a research interest. I was curious to explore the actual situation of the literature. I was aware that articles existed on some categories of clients; for example, we know that there has been a wealth of data on the character-disordered clients in recent years. I did not know how extensive the coverage might be. Have we clearly addressed in our literature the entire range of diagnostic variables customarily considered as being essential to effective treatment? Thus, beyond the wish to produce a book useful to practitioners, I was also interested in locating possible gaps in the literature, to point out strategic areas in which well-thought-out and carefully written articles are required. Some of the gaps which were located will be discussed in the introduction to each Part.

It was further hoped that by bringing together writings which set out our practice, concepts, and thinking in an easily accessible way, practitioners would be given an opportunity to test their "practice wisdom" against the opinions of their colleagues. In this way, we can assess what of our present thinking is still valid, what needs to be replaced with new insights, what can be refined by imaginative experimentation, and lastly, how our traditional understanding of clients can be enriched with new combinations of skills.

There was a further reason underlying this project. From time to time serious concerns have been exhibited as to the extent and diversity of our knowledge. It is hoped that the breadth of areas addressed in the literature and contained here will help to give a better appreciation of the richness of our practice knowledge. On the basis of this idea, I tended to select articles written by social workers over those written by our colleagues in other disciplines. This was not done exclusively, of course, but presuming the articles were judged to be comparable and relevant to the design of the book, authorship by a social worker was used as a criterion of selection. I realize that this can contribute to professional insularity of which we have suffered more than enough. My own conviction is that we are growing to even greater interprofessional collaboration at all levels. To do this effectively and responsibly necessitates that we know our own field well. It is to aid in this latter task that I have kept the book more social work oriented. I do hope, though, that the collection of readings will be of interest and use to members of other disciplines. Of course, some articles written by members of other disciplines were included. Such articles were selected in which the treatment methods discussed were clearly appropriate for social workers. Thus, for example, an article dealing with the pharmacological treatment of depression would not be considered here, although one discussing some form of treatment utilizing relationship therapy would be. In the same way, it is also hoped that some increased appreciation will be gained as to the complexity of client functioning and responsible therapy. Recent conferences and writings have devoted some attention to the possibility of a generic method of practice to be taught to all aspirants to the profession. Much has been said about the necessity for others without comparable training to be able to do some of the direct work with clients presently assigned to social workers. Obviously there is some merit in examining these ideas. It is known that some understanding of treatment principles can be learned by others. It is also obvious to those directly in contact with clients that *more* rather than *less* specialized knowledge and skill is required to understand, involve, and treat many of the persons who come or are referred to us for treatment. There is a growing need for practitioners of a very high level of competence, who have clear and demonstrated diagnostic and treatment skills.

In searching for articles and in selecting them an effort was made to cover all the professional journals which include articles of import to social work practitioners, as well as standard social work journals. I am aware that a considerable amount of data was missed. For example, frequently papers are given at conferences, speeches given to meetings, and reports made to agencies which do not find their way into the mainstream of professional reading. Many of these are of high calibre and should be more widely available. It is hoped that this book will serve to draw out some of these and to encourage people to make their views more broadly known.

Selecting a framework useful for organizing the wide range of topics located in the literature was difficult. The goal was to utilize articles dealing with a specific diagnostic variable or entity rather than a type of service or problem. Thus adoption, unmarried mothers, deserted wives, separated couples, or other problem or service classifications were not employed. It is not always easy to distinguish between a diagnostic variable with specific treatment implications and a problem classification with a multitude of causes so that little or nothing can be said about generic treatment implications. There are some types of situations which are both a problem for treatment and a variable in diagnosis affecting the method of treatment selected. For example, although treatment of unmarried mothers was not included I did include delinquent youth.

I was particularly interested in finding articles which discussed the therapeutic considerations which result from a precise part of our total assessment of the client. It is assumed that all treatment must be geared to the whole person and not to particular parts of that person. It is also understood that there are dangers in categorizing a segment of a client's total psychosocial functioning and selecting our treatment approach specific to that segment. The danger is the well-known one of stereotyping. It is the extent to which the individual person can be partialized and yet treated as a whole that determines the effectiveness of our treatment methods. It is clear that selective treatment skills are necessary with schizophrenic clients, yet there are no schizophrenic clients as such. There are young, recently married, working class, rural-oriented, dull normal, Irish Catholic schizophrenic clients. Our treatment will be most effective when we can begin to understand the significance of each of these variables and whatever others are important and the peculiar combination of treatment methods most appropriate for different constellations of variables.

The variables which were finally chosen were divided into the traditional biopsychosocial triad based on a framework of human growth and development stages. Obviously it would be much easier for all if a unitary theory of psychosocial functioning could be devised so that clients would only have to be assessed along one dimension. Unfortunately, we are a long way from this and for a long time to come we have to live with the problems arising from the fact that societal man is a most complex creature. To try to understand and explain him in a manner that will permit us to aid him effectively to achieve improved psychosocial functioning will demand a complex conceptual framework. Complex as is our present conceptual basis of human behavior, undoubtedly there are other dimensions whose significance we probably do not realize, such as some genetic, cosmotic, or time-space factors.

No apologies are made for utilizing traditional psychodynamic headings. It is true that there has been recent serious questioning of the utility of classical dynamic interpretations of behavior. No one denies these present difficulties. They require constant critical re-examination in the light of current practice. This doesn't mean that they are to be ignored; for they have supplied and will continue to supply a framework in which people can be understood and, even more importantly, effectively treated. When they are replaced, as is the lot of all theory, it must be done by validated reliable concepts.

In selecting the headings under which topics were gathered there was an additional difficulty that must always be considered in diagnosis. This is the different levels of precision which exist between and among the various diagnostic variables. The presence or the lack of precision affects the degree of exactness with which we can discuss the treatment implications of each variable. For example, our division of clients by socioeconomic classes is a much less precise variable than the distinction between the types of neuroses or between character-disordered and borderline clients.

As our knowledge about these variables grows and more specificity is developed, our precision in formulating treatment goals and methods will grow also. It is hoped that much of what has been written in these pages will be replaced with further experiences, new concepts, and generalizations. It is hoped that the ideas presented in the various articles will be subjected to the keen scrutiny of our colleagues who are secure in their practice and rich in experience. It is hoped that imaginative, responsible experimentation will provide us with new insights and suggest new therapeutic approaches for consideration. In such instances the most useful form of replacement would be by means of scholarly articles building on the past and adding the new. I would hope most seriously that this book would have to be re-edited in a few years, on the basis of new insights, further writing, and an increased acceptance of our responsibility to translate our knowledge into a form readily accessible to our colleagues.

Much remains to be done in improving our diagnostic categories, in clarifying their definitions and descriptions, in specifying commonly accepted indicators, and in developing optimum treatment approaches. In the meantime the practitioner must use the knowledge presently available to him, fully aware of its inherent limitations. It is the purpose of this book to make one segment of this knowledge more accessible to him.

Francis J. Turner
Graduate School of Social Work
Waterloo Lutheran University
Waterloo, Ontario, Canada

ACKNOWLEDGMENTS

This is the fourth time that I have turned to the pleasant task of acknowledging those many persons who have been the inspiration and help in preparing the various editions of *Differential Diagnosis and Treatment in Social Work*.

The immediate and operational help comes, as before from a fourfold perspective. First there are the students and research assistants, now colleagues, who participated in the locating and initial screening of the hundreds of articles, many in new journals, that have appeared since the last edition. In particular I want to mention Gail Wideman, Comfort Afari, and Jennifer Rodgers. Secondly, the journal editors and article authors were once again most cooperative in facilitating the complex process of republishing permissions. Thirdly, the enthusiasm, support and perceptiveness of The Free Press staff has ensured that the book remains relevant to the needs of our front-line colleagues. Those with whom I worked most closely are Susan Arellano, Jennifer Shulman, and Celia Knight. Fourthly and most particularly, I have long been, and continue to be, moved by the encouragement, and indeed helpful criticism that I have received as I meet colleagues in all parts of the world who have found this book to be useful in their learning and practice.

But overall the ongoing understanding and enthusiasm of the family remains the mainstay of inspiration and help. The four editions span some twenty-five years of our family history and have become a part of our tradition. Since the last edition much has changed for Joanne and me. Francis, Sarah, and Anne-Marie have all finished their education and are each pursuing their careers. Anne-Marie has married Greg. But throughout, as always, everyone remains interested and supportive.

To all, and for all, I am grateful.

FRANCIS J. TURNER
Collingwood, Ontario
April 1995

LIST OF CONTRIBUTORS

The contributors are identified by the professional positions they held at the time the articles were first published.

Leslie Rosenthal, M.S.W., is Chairman of the Group Analysis, Department of Manhattan, Center for Advanced Psychoanalytic Studies in New York.

Elaine Rubenstein is a Clinical Social Worker in private practice and Clinical Assistant Professor, Department of Pediatrics, Division of Adolescent Medicine, School of Medicine, University of Maryland, Maryland.

Glen Clifford, M.S.W., is a student at the Smith College of Social Work.

Katharine Odin is a graduate student at the Smith College School of Social Work.

Eileen M. Brennan is an Assistant Professor, School of Social Welfare, University of Kansas, Lawrence, Kansas.

Ann Weick is an Associate Professor, School of Social Welfare, University of Kansas, Lawrence, Kansas.

Roberta G. Sands, Ph.D., is Assistant Professor, College of Social Work, The Ohio State University, Columbus.

Virginia Richardson, Ph.D., is Assistant Professor, College of Social Work, The Ohio State University, Columbus.

Michàl E. Mor-Barak, Ph.D., is Assistant Professor, School of Social Work, University of Southern California, Los Angeles, California.

Margaret Tynan, M.S.W., is administrator, Beverly La Cumbre Convalescent Hospital, Santa Barbara, California.

Mickie Griffin is a practitioner at Aurora Community Mental Health Center, Aurora, Colorado.

Mildred Waller is a practitioner at Aurora Community Mental Health Center, Aurora, Colorado.

David P. Fauri is Professor and Associate Dean, School of Social Work, Virginia Commonwealth University, Richmond, Virginia.

Judith B. Bradford is a Doctoral Fellow at the School of Social Work, Virginia Commonwealth University, Richmond, Virginia.

Marielle Beauger is coordinator of services at the family medicine clinic of Sacré-Coeur Hospital in Montréal.

Michèle Dupuy-Godin, M.S.W., is employed as specialist in clinical activities at the family medicine clinic of Sacré-Coeur Hospital in Montréal and is also working in private practice.

Yolaine Jumelle is employed as human relations agent at the Metro Montréal Social Services Centre and is the national president of the Black Women's Congress of Canada.

Larry L. Smith, D.S.W., is an Assistant Professor, Graduate School of Social Work, University of Utah, Salt Lake City, Utah.

Doreen M. Winkler, M.S.W., is a Social Worker, Lakeshore Psychiatric Hospital, Toronto, Ontario, Canada.

Gene A. Brodland is Senior Outpatient Social Worker, Department of Psychiatry, University of Iowa College of Medicine, Iowa City, Iowa.

N.J.C. Andreasen, M.D., Ph.D., is an Assistant Professor, Department of Psychiatry, University of Iowa College of Medicine, Iowa City, Iowa.

Carleton Pilsecker, M.S.S.W., is Social Worker and Chairperson, Hospital Thanatology Committee, Veterans Administration Hospital, Long Beach, California.

Bernice Sokol is Supervising Clinical Social Worker, Department of Clinical Social Work, University of California, Los Angeles, California.

Helen Sloss Luey, M.S., A.C.S.W., L.C.S.W., is the Social Worker at Heaming Society for the Bay Area, Inc., San Francisco, California.

J. Dale Munro is at the Oxford Regional Centre, Woodstock, Ontario, Canada.

Mary W. Englemann is a Social Worker, Royal Alexandra Hospital, Edmonton, Alberta, Canada.

Kathleen Kirk Bishop is Assistant Professor, Department of Social Work, University of Vermont, Burlington, Vermont.

Alfred H. Katz, D.S.W., is Head of Division of Social Welfare in Medicine and Associate Professor, Social Welfare in Medicine, Department of Preventive Medicine and Public Health, University of California Medical Center, School of Medicine, Los Angeles, California.

Kathleen M. Hickey is Social Worker, Dialysis and Transplant Unit, Social Service Department, University of Minnesota Hospitals, Minneapolis, Minnesota.

Gary John Welch is an Assistant Professor in the Graduate School of Social Work, University of Texas, Arlington, Texas.

Kathleen Steven is Co-director of the Irving Counselling Center, Irving, Texas.

Joan Keizer is Coordinator of Consultation and Education at COPSA Institute for Alzheimer's Disease and Related Disorders, University of Medicine and Dentistry, Community Mental Health Center at Piscataway, NJ.

Linda C. Feins is Coordinator of Diagnostic Clinic, COPSA Institute for Alzheimer's Disease and Related Disorders, University of Medicine and Dentistry, Community Mental Health Center at Piscataway, NJ.

Mary Frances Libassi is Assistant Professor, School of Social Work, University of Connecticut, West Hartford, Connecticut.

Mona Wasow, M.S.W., is Clinical Assistant Professor, School of Social Work, University of Wisconsin, Madison.

Dorothy H. Coons, B.S., is Project Director, Institute of Gerontology, University of Michigan, Ann Arbor.

Kemal Elberlik is an Assistant Professor of Psychiatry and Director, Adult Psychiatric Clinic, Department of Psychiatry, University of Virginia Medical Center, Charlottesville, Virginia.

Alletta Jervey Hudgens, M.S.W., is a graduate student in Family Social Science and Relationship Counsellor in the Student Counselling Bureau at the University of Minnesota, Minneapolis, Minnesota.

Steven L. Taube, M.D., is at Arlington County Mental Health Center, Arlington, Virginia.

Nancy Harris, M.S.W., is a practitioner at Mental Health Services, University of Maryland, College Park, Maryland.

Shirley Conyard, M.S.W., is a Social Worker at the Jewish Hospital and Medical Center of Brooklyn, New York.

Muthuswamy Krishnamurthy, M.D., is attending Haematologist at the Jewish Hospital and Medical Center of Brooklyn, New York.

Harvey Dosik, M.D., is Chief of Haematology, Jewish Hospital and Medical Center of Brooklyn, New York.

Judith R. Singler is Clinical Social Worker, Youville Rehabilitation and Chronic Disease Hospital, Cambridge, Massachusetts.

Marie Cohen, M.S.W., is a Social Worker, Oncology Ward, U.C.L.A. Center for the Health Sciences, Los Angeles, California.

Irene Goldenberg, Ed.D., is Director of Psychological Services, Children's Division, U.C.L.A. Neuropsychiatric Institute, Los Angeles, California.

Herbert Goldenberg, Ph.D., is Professor of Psychology, California State University.

Julia B. Rauch is Associate Professor, School of Social Work, University of Maryland at Baltimore.

Carla Sarno is Clinical Assistant Professor, Department of Child Psychiatry, University of Maryland at Baltimore.

Sylvia Simpson is Assistant Professor, Department of Psychiatry, Johns Hopkins University School of Medicine, Baltimore, Maryland.

Elsa Marziali, Ph.D., is Professor of Social Work and Psychiatry at the University of Toronto, Toronto, Ontario.

Eda G. Goldstein is Associate Professor, New York University, School of Social Work, New York, New York.

Michael J. Scott is a Senior Research Social Worker and Senior Counselling Psychologist with the Liverpool Personal Service Society and Honorary Research Associate in the Department of Psychology at the University of Manchester, England.

Stephen G. Stradling is a Lecturer at the University of Manchester, England.

Margaret A. Fielden is Principal Clinical Psychologist, South East Staffordshire Health Authority and Lecturer, Keele University Department of Psychiatry.

Kenneth R. Wedel, M.S.W., is a Clinical Social Worker, Clinical Center, National Institute of Health, Bethesda, Maryland.

Harriette C. Johnson, Ph.D., is Associate Professor, School of Social Work, University of Connecticut, West Hartford, Connecticut.

Kaye H. Coker is a Social Worker at The Emory Clinic and Emory University Hospital, Atlanta, Georgia.

Bruce A. Thyer is Associate Professor, School of Social Work, University of Georgia, Athens, Georgia.

Fred R. Volkmar, M.D., is on the staff of the Department of Psychiatry and Behavioral Sciences, Stanford University School of Medicine, and the Palo Alto Veterans Administration Hospital, Stanford, California.

Sandra Bacon, M.S.W., is on the staff of the Department of Psychiatry and Behavioral Sciences, Stanford University School of Medicine, and the Palo Alto Veterans Administration Hospital, Stanford, California.

Saad A. Shakir, M.D., is on the staff of the Department of Psychiatry and Behavioral Sciences, Stanford University School of Medicine, and the Palo Alto Veterans Administration Hospital, Stanford, California.

Adolf Pfefferbaum, M.D., is on the staff of the Department of Psychiatry and Behavioral Sciences, Stanford University School of Medicine, and the Palo Alto Veterans Administration Hospital, Stanford, California.

Thomas J. Giancarlo is District Director, Amherst Regional Office, Child and Family Services, Buffalo, New York.

Monna Zentner is an Assistant Professor, School of Social Work, Renison College, University of Waterloo, Waterloo, Ontario, Canada.

William P. Gilmore is a Caseworker, Southwest Office, Family Service Association of Cleveland.

Sylvia B. Patten, M.S.W., is Assistant Professor, School of Social Work, Department of Sociology, Florida State University, Tallahassee, Florida.

Yvonne Gatz, M.S.W., is Assistant Professor, Department of Sociology and Political Science, University of North Florida, Jacksonville, Florida.

Berlin Jones, M.S.W., is Clinical Social Worker, Community Behavioral Services, Orange Park, Florida.

Deborah Thomas is Coordinator, Sexual Assault Center, Children's Crisis Center, Inc., Jacksonville, Florida.

Linda Jean Maloney, M.S.W., is a graduate student at Smith College School of Social Work.

Audrey Rosen Ely, M.S.W., is Clinical Director, Adult Outpatient Clinic, South Shore Mental Health Center, Quincy, Massachusetts.

Jody D. Iodice, M.S.W., is Clinical Social Worker, West Paces Ferry Psychiatric Center, Atlanta, Georgia.

John S. Wodarski, Ph.D., is Director, Research Center; Professor, School of Social Work; and Fellow, Institute for Behavioral Research at the University of Georgia, Athens, Georgia.

R.D.W. Taylor is Senior Lecturer in Social Work in the Department of Applied Community Studies, Manchester Polytechnic.

P.J. Huxley is Lecturer in Psychiatric Social Work, Department of Psychiatry, University of Manchester and Hospital Coordinator, Psychiatric Social Work, Manchester Social Services.

D.A.W. Johnson is Consultant Psychiatrist, University Hospital of South Manchester.

Judith C. Nelsen, D.S.W., is an Assistant Professor, School of Social Work, Hunter College of the City University of New York, New York, New York.

Carolyn Sandberg, M.S.W., is at the Mediplex Group Inc., White Plains, New York.

William M. Greenberg, M.D., is at Bergen Pines County Hospital, Paramus, New Jersey.

Joseph C. Birkmann, M.S.W., is at Bergen Pines County Hospital, Paramus, New Jersey.

William P. Sullivan is Assistant Professor, Department of Social Work, Southwest Missouri State University, Springfield, Missouri.

James L. Wolk is Associate Professor, Department of Social Work, Southwest Missouri State University, Springfield, Missouri.

David J. Hartmann is Associate Professor, Department of Social Work, Southwest Missouri State University, Springfield, Missouri.

Alice Ullman is Social Work Supervisor, New York Hospital and Assistant Professor of Social Work, Cornell University Medical College, New York, New York.

Peter Barnett is District Director at Family Services of Tidewater, Norfolk, Virginia.

Deborah W. Balak is a Social Worker at Family Services of Tidewater, Norfolk, Virginia.

Donald F. Krill, M.S.W., is an Assistant Professor, Graduate School of Social Work, University of Denver, Denver, Colorado.

Charles Zastrow, Ph.D., is a Professor in the Social Welfare Department at the University of Wisconsin, Whitewater.

Nancy Boyd Webb is at the Graduate School of Social Service, Fordham University in Westchester, Tarrytown, New York.

Mary Elizabeth Taylor Warmbrod is Assistant Professor, Psychological Service Center and Psychology, the University of Manitoba, Winnipeg, Manitoba.

Susan Krausz is a practitioner in New York, New York.

Susan A. Cho is program director, Consultation and Community Support Service, Shawnee Community Mental Health Center, Topeka, Kansas.

Edith M. Freeman is Assistant Professor, University of Kansas, School of Social Welfare, Kansas City, Kansas.

Shirley L. Patterson is an Assistant Professor, University of Kansas School of Social Welfare, Lawrence, Kansas.

Barbara V. Bulow is Director of Central Evaluation, Columbia Psychiatric Associates, and Assistant Professor of Clinical Social Work in Psychiatry, Columbia University, New York, New York.

Neal DeChillo is Senior Research Social Worker, Payne Whitney Clinic, New York, New York.

R.T.T. Morgan is a Post-graduate Research Scholar, School of Social Work, University of Leicester, Leicestershire, England.

G.D. Young, M.D., B.Sc., D.P.H., is Deputy Medical Officer of Health for London Borough of Barnet, London, England.

David J. Klugman, M.S.W., is Co-Chief Social Worker, Suicide Prevention Center, Los Angeles, California.

Robert E. Litman, M.D., is Chief Psychiatrist, Suicide Prevention Center, Los Angeles, California.

Carl I. Wold, Ph.D., is Chief Psychologist, Suicide Prevention Center, Los Angeles, California.

Dean H. Hepworth is Professor, Graduate School of Social Work, University of Utah, Salt Lake City, Utah.

O. William Farley is Professor, Graduate School of Social Work, University of Utah, Salt Lake City, Utah.

J. Kent Griffiths is Director, Alta View Center for Counselling, Intermountain Health Care, Sandy, Utah.

Sarah F. Hafemann is a Family Court Marriage Counsellor, Milwaukee County Department of Family Conciliation, Milwaukee, Wisconsin.

Catherine S. Chilman, Ph.D., is a Professor and Research Consultant, School of Social Welfare, University of Wisconsin, Milwaukee, Wisconsin.

Jon R. Conte, Ph.D., is Assistant Professor, School of Social Service Administration, University of Chicago, Chicago, Illinois.

Catherine K. Gagliano is a Clinical Social Worker and Senior Counsellor at Family and Children's Service, Inc., Tulsa, Oklahoma.

Wayne Scott, M.A., is a practitioner at Midwest Family Resource Assoc. Ltd., Chicago, Illinois.

Geraldine Faria is Assistant Professor/Wichita Coordinator, School of Social Welfare, University of Kansas, Lawrence, Kansas.

Nancy Belohlavek is Director, Community Support Program, Shawnee Community Mental Health Center, Topeka, Kansas.

Debra F. Brackner is a Social Worker at the Women's Therapy and Research Centre, Calgary, Alberta.

Peter E. Johnson is Counselling Psychologist, Alberta Vocational Center, Calgary, Alberta.

John W. Taylor is a Clinical Social Worker, Family Service Association of Orange County, California.

Caroline E. Sakai is a Psychiatric Social Worker, Kaiser Psychiatry Department, Kaiser Permanente Medical Center, and Men's Group Co-facilitator, Child and Family Service, Honolulu, Hawaii.

Jeffrey L. Edleson, Ph.D., is Assistant Professor, School of Social Work, University of Minnesota, Minneapolis, and Coordinator of the Research Unit at the Domestic Abuse Project of Minneapolis.

Deborah Bookin is Consultant, Protective Services Consortium for Older Adults of Cuyahoga County, Cleveland, Ohio.

Ruth E. Dunkle is Associate Professor, School of Applied Social Sciences, Case Western Reserve University, Cleveland, Ohio.

David Howe is lecturer at the University of East Anglia in Norwich, England.

Doris Bertocci, M.S.W., is Administrator for Clinical Services, Mental Health Division, Columbia University Health Services and Psychological Consultant, The Juilliard School, New York, New York.

Marshall D. Schechter, M.D., is Professor Emeritus, Child and Adolescent Psychiatry University, University of Pennsylvania School of Medicine.

Dory Krongelb Beatrice is a Clinical Social Worker, San Luis Valley Comprehensive Community Mental Health Center, Alamosa, Colorado.

Marquis Earl Wallace is an Assistant Professor, School of Social Work, University of Southern California, Los Angeles, California.

Sonya Rhodes is Adjunct Associate Professor, School of Social Work, Hunter College, New York, New York.

Robert M. Counts, M.D., is Program Director, Center for Marital and Family Therapy, New York, New York.

Anita Sacks, M.S.W., is Social Work Supervisor, Center for Marital and Family Therapy, New York, New York.

Richard R. Raubolt, Ph.D., is Staff Psychologist, Pine Rest Christian Hospital, Grand Rapids, Michigan.

Arnold W. Rachman, Ph.D., is in private practice in New York City.

Beverly B. Nichols is a caseworker, Family Counselling Service Region West, Inc., Waltham, Massachusetts.

Ann Wolbert Burgess, D.N.Sc., is an Associate Professor of Nursing, Boston College, Chestnut Hill, Massachusetts.

Lynda Lytle Holmstrom, Ph.D., is an Associate Professor of Sociology, Boston College, Chestnut Hill, Massachusetts.

M. Panneton, t.s., M. Serv.Soc., is a practitioner at the Centre des services sociaux, Richelieu, du Québec.

Michael J. Shernoff, M.S.W., is in private practice, New York City and Senior Clinician, Red Bank Outreach Center, Children's Psychiatric Center/Community Mental Health Center of Monmouth County, Red Bank, New Jersey.

J. Paul Fedoroff is a clinical Research Fellow in forensic psychiatry, Division of Forensics, The Clarke Institute of Psychiatry, Toronto, Ontario.

Rosemary Kiely, M.A., founding member of the Council for the Single Mother and her Child in Victoria, is a freelance journalist, writing on social welfare issues.

Geoffrey L. Greif, D.S.W., is Associate Professor, School of Social Work, University of Maryland at Baltimore, Maryland.

Martha Smith, M.A., is a practitioner at the Minnesota Department of Health, Minneapolis.

Roger Toogood, M.S.W., is a practitioner at the Children's Home Society of Minnesota.

Greta W. Stanton, M.S., is Associate Professor, School of Social Work, Rutgers University, New Jersey.

Wendy Glockner Kates, Ph.D., is a practitioner at the Kennedy Institute Family Center, Baltimore, Maryland.

Rebecca L. Johnson, Ph.D., is a practitioner at the Kennedy Institute Family Center, Baltimore, Maryland.

Mary W. Rader, M.S.W., is a practitioner at the Kennedy Institute Family Center, Baltimore, Maryland.

Frederick H. Strieder, Ph.D., is a practitioner at the Kennedy Institute Family Center, Baltimore, Maryland.

Shirley B. Schlosberg is Director of the Prevention Program, Parsons Child and Family Center, Albany, New York.

Richard M. Kagan is Director of Research, Quality Assurance and Training, Parsons Child and Family Center, Albany, New York.

Leonard J. Woods, M.S.W., is Supervisor, Alternative Program Associates, Family Therapy Unit, Pittsburgh, Pennsylvania.

Judith A.B. Lee is Associate Professor, New York University School of Social Work.

Susan J. Rosenthal is Supervising Social Worker, Victim Services Agency, Bronx, New York.

Mark S. Umbreit, Ph.D., is Assistant Professor, School of Social Work, University of Minnesota, Minneapolis, Minnesota.

Sally Johnson is a locum Social Worker for Wiltshire County Council.

Naomi Golan, Ph.D., is an Associate Professor, School of Social Work, University of Haifa, Haifa, Israel.

Manuel R. Gomez is at Florida International University, North Miami, Florida.

Anthony J. Marsella is in the Department of Psychology, University of Hawaii, Honolulu.

Judith Ann Schwartz, M.S.W., is a graduate student at Smith College School for Social Work.

Donald E. Gelfand is Professor at the School of Social Work and Community Planning, University of Maryland, Baltimore, Maryland.

Donald V. Fandetti is Associate Professor at the School of Social Work and Community Planning, University of Maryland, Baltimore, Maryland.

Ben A. Orcutt, D.S.W., is a Professor and Chairperson of the Doctoral Program, School of Social Work, the University of Alabama.

Dennis A. Bagarozzi, Ph.D., is on the staff of the Department of Family and Child Development, Kansas State University, Manhattan, Kansas.

Elizabeth Herman McKamy is a Psychiatric Social Worker, After-Care Services, the C.F. Menniger Memorial Hospital, Topeka, Kansas.

Francis J. Turner, D.S.W., is Dean, Faculty of Social Work, Wilfrid Laurier University, Waterloo, Ontario, Canada.

Patricia Sermabeikian, M.S.W., is Mental Health Coordinator, Barnert Hospital, Paterson, New Jersey, and Adjunct Lecturer, Rutgers University School of Social Work, New Brunswick, New Jersey.

Lita Linzer Schwartz, Ph.D., is a Professor at Pennsylvania Sate University, Ogontz Campus, Abington, Pennsylvania.

Florence W. Kaslow, Ph.D., is a Professor at Hahneman Medical College, Department of Mental Health Sciences, Philadelphia, Pennsylvania.

Arnold C. Bloch is Coordinator, Cult Clinic, Jewish Family Service of Los Angeles and is in private practice.

Ron Shor is a doctoral student, School of Social Work, University of Southern California and Social Worker, Jewish Big Brothers of Los Angeles, Los Angeles, California.

Alison Solomon is Coordinator, WomenReach, Jewish Family and Children's Service of Philadelphia, Pennsylvania.

E. Daniel Edwards is an Assistant Professor and Director of the American Indian Social Work Program, Utah.

Margie E. Edwards is a Professor, Graduate School of Social Work, University of Utah, Salt Lake City, Utah.

Donna R. Weaver is a Social Worker, Child Service and Family Counselling Center, Atlanta, Georgia.

May Tung, Ph.D., is in private practice in San Francisco, California.

Jeanne B. Robinson, Ph.D., is Lecturer, School of Social Services Administration, University of Chicago, Chicago, Illinois.

John A. Brown is Professor, School of Social Work, San Jose State University, San Jose, California.

Diane Drachman, D.S.W., is Associate Professor, University of Connecticut, School of Social Work, West Hartford, Connecticut.

Jon K. Matsuoka, Ph.D., is Assistant Professor, School of Social Work, University of Hawaii, Honolulu, Hawaii.

Sanford Schwartz, Ph.D., is Assistant Professor, Virginia Commonwealth University School of Social Work, Richmond, Virginia.

Herman Wood, M.S.W., is Director, Interstate Court Service, St. Louis, Missouri.

Anne Worral is lecturer at the Department of Applied Social Studies and Social Work at the University of Keele.

M.J. Cree is Visiting Fellow in the Department of Social Work, University of Canterbury, New Zealand, and Director of the Prison Aftercare Project.

J.A. Hoffman is Research Officer to the Prison Aftercare Project, University of Canterbury, New Zealand.

D.N. Riley is Senior Psychologist, Department of Justice and Consultant to the Prison Aftercare Project, University of Canterbury, New Zealand.

Nancy R. Vosler, Ph.D., is Assistant Professor, The George Warren Brown School of Social Work, Washington University, St. Louis, Missouri.

Madeleine R. Stoner is at the University of Southern California.

Gill Stewart is a Lecturer in Social Work and Social Policy in the Department of Applied Social Science at Lancaster University.

John Stewart is a Lecturer in Social Policy in the Department of Applied Social Science at Lancaster University.

Corinne Dufka is a Social Worker, Socorro Luterano Salvadoreno, San Salvador, El Salvador.

Burt Shachter, Ed.D., is Professor, School of Social Work, New York University, New York, New York.

Leona Grossman, M.P.H., M.S.W., is Director, Social Work Department, Michael Reese Hospital and Medical Center, Chicago, Illinois.

PART I

BIOPSYCHOSOCIAL DEVELOPMENTAL STAGES

Since social work is a profession committed to the healthy development of the human person from the first moment of life until death, it is fitting that the first section of this edition continues to focus on what we have so long called the "ages and stages" of development. The understanding of where our client or clients are from the perspective of psychological and social development has always been a key factor in the diagnostic and therapeutic components of practice. Indeed, for decades we have and continue to structure many of our programs and services along the various stages of human development. An integral part of all social work curricula includes some type of core course or sequence of courses that address this spectrum of human developmental stages. Where many of such sequences of course vary is in the content and perspective of what is to be taught.

In reviewing possible articles for inclusion in this edition, it was evident that we still continue to emphasize the need to understand this vast body of knowledge in as thorough and precise a way as is possible. However, we now do this with a growing awareness of the need to be careful about over-generalizing about the specificity of each stage. We are all much more aware of the extent to which we have tended to universalize our knowledge of developmental stages from a more narrow cultural perspective than is appropriate. As our knowledge of how variations in development occur in different parts of the world, perhaps the only thing about which we can be sure is that people are born very young and get older as the years go by. For example, it may well be that adolescence, important as it is in much practice in this part of the world, may be a life stage that does not have the same relevance, if indeed it exists at all, in some other parts of the world. If so, we may have to focus much more attention on the stage of young adulthood, which we have scarcely addressed in our literature.

Nevertheless, some generalizations can be made about these stages, and it is these data that we are trying to bring into our practice's purview.

Understandably, much of our literature focuses on problems in various developmental stages—on what goes wrong—rather than on normal and healthy development. For example, with our growing understanding of the prevalence of serious child abuse and neglect, we have produced a wealth of literature about this and other problems, and much less on normal and healthy childhood.

In this part we have tried to include a spectrum of articles that focus primarily on the stage of development itself rather than on what goes wrong in it, although understandably this was not fully possible. Inevitably some material addresses problem-influenced developmental stages. In such instances we tried to include articles that comment on the problem area from an understanding of healthy development.

Unlike earlier editions, in this part we did not include role-specific topics such as the student, marriage, parent, sibling, etc. Rather, we only included articles that touch on the stages through which we all are presumed to pass, separating out role issues for a different section.

Although it is understandable that in our writings we do focus more on what goes wrong than on how healthy development is fostered, it would be incorrect to overstate this. As we noted in the third edition, there is an even greater appreciation that such an important stage as adolescence or old age can be, and indeed should be, healthy and satisfying periods of life. It is wrong to correlate these periods with pathology, as we have tended to in the past.

As well, we were pleased to note in the literature a growing interest in understanding adulthood as an important and ongoing stage of growth and change, and not just as the end result of what happened in the earlier years. Thus, we were able to locate and include more articles on adulthood as a process from young adulthood through the frail elderly period.

Always our stress in diagnosis needs to be not only on what is wrong with our clients from a developmental perspective but as well on what their strengths are. In addition, we need to look for healthy patterns of functioning and build upon these. Always our goal is to seek to understand the complex yet patterned ways in which persons move through these stages of development in all parts of the world. Our goal in this search is to learn to tap these understandings of growth to assist others who are having difficulties to achieve and progress.

In conclusion, the stages of human development as a diagnostic variable requiring specific therapeutic consideration remain an important but certainly not exclusive part of the assessment process. Extended practice experience has clearly demonstrated patterns in behaviors and problems requiring specific and predictable treatment approaches in various stages of human life. It is also clear, and each author reminds us, that as knowledge of our client expands, and as our interventive plan emerges and is modified, a variety of other variables must be considered.

In recent years we have greatly enriched our specific understanding of many aspects of the stages of human development. As our knowledge has increased so has our awareness that there are many aspects of this dimension that as clinicians we have just begun to understand and address.

THE YOUNG CHILD

CHAPTER 1

QUALIFICATIONS AND TASKS OF THE THERAPIST IN GROUP THERAPY WITH CHILDREN

Leslie Rosenthal

A discussion of the tasks of the therapist in group therapy with children is akin to considering the varied responsibilities of a parent in a family. Within the family parental tasks will vary with the age of the children and their physical and emotional capacities at the different stages of development. The parent's life history, cultural, subcultural, and socio-economic affiliations will also shape the formulation and execution of these responsibilities. The assignments the therapist undertakes will be shaped by the age level of the group members and the structure and setting of the specific group modality he is using. The manner in which he carries out these tasks will be conditioned by his background, training, theoretical affiliations, and his life history.

In activity group therapy with latency youngsters, the therapist presents himself as accepting, nonlimiting, and primarily neutral. He seeks to create a group climate which is permissive, tolerant, friendly, and hospitable. With younger children, the therapist, mindful of their lesser controls and greater susceptibility to contagion, would be less permissive and would balance freedom of expression with appropriate restraints. In interview group therapy with young adolescents, the therapist orients himself more toward the center of the group's emotional network. Here he becomes, much more than in activity group therapy, an active and engaged participant as he questions, guides, becomes the object of negative transference, interprets, and seeks to facilitate the attainment of insight. Obviously, the very important differences in the ego structure of children at different ages makes differential treatment imperative.

Reprinted from *Clinical Social Work Journal*, Vol. 5, No. 3 (1977), pp. 191–199, by permission of the author and the publisher, Human Sciences Press.

There are however certain basic tasks which face the therapist in any group treatment endeavor with children. These are (1) that he know children; (2) that he be an individual therapist; (3) that he be a group therapist, one who can select the right members for the right group and utilize the therapeutic potential of the group setting for the benefit of all the members; and (4) that he know the child in himself.

KNOWING CHILDREN

The therapist's understanding of children is founded upon the inescapable realities of their physical and psychological incompleteness. He recognizes the child's relatively weak ego organization and the limits of its capacity to mediate between his inner and outer worlds. He is attuned to the primarily narcissistic quality of the child's libidinal functioning with its attendant self-indulgence, impulsivity, and strivings for omnipotence. He is aware of the inadequate protective barriers against excessive stimulation and the weakness of the child's emotional insulation. He sees that the child's capacities for repression are undeveloped as are his abilities to effectively sublimate; hence the more exposed nature of his unconscious. He understands that the child's identifications are labile, fluid, ambivalent, and malleable and that his capacity for change and reintegration is considerably greater than that of adults. The therapist's grasp of the emotionality of children would encompass the child's drive for motoric activity, which affords satisfaction of his impelling needs for play and the release of aggression. We may note that each of the children's group therapies devised and conceptualized by Slavson have sought to meet this maturational need for motor activity as a form of release, expression, and communication. Most of all he is related to the child's vulnerability and his urgent need for support and growth, thus enhancing emotional contact with significant others.

When working with adolescents in group therapy, our group therapist would have a consistent realization of their deep sense of incompleteness, their exquisite sensitivity to anxiety and emotional discomfort, and their compelling need to defend against feelings of inadequacy and damage. Alert to their emotional volatility and their propensity to swiftly convert impulse into action, he sets a high priority on helping group members put into language as early as possible their negative, skeptical, suspicious, and anxious feelings toward the group and himself. He is assured that this expression of negative feeling is the most effective deterrent to precipitous withdrawal from the group. He is alert to adolescents' sensitivities to premature (and too vigorous) attempts to establish contact and closeness or to efforts to help them and know them before they are ready to be helped and to be known. He is therefore prepared to curb his therapeutic zeal; to frustrate his own wishes for greater intimacy with his group members; to curb his impulses to re-enter his own adolescence by seeking emotional proximity to his adolescent patients (and by joining them as a peer in their struggles with authority).

BEING AN INDIVIDUAL THERAPIST

Given a basic appreciation by the developmental norms of childhood as related to treatment, what then are the tasks and qualifications of the group therapist? The first is that he be an *individual* therapist. Like individual psychotherapy, group therapy has as its *raison d'être* the benefit of the individual. It involves the understanding of individuals concurrent with the understanding and therapeutic exploitation of those forces and emotional currents which emerge when three or more individuals come together in the therapeutic group. The interest in the individual begins necessarily in the selection process where understanding of his dynamics is requisite to an evaluation of suitability for group treatment. Knowledge of the unique dynamics of the individual prior to his entry into the group is also essential to the formulation of a group treatment plan geared to his defensive structure and resistive patterns. If the prospective group member is a withdrawn and guarded child, should he be invited by the group therapist to participate and express himself? Would this invitation be gratefully received and enhance his self-image? Or would it be perceived as a demand for achievement or as a destructive maneuver by the adult to expose the child's weakness? If the youngster enters the meeting room silently with averted eyes, is he hoping for a warmly inviting greeting from the adult or is he asking that his hostility be accepted and that the therapist forbear from imposing the unwanted burden of his (the therapist's) positive feelings upon him. The indicated therapeutic response resides of course in the child's life history.

The principle of individualization geared to the nuclear dynamics of group members can be illustrated further. One boy, in marked oedipal rivalry with his father, is struggling to saw a long piece of wood. He neither requests nor receives any help from the therapist. Later in the session another member is in a similar situation and the therapist walks over and quietly holds the wood steady for the boy. This second youngster's father left the home when he was two and by his act the group therapist is supplying the maturational ingredient of active paternal interest. It is axiomatic that knowledge of the dynamics of the child's very first group, his family, is of significant predictive value to the group therapist; he knows that the role thrust upon the child in his family by psychologic exigency will be reenacted in the group family. Thus, the group member who was physically or emotionally expelled from his own family will invariably court expulsion from the group (a resistance which unfortunately all too often succeeds). The group therapist forearmed with study and comprehension of each of the individuals who compose his group is less likely to be caught off guard by the profound power of the repetition compulsion.

As a necessary prelude to group therapy the therapist will have had sound experience in treating individuals and thereby encountering the whole spectrum of human feeling within the intense and undiluted confines of the individual therapy setting. He will have developed a respect for defenses and an appreciation of their vital protective function. He will be prepared for the initial resistances of the individual members. He will know that these were initially conceived out of urgent psychological necessity and that these resistances represent the member's attempts to maintain his equilibrium under the stress of family living. He will thus value resistance in that it conveys, in indirect but richly emotional form, the life story of the child. As an individual therapist he will grasp the full import of Freud's statement that in its essense, resistance is nothing more than the character of the child.

SELECTING THE GROUP

The next task of the group therapist is to put together a viable group. Appropriate selection presupposes a clear appreciation of the very significant differences between the individual and group treatment arenas and the requirements, advantages, and limitations of each in relation to specific patient etiologies, character formations, and resistive patterns. Proper selection involves choice of those patients who possess that degree of ego strength essential to constructive group membership. Fundamental to this process is the recognition that the group setting involves certain stresses and imposes certain demands that are not inherent aspects of the dyadic treatment relation: the ever-present possibility of exposure to sibling hostility, the unavoidable necessity of sharing therapist, time, and in some settings food with other members, and the much greater degree of emotional stimulation. Thus, basic to the composition of a therapeutic group is the therapist's awareness that the child's capacity to enter and assimilate the world of multiple relations is based upon that which happens or does not happen in that first crucial dyad of child and mother. This embraces careful appraisal of the capacities of those children with marked oral deprivation to endure the built-in frustrations of the group setting. The therapist will also prudently evaluate the ability of impulsive children with minimal inner controls to withstand the permissive setting of activity group therapy where regressive and aggressive impulses can be swiftly mobilized and contagiously intensified throughout the group.

The establishment of group viability is also predicated upon group balance, which calls for a therapeutic equilibrium amongst the diverse personalities of the group, particularly with respect to the aggression and withdrawal polarities. Slavson has a clear statement here:

> The ability of any given group to withstand or absorb hostility and aggression has definite limits. Each individual and each aggregate of people has its own capacity to tolerate aggression or hostility density. When these limits are exceeded in groups, tension and anxiety set in which are expressed in hyperactivity or wanton destructiveness. (Slavson, 1948a, p. 318)

BEING A GROUP THERAPIST

Another task of the clinician who undertakes to simultaneously treat a number of individuals is that he be a *group* therapist. This involves the voluntary surrender of the therapeutic monopoly the therapist holds in individual treatment as the sole object of transference and identification. Being a group therapist embraces a readiness to yield some of his own therapeutic omnipotence as he accepts the concept that maximal therapeutic dividends are attained from the children's contact with each other. In a description of the role of the Activity Group Therapist, Slavson (1948b) stated, "He strives to remain outside the emotional flux of the group so as to allow a maximum interpersonal and intra-group emotional and physical activity" (p. 203). This is no easy task. One group of boys demonstrated their developing feelings of autonomy, competence, and mutual acceptance by busily working together on building a wagon at the far end of the room. The therapist described intense feelings of loneliness and loss in this situation.

Another aspect of being a group therapist is the capacity, usually developed with experience, to recognize and deal with subgroup and group resistances as they emerge. In a mixed group of adolescents, Jennie for several sessions regaled her fellow members with vivid and explicit descriptions of her sexual activity. The group-wide atmosphere of excitement and titillation and the members' overt and implicit encouragement for Jennie to continue labelled this an obvious group resistance on the level of exhibitionism-voyeurism. At the next session the therapist asked the group, "How would you all like Jennie to excite you today?" The anxiety generated by this question raised the developmental level of group functioning from one of perverse behavior to the healthier stage of neurotic functioning. The group members were then able to seriously explore with Jennie the self-damaging ramifications of her behavior.

Another example of successful resolution of a group problem is found in Slavson's first book, *Introduction to Group Therapy* (1943). In a group of thirteen-year-olds, two boys began to fight. Soon the entire membership had paired off in fights. The therapist said, "I think we'll have to get a license from the Boxing Commission for this club." The boys burst into laughter and the fighting stopped at once.

The group-oriented therapist is also aware that certain members can act as spokesmen for the whole group on crucial issues and can epitomize the major group concern with important constellations of feeling. One critical and argumentative member may represent the group's hostility to the therapist. An immature member may voice infantile yearnings for the others. An overstimulated youngster may therapeutically express feelings of sexuality for the more constricted numbers. The value of the group spokesman is reflected in this vignette:

The therapist of a girls' activity group was impatiently eager to convert the group to an interview group where talk would supplant play. In a session when this plan was being discussed, one girl began to sing a refrain from a popular song, "I don't want to grow up to go with a boy and be his toy." The other members began to hum along with her. The perceptive group therapist understood the message, relaxed her efforts, gave the group more time and subsequently a more successful transition was achieved.

Having formed the group the therapist faces the task of preserving it as a therapeutic entity and protecting the treatment of its members. To accomplish this he assigns highest priority to the resolution of group-destructive and treatment-destructive resistance. When one or more members engage in behavior that threatens continuation of treatment or when a member is exposed to potentially damaging contact, the group therapist becomes active to protect the integrity of the group family. The following illustration of a treatment-threatening resistance is drawn from an activity-interview group of 13- and 14-year-old boys which met in a school setting:

During a brief silence, Fred turned to John and asked when he is bringing in the dollar. John looked frightened and his voice quivered as he said, "I don't owe you any money." Fred retorted, "We made a bet playing baseball, remember?" Fred then warned John to bring the money tomorrow or he would get him after school, adding "maybe with my knife." John winced, said he was not bringing any money and that he might not come to school for a month.

The therapist asked, "What's going on here? It sounds like blackmail." Fred maintained that the money was owed to him, even if John had not agreed to the bet. The therapist asked Fred how what he was trying to do with John was connected to the purpose of the group. Fred looked embarrassed and said he didn't know. Another member, Kevin, said Fred was trying to con the other members instead of helping them. Fred turned to John and said he was only kidding anyway. John looked relieved.

In a subsequent session Fred talked about his father always cheating him and never keeping his promises to him. Thus, the therapist protected John's treatment and helped Fred enter treatment.

The participation of a whole group in a treatment-destructive resistance is illustrated in a natural group of predelinquent girls, which was referred as a unit by the school. The group was seen on an exploratory basis in meetings with an experienced group therapist. These several sessions were marked by vivid descriptions of acts of sadistic aggression and perverse sexuality. It was then discovered that group members met prior to sessions to plan a contrived agenda designed to shock the therapist. When exploration by the group therapist revealed little interest in understanding themselves or each other and continuing wishes to defeat authority, sessions were terminated by the group therapist. Subsequently several of the girls were able to use individual treatment constructively. In this case the task of the therapist was to evaluate the treatability of the group.

KNOWING THE CHILD WITHIN YOURSELF

As a final task the therapist should know the child within himself and be aware of the ways in which this inner child can interfere with his functioning appropriately as a group therapist. For example, a young therapist, unaware of his own deep fear of groups, in the course of one year rejected as unsuitable every single referral made to his proposed group. One therapist gratified his own unconscious craving for excitement by assembling a group composed exclusively of exhibitionistic and provocative youngsters who kept each other and the therapist in a constant state of titillation. Another reenacted his own sibling hostility as he permitted one very aggressive boy to drive three consecutive new members out of the group. A male therapist of a coed adolescent group paid scant attention as the boys drifted to the periphery of the group and then one by one dropped out in the face of his far greater interest in helping the female members.

The wish for a happy and serene group family is familiar to all of us who have worked with groups. In pursuit of this familial Eden one therapist intervened swiftly to settle any dispute, conflict, or disagreement amongst her group members by a toss of a coin. I recall an incident from my own practice of activity group therapy in the early 1950's. Morris, a withdrawn and suspicious boy, had delayed coming to the table for refreshments and was the last to sit down. I then observed that there was no cake left for Morris. Before he could utter a word I cut my own slice of cake in two and placed half on his plate. Morris accepted the cake silently but left most of it uneaten. Here the therapist's own need to maintain fair play and his overidentification with the youngster impelled him to precipitous intervention which deprived the child and the group of the opportunity to deal with the situation. An additional source of induced feeling in me in this situation was the presence in the observation room of Morris' individual therapist and her supervisor.

Impressed with the intense feelings aroused in myself and in my colleagues by our encounters with activity groups I wrote:

> The group is particularly fertile ground for testing the stability and maturity of the therapist. There is constant probing for his blindspots and the likelihood of reactivation of past traumata in his own familial relations is ever present. Inherent in the structure of activity group therapy are situations which activate and play upon the therapist's own feeling constellations around givingness, frustration, authority, aggression and passivity-activity. (Rosenthal, 1953, p. 440)

In a paper on the qualities of the group therapist, Martin Grotjahn (1971) stated:

> He should consider himself as his own favorite patient, one who has to learn as long as he lives. This thirst for knowledge, for truth and for learning belongs to his basic qualifications. (p. 757)

We are indebted to our groups for propelling us further along the lifelong road toward truth and greater maturity, and we are deeply indebted to S. R. Slavson for providing the stage for these encounters—so healing of children and so rewarding to their therapists.

REFERENCES

Grotjahn, M. The qualities of the group therapist. In H. Kaplan & B. Sadock (Eds.), *Comprehensive group therapy*. Baltimore: Williams & Wilkins, 1971.

Rosenthal, L. Countertransference in activity group therapy. *International Journal of Group Psychotherapy*, 1953, 3, 431–440.

Slavson, S. R. *An introduction to group therapy*. New York: Commonwealth Fund, 1943.

Slavson, S. R. Play group therapy for young children. *The Nervous Child*, 1948, 7, 318–326.(a)

Slavson, S. R. Group therapy in child care and child guidance. *Jewish Social Service Quarterly*, 1948, 25, 203–210.(b)

CHAPTER 2

AN OVERVIEW OF ADOLESCENT DEVELOPMENT, BEHAVIOR, AND CLINICAL INTERVENTION

Elaine Rubenstein

A dolescence is a time of rapid change, physiologically, cognitively, psychologically, and socially. Although adolescents tend to be grouped together in the popular press and in the eyes of the public, this developmental stage is not a single period. It is more clinically useful to divide adolescence into three developmental stages—early, middle, and late—each with its own characteristics. The changes in each of these stages occur at different rates and at different ages for each individual. Gender differences cause girls to enter puberty earlier than boys and to become emotionally mature earlier than their male peers. In addition, life circumstances, such as economic conditions, cultural influences, and family composition and interaction, clearly have an impact on individual development. Nevertheless, some overall patterns are important to keep in mind. This article highlights the important features of this life stage, presents an overview of adolescent problems, and discusses some clinical issues that have particular importance for professionals working with teenagers.

ADOLESCENT DEVELOPMENT
Early Adolescence

This first stage of adolescence usually occurs between the ages of 10 and 14 years. At this point, the young person begins to focus on independence and identity issues. Biological changes provoke concerns with body image, and the individual is increasingly

Reprinted from *Families in Society,* Vol. 72, No. 4 (1991), pp. 220–225, by permission of the publisher, Families International, Inc.

11

concerned with the peer group's values and codes of behavior. Teenagers become less interested in their parents' activities and begin to test their own ideas and values against those of their families. At this age, conflict may revolve around issues such as homework, responsibilities at home, and choice of friends. Teenagers are preoccupied with their physical development, particularly how they look compared with their friends, which often produces a high degree of narcissistic self-involvement. Young adolescents can spend long periods in front of a mirror looking for both flaws and reassurance. Along with their anxiety about appearance, adolescents begin to become sexually curious and need more privacy. Persons in this age group tend to have same-sex heroes and usually travel in groups (Conger, 1973).

Cognitive development dovetails with psychosocial development. Thinking at this stage is usually characterized in concrete terms. What is real and important happens in the present. It is very difficult for young people at this age to think about the future; they tend to think about events in terms of their own experience rather than hypothetically. Their ability to think in abstract terms is usually just beginning to develop. Egocentrism is at its peak at this stage. Young teenagers often have an "imaginary audience" and feel that they are on stage and the center of attention. They may be extremely self-conscious, which reinforces their need to fit in with the crowd. At the same time the young person feels special and unique. They may feel that no one understands them. They may also feel invulnerable to the usual problems in the world, which can lead to risk-taking behaviors (e.g., having unprotected sex) (Elkind, 1967).

Middle Adolescence

This stage usually occurs between 15 and 17 years of age. Independence and identity issues are highlighted and conflicts around these issues may reach their highest level. Teenagers may reject parental values (although they often return to embrace them in later years), may test limits (curfew, alcohol use, homework, and parties), and often feel the need to make independent decisions despite poor judgment and impulsivity. The advice and feedback of peers become very important, and the peer culture itself is very influential in determining a life-style that may or may not be in the teen's best interests. Many teenagers begin to have one-to-one heterosexual relationships at this time. They are usually more comfortable with members of the opposite sex than they were during early adolescence, and often more give and take occurs in their relationships. Finally, because most of their physical changes have already taken place, most teenagers become less concerned about their changing bodies but more concerned about attractiveness to the opposite sex and the meaning of masculinity and femininity in their particular culture (Conger, 1973).

Cognitive development proceeds with the teenager's ability to think abstractly and plan ahead. This ability is important in planning for high school completion and employment or further education. In addition, the adolescent is better able to perceive the relation between present actions and future consequences than he or she was at an earlier stage. This has important implications for the young person learning to take responsibility for his or her own behavior, especially in high-risk areas such as sexual activity, driving, and substance use.

Late Adolescence

This stage usually occurs between the ages of 18 and 21. Although independence and identity issues may not be fully resolved, many persons at this age are able to function independently. Although they may be able to make their own decisions, they are also able to listen to family advice and use it when appropriate, which helps to decrease family tensions and represents a return, in part, to family values. Identity issues and vocational or career plans tend to be more clear. Peers continue to be important, but the young person is able to evaluate peer influence and opinions. Finally, relationships with the opposite sex are usually more intimate and these relationships become as important as those with the family of origin.

Abstract thought is usually fully developed at this time. Past gains are consolidated, and the older adolescent focuses on and plans for the future. Both short-term and long-term goals are now achievable.

ADOLESCENT BEHAVIOR

Although adolescence can be a time of emotional highs and lows, most teenagers go through this period relatively well, even with their predictable experimentation and risk-taking behavior (Offer, Marcus, & Offer, 1970). Clearly, a young person's reserves of self-esteem and coping abilities, along with his or her support systems from earlier developmental periods, play important roles in influencing adolescent behavior. However, significant problems that do arise are not simply "outgrown" but may indicate a real need for help. Adolescents today face serious pressures and problems and they and their families are often without the resources to resolve them.

Two recent national surveys tried to assess the current state of American youth. The first survey presented information on the status of youth aged 16 to 24 (W. T. Grant Foundation, 1987) and the second surveyed more than 11,000 eighth and tenth graders in more than 200 public and private schools across the country (American School Health Association, 1989). The data in the following sections are drawn from these two studies.

The background against which many adolescent problems develop includes the fact that one-fifth of children younger than 18 live in poverty. This problem is compounded by homelessness and an increasing number of households headed by single women. Fourteen percent of children 10 to 14 years of age have no health insurance, further restricting access to resources. However, middle-class youth are not immune to problems. Most of the issues discussed here cut across economic lines, although they are certainly complicated by conditions of poverty.

Substance Use

Substance use is a serious problem among teenagers. Cigarette smoking is declining among adolescent males but not among females. More than one-half of eighth graders and two-thirds of tenth graders report having tried cigarettes. Approximately 80% reported having tried alcohol. About one-fourth of eighth graders and more than one-third of tenth graders reported having had five or more drinks on one occasion during the previous two weeks. Often peer pressure to drink is intense, and at many teen parties soft drinks are not available. Parents themselves may sometimes supply the alcohol at their son's or daughter's party.

Approximately 1 in 10 teenagers had smoked marijuana during the previous month, about 1 in 15 had tried cocaine, and 1 in 5 eighth and tenth graders had sniffed glue. Although drug use among high school seniors has declined nationally, high school dropouts are still at risk for substance abuse. Some drug use may start as self-medication, arising out of boredom, a wish to feel better about themselves, depression, or impulsivity.

Injuries

Unintentional injuries are the leading cause of death in the 15- to 24-year-old age group. Motor vehicle accidents account for more than 70% of these deaths. Adolescents are at high risk for injuries in car accidents for several reasons. More than half of students questioned reported that they did not wear seat belts the last time they rode in a car. In addition, more than 40% of tenth graders and approximately one-third of eighth graders reported that during the past month they rode with a driver who had used drugs or alcohol. Finally, impulsivity, risk-taking, and poor judgment, characteristics of adolescent development, do not add up to safe driving.

Violence

Violence is part of the lives of many teenagers. Violent crimes (rape, robbery, assault) occur at the highest rate among the 12-to-24 age group. This is true even for the youngest group, 12 to 15 years of age. Homicide is the leading cause of death for black males; approximately 77% of the teenagers surveyed reported that they had been in a fight in the past year. Approximately two-thirds had been robbed, threatened, or attacked at school in the past year. About one-fourth of the males reported that they had carried a knife to school at least once during the past year.

Sexuality, Pregnancy, and Childbearing

The onset of sexual activity is occurring at earlier ages. Approximately 50% of 15- to 19-year-old unmarried females and 70% of 17- to 21-year-olds have had sexual intercourse. Approximately 65% of males had experienced sexual intercourse at least once by age 18. Although progress has been made in promoting contraceptive use among sexually active teens, they are quite inconsistent in their use of effective birth control, again as a result of impulsivity, peer pressure, inability to plan ahead, and feelings of invulnerability. In addition, teenagers lack adequate knowledge about how their bodies function.

The teen pregnancy rate in the United States is the highest among developed countries. Since 1960, the number of births among 15- to 19-year-olds has dropped dramatically, but a similar decline has not been evident among teens 14 and younger. The younger the teen is at the time of first pregnancy, the more likely repeat pregnancies will occur. Approximately one-third of teenagers end their pregnancies in abortion.

Fewer young mothers are marrying today because of a pregnancy than was true in past years. Regardless of race, young women who are poor are three to four times as likely to become unwed mothers than are more affluent teens. The outcomes of a teen pregnancy are well known: the mother is likely to become a school dropout resulting in poor educational attainment and a reliance on public welfare support. She is likely to have subsequent pregnancies while unmarried and is at risk for delivering a low birthweight baby.

Depression and Suicide

Depression is a serious problem among youth. Depression may be evident in declining grades, loss of friends, self-destructive acting-out behaviors, eating and sleep disturbances, and lack of interest in or motivation for activities. Severe suicidal ideation increases in puberty and is correlated with severe depression. Within the past 25 years, the rate of adolescent suicide has more than doubled and is currently the third leading cause of death among 15- to 24-year-olds. One in seven teens reports attempting suicide. More than 30% of girls and 15% of boys say they often feel sad and hopeless. More than half of the students said that it would be difficult for them to tell a teacher or school counselor about a potentially suicidal friend.

Sexually Transmitted Diseases

The number of teens infected with a sexually transmitted disease (STD) is increasing. Approximately 2.5 million teenagers are infected annually. The majority of teens surveyed held misconceptions about how to prevent an STD, and approximately 75% were unsure about whether their parents had to be informed for them to obtain treatment (this requirement varies from state to state).

The most serious concerns regarding such diseases involve AIDS. Currently, approximately one-fifth of those with AIDS are in their 20s. Therefore, many were exposed to the virus in their teens. Most adolescents know that AIDS is transmitted by sexual intercourse and IV needles and most also know that condoms offer some protection and believe that they should be used. However, knowledge does not necessarily affect behavior, especially during this developmental period.

School

School is the natural environment for the teenager. However, the current school dropout rate is alarming. Students from poor families are three to four times as likely to drop out than are those from more advantaged families. In 1986, almost 40% of poor, white individuals ages 20 and 21 had not completed high school and almost 32% of poor blacks in the same age range had dropped out of school. Although the reasons for dropping out of school are complex and beyond the scope of this article, clearly the future of these adolescents is bleak with regard to earning capacity and occupational satisfaction.

CLINICAL WORK WITH ADOLESCENTS
Assessment

Clinical work with adolescents requires a developmental perspective. Clinicians need to assess the developmental age of the adolescent, recognizing that this does not always match chronological age. Teens with wide discrepancies in one or several developmental areas may face special problems. For example, those who become physically mature early are often faced with unrealistic expectations from others because they appear older or more mature. Conversely, those who lag behind physically may experience problems with peers and body image.

Another clinical issue that is particularly relevant for adolescents is distinguishing between dysfunctional behavior and normative development. For example, how does one distinguish excessive impulsivity and risk-taking behavior indicative of serious problems from normative experimentation with new behaviors? This issue is further complicated by the effects of stress, which often cause regressive behavior. Is the clinician observing the teenage client's true functioning capacity or is the teenager functioning at an earlier level because of stressful life circumstances that mask greater capacities?

Both of these issues can be addressed by taking a careful developmental history with particular focus on early independence/separation experiences, peer relations, peer culture, school adjustment, academic success or failure, family relationships, family economic standing, reactions to limit-setting, and symptom duration and intensity. In addition, the adolescent's strengths and typical coping mechanisms need to be assessed. A thorough review of current functioning in these areas, including the teenager's affect during the interview and how much he or she is interested in getting help, will complete the picture. Information from outside resources, such as teachers, school counselors, physicians, or previous therapists, is also essential.

How does the clinician obtain this information? When one is working with adults, the client provides the information. With young children, the parent usually provides the relevant information. With adolescents, however, obtaining relevant historical and clinical information depends on the age of the teenager. With young adolescents, the clinician should work closely with the parent or responsible adult while making the adolescent feel that he or she is part of the process. At the outset, the teen can be told what to expect during the assessment phase of treatment, including who will be seen and what information will be sought. The clinician can begin with an individual session with the teenager, first building a relationship, then exploring the adolescent's view of the problem. This can be followed by work with the parent or responsible adult and finally with the parent and adolescent together. This model allows the teenager the opportunity to be heard and to begin to form a relationship with the therapist while allowing the adult(s) to provide essential information and to be heard as well. All of this can be accomplished in the first session if it is extended to at least one and a half hours. However, the pacing may need to be slowed if the adolescent is reluctant to engage in treatment.

The situation may be less clear for older adolescents, who require more autonomy. In such instances, it is often best to start with the teenager him- or herself for one session, while acknowledging the need to involve the adult(s) early in the process. The extent of parental or adult involvement will depend on the age of the adolescent, whether the person is still living at home, the nature of the problem, and whether others should be involved (boyfriend or girl friend, spouse, or roommate).

Interviewing and Special Intervention Strategies

As in most clinical situations, establishing trust in the relationship is critical. Rather than starting with the presenting problem, the clinician should initially encourage the adolescent to talk about less threatening topics, such as interests, friends, positive and negative aspects of school, and the family constellation. After the adolescent begins to feel more comfortable, more difficult issues relating to the presenting problem can be addressed. This approach is particularly useful with adolescents who resist help by refusing to discuss "the problem" and for whom the therapist represents yet another authority figure making demands.

The adolescent's cognitive development must be carefully assessed. For the younger adolescent, who thinks in concrete terms, questions about the future, especially early in the treatment process, are not useful except as a clue to his or her cognitive development. Language should be at the adolescent's level because adolescents often do not ask questions when something is unclear. The adolescent may be unable clearly to link present behavior with future consequences. Short-term goals work best, enabling the adolescent to feel a sense of accomplishment and encouraging him or her to work further. At the start, goals should be concrete (attend school every day, eat dinner with the family) before moving on to affective goals (feel less sad, be more self-confident and less anxious).

Although abstract thinking may often be expected from older teenagers, in practice they are not always capable of it. Again, a careful assessment will reveal cognitive development. Questions about future employment or educational plans, about how their present behavior may affect them later (use of contraception, completing homework assignments), and about their ability to take responsibility for their behavior will yield important information that enables the clinician to distinguish between chronological and developmental age.

Confidentiality

Confidentiality is a complex issue when working with adolescents. It is essential that the teenager trust the clinician if treatment is to progress. Although the therapist can ensure general confidentiality, he or she must indicate that in some situations a parent or responsible adult may need to be given important information. The clinician can agree to discuss such situations with the teenager first. In addition, the teenager might be given several choices about how the information is revealed. For example, the therapist can help the adolescent discuss the issue with his or her parent(s) through rehearsal and role playing or the therapist can discuss it with the parents in the presence of the adolescent. Issues that clearly need to be disclosed include possible suicidal or homicidal behavior. Issues such as drug or alcohol use, pregnancy, school truancy, or sexually transmitted disease are more problematic. The therapist must weigh confidentiality against disclosure in the best interest of the adolescent.

Confidentiality may be further complicated when one considers the age and developmental capabilities of the adolescent as well as the degree of parental involvement in treatment. For the younger adolescent, parental involvement is almost always indicated and the adolescent is at high risk for making impulsive decisions. Thus, with younger clients, the therapist may need to include the parent or responsible adult in situations that would remain confidential if the client were older.

The older teenager may be more resistant to disclosure of confidential material, depending on his or her maturity, coping abilities, and the seriousness of the problem. Disclosure may sometimes be delayed until the choice is clear or until the teen has worked through a particular problem. Despite resistance, the adolescent is often relieved when the information is disclosed.

Issues related to sexuality pose special problems. Laws vary from state to state regarding the rights of an adolescent to confidentiality, and the clinician must be aware of these laws. Many have emancipated-minor laws with respect to pregnancy, allowing the teenager to seek treatment without parental permission. Although keeping her pregnancy secret is usually not in her best interest, the teenager may elect to do so until it becomes physically obvious. Other issues protected by confidentiality in many states include access to contraception and treatment for sexually transmitted disease. The clinician must help the teenager with decisions about disclosure while remaining especially sensitive to the developmental age of the young person.

Self-Awareness

Clinical work with adolescents requires a high degree of self-awareness and self-observation on the part of the clinician because of the often provocative nature of adolescents' behavior. Adolescents are able to "push buttons" in areas where adults are especially vulnerable, either as a parent of a teenager or as a result of unresolved conflicts from one's own adolescence. Adolescents may act out their feelings in ways that disturb the therapist. For the clinician who sees him- or herself as an empathic individual, being viewed with hostility by a resistant teen can be quite disturbing. The possibility of countertransference is always present. Thus, clinicians must constantly examine their therapeutic relationship with adolescent clients. Supervision, consultation, and ongoing training are useful tools to this end.

CONCLUSION

Adolescents are an interesting and exciting client group to work with, although they pose special treatment and ethical dilemmas. The clinician must have a thorough understanding of adolescent development and behavior as well as an arsenal of assessment and treatment strategies geared to the young person's particular cognitive and psychosocial developmental stage. In addition, a high degree of self-awareness is needed in order to avoid clinical pitfalls.

REFERENCES

American School Health Association. (1989). *National Adolescent Student Health Survey*. Reston, VA: Association for the Advancement of Health Education and Society for Public Health Education.

Conger, J. J. (1973). *Adolescence and youth: Psychological development in a changing world*. New York: Harper and Row.

Elkind, D. (1967). Egocentrism in adolescence. *Child Development, 38*, 1025–1033.

Offer, D., Marcus, D., & Offer, J. (1970). A longitudinal study of normal adolescent boys. *American Journal of Psychiatry, 126*, 917–924.

W. T. Grant Foundation. (1987). *American youth: A statistical snapshot*. Washington, DC: Author.

YOUNG ADULTHOOD

CHAPTER 3

YOUNG ADULTHOOD

A Developmental Phase

Glen Clifford and Katharine Odin

It is a striking fact that in comparison to the rich body of systematic knowledge concerning child and adolescent development, there exist far fewer studies of normative development in adulthood. Developmental shifts following adolescence, incompletely articulated and understood within the literature, warrant closer and more systematic attention. Since it has already been made clear in psychoanalytic literature that childhood and adolescent behavior may best be understood within a developmental context (Hartmann, 1958), it becomes necessary to have a clearer understanding of the developmental stages affecting adulthood in order to have a more complete context for interpreting adult behavior.

This study focuses on early adulthood, specifically ages 25 to 35. It is based on the premise that young adulthood may constitute a distinct developmental phase during which phase-specific tasks are negotiated. It also assumes that ego growth and development may extend and continue beyond the earliest years of life. The literature does not provide a coherent view of this period, but only a fragmentary sense that during early adulthood there are significant changes in how the individual views himself. This study is designed to explore the nature of those changes, as well as generate a theoretical framework within which these changes might be understood.

THEORETICAL PERSPECTIVES

Erik Erikson's work on the eight ages of man contains a widely known developmental treatment of adulthood. His two stages of adulthood, the stage of Intimacy versus Isolation and the stage of Generativity versus Stagnation, are both probably relevant to the

Reprinted from *Smith College Studies in Social Work*, Vol. 44, No. 2 (February 1974), pp. 125–142, by permission of the publisher.

age period of this study. Erikson's epigenetic conception advances the view that mastery of the tasks specific to each earlier stage is crucial to the mastery of those in the stages that follow. Thus, the tasks of the stage of Intimacy, the capacity for fusing one's identity with another, for committing oneself to concrete affiliations and for developing the ethical strength to abide by such commitments, require an identity solid enough to risk such affiliations without overwhelming the ego.

Successful mastery of the tasks of the stage of Intimacy then leads into the stage of Generativity: "The ability to lose one's self in the meeting of bodies and minds leads to a gradual expansion of ego interests and to a libidinal investment in that which is being generated" (Erikson, 1963, 267). This shift requires that the individual create for himself a continuing giving of himself in a creative, caretaking and participatory way that helps him avoid stagnation (Erikson, 1963).

Erikson's description of this particular shift is brief and skeletal, and he provides little in the way of concrete descriptive analysis. What seems implied in his notion of the expansion of ego interests and shift in libidinal investment is a broadening and integration of the individual's self-image, in a way that would incorporate the products of his concrete affiliations, specifically his work and his family and all external representations thereof. If so, the change in self-image would in some way be mirrored in the individual's capacity for and participation in concrete affiliations.

Other clues about adult development derive from research. Gould and his associates, for example, studied a population of 524 adults ranging in age from 16 to over 60. The subjects were asked to rate a series of statements in the order of greatest importance. Curves for each statement were plotted on the basis of the average rank ordering for the 20 subjects of each age.

Findings pertinent to this study are the number changes in the curve around age 30 from a relatively stable baseline at 20 with a return to another stable baseline at 40. Gould characterizes these curves as demonstrative of two major shifts. "There is a gradual peeling away of the magical illusions of omnipotence and omnipotentiality, and there is an identification of the self with the family" (Gould, 1972, 42). Gould's conclusions seem to offer some documentation for Erikson's theoretical notions of the shift from Intimacy to Generativity. Increased identification with the family would seem to support Erikson's notion of the widening sphere of ego interests as a defining characteristic of the stage of Generativity.

Buhler, who has spent a lifetime collecting individual biographies of creative and everyday people, found that the phasic phenomena of the life cycle, as reflected in her biographical studies, could best be described as a three-phasic process:

(1) a growth period from birth until the organism is fully developed; (2) a stationary growth period during which the organism's power to maintain itself and develop is equal to the forces of decline; and (3) a last period of decline (Buhler, 1968, 13).

She points to age 25 as the age at which phase one shifts to phase two.

This phasic orientation is important to the present study primarily because of the implication that the individual around age 25 experiences a shift from becoming to being, a shift that seems unique to this stage of development. One can infer that such a shift encompasses the loss of a sense of unlimited potential, a sense that had afforded fantasies of omnipotentiality as referred to by Gould, in the face of the encounters with personal and social realities.

Of the literature that focuses on the specific phase of early adulthood, Wittenberg provides the most coherent and detailed examination of the beginning phase of early adulthood: postadolescence. His work, which pertains roughly to ages 20 to 25, provides a backdrop to the period studied in this project.

Wittenberg describes as one characteristic of postadolescence a self-image crisis, during which the individual experiences conflict between superego and ego ideals, which includes the concept of a pseudoideal, "the expression of grandiose and megalomanic strivings" (Wittenberg, 1968, 3). The task involves the striking of a balance between these forces with the ego in full control. He postulates that since the ego is assailed by this and many other conflicts in postadolescence, the ego is usually not in the best position to reach this reasonable compromise and the process of resolution continues beyond postadolescence.

Wittenberg also describes a crisis occasioned by the end of role playing, an activity of adolescence that helps to assimilate anxiety about the mastery of reality. What is demanded of the postadolescent is that he begin to take on a permanent role, to assert the struggle for a persistent experience of sameness and to deal with the superego and ego ideal conflicts. Wittenberg states that some element of mourning accompanies this attempt which involves the holding off of the inevitable recognition of reality limitations. The young adult must take on a permanent role "which is to be his and can no longer be changed without new and often painful anxiety in adult life" (Wittenberg, 1968, 26).

Some of the anxiety experienced by the termination of role playing is related to an emerging awareness of time continuity. This cognition, of the extension of time and the continuity of time into the future, brings about an awareness that the individual determines the way he uses the time ahead of him. According to Wittenberg, this awareness prompts the postadolescent toward long-term commitments (Wittenberg, 1968).

Wittenberg's conceptions seem coherent with Erikson's formulation of the tasks of the stage of Intimacy and could characterize the kinds of crises from which the population in this study were probably beginning to emerge.

The limited developmental literature on adulthood suggests that the late twenties and early thirties is a period during which the individual experiences a change in how he feels about himself and how he defines himself. This project was designed as an exploratory, impressionistic study of the nature and course of such changes. How do these changes relate to age? How are they affected by the individual's capacity for and participation in concrete affiliations, as suggested by Erikson? Is there an experience of mourning in this process as suggested by Wittenberg?

METHOD

Direct interviews of persons within the 25 to 35 age range were elected as a means for obtaining data. The persons within the age group interviewed were selectively chosen for reasons of availability and capacity for introspection. The sample consisted of thirty psychiatric residents, child fellows and social workers. Other social characteristics of the sample are given in the accompanying table. The findings of this study thus reflect a relatively small and restrictive sample: highly educated, psychologically oriented, professional people.

Utilizing a guide based on the notion derived from the literature that the individual between the ages of 25 and 35 experiences a change in how he feels about and defines himself, the authors structured the interviews to obtain descriptive and affective data on how each individual viewed himself at his present age. The interviews were relatively unstructured, opening with the question, "How does it feel to be your age?" Subjects were encouraged to respond spontaneously and associatively to the question.

During each interview, the authors listened both for the respondent's descriptive feelings about himself as well as the affect accompanying that description. Near the end of the interview each subject over 25 was asked how he would have answered the same question at age 25. This question was asked to provide a perspective on his present view of himself and to elicit data concerning changes since age 25. Each subject under 35 also was asked how he thought he might answer at age 35, so as to obtain information on his ideas about the future and their relation to his present reality. The interviews were approximately one hour long.

The authors jointly interviewed each subject, one having the responsibility for posing questions and following the process of the interview, and the other the responsibility for process notes. This method allowed two perceptions of the same interview in order to provide more objective and reliable observations.

Content analysis was the method used to analyze the data collected. Following the interviews, each author individually summarized each interview in terms of predominant tone, content themes and affect. Shifts from past to present, as well as future fantasies were noted. The individual summaries were then compared. Differences in the summaries were found to be primarily due to omission on the part of one of the interviewers. There were 10 such incidents which were readily resolved by discussion, allowing inclusion of omissions in the final joint summaries.

The summaries were initially grouped for analysis according to age. Subsequently, the summaries were also studied when organized according to the sex of the subject, his marital status, parental status and discipline.

FINDINGS

In the analysis of the data that related directly to age, the authors identified some responses to the question, "How does it feel to be your age?" that apparently related directly to the description of the self typically occurring at each age level within the sample. This analysis suggested that it was indeed possible to speak of certain types of self-descriptions occurring more frequently during one range of ages than during another. It appeared that the respondents who were 25 and 26 described themselves differently than the older respondents. Also, it seemed that respondents from 27 to 31 described themselves in a way unique to that group. The respondents from the age of 32 to 35 constituted the final age group. In this report these three age groups will be referred to as early phase, middle phase and late phase.

Table 3–1
Selected Characteristics of the Sample

Age	25	26	27	28	29	30	31	32	33	34	35	Total
Number at each age	2	3	4	3	3	2	3	3	2	3	2	30
Number of males	1	3	3	1	2	1	1	2	1	2	1	18
Number of females	1	0	1	2	1	1	2	1	1	1	1	12
Number never married	1	1	1	1	1	1	2	1	1	1	1	12
Number married, no children	1	1	1	1	1	0	1	0	1	1	0	8
Number married, with children	0	1	2	1	1	1	0	2	0	1	1	10
Number social workers	2	0	1	2	1	1	2	2	0	0	1	12
Number psychiatric residents	0	3	3	1	2	1	1	1	2	3	1	18

AGE
Early Phase

The predominant tone of the interview of the 25- or 26-year-old was one of intensity and uncertainty. The first association to the question, "How does it feel to be your age?" tended to be a word or phrase like "unsettling," "uncertain," "in transition," or "a little scary." All of these respondents noted that one of their major struggles at this time was in being faced with and forced to grapple with their own limitations in the attempt to actualize adult roles. Within this context they spoke of an earlier tendency to see themselves in rather grandiose terms; two spoke of an earlier expectation that they would be "the new Sigmund Freud." Another described an earlier conviction that she would be a "phenomenal success" by age 25. Although they felt they were moving away from this earlier grandiose view, they expressed uncertainty about what could replace it. As one 25-year-old stated, "I feel I have nothing concrete to show for the past few years. It makes me feel inadequate because of my former fantasies about what I would be doing now." A 26-year-old commented that hearing one of his supervisors describe his interviewing techniques as "typical of a first-year resident" was one of the hardest blows of his first year of residency. In many ways, members of this group experienced confrontation with limitations as a severe blow to self-esteem.

A striking feature of these particular encounters with reality was the amount of sadness and disappointment expressed in regard to the relinquishment of earlier grandiose ideals. "It's sad to have to give up the utopian ideals of college and face the real business of being an adult. It's depressing." The 25-year-old woman mentioned above spoke of the fact that she was not the phenomenal success she had expected to be, as if something promised had been taken away from her. The affect accompanying this statement was a mixture of disappointment and anger. Thus, it appears that the passing of the grandiose inner image is affectively felt as a loss.

The data suggest that the members of this age group are in the process of integrating their private, inner view of themselves with their public, adult roles. In some instances the respondents expressed resentment about having to meet certain adult expectations. "I can't be as outrageous as I used to be. It's no longer age appropriate." One 26-year-old referred to being older and professional as a burden, and another seemed to mourn the loss of membership in a group with stability and cohesion that he had once experienced but no longer found available.

Within these interviews there were also references to new thoughts about the future. The respondents indicated that their former tendency to view the future concretely and in terms of deadlines and milestones was being altered. For many this change was precipitated by an inability to meet real or fantasized deadlines. The validity of deadlines was particularly challenged by the emerging awareness that the deadlines were derived from cultural and parental expectations often not in correspondence to the individual's real experience of life. Parents and their expectations were often referred to by this group. The desire to please their parents was still an issue. One married respondent mentioned that one of the major reasons he and his wife hoped to have children was for the pleasure of their parents.

The respondents over 25 who recalled how they felt about themselves at that age advanced descriptions quite similar to the associations given by respondents who were at that age. In addition, the retrospective data highlighted certain other aspects of this period. Several referred to a form of playacting of adult roles at that age. Others spoke of a different way of conceptualizing the decision-making process at 25. Decisions made at that age were not perceived as having the effect of closing off future options, although this eventually proved to be the case. This finding underlines the fact that people in this age range tend to view the future as existing outside the same rules of reality to which the present is subject.

Middle Phase

The respondents between ages 27 and 31 were in general much more confident in themselves and suffered less from feelings of immediate loss than the younger respondents. Instead, they communicated a feeling of transition and discovery which was less charged with the affects of anger and disappointment. Perhaps the tone of these interviews is best summarized in the statement of one 29-year-old: "I feel three-fourths through something. Things are beginning to fall into place."

In contrast to the younger group's expressions of inadequacy, most people in this group noted an emerging sense of competence and confidence with regard to their profession. They describe a new experience of personal gratification from their work which was becoming less dependent upon external approval and was less generated by external expectations. Several made statements similar to the following: "I feel a growing sense of competence and power. I'm giving up fantasies of power for the real thing. That's a lot tougher than I thought it would be." "I feel more willing to take risks, going out on a limb about what I know. It's getting easier to take criticism." "I now feel like I can still feel competent where I am and also be aware of where I want to go without invalidating the level I'm at." The actual experience of accomplishment by this group seems to have been a compensating factor for the feeling of loss so immediate to the younger group.

Another theme that emerged conspicuously throughout these interviews was reference to the process of aging. Almost all respondents noted that they were getting older. Often this was acknowledged in relation to their physical condition or to their diminished level of energy. Several references were made to old age: "Getting old, I mean haggard old, tired old is scary to me." "I wonder how I'll feel when I'm sixty?" A few married respondents queried what life would be like when their children were grown up and gone from home. Several of the unmarried respondents expressed concern about what life would be like in their fifties or sixties if they remained unmarried.

The death or decline of parents was often mentioned by this group and a few made direct remarks about their own mortality within that context: "I feel a little fearful about death. I mean I'm not really over the hump, but I realize the finality of death. My mother's death has affected my thinking." The awareness of mortality seems to be also reflected in this group's emphasis on and strong orientation toward the present. There were several references to the lack of control over events and the relinquishment of "master-plans" in favor of living more in the present. As one respondent stated, "I realize now that you can't make everything come out like a storybook. I don't have as many five-year plans, and I enjoy the present more. I enjoy just seeing how it's all going to come out."

Within this context was also the report that some things in life were becoming more fixed, and that it was becoming increasingly more difficult to change things. While several references were made to the awareness of options narrowing and possibilities limiting, the tone was more one of acceptance than in the younger group. At the same time, however, the past was often recalled in a reminiscent way that related to "the passing of my youth." The most significant amount of affect was expressed with regard to the age 30; apparently the experience of reaching this age stirred up again earlier feelings about the loss of grandiose fantasies. The age was not only anticipated with concern, "I'll really have to give up the things of my youth," but was experienced with some sadness: "At 30, I said to myself, look what Mozart was doing at 30, and look at me."

Within this group were two people whose responses to the initial question differed markedly from the others. One of these was a 31-year-old who impressed the authors as very depressed. He described a crisis around 30 when he realized that certain goals were not going to be reached and became aware that he was destined to lead a very ordinary existence. He felt unsatisfied about his career choices and his unmarried status. He saw parenthood as offering compensation for the loss of his own feelings of potentiality. He looked to age 35 with hopes that he would not be bitter and with the hope that he would find something to devote himself to.

This respondent differed from the others in this age range primarily in his lack of closure on any of the issues of adulthood: career choice, marriage and parenthood. While experiencing the loss of grandiose ideals and omnipotentiality similar to the other respondents, he had no commitments from which to gain self-esteem and enhance his life within a realistic context. This interview seems to highlight the importance of participation in concrete affiliations as a means of mourning or resolving the loss of omnipotentiality.

The other interview was with a 27-year-old married social worker, who having committed herself to both marriage and career, described her present feelings as "intolerable." This respondent reported deriving little satisfaction from her achievements and feeling haunted by the notion that "this isn't enough." Her orientation was continually toward the future and toward further achievement. She stated that she was aware that "what I really need to do is just be what I am."

This respondent impressed the authors as someone whose goals and commitments were highly determined by cultural and parental expectations. The lack of integration between these expectations and personal desires and goals seemed related to her limited capacity for personal satisfaction and self-esteem. This interview suggested some of the pitfalls of premature closure on the basic issues of adulthood, particularly if based largely on external expectations.

Late Phase

The interviews with the group between the ages of 32 and 35 were significantly marked by a tone of reflection and calm. One of the most striking features of this group was their tendency to view themselves from a historical perspective. Their first associations to the initial question, in fact, tended to include references to the past. These were statements like, "It's certainly better than 20." "That's an open question. The last ten years have been a big change." "I guess that has to do with where I've been."

In contrast to the expressions of inadequacy and loss advanced by the first group, and of transition and discovery by the second group, this group expressed feelings of integration, clarity and form. Respondents seemed to feel much more defined than the younger respondents and accepting of that definition. As one 34-year-old stated, "I feel more that who I am, I am, and that's not bad." The emergence of structure and form was described by one respondent as somewhat unconscious: "Whether conscious or not, decisions have been made, and you look around and realize you have a structure to your life. It's kind of a relief." Another referred to some of the components of the process that resonated with many of the issues highlighted by the younger groups: "It's been a process of sorting out who I am and what I want to do. You discover what's feasible, you limit and relinquish some of your ambitions—many of which were never real anyway, and you gradually begin to feel more formed."

Another feature of this group was their identification with those who had formerly been parenting figures. One respondent described the sudden realization that those whom she had formerly looked up to were now peers. This new identification seemed to bring to the surface the feeling of having something to offer others. "For awhile, I didn't feel like I belonged to any generation. There seemed to be no compensation for getting older and I had a feeling of loss. I guess I joined the older generation when I realized I had something valuable to offer." Within this context, respondents spoke of success as "a more personal thing," less defined by the environment. Their energy seemed to be focused less on new life plans and more on "making the most of what you've got." For many, this meant a stronger focus on their families and more emphasis on enjoying and appreciating life. Those who were unmarried spoke not only of gratification from teaching and supervising others, but of investing energy in activities outside their profession.

While several references were made to the issue of mortality, these were often made within the context of a lifetime perspective: "I see where I've been, but also where I'm going. My age is sort of a middle age. I think more of the end of life as a real possibility." It is this perspective on both past and future which was unique to this group. The frequent use of the word "process" by respondents of this group was also significant. Respondents communicated a sense of participation in a process that joined both the past and the future. "Before, I tended to look at the future in concrete terms, but now I feel more carried by and identified with an evolutionary process." Perhaps this identification with evolutionary and organic process can be viewed as a way of dealing with mortality.

The responses of younger subjects to the question of how they would feel about their age at 35 indicated that all of the respondents saw themselves as more settled and secure at 35 than they were now. Many saw this age as a vantage point from which they could evaluate their past performance. Those who lacked closure on pressing issues at their present age saw themselves as gaining closure before 35.

CONCRETE AFFILIATIONS
Parenthood

Ten of the 30 people interviewed were parents. One significant finding in analyzing the responses from this group alone was the conspicuous similarity in their expressions of feelings of form, comfort and clarity. Those with parenting responsibilities often sounded like the 32 to 35 age group regardless of their age. Having a child seems to be an affiliation of unique proportions that accelerates the process of getting in touch with real capacities, real limitations, and a reality based definition of self. Although most parents did not describe why they chose to have children or how the decision was made, parenthood brought with it very unexpected personal revelations. One respondent's comment may sum up the central theme of the experience. "Having a child is a conspicuous definition of who you are." The awareness of the force of that definition for many people precipitated shifts in their marriage and career affiliations.

One female respondent stated that, "having a child said something about myself, made me aware of new capacities . . . life suddenly had to do with me." It was this new sense of self that prompted her toward a new introspection and examination of her marriage. This experience led ultimately to a divorce several years later. For many the experience brought about within the marriage what is described by one respondent as "a renewed commitment in our marriage, a greater sense of closeness. There was something more final in our relationship then and a feeling that this is really it." One psychiatric resident, who had spent four years in another profession, traced his decision to change professions to the birth of his first child. "Having a child made me question what I was doing with myself. It was almost like being reborn." Another 29-year-old when describing himself stated that he had begun to experience the comfortable feeling of "settling into a groove," of giving up his former adolescent freedoms. When asked when this feeling began, he responded. "About ten minutes after my child was born. It was not there with the decision to have the child."

Marriage

Eighteen of the 30 people interviewed were married; 12 had never been married. The experience of marriage for most of the respondents has also been a reality experience requiring and precipitating struggle and change. Here, as with parenthood, the decision to get married was not well explained. A variety of reasons were expressed: "All my friends were getting married," "I was leaving the city, wanted her with me and felt it was the honorable thing to do," and "I was tired of being alone." It is important to note that all but one of our married respondents made the decision to marry before age 25.

Although many of the more personal marital details were not shared in the interviews, one struggle did emerge as a theme among the married respondents, the struggle with dependence and independence. Many people stated that they found it difficult to acknowledge their own dependency in marriage, to accept their own needs. As one respondent described it, "Accepting that dependency means giving up the notion that I'm superman; I guess that means beginning to accept myself."

Marriage for many brought about a change in relationships with parents. Respondents described a withdrawal on the part of their parents that made them feel more autonomous and responsible. This experience seemed to precipitate what many described as a greater capacity for dealing with the death of parents.

Two of the respondents had been married and divorced. Both were married in their early twenties and divorced after 25. Both described their marriages as relationships built on fantasy and role expectation: "I wanted to be the perfect Good Housekeeping wife." They both described a gradual process of getting in touch with their own true capacities and real potential that made the marriages no longer tenable.

To the respondents who were not married, the issue of marriage was an important one, but attitudes about marriage shifted throughout the age span of our sample. Those in the lower age range did not question whether they would eventually get married, but noted that they were facing new thoughts about it. One 25-year-old described a panicked feeling regarding the deadlines she had set for herself. "I always felt marriage should take place between 25 and 27 and now I'm faced with my deadline. I'm not sure what this means." One 26-year-old stated, "I used to be able to picture myself married, picture my wife and whole family. I can't picture this in my mind's eye anymore. I'm now aware that that has to develop, not just happen. I have a feeling about it now, instead of an image."

As the respondents progressed in age, a shift in thinking occurred away from cultural expectations and pictures of marriage to a more personal evaluation of whether marriage is desirable. Respondents between 28 and 31 spoke less about marriage itself and more about concerns with the quality of a relationship. There appeared a more serious and conscious awareness of the reality and demands of marriage resulting in more thoughtful discriminations about the kind of relationship desired. There also emerged some questioning about how needs could be met without the institution of marriage.

Those at the upper level of our age span, while leaving the question of marriage open, felt that not being married was a state compatible with their self-image. They viewed the unmarried state as a reality with which they had come to terms, a state that entailed a decision-making process as unconscious as that described by those who decided to marry.

Career

The most significant finding about the issue of career was that 8 of the 12 social workers in the sample decided to make social work their career and then took decisive steps to actualize their decision around the age of 25. Most traced this decision to a sudden pressure around that age to make a long-term career commitment. As one respondent described it, "I felt that the time had come to get serious about this. Although experimenting around with different jobs had been good for me, I was getting less and less gratification and felt I now wanted something definite."

The finding is significant not only in terms of what appears to be a pressure for closure on the career issue, but also in terms of the contrast to the psychiatric residents, the majority of whom made their career decision at age 21 or younger. What was a period of experimentation with career for one group was a period of intense preparation for career in the other group. The difference between the age at which career commitment is made raised two questions. What is the significance of choosing a career at 21 as opposed to at 25? What is lost or gained in delaying such a commitment until after a period of experimentation?

DISCUSSION

One aim of the present project was to explore the plausibility of viewing early adulthood as a developmental phase. To pursue this aim, it is useful to consider Erikson's criteria for a developmental stage. First of all, Erikson emphasizes that during each stage the person encounters certain phase-specific tasks and that out of these encounters new capabilities are realized (Erikson, 1963). Secondly, as part of this process, the person experiences a crisis because of "the necessity to manage the new encounters within a given time allowance" (Erikson, 1963, 105). Thirdly, he states that the negotiation of a phase has a "proper rate and sequence" (Erikson, 1968, 95). Fourthly, the successful negotiation of a phase will be experienced as, "an increased sense of inner unity, with an increase of good judgment and an increase in the capacity 'to do well' according to his own standards and to the standards of those who are significant to him" (Erikson, 1963, 95).

This study suggests that these four characteristics are present within the time period studied. First of all, the data point toward important shifts in descriptions of the self that begin at 25 and stabilize around 35; in addition, it seems possible to understand these shifts in terms of developmental tasks and emerging capacities. Second, most respondents report a pressure to reach closure on certain issues within a limited time. Third, the shifts in self-description with age could be grouped into three distinct, sequentially related stages, and that the rate of these changes is the result of aging and an interactional effect between aging and the concrete affiliations of parenthood, marriage and career. Fourth, the 31 to 34-year-old respondents and respondents who were parents, the two groups the authors postulate as most likely to have negotiated this developmental stage, describe themselves in terms consonant with Erikson's description.

The two atypical interviews described earlier may be understood as reflecting attempts to avoid the age-specific crisis by either premature or delayed closure on the issues of parenthood, marriage and career. The fact that engagement with the tasks of this stage was found even with these two subjects is further confirmation of the existence of a distinct developmental phase of young adulthood.

Many of the specific themes emerging from the present study seem related to generativity. The expansion of ego interests of these subjects is strongly suggested in the findings. Also, the older respondents begin to view themselves as having certain responsibilities toward the next generation and to prize their roles as parents and as teachers. An important source of self-esteem for those in the latter part of young adulthood came from caring for the next generation. It seems, then, that the stage of young adulthood described in this study corresponds in important ways to Erikson's stage of Generativity versus Stagnation.

A loss of omnipotentiality, that Buhler believed occurs at around 25, was found within our sample. Almost all of our respondents described a progression beyond the level of Wittenberg's postadolescent stage. This progression, which seemed to begin at around 25, included the element of mourning postulated by Wittenberg.

The results of this project can be summarized by a provisioned model of the tasks encountered in early adulthood and the new capacities realized by means of their successful negotiation.

TASKS:
1. Resolution, through mourning, of the loss of the grandiose self-image as the primary organizing element of life goals and self-esteem
2. Gaining closure on commitments to career, marriage, and parenthood
3. Acceptance of the person's ego boundaries in terms of realistic perceptions of one's capabilities, limitations, and the unique position of one's life cycle within history
4. Acceptance of one's self as a person now separate from the preceding and the next generation

NEW CAPACITIES:
1. Capacity to derive satisfaction from one's accomplishments within a realistic context
2. Capacity to value oneself as someone who makes a unique contribution to others
3. Capacity to integrate into the ego the experience accrued in the process of living with choices made in regard to career, marriage, and parenthood
4. Capacity to identify with life as an evolutionary process with a definite end and uncertain course

REFERENCES

Buhler, C. 1968. *The Course of Human Life*. New York: Springer Company.

Erikson, E. H. 1963. *Childhood and Society*. New York: W. W. Norton, Inc.

Gould, R. 1959. "The Phases of Adult Life: A Study in Developmental Psychology." *The American Journal of Psychiatry* VII.

Hartmann, H. 1958. *Ego Psychology and the Problem of Adaptation*. New York: International Universities Press.

Wittenberg, R. 1968. *Postadolescence*. New York: Grune and Stratton Company.

ADULTHOOD

CHAPTER 4

THEORIES OF ADULT DEVELOPMENT

Creating a Context for Practice

Eileen M. Brennan and Ann Weick

Until the 1970s, very little theoretical work underpinned the study of the majority of the human life span—adulthood.[1] Bernice Neugarten offered a fitting metaphor describing developmental theory prior to this decade—that of a circus: The child developmentalists sat too close to the entrance of the circus tent and the gerontologists too close to the exit; both groups missed the center ring (adulthood) and therefore lacked a view of the whole show.[2]

Recent advances in both the empirical description of adulthood and the building of developmental theory addressing the social psychology of the adult years have claimed the attention of students of human behavior and of human services practitioners throughout the United States. Signaled by the 1974 publication of *Passages*, Gail Sheehy's best seller that examined adulthood,[3] researchers have reported a series of major studies that investigated the years between adolescence and senescence. George Vaillant, Roger Gould, Daniel Levinson, and several other authors have all recently published works that attempt to describe and explain adult behavior by drawing upon extensive research studies.[4]

This article briefly describes the work of the three theorists Vaillant, Gould, and

Reprinted from *Social Casework,* Vol. 62 (January 1981), pp. 13–19, by permission of the publisher, Families International, Inc.

[1] Dorothy Rogers, *The Adult Years: An Introduction to Aging* (Englewood Cliffs, N.J.: Prentice-Hall, 1979), p. 4.
[2] Bernice L. Neugarten, "Adult Personality: Toward a Psychology of the Life Cycle," in *Human Life Cycle,* ed. William C. Sze (New York: Jason Aronson, 1975), p. 379.
[3] Gail Sheehy, *Passages: Predictable Crises of Adult Life* (New York: E. P. Dutton, 1974).
[4] George E. Vaillant, *Adaptation to Life* (Boston: Little, Brown, 1977); Roger L. Gould, *Transformations: Growth and Change in Adult Life* (New York: Simon and Schuster, 1978); and Daniel J. Levinson et al., *The Seasons of a Man's Life* (New York: Alfred A. Knopf, 1978). See also Henry S. Maas and Joseph A. Kuypers, *From Thirty to Seventy* (San Francisco: Jossey-Bass, 1975), and Jane Loevinger, *Ego Development: Conceptions and Theories* (San Francisco: Jossey-Bass, 1976).

Levinson, addresses the assumptions on which the theory of adult development is based, and proposes a view of social work intervention from a developmental framework.

ADULT LIFE-CYCLE THEORISTS

The three theorists named above acknowledge the pioneering work done by Erik Erikson, whose epigenetic model of the life cycle has often been taught as part of human behavior content in schools of social work.[5] Recently, Erikson has produced an interdisciplinary collection of papers in which he speculated that we may be entering the "century of the adult."[6] In a prior work, *Childhood and Society,* Erikson addressed the psychosocial aspects of developmental change throughout life, and had not confined himself to childhood and adolescence, as was largely true in earlier psychoanalytic and ego psychology formulations.[7]

Erikson postulated that adults go through four critical stages of development during which they struggle to adjust to the demands of the social environment and to master specific developmental tasks. The struggles are expressed in terms of striking a balance between polar qualities specified for each stage: adolescence (identity versus role diffusion), young adulthood (intimacy versus isolation), middle adulthood (generativity versus stagnation), and maturity (ego integrity versus despair).

Klaus Riegel argues that Erikson has built his theory so that it has a potentially dialectical framework, one that acknowledges the mutual influence of the active organism and the changing world in which the organism moves.[8] In Riegel's view of the developmental dialectic, growth comes through crisis and conflict, and every generation develops somewhat differently because of the historical events unique to it.

Each of the following theorists has proposed a view of development that marks out certain stages of the adult life cycle and also acknowledges the dialectic of development that encompasses each adult life.

George Vaillant

George Vaillant formulated his theoretical work *(Adaptation to Life)* in conjunction with an in-depth study of ninety-five men who served as subjects in a study of healthy adult development.[9] The men were investigated continuously from their sophomore year at an Ivy League college until age forty-seven by an interdisciplinary team of psychiatrists, psychologists, anthropologists, and social workers.

---

[5] See Sophie Freud Lowenstein, "Preparing Social Work Students for Life-Transition Counseling within the Human Behavior Sequence," *Journal of Education for Social Work* 14 (Spring 1978): 66–73.

[6] Erik H. Erikson, *Adulthood* (New York: W. W. Norton, 1978), p. vii.

[7] Erik H. Erikson, *Childhood and Society,* 2d ed. (New York: W. W. Norton, 1973), pp. 247–74.

[8] Klaus F. Riegel, "History of Psychological Gerontology," in *Handbook of the Psychology of Aging,* ed. James E. Birren and Klaus W. Shaie (New York: Van Nostrand Reinhold, 1977), pp. 70–102.

[9] Vaillant, *Adaptation to Life,* pp. 30–52.

Extending the theoretical notions of Norma Haan of Berkeley,[10] Vaillant conceptualized the passage of his subjects through life in terms of the maturation of the ego defenses, which he called adaptation mechanisms. He developed a hierarchy of adaptation mechanisms ranging from primitive (for example, denial and distortion) to fully mature (including sublimation and suppression) and found that as the men got older their ways of coping with reality became more mature. In his view, much behavior that is labeled pathological is actually healing; what appears in cross section to be "mental illness" can in the long run be quite adaptive, given an individual's personal and historical circumstances. Vaillant also found that the isolated traumas of childhood were not as important as predictors of later adaptation as the quality of sustained relationships.

Additionally, the men studied were found to pass through life stages in the sequence hypothesized by Erikson. Vaillant identified six stages of adult development that roughly corresponded to each of the six decades of life from the teen years to the sixties. Adults were successively involved in (1) identity formation, (2) achievement of intimacy, (3) career consolidation, (4) generativity, (5) keeping the meaning through "passing the torch" of culture, and (6) a search of ego integrity. Vaillant cautioned that women may go through a different sequence of stages than men do, especially when they are involved in balancing career consolidation, attaining intimacy, and achieving generativity. He also acknowledged the sociocultural biases of his work that concentrated on an elite population.

Roger Gould

Several large scale cross-sectional studies were conducted by Gould in an attempt to get a clear conceptualization of the sequential change that takes place with time in the lives of adults.[11] Gould used the empirical studies together with insights gained from his clinical practice as the basis for *Transformations: Growth and Change in Adult Life,* a book designed for the lay reader.[12]

His first informal study began with his search for patterns in over 125 life histories prepared by psychiatric residents. Gould next arranged for direct observation of fourteen therapy groups of outpatients who were assigned to age-homogeneous groups. The groups were observed by a ten-member interdisciplinary team who prepared descriptions of the psychological themes discussed by group members in each of seven age ranges.

In a follow-up study, 524 adult nonpatients completed questionnaires composed of salient statements heard in the age-homogeneous groups. The statements were arranged in sets of sixteen, according to theme (for example, sense of time, relation to parents), and each respondent rank ordered each set as to importance. Gould found similar responses clustered within seven distinct age groups: 16–17, 18–21, 22–28,

---

[10] Norma Haan, "Personality Development from Adolescence to Adulthood in the Oakland Growth and Guidance Studies," *Seminars in Psychiatry* 4 (November 1972): 399–414.

[11] Roger L. Gould, "Phases of Adult Life: A Study in Developmental Psychology," *American Journal of Psychiatry* 132 (November 1972): 521–31.

[12] Gould, *Transformations.*

29–36, 37–43, 44–50, and 51–60. Recognizing that cross-sectional studies can mask cohort differences, Gould nevertheless concluded that there was evidence that persons changed in their sense of time as they grew older, and that their attitudes toward themselves and others also changed in relation to time.

In *Transformations,* Gould theorized that adulthood is a dynamic time, full of change, in which each person moves away from childhood consciousness toward adulthood consciousness.[13] That is, with each forward movement toward adulthood, unfinished childhood business may intrude, impelling struggle toward further growth. At each stage of life the issues are different, and, as Gould points out, our responses to them are shaped by the social conditions that touch our world.

Daniel Levinson

The most comprehensive theoretical view of adulthood is offered by Levinson in *The Seasons of a Man's Life.*[14] Levinson and his co-workers based their theoretical work on intensive biographical interviewing of forty men, ranging from thirty-five to forty-five years of age. Ten men came from each of four occupational groups: (1) blue and white collar industrial workers, (2) business executives, (3) academic biologists, and (4) novelists.

Levinson traced the course of development of the *life structure,* which he defined as the underlying pattern or design of a person's life at a given time, for each man. The life structure is seen as having two aspects: *external,* referring to the person's pattern of roles, interests, memberships, lifestyle, and long-term goals; and *internal,* consisting of the personal meanings the external aspects have for the individual, as well as inner identities, values, fantasies, and psychodynamic qualities that inform one's engagement in the world.

Levinson pointed out that the life cycle can be divided into four eras, each lasting approximately twenty-five years: childhood and adolescence (birth–22 years), early adulthood (17–45 years), middle adulthood (40–65 years), and late adulthood (60 years and over). The eras are conceived of as seasons of life, each with its own distinctive and unifying qualities. As a person moves from era to era, transitions occur during which the outgoing era is terminated and the new era is initiated.

Of special interest to Levinson and his associates were the two middle eras. The eras of early adulthood and middle adulthood were each subdivided into two periods during which the life structure is relatively stable, and each of the two periods is seen as bounded by transitions. The transition is often a time of stress and crisis because the old life structure of the preceding stable period is reevaluated and new choices are often made. Each period and transition is posited as having proper developmental tasks and processes. Levinson's men were seen as passing through eight phases during the eras of interest: early adult transition (17–22), entering the adult world (22–28), age 30 transition (28–33), settling down (33–40), mid-life transition (40–45), entering middle adult-

---

[13] Ibid.
[14] Levinson, *Seasons of a Man's Life.*

hood (45–50), age 50 transition (50–55), and culmination of middle adulthood (55–60).

Using Levinson's theory, Wendy Stewart investigated the life structures of women in early adulthood.[15] She found that Levinson's stage divisions were supported, but that women had greater variability than men in the order in which they completed life tasks. For Stewart's female subjects, formation of a satisfactory, stable life structure was more difficult than for Levinson's men.

BASIC ASSUMPTIONS

It is possible to identify five basic assumptions that are common to the three theorists. The adoption of these assumptions paves the way for a developmental approach to the entire human life cycle and, therefore, to practice.

Assumption 1. Humans continue to develop throughout life.

The first assumption contradicts the prevailing view as surveyed by Richard M. Lerner and Carol D. Ryff that persons develop rapidly until the end of adolescence, reach a plateau during young adulthood, and then suffer an irreversible deterioration during the second half of the life span.[16] Much of the research done on intellectual development of post-adolescents has been based on the irreversible decrement model that draws on the prevailing view. But, recently, researchers have convincingly demonstrated that in one area, cognitive functioning, adults can continue to change positively throughout life.[17] It seems reasonable, given a continual interaction between self and world, to assume that all of the psychosocial aspects of persons (not just intellectual functioning) continue to develop through that interaction.

Assumption 2. Life unfolds in stages during the course of adulthood.

Erikson, Vaillant, Gould, and Levinson all propose that adult life is best understood in terms of a series of discontinuous stages during which certain dimensions of the person qualitatively differ from stage to stage. Each stage is logically built from the elements of past stages and emerges from those stages in a predictable fashion.

Bernice Neugarten criticized this assumption of adult stage theorists because she believes that evidence points to the recurrence of psychological themes and preoccupations throughout adult life without a single fixed order.[18] A dialectical view of development, however, does not preclude revisiting the issues of earlier stages, and, as

---

[15] Wendy Stewart, "A Psychosocial Study of the Formation of Early Adult Life Structure in Women" (Ph.D. diss., Columbia University, 1977).

[16] Richard M. Lerner and Carol D. Ryff, "Implementing the Life-Span View: Attachment," in *Life-Span Development and Behavior,* vol. 1., ed. Paul B. Baltes (New York: Academic Press, 1978), pp. 1–44.

[17] See ibid., for a brief review.

[18] Bernice L. Neugarten, "Time, Age, and the Life Cycle," *American Journal of Psychiatry* 136 (July 1979): 887–94.

Erikson points out, each element of the stages of development exists in some form before its critical time.[19]

Assumption 3. The stages are divided by transition periods that are sometimes punctuated with crises.

Levinson conceptualizes transitions as critical turning points during which persons are terminating one stage of life and simultaneously initiating the incoming one. When the transition involves considerable turmoil and disruption, a crisis may be said to occur. Although a smooth passage from one stage to another may occur for an individual, both Levinson and Vaillant found evidence that crises were by no means rare in their samples of men.

Assumption 4. Transitions provide opportunities for growth.

In successfully navigating through a transition period, one leaves behind a formerly comfortable way of relating to self and world and seeks new ways to relate. Levinson states that the primary tasks of transitional periods are to question and reappraise one's present life and to explore possibilities for change. Each transition, then, holds out the prospect of grieving and the possibility of growth.

Assumption 5. Adulthood is to be examined in terms of the underlying health and strength people have to cope with change.

Vaillant addresses the fifth assumption eloquently. He states, "Most of what is called illness in textbooks and in our diagnostic nomenclature . . . [is] merely outward evidence of inward struggles to adapt to life."[20] In his view then, those in the helping professions should devote much of their effort to identifying and supporting the natural healing processes.

A DEVELOPMENTAL CONTEXT FOR PRACTICE

One of the useful functions of behavioral theories is its role as context creator. In the process of linking together pieces of the human puzzle, theory establishes a context for understanding behavior and for applying that understanding to social work practice. Theory becomes an active ingredient in the helping process because the social worker may use it to reframe the client's experience and, thus, create the image of new possibilities and new choices. Clearly, the social worker's theoretical perspective is a significant determinant of the content of the reframing process.

The emergence of life-cycle theory is significant because its assumptions challenge

---

[19] Erikson, *Childhood and Society,* p. 271.
[20] Vaillant, *Adaptation to Life,* p. 369.

our understanding of the nature of human growth and change and, therefore, radically alter the theoretical context for practice. Because the process of change is a central issue in social work intervention, it is important to examine these assumptions in relation to the change process during adulthood. What the theory says about the process of change may ultimately be its most important contribution to social work practice. Let us examine the assumptions in light of the nature of change and their impact on our current thinking.

Persistence and Predictability of Change

The core assumption of adult life-cycle theory is the persistence of change throughout life. Focus on the adult years brings legitimate recognition to the significant development that continues to take place well beyond the period of childhood and adolescence. After reviewing evidence from life-span research, Lerner and Ryff find the data indicating "that change occurs across the lifespan and takes multidirectional forms."[21]

Adult life-cycle theory also posits as a basic position an appreciation of the normalcy and, indeed, predictability of change. Achieving adulthood does not signal an end stage. Rather, the theory is compatible with the notion that growth is an open-end process. It occurs through the stages and phases beginning to be outlined by adult life-cycle theorists. If achieving one's full potential is a respectable goal of human endeavor, and especially if that endeavor is linked with the needs of the larger human community, then challenge and change must become the accepted vehicles to achieve potential. The commitment of social work to the values of individual and social change makes this a felicitous assumption.

The acceptance of change as a predictable aspect of adult development requires a radical refocusing. In place of a sometimes exclusive preoccupation with the developmental dynamics of childhood, this acceptance requires that we become more finely attuned to the dynamics of change in adulthood. If change is to be seen as the norm, then we must pursue a more sophisticated understanding of the nature of the change process. Adult life-cycle theory, through its focus on change, contributes to that goal.

Crisis as a Mechanism of Change

Examining change as it occurs in situations of crisis has generated a substantial and useful literature. Because life stages are divided by transition periods that are sometimes laden with stress, crisis literature is a natural resource for extending an understanding of the process of change. One of its fundamental premises is shared by life-cycle theory, namely, its view of crisis as a healthy, rather than a pathological, phenomenon. To the extent that internal developmental changes or external circumstances present challenges that require new behaviors, an individual's familiar patterns of coping are subject to change. The shift from one pattern of behavior to another invariably carries with

---

[21] Lerner and Ryff, "Implementing the Life-Span View," p. 5.

it some element of crisis. However, it is through such periods of upset that positive growth can occur.[22]

Looking at crisis as a mechanism of change brings us closer to a complicated conceptual issue: whether our understanding of change is best served by the notion of homeostasis or by the notion of adaptation. The issue comes to light when crisis theory and adult life-cycle theory are compared in terms of their implicit positions on the dynamics of change. Crisis theory, as it has developed from Gerald Caplan's early conceptualization, is based on the notion of emotional homeostasis.[23] The perception of and response to crisis is directly related to an individual's habitual problem-solving skills. Only when those skills are insufficient to the situation does a crisis arise. The minimal goal of crisis intervention is "psychological resolution of the individual's immediate crisis and restoration to at least the level of functioning that existed before the crisis period."[24]

The notion of a system being in a homeostatic or steady state suggests a negative basis for change. Given this premise, change only occurs when the normative state fails, that is, when an individual's problem-solving skills no longer function. As a result, an individual's failure to cope may in itself be seen as a deficit, even though the failure may be the stimulus for the development of new and better coping skills. It is recognized, of course, that circumstances may be of such severity that even the most capable will experience a crisis-ridden upheaval. The point is that by establishing a homeostatic state as the normative one, the process of change is seen as unnecessarily negative.

In contrast to this, we can consider the state of change as the normative one. This position, as upheld by adult life-cycle theorists, views constant change as a more accurate describer of the human system. The quality and degree of change varies from moment to moment, day to day. The periods we ordinarily think of as change are the visible and demonstrable signs of this ongoing, dynamic state. However, the underlying state is one of continual change.

Drawing from the rich practice history of social group work, Hans S. Falck defines crisis in similar terms. Rather then viewing crisis as an event, he suggests that it could more profitably be viewed as a life-long process.[25] The goal of intervention is not to remediate the crisis but to strengthen coping skills through the ever-present structure of social groups.

If we entertain the notion of change as the norm, the concept that may ultimately prove more useful than homeostasis is adaptation. While homeostasis connotes fairly narrow boundaries within which a system can vary, adaptation suggests a system's ability to move and change in infinitely complex ways within much wider boundaries.[26] Homeostasis perhaps best speaks to very narrow and known conditions that must be present for survival. Adaptation speaks to the unmeasured and unrecognized potential for complex and continuous human change.

---

[22] For an extended discussion of this issue see, Lydia Rapoport, "The State of Crisis: Some Theoretical Considerations," in *Crisis Intervention: Selected Readings,* ed. Howard J. Parad (New York: Family Service Association of America, 1965), pp. 22–31; Naomi Golan, *Treatment in Crisis Situations* (New York: Free Press, 1978); Samual L. Dixon, *Working with People in Crisis* (St. Louis: C. V. Mosby, 1979); and Loewenstein, "Preparing Students."

[23] Gerald Caplan, *Principles of Preventive Psychiatry* (New York: Basic Books, 1964).

[24] Donna C. Agiulera and Janice M. Messick, *Crisis Intervention: Theory and Methodology* (St. Louis: C. V. Mosby, 1978), p. 21.

[25] Hans S. Falck, "Crisis Theory and Social Group Work," *Social Work in Groups* 1 (Spring 1978): 75–84.

[26] For a comprehensive discussion, see René Dubos, *Man Adapting* (New Haven, Conn.: Yale University Press, 1965).

Limits to Change

Establishing change as the norm opens up new considerations about the nature of change. At the same time, it presents new puzzles. While the notion of continual change and adaptation has an inviting openness, at the same time we must recognize that we have yet to learn the limits of the conditions within which human beings can grow and change. The human system does not have infinite adaptive capacity. The quality, duration, and intensity of change may be subject to some identifiable tolerances that set upper limits on human capacity for change.

The notion that growth is best characterized by a series of successive changes and that adult development—indeed, all development—is characterized by ongoing change shapes a new context for practice. Rather than asserting that equilibrium is desirable and that good coping skills last a lifetime, we must be willing to entertain the converse: that no human system can be expected to remain in persistent equilibrium and that problem-solving skills are time- and situation-linked. Not even a "normal" childhood guarantees the emotional psychological tools that will carry one throughout life.[27] No matter how successfully we have gained skills in our first physical and social interactions with our environment, those skills must be constantly improved and expanded. Facilitation of the change process, based on a more sophisticated knowledge of the related dynamics, becomes the focus of social work practice with adults.

Acceptance of change is a reminder that things do not remain the same, that a steady state is a false promise. Maturity is not a finite fact. One wonders parenthetically whether the reluctance to explore the vast changes of adulthood has been linked to the need to pretend that all the pain and change has been left behind in the turmoil of childhood and adolescence. In fact, the retreat to the skills used at an earlier period only demonstrates even more clearly that we can never return. Our personal and social world has changed, and the only recourse is to develop a view that allows us to break through the pretense.

The Need for Reappraisal

Exploring the changes occurring in adulthood forces social work practitioners to reexamine their notions about how human beings grow and develop. It is no longer possible to hold smugly to the belief that the quality and direction of all growth is established in the first few years of life and that attention to adults can only be remedial. Nor is it possible to claim an understanding of the dynamics of change in human behavior. The field has been cracked open, and those dynamics are once again subject to investigation.

The advent of this new theory tests practitioner's ability to deal with a reordering of old data. Minimally, it calls for an examination of current conceptualizations about how human beings develop. Potentially, it lays the foundation for a new synthesis. It is not that the emphasis on early periods of human development has been misguided or that the wealth of knowledge gained is useless. It is merely that those theories have not been large enough to embrace other important pieces of the puzzle. Now that data has

---

[27] Vaillant, *Adaptation to Life*, p. 369.

begun to accumulate about the process of adult growth and change, a way must be cleared for incorporating that information into our view of human behavior.

Social work practitioners have a much more practical and immediate investment in this process of synthesis. Because life-cycle theory embraces assumptions about change that posit, in essence, a nonpathological approach to intervention, it provides a new-found compatibility with the philosophical base of social work practice. At the same time, it challenges social workers to reexamine their notions of the change process both at conceptual and practice levels. This act of reexamination in itself is a positive one. By looking more closely at the linkages between a particular theory and its contribution to practice, and at its potential as a helpful guide for practice, the process will at once become more conscious and more open to critical analysis. The accumulating evidence on the adult life cycle deserves this conscious appraisal.

CHAPTER 5

CLINICAL PRACTICE WITH WOMEN IN THEIR MIDDLE YEARS

Roberta G. Sands and Virginia Richardson

Women in their middle years are at a crossroads in their developmental histories. Neither young and nubile nor old and feeble, they lack an image that represents their position. On the one hand, the portrayal of middle-aged women in the media suggests that as women get older they become less attractive and more dispensable.[1] On the other hand, research studies suggest that middle age is the prime of life, the time when one comes into one's own.[2]

Middle-aged women are of special interest to social workers, who inevitably find this population among their clients. Sandwiched between elderly parents and teenage children, middle-aged women are frequently involved in the treatment or planning for both generations.[3] Clinical services for marital and family problems are frequently initiated by wives and mothers who are in their middle years. Increasingly vulnerable to disease as they get older and caretakers when family members get sick, middle-aged women are both clients and family members seen at medical and psychiatric services.[4] Like women of other age groups, middle-aged women seek help for themselves for depression.[5] And the persons who provide social services to the population may be middle-aged social workers.

In recent years, the social work literature has been attentive to the developmental experiences of adults and to women's issues in particular.[6] Nonetheless, little attention has been given to clinical practice with middle-aged women. A few articles have discussed the psychological issues for mid-life adults of both sexes, and Strickler described crisis intervention with middle-aged men.[7] Yet the only article that focused specifically on clinical practice with middle-aged women examined medication abuse among this population.[8]

This article (1) describes various developmental perspectives on middle age and the difficulties inherent in applying developmental theories to women, (2) identifies and describes three developmental issues that are relevant to clinical practice with middle-aged woman, and (3) shows how these issues can be approached in clinical social work practice. The dilemmas of the middle-aged social worker will also be addressed.

DEFINING MIDDLE AGE

A working definition of middle age must first be established. Social scientists have differing ideas about how to define it. The terms "middle age," "middle years," and "middle adulthood" have been used to refer to the stage between young and older adulthood: "mid-life" refers to the approximate midpoint in the life span as well as to the entire middle period. This article uses all the above terms interchangeably.

The most common means of defining middle adulthood is age, but there is little consensus about the age parameters. Levinson and associates divided middle age into several phases: mid-life transition (age 40 to 45), building of a new life structure (45 to 50), age-50 transition (50 to 55), building a second middle-adult structure (55 to 60), and late-adult transition (60 to 65).[9] Frenkel-Brunswik discussed one period extending from the late twenties to the late forties, in which individuals are at the peak of their productive powers and highly involved in social activities. This is followed by another period, from the late forties to the early sixties, characterized by a decrease in activities and experiences of loss.[10] Havighurst stated that middle age spans ages 30 to about 55.[11] Human development textbooks consider middle age to cover the years from 35, 40, or 45 to 60 or 65.[12] Some writers believe that middle adulthood begins earlier for women than men and that for women it can begin as early as 30 or 35.[13]

Another approach to defining middle age is biological. According to Notman, women are especially sensitive to changes in their capacity for reproduction.[14] Those middle-aged women who have not had children will feel "up against the clock" as they assess the number of reproductive years that remain. Those who have already had children may decide to terminate their reproductive capacities surgically or abort unwanted children. Still other women will experience the menopause at its natural time which is, on the average, at age 50.[15] For women, middle adulthood is also accompanied by declines in estrogen and progesterone levels.[16]

Psychological and social factors are also used to define middle age. Neugarten suggests that two processes—a heightened sensitivity to one's position within a complex social environment and a reassessment of one's self—occur during this period. Middle-aged persons observe their status within the family, at work, and in other social contexts. They become more introspective than they were previously and think in terms of "time left to live" rather than "time since birth."[17] Events of the life cycle, such as children leaving home or becoming a grandparent, have also been regarded as indicators of middle age, particularly for women.[18] For men, experiences at work tend to be markers of their developmental progress.[19] To the extent that women begin to focus more on their careers, one can expect that they, too, will assess themselves in terms of work.

This article bases its concept of middle age on a number of factors. The chronological age period will be from 35 to 55, beginning with the closing phase of reproduction and nurturing children and ending with menopause. Middle age will be considered a period of transition in which persons experience and assess changes in biological, social, and intrapsychic functioning. However, the authors recognize the importance of a phenomenological approach in discussing the various definitions and theories of middle adulthood. Ultimately, it is the individual who defines and experiences middle age.

DEVELOPMENTAL PERSPECTIVES

Middle age is generally regarded as one of the series of developmental stages that characterize the human life cycle. According to major developmental theories, life progresses sequentially along a continuum of stages "from womb to tomb" with one stage built on the other. Deficits during earlier stages can hinder full development in later life. The life issues that emerge at each stage derive from biological, social, and psychological sources.

Jung was one of the first of the psychoanalytical theorists to discuss adulthood and particularly middle age. Some time between 35 and 40, Jung said, an individual begins to undergo an inner transformation during which aspects of the personality that were submerged during youth seek expression.[20] The obligations and social demands that were central during the first part of life no longer preoccupy the person; instead, the individual becomes introspective and concerned about the meaning of life. During middle age, individuals confront inner polarities and try to integrate both poles. This confrontation is often associated with "storm and stress," but successful resolution results in a sense of inner harmony. Jung also said that as a person grows older, she or he becomes more individuated,[21] that is, more integrated, whole, and androgynous.

Erikson, who built a conceptual framework for the life cycle on the foundation laid by Freud, is the prototype of a developmental theorist. He described eight life stages, each with its time of ascendancy and characterized by a conflict between two polarities of a psychosocial issue. According to Erikson, the conflict that occurs during middle age is the crisis of "generativity versus stagnation."[22] Generativity is the giving of one's energies to others. During this stage, one is intensely concerned about the welfare of the next generation, including, but not limited to, one's children. The generative person makes efforts to foster the development of others through responsible parenthood, mentoring, generating ideas, and productive activity. The other end of the spectrum is stagnation, or self-absorption. A person who successfully manages this stage resolves the conflict in favor of generativity but has been in touch with feelings of stagnation.

According to Havighurst, middle age is the period in which "men and women reach the peak of their influence on society, and at the same time the society makes its maximum demands on them for social and civic responsibility."[23] The specific developmental tasks of middle age are (1) achieving civic and social responsibility, (2) establishing and maintaining economic stability, (3) assisting teenage children to become responsible adults, (4) developing adult leisure-time activities, (5) relating to ones spouse and to oneself as individuals, (6) accepting the physiological changes in oneself, and (7) adjusting to aging parents. Although these tasks are the same for men and women, Havighurst recognized that they may be realized differently.

Levinson et al., who conducted a study of middle-aged men, stated that middle age is a period in which one reappraises the past, modifies one's life structure, and becomes more individuated. Four polarities are confronted—young versus old, destruction versus creation, masculinity versus femininity, and attachment versus separateness—in an effort to achieve a new sense of wholeness and order.[24] Levinson was highly influenced by Erikson, as was Vaillant, consolidator of a longitudinal study of Harvard men.[25]

Kohlberg, a cognitive psychologist, described a sequence of six stages of moral development.[26] Although the stages are not necessarily linked to age, they are hierarchical, with the higher levels of development appearing last, if at all. The stages are grouped in three consecutive pairs—the preconventional, conventional, and postconventional. The highest stage requires an orientation toward universal moral principles.

PROBLEMS IN APPLICATION OF THEORIES TO WOMEN

Several problems arise in applying developmental theories to women. Many of the existing studies of adult development make the assumption that men and women go through the same life stages in the same sequence and that the male life path is the model for women's development. Erikson, for example, applied his "eight ages of man" to women, even though he indicated in some of his work that men and women have qualitatively different inner experiences and sources of identity.[27] Douvan and Adelson provided evidence that during adolescence the two stages follow a different sequence for men than for women; for women, the achievement of intimacy (Erikson's sixth stage) appeared to be a prerequisite for the achievement of identity (Erikson's fifth stage).[28] Gilligan found that for women the issues of identity and intimacy are fused.[29]

Kohlberg's theory of moral development also made unfounded assumptions about the similarity of men's and women's life stages.[30] When studies comparing men's and women's moral development found women lagging behind men, the conclusion appeared to be that women were morally backward.[31] In a provocative study that considered women's unique developmental experiences, Gilligan concluded that women are not defective, but rather they assess moral issues in a manner congruent with their primary orientation toward caring interpersonal relationships, whereas men assess moral issues in relation to the ideal of autonomy.[32] The findings of Gilligan and Douvan and Adelson suggest that a linear model of distinct life stages occurring in a prescribed sequence disregards the uniqueness and complexity of women's experiences.

Aside from the false assumptions and omissions made concerning women in developmental studies, there is an ongoing debate on the value of the developmental approach itself. Neugarten, the eminent authority on middle age, has stated that the criteria of age and developmental stage are not relevant to the study of adults, although they are applicable to children.[33] Other social scientists have criticized the methodologies of developmental studies and argued that they overemphasize women's reproductive role and ignore their work experience.[34] Moreover, the emphasis on psychological conflict in the developmental theories ignores the powerful effects that nonnormative life events and lifestyles have on human experiences.

LIFE PROCESSES DURING MIDDLE AGE

The authors' perspective is Jungian insofar as they see a significant change in values and behavior during middle age. A distillation of existing theories, empirical studies, and clinical experience with middle-aged women suggests that during middle adulthood, women engage in transcending sex role stereotypes and become more androgynous. During early adulthood, women yield to social pressures and conform to the prevailing ideals of their day regarding womanhood and women's roles. When they reach middle age, they reassess earlier priorities and move toward a definition of self that is based on inner needs rather than external criteria. Stereotypically "masculine" strivings for achievements and "feminine" concerns with affiliation are reintegrated. This inner change is reflected in women's reassessment of their interpersonal relationships, their physical beings, and the meaning of work and achievement.

Reassessment of Interpersonal Relationships

During middle adulthood, women evaluate the various interpersonal relationships in their lives, reworking and redefining them. At this time, women assess the quality rather than the quantity of their relationships, particularly their most intimate ones, and think about the bases on which these relationships were founded. Women in their middle years ask whether their expectations of themselves and others are still valid when circumstances under which they were formed (such as the presence of young children or economic dependency) no longer exist. They consider how much involvement with others they want in the future and the prospects of achieving what they want.

The married woman will assess her relationship with her spouse. She will try to be objective about her husband as an individual with positive as well as negative qualities. The married woman will remember what she and her husband have been through together and consider past satisfactions in relation to her current needs. The needs for self-expression and self-actualization are paramount at mid-life.[35] These needs conflict with the sex role stereotype of the self-denying, all-giving wife. The extent of the woman's turmoil at this time is partly determined by her ability to recognize, articulate, and seek fulfillment of her needs and by her husband's ability to adapt to her changes.

During middle adulthood, women become more individuated or more differentiated from others and more whole as human beings.[36] Women become aware of their unique characteristics and separate needs and attempt new, autonomous activities. When children have become independent and women are working, the rationale for stereotypical sex roles no longer makes sense. Some couples are able to respond to the woman's inner changes and new circumstances by accepting differences and developing flexibility in sex role behaviors. These couples are able to achieve a renewed sense of closeness. Other couples find the transition very stressful. Mid-life divorces commonly occur when the couple cannot accommodate to individual differences.

The single woman will also assess her close interpersonal relationships. If she has a close relationship with a special person (heterosexual or lesbian), she will consider its strengths and weaknesses and the kind of commitment, if any, that she wants. On the one hand, women who have never married or who have been divorced for some time may consider mid-life a last chance to marry or remarry. On the other hand, newly divorced women may revel in their newfound freedom and enjoy a period of exploration without commitment.

During mid-life, mothers will find that their relationships with their children have changed. The middle-aged mother most often has adolescent or older children. Adolescent children are in the process of separation from their parents, a process that involves the differentiation from and rejection of their parents. Moreover, adolescents tend to be vibrant, attractive, and impulsive, qualities that challenge the image middle-aged parents are relinquishing. The behavior of adolescents can be a substantial threat to their parents and their parents' marriage.

Middle-aged women will also reassess their relationship with their parents. During middle adulthood, women experience increased independence and autonomy based on pride in past accomplishments and decreased dependence on others. They develop "filial maturity," resolving infantile needs in relation to parents, coming to terms with their own adulthood, and accepting parents and their parents' generation on a more equal basis.[37] During this period, middle-aged women develop a qualitatively different relationship with parents—one based on mutuality, or more giving on the part of the daughter, who no longer principally receives her parents' nurturance.

Middle-aged adults have been called the "sandwich generation" because they occupy a position between older parents and teenage children, and both of these groups make demands on the middle generation.[38] The principal caretakers for the old and the young are middle-aged women, who consequently experience increased stress, both emotionally and financially. The stress forces some women to ask themselves whether they are providing help out of feelings of guilt and obligation or love and concern. Women who have devoted much of their adult lives to caring for others will wonder how long they will continue doing so. Some women will resent the burden imposed by parents and feel conflict because of unresolved issues from the past. Those women who are involved in the world of work may experience a conflict between what they want for themselves and their obligations to their parents.

Relationships with friends are also reassessed during middle age. Friendships between women tend to be intense during adolescence and early adulthood, particularly prior to marriage. During marriage, friendships often are based on commonalities in regard to children, religious interests, or husbands' careers. These status-based friendships have little to do with the woman as an individual and are subject to dissolution if the bond (children, church membership, or marriage) is broken. Moreover, during early adulthood, relationships with spouses and children take precedence over other relationships, leaving some women wanting but unable to share experiences with other women. Friendships with men who are not their spouses can be problematic throughout adulthood because sexual issues can arise. During middle age, women assess the pattern of their friendships and consider modifying it to reflect inner preferences rather than external pressures. Some women will develop new friendships, possibly with people at work who share their new interests. This may mean that some married couples will have nonmutual friends during mid-life, further reflecting the ongoing process of differentiation.

Reassessment of One's Physical Being

Every day the body ages, but during mid-life, women seem to take particular note of these changes. The familiar signs—gray hair, dry skin, wrinkles, weight gain—are taken to indicate the end of youthful attractiveness and the approach of old age. Many women fight these changes by joining health clubs, dying their hair, and becoming nutrition conscious. In time, women accept changes in their body as part of the natural course of life.

Women's apprehensions about physical changes have much to do with the way they are perceived by others: The more physically attractive they are, the more desirable they are. Because a woman's sense of identity is linked with her body image, she feels a loss of self when external changes occur. Although these gradual changes are not necessarily accompanied by physical decline, women imagine that every gray hair is a sign of dwindling attractiveness. Actually, mid-life women lead healthy, vigorous lives and maintain or even increase their attractiveness. Moreover, many women come to realize that attractiveness has more to do with how they feel about themselves than with external appearance.

As mentioned previously, the capacity to bear children is another issue of concern during mid-life.[39] On the one hand, women who have not had children, either by chance or choice, now may consider whether or not they wish to remain childless. Currently, with many women marrying later, pursuing careers, and remarrying, mid-life pregnancies are not unusual. On the other hand, women who have had children may think about whether they want more and may consider having tubal ligations or other forms of sterilization.

Other women experience or anticipate menopause. During menopause, the ovaries stop producing eggs and menstruation ceases. It usually occurs in the forties or fifties, on the average at age 50.[40] A great deal of mythology surrounds this phenomenon, even though most women do not experience great psychological stress from menopause.[41] Some women believe that after menopause, they will lose their sex drive. Others believe that it causes mental illness. Normally, there are hormonal changes and some physical symptoms, such as hot flashes and night sweats.

Research has indicated a range of reactions by women to menopause. Some feel ambivalent, probably because menopause symbolizes to them that they are no longer capable of performing the socially valued function of childbearing. Other women feel relieved that they no longer have to worry about pregnancy or birth control. Some women have improved sex lives following menopause.[42]

The women who seem to be most vulnerable during mid-life are those whose husbands, during their mid-life crises, leave their wives for younger women. When a middle-aged woman feels that she is past her prime and her husband opts for a youthful woman, she experiences an assault on her self-esteem. The middle-aged woman feels helpless because she cannot compete with the younger woman. She has lost her husband and her status as a married woman, along with the attractiveness she had when she was younger.

Reassessment of Work and Achievement

Another area that women reevaluate during mid-life is work and achievement. Some time during their thirties or forties, women forego meeting others' expectations of them in favor of meeting their own needs to achieve. The need to achieve becomes particularly strong for those women who suppressed their competitiveness during young adulthood to raise children and manage households. When the children become older, women find that they have more time and increased energy and would like to channel it into meaningful activity.

During mid-life, many women struggle to realize a long-standing ambition. This may involve getting training, returning to college, or pursuing a new line of activity such as running for election or writing a novel. Women who worked in a particular field when they were younger may consider returning to the same line of work and may want to update their skills and knowledge. Working women may want to change jobs or develop a new career. Some middle-aged women experience vague, uneasy feelings of dissatisfaction, wanting to do something different but not knowing what. Such women might seek therapeutic help.

Involvement in the world of work requires that women be competent and aggressive. Aggression is stereotypically a masculine trait, a trait that women have difficulty accepting in themselves. Research on younger adult women has indicated that these women are afraid of exercising their abilities and succeeding.[43] Middle-aged women, however, find that the expression of aggressive impulses comes naturally at this time and that as they get older, they get even more aggressive.[44]

The women who refuse to accept their aggressive impulses experience the most conflict at this time. These women believe on some level that achievement negates their femininity. They recognize that men do not seem to like aggressive women, that the traits of passivity and compliance are more socially acceptable. The men with whom this is most likely to cause conflict are their husbands, who may object to their wives' working or seeking some other outlet such as returning to college. Under such circumstances, women may be told they are being selfish and are needed at home. But even single women may experience conflict over achievement and aggression. Achievements distinguish one as an individual; some women would just as soon cheer in the background.

Despite the conflicts some women have over achievement, research shows that employment is a key concern of women in their middle years. A large proportion of women, regardless of marital or parental status, are members of the work force. During mid-life, women can devote more energy to their work, developing a serious career orientation that endures for many years. A recent study by Baruch, Barnett, and Rivers compared married and divorced women with and without children and single women without children and found that regardless of marital or parental status, the women with the highest scores in "mastery" (self-esteem, control of oneself, absence of depression and anxiety) were employed. This was particularly true of women in high-prestige jobs. Moreover, married working mothers did not suffer from excessive role strain but had a particularly strong sense of well-being. The authors pointed out that prior research and theories about women's development have ignored or minimized the importance of work in relation to a woman's well-being. Marriage and other intimate arrangements may contribute to a woman's sense of pleasure but are not associated with mastery.[45]

Not all women return to work or change careers during mid-life. Some who have worked hard during young adulthood and perhaps married late, suddenly consider leaving the workplace as they approach 40. These women have decided that work is not enough, that they have needs for intimacy and a desire to nurture that are not fulfilled by paid employment. Friedan has described this phenomenon as exemplary of the "second stage" of feminism, which followed the strong career focus that characterized the earlier period.[46] These women seek to reconcile the desire to achieve with the need for intimacy by shifting their orientation toward intimacy and affiliation.

CLINICAL PRACTICE

The goal of clinical practice with middle-aged women is to help them resolve developmental conflicts. For example, women who have spent most of their adult years nurturing and caring for children must learn to recognize their assertive and active sides without guilt and uncertainty and to take pride in mastering new challenges. The aims of clinical practice are accomplished by increasing the clients' awareness of such issues, helping them integrate these conflicting urges, encouraging behavior change, and helping women cope with the consequences of these changes.

Awareness

Many middle-aged women begin treatment unaware of internal, conflicting urges, which they have usually suppressed for many years. The initial goal for the social worker is to increase the woman's awareness of these desires and to help her gain insight and understanding into these unexpressed aspects of herself.

In many instances, women seek help when their last child begins school or leaves home. As their children spend increasing amounts of time with their friends, some women feel a sense of loss and futility about their role in the family. They may become depressed and recognize no alternatives to their present situation. Although they may show symptoms of anger and frustration, they typically do not verbalize these feelings. They need help to understand and cope with anger and assertive tendencies and permission to verbally express their feelings within the safe boundaries of the therapy sessions.

Integration

Once a woman recognizes these conflicting desires, the aim of therapy is to enable her to integrate her contradictory impulses. The woman may feel sadness, depression, and anger because she has lost what she valued in the previous developmental stage. The social worker must help her express grief for this loss. If she spent her younger adult years primarily raising children, she must mourn the loss of this phase in her life and accept that her years of childbearing are almost over. A career woman who has focused her early adult years on achievement and working must also come to terms with her past. At mid-life, she, too, must acknowledge the impending loss of her potential childbearing years. This recognition is often accompanied by emerging desires for nurturance and affiliation that were previously subordinated to more compelling drives to achieve. She may also need help grieving her past and accepting sacrifices and choices already made. Unless the client truly grieves and accepts the pain of these losses, it will be difficult for her to progress to the next phase and to consider future alternatives realistically.

As grieving gradually subsides, the mother begins to recognize desires to assert herself or to work, while the career woman learns to confront her nurturant, affiliative needs. The social worker must encourage these women to explore their new feelings, to discuss them during sessions, and to tolerate them without feeling guilty or overly anxious. As these feelings become familiar, the women become able to accept them, and they gradually become integrated with earlier desires. The middle-aged woman ultimately appreciates both masculine and feminine aspects of herself and becomes more androgynous. During this phase, the social worker must also help the woman reflect on her future and consider constructive, growth-enhancing alternatives in preparation for the stage of behavioral change.

Behavioral Change

Once the client is aware of her conflicting wishes and has integrated them, therapy should become more task-oriented and focus on behavioral change. The social worker should gently nudge the client toward actively changing her situation. Courses on vocational alternatives, career exploration workshops, or reinvestment in a current work situation may be appropriate at this time. Some women may pursue a new hobby or develop recreational interests. Specific homework assignments can be assigned each week and reviewed during the therapy sessions. A client should be reinforced for any behavioral changes she makes toward the realization of her goals. In some instances, the social worker may have to model the appropriate skills and allow the client to rehearse them through role playing. A woman who has never interviewed for a job, for example, could practice in a simulated session before experiencing an interview in real life.

Coping with the Consequences of Change

In addition to implementing behavioral changes, these women need help coping with the consequences of these changes. For example, family members may resent women who reenter school after years of devoting themselves full time to the family. They may oppose her absence and make her feel guilty for expressing herself in this way. Family sessions are often necessary to help the client negotiate her new role with family members.

CASE HISTORIES

The following two case histories of Ms. Jones and Ms. Stewart illustrate this clinical process in greater detail. In both instances, the women had reached a turning point in their lives and were struggling with contradictory, internal impulses.

Case 1

Ms. Jones was a 42-year-old married woman with four children, the youngest of whom was 10 years old. She was referred for counseling because she was very depressed and felt suicidal. About six months prior to seeking help, Ms. Jones had become pregnant. Soon after learning this, she had had an abortion and had decided to have her tubes tied. She later regretted having made this decision and was sad that she would never be able to bear children again.

During the assessment phase of treatment, it was discovered that Ms. Jones was feeling lonely, unwanted, and alienated from her children, who, she believed, were interested only in being with their friends and no longer seemed to need her. She reported that her days were empty, and she felt no purpose in living.

During the early stages of treatment, the social worker provided Ms. Jones with the opportunity to express her feelings of loss surrounding the abortion, the tubal ligation, and her inability to have children. The client then began to realize that she was completing her role as a self-sacrificing mother. Although Ms. Jones saw the role of mother as one that provided meaning for her, she eventually admitted that her children were developing interests independent of her. She felt sad and depressed about these changes in the family.

As therapy progressed, Ms. Jones revealed that she enjoyed recreational sports and physical exercise but never had the time to engage in them. She admitted that lately she had been restless sitting around drinking coffee with the women in the neighborhood or being at home when no one was there. The social worker explored these feelings of restlessness in greater depth with Ms. Jones, who described earlier periods in her life when she had been active in sports, volunteer work, and other community activities. She mentioned that she had discontinued these involvements when she had married at the age of 20. This opened up the opportunity for the therapist and client to mutually assess this active side of herself and to help Ms. Jones become reacquainted with these unfamiliar desires. At this point, the aim of therapy was to increase Ms. Jones's awareness of these desires to be creative again outside of the home. Ms. Jones began to understand why she impulsively terminated the pregnancy and had had her tubes tied. She realized that on some level, she had not wanted to have more children but feared that she might refuse the surgery if she reflected about it too long.

Toward the end of this second phase, Ms. Jones recognized unexplored assertive aspects of herself. She commented on how she had always believed she had potential and could significantly contribute to the community. This recognition led to the next phase—behavioral change. At this point, the social worker suggested that Ms. Jones consider joining a community organization or becoming involved with local sports. Ms. Jones agreed to explore her alternatives and review her progress with the social worker during the next session. Soon afterwards, she joined the League of Women Voters and met two friends whom she had not seen since high school and whose children had also grown up. At the next session, Ms. Jones remarked that it felt good to get out and she was excited about her new friends and activities.

As Ms. Jones increased her involvement in the community and had more pleasurable experiences with friends and peers, her depression began to lift. Ms. Jones's husband and children initially resented her absence, but after she explained to them her new needs and they realized that she was more pleasant and less depressed than previously, they concurred that the whole family had benefited from the changes.

Case 2

Ms. Stewart was a 38-year-old single woman employed as the vice-president of a major company in a large midwestern city. She was very successful in her job and was doing well financially. Since becoming an executive of the company, however, Ms. Stewart had felt increasingly depressed and empty. She decided that she could not solve the problem on her own and sought counseling.

During the early stages of treatment, Ms. Stewart stated that she had considered marriage in the past but had never found the right man. Recently, she felt regrets about her decision not to marry, and now that her career was less demanding, new desires for nurturance and intimacy had emerged. For the first time, she felt ready to marry and raise a family—desires that earlier had remained subordinate to urges to achieve and succeed. She now wondered whether she should have married earlier and had children; she felt uncertain that she could be happy as a single woman for the rest of her life. At this stage, the social worker encouraged Ms. Stewart to express her feelings of grief over the loss of her young adult years and to accept the choices that already had been made. As this phase of therapy progressed, Ms. Stewart became more aware of her sad feelings about never marrying or having a family and actively experienced her feelings of loss surrounding these issues.

The next phase of treatment focused on helping Ms. Stewart integrate her desires for nurturance with her inclinations toward achievement and assertiveness without devaluing either preference. As treatment progressed, Ms. Stewart reconciled these two polarities into a new synthesis, recognizing and valuing both tendencies within herself.

During the latter stages of treatment, Ms. Stewart explored creative ways of becoming nurturant or affiliative by becoming a foster parent. Ms. Stewart later reported feeling that her life had become more balanced and that she now appreciated her work more than she had before treatment.

ACCEPTANCE AND GROWTH

Ms. Jones and Ms. Stewart were referred to treatment for different reasons. Ms. Jones sought help because she felt that her children no longer needed her and was guilty about new desires to assert herself. Ms. Stewart needed to reevaluate sacrifices she had made for her career and was struggling with her needs to nurture. Both women were grieving over the loss of time, youth, and childbearing as well as struggling with the emergence of unfamiliar developmental urges. Once these women grieved the loss of their young adult years and accepted the needs of mid-life, they were able to reconsider their future optimistically and make changes to improve the quality of their lives. Both women had become more integrated and androgynous.

Whatever their previous lifestyles, women in their middle years must come to recognize and accept those aspects of themselves that they expressed and repressed during early adulthood. The choices made during those years constitute past commitments that cannot be erased. As women enter middle adulthood, however, they do have the power to change their lives and fulfill previously suppressed aspirations. Responsibilities such as child rearing or achieving financial stability lessen, and women feel freer to pursue their own interests. During mid-life, women reassess their lives and reorganize their priorities. They come to accept their human strivings to be aggressive and nurturing, and they become more androgynous.

These observations about the mid-life experiences of women are relevant not only to women clients of social agencies but to the service providers as well. Today, when the war babies of the 1940s are in their middle years and more women are in the work force, the middle-aged woman client has a good chance of being treated by a middle-aged woman social worker.[47] Because the social worker may be in the process of evaluating her own inner polarities, she is in danger of overidentifying or underidentifying with the client, depending on the client's conflicts and lifestyle and the social worker's needs. This may be reflected in the social worker's thinking about the client a great deal outside of work, seeing the client more or less frequently than necessary, or engaging in acts of rejection. Middle-aged social workers should become aware of their own struggle to reconcile polarities during this time so that they can help resolve, rather than contribute to, the client's problem. The more the social worker accepts herself, the more effective she can be as a therapist to the client who is of a similar age.

NOTES AND REFERENCES

1. See S. Sontag, "The Double Standard of Aging," *Saturday Review,* September 23, 1972, pp. 29–38.
2. See B. L. Neugarten, "Adult Personality: Toward a Psychology of the Life Cycle," in W. S. Sze, ed., *Human Life Cycle* (New York: Jason Aronson, 1975).
3. D. A. Miller, "The 'Sandwich' Generation: Adult Children of the Aging," *Social Work,* 26 (September 1981).
4. G. S. Getzel, "Social Work with Family Caregivers to the Aged," *Social Casework,* 62 (April 1981), pp. 201–209.
5. M. Weissman and G. L. Klerman, "Sex Differences and the Epidemiology of Depression," *Archives of General Psychiatry,* 34 (January 1977), pp. 98–111.
6. See E. M. Brennan and A. Weick, "Theories of Adult Development: Creating a Context for Practice," *Social Casework,* 62 (January 1981), pp. 13–19; N. Golan, *Passing Through Transitions: A Guide for Practitioners* (New York: Free Press, 1981); Weick, "A Growth-Task Model of Human Development," *Social Casework,* 64 (March 1983), pp. 131–137; S. L. Rhodes, "A Developmental Approach to the Life Cycle of the Family," *Social Casework,* 58 (May 1977), pp. 301–311; Golan, "Wife to Widow to Woman," *Social Work,* 20 (September

1975), pp. 369–374; and "Special Issue on Women," *Social Work* (entire issue) 21 (November 1976).

7. S. H. Cath, "Some Dynamics of Middle and Later Years," in H. J. Parad, ed., *Crisis Intervention Selected Readings* (New York: Family Service Association of America, 1965), pp. 174–190; S. Wasserman, "The Middle-Age Separation Crisis and Ego-Supportive Casework Treatment," *Clinical Social Work Journal,* 1 (Spring 1973), pp. 38–47; H. Zacks, "Self-Actualization: A Midlife Problem," *Social Casework,* 61 (April 1980), pp. 223–233; and M. Strickler, "Crisis Intervention and the Climacteric Man," *Social Casework,* 56 (February 1975) pp. 85–90.

8. R. D. Borgman, "Medication Abuse by Middle-Aged Women," *Social Casework,* 54 (November 1973), pp. 526–532. For a nonclinical approach to the middle-aged housewife, see S. B. Klass and M. A. Redfern, "A Social Work Response to the Middle-Aged Housewife," *Social Casework,* 58 (February 1977), pp. 101–110.

9. D. J. Levinson et al., *The Seasons of a Man's Life* (New York: Alfred A. Knopf, 1978).

10. E. Frenkel-Brunswik, "Adjustments and Reorientation in the Course of the Life Span," in B. L. Neugarten, ed., *Middle Age and Aging* (Chicago: University of Chicago Press, 1968), pp. 77–84.

11. R. J. Havighurst, *Human Development and Education* (New York: Longmans, Green & Co., 1953).

12. See G. J. Craig, *Human Development* (3d ed.; Englewood Cliffs, N.J.: Prentice-Hall, 1983); L. B. Schiamberg and K. U. Smith, *Human Development* (New York: Macmillan Publishing Co., 1982); J. J. Bigner, *Human Development: A Life Span Approach* (New York: Macmillan Publishing Co., 1983); and J. T. Gibson, *Living: Human Development through the Lifespan* (Reading, Mass.: Addison-Wesley Publishing Co., 1983).

13. M. T. Notman, "Changing Roles for Women at Mid-Life" in W. H. Norman and T. J. Scaramella, eds., *Mid-Life: Developmental and Clinical Issues* (New York: Brunner/Mazel, 1980); and G. Sheehy, *Passages: Predictable Crises of Adult Life* (New York: E. P. Dutton & Co., 1976).

14. Notman, "Changing Roles for Women at Mid-Life."

15. P. Weideger, *Menstruation and Menopause: The Physiology and Psychology, the Myth and the Reality* (New York: Alfred A. Knopf, 1976).

16. C. W. Cooke and S. Dworkin, *The Ms. Guide to a Woman's Health* (New York: Berkley Publishing Corp., 1979).

17. B. L. Neugarten, "The Awareness of Middle Age," in Neugarten, ed., *Middle Age and Aging,* pp. 93–98.

18. A. Rossi, "A Transition to Parenthood," *Journal of Marriage and the Family,* 30 (February 1968), pp. 26–39.

19. Levinson et al., *The Seasons of a Man's Life.*

20. C. G. Jung, *Modern Man in Search of a Soul* (New York: Harcourt Brace, 1933). See also Jung, "The Stages of Life," *Collected Works,* Vol. 8 (New York: Pantheon Books, 1960).

21. C. G. Jung, *Collected Works,* Vol. 9 (Princeton, N.J.: Princeton University Press, 1969), chap. 6.
22. E. H. Erikson, *Childhood and Society* (2d ed., rev.; New York: W. W. Norton & Co., 1963).
23. Havighurst, *Human Development and Education,* p. 268.
24. Levinson et al., *The Seasons of a Man's Life.*
25. See G. Vaillant, *Adaptation to Life* (Boston: Little, Brown & Co., 1977).
26. L. Kohlberg, "Development of Moral Character and Moral Ideology," in M. L. Hoffman and L. W. Hoffman, eds., *Review of Child Development of Research,* Vol. 1 (New York: Russell Sage Foundation, 1964).
27. E. H. Erikson, "Womanhood and the Inner Space," reprinted in J. Strouser, ed., *Women and Analysis* (New York: Grossman Publishers, 1974).
28. E. Douvan and J. Adelson, *The Adolescent Experience* (New York: John Wiley & Sons, 1966).
29. C. Gilligan, *In a Different Voice* (Cambridge, Mass.: Harvard University Press, 1982).
30. Kohlberg, "Development of Moral Character and Moral Ideology."
31. C. Holstein, "Development of Moral Judgment: A Longitudinal Study of Males and Females," *Child Development,* 47 (1976), pp. 51–61; and E. L. Simpson, "Moral Development Research: A Case Study of Scientific Cultural Bias," *Human Development,* 17, No. 2 (1974), pp. 81–106. Both cited in Gilligan, *In a Different Voice.*
32. Gilligan, *In a Different Voice.*
33. B. L. Neugarten, colloquium, Ohio State University, Columbus, April 27, 1983.
34. A. S. Rossi, "Life-Span Theories and Women's Lives," *Signs: Journal of Women in Culture and Society,* 6 (1980), pp. 4–32; R. C. Barnett and G. K. Baruch, "Women in the Middle Years: A Critique of Research and Theory," *Psychology of Women Quarterly,* 3 (Winter 1978), pp. 187–197; and Notman, "Changing Roles for Women at Mid-Life."
35. Zacks, "Self-Actualization."
36. C. Jung, *Collected Works,* Vol. 9.
37. M. Blenkner, "Social Work and Family Relationships in Later Life with Some Thoughts on Filial Maturity," in E. Shanas and G. F. Streib, eds., *Social Structure and the Family* (Englewood Cliffs, N.J.: Prentice-Hall, 1966), pp. 46–59.
38. Miller, "The 'Sandwich' Generation."
39. Notman, "Changing Roles for Women."
40. Weideger, *Menstruation and Menopause.*
41. S. M. McKinely and M. Jeffreys, "The Menopausal Syndrome," *British Journal of Preventive Social Medicine,* 28 (1974).
42. B. L. Neugarten, "A New Look at Menopause," in L. R. Allman and D. T. Jaffe, eds., *Readings in Adult Development: Contemporary Perspectives* (New York: Harper & Row, 1977), pp. 308–314.
43. M. S. Horner, *Success Avoidant Motivation and Behavior: Its Developmental Correlates and Situational Determinants* (Cambridge, Mass.: Harvard University Press, 1973).

44. Neugarten, "Adult Personality."
45. G. Baruch, R. Barnett, and C. Rivers, *Life Prints* (New York: McGraw-Hill Book Co., 1983).
46. B. Friedan, *The Second Stage* (New York: Summit Books, 1981).
47. See "Membership Survey Shows Practice Shifts," *NASW News,* 28 (November 1983), p. 7, Tables E and F.

OLD AGE

CHAPTER 6

OLDER WORKERS AND THE WORKPLACE

A New Challenge for Occupational Social Work

Michàl E. Mor-Barak and Margaret Tynan

The beginnings of occupational social work in the United States are rooted in a form of sexism and racism (Brandes, 1976). Nineteenth-century America was a country of clearly defined roles, and the world of business was the world of white men. Consequently, as business grew and employers faced a growing number of female and immigrant employees, they found themselves at a loss about treating their workers' "peculiar" problems. One answer was to hire a "specialist" called the "social secretary" who was the predecessor of the occupational social worker (Popple, 1981). Today, ageism is presenting a challenge to occupational social work. Once again, companies need workers who have not previously been involved in the work force, and the social work profession is in the position to offer its skills and ethics to help both older workers and businesses meet their own, as well as each other's, needs.

Older adults' increased interest in employment is motivated by several factors. First, the American work force is aging. The baby boom generation is getting older and is being succeeded by a declining number of young people entering the work force (Johnson & Packer, 1987). Second, increased life expectancy rates combined with a continuing trend toward early retirement amplify the economic burden of retirement on society (Clark, 1988). Third, the economic reality for many older adults includes lack of sufficient income and benefits, which require older adults' continued involvement in the work force (Howard, 1986). Finally, many older adults can anticipate a prolonged and healthy aging and are interested in continuing their productive involvement in society (Hayward, Grady, & McLaughlin, 1988).

Reprinted from *Social Work*, Vol. 38, No. 1, by permission of NASW Press. Copyright 1993, National Association of Social Workers, Inc., *Social Work*.

Despite this interest in continued employment by employers and older adults, older workers are more likely to lose their jobs than younger workers in instances such as plant closings and corporate mergers (Beckett, 1988). Many businesses cannot adequately deal with some of the life events older workers face, such as widowhood and caring for ailing spouses, and as a result many older workers are forced to retire earlier than planned. Also, older adults seeking employment may be turned off by employers' attitudes or discouraged by the job-seeking process itself. Social workers who are trained in both occupational social work and gerontology are in a unique position to respond to these problems.

DEMOGRAPHICS OF THE WORK FORCE

The baby boom generation is getting older and will be in the over-55 age bracket by 2010. This generation is being succeeded by a declining number of young people entering the work force. This younger age group will continue to decrease as a percentage of the population through 2000. Figure 6–1 compares the demographic composition of American adults in 1986 with projections for 2000. The proportion of adults age 16 to

Figure 6–1
Individuals by Age, Projection for 2000

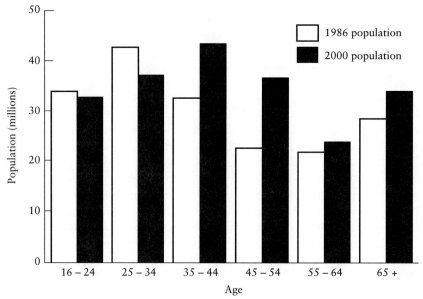

SOURCE: U.S. Bureau of the Census (1990). *United States Population Estimates* (Current Population Reports, P-25, No. 1057). Washington, DC: U.S. Government Printing Office.

34 will be smaller in 2000, whereas the proportion of adults age 55 and older will increase. In 1986, there were about 51 million adults age 55 and older, and by 2000 there will be about 59 million adults in that age bracket.

This population shift is coupled with a marked decrease in labor force participation among older adults. Although there are more elderly people in society now, they are less involved in work than they used to be. For example, in 1900, two-thirds of American men who were 65 or older were working, whereas in 1950, 45.8 percent of the men and 9.7 percent of the women who were 65 or older were part of the labor force. By 1980, the rate of labor force participation had been drastically reduced to 19.1 percent of the men and 8.5 percent of the women who were 65 or older (Kieffer & Flemming, 1980; U.S. Bureau of the Census, 1982).

This trend toward earlier retirement raises some questions about the impact of current public and private policies on the match between demographic trends and work force participation. Figure 6–2 demonstrates the declining labor force participation for men between 1960 and 1980 and projections for 2000. However, this pattern does not apply to women. Until recently, the life-cycle pattern of paid employment by women was influenced primarily by the presence of small children, and as a result, retirement, or the final withdrawal from the labor force, was not a distinct phase in the life cycle of most women. However, women's work patterns have recently become more similar to those of men, including the pattern of decline in labor force participation of women as they age (Clark, 1988).

Figure 6–2
Labor Force Participation by Age, Projection for Men to 2000

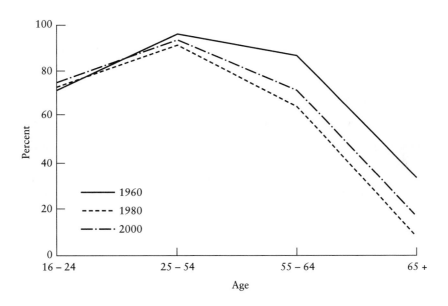

SOURCE: U.S. Bureau of Labor Statistics (1990). *Employment and Earnings*. 37(1). Washington, DC: U.S. Government Printing Office.

This trend of early retirement is partly a result of rising living standards in the United States and indicates improvements in economic well-being. However, it also reflects the inflexibility of the workplace. Until recently, industry did not actively recruit older people, nor did it make special efforts to accommodate the needs of older workers, such as part-time employment and flexible hours. In spite of the continued trend toward early retirement, there are indications that many retirees would welcome part-time or flexible jobs. Such continued activity corresponds to a wish to remain contributing members of society as well as to supplement incomes (Bourne, 1982; Sonnenfield, 1988).

Although high technology has enhanced worker productivity, it is anticipated that it will lead to changes in work force characteristics rather than size (Liebig, 1988). A work environment that requires education and work skills rather than manual labor can incorporate elderly people more readily than the pre-high-technology work environment. However, to facilitate this development, society in general and the workplace in particular must overcome the institutional barriers to employment of older adults that have been created over the years.

OLDER ADULTS AND THE WORLD OF WORK
Retirement

Society continues to expect and often require the majority of people older than 65 to retire. Historically, humane considerations were claimed to be the main reason. Because much of the labor in the early and middle stages of the industrial revolution consisted of heavy, physical effort over a long work day and work week, relief through retirement became a desirable goal. But, in fact, other factors than humane considerations have played a strong and persuasive part in the reduction of employment opportunities for older people.

Attitudes toward the past and, by extension, toward elderly people who are living repositories of the past, have changed markedly over the years, minimizing the contributions and perceived values of older people. The industrial revolution caused a dramatic change in society's views toward elderly people and what they represent by shifting away from traditional criteria of work assignments. Much of the population could no longer inherit occupations like their parents had because occupations had changed drastically. Industrial society required workers to be highly mobile and not bound to any locale or set of traditions. Industrialization represented a multifaceted attack on tradition, an attack symbolized by the words "change" and "movement" (Wilensky & Lebeaux, 1965). The attitudes resulting from these changes created an environment in which older adults found it difficult to keep up with the rest of the workers. Society has come to associate aging with decreased work and training capacity, with little or no regard for the heterogeneity of the 55 and older age group and with little or no knowledge of new and special work arrangements and retraining techniques.

However, during wartime increased numbers of minorities, women, and elderly people have left the ranks of the unemployed to join the labor force (Hinrichs, 1942; Stein, 1980). For example, World War II brought about significant changes in the labor force composition. The shortage in young male workers created employment opportunities and demand for both women and older adults, populations that have proven to be trainable, reliable, and productive. Between June 1940 and June 1942, increased job opportunities created by the mobilization for World War II contributed to a nearly 9 percent increase in the total number of workers older than 54 (Hinrichs, 1942). Conversely, employment rates among these population groups has decreased during peacetime periods, as represented by the trend for earlier retirements among older adults over the past several decades (Richardson, 1989; Stein, 1980).

Retirement at a specific age is an artifact of the Social Security laws that has acquired certain conveniences, leading to its perception and adoption as "normative" (*Work in America,* 1973). First, it enables employers to dispense with the services of older workers gracefully, avoiding the administrative difficulties of selectively firing often "'faithful" workers. Second, it enables older workers to salvage more self-respect when they are considered members of a class that is cut loose by compulsion from the work force than they would if they were individually removed. And third, it enables younger workers to look forward to both advancement and the benefits enjoyed by older workers in a system that shows preference to seniority.

However, these conveniences do not mean that the current retirement system is beneficial for everyone. Retirement, which was once seen as a great achievement for the worker, is now viewed as an obstacle by people who feel they can and want to continue participating in the work force. Improved health and longer life expectancy prolong the period in which older adults can be productive in society. In addition, the larger variety of jobs not demanding physical strength enables more older people to continue working. These changes call for policy alterations to provide older adults with options and real choices with respect to work and retirement.

Economic Realities of Old Age

In many respects, the majority of older people and their families have avoided the severe labor market and poverty problems of the 1980s. However, compared with younger workers, older people are more likely to become unemployed as a result of job loss and to experience greater difficulties in obtaining reemployment after they have lost their jobs.

The economic security package that emerged in postwar America was intended to give older workers a secure position in the economy. The ideal package included full employment, Social Security and private pensions, job-based health insurance, and seniority protection. Data confirm that the majority of today's older workers have secured the benefits of career employment, stable earnings, and adequate pensions. These relative advantages, however, are not evenly spread throughout the older population (Sum & Fogg, 1990). Specifically, four groups were identified as having experienced the most severe difficulties: ethnic minorities, women living alone, working poor people, and displaced workers. Unfortunately, these vulnerable groups are the most rapidly growing segments of the older population (Doeringer, 1990).

Although the poverty rates of all older people have declined absolutely and relatively over the past two decades, the poverty rates of women, blacks, and Hispanics remain well above the average for their age group. For example, in 1986 the poverty rate among older black families was four times as high as that of white families, and older Hispanic families experienced a poverty rate more than three times higher than that of white, non-Hispanic families. Older women, especially those living alone, have continued to live in poverty about 60 percent more frequently than men (Sum & Fogg, 1990). The changing demography of the nation's older population, including the growing numbers of racial and ethnic minorities, will complicate the task of combating future poverty problems among elderly people.

Work and Family. Older adults face life events, such as widowhood, loss of friends and relatives, and caring for an ailing spouse, that affect their health, life satisfaction, and work performance. In fact, caring for an aging spouse or relative has become a growing concern for middle-age and older workers as well as for the workplace (Brice & Alegre, 1989; Gadon & Serwin, 1989; Kola & Dunkle, 1988; Liebig, 1988; Piktialis, 1990). It is estimated that at least 20 percent of all employees currently provide assistance to elderly relatives, with some studies finding prevalence rates as high as 40 percent (Health Action Forum, 1989; Scharlach, Lowe, & Schneider, 1991).

Caregiving demands placed on middle-age and older adults create potential conflicts between family responsibilities and workplace obligations (Brice & Alegre, 1989; Gadon & Serwin, 1989; Kola & Dunkle, 1988). For example, elder care responsibilities often result in increased tardiness, absenteeism, and requested unscheduled days off (Kola & Dunkle, 1988). Studies have also indicated that caring for an elderly relative may negatively affect the caregiver's health. In addition, providers of elder care often report health problems such as weight fluctuations, sleeplessness, and depression (Gadon & Serwin, 1989). In spite of these circumstances, most businesses today do not offer work flexibility or support to workers caring for an elderly relative. As a result, many older workers caring for an ailing spouse or relative are forced to retire earlier than planned or desired.

Work and Well-being. Research to date has presented accumulating evidence that employment has a positive effect on the mental health, life satisfaction, marital satisfaction, and perceived health of older adults. For example, Bossé, Aldwin, Levenson, and Ekerdt (1987) examined psychological symptoms in a sample of 1,513 older men and found that retirees reported more psychological symptoms than did workers, even after controlling for physical health status. Another study found that the prestige associated with a spouse's employment had a positive effect on marital satisfaction among older adults (Cassidy, 1985). Further results of a nationally representative sample of elderly women indicated that employed women reported significantly higher levels of life satisfaction compared to members of the same cohort who were homemakers or retirees (Riddick, 1985).

A significant difference in perceived health between the older worker and the retiree was found in a randomized controlled study by Soumerai and Avon (1983). More than a third (36 percent) of the experimental group, who worked half-time in an urban park beautification program, reported their health as excellent compared with only 14 percent of the control group, who did not participate in the work program. Health status was reported as fair by only 8 percent of the experimental group compared with 45 percent of the control group. In comparing the control and experimental groups' individual scores, the overall effect on perceived health was highly significant. Perceived changes in health status were also measured, and the results indicated that improved health was reported more frequently by the experimental group and that declining health was more prevalent in the control group.

EXISTING PROGRAMS

Few programs specifically target low-income elderly people. One successful program is the Senior Community Service Employment (SCSE) program funded under the Older Americans Act of 1965, which has attracted many poor and near-poor older Americans into its part-time subsidized employment programs. For example, during the 1988 program year, the program provided job opportunities for 100,000 older Americans, and more than half of those remaining enrolled at the end of the program year were 65 years or older (Sum & Fogg, 1990). On the other hand, training programs for poor Americans, such as the Job Training Partnership Act (JTPA, 1982) Title IIA programs, have provided only limited services to elderly poor people. For example, during the 1987 program year, only 4 percent of JTPA participants were 55 or older (Sum & Fogg, 1990). Clearly, more programs are needed that target poor elderly people. As the experience of the SCSE indicates, such programs can make a difference in the income and in the quality of life of these people.

Older worker programs usually fall into two categories: programs facilitating linkages between the older adults and potential employers and programs that accommodate the needs of the older individual in the work environment, such as job modification, job training, and elder care. The resources available for both types of program are limited, drawing on public and community resources (for linkage and training programs), as well as some private industry resources (for linkage and accommodation programs).

Linkage Programs

In-house Programs. The trend toward early retirement, coupled with the diminishing numbers of youths entering the labor market as a result of lower birth rates, presents American industry with an impending shortage of available workers. However, few corporations are responding to this challenge with innovative programs to retain older workers or to encourage their return to active labor force participation. It has been estimated that only 4 percent of U.S. corporations offer such programs, whereas 62 percent encourage early retirement through various inducement programs (Ramirez, 1989).

Although there is little research in the area of the cost benefits to companies that implement such programs, several companies cited financial as well as intangible advantages (Jessup & Greenberg, 1989). The Travelers Company estimated that it saved $1 million a year by using retirees to fill temporary positions (Zetlin, 1989). A study of a large aerospace corporation found a savings of nearly $17,000 annually for each employee who retired after age 60 compared with employees retiring between ages 50 and 54. Builders Emporium credited reduction in annual staff turnover rates from more than 100 percent to approximately 70 percent to company implementation of older worker hiring and retention programs (Ramirez, 1989). Days Inns of America reported a similar outcome with turnover for positions filled by older workers falling from 40 percent to 1 percent (Holtcamp, 1989). Bankers Life and Casualty in Chicago has a history of hiring people older than 50 and has created a temporary workers pool made up of retirees that saved the company $10,000 in agency fees during its first year of operation (Root, 1985). Finally, Ames Department Stores, a large retailer, sends recruitment representatives from their human resources department to senior centers and other senior functions, and Western Savings and Loan Association in Arizona prefers older people to fill teller and customer relations positions because of their level of maturity and life experience (Goddard, 1987; Nye, 1988). Other advantages are difficult to measure monetarily, such as employee experience, loyalty, dependability, positive attitudes, and high morale.

Community-Based Programs. A review of community-based employment services to older adults reveals a variety of programs that focus on providing job referral, career counseling, and retirement planning to the older worker (Cronin, 1988). The majority of the job-referral programs, which create linkages between potential employers and older workers, are government funded. For example, the Senior Community Service Employment Program, a Title V program that provides older adults with work experience before employment placement, is government sponsored and provided free of charge. Other programs such as Forty-Plus, which is privately funded and focuses on job counseling and referral to executives, require a membership fee.

A variety of job-referral services are offered by older worker coordinating councils that link older workers and interested employers. These councils operate a hot line for older workers interested in employment and provide several employment services through a network of affiliated agencies. Some network members have job desks that match older workers with jobs, and others offer more elaborate services, called "job clubs," that provide practical help in resume writing, job interviews, and retraining. Self-employment services are often available through local chambers of commerce to assist those who wish to go into business for themselves. The Service Corps of Retired Executives is a national voluntary program that provides free advice on self-employment.

Career counseling services are affiliated with most private and public educational institutions. Vocational counselors are available through many state employment offices and through national organizations such as the American Society for Training and Development and American Personnel and Guidance Association. Career counseling is also included in some retirement-planning programs, which are increasingly being offered to employees by banks and other service industries as an important part of employee benefit packages.

Programs Accommodating Older Adults' Needs

Job Modifications. Work schedule modifications for older workers, including job sharing between two or more workers, flex-time schedules, and reduced work weeks, are in place at Stouffer Foods, Varian Associates, Warren Publishing Company, and Polaroid (Goddard, 1987; Ramirez, 1989). These programs encourage extension of the older worker's tenure with the company. In an effort to match the older worker with the appropriate program, Stouffer Foods instituted a participatory performance evaluation. The worker joins with management in deciding if the worker's current job status continues to be appropriate. Depending on the results of the evaluation, several choices are available to the older worker including job sharing, flextime, job transfer, incremental retirement plan, or assistance with family concerns.

Although only one in 100 U.S. corporations offers comprehensive job modification programs (Ramirez, 1989), a few companies offer gradual or incremental retirement plans to their employees. Varian's Retirement Transitions program offers a reduced workweek and the option of changing to a less stressful position (Holtcamp, 1989; Ramirez, 1989). Positive Transitions, Polaroid's gradual retirement plan, allows the older worker to try out retirement for a period of time while the company holds the work position open, giving the employee the option to return. Instron, a large manufacturing company, transfers the valuable talents of its retirees to younger sales people through a paid Sales Emeritus Program (Ramirez, 1989).

In some cases job demands may be difficult for the older worker to meet. Builders Emporium recognized that requiring heavy lifting as part of a salesperson's job duties discouraged older workers from participating in the labor force. By redistributing restocking duties to the night shift only, day employees could concentrate on sales. This modification facilitated an increase in older individuals among the company's employees (Ramirez, 1989; Taylor, 1989). Another approach to job modification, taken by Xerox, is a voluntary job downgrading program. Unionized older workers may bid on lower-stress positions at an adjusted rate of pay (Goddard, 1987).

Job enhancement programs also stimulate employee retention and discourage burnout. The Senior Associate program sponsored by Corning Glass Works recognizes outstanding employee performance with a pay increase and uses senior associates as advisors to newer employees (Ramirez, 1989). A unique Wells Fargo sabbatical program allows employees of 10 or more years up to three months at full pay to pursue their own interests. The company believes this program promotes company loyalty, which results in reduced employee turnover (Ramirez, 1989).

Flexible benefit packages often accompany programs that are geared toward retaining older workers. Benefits range from plans such as Varian Associates or Warren Publishing Company's prorated pension and health benefit plan for the retiree working part-time to full benefit plans with limited working hours such as the Travelers' plan (Goddard, 1987; Ramirez, 1989; Zetlin, 1989).

Training Programs. Training programs that upgrade employees' skills also target older workers. For example, General Electric's Aerospace Electronic Systems Department offers the Technical Renewal program to company engineers to keep them abreast of the latest technological science. The company estimates that retraining an employee costs only one-third of the expense of hiring a new engineering graduate (Nye, 1988). IBM offers a unique professional development program three years before and two years after retirement to employees and their spouses, paying their tuition for courses that either enhance skills or retrain for potential second careers (Goddard, 1987).

The Job Training Partnership Act (1982) mandated that states establish training programs targeting the older worker. Federal funds have been allocated to train dislocated workers. Employers who qualify to participate in the program are partially reimbursed for providing the older worker with on-the-job training.

Training for the older worker is also available through agencies that provide rehabilitation services. One example is the Projects with Industry program of Aging in America, which operates in several major cities in the country and offers job-skills training sessions targeting the older disabled adult (Cronin, 1988).

Elder Care Programs. A few corporations are responding to the growing needs of their caregiving employees, many of whom are older workers, by altering benefit packages to include assistance with elder care. The Travelers Company was one of the first corporations to look at the problem of elder care. Other examples of corporations with innovative programs are Philip Morris Companies and American Express, which offer counseling, referral services, education, and support groups for caregiving employees. Remington Products provides relief for the caregiver, freeing him or her to remain employed, by paying half the cost of the services of a visiting nurse. IBM supports employee caregivers through provision of a national network to find appropriate services for elderly people who need care (Gadon & Serwin, 1989).

Even though the few existing elder care programs appear to have positive outcomes for both the worker and the corporation, one corporate survey indicated that only 7 percent of these organizations planned to develop future policies and programs to address the problems of elder care. The reason for such a low percentage is attributed to the fact that caregivers tend not to relate their problems to their employers (Kola & Dunkle, 1988).

IMPLICATIONS FOR SOCIAL WORK

One obstacle to the proliferation of older workers' programs in the workplace are current policies in both the government and the private sector (Aging Work Force, 1989; Kauffman, 1987). The Travelers Company and Atlantic Richfield had to restructure corporate policies regarding pension rules and mandatory retirement to implement older worker programs. More difficult to change are ageist stereotypes that are part of corporate culture in many U.S. companies (Nye, 1988). It is hoped that the success of existing older worker programs will help dispel the stereotypes and myths and alter the corporate culture that generates policies adverse to the older worker. Corporations, businesses, work organizations, and society as a whole should be challenged to make the necessary changes in the workplace to accommodate the needs of older workers. The social work profession can promote awareness and facilitate change through interventions to promote continued employment and rehiring of older workers.

Promoting Hiring of Older Workers

Ending age discrimination in the workplace can discourage the trend toward early retirements and may bring retirees back to the work force. Practices such as mandatory
retirement, refusal to hire middle-age people, and preference for promoting younger
workers create barriers to the employment of older adults and constitute age discrimination. A congressional statute, the Age Discrimination in Employment Act of 1967
(ADEA), extends the concept of discrimination to age and prohibits most of these age-
related work practices (Levine, 1988). As stated by Congress, the purposes of the
ADEA are to promote employment of older people based on their ability rather than
age, to prohibit arbitrary age discrimination in employment, and to help employers and
workers find ways to meet problems arising from the impact of age on employment. On
the macro level, it should be made clear to employers that they cannot afford to waste
the talent and experience of men and women who have many active, productive years
ahead of them. On the micro level, emotional support and legal aid should be offered to
older adult victims of age discrimination.

Serving as a Resource for Managers

To encourage the continued employment of older adults, employers must initiate
changes in the workplace. The literature indicates that employers must increase their
knowledge and skills and change their attitudes to develop a more effective strategy to
manage a maturing work force (Liebig, 1988). Social workers trained in gerontology
can provide management with information about demographic trends and their implications for an aging society and can help management evaluate how current programs
and practices affect older workers and their families. Managers at all levels can prevent
and resolve work-related problems by using a variety of services within the organization or in the broader community. When services such as retraining, wellness programs,
and preretirement counseling are provided by the company they should be brought to
the attention of managers at all levels. In addition, managers should become familiar
with services in the community, such as older worker coordinating councils, job referral programs for older adults, retraining programs, career counseling services, retirement planning programs, rehabilitation agencies, and age discrimination information,
and should use these services to benefit older workers (Cronin, 1988).

Linking Job Seekers with Employers

Many older adults who are interested in obtaining a job do not actively seek employment, and although some companies may be aware of their need to hire older workers,
they rarely seek out those workers. Social workers can help bridge this gap in several
ways. The job-seeking process can be discouraging for a person who has not actively
looked for a job for several years. Social workers can help older adults cope successfully
with the job-seeking process by organizing support groups to help individuals prepare a
resume, rehearse for interviews, and exercise assertiveness in combating age discrimination. Social workers can also work with companies to set recruitment policies that are

sensitive to the older adults' needs. Activities can include job fairs aimed at older workers, advertisements that emphasize job flexibility and job options that may be attractive to older workers, and manager training in nondiscriminatory practices toward older people.

Advising Companies on Work Arrangements and Training Programs

Research in industrial gerontology has pointed to six job arrangements that can be used to effectively accommodate the work needs and preferences of older workers. These arrangements fall within two broad categories: part-time work schedules and job modifications for full-time older employees (Paul, 1988). The part-time category includes job-sharing (sharing one full-time job between two part-time workers), phased retirement (gradually reducing the number of hours until full retirement), and rehiring retirees part-time. The job modification category includes job redesign (restructuring the work to be performed or reshaping the physical environment surrounding the worker), job transfer (transferring the older worker to a less physically or mentally demanding job), and job retraining (updating the employee's job skills to keep pace with the changing technology). Employers may find it useful to offer older workers a choice of work arrangements that represent alternatives to the jobs they have held for years. A choice of work arrangements for older workers may permit those experiencing health problems or skill obsolescence to work more productively (Paul, 1988). Older employees and management can mutually benefit from these personnel practices.

Counseling and Supporting Older Workers and Their Families

Social work interventions focused on coping with both family and personal problems can enhance older adults' emotional and physiological well-being and facilitate their continued participation in the labor force. Elder care is one area in which social work can have a positive impact. Many older adults have spouses or parents who are disabled by Alzheimer's disease, stroke, and heart disease. Not only can social work programs provide support, counseling, and brokerage services to the individual and the family, but more importantly, they can also bring the severity of the problem to the attention of corporate America. Two exploratory studies reported by Kola and Dunkle (1988) indicated that employers and unions do not yet fully comprehend the effects of elder care concerns on the employees' health and well-being and, subsequently, on their work performance. Industrial social workers can provide counseling information and case management to alleviate problems experienced by individuals caring for elderly people. In addition, through documentation of the problem, social workers can educate management, thus influencing corporate policy.

Many older adults experience major life events such as widowhood, loss of friends and relatives, and forced relocation. Crisis intervention and bereavement counseling are, therefore, important areas for social work intervention in the workplace. Health deterioration is a concern for many older adults that can be alleviated by wellness programs in the workplace. Offering workshops, educational lectures, and support groups that focus on reducing health risks such as obesity, alcoholism, and tobacco use can enhance older workers' health and well-being, as well as their ability to continue their productive participation in the labor force.

Retirement planning is another important area for social work intervention with older adults in the workplace. Studies on retirement indicate that economic status and health issues emerge as major concerns for older adults (Beehr, 1986). Retirement planning aimed at reducing stress from retirement should focus on economic and health issues and should be available to those employees expressing the need for assistance (Safford, 1988).

CONCLUSION

There is a socioeconomic need for older adults to postpone their retirement and to continue their productive contributions to society. Research indicates that older adults who are in good health could benefit from a prolonged work experience, which may positively affect mental health, life satisfaction, and marital satisfaction. Some companies have initiated innovative older worker programs that seem to benefit both older workers and employers, but these programs are few and too limited to affect the lives of all older adults in this country.

In contrast to the ageist myth of feebleness and disability, many older people are interested and able to continue their productive involvement in the work force. As billions are spent on biomedical research to enable people to live longer, society must take measures to ensure that living is less onerous, financially and psychologically. Work organizations and society as a whole should be challenged to restructure the work environment in terms of work policies, social atmosphere, and physical conditions to accommodate the needs of older workers and to welcome them into the workplace. The social work profession can have an important role in raising awareness of the issues and initiating changes. Social work intervention can make a difference for the older worker by working with individuals, groups, and work organizations to change attitudes, initiate policies, and open up new options for older adults and work organizations.

REFERENCES

Age Discrimination in Employment Act of 1967, P.L. 90-202, 81 Stat. 602.

Aging Workforce. (1989). National Council on the Aging, 3(1).

Beckett, J. O. (1988). Plant closing: How older workers are affected. *Social Work, 33,* 29–33.

Beehr, T. A. (1986). The process of retirement: A review and recommendations for future investigation. *Personnel Psychology, 39,* 31–55.

Bossé, R., Aldwin, C. M., Levenson, M. R., & Ekerdt, D. J. (1987). Mental health differences among retirees and workers: Findings from the normative aging study. *Psychology and Aging, 2,* 383–389.

Bourne, B. (1982). Effects of aging on work satisfaction, performance and motivation. *Aging and Work, 5,* 37–47.

Brandes, S. T. (1976). *American welfare capitalism, 1880–1940*. Chicago: University of Chicago Press.

Brice, G. C., & Alegre, M. R. (1989). Eldercare as an EAP concern. *EAP Digest, 9*(5) 31–34.

Cassidy, M. L. (1985). Role conflict in the postparental period. *Research on Aging, 7*, 433–454.

Clark, R L. (1988). The future of work and retirement. *Research on Aging, 10*, 169–193.

Cronin, C. A. (1988). Resources for managers of an aging work force. In H. Dennis (Ed.), *Fourteen steps in managing an aging work force* (pp. 69–84). Lexington, MA: D.C. Heath.

Doeringer, P. B. (1990). Economic security, labor market flexibility, and bridges to retirement. In P. B. Doeringer (Ed.), *Bridges to retirement* (pp. 3–22). Ithaca, NY: ILR Press.

Gadon, B., & Serwin, S. (1989). Eldercare: Its impact in the workplace. *EAP Digest, 9*(5), 25–28.

Goddard, R. W. (1987). How to harness America's gray power. *Personnel Journal, 66*, 33–40.

Hayward, M. D., Grady, W. R., & McLaughlin, S. D. (1988). Recent changes in mortality and labor force behavior among older Americans: Consequences for nonworking life expectancy. *Journal of Gerontology, 43*, S194–S199.

Health Action Forum. (1989). *Employee elder caregiving survey*. Boston: Health Action Forum of Greater Boston.

Hinrichs, A. F. (1942). Problems of readjustment in the postwar labor market. *Annals of the American Academy of Political and Social Science, 224*, 157–164.

Holtcamp, R. (1989). At Varian, retirement transition program offers chance to ease into new life. *Aging Workforce, 3*, 7–8.

Howard, M. I. (1986). Employment of retired-worker women. *Social Security Bulletin, 49*(3), 4–18.

Jessup, D., & Greenberg, B. (1989, Summer). Innovative older-worker programs. *Generations*, pp. 23–27.

Job Training Partnership Act, P.L. 97-300, 96 Stat. 1322 (1982).

Johnson, W. B., & Packer, A. E. (1987). *Workforce 2000: Work and workers for the 21st century*. Indianapolis: Hudson Institute.

Kauffman, N. (1987). Motivating the older worker. AAM *Advanced Management Journal, 52*(2), 43–48.

Kieffer, J. A., & Flemming, A. S. (1980). Older Americans: An untapped resource. *Aging, 321*, 2–11.

Kola, L. A., & Dunkle, R. E. (1988). Eldercare in the workplace. *Social Casework, 69*, 569–574.

Levine, M. L. (1988). Age discrimination: The law and its underlying policy. In H. Dennis (Ed.), *Fourteen steps in managing an aging work force* (pp. 25–38). Lexington, MA: Lexington Books.

Liebig, P. S. (1988). The work force of tomorrow: Its challenge to management. In H. Dennis (Ed.), *Fourteen steps in managing an aging work force* (pp. 97–112). Lexington, MA: Lexington Books.

Nye, D. (1988, September). Writing off older assets. *Across the Board,* pp. 44–52.

Older Americans Act of 1965, P.L. 89–73, 79 Stat. 218.

Paul, C. E, (1988). Implementing alternative work arrangements for older workers. In H. Dennis (Ed.), *Fourteen steps in managing an aging work force* (pp. 113–122). Lexington, MA: Lexington Books.

Piktialis, D. S. (1990). Employers and elder care: A model corporate program. *Pride Institute Journal, 9,* 26–31.

Popple, P. R. (1981). Social work practice in business and industry 1875–1930. *Social Service Review, 55,* 257–269.

Ramirez, A. (1989, January). Making better use of older workers, *Fortune,* pp. 179–187.

Richardson, V. E. (1989). Social work practice and retirement. *Social Casework, 70,* 210–218.

Riddick, C. C. (1985). Life satisfaction for older female homemakers, retirees, and workers. *Research on Aging, 7,* 383–393.

Root, L. S. (1985). Corporate programs for older workers. *Aging, 351,* 12–16.

Safford, F. (1988). Value of gerontology for occupational social work. *Social Work, 33,* 42–45.

Scharlach, A. E., Lowe, B. F., & Schneider, E. L. (1991). *Elder care and the workforce.* Lexington, MA: D.C. Heath.

Sonnenfield, J. (1988). Continued work contributions in late career. In H. Dennis (Ed.), *Fourteen steps in managing an aging work force* (pp. 191–211). Lexington, MA: Lexington Books.

Soumerai, S. B., & Avon, J. (1983). Perceived health, life satisfaction, and activity in urban elderly: A controlled study of the impact of part-time work. *Journal of Gerontology, 38,* 356–362.

Stein, A. A. (1980). *The nation at war.* Baltimore: Johns Hopkins University Press.

Sum, A. M., & Fogg, W. N. (1990). Profile of the labor market for older workers. In P. B. Doeringer (Ed.), *Bridges to retirement* (pp. 23–32). Ithaca, NY: ILR Press.

Taylor, R. (1989). Builders Emporium tailors jobs to older worker strengths. *Aging Workforce, 3,* 9–10.

U.S. Bureau of the Census. (1982). *Population profile of the United States: 1981.* (Population characteristics, Series P-20; pp. 39–55). Washington, DC: U.S. Government Printing Office.

Wilensky, H. L., & Lebeaux, C.N. (1965). *Industrial society and social welfare.* New York: Russel Sage Foundation.

Work in America. (1973). *Report of a special task force to the Secretary of Health, Education, and Welfare.* Boston: MIT Press.

Zetlin, M. (1989, January). Help wanted: Life experience preferred. *Management Review,* pp. 51–55.

CHAPTER 7

GROUP THERAPY FOR THE ELDERLY

One Approach to Coping

Mickie Griffin and Mildred V. Waller

INTRODUCTION

The final developmental task of human life, as described by Erik Erikson (1963) is the acceptance of one's life as something that had to be, something that could not be changed. A certain gentle resignation about what has been can free us to explore fresh possibilities in the time that remains. Unfortunately, this potential is threatened in the aging process by inevitable change and, for many, a succession of losses. These experiences, common in the later stages of life, demand adjustments at a time when our capacity for adaptation is greatly reduced. Previous support systems—work habits, family patterns and value structures—are weakened or nonexistent, leaving us anchorless at a time of great stress.

Emotionally and physically drained by successive crises, many of us become susceptible to emotional problems. Depression, a pervasive state, sets in, leaving us useless and questioning the value of our existence. It is estimated that 10–20% of individuals over 65 years of age are afflicted with mental disorders and that prevalence of depression may range up to 65% in this age group (Blazer, 1980, p.52).

In years past, mostly in rural America, natural support systems given by families, neighbors, and clergy helped sad and lonely people to overcome depression. But with

Reprinted from *Clinical Social Work Journal,* Vol. 13, No. 3 (1985), pp. 261–269, by permission of Human Sciences Press, Inc.

With acknowledgment and appreciation to Myles Edwards, Ph.D., and Dawne Green, M.A., of the Aurora Community Mental Health Center for the review of this manuscript and to the four consortium agencies who sponsor this project, for their support and encouragement.

rapidly changing life styles and family patterns, who can be counted upon today, especially in crowded and impersonal neighborhoods of large, urban cities?

According to Rosen and Rosen (1982, p.21), only 4% of older adults seek treatment in public mental health clinics and even fewer, 2%, in private psychiatric care. Existing negative stereotypes of mental health agencies and personnel have been blamed for this underutilization of mental health services, though other reasons have been identified as well. It is no wonder that older persons account for 41% of all admissions to mental hospitals (even though this age group comprises only 11% of the United States population) and that, of all suicides, 31.5% are in this group (Busse & Pfeiffer, 1977). To counteract an escalation of these alarming statistics, much consideration has been given recently to alternative mental health service modalities which are more readily acceptable to the elderly than traditional clinic services. Group therapy in community settings is one of these alternatives.

Group processes for older adults have been in use since World War II. In a historical review of the development of group psychotherapy, Parham, Priddy, McGovern, and Richman (1982) point out that leader-focused, supportive group intervention evolved, mainly, from one-to-one approaches through trial and error. That process emphasized acquisition of daily living skills, not insight and personality change. The central focus of current work in group therapy stems from a model formulated by Yalom (1970), who discussed 11 curative elements which, he contended, apply to all forms of group treatment.

But until the mid-sixties, the predominant setting for this modality was in institutions. The greatest contributions to the application of this model have been in the area of social work, although nursing, psychiatry, and psychology have made significant contributions as well.

Among the first gerontologists to endorse group therapy were Butler (1975) and Busse and Pfeiffer (1977). They cited three specific advantages over individual treatment: (1) more efficient time-use of professional personnel; (2) exchanged learning among group members; and (3) group membership. They maintained that the development of social skills encourages group participants to reestablish membership in social groups, resulting in resocialization and problem-solving.

In 1978, Kaul and Bednar identified four factors which distinguished group from individual therapy approaches: (1) the group members learn by participating in the development and evaluation of a social microcosm; (2) they learn by giving and receiving feedback; (3) they serve both as helpers and helpees; and (4) they learn by the consensual validation of multiple perspectives. Thus, whatever the target problem addressed by the group, the way these four mechanisms are facilitated by the leader is very important.

Another study (Lakin, Oppenheimer, & Bremer, 1982) compared younger (ages 19–22) and older (ages 65–80) clients attending group sessions. These researchers found that older adults talked with relative ease about fears of abandonment, problems of widowhood, and feelings of rejection and vulnerability in the face of apparent indifference and hostility in the environment, while the younger clients were less disclosing and generally more defensive. Furthermore, the group process in the older age group was smoother than in the younger age groups.

These findings confirm our experience in the current project in which silence during the group session is minimized and discussion is usually continuous. Mutual reassurance and advice are offered, particularly in instances of illness and death of family members, at which time significant caring and concern are evident.

PROJECT OVERVIEW

Deep concern about the quality of life of depressed elderly residents of the Aurora suburb of Denver, Colorado, led to the initiation in 1979 of a project to aid depressed older adults. The Special Needs Project for Aurora Seniors, now in its fifth year, is sponsored by a consortium of four local agencies, the Aurora Community Mental Health Center being the anchor agency. The project's foundation consists of group process activities. Separate men's and women's groups are conducted weekly at the Aurora Senior Center by a clinical social worker and a retired public health nurse volunteer. In the Center's friendly, familiar environment, one serious risk factor, isolation, is counteracted by the provision of noon meals, social activities, and hobby classes. As Caplan (1963, p.61) advises, ". . . since there is reason to believe that social isolation is a potent factor in promoting mental disorder of the aged, a preventive program should emphasize communal social and recreational facilities."

Since in the beginning development of trust was the key issue, more leader involvement was necessary. With time, the members became open, self-disclosing, problem-solving oriented, and supportive of one another. One prime objective was the maintenance of emotional security along with a sense of personal dignity; the overall goal was to provide an appropriate environment which encouraged attainment of insight. Information sharing was common. Health issues were the focus at times, due to the input of the nurse co-leader, but this gradually became less important. Problem-solving was an integral part of most of the groups, although a social component, varying with time and need, existed as well. For example, at Christmas, the women's group exchanged inexpensive gifts and served light refreshments. In all of the groups, the members sent get-well cards or called a long-absent person.

At the outset, client referrals came from the county health department's well-oldster clinic. In time, referrals came from other sources as well: the consortium agencies, the community, and group members and their friends and relatives. Entry into the group has been voluntary and no fee has been charged.

Prospective clients are screened by the clinical social worker. Her evaluation has a two-fold purpose: (1) to determine the treatment of choice, and (2) to decide upon the appropriateness of the group for each individual. At times, marital or family therapy may be indicated as the more appropriate treatment modality. Medical, psychiatric, and social historical data are elicited in the structured interview. This interview forms a preliminary therapeutic alliance which helps to prepare the client for the group process.

A Hamilton Depression Inventory score rating for baseline data is completed after the client's first group session. In addition, two self-report forms are administered: the Beck Depression Scale and the Life Events Inventory (a geriatric version of the Social Readjustment Scale). Only mention is made here of these instruments; more discussion will take place later in this paper.

Although problems of aging are common to both sexes, the formation of men's groups was given priority, initially, because men generally lack available support services and are less communicative and more isolated than women. In time, additional groups were formed. Total project enrollment at this writing is 125 individuals, with an average weekly attendance of 25.

As stated earlier, the Aurora Community Mental Health Center, as the anchor agency, furnishes the two co-leaders, as well as research and evaluation guidance and computer services. A project Advisory Committee, composed of representatives of the consortium agencies and the therapy groups, plans and reviews each step of the project.

PROGRAM PARTICIPANTS

As of this writing, three groups are in session: two men's groups consist of five members in each group and one women's group is comprised of ten members. A second women's group is not included because it is just beginning. The members' ages range from 61 to 86 years, the median age being 70.5 years. Over one half (55%) are widowed; over one third (36%) are married; and 9% are divorced. An equal number (36%) of each sex lives alone or with an adult child and his/her family. Although most perceive their health status to be good, this does not coincide with the judgment of the co-leaders, who classify their health status as: fair—62%; good—24%; and poor—14%. Most of the clients have medical problems which are under control and so produce minor limitations in the life routine.

As for their psychiatric diagnoses, Dysthymic Disorders hold the highest rank (43%); Adjustment Disorders rank second (33%); Major Depression and Personality Disorders each shares third rank (14%); and Alzheimer's, Alcoholism, and Organic Disorders share the lowest rank (1% each). Overall, depressive states included in primary diagnoses affect 55% of all of the clients. These data confirm multiple areas of high risk, including age, health, and being widowed and alone.

This leads us to speculate on their probable psychiatric diagnoses prior to old age. Most would probably not have met the criteria for the diagnosis of Dysthymic or Major Depression earlier in their lives. This may confirm the need for preventive treatment in later life for avoidance of significant pathology.

GROUP STRUCTURE AND DYNAMICS

The groups meet weekly for 50 minutes in an informal setting at the Senior Center. Attendance has been consistently good, disrupted only by poor weather, illness, or vacation. Serious discussions evoke tears, especially in the women's group, but laughter is common as well. Confidentiality is sacrosanct. The leaders are directive at times or more peripheral, depending on the needs of the group. Limit-setting is necessary when members tend to monopolize. With the development of trust, the members are able to explore deeper feelings and pain, resulting in insight and awareness.

As stated earlier, the study of leadership strategies by Parham et al. (1982) noted that older persons prefer to talk about concrete issues such as personal isolation, financial difficulties, experiences of bereavement, or disadvantaged states of the aged as a class. Losses make emotional stress paramount. Often, people do not experience a normal grief process, especially if early losses predispose them to depression. Other issues of relevance in the discussion repertoire include death and dying, retirement, housing, depression, aging, politics, sex, family relationships, and intergenerational differences and conflicts. Life review is common, as are changes in family patterns and life styles.

Many of the clients moved to Colorado to be near a family member. Being in new surroundings with few, if any, friends, or connections results in weak support systems. At times, these forced relationships with family are disappointing. Time lags; anxiety and depression develop. For some, their only close friends are in the groups, where they share and receive more emotional support than elsewhere. Often, their lives lack intimacy and even if they maintain relationships, they are cautious, steeped in "old wounds," and unfulfilled. Group treatment gives them an opportunity to receive consensual validation for their feelings and to accept ideas and suggestions for coping and changing life patterns. Many clients have made significant changes, thus learning to deal better with later life issues. The classic phenomenon of seeing other members with worse problems gives them a broader perspective on their own lives. And since maintenance of stability in daily living is our goal for this high-risk population, we are convinced that the group experience provides for many an achievement of better quality of life.

PROGRAM SUCCESS

If older adults can transcend the initial trauma of fear in acknowledging that they need some help in coping, they become quickly committed to therapy. Once they realize the safety of a therapy group and recognize that they are not alone, they grow as a result of knowing that someone cares, that others have similar problems, and that therapists and group members listen.

The case of Jane (not her real name) is an example of the concepts presented above. Jane, a 66-year-old widow, was referred to the project by the Senior Center staff. Because of her mother's death at Jane's birth and the father's being unable to manage child care, she and her older sister were reared in an orphanage. Jane married and had one son. Several years prior to admission to the project, her husband's death resulted in her move to another state to live near her son. This move proved to be disappointing. When she came to us, she had just moved back to Colorado where she had been reared and where her sister lived. Unfortunately, the relationship between the two sisters was ridden with conflict.

A charter member of our first women's group, Jane became a dedicated participant. Her fears, depression, and isolation diminished with her involvement at the Senior Center in volunteer and other activities. In spite of the diagnosis of cancer (in remission), she is hopeful and happy with a better understanding of her family and her present limitations; a meaningful life has evolved for her. She brings her problems freely to the group, while helping others immeasurably as a positive role model.

Demographically, Jane is typical of many of the group members. Despite having had no previous psychiatric therapy, she has made considerable changes in her awareness and coping, particularly in regard to family relationships and socialization. As trust developed for Jane and other group members, along with the awareness that others share similar feelings and experiences, stability in group membership has been realized. Their frequent testimonies indicate a cohesive network, intimating how therapy works to assist them in better coping with life. They also recognize the need for a weekly forum to express themselves openly and confidentially.

Another factor we attribute to program success is the makeup and stability of the co-leaders. Our continuity as caregivers over a three-year period has taken on special importance for the clients during this time period of multiple losses and role changes of "significant others." This concept is vital for group dynamics.

As a clinical social worker with 13 years of mental health experience (the last six in gerontological practice) and a public health nurse volunteer (an age-peer of the clients), we comprise a balanced team. Our diversity in age is also complimentary, particularly for those with relationships to children—the volunteer being the age of the clients and the social worker closer to the age of their adult children.

The social worker's original training in group treatment was in psychoanalytical theory. Due to environmental constraints and client needs, her approach from the start was necessarily changed to a style which is more sociable, sharing, and directive. The special needs of this target population (who traditionally do not seek out mental health services) required innovative, nonconventional treatment modalities. This led to outreach as a key. As stated earlier, the first clients were known to the nurse volunteer who made their acquaintance in a health clinic. This relationship encouraged client commitment and lessened anxiety about trying a new involvement. As the project developed, the volunteer's understanding of similar life experiences gave the leadership more credibility. Frequently the co-leaders have been seen as Senior Center staff and not recognized as therapists connected with the Community Mental Health Center. This may be seen as an unobtrusive measure of the effectiveness of basing the services in a community setting.

Many therapists avoid treatment contact with older adults because they perceive them as depressing and unlikely to grow and change. In this project, both co-leaders have certainly experienced these feelings, particularly relative to high levels of physical pain experienced by patients and to patients' nearness to death. This is compensated, however, by observing significant attempts at change and growth of many of the clients, usually accompanied by an improved quality of life. Having experienced the aging process and its accompanying problems in themselves and their families, the project leaders' empathy with their clients becomes a two-sided sharing experience.

Perhaps a key stimulus of enjoying work with this age group is their wisdom. Their sense of history, perspective on societal changes, along with their views of life mistakes and successes are fascinating and enriching. Paramount to this work is the conviction of both leaders that older adults and their families benefit from treatment.

EVALUATION

In the early years of gerontological group experience, programs which were usually generic in nature were, generally, evaluated subjectively. But as programs became more diverse and as the state of the art became more sophisticated, commensurate research methodologies were developed for assessing clients and matching them with appropriate interventions. Since then, an increasing number of projects and studies with rigorous evaluation components are being reported. Still, problems of effective evaluation continue.

Parham et al. (1983) in a brief review of evaluation methodology reiterate the complexities of systematic, objective evaluation of the effectiveness of groups with older adults. This population group is difficult to assess effectively because of interfering accompanying influences such as chronic illness and the taking of medications. The authors summarize by saying that we know that groups work but little else.

It is for this reason that the Special Needs Project has been experimenting with the use of instruments established in the literature as validly measuring changes in depression over time as therapy proceeds.

From the onset of the project, attendance records and accompanying graphs displayed program growth. This sign of project success urged us to go on to other types of evaluation. Every six months we administered a self-report program evaluation questionnaire to elicit the clients' opinions on the value (to them) of the group experience. Feedback told us that the sessions were helpful. In response to the question, "What are the benefits that people may get out of a group such as this one?" clients answered, "To be helped and to help"; "It helped me to resolve many problems"; "The happiness of making friends"; and "This group helped me to come out of my depression."

Comments such as these convinced us that the program was successful but did not tell us why. We then began a search for reliable and valid instruments for measuring depression severity and change. With the realization that lengthy follow-up is crucial in prevention programs (because of the need to wait for the risk factors to develop), the instrument search was confined to short, self-report schedules. Data would be collected from the time of entry into the program and continued at six- to eight-week intervals throughout the life of the project. Early use of only the Zung (Zung, 1965) and Beck (Beck & Beamesderfer, 1974) Depression Scales contradicted the co-leaders' documented reports of depression symptoms, demonstrating the participants' denial of depression.

With the resultant preference for professional ratings to secure viable scientific measurement, the Hamilton Depression Inventory (Hamilton, 1960) was adopted. This scale of 21 variables assesses the symptoms of clients diagnosed as suffering from depression states. These variables are measured on two-point and four-point scales. The scores are then summed to produce a total score for each individual rated, ranging from 0–62. Higher scores denote a greater degree of depression. Two raters score each client independently. In the Special Needs Project, the raters are the two co-leaders.

In time, the recognition that other parameters would be required for correlation with the depression inventories' scores brought into use the internationally used Social Readjustment Scale (Amster & Krauss, 1974), which we call the Life Events Inventory (LEI), as well as the highly regarded Beck Depression Scale. Currently, data are being collected systematically (as stated earlier) with the Beck and LEI Inventories. A comparison group is composed of active Senior Center participants in physical fitness exercise classes not enrolled in the group therapy program. The identical measurement instruments, except for the HDI, are administered at the same time periods for members of this group and members of the ongoing therapy groups. Through Time 4 the return response rate for questionnaires administered to the comparison group has averaged a surprising 95%.

Only cursory, beginning tests have been carried out to this writing. Analysis will follow computer processing employing standard tests and others not yet finalized. In the project's early life, inter-rater reliability correlations between HDI-summed scores for the two raters yielded acceptable results (0.787 and 0.998) as compared with Hamilton's (Hamilton & White, 1960) range of 0.84 and 0.90. Preliminary testing by correlations and covariance on depression (HDI and Beck data) and stress (LEI data) was inconclusive, indicating the need for more data over time and possibly a restructuring of the research design. Final results will be reported in the literature at a future time.

SUMMARY AND FUTURE PLANS

In the Special Needs Project, our focus has been to understand better why group treatment has helped older adults to be less depressed and to function at a higher level emotionally as well as socially and interpersonally. Factors contributing to the success of this five-year-old program include its location, leader cohesion, stability of leaders and participants, leaders' personalities, and sponsoring agency support and commitment. Other contributing factors are that the stigma of mental health is minimized by the setting (Senior Citizens Center) and that there is no fee assessment.

Most of our clients have not had previous psychiatric treatment in spite of having experienced serious problems. With a major focus on prevention of emotional crises, the program is helping to limit the severity of regression in response to life stresses. Depression is an inherent response to the strains of later life; but the process and progression of time and loss can be eased by group treatment. As stated by Parham et al. (1982), older adults respond favorably to group treatment and, therefore, for many among this age group, it may be the treatment of choice.

Since its initiation five years ago and its step-by-step development, the Special Needs Project has evolved into one model of a viable program to assist older adults to maintain emotional stability in the face of life's changes and loss experiences. The project's demonstrated success has inspired us to share our experiences with personnel of other senior centers throughout Colorado and to consider doing so with other states.

One method of disseminating the information was a workshop sponsored in the fall of 1983 by the Denver Regional Council of Governments. Consultation services are available to assist agencies desiring to begin similar programs. A proposed forum would be teaching classes at senior centers or mental health centers on such issues as "Mental Health and Aging" and "As You and Your Parents Grow Older."

Finally, though a basic premise, we have learned that sharing with others helps us to understand and survive life's trials and tribulations, especially if we are facing a possible brief or uncertain future. We may even make sense of our pain, grow in our grief, and nurture the strength to begin again with new endeavors. Life is full of losses and changes. As older adults, our vast experience may enable us to incorporate life's traumas and go on. If we are fortunate to have a group of fellow travelers to listen, share, understand, and cheer us on, we are more likely to maintain stability, grow, and even become better people.

REFERENCES

Amster, L. E., & Krauss, H. H. (1974). The relationship between life crises and mental deterioration in old age. *International Journal of Aging and Human Development, 5* (1), 51–55.

Beck, A. T., & Beamesderfer, A. (1974). Assessment of depression: The depression inventory. *Psychological Measurements in Psychopharmacology, 7,* 151–160.

Blazer, D. (1980). The diagnosis of depression in the elderly. *Journal of the American Geriatrics Society, XXVII* (2), 52–58.

Busse, E. W., & Pfeiffer, E. (1977). *Behavior and adaptation in late life* (2nd ed.). Boston: Little, Brown and Company.

Butler, R. N. (1975). *Why survive? Being old in America.* New York: Harper and Row.

Caplan, G. (1963). *Principles of preventive psychiatry.* New York: Basic Books.

Erikson, E. H. (1963). *Childhood and society* (2nd ed.). New York: W. W. Norton & Co.

Gallagher, D. E., & Thompson, L. W. (1982). Treatment of major depressive disorder in older adult outpatients with brief psychotherapies. *Psychotherapy: Theory, Research and Practice, 19* (4), 482–490.

Hamilton, M. (1960). A rating scale for depression. *Journal of Neurology, Neurosurgery, and Psychiatry, 23,* 56–62.

Hamilton, M., & White, J. (1955). A rating scale for depression. *Journal of Mental Science, 105, 955.*

Kaul, T., & Bednar, R. (1978). Conceptualizing group research: A preliminary analysis. *Small Group Behavior, 9,* 173–191.

Lakin, M., Oppenheimer, B., & Bremer, J. (1982). A note on old and young in helping groups. *Psychotherapy: Theory, Research and Practice, 19* (4), 444–452.

Parham, I. A., Priddy, J. M., & Richman, C. M. (1982). Group psychotherapy with the elderly: Problems and prospects. *Psychotherapy: Theory, Research and Practice, 19* (4), 437–443.

Rosen, C. E., & Rosen, S. (1982). Evaluating an intervention program for the elderly. *Community Mental Health Journal, 18* (1), 21–33.

Yalom, I. D., & Terrazas, F. (1970). *The Theory and Practice of Group Psychotherapy.* New York: Basic Books.

Weiner, M. B., & White, M. T. (1982). Depression as the search for the lost self. *Psychotherapy: Theory, Research and Practice, 19* (4), 491–499.

Zung, W. W. K. (1965). A self-rating depression scale. *Archives of General Psychiatry,* 63–70.

OLD AGE

CHAPTER 8

PRACTICE WITH THE FRAIL ELDERLY IN THE PRIVATE SECTOR

David P. Fauri and Judith B. Bradford

Maintaining the independence of elderly persons who are frail, impaired, or vulnerable is becoming a critical element of social services for the elderly. Their longevity and psychological well-being benefit if they remain independent and continue their community social ties as long as possible. Long-term maintenance of the elderly in institutions is costly to individuals, to their families, and to public programs that pay for such medical care.

Community services have expanded for individuals qualified on the basis of limited income. Higher-income individuals with substantial savings or family resources can often purchase needed services. Neither of these kinds of services may be available to the middle-income elderly. People in this segment of the population may have limited resources or they may feel that accepting public services is inconsistent with their values. They may not wish to disclose the personal information that is required to establish eligibility for services.

This article explores the potential for social workers in private practice to respond to the needs of elderly persons for assessment of community service needs and facilitation of service provision. It explores the potential for increasing service options for frail elderly persons and their families and reviews concepts of the frail elderly, community-based support services, and case management.

Reprinted from *Social Casework,* Vol. 67, No. 5 (1986), pp. 259–265, by permission of the publisher, Families International, Inc.

THE FRAIL ELDERLY

The *frail elderly*—also referred to as the vulnerable elderly, high-risk elderly, and impaired elderly—face a higher than average risk of debilitating illness and accompanying institutionalization.

The Federal Council on the Aging found it necessary to identify special needs groups within the large mass of individuals labeled "elderly" and viewed those over seventy-five years of age as a target population with special needs by reason of their potential vulnerability. The council argued that it was at times necessary to use such criteria as "age status" in order to target benefits, even though this strategy might not be adequate for persons having additional minority statuses.[1] There is, however, a danger of overlooking the greatest commonality among older people, their individuality. It is necessary to realize that not all persons seventy-five years old or older are frail or vulnerable, but that at crisis points frailty may become a proper definition.

Specialized services for the frail elderly can help maintain them in independent living situations in their homes and communities. Social work services provided through the private sector to the frail elderly can expand available services while increasing diversity and sensitivity to specialized local needs. Diversity is desirable; providing community-based support services for the frail elderly in the not-for-profit sector, as well as in the public and private sectors of the economy, increases the sum total of services available.

COMMUNITY-BASED SUPPORT SERVICES

Community based refers to services delivered in community settings, not in institutions, although institutionally based, long-term care programs may also have explicit community components. Community-based support services provide assistance in private residences or accessible locations such as community centers. They are not limited to home health services and may be provided either in central locations or delivered to a person's home.[2]

The boundaries for community-based service to the frail elderly are often unclear.[3] Community-based support may be provided through such institutions as a hospital or nursing home with a home health care unit or through programs not connected with an institution. Differentiating between medical and nonmedical services and between long-term care and intermittent care may be difficult. A number of services are age-segregated; others are more universal or non-age-segregated.[4] Many community-based support services are available to elderly persons who are not frail and some are also

---

[1] National Council on the Aging, *Public Policy and the Frail Elderly* (Washington, DC: U.S. Department of Health, Education, and Welfare, Human Development Services, 1978), pp. 14–15. This publication presents statistics and characteristics as of 1978.

[2] Gloria Sorenson, Ed., *Older Persons and Service Problems* (New York: Human Sciences Press, 1981), p. 278.

[3] See Louis Lowy, *Social Work with the Aging* (New York: Harper & Row, 1979), p. 429. One definition of *home health care* is "a combined hospital-community responsibility"; also see Philip W. Brickner, *Home Health Care* (New York: Appleton-Century-Crofts, 1978).

[4] For listings of services, see Barbara Silverstone and Helen Kandel Hyman, *You and Your Aging Parent* (New York: Pantheon Books, 1976). Also see William Scanlon, Elaine Dipederico, and Margaret Stassen, *Long-Term Care: Current Experience and a Framework for Analysis* (Washington, DC: The Urban Institute, 1979).

Table 8–1
In-home and Centrally Provided Community-Based Services

In-home Services	Centrally Provided Services
Visiting nurses/Occupational therapy/ Rehabilitative therapy	Congregate meals
	Senior centers
Homemaker-Home health aide	Transportation (Dial-a-Ride)
Meals on Wheels	Day hospital/Day care
Telephone reassurance	Legal services
Escort and transportation	Special housing (domiciliary, congregate, adult homes, boarding houses, assisted residential living)
Chore services	
Friendly visiting/Companionship	
Sitting	Respite care for caregivers
Financial guardianship	Recreation
Respite care for caregivers	

available to other persons as well as the elderly. Table 8–1 lists a variety of community-based services, distinguished between those delivered in home and those centrally provided.

The need for more community-based support services has been identified in public hearings, public documents, and publications dealing with gerontology.[5] A federal government study found that 17 percent of the population over sixty-five years was greatly or extremely impaired and that 60 percent of them lived outside institutions.[6] Louis Lowy and Margot Helphand reported that 14 percent of 100,000 patients in licensed nursing homes did not need institutionalized care and that 23 percent needed only limited or periodic nursing care.[7] Richard Ham found that from 15 to 25 percent of institutionalized elderly persons could be living at home if home support services were available.[8]

Social workers practicing in the private sector have an important role to play in meeting this need for home support. Without access to professionals who can conduct psychosocial assessments, who assess the total needs of frail persons, and who are knowledgeable about community resources, elderly persons and their families are faced with devising care and support plans without assistance.[9]

[5] U.S. Congress, Senate Committee on Finance, Subcommittee on Health, *Comprehensive Community Based Non-Institutional Long-Term Care for the Elderly and Disabled* (Washington, DC: U.S. Government Printing Office, 1980); and U.S. Congress, House Select Committee on Aging, Subcommittee on Human Services, *Future Directions for Aging Policy* (Washington, DC: U.S. Government Printing Office, 1980).

[6] U.S. Government Accounting Office, *The Need for a National Policy to Better Provide for the Elderly,* Report to the Congress (Washington, DC: Publication No. HRD-78-19, December 30, 1977), p. 20.

[7] Louis Lowy and Margot Helphand, "Matching Community Resources and Patient Needs," in *Long-Term Care: A Handbook for Researchers, Planners and Providers,* ed. Sylvia Sherwood (New York: Spectrum, 1975), p. 349–89.

[8] Richard Ham, "Alternatives to Institutionalization," *American Family Physician* 21 (July 1980):14.

[9] Silverstone and Hyman, *You and Your Aging Parent,* p. 176.

Many elderly benefit, both in physical health and longevity, by remaining in their homes. A study of mortality that compared the institutionalized and noninstitutionalized elderly indicated a high mortality rate among older persons within one year of institutionalization.[10] The U.S. Government Accounting Office reported that individuals receiving expanded home health care services lived longer than those who did not.[11] An alternative care project in Georgia, in which community support services were provided by eighteen agencies, showed reduced deaths among those receiving services. Six percent of those in the program died within six months of enrollment, compared to 17 percent of the control group.[12]

Community-based support services also contribute to the mental health of the elderly. Lowy presented evidence indicating high levels of mental disorder and service need among noninstitutionalized elderly, ranging from 5 to 20 percent depending on the definition of impairment.[13]

CASE MANAGEMENT WITH THE FRAIL ELDERLY

Case management is a process relevant to private sector social work services with the elderly. Developed in the 1960s as a response to a maze of overlapping eligibility standards and services facing public welfare clients, it was later adopted in not-for-profit social service agencies. Case managers assess client needs, identify services relevant to alleviate problems, and assist in obtaining services for clients.[14] Case managers also monitor service delivery and evaluate effectiveness, serving to facilitate service delivery rather than to provide service. The phases of case management are assessment, service planning, brokerage, and community intervention.[15]

One case management service that private social work practitioners can provide to the frail elderly is identifying eligibility for entitlements and assisting the client in applying for such entitlements. For example, home health care for a frail elderly person may be paid for, depending upon employment history and income levels, by Medicare, Medicaid, sections of the Older Americans Act, Title XX of the Social Security Act, or through private auspices.

The effectiveness of case management with the frail elderly is demonstrated by Proj-

---

[10] Stanislav V. Kasi, "Physical and Mental Health Effects of Involuntary Relocation and Institutionalization on the Elderly—A Review," *American Journal of Public Health* 62 (March 1972):377–84. Also see Kenneth F. Ferro, "The Health Consequences of Relocation Among the Aged in the Community," *The Journal of Gerontology* 38 (January 1983):90–96.

[11] U.S. Government Accounting Office, *The Elderly Should Benefit from Expanded Home Health Care but Increasing These Services Will Not Insure Cost Reductions* (Washington, DC: Report B-208942, IPE-83-1, December 7, 1982), pp. 20–26.

[12] F. Albert Skellie, "The Impact of Alternatives to Nursing Home Care," *American Health Care Association Journal* 5 (May 1979):46; and F. Albert Skellie and Ruth E. Coan, "Community Based Long-Term Care and Mortality: Preliminary Findings of Georgia's Alternative Health Services Project," *The Gerontologist* 20 (June 1980):377–79.

[13] Louis Lowy, "Mental Health Services in the Community," *Handbook of Mental Health and Aging,* ed. James E. Birren and Bruce R. Sloane (Englewood Cliffs, NJ: Prentice-Hall, 1980), p. 828.

[14] Charles Rapp and John Poertner, "Public Child Welfare in the 1980's: The Role of Case Management," in *Perspectives for the Future: Social Work Practice in the 1980s,* ed. Kay Dea (Washington, DC: National Association of Social Workers, 1980), pp. 70–81.

[15] Ibid.

ect Triage, a public program for the frail elderly in seven counties of central Connecticut. The program provides client assessment, case planning, integration of services, and monitoring of quality and quantity of services delivered to clients.[16] It illustrates the usefulness of individual client assessment, coordination and monitoring of services, and assistance in making claims for health insurance reimbursement.

A rural, not-for-profit agency operating under contract with the State of Illinois Office of Aging offers another approach. The Shawnee Alliance for Seniors used centrally located case managers to conduct assessments and to plan services; subsequently, local case managers took over to link elderly clients to services in their towns or villages. This program split the case management functions, separating assessment and planning from linkage and follow-up, and spread scarce assessment skills over a large rural area while using on-site managers in individual communities.

Published studies focus on governmental and publicly funded case management services.[17] There is also in process a transfer of the case management concept to private social work practice with the frail elderly. In 1983, the New England Long-Term Care Center at Brown University identified twenty-two private providers of case management services for elderly persons.[18] The average cost of services was fifty dollars an hour or two hundred dollars a case. It was found that case managers were linking clients to such community-based support services as home aides and attendants, nurses, homemakers, occupational and physical therapists, geriatric physicians, psychiatrists, lawyers, and financial planners. They also helped clients process Medicaid and Medicare forms and counseled distraught relatives.[19] These providers were located primarily in the Northeast corridor, on the California coast, and in several large midwestern metropolitan areas.

SUPPORT TO CAREGIVERS

Families of the frail elderly also require assistance, and social work practitioners in the private sector can respond to their needs. Changes in family structures and roles, coupled with increased family mobility, may make it difficult for many families to assure care and support for elderly members. Certain factors are particularly relevant. The increase in the number of women who work has reduced the ranks of caregivers, a role traditionally filled by women in the home. An increase in the incidence of divorce limits family resources, emotionally and economically. The decline in family size, as seen in the rising number of single-parent families, often rules out possibilities for sharing the caregiving role.[20] A related demographic trend is the tendency for elderly persons them-

---

[16] Joan Quinn, Joan Segal, Helen Raisz, and Christine Johnson, Eds., *Coordinating Community Services for the Elderly* (New York: Springer, 1982).

[17] Raymond M. Steinberg and Genevieve Carter, *Case Management and the Elderly* (Lexington, MA: D. C. Heath, 1973), p. 34.

[18] Glenn Collins, "Care for Far-Off Elderly: Sources of Help," *New York Times,* 5 Jan. 1984, p. C1.

[19] Ibid.

[20] Howard H. Palley and Julianne S. Oktay, *The Chronically Limited Elderly* (New York: Haworth Press, 1980), pp. 6–8.

selves to have older parents, and the task of caring for older parents often falls to single or widowed women who are sixty-five years or older.[21] T. Franklin Williams, director of the National Institute on Aging, pointed out the importance of "supplementing and helping sustain the family members and neighbors who will continue, without doubt, to provide most of the care."[22]

Adult children, the so-called "sandwich generation," may require education and crisis intervention assistance during periods of acute and chronic illness of elderly parents.[23] Williams estimated that family members provided 75 percent of the care for older persons, with 25 percent being provided by home support services. A. H. Zimmer calculated that 80 percent of all services received by impaired older persons are provided informally by relatives and friends.[24] Lowy indicated that families give 75 percent of the care needed to keep the elderly in the community and stressed the need for assistance to family members to provide relief and respite.[25]

Organized efforts to provide support to caregivers are illustrated by a project of the Community Service Society of New York. Individualized and group services were provided to caregivers, using a task-centered approach.[26] Group services offered education and concrete information, provided peer support opportunities, and allowed groups to identify advocacy and social action functions.[27]

Practitioners working with caregiving family members find that the caregivers are under considerable sustained stress. A senile elderly individual who communicates on a limited or sporadic basis provides little positive reinforcement for the caregiver, and a helping professional's support may be critical. Assisting frail elderly persons with activities of daily living reduces the caregiver's leisure time and time for other family members. Adults may need help with feelings of guilt; the expression of "not doing enough" may indicate fear on the part of the adult child that he or she is shortchanging either the frail adult or other members of the immediate family. Unresolved child-parent problems may also be present.

POTENTIAL FOR PRIVATE SECTOR SERVICES

Families and communities often can only partially assist the frail elderly to remain in their homes, and no community can meet the needs of its elderly through public services alone.[28] Expansion of services can be achieved through a combination of public agencies, private and voluntary social service agencies, and private social work practice. In times of reduced public funding for social services, public interventions must

---

[21] Alida G. Silverman, Beatrice H. Kahn, and Gary Anderson, "A Model for Working with Multi-Generational Families," *Social Casework* 58 (March 1977):131–35.

[22] T. Franklin Williams, quoted in *AGEnda,* National Committee for Gerontology in Social Work Education (January 1984):1.

[23] Dorothy A. Miller, "The Sandwich Generation: Adult Children of the Aging," *Social Work* 26 (September 1981):419–23.

[24] A. H. Zimmer, "Community Care for the Aged: The Natural Support Program," *Journal of Gerontological Social Work* 5 (Fall-Winter 1982):149–55.

[25] Louis Lowy, "The Older Generation—What Is Due, What Is Owed," *Social Casework* 64 (June 1983):371–75.

[26] Daniel Reece, Thomas Walz, and Helen Hageboeck, "Intergenerational Care Providers of Non-Institutionalized Frail Elderly—Characteristics and Consequences," *Journal of Gerontological Social Work* 5 (1983):14.

[27] Zimmer, "Community Care for the Aged;" also see George S. Getzel, "Social Work with Family Caregivers to the Aged," *Social Casework* 62 (April 1981):201–09.

[28] Silverstone and Hyman, *You and Your Aging Parent,* p. 186.

continue to be supported to assist those persons who cannot pay for the services they need.[29] Yet private sector services also can be encouraged, thus increasing the diversity of service sources through a marketplace response to service needs.

The potential of private sector social work practice with the frail elderly depends in part on the number of social workers in private practice. Chauncey Alexander, while executive director of the National Association of Social Workers (NASW), estimated that one-third (30,000) of the members of NASW were in private practice, many of them on a part-time basis.[30] No figures are available on the number of social workers practicing in the private sector who assist the frail elderly.

Private practice with the frail elderly and their families varies from what may be usually thought of as private practice.[31] Private social work practice is often considered as clinical in nature, employing psychotherapy or other treatment approaches.[32] Practice with the frail elderly and their families is broader and includes individual counseling and community resource facilitation and interaction.[33] Alternatively, case management may be the focus of service. Another factor is the complexity of such payment reimbursement mechanisms as health insurance, which may favor institutional care over community care. An institutional bias, prevalent in medical services, can lead to competition between institutional care and community service.[34]

Social workers serving the frail elderly through private practice also assist relatives who are caregivers. This is an area of great potential, as community services for the frail elderly tend to be more available than are services to their caregiving children.[35] For example, assistance in locating respite programs may help children alleviate the physical and psychological costs of caregiving.[36] They may need assistance from workers who can link informal caregiving with community agency and professional services. Private social work practitioners can help families to use and strengthen existing family and social networks and also to recognize the limits of such networks. Workers are able to coordinate planning of formal and informal caregiving.

THREE SERVICES THAT HELP

One example of social work practitioners in the private sector who help the frail elderly to remain in their homes is the Aging Network Services in the Washington, D.C., metropolitan area. It locates social service for frail elderly individuals geographically separated from their relatives, who most often are adult children of the elderly person. The

---

[29] Jerry S. Turem and Catherine Born, "Doing More with Less," *Social Work* 19 (May-June 1983):209.

[30] Ronald Smothers, "Social Work Growth Is Reported Slowed by Cuts in Spending," *New York Times,* 28 Nov. 1981, p. A12.

[31] Other professions also offer specialized services for the elderly. For example, a law firm in New York City focuses on legal services to elderly individuals and their families regarding such matters as power of attorney, asset availability, and estate planning. See Collins, "Care for Far-Off Elderly."

[32] See, for example, Marquis Earl Wallace, "Private Practice: A Nationwide Study," *Social Work* 27 (May 1982):262–67.

[33] Max Siporin, "The Therapeutic Process in Clinical Social Work," *Social Work* 28 (May-June 1983):193–98.

[34] Robert L. Kane and Rosalie A. Kane, "Alternatives to Institutional Care of the Elderly: Beyond the Dichotomy," *The Gerontologist* 20 (June 1980):249–59. Also see Scanlon, Dipederico, and Stassen, *Long-Term Care.*

[35] Miller, "The Sandwich Generation."

[36] Lowy, "The Older Generation," p. 375; and Reece, Walz, and Hageboeck, "Intergenerational Care Providers of Non-Institutionalized Frail Elderly," p. 32.

personal experience of two social workers led to the development of this service; one of two partners was confronted with locating care for a frail elderly parent while engaged in a professional career at some distance from the parent, and the other identified the need through experiences with clients.[37] They assist long-distance caretakers of frail elderly individuals by locating appropriate geriatric social work case management services in the elderly persons' cities of residence. This is done by counseling with caretakers, obtaining consent of the elderly persons, and identifying in distant cities a social worker or agency with the appropriate geriatric and gerontological skills to provide effective case management service. Follow-up counseling services are also offered to the adult children. The service attracts young and middle-aged professionals who find it difficult and expensive to travel to meet recurring or emergency care needs of elderly parents in distant cities. Case management services also provided within the Washington metropolitan area include advocacy to assist in acquiring community services and entitlement benefits of elderly individuals. The brokerage cost of the case management location service is $250 for a four-week period. It includes the cost of linkage between elderly relatives and a geriatric social worker, interviews with the adult children to initiate the procedure, and long-distance telephone discussions with the parent.

A second example is Elderly Life Management Services in Richmond, Virginia. Case management services are provided to frail elderly individuals in their homes, and assistance is offered in locating appropriate nursing homes, foster homes, or adult homes. Other specialized services can also be provided, such as guardianship and emergency information service, which can be subscribed to by individuals who anticipate a possible need or feel that it will relieve the concerns of children or friends. Each client's file includes health and social data, information about medication and handicaps or limitations, data on financial resources and contacts, and family information. A wallet card and telephone decals are provided to expedite calls for assistance; the service will respond on a 24-hour basis. Service beyond an emergency incident can be purchased on a yearly retainer basis or on an incident-by-incident basis. Costs include a fifteen-dollar per person yearly charge for the emergency service subscription. Other services are charged at a scaled rate based on the kind of service and the time required, with professional services averaging about twenty-five dollars per hour. The service is operated by four professionals from different disciplines. One of the four, who is extremely active in the firm, is a social worker starting a second career after years of governmental and mental health work.

A third example is an in-home companion and helper service in the Washington, D.C., metropolitan area. It provides meal planning assistance, help with food preparation, transportation for or assistance with shopping, homemaker service, assistance with banking and financial record matters, bill paying, neighborhood escort service, and post-hospitalization, in-home nonmedical assistance. A few assistants are employed part time for selected duties. Fees vary depending on the particular service rendered. This venture, Home Independence, differs from the other two in not being a partnership or a firm of professional social workers and in functioning without an office location. The service began through a few crisis situation referrals. Knowledge of it

[37] For more information on this service, see *NASW News* 28 (October 1983):11.

spread by word of mouth, and the demand for its help increased to the point that its originator began to use selected assistants. Further expansion would be possible if employees or partners could be obtained to provide quality helping services. A key factor in the service is its emphasis on building relationships with its clients. As a result, clients find it preferable to the large home health care corporation services that are available in the metropolitan area.

PART II

PHYSICAL CONDITIONS

The physical dimension of our clients' lives has, of course, always been understood to be a component of the diagnostic process in social work practice, but for the most part not an important one for the profession in general. Certainly for our colleagues who practice in the health field this has not been so. For them an essential part of their practice begins from a knowledge of and a sensitivity to the physical condition, healthy or problematical, of clients, and the interaction of health with significant others in their clients' lives.

In an earlier day, the field of medical social work was an important specialty in the profession. Curricula of schools of social work included courses on medical information. Such courses usually focused on prevalent diseases of the time and their effect on bodily functions with which medical social workers would come into contact. However, for social workers not in specific "health" settings, the client's physical condition was rarely an area of interest except in the most obvious circumstances.

But this is no longer so. For a variety of important reasons, all social workers are beginning to realize that this earlier compartmentalization of the person into discipline- and problem-specific foci was a serious disservice to clients and their significant others, minimizing a potentially critical influencing factor in their day-to-day functioning. One of the unfortunate consequences of over-specialization is that we fail to translate what we have learned in specific situations to more general practice situations. For example, some practitioners in specialized medical settings have developed highly effective skills for communicating with persons with various limitations. There is much to be learned from this specialized knowledge that is of great utility in enriching our general communications skills.

Several factors have influences this rediscovery and our readiness to add "bio" to the "psychosocial" descriptor. Certainly the progress that has been made in opening up some of the once impermeable interprofessional boundaries has helped. This has been partially influenced by the enriched understanding of intersystems influence coming from systems theory. Further, our increased comfort with a pluralistic theoretical base for practice has also helped. For example, our growing acceptance of the important insights of some schools of meditation has helped us appreciate the powerful interconnections between mind and body far more than did the psychosomatic concepts of the earlier psychoanalytic tradition, important as these are.

A further contemporary factor is the expanding identification with the concept of "health seeking" rather than "pathology treating" that has permeated the health professions and, more and more, society in general. In our own practice, we have become increasingly sensitive to the interconnection between such things as stress, crisis, and posttraumatic responses and a range of physiological difficulties.

Another factor that is receiving much needed attention is the growing awareness of the complex and at times dramatic effects on biopsychosocial functioning of various medications and combinations of medications that are a part of a large number of our clients' lives. Being unaware of these potentially powerfully influencing agents can greatly distort our understanding of clients and their functioning.

How then are we to respond to all of these realities? Surely we are not expected to be, or to have the medical knowledge of, nurse practitioners, physicians, and pharmacists. Nor should we attempt to duplicate their proper competencies. But to ignore this material is irresponsible.

Rather, the task is to consider the extent to which the life patterns, problems, and potential for healthy functioning of an individual are influenced by his/her physical functioning. Our knowledge should focus on the impact of the client's physical condition and medical treatment on personality and on significant others, and on society's response to particular situations.

Always, of course, our task is to individualize. As in all situations, we need to ask how this client is the same as others in similar situations and how different. Certainly it is not, nor should it be, our responsibility to make medical diagnoses. However, since a client's denial or lack of information is often present, we do have a responsibility to be aware of obvious physical manifestations of illness or possible illness. For example, it would be tragic if we failed to recognize some obvious patterns of a mildly neurologically impaired child and to address the presenting problems as some type of reactive pattern to a family situation. In multidisciplinary settings, the interaction of many disciplines helps obviate this type of situation. It is much more difficult, and thus more crucial, for practitioners in primary settings to be attuned to these issues.

Thus, a more basic understanding of the physical components of our clients is needed so that we can be sensitive to the interconnections between body and psychosocial functioning. As well, we must develop skills and processes to ensure that in particular situations we know where and how to get specific knowledge. As a part of this we will need to develop an enriched body of practice-based clinical research on how to incorporate such knowledge into practice. We need to develop information and data banks that will permit us to find the information that is available to us, to ensure that we understand our clients, do not overlook important areas of functioning in our diagnosis, and formulate with them legitimate and appropriate interventive goals.

The articles selected for this part are arranged by subject matter and listed in alphabetical order. Our goal was to select a range of physical conditions to present an overview of the topic. Many more articles, touching on a host of other physical conditions, could have been selected; undoubtedly legitimate criticisms will be made as to what was omitted.

As mentioned in the last edition, writing in this general area is highly uneven, with some topics receiving much attention and others being totally untouched. Without doubt the day will come when there will be available practitioner-oriented texts that address only this topic. Until then, we present a range of topics with which practitioners in virtually all areas of practice will meet. This is meant to inform them about particular situations, but more importantly, to encourage colleagues to continue to enrich their knowledge of this aspect of the human condition so as to provide a more comprehensive and thus sensitive response to the persons we serve.

AIDS

CHAPTER 9

AIDS

A Clinical Approach

Marielle Beauger, Michèle Dupuy-Godin, and Yolaine Jumelle

AIDS is the most complex disease of this century. It evokes calamity, disaster, curse. It lays bare human vulnerability, both biological and psycho-social. It questions the values of yesterday and today. It challenges the roles of institutions such as hospitals, schools, social services and the legal system. It obliges us to cast doubt on the interactions between health and lifestyles, if not life itself.

In light of government statistics and the information transmitted by the mass media, it is easy to understand the hysteria, the panic and the devastation caused by the fear of the disease, the announcement of seropositivity and the confirmation of the disease itself. As in all great periods of stress, and in such a heavy bio-social context, the human animal will resort to all the weapons he has to defend himself: flight, aggressive over-statements, etc. Such behaviours add to the difficulty of dealing with the disease.

Placed at the junction of the relation between the practitioner and the person troubled or affected by the AIDS virus, we have developed a clinical approach comprising two very distinct stages:

- identification and appropriation, by health and social services professionals, of the fears and defence mechanisms related to AIDS and seropositivity;
- application of an intervention model favouring the right to dignity for the partners battling with AIDS; that is, the individual infected, the members of his network and the professional involved.

From conception, the human being must defend himself against death, and his immunity is formed progressively for the biological preservation of his life. At the same

From *The Social Worker,* Vol. 5-7, No. 1 (Spring 1989), pp. 23–27. Reprinted here with the permission of *The Social Worker/Le Travailleur Social.*

time, the initial and continuing anguish of death in him is countered by his psychological defence mechanisms. This both physical and psychological system of defence against death is indeed a necessity and a natural right for the person. The reality of dying from AIDS in the short or long term, and the sexual contamination threatening the very foundation of reproduction and survival of the human race, account for the panic triggered by the virus in human beings. Do the need and the right to protect oneself from dying psychologically and physiologically not derive from this panic? This protection is often expressed at the social level as myths to which biases are linked.

Because of its lethal nature and its patterns of transmission, AIDS creates, on its trajectory from functional immunity to the complete destruction of this immunity, sporadic crises. Fear, often obsessive, of being contaminated, prescription of the HIV test and expectation of the results, announcement of seropositivity, the watch for and appearance of the first symptoms, are all disruptive elements.

These crises erect barriers between the infected individual and the non-infected other, making more complicated and often impossible all personal and professional interaction. Each has specific characteristics and requires specific interventions. In this context, we have singled out three phases in the development of the AIDS situation during which therapeutic actions are essential: the pre-test, the announcement of seropositivity and the confirmation of the disease.

To illustrate in more concrete terms the interrelation between the person faced with the reality of AIDS and health and social services professionals, we propose three clinical pictures involving the three partners primarily affected. However, before presenting these pictures, we should discuss certain defence mechanisms prevailing in our society, popularly called myths.

MYTHS AND BIASES

The myth phenomenon was not formed in the 20th century. All societies have historically provided themselves, as do individuals, with defence mechanisms ensuring the survival of the rules established to govern community life. Not only has the 20th century inherited some of the myths of past centuries, it has also transformed these myths to adapt them to the phases of evolution. Nowadays, despite the liberalization of morals, we can see that some historical myths persist and continue to dichotomize reality between the legacy of mythical ideals and the credo of emancipation. If, according to Larousse, getting emancipated means freeing oneself from social constraints, a majority of persons infected with the AIDS virus can be associated with liberalization of sexual practices. However, these persons can easily be judged according to the code inherited from historical myths and thus be rejected because of social biases. In a society where human relationships are already powered by the requirements of profitability and technology, biases can only hinder services to clients bearing the burden of social contradictions.

Certain myths concerning AIDS should be recognized.

First is the myth of mutual fidelity in the couple, with reference to the need for emotional, material and social security. Loosened as a result of sexual revolution, which dragged infidelity out of the closet, this myth shows signs of mounting rigidity with regards to AIDS, since the disease threatens the human race with extinction.

Then comes the myth of mutual transparency, a utopian symbiosis, which controls separation between two individuals. In the case of AIDS, this form of defence is crystallized around the distrust associated with previous risky experiences: "I want to know your past, sexual and other, to reassure myself in the face of contamination; to a point, I want to know your HIV results". At the opposite, secrecy transgresses mutual transparency.

Social conformism is another of these myths. It has been used to maintain and justify the established order for centuries. Conformism is a protection against all deviation endangering structural stability since it sanctions marginalizing and isolating some elements that constitute a risk to its perpetuation.

There is also the myth of expiation. One could wonder if this myth derives from the three others already mentioned and if it serves to punish their transgressions. Well entrenched in most religious philosophies, does it not maintain its profound influence in spite of the liberalization of morals nowadays? In other words, would AIDS, a fatal disease, imply the punishment of an individual guilty of failing to properly protect himself physically and psychologically?

The myth of legal power is fundamental. Citizens rely on this power to protect themselves against all forms of danger, whether from the inside or the outside. If necessary, this protection is extended to counter the propagation of natural disasters. For example, quarantine was used to contain contagious diseases. With charters of rights and freedoms that ensure exclusive rights for the person, identifying limits between individual and collective rights becomes increasingly ambiguous. Moreover, in a reality filled with unknown factors (the period of time needed to document the virus with laboratory tests, the number of people carrying the virus who are not aware of their condition, the absence of cure), it would be extremely arbitrary to legislate in order to safeguard social safety. It is therefore each individual's responsibility to protect himself against AIDS. At the same time, this ambiguity of the legal power limits the intervention margin for the helping professional bound by a professional secrecy that sometimes interferes with his collective responsibility.

The myth of getting better linked with the historical reality of the healer is one of the most questioned surrounding AIDS. The power of the healer protects individually against the fear of dying and socially against the fear of extinction of the human race. The powerlessness accompanying the absence of drugs to cure AIDS weakens the myth of invincibility of the medical system and accentuates the anguish of death for individuals. This sort of powerlessness can nurture defence responses such as denial, rejection, desertion or isolation in partners battling against AIDS. This medical powerlessness impacts on social workers, since it increases the necessity of psycho-social intervention for persons suffering from the virus.

Today's social reality, dichotomized between mythical ideas and a faith in emancipation and loaded with the fear of death, therefore exacerbates the defence reactions in everyone. It introduces a struggle dynamic between persons infected with the virus and attending staff. It is essential that health and social services professionals recognize the complexity of their reactions with regards to AIDS and the urgent need to tame them. To this end, they must have access to human, space and time resources, to tools such as seminars, role playing, real-life situation exercises and psychodramas. Such resources will enable them to adjust and to plan, in very concrete terms, reassuring ways to protect themselves that hinder neither the intervention nor the right of the individuals infected with the AIDS virus to receive adequate services. Moreover, through this individual investigation process, professionals will discover the reactions of persons suffering from the virus and those of their environment, and see that they do not differ from their own.

THE PRE-TEST PHASE

Recently, X went to a medical clinic to consult for multiple symptoms: fatigue, digestive problems, occasional vomiting, insomnia, loss of appetite and limited attacks of anguish. Tests showed the presence of B hepatite virus, for which X is being treated medically. His doctor referred him to the social service for investigation of depressive signs. X is a homosexual. He is afraid of AIDS even though no indicator of the presence of seropositivity in his environment justifies the serosity test. A short time later, X leaves his friend, then has a brief sexual relationship with another man who, he knows, is suffering from the AIDS virus. X becomes obsessed by the fear of contamination and raises bluntly the question of the pre-test.

On the continuum of development of the disease, the pre-test phase is the one where the individual may have been in contact with the virus; contamination may have taken place without detection of the virus by test. The phase can last from three weeks to one year. This period of expectation is perturbing for X. The blame he addresses to himself as well as the shame that overcomes him add to his stress, expressed by states of confusion and elements of hypochondria. X has once gone through a deep crisis period when he had to assume his homosexuality, but this had taken place in the utmost isolation. At that time, X had put a distance between himself and his family and he is just as alone now to face the potential seropositivity.

At the pre-test phase, it is important to facilitate the step toward AIDS by clearly naming the disease and by associating in concrete terms the request for the test with the state of health and the risk factors. This allows the professional to determine precisely what the person knows about AIDS while opening the door to releasing underlying emotions. If necessary, these emotions can be empathetically proposed to the person to encourage their recognition. Intervention then becomes education. Waiting for the test, the intervenor discusses with X the necessity to protect his sexual partner to avoid transmitting the virus in the event he is infected, while at the same time protecting himself against eventual exposures. The sexual protection implies, of course, use of a preservative, with all related explanations and nuances. It can also mean knowledge and, from that moment, sexual practices that exclude vaginal, anal and oral penetration. The social practitioner also discusses with X the concepts of qualitative habits for everyday life (nutrition, exercise, leisure time, sleep) to preserve as much as possible his immunity defences. X takes care of himself and the others in making sure not to exchange body hygiene implements such as toothbrushes and razors. Information has been adapted to the state of panic dwelling in him. He is learning to love himself within new boundaries. He is learning to tame his fears and to bet positively on hope. The social practitioner's office becomes the only place where he can express his distress. The practitioner still must explore with him his solitude because, having learned early to be independent, he can easily withdraw into himself and act "as if", socially, nothing tragic has overcome him.

Progressively, X renews contact with his sexual partners. He can now discuss with them his precarious situation and let them decide if they want to have amorous relations with him that are protected and different.

Visits to the practitioner are less frequent. Later X comes back to talk about the test. The social practitioner thinks he is right and encourages him to get back to his doctor and request a HIV test. She schedules a visit once the results of the tests are known.

A pre-test intervention can take place in other circumstances. Whatever the conjunction, emotional stakes are associated with the turmoil, for which a psycho-social intervention must be located in a context of deterioration of the situation, that is, it must focus on prevention. Intervention at this stage is a good preparation, if needed, to the announcement of seropositivity and to facilitate both the progress of the infected individual and his interaction with health and social services environments.

ANNOUNCEMENT OF SEROPOSITIVITY

Z has been married nine years and has two children aged seven and five. Before his marriage, Z had many female as well as male partners. Three years after, he resumed his homosexual activities and has since had several male partners. His wife is not aware of his bisexuality.

Six months ago, following a loss of weight and the persistent increase in volume of his ganglions, Z saw a doctor. As a result of serosity tests, the doctor diagnosed seropositivity with a minor form of infection (AIDS-related complex). At the time of the first interview with the social worker, Z belonged to a mutual-help network. He has not yet told his wife or his immediate network about his disease. He feels ugly, bad and disorganized at the thought that he may have contaminated them. Since the announcement of seropositivity, Z never eats with his wife and only seldom comes home to sleep. In addition, he stays away from his friends and accuses them of having given death to him. He feels deceived, betrayed and is revolted by injustice. He feels quite helpless; anguish wakes him up at night in cold sweats. He is aggressive at work and still more during the few times when he sees his family. In the course of his first visit to the social practitioner, Z recognizes he uses distance and aggressivity to release his feelings of guilt.

In a first interview, the practitioner indicates she would like to be able to assess Z's knowledge about the life habits his condition requires. Z has a violent reaction. He accuses the practitioner of not understanding his feelings because she is not concerned. The practitioner accepts the rage in Z and bears with him that he wishes to be understood. Z cries and admits he is afraid to die. After allowing Z to centre himself upon his personal drama, the practitioner brings him back to the fact that he has two children. Z realises suddenly that he is still a father and that he must protect his family. After two interviews, Z cries over the feeling of "emptiness" that dwells in him. He can no longer fight alone. He expresses his need for support. Accompanying him in this "letting-go", the practitioner expands on his need of help for his family. She discusses with him his desire to announce his condition to his wife and asks how he plans to do it. Sanctioning

Z's right to be understood, she extends this right to his wife. She invites him to share with his wife his feeling of betrayal toward his family. Z asks to be accompanied in this process. He is hopeful. Z's wife heartily welcomes the practitioner. For the first time in seven months, he shows her pictures of the children, who are asleep. The practitioner directs the conversation towards the happy times the family has had together. After an hour, Z announces to his wife he suffers from a disease possibly diagnosed as fatal. He explains that nothing is definite, that there may be hope. The practitioner encourages him still in his endeavours. Z confesses to his wife he has AIDS. His wife cries, but she refuses the reality of AIDS. The practitioner allows her to express freely her protective denial. She joins the couple in a common battle against the enemy, the revolting disease that arouses by its very presence other ancient revolts. She allows the turmoil to express itself while appealing to the parents' responsibility toward their children and themselves.

Subsequently, Z's wife refused to meet again with the practitioner. The practitioner has therefore been unable to verify the state of contamination of the other members of the family, who moved a short time later to another city.

In most cases, announcement of seropositivity implies a rupture with others and a defence withdrawal into oneself. In the example presented here, the infected individual has succeeded, likely with the assistance of the mutual-help network, in coming in contact again with his need to be supported. Through the need to get out of isolation, the "letting-go" has become a force. The process does not always have such a happy ending. The need for support is not always recognized; grappling with the non-expressed revolt, some spouses convey it through rejection. Families of origin may do the same. In the case of Z's wife, what stands out most are the silent pauses, both before and after the announcement, about effects guessed to be present. It is as though she had to repress her emotions to protect herself making place only for a violent indignation followed by the challenge of AIDS itself. Through this challenge, she avoids questioning her own contamination; she does not question her faith in her husband, but she allows herself to go along with him in the deterioration. In other cases, the partner's anger and suspicion will elaborate and are expressed more bluntly. It is essential to recognize the loss of confidence and the rage associated with it. Expressing these feelings can be the requisite for the quality of the resumed relationship.

Major biases about bisexuality can at this point act on the helping professional, such as the absence of transparence and the many transgressions at the amorous and social levels. Before she has defined properly the seropositive individual's progress in the mutual-help network, the practitioner can herself feel manipulated by him and become a party to his manipulations. To be able to deal freely, it is therefore important for the practitioner to reach him in his shame and his fears and to recognize in the first place the impact of her own defence reactions.

In this seropositivity case, the follow-up shows quite well the conflictual dimension linked with the announcement. Together with the conflict, we sense the urgency of flight under any form: physical flight through distance, affective flight through denial. Autonomy that leaves one alone to cope, in isolation, as if one did "not need another", will accompany this flight.

Intended to break the loneliness, to reduce the stress and to normalize the way of life, social intervention enters here in the crisis period. Joining the infected individual in the announcement does not always result in reconciliation. The intervention can lead to separation and the search for a substitute network. It then implies more support to the desperate person. In this context, suicidal urges become more frequent. It is important at these times to centre intervention on the anger directed at the lack of comprehension. Whatever the outcome, the factors dignifying life must be redramatized.

CONFIRMATION OF AIDS

Y suffers from AIDS. Painful motor disorders are slowing him down. He is losing weight and becoming weaker. Since he has recurrent pneumonia, he must be hospitalized occasionally. Kaposi's syndrome makes his condition conspicuous. So many symptoms require the use of very expensive drugs. Y is well-informed and well-documented on AIDS, its development and its effects. He believes science will find a cure for his illness. He employs, therefore, his psycho-social defenses to fight against deterioration. He will even stay away from those who do not have the same faith in science and will sometimes break emotional ties to keep believing he will be cured. He also counts on a certain quality and a new way of life (vegetarian diet, avoidance of stress situations, professional reorientation to adapt his career to his condition, etc.). He is engaged in various activities directed toward solutions demanded by AIDS. The disease increasingly overcomes him in spite of his struggle against infection and the energy deployed through the whole reorganization of his life. Y shows aggressivity and revolt because of his state of dependence. When he allows himself to see his impending death, his spiritual discourse consists in ensuring, through his creations, that he will be remembered thereafter.

Y is one of the many examples of the progression of the AIDS-infected person towards death. Given individual characteristics, other reactions can take place. Psychosocial defences differ. Sublimation may happen at quite another pace or be non-existent.

Like any other chronic disease, AIDS is difficult to live with both for the infected individual and the people around him (network and intervenor). The psychotherapist sets the intervention within a bereavement process. Y moves constantly between aggressivity, denial of impending death, resignation, bargaining through material changes in his way of life, and sublimation, all valuable mechanisms preserving him from depression. In his case, the psychotherapist joins and supports him in his sublimation through a creative project. She defines his defence potential and helps him exploit it, thus taming his fear of death with the hope attached to a memory living beyond death. The psychotherapeutic intervention therefore invests, with the patient progressing towards death, in all forms of hope to be created and developed. However, because AIDS is specifically a stigmatizing disease, and because of the isolation frequently resulting from it, interactions can be more complex and give a particular coloration to intervention. The helping relation with the AIDS-infected person takes place in these circumstances. In a context of extreme loneliness, of sudden mood changes and often of physical degeneration, the intervenor must find and at times invent friendship and the support network.

CONCLUSION

In the context of AIDS, intervention can come within a continuum extending from the preparation for the HIV test to the accompaniment toward death. Each phase has specific characteristics and therapeutic approaches. For the person in the pre-test stage, a priority is the panic he expresses in different ways, from hysteria to frozen immobility and the feeling of helplessness related to death (fear of being contaminated oneself and of contaminating others).

In addition to accompanying the patient in his defence reactions against fear of contamination, the intervenor must at this time resort to an educative action aimed at the respect of herself and of the other person.

Announcement of seropositivity seems a very complex step, since it exposes the secret while indicating the possibility of death in the short or long term. It arouses the idea of betraying and being betrayed and invites isolation. The purpose of intervention is, more specifically, the disclosure so agonizing for the one and so revolting for the other. Intervention becomes a guarantee of accompaniment for better or for worse. At this stage, a family or substitute support network must be organized for the distressed person.

Confirmation of AIDS highlights the sad reality of an impending death, often in isolation and rejection. Psycho-therapeutic intervention comes within this dual context. The requisites for achieving such intervention are manifold. Availability and time; a capacity to receive the revolt, to be its target, to restrain it; a great capacity to live the other's helplessness and accompany him in this feeling; a great capacity also to practice with scarce substitute resources: all these personal and professional components should be part of the mediation. These conditions are also found throughout the continuum with different intensity. During the progress of the disease, the helping professional must combine hope with the fear of death. It is important, then, to question oneself about the intensity of one's own defence reactions, to take hold of them, to reorganize one's fears. This will release energies and make it possible to invent solutions to a socially catastrophic situation.

The clinical excerpts cited above force us to believe in the need of social services for persons suffering from the AIDS virus, in the necessity of agreements and collaboration between health and social services to this end, and in the urgency of training for the intervenors in the field of AIDS, a training that requires above all that the professionals open up to their own biases.

CHAPTER 10

HELPING TO MANAGE THE EMOTIONAL EFFECTS OF ARTHRITIS

Larry L. Smith

There are at least 50 million Americans with some type of arthritis. The Arthritis Foundation reports that 20 million of these people have arthritis severe enough to require medical care.[1] Although many Americans recognize the physical problems that may result from arthritis, especially the swollen and inflamed joints, few people understand the social and emotional concerns of arthritic patients. Despite the physical and psychosocial problems faced by arthritic patients, however, social workers, psychologists, and other therapists can help these patients and their families cope with the disease and live more productive lives.

DESCRIPTION OF THE DISEASE

There are many myths about arthritis. In order to dispel these myths and help patients gain a clearer understanding of the disease, social workers themselves must know something about it. According to the Arthritis Foundation, the term arthritis "is widely used to cover close to 100 different conditions which cause aching and pain in joints and connective tissues throughout the body, not all of them necessarily involving inflammation."[2] The five most common kinds of arthritis are (1) rheumatoid arthritis, (2) osteoarthritis, (3) ankylosing spondylitis, (4) systemic lupus erythematosus, and (5) gout.

Rheumatoid arthritis "is a systemic disorder of unknown cause in which symptoms and inflammatory change predominate in articular and related structures. The disease tends to be chronic and to produce characteristic, crippling deformities."[3] Rheumatoid

Reprinted from *Health and Social Work,* Vol. 4, No. 3 (1979), pp. 135–150 by permission of NASW Press, Copyright 1979, National Association of Social Workers, Inc., *Health and Social Work.*

arthritis is the most serious form of arthritis because it can result in crippling. Even though it attacks the joints primarily, it can also affect the heart, lungs, spleen, and muscles. The disease may subside and then flare up unpredictably, and it affects women three times more often than men. When it occurs in children, it is called juvenile rheumatoid arthritis and is extremely serious. Approximately 5 million Americans have rheumatoid arthritis.[4]

Osteoarthritis is a chronic disorder characterized pathologically by degeneration of articular cartilage and clinically by pain that appears with activity and subsides with rest.[5] It is primarily a wear-and-tear disease of the joints that comes with getting older. Although osteoarthritis is usually mild and not generally inflammatory, it is often painful and can cause mild to severe disability. Osteoarthritis does not affect parts of the body other than joints. It is estimated that over 12 million Americans have osteoarthritis.[6]

Ankylosing spondylitis is a chronic progressive disease of the small joints of the spine, which often begins in the teens or early twenties. Immobility of the spine ensues with the disease, and flattening of the lumbar curve is common. Studies indicate that 90 percent of those afflicted are men. The most important diagnostic indicator is radiologic evidence of spinal erosion and sclerosis of the sacroiliac joints.[7]

Systemic lupus erythematosus, called "SLE" or "lupus" or "lupus arthritis," is an acute systemic disease without a known cause.[8] It can damage and inflame joints and organs throughout the body, including the heart, lungs, kidneys, and brain. Females are affected more frequently than males, and the age of incidence is 20 to 40 years. It is often difficult to make a clinical diagnosis of SLE because its symptoms often are confused with those of other diseases such as rheumatic fever, viral pneumonia, and various disorders of the skin.[9]

Gout is an inherited metabolic disorder manifested by recurrent attacks of acute arthritis. It can inflame any of the joints of the body. Most victims are men, and the disease is extremely painful. The likelihood that gout will be inherited from one generation to another is often reported at 6 to 18 percent in the United States, although it may be higher. For example, studies in England suggest familial inheritance figures for gout as high as 75 percent.[10] When gout becomes clinically manifest, it often appears as arthritis of a peripheral joint, most often the big toe.

TREATMENT

Although there is no known cure for rheumatoid arthritis, effective treatment can control the disease and prevent deformities and crippling. The treatment for rheumatoid arthritis, as well as other forms of arthritis, may include all the following measures: (1) medication, (2) rest, (3) exercise, (4) splints, (5) walking aids, (6) heat, (7) surgery, (8) rehabilitation, and (9) rules of posture.[11] Anti-inflammatory drugs such as aspirin, ibuprofen, indomethacin, and phenylbutazone are often effective in treating rheumatoid arthritis because they reduce inflammation and the pain and swelling. Other drugs including corticosteroids, gold salts, and antimalarials also give relief to patients. Rest can also help reduce inflammation; yet moderate exercise can prevent stiffening of the joints.

There are also no known causes or cures for osteoarthritis. Although inflammation does not occur, considerable pain may exist around joints, and the patient often loses the ability to move the joints easily. Osteoarthritic joints should be protected from undue stress and strain. Any activity that leads to pain in an arthritic joint should be avoided, and overweight patients are encouraged to diet. Artificial hip joints have successfully relieved pain and restored movement in advanced cases of osteoarthritis of the hip. Because osteoarthritis is a chronic disease, treatment often continues throughout a patient's life.

Ankylosing spondylitis, which causes inflammation and deformities in the spine, has no known cause or cure. Medication, exercise, and methods to correct posture can help minimize the pain and control deformities. With prompt and proper treatment, most patients continue to lead productive lives. If the disease is not treated, curvature of the spine may develop, and the patient may be forced into a stooped posture.

Systemic lupus erythematosus affects the skin, joints, and internal organs and usually results in painful arthritis. Like rheumatoid arthritis, SLE follows an irregular course with painful flare-ups as well as periods of remission. Treatment varies considerably but usually includes rest and medication to control the pain and inflammation. If the disease is not treated, the patient can experience fever, skin rash, loss of weight, anemia and kidney problems.[12]

Although gout is extremely painful, treatment exists to control it effectively. This represents the first victory of medical science over a major form of rheumatic disease.[13] The treatment is designed to reduce the uric acid in the patient's system to tolerable levels, thereby preventing further painful attacks. Drugs and a special diet with moderate protein and little fat are used for this purpose, and they control rather than cure the disease for as long as the patient continues medication.

EMOTIONAL IMPACT

It is frustrating for a person to have a disease that can last a lifetime and has no known cause or cure. Arthritic patients struggle with a disease that can inflict excruciating pain one week and unexpectedly leave them free of pain the next. Arthritis often follows this roller-coaster course, which makes it difficult for a patient to plan ahead. A patient is often unable to follow through on plans because of the sudden onset of a painful flare-up. Living with such a disease may make a person temperamental, despondent, and angry.

One of the greatest frustrations arthritic patients encounter is with the physical restrictions forced on them by their disease. The author has spoken with many men and women who bitterly resent these restrictions. Men who once fished and hunted, played golf or bowled cannot now continue with these leisure activities. Other men who operated heavy equipment or worked as machinists have been unable to continue working and have had to find other employment. Women who painted, crocheted, and knitted often find it impossible to continue. These same men and women are sometimes severely hampered in the activities they can enjoy with their children and grandchildren. Children with juvenile rheumatoid arthritis struggle with these same restrictions, which may isolate them from other children and make their lives miserable.

These frustrations are sometimes too much for arthritic patients to endure. The author remembers one 50-year-old man who had not been able to fish for five years because of his arthritis. One summer he ignored his physician's warning and hiked out to some remote lakes in northern Utah for a week of fishing with some friends. The first three days were not too painful, but on the evening of the fourth day the pain became unbearable, and his companions had to bring him back to a Salt Lake City hospital on a stretcher. Mr. H still looks back fondly on that experience; he says he did it "to feel alive again." Mrs. P had a similar experience. Although, crippled with rheumatoid arthritis in her knees, she spent four hours kneeling one afternoon planting roses in her garden. She knew she would suffer pain the next day, but she did not care. It was her way of striking back at a disease that had plagued her for ten years.

Social workers who work with arthritic patients should encourage them to verbalize their frustrations and speak frankly about their feelings. This expression of frustration and anger often benefits the patient and may be a step toward helping the person cope with the disease. Patients also need to review what they can and cannot do because of their arthritis. Patients who can no longer hike, for example, need not give up the outdoors altogether. Scenic automobile rides in the country can help compensate for their lost activity. Arthritic patients who can no longer camp out with their families can still enjoy leisurely picnics in the park. Sometimes new interests can be substituted for old ones. One woman who could no longer knit because of her arthritis told the author that she became an avid reader on American Indians and started collecting Indian artifacts. She speaks to church and civic groups about her research and feels important and worthwhile once again. A sense of self-worth is difficult to maintain when many of the activities a person enjoys are suddenly taken away because of crippling arthritis. Social workers need to help arthritic patients in their quest for continued self-respect.

PAIN

Most people are unaware of the pain arthritic patients suffer each day. Many patients have told the author that their families and friends cannot understand how someone with arthritis "can look so well and still be in pain." Some patients have halfheartedly suggested that if they wore older clothes and appeared disheveled, people would be more compassionate. If social workers are to understand and help the arthritic patient, they must know something about the pain experienced. Some patients have described arthritic pain as a throbbing toothache that never goes away. Others have said that the pain comes unexpectedly and feels like "a thousand hot pins twisting in your shoulder." Still others describe a dull throb that is always there, morning, noon, and night. With some arthritics, the pain in their crippled and inflamed hands and knees is almost visible.

Some arthritic patients find it almost impossible to do even simple tasks without experiencing considerable pain. The author spoke with one woman who could not take the lid off a bottle of pickles without pain. This same woman had difficulty walking up a flight of stairs because of her inflamed knee joints. Another woman reported that she could not lift her arms above her shoulders. She found it impossible to comb her hair or give herself a permanent and said she was angry at her husband for needling her about her hair. Arthritic men have similar problems. One man confided how painful it was for him to shake hands with his business clients and friends. He had developed the habit of keeping his right hand in his pocket in self-defense. Another man mentioned how difficult it was to turn doorknobs or walk through revolving doors that sometimes slammed against his shoulders and arms. This same man also found it difficult to lift his beloved grandchildren.

The author encourages the arthritic patients he works with to let their families and friends know of their arthritis and that sometimes they have sudden painful attacks. The author is not suggesting that patients dwell on their illness. He is suggesting that arthritic patients be honest about their feelings. If shaking hands with other people gives a patient pain, he or she should let this be known so people do not interpret a reluctance or refusal as unfriendly or haughty behavior. If a father or mother cannot play with his or her children because of arthritic pain, the children should be told why and assured that the parent still loves them. Planning less painful activities with the children can help solve this problem.

PHYSICIANS

In helping the arthritic patient cope with pain, the social worker should encourage the patient to see a rheumatologist—a physician trained in managing arthritis—on a regular basis. If a rheumatologist is not available, the patient can be seen by an internist, family physician, or general practitioner who has experience in treating arthritic patients. Competent medical care is essential in helping the arthritic patient make the best possible adjustment to his or her illness.

After working with arthritic patients for three years, the author is convinced that many of them are not receiving the medical care they need. Some patients claim that their physicians are too busy to spend time with them. Others report how difficult it is to find a physician who is willing to add an arthritic patient to an already crowded work load. Still others criticize physicians because they cannot cure arthritis and only suggest ways to minimize rather than eliminate the pain. Some of these criticisms are justified; others are reactions that many patients with chronic illnesses voice against physicians.

Arthritic patients must become knowledgeable consumers of medical care if they are to work effectively with their physicians. Few Americans expect the same treatment from a physician that they do of other professionals, such as dentists, accountants, and lawyers, who dispense services. Arthritic patients are paying large sums of money for medical care and are entitled to certain services. Patients are entitled to the full attention of their physician during an office visit. It is not unreasonable to expect that a physician should spend fifteen minutes or more with a patient answering questions related to arthritis. The author even suggests to patients that they compile a list of questions prior to speaking with their physicians so they will not forget what questions they want to ask. The author has found that most physicians appreciate the patient's interest. If arthritic patients believe their physicians are not responsive to their needs, they should have a frank discussion with them. If the situation does not improve, the patients should consider changing physicians.

FAMILIES

The arthritic patient and his or her family do not always understand each other either. The author has listened to many patients who complain about the lack of concern shown to them by their family. One feisty patient even wished that his family could have arthritis for one day; they would then appreciate what he had been struggling with for fifteen years. Family members are equally frustrated with the arthritic patient. They want to help, but often everything they do seems to upset the patient and makes the problem worse.

The author believes a family must first know something about arthritis before they can begin to understand an arthritic family member. A family must understand that arthritis is a chronic disease with no known cause or cure that can cause great pain and crippling. Even though arthritis may begin with minor aches and pains, it is a serious illness that can lead to deformities of the hands, wrists, hips, knees, and feet. Family members also need to know that arthritis is not an old people's disease. Even though a brother or sister or parents may be less than 40 years of age, they may still suffer from arthritis. Arthritis can strike very early, and often first appears during the prime years of a person's life. Another myth that family members should recognize is the belief that nothing can be done for arthritis. With proper medication, much can be done for arthritic patients, especially in preventing further crippling and reducing pain.

As family members learn more about arthritis, they should be encouraged to discuss it with the patient. Family members should also ask the patient how they can be most helpful. One family resolved many of their problems when the patient finally agreed to let the family know when his arthritis was flaring up. This was a signal to the family that their father was in pain and could not be as helpful to them as he wanted. When the pain passed, the father said so, and they all went back to their regular routine. This example of open and honest communication should be seriously considered by all arthritic patients and their families.

SEX AND ARTHRITIS

Little has been written about the sexual problems arthritic patients encounter. Patients are reluctant to discuss the subject openly, but, based on private conversations with patients, the author knows it can be a serious problem: In "Sex and Arthritis and Women," Lachniet and Onder discuss this problem as it affects women. They believe open communication is one of the key ingredients in resolving sexual problems:

> Problems of mobility and flexibility caused by arthritis make it extremely important that the arthritic and her partner talk together. Whether the situation is a new sexual partner or is the onset of arthritis with an established sexual partner, the relationship will be strengthened if possible limitations in sex are discussed and interest indicated. For a woman to say, "Let's experiment and find out what we can do!" tells a man she is interested in sex and him. This is much more encouraging than saying, "I can't do much. I have arthritis."[14]

Lachniet and Onder believe a woman who wants to have sexual relations with a man must de-emphasize her reaction to arthritic pain. They offer the following suggestions:

> If a man feels he is hurting you every time he touches you (either in hugging, kissing, caressing, as well as intercourse), the fear of hurting you may keep him from having an erection and even from approaching you sexually or affectionately. If you think you may be unable to avoid saying "Oh!" or "Ouch!" when having sexual relations, it might be a good idea to tell the man something like this ahead of time: "Please don't worry if I say 'ouch!' I know you don't mean to hurt me. It sometimes gets to be a habit to say 'ouch' when I am touched. I don't want you to stop what you are doing."[15]

QUACKERY IN TREATMENT

This article would not be complete without discussing the problem of quackery in the treatment of arthritis. According to the Arthritis Foundation, "Arthritis sufferers are the most exploited of all victims of disease in the country today. They spend an estimated $485 million a year on worthless remedies, treatments, devices, and gimmicks. These fall into four general categories: (1) drugs and other medication; (2) devices; (3) dietary supplements; (4) advertised clinics."[16] Many of these products and treatments are harmful and even dangerous, while others only waste the patient's money. Even so, all worthless remedies are dangerous if they keep the arthritic person from seeking a qualified physician.

Why are arthritic patients so vulnerable to quackery? Many explanations probably exist, but the chronicity of the disease, the lack of knowledge about its cause or cure, and its infliction of great pain are certainly important factors. Very few people enjoy pain; most try to avoid it. The arthritic patient is no different and will try almost anything to stop the pain, including mysterious "cures." In addition, arthritis is an illness with periods of remission that follow periods of painful flare-up. If the arthritic patient happens to be wearing a copper bracelet or drinking vinegar and honey or following a special diet when a remission occurs, it is not difficult to understand why the patient might continue wearing the bracelet or drinking the mixture or following the diet, or why he or she might tell others the treatment "cured," his or her arthritis. Social workers need to be aware of the dangers of quackery and should encourage patients always to seek qualified medical help.

NOTES AND REFERENCES

1. *Arthritis: The Basic Facts* (New York: Arthritis Foundation, 1976), p. 2.
2. Ibid., p. 3.
3. Maxwell M. Wintrobe, ed. *Principles of Internal Medicine* (6th ed.; New York: McGraw-Hill Book Co., 1970), p. 1944.
4. *Arthritis: The Basic Facts,* p. 2.
5. Wintrobe, op. cit., p. 1949.
6. *Arthritis: The Basic Facts,* p. 2.

7. David N. Holvey, ed., *Merck Manual of Diagnosis and Therapy* (12th ed.; Rahway, N.J.: Merck Sharp & Dohme Research Laboratories, 1972), p. 1218.
8. *Arthritis: The Basic Facts,* p. 4.
9. Wintrobe, op. cit., p. 1965.
10. Ibid., p. 597.
11. *Arthritis: The Basic Facts,* p. 9.
12. Ibid., p. 18.
13. Ibid., p. 17.
14. Donna Lachniet and Jan Onder, "Sex and Arthritis and Women." Unpublished presentation, University of Michigan Medical Center, June 1973.
15. Ibid., p. 1.
16. *Arthritis: The Basic Facts,* p. 24.

BLINDNESS

CHAPTER 11

THE BLIND

Psychological and Emotional Needs

Doreen M. Winkler

Since formalized work with the blind began in North America about 1828, a good deal has been thought, written and said about their physical needs and how best to meet them. Much less attention has been paid to the psychological and emotional needs of blind individuals and their families. Perhaps this is because much less is known about these needs. Or, there may be a reluctance on the part of both blind and sighted people to become involved in discussions of them. The psychological needs created by blindness are important not only to blind people themselves but to all those who attempt to assist them.

This paper explores some of the psychological needs blind people and their families have: what they are, why they exist, and why they are often unmet. There are three major needs.

First, a person who is congenitally or adventitiously blind needs to know as honestly and objectively as possible the facts about his condition. The individual must be given accurate data and emotional help to accept and adjust. Second, a blind person needs to be rehabilitated according to the individual requirements of his personality and circumstances. He cannot be reconstructed according to a mold his rehabilitators have made for him. Third, in so far as possible, a blind person needs to have some control and power to shape his own destiny.

To achieve this third goal, he needs skilled intervention of an objective, knowledgeable worker to help him consider possible alternatives, to make realistic decisions for himself, and to attempt goals that are within his capabilities.

In part, all people have these needs. But with the advent of blindness, such psychological needs become intensified, urgent, and all-encompassing.

Reprinted from *Social Worker,* Vol. 40, No. 4 (December 1972), pp. 262–269, by permission of the publisher.

My observations and impressions have come from my personal experiences as a congenitally, totally blind person; and from my professional experiences as a social worker variously employed in a family service centre, a child guidance clinic, a medical clinic of a general hospital, a treatment ward in a psychiatric hospital, and, briefly, in the Social Service Department of the Canadian National Institute for the Blind in Toronto.

THE NEED TO KNOW

Dr. Louis Cholden, in his writings, argues that blind people need to know as quickly and as realistically as possible the unvarnished truth about their condition, and to adjust and accept that as a prerequisite to rehabilitation.[1] Secrecy is harmful to all concerned because it leads to distortions of reality.[2] Some sightless people begin and even successfully complete their education and training without accurate knowledge about their condition and without help in dealing with it emotionally. They do this, however, at great uncounted cost to themselves and, in some instances, to their families as well.

Parents of blind children are in need of special help. Their burden of anxiety and remorse is usually clearly evident. Because feelings are often irrational, most parents will inevitably blame themselves for what has happened to their child. If the marriage is not a strong one they will invariably blame one another for the occurrence. Such parents need a skilled counsellor to give factual information about their child's condition, and emotional support to sustain them in the crisis. Some form of marital or family therapy should always be made available to these parents for short periods of time.

Certain psychological factors account for information being withheld from the sightless and their families. Dr. Cholden suggests it may be partly due to society's concerted efforts to prevent such persons from accepting their blindness as a fact.[3] Such efforts may begin specifically with the attitude of the ophthalmologist. This physician has devoted his life to the conservation and preservation of sight.[4] Its loss in one of his patients may cause him to react emotionally rather than clinically.

Blindness in one of his patients may mean loss of self-esteem, loss of prestige among his colleagues, or injury to his reputation. His patient may no longer believe in his ability to treat him or he may hold him responsible for his blindness.[5]

Out of his own discomfort with blindness, or out of his need to spare the patient the pain he himself feels, he may distort or minimize information.[6] In fact, he may choose an even less desirable alternative and avoid the patient and his family altogether, assigning the task of information-giving to someone less qualified. If he does discuss the patient's condition at all the doctor's attitude will be conveyed by what he says, and the manner in which he says it.[7]

---

[1] Louis S. Cholden, M.D., *A Psychiatrist Works With Blindness,* American Foundation For The Blind, New York, 1958, p. 23.
[2] *Ibid.,* p. 16.
[3] *Ibid.,* pp. 76–77.
[4] *Ibid.,* p. 22.
[5] *Ibid.,* p. 23.
[6] *Ibid.*
[7] *Ibid.,* p. 25.

If the doctor holds out hope that his patient may live a full and productive life as a blind person that patient may be able to begin to think of his condition in a rather more positive light. If, on the other hand, he views blindness as a tragedy or as something akin to death, his patient will tend to reflect that attitude. If the experience of being informed is a negative one, the blind person may direct all the hostility he feels to the ophthalmologist and refuse further treatment which he may urgently need.[8] By being misinformed or misguided about his blindness, his family may have their worst fears confirmed and either blame themselves for what they do not know, or embark on an endless and painful search for miraculous cures.

If false hopes are repeatedly offered to the patient he may be prevented from coming to terms with his blindness and this will invariably hinder his adjustment to it.

RELUCTANCE TO DISCLOSE CONDITION

Some ophthalmologists may be reluctant to disclose information to a blind person because of what happens when he is told of his condition. Dr. Cholden described his initial emotional shock as a state of being "frozen," immobilized, unable to think or feel.[9] This is disturbing to the observer. Yet it is Dr. Cholden's belief that such a reaction on the part of a blind person is natural and essential, and must neither be prevented nor blocked. Time is needed by the blind person to recognize his inner strength to deal with the next phase of his adjustment. When his emotions return the first thing he feels is loss, the loss of his sight. Dr. Cholden describes the experience of a blind person that follows his initial shock as one of normal, reactive depression. His symptoms are those common to all reactive depressions: self-recrimination, feelings of hopelessness, self-pity, lack of confidence, suicidal thoughts, and psychomotor retardation. For a few days he may not want to get out of bed and he may have trouble eating and sleeping. In parents of blind children who experience this depression some genocidal fantasies may be present.

When this "expression of grief over the lost sense"[10] has run its natural course and the blind person begins to do some minor activities on his own he will be able, with skilled assistance from a counsellor or therapist, to start working on adjusting to his handicap.

At some time in his life the congenitally blind person must experience a process of mourning for his *lack* rather than his *loss* of sight.

In the initial stages of blindness a person will find contact with other sightless people very helpful to him. Dr. Cholden conducted group therapy with newly-blinded residents at the Kansas Rehabilitation Centre for the Adult Blind. He was impressed by the recurring themes around which discussions revolved. He found, for example, that many blind people felt their fears, anxieties, and emotional problems, were peculiar to themselves. He observed that "It is amazing to a blind person sometimes to know an-

---

[8] *Ibid.*, p. 22.
[9] *Ibid.*, pp. 25, 73–75.
[10] *Ibid.*, p. 20.

other feels uncomfortable in a silence, or that his blind friend is fearful when he is lost."[11]

A blind counsellor who has made a good adjustment to his own handicap is often better qualified emotionally and has greater depth of intellectual understanding of his newly or congenitally blind client than do his sighted colleagues. An early visit by a well-qualified blind worker to parents of a blind child is likely to give them more hope for their child's future than any number of visits by a sighted worker.

Dr. Cholden suggests that, in most cases, the blind person should be isolated from his family during his initial stage of depression as well-meaning members will tend to interfere with or try to prevent the mourning process.[12] The author is inclined, however, to share the opinion of Dr. Robert Scott that "a family crisis precipitated by the onset of blindness in one of its members is a family problem and not generic to blindness".[13] Experience in working with many families in crisis has been that whenever one member is suffering pain or loss all members feel that pain or loss in some way. The mourning process so necessary to a blind person's acceptance of his handicap is equally necessary to his family's acceptance of it.

FORCES BLOCKING ACCEPTANCE OF BLINDNESS

Even though adequate information has been given to blind persons and their families and they have received help in working through the first stages of shock and grief, many of them continue to have difficulty accepting and adjusting to blindness. Many external and internal forces thwart their efforts to do so.[14]

1. There is resistance to change in the human personality that makes it hard for everyone to accept a new self-concept. The sightless individual may feel that he will never be fully accepted by society. And he may see little need to reorganize himself in another, perhaps more painful way.

2. This observation underscores Dr. Cholden who writes that, according to his personality make-up, every individual will have his own individual reaction to blindness. Some reactions though are common to many For instance, people who have always depended on others will react in an even more dependent way to being blind. Blindness may be used by them to rationalize the gratification of those needs. They may try to prolong the period of regression that often accompanies the onset of blindness because they enjoy the attention and extra affection their family and friends have shown them because of it.[15]

Another person may see his blindness as a new way to controlling family members, or as a means of absolving him from family responsibilities. Some may use their blind-

---

[11] *Ibid.,* p. 37.
[12] *Ibid.,* p. 27.
[13] Robert A. Scott, *The Making Of Blind Men,* Russell Sage Foundation, New York, 1969, p. 76.
[14] Cholden, pp. 76–77.
[15] *Ibid.,* p. 19.

ness to punish themselves or their families in some way, or force sacrifices to be made on their behalf because of it. Still others may use their blindness to justify their recriminations against the world.

Sometimes a blind person who is enjoying his dependent role is encouraged in it by members of his family.[16] Many families sabotage a blind member's efforts to make a satisfactory adjustment.[17]

3. A blind person's adjustment may be hampered by the stereotypes he and others around him may believe concerning "the blind".[18] Some of the more common stereotypes are: (a) that of the blind beggar, completely dependent, constantly demanding charity in an inferior role;[19] (b) that of the blind genius, able to overcome all odds at great cost to himself, and magically able to do things no one else can;[20] (c) the notion that the blind have extra perceptions by which they can be guided, which the sighted do not have;[21] (d) the idea that the blind live in a "world apart", with spiritual qualities, aesthetic preoccupations and inner thoughts others cannot have;[22] (e) the assumption that blind people live in a "world of darkness" and that most of them are docile, melancholy, helpless and dependent.[23]

4. Closely linked with stereotype beliefs are what Dr. Cholden refers to as "the irrational feelings concerning blindness and its sexual meanings and historical connotation as punishment for sin."[24] Psychoanalysts' investigations have furnished proof of the close, unconscious connection between the eyes, vision, and sexual activity.[25] Child psychiatrists have often observed children in play therapy to expect punishment by blindness for masturbation or sexual curiosity. These unconscious connections often cause exaggerated, irrational responses by the sighted, and greatly affect the blind person's image of himself.

Out of these fears and irrational feelings the notion may arise that blindness is a stigmatized condition which causes the sighted to regard the sightless as their physical, moral and emotional inferiors, or, as somehow contaminating with the power to inflict physical or psychic damage.[26] Dr. Scott emphasizes that few blind people can ignore the stereotype beliefs of the sighted. Some actually come to believe in them themselves and so internalize them. Others try to insulate themselves against them or reject them as false. In either case, Scott's argument maintains that "these beliefs are a fact of life for the people who are blind". They must be reckoned with in some way.[27]

5. A blind person may be psychologically blocked in his adjustment by his knowledge

---

[16] *Ibid.*
[17] *Ibid.*, pp. 68–69.
[18] *Ibid.*, p. 21.
[19] *Ibid.*
[20] *Ibid.*
[21] *Ibid.*
[22] Scott, pp. 21–22.
[23] Cholden, p. 77.
[24] *Ibid.*, p. 20.
[25] Scott, pp. 18, 24.
[26] *Ibid.*, p. 117.
[27] *Ibid.*, p. 77.

that his blindness makes him part of a minority group which may represent to him a lowered social status and reduced self-worth.[28] It certainly means that he is different, and his encounters with the sighted are likely to confirm his feeling.[29]

More could be said about the obstacles to adjustment blind people encounter. The author's experience supports Gloria Sewell's conclusion, drawn from the findings of her study, that "every sightless person could benefit from professional help to build a sufficiently strong self-image to cope with community attitudes and his own feelings of difference" and to assist him in his integration into the sighted world.[30]

REHABILITATION IS NOT ALWAYS SUCCESSFUL

However, as Dr. Cholden suggests, a person who has been independent and mature, and accepts and adjusts to blindness, is not always successfully rehabilitated.[31] I share the view of Dr. Cholden that all blind persons are motivated to adjust to blindness, and to be rehabilitated, but there are many blocks that hinder the utilization of their motivation. As was indicated at the beginning of this paper, much is known about the physical needs of the blind. Much is known about their physical rehabilitation—how to teach braille and mobility skills, and so on. But, as Dr. Cholden has pointed out, much less is known about "making a frightened handicapped person courageous or a dependent client desirous of independence."[32]

Dr. Scott's sociological study vividly documented in his book, *The Making of Blind Men,* dramatically reveals that many sighted persons and workers in organizations for the blind clearly do not want to know the answers.

The thesis advanced by Scott is "that blindness is a learned social role. People whose vision fails will learn the attitudes and behavior patterns that the blind are supposed to have in their relationships with those with normal vision and in the organizations that exist to serve and to help blind people."[33] Further, "the needs of the blind are not determined from scientific studies of the impact of blindness on the functioning of the human organism. They are invented to justify the creation of programs and institutional arrangements required to palliate community reactions and fears about blindness."[34] Since the blind person must rely on the sighted for assistance in the most ordinary situations he finds himself automatically placed in the sighted person's debt and he may be restricted in his ability to reciprocate.[35] Therefore, as Scott emphasizes: "The blind person, by virtue of his dependency, is the subordinate in a power relationship."[36]

---

[28] *Ibid.,* p. 30.
[29] *Ibid.*
[30] Gloria Sewell, *The Adventitiously And Congenitally Blind,* School of Social Work, University of Toronto, unpublished master's thesis, Toronto, 1964, p. 98.
[31] Cholden, pp. 20, 67.
[32] *Ibid.,* p. 64.
[33] Scott, p. 71.
[34] *Ibid.,* p. 91.
[35] *Ibid.,* p. 36.
[36] *Ibid.,* pp. 118–19.

Within organizations for the blind there are also factors which prevent many blind people from receiving much-needed assistance. The findings of Scott's study indicate that, although there are many blindness agencies in the United States, only about one-quarter of the blind population is helped by them.[37] They are mainly blind children who can be educated and blind adults who can be employed. For the most part, the elderly unemployable, uneducable, and multiple-handicapped blind are excluded or minimally served.

Traditionally, blindness has meant or at least implied total absence of vision so that most of the programs of blindness agencies have been geared to the needs of the totally blind.[38] For example, in many agencies braille is taught to some who, with the aid of special lenses, can read enlarged or ordinary inkprint. People with partial vision are frequently trained to do jobs devised for totally blind people when, with a few minor adjustments, they might be able to continue in the jobs they held before their vision began to fail.

Scott's study also shows that when a person is legally "blind," he ceases to be "a sighted person with visual difficulty" and becomes "a blind person with residual vision".[39] His problems are seen not so much as medical ones but more as sociological ones pertaining to his adjustments to his disability, whether or not this is the case. Once accepted by the blindness agency, Scott's theory maintains, the person who has difficulty seeing is taught how to behave like a blind person.[40]

TWO APPROACHES TO REHABILITATION

Dr. Scott outlines two approaches adopted by blindness workers in rehabilitation agencies for the blind. The premise of the first is that blind people can be restored to a high level of independence enabling them to lead a reasonably normal life but this is only possible after they have come to fully accept the fact that they are blind, with the implication that this is a permanent role they must assume.[41] The second approach acknowledges that the first is noble but impractical for most blind people. It holds that blindness creates enormous obstacles to independence which can be overcome only by a few, highly-talented blind people through great personal effort. A more realistic objective is to provide an environment to which blind people can accommodate easily.[42] This "accommodative" approach assumes that most blind people are incapable of true independence, that most blind people prefer their own company, and that most blind people need to perform special kinds of work because of their disability.[43]

Scott's investigation shows that, as recently as 1968, although most agencies in America theoretically accept the "restorative" approach, most practise the "accom-

[37] *Ibid.*, p. 73.
[38] *Ibid.*
[39] *Ibid.*, p. 74.
[40] *Ibid.*, pp. 76–80.
[41] *Ibid.*, pp. 80–84.
[42] *Ibid.*, pp. 84–89.
[43] *Ibid.*, p. 93.

modative".[44] There are economic, political and sociological pressures which make this necessary.

When a sightless person comes for help with his blindness he has some definite ideas about his needs or about what problems he has that must be dealt with before he can cope with his situation. The place to which the blind person comes for help, and the means by which he is sent there, has significance in relation to his knowledge about it as well as how he is received. If his need for self-determination in planning his program of rehabilitation is ignored, he will react in a number of ways. His anxiety may cause him to present himself inappropriately as resistant or acquiescent. His views about his blindness are essential to an understanding of how best to help him with it. If, as so often happens, he is listened to very nicely and later finds his opinions have been discredited or dismissed as inaccurate or superficial, he may react with so much anger that he will leave the agency feeling more confused, frightened and frustrated than when he came to it. Thus he may fail to avail himself of the agency's services he needs, wants, must have, and indeed, to which he is entitled.

In the rehabilitation process, Scott discovered, "the blind person is rewarded for adopting a view of himself that is consistent with that of his rehabilitator's view of him, and punished for clinging to other self-conceptions. He is told that he is insightful when he comes to describe his feelings and personality as his rehabilitators view them and he is said to be blocking or resistant when he does not."[45]

Many clever blind people learn to behave as they are expected to and demonstrate "insightfulness" in order to receive tangible services or proceed through the agency's course of rehabilitation to make use of its programs. Such a person learns to play the rehabilitation game in much the same fashion as the prisoner learns to walk the straight line in order to be paroled, or the psychiatric patient learns to recite all the right responses in his therapeutic sessions in order to procure his discharge from hospital.

SUMMARY

This paper has identified three basic psychological needs I believe to be common to all unsighted or partially-sighted persons. The need to be informed as quickly and honestly as possible the facts of his condition and to receive professional help in accepting and adjusting to it. The need to be given rehabilitation assistance as an individual and not sociological reconstruction as a blind person having thoughts, feelings and abilities that sighted and many blindness workers believe he must have because he is blind. The need to be a partner with his rehabilitators in planning for a future as a sightless person and to be allowed some psychological autonomy in shaping his own destiny according to his personal preferences and desires.

Obstacles that hinder many blind people in their adjustment have been explored. The difficulties many blind people and their families encounter in meeting psychological needs have been examined primarily in the light of observations and research of Doctors Cholden and Scott.

[44] *Ibid.*, p. 90.
[45] *Ibid.*, p. 119.

Workers in rehabilitation agencies and educational institutions for the blind must employ great flexibility and imagination in their work with blind people. They use techniques and skills based on scientific knowledge of human behavior rather than on subjective experience with blindness and the unsighted. They must listen well to what each individual has to say about his problems with blindness as well as his feelings about being blind. The simple fact is that those who have difficulty seeing or who cannot see at all are, after all, individual persons who happen also to be blind persons. From this very simple fact comes the conviction that if a person's needs as an individual are not accounted for or met satisfactorily, his needs as a blind person will never be understood and total life adjustment will never be complete and happy.

CHAPTER 12

ADJUSTMENT PROBLEMS OF THE FAMILY OF THE BURN PATIENT

Gene A. Brodland and N. J. C. Andreasen

Patients who have been severely burned experience an intense and varied trauma involving catastrophic injury, severe pain, possible cosmetic or functional deformities, and a threat to their sense of identity and worth. Hospitalization is usually prolonged. During this time, the family of the burn patient often remains with him to comfort and console him. Because most of the attention of the medical staff is focused on the suffering patient, the family members remain in the background and few people are aware of their suffering and emotional needs. Yet, just as the patient himself must adjust to his injury, so the family must go through a complicated process of understanding, accepting, and adjusting to the illness and distress of the loved one.

The adjustment problems of the adult burn patient have been the subject of only a few studies, and the problems of his family have drawn still less attention.[1] Studies done in England have examined the grief reactions of parents of fatally burned children and pathology in the parents which may have contributed to behavioral problems in surviving children.[2] One follow-up study of ten children and their parents, an average of four and a half years after injury, discovered recognizable psychological disturbance (usu-

Reprinted from *Social Casework,* Vol. 55 (January 1974), pp. 13–18, by permission of the publisher, Families International.

[1] N. J. C. Andreasen, Russell Noyes, C. E. Hartford, Gene A. Brodland, and Shirlee Proctor, Management of Emotional Problems in Seriously Burned Adults, *New England Journal of Medicine,* 286:65–69. (January 13, 1972); David A. Hamburg, Curtis P. Artz, Eric Reiss, William H. Amspacher, and Rawley E. Chambers, Clinical Importance of Emotional Problems in the Care of Patients with Burns, *New England Journal of Medicine,* 248:355–59 (February 26, 1953); and David A. Hamburg, Beatrix Hamburg, and Sydney DeGoze, Adaptive Problems and Mechanisms in Severely Burned Patients, *Psychiatry,* 16:1–20 (February 1953).

[2] Helen L. Martin, J. H. Lawrie, and A. W. Wilkinson, The Family of the Fatally Burned Child, *Lancet,* 295:628–29 (September 14, 1968); Helen L. Martin, Antecedents of Burns and Scalds in Children, *British Journal of Medical Psychology* 43:39–47 (March 1970); and Helen L. Martin, Parents' and Children's Reactions to Burns and Scalds in Children, *British Journal of Medical Psychology,* 43:183–91 (June 1970).

ally depression) in eight of the mothers and nine of the children.[3] This morbidity is high, and it suggests that further examination of the reactions of families is needed.

The observations presented in this article are based on a study done over a period of approximately one year on the burn unit at the University Hospitals in Iowa City. A total of thirty-two adults and their families were evaluated psychiatrically on admission and were interviewed daily thereafter until the time of discharge. Initial evaluation was based on complete psychiatric and social histories and mental status examinations. The patients ranged in age from twenty to fifty-nine with a mean of thirty-six, in total body surface burn from 8 percent to 60 percent with a mean of 29 percent, and in duration of hospitalization from two and one-half weeks to three months with a mean of one month. Patients outside the age range of eighteen through sixty or with severe mental retardation were excluded.

The relatives of the burn patient appeared to go through an adjustment process, similar to that of the patients, involving two stages. The first stage was one of acute shock and grief analogous to the acute physical and emotional trauma experienced by the patient himself. In the second or convalescent stage, the relatives had overcome shock and disbelief; they rationalized and accepted the fact of the injury and its accompaniments and began to assist the patient in the process of recovery.

INITIAL REACTIONS OF RELATIVES

The family's first reaction on arriving at the hospital is usually relief that the patient has not died or been burned more severely. Rationalizations that "it could have been worse" provide an affirmative basis from which to begin coping with the stress that they face. In this first stage, the relatives express little concern about the potential scarring that might take place. Their primary concern is for the recovery of the patient, no matter what his appearance on recovery. The following case history illustrates the initial reaction of many families in the first stage of hospitalization.

> Mr. S, aged twenty-three, was severely burned in a car-truck accident. Having been pinned in the truck cab which caught fire, he sustained third-degree burns over 45 percent of his body. He was transferred to the burn unit two and one-half weeks after being burned and remained hospitalized for two and one-half months. His wife, who visited him daily, expressed her feeling that the scarring which might result was not important. She said she "would be happy if he could get well no matter what his condition is, so the kids will have a father." She demonstrated a considerable amount of quiet desperation; tears were often evident when she expressed her feelings.

Despite expressions of relief that the patient has not died, the fear that the injury might ultimately prove fatal lingers with many relatives. Sometimes this fear is expressed overtly. Interwoven with these feelings is a well-repressed wish by some rela-

[3] Aldo Vigliano, L. Wayne Hart, and Frances Singer, Psychiatric Sequelae of Old Burns in Children and Their Parents, *American Journal of Orthopsychiatry,* 34:753–61 (July 1964).

tives that the patient would die and thereby avoid the pain and frustration that lie ahead of him. Relatives of patients who die as a result of burns support this idea; when informed that a loved one has died, they often comment, "It is probably a blessing for he won't have to suffer any more now." Such feelings are usually suppressed because of the guilt they could arouse. The case of Mrs. K illustrates this reaction.

Mrs. K, aged twenty-four, was burned in a natural gas explosion in her home. Her husband suffered more severe burns and subsequently died. Her comments following his death indicate a degree of relief. She said, "I will miss him and it will be hard without him. He won't have to suffer for months and months. I'm glad God took him soon. I know he wouldn't want to live being terribly burned as he was. His death was a blessing." Mrs. K probably would not have said this before his death but as she rationalized in an attempt to face reality, these feelings were allowed to come to the surface.

During this early period, the relatives and the patients form feelings of trust or mistrust toward the medical staff. When a patient suffers from pain and fear, he and his relatives have to decide whether everything is being done medically to insure his comfort and recovery. Occasionally, patients and relatives question the competence of the staff and feel that the patient is the object of experimentation. The extended waiting period prior to skin grafting is often seen as abandonment and may lead to feelings of mistrust. Such feelings were expressed to the psychiatric social worker more often than to the medical staff. Relatives were concerned that by expressing angry feelings toward the staff they might jeopardize the patient's relationship with the staff.

Mr L. sustained a steam burn while working on a construction job. After skin grafting failed to take, the patient became suspicious and remarked that the resident doctor was practicing on him as if he were a "guinea pig." He requested that the social worker arrange for a transfer to a private doctor or to another hospital. He did not want to talk to the nurses or the staff doctor about this change, because it might cause hard feelings. It was determined later that his problem centered on the lack of communication between the resident and the patient. The problem was resolved when the resident made conscientious efforts to explain the treatment procedures more fully to the patient.

Soon after admission, a number of extensively burned patients experience confusion and disorientation as a result of an acute brain syndrome that often accompanies burn trauma. Many relatives found this reaction stressful. Sometimes a patient was verbally abusive or assaultive, and relatives had a difficult time in deciding whether this behavior represented his true feelings or whether it was the result of delirium. Relatives were frightened by this sudden "mental illness" and needed reassurance that delirium is a common occurrence in burn patients and that once the burn begins to heal, the delirium passes.

Mr. R, a twenty-eight-year-old farm hand, was burned over 60 percent of his body in a natural gas explosion. About a week and a half after admission to the burn unit, he became delirious. During his periods of confusion, he thought of a period during his second year of marriage when his wife had had an extramarital affair. Mr. R angrily expressed the belief that this affair was still going on. His bewildered wife thought that this problem had been resolved eight years before. Mrs. R needed reassurance that his accusations were a result of his delirium. After Mr. R recovered, he denied any feelings of suspicion toward his wife.

Another source of difficulty for relatives is the psychological regression that is often observed among the burn patients. Patients who have been quite self-sufficient in the conduct of their daily lives before being hospitalized often become complaining, demanding, and dependent during hospitalization. The family, unaccustomed to this behavior, becomes alternately confused and angry. They want to respond to the patient's needs but are confused by demands that seem so out of character. Relatives become angry when the patients do not give them credit for their efforts and continue with their childlike behavior.

REACTIONS AFTER INITIAL CRISIS

During the second phase of adjustment, the family is assured that the patient will survive and begins to consider the process of getting well. The family members begin to recognize that they and the patient still have many weeks in the hospital ahead of them. The patient and his relatives usually have no prior knowledge of the treatment and procedures required for recovery; now they begin to ask questions of physicians and nurses about the process of healing, dressing changes, grafting procedures, and so on. Often relatives of other patients on the ward are important sources of information, just as they are sources of reassurance. The family of the patient must prepare themselves psychologically for an extended stay in the hospital. From a practical standpoint, family members must make arrangement for their own physical well-being during this period and establish "a home away from home." This often involves spending days at the hospital and nights in a nearby motel.

The pain the patient suffers is a primary problem at this time, and it often results in a sense of helpless frustration in the relatives. The patient seems to become increasingly cognizant of his pain once the threat of death has passed. He then begins to verbalize the pain, at times in tones of desperation. The helplessness which relatives feel in handling this pain produces conflict. On the one hand, they try to do everything within their power to aid the patient by making him physically comfortable and providing emotional support. On the other hand, relatives sometimes feel the staff could relieve pain more adequately by the administration of analgesic medication. The relative often is in a precarious position, trying to maintain a good relationship both with the patient and with the medical staff. Few persons understand fully the principles followed in the use of pain medication. The following example illustrates the development in one relative of mistrust of the staff.

Mrs. B was burned when she and her family were trapped upstairs in their burning home. She broke her arm when she jumped from a second-story window to escape the flames. Because of the burns, the staff were unable to put her arm in the correct cast. The arm was very painful. Because of her complaints of pain and her mother's frustration in attempting to alleviate the pain, the mother confronted the nurse with the accusation that the staff was neglecting her daughter by not giving her enough pain medication. Once the problems inherent in using potent analgesics for long periods of time were explained in detail, the patient's mother was much relieved and could again be supportive to the patient.

Another source of pain occurring during this period is the process of autografting. The donor site, from which the skin for grafting is taken, often is more painful than the burn site itself, causing great distress to the patient. Further, the patient must lie quietly after the grafts have been placed, increasing the sense of helplessness felt by both patient and relatives. The fear of doing something that might disturb the graft is a significant cause of anxiety.

The frequent trips to the operating room for skin grafting are yet another source of anxiety. The fear of anesthesia must be faced each time the operative procedure approaches; the patient is anxious about being put to sleep and having to relinquish control. This anxiety is often sensed by the relatives.

REACTIONS DURING RECOVERY

Still later in the recovery period, the problem of pain is supplanted by one of itching, which creates a problem for the relatives who try to help the patient to tolerate each new stress. It often seems that total recovery will never arrive and that one discomfort is simply succeeded by another.

Another major problem faced during the recovery phase is fear of deformity. Most families initially expect grafting to restore fairly normal appearance. What medical personnel consider an excellent job of skin reconstruction is often viewed by the lay person as almost grotesque. Thus, patient and family tend to be disappointed by the results of grafting and to find a gap between their expectations and those of medical personnel. During this stage of recovery, the patient begins to prepare himself for facing the outside world by realizing that scarring and deformity may have made him unattractive and unacceptable to others with whom he has previously associated. He becomes hypersensitive to initial reactions and wonders what reactions he will find himself meeting the rest of his life. Relatives have similar fears.

The relatives' reactions are the first ones that the patient observes, and his distress is increased when he sees revulsion. A fairly typical case of family reaction was noted in a follow-up study of burn patients.[4] A young mother who had been hospitalized for three months eagerly anticipated seeing her children. She was greeted by her five-year-old with "Yuk, Mommie, you look awful." Adult family members, on the other hand, tend to recognize intuitively that they need to be supportive and to help the patient establish a denial system. Yet, providing a reassurance that they do not always sincerely feel is often quite stressful for them. Only with time and thoughtful support on the part of doctors, nurses, and relatives can the patient resolve his feelings about disfigurement

---

[4] N. J. C. Andreasen, A. S. Norris, and C. E. Hartford, Incidence of Long-Term Psychiatric Complications in Severely Burned Adults, *Annals of Surgery,* 174:785–93 (November 1971).

and come to realize that angry red scars eventually fade and that his appearance will gradually improve.

Sometimes relatives carry an additional burden because of their feeling that they have contributed to or caused the accident in which the patient was injured. Even when the relatives have had nothing to do with the injury, some feel guilty; they explain this feeling on the basis of not having foreseen the possibility of the accident and not having taken steps to prevent it. Eventually, the relative resolves his guilt feelings and achieves a rationalization that relieves him of full responsibility for the accident—for example, that the accident happened because it was God's will, because it would draw the family together, or because of the carelessness of others.

Notable throughout the recovery period is the difficulty that relatives have in dealing with the patient's need to express his feelings. They find it difficult to strike a balance between letting the patient describe his feelings about being burned and possibly handicapped and providing adequate emotional support. Sometimes relatives attempt to discourage the patient from expressing feelings of grief or fear and try to be constantly supportive and optimistic. In preserving their own comfort, they sometimes unwittingly deprive the patient of a necessary safety valve.

There are also relatives who become overwhelmed by the emotional stress of sitting at the bedside of a loved one and sharing his suffering. Many are reluctant to leave the bedside in the early stages of recovery, fearing that something might happen while they are gone. Occasionally, relatives become too depressed or anxious and must be asked to leave the ward temporarily to regain their emotional equilibrium. Remaining at the bedside of a burned patient is an unusually draining experience for his relatives. Much like a young child, the burn patient tends to focus only on himself and provides little support in return, leaving little opportunity for relatives to converse or receive support from others.

RECOMMENDATIONS FROM THIS STUDY

A burn injury is a traumatic experience for the uninjured relatives, as well as the patient himself. The families of the burn patients face multiple stresses and adjustment problems. They go through essentially the same phases of adaptation as the patients, for they must cope with anxiety about death, communication difficulties with the medical staff, fear of deformity, and the boredom of a prolonged hospital stay, as well as enduring the trauma of watching a loved one suffer. In some respects, their suffering may be greater than that of the patient. Although they do not suffer pain directly, they must stand by in helpless frustration, their guilt over the fact that the injury occurred at all further enhanced by their guilt about the anger which they must inevitably feel sometimes. Although they do not fear death or deformity for themselves directly, they must face these threats more immediately than the patient. Few patients are informed of their prognosis soon after admission and, if they were, their minds would be too clouded by trauma to comprehend it fully; however, relatives cannot be shielded from this information, and they must receive it when their minds are usually in a state of heightened sensitivity and alertness.

Relatives may provide valuable assistance on wards by helping to feed the patient, by providing companionship for him, and often by encouraging and assisting him with exercise and physical therapy. Nevertheless, nurses and physicians provide primary care, and the role of relatives must inevitably be simply a supportive one. This role is a difficult one to fulfill in such an emotionally draining situation unless the person providing the support receives support from others for himself. On the burn unit, this need was often met by the relatives of other patients. Although there was no formal effort by the staff to enhance such relationships, relatives often pooled their information about treatment methods, compared notes on the condition of the patients, and consoled one another when things were going badly.

Hospital burn units could learn a lesson from this phenomenon and formalize it in several ways. Relatives could be helped greatly if hospitals prepared a simple pamphlet to be given to them on arrival, explaining simple facts about injuries from burns and the operation of the unit. It should state the visiting hours established and describe the daily routine, the purpose of unfamiliar treatment methods such as the use of silver nitrate and sulfamylon, the rationale behind the use of milder and preferably oral analgesics, the usual course of recovery from a burn injury, the nature of the grafting procedures usually done, and so forth. A glossary of unfamiliar terms—*autograft, zenograft, debridement,* for example—should be included. Because of the complex nature of this type of injury, burn treatment units are often run quite differently from other hospital facilities, and relatives cannot carry over any prior hospital experience. For example, they find it difficult to understand the infrequent use of potent analgesics, although this practice usually becomes acceptable when they realize that the long-term use required in a burn injury might lead to dependence or addiction. On the affirmative side, on some burn units, rules about visiting hours are flexible and most relatives are permitted to remain with the patient as long as they wish.

A second way of providing communication and understanding among relatives would be the establishment of group support meetings. A group composed of family members or close friends of patients currently on the burn unit could meet at a regularly scheduled time once or twice weekly. The group would remain in existence, although the membership changed as the patient population changed. Ideally, this group would be conducted by a pair of group leaders—a psychiatric social worker and a nurse or physician who are members of the burn unit treatment team. A physical therapist, a dietitian active on the burn unit, and a psychiatrist familiar with the problems of adjustment to chronic illness would be other potential members or guest visitors.

The establishment of such a group would serve several purposes. It would demonstrate to the beleaguered relatives the interest and concern of the hospital staff, sometimes prone to leave relatives out of the picture because of their concern for primary patient care; regular group meetings would make efficient use of the professionals' time and experience. The meetings would also serve to educate relatives about problems of burn trauma, particularly when discharge draws near. Family members often take on primary responsibility for the patient at discharge and they greatly need adequate information about wound care, the need for continuing physical therapy, and the problems of emotional and social adjustment. The group discussions would provide relatives with an open forum for raising questions and for airing complaints. They would provide emotional support by strengthening the bonds formed between family members and alleviate some feelings of fear, frustration, futility, and boredom. Such a group would not be designed as therapy, but as a means of sharing strength and information.

Limited experience with such group meetings on burn units indicates, however, that often staff members also receive information and support from them.

A final way for social work staff to be effective on a burn unit is perhaps the most obvious. Families of patients often suffer significant financial expenses, and even after the patient is discharged the period of rehabilitation is prolonged. Family members and patients need to receive information about funds available to assist in the high cost of hospitalization, funds for care of dependents, and opportunities for vocational rehabilitation. An experienced and sensitive social worker can often provide subtle emotional support by demonstrating his concerned involvement as he offers his resources of information and interest to the family.

CHAPTER 13

TERMINAL CANCER

A Challenge for Social Work

Carleton Pilsecker

"Advances in cancer control . . . have nearly doubled the survival of American cancer patients over the last four decades. One and a half million who have had cancer are alive and well" (American Cancer Society, 1975). Surgery, radiation therapy, chemotherapy, and immunotherapy are contributing significantly to effective treatment of cancer. Great energy and sums of money are being devoted to research which promises one day to cure and even to eradicate this dread disease. Thus there is hope.

Hopefulness, however, is not usually associated with cancer. The initial reaction to a diagnosis of cancer is to be "scared to death", i.e., scared of death. There are two good reasons for such a reaction: (1) in spite of the "advances in cancer control", cancer remains the second-leading killer in this country and the death rate from cancer continues to rise (American Cancer Society, 1977), and (2) death by cancer is viewed as an ugly end to life.

If you could choose your way of dying, would your choice be cancer? Probably not, for cancer is seen as an insidious, debilitating, painful, drawn-out process. Most people want to die one of two ways: either suddenly and with as little prior trauma as possible (e.g., heart attack while at home, in bed, asleep) or peacefully and painlessly over a two to three month period in which life's business can be put in order, goodbyes can be said, and a dignified withdrawal from living can be made (Schneidman, 1971). Cancer, by contrast, threatens to hurt, to lay waste, to lead to physical dependence, to spread indecently so that, at last, one may even lose control of the excretory functions whose conquest first starts us on the way to becoming civilized and of the mental abilities which give *homo sapiens* its glory and its name.

Reprinted from *Social Work in Health Care,* Vol. 4, No. 4 (1979), pp. 369–380, with permission of the Haworth Press.

The wishes of human beings seem often to have little influence on the operations of nature, so over and over again people are seized by cancer. Though less often than in the past, frequently the medical armamentarium developed to combat cancer fails. The dying that few would choose takes place. And in that dying time there may well be opportunity for the social worker to provide important help, for there are crucial tasks which are amenable to social work intervention.

Before addressing those tasks, however, the social worker first needs to struggle with some basic questions.

PERSONAL REACTIONS TO DEATH

How do I react to dying and to death? For many people, including health professionals, these are morbid, frightening events. Hospital staff have been known to shy away from terminally ill patients, to attend to them quickly and perfunctorily when unable to avoid them, to refrain from significant conversation with them. The past decade has seen a considerable breakthrough in awareness of the needs of dying people and their significant others and some noble efforts to meet those needs. But death remains awesome and foreboding to many; to be in close proximity to it produces anxiety; to be starkly reminded that mortality afflicts us all is disquieting; to have previously experienced feelings about the deaths of significant others resurrected is painful. Can I manage my fear and anxiety in the presence of death while retaining my respect for the person who moves ever closer to it?

PERSONAL REACTIONS TO CANCER

What are my feelings about encountering the special sights and smells and sometimes twisted sounds emanating from the patient dying of cancer? Cancer and/or its treatments have a peculiar ability to produce results which are discomfiting to the senses. How do I feel knowing that I, as a social worker, cannot change those sights and smells and sounds—perhaps no one can—and that they are the products of a process which I do not like, which I dread, which I do not want to touch me or those I love?

When the cancer invades the brain and alters mental functioning, am I willing to try to sift through the confusion of words and phrases to find the patient's meaning? And am I able to forgive myself when the confusion overwhelms me and I stay away for longer and longer periods of time?

ABILITY TO TOLERATE UNCERTAINTY

How well can I tolerate uncertainty and ambiguity? Certainly they are part of the daily experience of every social worker, but the situation of the terminally ill cancer patient seems to conjure up an extra measure of each. First, there is often much uncertainty about the course of the affliction. Mr. W, mid 40's, had bronchogenic cancer which had widely metastasized. For weeks he hung on to a thread of life while the hospital staff wondered what kept him alive. On the other hand, Mr. S, early 50's, had battled cancer of the face and neck for over two years, submitting to a series of disfiguring surgeries, maintaining hope in the midst of pain and isolation. But, though in relatively good physical condition, when he learned that the new lump in his chest was malignant, he died within two days.

Then there is the ambiguity of the patient's emotional state. Much effort has gone into the creating of conceptual schemes which ostensibly eliminate this ambiguity and make the patient's overall course as well as his feeling state of the moment predictable. Kübler-Ross' five stages of dying (denial, anger, bargaining, depression, acceptance) (Kübler-Ross, 1969) is the most notable example. But patients have a knack for disrupting any schema, flitting from one emotion to another, challenging us to dare to discard our neat conceptualizations and find out what their feelings really are.

Underlying the ambiguity is the fundamental fact that one reacts ambivalently to imminent death. Mr. O was a living illustration. At age 56 he was hospitalized with a cancer which had begun in his bladder and then spread throughout his body. He was well aware of his terminal condition. The loss of control of many bodily functions, the distress at being unable to engage in the work and play which had once given him considerable pleasure, and the necessary distortion of his family relationships caused by the disease had prompted him to extract a promise from his physician that nothing would be done simply to prolong his life. One day when I entered his room, he pointed to the intravenous tube in his arm and expressed his anger at his physician for having it inserted during the night while he slept. The tube represented a breaking of the promise that no barriers would be erected to his dying. Immediately upon telling me this, he looked at the apparatus and noted that it was not working properly. His reaction was a quick: "Call the nurse," and as soon as the nurse arrived he informed her of the malfunction and relaxed only when it had been corrected. In those few minutes, Mr. O had dramatically expressed his ambivalence: I wish to die; I do not wish to die. He provides an important lesson.

SOCIAL WORK GOALS

Having decided that the anxiety and ambiguity which cancer and dying evoke are tolerable and that the cancer process is not necessarily one of ugliness and agony, what, then, are appropriate social work goals? Should a goal be, for example, to contribute to keeping the patient and his family as calm and outwardly peaceful as possible? Or, in contrast, should a goal be to facilitate the expression and exploration of strong feelings, feelings such as fear, anger, frustration, depression, which some people call "negative"?

Social workers seem to have less problem choosing the latter course than some other health professionals. Social work tends to attract people fascinated by tumultuous feelings; within social work the mental health world view is pervasive and offers continual encouragement to the ferreting out of such feelings. Yet even the social worker can be frightened by the depth of feeling which surrounds death, both within the patient and family and within herself. It may take several conversations with clients, proving that client and social worker can survive expression of these feelings, before the anxiety begins to abate.

Not all social workers will agree, however, that the solicitation of the patient's feelings about dying is appropriate. Ruth Abrams writes: "(As a result of) my study of the cancer patient at the terminal stage . . . I am convinced that the patient . . . should be permitted . . . to control his dying himself—to speak of it or not, as he wishes, without prompting . . . his caregivers must realize that perhaps it is they who wish to talk of death, even though the patient wishes to maintain silence" (Abrams, 1974, p. 77).

The inflicting upon the patient of what are needs for oneself is a primary hazard for any helping professional. In any given situation a discussion of death between patient and social worker may spring primarily from the social worker's inner demands. There is, however, strong reason for believing that, in this area, silence is more suspect than talk, for the rule of our culture in general and of the health care system in particular is still that death is not to be discussed. Silence, then, may well reflect the patient's bowing to what he believes is expected of him and, if this is the case, "prompting" may be necessary to help him realize that the rule need only apply if he himself so desires.

Another question about goals is whether or not the social worker should help the patient and his significant others move in the direction of accepting the patient's unhappy fate. A strong implication of Kübler-Ross' stages of dying, for example, is that acceptance is the natural, appropriate goal. The helper will recognize that some patients, perhaps many, will not get there, but this will be a falling short, a less than optimum result. If, however, you believe that one should "rage, rage against the dying of the light" (Thomas, 1973, p. 911), then your goal will be different: to permit the expression, in word and behavior, of that rage as long as there is energy to fuel it, and you will see acceptance as a deviant maneuver.

Social workers tend to be glib in response to this kind of issue. "Whatever the patient wants is all right with me. If he seeks to move toward acceptance, fine. If he wants to persist in being angry, that's fine, too." What this overlooks is that one's own priorities always influence the approach one takes to helping clients (Hardman, 1975). The only way to minimize this influence is to recognize what those priorities are. If, for example, you believe that an attitude of acceptance is the appropriate frame of mind with which to approach death, that belief will give some direction to your efforts no matter how eloquently you speak of client self-determination, unless you bring the belief clearly into view and consciously root it out of what goes on between you and the client.

A similar commentary can be made about the matter of whether or not we expect the patient to maintain hope for survival until the very end. There is a widely held belief that such hope is both ubiquitous and essential to a terminally ill person's emotional well-being. Kübler-Ross writes: ". . . all our patients maintained a little bit of it (hope for survival) and were nourished by it in especially difficult times" (Kübler-Ross, 1969, p. 123). For the cancer patient this hope presumably is formulated in terms of a cure that will surface just in the nick of time or an unfathomable natural process that will cause the hated tumor to disappear.

Another point of view, however, is that such "hope" is really an illusion which patients do not need nearly as much as those who deal with the patient. Perhaps it is the helper's discomfort with the reality and finality of the impending death that creates the idea that a patient must continue to hope. Or its source may be the professional person's need to keep death at a distance from herself.

The decision you make about the naturalness and/or necessity of hope will influence your action. Holding the first view, you will look for hope, encourage it, perhaps even try to plant some seeds if it seems missing. The other view will more likely lead you to try to learn if an expression of hope belongs to the real feelings of the patient (or family) or is his way of being nice to you, that is, by offering a commentary that he feels is expected of him.

Social Work Tasks

Having begun to struggle with these basic questions, it is then timely to consider the social work tasks appropriate to the helping of terminal cancer patients and their families. In essence they are the same as those which pervade all of social work, regardless of the kind of client served or the auspices under which the services are rendered; that is, people are helped to make contact with whatever will enable them to more fully and more effectively carry out one or more of their assignments. Specifically these tasks are: (1) Helping patients and their significant others to get in touch with their feelings and to recognize their behavioral options. (2) Assisting patients and their significant others to develop and/or maintain meaningful communication with one another. (3) Aiding patients and their significant others in locating and linking up with resources beyond themselves. (4) Helping health professionals, whose activities impinge upon the patient and his significant others, to acknowledge their own feelings, to understand the feelings and needs of those being served, and to learn effective and sensitive ways of meeting the recognized needs.

GETTING IN TOUCH WITH ONESELF

Once the social worker, in considering her goals, decides that it is worthwhile for the patient and those important to him to be given full opportunity to express and explore their feelings about the terminal cancer, one part of this task automatically follows. There is nothing automatic, however, about either the way it is to be carried out or the results which can be expected.

Some patients and families effectively avoid taking notice of their feelings by denying the terminal nature of the patient's cancer. In most cases the social worker will not want to challenge this denial but will want to be careful not to participate in it. There are few clients, however, who massively and continuously deny the illness and its attendant emotional turmoil. Most people, at least at times, admit to themselves what is going on within their body and their feelings (Weisman, 1972; Glaser and Strauss, 1965) but are selective about whom they will share these realities with. A patient's silence, therefore, may not reflect denial as much as politeness or conformity to the taboo against speaking of death and dying, or his belief that the social worker could not possibly be interested in his struggles.

To be most useful to the client, the social worker will do well to operate on three premises:

1. The client has a right to conceal or reveal whatever he chooses;
2. The client has a right to choose the person(s) to whom he will reveal himself (and being empathic will not guarantee the social worker that she will be one of those chosen);
3. A clear invitation by the social worker will likely be important to the client's decision to express himself freely to her. This invitation can be issued by (a) listening carefully to the client, (b) responding to the feelings and hints about feelings that come forth, (c) offering comments which explicitly state the expectation that strong feelings accompany serious illness; e.g., "Having a cancer like yours can be pretty scary."

This last technique seems to be the kind of "prompting" that Abrams inveighs against (Abrams, 1974, p. 77), but it is often necessary to combat the broad cultural expectation of silence, the health-care system's message that positive thinking and speaking are required of "good patients", and the caricature of the social worker as someone interested only in providing tangible services.

When does such "prompting" become the social worker's projection of her own needs onto the client? The answer to this question is only available in interaction with the patient or family member. As a general guideline, I usually allow myself two sequential promptings before deciding the patient is not interested in sharing his feelings with me.

PATIENT: I guess you know that my cancer is pretty far along.
SOCIAL WORKER: Yes, and I can imagine that's frightening to you. (Prompting #1)
PATIENT: Oh, I'm not scared.
SOCIAL WORKER: My guess is that most people in your situation would be. (Prompting #2)

If that does not call forth a response describing emotions of some kind, then the usual conclusion is that the client is not willing to open up at this time.

Part of the value of discussing feelings, particularly tumultuous ones, is the opportunity it provides to discover within oneself the ability to struggle with and obtain some measure of control over those feelings. "Though the cancer may kill me, the feelings won't." Alternative ways of thinking about one's situation as well as more comfort-producing behaviors may also evolve from conversations about feelings. When Mr. C's cancer finally metastasized to his brain, he occasionally had hallucinations in which he saw himself in places he had frequented when healthy. He could talk about how frightening these experiences were and, through the conversation, decided he could assure himself of being safely in his hospital bed when these hallucinations occurred by focusing on some specific pieces of the familiar hospital equipment which surrounded him.

As in Mr. C's situation, explorations of feelings and behavioral options are often intertwined. At times behavior in itself is a useful topic for discussion, enabling the patient to consider (1) how he wants to respond to his physical limitations, (2) means by which he can continue to exercise control over his life, (3) what treatment options are acceptable to him, and (4) the most comfortable ways for him to relate to his significant others and to health-care personnel. For family members, discussion of their options after the patient's death can be an important preparation for the difficult time ahead.

COMMUNICATING WITH OTHERS

Estrangement from others is a frequent concomitant of terminal cancer. The changes in the way the patient's body functions, the alterations in his appearance, and the aura of dread which cancer evokes can create severe obstacles to the maintenance of consistent and meaningful contact between patient and significant others. It can be an important social work task, therefore, to help those involved to maximize beneficial interaction while accepting their own and the other person's limitations.

When the cancer has reached the terminal stage, the patient may have limited endurance and be able to tolerate only carefully restricted visitation. Emotional limitations may exist as well. Mr. A, for example, needed to decide whether or not he wished further visits from his former golfing partners. Although it felt good to him to be remembered by them, their presence evoked in Mr. A very painful feelings about never again being able to engage in his once favorite pastime. Family members at times need recognition that they have a life apart from the patient, especially when he is being cared for at home, which needs their time and guilt-free attention.

Time spent together, however, is not usually the primary problem between the terminally ill patient and others. Rather, it is the kind of contact which they permit themselves that creates or reflects difficulties. "Let's pretend," is a common theme. "Let's pretend that you are not going to die." "Let's pretend that I, the patient, don't know about the deadly force which holds me; after all, the doctor hasn't really said there's no hope." "Let's pretend that by smiling and talking positively and saying what good care the health-care professionals provide and taking note of all the flowers and get-well cards and not mentioning cancer and definitely not talking about death, all of us will come through our meetings together unscathed."

The personality, life-style, and past relationship of patient and family members may make such pretending the only way they can deal with one another while the patient is dying. Then the social worker need not set herself to undo a lifetime of fixed behaviors. Frequently, though, patients and their family secretly wish to be able to share with one another their hurts and hopes, their frustrations and fears, their wishes and wonderings, but are blocked by a need to protect the other person as well as a concern that they themselves will be overwhelmed if they once open the door on the feelings and questions that surge within. In such situations the social worker may be able to help her clients express the wish they harbor and support them as they then, with trepidation, begin to talk and plan candidly with one another. Occasionally a very small amount of social work input can contribute to a considerable change in the way a patient and his significant others interact. Mrs. B, for example, told the social worker that she well knew that death was imminent for her husband who was hospitalized with lung cancer. Her distress was compounded by the fact that she had no idea what kind of funeral or burial arrangements he wished. "Of course," she said, "I can't talk with him about this because then he will know that he is dying." The social worker's brief comment that he and Mr. B had frequently talked together about Mr. B's dying was a revelation to Mrs. B, which enabled her to talk openly with her husband about the situation they faced, to the relief of both.

RESOURCES

Connecting clients with community resources is a well-recognized social work task. It can be carried out to the benefit of patient and family whether or not they allow the social worker to help with their feelings, behaviors, and relationships. Home-health agencies, American Cancer Society programs, self-help groups, financial assistances, and whatever other supplies and services the local community have available can be important means for maximizing the well-being of patient and family.

Another kind of resource for some patients is the formal opportunity for expressing wishes about the prolongation of their lives. California, for example, in 1976 became the first state in the nation to enact a law giving a terminally ill person a means by which he could direct his physician to refrain from using life-sustaining procedures when they "would serve only to artificially prolong the moment of my death and where my physician determines that my death is imminent whether or not life-sustaining procedures were utilized . . ." (California Health and Safety Code, paragraph 7188). Subsequently a number of other states have passed similar legislation (Friedman, 1978). Where such legislation has not been passed, a document such as the Living Will (Euthanasia Educational Council, 1974), although generally considered not legally binding, has the potential for guiding a physician, where he has discretion, to minister to the patient in a way compatible with the patient's desires when the patient can no longer express those desires.

For some patients, putting them in touch with religious resources meaningful to them can be a useful service. Calling the local minister or the hospital chaplain is an appropriate action for the social worker when it springs from the wishes of the patient. Wary of inflicting a religiously oriented visit upon an unreceptive person, social workers sometimes miss seeing that such a visit may provide considerable solace and support. Along with other resources, it is one that needs to be kept in mind and offered as an option to the patient.

Occasionally, however, a social worker will make a too quick referral to the clergy. The fact that a patient raises crucial existential questions such as: "Why is this cancer being visited upon me?" or "How can such a terrible affliction fit into a good God's plan?" does not necessarily mean that calling in a religious professional is indicated. Such questions may reflect a need to ventilate some of the feelings that accompany the patient's dire circumstances or a need to struggle through to his own answers or his own recognition that for him there are no answers. In either case the task is one that well fits within the purview of social work provided the social worker is clear that it is not her responsibility to provide answers. When the feelings have been expressed and the questions wrestled with, if the patient then wishes to hear the answers contained within a particular religious framework, the appropriate clergyperson can be sought.

HEALTH PROFESSIONALS

An increasing number of health professionals are finding themselves having significant contact with terminally ill patients and their families as health services are more and more provided to seriously ill people in their homes and as dying is transferred from the home to the hospital or nursing home. That many health-care personnel have a strong interest in learning about what was once a "taboo topic" (Faberow, 1963), is evidenced by the proliferation of workshops, courses, and writings on death and dying. Social workers have both informal and formal opportunities to contribute to their co-workers from other disciplines becoming more aware of their feelings in this area and knowledgeable about sensitive ways of meeting the needs of patients and families. Impromptu conversations, ward rounds, staff meetings, and educational programs can be vehicles for social work input. With social work leadership, some hospitals have developed a Thanatology Committee of multi-disciplinary membership, one of whose charges may be to provide education for the staff. The imaginative social worker, then, can find a variety of ways to contribute to the growth of her co-professionals.

There is a danger in assuming these several tasks: that continued immersion in the tragedy of terminal cancer may exact a heavy emotional toll from the social worker. The specter of possible burnout is ever present. The courage of patients and families and the love and concern shared by them will help diminish the drain on the social worker, but she will still need to be well aware of her own limits and of her own personal resources for renewal.

For many people cancer proves to be a deadly enemy. The social worker who is willing to work with patients engaged in this final struggle, and with their families, has some important questions to begin to answer, some difficult self-assessments to make, and some vital tasks to perform.

REFERENCES

Abrams, Ruth, *Not Alone with Cancer.* Springfield, Ill.: Charles C. Thomas, 1974.

American Cancer Society, "Cancer Research: Increasing Survival" (pamphlet), 1975.

American Cancer Society, *1978 Cancer Facts and Figures,* 1977.

California Health and Safety Code, Division 7, Part I, Chapter 3.9 (Natural Death Act).

Euthanasia Educational Council, "A Living Will." New York, 1974.

Faberow, Norman L., editor, *Taboo Topics.* New York: Atherton Press, 1963.

Friedman, Emily, "'Natural Death' Laws Cause Hospitals Few Problems," *Hospitals,* May 16, 1978, Vol. 52, pp. 124–130.

Glaser, Barney, and Strauss, Anselm, *Awareness of Dying.* Chicago: Aldine Publishing Co., 1965.

Hardman, Dale G., "Not with My Daughter, You Don't!" *Social Work,* July 1975, Vol. 20, No. 4, pp. 278–285.

Kübler-Ross, Elizabeth, *On Death and Dying.* New York: The Macmillan Company, 1969.

Schneidman, E. S., "You and Death," *Psychology Today,* June 1971, Vol. 5, No. 1, pp. 43–45.

Thomas, Dylan, "Do Not Go Gentle Into That Good Night," in Ellman, Richard, and O'Clair, Robert, editors, *The Norton Anthology of Modern Poetry,* New York: W. W. Norton and Co., 1973.

Weisman, Avery D., *Dying and Denying.* New York: Behavioral Publications, 1972.

CARDIAC DISORDERS

CHAPTER 14

INTERVENTION WITH HEART ATTACK PATIENTS AND FAMILIES

Bernice Sokol

A myocardial infarction (MI or heart attack) can serve as a model of the psychological reactions evoked by an acute medical illness in the "normal" patient. Some stresses, however, are more prominent than others at different transient points in the course of the illness, and social work interventions and goals must be adapted to each stage.

Many writers have referred to stages oriented toward recovery from illness. Herbert S. Rabinowitz and Spiros B. Mitsos, discussing rehabilitation as a process, orient their discussion of phases to the use of service, the preclient stage, followed by the client stage, and finally by a social reintegration phase, wherein the patient resumes normal functioning.[1] Laurence S. Kubie et al., have presented a useful formulation of the process of recovery; although not related specifically to the coronary patient, it is certainly relevant.[2] He suggests that a first phase is marked by initial shock, the second phase by appreciation of the full extent of the disability, and the third phase by recovery from the lure of hospital care. In the fourth or final stage, there is a facing of independent, competitive life.

A viable frame of reference is to think of the patients in terms of phases or transition points. This framework can also be helpful in communicating the innerworkings of the social work perspective on the patients in stress in their situation. This approach emphasizes six stages oriented toward recovery with the following major transition points:

Reprinted from *Social Casework,* Vol. 64, No. 3 (1983), pp. 162–168, by permission of the publisher, Families International, Inc.

[1] Herbert S. Rabinowitz and Spiros B. Mitsos, "Rehabilitation as Planned Social Change: A Conceptual Framework," *Journal of Health and Human Behavior* 5 (Spring 1964): 251.

[2] Laurence S. Kubie, cited by Jerome G. Kaufman and Marvin C. Beck, "Rehabilitation of the Patient in Myocardial Infarction," *Geriatrics* 10 (August 1965): 355–61.

(1) prehospitalization, symptoms experience; (2) hospitalization; (3) assumption of the sick role; (4) predischarge; (5) convalescence; and (6) relinquishment of the sick role. Each of these stages requires at least partial integration if the patient is to experience some forward movement toward recovery. Paralleling the classificatory phases are the kinds of behavior manifested in the patient and his or her family, and the social work intervention provided.

SEQUENTIAL PHASES
Prehospital

The first stage, prehospital, in which symptoms are experienced, is distinguished by physical, cognitive, and emotional aspects. The physical is related to the pain or discomfort felt by the patient; the cognitive is the patient's interpretation of his or her pain; and the emotional response is most often characterized by denial and apprehension or anxiety, as is felt in any situation in which a painful, unpleasant, and threatening circumstance is encountered. Some patients become especially anxious when they find themselves having to admit the existence of their discomfort. To these persons, their definition of independence depends on being active and never yielding to a physical discomfort. If the patients are men, the illness may be viewed as an emasculating process and thereby highly provocative of anxiety. Furthermore, there is a continuing folk tradition in some areas that suggests that illness is the just dessert of the sinner. Persons holding to this belief feel guilty when developing an illness and may even be impelled to pretend health rather than appear within the stigma of their perceived immorality.

Patients, therefore, may tend to underemphasize the pains that can occur in the chest, back, legs, arms, and jaws and they will deny that they are of any significance. They may interpret the pains as indigestion or gas or an upset stomach. The denial may be reinforced by engaging in more than routine activity. In this manner, patients seem to be reassuring themselves that if they can manage to be so active, there is nothing to fear—the whole affair is an illusion.

Examples of partial and major denial were found in the Arthur J. Moss and Sidney Goldstein study of patients' response to chest pains.[3] While one-third correctly interpreted the pain as being related to a heart attack, two-thirds of the group studied either minimized the importance of the symptoms by assigning benign or trivial causes to them or were unable to explain the nature of their pains.

This use of denial may cause many patients to delay calling for medical help when the pains occur. Prodromal symptoms (occurring between the earliest symptoms and the infarction) may be present for weeks before medical advice is sought. A study done by Henry A. Solomon, Adrian L. Edwards and Thomas Killip reported that, of 100 patients admitted to a cardiac care unit (CCU), 65 percent had experienced prodromal symptoms but had delayed calling for medical help anywhere from twenty-four hours to two months![4]

[3] Arthur J. Moss and Sidney Goldstein, "The Prehospital Phase of Acute Myocardial Infarction," *Circulation* (May 1970): 737–42.
[4] Henry A. Solomon, Adrian L. Edwards, and Thomas Killip, "Prodromata in Acute Myocardial Infarction," *Circulation* (October 1969): 463–72.

An example of the anxiety engendered in this stage was seen in Mr. Y, a sixty-two-year-old man who was admitted to the CCU with excruciating chest pains. He had suffered these pains for two weeks before entering the hospital. In subsequent interviews with him, the worker explored his cultural background to understand more clearly his reaction to the illness. He was born and raised in Poland, the oldest in a family of seven children. He was expected to assume a great deal of responsibility for his siblings; illness was frowned upon and thought to be a sign of weakness. During World War II, he was in a concentration camp, and the unwritten law was to hide any unpleasant feelings from the guards so that they would not know of their captives' suffering. These feelings resurfaced when he had chest pains and he could not call for medical help.

Hospitalization

When patients are admitted to the hospital, they are severely anxious. Once again, anxiety is aroused because of real and fantasized dangers as well as the unfamiliarity of the environment. Patients must deal with the realization that they have suddenly gone from feeling well, in control, working, living, and loving, to being very ill, in the hospital, facing possible disabilities, and maybe even death. Patients begin to show shifting degrees of denial and acceptance or there may be both denial and acceptance. At the center of this seeming contradiction is the familiar psychological concept that the ego copes with conflict between reason and emotion.

Patients may cope with this conflict in several ways. They may verbally acknowledge having had a heart attack, but ignore dietary and activity restrictions. They may deny any feelings associated with having had a heart attack or refuse to discuss what has happened to them and become withdrawn and noncommunicative. They may meet anxiety aggressively and become querulous and ill-humored. Or, they may try to allay their anxiety by passivity and behave in a happy-go-lucky manner, joking and assuming a euphoric attitude. All of these are evidence that they are not realistically integrating the situation.

It must be pointed out, however, that the denial mechanism can be functional and adaptive, providing patients with a hiatus from the full impact of the disease. Furthermore, by controlling the anxiety present in the situation, denial can help them progress to the next stage more effectively than if such a defense were not utilized at all. Indeed, Thomas Hackett and Ned Cassem found that, in the earliest stages of hospitalization, MI patients who used denial tended to gain control over their anxieties sooner than non-denying patients.[5]

Success in helping patients in this stage is dependent on recognizing their responses to their illness and understanding that their sense of self-worth and feelings of adequacy are shaken. They are in need of explanations and clarifications to help them understand what has happened, to answer questions on what the future will be like (Will I be the same person? What restrictions will be necessary?), and to have their concerns responded to in clear lay language. The doctor is perhaps the most important person to

[5] Thomas Hackett and Ned Cassem, "The Psychologic Reactions of Patients in Pre- and Post-Hospital Phases of Myocardial Infarction," *Postgraduate Medicine* 57 (April 1975): 43–46.

the patients now, and their relationship at this stage is crucial. There is much wisdom in the old medical dictum that in any contact between doctor and patient, there is room only for one anxious person . . . the patient.

For the social worker, contact with the patient's family generally has been initiated by this time; it continues to be developed during the patient's stay in the hospital. The focus is on the family members' reactions toward the patient, the illness, and the disruption caused by the sudden onset of the infarction. It is a joint endeavor between the family and the social worker to begin to establish the social work role with them and to identify resources needed from community agencies. Simultaneously, an initial assessment of their psychological resources is made in order to determine their capacity for coping with the sudden onset of the illness necessitating hospitalization .

The social worker has a linking as well as an interpretive position in the family intervention system. The assumption is that the family system is out of equilibrium by virtue of the illness of one of its members, and the situation has repercussions that affect the whole system. Not only does it affect the patient but it affects, in a complementary way, the other family members. They may have feelings of abandonment, fear of loss of the patient, fear of loss of income. The same kinds of fear may exist with the patient. It is the social worker's function to recognize these feelings on first contact, to interpret them and, as the situation develops, to provide a safe and protective climate for discussion, exploration, and explication of feelings. Many times, a family does not have the opportunity for this kind of interaction. It is crucial to remember that the way the family has communicated before the crisis has to be taken into account. The perception has to be very sensitively attuned to the family's potential and capacity, with the goal being to enhance members' particular modes of communication and style. Most people have never had the experience of being in a CCU; like all new experiences, preparation and familiarity, reassurance and support can act as the link to the social worker's beginning work with the patient and the family.

Assumption of the Sick Role

When patients view themselves as ill and abandon pretenses of health, they enter the third distinct time period and have moved toward assuming the sick role. This stage is generally the more propitious time for social work intervention. Patients have begun to make a shift from denial to realization of the actual occurrence and are beginning to understand the meaning of the crisis of the MI, which can lead to depression.

While depression can be an acute symptom, it frequently is a re-emergence of a personality characteristic that is quickly mobilized in time of crisis. Following a heart attack, most patients sense they have lost part of themselves. The depression looks like a grief reaction, and is reactive in nature, usually centering around a fear for the future with concerns about reduced earning power or premature old age, since it is assumed that a heart attack is an old person's affliction. In order to cope with the depression, patients may develop a variety of defenses—for example, minimization. "Oh, it isn't so bad; others have survived," they may say. Or suppression may be used, such as, "I simply won't think about it."

The important fact is that grieving is a necessary and natural reaction to loss. Patients must be encouraged to express whatever sentiment, sorrow, frustration, anger, or depression they feel.

The sick role, described by Talcott Parsons and Renee C. Fox as a social role, contains certain expectations in regard to behavior while ill.[6] Patients are expected to make an effort to get well, to seek help, and, in turn, therefore have the right to expect certain kinds of behaviors from other persons. These include provisional validation to relinquish their normal social role responsibilities. The sick role also means that patients must renounce a great deal of their autonomy. From the moment patients come into the hospital, they are expected to comply passively with myriad orders. They are separated from their families, friends, job, homes, beds. They regress to a transitional separation-individuation phase to the feelings they had at an earlier time, when they were struggling with separation issues. There is a shift in patients' behavior from supposed adulthood independency to a state of dependency.[7]

In contemporary society, regression and dependency are thought of as negative aspects of behavior, yet they serve a twofold adaptive purpose during illness: (1) Patients who are dependent and regressive are easier for the hospital system to manage physically; and (2) patients need to be receptive to other people's dealing with their particular dysfunctions at this particular time.

In the case of heart patients, if they can assume a passive dependent role, allowing themselves to be fed, bathed, and cared for, they have regressed adaptively, since this will help toward the recovery phase. If, on the other hand, they continue to experience the illness and enforced dependency as threats to their physical and emotional integrity, they may become very anxious and develop multiple fears which can be observed on an intrapsychic as well as on an interactive level.

Most MI patients experience a variety of fears. Intrapsychic-level fears are concerned with loss of life, loss of function, fear of bodily damage, and, in the case of male heart patients, the equating of the damaged heart with damaged masculinity. On the interactive level, there is fear of putting their lives in the hands of strangers, loss of love or approval, and the fear that the enforced idleness may be interpreted as weakness or bluffing. There may be guilt about their dependent self and that they are taking advantage of their situation, which could be followed by fear of retaliation. Fear of pain is also a prominent source of psychological stress that cuts across all of the fears discussed. Patients may particularly fear their inability to deal with pain as further evidence of loss of control.

The goal of social work intervention is to provide some understanding of how patients, with their personalities and life experiences, are responding to this particular distress process as well as to hospitalization.

Gordon Hamilton, a pioneer of social work, introduced a concept that has been the sine qua non of practice—"the person-in-his-situation."[8] To detail this concept as it relates to patients in the hospital setting, we must proceed on the premise that patients'

---

[6] Talcott Parsons and Renee C. Fox, "Illness, Therapy and the Modern Urban American Family," in *The Family,* ed. Norman Bell and Ezra F. Vogel (New York: Free Press, 1960), pp. 347–60.

[7] Margaret S. Mahler, "Mother-Child Interaction During Separation-Individuation," *Psychoanalytic Quarterly* 34 (October 1965): 483–98.

[8] Gordon Hamilton, *Theory and Practice of Social Casework,* 2nd ed. (New York: Columbia University Press, 1951.) Specific reference to phrase "person-in situation" appears on p. 153, but is cited on other pages.

psychological symptoms can be fully understood only if they are considered in relation to the nature and severity of the medical illness and to the hospital's environment, as well as to the particular history that the patients bring to this event. This complex inner relationship between psychosocial and physiological variables sets the tone for evaluation with treatment of patients.

The Crisis Model

One way of approaching patients is the crisis model. Briefly, this describes an event that has serious or major consequences to patients' functioning and equilibrium. This crisis necessitates a variety of social work interventions that will mobilize patients' inner resources to re-establish or enhance their overall functioning.

To gain an understanding of the patient in his or her individual situation, it is necessary to explore personal thoughts, fantasies, and feelings about the illness. The clinician will ask the patient to tell about the illness. What happened? What have the doctors said? What other illnesses has he or she had? How did he or she deal with the stress at that time? Has he or she known anyone else who has had a heart attack? How is the staff treating him or her and the family?

Further, the worker needs to gauge how accurately the patient has internalized the information that has been provided. Is further additional clarification necessary? What is this individual's capacity for this kind of dependency? Does he or she perceive the doctors and other caretakers as parents? Is he or she regressing to the period of childhood in the world of illness? The patient's responses here establish a baseline to help the worker decide where the patient is with stress at this moment, and if he or she is oriented as to time and place.

Many patients believe that having a heart attack is synonymous with death or invalidism. Discussing this reaction provides the beginning base for sensing how anxious they are, how guilty they might feel for becoming ill, and who they might blame for the illness—themselves, spouse, family members? The discussion will indicate the nature and extent of their fears. Not only is the content of the response important, but the nature or affect of the response is also essential to the assessment. A patient's tone may be cryptic, factual, guarded, or even exhibitionistic. It is the tonal quality of these responses that provides clues for further exploration into the meaning that the illness has for patients.

The social worker needs to know the events occurring in the patient's life, specifically in the premorbid state. The worker must ask what was happening in the family? At work? What losses have been experienced—death of a loved one, financial loss, job loss?

Equally important is the assessment of the patient's reaction to the illness. Is she or he optimistic or pessimistic? What life-style changes might be necessary, and how flexible is he or she in making these changes? How does he or she plan to make the changes? Moreover, the discussion provides important data in planning the discharge for the patient and identifies areas for further clarification. This would entail a joint conference with specific team members to offer their unique expertise to the patient—that is, psychiatric liaison, doctors, dietician, physical therapist.

During the interviews, the psychosocial assessment is simultaneously being formulated, with the ego indices being the focus of the assessment. These indices include intelligence, ability to relate, judgment, tolerance level, and capacity to understand fully what he or she is told. Further, how do cultural factors enter into the patient's perception of the illness? The assessment is also the basis for communicating the relevant information on the patient and his or her situation to the multidisciplinary team at the weekly patient progress rounds.

Case Illustration

Mr. B, a cardiac patient at a hospital, is a clinical example that illustrates the concept of the psychosocial assessment in the medical setting.

Mr. B, a sixty-year-old French Canadian, is married for the second time to a woman twenty-five years younger than he. He has two children from this marriage, ages five and seven. Prior to the heart attack, he had a life history of severe drinking bordering on alcoholism; he now regards this experience as the basis for his initial divorce and estrangement from his now adult children from the first marriage. He blames the lifetime pattern of drinking as the primary cause for his myocardial infarction, and feels it is direct retribution for his profligate ways.

Mr. B had been wrestling with his young children when he developed chest pains. He ignored the pains and continued wrestling to prove that the pain was a trivial indisposition. Several hours after dinner, he experienced more intense pains accompanied by sweating and nausea. Mrs. B insisted that she be "permitted" to call the paramedics, who brought the patient to the hospital. Mr. B was soon admitted to the CCU.

Initially, there was a reaction on Mr. B's part that clearly demonstrated his denial and fear of what was happening to him. This was further exemplified by his behavior on the ward. As soon as the pains abated and Mr. B became adjusted to the CCU routine, his boisterous behavior became evident. He called out to other patients, made comments to visitors who came to see other patients, hopped out of the bed against medical orders, and was flirtatious with the nurses, trying to fondle them and joking excessively.

During the initial evaluation, it became apparent to the worker that Mr. B was strongly defending against his emerging anxiety concerning his interfamilial role, and was truly frightened and anxious. He felt anxiety, guilt, and fear, and wondered how he would resume his work as a real estate broker and whether he would be able to play with his children again. In general, he was concerned about being able to manage his life as it had been before his heart attack. He equated his heart attack with damage to his masculinity and fantasized that sexual activity would precipitate a second attack.

Joint sessions with the doctor, Mr. and Mrs. B, and the worker were scheduled. The doctor explained that sex would not cause another heart attack, providing the reassurance needed. Plans were reviewed regarding his job as a real estate agent and what part of his activity he might be able to resume.

It was not possible, because of limited time, to explore the source of Mr. B's shaky sense of masculinity. Instead, the worker bolstered his sense of machismo, admired his fine young children, encouraged his interest in physical fitness and, in general, was supportive of his efforts.

The frequency of contact proved to be the ingredient that allowed Mr. B to begin to explore, understand, and ultimately synthesize the impact of the MI on his equilibrium. Before discharge he came to an adjustment that had to be made in view of his temporary limitations.

The social work task during this stage is to aid in the resumption of premorbid levels of functioning. Unique to this situation is the access to facets of the patient's personality that are brought into sharp focus by the physical event of the illness. But if intervention is terminated at this point, the ability to enhance functioning will be lost.

Predischarge

The predischarge stage gives prominence to preparing everyone for the patient's return home. Many patients become exceedingly anxious and irritable prior to discharge, and information provided daily during their hospitalization becomes vague and difficult to recall. A predischarge family conference will help to evaluate the patient's and family's understanding of the illness and the recovery process.[9]

The predischarge conference includes patient, family, physician, primary nurse, dietician, discharge planner, liaison psychiatrist, and clinical social worker. Medical staff members review what the patient has been told about medication, resumption of physical and sexual activity, rest, diet, and the possibility of either returning to work or the need to modify the work schedule. Discussion focuses on posthospital plans, what problems family members may anticipate, and how to meet these problems. The patient and the family learn that adjustment to a heart attack is an ongoing process that continues after hospitalization, and that anxiety and depression are commonly expressed by most post-MI patients . Such preparation can help to reduce the stressful experience of leaving the protected environment of the hospital and minimizes the difficulties of the convalescence phase.

Convalescence

After discharge from the hospital, most coronary patients return to their family settings. Very few patients can re-establish their premorbid equilibrium without the aid of significant others in their environment. It is essential that the family bonds existing prior to the myocardial infarction be identified, assessed, and mobilized to help patients in this convalescent stage in order to facilitate re-engagement with former roles.

The most pronounced concerns during this period are phobias or inhibitions related to work and sexual activities. The physician's support becomes even more important to prevent the exacerbation of psychological dysfunction by dealing with phobic reactions. As in all phases reviewed, explanations and clarifications are vital to dispel distortions and to provide correct information. Appointments with the doctor must be kept, and time must be given to answer questions and allay concerns.

The social work role in this stage is to assess the emotional climate in the home and to encourage conferences with the patient, family members, and the doctor; even to the point of scheduling such meetings.

[9] Charles Hollingsworth and Bernice Sokol, "Predischarge Family Conference," *Journal of the American Medical Association* 239 (February 1978): 740–41.

For the majority of convalescents, the broader scope of their healthy worlds is more attractive than the regressive pleasure of illness. With those patients who cannot respond positively to relinquishing the sick role, one would suspect that earlier neuroses have been revived by the trauma of illness. Theorists have suggested that there are structural and dynamic similarities between the convalescent and the adolescent. Like adolescents, convalescing patients have to leave a protected world in which responsibilities were minimal and the satisfaction of their self-centered needs were the major concern for themselves and those attending them. These pleasant aspects of illness attract convalescents so that they want to remain in this "regal home" of regression. Some patients may have difficulty giving up the attention, protection, and kindness of doctors, nurses, and family members to fend once more for themselves. Charles Lamb describes this phase: "Farewell with him all that made sickness pompous, the spell that hushed the household, the mute attendance, the inquiry by looks, the still softer delicacies of self attention. What a speck is he now dwindled into by his physical recuperation."[10]

Convalescence can be enhanced by the doctor's encouraging more activity and lifting restrictions on the patient's behavior from passivity to activity. Family members play a crucial role in cooperating with the physician's recommendations and by not being overprotective, which can foster a feeling of inadequacy and a fear of returning to health. It is important at this time also for the social worker to provide services to the spouse, encouraging ventilation and providing her or him with opportunities to express feelings about which she or he may have some inhibitions. In addition, the spouse must be encouraged to have time away from home, engaging in other activities. These brief interludes not only give necessary relief from the task of caring for the ill spouse, but also demonstrate to the patient that he or she is now able to function more independently than before.

Relinquishment of the Sick Role

The prerequisites for successful relinquishment of the sick role include the patient's ability to have regressed in the earlier stages in the service of recovery; the patient's ability to maintain adequate defenses against the stresses evoked by the illness and hospitalization; an effective support system; and trust in the medical caretakers.

Rehabilitation of patients begins in the hospital from the time they are encouraged to leave their beds, sit up in chairs, ambulate in the hall, and engage in an individually designed graduated exercise program.

Emotionally healthy patients will react constructively, and their initial anxiety will abate as their physical conditions improve. At this point patients have begun to face their problems realistically, accepting whatever limitations may be necessary and making suitable adjustments to their changed situations. They will have passed through each sequential stage of illness, and will have responded to the threat of illness as they have responded to other dangers in the past according to their characteristic patterns.

---

[10] Charles Lamb, "The Convalescent," *London Magazine* (July 1825): 8.

DEAFNESS

CHAPTER 15

BETWEEN WORLDS

The Problems of Deafened Adults

Helen Sloss Luey

eafness directly affects the interaction between an individual and his environment. By its very nature, then, this disability should hold special interest for social workers. Yet the whole field has been largely ignored in the professional literature.

Social workers may be called upon to help deaf people in a variety of situations. Sometimes people seek social work help to cope specifically with the impact of deafness. Deaf people, of course, are also vulnerable to all social and emotional problems, and they may seek help from a social worker in any area of practice. It is important, then, that all social workers have some understanding of the ramifications of deafness.

From the limited social work literature available, one might get the impression that deafness occurs primarily at birth or in infancy, and that most deaf people suffer the problems in language acquisition which stem from an early sensory loss. The few existing articles about deafness and social work deal almost exclusively with prelingually deaf people, or with individuals who lost their hearing before they had learned language (Chough, 1976; Hurwitz, 1969; Newbold, 1979; Silver, 1963). To be effective with this group of clients, a social worker must obtain highly specialized knowledge and an advanced level of sign language skill. The vast majority of deaf people, however, are not prelingually deaf. According to recent statistics, there are 1.8 million deaf people in the United States, of whom only 0.4 million lost their hearing before the age of nineteen (Schein, 1974, p. 4). In other words, 78% of all deaf people in the United States lost their hearing after having reached adulthood, long after having learned speech and language, and in most cases after having established a firm identity as a hearing adult. These people have a distinct set of problems and experiences which social workers have not addressed.

Reprinted from *Social Work in Health Care*, Vol. 5, No. 3 (1980), pp. 253–266, with permission of the Haworth Press.

For purposes of this discussion, the following definition of deafened adult will be used: "those individuals who at one time possessed enough hearing to learn language and oral communication through hearing, but who suffer with a loss of hearing so severe that audition is useless for purposes of receiving oral communication" (Krug, 1969, p. 99). The people discussed in this paper are those who would qualify as deafened by this definition, even when using the best amplification. This paper does not deal with prelingually deaf people, nor does it discuss hard of hearing people, i.e., people who have lost some ability to hear and understand speech but who, with proper amplification, good communication skills, and moderate adjustments in their social lives can reasonably be expected to participate in familiar pursuits. Because of their previous life experience, deafened people are quite unlike prelingually deaf people. Because of the severity of their hearing loss, they are also unlike hard of hearing people. They are between worlds.

SOME PROBLEMS FOR THE SOCIAL WORKER

In his first encounter with a deafened client, the social worker quickly perceives that his usual methods of communicating and of establishing relationship are ineffective. When he speaks at his normal rate and in his usual manner, the client understands virtually nothing. The client may aggressively demand repetition, may simply look pained and frustrated, or may nod politely and then reveal his lack of understanding with inappropriate responses. The social worker may not understand the reasons for these difficulties. He may think the client is inattentive, stupid, or hostile. Mutual frustration is inevitable.

A social worker in such a situation is likely to feel helpless, and helplessness may provoke anger at the client or guilt over one's own poor performance. Rejection is likely, and is damaging to the client, even when disguised by a conscientious effort to find some "more appropriate" agency.

If the social worker gets past the initial communication barrier, he may encounter deeper problems in diagnosis or countertransference. The client may be experiencing intense feelings related to his deafness. His social functioning may seem limited or inappropriate. Without specific knowledge about the impact of deafness in adult life and normal responses to this crisis, a social worker is unable to separate problems in adaptation to deafness from other issues in the client's situation, background, or personality.

A hearing social worker may also feel personally threatened by a deafened client. Unlike prelingually deaf people, the deafened person has grown up in a hearing world, and his life experience and cultural orientation may be similar to that of hearing people, perhaps that of the worker. The disability does not show in the person's appearance, nor is it necessarily obvious from his speech. The significance of the disability becomes apparent slowly, as the worker listens to the client's feelings. At that point, the worker has to face the fact that deafness can happen to anyone, and that he too is vulnerable to this devastating experience and to all of its permanent deprivations. Whether he expresses these feelings by outright rejection or compensates with overly solicitous behavior or over-protection, his personal discomfort will interfere with the quality and effectiveness of his service.

With some special knowledge, social workers can overcome the difficulties outlined above. This article will present information about deafness and its psycho-social ramifications. It will conclude with some practical suggestions for social workers.

LEVELS OF HEARING

In order to understand the impact of deafness in adult life, it is essential to understand the role of hearing in the person's previous life and, indeed, in all of our lives. Hearing has been divided into three levels, and a description of each level clarifies the different dimensions of sound in everyday life.

The symbolic level encompasses the part of hearing used to understand speech. In using language, we agree to accept certain sounds as symbolic of certain things or ideas. Conversation in the usual mode is dependent on hearing at the symbolic level (Ramsdell, 1970). Many aesthetic or inspirational experiences might also be considered part of hearing at this level. Music, the sounds of nature, and many religious experiences must be heard to be appreciated.

Contrary to popular opinion, lipreading skill can compensate for hearing at this level only to a limited degree. It is not possible to lipread all of the sounds of spoken language accurately. In fact, audiologists and lipreading teachers estimate that only one third of the sounds of English are clearly visible on the lips.

> Speechreading, whenever possible, must always be subordinated to hearing. It can supplement hearing, but it is no substitute for hearing. Most of the motor (muscular) movements involved in sound formation occur within the mouth and cannot be detected by the eye. The lip movements play a relatively minor part in the formation of sound. . . . Under usual viewing conditions, it is estimated that approximately 60% of the speech sounds are either obscure or invisible (Jeffers, 1974, pp. 14–17).

The lipreader learns to recognize some sounds from watching the speaker's lips, but he must guess the rest of the communication from the context and from visual clues. Lipreading is a skill which requires good vision, good knowledge of language, an ability to concentrate, and a certain mental agility and flexibility. Intelligence seems to be necessary, but it is not sufficient. Some people have a talent for lipreading; others do not. Even those people with good lipreading skill are limited to communication which is directed specifically to them. They must be able to see the speaker clearly. The light must be good. The speaker may need to talk more slowly than usual, to give the lipreader time to make the necessary guesses. In a group situation, the deafened person has difficulty knowing where to look, and he misses the rapid movement of the conversation. Lipreading itself is fatiguing, so the deafened person cannot converse for long periods of time. In all conversations, he misses the vital information transmitted through the tone of the speaker's voice. For those deafened people who are able to lipread, then, the skill helps to a degree, in some listening situations, for some of the time.

In addition to these significant deprivations from loss of hearing at the symbolic level, deafness involves losses in other dimensions. The warning or environmental level of hearing refers to the noises which alert us to circumstances in the environment.

Hearing is the one sense which enables us to scan our environment from all directions at once, regardless of our specific attention, of light, of obstacles between us and the source of sound, and even of whether we are asleep or awake. Hearing at this level enables us to anticipate changes in our environment, such as the approach of another person. The absence of unusual noise gives us constant reassurance that all is well.

The primitive level of hearing refers to the subtle, constant, connection with the rhythm of life which sound provides. Hearing at this level gives us a sense of being part of the environment and of other living things. It is impossible for a hearing person to simulate the absence of hearing at this level. But hearing at the primitive level gives us much of our sense of being alive (Ramsdell, 1970).

PSYCHO-SOCIAL IMPACT OF DEAFNESS
Communication Problems

When deafness interferes with communication, all human relationships are affected, and the person feels an overwhelming sense of isolation. He can see other people, but he feels as if he is locked behind a glass wall. He may be able to obtain some information by lipreading, or by persuading people to write. But lipreading requires great concentration and energy and, even with the greatest skill and the utmost attention, a great deal of misunderstanding will occur. Whenever the person is tired or preoccupied, his lipreading skill decreases. The sharing of ideas or experiences becomes a labored and sometimes impossible process. Easy, social intimate conversations become awkward. Casual interchanges with strangers are lost completely. The person is alone.

For many people, a sense of adequacy is connected with making appropriate responses to verbal information or to a social situation. When a person cannot understand what others have said, he is at a loss as to what to do. He feels awkward, stupid, and useless.

Much of the emotional content of conversation is transmitted by subtle changes in one's tone of voice, or in words which are deliberately said under one's breath. Humor, particularly, is often expressed in low tones, or while people are smiling, and thus hard to lipread. The deafened person misses many of the lighter moments, which are important in communication, and he also misses the discharge of tension and the feeling of closeness which shared laughter can bring.

All deafened people live with the reality that they misunderstand a great deal of what is said to them or around them. They often feel embarrassed by their mistakes, and terrified that others will label them as stupid. Hearing people often become impatient with the deafened person, and they sometimes react by excluding him from discussions and from decision-making processes. Some people actually take advantage of the person's deafness, by laughing at his misunderstanding, by talking about him in his presence, or by withholding information from him. One popular characterization of deaf people is that they are suspicious. Studies of the personalities of deafened people show that the incidence of paranoia is no higher in the hearing-impaired population than in the population at large. The suspicion shown by deafened people seems appropriate in view of the real responses they encounter from the public (Knapp, 1948; Levine, 1962).

The deafened person knows that other people have to go to some trouble to enable him to understand. Many people refuse to make the necessary accommodations, and the deafened person becomes angry at those individuals, and sometimes at society in general. Then, when people are willing to make the effort, the deafened person's sense of inadequacy is intensified by his awareness that others are going to some trouble for him.

> I took a cup of tea to a table to join four friends. When one of them asked me a question which I could not understand, the other repeated it for me, but I was still unable to lipread it. They paused while one of them wrote it down, and I was aware that the easy-going conversation they had been enjoying before my arrival was now disrupted ... within a few minutes two of them left and after a brief pause the others explained that they had to go because of pressing engagements. They were genuinely sorry and I understood, but it was small solace as I sat alone drinking my tea (Ashley, 1973, p. 149).

The deafened person almost inevitably loses some of his friends along with his hearing. Almost every individual's social group includes at least some people who are unwilling to accept the slow and labored communication of a newly deaf person. Other people are threatened or repelled by the sheer intensity of the deafened person's feelings. Also, the deafened person's style of socializing is limited. He can no longer enjoy his friends in large groups, or in noisy or visually distracting surroundings. He cannot converse socially for more than an hour or two at a time. His whole social life is altered. His loss in this area ranges from moderate to enormous, depending on the quality of his friendships and on his previous social habits.

Alienation from Self and Environment

In addition to the problems caused by difficulties in communication, deafened people suffer from alienation from their environment. Events are no longer announced for them in advance, by the sounds of footsteps approaching, brakes squeaking, or a door opening. A deafened person is forever being surprised, and is therefore in continual expectation of being caught unprepared. Nervousness, anxiety, and fear are common experiences. People who had been comfortable living alone can become fearful of their own safety. The sense of loss of control over the environment brings stress into all aspects of daily life.

Objects in the environment seem to lose their identities when they lose their characteristic sounds. When one cannot hear the sounds of one's own body, a person can feel detached even from himself. Breathing, coughing, walking, or turning over in bed become disorienting experiences when they are unaccompanied by sound. A deafened person may feel suddenly alienated from the world and from himself (Levine, 1962).

The deafened person not only misses sounds which are really in the environment, but often "hears" sounds which are not from outside, but which come from his own inner ear. Deafened people frequently suffer from tinnitus, or head noises. A truly deaf person may "hear" sounds which, to him, may be as soft as a distant hum, or as loud and intrusive as a clanging or roaring sound. Strong emotion may intensify the experience, but it is a physical phenomenon, caused by damage in the nerves within the ear. The deafened person, then, has lost the comforts of both sound and silence.

Some deafened people retain a small amount of residual hearing. Although useless for understanding words or perceiving warning sounds, this degree of hearing helps the person to feel alive. If that last shred of hearing is lost, a depression results which seems greater than even the losses outlined above can fully explain (Ramsdell, 1970). "That fragile wisp of hearing had maintained for me a slender contact with the ordinary world; it had given some sense of reality, a hint of that background of sound which, to a normal person, is so familiar as to be unnoticed. Without it, life was eerie" (Ashley, 1973, p. 136).

Identity Crisis

Implicit in the above discussion is a recognition that a deafened person has great difficulty functioning comfortably and competently with hearing people. His previous life style is drastically altered, and new skills, new social habits, and, in some cases, a new vocation must be found. A common misconception is that a deafened person is now like other deaf people, and able to find a satisfactory new sense of community in a society of prelingually deaf people. The first barrier to integration into the deaf community is language. Even after considerable effort to learn sign language, a deafened person may not have developed fluency in American Sign Language and his first encounter with a prelingually deaf person can be a frustrating and distressing experience. In addition to language problems, there are cultural differences. People deaf since birth have had a very different life experience from hearing people, and have developed attitudes and a culture of their own. Hearing people and deafened people can learn about the language and culture of deafness, but only with a great deal of time and careful attention. By the same token, many prelingually deaf people are understandably suspicious of hearing people, and a deafened person, after all, is essentially a hearing person who can no longer hear. A deafened person can encounter as much misunderstanding and suspicion from the deaf community as from many hearing people. Holly Elliott (1978) a professional counselor who is, herself, deafened, described the problem clearly:

> Even now I find myself wondering from time to time who I really am. Hearing people often think I am hearing because my speech is good; deaf people often think I am hearing because my signs are bad . . . Hearing people have their culture based on spoken language and deaf people have their culture based on sign language and we are caught between incomprehensible speech on the one hand and incomprehensible signs on the other. If only those hearies would talk more clearly! If only those deafies would sign more slowly! Who's taking care of us?

CRISIS

Along with these powerful and disturbing feelings, many of which will persist throughout his life, the deafened person at some point undergoes a crisis, and experiences all of the stages of adjustment which have been noted for people going through a catastrophic change (Kübler-Ross, 1969). The literature on reactions to crisis is enormous and there is no need to summarize it here. It is important, however, to examine the ways in which a deafened person experiences each stage.

Deafened people vary tremendously in the time they need to go through the stages of reaction to crisis. Some people remain in one stage for many years. There are some special reasons for the variation in time. Deafness is an invisible handicap and many uninformed people underestimate its significance. Deafened people are frequently reinforced by others for remaining in the stage of denial. Services for deafened people are scattered and inadequate, so many people are not offered the help they need to experience and cope with the various stages of adaptation. Also, even after achieving a high level of adaptation to deafness, an individual may at any time encounter a new experience which threatens his adjustment and plummets him into a stage he had long since mastered. For these reasons, it is impossible to predict what stage an individual might be in on the basis of the length of time he has been deaf.

The stage of denial is reflected in many people in feelings that there is a doctor or medical procedure somewhere which will make him hear again. Many people go from one doctor to another, then into acupuncture or other methods, all in the desperate hope of finding a cure. Sometimes people shop for the perfect hearing aid with the same desperation. Occasionally, as a person learns lipreading skills, he imagines how words sound, and he feels as if he is hearing again. His communication skills are likely to be uneven, and he may use his better moments to convince himself that the disability is not really significant. A sad by-product of the stage of denial is a refusal to learn useful skills, such as lipreading and sign language, and also a refusal to meet other deafened people. When a person remains in this stage, he can be immobilized for long periods of time, with devastating consequences to his rehabilitation.

The anger of a deafened person has many natural targets. First, there are doctors who have failed to restore hearing. Then there are audiologists and social workers, whose skills are never adequate to relieve the person's all-consuming pain and panic. And of course the general public knows all too little about deafness. The deafened person meets countless individuals who insist on talking with their backs turned, or with their mouths covered, who mumble, or who have the audacity to sport a mustache. There are still far too many people who think of deaf people as "deaf and dumb," and who associate deafness with stupidity or senility. Other people are convinced that, if a person can speak he can hear, and they act as if the deafened person is lying or malingering. These realities give the deafened person a legitimate basis for feeling that other people are to blame for his problems, and they make it difficult for him to move beyond this necessary phase of his adjustment.

Bargaining is occasionally expressed directly. One man said, "If only my ears hurt. I'd gladly stand the pain, if I could just have my hearing back."

Guilt is sometimes evident in a person's concern about the difficulties his deafness causes others. If the deafness was caused by an accident, some people view their deafness as fitting punishment for their carelessness. If the condition is hereditary, the person may feel responsible for passing the problems on to another generation. Until these feelings are worked through, rehabilitation is impossible.

The many reasons for a deafened person to be depressed have been given above. Another important dimension to depression for a deafened person is that it also interferes with learning and using communication skills. The depression, in itself, can block communication and intensify a person's sense of isolation.

> There is a great difference between grief and depression. Deafness is a frightening loss and grief is a natural response to loss, an active process that must be experienced to be resolved. Depression is a giving-up process, a long term withdrawal. The feeling of being 'left-out'—and not doing anything about it—is a feeling of depression. I have a hunch that depression interferes with communication more than deafness. The combination of deafness and depression makes communication very difficult (Elliott, 1978).

After the person acknowledges his loss as reality and experiences all of the feelings the loss inspires, he is able to adapt constructively to his deafness. He actively learns all appropriate communication skills. He starts to convey an interest in other people, a desire to communicate, and a sense of humor about his misunderstanding. As he learns to help other people feel comfortable with him, his social world expands considerably. He may be able to find compensations for the recreational and aesthetic experiences he misses. Holly Elliott (1978) for example, used to be a choral conductor; she now directs a sign language choir in her church. Joann Bartley (1978) also has found compensations which help her: "True, I can't hear music but I can still dance and watch someone sign a song. I can still go to parties and play sports. True, I can't hear, but I can still listen. Many people who can hear can't listen." Good adaptive skills enable a deafened person to have many satisfying experiences, and to feel some justifiable pride in the strengths he has found within himself.

When people talk about crisis, however, they often end with a discussion of acceptance, as if this is the goal the individual and his social worker should seek.

> We on the outside talk pretty glibly of 'accepting disability.' To accept sudden severe deafness is to accept the abrupt transition from pulsating life to the isolation, unreality, and flatness of a soundless world while at the same time straining to keep up with the demands of a hearing one (Levine, 1962, p. 304).

To ask another human being to accept such a global disruption to his whole existence seems arrogant indeed. A deafened person is never going to forget what his life was like when he could hear, and he will always miss many parts of his former world. One woman, who has become very successful personally and professionally in a community of hearing and deafened people, still gets tears in her eyes when she allows herself to think about music. Another person has maintained a continually positive attitude in recent years, and has found many activities which are fulfilling for her. But when playing happily with her new grandchild, she suddenly became deeply pained as she realized that she would never hear the child's voice. Acceptance, then, is never so complete that it cannot be shattered by some reminder of the past or an inadvertent expectation of an unimpaired future.

CLUES FOR ASSESSMENT

There is no real psychology of the deafened. Deafness has a particular set of difficulties which each person handles in his own way (Knapp, 1948, p. 208). To understand the meaning of deafness in the life of an individual, it is necessary to do a thorough assessment of that person's personality, his history, and his strengths. The social worker might well consider the same questions and issues as in any psycho-social assessment. Some additional questions might be raised, however:

- What is the history of this person's deafness? Was the loss gradual or sudden? How long has the person been deaf? What rehabilitation has been attempted?
- How has this person coped with other losses and crises? What are his defenses? What are his strengths?
- What are his social supports? Does he have close friends or relatives who will stay with him as he handles his problems?
- Which of the feelings associated with deafness are particularly threatening to him? Is he prone to anger and projection? Is it hard for him to ask other people to accommodate themselves to him? Is he generally insecure, especially sensitive to feelings of social inadequacy? Is he fearful? Is being alone hard for him?
- What was his style for socializing? Did he enjoy being with one or two people at a time, or was his social life primarily in large groups?
- Is his work dependent on his hearing? If so, can adaptations be made in his job responsibility, or will he have to find a new career?
- What is his aptitude for learning compensatory skills? How is his vision? How well does he know English, or his native language? Is he flexible enough to tolerate the imperfection of lipreading? Does he have the manual dexterity necessary for sign language? Does he enjoy learning?
- Does he have interests or hobbies which are not dependent on hearing? What meaning did music have in his life?
- Does he have a sense of humor? Is he able to laugh at some of his misunderstanding?
- What is his philosophical or spiritual perspective? Does he have the capacity to care about issues larger than himself? Is he able to appreciate positive experiences, beautiful sights, or moments of shared understanding, even in the midst of deprivation?

REHABILITATION

If a social worker is to help a deafened person cope with his disability, he must have a general idea about the different rehabilitative options available. The benefits and limits of lipreading have been discussed above. Some deafened people may be able to benefit from lipreading classes, or from individual instruction.

Most deafened people resist the idea of learning sign language at first, largely because their relatives, friends, and colleagues do not use it. If the person overcomes that mental barrier, he often finds that sign language gives him the opportunity for full, easy communication at least with the few other people he knows who use it. The social support available from other people who are learning the new language can be very valuable. One difficulty is that there are different forms of sign language. Deafened people tend to be most comfortable with Siglish (Signed English) or some form of sign language which follows the syntax and linguistic structure of English. Anyone with a solid knowledge of English finds such kinds of sign language easier to learn than the native language of deaf people, which is Ameslan (American Sign Language). Ameslan uses many of the same hand positions as Siglish, but grammar and word order are quite different. Also, Ameslan requires some use of facial expression and spacial relationships (Fant, 1977). A deafened person who learns Siglish may find himself unable to communicate with a prelingually deaf person, whose first language is Ameslan. If the deafened person can be assisted in clarifying his goals for the use of sign language, he can then be referred to the most appropriate program.

Deafened people, of course, cannot use a regular telephone, but there is special equipment which can provide some telephone communication. Teletype Devices for the Deaf (TDD's) are machines which enable a person to type messages through telephone lines. The equipment is expensive, and it enables the person to communicate directly only with other people who have compatible machinery. In some communities, there are TDD answering services, through which a deaf person can make telephone contact with people using voice phones only.

With a small amount of electrical work, homes can be wired for sound. Lights can be hooked up so that they flash when a doorbell rings or when a baby cries. There are alarm clocks which awaken a person with a flashing light, or with a vibrator placed under the pillow or in the bed frame. The American Humane Association is currently training "Signal Dogs," dogs who regularly alert their deaf owners to sounds in the environment.

SUGGESTIONS FOR THE HEARING SOCIAL WORKER

A social worker's first job is to establish communication with his client. Once this is accomplished, he is able to use all of his clinical and practical skills normally at his disposal. He no longer feels helpless. Many deafened people lipread to some extent, so clear, slow speech, in good visual contact with the client, may help a great deal. Minimizing background noise and visual distraction will help. If the client knows the subject under discussion, he has a better opportunity to lipread, so the worker might first establish the general subject, maybe by writing one or two words, or by restating that part of the communication until assured that the client understands. Some clients appreciate it if the worker writes at least some of the communication. Some clients prefer to use sign language, and would welcome a sign language interpreter. The only way for the social worker to know what is appropriate is to ask the client. Not only does the direct question yield essential information, it also opens up the whole area of communication style for frank discussion.

The lives of many deafened people are more limited than necessary, because of ignorance about the rehabilitative options discussed above. By its very nature, deafness limits a person's access to information, so special efforts are often necessary to keep the person informed. A social worker can be of tremendous help to a deafened client simply by obtaining accurate information about all available resources, their merits, and their limitations.

Social workers are accustomed to working at a certain pace. Communication with a deafened person is significantly slower than with a hearing client. It is also slower than working in sign language when the client and worker are fluent in manual communication. It is easy for a social worker to become impatient. The only answer to this problem is to accept a slower pace as a necessity, to budget time accordingly, and to remember that the deafened client is at least as impatient as the worker.

The social worker inevitably recognizes that deafness imposes real limitations upon the deafened person's functioning. It may be necessary and appropriate for the worker to engage in activities which he would normally expect his client to handle by himself. Because the worker can use the telephone and the client cannot, for example, the worker may need to make some phone calls for the client. Once involved in a client's personal phone call, however, it is all too easy for the worker to become active in areas of the client's life which do not warrant his intervention. The worker needs to be flexible, willing to go beyond the usual confines of a clinical role, when such activity is appropriate. But he must also remember that the client's inability to hear does not in itself interfere with his ability to make his own decisions. The worker's challenge, essentially, is to remain sensitive to the nature and scope of the problem of deafness and, at the same time, to maintain confidence in the client's capacity to manage his disability and his life.

There are few disabilities which affect a person's life as broadly and profoundly as deafness. Work with deafened clients is difficult, presenting a real test of a worker's flexibility of style, depth of understanding, and tolerance for pain. At the same time, deafened clients offer a social worker a rare opportunity when they allow him to share their intense experiences and participate in their struggle for a satisfying life in an altered world.

REFERENCES

Ashley, J. M. P. *Journey into silence.* London: The Bodley Head Ltd., 1973.

Bartley, J. Unpublished Speech, San Francisco, 1978.

Chough, S. K. Casework with the deaf: A problem in communication. In Francis J. Turner (Ed.), *Differential diagnosis and treatment in social work,* Second edition. New York: Free Press, 1976.

Elliott, H. Acquired deafness: Shifting gears. Unpublished Speech, San Francisco, 1978.

Fant, L. J. *Ameslan, an introduction to American Sign Language.* Northridge, California: Joyce Motion Picture Company, 1977.

Hurwitz, S. N. The contributions of social work practice to the mental health of the hearing impaired. In Kenneth Z. Altshuler and John D. Rainer (Eds.), *Mental health and the deaf: Approaches and prospects.* U.S. Department of Health, Education, and Welfare, 1969.

Jeffers, J., and Barley, M. *Speechreading (lipreading).* Springfield, Illinois: Charles C. Thomas, 1974.

Knapp, P. H. Emotional aspects of hearing loss. *Psychosomatic Medicine,* 1948, *10,* 203–222.

Krug, R. F. The relevance of audiologic data in planning mental health services for the acoustically impaired. In Kenneth Z. Altshuler and John D. Rainer (Eds.), *Mental health and the deaf: Approaches and prospects.* U. S. Department of Health, Education, and Welfare, 1969.

Kübler-Ross, E. *On death and dying.* London: Macmillan, 1969.

Levine, E. S. Auditory disability. In James F. Garrett and Edna S. Levine (Eds.), *Psychological practice with the physically disabled.* New York: Columbia University Press, 1962.

Newbold, H. S. L. Social work with the deaf: A model. *Social Work,* 24(2), March, 1979, 153–156.

Ramsdell, D. A. The psychology of the hard of hearing and the deafened adult. In Hallowell Davis and Richard S. Silverman (Eds.), *Hearing and deafness,* third edition. New York: Holt, Rinehart and Winston, 1970.

Schein, J. D., and Delk, M. T. *The deaf population of the United States.* Silver Spring, Maryland: National Association of the Deaf, 1974.

Silver, M. K. Casework with deaf clients. In U.S. Department of Health, Education, and Welfare, *Orientation of social workers to the problems of deaf persons.* Berkeley, California: University of California, 1963.

DEVELOPMENTAL DISORDERS

CHAPTER 16

COUNSELING SEVERELY DYSFUNCTIONAL FAMILIES OF MENTALLY AND PHYSICALLY DISABLED PERSONS

J. Dale Munro

Most families of mentally and physically disabled persons generally are supportive of their handicapped relatives and the professionals working with them. Nevertheless, in most helping settings, there always seem to be some families that might be described as being "severely dysfunctional." They need professional assistance, but often do not receive it.

In this article, a severely dysfunctional family is defined as a group of two or more blood relatives, at least one of whom is permanently disabled, that behave in an extremely self-destructive or resistant manner. These families pose one of the greatest dangers to the emotional growth of their disabled member and are a constant source of frustration for direct service professionals and agency executives. This article examines probable causes of severely dysfunctional family behavior, describes specific behavioral patterns manifested by these families, and proposes some pragmatic treatment interventions.

Reprinted from *Clinical Social Work Journal,* Vol. 13, No. 1 (1985), pp. 18–31, by permission of the author and Human Sciences Press.

CAUSES OF SEVERE FAMILY DYSFUNCTION

Professionals have long recognized that parents usually suffer extreme emotional pain when they first learn their child is disabled. The entire family is confronted with new demands that tax relationships both within and outside the family. Sieffert (1978) has skillfully described the parents' "normal coping process." First, there is the initial shock and grief of discovering the newborn baby will probably be permanently disabled. Second, initial numbness diminishes and is replaced by a sense of growing anger over feeling betrayed and deprived. Third, anger and denial gradually shifts to a growing desire to confront the reality of the disability. Coming to terms with this inescapable reality is necessary if parents are to avoid a prison of self-doubt, anger, guilt, and shame, and a need to punish themselves and others. Finally, as reality is confronted and the mourning period is worked through, the normal coping process is well under way. Now the parents can better focus on meeting the child's special needs.

Severely dysfunctional families differ from other families with disabled members in one salient way. Whereas most families gradually progress over time to some degree of acceptance of their disabled relative, severely dysfunctional families seem permanently arrested at an early stage in the normal coping process. Not surprisingly, siblings of the disabled person also become trapped in their parents' vicious cycle of grief and guilt. These disturbed families seem unable to "outgrow" initial nonacceptance.

Two factors may account for family members acting in a severely dysfunctional manner (Sieffert, 1978). First, the personality structure of individual family members may thwart the normal coping process. For example, parents or siblings who typically blame someone or something else about life problems, or who persist in blaming themselves, frequently will respond in an analogous manner when confronted with the birth of a disabled family member. Second, situational factors may negatively influence the personality factors. For instance:

(a) The quality of the parents' marital relationship can affect how the whole family responds to the presence of a disabled member. Relationships where "the marriage contract" (Sagar, Kaplan, Gundlach, Lenz, & Royce, 1971) has not been renegotiated after the disabled child's birth can result in general family dysfunction and scapegoating of the child (Bell & Vogel, 1968).

(b) The relatives' degree of disability along with the accessibility of outside professional resources can influence these families. In the absence of outside services, many parents become emotional wrecks after years of single-handedly trying to assist a severely disabled child.

(c) The large, bureaucratic, and somewhat oppressive nature of many helping agencies can frustrate families. Exacerbating this problem is the fact that some professionals behave in a less than caring manner when confronted by hostile family members. Professionals may show extreme symptoms of staff burnout (Munro, 1980; Pines & Maslach, 1978), or clash with family members because of differing cultural, religious, social class, or educational backgrounds. This adversarial relationship may intensify when either the family or the professional has unrealistic expectations about the other's needs or priorities (Sonnenschein, 1981; Hatfield, 1982; Gitterman, 1983).

SEVERELY DYSFUNCTIONAL FAMILY PATTERNS

Severely dysfunctional families seem overwhelmed by guilt, ambivalence, and hostility. These families usually deny these feelings when confronted directly, but show their emotional pain in a variety of overt or passive aggressive ways. They sometimes try to present a myth that "all is well" in the family (Ferreira, 1963), or mistakenly believe most of their problems are caused by the disabled relative. In response to tremendous family tension, the disabled person often begins to manifest maladaptive behavior. The disabled "identified patient" unintentionally becomes a spokesperson for the pathology present in the entire family system (Satir, 1967).

As professionals become involved to help the family with their problematic disabled member, they encounter enormous resistance. Family homeostasis depends on maintaining the disabled relative in the scapegoated problem role, in order that tension is not refocused on the real source of the conflict, the parental and family dysfunction. Behavioral improvement in the disabled person threatens the family since it creates disequilibrium in the family system.

Severely dysfunctional families show one or more of the following behavioral patterns.

1. *Loud, chronic complaining* is exhibited by some families. These families may:

   (a)   literally scream and create crises out of every minor concern, even when special efforts have been made to meet their needs. They seem preoccupied with the way agencies and professionals "should" and "must" provide quality and expanded services with little appreciation for large caseloads, high staff turnover, and dwindling agency budgets.

   (b)   telephone staff at home any hour of the day or night with minor problems, even when asked to call only during office hours.

   (c)   sometimes turn to lawyers, agency executives, local legislative representatives, special interest groups, or the mass media with complaints about service delivery, without first trying to resolve problems with direct service professionals.

   (d)   verbally attack professionals along racial, age, gender, religious, or personal lines, and demand other more suitable staff be provided to them.

2. *Program sabotage* is a trait of some families who tend to see professionals and agencies as adversaries. These families may:

   (a)   block attempts to provide treatment approaches (e.g., restrictions on family visits, time-out procedures, or pharmacotherapy) necessary for assisting extremely behaviorally disturbed individuals.

   (b)   refuse to support plans to place their institutionalized relative in an excellent community setting, or demand a disabled person be "discharged against advice" from a residential setting at the first sign of behavioral improvement.

   (c)   repeatedly break scheduled appointments with professionals, or appear an hour too early or too late for an appointment and demand an immediate interview.

(d)   have unrealistic or impossible expectations for their disabled relative, or at the other extreme impede program success by being overly pessimistic concerning the disabled person's prognosis.

3.   *Extreme overprotectiveness* is displayed by some families who seem overpowered by a ubiquitous sense of guilt. These families may:

(a)   infantilize and create dependency in otherwise capable, mildly disabled relatives. For example, parents may insist on still bathing their marginally retarded, adult child; demand a woman wear an undershirt rather than a brassiere; drive a person everywhere rather than allowing the individual to use public transportation; and insist on a hair style for the disabled person that is not age appropriate.

(b)   refuse to spend time away from their disabled family member (e.g., "During the first 25 years of Tom's life, I never was away from him for more than 3 hours at a time.") Family "martyrs" who devote their whole life to their disabled relative often secretly resent the life-long cost in time and money of caring for their relative.

(c)   take great personal risks when their disabled relative meets with a minor catastrophe to prove their undying love (e.g., elderly parents driving 30 miles through a blinding snowstorm after learning their institutionalized daughter had developed a minor physical ailment).

(d)   tolerate seemingly intolerable behavior. For instance, carrying out ridiculous requests from a disabled person to go for a car ride at 3:00 a.m., or to screw out every light bulb in the house. As well as, refusing to say "no" to a disabled person's compulsive eating of 14 chocolate bars at one time, or failing to seek assistance for a physically violent person who has repeatedly injured family members.

4.   *Hypochondriacal obsessions* are found in some families. Family members often talk incessantly about their own somatic problems and may:

(a)   "shop around" from one specialist to another to find some miracle cure for their relative's permanent disability. They may even demand that physicians perform unnecessary surgery or change the disabled person's treatment to some "medical breakthrough" described in sensationalized publications.

(b)   request that unnecessary laxatives or vitamins be given to their disabled relative, or constantly censure physicians for not finding undetectable ailments. They may also stockpile psychotrophic medication when their disabled relative is quiet and then overdose the person when behavior problems appear.

(c)   stubbornly deny the functional basis for many behavioral problems, while insisting their disabled relative's difficulties are caused entirely by some vague "brain disease" or obscure physiological problem.

(d)   continually ruminate about the probable etiology for their relative's disability (e.g., "She was developing normally until she had her tonsils out at age 2").

5. *Open warfare* is observed in some families. Overt hostility is the hallmark here. In these families:

   (a) parents seldom show warmth and closeness toward each other. Their marriage is characterized by sarcastic exchanges, violent arguments, extramarital affairs, and often ultimately divorce.

   (b) intense sibling rivalry occurs that lasts into adulthood. Brothers and sisters vacillate between displacing enormous anger onto their disabled siblings, to competing to prove who loves the person more (e.g., overindulgent gift-giving).

   (c) "shared family secrets" create considerable tension. These secrets involve knowledge the family is forbidden to talk about concerning incest, physical or sexual abuse, alcohol or drug problems (Karpel, 1980).

   (d) physical violence is common. Yet, the ever-present hostility can easily be projected onto professionals or agency officials who provoke family members in even minor ways. Professionals may be verbally threatened, sexually propositioned, or physically attacked by irate family members.

6. *Symbiotic relationships* are encountered in some families involving a pathologically close relationship between the disabled person and one or both parents, feeling uncanny sensitivity for the others' pain, and doublebind communication (Slipp, 1973). "Folie à famille" refers to cases where symbiotic fusion and a commonly shared delusion permeates the entire family (Wikler, 1980). Three such delusions may be found in severely dysfunctional families:

   (a) delusions of persecution in which the family socially isolates itself and develops a paranoid distrust of outsiders, be they neighbors or helping professionals.

   (b) delusions of grandeur in which one family member, sometimes the disabled person, is idolized beyond any realistic dimensions (e.g., the family may believe one member has magical healing powers, can forecast future events, or deserves most of the family's attention).

   (c) delusions of wish-fulfillment in which the family inaccurately believes their relative has been deliberately malingering a disability ("He puts on a fake retarded act in public"), or where families feel finding the right faith healer will cure their disabled relative.

7. *Avoidance of the disabled person* is demonstrated by other families. Sometimes:

   (a) family members completely terminate contact with the disabled individual after placing the person in a residential setting. They may never visit, write, or even acknowledge their relative's existence. Such total rejection can destroy the disabled person's self-worth, precipitate severe depression, and leave the person fantasizing about family that never comes. Other families may keep contact only until money from an inheritance or other source "runs dry."

   (b) family members make grand promises to disabled individuals (e.g., vow to visit or let the disabled person move in with them, or promise gifts) that are never kept.

(c) one parent will withdraw completely into vocational or spare-time activities, leaving the other parent to deal almost single-handedly with their disabled child.

(d) family members withdraw into severe depressions which effectively leads to little or no contact with the disabled relative (e.g., escape through psychiatric hospitalization, or alcohol and drug abuse).

8. *Psychosocial deprivation* characterizes some families frequently found in isolated rural or urban slum areas. In these multideficit families:

(a) little attention is paid to the special needs of the disabled person since all family members face day-to-day struggles meeting basic needs (Greene & Orman, 1981). A person's disability may never even be diagnosed, unless the degree of handicap is extreme or a major crisis arises. In some cases, environmental deprivation or genetic influences may result in limited intellectual capacities in several or all family members.

(b) there is often a distrust of professionals and helping agencies. Many of these socioeconomically disadvantaged families are frustrated after long-term contact (sometimes involving more than one generation) with welfare and social service establishments.

(c) incest and unwanted pregnancies sometimes run rampant. The disabled individual is particularly vulnerable to sexual exploitation by other family members.

(d) disabled relatives may still, even in this day and age, be found locked or hidden away in the home to minimize embarrassment or facilitate behavioral management.

INTERVENTION CONSIDERATIONS
Therapeutic Stance

Obviously professionals find working with severely dysfunctional families is emotionally demanding and sometimes extremely discouraging. Yet, frequently there are viable interventions which can be utilized, if the professional is really motivated to assist such troubled people. To a large extent, treatment success depends on the professional's persistence, high energy, optimism, and ability to be satisfied with small gains (Gourse & Chescheir, 1981; McKinney, 1970).

Sessions should focus on specific "here and now" strategies to assist the disabled individual and the family, since severely dysfunctional families tend to dwell on past problems and perceived injustices against them. Professionals should avoid using pedantic jargon and when appropriate employ humor to reduce anxiety. They should always be punctual for interviews, even if the family is not.

Professionals must be sensitive to, and empathize with, family feelings of despair, guilt, anger, and fear. But they also must be capable of adhering to constructive limits on family behavior when necessary. The short-term goal is always to keep the family's dysfunctional behavior under control so meaningful programs can be provided for the disabled individual. The long-term goal is to build a positive relationship based on consistency and trust with the family so they can feel like a partner on the team delivering services to their disabled relative (Hatfield, 1979).

Countertransference

The extreme resistance exhibited by severely dysfunctional families can elicit strong emotional reactions in professionals that destroy professional objectivity. The term "countertransference" is often used generically to cover not only unrealistic reactions on the part of a counselor towards a client, but also realistic responses that are countertherapeutic (Hollis, 1972).

Although no professional can avoid completely the effects of countertransference, some are more susceptible than others to having their feelings and behavior manipulated by severely dysfunctional families. Professionals should be particularly vigilant when they find that family members evoke strong reactions in them, such as hostility, repulsion, or overidentification with a particular family member. They should be prepared for family antagonism or mistrust without being provoked into defensiveness and power struggles.

Professionals must be cognizant of the distortion countertransference can create in their perceptions of severely dysfunctional families and strive to control its effect. Proper treatment of these families can begin only if the professional avoids colluding with punitive forces within the family (Nadelson, 1977). The professional should maintain a proper perspective in which the family's needs, not the professional's, guide their relationship.

Intervention Process

The family intervention process begins with the *assessment phase*. The disabled individual usually is identified as experiencing some need and is referred for professional assistance. Sometimes the referring agent indicates the family is "troublesome." Other times, family problems only come to light when programs are being developed for the disabled individual. If considerable difficulties are suspected, an experienced professional should become involved to assess the family.

The first contact with the family is important since it often sets the stage for future cooperation or conflict. The professional's assessment of the family begins (usually over the telephone) when arranging for the first interview. Clues can be picked up regarding family hostility, potential for cooperation, presenting problems, and previous contact if any with helping agencies and professionals. At this early stage, the professional is wise to remember Carl Whitaker's (1967) warning that all family intervention "has to begin with a fight" (p. 266). This is particularly apparent with severely dysfunctional families. It is important that professionals establish themselves early as authority figures who radiate an aura of knowledge, confidence, and compassion to the family. Professionals should carefully document all involvement with severely dysfunctional families in case the family considers lawsuits or creates bad publicity against the agency.

Family interviews should include all family members who regularly interact with or influence the disabled person. This symbolizes that problems belong to the entire family, not solely the disabled individual. The disabled person should be encouraged to fully participate in interviews. However, if the person cannot understand the proceedings or is too disruptive, or if the discussion focuses entirely on the parents' marital relationship, the professional may choose to exclude the disabled person.

Assessment of the family should include a brief family history and careful analysis of verbal and nonverbal interactions among family members. The family's perception of current problems should be explored and the professional should watch for evidence of marital dysfunction or other family pathology. As well, mental note should be made of areas of family strength, cohesion, and mutual support (Wikler, Wasow, & Hatfield 1983). During the assessment interview, professionals can outline services they are willing to provide, limits on services available, and possible restrictions to which family members must adhere. Finally, the professional should always attempt to instill some hope that current problems can change if everyone works together.

Once the family has been assessed, professionals should consult with their treatment teams to discuss all potential intervention alternatives. Then, the *contracting and treatment implementation phase* can occur. Here the professional, the disabled individual, and the family negotiate an explicit contract that lays out the treatment plan (Munro, 1981). It is important at this point to determine what type of family intervention format will be employed. There is the "one-shot interview format" in which the assessment and as much therapeutic impact as possible must be made in only one session. On the other hand, a "multi-interview format" is preferable if the family needs considerable support and is prepared for long-term professional intervention. The success of both one-shot and multi-interview formats can be augmented through occasional or regular use of a "telephone interview format." Here telephone discussions can be scheduled with the family to reinforce decisions made during face-to-face interviews, revise program decisions, share information, and provide emotional support (Ranan & Blodgett, 1983).

The *termination phase* completes the family intervention process. It may occur quickly in the case of one-shot interview formats. More often, where professionals provide long-term support to severely dysfunctional families, intervention approaches are gradually faded away. After many months or years of professional assistance, most of these families no longer can be termed dysfunctional. They are much more cooperative and motivated to follow any reasonable treatment regimen. Family members have worked through much of their hostility and guilt, see professionals and agencies in a more positive light, and have become a constructive force in the disabled person's life.

Supportive Approaches

All families of disabled persons require understanding and support. This is particularly true for severely dysfunctional families. However, these families seem caught in a bind. They desperately need professional help, but simultaneously push away professionals with their abusive or socially unacceptable behavior. Nevertheless, professionals attempting to assist severely dysfunctional families must saturate them with support. Such support often initially is rejected, but gradually is accepted after the family has had time to "test out" the professional's degree of commitment and concern for their problems. Several supportive approaches can be employed:

1. Interviews should be held in private, mutually agreeable settings. Home interviews can be particularly effective since they present the most realistic picture of the family's interaction and general environment. In addition, since the family perceives the home as their territory, it is less threatening for them. Home interviews often are interpreted by the family as proof the professional is really interested in their problems since an effort has been made to come to them (Ackerman, 1958). If office interviews are utilized, the professional can help the family relax by making tea and coffee available, having ashtrays handy, and having tissues ready for times when family members break into tears.

2. All promises or commitments the professional makes to the family must be faithfully adhered to and any constructive responses by the family should be positively reinforced in order to slowly shape their behavior. When necessary, the professional should model effective behavioral techniques which family members can utilize for managing their disabled relative.

3. When a disabled individual becomes involved with a residential program, day program, or other services, efforts should be made to identify one agency contact person from whom the family can obtain honest feedback regarding their relative's progress. Whenever possible, the professional counseling the family also should act as this contact person. Many agencies create a "systems dilemma" (Hoffman & Long, 1969) by having too many persons simultaneously imparting information, sometimes conflicting, to the same family.

4. Professionals must guard against treating the grievances of chronically complaining families too lightly. Usually, even the most pathological family has some legitimate concerns hidden amongst their perceived "bitching." Professionals should practice "active listening" (Gordon, 1970; Rogers, 1951). Being really listened to is a powerful supportive approach for severely dysfunctional families who have often been ignored, put off, or not taken seriously by overworked or insensitive professionals. Active listening can be combined with approaches to clarify and relabel feelings.

5. Smith (1975) suggests assertive training skills that can be combined to help sensitive professionals avoid becoming defensive when personally slurred or verbally attacked by hostile family members. "Fogging" is described as the acceptance of manipulative criticism by calmly acknowledging the probability of some truth in what your critic says ("Yes, I probably am a s.o.b. sometimes."). "Negative inquiry" teaches the active prompting of criticism in order to use the information, if helpful, or exhaust it if manipulative, while prompting your critic to become more assertive and less manipulative ("You've only made five complaints about your son's treatment. There must be something else we should be doing for him.") "Broken record" involves the professional calmly and persistently repeating a desired point while avoiding manipulative verbal traps ("I recognize your love for your daughter, but she's too disturbed to go home this weekend . . . I know you love her, but you can't take her home . . . etc.")

6. Professionals can "give permission" to families to take part in activities they seldom allow themselves. For instance, overprotective parents can be encour-

aged to strengthen their marital relationship by planning vacations, evenings or weekends away without the children. Professionals also can encourage parents to spend more time with the often-neglected siblings of the disabled individual.

7. Professionals should have knowledge of available resources (e.g., educational, residential, financial, vocational, speech therapy, baby-sitters, respite care, and medical services) in order to help the family make well-informed decisions regarding meeting their needs. At the same time, professionals can often serve as advocates and brokers in securing services for the family. Since severely dysfunctional families tend to be "crisis-prone" (Hill, 1965), professionals also should inform them of support services that can be expected for dealing with crises.

Confrontative Approaches

Professionals frequently experience uneasiness when called on to use authoritarian approaches with families. But with severely dysfunctional families the supportive measures just discussed must always be used in conjunction with confrontative interventions. Putting power politics, manipulations, bargaining, and persuasion to constructive use is necessary with such resistant clients (Gourse & Chesheir, 1981; Murdach, 1980). Professionals inadvertently reinforce family pathology by refusing to act in a firm manner with them. Before endeavoring to utilize such severe measures, however, it is wise to enlist the support of agency administrators. A supportive agency executive is the greatest asset when working with severely dysfunctional families (Frankenstein, 1982).

Confrontative strategies sometimes necessary when working with severely dysfunctional families include the following:

1. Interviews often must be conducted according to strict rules which enhance communication, while modelling order and mutual respect. For example, family members are confronted if they (a) interrupt the person speaking; (b) try to speak for others; (c) physically assault others; or (d) forget to turn off noisy radios and televisions in their home.

2. Family contact with particularly disturbed individuals occasionally must be limited or completely banned (Landesman-Dwyer, 1981). This occurs particularly in residential treatment settings where family members want to visit too frequently, thus stifling the disabled person's independence. This restriction also may be employed in cases where disabled persons react with severe maladaptive behavior in the presence of their family, or demand not to see them.

3. If the family is completely sabotaging their disabled relative's treatment, it sometimes is useful to orchestrate a one-shot "showdown" interview. The meeting should be very formal and take place in one of the agency administrative offices. High-profile agency representatives should be present to give the meeting an aura of importance. Sometimes such meetings help soothe the family's concern that everything possible is being done for their disabled relative. As well, the family can be confronted with ways they are sabotaging

programs. Program strategies can be reviewed or revised right in the interview and everyone's responsibility can be clarified. In rare situations where families still remain unmotivated to cooperate with agencies, it may be necessary as a last resort to withdraw professional services completely.

4. In carefully timed situations, skilled clinicians may utilize paradoxical intervention strategies in order to change disturbed family behavior (Whitaker, 1975; Fisher, Anderson, & Jones, 1981). Such "psychotherapy of the absurd" involves a deadly serious but tongue-in-cheek attitude on the part of the professional. The unreasonable quality of the family member's behavior is encouraged to escalate to the point of absurdity. For example, parents who encourage a disabled child's compulsive eating are told to feed him 10 milkshakes when they go to McDonald's rather than the usual 7, if they find this helpful.

5. The professional may find it necessary to confront family members with appropriate role expectations in order to resolve role conflict (e.g., disabled adults forced into frustrating infantilized roles). Role modification and clarification is an important function of professionals for reducing strain within severely dysfunctional families (Spiegel, 1968).

6. Hostile families sometimes must be confronted with a disconcerting truism. Namely, the way family members treat direct service professionals is often the way staff treat their disabled relatives. Thus, these families need to be counseled as to how best approach agency personnel to create the best results for their disabled relatives, as well as themselves.

CONCLUSIONS

Helping severely dysfunctional families requires innovative professionals—supported by enlightened agency executives—who are willing to experiment with novel and practical treatment alternatives. No longer can professionals simply blame, ignore, or stereotype these families as "untreatable." Refusing to reach out to help these families locks the family, the disabled individual, the professional, and the agency into a vicious cycle of tension, confusion, and wasted energy. It must be assumed that within every severely dysfunctional family is a core of love and constructive potential which can be put to positive purposes when molded in the hands of a skillful counseling professional. Severely dysfunctional families of disabled persons represent one of the most needy, but seldom recognized, client populations in the rehabilitation field today. Equipped with that deeper understanding, which can help to mitigate the probably inevitable negative counterreactions, professionals may arrive at flexibly adaptive approaches which will render them more effective in developing constructive working relationships with these families.

REFERENCES

Ackerman, N. W. (1958). *The psychodynamics of family life.* New York: Basic Books.
Bell, N. W., & Vogel, E. F. (1968). The emotionally disturbed child as the family scapegoat. In N. W. Bell & E. F. Vogel (Eds.), *A modern introduction to the family* (pp. 412–427). New York: The Free Press.

Ferreira, A. J. (1963). Family myth and homeostasis. *Archives of General Psychiatry, 9,* 457–463.

Fisher, L., Anderson, A., & Jones, J. E. (1981). Types of paradoxical intervention and indications/contraindications for use in clinical practice. *Family Process, 20,* 25–35.

Frankenstein, R. (1982). Agency and client resistance. *Social Casework, 63,* 24–28.

Gitterman, A. (1983). Uses of resistance: A transactional view. *Social Work, 28,* 127–131.

Gordon, T. (1970). *Parent effectiveness training.* New York: New American Library.

Gourse, J. E., & Chescheir, M. W. (1981). Authority issues in treating resistant families. *Social Casework, 62,* 67–73.

Green, M. J., & Orman, B. (1981). Nurturing the unnurtured. *Social Casework, 62,* 398–404.

Hatfield, A. B. (1979). The family as partner in the treatment of mental illness. *Hospital & Community Psychiatry, 30,* 338–340.

Hatfield, A. B. (1982). Therapist and families: Worlds apart. *Hospital & Community Psychiatry, 33,* 513.

Hill, R. (1965). Generic features of families under stress. In H. J. Parad (Ed.), *Crisis intervention: Selected readings* (pp. 32–52). New York: Family Service Association of America.

Hoffman, L., & Long, L. (1969). A systems dilemma. *Family Process, 8,* 211–234.

Hollis F. (1972). *Casework: A psychosocial therapy,* 2nd Ed. New York: Random House.

Karpel, M. A. (1980). Family Secrets: I. Conceptual and ethical issues in the relational context. II. Ethical and practical considerations in therapeutic management. *Family Process, 19,* 295–306.

Landesman-Dwyer, S. (1981). Living in the community. *American Journal of Mental Deficiency, 86,* 223–234.

McKinney, G. E. (1970). Adapting family therapy to multideficit families. *Social Casework, 51,* 327–333.

Munro, J. D. (1980). Preventing front-line collapse in institutional settings. *Hospital & Community Psychiatry, 31,* 179–182.

Munro, J. D. (1981). Utilization of written contracts to increase client self-determination. *Mental Retardation, 19,* 65–67.

Murdach, A. D. (1980). Bargaining and persuasion with nonvoluntary clients. *Social Work, 25,* 458–461.

Nadelson, T. (1977). Borderline rage and the therapist's response. *American Journal of Psychiatry, 134,* 748–751.

Pines, A., & Maslach, C. (1978). Characteristics of staff burn-out in mental health settings. *Hospital & Community Psychiatry, 29,* 233–237.

Ranan, W., & Blodgett, A. (1983). Using telephone therapy for "unreachable" clients. *Social Casework, 64,* 39–44.

Rogers, C. (1951). *Client-centered therapy.* New York: Houghton Mifflin.

Sager, C. J., Kaplan, H. S., Gundlach, M. K., Lenz, R., & Royce, J. R. (1971). The marriage contract. *Family Process, 10,* 311–326.

Satir, V. (1967). *Conjoint family therapy.* Palo Alto: Science and Behavior Books.

Sieffert, A. (1978). Parents' initial reaction to having a mentally retarded child: A concept and model for social workers. *Clinical Social Work Journal, 6,* 34–39.

Slipp, S. (1973). The symbiotic survival pattern: A relational theory of schizophrenia. *Family Process, 12,* 377–398.

Smith, M. J. (1975). *When I say no, I feel guilty.* New York: The Dial Press.

Sonnenschein, P. (1981). Parents and professionals: An uneasy relationship. *Teaching Exceptional Children, 14,* 62–65.

Spiegel, J. P. (1968). The resolution of role conflict within the family. In N. Bell & E. Vogel (Eds.), *A modern introduction to the family* (pp. 391–411). New York: The Free Press.

Whitaker, C. A. (1967). The growing edge. In J. Haley & L. Hoffman (Eds.), *Techniques of family therapy* (pp. 265–360). New York: Basic Books.

Whitaker, C. A. (1975). Psychotherapy of the absurd: With a special emphasis on the psychotherapy of aggression. *Family Process, 14,* 1–16.

Wikler, L. (1980). Folie à famille: A therapist's perspective. *Family Process, 19,* 257–268.

Wikler, L., Wasow, M., & Hatfield, E. (1983). Seeking strengths in families of developmental disabled children. *Social Work, 28,* 313–315.

DIABETES

CHAPTER 17

THE DIABETIC CLIENT

Mary W. Engelmann

Diabetes Mellitus is a common disease in North America. In Canada alone there are approximately 200,000 known diabetics. This figure will undoubtedly increase as detection methods improve, and as greater medical knowledge enables diabetics to enjoy longer and healthier lives. Social workers in both medical settings and community agencies can expect to see more individuals with this chronic condition in the future.

At first glance it would not seem that this handicap is particularly serious. Diabetes does not have a marked effect on the victim's appearance and no stigma is attached to it. The well-regulated diabetic can, with few exceptions, participate in most activities and he meets with relatively little discrimination in job-seeking.[1] Is it necessary then for the social worker—whether in a medical setting or not—to be concerned about the implications of this handicap? The answer can be found by examining the illness more closely.

In diabetes, more than in any other chronic illness, there is a delicate interplay between the victim's emotional life and satisfactions and his ability to live with and control his condition. The requirements for adequate diabetic control can affect the person's attitude to himself and his interpersonal relationships. Much depends on the previously existing personality patterns of the individual and the interaction of his family life. Those persons who have made reasonably satisfactory adjustments find it easier to cope with diabetes, though even in the best of circumstances, there are periods of stress, anxiety and anger. For the person with problems, whether emotional or environmental, diabetes can be particularly upsetting and difficult.

Reprinted from *The Social Worker,* Vol. 35 (February 1967), pp. 6–10, by permission of the publisher.

[1] A. H. Kantrow, M.D. "Employment Experiences of Juvenile Diabetics," *Diabetes,* Vol. 10 (1961), pp. 476–481. This article is a report on a survey of the employment experiences of the alumni of the camp for diabetic children in New York.

EMOTIONAL HEALTH AND CONTROL

An understanding of the interaction between emotional health and diabetic control, along with an understanding of some of the specific anxieties and problems encountered by the diabetic, should enable the social worker to assist him more skillfully.

There are varying degrees of diabetic severity. The older individual who develops diabetes generally has a milder form of the illness and his diabetes can be controlled through diet alone, or through diet and oral medication. In a person under forty years of age, diabetes is generally more severe, requires insulin therapy, and is often much more difficult to control.

DIABETES AND EMOTIONAL STRESS

While diabetes is generally considered to be an inherited condition, due to a metabolic defect, there is some indication that it can be precipitated by emotional stress. Some studies suggest that the onset of diabetes may have been preceded by a period of deprivation, particularly loss of emotional support, unconscious conflict and depression.[2] Obviously, in such situations, the individual is weakened in his ability to cope with the meaning of the diagnosis. The new diabetic may be shocked, frightened, and even have moments of panic. He may feel a sense of despair because he faces a lifelong incurable condition. The amount of technical information he must absorb about diet and insulin therapy can seem overwhelming, and he may have doubts about his ability to care for himself. Along with this great increase in anxiety can come feelings of inadequacy and insecurity as he is faced with the awareness of physical limitation, dependency on insulin and continuous medical supervision.

Parents of a diabetic child have many of the same reactions as the adult diabetic, and often have a great sense of guilt. Irrational feelings of having neglected their child, or of having passed on a hereditary defect are present in almost every instance. The parents of a diabetic child are often overwhelmed by the technical information given them. Parents, at such a time, need the opportunity to discuss their anxiety and receive supportive help in developing their strengths and capabilities.

Diabetes is controlled through a therapeutic regime consisting of a restricted diet, insulin injections, and regular exercise. Adequate rest and regularity in meals are important. As it is a condition which must be regulated on a day-to-day basis, diabetes must be controlled by the patient himself, or, in the case of a young child, by his parents. The doctor can determine the initial regulation, can advise, and can help in illness or emergency situations, but the diabetic himself is responsible for the actual treatment.

Emotional upsets, in addition to illness, will have a definite physiological effect, actually raising the blood sugar level, thereby adding to an already complicated job.[3] Diabetic coma and insulin reactions are two serious and immediate complications which

[2] P. F. Slawson, M.D., W. K. Flynn, M.D., E. J. Kollar, M.D., "Psychological Factors Associated with the Onset of Diabetes Mellitus," *JAMA—Journal of the American Medical Association,* Vol. 185, No. 3 (1963), pp. 96–100. E. Weiss and O. W. English, *Psychosomatic Medicine, A Clinical Study of Psychophysiologic Reactions,* 3rd Edition, 1957, pp. 334–335.

[3] D. G. Prugh, "Psychophysiological Aspects of Inborn Errors of Metabolism," in H. I., V. F., and N. R. Lief (eds.), *The Psychological Basis of Medical Practice,* New York, Harper & Row, 1963, p. 421.

can develop. In the former, the blood sugar level becomes too high, and the person loses consciousness after a period of time. In the latter, which can come on suddenly, the blood sugar level drops too low, and causes aberrant behaviour and, in the later stages, results in unconsciousness. Both, if untreated, can lead to death.

CONTROL CAN CREATE RESENTMENT

What meaning does this have for the diabetic individual and his family? The diabetic cannot "adjust" to his diabetes and forget about it. In order to control it effectively, he and his family must be constantly aware of and concerned about it. This situation can create resentment and irritation. The other members of the family find that, at times, their lives and social activities are limited by the diabetic's need to adhere to his regime. For children and adolescents this regime will add to already incipient feelings of being different. Diabetic women may have added concerns about their adequacy as it is difficult for them to carry pregnancies to completion. It is obvious that, even in the best of circumstances, there are going to be periods of rebellion, frustration and resentment.

In a disturbed situation diabetes can add to an already charged atmosphere and be used by both the diabetic and his family in an attempt to solve neurotic conflicts. The diabetic regime can become the focus for arguments which usually reflect existing and more deep-rooted personality conflicts. The anger and frustration that all diabetics and their families feel will be exacerbated, added to more basic hostility, and reflected in destructive ways towards self and others. This can result in the diabetic's denial of the illness and in a lack of adequate concern, manifested in deliberate over-eating or neglect of insulin requirements. In this way the diabetic can control, and indirectly hurt, his family. As he becomes ill, he gains attention and sympathy but, at the same time, adds to his guilt feelings of being a burden. All of this can create a vicious cycle of anger, illness, guilt and depression. The immature, dependent diabetic may use his poorly controlled diabetes and resulting illness as a way of meeting his emotional needs.

PERSONALITY PATTERNS IN DIABETES

Some observers say that dependent, passive behaviour is a frequent personality pattern in diabetes. Their views are summarized by Dr. David Hawkins:

> While a wide variety of individual personality patterns are seen in diabetes, clinicians have over and over commented on the frequency of marked passivity, masochism, extreme oral dependency, and frequent retreats into illness in these patients. Rosen and Lidz noted that the refractory diabetic patient "reacted to sibling rivalry by regressively seeking maternal attention by becoming helpless and demanding or negativistic rather than through more active measures." It is easy to see that this illness with its emphasis on diet would facilitate regression to whatever oral dependent behaviour was potentially present in the patient, and there is considerable evidence that in many individuals a passive dependent character structure antedated the onset of the clinical disease. Mirsky postulates that there

is an inborn, metabolic problem from birth, even though signs and symptoms of the disease do not become manifest until later, and that this interferes with the development of a confident and mature outlook.[4]

Other observers emphasize that these diabetic personality patterns are the result of and not the cause of the disease. Doctors Philip Isenberg and Donald Barnett, in writing about the personality of the juvenile diabetic, say the following:

What we have outlined above suggests that there are bound to be certain similarities in the group of diabetic children because of the traumatic effect of the onset of the disease on most families. The persistent vulnerabilities and character trends which have been studied and reported on are probably the consequence of the disease and not its cause. What has been reported is a certain suppression of emotions, a feeling of being oppressed by a frustrating outer world which forces the patients to subordinate themselves to its demands. As a group they feel somewhat restricted and have been shown to be less spontaneous and free in the expression of their emotions and fantasies. Since therapy aims to control the disease by imposing restrictions on diet and requiring certain routines to be fulfilled many claim this tends to increase the feelings of being oppressed and frustrated.[5]

Insulin injections can carry implications of self-punishment or self-mutilation to the diabetic. If injections must be given by a member of the family, similar fears with consequent guilt can result for the nondiabetic. The strict regime may carry the implication of punishment and authority and may reactivate in the diabetic earlier unresolved conflicts.[6] Diet restriction may be linked in the individual's mind to a restriction of love or affection, with the result that he may, denying the seriousness of this for his illness, have periods of over-eating, even gorging himself.[7]

The marital partner, fearing that the diabetic may become totally dependent on him, and perhaps resenting the inevitable partial dependency, may become over-solicitous and concerned, thus accentuating the diabetic's sense of being handicapped. Insulin reactions can come on suddenly, even in the best-regulated diabetic. They can be embarrassing as well as dangerous and can result in the diabetic being at times dependent for life or death on his marital partner, family or occasional associates.

REACTION MANIPULATION

Reactions can be used by both the diabetic and the non-diabetic for control and manipulation. A beginning insulin reaction has some resemblance to an anxiety attack. There have been instances when a diabetic thought he was suffering from fairly frequent reac-

[4] D. Hawkins, M.D., "Emotions and Metabolic and Endocrine Disease," Lief, op. cit., pp. 274–275.
[5] P. Isenberg, M.D., and D. M. Barnett, M.D., "Psychological Problems in Diabetes Mellitus," The Medical Clinics of North America, Vol. 49, No. 2 (1965), pp. 1127–1128.
[6] F. Upham, A Dynamic Approach to Illness, New York, Family Service Association of America, 1949, pp. 91–92.
[7] Lief, op. cit., p. 420.

tions but was actually suffering from anxiety (blood sugar levels were found to be normal or above normal).[8]

A case history reported in *Diabetes,* the journal of the American Diabetic Association, illustrates some of the interaction between neurotic disturbance and the control of diabetes.[9] A young woman diabetic was ensnared in a conflict between her parents and her husband. She was unable to decide whether to be the dependent child of her parents or develop a mature relationship with her husband. In spite of the fact that there were frequent arguments and scenes between all members of the family, the presence of tension was denied.

This young woman was admitted to the hospital five times in one year in diabetic coma, always following a family argument. There was ample evidence that there was no neglect of insulin treatment or diet, and that the comas were her attempt to escape from her problem. She could retreat into the relative safety and neutrality of the hospital and at the same time receive attention and sympathy. Psychiatric help enabled both her and her family to develop some insight and alleviate the tension-producing situations. As a result her diabetes came under much better control.

Much has been written about the particular problems that are encountered in the family with a diabetic child and about the importance of seeing that the child's emotional growth is not blocked by the condition. There are some particular problems that may be encountered when diabetes develops in a family where there is already a disturbed parent-child or marital relationship. All parents have some resentment about the extra care and responsibility required by the diabetic child. However, in some instances, the child himself may be resented and rejected. Parents may show this by using the diabetic regime in a punitive way under the guise of achieving good control. Over-protection and over-anxiety can accentuate the child's sense of handicap and may be an expression of hostility. Parents may, by using the rationalization that the child must become independent, give the child too much responsibility for his diabetic control and then blame him when things go wrong. A history from the records of the Social Service Department of the Royal Alexandra Hospital, Edmonton, illustrates this latter point.

A diabetic child, aged eight years, was the third of four children. There was much conflict between the parents. The mother, a nervous tense woman, suffered from asthma. The father, quiet and passive, was somewhat aloof from the family situation. Neither parent understood diabetes adequately and neither was able to enforce the necessary discipline concerning diet and rest. The child was given a great deal of responsibility for his own diabetic care. When difficulties developed and he had to be hospitalized, he was blamed by his parents for this.

It would appear essential that the social worker be aware of the ramifications of diabetes in working with afflicted clients. Recognizing this the New York City Diabetic Association has set up a special counseling service for diabetics. This service not only

---

[8] E. Weiss and O. S. English, *op. cit.,* p. 342.
[9] G. L. Schless, M.D., and R. von Laveran-Stiebar, M.D., "Recurrent Episodes of Diabetic Acidosis Precipitated by Emotional Stress," *Diabetes,* Vol. 13, No. 4 (July-August, 1964), pp. 419–420.

works directly with diabetics, but also provides specialized information on diabetes to community agencies.[10]

While many diabetics appear to be able to cope successfully with their condition, there are always a number who fail to do so and stumble through life with an increasing complex of physical and emotional problems. It is these people who are most likely to come to the attention of social agencies, and it is in working with them that a knowledge of the particular problems of diabetes is necessary.

[10] A. H. Kantrow, M.D., "A Vocational and Counseling Service for Diabetics," *Diabetes*, Vol. 12, No. 5 (1963), pp. 454–457.

CHAPTER 18

PSYCHOSOCIAL ASPECTS OF GENETIC DISORDERS

Implications for Practice

Kathleen Kirk Bishop

A social worker on an early intervention team makes a home visit to the M family to discuss services coordination issues. N, age two, is experiencing serious developmental delay and the suspected cause is medication taken during Mrs. M's pregnancy. As services are reviewed, the social worker learns that the M family has stopped visiting family and going out with friends. In fact, their friends don't know that N has not learned to walk. When Mrs. M takes N to the pediatrician's office, people ask "hurtful" questions about his development and Mrs. M doesn't know how to respond.

J, age 29, who is involved in a serious relationship with a man who has proposed marriage, seeks counseling at the community mental health center. She reports symptoms of sleeplessness, distractibility at work, and increasing anxiety about the relationship. As the social worker takes the family history, he learns that J has a brother, age 22, with hemophilia. J begins to discuss her concerns about having children with hemophilia and her inability to talk with her boyfriend about her genetic history.

Mr. B brings his two-month-old daughter, K, to the emergency room at their local community hospital, reporting that K seems to be in pain and cries uncontrollably at times. Upon examination, it is discovered that K has several fractures and the hospital social worker is contacted. Assuming that K has been physically abused, the social worker calls the county child protection team to investigate. Later, K is diagnosed with

Reprinted from *Families in Society,* Vol. 74, No. 4 (1993), pp. 207–212, by permission of the publisher, Families International, Inc.

osteogenesis imperfecta, a genetic disorder characterized by fractures at birth and fragile bones that can break very easily.

These examples, which will be reexamined in more detail in the practice section, represent potential psychosocial implications for individuals and families affected by genetic disorders. They also illustrate that regardless of social workers' field of practice, they may come in contact with people with genetic disorders.

This article discusses briefly some of the advances and issues in the field of genetics, the psychosocial implications of genetic disorders, and the role of social workers in providing services to individuals and families affected by genetic disorders.

ISSUES

Approximately 5,000 genetic disorders have been identified (McKusick, 1990), and the list continues to grow. It is estimated that 6% of the population, or 12 million Americans, suffer from diseases involving genetic factors. Moreover, genetic disorders have been identified as the cause of severe mental handicaps in a significant proportion of the population. In the area of reproduction, genetic disorders are present in nearly 5% of all live births; each couple in the United States has a 3% chance of having a child who is affected by a genetic disorder (Select Panel for the Promotion of Child Health, 1981).

Genetic screening and testing, including carrier, prenatal, newborn, and presymptomatic screening, are advancing rapidly. Holtzman (1988) suggested that the number of individuals screened for only a few common disorders could well exceed 10 million per year, entailing 18 million tests, of which approximately 1.2 million would be positive.

Perhaps the most dramatic developments to date are in the areas of human genome mapping and gene therapy. Scientists are currently engaged in an international effort to "map" every gene. Great progress has been made in locating the genes for various genetic disorders, such as cystic fibrosis, muscular dystrophy, fragile X syndrome (the most common inherited form of mental retardation), high blood pressure, and some immune system disorders. Gene therapy, an experimental procedure, treats the genetic disorder by restoring or replacing a missing or faulty gene. These new discoveries in the area of gene mapping and gene therapy provide hope in finding treatment for genetic disorders. According to Hirschhorn (1992), "Someday people will look back on the era before gene therapy in the same way we look back on the era before antibiotics and vaccines." (For a fuller discussion of social work and genetic issues, see Schild and Black [1984] and Rauch [1990]).

Concerns remain, however, as to how well informed the public is about these new discoveries and their implications, particularly in the areas of human genome mapping, increased use of genetic testing, and the potential for gene therapy. In a survey of 1,000 adults conducted for the March of Dimes Birth Defects Foundation by Harris and Associates (1992), 89% of Americans said they approve of using gene therapy to treat genetic diseases. Eighty-nine percent also favor continuing research into gene therapy. In the area of genetic testing, nearly 8 of 10 Americans say they would take a genetic test before having children to discover whether their future offspring would be likely to inherit a fatal genetic disease. Forty-three percent approve of using gene therapy to improve the physical characteristics that children would inherit, whereas 42% approve of gene therapy to improve the intelligence level children would inherit. And, by a margin of two to one, Americans believe genetic testing should be offered to everyone (65%), rather than limiting it to people who have a reason to think they may have a particular disease gene. In the answer to the question "Who else has the right to know?" the survey produced some rather surprising findings. Fifty-seven percent of the survey respondents stated that if someone is a carrier of a defective gene or has a genetic disease, then "someone else deserves to know." Persons who should be informed included a spouse or fiancé (96%), other family members (70%), insurance companies (58%), and employers (33%). In addition, 71% responded that if a physician of a woman who plans to have children discovers through preconception testing that her children might inherit a serious or fatal genetic disease, the physician has an obligation to inform the woman's husband.

In light of these attitudes toward support for genetic testing and continued support for research into the use of gene therapy, it was surprising to learn that relatively few Americans have even a basic knowledge of genetic testing or gene therapy. According to the survey, 68% know "relatively little" or "almost nothing" about genetic testing, and knowledge of gene therapy was more limited, with 87% reporting little or no information. One wonders if the respondents understood that informing an insurer or an employer about a potential employee's genetic condition could lead to discrimination in the workplace (see Weiss and Volner [1992] for a discussion of genetic discrimination, including employment and insurance issues).

Clearly, as the scientific and technological advances in medical genetics provide individuals with myriad choices and decisions regarding genetic issues, social workers must be knowledgeable, informed, and alert to these issues in order to address the ever-increasing psychosocial needs of people affected by genetic disorders.

PSYCHOSOCIAL ASPECTS OF GENETIC DISORDERS

Although the research literature examining psychosocial aspects of genetic disorders is not extensive, several research studies have examined these issues. Kiely, Sterne, and Witkop (1976), in their study of persons affected with osteogenesis imperfecta (OI), reported that although the adaptations of persons with OI "sometimes were remarkable," the constraints on their lives were evident in the areas of educational attainment, job placement, and job retention. Potential problem areas in families included feelings of guilt and inadequacy, a tendency to overfocus on and overprotect the child with the genetic disorder, propensity for marital discord and distress, and dysfunctional involvement of family members.

In the area of reproductive decision making and genetics, Donal, Charles, and Harris (1981) suggested that "genetic" terminations, although outnumbered by "social" ones, are very different, especially because genetic terminations end planned, or at least wanted, pregnancies. Interviews with women following abortion of abnormal fetuses showed that persistent adverse psychological and social reactions may be much more common in women undergoing termination of pregnancy for genetic rather than social indications. These results confirm Blumberg, Golbus, and Hanson's (1975) earlier study suggesting that the incidence of depression and marital disruption following selective abortion for genetic reasons may be as high as 92% among the women and as high as 82% among the men studied. Incidence of depression was greater than that usually associated with elective abortion for psychosocial indications or with delivery of a baby who is stillborn. Furlong and Black (1984) examined the impact of pregnancy termination on other family members, including children, and reported that the termination of these initially desired pregnancies are stressful on all family members, precipitating bereavement within the family.

Miller, Bauman, Friedman, and De Cosse (1986) assessed psychological and social adjustment in individuals with familial polyposis, a genetically transmitted disease placing one at risk for colon cancer. Concerns identified included fear about future health due to the high risk of cancer, guilt about transmitting a genetic disease to one's children, and concern about physical disfigurement resulting from surgery.

Ekwo, Kim, and Gosselink (1987) examined parental perceptions of the burden of genetic disease and found that perceived burdens associated with hypothetical congenital abnormalities leading to prolonged illness or early death were considered the most serious and problematical. Genetic conditions relating to physical handicap or facial abnormalities were perceived as being least serious, whereas genetic factors causing mental retardation fell between the two extremes. These findings highlight the importance of exploring parents' attitudes about specific genetic conditions, including their perceptions of how they would cope with the medical and social consequences of various conditions.

Conyard, Krishnamurthy, and Dosik (1980) studied psychosocial aspects of sickle cell anemia in adolescents and found that adolescents in the study group showed a high degree of isolation, dependence, fear of illness, and withdrawal from normal relationships with peers in school and their family members. Other emotional problems included poor self-image, depression, anxiety and preoccupation with death. They concluded, however, that these psychosocial aspects resemble the psychosocial aspects of other chronic illnesses. Morgan and Jackson (1986) hypothesized that adolescents with sickle-cell anemia experience difficulty in mastering the normal developmental tasks of adolescence because of the characteristics of their condition. Their results indicated that these adolescents experienced greater depression and social withdrawal and less body satisfaction than did their health peers.

In Weiss's (1992) study of support groups for persons with genetic disorders and their families, parents who were told that their child had a genetic disorder were "numb with shock, filled with apprehension, and shaken by feelings of guilt, albeit unjustified" (p. 13). Some of the members in the genetic support groups reported believing that they were "set apart" from society, especially if their condition was relatively unknown, and that they were at risk for stigmatization.

In summary, these studies as well as the work of Schild (1977, 1981), Weiss (1981), Black (1983), and Black and Furlong (1984) suggest that people with genetic disorders or at risk for genetic disorders experience very serious psychological and social issues. Thus, social workers can provide valuable services to these clients.

IMPLICATIONS FOR SOCIAL WORK PRACTICE

Given the dramatic advances in the field of genetics and the suggested psychosocial aspects of genetic disorder the three case illustrations introduced earlier are reexamined.

The M Family

In the M family situation, N's condition fell into the category of genetic disorders produced by exposure to particular environmental agents. Specifically, the genetic specialists suspected that a medicine Mrs. M used during her pregnancy may have caused N's developmental delay and other problems.

The social worker's efforts to help the M family adapt to N's diagnosis related to N, Mr. and Mrs. M, their other children, extended family members, various agencies that would provide services, and the community. Some of the issues the family faced and the social worker could help with included working with the early intervention team to access appropriate services for N, helping Mrs. M deal with potential feelings of guilt, exploring resources to assist with the extra and unexpected financial costs associated with having a child with special needs, providing support to deal with feelings of sadness and isolation, and suggesting a support group in which the Ms could talk with other families who were experiencing similar kinds of issues.

The Case of J

J's situation suggested the need for referral for genetic counseling due to her concerns and questions regarding her ability to bear children without hemophilia. The social worker's tasks included helping J explore her feelings about having a brother with hemophilia, explore her feelings about her impending marriage in relation to her fears about childbearing, understand the need to discuss her genetic history with her boyfriend as an important step in building a trusting relationship, and find a genetic counselor so that she could receive accurate information about available genetic testing for hemophilia and her risk of having a child with hemophilia. In this case, other family members may also need information, support, and counseling with regard to marriage and childbearing issues.

Mr. B and K

In the situation of Mr. B and K, the family learned that their presumably healthy child had a genetic disorder, thus altering permanently the plans, dreams, and expectations for K and her family. An additional and complicating issue occurred when the social worker, who lacked knowledge about osteogenesis imperfecta (OI, popularly referred to as brittle bone disease), inappropriately referred the family to child protection services, thus compounding the anguish of the B family.

The social worker, in this situation, needed to acknowledge quickly and respectfully her mistake and move quickly to provide the B family with information about OI, supportive counseling to help the family cope with the shock and confusion associated with learning that their child had a genetic disorder with serious and lifelong consequences, and referral to a genetic center where the family could receive genetic counseling and begin to understand the implications of the diagnosis for the entire family. With regard to the social worker's initial misdiagnosis of the problem, the social worker and the family needed to determine whether the family and social worker could continue to work together effectively.

These case examples suggest only a few of the many services, such as service coordination, assuring access to community resources, finding genetic services, working with school personnel, making referrals to family planning and adoption agencies, organizing and leading support groups, that social workers may offer to individuals and families affected by a genetic disorder.

SUMMARY AND RECOMMENDATIONS

Virtually all social workers are engaged with individuals and families who are at risk for or have genetic disorders. Whether a social worker is employed by a child welfare agency, nursing home, hospital, community mental health center, a shelter for the homeless, a family planning clinic, or in private practice, he or she is engaged with clients and client groups affected by genetic disorders. Regardless whether a social worker works with babies, couples who are trying to make reproductive decisions, young children, adolescents, adults, or the elderly, genetic issues span the life cycle and affect all ages and groups of people.

The following recommendations are suggested to assist social workers in identifying and meeting the needs of individuals and families who could benefit from genetic services:

1. Social workers must become knowledgeable about genetics, particularly the latest developments in genetic screening, human genome mapping, and gene therapy. See Forsman and Bishop (1980), Bishop (1983), Rauch (1984) for recommended areas of knowledge for social workers.
2. Social workers should use genograms that include three generations when taking a family history and doing a family assessment to help members see patterns of inheritance, disease, and other medical conditions that indicate reasons for referral for genetic services. See McGoldrick and Gerson (1985) for a more complete discussion of multigenerational assessments.
3. Social workers must be cautious in overemphasizing psychological issues (S. Roche, personal communication, November 4, 1992) to the exclusion of more biologically based explanations of individuals and family behavior (see the Mr. B and K case example).
4. Social workers must listen to the concerns of their clients with a "genetic ear" in order to identify and refer individuals and families who might benefit from genetic services.
5. Social workers must identify and become familiar with resources for genetic ser-

vices. They may wish to establish a consultative relationship with a genetic counselor in order to increase their understanding of appropriate reasons for referral.

6.   Social workers should consider referring anyone who has questions and concerns about diseases or traits in their family to genetic counseling. In addition, practitiners should consider referring individuals and couples with the following situations:

- Persons who have, or are concerned that they might have, an inherited disorder or birth defect
- Women who are pregnant or planning to be pregnant after age 34
- Couples who already have a child with mental retardation, an inherited disorder, or a birth defect
- Couples whose infant has a genetic disease diagnosed by routine newborn screening
- Women who have had two or more miscarriages or babies who died in infancy
- Persons concerned that their jobs, lifestyles, or medical history may pose a risk to pregnancy, including exposure to radiation, medications, chemicals, infection, or drugs
- Couples who would like testing or more information about genetic disorders that occur frequently in their ethnic group
- Couples who are close blood relatives
- Pregnant women who, based on an ultrasound test or blood tests for alpha-fetoprotein, have been told their pregnancy may be at increased risk for complications or birth defects (Harris & Associates, 1992)

Although genetic counselors play a critical role in helping people understand how inheritance works and in translating genetic knowledge into usable information, social workers must help individuals and families with the social and psychological consequences of genetic testing, the implications of a genetic diagnosis, and the possible choices and decisions available to them.

REFERENCES

Bishop, K. K. (1983). Social work needs in genetic education. In J. O. Weiss, B. A. Bernhardt, & N. W. Paul (Eds.), Genetic disorders and birth defects in families and society: Toward interdisciplinary understanding (pp. 27–30). *Birth Defects: Original Article Series,* 20(4). White Plains, NY: March of Dimes Birth Defects Foundation.

Black, R. B. (1983). Genetics and adoption: A challenge for social work. In M. Dinerman (Ed.), *Social work practice in a turbulent world* (pp. 193–206). Silver Spring, MD: National Association of Social Workers.

Black, R. B., & Furlong, R. M. (1984). Impact of prenatal diagnosis in families. *Social Work in Health Care, 9,* 37–50.

Blumberg, R. B., Golbus, M. S., & Hanson, K. H. (1975). The psychological sequelae of abortion performed for a genetic indication. *American Journal of Obstetrics and Gynecology, 122,* 799–808.

Conyard, S., Krishnamurthy, M., & Dosik, H. (1980). Psychosocial aspects of sickle-cell anemia in adolescents. *Health and Social Work, 5,* 20–26.

Donal, P., Charles, N., & Hanis, R. (1981) Attitudes of patients after "genetic" termination of pregnancy. *British Medical Journal, 282,* 621–622.

Ekwo, E. E., Kim, J., & Gosselink, C. A. (1987). Parental perceptions of the burden of genetic diseases. *American Journal of Medical Genetics, 28,* 955–963.

Forsman, I., & Bishop, K. K. (Eds.). (1980, January). *Education in genetics: Nurses and social workers* (DHHS Publication No. HSA 81-5120A) (pp. 15–27). Washington, DC: U.S. Government Printing Office.

Furlong, R. M., & Black, R. B. (1984). Pregnancy termination for genetic indications: The impact on families. *Social Work in Health Care, 10,* 17–34.

Harris, L., & Associates (April, 1992). *March of Dimes Birth Defects Foundation survey of public opinion of human genetics.* White Plains, NY: Author.

Hirschhorn, R. (1992, September 29). News Release. March of Dimes Birth Defects Foundation, White Plains, NY.

Holtzman, N. A. (1988). Recombinant DNA technology, genetic tests and public policy. *American Journal of Human Genetics, 42,* 624–632.

Kiely, L., Sterne, R., & Witkop, C. J. (1976). Psychological factors in low-incidence genetic disease: The case of osteogenesis imperfecta. *Social Work in Health Care, 1,* 409–420.

McGoldrick, M., & Gerson, R. (1985). *Genograms in family assessment.* New York: W. W. Norton.

McKusick, V. A. (1990). *Mendelian inheritance in man: Catalog of autosomal dominant, autosomal recessive and X-linked phenotypes.* Baltimore, MD: Johns Hopkins University Press.

Miller, H. H., Bauman, L. J., Friedman, D. R., & De Cosse, J. J. (1986). Psychosocial adjustment of familial polyposis patients and participation in chemoprevention trial. *International Journal of Psychiatry in Medicine, 16,* 211–229.

Morgan, S. A., & Jackson, J. (1986). Psychological and social concomitants of sickle cell anemia in adolescents. *Journal of Pediatric Psychology, 11,* 429–440.

Rauch, J. B. (Ed.). (1984, April). *Educating for practice in a changing world: Implications of the genetics revolution.* School of Social Work and Community Planning, University of Maryland.

Rauch, J. B. (1990). Genetic services. *Encyclopedia of social work* (18th ed.) (pp. 113–131). Silver Spring, MD: National Association of Social Workers.

Schild, S. (1977). Social work with genetic problems. *Health and Social Work, 2*(1), 59–77.

Schild, S. (1981). Social and psychological issues in genetic counseling. In S. R. Applewhite, D. L. Busbee, & D. H. Borgaonkar (Eds.), *Genetic screening and counseling: A multidisciplinary perspective* (pp. 131–141). Springfield, IL: Charles C Thomas.

Schild, S., & Black, R. B. (1984). *Social work and genetics: A guide for practice.* New York: Haworth.

Select Panel for the Promotion of Child Health. (1981). *Better health for our children:*

A national strategy, 1. Washington, DC: U.S. Department of Health and Human Services.

Weiss, J. O. (1981). Psychosocial stress in genetic disorders: A guide for social workers. *Social Work in Health Care, 6*(4), 17–31.

Weiss, J. O. (1992). Support groups for patients with genetic disorders and their families. *Pediatric Clinics of North America, 39*(1), 13–23.

Weiss, J. O., & Volner, M. W. (1992). *Genetic discrimination: A social work alert.* Chevy Chase, MD: Alliance of Genetic Support Groups.

CHAPTER 19

SOME PSYCHOSOCIAL PROBLEMS IN HEMOPHILIA

Alfred H. Katz

Hemophilia is a congenital, chronic illness, about which relatively little is known although it affects some 40,000 persons in the United States.[1] The medical problems it presents are far better understood than are its psychosocial aspects. The latter have received little attention in this country except for an early paper by Cohen and Herrman and a fragmentary outline for psychiatric research by Poinsard.[2] This discussion is an attempt, based on some years of association with the problems of hemophiliacs, to sketch some of these psychosocial factors, since social workers may encounter persons with this illness in the course of their work.

Hemophilia is a hereditary ailment characterized by excessive bleeding. It is not yet subject to cure, but in the past two decades various therapeutic advances have been made in the direction of stopping or controlling hemorrhaging and in the management of some resultant problems. Genetically, hemophilia is the product of a sex-linked recessive gene which is transmitted by females, but which primarily affects males. It also occurs, but quite rarely, as a result of genetic mutation. In recent years a number of related "bleeding disorders" have been found, which are milder in symptomatology than classical hemophilia, and which can be differentially diagnosed by refined laboratory procedures.

The severity of hemophilia varies from individual to individual although, generally speaking, severity remains comparatively stable among afflicted members of the same

Reprinted from *Social Casework,* Vol. 40 (June 1959), pp. 321–326, by permission of the publisher, Families International, Inc.

[1] Although the figures regarding the incidence and prevalence of hemophilia vary and are not definitive, this figure, given by Dr. Armand J. Quick of Marquette University, is the most commonly accepted estimate.

[2] Ethel Cohen and R. L. Herrman, "Social Adjustment of Six Patients with Hemophilia," *Pediatrics*, Vol. III (1949), pp. 588–596. Paul Poinsard, M.D., "Psychiatric Aspects of Hemophilia," in *Hemophilia and Hemophiloid Diseases,* Brinkhous, ed., University of North Carolina Press, Chapel Hill, 1957.

family. Some physicians (and patients) believe that there is a cyclical or seasonal variation in the onset and severity of bleeding episodes. Others believe that there is no such seasonal change, but that with maturation the affected individual learns to take better care of himself and is therefore less prone to situations where bleeding may be touched off.

With the introduction in the past twenty years of methods of banking blood, and particularly with the development of methods of processing human plasma through freezing or lyophilization, the treatment of hemorrhages has been greatly facilitated and the mortality rate among hemophiliacs has declined sharply. Owing to the volatility of the coagulative factor, the hemophiliac requires transfusions of blood or blood derivatives that have been freshly prepared, if the bleeding is to be stopped.

Although hemophilia is comparatively rare, it poses such severe problems of medical management and of psychosocial stress to the patient and his family that it must be considered a serious health problem for those affected and for the community. Not only does the moderately-to-severely affected individual have frequent, and at times almost uncontrollable, bleeding from external abrasions and sites, but even more serious forms of internal bleeding can occur from no apparent cause. Such bleeding episodes may be extremely painful, and often result in orthopedic problems. Hemophilic arthropathy, as it is termed, arises from such repeated bleedings into joint spaces. Orthopedic abnormalities and permanent damage to muscles and joints can occur from this type of bleeding. The approach of orthopedists and psychiatrists to appropriate measures of therapy and correction for such problems still varies considerably, and much of the therapeutic work that is being done is on an experimental basis.

SOCIAL PROBLEMS AND HEMOPHILIA

From this brief review of medical problems it can be understood that, both for patients and for their families, hemophilia reproduces many or most of the psychosocial problems of other forms of congenital chronic illness but with some added special features. Prominent among the latter are the extreme feelings of distress, guilt, and self-reproach experienced by the parents of newly diagnosed sufferers, especially by the approximately 50 per cent who are unable to trace a history of hemophilia in their families, but who are suddenly confronted with a child bearing this "hereditary taint," who forever after needs special care.

The protective care of the hemophilic infant and young child has to be extremely thorough to prevent the trauma that can result from normal childish exploration of the environment—crawling, body contact with furniture and floor, sharp-edged toys, and so forth. From a tender age the hemophilic infant must be protected from the more strenuous forms of physical contact with playmates and play objects; at the same time normal curiosity, growth, and socialization have to be fostered through stimulation by other means. *Thus the most general and pervasive psychosocial problem for these parents is to give their child physical protection and, at the same time, avoid making him overdependent and eventually a psychological invalid.* This all-pervading problem imposes tremendous burdens on the self-restraint and psychological maturity of the parents, siblings, and others in the hemophiliac's immediate environment. When he reaches school age, these problems are aggravated. The necessity of reaching a viable balance, of treading the narrow line between physical protection and psychological overprotection now involves teachers, playmates, and others in the child's environment.

The possibility of danger to the child is aggravated by the fact that frequently the young hemophiliac offers no external physical signs of his condition and thus appears to other children to be completely normal. Perhaps because of the difficulty of limiting the child's physical activity at this time, the school years are often the period of most frequent occurrence of hemorrhagic episodes. It is common for hemophiliacs to miss many weeks of the school term as a result of requiring rest and immobilization after, or between, periods of hemorrhage. Repeated bleeding can also lead to weakness and anaemia, with their effects on vitality and energy levels. The loss of time in school involves not only possible academic retardation and its important emotional concomitants, but the equally important loss of contacts with other children, of the socializing effects of play, and of the maturational benefits of social activity within a peer group.

It is also clear that if a hemophilic child is born into a family in which other male children are not affected by the disease, he tends to pre-empt major attention in the family, and there is a consequent withdrawal of attention from siblings.

Among the urgent and continuous pressures confronting the parents of a hemophilic child are the threat of being called upon at any moment to secure emergency medical attention for a hemorrhage; the consequent necessity of staying close to sources of such care; and the cost of such attention, not only in relation to the services of a physician, but particularly in relation to the replacement of blood or blood derivatives that may be used in transfusions. On the latter score, in some parts of the United States the American Red Cross does supply blood or blood products for hemophiliacs without requiring replacement by the individual user. In other localities the voluntary organization of hemophiliacs—The Hemophilia Foundation—may assume the responsibility and sometimes can cover the emergent needs of a particular family. Since, however, a hemophiliac may require as many as fifteen to twenty pints of whole blood to meet the exigencies of a single episode—and in the course of a year may require as many as one or two hundred pints of blood—this voluntary organization is usually overwhelmed and cannot meet all the requests. Thus, the drain on the finances and the energies of afflicted families is enormous. In those localities where blood or blood derivatives have to be purchased, the minimum cost to the family is $10 or $12 per unit, exclusive of administration fees. Therefore, the financial drains are constant, chronic, and severe; and these drains have important psychosocial consequences in increasing intrafamilial tensions and in promoting shame, withdrawal, and social isolation tendencies.

Other medical costs result from the frequent hospitalizations that are necessary for hemophiliacs. Although many of these families have hospital insurance, it is not at all uncommon that a hemophiliac will require repeated hospitalizations every few weeks and thus exhaust within a short time the coverage by hospital insurance for the whole year. In some states Crippled Children's programs may carry a portion of the cost of hospitalization, but eligibility for such aid is frequently defined by the state only in relation to the performance of corrective orthopedic procedures and is not available for the simpler procedure of treating a bleeding episode and its sequelae.

Such other emergent costs as those for transportation, ambulances, appliances, and braces for those orthopedically afflicted, and special fees of medical consultants are all constant accompaniments of this condition.

As indicated above, the area of schooling and vocational preparation is a critical one for the hemophilic child. In this regard, parents require much help, counseling, and support in order to understand the importance of maintaining the child's independence, autonomy, and self-reliance insofar as possible, and to handle the child appropriately.

PROBLEMS OF ADULTS

One of the striking observations regarding the hemophiliacs with whom I had contact was of the number of young adults in the group who lacked a stable occupation. When referrals of young men who were mild or even moderate sufferers were accepted by the State Division of Vocational Rehabilitation, the possibilities of their becoming self-maintaining were found to be excellent. However, this resource was little known and not widely utilized by the families of sufferers. It was my experience that social service assistance is rarely sought by or extended to adult patients in hospitals or attending clinics. The hospital social services for hemophiliacs tend to concentrate efforts on the problems of young children, their eligibility for assistance under Crippled Children's programs, and other such tangible services as camp arrangements, which are helpful and which carry a good deal of meaning for parents.

What has been found lacking, however, has been an approach to the hemophiliac through a program of counseling and advisement that would start at an early age, and that would tend to forestall the development of some of the special problems the hemophilic adolescents and young men encounter. The following case example illustrates some of these problems:

Harry B, aged 26, a sufferer from classical hemophilia of moderate severity, had lived in a small suburban community of New York all his life. He was a handsome young man, with no orthopedic involvements; yet he had been in and out of hospitals for years for treatment of hemorrhages and resultant internal complications. Harry was the only hemophiliac in a family of four sons. His father was a retired ship-building worker who received a pension. The three brothers—one younger and two older—worked at manual trades.

Of apparently normal intellectual capacity, Harry had finished two years of high school after an elementary schooling that was irregular owing to his frequent illnesses. He was 19 when he decided that he felt awkward with the younger high school students and simply dropped out. He had had no jobs, but amused himself at home by watching television and playing records. He did not go out socially, but had one close friend, a young man who had taken an interest in him and had attempted to arrange blood donations for him.

Harry played the piano and spoke of wanting to become a musician. He wanted to study at a school where he could learn to make transcriptions for jazz orchestras. He could not, however, afford to attend such a school, and did not know whether, after taking such training, he would be able to get a job in this field.

Harry verbalized his interest in such vocational planning, but had not followed through on suggestions that were made to him of discussing the plan with the State Vocational Rehabilitation Division. This failure to follow through seemed to be a characteristically apathetic approach to his own situation.

It is clear that casework help to Harry and his parents would have had to begin when Harry was much younger if realistic vocational counseling and referral were to take place. In extending casework help to his parents, the caseworker would have had to take into account the special medical and psychological problems experienced by the hemophiliac during various phases of his development. To be helpful, the caseworker would have had to be aware of the very special frustrations and anxieties that both Harry and his parents had encountered. As this case reveals, the caseworker must be particularly aware of the problems associated with the hemophiliac's adolescence. In addition to the maturational stresses of normal adolescence, the hemophiliac experiences growing awareness that he is afflicted with a chronic disease, one that has multiple implications for marriage and parenthood roles and for the highly valued role of worker in our culture.

The adolescent hemophiliac thus may call into question his own adequacy in relation to most of the important adjustment indices in the adult world. Unless he is helped to explore and understand the ramifications of these feelings and reactions by means of a professional relationship, he can easily lose his way, and, like Harry B, retreat into a chronic passive dependency which is not realistically related to his actual medical condition. I found particularly noteworthy the number of such apparently "lost," passively dependent, apathetic, and depressed personalities encountered among young adult hemophiliacs. That I also encountered a relatively small number of comparatively active and outgoing individuals, who had made what seemed to be a good adjustment to their illness and disability, should also be stated. In perhaps a majority of cases there were problems of overdependency and passivity. It should be possible for many hemophiliacs, through skilled casework help, to achieve a better adjustment that will involve coming to terms with limitations in relation to their image of themselves, their possibilities of becoming vocationally active, and their problems of social life.

A readily acceptable focus for such casework help to adolescents and young men would seem to be the area of vocational planning. The possible range of occupations that can be followed by the hemophiliac is limited by several factors: (1) the innate capacities of the individual; (2) the severity and frequency of occurrence of disabling episodes; (3) the presence and degree of correction of orthopedic defect; and (4) the attitudes of potential employers. Within a framework of such limitations, hemophiliacs have been able to function in the professions, in education, small businesses, and clerical occupations. Generally speaking, severe physical exertion is not advised, although one encounters hemophiliacs who are laborers, bus and truck drivers, machinists, and workers in other active trades. Awareness of the many vocational possibilities open to him and of available community resources for helping him secure employment in one of them can be decidedly therapeutic for the young hemophiliac, even without exploration of deeper, underlying feelings.

The problems of social life are also acute for the young adult who suffers from his constant awareness of the implications of his condition for marriage and parenthood. Awareness of such problems frequently imposes a pattern of withdrawal from group or individual relationships, which in turn intensifies his feelings of loneliness, isolation, and depression. Through simple encouragement, some young men have been helped to try, and have found considerable support from, planned participation in social and recreational activities with other handicapped or non-handicapped persons.

PROBLEMS OF FEMALE RELATIVES

One of the most serious areas of conflict is that experienced by the female members of a hemophilic family. Their conflict arises from the fact that they may be carriers of the defective gene, although they are not personally affected by the illness. Genetic data indicate that there is a fifty per cent chance that the daughter of a male hemophiliac will be a carrier of the defective gene. There is a 50 per cent chance that a male child born to a carrier will be a hemophiliac. *All* the daughters of a female carrier of the gene are themselves carriers. Thus, in the well-known instance of Queen Victoria, who was a hemophilic carrier, all her daughters were carriers; they married into the royal houses of Spain, Germany, and Russia, where, among their male children, several hemophiliacs were subsequently found.

There is at present no reliable test which indicates whether or not the daughter of a hemophilic male is herself a carrier of the defective gene.* Researchers are continuing to try to develop such a test but so far without success. In view of this, the psychological situation of the potential carrier is understandable. Attitudes range from shame, and the impulse to conceal the possible hereditary defect, to withdrawal from social contacts and extreme depression. It has been found that the daughters can be helped through professional or lay sources to face realistically the alternatives that confront them. Some daughters of hemophiliacs, for example, have been ready to take a chance on marriage and motherhood; they may rationalize their actions by the belief that, first of all, they have a "fifty-fifty" chance of having a healthy son; or that the care of a hemophilic child is not such a tremendous burden and is to be preferred to childlessness; or they may be convinced that the improvements in therapy developed over recent years, and the prospects of current research, give promise of more effective control or even a cure. Some women have sought to adopt children rather than to risk a perpetuation of the defective gene. Adoption has been arranged, to the writer's knowledge, in several instances, both within and outside the structure of social agency services. It is of interest to note that among hemophilic families known to me, there are several with two or more affected sons, and that such multiple-sufferer families are found in religious groups that do not have prohibitions against birth control practices.

Editor's Note: This article was published in 1959 and does not include recent developments in this research.

THERAPEUTIC ASPECTS OF HELP TO HEMOPHILIACS

Like other groups of the specially disadvantaged and handicapped, hemophiliacs and their families can draw great strength from group associations. In those communities where the voluntary agency concerned with their problems exists, these families have been able to work out generally superior arrangements for blood procurement, medical services, and special schooling. The less tangible advantages of participation in such "self-help" groups are also worth stating. Among these are: (1) overcoming the sense of isolation and overwhelming distress, frequently experienced by parents as a first reaction to the diagnosis of hemophilia; (2) provision of accurate information regarding problems of medical management, child care, blood procurement, and so forth; (3) socialization through contacts and exchange of experience with other families who can contribute to knowledge about developmental phases and problems that can be anticipated; (4) provision of organized or informal opportunities to discuss the parents' fears, frustrations, and satisfactions arising from the particular difficulties of caring for a hemophilic child; (5) opportunity to discuss broader and longer-range problems that can be anticipated on behalf of the child so that planning can be done; (6) possibility of securing through group action better facilities of a therapeutic and educational nature for their children; (7) cathartic effects of such personal participation, which helps to relieve anxieties by channeling them into constructive outlets.

As stressed in the foregoing, it seems to me that casework services are extremely important for both parents and patients, to help forestall and minimize some of the problems that have been described in this article. Such assistance can help to define and resolve for the parents some of the major feelings that may inhibit their handling their child in a way that combines necessary physical protectiveness with maximum psychological self-reliance. Early establishment of a relationship with a caseworker enables the hemophilic youngster to express his own perceptions, fears, anxieties, and wishes about himself, that for one reason or another cannot find adequate expression in his family group. Vocational planning can and should be instituted early in order to assist the hemophiliac to "capitalize his losses" by turning to academic or quiet hobbies, to make up for the fact that he cannot be an active participant in body contact athletics and rough games. Early counseling is particularly imperative for the individual who does not have the intellectual endowment suitable for pursuing academic courses of study, in order to steer him to an appropriate and consistently pursued course of preparation leading toward ultimate employment.

The older adolescent and the young adult need constant encouragement and opportunity to discuss their personal problems and reactions in other than the emotion-fraught home situation. One way social workers can also help in this area is by arranging special opportunities for group participation in existing social agencies, community centers, and informal clubs. Posing these problems and needs, however, does not answer the question of who in the community, that is to say, what professional group, will take responsibility on behalf of such patients. From my experience with hemophiliacs, I should estimate that not more than 20 per cent of the afflicted families in a large city have had contacts with social agencies. Although individual situations must be dealt with individually, it is apparent that once the definite diagnosis of hemophilia is made, the resultant psychosocial, educational, vocational, and other social problems of a patient and his family are numerous, diverse, long-continuing, and almost uniformly present. It would seem of great benefit, then, to have centers established for information, referral to appropriate resources, and, if possible, direct casework and related services—such as group counseling—that would utilize specific knowledge of the condition and its effects. The hemophilia associations are not yet strong enough nor do they have financial resources sufficient to provide such services, although they recognize the necessity for them. It would thus seem that in this, as in other fields of chronic illness, the community is in need of a new type of casework service, one that offers comprehensive information and knowledge of resources appropriate to meeting the needs of the chronically ill, along with some direct services of both a casework and a group character. The challenge of meeting the needs of the hemophilic patient and his family is a persistent and urgent one for social workers in all settings.

KIDNEY DISORDERS

CHAPTER 20

IMPACT OF KIDNEY DISEASE
ON PATIENT, FAMILY, AND SOCIETY

Kathleen M. Hickey

The National Kidney Foundation estimates that over seven million Americans now suffer disease of the kidney. More than 125,000 people in the United States die from kidney disease each year. If transplantable kidneys were available, seven thousand of these persons could be saved.

The long periods of chronic illness, repeated hospitalizations, and the overwhelming amount of stress placed on patients and families have implications for social work. It is the purpose of this article to provide information about kidney disease and methods of treatment and to point out some of the social problems in order that social workers might be better prepared to assist clients with kidney disease. The material in this article is drawn from experience at the Kidney Transplant Service of the University of Minnesota Hospitals, a teaching facility of 826 beds, with 125,000 outpatient visits each year. The Kidney Unit has 25 hospital beds and 220 patients attending the Transplant Out-Patient Clinic.

The person who is faced with the loss of kidney function manifests a state of crisis. Permanent kidney failure formerly resulted in death; choices today are limited to implantation of another person's kidney, kidney dialysis, or death. Two methods of treatment offer a chance for life—hemodialysis (use of artificial kidney machine) and kidney transplantation.

Hemodialysis has shown itself to be a feasible means of prolonging the lives of people with permanent kidney failure. The treatment procedure involves implantation of tubes (cannulas) into the arm or leg of a patient. The cannulas are inserted into the artery and vein and are connected by a shunt that lets the blood flow from one cannula to the other between treatments. When a patient comes in for treatments, the cannulas

Reprinted from *Social Casework*, Vol. 3 (July 1972), pp. 391–398, by permission of the publisher, Families International, Inc.

are connected to tubes leading to the artificial kidney machine that removes the impurities from the blood. The patient must spend several hours lying in bed attached to the machine, as a dialysis may take from four to twelve hours and is required two or three times a week.

Kidney transplantation, which involves grafting of an organ from one individual to another of the same species (homograft), has now advanced to the stage in which it is the treatment of choice for persons with permanent renal failure. Successful transplantation removes the patient from the "sick role"; dialysis does not. He feels better, sources of stress are lessened, and he is able to assume a functioning role. The aim of transplantation is to restore the individual to a normal functioning life.

Physicians have intensified research and study on kidney transplantation as a method of treatment for several reasons. (1) Deaths were numerous among young people; (2) kidney transplantation is technically the easiest method to perform; and (3) the kidney is the only vital paired organ of which a human being can lose one and still survive well. Also, if the body does reject the new kidney, the patient can be maintained on the artificial kidney machine. It is anticipated that improved immuno-suppressive drug therapy, organ preservation, and more accurate tissue typing will, within the next few years, greatly reduce rejection reactions and increase the chances of longer life.

The University of Minnesota Hospitals has a liberal admission policy. Although a patient must meet certain medical criteria, social and economic factors do not play roles in a patient's acceptance. Patients also do not have to be state residents. Those rejected by other centers and those with disease or complications, such as diabetes, are accepted. Because of these factors, social problems are perhaps more prevalent and severe.

In 1971, eighty patients received kidney transplants; of this number, sixty-three were adults, and seventeen were children under sixteen years of age. Of the group, thirty-four received cadaver (deceased, nonrelated donor) transplants. All the children and twenty-nine of the sixty-three adults received kidneys from blood-related donors. When a patient receives a kidney of a related donor, his chances for survival with a functioning kidney are much greater.

Surgical illness is a "human experience" and produces new adaptations that may or may not be pathological. The dramatic character of transplantation surgery diverts attention from social problems inherent in the medical procedures, such as failure of the operation to meet expectations of the patient and family, disruption of family equilibrium, and investment of public funds to meet these costs. Renal failure and transplantation precipitate a crisis that may be defined differently by the patient and family. The crisis situation may mobilize or it may incapacitate them.

The discussion that follows will be based on the experiences of the social worker assigned to the Kidney Transplant Unit. The social worker assists the staff by obtaining detailed information in the form of social histories concerned with the impact of the disease on the patient and his family. The major functions of the social worker are to help the patient face his current environment and work through his feelings, fears, and attitudes and to help him strive toward a realistic adjustment and plan for his future life after discharge. The social worker explores the interaction and dynamics of members of a family—their attitudes, ways of communicating, and patterns of coping. Adherence to the patterns of a past life is not always indicative of the future but may identify specific problem areas. The focus is on helping families retain their integrity and functions.

The social work role varies with each patient. It consists of (1) helping the individual to understand the extensive treatment plan, (2) counseling with the patient and family in working out acceptance of the medical problem and methods of modifying some of its aspects by exploring ways for more satisfying relationships, (3) assessing readiness for acceptance of help from community and similar resources, (4) acting as a resource person and liaison with community agencies, (5) providing casework services to assist the patient and family, and (6) offering public education.

In order to coordinate information to assist the physician so that the patient can receive maximum benefit of treatment at University Hospitals, the "Hospital Team Conference" was initiated and is concerned with a comprehensive program for total care. The team attempts to alleviate forces that interfere with the patient's ability to receive and accept medical care. There is also considerable interaction and intense involvement among patients and between patients and staff. Social systems that characterize hierarchy among the patients are evident. Codes and rules are established and patients redefine these roles and set up new expectations and responsibilities of which the staff must be aware in order to meet the needs. A therapeutic environment is encouraged by the staff through team conferences, physical therapy, occupational therapy, and diversional activities.

THE CHRONICALLY ILL PATIENT AND HEMODIALYSIS

Hemodialysis prolongs the life of patients by the use of the "artificial kidney." Patients unable to receive a kidney transplant, those awaiting a cadaver donor, and patients who have had rejected transplants are maintained on dialysis. The treatment procedure can return a patient to a reasonably normal existence but presents some physical side effects and psychological complications. Although hemodialysis alleviates the uremic syndrome and the patient generally feels better, there are diet restrictions, problems with blood pressure, feelings of weakness, impotence, periodic hospitalizations, and shunt complications (clotting), any of which may prevent participation in living activities. Most patients experience some degree of apprehension before dialysis and tend to become most anxious at the beginning and end of the treatment when the shunt is disengaged or when technical difficulties arise. Attention span is often short, and it has been noted that some patients defend themselves against their anxiety by intellectualization or through sleep. Dialysis can be a frightening experience as a patient is able to observe his blood leaving and returning to his body. He may experience various degrees of fantasies and distorted body imagery, and he may view himself as not wholly human. The dialysis technician and nurse, who are particularly close to the patient, must deal realistically with the patient's anxieties concerning the machine. After dialysis, temporary weakness and nausea from salt and water loss is present; this weakness is often accompanied by lethargy.

Thus, hemodialysis does not completely alleviate difficulties of renal failure, and patients may be faced with a future of chronic illness. Patients, however, may function adequately in the "sick role." The passive dependent person probably will make an adjustment to dialysis but may have difficulties in long-term adjustment after a success-ful transplant. Patients on dialysis are also placed in a dependent situation and may never accept the shunt as an integral part of themselves. The cannula is a constant re-minder of their condition and dependence on the dialyzer. A state of mental depression is not uncommon and follows the general grieving sequence of stages. At first patients tend to use denial; then they go through a period of grief and mourning, followed by anger and frustration, which may give way to depression or regression. Then construc-tive attempts are made to adjust to the illness and treatment plans. (A temporary de-pressive phase is also noted immediately following transplant.)

It is not uncommon for the patient on dialysis to violate a dietary or fluid restriction. Patients are carefully taught about permitted and forbidden food and its significance in relation to their illness and life. Nevertheless, patients frequently refuse to eat desig-nated foods, request foods they know they are not allowed, or eat in the hospital can-teen. Food can assume great importance for the patient under stress. The traditional methods for relieving anxiety and tension, other than food, are often not permitted for the dialysis patient. He may be advised to stop smoking or restrict alcoholic and fluid intake. He may not be allowed lengthy trips or participation in rigorous activity. These prohibitions may result in hostile feelings, and the patient may attempt to use his diet to control his situation, seek gratification, and release his stress. Another form of behavior that might be interpreted as an act of resentment, denial of illness, or desire for self-harm is the patient's neglecting to take care of his shunt.

Long-term dialysis requires sacrifices on the part of the patient and his family be-cause of the special requirements and frequent trips to the hospital for dialysis. The pa-tient and family members may resent this intrusion on family life and display open hostility and guilt, often directed at the staff. The patient's self-image and role can change greatly during this period.

The time of dialysis (day or night) and the distance to the center are important fac-tors in the patient's total rehabilitation and his ability to be gainfully employed or per-form household duties. Thus, chronic hemodialysis has a profound psychological impact on the patient and his family.

THE TRANSPLANT PATIENT AND HIS FAMILY

The transplant patient must plan to remain under medical supervision for an indefinite length of time. The prospect of transplantation presents freedom from pain and pro-vides an opportunity to engage in meaningful activity. Conflict may arise between the patient and family. The patient may feel more threatened by new independency in as-suming the "healthy role" than by facing death. The choice of a kidney donor requires family decisions that can produce a high degree of stress. This decision-making crisis in kidney transplantation is unique; all the members of the family know that one could be saved by the sacrifice of another. The act of donation may be inconsistent with other life patterns and may not follow a rational decision-making process. Man is used to identifying with a model, and the lack of norms and customs to use as guidelines would appear to cause a great amount of tension and stress. The patient knows that if he receives a kidney from a family member, his chances for survival are twice as good as they would be from a cadaver kidney. Reactions to receiving a cadaver kidney have been studied extensively; however, from observation, attitudes vary from curiosity about the person who donated and how his death occurred to indifference and relief that the patient does not have to be concerned about family responsibilities or obligations to the donor. Some relatives reveal a sense of grief about the inability of the family members to contribute toward saving the patient's life. The attitude regarding the donated cadaver organ seems to differ between recipient families and donor families, the latter probably viewing donation as a gift and sacrifice.

The length of the interval between the first knowledge that a transplant is needed and the time of the surgery influences psychological attitudes. The patient exhibits various degrees of psychological decompensation pertaining to the donated kidney, based on intrafamilial relationships and personality makeup. Particularly if the recipient is an adult, he will look beyond his immediate family for a potential donor. Role obligations for family members (siblings, aunts, or other close relatives) are unclear in our culture with the possible exception of parents' donation to children. Parents who donate seem to feel that their donation is not so spectacular or extraordinary but something natural to do for their child. Siblings appear unclear about this obligation to donate a kidney. Realistically, the donation of a kidney would cause the donor discomfort, loss of work time, and a small risk of kidney loss for himself later in life. Some families are subjected to many pressures, and the decision to donate a kidney may be a very stressful process. Many of the patients do not approach the entire family but request another member to do so, and this member may play a key role in the recruiting of donors. The patient usually has a good idea if a family member will not volunteer because of ambivalent family relationships; he accepts this fact and is satisfied to wait for a cadaver donor. However, in less close relationships, decision making can be very difficult. Studies are currently being conducted by Dr. Roberta Simmons of the Sociology Department at the University of Minnesota on the nature of this crisis, focusing on the extended family and on the relative who does not donate a kidney. It has been observed that some relative donors, however, may question their responsibility for the recipient's life; likewise, the recipient may feel threatened in taking the kidney. There is also some indication of feelings of greatness versus hypochondrism on the part of the recipient and donor. In general, donors postoperatively display pride and increased self-esteem and handle their emotions and physical discomfort well.

Patients, both adult and child, become quite sophisticated and knowledgeable about their medical conditions. The patient takes an active part in his treatment program and is able to understand and speak the medical terminology. He learns about the detailed functions of the kidney and about the complex medications and their purposes. "Dialysis and transplantation" are explained thoroughly to him. The kidney disease patient understands his medical diagnosis and prognosis and the reasons for this renal failure in more detail than do most chronically ill patients. The medications given after transplant are essential for the life of the new kidney and the patient's life. The patient knows this and must accept the medications, which may produce observable side effects and impose psychological implications. The first year posttransplant is probably most crucial; problems such as rejection of the organ will most likely occur during this time period. Thus, even after discharge from the hospital, patients often must be readmitted for rejection episodes. This threat, which continues to cause work and home disruptions, adds to the patient's fears.

The high level of emotional involvement in regard to the donation and possible rejection of the new kidney may arouse great anxiety, grief, and disruption of family equilibrium. Rejection of a transplanted kidney produces changes in relationships and a breakdown in defenses. Changes in roles in the patient's total life situation may be consequences of chronic illness or kidney rejection. Successful transplantation, however, also may produce new life situations and adaptations that do not automatically insure total social and psychological rehabilitation.

The changes in total life situation and attitudes of the transplant recipient may, for example, influence women to change their attitudes in regard to childbearing as against adoption of a child. Marital and sexual relations that have been altered drastically because of the patient's uremic condition during dialysis treatment may make the posttransplant adjustments difficult. Employment retraining may be indicated. Conflicts or problems existing prior to transplantation, on the other hand, may be resolved following a successful transplant.

Teen-agers who receive a transplant have special problems. Absences from school, loss of friends, and conflicts in regard to sex and dating appear to be common. The adolescent is apt to find his body image and identity more of a problem than he can handle.

The social problems a child with kidney disease faces differ from those of the adult. His lack of knowledge and immaturity make the medical treatment plan less well understood and more frightening. Often the child's personality is formed during lengthy and recurrent hospitalizations. The parents' fears and concerns and the limitations of the illness influence the child's development.

Children frequently identify very strongly with a kidney that has been received from a parent donor. For example, a thirteen-year-old boy who received a kidney from his father stated, "I have the only kidney for a boy my age that flew forty missions over Germany."

The parents of a child who has a successful kidney transplant must learn a whole set of new adjustments. Their general concerns and overprotection must be modified to enhance the child's normal development. Siblings who have had competitive feelings and resentment because of special favors and privileges accorded the ill child may add to the difficult readjustment of parents and patient. At times, even the marriage itself must be rebuilt and the entire family relationships recast, requiring assessment, time, and work. Most families need the services of a caseworker during this process.

The social workers in hospitals need to be sensitive to the reactions of patients and relatives so that they can provide guidance and support when needed. During the patient's hospital course, he usually seeks out other patients and compares progress. Strong friendships may form, offering each other a great deal of support. On the other hand, inaccurate information is often exchanged. Relatives, too, may misinterpret another patient's medical status and assume that the same fate is in store for their relative. When a patient becomes acutely ill or dies, the other patients generally become agitated, withdrawn, and depressed; feeling tones are easily picked up and transferred one to another and should be discussed. Because of the critical nature of the illness, the social worker must be able to understand and recognize his own feelings about death and have substantial medical knowledge so that he can empathize with and relate to all patients' families.

FINANCIAL COSTS AND COMMUNITY RESPONSIBILITY

The cost of medical care for kidney transplant patients ranges from $10,000 to $80,000. The average cost at the University Hospitals is approximately $16,000 for total inpatient care exclusive of professional fees. Chronic dialysis treatment may amount to between $5,000 to $15,000 on a yearly basis, whereas it is hoped that transplantation is a one-time expense. Eventually, these costs will decrease because of shorter hospital stays and medical advances. The principal sources of financial help at the present time are private insurance, federal research grants, and public welfare programs. Thus, the financial costs entailed by chronic hemodialysis and transplantation impose a problem for the patient, his family, and society. Loss of economic, social, or personal status can become a serious problem and can greatly affect the patient's adjustments and capacity to function. Economic variables directly influence family attitudes as do those of culture, religion, sex, age, and length of illness.

The middle-class patient, who may have insurance coverage and a fairly adequate and stable salary prior to hospitalization, may be required, when his insurance coverage is less than his expenses, to apply for welfare assistance—a plan difficult for many to accept. Furthermore, because they own property and have financial assets, many are ineligible for public assistance until legal income requirements are met. The tragedy is compounded for farm patients who are faced with the necessity of selling their land and sacrificing their livelihood and financial independence. For patients residing outside the metropolitan area, there is the additional financial strain of transportation and maintenance costs. Most welfare departments and communities are not able to authorize funds to meet these expenses.

Major financing for the medical expenses of these patients comes from public funds under Title XIX of the Social Security Act. The provisions of the act make it possible to provide complete care for these patients. However, state plans, the interpretation of the act, and procedures by local community agencies impose limitations that create difficulties. The large amount of money required to provide medical care for patients who have severe renal disease, moreover, may be more than a community considers justifiable for one individual. The alternatives are for those in medical practice to refine technical methods to reduce costs and for the federal government to grant financial assistance to institutions involved in development of new methods of medical care. Kidney disease is a major community health problem and thus has serious implications for every community whose social agencies cannot offer constructive services to help these patients.

Among men and women under twenty-five, kidney diseases are the second highest cause of work loss in the United States today. From age twenty-five on, these kidney-related diseases are the fourth highest cause of work loss. The Kidney Foundation, the only major voluntary agency relating itself to the total problem, states that one of every twenty-five persons in any community suffers from some form of kidney disease. Thus, in order for the patient to receive maximum benefit from medical care, his financial, social, and psychological needs must also be met by the community and society.

EMPLOYMENT

Generally, when the patient who has had a successful kidney transplant is ready for discharge from the hospital, he has no vocational restrictions imposed upon him. Ideally, the patient can return to his former job. Realistically, however, his former job may not be available. The prolonged treatment and hospitalization, the financial costs, complexity of medications, periodic checkups at the hospital, and drastic changes in the patient's life situation may have interfered with work performance and resulted in loss of his job. Overprotection is often manifested by family members; it impedes the patient's return to work and independency and interferes with his rehabilitation. Patients, too, fear that harm may come to the new kidney if they engage in strenuous work or extracurricular school activities. Because the majority of patients receive Social Security Disability or county assistance, it is difficult for them to relinquish this aid until they are secure in a new job. Employers hesitate to hire persons who receive Social Security Disability. Many employers do not understand the nature of kidney transplants and do not wish to risk employing someone who might be readmitted to a hospital at any time. Thus, patients may be rejected because they have received an organ transplant. The primary reason generally given is the restrictions imposed by insurance and union policies of large companies.

Physical side effects produced by medication, such as cushioned face, may also prevent patients from seeking the type of employment they want or from resuming past activities. Family relationships and support are important in determining the patient's successful rehabilitation and his return to a level of activity that is equal to, or surpasses, the level prior to the onset of kidney disease.

Vocational rehabilitation and counseling services should be enlisted prior to the patient's discharge from the hospital. Studies focused on defining "rehabilitation" and "adjustment" pretransplant and posttransplant would be useful with the recognition that definitions vary. The mere fact that a person has returned to work following transplantation does not automatically conclude that he is "rehabilitated." The quality of the individual's functioning must be explored. When the gainful employment he has returned to is satisfying to him and to his needs, employment can be used as an indicative factor of rehabilitation.

MORAL AND ETHICAL ASPECTS OF TRANSPLANTATION

Transplantation of human organs is a new era in medical history. The availability of new surgical techniques that prolong and save the lives of thousands of individuals makes it necessary to examine current beliefs concerning the use of organs from the bodies of other people. There are fears within the population regarding the donation of organs, as evidenced by the customs and the mass media. The value of the body, fear of mutilation, sickness, and future health are all considerations and should be correlated with religious beliefs, socioeconomic status, sex, age, race, and culture.

The development of living organ banks is an attempt to institutionalize societal fears. The signing of a donor card may represent a wholesome impersonal aspect, although it is questionable whether people view this action realistically or view it as socially desirable. In the past it has been thought that people who sign cards donating vital organs to a medical center to be used for others are from the better educated, higher socioeconomic groups and view this act as humanitarian. Recent studies, however, indicate that people in the lower socioeconomic groups also wish to make a donation of parts of their body—possibly as a contribution to society or from religious motivation.

The use of organs from the body of a healthy, functioning individual raises moral questions. The extent to which one individual may impose on another is an ethical consideration. The rights of people to safeguard their own bodies can never be denied. In some of these instances the moral and family pressures on donors impose obligations that deny this right.

Another ethical aspect of the procurement of organs involves the purchase of organs for transplants when immunological techniques are perfected. More organs would then be available on a case-negotiation basis. Because American culture is based on paying for what one receives, this action might not be disturbing to the population. If purchase of organs were authorized, the use of family and cadaver donors would be less of a necessity. However, purchase of organs raises the difficulty of determining price. A high price for organs would certainly discriminate against the poor. The selling of organs might also be interpreted as a partially suicidal gesture. Through laws, it is likely that attitudes and customs regarding transplantation and donation may change, and donation may come to be viewed as a social obligation rather than as a gift or sacrifice.

At the University of Minnesota Hospitals the criteria used for selection of people to receive a renal transplant or to be maintained by hemodialysis are based primarily on medical decisions. As yet, the quality of life the patient will be able to lead or the contributions he can make cannot be determined or defined without enlisting value judgments. Transplantation provides a "potential" life with a new organ. The moral issue is, "Are we doing what we are supposed to do?" Focusing on the quality of life and on transplantation and developing ways of improving present situations are needed.

Other questions raised pertaining to the moral and ethical aspects of transplantation might include the high costs of maintaining dialysis and transplant units of equipment and of training of specialized personnel. People undoubtedly will question the future of transplantation and the possible creation of genetic pools. There are also ambiguities concerning whether to view transplantation as research or treatment, thereby affecting the cost-benefit ratio.

Technical problems of transplantation are now being surmounted and the risk of death reduced. Perhaps we should also look at what technology has not accomplished. Technology may change or eliminate some of the forementioned problems. For example, selection criteria may never have to be defined if the use of mechanical or animal organs replaces the use of human organs in transplantation.

Kidney transplants are successful and are becoming a socially approved procedure. Society lags behind the technological aspects of transplantation, and we must prepare ourselves to meet the psychological and social needs imposed by transplantation in order for these members of society to return to a functional life. The social worker, who has direct contact with the patients, staff, and community agencies, has a professional obligation to transmit accurate information to the public and inform agencies of the needs of certain groups of people in an attempt to establish new resources or change existing attitudes and conceptions.

CONCLUSIONS

Social factors are being recognized as important components of kidney disease. Extreme importance is attached to the period following acute illness when the patient regains his health. The patient's attitudes toward kidney disease range from acceptance, resentment, and feelings of inadequacy to withdrawal and exclusiveness. Attitudes of the family members can result in increased dependency, overprotection, and unwanted sympathy. The patient who returns to the community sometimes needs complete economic and social rehabilitation, or he may undergo only relatively minor adjustments. The psychological manifestations are manifold, especially in patients and families when transplantation has failed. The threat or fear of rejection and the high degree of emotional involvement can prevent the patient from resuming his normal life.

In describing some instances of family conflict, decision making, stress, and the impact of kidney disease on the patient, on his family, and on our society, is not intended to imply that the information presented is valid for all potential transplant candidates. In many instances, dialysis, donation, and transplantation run a fairly smooth course and only minimal amounts of rehabilitation are required in order for the patient to resume a fully functioning life.

A program of early social evaluation in the course of the illness should be designed to detect patients whose defenses and coping patterns seem ineffective. The degree of personality disintegration that may accompany organ transplantation has made it evident to medical personnel that a more comprehensive program must be developed to meet the total needs of these patients.

This is a new era in medical history, which offers an opportunity for health to thousands of people with kidney disease. The social worker has an essential contribution to make to the total treatment plan. The new developments present a challenge to social workers to use their skill and knowledge to assist patients to obtain the greatest benefits from medical care and to participate in the healthful living that new treatments promise.

CHAPTER 21

GROUP WORK INTERVENTION WITH A MULTIPLE SCLEROSIS POPULATION

Gary John Welch and Kathleen Steven

For several decades we have seen the development of parallel movements in group rehabilitation care: a professional care approach utilizing techniques of counseling and psychotherapy, and a self-help approach. While there is a wealth of information available concerning the theory and practice of group methods to promote personal and interpersonal change (e.g., Cartwright & Zander, 1968; Ohlsen, 1970; Shaffer & Galinsky, 1974; Yalom, 1975), little attention has been focused on the use of group methods to meet the specific needs of disabled individuals. The nature of the self-help process has likewise been discussed at length (e.g., Grosz, 1972, 1973; Hurvib, 1970; Jacques, 1972; Jacques & Perry, 1974; Katz, 1965, 1967, 1970; Mowrer, 1972; Reisman, 1965; Wechsler, 1960; Wright, 1971; Yalom, 1970), but there has been little attempt to provide a bridge between the professional care and self-help models.

In the current study the two approaches are combined in that a self-help organization for individuals with Multiple Sclerosis requested professional guidance in the supervision of a therapy group for its members. The intervention program described below was developed in response to that request. The organization's leadership had identified the problem areas among group members: self-imposed social isolation, negative self-image, and stressed family relationships. The intervention program was formulated within the context of the organization and its operating philosophy, that of self-help and mutual aid.

Prior to discussing the group members and the intervention setting, it is important to discuss how the term 'self-help group' is being employed in the current study. Tracy and Gussow (1976) note that there are two basic types of self-help groups: groups that are truly mutual-help associations (e.g., Emphysema Anonymous, Mending Hearts,

Reprinted from *Social Work with Groups*, Vol. 2, No. 3 (1979), pp. 221–234, with permission of the Haworth Press.

Reach to Recovery, A.A.) and groups that are more foundation-oriented with the emphasis on promoting biomedical research, fund raising, public education, and legislation (e.g., The National Heart Association, American Diabetes Association, The Muscular Dystrophy Association). The self-help group in the current study is of the first type of self-help group. The organization was not affiliated with the National Multiple Sclerosis organization and was therefore dependent on local support for funding and operational assistance.

The core members of the treatment group included nine Multiple Sclerosis victims (five female, four male). Three individuals were chair bound and six were to some extent ambulatory. Ages ranged from mid-20s to late 40s. In addition to the regular group members, parents, spouses, and other interested parties attended intermittently. The average group attendance was 15 individuals. The setting for the group was the self-help organization's small offices. The meeting area was cramped and attendance was often limited due to lack of space.

In addition to the problem areas identified by the organization's leader, mentioned above, the professionals identified deficits in the areas of self-management skills and assertiveness as major problem areas for Multiple Sclerosis victims. Multiple Sclerosis is rarely fatal, but is usually a progressively disabling disease. It is one of the most common organic diseases affecting the nervous system and disables primarily by interfering with motor activities. Multiple Sclerosis almost invariably strikes individuals between the ages of 20 and 40. As there is no known cure for Multiple Sclerosis, individuals are left to reconcile themselves to the illness and learn to cope with its numerous and varied effects. The intervention program described below combines cognitive restructuring, modeling and behavior rehearsal, homework assignments, the presentation of didactic material, and group process in an attempt to overcome the deficits identified above.

METHOD

Group sessions were conducted weekly for 10 weeks, two hours per meeting, with each successive session devoted to a new topic. Topics were either leader or group member generated. The specific format of individual sessions varied depending upon content and purpose; however, a general procedure was followed weekly.

Each session began with a 30 to 45 minute didactic introduction to the content area under consideration. Content was presented by group leaders, guest speakers, or group participants. Identified were common dilemmas in the content areas, factors potentially influencing individual adjustment, and new ways of coping with the experience of a progressive debilitating disease. After the content was presented, the remainder of the group time was devoted to group discussion, problem-solving, modeling, and role rehearsal. As an example of didactic content and homework assignments an outline of weeks four and five is presented in Table 21–1.

Table 21–1
A Two-Week Sample Outline of Group Meeting Content and Homework Assignments

Week 4

Content Areas:

1. A physical therapist discussed and demonstrated a program of exercises for M.S. patients. The exercises were tailored to the needs of specific members.
2. There was a discussion of how to incorporate appropriate exercises into individual group members' daily routine.
3. Participants presented the previous week's homework assignments.

Homework Assignment:

Each group member was asked to select two or three of the exercises appropriate for his/her specific condition and incorporate them into their daily routine. He/she was to record (mentally note, write down, or have someone else record) the exercise, when and how often it was performed, and to list any noticeable effects or problems.

Week 5

Content Areas:

1. Discussion and review of last week's homework assignment.
2. A didactic presentation was given on various relaxation techniques using imagery, diaphragmatic breathing, and self-hypnosis as a possible means of pain and anxiety control.
3. Group practice of several specific exercises was undertaken, and was followed by a discussion of their potential usefulness for individual group members.

Homework Assignment:

1. Each group was asked to select one of the relaxation exercises and apply it when he/she became aware of the onset of anxiety, tension, or pain. Group members were asked to record the results of both their ability to recognize the onset of the above and the impact of relaxation.
2. An ongoing concern of group members was the lack of public acceptance of M.S. victims and the resulting lack of recognition and support for their organization. As a result of this concern, individuals with particular abilities were given individual homework assignments to facilitate the group goal of greater public acceptance and support (e.g., one individual volunteered to write a short speech which could be presented by group members to civic and religious organizations; others agreed to contact individuals in the media in an effort to educate the public regarding the organization).

INTERVENTION PROCEDURES

Group Process. Attention is given below to the intervention procedures implemented in the treatment program. The procedures are outlined and presented as if somehow operating in a state of mutual exclusion. This is due to the limits of written expression and for the benefit of clarity. In practice there is interaction among the intervention approaches in that affective, cognitive, and behavioral functioning are interrelated and the timing of several intervention procedures coincide.

In addition to the specific intervention procedures discussed below, a major variable influencing outcome may be labeled group process. The following discussion is an attempt to identify some aspects of group process (e.g., the catalytic effect, vicarious learning, and social reinforcement) which are assumed to have contributed to treatment outcomes. First a catalytic effect was observed in the group as individual participants began to share experiences. Consistent with previous research (Jourard, 1971; Kangas, 1971) participant response to self-disclosure was self-disclosure, the consequence of which was the realization of similarity. The sense of being faced with the possibility or certainty of some degree of permanent disability precipitated serious emotional reactions which demanded basic psychological readjustments. Participants realized their commonality with others who, like themselves, were confronted with the pervasive changes and accommodations inherent in attempting such major readjustments. Exposure to other individuals who had coped or were successfully coping with such adjustments functioned to provide positive adaptive models to several group members. For example, a sense of community developed as group members began to verbalize their feelings of alienation and isolation (frequently self-imposed). As specific personal experiences of embarrassment or rejection were shared, members became aware of their similarities and were able to focus their energies on constructive problem-solving.

Second, the Multiple Sclerosis group, with its problem-solving focus and extensive discussion time, was designed to promote vicarious learning. Many group participants maintained strong negative self-evaluations based on changed physical abilities and possible wide mood swings that can accompany Multiple Sclerosis. Personal disclosure by participants who were attempting to continue to live meaningful and full lives offered constructive ways of viewing self in relation to the disease process. The value of attempting to capitalize upon changed physical and non-physical capacities was strongly emphasized. These alternatives were important in motivating participants to take steps in their own behalf. The intervention program was structured so as to provide group members with responsibilities which focused on their capabilities rather than disabilities. Additionally, group members' efforts directly benefited the individual, the group, or the self-help organization which provided direct reinforcement for effort expended. For example, two group members, no longer able to actively practice their professions, wrote newspaper articles intended to provide the public with a more accurate compassionate picture of the Multiple Sclerosis patient. Each of their articles was published in a local newspaper.

Third, participants, as well as group leaders, functioned as social reinforcers for other participants. The group was structured to allow each participant numerous opportunities to receive the attention of others. There were frequent expressions of peer understanding and support. Such expressions were of particular value to Multiple Sclerosis patients engaged in comprehensive change and concomitant self-doubt. The homework assignments were designed and implemented to accomplish these objectives. Time was allotted in each group meeting for individual presentations of the assignment and for group response. For example, in the eighth week group members had been asked to use specific assertive communication skills in an interaction with an authority figure (viz., V.A. or social security personnel, landlords, physician). The following week, each group member shared his experience and received feedback from the group.

Feedback included support for attempts to complete the assignment, suggestions as to alternative approaches, and recognition for "success."

Cognitive Restructuring. Though the adjustment problem presented by Multiple Sclerosis can be severe, many participants exacerbate their situation with irrational, catastrophizing beliefs. A number of authors (e.g., Beck, 1970; Ellis, 1962; Goldfried, Decenteceo, & Weinberg, 1974; Kelly, 1955; Meichenbaum, 1974) have developed therapeutic procedures based on the assumption that behavioral and psychological change can be brought about by modifying an individual's assumptions and expectations about the world around him and his consequent internal verbalizations. The concepts "expectancy" and "assumption" can be translated into what is generally known by experimental investigators as cognitive set. The treatment goals of cognitive restructuring involve the alteration of negative cognitive set, irrational assumptions, and internal verbalizations.

The group leaders employed a modified version of Goldfried and Goldfried's (1975) systematic guidelines for cognitive restructuring. The steps followed included: (1) presenting a rationale; (2) presenting a method for identifying irrational assumptions; (3) self-intervention; and (4) creative problem-solving.

As a framework for cognitive restructuring, the authors utilized Ellis' (1962) Rational-Emotive Therapy (RET). Rational-Emotive Therapy was selected for its practical straightforwardness and its demonstrated efficacy in a number of controlled outcome studies (DiLoreto, 1971; Meichenbaum, 1972; Meichenbaum, Gilmore, & Fedoravicius, 1971; Trexler & Karst, 1972). A short introductory lecture was provided outlining RET's A-B-C method of viewing human psychological functioning and its disturbances. Starting with C (the upsetting emotional consequence, perhaps feelings of worthlessness, anxiety, or depression), and moving to A (the activating experience), group members were shown that between A and C there is the intervening variable which Ellis labels B (the individual's belief system). The belief system may be rational or irrational, but either case provides the basis for the connection between A and C through internal dialogue.

The method for training participants to the identification of irrational assumptions was based upon an analysis of Ellis' (1962) typical irrational beliefs. Understanding these tenets of rational judgement was considered requisite for corrective mediation and resulting behavior change. Group discussion and homework assignments were used to facilitate understanding. Homework involved participants in an attempt to apply the appropriate "rational point" to a current adjustment problem through the device of writing a short essay in which irrational cognitions were actively refuted. (For several Multiple Sclerosis group members it was not possible to write and an alternate assignment involving tape recording the essay was substituted.)

After the groundwork was laid and group members began to understand how irrational internal dialogues precipitated emotional disturbance, the participant could use his emotional reactions as "cues" to consider the question: "What am I telling myself about the situation that might be irrational?" As with any new skill there was an initial period of awkwardness and a pervasive sense of artificiality. With continued practice, however, the new response pattern of rational self-appraisal became habituated.

There are adjustment difficulties which required more than a rational self-appraisal.

To be optimally effective as an intervention technique, cognitive restructuring was combined with the emission of specific behaviors which were incompatible with the irrational belief system. In this treatment program, group members were required to emit behaviors which were incompatible with their sense of isolation, negative self-image, and sense of powerlessness over self and environment (refer to Table 26–1). Some situations required the development of creative solutions to actual problems. In addressing these situations, the current authors adapted a technique employing four sequential steps to provide a learning experience in creative problem-solving. The procedure discussed below was first suggested by Roosa (1973) for application to family therapy. The steps include: (1) the statement of a problem situation in clear, unambiguous language; (2) the suggestion of possible options for solution of the problem; (3) an analysis of possible consequences for each solution; and (4) the simulation of the skills required to put the solution into action. Step 4 was employed only if a skill deficit was evident. These four steps were applied by the group to organizational problems which were of major concern to group members; that is, the lack of effective public relations and lack of funding.

Although the acquisition of problem-solving skills was programmed into the homework assignments, the usefulness of the procedures was occasionally demonstrated in the meetings themselves. A case in point is a disagreement over household responsibilities which erupted between two married group members. The leaders modeled the application of problem-solving skills to a "real" problem. Group members contributed by suggesting possible options and discussing possible consequences of the various options.

Modeling and Behavior Rehearsal. As problems were specified and desirable courses of action identified, participants frequently communicated an inability to perform actions leading to problem solution. To facilitate the participants' incorporation of the desired behavioral action/response, specified behaviors were modeled by the authors assuming the role of the participant whose problem was under consideration. That participant assumed the role of interactor while remaining group members either played significant others in the situation or observed the interaction.

The modeling role playing situation was repeated two or three times. Then the roles were switched to allow the participant an opportunity to begin practicing the desired behavior. As the participant became comfortable with the behavior, other group participants were enlisted in the role of responder. With the instruction of the group leaders, responders presented successively greater demands of skill incorporation on behalf of the participant. This procedure reinforced the participant in his skill development, shaped the participant into more sophisticated skill performance, and supported generalization of the skill.

After completion of behavior rehearsal the participants discussed the anticipated consequences of the newly incorporated skill. Group members provided further reinforcement to the participant in training through positive verbal feedback and encouragement to try the skill in vivo. For example, group members rehearsed various ways of responding to others' perceived negative response (e.g., avoidance, rejection, ridicule) to their illness. Individuals would report to the group their efforts to practice these responses in vivo. These attempts would frequently stimulate others to initiate their own efforts.

Homework Assignments. While skill development and practice are legitimately accomplished in the group, the goal of intervention is the performance of the behavior in its natural context. The promotion of behavior transfer and generalization was accomplished through homework assignments. This procedure has been found to be most efficacious with educational and skill building treatment approaches in which the individual practices new behaviors and attitudes (Shelton & Ackerman, 1974). Consistent with Rose (1974, p. 103), the homework assignments were designed and implemented as follows:

1. Assignments were highly specific. Participants were aware of the exact actions/responses to be displayed, the conditions under which the behaviors were to be performed, and the appropriate alternatives should the appropriate condition fail to occur.
2. Assignments were realistic and supportive of reasonable change. The probability of success was high, and yet the assignments were challenging.
3. Participants made a verbal commitment in the presence of peers to attempt performance of the assignment.
4. Participants reported to the group their attempts to carry out the assignment. Monitoring of the change effort by the group provided an opportunity for positive reinforcement for trying to implement the behavior. This procedure provided an opportunity to evaluate the behavioral response against the reality of natural circumstances. The outcome of such an evaluation at times led to slight modification of the behavioral response. Although modifications were not great, occasionally a reinitiation of behavior rehearsal was indicated. Thus, reporting to the group was an effective way to gain corrective input.

RESULTS AND DISCUSSION

The Multiple Sclerosis group, combining the self-help model with professional supervision, was evaluated based on client satisfaction and completion of homework assignments. Client satisfaction was assessed in the last group meeting during which individual group members were asked to rate the value of the group to them personally along several dimensions from the value of group homework assignments to participant evaluation of group size. As Table 21–2 indicates, all group members highly rated the value of the group experience along all dimensions.

Due to the nature of the group, which was an attempt to combine self-help concepts with the technical expertise of trained therapists, client satisfaction is regarded as the most relevant outcome measure employed. Group members established individual goals, suggested and occasionally provided content, and were generally responsible for the group experience. Under these conditions their satisfaction is of primary importance. The therapist-led self-help group operated on the ideas that both group members and therapist were equal partners in the change effort, and that the value of a particular therapist to the group was a function of the results of therapeutic procedures employed.

Completion of homework assignments was selected as a less subjective outcome

Table 21–2
Client Evaluation of Program Usefulness

Areas Evaluated	Rating By Group Members*					Number Participants
	Not at all Helpful	Not Very Helpful	Neutral	Helpful	Very Helpful	
1. Group Homework Assignments				44%	56%	9
2. Individual Homework Assignments			11%	33%	56%	9
3. The Use of Co-leaders					100%	9
4. The Use of Non-M.S. Leaders				22%	67%	8
5. Presentations by Guest Speakers				11%	89%	9
6. Presentations by Group Members				33%	67%	9
7. Meeting Format				11%	89%	9
8. Involvement of Family Members in Group Activities			22%	33%	44%	9
9. Contributions (input) of Group Leaders				11%	89%	9
10. Contributions (input) of Group Members				11%		9
11. The Size of the Group in Relation to: a. Your willingness to self-disclosure b. Your ability to have input		11% 11%	22%	22% 78%	33% 11%	8 9

*Each group member rated the usefulness of each component of the intervention program. The results indicate the percentage of group members who rated the experience in a particular category.

measure as it was in keeping with the nature of the self-help group that members be actively involved in the process of change for themselves and other group members. Each week group members were given a common homework assignment. Occasionally individual group members were given specific homework assignments in keeping with individual objectives, interests, or capabilities. Combining group and individual assignments, 27 homework assignments were given. Of these, 23, or 85%, of the homework assignments were completed. This result suggests the group was successful in motivating self-help activity.

In addition to the above, several preliminary conclusions have been reached regarding maximizing the efficacy of the professionally guided self-help group approach to intervention with the Multiple Sclerosis population. The opinions expressed here are based upon observation of one group and must, therefore, be regarded as tentative. These early conclusions regarding treatment methodology may function as guidelines for other practitioners contemplating such treatment groups. Furthermore, until such time as data derived from controlled experimental studies is available, the following observations may be of heuristic value.

Problem-solving Focus. Pervasive change is inherent in the process of Multiple Sclerosis. Such change results in problem-solving which is either haphazard or planful, active or passive. With large, time-limited groups it is desirable to train participants in individual problem-solving. Through the problem-solving orientation, the group functioned to provide services to its members. Information regarding social outlets was shared, a network for exchanging self-care information was established, and creative ways of coping with loneliness and uncommitted time were developed. The group created a vital social/interpersonal network for solving special problems.

As specific problems were considered in the group, the expectation was established that most problems are manageable. It was determined from participants through self-report (verbal feedback) that the cognitive restructuring generalized from the exercises in group problem-solving to individual problem-solving outside the group.

Heterogeneous Versus Homogeneous Grouping. The Multiple Sclerosis group was heterogeneous in terms of participant age, time since onset of the disease, and major adjustment problem area. Heterogeneous grouping enabled participants to view problems of Multiple Sclerosis as they might emerge over time and provided exposure to long-term problem-solving. The homogeneity of the group was emphasized through designing the program around several topical areas of adjustment that allowed participants to confront specific problems with others in similar situations. The advantages of heterogeneity and homogeneity were thus combined to serve the objectives of the program.

Use of Co-leaders. While a co-leader is not essential, participants indicated their preference for co-leaders. The presence of two leaders facilitated more specific problem focus and enabled the provision of more individualized attention. Furthermore, there was benefit from the diversity of experience and expertise of each leader.

Group Versus Individual Treatment. For the Multiple Sclerosis victim, the group offers several advantages over individual treatment. First, the group described was designed to emphasize vicarious learning through the provisions of extensive group discussion time. Second, the benefits of peer understanding and support, characteristic of many treatment groups, are particularly valuable to individuals engaged in comprehensive change and concommitant self-doubt that are typical of one in the process of adjusting to Multiple Sclerosis. Third, the group served to motivate individual participants toward productive and regenerative change. As participants report successful resolution of problems, motivation toward individual change was enhanced. Finally, the group facilitated the development of a viable social/interpersonal network for the participants.

REFERENCES

Beck, A. Cognitive therapy: Nature and relation to behavior therapy. *Behavior Therapy,* 1970, *1,*184–200.

Beck, D. F., & Jones, M. A. Progress on family problems: A nationwide study of clients and counselors' view on family agency services. *Family Service Association Census Report,* 1970.

Cartwright, D., & Zander, A. *Group dynamics: Research and theory.* New York: Harper and Row, 1968.

DiLoreto, A. O. *Comparative psychotherapy: An experimental analysis.* Chicago: Aldine-Atherton, 1971.

Ellis, A. *Reason and emotion in psychotherapy.* New York: Lyle Stuart, 1962.

Goldfried, M. R., Decentaceo, E. T., & Weinberg, L. Systematic rational restructuring as a self-control technique. *Behavior Therapy,* 1974, *5,* 247–254.

Goldfried, M. R., & Goldfried, A. P. Cognitive change methods. In F. Kanfer & A. Goldstein (Eds.), *Helping people change.* New York: Pergamon Press Inc., 1975.

Grosz, H. J. *Recovery, Inc., survey: A preliminary report.* Chicago: Recovery, Inc., May 1972.

Grosz, H. J. *Recovery, Inc., survey: Second report.* Chicago: Recovery, Inc., 1973.

Hurvitz, N. Peer self-help psychotherapy groups and the implications for psychotherapy. *Psychotherapy: Theory, research, and practice,* 1970, 7(1), 41–49.

Jacques, M. E. Rehabilitation counseling and support personnel. *Rehabilitation Counseling Bulletin,* 1972, *15* (3), 160–171.

Jacques, M. E., & Perry, J. W. Education in the health and helping professions: Philosophic context, multi-disciplinary team models and cultural components. In J. Hamburg (Ed.), *Review of allied health education,* vol. I. Lexington, Ky: University Press of Kentucky, 1974.

Jourard, S. M. *Self disclosure: An experimental analysis of the transparent self.* New York: John Wiley and Sons, 1971.

Kangas, J. A. Group members' self-disclosure. *Comparative Group Studies,* 1971, *2,* 65–70.

Katz, A. Application of self-help concepts in current social welfare. *Social Work,* 1965, *10* (3), 68–74.

Katz, A. Self-help organizations and volunteer participation in social welfare. *Social Work,* 1970, *15* (1), 51–60.

Katz, A. Self-help in rehabilitation: Some theoretical aspects. *Rehabilitation Literature,* 1967, *28* (1), 10–11, 30.

Kelly, G. A. *The psychology of personal constructs.* New York: Norton, 1955.

Meichenbaum, D. H. *Cognitive behavior modification.* Morristown, N.J.: General Learning Press, 1974.

Meichenbaum, D. H. Cognitive modification of test anxious college students. *Journal of Consulting and Clinical Psychology,* 1972, *39,* 370–380.

Meichenbaum, D. H., Gilmore, J. B., & Fedoravicius, A. Group insight versus desensitization in treating speech anxiety. *Journal of Consulting and Clinical Psychology,* 1971, *36,* 410–421.

Mowrer, O. H. Integrity groups: Basic principles and objectives. *Counseling Psychologist,* 1972, *3* (2), 7–33.

Ohleen, M. *Group counseling.* New York: Holt, Rinehart and Winston, 1970.

Reissman, F. The "helper" therapy principle. *Social Work,* 1965, *10* (2), 27–32.

Roosa, J. B. *Situation, options, consequences, simulation: A technique for teaching social interaction.* Paper presented at the annual meeting of the American Psychological Association, Montreal, Canada, 1973.

Rose, S. D. A behavioral approach to the treatment of parents. In J. Thomas (Ed.), *Behavior modification procedure: A sourcebook.* Chicago: Aldine Publishing Co., 1974.

Shaffer, J., & Galinsky, M. D. *Models of group therapy and sensitivity training.* Englewood Cliffs, N.J.: Prentice-Hall, 1974.

Shelton, J. L., & Ackerman, J. M. *Homework in counseling and psychotherapy.* Springfield, Ill.: Charles C. Thomas, 1974.

Tracy, G., & Gussow, Z. Self-help health groups: A grass roots response to a need for services. *Journal of Applied Behavioral Science,* 1976, *12* (3), 381–397.

Trexler, L. D., & Karst, T. O. Rational-emotive therapy, placebo, and no-treatment effects on public speaking anxiety. *Journal of Abnormal Psychology,* 1972, *79,* 60–67.

Wechsler, H. The self-help organization in the mental health field. Recovery, Inc., a case study. *Journal of Nervous and Mental Disorders,* 1960, *130* (4), 297–314.

Wright, M. E. Self-help groups in the rehabilitation enterprise. *Psychological Aspects of Disability,* 1971, *18* (1), 43–45.

Yalom, I. *The theory and practice of group psychotherapy.* New York: Basic Books, 1970.

Yalom, I. *The theory and practice of group psychotherapy.* New York: Basic Books, 1975.

NEUROLOGICAL DISORDERS

CHAPTER 22

INTERVENTION STRATEGIES TO USE IN COUNSELING FAMILIES OF DEMENTED PATIENTS

Joan Keizer and Linda C. Feins

INTRODUCTION

This paper describes a method of counseling families that combines intervention strategies with assessment techniques during the evaluation procedure for diagnosis of dementia. Various interventions are identified (Table 22–1) and how they are integrated with assessment of the patient and family is described. The list of interventions is not exhaustive but the ones described are those most often used during the evaluation interview at the COPSA (Comprehensive Services on Aging) Institute for Alzheimer's Disease and Related Disorders. Observations used in this paper are based on practice with over 300 patients and families who have been seen at the COPSA Diagnostic Clinic over the last three years. It is not within the scope of the paper to present the family systems theory that forms the matrix for assessment and treatment, but rather, to provide a practical method for employing helping interventions early in the family's contact with the Institute. All families experience problems related to the dementing illness, and the interventions described can provide them an opportunity to change dysfunctional patterns and empower them to cope more effectively with the stresses of caregiving.

Reprinted from *Journal of Gerontological Social Work,* Vol. 17, No. 1/2 (1991), pp. 201–216, by permission of the Haworth Press.

Table 22–1
Interventions

1. Establishing a collaborative relationship	11. Giving suggestions
2. Listening	12. Evaluating the client/family situation
3. Being available	13. Using the genogram to expand context of the illness
4. Normalizing feelings	
5. Validating feelings	14. Using additional family meetings
6. Giving credit to caregivers	15. Interviewing family members separately
7. Educating family members about the illness, about therapy & what it can offer	16. Increasing family support network
	17. Using crisis intervention strategies
8. Referring to caregiver support groups	18. Making frequent telephone contacts
9. Recommending reading material	19. Referring to other community resources
10. Exploring alternative solutions	

Program History

COPSA, a unit of the Community Mental Health Center at Piscataway, University of Medicine and Dentistry of New Jersey, was established in 1975 to provide outreach services to older adults and their families whose psychiatric and social needs were not being met by more traditional models of service delivery. By 1982, services available through COPSA in the catchment area included information, counseling and referral, individual and family therapy, psychosocial assessments, advocacy, a day hospital for demented elderly, family support groups, consultation and education services.

In 1983, the Alzheimer's Disease Study Commission was established in New Jersey by Governor Kean. It recommended that state-wide services for Alzheimer's patients and their families be developed and in 1985, the COPSA Institute for Alzheimer's Disease and Related Disorders was established. Funding is provided through a legislative appropriation administered by the New Jersey Department of Health. A Resource Center, Diagnostic Clinic for dementia evaluations and consultation and training of service providers working with dementia patients became available, along with the day hospital program, through the COPSA Institute.

THE EVALUATION PROCEDURE FOR DEMENTIA

The COPSA Diagnostic Clinic is available to any resident of New Jersey requesting an evaluation of a memory problem or confusion, or seeking a second opinion about such symptoms. After an intensive telephone interview to rule out an acute problem needing immediate intervention, the initial diagnostic evaluation is scheduled. The evaluation includes laboratory studies, EKG, EEG, neuro-psychological testing, psychiatric and neurological screening, a medical history, physical examination and psychosocial assessment. The evaluation team consists of a family practice physician who evaluates the patient's medical status and a gerontological nurse or social worker who assesses the psychosocial needs of the patient and family and serves as case manager. During part of the session, both physician and case manager interview the patient and family. Later, the case manager meets with the family while the patient receives a physical exam.

In this setting, the nurse and social worker perform the same assessment and case management tasks. Over the years of working together there has occurred some overlap in knowledge and skills in working with families of demented elderly. Each, as part of the team effort, has educated the other about their different disciplinary perspectives so that a broad-based approach to assessment and intervention can be utilized. The nurse, certified in Gerontology, has acquired extensive knowledge and skill in family dynamics and family counseling. The social workers, with expertise in family therapy, have acquired valuable medical information and skills in educating families about chronic illness, preventive health and safety factors.

After the initial interview the evaluation team, in consultation with other team members, formulates an initial treatment plan based on data gathered thus far. The physician and case manager meet with the patient and family to recommend further testing that may be needed, such as, CT scan (computer tomography) or MRI (magnetic resonance imaging) and to make necessary referrals to social services. The entire multidisciplinary team, comprised of representatives from nursing, social work, family medicine, neurology, gero-psychiatry and neuro-psychology meets when all test results have been received and a master treatment plan is developed. A diagnostic feedback session with the patient and family is then scheduled to discuss test results, diagnosis, management issues and future planning.

INTEGRATING ASSESSMENT AND INTERVENTION

Dementia interferes with the dignity and independence of the person while causing much stress on the family. Two-thirds of all people with dementia are cared for by their family. Psychosocial issues can be overwhelming and their identification is a crucial part of a good evaluation (Rabins, 1988). The case manager collects data pertinent to diagnosis and assesses the needs of the family using a psychosocial assessment questionnaire. The questionnaire combines a family systems theoretical framework with cognitive and behavioral assessment scales. It focuses assessment on understanding the patient within his family system and the family in relationship to structure, racial background, ethnicity and socio-economic level. Family stressors, patient care and safety factors are also assessed. Tables 22–2 through 22–4 contain portions of the questionnaire.

The variability of families of individuals with a dementing illness necessitates a flexible approach to data collection that permits a focus on why the family is seeking an evaluation and what they want to obtain from it. The primary concern of families is diagnosis and possible treatment, but also important to many is the need for information about dementia, help with management problems and concerns about future planning. Many seek help for their emotional distress. During the evaluation interview, the case manager must assess the nature and extent of family and caregiving problems and decide what interventions will be most effective in their resolution. Effective use of interventions is also determined by an understanding of the family's own problem-solving style, coping mechanisms and values.

The initial evaluation interview begins the forming of the relationship between the family and case manager. If the task of gathering data is carried out in a way that is responsive to the family's needs, a positive connection will be made. To be viewed as helpful by the family, the case manager must be empathetic, nonjudgmental, knowledgeable about the disease, have a good understanding of family dynamics and be able to do effective management counseling. Once a good relationship has formed, the family will not hesitate to call seeking guidance and support as symptoms change or worsen during the course of the disease.

1. Intervening During Assessment of Family Structure

When changes in the family homeostasis stimulate interpersonal conflicts, relationships are affected negatively between husbands and wives, among adult siblings, and across the generations . . . filial care of the elderly has become normative but stressful [and] affects the entire family (Brody, 1985). Having other family members, in addition to the caregiver, present during the psychosocial evaluation is a useful intervention in identifying, assessing and resolving family conflict and reducing the stress on family members resulting from the illness. Others the caregiver identifies as important sources of support or assistance can be included as well (Zarit, Orr, Orr, 1983). Often during family meetings, adult children frustrated in their attempts to deal with their parent's anger at the ill spouse have gained greater understanding of the complexity of emotions with which the well parent is struggling. They become sensitized to the caregiving parent as they hear him describe intense feelings of anger, sadness and loneliness resulting from changes that have occurred.

Some parents and children are reluctant to "open up" in front of each other and express feelings of loss and frustration. In other families adult children have so much anxiety about the situation they see both parents as incompetent and begin to make

Table 22–2
History and Assessment of Illness

When did you first notice any change in your family member?
    What changes did you observe?
Describe any behavioral changes in the past six months.
Describe previous personality and/or behavior.
Language Function:
    Any problem with language?
    Word-finding? For how long?
    Understanding what you are saying?
    Finishing sentences?
    Can the patient read?
Has there been a significant weight loss or weight gain? Period of time?
    Amount?
Has there been any change in sleep habits? If so, please describe.
    (Insomnia? Hypersomnia?)
Is there confusion or agitation when it gets dark?
Is there a decrease in interest and enjoyment of usual activities?

Table 22–3
History and Assessment of Illness

Driving History (omit if never drove):
    Has stopped driving?_____ Reason:
    Any problem with getting lost? When?
    Any problem with reading road signs?
    Has your family member been in an accident? When?
    Have they scraped the sides of the car?

Orientation:
    Is family member oriented to home?
    Any episodes of getting lost? When?

Legal Status:
    Does someone have power of attorney?
    Durable power of attorney?

decisions for the well parent. The well parent feels threatened and resentful toward the children who appear to be taking over the parents' lives. In such cases it can be useful to separate family members to further assess the relationship and clarify the situation. Through separate interviews the case manager can validate the views of all family members while reinforcing the generational boundaries. The case manager can educate the children about the impact of their behavior and suggest and encourage meetings with the entire family for joint decision-making. Use of separate meetings and additional family meetings in this way can facilitate the resolution of conflicts and the family's need to reorganize and adapt to its member's illness (Minuchin, 1974).

The stress on the caregiver and the family system can be intensified when unresolved conflicts and feelings of anger and resentment from past experiences exist. Likewise, an adult child still seeking nurturance from his parent, may be unable to make the change to an effective caregiver. It has been suggested that when a parent is no longer emotionally available to the adult child due to a dementia, the caregiver and other family members could become "stuck" in wanting the parent to be the source of nurturance, or to be available to rectify past injustices, unresolved conflicts and disappointments (Pett, Caserta, Hutton, Lund, 1988). When such a situation is assessed, scheduling additional family meetings to work through these issues or referral to a trained counselor may be indicated.

Table 22–4
Assessment of Caregiver Stress/Social Supports

What is a typical day like for you?
What is the most difficult part of caregiving?
Can patient be left alone?
    If so, for how long?
How have you been handling the changes in your relative?
Does anyone help you with caregiving?
Who do you turn to for emotional support in caring for your relative?
Are you utilizing any social services?

Family therapists with a Bowenian systems approach have been using genograms for many years as a primary tool for assessment and for designing therapeutic interventions (McGoldrick & Gerson, 1985). During the psychosocial assessment for evaluation of dementia, the genogram is used to widen the context of the illness, record the family history of illness, assess the structure and quality of family relationships and identify sources of support for the patient and the caregiver. Areas of family dysfunction and stress that may present obstacles to care can also be identified. For example, that a long-standing conflict exists between patient and his spouse, or that a member of the household is an alcoholic may be learned by use of the genogram. When the dementing illness coincides with life-cycle events such as the launching of a child or retirement, a caregiver and family are often doubly stressed.

Expanding the focus of assessment beyond the patient to the caregiver and family system via the genogram gives credibility to the caregiver and conveys the message that the patient-caregiver relationship and the illness are not occurring in isolation. The use of the genogram can provide families with insight into family relationships, serve to engage them in assessing for themselves who may be available for support and stimulate them to begin problem-solving around future health care needs. Use of the genogram provides a non-threatening format for establishing a collaborative relationship with the family as the case manager learns about their ethnic background, lifestyle, values and unique way of relating (McGoldrick & Gerson). It will stimulate families to reveal their concerns and fears about their relative's illness and provide the case manager an opportunity to educate the family about the illness.

2. Intervening During Assessment of Family's Reaction to Illness

That some family members use denial as a defense for coping with the pain of their relative's dementia has been well documented (Cohen & Eisdorfer, 1986; Powell & Courtice, 1983). Although denial is often viewed as an obstacle in engaging the family in planning for the care of their relative, it serves as a protective mechanism for families and must be confronted with respect. When families bring their relative for an evaluation they indicate a willingness to deal with the possibility of illness and an openness to explore treatment and care options.

The experience of the evaluation process itself becomes an intervention for confrontation of denial as the family faces the reality of their relative's limitations. Reviewing areas of functioning as noted in Tables 22–2 and 22–3 often makes the family conscious of changes in their relatives' cognitive and behavioral abilities. Likewise, when family members are present during the evaluation, they observe first-hand the patient's performance on the Folstein mini-mental status exam (Folstein, Folstein, McHugh, 1975). Afterwards many have remarked when alone with the case manager, "I didn't realize his memory was so bad." Even family members who have given many rational explanations for the memory loss such as, "He never was good at remembering dates" or "I have trouble with that too," will be impressed by the performance of the patient on the Folstein. This subtle, indirect confrontation of denial can be very powerful, and often the family's awareness can be a turning point that enables families to engage in decision-making about care of the patient for which they previously were not ready.

For many families, denial has given way to anger and grief over the losses resulting from the illness. While they respond to questions about the history of the symptoms (Table 22–2) asking, "What is that like for you?" provides them with an opportunity to express feelings and use the interview to address their needs. When the patient has undergone a personality change, even when there has been a history of a positive relationship, the caregiver may react with resentment and anger toward the patient. In a recent study of middle-aged women caring for demented older relatives, it was found that dramatic changes occurred in feelings toward the affected relative, and the caregivers experienced "turmoil and psychic pain when the personality lost its constancy and coherence" (Pett et al.). For many family members the evaluation interview is the first time they have discussed their reactions to the illness. The case manager can intervene by listening, validating and normalizing their feelings and allowing them time to grieve.

Discussing the marital relationship can reveal feelings of deep disappointment on the part of the well spouse. Some are resentful about changes in retirement plans. Others are angry about role changes that have placed increasing responsibility on them. Where there are remarriages later in life, there may be little history of shared positive life experiences. These marriages often are more vulnerable to possible collapse as the dementia progresses (Cohen & Eisdorfer).

In some cases anger may be intense and directed at the patient. It then becomes necessary to further assess the potential for physical abuse. The case manager can ask, "What do you do when you are so angry?" When the family member states, I "yell at" the patient or "argue with him," the case manager can reply, "Have you become so upset that you have lost control of yourself? Have you ever been so angry that you have struck him?" Gathering such information clarifies the situation and may indicate that crisis intervention is needed.

Case example: Mr. R. cared for his first wife for a long time until her death from cancer. He then met Mrs. R. and was attracted to her vivacious personality, sociability and love of dancing. Shortly after their marriage she developed memory problems, began hiding things and had episodes of wandering. A few years later Mr. R. brought her to the Diagnostic Clinic for evaluation. He appeared depressed and overwhelmed. He resented caring for Mrs. R. and was also worried about his 100-year-old ill mother. Through discussion it became apparent he had little understanding of dementia and needed help with management.

When alone with the case manager Mrs. R. stated, "I want to show you something," and she pointed to several bruises on her arms. She stated Mr. R. frequently became upset with her and pinched her. The case manager asked Mr. R., in a non-threatening way, if he ever lost his temper with his wife. He began to cry and reported episodes of abuse for which he was sorry. By listening non-judgmentally and letting him know she understood how difficult this situation was for him, the case manger began to form a relationship with Mr. R., educated him about dementia and provided management counseling. Being supportive without overwhelming him, she advised him to call if he felt he was losing control of his anger. Mrs. R. was immediately placed in the Institute's day hospital as respite for Mr. R. and he began attending a caregiver support group. Only one more episode of abuse occurred. The case manager maintained daily contact with

Mr. R. by phone and office interviews, and meetings were held with extended family to increase sources of respite.

Interventions utilized included crisis intervention, establishing the collaborative alliance, listening, educating, giving suggestions, being available, increasing the family support network, frequent telephone contact, validating feelings and referral to a caregivers support group and day care program. Interventions in such cases are aimed at calming down the family system by providing both supportive assistance to the caregiver and a safe environment for the patient. Where there is intense emotion on the part of caregivers, joining with them is crucial to the effectiveness of interventions. Providing information about the illness and educating them about management techniques adds to their self-confidence and reduces their anxiety and, consequently, that of the patient (Anderson, 1983). At times, a referral for counseling for long-standing, unresolved marital conflicts may be indicated even if only one spouse is capable of participating. Some marital and family conflicts complicated by chronic patterns of alcohol abuse, psychiatric illness or violence may require the intervention of a skilled psychotherapist as well.

Family members can be emotionally overwhelmed and physically exhausted by demands of care of the patient. "Some people experience financial hardship and some experience decline in their physical health—study after study has identified the most pervasive and most severe consequences as being in the realm of emotional strains" (Brody). By asking the questions in Table 22–4, family members who are feeling depressed or those at risk of becoming physically ill can be identified. The case manager can convey concern for the caregiver and let him know that it is common for caregivers to become ill or feel depressed in this situation. Depending on the degree of depression, she can suggest involving family or community resources and encourage the caregiver to pursue respite services. At times a referral to a psychotherapist who has specialized knowledge of dementia, and the issues of care and loss characteristic of the disease, is the appropriate intervention.

Focusing on the caregiver's needs conveys the message that he is important as an individual as well as a caregiver. Giving family members credit for the good job they are doing is helpful also (Minuchin). For indeed, the tireless efforts of families of demented individuals is most impressive.

3. Intervening During Assessment of Patient Care

It is often in response to financial and legal questions that the complexity of the family's thoughts and feelings become so obvious and poignant as they confront both the practical and ethical dilemmas of care (Table 22–3). Many struggle with not only "Who should manage the finances?" but, "What will be the impact of this decision?" The family's concern about whether the patient should continue to drive a car is often raised as well. Some families are so caught up in day-to-day care that they haven't yet thought about long-range plans. By discussing these concerns they begin to be aware of ramifications for themselves and the patient should the presence of an irreversible dementia be confirmed. The case manager can provide information on legal aspects of care such as power of attorney and guardianship. The advantages for the patient and the family of early planning, including possibly less financial expense, minimizing loss of legal rights, and patient safety, justifies time spent during the initial evaluation on these concerns. Suggestions can be made for ways to involve the high-functioning patient in the decisions about his care in order to maintain his self-esteem. Thus the interview can provide a forum for discussion and serve as a model for the family for future problem-solving.

Exploring symptomatology (Table 22–2) and asking open-ended questions about bathing, toileting, dressing and eating can provide the case manager an opportunity to do management counseling and offer support. A family's reaction to symptoms provides insight about the most problematic behaviors and how the family manages and copes with them. If family members find a symptom particularly distressing, they are likely to be upset when it occurs (Rabins). When discussing symptoms it can be helpful to ask "What is that like for you?" and "How did you handle that?"

Case example: A patient with severe word-finding problems is brought to the diagnostic clinic by her daughter who is a teacher. The case manager asks, "What do you do when your mother searches for the right word?" The daughter replies, "I make her think of the right word to challenge and stimulate her. She cannot always come up with the word and gets frustrated." The case manager explains that word-finding is a common problem in dementing illness which often can frustrate and anger the patient. She points out it can be less stressful for the patient if the caregiver tries to come up with the word she needs. Reading material such as *The 36 Hour Day* (Mace & Rabins, 1982) that provides information on patient care is recommended as well as a caregiver support group.

Case example: A son explains that his mother lives alone in a senior citizen building and, since her memory problem has become worse, has lost over 20 pounds. When she visits him in his home she eats well. He wonders why the food he brings into her apartment is left in the refrigerator uneaten. He is adamant about wanting his mother to live alone for as long as possible. The case manager explains that cooking is a difficult process for someone with a dementia since it involves many steps that may be too complex for his mother to accomplish. After discussion of alternatives with the son, she assists him to obtain "meals on wheels" and daily home health aide to prepare an evening meal.

Case example: A husband states he feels the reason for his wife's frequent episodes of incontinence is that she always answers "no" when he asks if she has to go to the bathroom. The case manager commends his attempts to toilet his wife frequently and explains she may not understand his questions. She suggests he just say to her, "Let's take a walk," and gently assist her into the bathroom. A few days later the husband is contacted to see if he has followed the suggestion and whether it has been effective. If this management suggestion was not successful, other options would be explored.

In these examples, the case manager intervened by listening, educating, exploring other alternative solutions, recommending reading material, referring to caregiver support groups and other community resources. Not unlike the psychoeducational approach to treatment used in work with families of the chronically mentally ill, this approach is designed "to increase the predictability and stability of the family environment by increasing their self-confidence and knowledge about the illness, thereby decreasing family anxiety about the patient and their ability to react helpfully to him" (Anderson). Referral to caregiver support groups is one of the most effective interventions for empowering families to resolve their problems. Members can identify with each other and through sharing common problems and emotional support acquire the knowledge and skills they need to manage and cope effectively during the course of the illness (Mace, 1990).

As many family members as possible are encouraged to attend the diagnostic feedback session held about one month after the initial evaluation interview. The diagnosis and its implications for the patient and family is discussed and the case manager has another opportunity to educate the family about dementia and provide information about resources for long-term care. Families report great relief when advised the case manager is available for phone counseling or family meetings should nursing home placement be considered. Understandably all families need support during this difficult time (Zarit et al.). Many families report having "peace of mind" after a thorough workup has been done and will state, "I know I did everything I could to help him be better." The case manager can validate their feelings by agreeing with and giving them credit for acting on their desire to obtain the most comprehensive evaluation possible for their family member.

CONCLUSION

Dementing illness is devastating and family members draw on their own strength and on each other to cope. When case managers develop a repertoire of interventions to use during the psychosocial assessment they also become a valuable resource for families experiencing the stress of caregiving. They can facilitate the family's need to reorganize and adjust to the illness while providing a model of problem-solving that can be used in the future should new symptomatology develop. Through effective application of interventions, families can acquire the knowledge, management skill and confidence they need to move beyond being overwhelmed. They can be empowered to resolve their problems and make the necessary decisions about care of their family member that confront them.

REFERENCES

Anderson, Carol M. A psychoeducational Model of Family Treatment for Schizophrenia. *Psychosocial Intervention in Schizophrenia, an International View.* New York: Springer-Verlag, 1983.

Brody, Elaine M. Patient Care as a Normative Stress. *The Gerontologist*, 1985; 25:19–29.

Cohen, Donna, Ph.D., and Eisdorfer, Carl, Ph.D. *The Loss of Self*. New York: W. W. Norton and Co., 1986.

Dementia. *JAMA*, 1986; 256:2234.

Differential Diagnosis of Dementing Illness. NIH Consensus Development Conference, NIA, 1987. Final Report of the New Jersey Alzheimer's Disease Study Commission. July, 1986.

Folstein, M.D., Folstein, S. E., and McHugh, P. R. Mini Mental State. *J. Psychiatric Research*, 1975; 12:189–198.

Mace, Nancy L., and Rabins, Peter V., M.D. *The 36 Hour Day*. Baltimore: Johns Hopkins University Press, 1982.

Mace, Nancy L, ed. *Dementia Care, Patient, Family, and Community*. Johns Hopkins University Press, 1990.

McGoldrick, Monica, and Gerson, Randy. *Genograms in Family Assessment*. New York: W. W. Norton and Co., 1985.

Minuchin, S. *Families and Family Therapy*. Cambridge, MA: Harvard University Press, 1974.

Pett, Marjorie A., Caserta, Michael S., Hutton, Ann P., and Lund, Dale A. Intergenerational Conflict: Middle-Aged Women Caring for Demented Older Relative. *American Journal of Orthopsychiatry* 58(3), July 1988.

Powell, Lenor S., and Courtice, Katie. Alzheimer's Disease, *A Guide for Families*. Reading, MA: Addison-Wesley Publishing Co., 1983.

Rabins, Peter V., M.D. Psychosocial Aspects of Dementia. *J. Clinical Psychiatry*, 1988; 49:29–31.

Zarit, Steven H., Orr, Nancy K., and Orr, Judy M. *Working with Families of Dementia Victims: A Treatment Manual*. U.S. Department of Health and Human Services, 1983.

CHAPTER 23

THE CHRONICALLY MENTALLY ILL

A Practice Approach

Mary Frances Libassi

Persons with chronic psychiatric disabilities have received increasing attention in the past few years. As a result of deinstitutionalization, community services have expanded in many areas of the country and the chronically mentally ill are a growing part of the service population in mental health agencies However, many professionals are resistant to work with this group of clients, and community services are often inadequate.[1]

The present article presents a conceptual framework for practice with this population that was tested by a group of graduate social work students who found it useful and effective. The approach is illustrated through practice examples of work with clients with chronic psychiatric disabilities The article provides suggestions and guidelines for practice that may influence attitudes and values of mental health professionals toward persons with psychiatric disabilities and that may stimulate their interest in this underserved population.

The chronically mentally ill have been referred to as an "abandoned population."[2] A major public policy initiative for the past twenty years has been that of the deinstitutionalization of the chronically mentally ill, and increased attention is being paid to their plight. Although the original motivation for deinstitutionalization was well-intentioned and humane, its consequences have at times been unexpected and even harmful.[3]

Reprinted from *Social Casework,* Vol. 69, No. 2 (1988), pp. 88–96, by permission of the publisher, Families International.

[1] Ursula C. Gerhart, "Teaching Social Workers to Work with the Chronically Mentally Ill," in *Education for Practice with the Chronically Mentally Ill: What Works?* ed. Joan P. Bowker (Washington, D.C.: Council on Social Work Education, 1985) pp. 50–66.

[2] "Abandoned," *Newsweek,* 6 January 1986.

[3] Leona L. Bachrach, "Asylum and Chronically Ill Psychiatric Patients," *American Journal of Psychiatry* 141 (August 1984): 975–78.

For many clients with a psychiatric disability, deinstitutionalization has been a brutal hoax.[4] Professionals are increasingly asking what went wrong.

THE CHRONICALLY MENTALLY ILL: AN UNDERSERVED GROUP

Various factors are associated with the plight of the chronically mentally ill. First, the development of community programs has not kept pace with the level of deinstitutionalization. Although community programs are now being developed, spurred on by planning and service dollars from the federal government[5] as well as increased funding by some state governments, systems of care that meet the complex needs of this group of clients are still the exception rather than the rule.

In addition, mental health professionals, including social workers, have not fully accepted responsibility for service to this client population. Nancy Atwood documented a professional prejudice toward psychotic clients in social workers as well as other professionals.[6] Others have discussed the resistance of practitioners toward this client group and have provided detailed reasons for this resistance.[7] For example, practitioners dislike working with the chronically mentally ill because psychotherapy or high status work is usually not appropriate; progress is slow and frequently minimal; and practice, especially case management, requires assertive outreach and environmental intervention. Similarly, a study conducted by Peter Johnson and Allen Rubin on the direct-practice interests of students enrolled in a master's degree program in social work revealed not only a lack of interest in case management interventions, but also a disinclination for work with the chronically mentally disabled. In fact, out of sixteen client groups that the students were asked to rank in terms of preference, the least appealing was the chronically mentally disabled.[8] Thus a host of factors result in a lack of motivation on the part of professionals to accept service responsibility for this important and needy segment of our population .

CONCEPTUAL FRAMEWORK

Practice with persons who have a chronic psychiatric disability requires a conceptual framework that fully accounts for the complexities of human beings, the environments in which they live, and their transactions with these environments. The ecological perspective is a basic component of such a conceptual framework.

A central feature of the ecological perspective is its view of people and environments as parts of a unitary system in which each continually shapes the other.[9] The person

---

4. "Abandoned."
5. Judith C. Turner and William J. Tenhoor, "The NIMH Community Support Program: Pilot Approach to a Needed Social Reform," *Schizophrenia Bulletin* 4 (4, 1978): 319–48.
6. Nancy Atwood, "Professional Prejudice and the Psychotic Client," *Social Work* 27 (2, 1982):172–77.
7. Gerhart, "Teaching Social Workers"; and Allen Rubin, "Effective Community-Based Care of Chronic Mental Illness Experimental Findings," in *Education for Practice with the Chronically Mentally Ill,* pp. 1–17.
8. Peter J. Johnson and Allen Rubin, "Case Management in Mental Health: A Social Work Domain?" *Social Work* 28(1, 1983): 49–55.
9. Carel B. Germain, "Ecology and Social Work," in *Social Work Practice: People and Environments,* ed. Carel B. Germain (New York: Columbia University Press, 1979), pp. 1–22.

and the environment are understood to be complementary, interdependent parts of a whole—whether one is looking at a person and the family, a patient and the ward, roommates in a residential facility, or any type of community support program within its neighborhood. The development and survival of both the person and the environment depend upon the nature of their transactions or interchanges. The ecological perspective is particularly useful in lifting the environment out of its customary background position and placing it, along with the person, in the foreground. Research on effective practice with persons with psychiatric disabilities increasingly documents the critical importance of an appropriate level of environmental stimulation as well as environmental resources and supports in maintaining clients in the community and in preventing a return to the hospital.[10] The ecological perspective enables practitioners to understand the impact of environment, both social and physical, on a client's mental health, and more important, to use the environment to support the coping and adaptive efforts of individual clients and groups of clients in dealing with the stress of daily living.

Flowing from the ecological perspective are ideas about *stress* and *coping* that are congruent with emerging theoretical notions regarding chronic psychiatric disability. For example, the concept of *stress* refers to upsets that occur in the characteristic adaptive balance between person and environment.[11] Some stress is zestful and challenging, contributing to growth and development; other stress is problematic and unmanageable, because it exceeds the usual coping limits or because the person perceives a discrepancy between the coping demands and his or her coping capacity. What is defined as stress and how it is defined or experienced varies from person to person and is affected by such factors as vulnerability, previous experience, culture, and so forth. Although it may arise from the environment, it may also arise from internal processes, both physical and psychological. In his discussion of schizophrenia, Gerard Hogarty reports on the "stress-diathesis" model.[12] The "diathesis" side of the equation refers to a constitutional "vulnerability" or disposition to severe mental disorders related to altered neurotransmission processes in the brain. The midbrain systems are uniquely involved in processing information about both the internal and external world, in regulating emotion and cognition, and in facilitating adaptive behavior. Environmental stress is implicated, interactively, in the tendency toward recurrent episodes or sustained social dysfunctioning, or both.[13]

In ecological terms, environmental stress in transaction with a vulnerable individual is experienced as unmanageable and responses to that stress become dysfunctional. Interventions must necessarily address the vulnerability of the individual as well as the en-

[10] Margaret Linn et al., "Foster Home Characteristics and Psychiatric Patient Outcome," *Archives of General Psychiatry* 37 (1980): 129–32; Margaret Linn et al., "Day Treatment and Psychotropic Drugs in the Aftercare of Schizophrenic Patients," *Archives of General Psychiatry* 36 (10, 1979): 1055–66; Gerard E. Hogarty, "Aftercare Treatment of Schizophrenia: Current Status and Future Direction," in *Management of Schizophrenia*, ed. Herman M. Pragg (Assen, Netherlands: Van Gorcum, 1979), pp. 19–36; and Patrick Crotty and Regina Kulys, "Social Support Networks: The Views of Schizophrenic Clients and Their Significant Others," *Social Work* 30 (4, 1985): 301–309.

[11] Germain, "Ecology and Social Work."

[12] Gerard E. Hogarty, "Curricula and Administrative Issues Addressed to the Needs of the (Chronic) Mentally Ill" (paper presented at the NIMH Division of Human Resources' Workshop, July 1984, Rockville, Md.).

[13] Ibid.

vironmental stress. Research studies on effective treatment have borne out the importance of a combination of both types of interventions for effective social adjustment of the chronic psychiatric client.[14] Clients who received combined treatments of drugs and sociotherapy adjusted better than did those who received drugs or sociotherapy exclusively. In fact, sociotherapy appeared ineffective, even toxic, without the drug therapy. The enriched cognitive field and the increased expectations for responsibility and productivity of some sociotherapy programs were found to be overly stressful for some vulnerable individuals who did not have the benefits of drug therapy as well.[15] The ecological perspective is a theoretical orientation that helps practitioners appreciate more fully this dual attention to person and environment.

APPROACHES TO PRACTICE

From the ecological perspective emerge approaches to practice that are useful in work with clients with psychiatric disabilities. These approaches include the life model[16] and competence-oriented social work practice.[17] The life model of practice assumes that the social worker's intervention into a client's situation is patterned after life itself: the approach provides concepts and principles based on life processes that are designed to strengthen coping patterns by changing transactions among people and their environments. In competence-oriented practice, the promotion of competence in the transactions is viewed as a special goal of social work intervention. For persons with chronic psychiatric problems whose competence may be low, social work practice that focuses on the rebuilding of competent functioning to the greatest degree possible is particularly appropriate. These approaches to practice have much in common with developing frameworks for psychiatric rehabilitation treatment.[18]

Several guidelines that are especially valuable in effective practice with clients with psychiatric disabilities can be gleaned from the approaches mentioned above.

Humanistic Perspective

Humans are active and purposeful beings who are capable of achieving their potential when necessary environmental resources are made available. In working with clients with psychiatric disabilities, this humanistic orientation leads the practitioner to acknowledge but deemphasize the disability and to emphasize strengths, assets, and potentialities. The focus of intervention is not on treatment or cure of the illness but on

---

[14] Gerard E. Hogarty, "Aftercare Treatment of Schizophrenia"; Carol M. Anderson, Gerard E. Hogarty, and Douglas J. Reiss, "Family Treatment of Adult Schizophrenic Patients: A Psycho-Educational Approach," *Schizophrenia Bulletin* 6 (3, 1980): 490–502; and Carol M. Anderson, Douglas J. Reiss, and Gerard E. Hogarty, *Schizophrenia and the Family* (New York: Guilford Press, 1986).

[15] Gerard E. Hogarty, "Curricula and Administrative Issues."

[16] Carel B. Germain and Alex Gitterman, *The Life Model of Social Work Practice* (New York: Columbia University Press, 1980).

[17] Anthony N. Maluccio, "Competence-Oriented Social Work Practice: An Ecological Approach," in *Promoting Competence in Clients: A New/Old Approach to Social Work Practice,* ed. Anthony Maluccio (New York: Free Press, 1981) , pp. 1–26.

[18] William A. Anthony, Mikal Cohen, and Marianne Farkas, "A Psychiatric Rehabilitation Treatment Program: Can I Recognize One If I See One?" *Community Mental Health Journal* 18 (2, 1982): p. 83–96.

supporting or releasing the client's adaptive potential so that he or she can cope with the disability as well as improve his or her social functioning in the environment. This practice guideline suggests that success, that is, effectiveness with clients, should be measured by improvement in the person's competence and functioning in the environment, not by cure of illness. This guideline is especially useful in work with persons with chronic psychiatric disabilities, because much of social work practice activity is focused on enhancing living conditions and promoting competent role performance. As Allen Rubin reflects, "In a hospital setting, social workers are not expected to cure physical disabilities; their job is to help individuals and families cope with them. Cannot the same be said for mental disabilities?"[19]

Problem Definition and Assessment

A second guideline flows logically from the first and relates to the way in which problems are viewed. In contrast to the emphasis on pathology in more traditional practice approaches, this approach suggests that problems occur when there is not a good match between the person's needs and skills and the demands and resources in the environment.[20] Accordingly, problems do not represent weaknesses in the person but rather are outcomes of the transaction of the person with the environment.[21] The units of attention for both assessment and intervention include the person, the environment, and the transactions between them.

For example, in competence-oriented practice, assessment is redefined as competence clarification—the process of identifying and understanding the person's capacity to deal with environmental challenges at any one time.[22] Through this technique, the competence of the client system is assessed together with the characteristics of the impinging environment that influence the client's coping and adaptive patterns. The purpose of competence clarification is to determine where to intervene in order to enhance the person-environment transactions and thus improve social functioning. Interventions into the person system, the environment, or both are equally important.

Psychiatric rehabilitation programs utilize similar techniques by assessing a client's strengths and deficits in relation to the demands of the particular environment in which the client wants or needs to function.[23] In addition, such programs assess environments to ensure that proper resources and supports are available to facilitate the client's success within them. As in competence-oriented practice, interventions may relate to teaching new skills to clients or to modifying environments. Utilizing such sophisticated skills of assessment as guides for intervention is another way to ensure success for both clients and practitioners.

[19] Allen Rubin, "Effective Community-Based Care of Chronic Mental Illness," p. 4.
[20] Germain and Gitterman, *The Life Model of Social Work Practice.*
[21] Maluccio, "Competence-Oriented Social Work Practice."
[22] Anthony N. Maluccio and Mary Frances Libassi, "Competence Clarification Social Work Practice," *Social Thought* 10 (2, 1984): 51–58.
[23] Anthony, Cohen, and Farkas, "A Psychiatric Rehabilitation Treatment Program."

Emphasis on Environmental Work

The emphasis on environment is a natural outgrowth of the ecological perspective and its dual focus on person and environment. This guideline for practice is congruent with the emphasis on the importance of environmental resources and support in much of the literature on services for persons with chronic psychiatric disabilities. These environmental resources "include significant others (e.g., family, other practitioners), services (e.g., transportation), and things (e.g., money)."[24] For example, practitioners working with clients who are schizophrenic speak of the "nitty gritty stuff": intervention with housing and money management issues, advocacy to secure appropriate benefits, and helping clients to find employment and be successful on the job.[25]

Case management is widely regarded as an essential component for pulling together these environmental resources. The psychiatrically disabled have multiple needs. The principle underlying the case management approach is that one worker—the case manager—will link the client to the complex service delivery system and be responsible for ensuring that the client receives appropriate services in a timely fashion.[26] James Intagliata describes various functions that are required of case managers including outreach, client assessment, case planning, referral to service providers, advocacy for clients, direct casework, developing natural support systems, reassessment, advocacy for resource development, monitoring quality, public education, and crisis intervention.[27] Leonard Stein and Mary Ann Test describe the work of case managers in developing support systems to motivate and encourage patients, educating community residents involved with patients, and assertively persevering in outreach and continued contact with clients.[28] These case management activities are examples of the kinds of environmental interventions that are necessary in work with clients with psychiatric disabilities. Evaluation of programs that provide case management have consistently shown that these programs are effective in creating and modifying environments and in promoting the client's effective social functioning.

Johnson and Rubin make an excellent argument in support of implementation of the broad interventions of case management in social work.[29] The focus on the person–environment transaction and commitment to enhanced quality of life social responsibility and relatedness are compelling arguments for social work activity in the broad area of environmental modification. When these values and ideals are combined with positive results with regard to enhanced client competence, social workers may indeed begin to take pride in providing (environmental) resources for this client group.[30]

---

[24] Ibid., p. 90.
[25] Jerry Dincin, "Psychiatric Rehabilitation Today," in *Education for Practice with the Chronically Mentally Ill*, pp. 18–31.
[26] Johnson and Rubin, "Case Management in Mental Health."
[27] James Intagliata, "Improving the Quality of Community Care for the Chronically Mentally Disabled: The Role of Case Management," *Schizophrenia Bulletin* 8 (4, 1982): 655–74.
[28] Leonard I. Stein and Mary Ann Test, "Alternative to Mental Hospital Treatment: Conceptual Model, Treatment Program, Clinical Evaluation," *Archives of General Psychiatry* 37 (April 1980): 392–97.
[29] Johnson and Rubin, "Case Management in Mental Health."
[30] Ibid.

Redefinition of Client and Practitioner Roles

A fourth guideline relates to the role of clients and workers in the helping process. In both the life model of practice and the competence-oriented approach, clients are viewed as resources and as partners in the process. They are encouraged to play active roles in the helping process and to meaningfully participate in such areas as assessment, goal formulation, and selection of interventive strategies.[31] Practitioners currently working with the chronically mentally ill propose similar roles. For example, Charles Rapp suggests that workers form a helping relationship whereby the client is the principal director of the efforts.[32] Courtenay Harding, a noted researcher on effective practice with persons with prolonged psychiatric disorders, suggests asking clients themselves what they need and what works for them.[33] William Anthony and co-workers state that client involvement in assessment and intervention is an essential ingredient in a psychiatric rehabilitation program.[34]

This redefinition of client and worker roles has implications for the therapeutic relationship. Qualities such as mutuality, authenticity, reduction of social distance, honesty, and "human caring" are emphasized.[35] Walter Deitchman has captured what this might mean for work with clients with a chronic disability:

> The chronic client in the community needs a traveling companion, not a travel agent. The travel agent's only function is to make the client's reservation. The client has to get ready, get to the airport, and traverse foreign terrain by himself. The traveling companion, on the other hand, celebrates the fact that his friend was able to get seats on the plane, talks about his fear of flying, and then goes on the trip with him, sharing the joys and sorrows that occur during the venture.[36]

Focus on Life Processes and Experiences

Effective practice with clients with psychiatric disabilities requires the use of natural (real) life experiences and events as instruments for change. Life experiences, events, and processes can and should be used to promote personal growth, learning of new social skills, and the promotion of competence.[37]

Community support programs, particularly psychosocial rehabilitation programs, often utilize this approach in trying to facilitate successful experiences for their mem-

---

[31] Maluccio, Competence-Oriented Social Work Practice."

[32] Charles A. Rapp, "Research on the Chronically Mentally Ill: Curriculum Implication," in *Education for Practice with the Chronically Mentally Ill,* pp. 32–49.

[33] This suggestion was made by Dr. Courtenay Harding in an address to the State Board of Mental Health, Wallingford, Connecticut, March 1986.

[34] Anthony, Cohen, and Farkas, "A Psychiatric Rehabilitation Treatment Program."

[35] Germain and Gitterman, *The Life Model of Social Work Practice.*

[36] Walter S . Deitchman, "How Many Case Managers Does It Take to Screw in a Light Bulb?" *Hospital and Community Psychiatry* 31 (November 1980), p. 789.

[37] Maluccio, "Competence-Oriented Social Work Practice."

bers. Members need rebuilding exercises that slowly increase their level of confidence.[38] Behavioral techniques such as shaping (breaking skills into smaller increments), the use of positive reinforcement, modeling, and role playing are often used to improve competence and social functioning in real-life situations.[39]

A corollary of this focus on life processes and experiences is the emphasis on practice within the environments of clients. Teaching social skills and improving social functioning is best done in *in-vivo* situations rather than in contrived environments. Bruce Hall and John Valvano suggest that "life space social work uses the immediate experiences of the client system to pursue developmental goals, maintaining a sense of proportion and optimism for clients' encounters with obstacles to achievement."[40] Effective practice with clients with psychiatric disabilities requires that workers move out of their offices into the places where clients live and congregate.

The Family, a Critical Focus for Practice

From an ecological perspective, the family is a major "environment" that affects the functioning of individual clients. Studies on community-based alternatives to institutional care for those with chronic psychiatric problems support the crucial role that families can and do play in preventing rehospitalization and maintaining a client in the community.[41] In some programs, a psychoeducational approach to family intervention is used. Families are encouraged to discuss their anxieties, are provided with information to increase their understanding of the patient's illness, and are taught skills of crisis management that enable them to better cope with schizophrenic symptomatology.[42] Agnes Hatfield has been an advocate and a leader for this approach. Her monograph discusses such topics as understanding chronic mental illness, the treatment of mental illness, creating a low-stress environment, managing disturbing behavior, and promoting growth and rehabilitation.[43]

The emphasis on family education and intervention is yet another guideline that flows from the conceptual framework and the approaches to practice described herein. As noted above, it is also congruent with theoretical approaches currently utilized by those who work with clients with a chronic psychiatric disability.

PRACTICE ILLUSTRATIONS

The conceptual framework and the practice approaches presented above were tested by a group of graduate social work students placed in a community mental health training

---

[38] Dincin, "Psychiatric Rehabilitation Today."

[39] Rapp, "Research on the Chronically Mentally Ill."

[40] Bruce Hall and John Valvano, "Life Space Social Work: A New Level of Practice," *Social Casework* 66 (November 1985): 515–24.

[41] Donald G. Langsley, Kalman Flomehaft, and Pavel Mochotra, "Follow-up Evaluation of Family Crisis Therapy," *American Journal of Orthopsychiatry* 39 (5, 1969); 753–59; and Joan D. Rittenhouse, *Without Hospitalization: An Experimental Study of Psychiatric Care in the Home* (Denver: Swallow Press, 1970).

[42] Anderson, Hogarty, and Reiss, "Family Treatment of Adult Schizophrenic Patients."

[43] Agnes Hatfield, *Coping with Mental Illness in the Family: A Family Guide* (Washington, D.C.: National Alliance of the Mentally Ill, 1982).

unit.[44] The value of the practice guidelines is illustrated through the following examples, which draw from the work of the students who worked in agencies both institutional and community, that served clients with chronic psychiatric disabilities.[45] The students found that it was essential to reframe their practice along the lines of the conceptual approaches discussed above.

MSG Group

A student placed in a psychosocial rehabilitation center was asked by staff to develop an educational group that would focus on the development of employment skills to facilitate the reentry of psychiatric clients into the job market. Despite his efforts and staff efforts, the group was not successful. Membership was small and attendance poor. In evaluating the group intervention, the student solicited input from client group members and discovered several important reasons for the failure of this group. First, the focus of the group was on problems and deficits; the members felt that enough attention was already directed to their weaknesses. Second, the group met in the rehabilitation center, which intensified the feeling among members that the group was a problem-focused group. Finally, the comments of the clients suggested that much of the difficulty in obtaining employment stemmed from systems or environmental problems. The opportunities for employment for an ex-psychiatric client were almost nonexistent. The problems experienced in obtaining employment were just as much an outgrowth of systems and environmental issues as they were of personal deficits. By zeroing in on personal problems only, the group fed the low self-esteem of the clients.

With this evaluation in mind, the student began to reframe his work with the group utilizing the guidelines presented here. First, he made a conscious effort to start with the clients' definitions of their problems. In addition, he changed his focus to client strengths and competencies. The goal became to foster the social competencies that each group member already possessed as well as the competencies of the group as a whole. The group was described to potential members as a social group that would explore any activities *they* wished to pursue in the community. Instead of focusing on problems in self (internal problems), the group focused on the interests, knowledge, and strengths that members already possessed. No restrictions were placed on membership. Anyone who wished to be a part of the group was welcome. The student saw his role as facilitator and encouraged group interaction rather than leader-participant interaction.

Student process notes highlight many of the practice guidelines delineated above.

> T, a group member, volunteered to hold a television-viewing party at his house after the group had elected that activity as the program for the next meeting. T's fears about being a host surfaced and he started to back down. Group members

[44] Mary F. Libassi and Anthony N. Maluccio. "Teaching the Use of the Ecological Perspective in Community Mental Health," *Journal of Education for Social Work* 18 (3, 1982): 94–100.

[45] These practice examples were contributed by Richard Forleo, Christine Nicols, and Kathy Little, former students at the University of Connecticut School of Social Work.

offered their support, and one member volunteered to help him prepare for the coming meeting.

On the day of the meeting, I drove to the party with some of the group members. They mentioned how scared T must be and how hard it would be for any of them to host the meeting. When we arrived, we were all amazed at the snacks that T had prepared. People quickly prepared their plates and sat down. Little, if any, conversation followed. At first I defined the silence as a symptom of the ex-psychiatric clients' deep-seated problems and became anxious to intervene. However, I quickly recognized that I was falling back into my old deficit mind set and began to reframe what was happening. I recognized that silence can occur in any group and began to relax. T was also upset and suggested to the group that he was a poor host. I responded that the best of hosts had silent parties at times and that it wasn't the host's responsibility to *make* the party work. This comment seemed to break the ice for everyone. It served to normalize the experience. T and the others began to talk. When the meeting was over, they all felt good at how well it had gone and another member volunteered to use her house for a potluck supper at the next group meeting.

This group, which was initiated five years ago, was the first of its type in the rehabilitation center. It still exists today; it has become the prototype for several other similar groups, all of which enhance the life of the participants. Social competencies are enhanced in natural situations. Self-esteem has grown, and clients with psychiatric disabilities have been helped to move from the role of patient to that of person.

A Resistant Client

A student placed in a psychiatric hospital setting was assigned to work with J, a patient who had attempted suicide. The client had a history of hospitalizations and of long periods of therapy. She was described as hostile, manipulative, resistant, and unmotivated. The student's first task was to complete a psychosocial history. Although J had been hospitalized a number of times, her history was incomplete. There was no clear agreement on what kind of person J was, what had caused her psychosis, or how she perceived herself and her world.

The student's process notes highlight her approach to engagement and her determination to reframe her work with J along the general guidelines presented in this article.

Before I met J, I was determined to circumvent resistance and fill in the blanks in her history. I felt pressure by the hospital requirement to prepare an interim history for the treatment meeting. However, I decided that I should not allow my sense of unmet responsibility to the hospital procedures to interfere with my work with J.

I approached J with the intent to convey my respect for her choice of utilizing my services rather than to obtain information from her. I hoped to establish a relationship with her by agreeing to work on discharge plans. When I knocked on her door, she asked me to leave her alone. I did, but left her a note explaining my role as her social worker and stating that I'd be back the next day. When I returned, she was reading in her room. "What do you want?" she asked, without looking up. I introduced myself. There were no chairs, so I sat on the floor. "You don't want to be here?" I asked. She responded with a chaotic outburst directed toward the people who ran the transitional living facility where J had been and the psychiatrist on her ward. I was frightened, less by the language than by the intense energy behind the language. I couldn't think of anything to say. I asked J if she minded if I had a cigarette and offered her one. We sat in silence, smoking. She seemed to forget that I was there. She appeared to be listening to something. She shook her head and shoulders rapidly. "Were you hearing voices?" I asked her. "Get out of here," she replied, "You think I'm loony, too." I said, "I think you are angry and sad and that you don't want to be here. I don't know whether that's loony or not. You know where you are and why you are here. What do you think?"

I sat with her for almost two hours, saying very little. When she spoke, I had difficulty following her train of thought, references to people, and references to politics. I was fascinated by the images she used to illustrate her despondency with the world.

When I left, she asked if I planned to write up her "loose associations" in her chart. I told her that even though they didn't help us deal with her present issues, they helped me to get an idea of what she cared about and how she thought. I told her that I would write that she exhibited an imaginative use of language and that she attributed her depression to external things. She agreed to another meeting, and we shook hands.

I saw J twice a week for almost three months. At first our meetings were erratic in that she continued to refuse to talk to me at times. We met in different places— my office, the ward, and so forth. I realized she was most hostile when we met in my office and commented on this. She said that being there made our talks feel like therapy, which she had no use for. We agreed to have coffee together in the mornings, then talk in the visitors' lounge. It was here that an emotional connection occurred; a working contract was developed that eventually led to discharge and acceptance to a transitional living program.

This humanistic approach to the helping relationship showed respect for the client as a person, allowing the student to give direction to the process and practice effectively with a client who had always been viewed as resistant, unmotivated, and unlikely to succeed in any environment other than an institutional setting.

Life Space Intervention

A public health nurse referred M to a student placed in a community mental health multiservice agency. M had a history of multiple hospitalizations but had been living in the community for about six months. The public health nurse felt M needed support and direction in achieving his goal of obtaining his graduate equivalency diploma (GED). M's goal was to make something of himself and to support himself like other young men his age. He was concerned about the stigma associated with his mental illness and wished to be viewed as one who not only had a mental illness but also had much in common with normal young adults his age. The student assured M that she would attempt to view him as a young man working to achieve his potential, not just as an ex-psychiatric patient.

To assess M and his life space, the student used ecomapping.[46] As she and M developed the ecomap, activities for intervention became clear. For example, M's first goal was to become employable. Therefore his work on the GED was a primary activity. The student assumed the role of tutor, assigning specific chapters in the GED manual for work, assessing M's capacity in each area, and working with him on specific deficits. For leisure activities, M was encouraged to pursue his interest in basketball in a program offered by a local church. This activity not only helped him structure his leisure time but also allowed him to meet young men his own age who were not ex-psychiatric clients. To ensure success in this endeavor, the student and M role-played early encounters with members of the new group and also made sure M had adequate directions to get to the church where the program was held. In addition, the student offered to meet the priest with M so that the experience would be less stressful.

Reading was chosen as an area for intervention. The student helped M acclimate himself to the local library, learn how to get there by bus, how to find books he enjoyed, how to solicit aid from the librarian, and so forth. When M found the branch library in the neighborhood inadequate, the student helped him learn how to use the main library.

M's family history indicated overinvolvement by his mother and neglect by his father and brothers. The student helped educate the family about M's potential. In addition, she helped them identify the type of support that would benefit him most.

The practice approach proved effective; two years later M had obtained his GED, was employed, had rented his own apartment, had learned to drive, and was a leader in a social support group at the local social club. He did not require any additional hospitalizations. Currently, M is on the Board of Directors of the social club.

CONCLUSION

The ecological perspective and practice approaches such as the life model and competence-oriented perspective allow comprehensive assessment of problem situations and multiple approaches to interventive activities. Together, they form a rich conceptual framework that enriches practice with those who have a chronic psychiatric disability. The conceptual framework here provides an alternative to the disease or medical models and is congruent with a psychosocial rehabilitation focus. It emphasizes the practitioner's responsibility to identify, mobilize, and ally him- or herself with the potential of the client. It focuses on the interface between the person and the environment, on the practitioner's role in facilitating the person's life and goals, and on matching the client's needs with environmental supports. It emphasizes the need for the availability of services in the person's environment and stresses the importance of the family as a major part of that environment.

These guidelines have been tested by a group of graduate social work students. The

---

[46] Ann Hartman and Joan Laird, *Family-Centered Social Work Practice* (New York: Free Press, 1983), pp. 157–86.

response of clients to such practice approaches has been most encouraging and suggests that the practice guidelines may be applicable to work with clients with chronic psychiatric disabilities. The ecological perspective and the approaches to practice from which these guidelines flow are receiving wide acceptance and attention in the field of social work. Explicating services to the chronically mentally ill in conceptual and practice terms that are widely accepted in the field is one way to increase workers' motivation to practice with this undeserved population.

NEUROLOGICAL DISORDERS

CHAPTER 24

WIDOWS AND WIDOWERS OF ALZHEIMER'S VICTIMS

Their Survival After Spouses' Death

Mona Wasow and Dorothy H. Coons

Future problems related to serious emotional stress tend to develop when grief is intense, prolonged, and largely unresolved. This is particularly true when the grief and loss have been long, complicated, and associated with negative feelings, as is often the case when dealing with the dementias.

Dementias create dreadful burdens for caregivers. The grief tends to be compounded with anger and guilt, and our culture usually does not recognize that the caregivers are grieving. There are no rituals or opportunities to "normally" grieve during this long, devastating illness. For these reasons we wonder if caregivers, especially spouses, are often prone to future emotional troubles after the death of their partner.

Dr. C. Murray Parkes and R. S. Weiss (1983), leading authorities on bereavement reactions, report that many physical symptoms in family members increase by 50% following a death in the family, and that following the death of a spouse seven times the normal amount of women and four times as many men enter psychiatric care. Dr. Jerome Frederick (no date), a biophysiologist, writes:

> There seems to be little doubt that people undergoing unresolved grief, who at one time had arrested T.B., during . . . bereavement redeveloped active T.B. (p. 8).

Reprinted from *Journal of Independent Social Work,* Vol. 2, No. 3 (Spring 1988), pp. 51–62, by permission of author and publisher.

The authors express their appreciation to the following interviewers for this project: Shari R. Glickman, Nancy K. Henderson, Nancy D. Miller, and David L. Staude in Wisconsin; and to Glynis Cullens, Tom Gaughan, Anthony Gensterblum, Lena Metzelaar, Chaplain H. Miller, and Michelle Stone in Michigan. To request reprints of Appendices A and B, please address correspondence to Mona Wasow, School of Social Work, University of Wisconsin-Madison, 425 Henry Hall, Madison, WI 53706.

Physicians now speak of grief as the hidden illness, and think it may account for many of the physical symptoms they see in their daily practice. There is a higher than average mortality rate for widowers in the first year of their bereavement.

When Warden (1982) did his studies on anticipating grief, which is what spouses of dementia victims go through, he felt that data was inconclusive as to whether anticipation was helpful or not. For many, he said, anticipatory grief increased anxiety and also increased personal death awareness in the caregiver. So even the often assumed notion that anticipatory grief is helpful comes under question.

Silver and Wortman (1980) did an extensive literature review on coping strategies of people under severe, prolonged stress, and came to the following conclusion:

> Clearly, the evidence reviewed suggests that a simple expectation of acceptance or recovery from a serious life crisis is unwarranted for a large minority of people. Most studies find significant levels of distress or disorganization after a year, and those that have continued to follow their sample for a longer period of time have not typically found substantial improvement. . . . There are relatively few studies that have documented reactions to life crises several years after the event has occurred. Nevertheless, there is a clear suggestion from the available evidence that for many people acceptance or recovery is not apparent despite the passage of a long period of time.
>
> In conclusion, it is clear that prevailing notions of recovery need to be reconsidered. There is evidence that a substantial minority of individuals exhibit distress for a much longer period of time than would be commonly expected. There are also a number of indications that people continually re-experience the crises for the rest of their lives (pp. 307–308).

Our rationale for this project, then, is based on the notion that widows and widowers of dementia victims, because their bereavement process is unique, may be having a rough survival period, about which we know very little. By talking with them, we hoped to learn more. We specifically hoped to learn how support groups for caregivers might better address the present and future needs of the members.

Hospice care has long recognized the need for after-care with the bereaved, and as a national policy builds this care in for a minimum of one year after the death. We are suggesting the same model for spouses of dementia victims. Our hypothesis is that future problems could be ameliorated by counseling before or soon after the death of the spouse.

INTRODUCTION

Our exploratory study was based on 40 two-hour interviews with widows and widowers of dementia victims (Appendix A). Our subjects were from Wisconsin and Michigan, ranged in ages from 50 to 93, were all white, and were largely from Alzheimer's Disease and Related Disorders Association (ADRDA) support groups. Our sample consisted of 27 females and 13 males whose spouses had died between three months and three years prior to the interview.

Our sample is biased: people who belong to ADRDA and other support groups are probably better off in many ways than those who do not belong; our people were all white, largely middle class, and from the midwest. So while our sample is far from perfect, the responses of the interviewees provide a beginning for understanding the difficulties and emotions experienced during this vulnerable period. We are aware that three months after death looks very different from three years after death, as do all the many stages in between. We were asking for their expertise and advice: "What has this survival been like for you? What advice do you have for us, for today's caregivers and support groups?"

In addition to our 40 interviews, we did an extensive literature review on caregivers of dementia victims, and on coping strategies of people under stress. We also reviewed 80 questionnaires completed by relatives of deceased Alzheimer victims from a previous study by Coons et al. (1983) (Appendix B). A number of the questions from this questionnaire were directly related to the present study, in that the 1983 study dealt with the subjective experiences of families dealing with Alzheimer's Disease.

From the moment of inception we had two main goals in mind: (1) What could we learn from our study to incorporate into the running of support groups that might prove helpful to caregivers, both in their present and future lives? And, (2) Are there any clinical or policy implications in our findings?

LITERATURE REVIEW

There has been much literature in recent years about family caregivers of dementia victims as they care for their relatives. There are also bodies of literature on grieving, stress, and recovery from loss. What we have not been able to find is any literature dealing specifically with the survival of caregivers *after* the death of their spouse from dementia.

We have attempted to draw from some of the literature about grieving, stress, and loss, that which seems relevant to our present study of widows and widowers. In our study we present a tentative exploration of a recovery process for spouses of dementia victims.

Sudden vs. Expected Death

There is a commonly held view that sudden death produces more disturbed survivors than does gradual, expected death. In a study by Fulton and Cottesman (1980) of older men and women, there was a negative correlation between length of illness and the emotional response of the survivors. The longer the terminal illness, the more likely there was for a poor outcome for the surviving spouse. Rando (1984) comes to the same conclusion:

Despite the importance of a period of preparation prior to death, there is some evidence that too long a period of forewarning can also predispose grievers to poorer bereavement outcomes (p. 52).

Rando writes that the longer the illness, the angrier caretakers become, and consequently the more typical grief responses they evidence after the death. A long, drawn-out illness leads the caretaker to decathect from the patient, which often causes guilt feelings.

A 1984 study done by the Committee for the Study of Health Consequences of the Stress of Bereavement (Osterweis, Solomon & Green), comes to a similar conclusion:

> But if life is prolonged for someone who is unconscious or in pain, or whose personality and mental function have been dramatically altered by the illness or treatment, then such extensions of life may make the anticipation of death and the subsequent bereavement more difficult for survivors (p. 4).

Simos (1979) points out that a long, drawn out illness can cause depletion in the caregiver.

> In depression, narcissistically important goals are still maintained; in depletion they are altered, if not altogether abandoned (p. 241).

It is not clear what we are seeing when caregivers express resignation and apathy. Is it depression, or true depletion? What seems like resignation and acceptance, Simos writes, may in reality be a defense mechanism against overwhelming threat and loss.

Depletion, apathy, resignation, and helplessness were all dominant themes that showed up in connection with prolonged grieving, both in the literature and in our interviews. Most studies on bereavement focus on the first year. Anticipatory grieving, particularly when it is prolonged, deserves more rigorous study.

Bowling and Cartwright (1982) studied a random sample of 361 elderly widowed people in England. For these people practical problems caused the most serious adjustment difficulties. Those most frequently listed were: adaptation to living alone, coping with new household tasks, and adjusting to less money.

Complicated Grief

Both Parkes (1983) and Warden (1982) found that spouses who were angriest following the death of their partner also experienced the highest degree of social isolation. Warden discusses *failure* to grieve as a predictor of future difficulties. Much of this failure to grieve is traced to the absence of social sanctions for expressing one's negative feelings. He lists three social conditions which may give rise to complicated grief reactions:

1. When the loss is socially unspeakable, as many in our society feel dementia is.
2. When the loss is socially negated. This is true with dementias, both in our lack of medicare and medicaid services, and in our social isolation of victims and their caregivers.
3. When there is an absence of social support networks.

In addition to the absence of social sanctions to grieve, Warden mentions several other reasons why people might fail to grieve:

1. Relationship factors, especially if they were highly ambivalent or highly dependent.
2. Circumstantial factors, especially poverty.
3. Historical factors, especially if a person has had a history of previous losses and separations or a history of depression.
4. And last, but in our opinion an important factor, people are different—with different capacities for tolerating stress.

He goes on to list grief reactions that he considers complicated and in need of resolution: chronic, delayed, exaggerated, and masked. An atmosphere of support, compassion, and acceptance for expressing negative thoughts and feelings, he feels, will help resolve some of the grief.

Weisman (1984) makes this same point as the central theme in his book *The Coping Capacity*. He believes that life is full of unpredictable, uncontrollable events that upset us. The notion that one can control and direct one's life is irrational. The best people can do is learn to cope well.

> Many human problems have no discernible solutions., Our morale and self-esteem are exposed to a variety of erosions and explosions, and distress is almost a natural state of being (p. 63).
>
> We can cope, and learn to cope better. We cannot eliminate problems and eliminate death (p. 30).

Institutionalization

Since most of our interviewees expressed very high levels of stress around the issue of institutionalizing their husband or wife, we were interested in literature on nursing home decisions.

Study after study suggest that caregivers resort to nursing home placement only after they have totally exhausted their own physical and emotional resources (Crossman et al. 1981). The decision to place a relative in a nursing home is a very difficult one for many caregivers. Informants say that they make the decision when they just can no longer endure the situation. Either the caregiver realizes that he or she is totally exhausted and out of control, and no longer able to manage, or else someone who is close to the caregiver advises that the time has come. Since dementia patients' physical needs often escalate, it becomes more and more difficult to care for them without the professional help that a nursing home provides.

Powell and Courtice (1983) say that institutioning a dementia victim forces the spouse to face her own aging and even the chances of getting Alzheimer's disease herself. These thoughts are sometimes too much to bear.

As mentioned in the beginning of this literature review, we have been able to find only related writings, not literature specifically on widows and widowers of dementia victims. One of the most meaningful articles was written in the context of why adult children have so much guilt and difficulties around nursing home placement (Brody, 1985). Although we are concerned about spouses, what Brody has to say seems most relevant. She hypothesizes that the disparity between the standards and expectations of devotion we think we should feel, and the unavoidable mixed and/or negative feelings we do have, leads to guilt. Most people carry a fantasy that they should somehow do more for their loved one. Placing someone in a nursing home is experienced "as the ultimate failure to care." This was a theme we found repeatedly as our interviewees expressed trauma over nursing home placement.

DISCUSSION AND IMPLICATIONS
People Are Different

Whether it is death and dying, successful sex, coping with life's many stresses, or baking zucchini bread—it seems that what we all want is a recipe, a neat package of stages or skills that says this is how it is. With the exception of zucchini bread, this does not seem to be the case. And so it is with our survival study of widows and widowers of dementia victims. We looked for patterns of coping or predictable stages of recovery from the caregiving experience. In part, we wanted to find a package of answers that would enable us to say to existing groups of caregivers: here is what is apt to happen and this is what you can do to best prepare yourselves. Warden (1982) suggest a nine-step therapeutic procedure (pp. 67–73):

1. *Rule out physical disease.* Since grieving people often experience physical symptoms of stress, it is important to rule out physical disease behind the symptom, if at all possible.
2. *Set up a contract* of how you will work together to reexplore his or her relationships with the person involved in the loss. Relationships are explored only if they affect the response to the immediate bereavement.
3. *Revive memories of the deceased,* particularly about positive experiences, to help the patient later on if he or she is experiencing some of the more negative effects. This provides some balance and enables the patient to face some of the negative areas.
4. *Assess which grief tasks are not completed,* and try to work on those in hopes that the patient will be emancipated from a dysfunctional attachment to the deceased, and thus be free to move on to other relationships and activities.
5. *Deal with affect* (or lack thereof) stimulated by memories, particularly the more ambivalent feelings. The goal here is acceptance of all feelings, positive, negative, and mixed. Guilt is often an area that needs a lot of attention and "working through."
6. *Explore linking objects,* that is, symbolic objects that the survivor keeps to provide a way of maintaining a relationship with the deceased. Understanding the meaning behind these objects, other than as keepsakes, is often very important.
7. *Acknowledge the finality of the loss.* Some people hang on to the notion that somehow the person will come back in one form or another, and this keeps them from moving on with their lives
8. *Deal with the fantasy of ending grieving,* or what they would lose in giving

up their grief. This, says Warden, is a simple procedure, but one that is often helpful.

9. *Help the patient say a final good-bye.* Warden believes that when the unfinished business is completed the patient will know he or she is ready.

Although some of the procedures may seem simplistic and a means of providing the counselor with "neat packages," they touch upon sensitive and difficult areas that face those who are grieving and must be dealt with by counselors.

Osterweis et al. (1984) also mention lack of social support and ambivalence in marital relationships as predictors of poor bereavement outcomes. They describe a bereavement intervention program in which the goals centered around change, not "recovery."

> It was discovered in talking to widows that they never 'recovered' in the sense of returning to all prebereavement baselines, but that a successful outcome depended upon their ability to adapt and alter their images and roles to fit their new status (p. 267).

In other words, the most fundamental need for survival was learning how to cope and change.

In rereading the quantity of subjective interviews before us, perhaps all that can be said for sure is that the coping mechanisms for survival seem as infinite as the number of respondents. Before abandoning the whole project as an exercise in futility, it occurred to us that perhaps this is what we have found and should say—as obvious as it seems— that people are very different. The clinical implication of this is: do not make assumptions about how it ought to be—just listen carefully and try to be helpful. As one interviewee said in response to our asking him if he had advice for families on how to cope: "I think it is impossible to generalize, since each case is so different."

A few key issues did emerge. Transition into a nursing home seemed to be the most consistent trauma for caregivers. It was a decision often made out of desperation. Responses about placement ranged all the way from "I'd never place him in a home, no matter what," to "A good nursing home is the only solution. Don't try to be 'superfamily.'"

Experiences with nursing home placement also varied from the extreme positive to the most negative. On the negative side the most often expressed complaints were: the nursing home was understaffed; the workers did not know enough about dementias; patients were overdrugged; and there was not enough for the patient to do. On the positive side: "Church nursing homes are the best," good care was given to the patient, and staff was pleasant to family members.

When we asked spouses: "How has this whole experience affected your development as a person?" we again got responses that varied from the most positive ("It made me stronger; increased my faith in God"), to the very negative ("It made me very bitter; weaker; nervous"). For some it seemed as if the martyr role was the only possible reward left.

A number of people had combined and mixed feelings on the subject, and expressed their reactions to the question in a number of ways. In one form or another 25 of our sample of 40 said the experience made them "stronger;" 15 said it made them "more accepting;" 9 said it made them "bitter;" and 10 used the word "weaker."

For those spouses who remained in support groups after the death of their victim, there were three gains that were frequently mentioned: it was meaningful for them to try and help others, they were interested in information about dementias, and there was still the comfort of feeling understood by others in the group.

A central question we were interested in is what advice, if any, they had for caregivers, to help them with their adjustment. That is, given what they had been through, did they have words of wisdom for people to prepare themselves for life after the death of their spouse?

Their advice reconfirms the concept that people are different, and we cannot find neat packages in which to frame this process. Some people took a rather positive stance and advised others: "Be accepting, it is God's will, take one day at a time, be patient." Others had an eye to future adjustment, and warned: "Family members have rights, too, and must not give all of themselves for the 'cause';" "Be good to the patient, because you will suffer regrets and guilt if you don't;" "Try not to rage because it will only make you feel guilty later on;" "Don't be proud—Ask for help;" "Continue to visit in the nursing home so you don't feel regrets afterwards;" "Stay tender and loving;" "Get support to alleviate the guilt around nursing home placement;" "Be honest with yourself;" and "Join a support group and take care of yourself."

Some people stressed practical advice: "Be sure to get control of property and other finances; get legal issues taken care of;" "Education abut dementias in all its stages is most important; support groups are a must;" and "Specify to the doctors not to attach life-support equipment towards the end."

And still others found advice giving beyond them: "I don't know; it was such a nightmare;" "I've asked my daughter to shoot me if I get it;" or, "I just didn't want to lose him, no matter what." One caregiver put it succinctly: "You can't give advice. It depends on whether you place your own life and happiness foremost, or your victim's." "Advice, I really don't know. All I know for sure is that it was very sad and hard on me to see her deteriorate that way." One person summarized this question beautifully: "Each family, and more specifically each family member, has a wide variety of coping and tolerance levels. Therefore, I find it difficult to presume that I could advise others based on my own experience. I don't advise others, I just listen carefully and assure them I understand what they are going through." Sage advice for all us!

Another issue that came up frequently was one of genetic concern, either for their children or themselves. This is a particularly difficult issue, because we have no answers beyond statistical probabilities. But we must be aware of the fact that many people are worried about genetic factors, and provide an opportunity for discussion. Unspoken fears are probably worse than those that can be discussed openly.

In many ways our central question remains: is dementia bereavement different from and more difficult than other bereavement situations? One hypothesis is that it is. Because dementias destroy the brain, the very essence of a person, we wonder if the problems and stresses for spouses are not more complicated than in other terminal diseases.

Summary

The most significant finding from our exploratory study with widows and widowers of dementia victims is that you cannot make generalizations about their recovery process.

It follows, then, that the most important implication for practice is to sharpen our skills at listening very carefully to what we are being told. On some level, this is a self-evident statement. But sometimes we all need to be reminded of it, as we search for neat packages of explanations for human behavior—in order to make us feel more secure in our work.

Our interviewees did spell out the helpfulness of support groups for caregivers, both during the long course of the illness, and after the death of their spouse. Most people benefit from remaining in a support group, or from getting some kind of supportive counseling, during the recovery period after the death of their spouse. It is our recommendation that this after-care service be routinely offered. To lose a spouse from dementia may be one of the most difficult and complicated bereavement processes there is.

Our sample stressed three main areas they felt should be incorporated into caregiver support groups.

1. Practical issues, i.e., legality and financial concerns; letting the doctor know whether or not the family wishes life supports to be used at the end; knowing as much as possible about the dementias and their course, from beginning to end.
2. Caregiver needs, both emotional and practical.
3. Help with nursing home placement: both the practical and financial side, and the emotional one of making that decision and then living with it. People seem to feel the whole gamut of responses from relief to burdensome guilt.

According to Morycz social support is the most important variable in reducing stress for caregivers, so it stands to reason that support groups are of paramount importance.

... dementia will be the most common cause of institutionalization in this country. It therefore will be crucial for health care providers and social policymakers to be better informed about the nature of social costs of family support to the aged with mental impairment (Morycz, 1985, p. 356).

Last, but surely not least, we were touched by the eagerness of so many caregivers to give of themselves. They gave to their spouses and were eager to help others in support groups. Their willingness to participate in this study reflects a wish to offer their valuable help and advice to present and future caregivers.

REFERENCES

Bowling, A., & Cartwright, A. (1982). *Life after death—A study of the elderly widowed.* London: Tavistock Publications.

Brody, E. M. (1985). Parent care as a normative family stress. *The Gerontologist, 25* (1), 19–29.

Coons, D., Chenoweth, B., Hollenshead, C., & Spencer, B. (1983). Report to families of the study, Alzheimer's Disease: Subjective experiences of families. Ann Arbor: Institute of Gerontology, The University of Michigan.

Crossman, L., London, C., & Barry, C. (1981). Older women caring for disabled spouses: A model for supportive services. *The Gerontologist, 21* (5), 464–470.

Frederick, J. (no date). Physiology of grief. *Dodge Chemical Magazine.*

Fulton, R., & Gottesman, D. J. (1980). Anticipatory grief: A psychosocial concepts reconsidered. *British Journal of Psychiatry, 137,* 45–54.

Morycz, R. K. (1985). Caregiving strain and the desire to institutionalize family members with Alzheimer's Disease. *Research on Aging, 7* (3), 329–361.

Osterweis, M., Solomon, F., & Green, M. (eds.) (1984). *Bereavement: Reactions, consequences, and care.* Washington, DC: National Academy Press.

Parkes, C. M., & Weiss, R. S. (1983). *Recovery from bereavement.* New York: Basic Books.

Powell, L., & Courtice, K. (1983). *Alzheimer's Disease: A guide for Families.* Menlo Park, CA: Addison-Wesley Publishing Company.

Rando, T. A. (1984). *Grief, dying, and death: Clinical interventions for caregivers.* Champaign, IL: Research Press Co.

Silver, R. L., & Wortman, C. B. (1980). Coping with undescribable life events. In J. Garber & M.E.P. Seligman (eds.), *Human helplessness: Theory and applications.* New York: Academic Press, 307–308.

Simos, B. G. (1979). *Time to grieve: Loss as a universal human experience.* New York: Family Service Association of America.

Warden, W. J. (1982). *Grief counseling and grief therapy: A handbook for the mental health practitioner.* New York: Springer Publishing Co.

Weisman, A. D. (1984). *The coping capacity: On the nature of being mortal.* New York: The Human Sciences Press.

CHAPTER 25

ORGAN LOSS, GRIEVING, AND ITCHING

Kemal Elberlik

BODY IMAGE

A teacher once asked his students where they would choose to have a third eye if it were possible to have one. Some replied that a third eye in the center of the occipital region would be useful because with it they could see the back of the body. Some favored placing it in the abdomen or in the stomach to permit a view of the inside of the body.

One, however, said that having a third eye on the tip of the index finger would be ideal; he pointed out that then he could point it in any direction he wanted, and could see inside and back of his body and objects in the environment, and could touch most of the things he could see and see what he was unable to touch. All the students were eager to see the parts of the body invisible to them in ordinary circumstances, and they all expressed a need to know the total body. Optic experience is important in acquainting us with the nature of the external world and our relationship to it, and it also plays a dominant role in the creation of the body image.

Schilder[1] speaks of the body image as being, in simple terms, the picture of one's own body that each of us has formed in his own mind, and he stresses the special contribution of the senses of sight and touch in determining what that picture will be. But we also experience movement, both fine and gross, with the body and within it, and the kinesthetic gives further dimension to the self. Thus a *third eye* on the index finger would be a prime refinement of the individual's ability to know his environment and his self, action and touch giving final shape to the bodily self as it appears to him and as he believes that others perceive it.

Reprinted with permission from the *American Journal of Psychotherapy*, Vol. 34, No. 4 (October 1980), pp. 523–533.

The effect of body image on the emotions can be illustrated at one extreme by children so effectively "pretending" to be giants that they suddenly become unwontedly "brave" on the playground; and at another extreme by the sensibility of the orchestral conductor Giulini, who says of music, "Until I feel it in my physical body I cannot conduct it." It follows that when the body is damaged and a new, flawed body image must be acknowledged, emotional and behavioral alteration can be expected, although it may be manifested so subtly as to require careful clinical scrutiny.

Niederland[2] suggests that an early body defect tends to leave an aura of unresolved conflict because of its concrete nature, its permanence, and its cathectic significance. Greenacre's[3] work supplements this view; she talks about a primitive "body disintegration anxiety" in serious disturbances of the early body image, and proposes that defective development of the body image contributes significantly to the establishment of fetishism.

Volkan[4] refers to the importance of the mother's role in the crystallization of the child's image of his own body. The mother's perception of a child's physical deformity may persist long after the deformity has been corrected, and may thus be conveyed to the child in the interaction of the mother-child unit. The mother of a child with a body defect can further traumatize her child if the mother-child unit functions poorly and she overstimulates the child's body or attempts to perform physiotherapeutic or orthopedic maneuvers.[5]

The evaluation of the body image is important in facilitating and completing the process of separation-individuation. Separation begins with the discovery of a world beyond the mother-me, and is activated by the beginning crystallization of body boundaries during the symbiotic period and thereafter. Growing intrapsychic awareness of separation, and the continuing practice of differentiation promote the formation of appropriate representations of self and object essential to the development of the ego.

The infant assimilates aspects of the key persons in his environment as his ego and superego by introjecting and incorporating them, then depersonalizing these introjects and identifying with them. They become part of his self. Early separation is dealt with by introjection-identification. Since humans change greatly from birth to adulthood to old age, body image is not constant.[6] Nonetheless, the effect of early experiences of separation-individuation and psychosexual development upon the body image—and even to a certain extent upon the physical body itself—is evident.

The early body image begins with contribution from all of the senses, and from all available emotional resources. The construction of the early self-representation is accomplished through the first autonomous ego functions, i.e. sensation and perception, both of which are strongly influenced by libidinal as well as aggressive drive derivatives. The infant soon becomes able to connect sensation with the appropriate body part, and is early engrossed in enjoyment of feedback mechanisms as he obtains gratification from touching and being touched. Those parts of the body accessible to his searching hands will take on unique importance for him, and as he makes contact with them and with objects in the environment, introjection and identification come into play in the determination of the postural model.

The discovery of erotic zones, and the ability to eroticize, play a significant part in the investment in the body. Those body parts that can easily be reached by the hands come to have a psychological meaning that does not pertain to parts that are out of sight and out of reach. At different stages of early development different areas of the body have different values and carry differential loads of emotional reference. Such progression from one bodily focus to another is recognized in our reference to the oral, anal, and phallic stages and their corresponding types of personality. Early experience and the degree of identification shape the perception of any given body part as good or bad,[7] pleasing or repulsive, clean or dirty, loved or disliked; and such attitudes and values help to determine what the body image will be.

ORGAN LOSS

It is self-evident that the individual's reaction to organ loss will substantially depend on what the significance of the lost organ has been to him, both realistically as a functional body part and unconsciously as a symbol. Nevertheless, one must anticipate emotional reaction to a physical change in the body, whether gradual or sudden, and this is much like the loss of a key figure whose disappearance alters the individual's immediate environment; although mediated by the nuclear personality, this reaction is likely to involve acute anxiety and grief, even among the so-called well-adjusted, and the physician who fails to appreciate his patient's emotional distress in such circumstances is falling short of meeting his patient's needs.

It is now clear that unless there are complications, the process of mourning goes through predictable phases.[8-10] After an acute phase, well described by Lindemann,[11] the "work of mourning"[12] takes place. There is shock and denial, then anger, then a search to regain the lost object and disorganization, which, in the absence of complications, gives way to new organization that includes both inner and outer adaptation to the loss. Freud[12] indicated that this process is likely to take two years.

Such manifestations—the progress through different phases—may also appear in "established pathological grief,"[13] and extreme ambivalence and conflict concerning separation and union are present, and an introject and "linking objects" are established. Of course, if the patient disruptively identifies with the lost object, he presents a clinical picture of depression, as Freud[12] has established.

The loss of a key person is often expressed as a physical loss: "When my husband died it was as though an arm or a leg had been torn from my body." In the ensuing inevitable mourning and depression the mourner may express a sense of painful emptiness in the chest or epigastrium when the reality of the loss penetrates the consciousness. It is interesting that in a single study of grieving Parkes[14] observed a group of widows with a group of amputees. All of these subjects had suffered severe loss, and half of them experienced the same reactions, being numb at first, and then showing a strong tendency to deny the loss. Fifty-two percent of the amputees and 62 percent of the widows said they could not believe what had happened.

Then came anxiety and distress, often severe and readily evoked by any reminder of the loss. Fifty-nine percent of the amputees and 72 percent of the widows said they made a conscious effort to avoid thinking of or being reminded of their loss. At last the pangs diminished, and the subjects began to surrender hope of getting back what they had lost. They felt depressed and apathetic. Even a year after the loss, 63 percent of the amputees and 76 percent of the widows still felt disinclined to think of the future, but there were signs of improvement and reorganization, and a redirection of feelings and behavior finally took place.

The reaction to either kind of loss was seen to have two aspects: a feeling of external loss, and a feeling of internal change. External loss elicits separation anxiety and grief, separation anxiety being the principal emotion to arise after any major loss for which one is not fully prepared. Parkes's patients who had lost limbs exhibited grief in much the same way as those who had lost important others; the typical dream of the bereaved dealt with seeing the dead person alive again, and 38 percent of the amputees dreamed of the restoration of the lost limb.

Volkan's[15] work with "established pathological mourning" indicates, however, that this is only half the story, since the typical dream of seeing the dead alive also includes elements that indicate the wish to "kill" him, as it were, in order to end the process of mourning. Similarly, it can be said that the person who has lost a part of his body wants to have it back, but at the same time wants, under the influence of the reality principle, to "lose" it in order to finish his mourning process. The individual coming to terms with loss will experience sadness before his new model has developed to the point at which he seeks out and relates in a satisfactory way to new external objects. And the process may not move toward a satisfactory outcome, but be exaggerated, delayed, or distorted.

Parkes's study points to the existence of phantom husbands as well as phantom limbs. The persistence of either may do no harm, but there are other residues of the old working models that need to be replaced or modified in such a way that they contribute to affective functioning rather than interfering with it.

CASE REPORTS

CASE 1

The problem of the first patient I will present in this connection was far less obvious than an amputated limb. Bill was a 31-year-old, well developed and well nourished white man who disavowed any major emotional problem but spoke of having had bad blackouts and being unable to work, to concentrate, or to keep up any continuing relationships. He spoke also of shunning any intellectual or emotional involvement, feeling strange about his body, and being curious as to why he had so little interest in life. He had gone several times to the emergency room because of fainting, disorientation, and vomiting, and he continued to suffer from heartburn, headache, and occasional *itching* all over his body. He reported having had chest surgery in the recent past. I then learned from his physician that Bill had been a patient in his hometown hospital on several occasions, complaining of abdominal and chest pains. Although his physician had diagnosed musculoskeletal chest pain and panic reactions, the crucial disclosure was that Bill had Klinefelter's syndrome. Questions of a possible vascular origin of his headaches and hysterical personality had been raised during hospitalizations a year or two before I saw him.

He had been married for ten years, and although his marriage had had its stormy moments, there had been no recent turmoil. The couple was untroubled about the absence of children; indeed, the wife herself had been told by a gynecologist that she was unable to have a child. The revelation that Bill's "chest surgery" had been done for the correction of gynecomastia, with mammectomy on both breasts, led to an account of his attempts to accommodate to the effects of Klinefelter's syndrome on both his functioning and his body image.

Bill told me that after puberty he was very restless, and constantly acted out in an effort to demonstrate his masculinity. He always sought work in jobs available only to strong, masculine men, in which physical strength (power) was required. He dated heavily, drank a great deal, and was often engaged in physical combat of some kind. His first hospitalization took place when he had a problem with one knee. The physical examination made at that time disclosed not only an infectious process in his right knee, but gynecomastia and bilateral hypoplasia He had always felt concern about the overgrowth of his breasts, but this was the first time he had had to face a medical verdict concerning his condition. It took six years for him to make up his mind to submit to a mammectomy. Surgery for hiatal hernia was performed soon after this, and was followed by several more operations to correct postsurgical complications on the chest.

He had exhibited hysterical physical symptoms for two years, wandering pains and itching foremost among them. Psychological tests given at this time pointed to the possibility of feelings of inadequacy and difficulties in interpersonal relationships. His defensive style was effective only in a very limited way, and the prospect of his being able to deal effectively with periods of increased life stress was poor. He was suffering from a continuing need to act out on account of his complex sexual identities, and he was unable to deal adequately with the reorganization of body image after his chest surgery. His history of acting out during his postpubertal stage was related to his genetic characteristics and his gynecomastia.

His inability to form a cohesive body image or stable identity was an important factor in his inadequate coping with his mammectomy, which affected both his physical and emotional equilibrium. His postoperative complications and emotional disorientation continued as an accompaniment to ego impairment. He could not deal with the change in his body, and expressed his frustration and anger by blaming the surgeon and the complicated surgery he had performed. His hysterical behavior and acting out actually related to the fragility of his nuclear identity. Denial and anger were the affective roots of his pathological reaction to the loss of the already delicate balance between body and self-image. His wandering pains and *itching* were probably attempts to reorient himself and to work through toward the formation of a new body image, which in turn might be expected to foster a stable identity. The inability to form the necessary new body image brings with it the threat of disintegration, and Bill's great anxiety and mild depersonalization and anger reflected his frustration over his incapacity. Any realistic orientation to his bodily state was unfortunately being blocked by his denial, anger, and extreme frustration.

CASE 2

Joe was a 46-year-old white man who was unemployed and divorced. His chief complaint was insomnia, headache, and spells of *itching*, mostly on the upper extremities and the face. He was also depressed. When 13 years old, he had sustained a fractured pelvis and rupture of the bladder in a truck accident. His injuries had led to 30 hospital stays, and several operations, both major and minor. Complications in his urinary tract had finally been corrected by major surgery two years before he came to our attention. An artificial ureter and the construction of an artificial orifice in the perineal area made it necessary for him to sit down to urinate, and to devote considerable time to cleaning himself in the absence of adequate sphincter control. He could seldom go for more than a few hours without urinating. He had abdominal and gastrointestinal disturbances, and a large inoperable inguinal hernia for the discomfort of which he wore a brace.

Joe had married at 20. At that time his physical condition was adequate, and he and his wife had three children. When the corrective surgery for the urinary tract became necessary a few years after his marriage he became impotent, and his wife left him on that account when he was 33 years old. After her departure he lived with his mother and a bachelor brother, who died four years before we saw Joe. His mother died during the following year, and he was unable to work after her death, moving in with an older brother and his wife with whom he continued to live, doing their domestic work and driving them to their places of employment. He became responsible for all of the household tasks that usually fall to a woman's lot, and gradually dropped all other interests and contacts, occupying himself altogether with the feminine role. He was passive-dependent and very fragile. Although he expressed hopelessness, he denied any suicidal ideation and had no history of attempted suicide.

The losses he had suffered were major; although he still had a penis it was not functional, and he had to accommodate to the artificial urinary tract and orifice in the perineal area. In addition, he was obliged to function in the role of a helping mother, and to reorganize his body image to take into account not only physical alteration but also the disturbance in and alteration of gender role.

Joe's losses—the loss of sexual function resulting from several ureter dilations and the final surgical construction of a new orifice, and the death of his mother—threatened his identity and his feelings of integrity. He was unable to make any real effort to return to his active role, but accepted a passive posture continuing to be a housekeeper instead. From time to time his pain would become acute and his constant itching intolerable; his distress led him to visit the emergency room often. His frequent touching suggested the "eye on the index finger," since it served many purposes and activated the integration possible after mutilation. He had to keep the orifice of the ureter clean, and he became obsessed with this process, feeling the need to touch the orifice more often than was necessary. This constant need to touch reflected the need to know the new opening of his body, and was also a replacement of his need to see it. Although his penis was not functional, it was still physically present.

Joe's constant preoccupation with his dead mother minimized the affective reality of the loss of a functioning penis. His unresolved grief for her combined with his grief for what had been lost to him through the mutilation of his body. He had recurrent dreams of going fishing with his mother, although in reality they had never fished together; the lost penis seemed to be symbolically displaced by the fish they caught in the dreams. His denial of the loss of sexual integrity and his earlier physical image was displaced and extended in the concomitant mourning process.

The constant itching of Joe's face was a kind of testing related to his gender identity as it involved touching and seeing his beard and his features. It was necessary for him to test and assimilate these visual and tactile perceptions of his physical self. Itching and pain were important in supporting the redistribution and reintegration of what had been his in the past and what was still available to him. They were essential to the formation of a new image for the present and the future. He kept hoping for some quick benefit from medication, and I saw him only six times. Dependent on his brother and sister-in-law, he kept using denial, somatization, and passivity as major defenses in his unresolved grieving for his losses.

CASE 3

Tom was a 69-year-old black man with bilateral amputation of the legs below the knee. He had suffered from diabetes mellitus since 1951, and was an inpatient when I saw him. He had lost his left leg from gangrene in 1974, and his right in 1975, but was under regular treatment that included careful management of his diet. At the time he was hospitalized because of severe depression and isolation—several months after the second surgical procedure—he was living with his son but was unable to care for himself or to function adequately. He recalled having suffered severely from phantom-limb pain for some time, and being disturbed by occasional itching in the stump and upper extremities.

His wife had died in 1954, leaving him with two children whom he cared for and educated. After his son moved out of their home in 1976 Tom tried to commit suicide. He lived alone after that, dependent on outside help because of has inability to care for himself. A year later he made a second suicide attempt and was taken to the hospital with severe depression. After treatment there he went to live with his son and daughter-in-law, but was taken to the State Hospital in 1978 in a depressed state.

When I saw him he was totally amnesic, negative, and uncooperative, but after regular contact with him was established he became communicative, although his hopelessness never abated. He had no place to go, and on the basis of past rejection feared being rejected again. His amnesia about his operations, etc., continued. He could remember the pain of his phantom limbs and has trouble with itching, but not his attempts at suicide, the events of his hospitalization, or other experiences of that period. I saw him for only a short time in the hospital since he rejected therapeutic contact. He refused to consider a prosthesis.

Tom had undergone what were surely drastic organ losses, but he was suffering also from the rejection by his children, during the time of his incomplete recovery from the grief of his amputation. So he continued in a state of delayed and unresolved grief, with marked hopelessness and helplessness. His behavior continued to be passive-aggressive, and his negativistic attitude continued to reflect the impulse to self-destruction that had been exhibited in his two attempts at suicide. The total physical structure is important for total and effective functioning. Injuries, illness, and the loss of an organ often disturb emotional balance.

DISCUSSION

All three of the patients described suffered from some degree of alteration in their relationships with others, and exhibited denial, displaced anger, dread of dependence on others, phantom phenomena, a loss of social and professional orientation, and marked regression, all of which closely parallel the symptoms (fixation) of complicated pathological grief reactions, and relate to major organ losses in these cases. The *itching* and wandering pains, characteristic and persistent symptoms, were the dominant psychophysiological reactions, and will be examined from the point of view of bringing back or giving up the lost parts in the psychodynamics of established pathological mourning.

The phenomenon of the phantom member is described by Kolb[16] as usually disappearing within two years, but it seems probable that the inability to reorganize the body image after the phantom disappears lasts much longer than is supposed. Jarvis[17] and Simmel[18] found the phantom manifested chiefly in sensations of itching; and Hoffman[19] reports a phantom eye that manifested itself in itching of the brow. Kolb indicates that pain in a phantom member, or in the area of physical disturbance, may serve as symbolic expression of anxiety over the loss of a member and the threat to dependency needs that the issue has brought about. He postulates also that the phantom may express sadomasochistic identification with a depressive equivalent, as is seen in the second and third cases described here.

The ability to exert voluntary control of a member's movement is an important factor in the construction—and reconstruction—of the body image. Löfgren[20] notes that the normal autonomous motility of the penis is in itself anxiety provoking. The mouth and the anus are genetically highly erogenous zones in their developmental period, and before long they become part of the voluntary system, whereas the penis does not.

Moreover, because it is anatomically less firmly attached than most other parts of the body, it is not surprising that fantasies about its possible loss occur. The rarity of a phantom penis, the organ's peculiar sensitivity to touch, and the changes it undergoes in puberty support the conclusion that one cause of castration anxiety is its failure to become a securely anchored part of the body ego. The second patient I described, who had a penis without function, never developed a phantom penis but manifested persistent and overwhelming castration anxiety as well as depression.

In an article on organ transplants and their relation to body image and psychosis, Castelnuevo-Tedesco[21] noted that recent experience with organ transplantation has contributed to our understanding of the phenomenon of body image, particularly to the concept one has of the arrangements within the body. He goes on to say that life-saving operations that remove some diseased body part seem to restrict or limit the body image; the patient, having experienced a loss, is often depressed. Many have a tendency to retain the lost member or organ in fantasy, as is evidenced by the phantom phenomenon.

The life-extending surgery of transplantation, however, enlarges the body image. Something has been added, and the patient must make room for it so that something previously exterior to the self can be felt as included within the ego. This investigator feels that body image is maintained by a rather fluid process that is strongly influenced by—and that in turn influences—the level of ego integration, including the degree of regression present at any given time. The first case here demonstrates acute anxiety and mild depersonalization as signs of marked regression and extreme ambivalence.

The individual whose completeness of body image is disturbed by a sudden physical change or loss of function faces a situation that is without precedent in his experience. After some time he may be successful in reconstructing a new body image by reactivating all perceptive systems and continuing to reintegrate and reorganize his feelings and attitudes. The reorientation to the new situation with what remains constitutes an attempt to accept a new image. However, pain or physical irritation will change the postural model of the body, and whatever area of the body has been attacked or mutilated can become the focus of the self and the object of attention not only for the sufferer but for those in the environment as well. Such a powerful concentration of internal and external emotion when centered in that part of the body is overloaded with the early integrated emotional experiences, and these will activate and mobilize early unresolved conflicts and fantasies. Such regression may disturb the successful orientation to the loss, and cause impairment of the ego. The restoration of satisfactory function depends psychologically on the resolution of the early unresolved experiences and their presently existing sequelae. Constructive medical care on a continuing base is often the determinant of successful physical and psychophysiological reorientation.

ITCHING AND SCRATCHING

As noted, all three of the cases described exhibited itching. It seems that itching and/or scratching, accompanied by phantom phenomena or wandering pain, become the core of experimentation in the restructuring of the mental image of the body. Itching makes for restlessness, and it is painful. Scratching may comfort the surface of the body, but dealing with an irritated part of the body by scratching it can activate sadomasochistic tendencies. According to Musaph[22] many people scratch without actually having an itch. Scratching may be simply a motor discharge of such emotional tension as might appear in someone embarrassed or lost in concentration. In some cases scratching can produce itching.

The element of pleasure in such a largely unconscious movement is evident. Some people develop a way of scratching that produces sensations of mild pain that they enjoy; this might be compared to masturbation. In this connection the element of skin eroticism should be considered. Itching and scratching may provide dermal erotic gratification. Each phase of infantile sexuality can give dermal eroticism its special color.

Thus itching can be a sign of repressed anxiety, repressed rage, or repressed sexuality. Certainly we cannot ascribe to any one single psychological meaning all occurrences of itching, particularly since it may indeed be symptomatic of some physical illness.

Nonetheless, the emotional libidinal exchange involved in ministering to the body's needs by "scratching where it itches" contributes to the knowledge of the total body. In each of the cases described here, wandering pain and itching appeared in other parts of the body than those from which a member had been lost. The total body image must be reconstructed by rechecking what remains. Optical and tactile perceptions, along with motility, are the most important elements in such reconstructive attempt, and the grieving is a normal emotional process in reconstruction after internal loss.

It is interesting to note how common it is for the geriatric patient to complain of itching, which, however much it may be due to the dryness of aging skin, is also evidence of the need to recheck the boundaries of a body that is undergoing profound alteration from the body image to which the aged person was so long accustomed. The old can tolerate no further loss; what remains to them must be constantly checked. Their limited control of voluntary movement and their dread of further loss make it necessary to monitor what is still there, and touching can very well be a sign of the power of the body image to galvanize the individual's resources.

SUMMARY

Three cases in which the patients had to modify their body images because of surgical change are described. In their postsurgical period all gave evidence of undergoing complicated mourning. This article examines itching and scratching manifested in all three from the point of view of its contribution to the patient's exploration of his new body image.

REFERENCES

1. Schilder, F. *The Image and Appearance of the Human Body.* International Universities Press, New York, 1950.
2. Niederland, W. C. *Narcissistic Ego Impairments in Patients With Early Physical Malformations.* Psychoanal. Study Child, Vol. XX, 1965, 518–34.
3. Greenacre, P. Certain Relationships between Fetishism and the Faulty Development of the Body Image. (1953) In *Emotional Growth,* International Universities Press, New York, 1971, pp. 9–30.
4. Volkan, V. D. *Primitive Internalized Object Relations.* International Universities Press, New York, 1976.
5. Freud, A. The Role of Bodily Illness in the Mental Life of Children. In *The Writings of Anna Freud,* Vol. 4, International Universities Press, New York, 1952, pp. 260–79.
6. Abse, D. W. *Hysteria and Related Mental States.* Williams and Wilkins, Baltimore, 1966.

7. Schoenberg, B. and Carr, A. Loss of External Organs: Limb Amputation, Mastectomy and Disfiguration. In *Loss and Grief: Psychological Management in Medical Practice*. Columbia University Press, New York, 1970.

8. Hartmann, H. *Ego Psychology and the Problem of Adaptation*. International Universities Press, New York, 1939.

9. Bowlby, J. Process of Mourning. *Int. J. Psycho-Anal.* 42:317, 1961.

10. Pollock, G. Mourning and Adaptation. *Int. J. Psycho-Anal.* 42:341, 1961.

11. Lindemann, E. Symptomatology and Management of Acute Grief. *Am. J. Psychiatry* 101:141, 1944.

12. Freud, S. *Mourning and Melancholia*. (1917). Standard Edition, Vol. XIV, London, Hogarth Press, pp. 237–58, 1957.

13. Volkan, V. D. Death, Divorce and the Physician. In *Marital and Sexual Counseling in Medical Practice*. 2nd ed. Abse, D. W., Nash, E. M. and Louden, L. M. R., Eds. Harper and Row, New York, 1974.

14. Parkes, C. M. Components of the Reactions to Loss of a Limb, Spouse or Home. *J. Psychosom. Res.*, 16:313, 1972.

15. Volkan, V. D. Typical Findings in Pathological Grief. *Psychiat. Q.*, 44:231, 1970.

16. Kolb, L. D. Disturbance of the Body Image. In *American Handbook of Psychiatry*, 2nd ed., Arieti, S. E., Ed. Basic Books, New York, 1975.

17. Jarvis, J. H. Post-Mastectomy Breast Phantoms. *J. Nerv. Ment. Dis.* 144:266, 1967.

18. Simmel, M. L. Phantom, Phantom Pains and Denial. *Am. J. Psychother.*, 13:603, 1959.

19. Hoffman, J. Facial Phantom Phenomenon. *J. Nerv. Ment. Dis.*, 122:143, 1955.

20. Löfgren, B. Castration Anxiety and the Body Ego. *Int. J. Psycho-Anal.*, 49:408, 1968.

21. Castelnuevo-Tedesco, P. Organ Transplant, Body Image, Psychosis, *Psychoanal. Q.*, 42:349, 1973.

22. Musaph, H. Psychodynamics in Itching States. *Int. J. Psycho-Anal.*, 49:336, 1968.

CHAPTER 26

FAMILY-ORIENTED TREATMENT OF CHRONIC PAIN

Alletta Jervey Hudgens

Health care practitioners are coming to realize that even chronic pain can be understood and treated within a family system perspective. If the family operates as a system to enlarge or to maintain a pain problem, then the family needs to be treated to bring the pain problem under control. As a result, programs have been developed which integrate a family-oriented and behavioral treatment program for chronic pain.

The family-oriented pain treatment program discussed in this paper involved 24 patient-families completing the treatment program in 1974 and 1975, in the Physical Medicine and Rehabilitation Service at the University of Minnesota Hospitals. A detailed description of the clinical treatment program process has been published elsewhere (Anderson, et al. 1977; Hudgens, 1978). The program is modeled after one at the University of Washington at Seattle (Fordyce, 1976).

UNDERSTANDING CHRONIC PAIN: A SOCIAL LEARNING APPROACH

Pain normally serves as a warning signal that something in the body's system is not right. However, when pain persists more than four to six months and becomes chronic, it is useful to consider the possibility that the pain may have come under the influence of powerful learning or operant mechanisms (Skinner, 1953). Pain responses or signals, such as moaning, grimacing, limping, and complaining, which occur over a long period

Reprinted from the *Journal of Marital and Family Therapy,* Vol. 5, No. 4 (October 1979), pp. 67–77. Copyright 1979 American Association for Marriage and Family Therapy. Reprinted by permission of the Association and the author.

of time, can become systematically followed by favorable consequences (positive rein-forcement) in the family and surrounding environment (Fordyce, 1976). For example, a patient might get more attention from family members, be able to avoid work, or ob-tain financial compensation.

Pain that began as a physiological response can later be experienced as a learned re-sponse or a mixture of the two. When healthy behavior (patient does not demonstrate pain) is not reinforced or rewarded, or when healthy behavior is followed by unpleas-ant consequences, it is even more likely that the pain behavior will be maintained or even be increased.

According to social learning theory, if pain behavior is learned it can also be un-learned. Using an operant conditioning approach, new behaviors that indicate activity and health can be consistently and systematically rewarded and pain behaviors ignored. As a result, new behaviors can be taught which can provide a more satisfactory life for the pain patient and family. There is precedent for the effectiveness of behavioral sys-tems therapy for families (Olson, 1976).

FAMILY SYSTEMS AND CHRONIC PAIN

The systems model views the family as a complex unit of interacting personalities and forces. When pain enters a family it is a powerful force that often controls the structure, the actions, and reactions of family members. Pain can effect sweeping changes in fam-ily roles, realign subsystems within the family, and isolate family members from each other and from outside influences. Consequent anger and guilt can change a normally functioning family into a frustrated, rigid, and unhappy group of people.

To bring about a change in such a family there must be a change in the entire system. The family system seeks balance, and a change in the patient alone will result in efforts by the rest of the members to return the system to its prior way of operating, with pain as the controlling force.

This paper will demonstrate the importance of a supportive family unit, and of working with the entire family to bring about behavioral changes that will result in sat-isfactory functioning for the family system.

DESCRIPTION OF PATIENTS AND FAMILIES
Selection Criteria

General criteria for admission to the program were the following:

1. There was at least one "significant other" who had sufficient contact with the patient to constitute a social system for effective support and change, and who was willing to work with the program.
2. The patient and family understood the program and wished to undertake it.
3. There were significant, identifiable behaviors associated with the pain, and considered modifiable by the staff.
4. There were identifiable reinforcers for healthy behaviors.
5. All other treatment methods had been unsuccessful or were not feasible.

6. Chemical dependence was not a primary problem.
7. The patient was not suffering from overt or underlying schizophrenia which might have affected his/her ability to benefit from the program.
8. There was no pending litigation in regard to the pain problem.

In the two years of this study, 86 patients (50 women and 36 men) were evaluated for admission to the program. Using the aforementioned criteria, 29 (33%) were accepted in the program. Three of these chose not to undergo treatment, and two who entered dropped out before completing treatment. Thus, the final group in this study (N=24) consisted of 18 women and six men who completed the program.

Other demographic data are as follows: Age ranged from 23 to 72, the mean age being 46. There was one black female patient, the rest were white. Nineteen (79%) of the patients were married, four were widowed, and one was single. Fifteen (65%) of the patients had some high school education, eight (33%) had some college education, and one patient had a graduate degree. Seventeen patients (71%) came from large families of four or more children. As to socioeconomic status, eight patient-families were professional or managerial, four were clerical or sales, nine were laborers, and three were farmers. This assumes that the seventeen housewives identified with their husband's socioeconomic status.

The social histories given by the patients revealed a number of factors present in patients' childhood homes. Ten reported harsh, demanding, or distant parents. Seven had lost one or both parents in childhood. Thus raises the question whether pain patients may show a significant lack of healthy, emotionally giving parent figures in early life.

In seven cases, the patient had experienced a significant amount of illness as a child, and in another seven cases one parent had been chronically ill or disabled. Merskey and Spear (1967) and Tuohy (1972) noted that pain patients frequently have an immediate family member who was injured or severely physically disabled.

Table 26–1 lists problems observed in the families by staff during counseling and in other family interactions. Each family had two or three problem areas and the most common problems were high patient dependency, indirect communications, narrow social contacts, and difficulty handling anger. The number of families who experienced sexual conflicts might be an underestimate because pain patients often deny sexual functioning problems. The narrowing of social life occurred in 60% of the families.

INITIAL DIAGNOSTIC ASSESSMENT
Medical Diagnosis

In the group of 24 patients studied, nineteen (79%) experienced lower back pain. Of these nineteen patients, five had additional pain in other body areas. There were two patients with upper back and neck pain, two patients with headaches, and one with perineal pain after prostatectomy. Patients had an average of 2.5 surgeries each. All had been unable to work, to be satisfactorily active, or to function adequately in social relationships for an average of four years.

Sixteen (two thirds) of the group had a significant problem with overdosing on pain medications, and half of these (N=8) currently or formerly had severe problems with chemical dependency.

Table 26–1
Problem Areas and Improvement for 24 Pain Patients and Families*

Problem Area	No. of Families with Problem Before Treatment	No. of Families Improved After Treatment
Patient very dependent on spouse or significant other	18	18 (100%)
Indirect communications	18	11 (61%)
Narrow social contacts	16	13 (81%)
Inability to handle anger appropriately	15	13 (87%)
Sexual conflicts	11	7 (64%)
Power struggle between spouses	10	7 (70%)
Spouse of patient had difficulty expressing warmth and affection	10	7 (70%)
Spouse of patient openly resentful of patient's illness	10	8 (80%)
Conflict over male-female roles	7	5 (71%)
At least one child in the family had adjustment problems (stealing, bowel control, setting fires)	6	4 (67%)
Large debt due to pain problem	6	5 (83%)**

*The number of problem areas was not the same for all families. Families had an average of five problems each.
**No more debt added and plans underway to reduce former debt.

Minnesota Multiphasic Personality Inventory

The mean MMPI profiles for the group appear similar to those found by Sternbach (1974). The "conversion V," or neurotic triad, with elevations on hypochondriasis, depression, and hysteria (scales 1,2,3) as shown in Figures 26–1,2,3, generally reflects the tendency to preoccupation with bodily functions and complaints. Clinicians familiar with the scales commonly note repression and denial as defenses against anxiety and depression. The majority of the sample refused to consider any psychological explanation for their pain, although some were able to do so after the pain behavior lessened in treatment, and they could function more adequately.

There was not any distinctive personality type associated with chronic pain patients. The patients did tend to be hysteroid (scale 3) or naive, self-centered, and immature in their communications with their surrounding social system. One group of ten patients (42%) were very demanding of themselves and allowed themselves little or no pleasure, which was reflected by a high score on compulsivity (scale 7).

Curiously, life histories tend to show that most chronic pain patients functioned adequately before they had pain problems (Sternbach, 1974). It appears likely that the pain produces the neuroticism and the increased awareness of physical symptoms that we see in them.

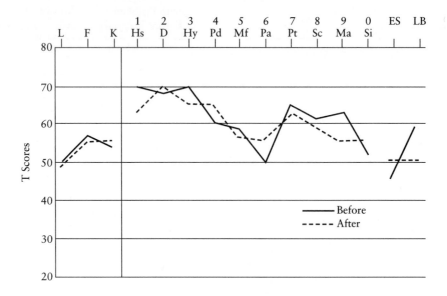

Figure 26–1
Composite MMPI profile of 6 male patients who showed significant
long-term improvement in the Pain Treatment Program

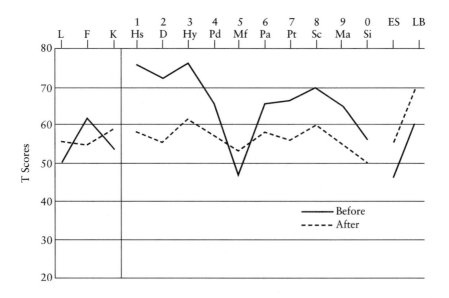

Figure 26–2
Composite MMPI profile of 12 female patients who showed significant
long-term improvement in the Pain Treatment Program

Figure 26–3

Composite MMPI profile of 6 female patients who did not achieve significant long-term improvement in the Pain Treatment Program

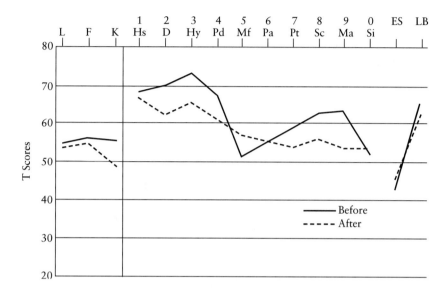

Assessing Reinforcement of Pain

In assessing the function and reinforcement of pain, staff observations were gathered from charts and conference notes. They included present behavior related to former behavioral patterns, satisfactions, and problems as described by patients and families.

In all cases pain functioned to obtain medical attention. Likewise, medical treatment, surgery, and the administration of pain medications often reinforced and maintained pain behavior.

Most patients appeared to have several functions for pain in their lives. The most common one, controlling/manipulating others, was observed in half the patient-families (N=12). An equal number of patients (N=11) seemed to use pain to justify dependency. Other functions observed included earning rest, avoiding sex, gaining attention, punishing others, controlling anger, and avoiding close relationships.

GOALS AND PLAN OF THE FAMILY-ORIENTED PROGRAM

Goals for treatment for the 24 patient-families in this study were to increase family interactions around issues other than pain, to improve family relationships, to regain occupational roles, to eliminate the use of prescription pain medication, to increase tolerance for selected exercises, and to reduce use of the health care system.

Since pain was treated as learned behavior, the pain behaviors were the initial focus of treatment. The aim was to decrease specific pain behaviors and increase healthy be-

Table 26–2
Reinforcers for Pain Behavior

	No. of Families
Attention from others	16*
Spouse gives negative attention (fusses about inactivity or intake of pain medications)	9
Financial gain for disability	9
Others take over duties	7
Community mores sanction social discussion about pain and medical problems	6

*Family members used an average of two reinforcers for pain behavior in the patient.

haviors. The inpatient program lasted seven to nine weeks, followed in most cases by an outpatient program of one to five weeks.

One major goal was to change family interactions so that the patient did not use pain in communication and interaction with others. The social worker and family developed a contract to help the family focus on specific objectives to be pursued with the patient.

Each family had at least one "significant other," usually the spouse of the patient, who came into the hospital two or three times a week for an hour to work with the social worker in retraining to ignore pain related behavior and to reinforce health related behavior of the patient. Later in the program joint interviews with the patient and spouse, and then with the entire family, served to examine and to treat problems, such as maintaining well behaviors, in the transition to the home environment. [This aspect of the problem has been discussed in detail elsewhere (Hudgens, 1978).]

While the social worker worked with the entire family, other hospital staff members worked with the patient in the hospital. Again, all pain behaviors were consistently and systematically ignored and well behaviors reinforced. Occupational therapy and physical therapy helped to slowly strengthen muscles weakened by pain and disuse. Pain medications were given on a time contingent basis and slowly reduced to zero. Work activities were introduced. Work evaluation and counseling psychology often were involved in helping the patient plan to resume meaningful activity, paid or unpaid, upon returning home. The patient kept daily graphs of exercise and activity progress for him/herself and others to see. This helped the patient and others to see him/herself as a responsible, adequate, functioning person.

The rehabilitation setting, which emphasized increased physical activity and visible, attainable goals, played a critical role in family motivation and expectations. Patients and their families were assured that the rehabilitation team believed the pain was real and treatable, regardless of the etiology of the pain problem. Staff emphasized that the program was not designed to eliminate pain, but to change behavior in order to more effectively cope with pain.

METHODS AND DESIGN

This paper describes changes in the 24 patients and family members before and after treatment. A social history was obtained from the patient and family, staff observation, family interviews, physical examination, medical records, and the Minnesota Multiphasic Personality Inventory. Reports of the community physician also contributed to the data base.

There were six variables that measured success in the program. Family relationships were measured relative to the problems listed in Table 32–1 and measurement was effected through self-report of the patient and other family members and observed behavior reported by staff and family members. Occupational role improvement was measured in the same way. Personality changes were measured by the MMPI. Activity level was assessed by changes in exercises prescribed for patients, and by reports of patients and family regarding activity outside the hospital setting. Medication intake was measured by the staff-monitored and recorded medication program. Use of the health care system was measured by interactions with the hospital staff and by the quantity and nature of contacts with the family's community physicians, reported by the family and the physicians.

Follow-up data were obtained six months to two years later in personal interviews for twelve patient-families, by telephone interviews for eight others, and by letters or second-hand reports for four patient-families.

EFFECTIVENESS OF THE PROGRAM AT DISCHARGE
Improvement in Family Relationships

Changes in the family system were often dramatic. An eight-year-old child, seeing her patient-mother walk for the first time without crutches, rushed into her arms with reinforcing hugs. A man unable to work for five years returned to his former job as a construction worker and regained his former role as a laborer and family provider. A grandmother, who had used pain to gain sympathy and resentful attention from her grown children, renewed her role as the "best cook in the family" and enjoyed visits from her grandchildren and family once again.

Table 32–1 gives the percentage of families for which problem areas significantly improved after treatment. These figures were obtained from chart notes regarding observations of behavior by staff and from self-report of patients and families.

In addition to these improvements in previously assessed problem areas, three-fourths (N=18) of the families reported a significant increase in recreation and leisure time spent within the family circle and in visiting friends and relatives.

Other individual patient gains had a positive effect on the satisfaction with family life reported by their families. Almost two-thirds of the patients reported a more optimistic and happy outlook on life (N=17), feeling more in control of their lives (N=7), and having a more positive self-concept (N=16). Over half the group (N=14) also demonstrated more assertive behavior.

Improvement in Occupational Roles

The most frequently observed and reported occupational improvement was the patient's return to some type of useful work, paid or unpaid, that was satisfactory for the patient and family. At the time of discharge this was true for 83% (N=20) of the patient-families. Home-making was the most common undertaking for fourteen patients; six returned to full-time paid employment. Of these same twenty patients, six began education or retraining programs, and three found volunteer work.

MMPI Changes

As illustrated in Figures 32–1, 2, and 3, post-treatment MMPI profiles tended to drop into a normal range, especially for the women. There was a dramatic drop in the neurotic triad (scales 1,2,3) for the women, indicating less concern with bodily functioning, less depression, and fewer hysteroid characteristics. Since the scales retain the "conversion V" pattern, one would still expect the patients to dwell on physical functioning under stress. There was less dependence (lower scale 3) and less anxiety (lower scale 7). The drop in scales 3,7, and 9 together reflect a reduction in anxiety and agitation. Ego strength (ES scale) increased, indicating greater feelings of self worth.

The profiles of the men showed that they did not change as much as the women. They had fewer bodily complaints (scale 1) and denied less (scale 3), but male depression scores (scale 2) were a bit higher after treatment, indicating their morale had not changed. This might be explained by the following. In our society it is highly valued for men to have paid employment. Employment for former back patient males is not easily attainable, and therefore work was not available as a reinforcer immediately after treatment. In comparison, almost every woman in the sample was a housewife who could return immediately to what she and society considered a productive life over which she had more control.

Activity Level and Exercise Tolerance

At the time of discharge, each patient demonstrated an activity level normal for his/her age and sex. Patients reported that weekends at home were quite different from before treatment; the patient and family lived a normally active life, interacting and enjoying each other without reference to pain or other physical complaints.

Exercise tolerance rose considerably, as shown in Figure 26–4, which compares the beginning and end of the inpatient treatment for the four more often prescribed treatment activities. At the time of discharge, each patient was given an exercise program to continue daily for the rest of their lives.

Medication Intake

Chronic pain patients relied heavily on pain medications, and overdosing was common. The use of medication differed widely in number, type, and frequency. Only one of the twenty-four patients took no medication before the program. As a group, they were

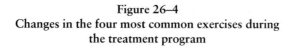

Figure 26–4
**Changes in the four most common exercises during
the treatment program**

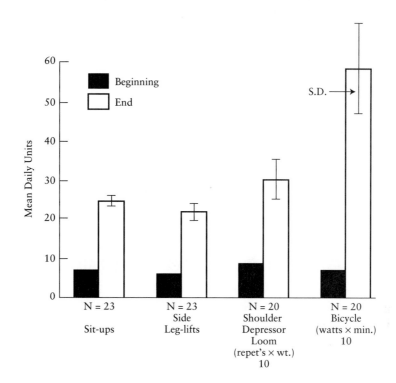

using forty different types of medication. Eighty-three percent (N=20) were on some type of pain medication, and 75% (N=18) of this group were taking narcotic analgesics. During the course of the program, the amount of medication given was reduced until, by the last two weeks of the program, all patients had no pain medication. The increases in activity level and exercise tolerance, despite the elimination of all pain medications, supported the program assumption that an operant conditioning approach can effectively reduce dependence on drugs.

Use of the Health Care System

During the treatment period, staff worked with the patient's community physician to continue the well behavior reinforcement program, insuring the maintenance of appropriate well behavior after treatment. This was an extension of a systems approach to the community system which interacts with the family system. At discharge, 20 (83%) of the patients and families were using the health care system appropriately.

FOLLOW-UP EVALUATION

At the time of the follow-up six months to two years after treatment, eighteen (75%) of the patient-families had maintained their gains as demonstrated in continuing satisfactory family relationships and occupational roles, continued exercise and activity, absence of prescription pain medication, and normal use of the health care system.

Six women did not maintain these gains. The most salient feature of this group was the lack of a strong social support system. Three were widows living alone. Two lived with spouses who did not consistently reinforce well behavior and ignore ill behavior. Only one of these six women had an adequate support system.

Differences on the MMPI were also obvious between the women who continued to do well six months to two years after the program and those women who did not maintain their gains. In comparing the women who did well (Figure 26–2) with those who did not (Figure 26–3), one observes that the former were initially more passive-aggressive and manipulative (the 4, 5, 6 "V") than the latter women who appeared more depressed. It may be that women who show a dramatic neurotic triad and complain more might more easily learn different coping methods than depressed women.

SOCIAL FACTORS IN SUCCESS AND FAILURE

A strong support system seems to be the most salient factor in the long-term successful functioning of the patient-family. Sternbach (1974) noted that married patients with family support did better in a pain treatment program. He found that in a strong supportive family, the prognosis for constructive adjustment to pain was better. Strengths included mature caring for each other, a satisfactory marriage, flexibility, and the ability to use help in readjustment. Where outside resources were also available, prognosis was even better. Friends and relatives who were open to change and who were basically mature strengthened the family support system. Community opportunities for increased social contacts and supportive services were also helpful.

The willingness of the spouse or "significant other" to modify his/her behavior toward the patient was one criterion used in acceptance to the program. Two-thirds (N=16) of the families demonstrated this by their understanding and acceptance of the program and by showing evidence of concern for the patient and desire to help. In the eight families where the families did *not* modify their behavior, half the patients did not succeed in maintaining treatment gains six months or more after the program. Three of these four were widows living alone, so that their families were tangential to the living environment. Only one widow in the program succeeded, and her "significant other" was a 20-year-old son who still lived with her part time. The four patients who succeeded in keeping their gains despite the inability of the family to modify behavior exhibited at least one of the following factors: unusual strength in assertiveness and independence, illness of the spouse enabling the former patient to feel needed, and the return of one patient to a desired job.

The problems of middle age appear important in chronic pain development and management. The median age of the sample was 44. Older men and women facing the crisis of middle age might use pain as a reaction to numerous frustrations: children leaving home, a couple's inability to deal with increased time with each other, facing unachieved dreams and improbable hopes. A study cited in Soulairac (1968) of 430 patients with somatic pains for which the clinician found no physiological evidence, observed a preponderance of patients between the ages of 30 and 50.

A look at the large group of housewives (N=17) in this sample is instructive. Skolnick (1973) noted that more married women than single women were bothered by physical pains and ailments. In a study by Pratt (1973), two-thirds of the mind-affecting drugs prescribed were to women.

The importance of returning to useful work, whether paid or unpaid, was seen in the lasting results in a family system. In the United States, usefulness and productivity are important values. If these values are strong in a family, the feasibility of useful work as a target goal in pain treatment should be considered in undertaking such an expensive and difficult program.

A number of interesting questions could be researched in the future. Do family structure and function influence the emergence of pain as a health problem? How does a family's belief about illness and its treatment affect the development and treatment of pain problems? What factors enable a family to manage pain constructively without intervention?

CONCLUSION

Of those family factors that predict success in an operant conditioning program, two factors appear to be important. Every patient-family in this sample who remained well demonstrated at least one of these features: 1) the family with whom the patient lived was supportive and amenable to retraining, 2) the patient was able to learn assertiveness and to develop control over his/her own environment. Community agency support often helped to reinforce family strengths, though in no instance could it replace family support.

It also appears that maintaining gains in the long run occurred more often where the families attended to and improved their skills in communication, such as awareness and expression of feelings, when they learned appropriate, assertive behaviors.

In summary, this study demonstrated the importance of treating the whole family in changing the management of the chronic pain of one member within the family system. Patients with a closely interacting and supportive family system that cooperated in learning to manage pain constructively maintained their gains after a retraining program, whereas those patients without a participating and cooperating, supportive family system did not maintain their gains. It is also important to enlarge the system approach to include in the treatment plan such resources as physicians, ministers, employers, and relatives interacting with the patient and family.

REFERENCES

Anderson, T. P., Cole, T. M., Gullickson, G., Hudgens, A., Roberts, A. H. "Behavior Modification of Chronic Pain: A Treatment Program by a Multidisciplinary Team," *Clinical Orthopedics,* Nov.–Dec., 1977, *129,* 96–100.

Fordyce, W. E. *Behavioral Methods for Chronic Pain and Illness.* St. Louis, Mo.: C. V. Mosby Co., 1976.

Hudgens, Alletta, "The Social Worker's Role in a Behavioral Management Approach to Chronic Pain," *Social Work in Health Care,* Winter, 1978, *3,* 149–157.

Merskey, H., and Spear, F. G. *Pain: Psychological and Psychiatric Aspects:* London: Bailliere, Windall and Cassell, 1967.

Olson, D. *Treating Relationships.* Lake Mills, Iowa: Graphic Publishing Co., 1976.

Pratt, L. "The Significance of Family in Medication," *Journal of Comparative Social Studies,* 1973, *1,* 13–31.

Skinner, B. F. *Science and Human Behavior.* New York: Macmillan Company, 1953.

SEIZURE DISORDERS

CHAPTER 27

THE PSYCHOTHERAPY OF PATIENTS WITH COMPLEX PARTIAL SEIZURES

Steven L. Taube and Nancy Harris

Patients with complex partial seizures (CPS) have unique psychological problems that may not be addressed in conventional psychotherapies (*Blumer & Benson, 1982*). The episodic but pervasive nature of these seizures may distort their present existence, their memories, their personalities and their interpersonal relationships. Their psychological healing often requires a psychotherapy based on the distinctive nature of their experiences.

There is a large body of scientific literature describing the psychiatric effects of seizures (*Hermann & Whitman, 1984*). Many of these articles discuss the psychosocial impairment of individuals with seizures (*Goldin & Margolin, 1975*). However, the literature on the psychological treatment of adults has focused on seizure reduction (*Feldman & Ricks, 1979*). Until Blumer (*1977*), the treatment of these patients' special emotional needs had not been addressed. He reported the use of psychotherapy to help a patient comprehend the behavioral consequences of his illness. Subsequently, Dorwart (*1984*) elaborated on the interaction between seizures and emotional difficulties, but his goal was still primarily seizure reduction. Messner (*1986*) outlined the use of psychotherapy to alleviate the psychological suffering of patients with CPS. Drotar (*1981*) emphasized "the unique stresses posed by each individual disease and its treatment regimens." He suggested that the behavior of patients with chronic illnesses is understood best in terms of the adaptive tasks required of these patients.

We could find no article that based the psychotherapy of patients with CPS on a systematic presentation of the adaptive difficulties and psychological stresses caused by the seizures. In this paper, the psychological impact of CPS is described and a psychotherapeutic model offered. We concentrate on the problems of those with undiagnosed

Reprinted from *American Journal of Orthopsychiatry,* Vol. 54, No. 1 (January 1984), pp. 156–161. Copyright 1984 by the American Orthopsychiatric Association, Inc. Reproduced by permission.

seizures arising in childhood, then discuss the generalization of this approach to other patients with seizure disorders.

CPS are common, with an estimated prevalence of 1–8 per 1000, affecting males and females equally *(Zielinski, 1984)*. Of those affected, 30%–40% are estimated to have persistent psychiatric symptoms; psychotherapists are likely to see such patients *(Pritchard, Lombrosco, & McIntyre, 1980)*. In 25% of those with CPS, the epilepsy is undiagnosed *(Zielinski, 1984)* and these patients may not even be aware of the existence of a pathological process, presenting themselves as maladaptive. These patients are dependent on the psychotherapist to be aware of the possibility of seizures *(Adebimpe, 1977; Stern & Murray, 1984)*.

THE NATURE OF SEIZURES

Partial seizures are caused by a paroxysm of abnormal electrical activity in a localized area of the brain. When there are changes in consciousness during the partial seizure, the episodes are classified as complex partial seizures (CPS) *(Neppe & Tucker, 1988)*. "CPS can mimic, distort or inhibit any brain function" *(Williams, 1956)*. There can be changes in sensation, perception, cognition, speech output and analysis, arousal, affect, memory storage and retrieval, motor activity, and behavior *(Neppe & Tucker, 1988)*.

Modulation of affect, particularly, is disturbed *(Williams, 1956)*. Spontaneous seizures, isolated from any causal external event, may produce bursts of strong affect. Although many emotions, pleasant and unpleasant, have been described, those of unhappiness, fright, or a vaguely disconcerted feeling are the most common. The affects generated by seizures may persist for several days after the ictal event.

Not only can seizures cause strong affects but strong emotions generated by external events can precipitate seizures that distort or replace the original feeling *(Bear, 1979)*; the result is "peculiar" responses to emotional situations. Happy occasions may paradoxically produce unexpected feelings of sadness or dread. CPS can produce distortions of perception or frank hallucinations. Accustomed surroundings can seem unusual and foreign, new environments can be strangely familiar. The events around one can have no more reality than a play or a movie. Parts of one's body can be thought to be "alien," as if they belonged to someone else. Visceral activity can be affected and may be accompanied by peculiar abdominal sensations. Memories may be fragmented, or distorted in their storage or retrieval. The patient's sense of the chronological sequence of events may be incomplete.

During a seizure, some people engage in automatic behavior that simulates eating or dressing; some may wander away in the midst of a seizure, appearing purposeful but unaware of their own activity. Some may have mystical experiences that they interpret as religious *(Neppe & Tucker, 1988; Williams, 1956)*.

One patient described her seizures thus:

> Since childhood I have experienced episodes of depersonalization, auditory hallucinations (bells ringing or indistinct voices), strange feelings in my stomach, sudden instances of fear, sadness or dread, visual distortions of others' faces, deja vu, jamais vu, and persistent preoccupation with death and eternity. I wrote poetry

and extensive journals. I often felt panicky that I would lose part of myself. The writing temporarily assuaged the panic. From the age of 18 I noted periods of depression that lasted two or three months. I had mystical experiences and visions in periods of stress. I remember projecting myself into the corner of the room, watching the corner get larger and larger, swallowing me, expanding the inside of my head.

Effect on Development

The adaptive tasks of children who suffer from covert seizures is complex. The episodic events that occur within them, as well as their attempts to find equilibrium, take place within a changing and evolving psychobiological matrix. These children must master each of the tasks of development despite the extra burden of perceptual, cognitive, and affective turbulence *(Perrin & Gerrity, 1984)*.

Like the child with dyslexia, these children may appear bright, but somehow they do not function as well as they should *(Long & Moore, 1979)*. Their failures and limitations lead to a sense of inadequacy and shame *(Ziegler & Holden, 1988)*. Ignorant of the true nature of the problem, their parents and teachers may add to the children's difficulties *(Hoare, 1984)*. However, unlike the dyslexic children, who may function least well inside the classroom, children with CPS lead an unpredictable existence and may find it hard to know their true skills and deficits *(Margalit & Heiman, 1983; Matthews, Barabas, & Ferrari, 1982)*.

Subjective experience, which for others is a touchstone, is disrupted for those with CPS by the seizure process. Events are distorted in their occurrence and garbled in their storage as memories. These patients may describe a resultant sense of "fragmentation," an "alienation" from themselves. They may not develop a cohesive sense of themselves acting upon an external world; i.e., they may lack a strong observing ego.

Simultaneously, and on another level, the seizures have an effect on the patients' self-concept. The individuals affected early in life may not even recognize that they have an illness *(Zielinski, 1984)*. Not recognizing the discrete nature of the seizure events, they may be burdened by a sense that something is psychologically wrong with them, an idea that may be supported by their family members and their doctors. Often these patients include their peculiarities and perceived limitations in their self-concept.

Not only do they have a sense of alienation from themselves, these children experience isolation from others for several reasons. Coping strategies that they adopt to diminish seizures may involve restrictions on their behavior that deprive them of the opportunity to share certain activities with others. For example, one patient was afraid to sleep away from home as a child, possibly because sleep-onset seizures aggravated the usual childhood bedtime anxieties. On various occasions, she either avoided overnight activities or was so preoccupied with her anxiety that she did not enjoy them.

Discussing these problems with adults who are ignorant of the underlying difficulty but who offer misguided reassurance may leave the children not only not reassured, but convinced that they are incomprehensible. Further, the idiosyncrasy of these children's responses leaves them feeling different from and frustrating to others, heightening their sense of separation.

People who develop seizures later in life have several advantages over those with an early onset. Their development and relationships progressed without the distorting effect of the illness upon their personality and social skills *(Lewis & Rosenberg, 1990)*. Having a more coherent sense of themselves, they may be able to distinguish the episodic, "alien" effects of the seizures. However, even these individuals find themselves responding to affects about whose validity they may be skeptical but by which they are nonetheless moved.

Diagnostic Difficulties

Even though they do not realize that they have seizures or even that there is an episodic problem, many patients recognize differences between themselves and others. Initially, they may be misdiagnosed as having various Axis I or personality disorders, especially an affective disorder *(Stern & Murray, 1984)*. Some of the medications prescribed for these conditions exacerbate seizures, while others are weakly anticonvulsant and may be incompletely and temporarily helpful. Psychotherapy that is based on the inaccurate diagnosis may also be marginally helpful but ultimately frustrating.

Whether medicated or not, such patients may spend years in psychotherapy, attempting to relieve their symptoms by understanding themselves or changing their behavior. Dynamic psychotherapies may lead to a futile search for the unconscious secrets that undermine the patients' mental health. Often, by the time the correct diagnosis is made, patients have been searching for a solution to their problems for many years, and their lack of success has compounded their sense of impotence and self-denigration.

THERAPEUTIC STRATEGIES

Therapy begins with the diagnosis. Those patients whose seizures were undiagnosed must start the process of seeing themselves as suffering from a neurological disease. Those with known seizures must develop a more thorough understanding of CPS. Patients in both groups must abandon previously held, often self-deprecating, notions that they had "emotional problems" or "character defects" *(Geist, 1979)*.

The tasks of the therapy include: *1)* controlling the seizures with anticonvulsants; *2)* helping the patient to accept the disorder and to collaborate in taking medication; *3)* teaching the patient to distinguish among seizure symptoms, medication side effects, and psychological responses; *4)* encouraging a reassessment of the choices and restrictions the patient has made in current behavior; *5)* obtaining family support for the therapy; *6)* assisting in the reevaluation and reintegration of the past; and *7)* undertaking the formation of an integrated sense of self. The first five tasks must be substantially under way before moving on to the last two.

Control of the Seizures

The organic problems must be alleviated first. After reducing the seizure symptoms to a minimum, an evaluation can be made of any remaining neurological, cognitive, or psychological problems.

Anticonvulsants can eradicate or reduce CPS, but the dose required may be higher than that for other seizure types *(Schmidt, Einicke, & Haenel, 1986).* The therapist should be aware of two medication problems that may arise: The therapeutic ratio of the anticonvulsants is small and the patient may be inadvertently intoxicated *(Rodin, 1984);* the common signs of toxicity may be confused with seizure symptoms. The medications also change the seizures *(Engel, 1989);* they may alter the familiar stereotyped progression, or new symptoms may emerge. The therapist helps the patient correctly to identify both situations.

The healing process accelerates after the anticonvulsants have been properly titrated. Patients notice that their responses have become more predictable, and that "weird" responses have diminished. Memories become less fragmented and distorted, and can be stored and retrieved coherently. Patients, in some cases for the first time in their lives, have a cohesive, chronological trace of events.

Acceptance and Collaboration

Taking medication is the first task that doctors and patients have to accomplish collaboratively *(Gutheil, 1982).* Although the medication will be prescribed by a neurologist or a psychiatrist, nonmedical psychotherapists should discuss medication issues as a regular part of the psychotherapy. The endeavor affords psychotherapists a chance to evaluate the patients' acceptance of the diagnosis and motivation level. Transference issues can be assessed initially here. Taking medication as an autonomous partner is therapeutic, becoming one of the most important ways in which patients learn to accept the illness and to take care of themselves. Psychotherapists must deal with patients' attitudes and misconceptions about epilepsy. Considerable social stigma still exists. Therapists should provide information about the condition, its treatment, and the prognosis. Patients may have hoped that they would outgrow their problem or be able to change themselves, and a medical diagnosis may seem immutable. Further, if they hold certain religious beliefs, patients may interpret illness as a punishment. Therapists should explore these issues.

Patients who cannot accept the diagnosis of CPS often do not adhere to the medication regime, and a vicious cycle may ensue. Missed medication may result in an increase in seizures, followed by an increase in feelings of hopelessness or denial, with concomitant decreases in medication taking. Some patients, whether or not they accept the diagnosis, may have difficulty accepting the idea that they must take medication for an indefinite period.

On the other hand, patients may take excess medications hoping to stop any remaining symptoms, especially during the early stages of the therapy. Such patients may decide that every negative feeling is a seizure that needs to be medicated away, denying the existence of emotional issues to be worked through. Family treatment, described below, can help family members and, in turn, the patient to accept the diagnosis.

Distinguishing Among Responses

It is necessary for patients to learn to distinguish not only between seizure symptoms and medication toxicity, as described above, but also between seizures and valid thoughts and feelings. They must learn not to respond to the affective bursts and the distortions of cognition and memory of the seizures as though they were valid guide-posts to the comprehension of themselves and their circumstances. As a rule of thumb, we have found it useful to consider untoward responses as seizures first, medication problems second, and as genuine only last.

In discussing these distinctions, therapists should encourage patients to develop skepticism about the validity of unusual responses. As they learn to distinguish seizures from genuine emotions, patients need no longer react to stray feelings or search for their meaning, thus minimizing the seizures' impact on their lives.

Reassessment of Behavior

As patients develop confidence in their responses and are able to modulate their behavior according to their own valid reactions, they and their psychotherapists should begin to examine the patients' current functioning.

Seizure patients often seek order and avoid change. Some patients do not like to travel, for example. It is probable that when patients' inner worlds are disrupted by seizures, they can only achieve equilibrium by diminishing external changes *(Hutt & Hutt, 1968)*. As internal disruption diminishes, patients become free to abandon the be-havioral restrictions that were previously adaptive. They can then be encouraged to ex-pand their behavioral repertoires.

The mastery of previously avoided situations contributes to patients' growing sense of self-acceptance. As they comprehend the impact the CPS have had upon their lives and begin to accept themselves as people struggling with seizures, they are able to shed their earlier self-concepts. While discarding the unnecessary restrictions, however, pa-tients must also learn to be realistic about the impact the disease has upon their lives, and to accept whatever limitations it may impose. For example, they may have to avoid situations in which a seizure could compromise either their own safety or that of others. They may not be able to drive until their seizures are under good control.

Many patients notice an increase in seizures when they are tired, hungry, or under stress. They must learn to avoid or minimize these situations. They should be advised to avoid drugs of abuse and excessive alcohol consumption because these can aggravate the seizures. A life style of moderation and adherence to a medication regimen can bring the reward of neural stability *(Engel, 1989)*.

Obtaining Support of the Family

As is true in many conditions, acceptance of the diagnosis and the treatment by the pa-tient's family and their willingness to collaborate is vital to the success of the therapy. Their family's support may help patients to overcome their own hesitation about ac-cepting the diagnosis. On the other hand, their family's rejection of the diagnosis may undermine patients own acceptance of their condition. Family sessions should help families to make necessary changes in their concept of the patient's condition, to avoid blaming the patient for the illness, and to achieve a new homeostasis *(Appolone, 1978; Lechtenberg & Akner, 1984; Ziegler, 1982)*.

To encourage their collaboration, families should be involved in the treatment from the beginning, i.e., from the time of the diagnosis. They should participate in all decisions, including those about the medications.

Family members should be taught how to recognize seizure symptoms. For example, spouses who learn to distinguish affective symptomatology could minimize their responses to their partner's seizures, thereby restoring family equilibrium more quickly.

It is important that families support patients in taking anticonvulsants. When patients fail to adhere to the medication regimen, especially when they are caught in the vicious spiral of nonadherence leading to further seizures leading to further nonadherence, families can help them to take the medication or can notify the therapist of the problem.

Reevaluation and Reintegration

After psychotherapists and patients have addressed the current situation together, they are ready to reexamine the past through the prism of the new diagnosis. Patients should be encouraged to develop a new understanding of their previous behavior and a new acceptance of the reactions of others. They may experience a variety of emotions during this painful process.

As they follow the thread of the illness through the past, patients and therapists must try to understand the direct and indirect effects of the seizures on the patients' development. As they identify those events altered by seizures, they attempt to distinguish the direct results of seizures from valiant but often misconstrued attempts to cope with seizures. This is analogous to the process of learning to discriminate between seizures and other influences upon behavior. The expectation is that patients will develop a more informed, more compassionate understanding of their past, not that they will be able to recognize every occasion on which they had seizures.

The most important aspect of this process is the attempt to detect and correct mistaken ideas patients have had about themselves. Patterns of behavior engendered by these mistaken notions are identified and modified. Patients are encouraged to become less harsh and judgmental toward themselves as they realize that they were struggling against an unknown condition.

Patients must also reevaluate others from their past, none of whom knew the nature of their difficulties, many of whom added to their problems through that ignorance. In addition, patients should be encouraged to explore and to cope with their feelings toward any previous therapists who may have compounded their problems by misdiagnosis of the condition, by treatment with medications that caused an increase in seizures, or by the offer of case formulations that sent patients searching for past traumas and current character flaws. Patients may have had intense relationships with these therapists *(Bear, 1979)*.

Forming an Integrated Sense of Self

Replacing the disturbing sense of fragmentation, the alienation from oneself, and the isolation from others with a sense of integration will happen gradually as the therapy progresses. This results as seizures are reduced, and as patients understand what has been happening to them, gain confidence in their executive abilities, feel in greater control, and internalize the process of distinguishing seizures from normal feelings .

The psychotherapists' understanding and acceptance allow patients, perhaps for the first time, to discuss all their symptoms. They are able to dismantle earlier false explanations as their "new" self is defined. At this critical juncture, therapists must help patients to avoid substituting an "epileptic" self-concept for their previous negative self-view.

Until the seizures are in remission, therapists should expect an intense attachment by the patient *(Bear, 1979)*. Those experiencing CPS feel a real dependency on their psychotherapists, perhaps on a direct neurological basis or because of the intense, unpredictable, internal changes they experience. The turmoil that these patients experience until their seizures are under control and are understood can be quite confounding .

Clinicians can promote the integrative process by conducting reality-based psychotherapy that strengthens the boundary between subjective and objective reality *(Winston, Pinsker, & McCullough, 1986)*. Psychotherapists should minimize the transference, at least initially, to avoid burdening patients further with a counterproductive, intense transference. Therapists can accomplish this by meeting less frequently, by focusing discussions on reality issues such as the medication, by being more active and self-revealing, and by not analyzing the transference .

CONCLUSION

Patients with covert CPS arising in childhood have unique experiences and psychological needs. They suffer from an illness that is hidden but often results in overt behavioral changes, one that is episodic and fleeting in its direct effects but pervasive in its consequences.

The therapeutic model described above is generalizable to those with other seizure manifestations. It applies to patients with grand mal seizures, which may occur alone or infrequently in over 50% of patients with CPS *(Engel, 1989)*. These patients have added problems. They have to cope with the unpredictability of the attacks, their own helplessness and vulnerability during the episode, and the restrictions on their lives; the frightening nature of the seizures influences their social relationships; and their families tend to be overprotective, especially when they are children *(Long & Moore, 1979)*. Generalized seizures may leave patients dependent upon the "kindness of strangers." The seizures can be humiliating, frightening, and stigmatizing *(Goldin & Margolin, 1975)*, and people who suffer them have long been thought of as defective or evil.

Even though the generalized grand mal seizures are not covert, those with combined partial and generalized seizures may not be aware of the range of seizures from which they suffer. Some CPS arising as an aura may be recognized as presaging a seizure; others may not be recognized at all. One patient, a physician knowledgeable about seizures, did not realize that the brief bursts of hopelessness and helplessness arising without any external provocation were, in fact, seizures.

Seizures arising later in life create problems similar to those arising earlier, as discussed above, but the development and the interpersonal relations of these patients are often less affected. Although their treatment is very similar to that presented above, there is usually less need for reexamination of the past and they may not need help with self-integration.

All psychotherapists need to be aware of the protean manifestations of CPS. Patients with CPS often present, undiagnosed, for psychiatric help. The clinician must be prepared to recognize the underlying disorder and to refer the patient when appropriate. Although the diagnosis is clinical, less experienced psychiatrists and neurologists are often uncomfortable making the diagnosis on clinical grounds in the absence of corroborative EEG findings. Unfortunately, the EEG is an insensitive tool and initially is falsely negative in 30%–70% of cases *(Fenwick, 1981)*. The diagnostic discomfort is heightened by the lack of standardized criteria for these conditions in the *DSM-III-R (American Psychiatric Association, 1987)*.

We believe the model described herein can be applied to other organic illnesses with psychological complications. The methodology for the evaluation of the effect of the illness on the patient's existence and development is similar to that described above. The influence, if any, of the basic disease pathology (or the treatment) on neurological function must be appreciated, and any consequent cognitive or psychological changes assessed. The effect of these changes on the patient's experiences and relationships must next be considered in conjunction with the patient and the patient's family. Two recent articles concerning psychotherapy with persons suffering from schizophrenia and acquired brain damage, respectively, contain elements in common with our model *(Coursey, 1989; Lewis & Rosenberg, 1990)*. Clinicians are beginning to recognize the need to put organic and neurological problems into a human matrix, focusing more on the personal experience of the illness *(Sacks, 1985; Gazzaniga, 1988)*.

REFERENCES

Adebimpe, V. R. (1977). Complex partial seizures presenting as schizophrenia. *Journal of the American Medical Association, 237,* 1339–1341.

American Psychiatric Association. (1987). *Diagnostic and statistical manual of mental disorders* (3rd ed.-rev.). Washington, DC: Author.

Appolone, C. (1978). Preventive social work intervention with families of children with epilepsy. *Social Work Health Care, 4,* 139–148.

Bear, D. M. (1979). Temporal lobe epilepsy: A syndrome of sensory-limbic hyperconnection. *Cortex, 15,* 357–384.

Blumer, D. (1977). Treatment of patients with seizure disorder referred because of psychiatric complications [special issue]. *McLean Hospital Journal, 2,* 53–73.

Blumer, D., & Benson, D. F. (1982). Psychiatric manifestations of epilepsy. In D. F. Benson & D. Blumer, (Eds.), *Psychiatric aspects of neurological disease* (Vol. 2). New York: Grune & Stratton.

Coursey, R. D. (1989). Psychotherapy with persons suffering from schizophrenia: The need for a new agenda. *Schizophrenia Bulletin, 15,* 349–353.

Dorwart, R. A. (1984). Psychotherapy and temporal lobe epilepsy. *American Journal of Psychotherapy, 38,* 286–294.

Drotar, D. (1981). Psychological perspectives in chronic childhood illness. *Journal of Pediatric Psychology, 6,* 211–228.

Engel, J., Jr. (1989). *Seizures and epilepsy.* Philadelphia: F. A. Davis.

Feldman, R. G., & Ricks, N. L. (1979). Nonpharmacologic and behavioral methods. In G. S. Ferriss (Ed.), *Treatment of epilepsy today.* New Jersey: Medical Economics.

Fenwick, P. (1981). EEG studies. In E. H. Reynolds & M. R. Trimble (Eds.), *Epilepsy and psychiatry.* Edinburgh: Churchill Livingston.

Gazzaniga, M. S. (1988). *Mind matters: How the mind and brain interact to create our conscious lives.* Boston: Houghton-Mifflin.

Geist, R. A. (1979). Onset of chronic illness in children and adolescents: Psychotherapeutic and consultative intervention. *American Journal of Orthopsychiatry, 49,* 4–22.

Goldin, G. J., & Margolin, R. J. (1975). The psychosocial aspects of epilepsy. In G. N. Wright (Ed.), *Epilepsy rehabilitation.* Boston: Little, Brown.

Gutheil, T. G. (1982). The psychotherapy of psychopharmacology. *Bulletin of the Menninger Clinic, 46,* 321–330.

Hermann, B. P., & Whitman, S. (1984). Behavioral and personality correlates of epilepsy: A review, methodological critique and conceptual model. *Psychological Bulletin, 95,* 451–497.

Hoare, P. (1984). Does illness foster dependency? A study of epileptic and diabetic children. *Developmental Medical Child Neurology, 26,* 20–24.

Hutt, S. J., & Hutt, C. (1968). Stereotypy, arousal and autism. *Human Development, 11,* 277–286.

Lechtenberg, R., & Akner, L. (1984). Psychological adaptation of children to epilepsy in a parent. *Epilepsia, 25,* 40–45.

Lewis, L., & Rosenberg, S. J. (1990). Psychoanalytic psychotherapy with brain-injured adult psychiatric patients. *Journal of Nervous and Mental Disease, 178,* 69–77.

Long, C. C., & Moore, J. R. (1979). Parental expectations of their epileptic children. *Journal of Child Psychology and Psychiatry, 20,* 299–312.

Margalit, M., & Heiman, T. (1983). Anxiety and self-satisfaction in epileptic children. *International Journal of Social Psychiatry, 29,* 220–224.

Matthews, W. S, Barabas, G., & Ferrari, M. (1982). Emotional concomitants of childhood epilepsy. *Epilepsia, 23,* 671–681.

Messner, E. (1986). Covert complex partial seizures in psychotherapy. *American Journal of Orthopsychiatry, 56,* 323–326.

Neppe, V., & Tucker, G. J. (1988). Modern perspectives in epilepsy in relation to psychiatry: Classification and evaluation. *Hospital and Community Psychiatry, 39,* 263–271.

Perrin, E. C., & Gerrity, P. S. (1984). Development of children with a chronic illness. *Pediatric Clinics of North America, 31,* 19–31.

Pritchard, P., Lombrosco, C., & McIntyre, M. (1980). Psychological complications of temporal lobe epilepsy. *Neurology, 30,* 227–232.

Rodin, E. (1984). Medical treatment of epilepsy patients. In D. Blumer (Ed.), *Psychiatric aspects of epilepsy.* Washington, DC: American Psychiatric Association Press.

Sacks, O. (1985). *The man who mistook his wife for a hat and other clinical tales.* New York: Summit Books.

Schmidt, D., Einicke I., & Haenel, F. (1986). The influence of seizure type on the efficacy of plasma concentrates of phenytoin, phenobarbital and carbamazepine. *Archives of Neurology, 43,* 263–265.

Stern, T. A., & Murray, G. B. (1984). Complex partial seizures presenting as a psychiatric illness. *Journal of Nervous and Mental Disease, 172,* 625–627.

Waxman, S. G., & Geschwind, N. (1974). Hypergraphia in temporal lobe epilepsy. *Neurology, 24,* 629–636.

Williams, D. (1956). The structure of emotions reflected in epileptic experiences. *Brain, 79,* 29–67.

Winston, A., Pinsker, H., & McCullough, L. (1986). A review of supportive psychotherapy. *Hospital and Community Psychiatry, 37,* 1105–1114.

Ziegler, R. (1982). Epilepsy: individual illness, human predicament and family dilemma. *Family Relations, 31,* 435–44.

Ziegler, R., & Holden, L. (1988). Family therapy for learning disabled and attention deficit disordered children. *American Journal of Orthopsychiatry, 58,* 196–210.

Zielinski, J. (1984). Epidemiologic overview of epilepsy: Morbidity, mortality, and clinical implications. In D. Blumer (Ed.), *Psychiatric aspects of epilepsy.* Washington, DC: American Psychiatric Association Press.

CHAPTER 28

PSYCHOSOCIAL ASPECTS OF SICKLE-CELL ANEMIA IN ADOLESCENTS

Shirley Conyard, Muthuswamy Krishnamurthy, and Harvey Dosik

Sickle-cell anemia is a chronic hereditary, hemolytic anemia found in descendants of Africans, Italians, Greeks, and others from the area near the Mediterranean Sea. In the United States, it is found most commonly in Blacks, occurring in about one of four hundred births of Black babies.[1] An estimated fifty thousand Blacks in the United States alone have sickle-cell anemia.[2] This disease is not a new problem. The basic clinical conditions were observed as early as 1910 by James B. Herrick, a physician, in the bloodstream of a Black West Indian student.[3]

Sickle cells are elongated red blood cells with sharp double points, giving the cell a crescent shape rather than the round, disc shape of normal red blood cells. The cells resemble the narrow, curved blade of a sickle used to cut grass, hence the name, sickle-cell anemia. Sickle-cell anemia is characterized by a chronic hemolytic anemia, that is, a deficiency of red blood cells due to their excessive destruction, and intermittent crises of variable frequency and severity involving fever and pains in bones, joints, and abdomen. In addition, there is an increased incidence of bacterial infection. A multiplicity of symptoms may occur with gradual involvement of many tissues and organ systems, for example, splenic congestion and a somewhat enlarged liver. Life expectancy is reduced; many sufferers succumb in infancy or early childhood, and most do not survive their fourth decade. The clinical picture is quite varied, however. Some patients remain relatively asymptomatic for many years, whereas others become severely disabled or die at an early age.[4]

Although some features of the disease may be seen at any age—for example, anemia, painful crises, and bone infarcts—others occur characteristically in certain age groups. For example, clinical manifestations are generally first noted between 6 months and 2

Reprinted from *Health and Social Work*, Vol. 5, no. 1 (1980), pp. 20–26, by permission of NASW Press. Copyright 1980, National Association of Social Workers, Inc., *Health and Social Work*.

years of age. The most common problems present in this age group and throughout childhood are infections and dactylitis, that is, joint pains, swelling, and limited motion. In adolescents and young adults, leg ulcers, aseptic necrosis of the femoral head, and retinal lesions are usually seen.[5]

In the past, treatment has been supportive and limited to the symptoms, only attempting to alleviate pain or combat infections as they occur, since there is no treatment of the disease itself. For example, when pain is severe or if vomiting and dehydration supervenes, hospitalization is necessary. Fluids are then given intravenously along with analgesic drugs such as codeine or meperidine. A variety of intravenous fluids such as electrolyte solutions, dextrose, dextran, and plasma have reportedly been effective in alleviating pain, presumably through their ability to mobilize trapped sickle cells. However, severe pain may persist for days or even weeks in some cases despite these measures.[6] This treatment produces little or no side effects.

However, the physical aspects of sickle-cell anemia constitute only one facet of the health problem. Sickle-cell anemia also causes severe social and emotional problems. The normal adolescent is characterized psychologically as attempting to achieve emancipation from their parents and increasing independence.[7] However, Whitten and Fischoff described the chronically ill adolescent as afraid to be an autonomous individual, withdrawn from relationships, having limited aspirations and poor self-esteem, feeling depressed, helpless and fearful, and preoccupied with death.[8] Singler described chronically ill patients as fearful, nonverbal, and having damaged self-esteem.[9] Whitten and Fischoff postulate the existence of similar emotional and social problems in patients with sickle-cell anemia, but this has never been documented.[10] With this in mind, the authors investigated the behavior patterns of twenty-one adolescents with sickle-cell anemia to see whether they resembled the patterns found with other chronic diseases.

EVALUATION OF ADOLESCENT PATIENTS

In 1972, with the aid of funding from the National Institutes of Health and the National Heart and Lung Institute, a comprehensive sickle-cell clinic was established at the Jewish Hospital and Medical Center of Brooklyn, New York. A social worker was assigned to study the emotional problems of persons suffering from sickle-cell anemia and to carry out emotional rehabilitation when it was needed.

The social worker evaluated a total of twenty-one adolescents, nine males aged 14 to 19 and twelve females aged 13 to 19. All the adolescents in the study were in school, and all came from the same social and economic background, that is, they lived in ghetto areas and came from low-income, one-parent families with three or more siblings. Table 28–1 describes the composition of the group, according to age, sex, and type of hemoglobinopathy.

There are two types of sickle-cell anemia of differing severity. Individuals with SS hemoglobin have inherited sickling hemoglobin (S) from both parents. Individuals with SC hemoglobin have inherited sickling hemoglobin (S) from one parent and a different type, crystallizing hemoglobin (C), from the other parent. Hemoglobin SS disease and

Table 28–1.
Patients Studied, According to Sex and Hemoglobinopathy

Hemoglobinopathy	Male	Female	Total
SS	6	9	15
SC	3	3	6
Total	9	12	21

hemoglobin SC disease are both characterized by a chronic hemolytic anemia. However, the clinical manifestation from intravascular occlusion and vaso-occlusion is generally less severe in those with SC disease than in those with SS disease. The incidence of bacterial infections is also much less in individuals with SC disease, but they have a greater frequency of aseptic necrosis of the femoral head, retinal infarcts, and renal papillary necrosis.[11]

Each patient and his or her family were seen by the social worker in the clinic and on admission to the hospital to evaluate the patient's needs, to assist in discharge planning, to provide casework treatment, and to serve as liaison between the patients and other helping agents such as nurses and physicians. To further assess the patients' emotional and social problems, the study also included evaluations by the patients' parents and their schoolteachers. Each patient was rated good, fair, or poor on the following criteria: leadership, mental response and/or communication, relationship with peers, relationship with teachers, adjustment to school, participation in school activities, independence, reaction to suggestions and criticisms, responsibility, reaction to own illness, neatness, and attendance record (other than for acute illness). Each evaluator was unaware of the others' ratings. The evaluations of the parents and the schoolteachers for each patient concurred with the worker's findings. The results were compiled at the end of the study by averaging the ratings of all three evaluators, and these results are shown in Table 28–2.

PSYCHOSOCIAL PROBLEMS OF PATIENTS

Patients in the study showed a high degree of isolation, dependence, fear of illness, and withdrawal from normal relationships with peers in school and their family members. Other emotional problems included poor self-image, depression, anxiety, nonverbalization, and preoccupation with death. All the patients showed an overall poor performance on the criteria, although the females fared better than the males in certain areas such as responsibility, adjustment to school, leadership, and neatness. The sex variation shown in this study is probably due to natural maturation, since girls mature earlier than boys, and to social environment, since girls are encouraged early to develop their skills.[12] There appeared to be little or no difference in performance between patients with SS disease and patients with SC disease.

The study confirmed the hypothesis that the psychosocial aspects of sickle-cell disease resemble those of other chronic illnesses. However, this psychosocial profile does

TABLE 28-2.
Results of Evaluation of Adolescents with Sickle-Cell Disease

	Number of Subjects											
	SS Disease						SC Disease					
	Male			Female			Male			Female		
Criteria	Good	Fair	Poor	Good	Fair	Poor	Good	Fair	Poor	Good	Fair	Poor
Leadership		2	6	1	3	5			3		2	1
Mental response and/or communication		2	4	1	3	5		2	1		2	1
Relationship with peers		1	5	1	0	8			3		3	
Relationship with teachers		1	5	4	4	1		1	1		1	2
Adjustment to school		2	4	3	2	4		3			1	2
Participation in school activities			6	1	1	8	1	1	1		1	2
Independence		1	5	1	1	7			3		1	2
Reaction to suggestions and constructive criticisms		4	2		4	5		2	1		2	1
Responsibility			6	3	2	4		1	2		1	2
Reaction to own illness		2	4	1	4	4		1	2		1	2
Neatness	3		3	6	2	1	2	1		2	1	
Attendance record		2	4	4	1	4	1	2		1	2	

289

not have the same cultural, social, and environmental impact on patients with other chronic diseases that it has on patients with sickle-cell anemia. First, sickle-cell anemia is primarily a disease of Black people. Second, most information concerning sickle-cell anemia is presented in negative terms, for example, that people with the disease have short life spans, are unable to work, should not have children, and should not take part in activities such as sports. Third, parents who have children with the disease experience feelings of guilt. Finally, professional people in the medical and social sciences have inadequate training or background to deal comfortably with the problems of counseling and medical treatment of the sickle-cell patient. In other words, patients, parents, and medical professionals all experience a feeling of hopelessness. Hope is offered by society to patients with other chronic diseases but not to sickle-cell patients.

TASK-ORIENTED GROUP

The study unmasked many emotional and social problems experienced by sickle-cell patients. Since there is no effective medical treatment for relatively asymptomatic patients with uncomplicated sickle-cell anemia, the authors believe that these individuals would benefit greatly from counseling.[13] In the past, individual casework was utilized to meet the patients' severe emotional and social needs and to enable them to grow emotionally. However, this method tended to compound patients' feelings of uniqueness and did not provide them with the experience of peer relationship and peer socialization. It also fostered the patients' dependence, which at times would shift from the parents to the social worker. The authors felt that a group approach would be a successful alternative method of treatment, and initiated a pilot study to test this hypothesis.

By design, the group was a closed, task-oriented group. "Task-oriented" is defined here as putting into practice the concerns of the group as expressed in its discussions through the carrying out of assigned tasks. The group's aims were to build on the strengths and knowledge that the adolescent patients already had in order to reduce anxiety, enhance social functioning, achieve self-fulfillment, and if possible, resocialize the patients emotionally so that they could enter the "normal" mainstream of life. The authors believed this could be accomplished by freeing each patient from the myths and misconceptions he or she held about the illness.

Scheduled meetings were held once a week for 1½ hours from September 1973 until May 1975. The interviewing and evaluating of the adolescents chosen for the group have already been described. The six patients selected from among the twenty-one in the study had been rated fair and poor on all the variables in the evaluation. They were also chosen because they showed a positive interest in improving themselves and agreed to take part in group counseling. The group was made up of three males and three females ranging in age from 13½ to 15. Four of the group members had SS disease, the other two had SC. The group attendance was very good, no more than one member ever being absent at one time. Member participation was one of the group's most important features, since the social worker was trying to develop peer-group identity and group cohesiveness to create free-flowing group communications and participation.

ROLE OF THE SOCIAL WORKER

To begin with, the social worker had to remove all barriers that would keep patients from attending the group meetings, such as problems with carfare or fear of traveling alone. During the group process, the social worker acted as a catalyst, creating stimuli for group interaction. Initially, the social worker led the sessions, giving some guidance, arranging for the various group tasks, and choosing some of the topics for discussion. Other topics for discussion were chosen by the group. As time passed, the social worker's role developed into that of an observer, except for explaining medical data, intervening for the protection of a group member, or restructuring the sessions when the group strayed from the topic of that session.

The group discussions focused on two types of problems experienced by the members: medical problems and social problems. Discussions of medical problems dealt with (1) members' knowledge about sickle-cell anemia; (2) their ability to handle themselves during crises and when asymptomatic; (3) members' growth and development, including delay in development, sex characteristics, and physical growth; and (4) feelings about having the disease, including fears and myths concerning early death and feelings about physical activities, being alone, and traveling alone. Topics relating to social problems included the following: (1) adjustment to school, for example, fear of being ill in school, difficulty in keeping up with homework, absences, and relationships with peers and teachers; (2) members' feelings about themselves as persons, in particular about their uniqueness and handicap, and about being stigmatized or socially outcast; (3) effects on social life caused by the illness, including feelings of embarrassment and rejection, relationships with peers and family members, blaming of parents for the illness, and feelings of guilt toward healthy siblings, who often had to wait for parents' attention while it was focused on the patient; and (4) members' perception on the future in relation to college, marriage, and children.

TASKS

For the first twelve weeks the group members were still apprehensive about exposing and sharing their feelings with each other, which limited group interaction. Not until discussions were accompanied by performance of tasks did the members begin to function as a group.

The first task was a project for the entire group—organizing a party for the entire population of the sickle-cell clinic. It was carried out quite successfully with some help from the social worker. Besides creating a few inflated egos, this task provided the group with three very important factors, namely, group interaction or free-flowing communication, interest in the group, and motivation to carry out other tasks.

Next, the entire group went on a field trip, and each member was supposed to bring a friend. This task was difficult and created a lot of anxiety because it called for the members to share themselves with people other than those in the group. Once their anxiety was worked through, the second task was carried out over and over again on other field trips and outings. The group went to such places as museums, libraries, plays, baseball and football games, the United Nations, colleges, parks, zoos, and several restaurants. As a result, the group members began to form independent peer relationships. Through these group outings, the members learned how to travel by themselves, and their minds and eyes were opened to aspects of life other than those in front of their house or just up the block.

The third task involved removing the adolescents from classes for the handicapped in school and also having them participate in gym classes if their physician approved. This task began to work away at the fears and myths surrounding physical activity and the feeling of physical handicaps. It also made each group member aware of his or her limitations and began to build positive coping mechanisms. Parents and teachers reported that the adolescents became more outgoing and experienced no ill effects from participating in gym and being placed in regular classes.

The next task was designed to test the progress made during the group sessions that dealt with independence and ego strength in relation to sociability. After this discussion, the group members began to search for something of interest to take on as an independent project. Among the female members, one began music lessons, the second took dance lessons, and the third became vice-president of a handicapped group in her neighborhood. One male joined the Salvation Army band and a second got a part-time job. The third male, whose emotional growth lagged behind the other members, felt that he needed more time before selecting an outside activity.

The fifth group task was to attend a normal "sleepaway" camp. The members participated in all camp activities, including learning how to swim. No one became ill, and all members stayed for two weeks. The group members were given excellent ratings by the counselors at the camp, leadership, relationships with other campers and counselors, participation in camp activities, independence, reaction to their handicap, temperament, and responsibility.

For their final task, all group members, except the one who was lagging behind, obtained summer jobs. Their employers found them to be good workers, and they have worked every summer thereafter.

DISCUSSION

The major emotional factors describing the characteristics of sickle-cell patients were depression, feelings of helplessness, fear, poor self-esteem, and poor self-concept.[14] Treatment of these problems involved participation in the task-oriented group, which gave the adolescents the opportunity to verbalize their feelings, receive constructive education, and actually test themselves in situations that they most feared. It also helped them to move toward what may be termed "social responsiveness," or taking part in normal social activities and responsibilities. As Parsons stated, the sick person is exempt from normal social responsibilities.[15]

The first two tasks, giving a party and going on outings with a friend, were important because they put each member into a position of exposing him- or herself. These tasks covered a wide range of the group members' fears, such as communicating, that is, relating to another person; carrying out tasks; forming peer relationships with group members, schoolmates, or neighbors; and, most of all, being accepted. All adolescents need to feel they have some acceptance by their peers and will withdraw from social relationships if they feel acceptance does not exist.[16] The success of the first two tasks helped the group members to gain some self-esteem and confidence in their ability to carry out a specified task and succeed. Members were motivated to take on the third task which challenged their limitations and imperfections.

This task, participating in normal classes, enabled the group to continue with the last three tasks by reinforcing confidence in themselves and boosting their self-esteem. At this point, they began to enjoy life, going to school, and relating to their peers. Their attitude at home and school improved. Adolescents with sickle-cell anemia may place themselves in a stressful situation to prove that they are like other adolescents if they are not allowed to prove their capabilities in planned supervised activities, such as the ones provided by this task.[17]

The final three tasks can be described as emancipating and future-oriented tasks. These allowed the group members to begin experiencing a certain amount of independence and to start reaching for self-fulfillment. Most of all, these tasks helped the group members to become a part of society, enhancing their sociability and developing their talents, from camping to earning money. To sum up, all six tasks helped the individuals in the group to reach more of an emotional and social balance, hence, "normalcy."

SUMMARY

The task-oriented group method used in this study was more successful than individual casework or a discussion group. The tasks that the group members were asked to do required them to modify certain patterns of social behavior, demanded taking of risks, and clearly spelled out the behaviors to be undertaken. In making a commitment to carry out the tasks, each member recognized that he or she had to make a choice between action and inaction. By acting, each individual was saying, "This is what I am willing to try to achieve," thus beginning immediate action to solve his or her problem.[18] This advantage is not present in the individual casework method, where socialization and interaction with peers are limited. Similarly, a discussion group with no action will often leave the members with their problems unresolved.

The ideal number of participants for a group is not clear. The group described contained six members, enough for an adequate amount of interaction, but not so many that members would be neglected. The two-year period of interaction provided enough time to research and discuss topics and to find social resources for group tasks. This period enabled the group to develop better feelings about and understanding of themselves and their illness. It enabled the authors to gain a better understanding of the psychosocial makeup of adolescents with sickle-cell anemia. This successful group approach to adolescents with sickle-cell anemia should lead others to try a similar approach and to apply it to groups of children and adults as well.

NOTES AND REFERENCES

1. *Sickle Cell Counseling: A Committee's Study and Recommendations* (Los Angeles: Los Angeles County Department of Health Services, Chronic Disease Control Division, Community Health Services, March 1973), p. 8.

2. Marion Barnhart, Raymond L. Henry, and Jeanne Lusher, *Sickle Cell* (Kalamazoo, Mich.: Upjohn Co., 1974), p. 7.

3. *See* Stanley H. Smith, "The Sociopsychological Aspects of Sickle Cell Anemia," *First International Conference on the Mental Health Aspects of Sickle Cell Anemia* (Rockville, Md.: U.S. Department of Health, Education & Welfare, 1974).

4. Barnhart, Henry, and Lusher, op. cit., 36.

5. Ibid., pp. 36–37.

6. Ibid., p. 86.

7. H. Thornburg and D. Ershel, "Behavior and Values: Consistency or Inconsistency," *Adolescence,* 8 (Winter 1973), pp. 513–520.

8. Charles Whitten and Joseph Fischoff, "Psychosocial Effects of Sickle Cell Disease," *Archives of Internal Medicine,* 133 (April 1974), pp. 681–689.

9. Judith R. Singler, "Group Work with Hospitalized Stroke Patients," *Social Casework,* 56 (June 1975), pp. 348–354.

10. Whitten and Fischoff, op. cit.

11. Barnhart, Henry, and Lusher, op. cit.

12. R. G. Wiggins, "Difference in Self-Perception of Ninth Grade Boys and Girls," *Adolescence,* 7 (Winter 1973), pp. 491–496.

13. William J. Williams et al., *Hematology* (New York: McGraw-Hill Book Co., 1972), p. 421.

14. Ibid.; Talcott Parsons, *Social System* (New York: Free Press of Glencoe, 1951); and Santosh Kumar et al., "Anxiety, Self-Concept and Personal and Social Adjustments in Children with Sickle Cell Anemia," *Journal of Pediatrics,* 88 (May 1976), pp. 859–863.

15. Parsons, op. cit., p. 23.

16. Whitten and Fischoff, op. cit.

17. William R. Montgomery, "Psychosocial Aspects of Sickle Cell Anemia," *First International Conference on the Mental Health Aspects of Sickle Cell Anemia,* pp. 31–39.

18. *See* William J. Reid and Laura Epstein, *Task-Centered Casework* (New York: Columbia University Press, 1972), p. 147.

CHAPTER 29

GROUP WORK WITH HOSPITALIZED STROKE PATIENTS

Judith R. Singler

Each year in the United States, thousands of persons suffer cerebrovascular accidents—strokes. Many of these persons require hospitalization for extensive rehabilitation therapy, including physical, occupational, and speech therapies. For some, the reward for weeks of physical and emotional toil is a return home to family and friends; for others, the long hours of struggle lead to a nursing or rest home; still others find themselves confined indefinitely, perhaps permanently, to hospitals for the chronically ill.

To meet the needs of severely handicapped patients, social workers have long utilized casework skills. In 1961, Esther White described the difficulties of casework in the early stages of illness, noting that patients (in her experience, adult polio patients hospitalized for six to twelve months) were often nonverbal with staff and family, as well as with other patients, in areas that related to their illness.[1] She ascribed this lack to a dual fear on the part of the patient: a fear of antagonizing staff by negative comments and a fear of confirming in their own minds what they feared most about the illness. Other writers[2] have noted the reactions of patients to catastrophic illnesses, citing anxiety and depression, as well as the damage to the individual's self-esteem, all of which combine to isolate him from people around him. Thus isolated, the patient may feel his condition is unique, so that others, especially those who are well, are unable to understand

Reprinted from *Social Casework*, Vol. 56 (June 1975), pp. 348–354, by permission of the publisher, Families International, Inc.

[1] Esther White, The Body Image Concept in Rehabilitating Severely Handicapped Patients, *Social Work*, 6:51–58 (July 1961).

[2] See, for example, Samuel B. Kutash, *The Application of Therapeutic Procedures to the Disabled,* Office of Vocational Rehabilitation Services Series, No. 343 (Washington, D.C.: U.S. Department of Health, Education, and Welfare, 1956), pp. 10–14; and Shirley London, Group Work in Limited Therapy Situations, in *Social Work with Groups: Selected Papers from the National Conference on Social Welfare* (New York: National Association of Social Workers, 1959), pp. 41–51.

his predicament and are unable to help him. For this type of patient, casework early in his hospitalization may have limited value.

An alternative method of treatment is, of course, the group. Use of group work in this situation offers several benefits, perhaps the most significant of which was stated by Gisela Konopka: "Human beings cannot stand alone. The group is not just one aspect of human life, but it is life blood itself because it represents the belonging to humanity."[3] Thus, for the stroke patient, separated from much of his former world, the group becomes a potential vehicle of return to self, to others.

Youville Hospital is a private, nonprofit, 305-bed rehabilitation and chronic disease hospital in Cambridge, Massachusetts, receiving patients from the greater Boston area. In 1971, it was decided by the social service department of the hospital to initiate a discussion group for rehabilitation patients who had suffered cerebrovascular accidents. The writer was involved from its inception in December 1971 to December 1972. There were sixty-five beds on two wards devoted to patients admitted specifically for rehabilitation. Each patient and his family were seen on admission by a social worker, who remained on the case throughout the patient's hospital stay, acting as liaison between patient, family, and the hospital, providing direct casework treatment when needed, assisting in discharge planning, and providing staff consultation when indicated.

GROUP STRUCTURE

By design, the group was open-ended and had an open membership system. Its aims were to provide support for members, to reduce anxiety, and to promote increased self-acceptance. Any hemiparetic or hemiplegic patient (that is, one who had suffered partial or total paralysis on one side of his body) who was able to speak and be understood by others, as well as to comprehend others, was invited to attend. Each was on the rehabilitation program for one week prior to attending his first group meeting. This plan allowed the patient to acclimate himself. Meetings were held once weekly for one hour, apart from the regular therapy schedule. New members were expected to attend three sessions as a part of their total rehabilitation program; after that, the decision to continue was up to the individual.

Members ranged in age from thirty-two to eighty-eight for women and from forty-one to seventy-nine for men. The actual number of patients attending any one meeting varied from three to twelve. The total number of patients served in the first thirteen months of the program was sixty-one; of this group, fifty-nine had suffered strokes. There was no maximum on the number of sessions an individual could attend, but membership ceased on discharge from the hospital. In practice, attendance ranged from three to seventeen sessions.

With new patients joining and older members leaving almost weekly, the group membership was quite fluid. This open membership system was given careful consideration before the group was begun. The continuous admission and discharge procedures of the hospital favored such a system, because every stroke patient had an opportunity to join the group. The system was recognized as having limitations, most obviously that

[3] Gisela Konopka, *Group Work in the Institution* (New York: Association Press, 1972), p. 22.

of stunting potential group movement, as well as the difficulty of obtaining group cohesion. It should be noted, however, that primary consideration was not the development of an intense group identity but individual growth through the group process. Aware of the fluctuating stroke patient population within the hospital and variable lengths of patient hospitalization and encouraged by the success of a like-structured group in reducing isolation and depression among parents of handicapped children,[4] the writer began an open-ended group for stroke patients and other hemiparetic or hemiplegic patients.

ROLE OF THE SOCIAL WORKER

The role of the social worker in the position of group leader was, as noted by Hans S. Falck,[5] to act as a catalyst to the members, to provide stimulus and some guidance to their interaction, and to answer questions on hospital policy or other objective or technical matters. The worker was also the planner of the meetings, arranging for the room and for refreshments. In practice, the worker initially led the meetings, beginning the discussions and choosing topics for discussion. In time, the members began to introduce their own concerns, seeking responses not from the worker, but from each other. At this point, the worker saw her role become that of an observer, watching for any adverse reactions on the part of any member, and occasionally intervening to return the members to the topic of that session.

CONTENT OF THE MEETINGS

A working pattern arbitrarily established by the worker in the initial meetings received support from the members and continued for over a year. This pattern provided each member with the opportunity, at his first meeting, to tell the circumstances of his stroke. No one declined to do so. Each member could begin to express himself in the group and, more important, to answer what seemed to be a need for such a recitation, seen commonly in these patients in this early, self-centered stage of adjustment. It also provided the opportunity for the members who had been in the group longer to disassociate themselves to see the problems that others were experiencing.

Discussion among members can be divided into several areas: (1) gathering of information about strokes, the hospital, and therapy; (2) sharing of experiences and feelings; and (3) identification of fears and problems. In all of these areas, the members tended to support one another and to test their perceptions of themselves against the others. Gathering of information often overlapped with the sharing of experiences, providing insight for both patients and worker.

Two men were discussing the difficulties of putting on a brace, then shoes, and, finally, a T-shirt. Mr. C recounted, very humorously, a tale of how he had one day become hopelessly entangled in his shirt, requiring a nurse to extricate him. Mr. K, who had been quietly listening to the entire exchange, suddenly uttered a great

---

[4] Ann Murphy, Siegfried Pueschel, and Jane Schneider, Group Work with Parents of Children with Down's Syndrome, *Social Casework,* 54:114–19 (February 1973).

[5] Hans S. Falck, The Use of Groups in the Practice of Social Work, *Social Casework,* 44:63–67 (February 1963).

sigh of relief, stating, "I thought I had to be the only one who couldn't get a shirt on right." He added that he had not mentioned it before, even to his therapist, because he was so embarrassed by his failure. Now obviously relieved, he went on to emphasize that for him such items as his inability to wind a watch, scratch his shoulder, and comb his hair were more discouraging than his loss of ambulation. Mr. C agreed. "It's just one more thing we have to depend on someone else for. The big things are much easier to take. These little things, they are really hard."

Here a man's self-esteem, battered down by his inability to perform what had once been an elementary task, was boosted by the knowledge that he was not alone in this difficulty. Embarrassed by his failure and perceiving this problem as unique to himself, he had not mentioned it and, thus, had created a situation which further isolated him from others. The additional activities he mentioned were quickly picked up by another member as relating to personal independence, an insight which provoked considerable discussion.

Members, especially when first attending, appeared to gain considerable satisfaction from sharing their own experiences. Indeed, they would often seem to vie with one another, each wanting to tell a tale of greater frustration or greater success. An obvious expression of their self-centered state, such a recitation also seemed to enable many individuals to begin to identify both strengths and weaknesses and, in some measure, to begin to come to grips with them. It is interesting to note that as each patient began to adjust to his own disability and to accept himself as he had become, a move away from this competition could be seen, with members more frequently commenting on the progress or successes of others. One patient put it this way: "At first all you can see is what you can't do, but after a bit, you find yourself doing some new things. After that worries seem less, and you can look at other people and at the rest of the world again."

GROUP SUPPORT

Although physical disabilities are the ones most apparent to other persons, for the stroke patient himself heightened emotionalism is often a frustratingly incapacitating feature of his disability.

Mrs. G., attending for the first time, told the others of her experience in suffering the stroke. While doing so, she began to sob uncontrollably, tried to apologize, but only cried even more. Mrs. M and Mrs. K immediately came to her support, both with tears in their eyes. Mrs. M explained that a tendency toward crying "just seems to be a part of the total effect of a stroke, as if the mind just can't believe what has happened to the body."

In the early weeks of the group, the writer pointed out to members, in response to questions, the fact of heightened emotionalism's often accompanying a cerebrovascular accident. The members quickly learned to explain this fact to each other, thus helping to allay the anxiety of their fellow patients, while gaining some mastery over the mysteries of their own conditions.

Just as they shared their successes and helped each other to cope with some of the frustrations of living with handicaps, the members also slowly began to confront the negative attitudes, feelings, and experiences of some members. This process began with a single member's wondering aloud if the others ever became depressed, noting that he was very discouraged about his minimal progress. Others agreed that they had felt the same way at times, suggested activities for leisure time to avoid thinking only of one's own problems, and emphasized that it was important to find someone to talk with about these feelings. Gradually, they began to see the group as the "someone" who would listen. Once this realization occurred, a solution for the problems voiced became less crucial; the sharing of the feeling was the important factor, with longer-participating members most often providing advice and guidance for the newer members. In the weeks after this step, members began to bring up regularly such questions of feelings and attitudes.

Their greatest challenge as a group came in a session that brought into the open perhaps their greatest fears.

> Mr. F, usually amiable and jovial, suddenly blurted out, "The work isn't really worth anything when you have nothing to live for. There's no sense in going through all this if things aren't going to change. Me, I have nothing to live for. I might as well die." The others appeared stunned and sat silently staring at the table. Mrs. P., an eighty-eight-year-old widow, tried to support him, saying she, too, had felt this way. The response from Mr. F was an angry, "But you can walk: I can't even pull up my pants. And I don't even have a mind: I'm of no use to anyone anymore." Others tried to respond but were overwhelmed by the intensity of Mr. F's remarks. Finally, Mrs. P tried again. "You seem to be comparing yourself to the past, to the way you used to be. I think that we have to go day by day, not remembering the past too much or worrying about the future. And you can be useful—even just by talking or listening you can help someone else." By this time some of the others had recovered sufficiently to voice added support, emphasizing that activities were secondary to being alive. Others added that they, too, often wanted to give up, that daily therapy often seemed futile. Mr. F gradually relaxed and tearfully thanked the others for helping him, adding that he "just had to get it out into the open" and expressing relief that the others shared his feelings.

In this manner, members gradually began to confront themselves and each other with the reality of their handicaps. Sharing their successes had been easy for most of them and had, in some cases, enabled them to avoid consideration of their own failures. Mr. F, in the meeting described above, brought out what probably had occurred to all of them at some time. They could not provide a solution for his lack of progress in therapy or for the severity of his stroke, but they could and did listen and voice support. The recitation had a visibly cathartic effect on Mr. F. The isolation he had felt was revealed as a self-imposed burden. In addition, his directness had forced others to confront their own situations and to examine their own feelings.

> Mrs. M. was depressed and tearful over her slow progress in therapy. Others had tried to comfort her and share their similar feelings. Finally, Mr. R, began speak-

ing loudly and rapidly to avoid her interruptions. "Look lady, quit feeling so sorry for yourself. All of us are going through the same thing. You can do more than I can do. You have enough guts to pick yourself up right now and face your situation and begin to adjust. We can't do it all for you. We'll all help each other, but we have to learn to help ourselves, too. And if you or I will never walk again, well, we had just better learn to face it instead of making ourselves and everyone else miserable wishing for something that we will never have."

These two incidents also illustrate a prime benefit of this type of membership pattern: the development of a nurturing and supportive role for the older members, through which they could guide, chastise, praise, and empathize with the newer members. Such comments, far from being rejected even when harsh, were almost always well received by the group members.

CONFRONTING FEARS

In the early weeks of group life, the members dealt largely with such concrete matters as techniques learned in therapy, circumstances of their own strokes, hospital policies, and shared experiences of weekend visits home. In these weeks, the group included two patients who were hemiparetic as a result of externally caused injuries rather than strokes. Because their handicaps were in large measure the same, they were included in the group. However, an occurrence at one meeting in the third month of the group points up an important difference in their respective adjustment patterns.

Mr. O, who had suffered a rather mild stroke, hesitantly asked if he could "talk about something no one seems to ever mention. I was afraid to ask my doctor . . . but what are the chances of any of us having another stroke?" Everyone looked to the worker for an answer, and she referred the question back to the group itself. Several members commented that they had not asked their doctors because they thought it "would just be more bad news." Two members, however, the non-stroke hemiparetics, were puzzled by this attitude, saying, "If it happens, it happens, but you can't worry about it." The remaining members sought a response from the worker, who answered in very general terms about the various causes of strokes and means of protecting oneself beforehand and mentioned the importance of discussing this query thoroughly with their own physicians. The group became very subdued, and several comments were made on the difficulty of continuing in therapy with such a threat over their heads. This discussion went on for some time, until the two hemiparetic patients again blurted out their disagreement with this attitude. The stroke patients were quiet, almost embarrassed by their earlier comments. Mr. O said, "I guess if you haven't had a stroke you can't really know what it is like. I just don't know if I could bear to start all over again with hospitals and therapy. It would be too much to ask of a person."

In subsequent meetings, this fear of a second stroke was brought up repeatedly. At times, the members discussed it at length; at other times, they simply alluded to it. It became obvious to the writer that this fear of another stroke underlay much of the members' conversation while in the group and, thus, perhaps some of their behavior. This fear was an area of concern which the nonstroke hemiparetics did not share, and they found it difficult to relate to the profound, very visible effect its mention had on the others. As in the incident above, their inability to comprehend this reaction in those who had suffered a stroke caused the other patients to become embarrassed and concerned over these very honest feelings. Because of the important role this fear seemed to play in the lives of these patients, the writer decided to restrict the group thereafter to persons who had suffered a stroke.

Another cause of anxiety for these patients was concern over acceptance by the nonhospital world. From the early days of hospitalization, when a patient's image of himself was so dependent on the staff, a bond was formed. This bond gave support and encouragement that was felt and recognized by these patients when they approached discharge, became increasingly anxious about how the "outside world" would receive them. White, in writing on the rehabilitation of the severely handicapped, saw the hospital as a microcosm, reflecting attitudes of the community and preparing the patients for posthospital adjustments.[6] The patients in the stroke group, however, discerned a definite distinction between the attitudes of the hospital staff and those of individuals in the community. They felt that the understanding and supportive attitudes of the staff would not be found after their discharge, and all were concerned about this problem. The open membership system greatly facilitated the intense quizzing of members who went home for weekends about the reactions of people to their presence in stores, churches, parks, and other public places. The interpersonal relations in the hospital as well as in the group had made the difference in their movement toward acceptance of their limitations, and they despaired of finding such relationships in the community.

COMPLAINTS

Members tended at times to voice complaints about such things as hospital policies, food, ward difficulties, and nursing or therapy procedures. These complaints usually occurred in cycles, most often when the group members were in periods of little progress in therapy. Such occurrences may be viewed as a means of venting frustration incurred in their necessarily regimented lives. Anxieties concerning discharge and weekend visits were also vented here, as well as the periodic irritations of daily life. What is important is that the group provided, for both patients and staff, a setting in which anger and frustration could be freely voiced, with little risk of offending anyone. Patients were vividly aware of their dependence on the staff and were often reluctant to voice complaints directly to them. Hence, the group provided a useful vehicle for them.

[6] White, The Body Image Concept.

DISCUSSION

The major purpose of the meetings was to provide a means of regular and continuing support for persons who had suffered a stroke. The members accomplished this aim in discussion of their fears and anxieties and in the sharing of experiences both in and out of the hospital. Initially, patients were depressed and discouraged, still bound and isolated by the initial terror of suffering the stroke, yet also fearful of what the future would hold. As each patient recounted the circumstances of his stroke to the others, he gained his first measure of group support. That feelings of depression and anger, as well as joy over improvement, were voiced illustrates the value of the group in providing an opportunity for the members to test their new images of themselves in a comfortable setting. In addition, the regular influx of new members provided an input of opinions and attitudes which were an added source of material for discussion.

The most readily observable effect of the open-ended membership system was the development of an almost parentally supportive spirit among the members. A newer member, often just beginning to realize the extent of his impairment, was frequently jolted by the information given him by the others. The myth of a miracle cure was dispelled and replaced with the hard reality of the work of therapy. It was not uncommon to find this same member several weeks later coming to the aid of a newer patient, struggling to cope with the same frustrations that had earlier perplexed and dismayed him. The satisfaction individuals gained from these exchanges should be viewed in the light of an often-voiced fear—that of becoming useless. The fact that, while gaining in the understanding of their own conditions, members were apt to achieve a measure of utility should not be underestimated.

This method of membership rotation did have limitations. The primary difficulty involved the depth of discussion. During periods when several new members entered simultaneously, much of the group time was spent in the introductory stage. In general, the longer-term members were more concerned over specific problems in their adjustment and wanted to discuss these with the other members. With new members entering weekly, this effort was hampered. In view of this fact, the membership system might be modified by allowing new members to join at established intervals, perhaps once every three or four weeks. This change would permit the advantage of developing support but would limit the problem of frequent repetition and thus allow more time for discussion of substantive issues of concern to the longer-participating members.

The anticipated problem in group cohesion was of less importance than expected, especially after the restriction of the group to stroke patients. Apparently, the fact of the stroke provided a bond of its own, with a strength that overcame some of the difficulties of the membership rotation.

CONCLUSIONS

The open-ended group of hemiplegic and hemiparetic patients discussed here presents a viable alternative to the time-limited group, especially in settings where individuals remain for an extensive and indeterminate period of time. Meeting weekly, the group became a vehicle for the discussion of fears, frustrations, and practical concerns for the future. Although all hemiplegics shared certain practical adjustment problems, those who had suffered a stroke were found to have such a strong and specific fear of its recurrence that the decision was made to limit the group to stroke patients.

This membership pattern found a special benefit in the development of a nurturing, protective system in which the more experienced members aided the newer members in their initial adjustment stages. The results included a decrease in individual isolation as evidenced by increasing interest in others and simultaneous gains in self-esteem and personal satisfaction.

CHAPTER 30

TREATING FAMILIES OF BONE MARROW RECIPIENTS AND DONORS

Marie Cohen, Irene Goldenberg, and Herbert Goldenberg

A recent dramatic medical breakthrough in the treatment of acute leukemia and aplastic anemia involves replacing the patient's bone marrow with fresh marrow of a matching type from a donor, typically a close relative. Because the technique is fraught with numerous physical dangers, the UCLA Bone Marrow Transplant Center, one of six such centers in the United States, utilizes the skills of oncologists, radiologists, microbiologists, immunologists and in the case of children, pediatricians. The need for social work and psychological services is increasingly recognized.

This paper is directed specifically at the team management of these disorders, and by implication, of a wide variety of serious, threatening, or terminal illnesses. Few human experiences are filled with such suffering and anguish to both family and hospital staff as those involved with malignancies, especially when the patient is a child and there is the imminent threat of a premature separation and an unfulfilled life (Ablin, Binger, Stein, Kushner, Zoger and Mikkelson, 1971). Nevertheless, with few exceptions (Lansky, 1974; Spinetta, 1974), little attention has as yet been directed at the potential usefulness of social-psychological interventions on an oncology ward. In this paper, we intend to describe a crisis-focused family therapy approach involving the patient and his or her family, to offer several relevant case histories from among the ten families already seen, and to draw some conclusions regarding the best utilization of a physician-therapist team concept for families where one member is terminally ill.

Reprinted from *Journal of Marriage and Family Counseling,* Vol. 3, No. 4 (October 1977), pp. 45–52, by permission of the publisher.

HISTORY OF THE PROBLEM

The general literature on death and dying, once a taboo subject, has burgeoned in the last two decades (Feifel, 1959; Fulton, 1965; Kübler-Ross, 1969). Attitudes toward the prospects of one's own death, unspoken fantasies that it can be resisted and cajoled, the reliance on denial of the inevitable, and coming to terms with the process and finality of death have all been investigated (Weisman, 1972).

Fear, anger, depression, resentment, even relief, are common responses to receiving a fatal diagnosis (Kübler-Ross, 1969). Hamburg (1974) has outlined a common sequence of responses in family members who must learn to cope with such news; guilt; self-blame (perhaps if the diagnosis had been made earlier, the chances of successful treatment would increase); hope (perhaps a curative miracle drug will be discovered in time to save the person's life). As the disease progresses, as hope diminishes, relatives live on a day-to-day basis, wishing for one more remission of symptoms before death. Finally, there is a resignation to the inevitable outcome, in preparation for the eventual loss.

While hospital personnel—doctors and nurses—are trained in the technical aspects of dealing with a patient's illness, they receive little training regarding the disclosure of an impending death, or even how to approach the subject with the patient and his/her family members (Glaser and Strauss, 1965). Dying is a temporal process, as much a social phenomenon as a biological one. That is, death of a family member takes place over a period of time and calls for a series of social readjustments. Death expectations are a key determinant in how others (family, hospital staff) act during the dying process (Glaser and Strauss, 1968). It is our contention that an approach to the entire family experiencing this crisis may facilitate the necessary, if painful, readjustments to death in one of its members.

THE BONE MARROW TRANSPLANT

Both leukemia and aplastic anemia are ordinarily fatal diseases of the bone marrow, the blood-forming organs. In the former, frequently referred to as cancer of the blood, there is an abnormal proliferation of white blood cells. In the case of the latter, there is a defective production of red and white blood cells and platelets. Three types of medical intervention are possible: drug therapy, radiation therapy, and bone marrow transplant. Unfortunately, each has certain potential deleterious effects. For example, to be effective against leukemia cells, drug therapy must be of such high dosages that bone marrow may be destroyed in the process. A similar consequence may result from high doses of radiation therapy. A third possibility is to use these powerful therapeutic agents and then give the patient new marrow cells through a bone marrow transplant from a compatible donor.

The medical procedure is a drastic one, calling for the complete suppression of his or her bone marrow. After matching for genetic factors through tissue typing, the marrow recipient receives the new marrow from a closely-matched sibling and then receives continual supportive blood transfusions from other family members. If successful, the patient is rescued from death for an undetermined period of time; in rare cases this extension of life may be the length of the patient's normal life span.

A FAMILY-FOCUSED CRISIS

Family members inevitably are participants in every phase of the patient's treatment. Frequently, they must interrupt their employment and home routines, sometimes for several weeks, in order to relocate in an unfamiliar city (in this case Los Angeles). Once there, donors must devote most of their days to traveling between their hotel room, the patient's room, and the Red Cross cell separating machine. The patient must spend six to eight weeks or more on "reverse isolation" while undergoing this medical procedure. He or she is kept in a private room and is severely restricted in contact with the outside world. Those few family members who are permitted to visit must wear caps, gowns, masks, and gloves. Since the patient must be kept immune to infection, no intimate physical contact is possible.

Several severe psychological stresses must be coped with by the patient in this isolated-bed "life island": inhibition of motor activity, loss of intimacy with loved ones, dependency on others, physical and social isolation, separation from family and, finally, confrontation with the severity of the illness. (Köhle, Simons, Weidlich, Dietrich and Durner, 1971). The parent who is a patient cannot have contact with his or her children because the children might introduce infections which could be fatal since the parent has no functioning immune response or body defense. This has severe intrapsychic and interpersonal repercussions, not merely for the patient, but for the entire family unit.

Each participating family member is in a highly stressful situation. In particular, the bone marrow donor's commitment is usually intense and extremely personalized ("flesh of my flesh, bone of the bone"). All members experience a disruption of family life as well as share in the fantasy that somehow their loved one will be saved from imminent death.

To date, the transplant procedure has extended lives from one to eleven months, with a mean thus far of seven months. One patient apparently has returned to normal health.

THE ROLE OF FAMILY THERAPY

While major attention of necessity is directed at those medical procedures that are life-supporting, there is also an important role for psychotherapeutic intervention. Lansky (1974), focusing on childhood leukemia, points out how patient management becomes more complex with some of the newer medical treatments which prolong remissions. Such remissions frequently allow the parents to stop grieving, deny to themselves that their child is fatally ill, perhaps even become elated; unfortunately, such hopes are short-lived and sooner or later they must be reoriented to reality. While Lansky notes typical family disruptions—fathers spend increasing amounts of time away from home, siblings develop adjustment problems, the family is deserted by friends, relatives and neighbors who themselves fear death—he advocates crisis-oriented individual sessions with disturbed members. On the other hand, Ablin et al. (1971) describe family conferences with the hospital staff that parents later rated as highly significant in helping them cope with the crisis of discovering their child's diagnosis of leukemia and his/her eventual death. Such conferences are essentially supportive as well as informative regarding etiology, therapy and prognosis.

We have followed a family crisis model in such situations because we assume that all the family members function in the shadow of their loved one's death, although commonly they deny and repress affect in their daily behavior, feelings and attitudes. Typically, the family dysfunction is blamed on the disease rather than the maladaptive family response to the crisis brought on by the patient's life-threatening illness.

One purpose of the family therapeutic approach (Goldenberg and Goldenberg, 1975) is to ease the psychological impact of the severe medical procedures on all concerned. Frequently, the crisis may exacerbate previous underlying pathological interactions among family members, and these must be recognized and resolved. All must help in coming to terms with the possible impending death of the patient, while still maintaining hope. The family therapist must help frightened, confused, distrustful relatives to mobilize their existing coping mechanisms and learn new, more adaptive ones appropriate to the immediate crisis situation. The family must work through together the issues of forthcoming separation and loss, overcoming the wish to avoid or deny the inevitable. This is complicated by the magical fantasies of the physician, the psychotherapist, and the family, each of whom needs or wants to believe death can be forestalled.

SOME FAMILY CASE HISTORIES

Disequilibrium in both family structure and function are inevitable consequences of the illness, hospitalization, and bone marrow transplant. For example, a 12-year-old girl is forced to assume the role of homemaker and surrogate mother to her four-year-old sister in the absence of her mother, hospitalized for months at a time with acute myelogenous leukemia. At the same time she becomes a confidante of her lonely, uncertain, 26-year-old stepfather. Another adolescent, a 13-year-old boy, living alone with his divorced mother, must take on the role of a substitute husband when she falls ill with leukemia. Despite the circumstances, she clearly is delighted, as is he, with his newfound adult status. Such role changes among family members are typical and in most cases need not necessarily prove maladaptive in the long run. In most cases we have seen, shifts in function are appropriate, provided that the child's psychological and social development are not stunted and provided, too, that he or she does not become the sole keeper of the family's sudden burdens.

The following case study illustrates such shifts in roles within the family:

In Tom G.'s family, the family caretaker role was adopted by the 16-year-old sister, Dee, who also was the marrow donor for Tom, an 18-year-old, black adolescent who had marrow aphasia. Their father, physically disabled, held little status in the family, was generally devalued by all family members. Mrs. G., an anxious, hypertensive person, had been married and divorced several times prior to her current marriage. Dependent and insecure, she openly stated that her children would have to take care of her during this family crisis. Ordinarily the therapist, one of the authors, would have attempted to block this abandonment of "normal" role functioning. However, in this family and under these circumstances it appeared as though Dee could assume a great deal of the emotional support functions for her mother, her two brothers, and herself. She also appeared able to ask for additional support when she needed to be less "grown up." The therapist thus gave her encouragement to pursue this new role.

The continuing experience with families of transplant candidates has taught the hospital staff some diagnostic indices of "elasticity" in family functioning. It is helpful to know if the family can identify those members who emerged as leaders and followers in prior family crises. A family can profit from interventions if they have insight into their prior functioning. It is also often profitable for families to become aware of how in the past they may have scapegoated a member as being solely responsible for their problems. The following case illustrates how scapegoating and denial are common strategies for avoiding confronting the painful truth of a family crisis situation, while presenting to the world a picture of a fraudulently warm family atmosphere:

The S. family came to UCLA Hospital from a neighboring state in order to get a bone marrow transplant for Carol, age 16, their eldest daughter. She had been diagnosed as suffering from acute myelogenous leukemia four months earlier, and her condition had been refractory to all other therapeutic intervention. Carol was accompanied by her parents and three younger siblings. The family described themselves as warm and close, the proof being their leaving for California as soon as they heard that Carol had been accepted for the transplant procedure. They down-played their lack of financial and social resources in the new city, denied that Mr. S.'s unemployment of four months' duration was a strain on him and them. They were here to do all they could for Carol.

The cracks in this warm and supportive family veneer first appeared when they had to sign for Carol's transplant. The informed consent form clearly mentions the possibility of the patient's death. Though everyone continued to support their desire for the transplant, Mr. S. began appearing at the hospital drunk, and his wife began losing weight rapidly while denying that her husband's behavior or anything else bothered her.

In family therapy sessions, Carol expressed her feeling that she was the sole cause of her family's "new" problems, and admitted that she felt her death would bring relief to the family, feeling she had been an emotional and financial burden on them since the time of the original diagnosis. Her brother and sister were finally able to voice the forbidden expressions of resentment toward Carol for becoming ill and causing their travels to this strange city with no friends. They held her responsible for their parents' fights, daddy's drinking, and their missing graduation day at school.

Family therapy was directed first at uncovering the many deeply held but largely unexpressed feelings experienced by each of the family members—feelings of grief, depression, caring and hostility. As these previously forbidden feelings were expressed, the therapist was able to reassure all the family that such reactions were common in attempting to deal with a possible impending death. Each member learned to accept his or her own ambivalence toward Carol's condition—a combination of positive love and concern along with negative feelings of resentment and irritation. Finally, the therapist helped them, collectively, to accept the leukemia as a family crisis that required an allied family effort to cope with satisfactorily.

COPING STRATEGIES

Coping effectively involves far more than self-protection from stress. The adaptive person (or family) must approach the situation with plans, calculate risks and opportunities, seek information to prepare for probable difficulties and keep all possible options open (Hamburg, 1974). Typical for families of bone marrow recipients and donors is this sequence: denial; acceptance of the diagnosis but not the prognosis; acceptance of the prognosis.

To be effective, family therapy must be tailored to the point in this sequence which reflects the family's current set of attitudes and expectations. For example, the therapeutic approach differs widely if the patient is newly admitted to the hospital or admitted for the last time because death is imminent. Similarly, whether the patient is to receive an immediate transplant or such a decision may be postponed may have an impact on the course and thrust of family therapy. Finally, of course, the degree of physical illness and patient availability influences the form and content of the psychotherapeutic intervention.

Typically, all concerned first attempt to cope with the reality of impending death through denial; they wish to screen it out of awareness or reverse it. Family behavior during this phase may be characterized by hostility toward physicians or other staff and refusal to accept or understand the diagnosis. At this point, usually following hospital admission, the social worker is likely to focus on concrete problems such as family finances and living arrangements and not on the patient's possible death.

Osgood (1964) has suggested that physicians adopt a psychotherapeutic stance, providing the entire family with a full explanation of the disease and its treatment, removal of unwarranted fears or guilt feelings, and above all, helping to instill a thread of hope and comfort that somebody cares. To preserve hope, Osgood even offers the initial possibility that the diagnosis is incorrect and that a cure may be found in time. However, in our experiences, one consequence of Osgood's last suggestion is that all involved (physician, therapist, family members) will in all probability have to relinquish that hope fairly soon. Hospital personnel in particular must do so with each succeeding patient, so that cynicism and hope need to be carefully balanced.

During the second phase, the patient and his/her family come to accept the reality of cancer, while still denying its implied terminal prognosis. Not uncommonly, physicians may unconsciously foster the fantasies of family members concerning the patient's life expectancy. Frequently, this may be an attempt on the physician's part to diminish his/her own personal distress regarding the loss of the patient through death and one's helplessness to reverse its inevitability. However, if the physician refuses to deal with the medical reality, the family does too. The family may resist accepting the prognosis if they see the physician resisting it. The task for the family therapist during this second phase is often to become the insistent bearer of reality which, in effect, means the bearer of bad news.

In the third and final phase, hopefully, the patient, family, and staff arrive at a realistic acceptance of the medical reality and its inevitable outcome. If death occurs before both the family and staff have worked through this separation process, there may be serious consequences for all concerned. The family will be set back in its efforts to restructure, remobilize, and return once again to the real world. Staff, still grieving, will find it difficult to take on new patients with similar prognoses.

THE FAMILY THERAPIST: ROLE AND CONFLICT

We have seen that in the general therapeutic process with dying patients, the position of the therapist as both part of the family and separate from it is imperative for effective intervention. This phenomenon is one of the most delicate therapeutic problems in working with oncology patients. The therapist must be empathetic with the patient who is being blamed and rejected. At the same time, he or she must be on guard against being caught up in, and thus aiding and abetting, the family's *mythification of death:* the process in which the incipient pain of separation and loss is denied, and in which it is expected that the dying person will deny his experience in order to spare others a confrontation with their own mortality (Pattison, 1975).

One conflict necessarily faced by all therapists dealing with oncology patients is the therapist's feelings and attitudes regarding his/her own ultimate death. Another is how not to succumb to the family's (or one's own) wish that the therapist be omniscient and omnipotent.

The family therapist stands for a degree of reasoned intervention in an environment which appears arbitrarily to give and take lives by magical means. The patients cannot do without the physician and are out of control in their physical functioning. The psychotherapist intervenes to strengthen the existing psychological coping mechanisms of the patient and his/her family members. He/she moves into the family's system and assists the family in using its own coping mechanisms for support. Such direct interventions are designed to help family members and support them as individuals even if that means they may have to recognize their end as a family unit due to a member's imminent death. The therapist has to function in the "family unit" within the hospital ward, supporting individuals and the system itself to allow the unit once again to take on a new member-patient.

Finally, the therapist must recognize the primary physician's need for a delicate balance of hope and reality orientation. The therapist helps to guide the physician toward the acceptance of the loss of a patient by helping the physician to reject the magical omnipotence with which the family invests him and which turns into inevitable rage at the death of the patient.

REFERENCES

Ablin A. R., Binger, C. M., Stein, R. C., Kushner, J. H., Zoger, S., & Mikkelson, C. A conference with the family of a leukemic child. *American Journal of Diseases of Children,* 1971, *122,* 362–364.

Feifel, H. (Ed.) *The meaning of death.* New York: McGraw-Hill, 1959.

Fulton, R. (Ed.) *Death and identity.* New York: Wiley, 1965.

Glaser B. G., & Strauss A. L. *Awareness of dying.* Chicago: Aldine, 1965.

Glaser B. G., & Strauss, A. L. *Time for dying.* Chicago: Aldine, 1968.

Goldenberg I., & Goldenberg, H. A family approach to psychological services. *American Journal of Psychoanalysis,* 1975, *35,* 317–328.

Hamburg, D. A. Coping behavior in life-threatening circumstances. *Psychotherapy and Psychosomatics,* 1974, *23,* 13–26.

Köhle K., Simons C., Weidlich, S., Dietrich M., & Durner, A. Psychological aspects in the treatment of leukemia patients in the isolated-bed system 'life island.' *Psychotherapy and Psychosomatics,* 1971, *19,* 85–91.

Kübler-Ross, E. *On death and dying.* New York: Macmillan, 1969.

Lansky, S. B. Childhood leukemia: The child psychiatrist as a member of the oncology team. *Journal of the American Academy of Child Psychiatry,* 1974, *13,* 499–508.

Osgood, E. E. Treatment of chronic leukemias. *Journal of Nuclear Medicine,* 1964, *5,* 139–153.

Pattison, E. *The fatal myth of death in the family.* Presented at the American Psychiatric Association's 128th Annual Meeting, May 5, 1975.

Spinetta, J. J. The dying child's awareness of death: A review. *Psychological Bulletin,* 1974, *81,* 256–260.

Weisman, A. D. *On dying and denying.* New York: Behavioral Publications, 1972.

PART III

PSYCHOLOGICAL PROBLEMS

The psychological functioning of our clients has been the essence of clinical social work practice since its earliest beginnings. Increasingly, social work plays a leadership role in the provision of a broad spectrum of psychotherapies to a vast number of clients whose presenting symptomatology covers the total range of psychopathological functioning.

Although we have frequently quarreled, both within the profession and with colleagues in other professions, as to the extent, depth, sophistication, and exclusivity of our role in this essential area of the human condition, we have never denied our responsibility in it. We have, as well, spent far too much energy (in this author's opinion) in fruitless agonizing rumination on how our spheres of interest are like and how they are different from those of colleagues in other professions, but gratefully never to the point of denying a commitment to the provision of a therapeutic service. If we are going to take responsibility for a client in a particular situation we have an equally compelling responsibility to know that client. Hence a social work-based psychological diagnosis has always been, and will continue to be, of importance to us!

Much discussion, of course, has taken place around the terminology to be used in describing our clients' psychological state. We have been accused and have accused each other of mimicking other professions, of being too timid in developing our own paradigms, and in recent years of over-stressing pathology and using "labels" in improper and disempowering ways.

Such debates will continue long into the future, as we seek to find more accurate ways of describing clients that build on strength, that take into account weaknesses or problems, that recognize the potential risks of some persons to themselves and others, that ensure that persons obtain the resources that best suit their needs and wishes and do not subject them to inappropriate or dehumanizing interventions.

In recent years, the tremendously influential *Diagnostic and Statistical Manual* and its various editions and revisions have been most helpful in developing a common multiaxis and cross-disciplinary approach to this challenge. Certainly this is a system that is not free from criticism and politicization. Just as certainly, as it emerges and develops it is not the final word. It is the view of this writer that this manual has served us well, and although it isn't perfect we should make use of its strengths.

Again, because this is such an important area with such a long history in our profession, the social work literature is rich. Indeed, it is an area of practice in which specific social work textbooks have been written. Thus, the selection of articles for this edition was challenging in the extreme. As we have noted in other sections, and as we have observed in preparing other editions, our writing in this field has been highly uneven. Understandably, some topics receive much more attention than others. Topics or situations with which we frequently come into contact in practice are stressed. Hence topics such as schizophrenia, depression, borderline conditions, substance abuse, and the newly identified post-traumatic stress disorders are most frequently addressed in the literature of recent years. This is understandable. These are the situations in which social workers are frequently found to play a critical role in practice. Partly because of their prevalence in society, partly because they are situations that tend to be ongoing and only infrequently alleviated in any but a minor way, and partly because of the impact of persons with these conditions on significant others and on societal systems, clients with these problems are frequently found in the caseloads of social workers in virtually all settings.

This does not mean that other diagnostic categories are not important. It does mean that many of these other topics have not been addressed by social workers in our practice literature. This is unfortunate. Many of our colleagues have considerable experience with a much wider range of patterned psychological disorders than is reflected in the literature of the last two decades. Interestingly, one topic that has rarely been discussed in social work literature is paranoia. There are few caseloads in our profession that do not include some persons who manifest some degree of difficulty in functioning related to this very complex condition. It is an area in which I believe we have had considerable experience and have developed some very helpful skills for assisting clients and persons close to them, but we have rarely written about this knowledge.

Undoubtedly, many reasons for our avoiding particular topics could be postulated. This is not the place for this analysis, except to comment on one point. It is evident that in recent years, at least in North America, there has been a very strong and oft-repeated critical challenge to what is referred to as "labeling." Although this issue could also be raised in regard to other sections of this volume, it is mentioned here because it seems most frequently connected to "things psychiatric." It is true that much harm has been done as a result of the misapplication of labels to clients and their subsequent misuse. But just as much harm has been done, though this is frequently forgotten by the denouncers of labeling, by the failure to use labels appropriately. Thus, clients can be underserved, can harm themselves or others, and can be deprived of needed, appropriate, and available services and resources as a result of the failure to make legitimate use of diagnostic categories. Our challenge, in social work and indeed in all professions, is to learn how to make appropriate and helping use of labels and to wage war relentlessly against their misuse. The reality is that labels are powerfully helpful but equally powerfully dangerous.

One other challenge in this section was, once again, the ordering of the topics. As in other sections, after several false starts, the decision was made to stay with the alphabetical strategy.

There is probably no area of practice to which social work could make a more critical contribution than the psychosocial aspects of the range of psychological problems that our clients of all cultures manifest. Yet there seems to be no other area of practice in which there is more discomfort about teaching each other and our colleagues in other disciplines what we know to be helpful and effective, and equally important, what we know to be harmful and what we do not know.

One aspect of this component of our clients' lives that we have not as yet addressed in an adequate manner is the role of medication in the management of many of the diagnostic categories with which we come into contact. This was mentioned in the introduction to the previous section on physical conditions, and it needs to be underscored once again. This is of particular importance, since so many who manifest various psychological patterns of upset, and who in an earlier day would have been institutionalized, are found in our caseloads. Many of these persons are able to maintain a level of functioning that permits them to benefit from the range of interventions and resources available to us only through a carefully regulated and supervised regimen of medication. Hence, once again, it is critical that all practitioners have a general knowledge, and sometimes a very detailed understanding, of the role and limitations of medications. Without it we can greatly underserve, misdiagnose, and deprive clients of access to resources.

CHAPTER 31

SCREENING FOR AFFECTIVE DISORDERS

Julia B. Rauch, Carla Sarno, and Sylvia Simpson

Practitioners in family and children's services need skills for assessing mood disorders and for referring symptomatic individuals for psychiatric evaluation. The personal and social costs of mood disorders are high and include suicide; increased mortality from physical disease; drug and alcohol abuse; and disruption of relationships, education, and careers (Akiskal & Weller, 1989; Boyd & Weissman, 1985; Brent, 1987; Goodwin & Guze, 1989; Goodwin & Jamison, 1990, Stoudemire, Frank, Hedemark, Kamlet, & Blazer, 1986; Whybrow, Akiskal, & McKinney, 1984). Unfortunately, these illnesses are underrecognized and undertreated, resulting in preventable, needless suffering for both afflicted individuals and their families (Costello, 1989). Family and children's workers are strategically positioned to screen for affective disorders and to assist affected clients and their families to secure needed psychiatric care, support services, and entitlements.

Sound assessment is a prerequisite to selection of effective intervention. Careful appraisal is particularly critical with affective disorders because they can be life threatening. Failure to diagnose a severe affective disorder may end in suicide or even homicide. Further, workers who do not recognize possible mood-disordered clients or who do not refer them for competent psychiatric evaluation are at risk for malpractice, as are their employers.

Scientific understanding of affective disorders is increasing rapidly (Keller, 1989). Etiological paradigms are changing as a result of evidence that these conditions are often inherited biological diseases and are amenable to pharmacological treatment (Akiskal, 1989; Engel, 1977; Kupfer, 1982; Group for the Advancement of Psychiatry,

Reprinted from *Families in Society*, Vol. 72, No. 10 (December 1991), pp. 602–609, by permission of the publisher, Families International, Inc.

1989, Marmor, 1983; Sabelli & Carlson-Sabelli, 1989). Screening for affective disorders should be a routine part of initial assessment in family and children's agencies. Additionally, workers should know how to monitor mood-disordered clients (and/or their significant others), how to assess the risks of harm to themselves or others, and when to contact the treating psychiatrist about possible changes in medication or the need for a more protective environment.

The purpose of this article is to update clinicians about current developments in affective disorders. It also provides guidelines for screening. The need for partnerships between family and children's services and psychiatrists is discussed.

BIOLOGICAL ASPECTS OF AFFECTIVE DISORDERS
Inheritance

Five decades of epidemiological research have (1) documented that affective disorders run in families and (2) provided evidence of biological inheritance (Blehar, Weissman, Gershon, & Hirschfeld, 1988; Gershon, 1989; Gershon, Berrettini, & Goldin, 1989; Mendlewicz, 1985; Nurnberger, Goldin, & Gershon, 1986; Tsuang & Faraone, 1990). Studies have compared (1) the incidence of mood disorders in families of unipolar or bipolar patients with control groups, (2) concordance for affective illness in identical and fraternal twins, (3) the frequency of affective illness in biological and adoptive parents of afflicted adult adoptees and in adopted children of ill mothers.

Despite methodological difficulties, findings of these studies consistently provide evidence for genetic factors in affective disorders. Relatives of bipolar and unipolar patients have higher prevalence of mood disorders than do relatives of control groups (Mendlewicz, 1985; Gershon, 1989; Wender, Kety, Rosenthal, Schulsinger, Ortmann, & Lunde, 1986). Several studies documented higher concordance for affective disorders among identical twins than among fraternal twins (Tsuang & Faraone, 1990). Although family, twin, and adoption studies provide evidence for genetic factors in affective disorders, they also document the power of environmental factors. All families had unaffected as well as affected members.

CLINICAL ASPECTS OF AFFECTIVE DISORDERS
Characteristics

The primary symptoms of mood disorders are depression, elation, or mood swings between the two. However, disturbed mood itself is not diagnostic. Affective disorders are clinical syndromes, or clusters, of symptoms. The *Diagnostic and Statistical Manual of Mental Disorders* (DSM-III-R) (American Psychiatric Association, 1987) identifies three categories of these conditions: (1) major affective disorders and syndromes, (2) other specific affective disorders, and (3) atypical affective disorders. This article focuses on the first group, major affective disorders such as unipolar (depressive) and bipolar (manic depressive) syndromes. These disorders are the most common and most likely to be seen in family and children's agencies.

Affective disorders vary on several dimensions (Whybrow, Akiskal, & McKinney, 1984).

- Mood—depression, elation, or both
- Time—acute or chronic, age of onset, duration of episodes and intervals between episodes, episode frequency
- Severity—psychotic or nonpsychotic
- Etiology—symptoms primarily caused by affective disorders or by another condition (i.e., medical illness)
- Apparent response to environmental change and intervention (responsive or nonresponsive)

Thus, individual pictures vary considerably even within the same disease category. For example, one person may have a first episode of major depression in adolescence and recurrently throughout life. Another person may have only a single episode in late adulthood.

Unipolar Affective Disorders

Unipolar affective disorders in which patients experience recurrent episodes of depressed mood are the most common. In depression, the "down" mood differs from ordinary sadness or "blues" and includes painful emotions and the absence of pleasure (anhedonia). The painful dimension is usually related to anxiety, guilt, anguish, and restlessness.

A diagnosis of major depressive episode is assigned when an individual has at least five of the nine symptoms listed below for at least two weeks:

- depressed mood . . . most of the day, nearly every day
- markedly diminished interest or pleasure in all, or almost all, activities
- significant weight loss or weight gain when not dieting . . . or decrease or increase in appetite
- insomnia or hypersomnia nearly every day
- psychomotor agitation or retardation
- fatigue or loss of energy nearly every day
- feelings of worthlessness, or excessive or inappropriate guilt
- diminished ability to think or concentrate, or indecisiveness
- recurrent thoughts of death . . . recurrent suicidal ideation with a specific plan, or a suicide attempt or a specific plan for committing suicide (American Psychiatric Association, 1987, pp. 222–223).

A diagnosis of melancholia (endogenous depression) requires at least five symptoms but also a history of (1) one or more major depressives episodes followed by complete, or nearly complete, recovery and (2) previous good response to specific and adequate somatic antidepressant therapy (American Psychiatric Association, 1987).

Dysthymia, according to DSM-III-R,

is a less severe form of unipolar illness characterized by depressed mood for most of the day, more days than not, for at least two years and the presence of at least two of six other symptoms: (1) poor appetite or overeating, (2) insomnia or hypersomnia, (3) low energy or fatigue, (4) low self-esteem, (5) poor concentration or difficulty making decisions, (6) feelings of hopelessness (American Psychiatric Association, 1987, p. 230).

Bipolar Affective Disorders

Bipolar diagnoses are based on the presence of episodes of elevated mood, with or without intervening depression. In mania, a distinct period of abnormally and persistently elevated, expansive, or irritable mood is present. During the period of mood disturbance, at least three of seven symptoms must persist:

- inflated self-esteem or grandiosity
- decreased need for sleep
- more talkative than usual or pressure to keep talking
- flight of ideas or subjective experience that thoughts are racing
- distractibility
- increase in goal-directed activity (either socially, at work or school, or sexually) or psychomotor agitation
- excessive involvement in pleasurable activities which have a high potential for painful consequences, e.g., unrestrained buying sprees, sexual indiscretions or foolish business investments (American Psychiatric Association, 1987, p. 217)

The diagnostic criteria for manic episodes require sufficient symptom severity to cause marked impairment in occupational functioning or relationships, or to necessitate hospitalization to prevent harm to self or others. The person may be psychotic.

In hypomania, individuals meet all the criteria for a manic episode but without significant impairment. A diagnosis of cyclothymic disorder is assigned if numerous episodes of hypomania occur during a two-year period, along with numerous periods of depressed mood that did not meet criteria for major depression (American Psychiatric Association 1987).

Differential Diagnosis

One complexity of differential diagnosis is distinguishing mood disorders from the normal emotional ups and downs that everyone goes through and from expected responses to loss and other psychosocial stressors. The line between normality and psychopathology is blurred. Some experts contend that affective disorders vary along a continuum; others assert that affective disorders are qualitatively different from other variations in mood (Whybrow, Akiskal, & McKinney, 1984). In addition, normal reactions to catastrophic losses may include severe, disturbing symptoms similar to those found in affective disorders. For example, bereaved people may report seeing and hearing the lost loved one and express fears that they are going crazy.

The concept of *autonomy* helps to define the boundaries between normality and psychopathology (Whybrow, Akiskal, & McKinney, 1984). Autonomy refers to the phenomenon that the illness develops according to its own characteristics; it may emerge suddenly without any discernible reason for onset and may manifest mood and symptoms that are inappropriate to the person's situation.

Differential diagnosis is also complicated because symptoms of different mental illnesses can overlap. For example, symptoms of hallucinations and delusions can occur in both bipolar illness and schizophrenia. In those instances, it is useful to look at the course of the person's illness and the family history. Making the correct diagnosis has important treatment ramifications. Increasing knowledge of the biology of affective disorders may make it possible in the future to diagnose on the basis of biochemical laboratory tests (DePaulo, Simpson, Folstein, & Folstein, 1989).

Masking of depressive symptoms may also hinder differential diagnosis. Depression may manifest as stomach pains, headaches, backaches, palpitations, and a host of other physical complaints. People with masked depression may claim to have no sad feelings, although they may admit to being upset about their health. According to one study, one-third to two-thirds of all hospitalized medical and surgical patients older than 40 are suffering from masked depression and not the disease for which they are receiving treatment (Hamilton, 1989). Drug and alcohol abuse, eating disorders, and antisocial behavior may also conceal underlying depression.

Differential diagnosis in children and adolescents is also complex. Early symptoms of bipolar illness in children may appear as attention deficit hyperactivity disorder (Schmidt & Friedson, 1990). Adolescents who appear to be angry and conduct disordered may have a mixed state, that is, simultaneous presentation of significant symptoms of depression and mania (Puig-Antich, Ryan, & Rabinovich, 1985).

Medical disorders accompanied apparently by psychiatric symptoms also complicate differential diagnosis. Depressed mood and allied symptoms appear with numerous medical "mimickers." These include hypothyroidism, diabetes, and other endocrine diseases; neurological problems such as multiple sclerosis, stroke, and Parkinson's disease; some cancers; heart disease; infectious diseases such as mononucleosis and infectious hepatitis; and autoimmune disorders (lupus).

Drugs and alcohol are powerful mood-altering substances; licit drugs (such as birth control pills) and illicit drugs (such as cocaine) can cause symptoms that mimic depression and mania and can also trigger episodes of these illnesses. A relatively common but underrecognized cause of depressed feelings is undernutrition, particularly in poor people and others with poor diets (Belle, 1982; Cassel, 1987; Wortis, 1985).

GUIDELINES FOR SCREENING AFFECTIVE DISORDERS
Probing for Symptoms

Although psychiatric expertise is required for full diagnosis of complex conditions involving affective disorders, nonpsychiatric clinicians can provide a valuable service to their clients by screening for these disorders. Clients' presenting problems may include disturbed mood, for example, persistent depressed feelings or unusual irritability. Much information may be obtained by probing clients' statements while using diagnostic criteria as a guide (Tables 31–1 and 31–2). For example,

Table 31–1
Screening Questions for Depression.

Over the past two weeks:

Has your mood been sad or irritable most of the time?

Do you have less interest or pleasure in doing things, most of the time?

Have you lost or gained weight? If so, how much?

Are you sleeping too much or too little?

Do you feel restless or tired?

Do you feel tired or run down nearly every day?

Are you having feelings of worthlessness or severe guilt?

Are you having trouble concentrating or having a hard time making up your mind?

Have you been thinking about death or suicide?

Have you lost a close relative or loved one within the past year?

Are you taking any medicines? If so, what are they?

Do you use alcohol or drugs? If so, what do you use and how often do you use it (them)?

Have you ever been treated for depression or had a psychiatric hospitalization? If so, how often and when?

You say that you are feeling pretty low. Could you tell me more about that? When did you start feeling this way?

If a client's narrative omits important symptom clusters, the worker should ask directly about specific symptoms to make sure that the possibility of an affective disorder is not overlooked.

I would like to ask you about something that we haven't talked about yet—your appetite. Have your eating habits changed since you began to feel blue? That is, do you eat more than you used to, are you eating less, or are you eating about the same?

When obtaining data for assessment, workers should ask about mood, even if the client has not mentioned disturbed feelings.

Many people who are having trouble with their children feel pretty down, pretty hard on themselves. What about you? Have you been feeling more depressed than you usually do?

As mentioned above, disturbed mood itself is not diagnostic; in some cases, a person with an affective disorder may not report disturbed mood. For this reason, workers should systematically explore whether symptoms are present.

Table 31–2
Screening Questions for Mania.

Have you ever felt unusually excited, energetic, or irritable?

If the person answers "yes" to this question, proceed with the questions below. Even if the person clearly answers "no," proceed with the additional screening questions if you suspect that the person may have been manic. If you are confident that the person has never been manic, you may stop here.

During the time your mood changed, did you ever feel that you had special powers or gifts?

Did you ever feel that you needed less sleep? For example, you felt rested after three hours of sleep?

During the time you felt unusually excited or energetic, did people tell you that you talked too much or too fast?

Did you feel your thoughts were racing or going too fast?

During the time when your mood changed, did you feel easily distracted or drawn to unimportant details?

Did you ever feel that you had so much energy that you needed to keep moving?

Did you ever do things that could have hurt or injured you?

Did you lose a job or friend during the time you felt unusually energetic?

Assessment of Danger

Dealing with risk of suicide is difficult but essential. Practitioners should ask directly whether the depressed client is thinking about killing him or herself. Such questions can be asked tactfully in response to the client's description of low mood:

> You say that you've been feeling pretty low recently. Have you been feeling so badly that you think about killing yourself?

Some workers may worry that asking a client about suicide will "plant" the idea. However, clients are usually relieved that someone takes them seriously and appreciates how badly they feel (Puryear, 1984; McAlpine, 1987).

The client's response should be probed in some detail. If the client has a specific plan, the means for carrying it out (gun, pills, rope), and the intention of implementing the plan, suicide risk is high. Workers should also determine whether clients have previously attempted to kill themselves and if they have known anyone who committed suicide. Famous people (e.g., Janis Joplin or Jimi Hendrix) may be role models for the potentially suicidal person. Social contagion may occur, as has happened in some high schools and communities in which "epidemics" of self-inflicted deaths have occurred (Brent, Kerr, Goldstein, Bozigar, Martella, & Allan, 1989).

If the person has a plan and the means to commit suicide, the practitioner must act quickly. The worker should not attempt to resolve the situation alone but should consult with colleagues. If the client will not agree to see a psychiatrist or go to a hospital, the worker should notify relatives (or other legally responsible persons) of the danger.

Significant others should be advised of (1) the client's need for evaluation and hospitalization and (2) the process for obtaining an emergency petition, if the person is unwilling to seek help voluntarily. They should be told to remove instruments of suicide from the home and to not leave the person alone. The worker should stay closely in touch with the family until hospitalization is achieved.

If the client has no relatives or if the family is unwilling to cooperate the practitioner may need to file for an emergency petition and call the police to transport the client to a psychiatric emergency service. Because the person should not be left alone, the practitioner may need to cancel other appointments and stay with the person until other arrangements are made.

Practitioners should continue to monitor risk for suicide, even if the client protests that she or he is OK. Paradoxically, some people commit suicide when they are recovering from a depressive episode. Severely depressed people may not have enough energy to act. However, when the antidepressants kick in, the person is energized and thus may take the steps necessary, such as buying a gun, to implement the plan.

Clients may insist that they will never kill themselves. However, commission of suicide is "state dependent." Although the client may not be planning death *now,* he or she may become more deeply depressed and suicidal in the future. It is better to err on the side of overestimating risk than minimizing it. For example, some clients use talk about suicide as a histrionic, emotional, and frequently manipulative tactic. It may be tempting to believe that the client does not "really mean it." Such clients, however, may kill themselves impulsively, their gesture inadvertently proving lethal. A common method is overdose with antidepressants.

Several variables are associated with increased risk of suicide (Mollica, 1989; Hirschfeld & Cross, 1982; Roy, 1989):

- Age 45 years or older
- Male
- Divorced or widowed
- Unemployed or retired
- Conflictual interpersonal relationships
- Chronic illness and/or hypochondriasis
- Family history of suicide
- Substance abuse
- Severe personality disorder
- Frequent, intense, and prolonged suicidal ideation
- Previous suicide attempts
- Suicide plan, especially one that makes rescue before death unlikely
- Unambiguous wish to die
- Method lethal and available
- Feeling of guilt and self-blame
- Poor achievement, lack of success
- Poor insight
- Social isolation
- Unresponsive family

Each suicide is idiosyncratic, of course. Nonetheless, if a client reports, for example, that she is worried about her 67-year-old retired, recently widowed father who is losing weight and not sleeping well, the worker should be instantly attuned to the possibility of the father's suicide.

RISKS WITH MANIA

People who are in manic states are unlikely to cooperate with mental health professionals and may be dangerous. At first, changes in mood are not seen as problematic and may be welcomed if the person has been depressed. The individual is cheerful, enthusiastic, and appears to relish life. This zest may be infectious, and other people may enjoy being with the manic person. Thus, the manic individual (and significant others) may see no need for intervention. Only if there is family history of mania are members likely to view apparent well-being as a warning.

The euphoric mood is volatile and can quickly change at the slightest frustration into anger, resentment, hostility, and unpredictable behavior. Manic people may be delusional or hear voices telling them to harm or kill themselves or others.

Family members and clinicians involved directly with manic individuals should follow safety precautions (Hirsh, 1988). First the potential for violence should be assessed. Predictors include a recent history of violence, recent acquisition of a weapon, presence of command hallucinations, preoccupation with thoughts of death, and a culture of violence in the individual's family or neighborhood. It is important that the manic individual, family members, and/or clinician all have the ability to escape a dangerous situation. The ability to secure help, for example, the police, is critical when dealing with unpredictable and potentially violent people.

DEVELOPING PARTNERSHIPS
Contemporary Treatment

Treatment of affective disorders has progressed since the days of leeching by the ancient Greeks (Goodwin & Jamison, 1990). More new treatments have been developed in the 20th century than in all preceding epochs. An important change is the way in which psychiatric symptoms are classified (Levy, 1982). In the past, categorization was based on inferences about unconscious processes. Reliance on inferences rather than observable, measurable characteristics created much disagreement among researchers and hindered research. Today, agreement about diagnoses is easier to achieve because clusters of symptoms are used as the basis for classification. Because diagnostic categories are based on measurable observation, they can be tested for usefulness in communication, etiological research, and prediction of clinical course (Hirschfeld & Shea, 1989).

Contemporary psychiatric classification is particularly useful in assessing the effectiveness of particular medications and psychotherapies for specific conditions because before and after measurements can be obtained. Psychotherapies have been developed and evaluated for their effectiveness (Hirschfeld & Shea, 1989). Most therapies are short-term and aim to correct specific aspects of depression, including cognition, behavior, and affect. Psychoanalytic, interpersonal, behavioral, and cognitive models have been formulated and used (Hirschfeld & Shea, 1989). Most people with mood disorders respond to the first antidepressant with which they are treated. New antidepressants and mood stabilizers are now available for treating persons with more persistent forms of mood disorders.

Moving from Consultantship To Partnership

Nonpsychiatric clinicians have and will continue to have an important psychotherapeutic role, especially with clients who do not require hospitalization and can be seen in community settings. They will also continue to play other roles, such as case manager, needs assessor, program developer, and program administrator. However, a clinician/psychiatric *partnership* must be nurtured.

A thorough psychiatric and medical history and examination of individuals with symptoms of affective disorders are necessary to detect any potential medical causes of symptoms before psychosocial interventions can be selected. In some instances, no services may be required; in other instances, multiple services may be needed.

Family and children's agencies historically have utilized psychiatric consultation. In the past, consultants tended to be psychoanalytically oriented. The psychiatrist provided insight into psychodynamic factors and suggested appropriate psychotherapeutic methods. Advice was usually given in response to case presentations, and the psychiatrist did not interview the client. Current knowledge of biological determinants of affective disorders requires that the role of the agency-affiliated psychiatric consultant be redefined. The agency must assure that symptomatic clients obtain a *competent* medical and psychiatric evaluation.

In some cases, clients may have a regular source of medical care and may have recently had a diagnostic work-up. However, relying on client's health care providers can be risky. Some clients do not have adequate health care coverage and may not have access to quality health care. Busy physicians may not keep up to date on new developments and may have little time to spend with patients. Thus, the examination may be superficial, the right questions may not be asked, and potentially helpful tests may not be administered. It may be advisable to suggest that the client obtain a second opinion.

In selecting psychiatric consultation, the agency and/or clinician should inquire about psychiatrists' training, type of practice, hospital affiliations, illness model, approach to treatment, and, of course, attitudes toward nonpsychiatric mental health practice. The goal should be to obtain competent consultants who have a *biopsychosocial* perspective.

Once a diagnosis is established and a treatment plan is designed, agencies can offer the specific counseling and support services to enable mood-disordered individuals and their families to cope with the disease. Achieving this goal, however, depends upon schools of social work and agencies providing the needed foundation knowledge, inservice training, and continuing education to prepare practitioners for their role in this emerging partnership.

REFERENCES

Akiskal, H. S. (1989). New insights into the nature and heterogeneity of mood disorders. *Journal of Clinical Psychiatry, 50* (supplement), 6–10.

Akiskal, H. S., & Weller, E. (1989). Mood disorders and suicide in children and adolescents. In H. I. Kaplan & B. J. Sadock (Eds.), *Comprehensive textbook of psychiatry* (vol. 2, 5th ed.) (pp. 1710–1715). Baltimore: Williams & Wilkins.

American Psychiatric Association. (1987). *Diagnostic and statistical manual of mental disorders* (3rd ed., rev.). Washington, DC: Author.

Belle, D. (1982). *Lives in stress: Women and depression.* Beverly Hills, CA: Sage Publications.

Blehar, M. C., Weissman, M. M., Gershon, E. S., & Hirschfeld, M. A. (1988). Family and genetic studies of affective disorders. *Archives of General Psychiatry, 45,* 289–292.

Boyd, J. H., & Weissman, M. M. (1985). Epidemiology of affective disorders. In R. Michaels, J. O. Cavernar, H. K. H. Brodie, A. M. Cooper, S. B. Guze, L. L. Judd, G. L. Klerman, & A. S. Solnit (Eds.), *Psychiatry* (vol. 3, rev.) (pp. l–16). Philadelphia: J. B. Lippincott.

Brent, D. A. (1987). Correlates of the medical lethality of suicide. *Journal of the American Academy of Child and Adolescent Psychiatry, 26,* 87–91.

Brent, D. A., Kerr, M. M., Goldstein, C., Bozigar, J., Martella, M., & Allan, J. (1989). An outbreak of suicide and suicidal behavior in a high school. *Journal of the American Academy of Child and Adolescent Psychiatry, 28,* 918–924.

Cassel, R. N. (1987). Use of select nutrients to foster wellness. *Psychology: A Quarterly Journal of Human Behavior, 24,* 24–29.

Costello, E. J. (1989). Developments in child psychiatric epidemiology: Introduction. *Journal of the American Academy of Child and Adolescent Psychiatry, 28,* 836–841.

DePaulo, J. R., Jr., Simpson, W., Folstein, S. F, & Folstein, M. F. (1989). The new genetics of bipolar affective disorder: Clinical implications. *Clinical Chemistry, 35,* B28–B32.

Engel, G. L. (1977). The need for a new medical model: A challenge for biomedicine. *Science, 196,* 129–135.

Gershon, E. S. (1989). Recent developments in genetics of manic depressive illness. *Journal of Clinical Psychiatry, 50* (supplement), 4–7.

Gershon, E. S., Berrettini, W. H., & Goldin, L. R. (1989). Mood disorders. In H. I. Kaplan & B. J. Sadock (Eds.), *Comprehensive textbook of psychiatry* (vol. 1, 5th ed.). Baltimore: Williams & Wilkins.

Goodwin, D. W., & Guze, S. B. (1989). *Psychiatric diagnosis* (4th ed.). New York: Oxford University Press.

Goodwin, F. K., & Jamison, K. R. (1990). *Manic depressive illness.* New York: Oxford University Press.

Group for the Advancement of Psychiatry. Committee on the Family (1989). The challenge of relational diagnoses: Applying the biopsychosocial model in DSM-IV. *American Journal of Psychiatry, 140,* 1492–1494.

Hamilton, M. (1989). Mood disorders: Clinical features. In H. I. Kaplan & B. J. Sadock (Eds.), *Comprehensive textbook of psychiatry* (vol. 1, 5th ed.). Baltimore: Williams & Wilkins.

Hirsch, P. R. (1988). Psychiatric emergencies for nonpsychiatrists. *Treatment trends. A newsletter of Taylor Manor Hospital, 3*(2), 1–7.

Hirschfeld, R. M. A., & Cross, C. K. (1982). Epidemiology of affective disorders: Psychosocial risk factors. *Archives of General Psychiatry, 39,* 35–46

Hirschfeld, R. M. A., & Shea, M. T. (1989). Mood disorders: Psychosocial treatments. In H. I. Kaplan & B. J. Sadock (Eds.), *Comprehensive textbook of psychiatry* (vol. 1, 5th ed.) (pp. 933–944). Baltimore: Williams & Wilkins.

Keller, M. B. (1989). Current concepts in affective disorders. *Journal of Clinical Psychiatry, 50,* 153–162.

Kupfer, D. J. (1982). Toward a unified view of affective disorders. In N. I. Zale (Ed.), *Affective and schizophrenic disorders* (pp. 225–262). New York: Brunner/Mazel.

Levy, R. (1982). *The new language of psychiatry.* Boston: Little, Brown and Company.

Lipton, M. A. (1982). The evolution of the biological understanding of affective disorders. In M. R. Zales (Ed.), *Affective and schizophrenic disorders* (pp. 5–28). New York: Brunner/Mazel.

Marmor, J. (1983). Systems thinking in psychiatry. *American Journal of Psychiatry, 140,* 833–838.

McAlpine, D. E. (1987). Suicide: Recognition and management. *Mayo Clinic Proceedings, 62,* 778–781.

Mendlewicz, J. (1985). Genetic research in depressive disorders. In E. E. Peckham & W. R. Leber (Eds.), *Handbook of depression: Treatment, assessment, and research.* Homewood, IL: Dorsey Press.

Mollica, R. F. (1989). Mood (affective) disorders. In H. I. Kaplan & B. J. Sadock (Eds.), *Comprehensive textbook of psychiatry* (vol. 1, 5th ed.) (pp. 859–867). Baltimore: Williams & Wilkins.

Nurnberger, J. I., Goldin, L. R., & Gershon, E. S. (1986). Genetics of psychiatric disorders. In G. Winokur & P. Clayton (Eds.), *The medical basis of psychiatry* (pp. 486–522). Philadelphia: W. B. Saunders.

Puig-Antich, J., Ryan, N. D., & Rabinovich, H. (1985). Affective disorders in childhood and adolescence. In J. M. Wiener (Ed.), *Diagnosis and psychopharmacology of childhood and adolescent disorders* (pp. 152–173) New York: John Wiley.

Puryear, D. A. (1984). *Helping people in crisis.* San Francisco: Jossey-Bass.

Roy, A. (1989). Suicide. In H. I. Kaplan & B. J. Sadock (Eds.), *Comprehensive textbook of psychiatry* (vol. 2, 5th ed.) (pp. 1414–1426). Baltimore: Williams & Wilkins.

Sabelli, H. C., & Carlson-Sabelli (1989). Biological priority and psychological supremacy: A new integrative paradigm derived from process theory. *American Journal of Psychiatry, 146,* 1541–1551.

Schmidt, K., & Freidson, S. (1990). Atypical outcome in attention deficit hyperactivity disorder. *Journal of the American Academy of Child & Adolescent Psychiatry, 29,* 566–569.

Stoudemire, A., Flank, R., Hedemark, N., Kamlet, M., & Blazer, D. (1986). The economic burden of depression. *General Hospital Psychiatry, 8,* 387–394.

Tsuang, M. T., & Faraone, S. V. (1990). *The genetics of mood disorder.* Baltimore: Johns Hopkins University Press.

Wender, P. H., Kety, S. S., Rosenthal, D., Schulsinger, F., Ortmann, J., & Lunde, I. (1986). Psychiatric disorders in the biological and adoptive families of adopted individuals with affective disorders. *Archives of General Psychiatry, 43,* 923–929.

Whybrow, P. C., Akiskal, H. S., & McKinney, W. T., Jr. (1984). *Mood disorders: Toward a new psychobiology.* New York: Plenum Press.

Wortis, J. (1985). Irreversible starvation. *Biological Starvation, 20,* 465–466.

BORDERLINE CLIENTS

CHAPTER 32

BORDERLINE PERSONALITY DISORDER

Diagnosis, Etiology, and Treatment

Elsa Marziali

INTRODUCTION

Patients with borderline personality disorder experience severe and disabling symptoms. When they seek help they are frequently in an acute state of suffering and are at risk of engaging in self-destructive behaviors if relief from their distress is not speedily forthcoming. More often than not, for the borderline patient, the current clinical contact is one in a series of attempts to engage in a therapeutic encounter, ever hopeful that this time the treatment will be effective. Unfortunately, we know from clinical experiences with these patients that treatment success is not predictable; that is, we cannot predict with confidence what form, duration, or combination of treatments will be effective. Various theoretical perspectives on the diagnostic and etiological features of borderline pathology have not led to more effective clinical processes. In fact, studies to date have failed to support the discriminant validity of the diagnosis, the validity of etiological hypotheses about early developmental precursors, or the predictive validity of long-term psychoanalytic psychotherapy which, until recently, has been the treatment of choice for borderline personality disorder (Gunderson, 1984; McGlashan, 1986).

Rationale for an Empirical Approach to the Study of Borderline Personality Disorder

While diagnostic criteria and etiological factors should predict course of illness, treatment type, and outcome, clinical experiences with borderlines show that other influ-

Reprinted from *Smith College Studies in Social Work,* Vol. 62, No. 3 (June 1992), pp. 205–227 by permission of the publisher.

ences are operative. For example, borderline patients comprise 13–15% of psychiatric outpatient caseloads, yet long-term treatment is rarely provided because government subsidized clinical resources are limited and parsimoniously allocated to those patients who are expected to benefit most. Second, clinicians tend to avoid treating borderlines because they are so difficult to manage and treat successfully. Third, follow-up studies show that 50% of borderline patients who begin dynamic psychotherapy drop out within the first six months of treatment. Only one-third of those who remain complete treatment and of these only 10% have moderately successful outcomes. Finally, even when patients engage in intensive long-term treatment with highly experienced and talented therapists, changes reflect improvement in adaptive responses rather than in structural changes to the personality (Waldinger & Gunderson, 1984). Although these findings are in part discouraging, borderlines continue to be the focus of considerable clinical and research effort. Study results are beginning to challenge previous formulations about the nature of the disorder, and to show the effects of alternate treatment approaches which are not psychoanalytically based. In particular, cognitive behavioral (Linehan, 1984; 1987) and non-interpretive (Dawson, 1988; Munroe-Blum & Marziali, 1987–1992) methods of intervention have been tested in treatment comparison trials with borderlines. Reviewed are studies of diagnostic, etiological, and treatment approaches to borderline personality disorder.

BORDERLINE DIAGNOSIS
Objective Criteria Method—DSM III Axis II-R

As a diagnostic category, borderline personality disorder (BPD) does not fit clearly into either Axis I or Axis II of the DSM III-R, even though the diagnosis is assigned when any five of eight Axis II criteria are present. The eight criteria include:

1. A pattern of unstable and intense interpersonal relationships;
2. Impulsiveness in at least two areas that are potentially self damaging;
3. Affective instability;
4. Inappropriate, intense anger and lack of control of anger;
5. Recurrent suicidal threats, gestures, or behavior, or self-mutilating behavior;
6. Marked and persistent identity disturbance;
7. Chronic feelings of emptiness or boredom;
8. Frantic efforts to avoid real or imagined abandonment.

A closer examination of these criteria shows a mixture of symptoms and traits. The symptoms overlap with criteria used to make Axis I diagnoses and the traits overlap with other Axis II disorders. In other words, the set of descriptors used to distinguish borderline disorder from other psychiatric syndromes confuses current symptomatic state with enduring personality traits.

In an attempt to clarify which of the Axis II criteria are most frequently used to determine the presence of BPD, Clarkin, Hurt and Hull (1991) used an agglomerative cluster analysis to generate subsets of criteria used in the clinical diagnosis of 451 borderline patients. Three clusters were identified: an Identity Cluster which included two criteria (identity disturbance and chronic feelings of emptiness); an Affective Cluster which included three criteria (labile affect, unstable interpersonal relationships, and inappropriate anger); and an Impulsive Cluster which included two criteria (self-damaging acts and impulsivity). When the observed prevalence of cluster pairs was assessed for each patient, the Affective-Impulse cluster pairing occurred much more frequently than could be expected by chance. Thus, the borderline is best defined by symptom-based criteria (labile affect, inappropriate anger, self-damaging acts) and two trait-based criteria (impulsivity and unstable interpersonal relationships).

Reliability and Validity of the BPD Diagnosis

Studies of the reliability and validity of the BPD diagnosis have addressed several questions: Is the reliability of clinical diagnosis of BPD enhanced by the use of instruments developed for assessing the disorder? Is the BPD disorder distinct from Axis I disorders? Is it distinct from other Axis II personality disorders? Several diagnostic instruments have been developed and tested. The most frequently used, the Diagnostic Interview for Borderlines (DIB) (Gunderson, Kolb, & Austin, 1981), is specific to the borderline diagnosis. Its construct, concurrent, and discriminant validity have been demonstrated. Other instruments have included diagnostic criteria for all eleven Axis II disorders. Examples include two self-report measures; the Millon Clinical Multiaxial Inventory (MCMI) (Millon, 1982) and the Personality Disorder Questionnaire (PDQ) (Hyler, Rieder, Williams, Spitzer, Hendler, & Lyons, 1987); and two coded interview schedules; the Personality Disorder Examination (PDE) (Loranger, 1988) and the Structural Interview for DSM-III-R (SCID) (Spitzer, Williams, & Gibbon, 1987). While each of these diagnostic systems has demonstrated good reliability, their discriminant validity has not been demonstrated. In a study of the overlap between BPD and other Axis II disorders, patients who met the criteria for BPD on the Personality Disorder Exam also met the criteria for one or more other personality disorders (Angus & Marziali, 1988). The Axis II disorders most frequently associated with BPD were histrionic and antisocial.

In addition to meeting criteria for other Axis II disorders borderline patients frequently have concomitant Axis I affective disorders (Akiskal, 1981; Frances, Clarkin, Gilmore, Hurt, & Brown, 1984; Perry, 1985; Soloff, 1987; Zanarini, Gunderson, & Frankenberg, 1989). However, BPD patients with affective disorders can be distinguished from other patients with affective disorders; BPD subjects are more impulsive, self-destructive, and angry than depressed patients. In contrast, other studies have not shown any overlap between BPD and schizophrenia (Barasch, Frances, Hurt, Clarkin, & Cohen, 1985; Jonas & Pope, 1984; Pope, Jonas, Hudson, Cohen, & Gunderson, 1983). The results of these studies suggest that a diagnostic assessment of BPD must include an assessment of the presence or absence of other diagnoses, either Axis I or Axis II.

Follow-up studies show that the BPD diagnosis remains stable over time (Barasch et al., 1985; Pope et al., 1983; McGlashan, 1986). The associations between BPD and affective disorder at follow-up vary; many BPD patients who do not initially present with affective disorder may develop affective symptoms. Patients with BPD do not develop schizophrenia. However, the overlap with other Axis II disorders remains an unresolved problem.

Psychodynamic Diagnostic Criteria for BPD

The main challenge to the DSM III-R diagnostic perspective of borderline personality disorder has been formulated by Kernberg (1975). Kernberg describes borderline pathology according to metapsychological principles of personality organization. Borderline personality organization includes a heterogeneous group of patients who experience identity diffusion, utilize primitive defenses (projective identification, splitting), and whose reality testing is intact. Even though this dynamic formulation of BPD is difficult to measure reliably, it has clinical appeal because the manifest equivalents of identity diffusion and primitive defensive operations are "experienced" by the clinician in vivo in any exchange with a borderline patient. Validation of Kernberg's diagnostic system requires alternate systems to the DSM diagnostic criteria for determining the unique interpersonal and defense features of borderline disorder. Recent studies of these factors provide some support for Kernberg's formulation of borderline personality organization.

Using a circumplex model of social behavior, Lorna Smith Benjamin (1992) has shown differences in the interpersonal patterns of several patient groups: BPD, antisocial personality, and affective disorder. Other investigators have developed systems for distinguishing the quality of object relations in BPD. The tests have successfully differentiated borderlines from affective, schizoaffective, and schizophrenic groups (Bell, Billington, & Becker, 1986; Bell, Billington, Cichetti, & Gibbons, 1988); from neurotics and schizophrenics (Burke, Summers, Selinger, & Polonus, 1986); and from non-psychiatric subjects (Marziali & Oleniuk, 1990). Perry (1986) and Perry and Cooper (1986) have studied ego defenses and conflicts in borderline patients. They found that eight "borderline" level defenses tended to predict negative outcomes for the borderline group in terms of work stability, interpersonal relating, and personal satisfaction.

What conclusions can be drawn from the diagnostic studies of BPD? The bulk of the evidence suggests that BPD is a reliable DSM III-R diagnostic category with a stable picture over time. There is an association between BPD and affective disorder but its exact nature requires further exploration. There is also overlap between BPD and other personality disorders but the pattern and consistency of this overlap is unknown.

More recent studies show that the DSM III-R, Axis II system is inadequate for capturing the relevant interpersonal features and defense structure of BPD. The criteria which most systematically distinguish the disorder from other diagnostic entities (impulsivity, self-damaging acts, and unstable relationships) describe behaviors which can be understood as core features of personality development. Impulsivity and self-damaging acts suggest failures in the capacity to process information, including affective contents which emerge in the context of erratic patterns of interpersonal relating. Clarifications about deficits in defensive function and their impact on interpersonal relating would contribute to the management of the treatment relationship. While the DSM III-R criteria provide one system for reliably identifying BPD they contribute little to the clinical management of these difficult-to-treat patients. Other criteria systems are needed, in particular systems which provide operational definitions of defense structure and interpersonal features which are unique to BPD.

ETIOLOGY

Historically, the most persuasive postulates regarding the etiology of the borderline syndrome have come from psychodynamic models of personality development. Here, emphasis has been placed on inferring from the adult patients' reconstructions of past experiences, possible intra- and inter-psychic models of separation-individuation and identity formation. In the last decade clinical investigators have begun to explore the relevance of neurological impairment (minimal brain disfunction, traumatic brain injury) and early life experiences (parental abuse, neglect, separation, and loss) for explaining onset of the disorder and its behavioral manifestations in the adult borderline patient. Reviewed are three etiological perspectives of borderline pathology: psychodynamic, neurobehavioral, and early childhood neglect/abuse.

Psychodynamic Perspective

In psychoanalysis, developmental-diagnostic hypotheses are inferred from observations of the patient, reported symptoms, and interview material which includes recollections of early life experiences with caregivers. While different psychoanalytic theorists are at variance as to the specific factors which contribute to the development of borderline personality disorder, most locate the occurrence of developmental failures/conflicts in the first two years of life (Adler, 1985; Gunderson, 1984; Kernberg, 1975; Mahler, 1971; Mahler, Pine, & Bergman, 1975; Masterson & Rinsley, 1975).

According to Kernberg, certain constitutional phenomena combined with deficiencies in the environment contribute to the formation of early developmental conflicts which fail to be adequately resolved. An excessive aggressive drive coupled with a deficiency in the capacity to neutralize aggression and/or a lack of anxiety tolerance are associated with a failure to integrate good and bad self-other object representations. Primitive defenses (denial, projection, and splitting) are mobilized to keep separate the conflicted perceptions of self and other. Kernberg underemphasizes the role of the parent in determining the pathological outcome of the borderline's identity formation. Rather his focus is on the progressively integrative aspects of ego development which are based on Mahler's stages of separation-individuation.

Other psychoanalytic developmental hypotheses are similarly based on Mahler's formulations about early development. Adler (1985) and Gunderson (1984) believe that the borderline patient has not experienced an environment which could support the development of a stable self-identity in relation to a perception of an independent other. Adler (1985) suggests that the aloneness experienced by borderlines may be associated with the absence of good-enough mothering during the phases of separation and individuation. He believes that borderlines experience a primary emptiness due to the absence of stable images of positive introjects; that is, in the absence of these positive introjects a holding, soothing sense of self does not develop. In contrast, Kernberg's developmental model presumes that sufficient positive introjects have been developed and that the defensive undertaking for the borderline is to keep separate positive and negative images of the self and of the object.

Psychodynamic formulations about the etiology of borderline pathology have not been empirically validated. There is no verifiable association between constitutional predisposition (Kernberg, 1975) and the development of personality disorders in adults. Also, Mahler's observational study of child development yielded results which were interpreted from an ego-psychological perspective; these results would now need to be interpreted in the light of infant observational studies and subsequent longitudinal studies of children in interaction with their caregivers. The infant studies show that the neonate plays a significant role in determining the quality and quantity of interactions with caregivers (Stern, 1985). Longitudinal studies show the powerful role played by constitutional, biological, and environmental factors in determining the outcome in adults of early childhood experiences (Werner & Smith, 1982).

In a review of studies of early child development, Emde (1981) made the following observations: Infants construct their own reality; therefore, what is reconstructed in the psychoanalytic situation may never have happened. Since discontinuities are prominent throughout, developmental experience is reorganized to fit with new demands. There is a strong tendency in children, even very young children, to recover from trauma; thus, not all traumatic events predispose to psychopathology. The adverse effects of early childhood experiences, such as neglect and abuse, are reversible and responsive to changes in the environment.

It is likely, that for every borderline patient who reconstructs a history which confirms the problematic separation-individuation hypothesis, there is an individual with a comparable early history who did not develop the disorder. Longitudinal studies of childhood development have shown that although some children and adolescents experience highly conflicted interactions with their caregivers they do not develop behavior disorders as adults. For example, Werner and Smith (1982) found that children who were particularly at high risk due to their exposure to poverty, family instability, and mental health problems in their caregivers remained "invincible" and developed into competent, autonomous young adults. Thus, a linear association between phase-specific developmental problems and borderline personality disorder in adults cannot be supported.

Neurobehavioral Perspective

The neurobehavioral etiological perspective suggests a connection between the negative developmental effects of childhood brain dysfunction and the development of borderline symptomatology. For the neurologically-impaired child, developmental symptoms appear in the form of hyperactivity, short attention span, distractibility, mood oscillation, and high impulsivity. The resultant behavioral syndrome includes problematic social interactions, academic difficulties, and low levels of achievement. Several authors (Hartocollis, 1968; Murray, 1979) postulate an association between the distorting effects of minimal brain dysfunction (MBD) and the child's perceptions of his own behaviors and interactions with his caregivers. The outcome is one of confused cognition, affect regulation, and impulse control which may lead ultimately to borderline ego development and behavior. Some studies have explored empirically the MBD and adult psychopathology hypotheses (Milman, 1979; Quitkin, Rifkin, & Klein, 1976; Weiss, Hechtman, Perlman, Hopkins, & Wener, 1979; Wender, Reimher, & Wood, 1981). Only a few have examined factors specific to the development of borderline pathology

(Akiskal, Chen, Davis, Puzantian, Kashgarian, & Bolinger, 1985; Andrulonis, Gluek, Stoebel, Vogel, Shapiro, & Aldridge, 1981; Andrulonis & Vogel, 1984; Soloff & Millward, 1983).

A frequently quoted study by Andrulonis et al. (1981) is one of few which examined neurological factors specific to the development of BPD. A retrospective chart review was conducted of 91 subjects meeting DSM III criteria for the borderline diagnosis. Andrulonis and colleagues were able to subdivide the subjects into three groups: a non-organic group, a minimal brain dysfunction (MBD) group with a history of attention disorder deficits or learning disabilities, and an organic pathology group comprising subjects with a history of traumatic brain injury, encephalitis, or epilepsy. Overall, 38% of the subjects had a history of organicity, either MBD or organic pathology. In a subsequent study (Andrulonis et al., 1985), four subcategories of borderline personality disorder were identified, two of which included organicity factors: attentional deficit/ learning disabled, and organic. Of particular interest were the results showing differences between male and female borderlines. Forty percent of the males compared with only 14% of the females suffered from an attentional deficit disorder and/or learning disabilities. Also, 52% of the males compared with 28% of the females had either a current or past history of organic insults such as head trauma, encephalitis, or epilepsy. Andrulonis concluded that borderlines with minimal brain dysfunction are predominantly male and have an earlier onset of emotional and functional difficulties based in part on a constitutional deficit.

In a study of 100 borderline patients Akiskal (1981) and Akiskal et al. (1985) showed that in addition to overlapping affective diagnoses for almost half of the group, 11% had organic, epileptic, or attention deficit disorders. Other studies of neurological hypotheses for inferring onset of BPD have shown similar results; that is, between 10% and 30% of the subjects provided reports of early or current neurological impairment. However, the use of developmental histories to infer neurobehavioral factors may explain the variations in the findings. Historical methods are limited by inaccuracies and incompleteness of recall and by distortions associated with the patients' psychological state at the time the histories are taken.

Neglect/Abuse Perspective

In the last decade, the results of a series of studies provide some support for an etiological hypothesis which links early childhood neglect and/or abuse with the development of borderline personality disorder in adults. These studies can be viewed as partial attempts to test psychodynamic, developmental theories about borderline pathology; that is, what associations, if any, exist between children's early experiences with their caregivers and later onset of borderline personality disorder?

Soloff and Millward (1983) used a retrospective historical method to compare the early life separation experiences of borderlines with those experienced by schizophrenics and patients with major depressive disorders. The borderline group had experienced more parental loss due to death and divorce but there were no between group differences for separations experienced due to either parent or child illnesses. The borderlines reported more problems in coping with normal separations such as attending school, transferring to a different school, and normal school transitions (public to high school).

Several investigators (Goldberg, Mann, Wise, & Segal, 1985; Paris & Frank, 1989) have examined qualities of parental bonding experienced by borderlines. Paris and Frank (1989) assessed subjects' recollections of the quality of care and protection received from parents during early childhood. The results showed that the degree of perceived maternal care significantly differentiated borderlines from non-borderline patients. In a similar study, Goldberg et al. (1985) compared the responses of borderlines to a parental bonding instrument with the responses of patients with other psychiatric disorders and those of non-psychiatric subjects. The borderlines perceived their parents to care less than the two control groups. The borderlines also perceived their parents to be more overprotective than the non-psychiatric group but did not differ on this dimension from the psychiatric controls.

Due to a changing social climate which is more receptive to examining the incidence and effects of child sexual abuse, there has been a proliferation of studies concerned with these issues. There is increasing evidence for associating sexual abuse trauma in childhood with psychological difficulties in adults. Briere and Zaidi (1989) reviewed 100 charts of female patients seen in a psychiatric emergency service for histories of sexual abuse. Fifty of the charts were selected randomly from files where the clinician had not been directed to enquire about sexual abuse. These were compared with 50 charts selected randomly from files written by a clinician who had been instructed to enquire about early childhood sexual abuse. The charts were coded for demographic variables, incidence of sexual abuse, and for the presence/absence of three personality disorder clusters (DSM-III-R). The most revealing finding was the very large discrepancy in the rate of reported abuse between subjects who had not been specifically asked about experiences of sexual abuse (6%) and those who had been asked (70%). For the subjects reporting sexual abuse, three times as many abused versus nonabused subjects had been given diagnoses of personality disorder. Also, five times as many of the abused patients received specific diagnoses of borderline personality disorder or borderline traits.

Three recently reported studies (Herman, Perry, & van der Kolk, 1989; Shearer, Peters, Quaytman, & Ogden, 1990; Zanarini, Gunderson, Marino, Schwartz, & Frankenberg, 1989) compared reports of childhood trauma provided by borderline patients with those provided by several cohorts of patients with other psychiatric disorders. Zanarini et al. (1989) compared borderlines with antisocial personality disorder and dysthymic disorder. Two semi-structured interviews were used to obtain histories of family pathology and early separation experiences. The reported neglect/abuse experiences were segmented into three childhood periods, early (birth to age five), latency, and adolescence. A significantly higher percentage of borderlines than controls (antisocial and dysthymic) reported being abused (verbal, physical, or sexual) during all three childhood periods. The borderlines were more likely than the dysthymic group to have been sexually abused during latency and adolescence and to have been physically abused during early childhood. A history of neglect, emotional withdrawal, and disturbed caretaker behavior discriminated the borderlines from the antisocial controls in each of the childhood phases. More borderlines than dysthymics reported early childhood prolonged separations, but the borderlines did not differ from the antisocial group on this dimension. The authors conclude that, although their results lend support to hypotheses which link the development of borderline disorders with early life experiences of abuse, neglect, and loss, there is insufficient evidence to suggest that any one type of childhood experience predicts to the development of the disorder.

In a similar study (Herman, Perry, & van der Volk, 1989), childhood traumas reported by subjects in an ongoing study of borderline personality disorder (N=21) were compared with reports provided by subjects with related diagnoses (schizotypal and antisocial personality disorders, and bipolar II affective disorders; N=23). Eighty-one percent of the borderline patients gave histories of major childhood trauma; 17% had been physically abused, 67% had been sexually abused, and 62% had witnessed domestic violence. The borderlines also reported more types of trauma which lasted for longer periods of time. To be noted are the overall gender differences: women had significantly higher total trauma scores and they reported more physical and sexual abuse in childhood.

In summary, the research evidence suggests multiple etiological pathways to several, if not numerous, subgroups of borderline personality disorder. Not all borderlines have neurological deficits; not all borderlines have early life experiences of sexual/physical abuse, neglect, or loss; and not all borderlines show evidence of unresolved early developmental conflicts associated with Mahler's rapprochement subphase of separation-individuation. If these observations have currency, it follows that the approaches to treatment and management of the disorder must be as flexible and as varied as the subtypes of the disorder.

TREATMENT

Until relatively recently the treatment of choice for borderline personality disorder has been long-term psychoanalytically-oriented psychotherapy. The aim of the therapy is change in the structure of the personality. Follow-up studies of this form of treatment show that some patients benefit (Gunderson, 1984; McGlashen, 1986; Waldinger & Gunderson, 1984). However, there is a paucity of treatment comparison trials demonstrating the process and effectiveness of any form of treatment for borderline personality disorder. In the last five years, three studies of different models of treatment for borderline personality disorder have been initiated and are still in progress: Kernberg's psychodynamic psychotherapy (Clarkin, Koenigsberg, Yeomans, Selzer, Kernberg, & Kernberg, 1992), Linehan's cognitive behavioral approach (Linehan, 1984, 1987), and the relationship management psychotherapy of the McMaster University group (Munroe-Blum & Marziali, 1987–1992). A comparative analysis of the three approaches to treatment of BPD is presented. For each of the three models the following treatment factors are discussed: treatment contract and induction into treatment, management of anger and self-destructive impulses, the use of extra-therapy contacts, and the central work and aims of the therapy.

Kernberg's Psychoanalytic Psychotherapy

In their treatment manual, Kernberg, Selzer, Koenigsberg, Carr and Appelbaum (1989) discuss at some length the theoretical and clinical hypotheses which determine the treatment strategies to be used with borderlines. Their approach to developing a treatment contract requires from the onset a clear statement of the roles of patient and therapist and the nature of their work together. The goals of the therapy are stated and the activities of the therapist are outlined. The therapist emphasizes a commitment to understanding feelings, thoughts, and behaviors and their relationship to one another. The patient is expected to collaborate in an exploratory process with the aim of understanding self-destructive behaviors which in the past have undermined efforts to benefit from psychotherapy. The role of the patient is to organize, remember, and present personal experiences related to self-destructive impulses. Thus, in the first session the patient is informed about the shared responsibility for the therapeutic work. By explaining the process, the therapist provides a framework intended to help the patient achieve self-restraint and make a commitment to the therapeutic work. This inductive process communicates implicitly to the patient that a regularly scheduled treatment contact is the only arrangement that will produce the desired results. The early sessions are especially focused on exploring and interpreting the patient's fears and anxieties about the treatment situation; that is, every effort is made to protect the patient from the impulse to bolt from therapy.

With borderline patients, the management of anger and self-destructive behaviors constitutes the major challenge to the therapeutic work. The Kernberg group believes that if such behaviors are not explicitly identified and managed the patient will continue to express anger in forms which are threatening to the patient and to the continuance of treatment. The therapist specifies the limits of his or her involvement with the patient's self-destructive behavior as it occurs outside of the therapy hour. Rather than attempting to intervene to prevent possible death, the therapist suggests alternative means of seeking help such as going to hospital emergency departments. The therapist acknowledges the difficulty of this task for the patient as well as the disappointment with the therapist. The therapist states clearly that he or she cannot prevent the patient's self-destructive behavior and conveys that although the patient's death would sadden the therapist, the therapist's life would not be altered significantly by this event. The aim of these explicit statements is to limit the patient's power over the treatment and to force a choice between continuing treatment or ending life. In tandem with this explicit process, the patient is encouraged to bring to therapy all thoughts and feelings related to self-destructive impulses so that the material can be explored and understood.

Another main issue in the treatment of borderline patients is the amount of support given either verbally in sessions or by providing contacts beyond the regularly scheduled sessions. Kernberg and his group recommend therapeutic neutrality. The giving of advice is avoided and concrete information is given when needed in as neutral a format as possible. Therapists trained in the Kernberg method explicitly forbid any contact between sessions and instead discuss, within the therapy hour, the requirement that the patient utilize other services as needed without involving the therapist. Extra session contact is disallowed since it would require the therapist to forgo the original treatment contract of helping the patient to understand his anxieties and concerns rather than act on them. If the therapist were to assume an active posture at times of emergency, the primary task of the therapy would be violated. In the face of these limitations the patient is assured that the twice-a-week scheduled sessions are protected for his or her use. This structure creates a situation in which the therapist becomes a major figure in the patient's life and thereby the recipient of transferential feelings. The approach taken by the Kernberg group to the management of the structure and limitations of the therapy promotes the early development of strong transferential responses which provide fertile ground for understanding and interpreting the patient's thoughts, feelings, and behaviors.

The Kernberg group recommends a model of psychoanalytic psychotherapy which is intensive, long-term, and aimed at altering basic structures of the personality. Their treatment approach relies principally on the techniques of clarification, confrontation, and interpretation within the context of a therapeutic relationship much influenced by transference distortion. They believe that the split-off aspects of the patient's identity contain polarized emotions which fail to be adaptively processed. Shifts in the processing of emotional contents occur when facets of the patient's identity are interpreted in the context of the evolving transference relationship. This interpretive process becomes the central focus of the therapy. Defense, affect, and the fragmented aspects of the personality are addressed repeatedly as they emerge in the here and now context of the treatment relationship. The Kernberg group are attentive to how the patient manifests disparate and contradictory aspects of the self in the treatment relationship. The therapeutic strategy of confrontation is used to address the contradictory nature of the patient's experience and to help the patient integrate split off features of the self. This, then, is the ultimate aim of the Kernberg form of psychoanalytic psychotherapy for BPD. When the patient achieves a more integrated and thereby a less fragmented sense of self-identity, the primitive defenses which had previously played a role in supporting self-destructive behaviors will have been altered. Similarly, the accompanying symptoms and other behavioral manifestations of the disorder will have changed in a favorable direction.

Linehan's Cognitive Behavioral Psychotherapy

Linehan's cognitive behavioral treatment strategy relies principally on the cognitive and behavioral techniques of support, education, contingency management, and construction of alternatives. The principal aim of the treatment is to reduce or extinguish parasuicidal behavior. A combined format of individual and group psychotherapy is used. The two forms of therapy are conducted concurrently and attendance at all sessions is mandatory. Missing four sessions of group or individual therapy in a row will result in termination of the treatment. The program is contractual and time-limited (one year); however, the contract can be renewed if progress has been made. In the initial sessions Linehan provides information about the treatment program and specifies the roles of patient and therapist. The educational structure of the program is explained. Patients are encouraged to ask questions and to understand their personal experiences in the context of the educational materials provided. For example, in Linehan's program there is an explicit focus on the underlying theory of parasuicidal behavior and an emphasis on bibliographic materials. Each patient is expected to discuss the materials and to acquire an understanding as to the reasons for their own self-destructive behaviors.

Linehan provides a careful explication, at the beginning of treatment, as to how angry and self-destructive behaviors will be handled. The patient is asked to contract to try to reduce suicidal behavior and is told that the therapist assumes that such behavior will not immediately subside. Through the use of a combined treatment format, Linehan encourages patient contact with a number of people (other patients, and both individual and group therapists), which may help diffuse anger toward either therapist and which may provide additional time and support for developing adaptive coping strategies. Since the main focus of Linehan's cognitive behavioral model of treatment is on understanding and extinguishing parasuicidal behavior information about the cognitive/behavioral conceptualizations of self-destructive behavior is provided in the first session. Patients are expected to commit themselves to a treatment focus concerned with preventing self-destructive behaviors.

Linehan reinforces the role of the therapist in controlling the patient's parasuicidal behaviors by encouraging the patients, during emergencies, to contact the therapist. Emergency consultations between sessions are used to help the patient actively solve an immediate problem in order to avoid hospitalization or medical treatment. In Linehan's view, these extra sessions serve to increase the strength of the relationship by encouraging the patient to use new coping strategies with the support and guidance of the therapist. Linehan also views the provision of educational material about self-destructive behavior as supportive to the patient; that is, this information can be used by the patient to reflect on the reasons for his or her own behavior.

This model of psychotherapy is primarily concerned with helping patients diminish their self destructive behaviors. Patients are educated about the maladaptive nature of such behaviors which are defined as "habits" and thus difficult to change. The therapy provides the patient with alternative means for tolerating and expressing distressful affects. Also, patients are encouraged to actively engage in problem-solving strategies for coping with these life-time maladaptive patterns for processing emotions. The therapist uses all available contingencies to reinforce adaptive responses and to discourage maladaptive ones. The relationship between therapist and patient plays an important role in supporting contingency management.

The first topic of any psychotherapy session is the occurrence of any parasuicidal behavior since the last session. The patient is helped to gain insight into the reasons for the suicidal behavior and to learn new skills for coping with suicidal impulses. The patient is informed of the therapist's rights to assess the potential risk involved in a patient's self-destructive behavior, and to insist on hospitalization or other unwanted interventions if the patient convinces the therapist that death by suicide is imminent. The purpose of a structure which emphasizes, so strongly, parasuicidal behavior is to alter the patient's maladaptive responses within the time-limited course of the therapy. Disruptions to the therapeutic framework which derive from impulsive self-destructive behaviors require an immediate response. Also, the activity of the therapist reinforces the commitment to the therapeutic relationship and the work of therapy. Given the particular orientation of Linehan's model of cognitive behavioral treatment the outcome to be achieved is the extinction of parasuicidal behaviors. Accompanying this change is the patient's enhanced understanding of the function of maladaptive, habitual responses to stress as well as the acquisition of new coping skills.

The McMaster Relationship Management Group Psychotherapy

The treatment strategy of the McMaster University group (Relationship Management Group Psychotherapy [RMGP]) is focused on observing and processing the meanings of the contextual features of the patient-therapist interactions (Dawson, 1988; Munroe-Blum & Marziali, 1987–1992). According to this perspective, the borderline has a self-system that contains conflicting attributes resulting in a state of instability and ambiguity which the patient seeks to resolve in the context of interpersonal relationships, including the therapeutic relationship. In the McMaster approach, patients are seen in a co-therapist led group which meets weekly for 30 sessions.

In contrast to both Kernberg's and Linehan's beginning strategies, the RMGP approach places less emphasis on the development of a treatment contract. RMGP does not focus on self-destructive behaviors or any other patient actions or threats which Linehan and Kernberg view as potentially disruptive to therapy. The patient is told about the structure of the group; that is, its time boundaries and the frequency, time, and place of the meetings. In addition, each patient is offered the opportunity to meet with the group therapists individually prior to the first group meeting. Each patient is free to either take up or ignore this option. Of importance is the fact that the therapists do not attempt to structure these pre-group sessions and the patient has full control over how they wish to use the session. In taking this stance, RMGP affirms the patient's control over whether or not to accept treatment.

The objectives of the initial group sessions are similar to those established for any psychotherapy group: engagement, testing the group parameters, developing connections, and forming some commitment to group membership. The therapists are actively involved in the process but their interventions are largely exploratory, open-ended questions which are phrased tentatively. When challenged, the therapists acknowledge and affirm the patients' doubts about the ultimate benefits that might be gained from participating in the group. Similarly, patients' frustrations with the futility of previous treatment experiences are affirmed. Behaviors which could disrupt the treatment process are not explained or interpreted. Attendance at group is voluntary; participation is voluntary; silences are accepted.

RMGP does not attempt to explain or interpret the patient's anger and potentially self-destructive behaviors. No attempt is made to help the patient gain insight about what motivates maladaptive and self-destructive behavior. The therapist does not educate or attempt to exert control over the patient through therapeutic management of behaviors that threaten disruption of the therapy. In contrast to the approaches of Kernberg and Linehan, it is hypothesized that the act of focusing on self-destructive behaviors allows the intensified concern for the behaviors to rule and possibly derail the therapeutic encounter. RMGP is based on the assumption that only by responding in a neutral fashion to potentially self-destructive behaviors will they diminish in influence. If a patient reports engaging in potentially life-threatening behaviors the therapist responds, empathically stating that he or she does not want the patient to come to any harm but realistically cannot do anything to stop the patient; help is always available at a hospital emergency service.

Since RMGP is not concerned with controlling the patient's potentially self-destructive behaviors the initial therapeutic phase parallels the beginning of any psychotherapy group. The therapists attend carefully to group member efforts to place the therapists in the expert position and themselves in a position of having no control, no answers, and at risk of being humiliated. The therapists achieve a shift in this polarization by being interested but non-directive and by taking the non-expert role; the patients respond by assuming responsibility for developing a collaborative working environment in the group. It is the patients who then begin to exert control over each other's potentially destructive behaviors.

RMGP neither prescribes nor prohibits between-session contacts with the therapists. Within the parameters of RMGP, between-session contacts are not discussed during group sessions unless raised by one of the patients. The therapists tell the patients that they can call if they wish, but that this might result in frustration because they often will not be able to reach the therapist immediately. If the concern is with suicidal risk, the patients are told that hospital emergency departments are available to them.

The RMGP model of treatment is based on the belief that borderline patients enhance their capacity for self-regulation when they are given the opportunity to exert control over the therapeutic situation. The therapist's task consists of tolerating the patient's anger, suicidal threats, and vacillating affective states while maintaining simultaneously an intense interest in the patient's view of the world. As in other relationships, the borderline patient externalizes conflict in the therapeutic dialogue. If the therapist takes up one side of the dialogue by being supportive and optimistic the patient will assume the other side by being argumentative and pessimistic. As long as the therapist replicates with the patient the self-system conflict no resolution takes place. Since the patient has little knowledge of how internal conflict is externalized in the therapeutic interaction, it is the therapist who must behave in a manner which will alter the dialogue and disconfirm the patient's distorted expectations. In psychodynamic psychotherapy the self-system conflict is addressed when the therapist explores and interprets the nature of the conflict, its developmental antecedents, and its manifestations in the treatment relationship. The McMaster University group argues that these dynamic therapeutic strategies perpetuate the conflict because they reinforce the patient's "helpless, hopeless" role and maintain the therapist in the "healthy, responsible" role. In RMGP the therapist avoids the patient's projected expectations (rescue, protect, admire, control, humiliate, devalue) by attending to the process rather than the content of the interaction. It requires of the therapist a neutral stance in which the patient's propositions are acknowledged, reflected, and affirmed. The therapist admits to not having answers to the patient's dilemma and, like the patient, is frequently confused. These therapist responses are provided in the context of an unwavering interest in the patient's dialogue. When the patient castigates the therapist for being unhelpful, the therapist acknowledges that therapy might not help; when the patient threatens disruption of the therapy the therapist states that he or she will be at the next session and the patient can decide if he or she wishes to use it. It is the patient who has control and it is the therapist who communicates uncertainty and confusion while maintaining a "working" therapeutic stance.

The group form of RMGP follows the typical stages of group formation and commitment. The unique difference is that much of the focus of the working phase of the therapy is on recognizing and mourning the loss of the wished-for fantasies which are imbedded in interpersonal relations. Historically, when these fantasized wishes were frustrated and the borderline responded with impulsive self-destructive behaviors, the mourning process and the accompanying pain was circumvented. In the group the fantasized wishes are expressed and measured against the reality of each patient's personal life situation. Each patient has the opportunity to give and receive empathic understanding for their shared loss of wishes that cannot be realized.

The ultimate aim of RMGP is to help the patient make changes in the concrete behaviors of everyday living; that is, improved and more stable living arrangements, stable employment, and a more predictable and satisfying social life, including improved relations with intimate others.

In summary, there is no evidence as yet to suggest that any one of the treatment models described is more effective in promoting change in patients with BPD. It may be that the most effective and parsimonious model is a staged approach which combines all three models. BPD patients with extensive histories of impulsive and self-destructive behaviors coupled with no fruitful work experience may need either the structure, support and direction of the behavioral approach or the neutrality and support of the RMGP approach in order to achieve control over these behaviors. Once this is accomplished, the dynamic, interpretive approach may add depth and stability to changes in behavior and understanding of the self. Future research could add useful information regarding the optimal match of patient profile and treatment strategy as represented by these three approaches to treating BPD.

CONCLUSIONS

An empirical exploration of the features of borderline personality disorder has been compared with clinical and theoretical approaches to the diagnosis and treatment of the disorder. In assessing the diagnostic criteria for BPD more emphasis needs to be placed on the nature of the interpersonal and defensive behaviors which are associated with self-destructive behaviors. Thus, assessment interviews should provide patients with the opportunity to describe their perceptions of themselves in relation to significant others. What are their hopes and wishes, how are they repeatedly frustrated, and what are their typical responses to these failed interpersonal encounters? This information will be immediately relevant for understanding BPD patients' behaviors both in assessment interviews and subsequently in treatment sessions.

The findings of the etiological studies suggest that the assessment of patients with a clinical diagnosis of BPD should include a careful history of early family life experiences, particularly neglect, and physical and sexual abuse. Also, the history taking should include an exploration of the occurrence of traumatic brain injury and/or the presence of learning disabilities during childhood. When organic features are suspected an adequate neuropsychological examination is warranted. The exploration of these factors has direct implications for treatment planning; that is, a specific treatment approach could be selected to address the particular residual effects of the early life experiences of the borderline patient.

The comparative analysis of three treatment approaches to BPD suggests that all three include important strategies for the management of these difficult-to-treat patients. Not surprisingly, attending to the development and maintenance of a constructive therapeutic alliance seems paramount to the success of each approach. As was suggested, the optimal treatment for BPD may need to integrate the strategies of all three therapies, but in what proportion, or in which order of presentation, is unknown and remains to be tested clinically and empirically.

Missing in the review of treatments are family approaches to the management of BPD. There is a paucity of reports of family interventions with adult borderline patients. Yet family members, friends, and co-workers might benefit from a psychoeducational approach which would explain the disorder and suggest strategies for coping with the interpersonal distress experienced by borderline patients and their families.

REFERENCES

Adler, G. (1985). *Borderline psychopathology and its treatment.* New York: Aronson Press.

Akiskal, H. S. (1981). Subaffective disorders: Dysthymic, cyclothymic and bipolar II disorders in the borderline realm. *Psychiatric Clinics of North America, 4,* 25–46.

Akiskal, H. S., Chen, S. E., Davis, G. C., Puzantian, V. R., Kashgarian, M., & Bolinger, J. M. (1985). Borderline: An adjective in search of a noun. *Journal of Clinical Psychiatry, 46,* 41–48.

Andrulonis, P. A., Gluek, B. C., Stoebel, C. F., Vogel, N. G., Shapiro, A. L., & Aldrige, D. (1981). Organic brain dysfunction and the borderline syndrome. *Psychiatric Clinics of North America, 4,* 47–66.

Andrulonis, P. A., & Vogel, N. G. (1984). Comparison of borderline personality subcategories to schizophrenic and affective disorders. *British Journal of Psychiatry, 144,* 358–363.

Angus, L., & Marziali, E. (1988). A comparison of three measures for the diagnosis of borderline personality disorder, *American Journal of Psychiatry 145,* 1453–1454.

Barasch, A., Frances, A., Hurt, S., Clarkin, J., & Cohen, S. (1985). Stability and distinctness of borderline personality disorder. *American Journal of Psychiatry, 142,* 1484–1486.

Bell, M., Billington, R., & Becker, B. (1986). A scale for the assessment of object relations: Reliability, validity and factorial invariance. *Journal of Clinical Psychology, 42,* 733–741.

Bell, M., Billington, R., Cichetti, S., & Gibbons, J. (1988). Do object relation deficits distinguish BPD from other psychiatric groups? *Journal of Clinical Psychology, 44,* 511–516.

Briere, J., & Zaidi, L. Y. (1989). Sexual abuse histories and sequelae in female psychiatric room patients. *American Journal of Psychiatry, 146,* 1602–1606.

Burke, W. F., Summers, F., Selinger, D., & Polonus, T. W. (1986). The comprehensive object relations profile: A preliminary report. *Psychoanalytic Psychology, 3,* 173–185.

Clarkin, J., Hurt, S., & Hull, J. (1991). *Subclassification of borderline personality disorder: A cluster solution.* Unpublished manuscript, New York Hospital-Cornell Medical Center, Westchester Division, White Plains, NY.

Clarkin, J., Koenigsberg, H., Yeomans, F., Selzer, M., Kernberg, P., & Kernberg, O. (1992). Psychodynamic psychotherapy of the borderline patient. In J. Clarkin, E. Marziali, & H. Munroe-Blum (Eds.), *Borderline personality disorder: Clinical and empirical perspectives*. New York: Guilford Press.

Dawson, D. (1988). Treatment of the borderline patient, relationship management. *Canadian Journal of Psychiatry, 33*, 370–374.

Emde, R. N. (1981). Changing models of infancy and the nature of early development: Remodelling the foundation. *Journal of the American Psychoanalytic Association, 29*, 179–219.

Frances, A., Clarkin, J., Gilmore, M., Hurt, S., & Brown, R. (1984). Reliability of criteria for borderline personality disorder: A comparison of DSM-III and the diagnostic interview for borderline patients. *American Journal of Psychiatry 141*, 1080–1084.

Goldberg, R. L., Mann, L. S., Wise, T. N., & Segall, E. A. (1985). Parental qualities as perceived by borderline personality disorders. *Hillside Journal of Clinical Psychiatry, 7*, 134–140.

Gunderson, J. G., Kolb, J., & Austin, V. (1981). The diagnostic interview for borderline patients. *American Journal of Psychiatry, 138*, 896–903.

Gunderson, J. G. (1984). *Borderline personality disorder*. Washington, DC: American Psychiatric Press.

Hartocollis, P. (1968). The syndrome of minimal brain dysfunction in young adult patients. *Bulletin of the Menninger Clinic, 32*, 102–114.

Herman, L. H., Perry, J. C., & van der Kolk, B. A. (1989). Childhood trauma in borderline personality disorder. *American Journal of Psychiatry, 146*, 490–495.

Hyler, S. E., Rieder, M. D., Williams, J. B., Spitzer, R. L., Hendler, J., & Lyons, M. (1987). *Personality diagnostic questionnaire—revised (PDQ-R)*. New York: New York State Psychiatric Institute.

Jonas, J., & Pope, U. (1984). Psychosis in borderline personality disorder. *Psychiatric Developments, 4*, 295–308.

Kernberg, O. (1975). *Borderline conditions and pathological narcissism*. New York: Aronson.

Kernberg, O., Seizer, M., Koenigsberg, H., Carr, A., & Appelbaum, A. (1989). *Psychodynamic psychotherapy of borderline patients*. New York: Basic Books.

Linehan, M. M. (1984). *Dialectical behavior therapy for treatment of parasuicidal women: Treatment manual*. Unpublished manual, University of Washington.

Linehan, M. M. (1987). Dialectical behaviour therapy: A cognitive approach to parasuicide. *Journal of Personality Disorders, 1*, 328–333.

Loranger, A. W. (1988). *Personality disorder examination (PDE) manual*. Department of Psychiatry, Cornell University Medical College, Westchester, New York.

Mahler, M. S. (1971). A study of the separation-individuation process and its possible application to borderline phenomena in the psychoanalytic situation. *Psychoanalytic Study of the Child, 26*, 403–424.

Mahler, M., Pine, F., & Bergman, A. (1975). *The psychological birth of the human infant*. New York: Basic Books.

Marziali, E., & Oleniuk, J. (1990). Object representations in descriptions of significant others: A methodological study. *Journal of Personality Assessment, 54*, 105–115.

Masterson, J. F., & Rinsley, D. B. (1975). The borderline syndrome: The role of the mother in the genesis and psychiatric structure of the borderline personality. *International Journal of Psychoanalysis, 56,* 163–177.

McGlashen, T. H. (1986). The Chestnut Lodge follow-up study, III: Long-term outcome of borderline personalities. *Archives of General Psychiatry, 43,* 20–30.

Milman, D. H. (1979). Minimal brain dysfunction in childhood: Outcome in late adolescence and early adult years. *Journal of Clinical Psychiatry, 40,* 371–380.

Millon, T. (1982). *Millon multiaxial clinical inventory manual.* Minneapolis: National Computer Systems.

Munroe-Blum, H., & Marziali, E. (1987–1992). *Randomized clinical trial of relationship management time-limited group treatment of borderline patients.* Funded by Ontario Mental Health Foundation, and National Health and Research Development Program.

Murray, M. E. (1979). Minimal brain dysfunction and borderline personality adjustment. *American Journal of Psychotherapy, 33,* 391–403.

Paris, J., & Frank, H. (1989). Perceptions of parental bonding in borderline patients. *American Journal of Psychiatry, 146,* 1498–1499.

Perry, C. J. (1985). Depression in borderline personality disorder: Lifetime prevalence at interview and longitudinal course of symptoms. *American Journal of Psychiatry, 142,* 15–21.

Perry, C. J. (1986). Preliminary report on defenses and conflicts associated with borderline personality disorder. *Journal of American Psychoananalytic Association, 34,* 865–895.

Perry, C. J. & Cooper, S. (1986). What do cross-sectional measures of defense mechanisms predict? In G. Vaillant (Ed.), *Empirical studies of ego mechanisms of defense* (pp. 31–46). Washington, DC: American Psychiatric Press.

Pope, H., Jonas, J., Hudson, H., Cohen, B., & Gunderson, J. (1983). The validity of DSM-III borderline personality disorder: A phenomenologic, family history, treatment response, and long-term follow-up study. *Archives of General Psychiatry, 40,* 23–30.

Quitkin, F., Rifkin, A., & Klein, D. (1976). Neurological soft signs in schizophrenia and character disorders. *Archives of General Psychiatry, 33,* 845–853.

Shearer, S. L., Peters, C. P., Quaytman, M. S., & Ogden, R. L. (1990). Frequency and correlates of childhood sexual and physical abuse histories in adult female borderline patients. *American Journal of Psychiatry, 147,* 214–216.

Smith Benjamin, L. (1992). An interpersonal approach to the diagnosis of borderline personality disorder. In J. Clarkin, E. Marziali & H. Munroe-Blum (Eds.), *Borderline personality disorder: Clinical and empirical perspectives.* New York: Guilford Press.

Soloff, P. H., & Millward, J. W. (1983). Developmental histories of borderline patients. *Comprehensive Psychiatry, 24,* 574–588.

Soloff, P. (1987). Characterizing depression in borderline patients. *Journal of Clinical Psychiatry, 48,* 155–157.

Spitzer, R. L., Williams, J., & Gibbon, M. (1987). *Instruction manual for the structured clinical interview for DSM-III-R (SCID).* New York: Biometrics Research Department, New York State.

Stern, D. N. (1985). *The interpersonal world of the infant: A view from psychoanalysis and developmental psychology.* New York: Basic Books.

Waldinger, R., & Gunderson, J. G. (1984). Completed psychotherapies with borderline patients. *American Journal of Psychotherapy, 88,* 190–202.

Wender P. H., Reimher, F. W., & Wood, D. R. (1981). Attention deficit disorder ('Minimal Brain Disfunction') in adults. *Archives of General Psychiatry, 38,* 449–456.

Werner, E. E., & Smith, R. S. (1982). *Vulnerable but invincible.* New York: McGraw-Hill.

Weiss, G., Hechtman, L., Perlman, T., Hopkins, J., & Wener, A. (1979). Hyperactives as young adults. *Archives of General Psychiatry, 36,* 675–681.

Zanarini, M. C., Gunderson, J. G., Marino, M. F., Schwartz, E. O., & Frankenberg, F. R. (1989). Childhood experiences of borderline patients. *Comprehensive Psychiatry, 30,* 18–25.

Zanarini, M., Gunderson, J., & Frankenberg, F. (1989). Axis I phenomenology of borderline personality disorder. *Comprehensive Psychiatry, 30,* 149–156.

CHAPTER 33

CLINICAL AND ECOLOGICAL APPROACHES TO THE BORDERLINE CLIENT

Eda G. Goldstein

Increasing numbers of young people show inconsistent and inadequate school and work performance, drug and alcohol abuse, and impulsive, self-destructive, or anti-social behavior. They engage in chaotic, dependent, volatile, self-centered, or ex-ploitive interpersonal relationships, or they withdraw from others. They experience apathy, emptiness, shallowness, anger, depression, anxiety, and confusion in their emotional lives. They seem unable to evolve and consolidate an identity, or they assume one that puts them at odds with their families and society. Many of these young people can be helped, but instead they develop chronic personal and social difficulties.

Social work practitioners have relied on a psychodynamic and individually oriented clinical model in assessment and intervention with this client population.[1] The general term "character disorder" and the more specific diagnosis of borderline personality are applied to many of these individuals, who are viewed as having severe ego deficits caused by early developmental arrests. Practitioners stress individual treatment, some-times with hospitalization or residential treatment, that is aimed at supporting or build-

---

Reprinted from *Social Casework,* Vol. 64, No. 6 (1983), pp. 353–362, by permission of the publisher, Families International, Inc.

[1] For discussion of the treatment of borderline clients in the social work literature, see, for example, Anne O. Freed, "The Borderline Personality," *Social Casework* 59 (November 1980): 548–58; Irving Kaufman, "Therapeutic Consideration of Borderline Personality Structure," in *Ego Psychology and Dynamic Casework,* ed. Howard J. Parad (New York: Family Service Association of America, 1958); Richard Stuart, "Supportive Casework with Borderline Patients," in *Differential Diagnosis and Treatment in Social Work,* ed. Francis J. Turner (New York: Free Press, 1968); and Jerome L. Weinberger, "Basic Concepts in Diagnosis and Treatment of Borderline States," in *Ego Psychology and Dynamic Casework,* ed. Howard J. Parad (New York: Family Service Association of America).

ing ego, correcting for earlier developmental pathology or modifying pathological defenses and character traits.[2] The assessment of and intervention with the family and the social environment of the borderline client has not been emphasized or well-conceptualized.

THE ECOLOGICAL PERSPECTIVE

In contrast to the individual developmental focus of such a clinical model, an ecological perspective stresses the "goodness of fit" between an individual's adaptive capacities and environmental conditions in assessment. It reconceptualizes individual psychopathologies as "life-space transactions," and redefines individual pathology as a mismatching of individual needs and coping capacities with environmental resources and supports.[3]

An ecological perspective focuses on promoting people's adaptive capacities and enhancing the mutuality between people and environments. It relocates the social work point of entry to the transactional area, "at points where dyadic role relationships, family processes, organizational processes, and societal attitudes and constraints interact to maintain pathological structures."[4] While Carel B. Germain writes that "such a view in no way denies the importance of personality in social functioning,"[5] others have viewed this perspective as replacing a depth dimension with a breadth dimension.

An ecological perspective is valuable in broadening the scope of social work practice with the so-called borderline client. Such a broadened view, however, does not obviate the need for understanding intrapsychic and developmental factors in personality. Environmental phenomena affect the individual's values, identity, character, ego functioning, and sense of self-esteem and competence. They also provide opportunities for, stresses on, and obstacles to successful individual adaptation. At the same time the individual's personality, through a combination of innate endowment, internalization, and socialization, takes on a structure of its own that shapes the way the external world is experienced, assimilated, and acted upon. The assessment of the borderline client must encompass developmental and transactional elements. Intervention must proceed from a determination of where and how to enter the complex person-environment system to set improved adaptation in motion.

ORIGINS OF BORDERLINE PERSONALITY

The writings of Otto F. Kernberg, Margaret Mahler, and James Masterson are of particular significance in the current literature on borderline conditions. Kernberg attributes the development of the stable pathological ego structure of the borderline

---

[2] See, for example, Gerald Alder, "Hospital Treatment of Borderline Patients," *American Journal of Psychiatry,* 130 (January 1973): 32–36; Burt Shachter, "Treatment of Older Adolescents in Transitional Programs: Rapprochement Crisis Revisited," *Clinical Social Work Journal,* 6 (Winter 1978): 293–303.

[3] Carel B. Germain, *People and Environments* (New York: Columbia University Press, 1979); Carel B. Germain and Alex Gitterman, *The Life Model of Social Work Practice* (New York: Columbia University Press, 1980).

[4] Ibid., pp. 150–51.

[5] Ibid.

personality in some children to their inability to integrate good and bad images of themselves and of others. Splitting—a defense mechanism that serves to maintain this lack of internal integration of good and bad self and object images—continues beyond its phase-appropriate emergence along with other primitive defenses such as projective identification, denial, idealization, devaluation, and omnipotent control. Although the individual is able to differentiate herself or himself from others, a capacity that permits the development of reality testing and ego boundaries, identity does not consolidate but remains diffuse. Other ego functions such as impulse control, anxiety tolerance, the management of affects or feelings, and sublimatory capacity do not mature fully. Kernberg is equivocal as to whether constitutional or environmental factors predispose children to the excess aggression that accounts for this lack of ego integration.[6]

Mahler's view of the sequential development of the borderline's difficulties is generally similar to that of Kernberg. In the genesis of borderline conditions, however, she draws attention to the importance of the mother's emotional unavailability and not being attuned to the child's unique characteristics and phase-appropriate needs for separation-individuation. Borderline individuals become preoccupied with fears about engulfment and abandonment. She concurs that the child who becomes borderline does not overcome the defensive splitting which maintains identity diffusion, but she sees this as arising from the mother's emotional withdrawal from or negative attitudes toward the child during the second and third years of life. The failure to master the rapprochement crisis after the child has achieved some differentiation from the mother—but before he or she attains object constancy (a stable, internal, three-dimensional representation of the mother)—leaves the child impaired with respect to the consolidation of a solid and integrated sense of self and significant others. This cripples the child's ability to function autonomously, neutralize aggressive feelings, and engage in mature interpersonal relationships.[7]

Drawing in part on Kernberg's and Mahler's writings, Masterson argues that the mother's withdrawal from the child during the separation-individuation process results in an abandonment depression. Thus the child experiences his individuation as resulting in aloneness and abandonment with concomitant feelings of fear, anger, guilt, depression, helplessness, and emptiness. Maladaptive defenses and coping mechanisms develop to ward off these painful feelings that, in turn, block successful movement through later developmental stages. Because of the faulty internalization process, optimal ego development does not occur. Not only does the individual suffer from a developmental arrest that limits functioning, but he or she also reexperiences the abandonment depression at later points in life that call forth more autonomous functioning.[8]

These authors agree that borderline ego pathology is stable within the person. Intervention therefore focuses on aiding separation-individuation, modifying pathological defenses, fostering identity integration, and building ego. Intervention in dyadic or fa-

[6] Otto F. Kernberg, *Borderline Conditions and Pathological Narcissism* (New York: Jason Aronson, 1975).

[7] Margaret S. Mahler, "A Study of the Separation-Individuation Process and Its Possible Application to Borderline Phenomena in the Psychoanalytic Situation," *Psychoanalytic Study of the Child* 26 (1971); and Margaret Mahler, Fred Pine, and Anni Bergman, *The Psychological Birth of the Child,* (New York: International Universities Press, 1975).

[8] James Masterson, *Treatment of the Borderline Adolescent: A Developmental Approach,* (New York: John Wiley, 1972).

milial relationships or in the social environment is not discussed. In attributing the pathogenic features that generate borderline conditions to inadequate mothering or to the pathological personality of the mother, Masterson and others ignore the idea that growth-enhancing mother-child transactions are affected not only by the personality of the mother but also by the degree to which the surrounding interpersonal and social environments mesh with the phase-specific needs of the mother herself.

Pathological Family Characteristics and Transactions

Despite the proliferation of family diagnostic and treatment models, there are few linkages between the clinical assessment of borderline pathology and family assessment. The literature on family characteristics of borderline individuals is largely anecdotal, and the studies that do exist are too discrepant to permit definite conclusions to be drawn.[9] An important contribution comes from Edward R. Shapiro and his colleagues. They observe that both parents of borderline offspring show similar difficulties as do the offspring themselves. They hypothesize that such parental characteristics represent stable structures that generate patient pathology during an offspring's early separation-individuation phase. These structures are reactivated in the parents during the adolescent's second separation-individuation phase, exerting additional pressure on the already disturbed adolescent and creating a family regression. Certain parental traits are disavowed or not integrated into their own self-images and are projected onto the child and adolescent, who acts in accordance with the projections. The families they studied appeared highly overinvolved, and primitive defenses dominated family transactions.[10] In contrast, Roy R. Grinker, John G. Gunderson, Diane Woods Englund, and Froma Walsh have found more evidence for patterns of rejection, nonprotectiveness, covert hostility, and unrelatedness in their studies.[11]

In the author's own work three main family patterns revealed themselves: triangulated, highly involved families, rejecting or distant families, and idealizing families. Overcontrol and the long-standing specialness of the identified patient were noted. Family members also showed extensive use of primitive defenses and problems in defining their capacity for empathy with the specific needs and total personality of the borderline offspring.

Although other conclusions can be drawn, the data lend support to the view of Shapiro and his colleagues. Parents of borderline youngsters appear to project either their disavowed badness, idealized goodness, or some combination of the two onto a

[9] John C. Gunderson and Diane Woods Englund, "The Family Characteristics of Borderline Patients: A Literature Review," unpublished.

[10] Edward R. Shapiro, John Zinner, Roger L. Shapiro, and David A. Berkowitz, "The Influence of Family Experience on Borderline Personality Development," *International Review of Psychoanalysis* 2 (1975): 399–411; John Zinner and Edward R. Shapiro, "Splitting in Families of Borderline Adolescents," in *Borderline States in Psychiatry,* ed. John Mack (New York: Grune and Stratton, 1974); John Zinner and Roger L. Shapiro, "Projective Identification as a Mode of Perception and Behavior in Families of Adolescents," *International Journal of Psychoanalysis* 53 (1972): 523–30.

[11] Roy Grinker and Beatrice Werble, *The Borderline Patient* (New York: Jason Aronson, 1977); John G. Gunderson, John Kerr and Diane Woods Englund, "The Families of Borderlines: A Comparative Study," *Archives of General Psychiatry* 37 (January 1980): 27–33; Froma Walsh, "Family Study 1976: 14 New Borderline Cases," chap. in Grinker and Werble, *The Borderline Patient.*

particular offspring. The projections, and consequent lack of full empathy with the child, often seem to begin shortly after birth. These continue, remain active, and are reinforced by the child's behavior, which conforms to the parental projections. The child's acceptance of a particular identity such as the "bad" one or the "good" one is at the expense of his ego integration. With the demands for increased autonomy in adolescence, the underlying ego pathology emerges. The adolescent cannot separate or consolidate his identity both because of family pressure and the fact that by now internalized difficulties and impaired ego functioning have crippled adaptive capacity.

An emphasis on family pathology in the etiology and maintenance of borderline personality fails to connect individual developmental needs to the family life cycle or to other aspects of the social environment. Symptomatology or difficulties in an individual may result from clashes between individual phase-specific needs and family life cycle needs or from environmental factors.

The difficulties evidenced in the families of borderline individuals observed by the author rarely represented deliberate, willful efforts to neglect, exploit, enmesh, and control the patient. Nor did they represent a total parental incapacity to be responsive to the needs and characteristics of the patient. While personality and marital difficulties of the parents were significant in most cases, these families experienced multiple external stresses due to employment problems, financial instability or dependency, career pressures, physical or emotional illness, distance by death or geography from significant family members, or nonsupportive relationships with the extended family during the early child-rearing years. It is likely that such stress contributed to the parenting difficulties shown in these families as well as to problems in providing a sufficiently growth-enhancing family environment.

The Person-Environmental Fit

There may be a lack of fit between the borderline individual's ego capacities and the stresses, expectations, resources, and rewards of the social environment. A person who consistently faces situations that demand more than he or she can possibly deliver will not only experience failure but also an erosion of self-esteem that may have profound effects. Similarly, an individual who has no realistic chance of finding outlets for the use of particular capacities or little hope of reward for efforts at fulfilling social roles may become apathetic and despondent. The effects of poverty and the assaults on, negative expectations of, and discrimination against certain groups of individuals in society contribute to disturbances of identity and self-esteem. For example, strains on racial and ethnic minorities, dysfunctional societal attitudes toward women, the negative labeling of those whose sexual orientations and life-styles differ from the norm, and the lack of social support to important segments of society can be expected to have serious repercussions on personality functioning.[12]

Beatrice Simcox-Reiner has noted that the conditions of our increasingly inhuman, depriving social environment and the discrepancies between values, expectations, and

---

[12] See, for example, Eda G. Goldstein, "Mothers of Psychiatric Patients Revisited," *People and Environments*, ed. Carel B. Germain (New York: Columbia University Press, 1979).

the realities of life lead to personal difficulties. While a basic sense of irrelevance may originate in childhood, she believes that it is intensified in later life by the struggle to survive in a society that provides few supports during developmental crises or at other stressful points in life.[13] Society's current attack on the needs of its underprivileged and less than privileged can be expected not only to deprive people of essential material resources but also to aggravate emotional neglect and profound feelings of despair and worthlessness. Such a social context is inimical to optimal parenting, ego development, and social functioning.

ASSESSING THE BORDERLINE PERSONALITY

The assessment of borderline adolescents and young adults must integrate an understanding of the person with that of person-environmental transactions and social resources. While all of the factors within an individual's life space are interconnected and overlapping, schematically five major areas to be included in a full assessment can be identified (see chart, Assessment Factors in Borderline Cases).

Utilizing the schema as a guide, the practitioner should consider the following questions in the assessment process:

Assessment Factors in Borderline Cases

The Person

1. Individual life cycle tasks
2. Ego functioning and coping mechanisms
3. Personality characteristics
4. Developmental accomplishments

The Family Life Cycle	The Social Environment	The Parental Dyad
1. Stage	1. Stresses and demands	1. Life cycle needs
2. Needs and difficulties	2. Rewards	2. Personality characteristics
	3. Societal or cultural values, attitudes, and norms	3. Marital relationships
	4. Resources	4. Parent-child relationships

The Family System

1. Communication
2. Roles and structures
3. Interpersonal relationships
4. Coping strategies

[13] Beatrice Simcox-Reiner, "A Feeling of Irrelevance: The Effects of a NonSupportive Society," *Social Casework* 60 (January 1979): 3–10.

1. What are the specific life cycle tasks faced by the adolescent or young adult?
2. How well are these tasks being met?
3. What ego capacities, coping mechanisms, and personality characteristics does the adolescent or young adult bring to the life tasks?
4. What developmental difficulties are interfering with task mastery?
5. What is the nature of the parents' life cycle phases, personalities, marital relationships, and the nature of parent-child relationships?
6. Are there significant problems or conflicts in the parent-child relationships that help in the understanding of the adolescent's or young adult's difficulties?
7. What is the nature of family communication, roles and structure, interpersonal relationships, and coping strategies?
8. Are there significant problems or conflicts in the family system that help in the understanding of the adolescent's or young adult's difficulties?
9. What environmental stresses, demands, rewards, values, mores, and attitudes are affecting the adolescent or young adult and his or her family?
10. What social resources are available?

Difficulties generally will be manifest both within the individual and among the person, family, and environment. In such instances, intervention must have a fourfold focus: (1) promoting individual developmental mastery; (2) enabling more growth-enhancing marital, parent-child, and family transactions; (3) improving the fit among individuals, families, and the social environment; (4) promoting self-esteem and competence in the individual and family.[14] Intervention with the individual generally is indicated, but the failure to include work with the family or the social environment in cases where the transactional field is a significant part of the problem results in treatment impasses or failures. There are many cases in which problems that may appear as developmental deficits actually reflect transactional difficulties or a difficulty in fit between individual needs and resources. Family or social intervention may be the optimal approach. Further, even in cases in which individual treatment may be desirable, it may not always be feasible, and work with the family or social environment provides a crucial entry point.

THE CASE OF THE F FAMILY

Doug, age fifteen, and his parents, Mr. and Mrs. F, a middle-aged Catholic couple of Irish-English descent, were referred to the social worker after Doug's discharge from a psychiatric hospital. He had been taken there by his reluctant parents one week earlier at the urging of Doug's high school counselor, who thought he was becoming "psychotic." This episode followed a year of increasing marijuana and alcohol abuse, tru-

[14] Eda G. Goldstein, "Promoting Competence in Families of Psychiatric Patients," in *Building Competence in Clients—A New/Old Approach to Social Work Intervention,* ed. Anthony N. Maluccio (New York: Free Press, 1981).

ancy, erratic and failing school performances, lying, and minor antisocial acts. Mr. F was angry and confused as to how "Doug could be stupid enough to throw away all the chances he's been given." Mrs. F saw Doug's behavior as further indication of "his always being headed for trouble." They disagreed as to the best way of dealing with Doug, alternating between setting inappropriately strict and ineffectual limits and abdicating their parental authority totally.

The hospital team diagnosed Doug as a borderline personality and discharged him, recommending individual treatment. He refused to see a psychiatrist. In desperation the parents accepted a referral to a social worker for themselves; at the social worker's urging, Doug unexpectedly agreed to attend the sessions. In the first session he screamed, "Make them stop bugging me. If I'm sick, they're sick." In fact, anger seemed to be the main emotion that Doug experienced. While good-looking, he was very nervous; his body was taut and seemed to be bursting out of itself.

Doug regarded his parents as enemies who were trying to control him, and was quick to accuse them of being hypercritical, stupid, and rigid. He was intelligent and talented in sports but was failing courses and had been kicked off the wrestling and football teams, his main sources of self-esteem. His ambitions to attend college or become a pilot were disassociated from his everyday life, and he showed no concern that his actions were undermining his future plans. Extensive marijuana and alcohol abuse contributed to the numbing of his feelings. He associated with semidelinquent peers, and his only real friend was a loner who had dropped out of school. It was impossible to get a sense of who Doug really was and what he thought and felt; his inner life reflected a confusion and turbulence that he tried to ward off.

Doug, the only natural child, was named for Mrs. F's father. Thinking they could not have children, Mr. and Mrs. F had adopted a daughter—a boy was not available—several years before Doug's birth. Both children were born in a foreign country where the couple lived as a result of Mr. F's work in the financial field. Mrs. F described how happy she was when Doug was born, how close she felt to him, and how rejected she was when he would push out of her arms as he became more active. His increasing independence and aggressiveness frightened her, and she wondered if she had "created a monster."

Mr. F's business was precarious during this period, and he spent long hours at work. The family moved back to the United States when Doug was two-and-a-half years old; finances were tight and they lived with Mrs. F's parents until they were self-sufficient. Mr. F busied himself with career rebuilding, and Mrs. F was depressed. By this time Doug had become a "bad" boy who could not be controlled easily. At times Mrs. F would withdraw; at others she would assert her control. At still other times she would marvel at Doug's mischievous exploits, but then would feel guilty and angry when he got into minor accidents. When home Mr. F doted on Doug and accused his wife of being too strict. Doug went to a highly structured small Catholic school where he adjusted surprisingly well, although he often got into minor difficulties because of his role as the class comic. Doug's relationship with his sister was turbulent. He felt she was a "goody-goody" who had to be perfect to please their parents, and that he was always being blamed for her secret misdeeds. When Doug was thirteen-years-old he had to change schools and attended a large, impersonal public school. His sister soon left for college, and his recent difficulties began.

Troubled Familial Relationships

At the time of the first interviews, the parents' attitude toward Doug vacillated between rage for disappointing them and guilt over being too hard on him. Similarly, they alternated between getting him "to shape up or ship out" and giving him another chance. At times they felt victimized and controlled by Doug. At others they asserted their authority and overpowered him. They had difficulty seeing or relating to his good qualities.

The Fs' relationship with one another also reflected extreme oscillation. Mrs. F. felt victimized by Mr. F. She complained bitterly of his long working hours and his lack of physical demonstrativeness. She accused him of "lording it over her" because he was the "man and the breadwinner." She felt demeaned and treated as the "maid in the family while he has all the fun"; she withdrew into her room or threatened to leave and get a separation. Mr. F panicked, felt helpless, tried to please his wife, pleaded for another chance, pointed out that things could be a lot worse, and pledged his devotion to her. As they reestablished a truce, he again occupied himself with work and the cycle repeated itself.

The parents' attitudes toward themselves also showed contradictory swings. On the one hand Mr. F berated himself for not doing better in his career, for being a spendthrift and not saving any money, and for not getting enough fun out of life. On the other hand he indulged himself with expensive vacations and impulsive buying sprees, both of which led to remorse. Mrs. F also berated herself at times for being mean, a wet blanket, too practical, too demanding, and longed "to kick up her heels and have a good time." At other times she felt she was too frivolous, impractical, romantic, and irresponsible.

Recently, work pressures on Mr. F had escalated as his business is youth-oriented, and he received little help from his company in getting new accounts. He still brought in a great deal of business but had to work much harder. Mrs. F also had experienced more distress. Her mother had died a short time ago. She felt her life was empty and wondered if she would ever really live before she died. She rarely saw her sisters and father. The couple had withdrawn from friends because of Doug's problems and increasing financial pressures that made it hard for them to entertain or participate socially.

Significant in the parental histories was the fact that Mr. F is an only child whose father abandoned his family when Mr. F was four-years-old. Mr. F was on his own at an early age. He attended military school, rarely saw his mother—who "lived a high life"—and only saw his father once after the separation. He denied anger at his mother and was very obedient when home with her. At school he frequently was caught and punished for his exploits, which he discussed with some relish. He always yearned for a stable home life, and Mrs. F was his high school sweetheart. His career had been successful intermittently, but he ruminated about his lack of self-assertion and risk taking.

Mrs. F was the oldest of four daughters; looking after her sisters was a major responsibility for her. Like her mother, she was quite serious and strict. Her father was jovial but preferred Mrs. F's younger sister to her, a fact that his oldest daughter greatly resented. She was angry at and felt rejected by her father and allied herself with her mother. She yearned to be more fun loving and to become a dancer. She had rebelled somewhat and did perform in high school, but she yielded to her mother's wishes and became a nurse. She had worked periodically. Mrs. F suffered intermittent depressions in her life; the worst occurred after she finished nursing school and another after she married and moved away from her family.

A Failure in Developmental Tasks

At fifteen, Doug was failing miserably in achieving his phase-appropriate developmental tasks and was at risk of becoming chronically and pervasively disturbed in his personal and social functioning. He lacked even a rudimentary sense of a solid and positive identity. He could not utilize his intelligence and talents. Riddled with anxiety, highly impulsive, and lacking judgment, he had difficulty sustaining the kind of behavior that leads to a sense of competence and self-esteem. He had little in the way of satisfying relationships with others. He was filled with unneutralized anger that was barely contained and he utilized a good deal of denial and projection. While he felt controlled by people, his behavior had powerful effects on others.

Doug's problems began in adolescence, but they appeared in part to be rooted in developmental difficulties in childhood. Doug was a special child. In naming him for her father, it is likely that Mrs. F brought some of her frustrated expectations in her relationship with her father to her relationship with Doug. It also can be inferred that Doug's toddler efforts to push out of his mother's arms represented another rejection to her. His early aggressiveness may have been an innate characteristic or a response to his mother's difficulties in helping him move out of the symbiotic relationship she enjoyed. Her reaction to Doug's initial efforts at differentiation equated his assertiveness with rejection; she in turn alternated between rejecting and trying to control Doug and to keep him from separating from her. She may have displaced onto Doug her anger at her father, but she also projected onto him aspects of her own sense of badness as a result of having been rejected by her father.

Mr. F, unfortunately, was unavailable to foster the separation-individuation process and to support his wife. When he was home his overindulgence of Doug may have represented efforts to make up for his own neglected childhood. Seeing himself in Doug he was unable to set appropriate limits, to support his wife in her treatment of Doug, or to encourage Doug in being autonomous. The absence of extended family and the alien culture in which Mrs. F found herself contributed to her aloneness.

The return of the family to the United States placed additional strains on the parents that made them both less emotionally available to Doug who, at two-and-a-half, had already acquired the reputation of being headed for trouble. The small, highly structured Catholic school seemed to foster some aspects of Doug's ego functioning while masking other problems. A rigid and authoritarian structure that rewarded compliance may have reinforced the split between Doug's good and bad sense of self; its repressive aspects did not help him develop mastery of his impulses. In adolescence the pressure of new developmental tasks, the upsurge in drives, a nonempathic, inconsistent, and unrelated family environment, and a new school that was impersonal and bureaucratic while filled with constant temptations aggravated his underlying ego fragility.

At the same time, current family dynamics appeared to be aggravating and perpetuating Doug's problematic behavior. His "badness" usually involved giving vent to the fun-loving impulses that his parents yearned for but could not integrate or tolerate and sought to control. His behavior enabled the parents to experience the disavowed parts of themselves vicariously through Doug. They had showed secretly rebellious behavior as children, adolescents, and adults that they both relished and renounced in themselves. Their daughter became their "good" selves while Doug represented the badness they needed, admired, and felt guilty about. Doug's badness was essential to the parents' ability to maintain their equilibrium. Thus his difficulties, in addition to reflecting developmental impairments, also served the important function of fulfilling parental needs. Another aspect of the transactional dynamics that seemed to be operating was that Doug's behavior diverted his mother and father from fully experiencing the vacuum in their relationship. When he was the focus of attention, at least there was some excitement and communication at home.

Separation-Individuation Issues

It does not seem coincidental that Doug's difficulties became apparent at a time when adolescent separation-individuation issues were paramount. While this stage placed new demands on Doug that he was ill-equipped to meet because of ego deficits, it also may have stimulated Doug's fear that his family would break up if he were to become independent. Thus his behavior may in some measure have been designed to maintain the family equilibrium. Further, this stage imposed new demands on his parents to help Doug become independent. Yet they needed him desperately. Old struggles around autonomy and control were reactivated, but there also were new pressures on the parents due to their life stage. Each felt robbed of important sources of self-esteem. The impact of aging, time passing, personal losses, increasing business pressures, shrinking opportunities, and the awareness of unrealized ambitions and goals made them more vulnerable, decreased their sense of autonomy and control, engendered feelings of frustration and hopelessness, and made it more difficult to be appropriately nurturing of Doug.

The Nature of Intervention

In the case of the Fs, there was a complex interplay among current difficulties in meeting life cycle tasks, problems in ego functioning and developmental deficits, marital discord, dysfunctional family patterns, conflicts between family life cycle and individual stages, and discontinuities between individual and family needs and social conditions and resources. A combination of interventive approaches including individual, marital, family, and social intervention seemed indicated, yet Doug refused to attend individual sessions. The family was the most feasible entry point in the case. The goal was not to modify Doug's maladaptive patterns or to correct for his ego and developmental deficits but to improve the transactions among Doug, other family members, and the social environment in the hope that all the Fs' adaptive functioning would be enhanced.

The purposes of the biweekly family meetings including Mr. and Mrs. F, Doug, and his sister when she was available were: (1) to provide an environment in which family members could recognize and learn to empathize with each other's needs, perceptions, and views; (2) to identify dysfunctional parent-child transactional patterns; (3) to develop alternative modes of relating; (4) to promote joint problem solving, particularly around the areas of appropriate parenting; and (5) to mobilize the family to create or utilize environmental supports to foster Doug's and other members' functioning.

The couple's sessions that took place on alternate weeks included the above goals but had the more specific foci of: (1) helping the parents identify how they might deal with Doug at home and strengthening the couple's ability to act as a team; (2) identifying the needs, frustrations, and dysfunctional patterns in the marriage; (3) identifying how the parents' individual histories were affecting the current parent-child and marital relationships; (4) promoting more adaptive marital transactions; and (5) identifying the external and life cycle stresses impinging on the couple and finding better ways of gratification outside the marriage.

Dissolving Misperceptions

The initial family meetings were volatile. No one listened to anyone else, and acrimonious accusations dominated the atmosphere. The meetings were structured to help each member share perceptions, feelings, and needs. Distortions and impasses in communication were pointed out as were the repetitive ways in which misperceptions escalated into battles within the family and Doug's acting out on the outside. In the couple's sessions the parents were helped to relate their own histories; they were able to make connections between their own personal experiences and the way they perceived and reacted to Doug and to each other. The two critical issues were: the difficulties each had in integrating her or his good and bad aspects (particularly around the areas of gratification of pleasurable impulses) and the mutual displacements of past relationships and conflicts around their own parents onto their relationships with one another and Doug.

In family sessions Doug initially refused to acknowledge his parents' efforts to see him more realistically and to reach out to him, but he sensed them. Gradually he revealed more of himself, which in turn helped his parents see him in more three dimensional ways. This enabled the correction of familial distortions as well as the creation of more positive connections.

With energy freed, the family engaged in problem solving particularly with respect to how to handle autonomy and responsibility issues with Doug, how his parents could be helpful to him, and the nature of his obligations. Sessions with the couple examined the difficulties they had in implementing new behaviors with Doug and in strengthening their ability to work as a team. This led to the identification of more complex dynamics—the fear the parents had in anticipating Doug's growing up because of their lack of pleasure, their loneliness, and marital friction—as well as Doug's fear that the family would be destroyed as he grew up. Sessions with the couple aided this process as they focused on marital difficulties and the way Doug was used to ease the union.

Changes in Doug

After approximately four months the parents' relationship with Doug had improved considerably; he was more able to spend time at home with them rather than being driven to escape. The parents mobilized to help create opportunities at school that might enhance Doug's self-esteem and competence and decrease his isolation from peers who were "making it." They arranged for tutoring and Doug was permitted to rejoin the wrestling team if he remained drug free. Doug took flying lessons with the understanding that he would curb his marijuana abuse.

As both parents related to the positive side of Doug, he began to risk himself more with them. His school attendance and academic work improved so that he was passing his courses. When the wrestling season was over, Doug joined the football team and did very well. With his improved functioning Doug stopped attending sessions regularly, but the parents continued.

The lessening crisis with Doug motivated the parents to confront more clearly the need for change in their marital relationship. The social worker advocated new behaviors within the relationship and outside of it. One critical issue was the couple's inability to accept pleasure. As they received more permission to risk having fun, they were helped to find ways of building fun into their lives. Their concerns about Doug's drug use led them to mobilize the principal at the high school to help parents of drug abusers form a self-help group. This provided Mr. and Mrs. F with a much-needed source of competence as well as a network of new acquaintances that relieved their social isolation.

As the couple spent more time with each other and with others, pressure on Doug subsided. He was given increasing autonomy and used it fairly well. He also began to date a girl the family liked considerably. The parents remodeled the basement so that Doug could have his own space, which he wanted desperately. They were surprised at how lonely they were at first with him "gone" and pleased when they all survived. Doug now engaged in more phase-appropriate behavior, but his ego fragility remained and required individual treatment aimed at ego building. After his girl friend broke up with him, he was devastated and there was a flare up of his previous maladaptive behavior. His parents were able to overcome their disappointment and anxiety and reached out to him sensitively. He accepted their help and was able to "pull himself together" when they provided more structure for him. Some time later Doug agreed to his father's suggestion that it might be good to talk things over "man to man" with someone outside the family. He seems to have made a positive connection to a male therapist the social worker recommended.

AN ECOLOGICAL APPROACH

While the approach used with the Fs is not a model for what should be done in all such cases, it reflects the importance of work with the family and the social environment of borderline young people in correcting the developmental process and in fostering improved adaptation. It does not portray a situation in which the family or social environment were particularly depriving or pernicious in their failure to provide opportunities for physical or emotional growth. In many instances the social environment is so obstructive that social intervention must be the first order of business. Similarly, some families are so entrenched in their pathological transactions that more creative approaches to dislodging dysfunctional patterns must be attempted.

Adolescents and young adults with borderline personalities must be viewed from a perspective that encompasses both developmental and transactional formulations. The case example reflects the interplay of individual, familial, and social factors in the maintenance of borderline pathology. It illustrates an intervention approach that focused on improving the transactions among the individual, the family, and the social environment in order to promote more adaptive functioning. It also acknowledges the importance of individual intervention aimed at more extensive personality rebuilding.

DEPRESSION

CHAPTER 34

THE COGNITIVE–BEHAVIOURAL APPROACH WITH DEPRESSED CLIENTS

Michael J. Scott and Stephen G. Stradling

The origins of Cognitive–Behaviour therapy may be traced back to the philosopher Epictetus, who in the first century AD wrote 'People are disturbed not so much by events as by the views which they take of them'. More recently this notion has been systematized into the various forms of Cognitive–Behaviour Therapy, the most popular of which are Cognitive Therapy (Beck *et al.*, 1979), Rational–Emotive Therapy (Ellis, 1962), and Stress–Inoculation Training (Meichenbaum, 1985). The Cognitive–Behaviour Therapies share a central assumption that the response of a person to a situation is not simply a product of external rewards and punishments but is influenced by the individual's idiosyncratic interpretation of their situation.

The Behaviourist's stimulus response, S → R, model of human behaviour is thus extended to include a mediating variable: stimulus → appraisal → response. To take an example, suppose two mothers regularly go for coffee in each other's homes and take along their respective toddlers, and that one parent gets quite distressed at the children running riot around the house whilst the other is seemingly oblivious. Here the situations are the same for both but their response is different—one parent may be up and down shouting requests and injunctions to the children, whilst the other sits calmly drinking coffee. In Cognitive–Behaviour terms these parents' emotional responses would differ because their appraisals of the situation differ. The development and maintenance of the *distressed* parent's emotional state may be represented by Figure 34–1.

The sequence in Figure 34–1 begins with the children's boisterous behaviour. The distressed parent then has an automatic thought that, since she cannot control their behaviour, she is a bad person. (Automatic Thought 1 may be traceable to a more wide ranging silent assumption that to be worthwhile she must get everything 'just right'.)

Reprinted from *British Journal of Social Work*, Vol. 21, No. 5 (1991), pp. 533–544, by permission of Oxford University Press.

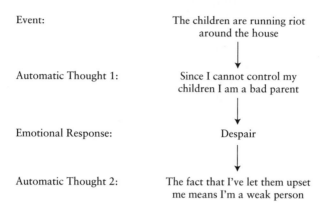

Figure 34–1.
The Development and Maintenance of a
Distressed Parent's Emotional State

Event: The children are running riot around the house

Automatic Thought 1: Since I cannot control my children I am a bad parent

Emotional Response: Despair

Automatic Thought 2: The fact that I've let them upset me means I'm a weak person

This global negative self-statement brings emotional distress which is intensified and maintained by Automatic Thought 2 'that to be distressed is a sign of weakness'. Figure 34–2 indicates that cognitions—memories, thoughts, images—can have an important influence on emotional state. However, current emotional state can, itself, influence what is remembered from the past—a phenomenon known as mood congruity (Blaney, 1986). In depressed mood compared with elated or neutral mood, the relative probability of

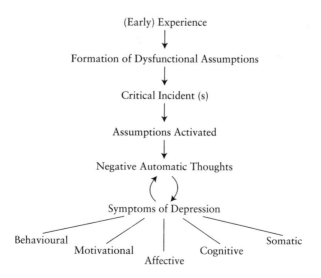

Figure 34–2.
Beck's Cognitive Model of Depression (Beck 1976)

(Early) Experience

Formation of Dysfunctional Assumptions

Critical Incident (s)

Assumptions Activated

Negative Automatic Thoughts

Symptoms of Depression

Behavioural   Motivational   Affective   Cognitive   Somatic recall of material of negative tone is enhanced, whereas the relative probability of recall of positive material is decreased. There is then a reciprocal interaction between cognition and affect and one can, in principle, influence this interaction through either.

In Cognitive–Behaviour Therapy, the chosen path of influence is via cognitions. To return to the example, the non-distressed parent may choose to make explicit to the friend her own thinking, such as 'well, the children do usually obey us and every parent gets wound up from time to time with their child'. The non-distressed friend would here be in the role of a social worker inviting the distressed friend to consider a possible alternative interpretation of the situation.

The Cognitive–Behavioural approach encourages clients to check out how accurate their representation of a situation is. The social worker helps clients become aware of information processing biases that can distort the sense they make of a situation.

An example of a processing bias would be the use of a mental filter—characteristically homing in on the negative in a situation and leaving the positive out of account. The biases in information processing can lead to dysfunctional beliefs. For example, people who habitually discount compliments are likely to form negative beliefs about themselves. The modification of dysfunctional attitudes is a key concern in Cognitive–Behaviour Therapy. However, often the best way of challenging a dysfunctional attitude is to test out the validity of the attitude, for example a client who believed he could not stand going to a party might be invited to test this belief out by going, for at least part of the time. In this way behavioural assignments form an integral part of Cognitive–Behaviour Therapy.

This approach suggests that experiences, often occurring in childhood, may lead people to the formation of dysfunctional assumptions about themselves and their world. See Fig. 34–2. These assumptions form a template or schema with which the information about environmental events and self is processed. If subsequently a critical incident happens which is pertinent to the individual's particular dysfunctional assumption, then, rather like a key fitting into a lock, the dysfunctional assumptions are activated. For example, a person who early on in life formed the assumption that they had to have everybody's approval in order to be happy, could become depressed if they did not subsequently secure the approval of someone important to them. They may, for example, have suffered redundancy or have difficult financial problems, but these events would not be directly impinging on their particular vulnerability. However, a person who based his or her sense of worth entirely on achievement would be much more likely to succumb to depression in the event of such employment problems. Once activated, dysfunctional assumptions produce 'negative automatic thoughts'—'negative' in that they are associated with unpleasant emotions and 'automatic' in that they pop into people's heads rather than being the product of any deliberate reasoning process. These may be interpretations of current experiences, predictions about future events, or recollections of things that have happened in the past. They, in turn, lead on to other typical signs of depression: behavioural symptoms (for example, lowered activity levels, withdrawal); motivational symptoms (for example, loss of interest, inertia); emotional symptoms (for example, anxiety, guilt); cognitive symptoms (for example, poor concentration, indecisiveness); and physical symptoms (for example, loss of appetite, loss of sleep). The lowered mood itself increases access to negative memories, serving to maintain the depression. In this way a vicious circle is set up.

AN OUTLINE OF COGNITIVE THERAPY

Cognitive therapy is aimed primarily at modifying the dysfunctional silent assumptions held by Beck *et al.* (1979) to underpin depression. Typically, individual therapy involves 12–20 sessions of 45–60 minutes over a three-month period. In the first phase of therapy the emphasis is behavioural, aimed at increasing the client's sense of mastery and achievement. The second phase is more cognitive, aimed at the identification and modification of the dysfunctional silent assumptions. In part this is achieved by setting up 'behavioural experiments' to test out the silent assumptions and in part by 'Socratic dialogue' with the client as to the validity, consistency and utility of these assumptions. For homework, clients are encouraged to complete a daily record of dysfunctional thoughts in which the situations that lead to emotional upset are recorded, automatic thoughts that lead to the upset are set down, and rational responses to the dysfunctional thoughts are recorded. Unless the client has something very pressing, that it is agreed must take precedence, the thought records from the previous week are reviewed at the beginning of the session.

A Case Example of Cognitive Therapy for Depression—Enid

Enid was 47, married with three children at home, and was referred to the social worker by her GP for help with her depression. At assessment she was found to be severely depressed with a score of thirty-two on the Beck Depression Inventory (Beck *et al.*, 1961)—into the severe depression range. She hated her job as a typist which she found boring, and there were financial difficulties as her husband was a self-employed handyman. Her husband became irritable when he was not working. She had had no previous treatment for any emotional difficulties.

She was sexually assaulted as a child and the recent publicity had brought it all back to her. In her words 'I find myself blaming this for my self-hate, my lack of confidence, my feeling of, "how can anyone love me".' She had kept this a secret and this was the first time it had been put on paper.

At the end of the initial assessment interview, Enid was given a copy of Beck and Greenberg's (1974) 'Coping with Depression' article which provides a summary of the rationale for cognitive therapy and an outline of the counselling programme. She was also asked to keep a diary of her week, monitoring the extent of her sense of achievement and pleasure in the various situations she was in. The second individual session began, as do all sessions, with a review of the homework assignment. Enid's response to the 'Coping with Depression' article was very positive, and this is usually predictive of a good response to counselling in the long term (Fennell and Teasdale, 1987). She felt reassured from the article that other people suffered the same symptoms as she did, and could already identify her own propensity to jump to the conclusion that people looked down on her in the absence of any hard evidence.

Inspection of Enid's diary, however, showed that there was very little in her week that gave her a sense of achievement or pleasure. A list was drawn up of events that had, prior to depression, given her a sense of achievement and pleasure. They included taking lessons for her advanced driving test, watercolour painting and gardening. The social worker discussed with Enid the possibility of planning such events into her week. Enid felt she did not have the concentration for advanced driving or painting but thought she could probably try gardening. However, when the practicalities of gardening were examined, it was difficult for her to timetable it in.

On the one hand she thought she would possibly enjoy a hour's gardening when she came home from work and that it would help her unwind, but on the other hand her adult children and her husband would expect tea at 6 p.m. The social worker helped her examine more closely the cognitive 'roadblock' to action, and she conceded that she was jumping to conclusions that they would be annoyed with her if she postponed tea until 7 p.m. However, whilst agreeing they might not be annoyed with her, she thought she would feel guilty if she did not start tea until 6 p.m. At this point the social worker introduced the notion of emotional reasoning, which suggests that 'feelings of guilt are not necessarily evidence of guilt'. Though the early stages of cognitive therapy are primarily behavioural, one often has to introduce cognitive material in order to facilitate tasks. The latter stages of cognitive therapy are more explicitly cognitive and clients are asked to monitor their down-turns in mood using a Thought Record. The following is an example of one of Enid's Thought Records:

1. *Situation:* Describe
   a) Actual event leading to unpleasant emotion, or
   b) Stream of thoughts, daydreams or recollections leading to unpleasant emotion.
   Recollection of promotion interview and doubts about how well I answered questions.
2. *Emotions:*
   a) Specify sad, anxious, angry, etc.
   b) Rate degree of emotion, 1–100
   Anxious, 80 per cent
3. *Automatic Thoughts:*
   a) Write automatic thought(s) that preceded emotion(s)
   b) Rate belief in automatic thought(s) 0–100 per cent
   a) I must have sounded stupid in the interview
   b) 80 per cent
4. *Rational Response:*
   a) Write rational response to automatic thought(s)
   b) Rate belief in rational response 0–100 per cent
   a) I felt quite pleased immediately after the interview. What am I worried for? No one likes interviews. I did well to get down to the last six. If I didn't get the job the interviewer said my references were excellent.
   b) 60 per cent
5. *Outcome:*
   a) Re-rate belief in automatic thought(s) (0–100 per cent)
   b) Specify and rate subsequent emotions (0–100 per cent)

a)   *25 per cent*
b)   *Anxious, 50 per cent*

After four weeks into cognitive therapy Enid was only mildly depressed with a Beck Depression Score of fourteen—in the mild depression range (10–20). However she indicated that she still felt guilty a good part of the time. The guilt feelings related in part to the sexual abuse in childhood. There were a number of aspects of the abuse that bothered Enid, particularly that she 'should' have played the whole situation differently, telling her mother about her father as soon as it started. The social worker helped her question her self-blame:

SOCIAL WORKER: What stopped you telling your mother?
ENID: My father said I would be sent away if I told her. I liked it at home and didn't want to go away.
SOCIAL WORKER: That sounds a good reason for a 9-year-old not to tell her mother.
ENID: I suppose it was.
SOCIAL WORKER: Then how could you have played it differently?
ENID: I don't know.
SOCIAL WORKER: Can you be guilty of something if you don't have any other choices?
ENID: Well no, but I feel guilty.
SOCIAL WORKER: Does feeling guilty make you guilty?
ENID: No, but I did get some pleasure from the abuse.
SOCIAL WORKER: Why is experiencing some pleasure in that situation blameworthy?
ENID: You shouldn't because it is wrong.
SOCIAL WORKER: It may be wrong, but you couldn't then make your body not a body which was the only way then you could make yourself not experience some pleasure.
ENID: I see what you mean.
SOCIAL WORKER: If a 9-year-old was sitting next to you expressing the guilt you have expressed, what would you do or say?
ENID: I would just give them a big hug and tell them not to be silly.

Dialogues such as the above are central to cognitive therapy, focusing on the client's negative view of themselves, the future and the world—Beck's Cognitive Triad (Beck *et al.*, 1979). In this extract the social worker focuses on the first aspect of the triad and explores with the client whether she is consistent in their guilt reaction. The social worker finds the client applies one set of rules to herself and a very different set to other people.

The Results of Two Cognitive Therapy Outcome Studies

We have conducted two studies on the outcome of Cognitive Therapy treatment for depression by a social worker, the first using referrals from general practitioners at an inner-city health centre, the second from the occupational health services of large local employers. Both were in Liverpool and covered a total of 103 clients suffering primary major depressive disorders. In both studies those referred were preponderantly female and working class as defined in Brown and Harris's study (Brown and Harris, 1978). Those in the Health Centre study were also mainly single and unemployed, as well as being female and working class. In both studies we compared the effectiveness of Cognitive Therapy presented in Individual and Group modes. In the Individual mode clients received 12 weekly 45 minute sessions, while those treated in small groups (4–8 persons) attended 12 weekly 90 minute group sessions which ran alongside an initial three individual sessions each. (See Scott, 1989a, for more details.)

In the first study we were able to show that clients treated in either mode were significantly less depressed at the end of treatment than those held on a waiting list for the same length of time (Scott and Stradling, 1990), and that this reduction in symptoms was maintained for up to 12 months post treatment—see Figure 34–3. The only previous controlled trial of social work help for depression (Corney, 1981) had found it no better than treatment-as-usual from the GP. All our clients—both treated groups and waiting list group—were receiving treatment-as-usual and Figure 34–3 shows that Cognitive Therapy by a social worker, in combination with GP treatment, was clearly more efficacious here than GP treatment alone.

In our second study we sought to confirm our findings that group and individual cognitive therapy were equally effective. Using clients referred from across the city, they were assigned to either ICT or GCT and followed up at one, two, three, and six months. Again we found both modes equally effective. In both studies, then, we were

Figure 34–3.
Treatment follow-up

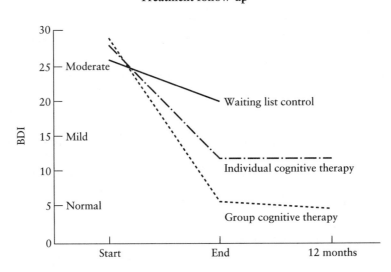

able to show that the results for Group treatment were just as good as those for Individual treatment—and, thereby, more cost effective in use of worker time. Simply getting depressed clients to work in groups and focus on their problems in living has been found not to effect significant changes in level of depression (Nezu, 1986). This suggests that our results are not solely due to being in a group but depend upon some 'active ingredients' for effective change inherent in the Cognitive–Behavioural approach.

DISCUSSION
The Breadth of Applications of Cognitive–Behaviour Therapy

In this paper particular mention has been made of the application of Cognitive–Behaviour Therapy to depression. In this area a substantial number of well-designed outcome studies testify to the efficacy of Cognitive–Behaviour Therapy. Indeed, a number of studies have shown that the rate of relapse following CBT is only half the rate for clients taking anti-depressants. It is now virtually impossible to find a disorder that Cognitive–Behaviour Therapy has not been applied to. But depending upon the particular disorder focused on there are varying bodies of evidence as to the efficacy of Cognitive–Behaviour Therapy for that problem. It should be noted also that Cognitive–Behaviour Therapy has been applied beyond psychiatric disorders to the problems of offenders and to people with learning difficulties.

The social worker utilizing Cognitive–Behaviour Therapy should be wary of its indiscriminate use. The disorders of bulimia nervosa and anorexia nervosa are a case in point. The evidence of three recent controlled studies indicates that clients with bulimia nervosa can benefit to a similar degree from treatments which cannot be regarded as forms of Cognitive–Behaviour Therapy (Fairburn and Cooper, 1989). With regard to anorexia nervosa, Cognitive–Behaviour Therapy has yet to be evaluated. Cognitive–Behavioural treatments have been the most extensively evaluated interventions of all the psychotherapeutic schools in relation to these disorders and they do indicate that clients benefit in the short term, but little is known about the maintenance of change in the long term.

The research base is more substantial in areas such as Cognitive–Behavioural Marital Therapy, but here, again, some caution is necessary. Though Cognitive–Behavioural Marital Therapy has consistently been found to be as or more effective than any other type of marital therapy, nevertheless in terms of the proportion of clients that actually improve, the results are quite modest. Jacobson *et al.* (1984) found that by the end of therapy about half of couples showed significant improvement and approximately one-third of couples appeared to be non-distressed. However, clinically significant improvements were often limited to just one spouse in the couple.

Though the standard approach to agoraphobia is an overtly behavioural one of graded exposure, many of the aspects of exposure that used to be described as 'non-specific', such as arriving at a realistic interpretation of the week's events, or at accurate expectations for the future, or dealing with reservations about treatment, are now described in cognitive terms. Thus, though exposure-based treatments for phobias have been very successful (for example, Marks, 1987) it is problematic as to what are the 'active ingredients for change'. In some cases the efficacy of behavioural programmes has been potentiated by adding explicit cognitive procedures (Mattick and Peters, 1988).

Cognitive therapy has sometimes been accused of being only applicable to the 'intellectual' client. Williams and Moorey (1989) have provided a convincing rebuttal of this notion with their description of its use with clients who have a mental handicap. They show how the complexity level of the techniques used can be varied to suit the client.

Social workers are often left to deal with those clients who are most difficult to engage in any treatment and most likely to relapse such as drug abusers and offenders. The cognitive behavioural strategies for the engagement, treatment, and relapse prevention of drug abusers has been described fully in Scott (1989a) and Scott (1989b), whilst Cole (1989) has detailed the specifics of cognitive-behavioural approach to the problems of offenders.

Cognitive–Behaviour Therapy is sufficiently detailed to equip a social worker with a wide range of strategies he/she can adopt with almost any emotional problem. Encouraged by the demonstrated efficacy of CBT with disorders such as depression, the social worker can consider that it is at least plausible to use similar strategies with other client difficulties. Nevertheless, CBT has, ultimately, to be evaluated with each disorder in turn.

If such trials are successful, attention will then turn to examining the mechanisms by which CBT achieves its goals and whether they are in accord with the hypotheses of the theorists.

REFERENCES

Beck, A. T. (1976) *Cognitive Therapy and the Emotional Disorders,* New York, International Universities Press.

Beck, A, T. and Greenberg, R. L. (1974) *Coping with Depression.* Available from Centre for Cognitive Therapy, Room 602, 133 South 36th Street, Philadelphia, PA 19104–32406, USA.

Beck, A. T., Rush, A. J., Shaw, B. F. and Emery, G. (1979) *Cognitive Therapy of Depression,* New York, Guildford Press.

Beck, A. T., Ward, C. H., Mendelson, M., Mock, J. and Erbaugh, J. (1961) 'An Inventory for Measuring Depression', *Archives of General Psychiatry,* 4, pp. 561–71.

Blaney, P. H. (1986) 'Affect and Memory: A Review', *Psychological Bulletin,* 99, pp. 229–46.

Brown, G. W. and Harris, T. (1978) *The Social Origins of Depression,* London, Tavistock Press.

Cole, A. (1989) 'Offenders' in Scott, J., Williams, J. M. G. and Beck, A. T. (eds.) *Cognitive Therapy in Clinical Practice: An Illustrative Casebook,* London, Routledge and Kegan Paul.

Corney, R. H. (1981) 'Social Work effectiveness in the Management of Depressed Women: A Clinical Trial', *Psychological Medicine,* 11, pp. 417–23.

Ellis, A. (1962) *Reason and Emotion in Psychotherapy,* New York, Lyle Stuart.

Fairburn, C. G. and Cooper, P. J. (1989) 'Eating Disorders' in Hawton, K., Salkouskis, P. M., Kirk, J. and Clark, D. M. (eds) *Cognitive Behaviour Therapy for Psychiatric Problems: A Practical Guide,* Oxford, Oxford University Press.

Fennell, M. J. V. and Teasdale, J. D. (1987) 'Cognitive Therapy for Depression: Individual Differences and the Process of Change', *Cognitive Therapy and Research*, 11, pp. 253–71.

Jacobson, N. S., Follette, N. C., Revenstorf, D., Baucom, D. H., Hahlweg, K. and Margolin, G. (1984) 'Variability in Outcome and Clinical Significance of Behavioural Marital Therapy: A Re-analysis of Outcome Data', *Journal of Consulting and Clinical Psychology*, 52, pp. 497–504.

Marks, I. M. (1987) *Fears, Phobias and Rituals: Panic, Anxiety and their Disorders*, New York, Oxford University Press.

Mattick, R. P. and Peters, L. (1988) 'Treatment of Severe Social Phobia: Effects of Guided Exposure with and without Cognitive Restructuring', *Journal of Consulting and Clinical Psychology*, 56, pp. 251–60.

Meichenbaum, D. (1985) *Stress Inoculation Training*, New York, Pergamon Press.

Nezu, A. M. (1986) 'Efficacy of a Social Problem Solving Therapy Approach for Unipolar Depression', *Journal of Consulting and Clinical Psychology*, 54, pp. 196–202.

Scott, M. J. (1988) *An Evaluation of Individual and Group Cognitive Therapy for Depression and an Examination of the Process of Change*. Doctoral Thesis. University of Manchester.

Scott, M. (1989a) *A Cognitive-Behavioural Approach to Clients' Problems*, London, Tavistock/Routledge.

Scott, M. (1989b) 'Relapse Prevention', in Bennett, G. (ed.) *Treating Drugs Abusers*, London, Tavistock/Routledge.

Scott, M. J. and Stradling, S. G. (1990) 'Group Cognitive Therapy for Depression Produces Clinically Significant Reliable Change in Community-based Settings', *Behavioural Psychotherapy*, 18, pp. 1–19.

Williams, J. M. G. and Moorey, S. (1989) 'The Wider Application of Cognitive Behaviour Therapy: the end of the beginning', in Scott, J., Williams, J. M. G. and Beck, A. T. (eds.) *Cognitive Therapy in Clinical Practice: An illustrative casebook*, London, Routledge.

DEPRESSION

CHAPTER 35

DEPRESSION IN OLDER ADULTS

Psychological and Psychosocial Approaches

Margaret A. Fielden

A discussion of 'depression in older adults' may imply that when people age they in some way change and become a separate subgroup. However, the intention of this article is not to suggest that the elderly form a different population, but to point out the particular vulnerability of this group of adults, to look for explanations for this vulnerability, and explore the sensitivity of psychological and psychosocial approaches to special problems facing the elderly.

Busse (1985) in the USA Duke Adaptational study looked at groups of people over long periods of time and suggested that few elderly people escape the experience of depression at some time in their later years. Colman (1986) states that depression is almost a 'normal' part of ageing. This suggests that the experience of ageing, with associated physical, economic, and social role changes and the likelihood of experiences of loss, including bereavement and the loss of status, exposes vulnerability to depression in many people. This article reviews therapeutic responses to depression in later life focusing on psychological and psychosocial approaches to treating and preventing depression.

Problems in Diagnosing Depression in Older People

In our society severe life events are often concentrated in later years and distinctions between 'reactive' and 'endogenous' depressions may be irrelevant. Indeed, in elderly people certain depressive features seem to be predominant which combine the symptoms attributed to reactive and endogenous depressions: apathy, poor self-care, weight loss, low mood, anxiety. Agitation is more common than retardation and may give an im-

Reprinted from *British Journal of Social Work*, Vol. 22, No. 3 (June, 1992), pp. 291–307, by permission of Oxford University Press.

pression of cognitive impairment or 'pseudodementia'. There may be delusions of bodily decay or paranoid ideations and a pre-occupation with somatic complaints and suicide or death (Bergmann, 1982). Reoccurrence is common in older people and it is less likely to be associated with a family history of depression. Distress at adverse psychosocial factors cannot be separated from the expression of depressive symptoms.

A distinction between primary depressions and secondary depressions made by Robins-Guze (1970) may have particular significance for the elderly. Many people have severe illness or incapacitation in old age and Bergmann (1982) and Murphy (1982) have found strong associations of physical illness and secondary depression. Bergmann found that, sadly, these depressions were often overlooked by medical staff who described their patients as 'not wanting to get well'.

Gurland *et al.* (1988) describe the links between depression and disability as reciprocal; depression may increase complaints about physical symptoms and physical illness may precipitate depression.

The general hospital social worker will be familiar with the client whose recovery appears to have halted. This elderly person may be presenting problems for physical care staff who feel frustrated in their attempts to improve the client's condition for discharge. For the social worker consideration of the elderly person's future living arrangements can be complex when the physical condition fails to improve as expected. It is vital that the psychological needs of the elderly person in hospital are acknowledged. Not only is that individual vulnerable to depression associated with physical illness and disability which may reflect fears of increased dependency and imminent death, but also, he or she is subject to the consequences of hospitalization. 'Good' patient behaviour tends to be preferred by busy staff but the compliance and passivity associated with this style of behaving can lead to learned helplessness and an inability to digest or offer condition-relevant information. Feelings of loss of control, denial, or fatalism are commonly expressed and the person's affective state appears anxious and depressed. Taylor (1979) suggests that helplessness is related to sudden death and to gradual erosion of the person's health.

Again, when an elderly person has a progressive organic syndrome the presence of a superimposed depression should not be overlooked; treatment of depressive symptoms can lead to improvements in cognitive impairment. Depression may co-exist with an early Alzheimer's dementia when the person is aware of failing memory and may persist with the more patchy decline in multi-infarct dementia.

Where the elderly person suffering from a dementia is institutionalized, paucity of the social environment can isolate the individual and reduce personal skills further. Harrison *et al.* (1990) in a survey of depression and disability amongst elderly people in receipt of services in a London Borough found that in Part III and private or voluntary accommodation 28 per cent and 35 per cent respectively were suffering from depression. This was often in conjunction with dementia. National Health Service departments fared better, but the elderly people in their care still showed unacceptably high levels of depression. There is evidence to suggest that residential or nursing staff may be unwittingly contributing to the creation of an impoverished environment which heightens the vulnerability of these people to depression. In a comparison of nursing staffs' interactions with confused and lucid patients on two geriatric wards Armstrong-Esther and Browne (1986) found that whereas lucid patients were occupied in some purposeful activity for 30 per cent of the observed time, confused patients were occupied only 18 per cent of the time. Similarly, nurse/patient interactions occurred 15 per cent of the observed time with lucid patients and only 5.6 per cent of the time with confused people.

The history provided by the social worker may clarify diagnosis where depression mimics an organic dementia by showing that onset was rapid, in contrast to the slow progression of common organic syndromes. Depressive retardation or hypomania seriously disrupt cognitive function but the depressed person is likely to retain insight and may seem sad whereas in dementia mood may be shallow. The person may fail to answer questions rather than confabulate answers and show patchy performance on cognitive tests rather than a general decline. Hypomanic patients may appear to be making gross errors in testing but may express an elated mood. Grossberg and Nakra (1986) point out that failure to identify depression in these cases may lead to inappropriate institutionalization but that with treatment many cases of cognitive impairment in this 'pseudodementia' make dramatic improvements.

Diagnosis of depression in elderly people is complex. The existence of physical or organic disease may draw attention away from the depression, as will the emphasis some older people place on somatic symptoms. The depression may mimic dementia and therefore go unrecognized. Other patients with 'smiling' depressions will fail to seek help, their attempts to mask their feelings expressing their socio-cultural experience of the need to 'soldier on'. Diagnosis requires a global approach to understanding the present position of each individual person.

Akiskal and McKinney (1975) suggest that it is now considered preferable to define types of depression in terms of patterns of psychological, social, somatic, and psychomotor presentations and genetic vulnerability and thereby to predict implications for treatment and outcome. If a diagnostic label of depression is to have value it must describe the presentation, point to the aetiology, have implications for treatment, and predict prognosis. It seems unlikely that dichotomous labels meet these criteria but an holistic view of each individual in terms of psychosocial, somatic, psychomotor, and biological factors may prove a more sensitive approach.

Psychosocial Approaches to Understanding Depression in Old Age

Elderly people have long years of experiences which have influenced their learning and personality development, yet, in half of those who present with depression, evidence of a previously unstable personality or maladaptive learning will be slight (Murphy, 1982). Apparently, social and physical experiences and psychological tasks of old age are sufficient to awaken or create vulnerability to depression in some individuals.

Particularly vulnerable are those who have no confidant and who have not developed a capacity for intimacy in their lifetime. Murphy (1983) suggested that lack of a confiding intimate relationship was a key factor in the onset of depression in old age, and Surtees (1980) claimed that a reciprocally confiding relationship could offer partial immunity from the effects of severe life events in recovering depressives. However, diffuse social networks were not sufficient, perception of intimacy was the vital ingredient (Murphy, 1983). Since losses of family, friends, and of the energy for daily living are liable to lead to reduced social contacts in some elderly people, depression is more likely to occur. An inability to re-establish close relationships when depressed may lead to the reoccurrence of depression which is so common in old age.

An indication of the importance of intimate relationships in preventing depression was given by Clayton *et al.* (1972) who reported on interviews with 109 people who had been recently bereaved. They found that, for 35 per cent of their subjects, grief reactions experienced were similar to primary depressive symptoms. However, these were self-limiting except where the widowed individual had no other close relationship.

Murphy (1982) found that social problems were experienced both by those having psychiatric treatment in hospital and by a group of depressed people within the community, but the latter were more likely to have experienced severe life events and health problems; this factor and the tendency for the patient group to show more florid symptoms led Murphy to suggest that biological factors play a part in about 15 per cent of elderly depressed psychiatric patients. However, overall, social factors were as important in the development of depression in the elderly as in the young, and social problems were often concentrated in old age. Murphy states that whilst some personalities may be vulnerable to depression, these people are no more at risk than the well adjusted until faced with a sudden life crisis, major social problems, or loss of health. These individuals require a pro-active approach to prevent onset of depression by confronting social and health problems and facilitating the development of protective intimate relationships. The area of preventing depression by encouraging the development of new relationships is better addressed by social workers than other health professionals. Their knowledge of their clients' social backgrounds and of the local possibilities of developing social relationships which may lead to intimate friendship for the client is invaluable.

THERAPEUTIC APPROACHES

Preventing onset of depression should be the aim of all professionals working with vulnerable individuals. Post (1985) reporting on long-term studies of outcome, states that 53 per cent of elderly patients had relapsed or failed to recover fully, 15 per cent had remained disabled by their depression, and only 32 per cent had fully recovered. Sadly, as Post states, depressive symptoms seem to become habitual for some people.

Since areas of vulnerability have been identified attention must be paid to early response to physical disability, early diagnosis of depression concomitant with physical illness, early provision of counselling for those elderly people who have experienced losses, maximizing of opportunities for developing new intimate relationships, enriching institutional environments, and redressing the balance of lost social status for our elders. However, the need for effective treatment of depression in older people remains.

Somatic Treatments

Treating depression in older people with somatic therapies requires special care. Elderly people commonly take a number of medications, prescribed or otherwise, and the social worker needs to be aware of the possibilities of drug interactions and side effects.

Beck (1967) found that around 60–65 per cent of all depressed patients have a definite therapeutic response to medication; for the rest medication is ineffective. Effectiveness of medication may be reduced in older people. A study by Gerner *et al.* (1980) found a 50 per cent reduction in depression scores following anti-depressant medication over twenty-six weeks with the elderly patients tending to show a great improvement or none at all.

In elderly people with complex physical problems medication may be contra-indicated and treatment of the physical condition may be effective in lifting mood. This highlights the importance of attending to physical symptoms in the elderly, both to avoid and to treat depressive symptoms.

However, the evidence given indicates that some people will respond well to medication and indeed where the individual is severely ill a psychotherapeutic approach may be ineffective until their symptoms have been sufficiently controlled by medication. Electro-convulsive therapy shows some success in studies with elderly people with psychotic symptoms where food refusal or threat of suicide endangers life but early relapse is common (Post, 1985). The evidence of relapse in one-third of elderly people treated with somatic therapies (Murphy, 1983) may indicate that they merely control symptoms in some people. Long reliance on psychoactive medication, as well as a severe crisis or series of problems, can undermine the elderly person's own coping strategies. Therapies are needed which develop the person's capacity to cope with their present circumstances and hopefully to cope with any further distressing circumstances without relapse.

Psychological Therapies

Psychological therapies may have a useful role in treating depression in elderly people by reducing psychological vulnerability in addressing the developmental tasks of ageing: the acceptance of role, status, and income change through retirement, adapting to physical disability, adapting to bereavements and losses, affiliation with new social groups, developing flexibility in social roles, and establishing satisfactory living arrangements. Problems which may be lifelong or have arisen through age-related changes in circumstances are amenable to psychological therapies, for example in altering underlying depressive belief systems, in re-establishing socialization and self-esteem, and in resolving conflicts, both internal and those caused by changes in relationships.

Broadly psychological therapies fall into 'interpretive' and 'directive' traditions with differing origins for models of depression and orientations for therapy. Here therapies based on psychodynamic and cognitive behavioural approaches are reviewed and consideration is given to some developments and adaptations specifically designed to be therapeutic with elderly people.

Therapy with Older Adults Based on Psychodynamic Traditions

Freud himself considered elderly people too rigid after the age of fifty to benefit from psychoanalysis. However, the psychodynamic approach does have something to say about the particular experiences of elderly people and psychological response to those experiences. Reminiscence work and group work on specific themes of loss and relationship needs could prove to be a way forward in treating depression in older people.

Woods and Britton (1985) suggest that, as yet, no coherent model for psychodynamic psychotherapy with the elderly has emerged but some success has been reported by Hildebrand (1982), Cooper (1984), and others. Adaptations have been made by these therapists to suit the needs of older people.

Hildebrand (1982) disputes Freud's claims of 'rigidity' which he suggests is not a problem with older people who 'possess a demonstrable capacity to use experience, varying frames of reference in a creative and plastic way' (p. 22). He finds older people are often ready to concentrate work on particular themes, frequently concerned with losses (Cooper, 1984) or the need for mutually satisfying relationships (Bergmann, 1978). Hildebrand suggests that, because they are aware of the shortness of time left to them, older adults respond well to brief psychotherapy of around fifteen sessions. This may give the opportunity for a depressed elderly person to resolve conflicts and needs which have not been allowed to surface previously.

Saracino (1978–9) modified the therapist's role to become more directive, open, and empathic; this is advocated by Burnside (1970) in group psychotherapy with the elderly. This is intended to make the therapy more accessible and to allow direct intervention into the patient's life if appropriate. This 'supportive psychotherapy' is the approach probably most commonly used with the elderly, attempting to make symptoms ego-syntonic, increasing personal comfort, rather than ego-dystonic, decreasing personal comfort, as with traditional psychoanalysis.

Group work offers possibilities of a shared experience with other elderly people, but a modified approach may be more appropriate since traditional psychoanalytic groups do not encourage the friendships which can be important in preventing further episodes of depression. Social workers have access to a number of environments where they can facilitate group work. A skilled group facilitator can allow common ground to emerge, focusing the group on themes relevant and universal to the ageing experience.

Reminiscence Therapy

An innovative development from the psychodynamic tradition has been the use of reminiscence as a therapy for depression. This was originally based upon Butler's (1963) concept of 'life reviewing' taken from Erikson's (1950) developmental theory focusing on the psychological 'tasks' involved in the final stage of conflict between ego-integrity, acceptance of life and death, and despair. Butler (1963) suggests that this ego-despair explains the appearance of late life depression and the 'thousand little disgusts' of the unhappy older person dissatisfied with their life.

Hildebrand (1987) suggests that older people need to explore and evaluate their past in therapy. Reminiscence gives this opportunity and can be used very successfully in a group format and is a popular activity. It has advantages over more traditional psychoanalytic approaches in its inherent acceptability to people unused to self-analysis. It is an easily accepted method of using past experiences to promote understanding of present emotional distress. By enabling group members to develop their psychological and social resources for coping with present and future life stresses, reminiscence may have therapeutic and preventative value. This type of group is popular and can be developed in residential, sheltered housing or localized community settings to promote mental health in elderly participants giving ready access to mutual ground for developing new relationships. Relationships can become intimate through the sharing of personal information which participants choose to disclose about themselves in group sessions.

Studies of reminiscence therapy for depression offer conflicting evidence for its efficacy. Fry (1983) found that individual reminiscence therapy was effective in improving self-reports of depression as measured by the Beck depression inventory, particularly when reminiscence was structured and guided. Perrotta and Meacham (1981) used a short-term group intervention with no success; however, unlike Fry, they failed to define levels of pre-treatment depression and they reduced Fry's session time by half. This suggests that Fry's work is a fairer test of the effectiveness of reminiscence as a therapeutic intervention for depression.

Research comparing reminiscence and a therapy focusing on coping with current life experience as a group intervention with sheltered housing residents showed very significant improvements in perceptions of psychological well-being in individuals with borderline depressions (Fielden, 1990). One gentleman, a widower of seventy-three with heart problems, showed the highest levels of psychological distress of all participants. He knew no one well and feared mixing with other residents. He kept a shrine to his long dead wife and claimed that his life was not worth living without her. After this gentleman had attended group sessions of reminiscence, he developed new relationships which he has maintained and his psychological well-being has been dramatically improved. Reminiscence in group sessions enabled him to overcome his social anxiety, because the inherent nature of reminiscence provides common ground for re-engagement with others (Lewis, 1971). He also worked through his unresolved grieving and allowed himself new opportunities to establish a more rewarding pattern of life.

A sociometric measure used in the study mentioned showed that the elderly people involved perceived great changes in relationships within the sheltered housing complex with large numbers of new friendships developing. Reminiscence may facilitate development of confiding relationships which Murphy (1982) stresses may be a key to preventing onset of depression.

Cognitive Behavioural Approaches

Cognitive behavioural models of depression regard the individual as having a cognitive disposition towards depression, developed as a lifetime pattern or as a response to changes experienced in reinforcement patterns or through perception of loss of control over life experiences. This approach to understanding the development of depression differs from the psychoanalytic emotional conflict theory of depression and, in contrast, emphasizes the role of thought disturbance underlying these emotional states. Thus, depression is characterized by 'helplessness and hopelessness' reflecting a 'cognitive triad' of negative beliefs about the self, experiences, and the future.

Beck's (1967) cognitive theory of depression is based on the assumption that people who become depressed have an habitual and resistant negative cognitive bias to the processing of life experiences which results in internal negative attributions. Whilst cognitive behavioural approaches do not offer specific explanations of problems of ageing, it is often appropriate to conceptualize depression in the elderly in cognitive behavioural terms. A vulnerability to develop depression may relate to an habitual negative cognitive set which may only become apparent when the stresses of life are too high.

Vulnerability could also be created by an increase in frequency of aversive events leading to 'learned helplessness' (Seligman, 1975) or by a decrease in access to reinforcing situations, through role loss, bereavement, physical illness, etc. (Lewinsohn, 1981). Such experiences are common for the elderly since the changes and losses of ageing may 'overload' the coping system or result in the reduction of opportunities to meet others or perform activities which give pleasure or reduce anxiety (Lazarus, 1968; Wolpe, 1971).

Therapeutic attempts at changing a negative cognitive set are usually accompanied by behavioural methods which aim to increase activity and reinforcing experiences. Recently, a client with severe tinnitus was referred to psychological services suffering from anxiety and depression. This lady, in her sixties, had suffered from tinnitus for nine years. Her case illustrates the particular vulnerability of elderly people to become depressed because of an accumulation of physical problems and social change. She had moved to a new home following her husband's retirement and her tinnitus had worsened. She and her husband had always had different needs socially, she enjoying company whereas he preferred solitude. She now felt imprisoned in isolation, by her new environment, her tinnitus, and her lifetime obligation to put others' needs before her own, in this instance her husband's.

Cognitive methods have been useful in establishing the reality of her need to learn to live with her tinnitus and in exploring her automatic thoughts about herself, for example: 'The noises are bad this morning, I will have a dreadful day', 'I am a bad person if I want something for myself'. She has begun to accept the inevitability of her physical condition and her need to cope with it rather than search for cures (she has had specialist treatment which was unsuccessful). She now uses coping statements to help her through difficult periods of each day. She has also begun to balance the evidence for and against her distorted thinking; for example, accepting that she has given much in her life and that making some demands does not make her a bad person. Behavioural techniques are helping her to see associations between her thoughts, emotions, and behaviour. She has recorded her activities, the level of enjoyment, and the levels of tinnitus experienced and it has become apparent to her that she can enjoy activities when her tinnitus is severe, and that positive or negative cognitions determine whether she can find pleasure in spite of her physical symptoms. She has increased her activity levels, choosing some pleasures shared with her husband and others which please her. She is developing the ability to be assertive without feeling guilty.

Emery (1981) reports success in using individual cognitive therapy with elderly people and Steur and Hammen (1983) discuss group work with four elderly depressed people. Again group work may prove valuable in helping withdrawn depressed people regain the skills needed for building the protective intimate relationships described by Murphy (1985). Akiskal and McKinney (1975) suggest that the process of altering negative thinking is likely to 'fortify the individual against future attacks', therefore giving cognitive therapy preventative value. Hussian and Lawrence (1981) developed a model of problem solving to teach skills which could be used in decision making when the individual is faced with problems in the present or future. This involves brainstorming and evaluating the consequences of alternative choices. A brief evaluation study by Hussian and Lawrence (1981) suggested more improvement in depressive symptoms for patients taught problem solving than for those experiencing social activity alone.

Cognitive behavioural techniques have been appropriate for the lady described because she needed to re-establish a pattern of reinforcing activity in her life and re-evaluate her negative beliefs about herself. Other methods and interpretations of her problems might have been equally successful, but there is a need to consider the effectiveness of techniques in preventing further depressive episodes. Some evidence suggests that there are differences in the long-term effectiveness of certain therapeutic methods used with depression in the elderly.

A Brief Comparison of the Effectiveness of These Approaches

Gallagher and Thompson (1983) and Thompson *et al.* (1987) have evaluated some of the therapies discussed here in comparative studies. In both studies elderly people suffering from depression were allocated to one of three psychotherapy groups, behavioural, cognitive, or insight-oriented psychodynamic. In the first study sixteen individual sessions ranged over a twelve-week period and in the second study sixteen to twenty sessions ranged over six weeks. The immediate outcome for all three therapies was similar, significant improvements had been made. However, in the earlier study, those patients who received insight-oriented therapy were significantly more depressed and showed a greater number of relapses at a one-year follow-up than those having the structured therapies.

A comparison between cognitive-behavioural and psychodynamic group therapy by Steur *et al.* (1984) showed significant improvements in reported and observed depressive symptoms in older adults in nine months of both types of treatment. Scores on the Beck Depression Inventory were better for the cognitive-behavioural group but this may have been an artefact of this measure which is designed to assess the negative thought patterns which cognitive therapy specifically addresses.

This research shows that psychological therapies can successfully treat depression in older people. There may be some evidence that more structured therapies are preferable with elderly people; perhaps the reconstruction of activity patterns in conjunction with attempting to alter negative cognitions can give some immunity to future depression. Hildebrand (1982), whilst using a psychodynamic approach, suggested that elderly people are often more willing to 'get on' with therapy than younger. Therefore, whilst more session time may be needed and encouragement to stick to the session content, a structured approach with goals clearly defined may be readily accepted.

RESPONDING TO DEPRESSION IN THE ELDERLY: WORKING WITHIN HOSPITAL AND COMMUNITY SETTINGS

The particular problems of elderly people range from their increased likelihood of experiencing ill-health and disability, with the associated risk of depression and possibility of idiosyncratic reactions to psychoactive drugs, to increased experiences of loss by bereavement or separation, by moving home, by losing status, by financial insecurity, and social role and activity reduction, many of which characterize the tasks of old age.

Multi-disciplinary teams can ensure that all agencies involved with the social, psychological, and medical needs of an elderly person are fully informed of problems which pre-exist, or develop during hospitalization, and of each agency's response to these problems. The multi-disciplinary team can challenge assumptions about the elderly person's functioning and needs. How often do we find that an individual cannot hear well yet has no hearing aid or discover that an individual has skills which are not being used?

The social worker may be in a strong position to help a depressed institutionalized client who suffers from a dementia. Their knowledge of the individual's family situation can be a tool for change. Families can feel that they are intruding on the institution's care of their elderly relative and this reduces their motivation to stay involved. Sometimes the social worker can negotiate with staff and family to find roles and responsibilities which relatives can undertake to provide social stimulation for the elderly person. Again the social worker can provide information on the person's background which can enable staff to relate to the individual's experience and preferences or to create an 'information pack' unique to that individual for reminiscence work.

Group work can be used to re-establish social functioning in depressed people, paying particular attention to group cohesion and group members' concern for one another. During hospitalization it is possible for the social worker to work with the individual and his or her family or friends, to encourage existing relationships to be perceived as more fulfilling and to develop them to assume a protective function against further depressive periods.

However, for many elderly people who have suffered multiple losses, or whose family relationships are poor, this may not be possible. Therefore, to offer effective treatment which may provide some immunity, the social worker may need to provide links with the community on an individual basis and to establish means of facilitating the development of intimate close relationships within the local community.

A community service providing for these needs must be locally based; proximity, with perceived age homogeneity and compatability being key factors in the development of strong relationships (Carey and Mapes, 1972). Health Centres may have facilities for therapeutic groups for depressed or bereaved elderly people. Such groups could both support patients following release from hospital and help to prevent admission for outpatients.

Prevention

The social worker is a rare breed and cannot reach all needy elderly people. However, there is a real need to act at a very early stage to prevent the onset of depression in vulnerable people and this may be achieved by making use of community resources and professional, voluntary, or self-help. Whilst the social worker cannot expect to teach therapy skills to everyone interested in working with the elderly in their area, workshops for interested statutory and voluntary agencies are a cost-effective method of increasing knowledge about experiences of ageing and encouraging the development of facilitating environments and activities. For example, introducing small changes such as arranging chairs in small groups for tea to encourage conversation, or encouraging listening to and valuing the elderly person's memories can create a more facilitating atmosphere for psychological health.

The use of group sessions such as reminiscence groups is not stigmatizing and these are easily run by non-professionals with some training and access to professional support, and can enable participation in a more personal way than the social events often organized for the elderly. A social event may not be sufficient stimulus to creating friendships and ineffective in addressing depression (Ames, 1990).

Getting to know something about another person's life can foster a sense of intimacy from which close relationships can develop. Learning about the experiences which the elderly person has lived through can change the attitude of people working with the elderly (Cook, 1986) leading to greater respect and understanding.

Many older people feel they have a devalued status; reminiscence groups can give back to the older person the 'expert' role by acknowledging their greater experience. In a similar way drama therapy has used story building from reminiscences to enable elderly people to regain a sense of self-esteem (Mazor, 1982). Mazor describes how by reenacting scenes from her past life a severely depressed woman was enabled to regain lost assertiveness.

For some elderly people their world may seem constricted to their own four walls. Lomranz et al. (1988) found that in older men levels of outdoor activity were related to well-being and indoor activity to depression. This stresses the need to enable older people to continue to get out to enjoy interests and social meetings even when physical disability makes walking or use of public transport difficult.

Scoggin et al. (1989) describe significant effects in aiding mild to moderate depression in older adults using a self-help cognitive therapy manual. This type of approach could be used to help individuals to understand their response to stressful situations and to use their coping skills to respond to them.

CONCLUSION

It is necessary to understand the past and present experiences, psychological, physical, and social, of an older person suffering from depression. Psychological treatments have been successful in alleviating symptoms, but, without sensitivity to the multiple influences upon that person, treatment is less likely to prevent reoccurrence.

The association of physical ill-health, frequent severe life events, and lack of a confiding relationship with onset of depressive symptoms requires a preventative and multi-disciplinary approach to work with the elderly; offering early attention to medical problems, support through difficult periods, and help to re-establish close relationships which may give protection from life's stresses.

REFERENCES

Akiskal, H. S. and McKinney, W. (1975) 'Overview of recent research into depression', *Archives of General Psychiatry*, 32, pp. 285–305.

Ames, D. (1990) 'Depression among elderly residents of Local Authority residential homes: Its nature and efficacy of intervention', *British Journal of Psychiatry*, 156, pp. 667–75.

Armstrong-Esther, C. A. and Browne, K. D. (1986) 'The influence of elderly patients' mental impairment on nurse–patient interaction', *Journal of Advanced Nursing,* 11, p. 397ff.

Beck, A. (1967) *Depression: Clinical, Experimental and Theoretical Aspects,* New York: Harper and Row Publishers Inc.

Bergmann, K. (1978) 'Neurosis and personality disorder in old age', in Isaacs, A. D. and Post, F. (eds.) *Studies in Geriatric Psychiatry,* Chichester, Wiley, pp. 41–77.

Bergmann, K. (1982) 'Depression in the elderly', *Recent Advances in Geriatric Medicine,* pp. 159–80.

Bibring, E. (1965) "The mechanism of depression', in Greenacre, P. (ed.) *Affective Disorders,* New York. International Universities Press.

Burnside, I. M. (1970) 'Loss: A constant theme in group work with the aged', *Hospital and Community Psychiatry,* 21, p. 173.

Busse, E. W. (1985) 'Normal aging: The Duke longitudinal studies', in Bergener, M., Ermini, M. and Stabelin, H. B. (eds.) *Thresholds in Aging,* New York, Academic Press.

Butler, R. (1963) 'The life review: An interpretation of life review in the elderly', *Psychiatry,* 26, pp. 65–76.

Carey, L. and Mapes, R. (1972) *The Sociology of Planning, a Study of Social Activity on New Housing Estates.* London, George Allen and Unwin.

Clayton, P., Halikas, J. and Maurice, W. (1972) 'The depression of widowhood', *British Journal of Psychiatry,* 120, pp. 71–7.

Coleman, P. G. (1986) *Ageing and Reminiscence Processes, Social and Clinical Implications,* Chichester, John Wiley.

Cook, D. A. (1986) *The Effect of Participation in Reminiscence Groups on Nurses' Attitudes,* Unpublished M.Sc. Thesis, Leicester University.

Cooper, D. E. (1984) 'Group psychotherapy with the elderly: Dealing with loss', *American Journal of Psychotherapy,* 38, pp. 203–18.

Emery, G. (1981) 'Cognitive therapy with the elderly', in Emery, G., Hollon, S. D. and Bedrosian, R. C. (eds.) *New Directions in Cognitive Therapy,* New York, Guildford.

Erikson, E. (1950) *Childhood and Society,* New York, W. W. Norton.

Fielden, M. (1990) 'Reminiscence as a therapeutic intervention with sheltered housing residents', *British Journal of Social Work,* 20, pp. 21–44.

Freud, S. (1917) 'Mourning and Melancholia', in *Collected Papers,* Hogarth Press 1950, 4, pp. 152–72.

Fry, P. S. (1983) 'Structured and unstructured reminiscence training and depression among the elderly', *Clinical Gerontologist,* 1(3), pp. 15–37.

Gallagher, D. E. and Thompson, L. W. (1983) 'Effectiveness of psychotherapy for both endogenous and nonendogenous depression in older adult outpatients', *Journal of Gerontology,* 38(6), pp. 707–12.

Gerner, R., Estabrook, W., Steur, J. and Jarvik, L. (1980) 'Treatment of geriatric depression with trazodone, imipramine and placebo—a double blind study', *Journal of Clinical Psychiatry,* 41, pp. 216–20.

Grossberg, G. T. and Nakra, B. R. S. (1986) 'Treatment of depression in the elderly', *Comprehensive Psychiatry,* 12(10), pp. 16–22.

Gurland, B. J., Wilder, D. E. and Berkman, C. (1988) 'Depression and disability in the elderly: Reciprocal relations and changes with age', *International Journal of Geriatric Psychiatry*, 3, pp. 163–79.

Harrison, R., Saula, A. and Kafetz, K. (1990) 'Dementia, depression and physical disability in a London borough: A survey of elderly people in and out of residential care and implications for future developments', *Age and Ageing*, 19, pp. 97–103.

Hildebrand, P. (1982) 'Psychotherapy with older patients', *British Journal of Medical Psychiatry*, 55, pp. 19–28.

Hildebrand, P. (1987) *Psychotherapy with the elderly*, Unpublished lecture, Tavistock Clinic, London.

Hussian, R. and Lawrence, P. (1981) 'Social reinforcement of activity and problem-solving training in the treatment of depressed institutionalised elderly patients', *Cognitive Therapy and Research*, 5(1), pp. 57–69.

Jones, R. (1986) *Depression in the elderly*, Unpublished lecture, Nottingham University Medical School.

Kendell, R. (1970) 'Relationship between aggression and depression: Epidemiological implications of a hypothesis', *Archives of General Psychiatry*, 22, pp. 308–18.

Lazarus, A. (1968) 'Learning theory and the treatment of depression', *Behaviour Research and Therapy*, 6, pp. 83–9.

Leff, M., Roatch, J. and Bunney, W. (1970) 'Environmental factors preceding the onset of severe depressions', *Psychiatry*, 33, pp. 293–311.

Lewinsohn, P. (1981) 'A behavioural approach to depression', in Friedman, R. and Katz, M. (eds.) *The Psychology of Depression: Contemporary theory and research*, Washington DC, US Government Printing House.

Lewis, C. (1971) 'Reminiscing and self-concept in old age', *Journal of Gerontology*, 21, pp. 240–3.

Lomranz, J., Bergman, S., Eyal, N. and Shmotkin, D. (1988) 'Indoor and outdoor activities of aged women and men as related to depression and well-being', *International Journal of Aging and Human Development*, 26(4), pp. 303–14.

Mazor, R. (1982) 'Drama therapy for the elderly in a day care center', *Hospital and Community Psychiatry*, 33(7), pp. 577–9.

Murphy, E. (1982) 'Social origins of depression in old age', *British Journal of Psychiatry*, 141, pp. 135–42.

Murphy, E. (1983) 'The prognosis of depression in old age', *British Journal of Psychiatry*, 142, pp. 111–19.

Murphy, E. (1985) 'The impact of depression in old age on close social relationships', *American Journal of Psychiatry*, 142, pp. 323–7.

Perotta, P. and Meacham, M. (1981) 'Can a reminiscing intervention alter depression and self-esteem?' *Aging and Human Development*, 14(1), pp. 23–30.

Post, F. (1985) 'Psychotherapy, electro-convulsive treatments, and longterm management for elderly depressives', *Journal of Affective Disorders*, Supplement 1, pp. S41–S45.

Robins, E. and Guze, S. (1970) 'Establishment of diagnostic validity in psychiatric illness: Its application to schizophrenia', *American Journal of Psychiatry*, 126, pp. 983–7.

Roth, R., Gurney, C. and Garside, R. (1972) 'Studies in the classification of affective disorders: The relationship between anxiety states and depressive illnesses', *British Journal of Psychiatry,* 121, pp. 147–66.

Saracino, J. (1978–79) 'Individual psychotherapy with the aged: a selective review', *International Journal of Ageing and Human Development,* 9(3), pp. 197–217.

Scoggin, F., Jameson, C. and Gochneaur, K. (1989) 'Comparative efficacy of cognitive and behavioural bibliotherapy for mildly and moderately depressed older adults', *Journal of Consulting and Clinical Psychology,* 57(3), pp. 403–7.

Seligman, M. (1975) *Helplessness: on Depression, Development and Death,* San Francisco, W. H. Freeman.

Steur, J. and Hammen, C. L. (1983) 'Cognitive behavioural group therapy for the depressed elderly: issues and adaptations', *Cognitive Therapy and Research,* 7, pp. 285–96.

Steur, J., Mintz, J., Hammen, C., Hill, M. A., Jarvik, L. F., McCarley, T., Motoike, P. and Rosen, R. (1984) 'Cognitive behavioural and psychodynamic group psychotherapy in treatment of geriatric depression', *Journal of Consulting and Clinical Psychology,* 52(2), pp. 180–9.

Storr, A. (1979) *The Art of Psychotherapy,* London, Secker and Warburg.

Surtees, P. (1980) 'Social support, residual adversity and depressive outcome', *Social Psychiatry,* 15, pp. 71–80.

Taylor, S. E. (1979) 'Hospital patient behaviour: Reactance, helplessness, or control?' *Journal of Social Issues,* 35, pp. 156–84.

Thompson, L. W., Gallagher, D. and Steinmetz-Breckenbridge, J. (1987) 'Comparative effectiveness of psychotherapies for depressed elders', *Journal of Consulting and Clinical Psychology,* 55(3), pp. 385–90.

Weissman, M., Fox, K. and Klerman, G. (1971) 'Hostility and depression associated with suicide attempts', *American Journal of Psychiatry,* 130, pp. 450–5.

Wolpe, J. (1971) 'Neurotic depression: experimental analog, clinical syndromes and treatment', *American Journal of Psychotherapy,* 25, pp. 362–8.

Woods, R and Britton, P. (1985) *Clinical Psychology with the Elderly,* London, Croom Helm.

CHAPTER 36

A THERAPEUTIC CONFRONTATION APPROACH TO TREATING PATIENTS WITH FACTITIOUS ILLNESS

Kenneth R. Wedel

Factitious illness has received attention in the medical literature for a number of years. Broadly defined, this diagnosis includes patients who, for a variety of little-understood reasons, simulate real patterns of illness and/or symptomatology suggesting real illness. The illness ranges in severity from the so-called "Munchausen's syndrome," a term applied to patients who chronically wander from hospital to hospital seeking admission by distorting their medical histories, to self-induced simulated disease or common malingering.

Petersdorf and Bennett have described the most commonly used methods of creating factitious fevers.[1] Patients may hold the thermometer next to a hot water bottle, steam pipe, light bulb, flame, and the like; shake it; or produce a higher reading by rubbing the teeth, gums, or anal sphincter. Another method is to substitute the thermometer offered by the nurse with one from a cache of thermometers that the patient has set at various readings. Patients have also been known to inject themselves with vaccines, toxoids, and pyrogenic substances to produce a real fever.

A comprehensive review of the literature on factitious illness has been made by Spiro, who found the psychiatric literature contained only three reports of factitious illness.[2] The medical literature, however, described thirty-eight cases with various pre-

---

Reprinted from *Social Work,* Vol. 16, No. 2 (1971), pp. 69–73, by permission of the publisher.

[1] Robert G. Petersdorf and Ivan L. Bennett, "Factitious Fever," *Annals of Internal Medicine,* Vol. 46, No. 6 (June 1957), pp. 1039–1062.

[2] Herzl R. Spiro, "Chronic Factitious Illness," *Archives of General Psychiatry,* Vol. 18, No. 5 (May 1968), pp. 569–579.

senting symptomatology. The behavior of these patients in the hospital was characterized by uncooperativeness and hostility. Following diagnosis of factitious illness, their
most common reaction was to sign out of the hospital against advice. Only sixteen of
the thirty-eight patients were seen by a psychiatrist, and generally the motivating factors for the illness were not discussed.

A central theme in the literature is the hostility of hospital staff toward the patient
that is common when factitious illness is diagnosed, with immediate hospital discharge prompted by either the patient or the physician as the result. One approach to
the control of serious factitious illness is the "blackbook"—a list of names kept in
hospital emergency rooms to identify patients who chronically wander from hospital
to hospital. English physicians have sometimes initiated legal action when all other
methods have failed.[3] In general, the literature emphasizes both the waste of valuable
medical resources and the human and economic loss to such patients and their families.[4]

THE STUDY

Ten patients took part in the clinical study of fever of unknown origin conducted at the
Clinical Center, National Institute of Allergy and Infectious Diseases, National Institutes of Health.[5] Seven of the patients were female and ranged in age from 16 to 41
years. The three male patients were much younger: two were 11 years old and the
other was 13. Five of the patients worked in medically oriented occupations: three
were registered nurses, one was a pharmacist, and one was a medical laboratory technician. Psychiatric diagnoses and social histories did not reveal any common characteristics among the patients, but five of them had recently experienced a death, tragic
accident, or severe illness in the family. Follow-up data were available for five patients;
of that group, four made a satisfactory readjustment, as measured by completion of
recommended psychotherapy and freedom from factitious illness, and one patient refused to be seen by the consulting psychiatrist and left the hospital against medical advice when her factitious illness was verified. She later died under circumstances that
suggested suicide.

At the Clinical Center it has been found that a multidisciplinary approach involving
medicine, nursing, social work, and psychiatry is most successful in working with patients exhibiting factitious illness. Central to the approach is the recognition that factitious illness represents the patient's attempt to cope with emotional problems. Although
the patient may not acknowledge or recognize that his problems are emotional, he
has managed to convey his desperate need for help by placing himself in the hands of
physicians and other hospital staff. An understanding response by the staff makes it
possible for this disguised request to become more direct and opens the door to treatment planning.

---

[3] P. Blackwell, "Munchausen at Guy's," *Guy's Hospital Report,* Vol. 114, No. 3 (1965), pp. 257–277.
[4] Joseph J. Bunim et al., "Factitious Diseases: Clinical Staff Conference at the National Institutes of Health," *Annals of Internal Medicine,* Vol. 48, No. 6 (June 1958), pp. 1328–1341; and Spiro, op. cit.
[5] The study began in 1960, and of the 175 patients seen to date, ten were found to have factitious illness.

CONFRONTATION PROCESS

The first step in the confrontation process is the search for organic disease. As organic causes for fever are ruled out, suspicion grows that the illness may be factitious. Clues that signal the possibility of factitious fever to the ward physician are the absence of laboratory data to substantiate fever and an unusual fever pattern. To determine whether the patient may be switching thermometers or manipulating them in order to produce a high reading, the nurse remains with the patient while his temperature is being taken. The serial numbers of thermometers also may be checked. A room search by the ward physician and head nurse has revealed substitute thermometers, unauthorized drugs and chemicals, and needles and syringes in some cases.

Following the verification of factitious illness, the ward physician requests a psychiatric evaluation. The psychiatrist is asked for (1) an analysis of the patient's personality dynamics together with a diagnostic impression, and (2) advice and assistance when the patient is confronted with his factitious illness. Particular attention is paid to any contraindications to confrontation, such as the risk of suicidal or psychotic behavior.

After the psychiatric evaluation is completed, a meeting of the patient, senior staff physician, ward physician, head nurse, social worker, and psychiatrist is held so that the senior staff physician (who has primary responsibility for the patient) can confront the patient with the factitious nature of his illness. The patient is given an opportunity to react after the confrontation. Frequently his reaction will be one of defensive anger, which is usually directed at the confronter, i.e., the senior staff physician, who serves as a lightning rod for the patient's emotions. Because the patient's intense initial need to storm and protest is accepted, he usually will not need to vent his angry feelings later on staff members who must give him day-to-day care. As a result, they are able to offer support to the patient as he goes through the difficult period of readjustment. At the conclusion of the meeting, the patient is reassured that he will have time to come to terms with the experience and plan for his return home.

During the confrontation a redefinition of the illness takes place for both patient and staff. Prior to this, the major goal was to diagnose an organic cause for the fever. Following confrontation, the goal of medical care is to interrupt effectively the patient's maladaptive behavior pattern. To be successful in this, the confrontation process must be firm, but gentle and nonpunitive. The patient must be helped to remain in the hospital long enough to work through the worst of his feelings of rage and shame, to begin reconstructing his shattered self-image, and to experience the staff's continued acceptance of him as a person who is worthy of concern and has not wholly forfeited the staff's trust.

SOCIAL WORK PRACTICE

Social work services are provided for all patients admitted to the study. Contacts early in the patient's hospitalization are valuable because (1) the broad diagnostic category "fever of unknown origin" may encompass a number of serious illnesses or it may mask emotional problems, (2) a final diagnosis of factitious illness is a possibility, and (3) the exhaustive medical workup may in itself be a source of anxiety and stress. The casework relationship is an important tool in cases of fever of unknown origin, but the worker recognizes that most of these patients are unable to form mature and trusting interpersonal relationships and they will relate in different ways—some will be guarded and defensive, while others will reach out for understanding and sympathy. The worker also avoids probing to uncover the patient's underlying feelings in order to minimize disruption of emotional defenses essential to the patient's functioning. Attacking these defenses would only increase the patient's resistance and blunt the relationship. Thus the initial treatment goal is to support the patient through the medical diagnostic workup, to convey the worker's commitment to him as a person, and to develop a contact with enough meaning to the patient so that the worker can help him when his defenses are breached by the confrontation procedure.

If the social worker has succeeded in developing a firm supportive relationship with the patient, it is helpful for him to be present at the actual confrontation. His presence can be regarded as a commitment to be with the patient during a difficult time. The worker has heretofore been accepting of the patient's emotional defenses and is not an active participant in the confrontation, but his presence symbolizes his alliance with the goal of medical treatment—the interruption of maladaptive behavior patterns. As a witness, he is better able to handle the patient's subsequent need to distort the intent of the confrontation.

Once the confrontation has taken place, the social worker shares with the rest of the staff a number of therapeutic tasks, all of them carried out in a spirit of acceptance and continuing concern. The patient feels stripped and may be tearful, anxious, or storming. He may cloak his sense of shame and helplessness in attacking or defensive behavior, or he may withdraw; however, his feelings of being worthless and untrustworthy nevertheless come through. The social worker and other staff members can help the patient handle his sharp and conflicting feelings about the confrontation. He will need a "winding down" period for self-reassessment and for consideration of the treatment recommendations, and his heightened anxiety often can be used constructively to help him accept psychotherapy—a concrete step in relinquishing old patterns. Arrangements for psychotherapy after discharge are usually made by the patient and the local referring physician. In some cases the social worker may assist with these referral arrangements, but his most important function is to be a source of support and encouragement to the patient. He may also be called on to help the patient's family understand the patient's illness in terms of his emotional needs and problems.

ILLUSTRATIVE CASE

The case of Mrs. A, a 39-year-old registered nurse admitted for fever of unknown origin, illustrates the confrontation approach to treatment. Her medical history revealed numerous hospitalizations in the past for excision of a benign cyst of the breast, hysterectomy, suture granuloma of the colon, hiatal hernia, cystitis, gastritis, and fever of unknown origin. During the year prior to her most recent admission, the patient suffered from fever with associated aches and pains and had been unable to work.

Social work contacts with Mrs. A began at the time of admission. In early interviews she was friendly but guarded when talking about her life situation. As the casework relationship developed, she expressed concern that even the experts would not find the source of her illness. She also disclosed that she had not advanced professionally to her satisfaction because she was unable to get along with superiors. However, she was quick to deny that her medical or employment history indicated any adjustment problems. Despite the system of denial and superficiality maintained by the patient, she seemed to regard the social worker as a safe person with whom she could share negative feelings about the unpleasant aspects of hospitalization.

Shortly after admission, the nursing staff discovered that Mrs. A was substituting thermometers each time her temperature was taken. In order to confirm this, the serial numbers of thermometers given to the patient were compared with those on the thermometers handed back. This documented information was kept in the patient's medical record.

The diagnostic medical evaluation revealed no organic basis for the patient's fever. The psychiatric evaluation described her as a fairly rigid individual with many dependency needs and a strong defense of denial concerning her psychosomatic illness. No evidence of psychotic or prepsychotic behavior was found.

In a meeting with the senior staff physician, ward physician, head nurse, and social worker, the patient was confronted with the fact that she had been switching thermometers. A nonaccusatorial, understanding, straightforward approach was used by the senior staff physician to describe the staff's concern about her. The patient was told that there were no physiological findings to explain her illness and her behavior indicated she needed therapy for her emotional problems. Furthermore, she would be given ample time to consider the recommendation for therapy and to make plans for her return home.

During the confrontation the patient maintained her composure and insisted that she did not understand the matter of differing serial numbers because she had not switched thermometers. She was not questioned further about this and was allowed to save face when the senior staff physician indicated that several laboratory tests would be repeated to confirm past findings.

Following the confrontation, Mrs. A became markedly anxious, began weeping, and remained in her room. After she had regained her composure somewhat, she verbalized to the social worker her anger toward the senior staff physician for saying that she had switched thermometers. She continued to deny that she had switched them and wondered how anyone could now believe her. How could she face the nurses who would soon arrive for the evening shift? Several hours after the confrontation, however, she confided individually to the head nurse, senior staff physician, and social worker that she actually had switched thermometers because she believed she must have a fever if her physical ailment were to be given sincere consideration.

Following the confrontation, hospital care was continued for several days so that Mrs. A could prepare for her return home and make preliminary plans for the future. She was able to make constructive use of the casework relationship by discussing her fears and misconceptions concerning psychotherapy, which helped to reduce her ambivalence about accepting the recommended treatment. She was doubtful that her former supervisors would approve of her undertaking psychiatric treatment and felt her future employability would be jeopardized if she did so. With encouragement, however, she contacted her own physician, who assured her he would not divulge the factitious nature of her illness to her former employer and would arrange for her to obtain therapy in her own community.

CONCLUSION

Factitious illness is an expression of a complex network of psychosocial and physiological factors that are not clearly understood. It is clear, however, that this illness is not merely a malicious hoax perpetrated by the patient; it is the desperate plea for help of a person who has been unable to devise a better solution for his emotional problems.

A hospital team that understands the message of the patient's behavior and has a treatment plan geared to his emotional needs will not react with hostility toward the patient or punish him through premature discharge. The primary social work contribution to treatment is to develop a relationship with the patient that will help carry him through the difficult period of confrontation with the factitious nature of his illness. Following confrontation, this sympathetic but reality-based support sustains the patient as he struggles to abandon modes of behavior that have been so damaging to him.

CHAPTER 37

DRUGS, DIALOGUE, OR DIET

Diagnosing and Treating the Hyperactive Child

Harriette C. Johnson

For the past two decades, the hyperactive child has generated controversy. Debates have centered around whether a hyperactive syndrome exists[1]; whether its etiology is physiological or psychogenic[2]; and whether medication, diet, behavior modification, cognitive therapy, family systems therapy, or psychodynamic psychotherapy is the treatment of choice.[3]

Children with attention deficits, hyperactivity, and associated characteristics are seen in a multitude of settings. An inventory of the settings in which social workers practice undoubtedly would reveal that most social workers are likely to encounter children with attention deficit hyperactivity disorder (ADHD). ADHD is common. According to DSM-III-R estimates, approximately 3 percent of children have been diagnosed as having the disorder. Other estimates have ranged from less than 1 percent to 14.3 percent. ADHD occurs more frequently in boys than in girls (3:1 to 10:1).[4]

WHAT IS ADHD?

According to DSM-III-R criteria, ADHD refers to a condition in which developmentally inappropriate degrees of inattention, impulsiveness, and hyperactivity are evident.[5] Children diagnosed with the disorder generally display disturbance in each of these areas, but to varying degrees. These disturbances can be pervasive, appearing at home, at school, at work, or in social situations. Sometimes they are situational, occurring in only one situation; that is, only at home or only at school.

Reprinted from *Social Work,* Vol. 33, No. 4 (July–August 1988), pp. 349–355, by permission of NASW Press. Copyright 1988, National Association of Social Workers, Inc., *Social Work.*

Opinions vary as to whether there is a distinct hyperactive or attention deficit syndrome.[6] The DSM-III-R classification represents an interim working hypothesis that such a syndrome can be defined. The author uses the DSM-III-R definition despite recognition that the medical model might better be replaced by a systems (biopsychosocial or ecological) conceptual framework. In addition, the author recognizes the concerns raised by Kutchins and Kirk about the possible pitfalls of assigning DSM-III labels.[7]

Nevertheless, there are several reasons for using the DSM-III-R typology of ADHD. First, there is no other well-developed definition. The dimensional approach advocated by Shekim and colleagues may become an alternative.[8] Their approach involves obtaining a behavioral profile of the child that emphasizes dimensions of social competence, as compared with the categorical approach of DSM-III-R. However, the dimensional approach needs further development and validation.

Second, social and cultural factors appear not to influence significantly the manifestations of ADHD. Children meeting criteria for ADHD in affluent suburbs look remarkably similar to ADHD children in poor, inner-city schools.

Third, the diagnosis of ADHD is related strongly to treatment recommendations. Children who meet criteria for ADHD respond predictably to certain treatments.

Fourth, despite varying opinions about DSM-III-R classifications, these groups represent a consensus among many clinicians who deal continually with ADHD children and who comprise reputable researchers and clinical practitioners in the area of ADHD. There is no equivalent work or even an approximation of it by social workers. For these reasons, our consideration of ADHD is based on DSM-III-R criteria.

Manifestations

ADHD appears first in early childhood. Often the condition is not recognized until the child enters school although characteristics of ADHD may be present during the preschool years. Children with ADHD talk excessively and loudly, interrupt adults and other children, blurt out answers to questions before the question has been stated completely, do not listen, are poor at following directions, produce careless or messy work, fail to wait for their turn in group situations or to follow the rules in structured games, fidget, wiggle, and manipulate objects. ADHD children may shift frequently from one activity to another and intrude on other family members. Often, ADHD children show accident-prone behavior. They may knock items over, grab objects (not maliciously), and engage in potentially dangerous actions without stopping to think about the consequences, such as running into the street without looking or riding a skateboard over rough terrain. Adolescents often display impulsive behavior by initiating spur-of-the-moment activities instead of carrying out previous commitments (for example, going for a ride with friends instead of doing homework).

Other characteristics of children with ADHD often include low self-esteem, mood lability, low frustration tolerance, temper tantrums, and poor social judgment. Most ADHD children are underachievers academically.[9]

Two brief vignettes represent typical ADHD histories:

Karen is a 6-year-old girl referred to a local child guidance clinic by the school social worker. She jumps out of her seat, talks out of turn, picks fights with other children, and does not listen to the teacher. She is rude frequently to adults as well as children.

Joey is a 9-year-old boy with a lifelong history of overactivity, temper tantrums, distractibility, disruptive behavior at school, frequent fighting, and argumentativeness with adults. He torments his sisters. He threw a brick at his 7-year-old sister in a fit of temper, narrowly missing her head. He scares his 2-year-old sister by telling her a bear is going to eat her up. Joey often lies and appears to enjoy getting other children into trouble. Sometimes he steals money from his parents. He has been caught shoplifting twice. Joey has been staying out at night, throwing soda cans on the next door neighbors' front walk, and teasing their dog by tying a tee shirt around its head.

In the case vignettes, ADHD is Karen's sole diagnosis. Joey, however, has overlapping diagnoses. He meets criteria both for conduct disorder and ADHD.

ADHD typically persists throughout childhood and frequently continues into and through adulthood. Adults with ADHD have problems with inattention and impulsivity, difficulty organizing and completing work, and trouble in following instructions. A childhood history of ADHD is sometimes a precursor to adult diagnosis of borderline personality disorder.[10] Some predictions of a poor outcome of childhood ADHD are coexisting conduct disorder, low intelligence quotient, and severe mental disorder in the parents.[11]

ETIOLOGY OF ADHD

Although a few reviewers are unconvinced about the biological etiology of ADHD, there is vast evidence pointing to biological underpinnings for ADHD.[12] However, currently it is unknown which biological etiologies give rise to particular behaviors or clinical symptoms. The lack of specific association may mean that the hyperkinetic syndrome is not a unitary disorder on a biological level, and therefore should be subdivided into etiological categories. The hyperkinetic outcome may represent a common pathway of biological disturbance resulting from exposure to toxins, brain damage, genetic transmission, and even early social deprivation.[13] Many technologies developed recently have added new evidence to support the belief that brain dysfunction is a major determinant of ADHD symptomatology.[14]

A wide range of possible etiological events and conditions can lead to ADHD. Perinatal hypoxia (insufficient oxygen around the time of birth) or hypoxia at later ages can cause minimal brain damage that shows up several years later as ADHD. Genetic factors also have been related to ADHD. Other causative factors have included head injury, environmental toxins, such as lead and radiation, maturational lag, food sensitivity, malnutrition, hormone imbalance and other disturbances of body chemistry, and several specific medical and neurological syndromes. Reviews of literature on the etiology of ADHD are available elsewhere.[15]

ADHD ASSESSMENT AND DIAGNOSIS

Several methods are used to assess children who exhibit characteristics of ADHD: interviews with the parents; interviews with and observation of the child; behavior-rating scales completed by parents, teachers, and significant others in the child's life; physical examination; neurological examination; allergy evaluation; psychological testing; and laboratory studies. Parent and child interviews and behavior rating scales are used most often.[16] Psychological testing is valuable for determining the specific nature of the child's deficits and strengths.[17]

To be diagnosed as having ADHD, a child must display a certain number of characteristics typical of ADHD and must not meet criteria for certain other diagnoses (notably pervasive developmental disorder and manic depressive disorder). That is, the latter diagnoses preempt a diagnosis of ADHD. Other diagnoses, such as conduct disorder and oppositional defiant disorder, are carried concurrently with ADHD.[18]

The basic tools for making a diagnosis are history and description of the problem. A careful medical, behavioral, and psychosocial history is necessary in all cases of overactivity, attention deficit, or disruptive behavior. Behavior rating scales, which the parents and teachers complete, are an important tool for recording the child's history.

Neurological Examination

The neurological examination has been the subject of ongoing debate. It is used to identify brain lesions caused by trauma, stroke, tumor, or other diseases. The neurological examination includes several procedures: physical examination; special-instrument tests (electroencephalogram [EEG], computed axial tomography [CAT], or positron emission transverse tomography [PETT]); and tests requiring minor surgical procedures (lumbar puncture, Wada test, pneumoencephalogram, angiogram, brain surgery, and biopsy).

There are arguments against routine use of the neurological examination. First, when lesions are present in ADHD (there are many causes of ADHD other than brain lesions), the lesion is likely to be subtle. Consequently, the standard examination often produces negative findings even when brain lesions are suspected based on other evidence.

Second, EEG provides limited information. Only about one-third of the brain is available to electroencephalography; 5 to 15 percent of normal adults show deviant EEGs, and EEG recordings are affected by many factors other than brain pathology. More specialized EEG techniques do produce findings with higher validity. The CAT scan and PETT scan are composite X-ray pictures that allow the structures and physiological processes of the brain to be viewed, respectively. These tests are potent but expensive tools for diagnosing brain lesions. Consequently, it is doubtful whether they should be used when the choice of treatment does not differ according to the findings, as is frequently the case in ADHD. Because minor surgical procedures can be extremely uncomfortable and anxiety-provoking, their use is justified only in the minority of cases in which the outcome makes a difference in treatment. If treatment is stimulant medication plus additional psychological services, knowing the results of such tests might satisfy the provider but not really benefit the client.

On the other hand, the neurological examination appears to be indicated when history suggests seizure activity that warrants consideration of anticonvulsant medication. Also, there is the rare situation in which an expanding lesion is present and detecting it may be crucial to treating a potentially life-threatening condition. Several conditions suggest the need for neurological examination—history of head injury, perinatal hypoxia, or other neurological insult—are not uncommon for ADHD children.[19] Symptoms such as loss of balance, altered state of consciousness, memory lapse or blackout, unusual sensory or motor experience, automatic behavior (petit mal seizure) suggest subtle seizure phenomena.[20] Other indicators for neurological examination are marked discrepancies in psychological test data on the Wechsler Intelligence Scale for Children (WISC), Bender Gestalt, lateralization tests, projective tests, or in neuropsychological testing; a disruptive emotional state or sudden emotional change not commensurate with precipitating events; and physical symptoms such as sleep disturbance.[21] Ravenous hunger or thirst, alteration in sexual appetite, or a report by the patient of a gradual alteration in vision, hearing, touch, motor control, or skills such as driving, typing, or playing a musical instrument are other conditions that may warrant a neurological examination.[22] The author concurs with Small that the nonmedical service provider should develop a working relationship with a neurologist to obtain telephone consultation before referring a client for a neurological examination, thus avoiding unnecessary referrals.[23]

Also controversial are the "soft signs," indicators that arouse suspicion of neurological pathology, but are associated with very slightly discernible dysfunction only. The list of possible soft signs is long. In general, it includes minor physical anomalies of the head, face, feet, and hands; minor motor abnormalities or poor coordination; impaired perception of symbols or objects; visual or hearing deficits; grimacing; involuntary movement; abnormally weak or strong muscle, clumsiness, or tremor. Small argues that identification of soft signs has value in pointing at times to serious conditions.[24]

Psychological Testing

Now, psychological tests used to assess children with ADHD are numerous, varied, and highly specific. Psychoeducational testing (not to be confused with psychoeducational approaches to family therapy) explores cognitive functioning in relation to patterns of lateral cerebral dominance (that is, which side of the brain manages which functions). Psychodiagnostic testing reveals the emotional impact of ADHD. Neuropsychological tests illuminate an array of brain–behavior relationships, notably sensory, motor, intrasensory, language, and other higher-level cognitive processes. Intelligence tests are used in relation to these other three areas of exploration.[25]

Allergy Evaluation

If a child diagnosed with ADHD also has a history of allergy, the practitioner should explore a possible connection between the child's problem behavior and sensitivity reaction to ingested or environmental substances. Allergy or idiosyncratic toxic reaction can be a major or contributory factor to ADHD symptoms.

Two types of specialists evaluate allergy: (1) traditional allergists who use widely accepted procedures, such as skin tests to discover the allergens; and (2) holistic practitioners, who use, in addition to traditional methods, more controversial methods, such as hair analysis (to detect high levels of heavy metals); sublingual testing (in which the child holds soluble extracts of substances under the tongue to see if allergic responses occur); and cytotoxic testing (white blood cells are mixed with various food extracts and the chemical responses noted).[26] Holistic practitioners criticize traditional allergists for overlooking many possible factors; traditional allergists criticize holistic practitioners for using invalid and unreliable testing procedures. Some traditional allergists do not attribute symptoms of behavioral disturbance to an allergic process. As with most practitioners, individual biases often determine etiological inferences and treatment recommendations.

The four-day fast is the most reliable and valid method for detecting ingested allergens that can be implemented at home (four days is usually required for the body to eliminate traces of foods). Foods are reintroduced one-by-one to determine which ones produce allergic symptoms. The fast is difficult to implement because of the discomfort the individual experiences by not eating. A trial-and-error method involving elimination of food while continuing to eat other foods, then reintroducing the eliminated foods, sometimes is successful in detecting culprits. Because a person usually is allergic to more than one substance, identifying the culprits through trial and error is difficult.

TREATING ADHD

Many studies have been conducted on treatment for ADHD. More than 100 controlled studies were completed before 1977 and unknown numbers more have been completed since that time.[27] The findings of several of the best designed and most rigorously controlled studies support numerous conclusions.[28]

Stimulant Medication

Stimulant medication is the most effective single treatment for ADHD. No other single treatment approaches the use of stimulants in efficacy. Although no precise information on the rate of agreement concerning this finding is available, it is a view accepted by most researchers and clinicians working with ADHD.[29] Among the stimulants, methylphenidate (RITALIN®) generally is considered the drug of choice.

Methylphenidate is available now in generic form at half or less the cost of RITALIN. About 70 to 80 percent of children diagnosed with ADHD respond favorably to stimulants; many show dramatic improvement.[30] Stimulants decrease motor activity, fighting and provocative behaviors, negativism and argumentativeness, and increase attention span and ability to listen. That is, they make hyperactive children more like other children.

Parents often tell practitioners they tried medication for a while but it did not work. The statement may be accepted as evidence that medication should not be considered as a treatment option, without first questioning the dosage; whether the treating physician had titrated the dosage until a therapeutic level (favorable response) was achieved; whether some interference with absorption of the medication had occurred, due to drinking milk around the time of administration, and whether the parents had complied with the instructions for administering the medication.

Most persons who have seen the dramatic effects of stimulant medication on a stimulant-responsive child are impressed by the difference before and after medication. The
unmedicated child typically is heard above all the others in the room; frequently provokes or teases other children; often is the center of turmoil; seems impervious to
instructions from adults; demands immediate gratification; and often is defiant, negativistic, and bossy.

When children take medication, they respond appropriately, and are able to follow
directions and complete tasks. Oppositional, argumentative, and noisy behavior subsides. If the correct medication or dosage is prescribed, they are not apathetic and sad—
they retain a normal level of animation and interest. There is no evidence that either
stimulant medication or behavior therapy transforms hyperactive children into overly
compliant, unspontaneous children.[31] Lethargy may indicate too high a dosage or the
wrong medication.

Methylphenidate

Methylphenidate has positive rippling effects on interpersonal relationships as it reverses a spiral of negative interactions between ADHD children and their parents,
teachers, and peers. Barkley, Karlsson, and colleagues wanted to test the hypothesis
that mothers' childbearing practices generated the ADHD behaviors in their children.[32]
They observed that children diagnosed with ADHD who were not on medication were
less compliant, more obstinate, negativistic, and resistant to commands, and that they
spent more time in off-task behavior than did normal controls. Their mothers, by contrast, were more controlling and directive than were mothers toward normal children.
Mothers of hyperactive children were more depressed, had more marital discord, and
more family psychiatric disturbance than did mothers of controls.

The investigators found that children greatly improved when treated with methylphenidate, and, as a result, their mothers decreased their commands and increased
expressions of approval and rewards. That is, the mothers' unfavorable behaviors
were a response to, not the cause of, the children's oppositional and negativistic behavior. The use of methylphenidate to treat the children also produced positive changes in
mothers' behavior.

In another study of the effects of methylphenidate on interpersonal relations, 42
boys diagnosed with ADHD were compared with 42 normal controls. The boys
diagnosed with ADHD were controlling and dominating, overactive, and off-task before receiving the medication. After receiving the medication, their controlling and
dominating behavior decreased, on-task behavior increased, activity level decreased,
and the boys showed improved visual–motor performance. Normal peers displayed reciprocal reductions in controlling and dominating behavior, activity level, and on-task
behavior. That is, improving the interpersonal behaviors of the ADHD boys also improved the responses of normal peers to those boys.[33]

Medication can reverse negative feedback loops into positively reinforcing interpersonal sequences—one indication that withholding medication can be very toxic psychologically. Collusion between parents fearful of medication and clinicians opposed to its
use may create a situation in which medication is never given a carefully monitored
trial; rather, it is dismissed quickly as not working or just suppressing symptoms, not

treating the causes. Hence, the child and family may be deprived of effective treatment, and the child may suffer years of social rejection or academic failure, which could have been avoided or lessened by medication. Clinicians are justified in being concerned about the use of medication; however, withholding medication from the 70 to 80 percent of stimulant-responsive children can have very damaging psychosocial effects.[34]

Other Medications

In addition, other medications have been used with ADHD: tricyclic antidepressants; pemoline (CYLERT®); clonidine; neuroleptics; and amino acids. When methylphenidate is ineffective or inappropriate, other medications are tried.[35]

Multimodal Interventions

Multimodal interventions that include medication lead to more favorable outcomes than treatment by medication alone. ADHD children have multiple difficulties (behavioral, cognitive, social, and emotional) requiring multifaceted responses.[36] Recent research strongly supports multimodal treatment for ADHD. The Satterfield group demonstrated that a combination of treatment is more effective.[37] Generally, the treatments are selected according to the apparent needs of each child and family. Although proponents of behavior therapy have reported benefits, evidence suggests that behavior therapy is helpful only when combined with medication.[38] Cognitive problem-solving skills training also has proven useful in conjunction with medication.[39] However, there is no support for the claims that either psychodynamically oriented therapy (play therapy) or structural and strategic family therapy have positive effects on manifestations of ADHD. Psychodynamic and family systems therapies should be used cautiously, if at all, when the presenting problem is symptoms of ADHD because of several possible iatrogenic effects.[40] Reframing ADHD as a family problem victimizes parents by reinforcing feelings of guilt and inadequacy, and harms children by emphasizing a treatment approach that is ineffective for ADHD in lieu of other treatments that are. By contrast, psychoeducational family therapy that emphasizes parent education and instruction in management techniques offers promise as part of a multimodal approach to treating ADHD.[41]

Side Effects

Serious side effects are almost unknown. Practitioners, especially from nonmedical disciplines, often are reluctant to prescribe medication for children. However, emphasis is very strong that the only long-term side effect of methylphenidate and amphetamine, in some children, is minor delay in growth, a consequence of long-term use of the medication that can be overcome by drug holidays. Short-term effects may include appetite suppression or difficulty getting to sleep. Both problems can be minimized by management, that is, taking the medication after meals and giving the last dosage in the early afternoon so that it has worn off by bedtime.[42] Very rare side effects, such as tachycardia, and stereotyped behavior, such as nailbiting, have been reported but were eliminated by discontinuance of the drug.[43] The negative response that methylphenidate has received in the popular media is unwarranted by the evidence, but unfortunately is likely to deter families and uninformed professionals from using a treatment that can dramatically improve the quality of life for both the child and his or her family.

Diet

Treatment by diet may help a few ADHD children. This method is appealing because of legitimate concern about the possible harmful effects of medication. For children in which ADHD is a reaction to substances in the diet, it is clearly desirable to treat with diet rather than with medication. However, the symptoms of most children diagnosed with ADHD arise from one of many possible causes other than allergic or toxic responses to substances in food. For these children, the Feingold diet (or other diets) will not alleviate symptoms of ADHD. However, stimulants may be effective even when an unknown food sensitivity is the cause, because the chemical properties of stimulants that diminish chemical imbalances arising from, for example, genetic propensity or the presence of scar tissue in the brain, also may diminish the chemical imbalances arising from allergic or toxic reactions.

There is a possible danger that medication may conceal a food sensitivity by suppressing symptoms. The only way to find out is to withhold medication and implement the stringent four-day fast.

In addition to the difficulty in carrying out this detective work, treatment by dietary restriction usually is hard to enforce. A single infraction may bring on ADHD symptoms, and few children can resist goodies that others are having. Children do not like the Feingold diet,[44] and predictably also will dislike other restrictive diets. However, Wender[45] and Varley[46] do not recommend contravening parents' wishes to pursue diet as a treatment, because cursory dismissal of the diet is likely to prevent development of a therapeutic alliance with parents.

Short-Term Effects

The positive effects of stimulants on the behavior itself are limited to the time period during which the medication is active (between two-and-one-half to four hours unless sustained release form is used). These effects are reversible; as soon as the medication wears off, the child reverts to the premedication state. There is no cure for most cases of ADHD.

Long-Term Outcomes

Young children treated with stimulant medication for at least three years did better in some areas as young adults than hyperactive children who had not received medication. They had fewer car accidents, a more positive view of their childhood, and better social skills and self-esteem than untreated counterparts. However, they functioned similarly to untreated hyperactives in school, work, and with respect to prevalence of personality disorders.[47] The failure of medication to improve long-term prospects in these areas, when used without other services and only for certain periods during the growing up years, should not be surprising. Children with ADHD have multiple difficulties over many years of childhood and adolescence that require multimodal, not single, interventions.

About 50 percent of hyperactive children have continuing difficulties as adults, particularly with impulsivity, restlessness, and poor social skills that range from mild to severe.[48] Yet most hyperactive children do grow up without major psychopathology. Almost none becomes psychotic; a few develop antisocial personality disorder.

Antisocial Behavior

The antisocial behavior of most hyperactive adolescents appears transitory. High rates of antisocial behavior are seen in hyperactive children during adolescence (25 to 50 percent); but this rate drops significantly in adulthood, in contrast to rates of adult antisocial behavior for antisocial children.[49]

Contrary to popular belief, methylphenidate continues to be effective in adolescent ADHD in reducing inattentiveness, disobedience, and aggressivity.[50] Side effects are rare, and there is no evidence that stimulant therapy predisposes to illicit drug use. In addition to the practice implications for use of medication, psychotherapeutic approaches, and diet, some general principles of practice should be noted.

ADDITIONAL IMPLICATIONS FOR SOCIAL WORK PRACTICE
Multiplicity of Causes

To do competent assessment, treatment planning, referral, advocacy, and therapy with ADHD children and their families, knowledge of its many possible origins is essential. The practitioner can become familiar with these possible causes by reading literature surveys.[51] Curricula in schools of social work need to be expanded and updated to include this type of information, given the prevalence of ADHD and the frequency with which it is encountered by practitioners in diverse settings.

Locating Diagnostic and Treatment Services

The first major task that often confronts a practitioner working with a child behavior problem is to find the cause or to find effective responses even if careful investigation fails to disclose an identifiable cause. The practitioner who sees the child initially needs to know what types of diagnostic and assessment procedures are indicated and where they can be obtained. The specialities involved in the assessment of these problems include pediatrics, neurology, special education, psychiatry, allergy, psychology, nutrition, and, sometimes, endocrinology. Locating appropriate treatment resources is a later and sometimes even more difficult task.

Case Management

Once a treatment plan has been developed and implemented, one person should take responsibility for managing the case. This person should coordinate services of specialists involved in prescribing medication (for example, psychiatrists, neurologists, or pediatricians); school personnel, including the child's teacher; learning disabilities specialist; providers of supportive services, such as remedial reading or math; and the parents.

The specialists often do not communicate with one another. They also frequently work at cross-purposes unless someone is taking responsibility for coordination of services. A case manager may perform such functions as monitoring the effects of various dosage levels of medication by coordinating observations of teachers and parents; acting as a coordinator to transmit information between physician, school personnel, and parents; responding in a crisis situation by contacting all the people who need to be informed about what is happening; and ensuring accountability to the child and the family by all service providers.

Advocacy

Parents and children may not be receiving services to which they are legally entitled because school districts, in an effort to avoid expenditures, may not inform them of all available options. Parent support groups and advocacy groups have been formed in many communities to monitor schools, boards of education, and state agencies to ensure that handicapped children receive the services to which they are entitled.

A practitioner should be knowledgeable about the rights of children and parents, and should routinely inform families of these rights. Many professionals are subject to conflicts of interest; in some instances, giving a parent the best possible advice might threaten the practitioner's job. School districts often prefer to provide less expensive as well as less desirable services. It is frequently in the interests of the school administration, politically, to convince as many parents as possible to accept cheaper (and often inferior) services. Generally, school budgets do not provide for optimum educational services.

Parent Support Groups

Parent support groups can collect and disseminate information without threat of reprisal. They can organize and exert political pressure and they can provide parents with the often desperately needed support that comes from finding out that many others have similar problems and that such problems do not always have to be defined in terms of the failure of individual parents and individual children. Unless some circumstances strongly contraindicate it, parents should be referred routinely to parent support groups to provide mutual support, mutual assistance in problem solving, access to useful information, and to break down the social isolation that often accompanies being the parent of a behaviorally disturbed child. If such a group does not exist in the community, formation and development of such a group is an important social work task.

In addition to these general principles, specific treatment recommendations must of course be targeted on the various dimensions of ADHD. Although much remains to be learned, research on ADHD has given practitioners some specific guideposts to follow in assessing behavior problems, choosing appropriate interventions, and implementing these interventions.

NOTES AND REFERENCES

1. J. S. Werry, J. C. Reeves, and G. S. Elkind, "Attention Deficit, Conduct, Oppositional, and Anxiety Disorders in Children: I. A Review of Research on Differentiating Characteristics," *Journal of the American Academy of Child and Adolescent Psychiatry,* 26 (1987), pp. 133–143; G. Weiss, "Hyperactivity: Overview and New Directions," *Psychiatric Clinics of North America,* 8 (1985), pp. 737–753; N. M. Lambert and C. S. Hartsough, "The Measurement of Attention Deficit Disorder with Behavior Ratings of Parents," *American Journal of Orthopsychiatry,* 57 (1987), pp. 361–370; and P. Schrag and D. Divoky, *The Myth of the Hyperactive Child* (New York: Dell Publishing, 1975).

2. H. C. Johnson, "Human Behavior and the Social Environment: New Perspectives," in *Behavior, Psychopathology, and the Brain* (Vol. 1; New York: Curriculum Concepts, 1980); and D. R. Dubey, "Organic Factors in Hyperkinesis: A Critical Evaluation," *American Journal of Orthopsychiatry,* 46 (1976), pp. 353–366.

3. H. C. Johnson, "Behavior Disorders," in F. Turner, ed., *Child Psychopathology.* To be published in a forthcoming book by Free Press.

4. M. Rutter et al., "Attainment and Adjustment in Two Geographical Areas. I. The Prevalence of Psychiatric Disorder," *British Journal of Psychiatry,* 126 (1975), pp. 493–509; and R. Schachar, M. Rutter, and A. Smith "The Characteristics of Situationally and Pervasively Hyperactive Children: Implications for Syndrome Definition," *Journal of Child Psychology and Psychiatry,* 22 (1981), pp. 375–382.

5. *Diagnostic and Statistical Manual of Mental Disorders, Third Edition, Revised* (Washington, D.C.: American Psychiatric Association, 1987).

6. Johnson, "Behavior Disorders."

7. H. Kutchins and S. A. Kirk, "DSM-III and Social Work Malpractice," *Social Work,* 32 (May–June 1987), pp. 205–211.

8. W. O. Shekim et al., "Dimensional and Categorical Approaches to the Diagnosis of Attention Deficit Disorder in Children," *Journal of the American Academy of Child Psychiatry,* 25 (1986), pp. 653–658.

9. *Diagnostic and Statistical Manual of Mental Disorders, Third Edition, Revised.*

10. P. A. Andrulonis et al., "Organic Brain Dysfunction and the Borderline Syndrome," *Psychiatric Clinics of North America,* 4 (1981), pp. 47–66.

11. *Diagnostic and Statistical Manual of Mental Disorders, Third Edition, Revised.*

12. Dubey, "Organic Factors in Hyperkinesis"; S. E. Shaywitz et al., "Monoaminergic Mechanisms in Hyperactivity," in M. Rutter, ed., *Developmental Neuropsychiatry* (New York: Guilford Press, 1983); J. L. Rapoport and H. B. Ferguson, "Biological Validation of the Hyperkinetic Syndrome," *Developmental Medicine and Child Neurology,* 23 (1981), pp. 667–682; Johnson, *Human Behavior and the Social Environment,* 1980; A. S. Brickman et al., "Neuropsychological Assessment of Seriously Delinquent Adolescents," *Journal of the American Academy of Child Psychiatry,* 23 (1985), pp. 453–457; and M. G. Tramontana and S. D. Sherrets, "Brain Impairment in Child Psychiatric Disorders: Correspondencies Between Neuropsychological and C.T. Scan Results," *Journal of the American Academy of Child Psychiatry,* 24 (1985), pp. 590–596.

13. Rapoport and Ferguson, "Biological Validation of the Hyperkinitic Syndrome."

14. G. A. Rogeness et al., "Near-Zero Plasma Dopamine-Beta-Hydroxylase and Conduct Disorder in Emotionally Disturbed Boys," *Journal of the American Academy of Child Psychiatry*, 25 (1986), pp. 521–527; A. J. Zametkin et al., "Phenylethylamine Excretion in Attention Deficit Disorder," *Journal of the American Academy of Child Psychiatry*, 23 (1985), pp. 310–314; B. P. Rourke, J. L. Fisk, and J. D. Strang, *Neuropsychological Assessment of Children* (New York: Guilford, 1986); A. L. Stewart et al., *Relation Between Ultrasound-Appearance of the Brain in Very Preterm Infants and Neurodevelopmental Outcome at 18 Months of Age.* Paper from the second Perinatal Intracranial Conference, Washington, D.C. (Columbus, Ohio: Ross Laboratories, 1982).

15. Johnson, *Human Behavior and the Social Environment;* and Johnson, "Behavior Disorders."

16. Shekim et al., "Dimensions and Categorical Approaches to the Diagnosis of Attention Deficit Disorder in Children."

17. L. Small, *The Minimal Brain Dysfunctions: Diagnosis and Treatment* (New York: Free Press, 1982).

18. *Diagnostic and Statistical Manual of Mental Disorders, Third Edition, Revised.*

19. Small, *The Minimal Brain Dysfunctions.*

20. Ibid.

21. Ibid.

22. Ibid.

23. Ibid.

24. Ibid.

25. Ibid.

26. D. Sheinkin, M. Schachter, and B. Hutton, *The Food Connection* (Indianapolis, Ind.: Bobbs Merrill, 1979).

27. R. A. Barkley, "A Review of Stimulant Drug Research with Hyperkinetic Children," *Journal of Child Psychology and Psychiatry*, 18 (1977), pp. 137–166.

28. R. Gittelman, "Hyperkinetic Syndrome: Treatment Issues and Principles," in Rutter, *Developmental Neuropsychiatry;* Weiss, "Hyperactivity"; G. Weiss and L. T. Hechtman, *Hyperactive Children Grown Up* (New York: Guilford Press, 1986); and J. L. Rapoport, "The Use of Drugs: Trends in Research," in Rutter, *Developmental Neuropsychiatry.*

29. Ibid.

30. J. M. Halperin et al., "Relationship Between Stimulant Effect, Electroencephalogram, and Clinical Neurological Findings in Hyperactive Children," *Journal of the American Academy of Child Psychiatry*, 25 (1986), pp. 820–825.

31. R. Gittelman et al., "A Controlled Trial of Behavior Modification and Methylphenidate in Hyperactive Children," in C. Whalen and B. Henker, eds., *Hyperactive Children: The Social Etiology of Identification and Treatment* (New York: Academic Press, 1980).

32. R. A. Barkley, J. K. S. Pollack, and J. V. Murphy, "Developmental Changes in the Mother–Child Interactions of Hyperactive Boys: Effects of Two Dose Levels of Ritalin," *Journal of Child Psychology and Psychiatry*, 26 (1985), pp. 705–715.

33. C. E. Cunningham, L. S. Siegal, and D. R. Offord, "A Developmental Dose-Re-

sponse Analysis of the Effects of Methylphenidate on the Peer Interaction of Attention Deficit Disordered Boys," *Journal of Child Psychology and Psychiatry,* 26 (1985), pp. 955–971.

34. H. C. Johnson, "Biologically Based Deficit in the Identified Patient: Indications for Psychoeducational Strategies," *Journal of Marital and Family Therapy* (October 1987); H. C. Johnson, "Emerging Concerns in Family Therapy," *Social Work,* 37 (July–August 1987), pp. 299–306; and P. H. Wender and E. H. Wender, *The Hyperactive Child and the Learning Disabled Child* (New York: Crown Publishers, 1978).

35. S. R. Pliszka, "Tricyclic Antidepressants in the Treatment of Children with Attention Deficit Disorder," *Journal of the American Academy of Child and Adolescent Psychiatry,* 26 (1987), pp. 127–132; P. Wender, F. W. Reimherr, and D. R. Wood "Attention-Deficit Disorder (Minimal Dysfunction) in Adults," *Archives of General Psychiatry,* 38 (1981), pp. 449–456; R. D. Hunt, R. B. Minderaa, and D. J. Cohen, "Clonidine Benefits Children with Attention Deficit Disorder and Hyperactivity: Report of a Double-Blind Placebo-Crossover Therapeutic Trial," *Journal of the American Academy of Child Psychiatry,* 24 (1985), pp. 617–629; A. Weizman et al., "Combination of Neuroleptic and Stimulant Treatment in Attention Deficit Disorder with Hyperactivity," *Journal of the American Academy of Child Psychiatry,* 23 (1984), pp. 295–298; E. D. Nemzer et al., "Amino Acid Supplementation as Therapy for Attention Deficit Disorder," *Journal of the American Academy of Child Psychiatry,* 25 (1986), pp. 509–513.

36. Weiss, "Hyperactivity"; J. H. Satterfield, B. T. Satterfield, and A. M. Schness, "Therapeutic Interventions to Prevent Delinquency in Hyperactive Boys," *Journal of the American Academy of Child and Adolescent Psychiatry,* 26 (1987), pp. 56–64.

37. Satterfield, Satterfield, and Schness, "Therapeutic Interventions to Prevent Delinquency in Hyperactive Boys."

38. R. Gittelman et al., "A Controlled Trial of Behavior Modification and Methylphenidate in Hyperactive Children," in Whalen and Henker, eds., *Hyperactive Children;* and K. D. O'Leary et al., "Behavioral Treatment of Hyperactive Children: An Experimental Evaluation of its Usefulness," *Clinical Pediatrics,* 15 (1976), pp. 510–15.

39. Gittelman, "Hyperkinetic Syndrome"; Satterfield, Satterfield, and Schness, "Therapeutic Interventions to Prevent Delinquency in Hyperactive Boys"; and V. I. Douglas, "Attentional and Cognitive Deficits," in Rutter, *Developmental Neuropsychiatry.*

40. Johnson, "Biologically Based Deficit in the Identified Patient."

41. Johnson, "Emerging Concerns in Family Therapy."

42. P. H. Wender and E. H. Wender, *The Hyperactive Child and the Learning Disabled Child;* and L. B. Silver, *The Misunderstood Child* (New York: McGraw Hill, 1984).

43. M. S. Sokol et al., "Attention Deficit Disorder with Hyperactivity and the Dopamine Hypothesis: Case Presentations with Theoretical Background," *Journal of the American Academy of Child and Adolescent Psychiatry,* 26 (1987), pp. 428–433.

44. M. D. Gross et al., "The Effects of Diets Rich in and Free from Additives on the Behavior of Children with Hyperkinetic and Learning Disorders," *Journal of the American Academy of Child and Adolescent Psychiatry*, 26 (1987), pp. 53–55.

45. E. H. Wender, "The Food Additive-Free Diet in the Treatment of Behavior Disorders: A Review," *Developmental and Behavioral Pediatrics*, 7 (1986), pp. 35–42.

46. C. K. Varley, "Diet and the Behavior of Children with Attention Deficit Disorder," *Journal of the American Academy of Child Psychiatry*, 23 (1984), pp. 182–185.

47. Weiss and Hechtman, *Hyperactive Children Grown Up*.

48. Weiss et al., "Psychiatric Status of Hyperactives as Adults: A Controlled Perspective 15-Year Follow-Up of 63 Hyperactive Children," *Journal of the American Academy of Child Psychiatry*, 24 (1985), pp. 211–220.

49. Weiss and Hechtman, *Hyperactive Children Grown Up*.

50. R. Klorman, H. W. Coons, and A. D. Borgstedt, "Effects of Methylphenidate on Adolescents with a Childhood History of Attention Deficit Disorder: I. Clinical Findings," *Journal of the American Academy of Child and Adolescent Psychiatry*, 26 (1987), pp. 363–367.

51. Johnson, *Human Behavior and the Social Environment*.

CHAPTER 38

SCHOOL- AND FAMILY-BASED TREATMENT OF CHILDREN WITH ATTENTION-DEFICIT HYPERACTIVITY DISORDER

Kaye H. Coker and Bruce A. Thyer

Attention-deficit hyperactivity disorder (ADHD), as defined in the *Diagnostic and Statistical Manual of Mental Disorders* (DSM-III-R), is part of a subclass of disorders characterized by behavior that is socially disruptive (American Psychiatric Association, 1987). The essential features of this disorder are developmentally inappropriate degrees of inattention, impulsiveness, and hyperactivity. The disorder is usually evident at school, at home, and with peers, but it may vary in degree. Low self-esteem, mood lability, low frustration tolerance, academic underachievement, and temper outbursts are associated features of this disorder. Symptoms associated with oppositional defiant disorder, conduct disorder, and specific developmental disorders may also be present. Onset of ADHD occurs before age four in approximately half the cases, and the condition usually continues throughout childhood. Oppositional defiant disorder or conduct disorder more often occurs initially in late childhood. Studies have shown that approximately one-third of the children with ADHD continue to exhibit symptoms of the disorder as adults. Disorganized or chaotic environments, child abuse and neglect, and certain neurological abnormalities are possible predisposing factors. The disorder may occur in as many as 3% of children; it is more common in males than in

Reprinted from *Families in Society,* Vol. 71, No. 5 (1990), pp. 276–282, by permission of the publisher, Families International, Inc.

females. The disorder is also believed to be more common in first-degree biologic relatives of persons with the disorder than in the general population (American Psychiatric Association, 1987).

Many hyperactive children are identified as having problems when they reach school age, a time when they encounter rules, regulations, and restrictions that may be very different from those imposed in the home environment or in day-care situations. These children's high rates of motor activity, impulsiveness, and fidgety, squirmy behaviors may be either accepted as "normal" or regarded as the behaviors of a "spoiled" child by the family. One mother mentioned that she had no idea that her six-year-old son's behavior was so different from the other children's behavior until they went to a Boy Scout meeting and she noticed that all the other boys his age were sitting quietly during the meeting.

PRACTICE AND THE CHILD WITH ADHD

School is one of the most important components of the child's ecosystem. For the majority of children, school is the most important socialization experience outside the family (Bronfenbrenner, 1979). Failure to achieve in school has a direct influence on a child's self-esteem. The restless, noncompliant, frequently disruptive behaviors of the hyperactive child create difficulties both academically and socially.

Much of the practice research regarding children with ADHD has been conducted by child psychologists and psychiatrists, usually for the purpose of controlling classroom behavior (Patterson, 1965; Madsen, Becker, Thomas, Koser, & Plager, 1968). Behavior therapy has emerged as the treatment of choice; it is often combined with psychostimulant medication (Pelham, Walker, & Milich, 1986). Parent training in behavior therapy techniques to improve child-management skills has also been shown to be beneficial.

Practitioners often integrate behavioral techniques into more traditional treatment modalities and include work with families in addition to intervening in school settings. When behavioral techniques were introduced by social workers in classes for emotionally disturbed or socially maladjusted children, the positive results brought increasing requests for similar programs from teachers in the regular classes (see Wadsworth, 1970, 1971). Canter and Paulson (1974) designed a consultation seminar for implementing behavioral techniques in elementary school classrooms. Teachers were taught to modify the disruptive behaviors of students by using behavioral techniques. Positive results were obtained in 11 out of 12 children.

Barth (1979, 1980) developed a daily report card system that kept parents informed of their children's behavioral and academic achievements, providing more potent reinforcement (i.e., immediate feedback) than did quarterly report cards. Parents were also involved in the psychosocial treatment program described by Goff and Demetral (1983), in which students received reinforcement at home for appropriate behavior at school. During the baseline period, teachers praised appropriate behavior but avoided use of any other rewards or punishment. During the treatment phase, the children were awarded stickers on cards after periods devoid of selected problem behaviors. This reward was coupled with praise for appropriate social and educationally on-task behaviors. The stickers could then be exchanged at home for certain privileges, with the required number of stickers increasing as the classroom behavior continued to improve. The privileges used as rewards were selected by the parents, who received frequent support and reinforcement (praise) from the social worker. The program proved highly successful in reducing the targeted problem behaviors. It was further noted that the parents' attitude and behavior toward their children were major factors in this program.

In one family seen by the senior author, combining rewards for compliance at school and at home was successful in reducing aggressive classroom behavior in a seven-year-old boy with ADHD. In a previously developed program, points earned daily for appropriate behaviors in the classroom were exchanged for money that the boy used at the end of the week to purchase miniature cars. When the aggressive behavior appeared and other interventions were attempted and discarded, including corporal punishment by his father, the parents sought family counseling. An intervention was devised that required "payback"; the boy was required to pay back or forfeit an agreed-upon sum for each reported incident of aggressive behavior. He soon realized he would not be able to purchase his miniature cars if the aggressive behavior continued. Follow-up reports indicated that the aggressiveness was reduced after the first week and eliminated three weeks later. This intervention had the additional benefit of improving the relationship between the father and son by eliminating the use of corporal punishment.

IMPROVING ACADEMIC PERFORMANCE

The practice-research literature indicates that various psychosocial methods can be effectively employed to improve the academic performance of children with ADHD. For example, in a study of three children diagnosed as hyperactive who were receiving drugs to control their hyperactivity, behavioral techniques were used to reinforce academic performance, which *also* reduced hyperactive behaviors (Ayllon, Layman, & Kandel, 1975). Each student's daily level of hyperactivity and academic achievement, both on and off medication, was observed and recorded before the reinforcement program began. When the medication was discontinued, the level of hyperactivity increased by 200% to 300% above its initial level. The next phase involved reinforcing correct responses in math by rewarding the children with check marks, which could later be exchanged for back-up reinforcers. Their hyperactivity decreased, and their performance in math got better. In the last phase, the children were reinforced for their performance in reading as well as math. The hyperactivity decreased to levels comparable to the initial period when it was controlled by the drug, and academic performance levels were dramatically higher. These results suggest that children on stimulant medication may be removed from drug regimens and treated with psychosocial alternatives, or that a combination of medication and behavioral methods may be beneficial.

More than 10 years later, Pelham, Walker, and Milich (1986) measured the learning abilities of 30 children with attention-deficit disorder. The children were given the task of learning to spell nonsense words; the effects of two behavioral reinforcement schedules (partial and continuous) and the effect of a dosage of 0.3 mg/kg methylphenidate (Ritalin) were assessed. Three reinforcement groups were used: no reinforcement, continuous reinforcement, and partial reinforcement. The children performed the spelling task twice, once after taking the medication and once after taking a placebo pill. It was found that the reward conditions produced significantly lower error rates and that in combination with the medication, spelling performance was improved by 43%. This study suggests the value of combined medication therapy and behavioral procedures in improving the academic performance of children with ADHD.

HELPING HYPERACTIVE CHILDREN AND THEIR FAMILIES

McPherson and Samuels (1971) found that educational groups for parents of hyperactive children not only were effective in teaching parents behavioral methods for improving their children's behavior but proved helpful in eliciting support from other parents and led to their further involvement in traditional forms of therapy. In this project, the authors included a psychologist, who evaluated the children, and a social worker, who assessed the parents. The subsequent group meetings were led by both professionals: the psychologist presented training materials in a didactic fashion, and the social worker focused on feelings and group dynamics. At the conclusion of the training program, other needs were identified and several of the families elected to continue therapy. Some of the children were seen individually by the psychologist, and several of the parents received marital counseling and family counseling with the social worker. All of the families involved in the project indicated improvement in coping with their children's behavior problems.

Training parents in behavioral techniques is a well-established method for controlling children's behavior in the school setting (Dangel & Polster, 1984). Such practice research has focused on families, the *reciprocal* nature of interactions between parents and children, and the ways in which inappropriate behavior can be inadvertently negatively reinforced. A representative study by Barkley and Cunningham (1980) involved four observational sessions of a pair of hyperactive identical twin boys and their mother, with the children placed on and off stimulant medication. The mother's reactions to the nonmedicated hyperactive behaviors were more negative and directive, and the children were more negative and noncompliant than they were during sessions when they were on medication. The study indicated that

> the parent–child behaviors are best viewed as a reciprocal feedback system in which the behavior of one person serves as both a controlling stimulus and a consequating [sic] event for the responses of the other. It further serves to underscore the notion that the child's behavior exerts a great deal of control over parental responses, in addition to the traditional view that parental behaviors influence child responses (Barkley, 1981, p. 60).

Patterson (1982) found that parental punishment may inadvertently *increase* negative behavior of children and that teaching parents to ignore the behavior may also serve to transiently increase such problems. This result is likely due to negative reinforcement, which occurs when an aversive event is terminated by the use of a particular behavior. When parents and others behave in an aversive fashion, using commands, disapproval, and other negative responses to the aggressive child, the child may respond with aversive behavior as a way of coping. If the child's aversive behavior is even partially effective in getting the parent to cease his or her demands or nagging, the child is negatively reinforced for reacting in this fashion. Such interactions have a way of escalating and increasing the chances for recurrence. Patterson also found that these interaction patterns do not always generalize to other settings. The occurrence is dependent on the reactions of the person with whom the child is interacting.

The hierarchy of response progression by the parents of hyperactive children described by Barkley (1981) explains how some parents arrive at a state of "learned helplessness" with respect to parenting skills. As parents try to cope by ignoring or withholding attention during hyperactive behavior, the child's behavior intensifies. At this point, the parent issues commands, usually several times. If the child does not respond positively, threats of discipline are added. Physical discipline may interrupt the behavior, or the parent may back away from enforcing the threats, perhaps even complying with his or her own command (e.g., cleaning the child's room him- or herself). Over time the parent begins to omit the unsuccessful behaviors and attempts to control the child's behavior by beginning at the level at which he or she has previously been successful in either reducing the behavior or the level of tension in the family. Thus, either intensely angry, punitive actions are taken or the parent seemingly acquiesces, making few, if any, attempts to enforce the commands. The latter behavior is seen in families with severe management problems and in which parents have become progressively more disengaged from the children.

Many of the coercive behaviors observed in Patterson's (1982) research with aggressive children and their families are also descriptive of behaviors of hyperactive children. These behaviors include command negative (immediate compliance demanded); dependency (request for unnecessary assistance); destructiveness; high rate of repetitive, physically active behavior; noncompliance (not doing what is requested within 12 seconds of the request); and teasing, whining, and yelling. It was found that these coercive behaviors were often maintained by the child to ensure continued attention from the adult.

These findings have implications for the assessment and subsequent treatment of hyperactive children and their families. Barkley (1981) notes that certain consequences are developed from long-term patterns of coercion, whereby reduced levels of positive consequences are exchanged among family members. The tension level in the home is high, and family members tend to disengage and withdraw from one another. Low self-esteem and depression may develop, especially in the mothers, who are usually the most involved in the coercive interactions with the child. Marital difficulties are not uncommon. Patterson (1982) has also shown that due to the history of negative, aversive, and coercive interaction patterns, the child is likely to devalue parents' positive attention when it does occur. The most useful treatments, then, are those that focus on modifying the parent–child interactions and helping the child become more responsive to and compliant with adult instructions.

Noncompliance with parental requests and commands has been cited as one of the most frequent complaints of parents seeking help with their problem children (Wilson, Franks, Kendall, & Foreyt, 1987). This may involve not performing the requested behavior, doing it too slowly, refusing to comply, or promising to do it later but not following through. Barkley (1981) discusses noncompliance not only with parental commands, but with "rules known through actual experience to govern behavior in a situation, or with given rules of conduct and etiquette while interacting with others" (p. 12), as a significant part of the symptomatology of hyperactivity, which includes inattention, overactivity, and poor impulse control.

The program devised by Barkley for treating noncompliance deals with the development of the children's rule-governed behavior. The program emphasizes six principles that are stressed throughout the eight sessions. Parents are taught the importance of immediacy of consequences (positive or punitive); the specificity of consequences; consistency over time, setting, and between parents; using positive before negative consequences; and the axiom of reciprocity of interactions. Throughout the program, parents are reminded that what they are being taught is a way of coping, not a cure. The eight training sessions begin with a general orientation about hyperactivity, then move from a focus on parent–child interactions through parental attention strategies and reinforcers to punishment and noncompliance. The last session focuses on developing skills for handling future problems. A follow-up session is held a month later; more sessions can be added if necessary.

The clinical research by Forehand et al. (1979) indicates that dealing with noncompliance serves as the foundation for working with many other problem areas. Their program begins with training sessions on hyperactivity and parent–child interactions, and includes managing public behavior and increasing independent play. Later sessions are tailored to the needs of the individual child and family, which may include problems such as encopresis or enuresis.

Patterson (1982) developed a program that focused on teaching family-management skills for families with antisocial children. Because many of the behaviors of antisocial and aggressive children are similar to those of hyperactive children, the techniques for change are often equally applicable. By changing the psychosocial environment and the interactions among family members, Patterson found that problem behaviors in more than 200 children were reduced. The fundamental premise of this program is that the parents are the ones who must change the problem child; the therapist plays the role of teacher and facilitator. The families were found to be deficient in four basic skills: devising clearly stated "house rules"; monitoring behaviors; providing contingent consequences; and problem solving, which includes crisis management and negotiating compromises. These skills are carefully role-played and supervised, with a significant amount of in-home contact.

In a more abbreviated intervention, Pinkston (1984) used social learning theory and behavior analysis to teach parents to alter their interactions with their children. Their Parent Education Program begins with an initial telephone contact between the parent and human service professional. Upon receipt of a completed assessment questionnaire, the practitioner schedules an initial interview, during which the program is explained and the parents are taught how to define target behaviors and collect baseline data. A home visit by the human service professional follows in order to assure reliability of the data and to reassess the target behaviors. A two- to three-hour intensive training session takes place in the clinic, focusing on establishing positive patterns of interpersonal interaction within the family. Contracting and behavioral contingencies are modeled and rehearsed, and overcorrection and time-out procedures are presented if necessary. The program can be modified to meet the needs of different family situations and structures. The Single-Parent Program was designed to include an extra training session and more practitioner support for the parent.

COGNITIVE-BEHAVIORAL TRAINING

The notion of teaching hyperactive children to control their own behavior by use of self-verbalization is a promising area of practice research. The process involves modeling, cognitive rehearsal, self-instruction, and self-reinforcement. Meichenbaum and Goodman (1971) describe one cognitive training technique as follows: The trainer performs a task talking aloud while the child observes. The child then performs the same task while the trainer instructs the child aloud. Next the child is asked to perform the task again while instructing him- or-herself (lip movements), then covertly (without lip movements). The authors found this program effective in improving 15 children's behavior on various psychometric tests assessing cognitive impulsivity, performance IQ, and motor ability.

This approach is attractive for several reasons, one being that it offers hope for an alternative to stimulant drug therapy. Also, because these children are viewed as impulsive and having poor self-control, concentration on problem-solving and self-guidance seems an appropriate focus. However, subsequent outcome studies have found that the results of cognitive–behavioral therapy with clinically diagnosed attention-deficit disorder children are not very strong, somewhat inconsistent, and difficult to replicate (c.f., Whalen, Henker, & Hinshaw, 1985). A review of such outcome studies may be found in Kendall and Braswell (1984) and Meyers and Craighead (1984).

Combining behavioral parent training and cognitive–behavioral self-control therapy does not produce better results than does either treatment when used alone, nor does the combination produce treatment effects that generalize from the home to classroom (see Horn et al., 1987). In a study of 24 elementary school children with ADHD, these authors found improvement in home behavior and were able to derive some conclusions concerning the children's characteristics and attitudes. The most improved children were those who had a greater ability to reflect when given a problem-solving task, were better able to recognize that they did have self-control problems, and had a greater sense that they could exert control over their own behavior. There was no involvement of school personnel or use of psychostimulant medication, leading the authors to call for further research to determine the effects of these variables on generalization across settings.

USING SOCIAL SKILLS TRAINING

The well-documented peer-relationship problems of children with ADHD arise from several elements native to their disability. Difficulty with attention hampers sustained play. Impulse-control problems and aggressive behaviors may cause children to settle differences with peers by physical means. An inability to accept responsibility for one's actions and attributing blame to others further diminishes the child's acceptance by peers. Peers may complain that the child is "bossy" or controlling. Carlson, Lahey, Frame, Walker, and Hynd (1987) found that a group of ADHD and a group of

ADD/WO (without hyperactivity) children were least liked and had lower social preference scores from their classroom peers than did children in a normal control group. The ADHD group also scored higher in the "fights most" category.

Social skills are defined by Rinn and Markle (1979) as

> a repertoire of verbal and nonverbal behaviors by which children affect the responses of other individuals in the interpersonal context. This repertoire acts as a mechanism through which children influence their environment by obtaining, removing, or avoiding desirable and undesirable outcomes in the social sphere. Further, the extent to which they are successful in obtaining desirable outcomes and avoiding or escaping undesirable ones without inflicting pain on others is the extent to which they are considered "socially skilled" (p. 108).

Asher (1977) found that children who are disliked and isolated emit a high rate of aversive stimuli (e.g., commands, criticisms, and hits), and a low rate of positive stimuli (e.g., praise, sharing, and helping).

Training in social skills employs instructions, modeling, behavior rehearsal, coaching, and feedback in analogue situations. In Rinn and Markle's model, the children are taught self-expressive skills, other-enhancing skills, appropriate assertive skills, and communication skills. The practice implications of using these techniques for fostering better relationships in the family, in the classroom, and on the playground are evident and important in building the child's self-esteem. Early intervention, however, would appear to be critical. Patterson (1982) found that the child develops an extremely negative view of others as a result of his or her coercive behavior and its effects on family interactions. Perhaps by adding a social-skills training component to behavioral methods taught to parents and children, a foundation could be built that would improve positive peer relations and strengthen positive family relations.

SUMMARY

These positive findings in practice research suggest increased interest and concern for treating the hyperactive child in the family as well as utilizing the social systems outside the family. Many of the stressors that affect families without hyperactive children, such as life-cycle issues, economic pressures, work-related problems, and child-care concerns, may exacerbate feelings of helplessness, guilt, anxiety, and depression of parents who are not effectively coping with their hyperactive child. Changing the interactions between parent and child is one of the most significant focal points for treatment; early intervention is crucial. It is further evident that effective analysis and treatment of these problems should take place in the natural environments of the home and school rather than solely in a clinic setting. Using natural environments can lead to solutions to problems of maintenance and generalization encountered when treatment is provided only in an agency-based setting.

It is important to continue developing effective psychosocial interventions to help these children and their families cope. Through participation in education and support groups and training in behavior-management techniques, families can begin to feel empowered in that they are the interventions that produce therapeutic changes.

REFERENCES

American Psychiatric Association. (1987). *Diagnostic and statistical manual of mental disorders* (3rd ed., rev.). Washington, DC: Author.

Asher, S. R. (1977, December). *Coaching socially isolated children in social skills.* Paper presented at the annual meeting of the Association for Advancement of Behavior Therapy, Atlanta.

Ayllon, T., Laymon, C., & Kandel, H. (1975). A behavioral–educational alternative to drug control of hyperactive children. *Journal of Applied Behavior Analysis, 8,* 137–146.

Barkley, R. (1981). *Hyperactive children: A handbook for diagnosis and treatment.* New York: Guilford Press.

Barkley, R., & Cunningham, C. (1980). The parent–child interactions of hyperactive children and their modification by stimulant drugs. In R. Knights & D. Bakker (Eds.), *Treatment of hyperactive and learning disordered children.* Baltimore, MD: University Park Press.

Barth, R. (1979). Home-based reinforcement of school behavior: A review and analysis. *Review of Educational Research, 49,* 436–458.

Barth, R. (1980). Report cards in a home–school communication system. *Social Work in Education, 2,* 44–58.

Bronfenbrenner, N. (1979). *The ecology of human development.* Cambridge, MA: Harvard University Press.

Canter, L., & Paulson, T. (1974). A college credit model of in-school consultation: A functional behavioral training program. *Community Mental Health Journal, 10,* 268–275.

Carlson, C., Lahey, B., Frame, C., Walker, J., & Hynd, G. (1987). Sociometric status of clinic-referred children with attention deficit disorders, with and without hyperactivity. *Journal of Abnormal Child Psychology, 5,* 537–547.

Dangel, R., & Polster, R. (Eds.). (1984). *Parent training: Foundations of research and practice.* New York: Guilford Press.

Forehand, R., Sturgis, E., McMahon, R., Aguar, D., Green, K., Wells, K., & Breiner, J. (1979). Parent behavioral training to modify child noncompliance: Treatment generalization across time and from home to school. *Behavior Modification, 3,* 3–25.

Goff, G., & Demetral, D. (1983). A home-based program to eliminate aggression in the classroom. *Social Work in Education, 5,* 5–14.

Horn, W., Ialongo, N., Popovich, S., & Peradotto, D. (1987). Behavioral parent training and cognitive–behavioral self-control therapy with ADHD children: Comparative and combined effects. *Journal of Clinical Child Psychology, 16,* 57–68.

Kendall, P., & Braswell, L. (1984). *Cognitive–behavioral therapy for impulsive children.* New York: Guilford Press.

McPherson, S., & Samuels, C. (1971). Teaching behavioral methods to parents. *Social Casework, 52,* 145–153.

Masden, C., Becker, W., & Thomas, D. (1968). Rules, praise, and ignoring: Elements of elementary classroom control. *Journal of Applied Behavior Analysis, 1,* 139–150.

Meichenbaum, D., & Goodman, J. (1971). Training impulsive children to talk to themselves: A means of developing self-control. *Journal of Abnormal Psychology, 77,* 115–126.

Meyers, A., & Craighead, W. (Eds.). (1984). *Cognitive behavior treatment with children.* New York: Plenum Press.

Patterson, G. (1982). *A social learning approach, vol. 3, Coercive family process.* Eugene, OR: Castalia Publishing.

Patterson, G. R. (1965). An application of conditioning techniques to the control of a hyperactive child. In L. Ullmann & L. Krasner (Eds.), *Research in behavior modification.* New York: Holt, Rinehart & Winston.

Pelham, W., Walker, J., & Milich, R. (1986). Effects of continuous and partial reinforcement and methylphenidate on learning in children with attention deficit disorder. *Journal of Abnormal Psychology, 95,* 319–325.

Pinkston, E. M. (1984). Individualized behavioral intervention for home and school. In R. Dangel & R. Polster (Eds.), *Parent training: Foundations of research and practice.* New York: Guilford Press.

Rinn, R., & Markle, A. (1979). Modification of social skill deficits in children. In A. Bellack & M. Hersen (Eds.), *Research and practice in social skills training.* New York: Plenum Press.

Wadsworth, H. (1970). Initiating a preventive–corrective approach in an elementary school system. *Social Work, 15,* 60–66.

Wadsworth, H. (1971). Social-conditioning casework in a school setting. *Social Casework, 52,* 32–38.

Whalen, C., Hinker, B., & Hinshaw, S. (1985). Cognitive–behavioral therapies for hyperactive children: Premises, problems, and prospects. *Journal of Abnormal Child Psychology, 13,* 391–410.

Wilson, G., Franks, C., Kendall, P., & Foreyt, J. (1987). *Review of behavior therapy treatment: Theory and practice* (Vol. 2). New York: Guilford Press.

CHAPTER 39

GROUP THERAPY IN THE MANAGEMENT OF MANIC-DEPRESSIVE ILLNESS

Fred R. Volkmar, Sandra Bacon, Saad A. Shakir, and Adolf Pfefferbaum

INTRODUCTION

Patients with bipolar affective illness have been viewed as poor candidates for both individual and group psychotherapy. Before the advent of lithium therapy most psychotherapists viewed manic-depressive patients as resistant to both individual and group psychotherapeutic approaches even during the euthymic phase of the illness. A number of factors seemed to militate against psychotherapy with such patients. Manic-depressive patients were felt to exhibit a facade of conventionality and sociability which, in fact, served as a defense against true intimacy and the anxiety entailed by such intimacy. These patients were thought to exhibit superficial and conventional relationships with strong underlying feelings of dependency, hostility, envy, and competition. The patients' inability to tolerate anxiety or intimacy and their use of massive denial and manipulation were seen as precluding the formation of a treatment alliance even during the euthymic phase of the illness.[1]

Yalom[2] has referred to the presence of a manic-depressive member in a mixed outpatient therapy group as "one of the worst calamities that can befall a therapy group." The recurring nature of the patients' illness and their inability to tolerate closeness and their superficiality present major and very significant obstacles to their successful integration into a heterogeneous therapy group.

Many clinicians have, therefore, been discouraged from using psychotherapeutic approaches with these patients and have, instead, relied exclusively on lithium prophy-

Reprinted from *American Journal of Psychotherapy,* Vol. 35, No. 2 (April 1981), pp. 226–234, by permission of the publisher.

laxis as the major treatment modality for them. The efficacy of such treatment has been shown in over 100 single- and double-blind studies. For example, in one study 50% of patients with bipolar affective illness who were receiving lithium relapsed over a two-year-period as compared to 90% of control patients receiving placebo.[3] With the advent of this effective psychopharmacological treatment, interest in psychotherapeutic approaches has declined markedly, with but a few exceptions.[4]

Unfortunately, despite its proven efficacy, many patients receiving lithium prophylaxis will relapse, and a significant number of patients will remain chronically ill.[5] The most positive studies of lithium prophylaxis report failure rates of 20–23% with many, if not most, of these failures occurring early in treatment. In a careful follow-up study of 47 bipolar manic-depressive patients, Carlson, et al. report that one-third of their sample remained impaired with moderate-to-severe symptoms which interfered with social and work adjustment.[6] It was their impression that even though lithium could control extreme mood fluctuations and keep patients out of the hospital, it might not control the illness sufficiently to enable many patients to return to former levels of functioning.

In many cases relapse requiring rehospitalization is associated with cessation of lithium use or inadequate maintenance doses of medication, with a subsequent re-emergence of the natural course of the illness. Lack of adherence to lithium maintenance treatment has been related to several factors.[7] Patients' use of denial may lead them to deny the reality of the illness and the need for medication and may lead them to ignore early signs of recurrence. Additionally, patients may miss the euphoria which lithium use sometimes entails. Interpersonal or family problems may also lead to poor compliance, especially in settings which provide little support for the patients' treatment. A further complicating factor may be the patients' attribution of responsibility for the successful management of treatment to the physician.

In their review of the course and outcome of bipolar manic-depressive illness, Welner, et al. concluded that even with lithium treatment the illness has a less favorable outcome than is generally believed and that a substantial minority of patients remain chronically ill.[8] Clearly, despite its proven effectiveness, many patients receiving lithium will relapse; most of those relapsing will do so in situations where their clinical state and perhaps their lithium levels are not being closely monitored, and in which they are receiving little support or encouragement for adhering to long-term lithium maintenance therapy.

In an effort to provide (a) close follow-up for patients on lithium, (b) support for continuing treatment, and (c) the opportunity for psychotherapy, we formed a long-term therapy group composed entirely of patients with a diagnosis of bipolar affective illness. Many of these patients had histories of poor adherence to lithium maintenance treatment. This group is now in its fourth year of existence. A preliminary report based on two years' experience with this group has appeared elsewhere;[9] in this report we shall focus more specifically on the problems and issues raised by patients in a long-term therapy group of this kind.

GROUP COMPOSITION

All members of the group had diagnoses of manic-depressive illness, bipolar type; these diagnoses were established by at least two psychiatrists on the basis of history and mental status examination. Referrals came from inpatient psychiatric wards at the Palo Alto Veterans Administration Hospital. All patients had responded acutely to lithium treatment prior to entering the group. A majority of the patients had histories of poor adherence to lithium maintenance. Patients were screened individually by the two group therapists before they were admitted to the group. During this screening the general purpose and rationale of group psychotherapy and the group format were discussed with the prospective member. When the patients with a primary diagnosis of bipolar affective illness and with a history of responsiveness to lithium were screened, their interest in group treatment was discussed. Only those who expressed at least a tentative interest in group treatment were included in our groups. Many of the patients selected were initially skeptical of the benefits of group therapy; often this was in response to their previous "failure" experiences with heterogeneous therapy groups. Any questions or concerns the prospective member had about the group were addressed as honestly as possible, and the therapists attempted to anticipate problems they thought the prospective member might encounter in the group. At the time of entry patients were generally euthymic; occasionally referrals were made while patients were still hospitalized. Baseline laboratory studies and EKG were obtained on all patients.

To date twenty patients (eighteen male and two female, with a mean age of 41.7 years and a range from 18 to 63 years of age) have participated in the group. The average duration of treatment prior to the patient's entry in the group was 17 months. Four of the members fit the bipolar type II description of Fieve;[10] the other sixteen fit the bipolar type I description. A minority of the patients had histories of episodic alcohol abuse, a majority had family histories suggestive of affective illness.

GROUP FORMAT

In designing our group, we hoped to provide a weekly meeting that would present the members with the opportunity for interpersonal learning and support as well as providing for close follow-up of medications. The group met for 75 minutes weekly and was conducted with an interactional, interpersonal "here and now" approach as described by Yalom.[2] Thus, the focus of the group was on expression of affect, reality issues, and immediate problems and concerns rather than on past history. The therapists (a psychiatric resident and social worker) attempted to discourage intellectualization, superficiality, and rationalization as much as possible, i.e., to focus on affect rather than semantics. The group norms that became established encouraged honesty and support with occasional limit-setting by either group members or one of the therapists.

Lithium carbonate was dispensed monthly during a group meeting; lithium levels were maintained in the range of 0.8 to 12 mEq./1. Group members were free to discuss concerns or problems with lithium at any time. If a member began to exhibit signs of either mania or depression, other members would discuss this openly in the group and provide support and encouragement, while medications would be adjusted as necessary.

Occasionally patients who were not regular group members were allowed to visit a meeting. Often this was in response to the nonmember's wish to meet other patients receiving lithium.

COURSE IN GROUP TREATMENT

Most patients appeared to exhibit substantially the same course during their participation in the group. Initially new members remained somewhat aloof and remote from others in the group. Typically the patient would greatly minimize his or her problems and attempt to relate to other members and the therapists in very superficial ways. The group encouraged new members to focus on affective and reality issues. During this initial period attendance was often somewhat unpredictable. The responsibility for the efficacy of lithium maintenance would generally be attributed to the therapists (especially the psychiatrist), and patients typically gave little indication of more than a passing interest in their lithium levels, etc. The therapists had the impression that this initial period of wariness was more prolonged than that typically associated with a new members' joining a heterogeneous therapy group.

After about ten sessions attendance generally became more regular as the group members became interested in and committed to the group. Increased interest in lithium maintenance and its risks and benefits often seemed to serve as the focus of the member's interest during this period and seemed to indicate the integration of the patient in the group. The new member was often surprised to discover that other members were the source of a great deal of information about lithium use; other group members provided support and reassurance to the new member during this period. The new member would begin to show more interest in his own treatment, e.g., inquiring about blood levels, describing his various side effects, etc. The common interest in lithium served to foster cohesiveness in the group. Other common themes included the patient's sense of loss of the periods of mild-to-moderate euphoria he is less likely to experience when being maintained on lithium.[7] Members often found that they were forced to make changes in their work and social habits as a result of the loss of these periods.

By the sixth month of participation in the group, patients were generally active in the group and committed to it; they served as "culture carriers" for new members. Participants became progressively more open during the course of their time in the group. Common themes during this period included fears of recurrence of mania or depression and the consequent social disruption. Marital and family difficulties often were discussed as well as concerns about feelings of dependency and hostility. Less time was spent discussing medication issues in the group, although there would be a resurgence of interest in lithium-related issues when a group member experienced either a period of depression or euphoria or when a new member joined the group.

During their last months in the group, members expressed increased concerns over the effect of their illness on family members and friends. Representative comments made during this period included statements like: "I feel like I am an introvert trapped in an extravert's body," and "When I'm high I live in the future, when I'm low I live in the past—my problem is learning to live in the present." Patients during this stage of group participation seemed much like other patients in long-term group therapy, i.e., much time was spent in interpersonal learning, instilling of hope, and the experience of mutual sensitivity.

If a member began to exhibit signs of either mania or depression, a considerable portion of the group meeting would be devoted to discussing this. Other members were particularly acute in responding to any indication of an impending manic or depressive episode. Members were especially sensitive to increased need for attention in the group as well as problems of increased activity, unrealistic plans, unexpected hostility, etc. These occasional episodes were less disruptive in this group than they would have been otherwise, since the other members could provide support and encouragement and the sense that they had experienced what the member was experiencing.

OUTCOME

Members attended an average of 47 sessions during their time in the group. With the exception of three participants who left the group during the first three months of membership, participants typically left the group only after returning to full-time employment. These "graduates" of the group were invited to return periodically for medication follow-up; these members served as models of lithium efficacy to other members.

In the two-year period prior to their participation, fourteen of the members had been hospitalized for mania or depression. Only six members were continuously employed during this period. During the two-year period following their entry in the group, four of the participants have been rehospitalized for treatment of affective episodes. The group as a whole has averaged 3.6 weeks per year in the hospital during the period as compared to the average of 16.8 weeks per year in the two-year period prior to their entering the group. In two of these four cases, the rehospitalization occurred some months after the patient had terminated the group and had stopped lithium prophylaxis. The preponderance of group members indicated that they felt a more satisfactory and adequate social and occupational adjustment at the time they ceased full-time participation in the group. While only six members had been continuously employed in the two-year period prior to their participation, in the subsequent two years sixteen members secured continuous full-time employment or full-time student status. Lithium levels in the two-year period prior to group participation averaged 0.62 mEq./1. In the subsequent two-year period mean lithium levels averaged 0.96 mEq./1.

DISCUSSION

Davenport et al.[11,12] have described the use of a couples group in the long-term treatment of manic-depressive patients. The patients followed in couples group therapy generally had more benign hospital courses than those who received the usual medication follow-up. Rosen[13] has reported on two and a half years of experience with monthly "lithium group" meetings aimed primarily at promoting lithium compliance. The patients in that group were homogeneous only in that they were receiving lithium therapy and were not uniformly bipolar patients. In that group a majority of the patients at follow-up were managed successfully in the group.

Although some investigators[14] have recently questioned the existence of character pathology in the euthymic phase of this illness, the consensus of psychotherapeutic opinion has tended to support the notion that these patients have character pathology that makes psychotherapy difficult, at best. These patients have been generally thought to have problems with dependency, hostility, impulsivity and the frequent use of denial as a defense. They have been viewed as being capable of forming only the most superficial of relationships.[1] Characteristic interpersonal patterns have been found to occur in acutely manic patients, e.g., projection of responsibility, sensitivity to others' vulnerabilities, etc.[15] Our experience has been that many of these patterns are also present, at least initially, during the course of a patient's participation in a homogeneous group of this kind.

We found that even though such problems may arise, they are not insurmountable obstacles to group treatment. The attempts of the patient to project responsibility on the therapists and to avoid focusing on a sometimes painful reality are readily dealt with in a group setting. The advantages of such an approach are numerous. The use of lithium is demystified, and patients are forced by other members to accept responsibility for lithium maintenance; indeed, in this setting their "conventionality" encourages compliance. Close follow-up is obtained with both the patient's clinical state and lithium levels being regularly monitored. The occasional episode of euphoria or depression can be handled in a much more supportive and empathic fashion than would be the case in a mixed therapy group. Finally, the patient is unable to say, "You can't understand what I'm going through" since the other members have experienced the same problems and feelings.

Davenport, et al.[11] remind us that even though lithium can stabilize mood swings, the patient's interpersonal difficulties can remain and interfere with successful lithium prophylaxis; lithium use does not solve all the patient's problems. Our experience is that cessation of lithium use seems more often to result from denial of illness and lack of information about lithium and lack of support from family members or friends, rather than from a conscious desire to precipitate a manic episode.

Despite our patients' histories of poor adherence to lithium maintenance, the relapse rates we report compare favorably to those reported in other studies of lithium maintenance.[8] It is not clear whether the high rate of compliance is secondary to the effects of group therapy as such or to the close follow-up patients received or to the interaction between the two; such interactions have been reported between antidepressant medications and psychotherapy.[16] Certainly the modeling of lithium compliance and effectiveness provided by the attendance of "graduates" of the group encouraged compliance, as did the support they received each week from other group members.

Contrary to expectation, we found that these patients worked well in a homogeneous therapy group of this kind. The common experience of manic-depressive illness made the episodes of hypomania or depression much less disruptive than would have been the case in a heterogeneous therapy group. The same therapeutic factors are presumably at work in groups of this kind as in other groups, e.g., instillation of hope, interpersonal learning, support, mutual sensitivity, universality, and imparting information.[2] The benefits of this kind of psychotherapeutic approach included the demystification of lithium treatment with a consequent lessening of the patient's unrealistic expectations as well as the involvement of the patient in the treatment process and an increase in the patient's sense of control over his illness. Groups of this kind may serve as a simple, efficient, and cost-effective adjunct to lithium maintenance therapy, especially for patients with a history of poor adherence to lithium prophylaxis. They may also offer a way of providing the benefits of psychotherapy to a group of patients generally seen as poor candidates for such treatment.

SUMMARY

Because patients with bipolar affective illness have generally been viewed as poor candidates for psychotherapy, many clinicians have relied on lithium prophylaxis as the major treatment modality. However, even with lithium prophylaxis many patients still relapse, often in settings providing little support for maintenance treatment. This report presents the results of a long-term therapy group composed exclusively of bipolar manic-depressive patients, many of whom had histories of poor adherence to lithium maintenance. The group met weekly and was conducted with an interpersonal, interactional "here and now" format. Patients attended an average of 47 sessions. Members were initially somewhat aloof and remote and minimized their problems. Over the course of their participation, members became more open and began to discuss their concerns about their illness and lithium maintenance treatment; during this time they functioned much as members in any long-term psychotherapy group. In the two-year period prior to entering the group, patients averaged 16.8 weeks of hospitalization; in the subsequent two-year period they averaged 3.6 weeks of hospitalization. Groups of this kind may offer a simple, cost-effective adjunct to lithium maintenance treatment and may provide the advantages and opportunities of psychotherapy to a group of patients generally seen as resistant to such approaches.

REFERENCES

1. Cohen, M., Baker, C., Froom-Reichmann, F., et al. An Intensive Study of 12 Cases of Manic-depressive Psychosis. *Psychiatry*, 11:103, 1954.
2. Yalom, I. D. *The Theory and Practice of Group Psychotherapy*. Basic Books, New York, 1975.
3. Stallone, F., Shelley, E., Menlewicz, J., et al. The Use of Lithium in Affective Disorders: III. A Double-blind Study of Prophylaxis in Bipolar Illness. *Am. J. Psychiatry*, 130:1006, 1973.
4. Benson, R. The Forgotten Treatment Modality in Bipolar Illness: Psychotherapy. *Dis. Nerv. System* 36:634, 1975.
5. Clayton, P. J. Bipolar Affective Disorder—Techniques and Results of Treatment. *Am. J. Psychother.* 32:81, 1978.
6. Carlson, G. A., Kotin, J., Davenport, Y. B., Adland, M. Follow-up of 53 Bipolar Manic-depressive Patients. *Br. J. Psychiatry*, 124:134, 1974.
7. Van Putten, T. Why Do Patients with Manic-depressive Illness Stop Their Lithium? *Comp. Psychiatry*, 16:179, 1975.
8. Welner, A., Welner, Z., and Leonard, M. Bipolar Manic-depressive Disorder: a Reassessment of Course and Outcome. *Comp. Psychiatry*, 18:327, 1977.
9. Shakir, S., Volkmar, F., Bacon, S., Pferrerbaum, A. Group Psychotherapy as an Adjunct to Lithium Maintenance. *Am. J. Psychiatry*, 136:455, 1979.

10. Fieve, R., Kumbarci, T., and Dunner, D. Lithium Prophylaxis of Depression in Bipolar I, Bipolar II, and Unipolar Patients. *Am. J. Psychiatry,* 133:925, 1976.

11. Davenport, Y., Ebert, M., Adland, M., et al. Couples Group Therapy as an Adjunct to Lithium Maintenance of the Manic Patient. *Am. J. Psychiatry,* 47:495, 1977.

12. Ablon, S., Davenport, Y., Gershon, E., et al. The Married Manic. *Am. J. Orthopsychiatry,* 45:854, 1975.

13. Rosen, A. M. Group Management of Lithium Prophylaxis. Paper presented at the 133rd annual meeting of the American Psychiatric Association, San Francisco, CA., May 6, 1980 (mimeo).

14. MacVane, J., Lange, K., Brown, M., et al. Psychological Function of Bipolar Manic-depressives in Remission. *Arch. Gen. Psychiatry,* 35:1351, 1978.

15. Janowsky, D., El-Yousef, M., and Davis, J. Interpersonal Maneuvers of Manic Patients. *Am. J. Psychiatry,* 131:250, 1974.

16. Kierman, G., DiMascio, A., Weissman, J., et al. Treatment of Depression by Drugs and Psychotherapy. *Am. J. Psychiatry,* 131:186, 1974.

MULTIPLE PERSONALITY

CHAPTER 40

MULTIPLE PERSONALITY DISORDER

A Challenge to Practitioners

Thomas J. Giancarlo

M uch has been written about multiple personality disorder in the past 10 years. Forms of multiple personality disorder have appeared throughout history; often it was considered proof of demonic possession. Reported cases go back as far as 1646 (Bliss, 1980). Numerous cases have been reported since that time, as students of the human psyche became interested in the mechanisms of the mind, especially dissociation. In the early part of the 20th century, however, the psychiatric profession showed less interest in dissociation and multiple personalities as a result of the psychoanalytic model's emphasis on repression. Moreover, the diagnosis of schizophrenia was used more often in the United States in the 1920s, resulting in a decline in the diagnosis of multiple personality. Bleuler states that "schizophrenia produces different personalities existing side by side" (Rosenbaum, 1980, p. 1384). The lay public's view of schizophrenia as being a form of "split personality" evolved during this period (Bernheim & Levine, 1979). It wasn't until the 1970s that interest in dissociation and multiple personality was renewed, partly as a result of the publication of *Sybil* (Schreiber, 1974)—a book that reintroduced the public and the mental health profession to multiple personalities.

The *Diagnostic and Statistical Manual of Mental Disorders* (DSM-III-R) (American Psychiatric Association, 1987) defines multiple personality disorder as follows:

A. The existence of two or more distinct personalities or personality states (each with its own relatively enduring pattern of perceiving, relating to and thinking about the environment and one's self).

Reprinted from *Families in Society,* Vol. 72, No. 2 (1991), pp. 95–102, by permission of the publisher, Families International, Inc.

B. Each of these personality states at some time, and recurrently, takes full control of the individual's behavior (p. 106).

This definition is different from the 1980 edition of the manual (American Psychiatric Association, 1980), which stated that "each individual personality is complex and integrated with its own unique behavior patterns and social relationships" (p. 259). Putnam (1989a) reminds us that many secretive alter personalities actively avoid the "social relationships" mentioned in this definition. In addition, many of the alter personalities are "personality fragments," that is, entities with a persistent sense of self and a characteristic, consistent pattern of behavior but "with a more limited range of function, emotion, or history" (Kluft, 1984b, p. 23). These fragments might appear only in specific contexts, such as a guardian personality that emerges to protect the body from injury or threat. However, as Lowenstein (1989) pointed out, current thought focuses less on the personalities as reified constructs and more on multiple personality disorder as a complex dissociative process, only one aspect of which is the creation of alter personalities.

ETIOLOGY

Several models have attempted to describe the development of multiple personality disorder. Kluft's (1984a) four-factor theory posits that a person is a candidate for multiple personality disorder if he or she is sufficiently influenced by the following factors:

1. He or she has the biological and psychological potential to disassociate.
2. He or she is exposed to traumatic experiences that overwhelm normal means of coping with stress, thus causing the person to dissociate.
3. These dissociations assume forms such as the development of imaginary companions.
4. Significant others do not protect the individual from overwhelming stimuli and/or do not provide adequate soothing and other restorative experiences (e.g., a parent who does not recognize a child's stress and trauma and does not comfort the child in some way).

Putnam (1989a) believes that "we are all born with the potential for multiple personalities and over the course of normal development we more or less succeed in consolidating an integrated sense of self" (p. 51). He explains that in infancy our behavior is organized into a series of discrete states. Over time, and with the help of healthy caretakers, we learn to modulate the transitions between these behavioral states. Our success with this process allows us to sustain a given state longer and to present a "more unified sense of self across contextual changes" (p. 51).

Children are able to more easily enter dissociative states than are adults. Children are able to fantasize and to project feelings, motives, and thoughts onto objects such as dolls. An extension of this is the development of imaginary companions. Imaginary companions are often seen in normal children. However, many researchers believe that in children who are predisposed to multiple personality disorder, imaginary companions may be the prototypes for alter personalities. It may be that these imaginary companions are endowed with certain characteristics and linked to specific types of circumstances, feelings, or experiences. Similar experiences occurring over time reinforce this process, building a kind of "life history" for that personality part (Putnam, 1989a). Putnam (1989a) further states that "the number of different alter personalities in adult MPD victims is significantly correlated with the number of different kinds of trauma suffered in childhood, suggesting that a child enters into different dissociative states depending upon the circumstances" (p. 54).

In general, then, a child with potential and predisposition for dissociation may use that naturally occurring psychological mechanism to cope when exposed to overwhelming stress. If similar circumstances recur, the child's dissociation may solidify into an alter personality system, especially if significant caretakers in that child's life fail to relieve that stress or, worse, contribute to the continuation or recurrence of that stress.

In a National Institute of Mental Health study of 100 cases of multiple personality disorder, Putnam, Guroff, Silberman, Barban, and Post (1986) found that 97% of the cases reported significant childhood trauma, 68% reported incest, 85% reported sexual abuse, and 80% reported physical abuse. Confinement abuse was common. In addition, various forms of emotional abuse were commonly reported, including threats of violent punishment or actual abuse of siblings or pets in the presence of the child. Approximately 40% reported witnessing a violent death. Clearly, the vast majority of persons with multiple personality disorder grew up in highly dysfunctional families where violence was common.

DIAGNOSIS

The classic presentation of multiple personality disorder is a client who is depressed, anxious, with blunted affect, a constricted range of feelings, often guilt ridden and masochistic, suffering both psychological and physiological symptoms, as well as time loss or distortion (Kluft, 1984a). Prior to being diagnosed with multiple personality disorder, these clients have usually been in and out of the mental health system for many years (seven years on average) (Putnam et al., 1986) and have received several different diagnoses, for example, depression, schizophrenia, manic-depressive illness, or borderline personality disorder. They may have been hospitalized and medicated for these diagnoses but typically have not improved with treatment. At least 75% have made one or more serious suicide attempts, and approximately 33% have mutilated themselves (Putnam et al., 1986). Substance abuse is also quite common (Coons, 1984).

Trust is a major issue for persons with multiple personalities, just as it is for other victims of abuse. Self-protection and secrets are part and parcel of multiple personality disorder. Thus, much of the personal data needed to confirm the diagnosis is not readily available to the therapist early in treatment. The presenting personality may actively withhold information in order to protect the multiple personality system or because important personal material may just not be available to a given personality.

Most reports of clinical experience indicate that fewer than 10% of cases present with abundant evidence of the disorder (Kluft, 1985). Usually, it is only after some time in therapy that a therapist may begin to suspect multiple personality disorder. In addition to the criteria described earlier, Greaves (1980) noted several signs that may suggest the possibility of multiple personality disorder. These signs may appear only gradually and sporadically and can be easily overlooked.

> 1) Time distortion or time lapses, 2) Being told of disremembered behavior, 3) Observers' reports of notable changes, 4) Other personalities elicitable by hypnosis, 5) Use of "we" in a collective versus editorial sense, 6) Discovery of productions (such as writing or art) or objects among one's possession [sic] which neither can be recognized nor accounted for, 7) Severe headaches, 8) The hearing of voices, originating within, but separate, entreating toward good or bad deeds (Kluft, 1984b, p. 23).

Once the possibility of multiple personality disorder or other chronic dissociative disorder is suspected, the clinician should seek out information that will clarify the diagnosis. The therapist will need to explore with the client issues regarding "time loss" or other time distortion. For example, these might include time unaccounted for; behavior that can't be explained, such as purchases made and forgotten; connections with people unknown to the host or presenting personality; and fugue-like experiences wherein the person cannot account for why he or she is in a certain place or how he or she got there.

Such inquiries may begin to elicit in the client a pattern of experiences over his or her lifetime that describes the person's disjointed history. This may include an erratic work history, with abrupt job changes, or equally erratic social and emotional relationships. The person may have been described as "moody" by friends or family and may have been accused of being a liar as a child. The person may evince some knowledge or skill—such as the ability to paint or to write creatively—and not know how he or she acquired it.

Fagan and McMahon (1984, p. 29) summarize the signs of multiple personality disorder or incipient multiple personality disorder in children. Because many of these indicators are seen in other diagnostic groups, the clinician needs to look for a pattern of these signs:

- "In another world." This may be evidence of the person switching back and forth among personalities.
- Responds to or uses more than one name and may seem confused about other names or use the third person to refer to him- or herself.
- Shows marked changes in personality, swinging from one set of characteristics to the opposite (shy to belligerent, demure to seductive, feminine to masculine, etc.).
- Peculiar and perplexing forgetfulness. Confused about basic things such as possessions, teachers' names, and so forth.
- Odd variations in physical skills and attributes: right handed vs. left handed, artistic ability, food preferences.
- Inconsistent schoolwork.
- Disruptive, delinquent, or peculiar behavior.
- Perplexes professionals. They are unable to diagnose the problem or to help child change behavior with usual therapeutic approaches.
- Lies. Denies lying in spite of clear evidence.

- Discipline has little or no effect.
- Discipline responded to by strong protestations of innocence or stoical detachment.
- Delinquent behavior far beyond normal childhood acts.
- Self-injurious, self-mutilating, reckless, takes physical risks.
- Homicidal. Has severely injured other children or adults or attempted assault with a deadly weapon.
- Suicidal—overt, serious attempts.
- Precocious sexuality.
- Truant.
- Lonely. Often ignored, avoided, teased, or rejected by other children.
- Many physical complaints, illnesses, or injuries. These may be hypochondriacal complaints or evidence of physical abuse.
- Hysteric symptoms (sleepwalking, sudden blindness, epileptic-like seizures, paralysis, loss of sensation).

The child may experience some or all of the following:

- Loses track of time, is disoriented with respect to time and/or place.
- Believes he or she is called by the wrong name.
- Hears voices inside his or her head.
- Feels as if he or she is frequently punished when innocent.
- Has imaginary playmates.
- Is lonely.

ALTER PERSONALITIES

A person may have two personalities, as was the case in early reports, or as many as several hundred, although many of these do not fit the definition of "personality" and are actually personality fragments. The average number found in several studies was 13 to 15 (Kluft, 1984c; Putnam et al., 1986). One major study (Putnam, 1984) explored the range of characteristics of alter personalities. One third of the therapists surveyed had seen patients change from being right-handed to left-handed and vice versa. One half of the subjects had personalities that responded differently to medication; 75% had personalities with different physical symptoms; 25% had alternate-personality-specific allergies; 75% had personalities claiming to be younger than 12; and 50% had opposite-sex personalities.

Tests were performed with multiple personality disorder patients versus a control group told to "fake" having alter personalities and switching between them (Putnam, 1989b). Tests on both groups included electroencephalograms (EEGs), galvanic skin response tests, and positron emission tomography (PET) scans.

Results indicated that the control group's faking did not sufficiently alter mental and physical results of the tests, whereas the multiple personality disorder group did. The various personalities of the multiple personality disorder patients showed real changes in all the tests as well as during the switching process.

Several types of alter personalities are common in multiple personality disorder. The personality that is most often in control of mind and body is considered the host personality. It is this personality who often presents for treatment and will typically fit the classic presentation described above.

Most people with this disorder have personalities that protect and help the person. Often they serve to protect the individual from persecutor personalities, which are also common in multiple personality disorder patients. The persecuting personality may be self-destructive and may consider him- or herself separate from the host and other personalities.

Sometimes patients have a special helper personality called the *inner-self helper* (Allison, 1974). This personality may be able to provide insight into the workings of the multiple personality system and may also help influence other personalities to cooperate with the therapist. This personality can become a great ally in the treatment process.

Child personalities are very common in multiple personality disorder systems. Some patients may have many child personalities, each of whom retains a tragic memory of the patient's childhood. A lot of the therapeutic work focuses on the child personalities in an effort to gain their trust and to work through long-stored and repressed memories.

Some of the alter personalities may not be aware of other personalities. Other personalities may be aware of all of them but still not know why they exist. Some personalities express the bond of sharing the same body with other personalities, whereas others consider themselves completely independent. Some memories are shared among some of the alter personalities. Other memories are held within an individual personality. The helper personalities often play a nurturing, almost parental role, with one or more of the child personalities. Often, the host does not know about the other personalities.

TREATMENT

In discussing therapeutic goals with multiple personality disorder patients, Caul stated, "It seems to me that after treatment you want to end up with a functional unit, be it a corporation, a partnership or a one-owner business" (Hale, 1983, p. 106). The treatment goal for most cases of multiple personality disorder is fusion or integration of the personalities into a single unified personality with the concomitant goal of ending the time loss, amnesias, and physiological effects, such as headaches, that these patients experience.

Allison (1974), Braun (1986), Caul (1978) and Putnam (1989a) have presented guidelines for treatment of this disorder:

1. Establish an atmosphere of safety and trust. This is essential to treatment because the client has been severely victimized in the past.
2. Make the diagnosis and share it with the available personalities.
3. Establish communication with the accessible personalities. This may be done directly or through hypnosis or keeping a journal.
4. Develop a contract with regard to therapy (i.e., limits, avoidance of self-harm, etc.).
5. Gather history on the individual and the system to determine the origin, functions, and problems of each alter personality.
6. Begin to work on the alter personalities' issues.

7. Map the system (i.e., the structure, relationships of the various personalities).
8. Increase communication among the alter personalities. This breaks down the amnesia barriers and the need for separateness is diminished.
9. Work toward recovery and integration of traumatic material.
10. Help patient to develop new coping skills and social supports.
11. Solidify the gains made.
12. Long-term follow-up.

The treatment process is dynamic; most of these steps are overlapping and ongoing. No one right way exists to do therapy with multiple personality disorder patients. Most experts agree that therapeutic effectiveness mainly requires good psychotherapy skills and knowledge about the particulars of the disorder.

The therapist needs to understand the degree of commitment needed for the therapeutic process of treating a multiple personality client. Most therapy lasts a year or longer, and many experts recommend that the client be seen more than once a week. In order to manage this therapy properly, the therapist needs to contract with the client regarding the limits of treatment, the safety of both the therapist and the client, the therapist's privacy, and the safety of the therapist's property. The contract should be negotiated with as many of the alter personalities as possible. Putnam (1989a) recommends a written contract.

Watkins and Watkins (1984) offer several bits of wisdom regarding the therapist–client relationship. In order to build and keep the trust necessary to complete this difficult work, "the patient must perceive the therapist as friendly, strong and unafraid" (p. 116). Eventually, all the alter personalities must believe that the therapist can handle anything that comes up in the treatment process. Moreover, "it is vitally important that the therapist remain on good terms with every ego state" (p. 114). The therapist should keep the following principle in mind:

> The first essential to be recognized by a therapist is that each personality has been created for a purpose to fill a need of the individual, and that one can seldom eliminate it, however malevolent it appears to be, unless the basic need or purpose is met in some more constructive way (p. 113).

This caveat corresponds to Kluft's (1984c) reminder that the therapist should treat all personalities similarly and that "treatment will sink or swim on the quality of the therapeutic alliances developed with the personalities" (p. 14).

The demands on the therapist can be very great, especially when treating his or her first multiple personality client. Because the disorder is relatively rare, most therapists will not have been exposed to extensive literature on the subject. When confronted with his or her first case, the practitioner may attempt to absorb as much knowledge as possible in a short period, which may create a crisis of competence for the therapist. Although it may be difficult to find a supervisor with more experience than the treating therapist, finding someone with experience with such cases can be invaluable. Also, diagnosis of this disorder will be met with skepticism by one's colleagues, resulting in feelings of professional isolation. One's own belief in the diagnosis may also falter from time to time.

These clients may need to be seen two or three times per week. Often, the process of contacting alter personalities and working through the traumatic experiences held in their memories is not easy to fit into a 50- or 60-minute session. The therapist must schedule carefully in order to accommodate other clients and to allow time to process the events of the session. In addition, because journaling is an excellent way for clients to continue therapeutic work outside of the sessions and for alter personalities to "contact" the therapist, the therapist may find him- or herself spending additional time reading the journals of a cooperative client. When added to the time spent keeping notes, talking with colleagues about the case, and just thinking about it, the treatment process can begin to feel quite overwhelming.

The actual experience of being with a multiple personality disorder client—witnessing the switches from one personality to another, often several times in a session, and watching a person relive, from several different perspectives, horribly traumatic episodes of abuse—can be very draining indeed. Being with a person who changes from a tough, swaggering male personality to a cowering, thumbsucking child to a lilting, hopeful "flower child" to a depressed, bland, woeful host personality in a matter of minutes can cause one to question his or her own sense of reality. My experience was echoed by a colleague who described being in an "altered state" during and after sessions with such a client and needing to "come down" and reorient before moving on to another activity. A combination support group and study group of therapists who work with multiple personality disorder clients may help the therapist to cope with these effects.

Therapists should have access to a psychiatrist, who can act as a supervisor or consultant, especially if the psychiatrist has some experience with multiple personality disorder. Although "there is no good evidence that medication of any type has a direct therapeutic effect on the dissociative process as manifested in MPD" (Putnam, 1989a, p. 253), medication may be used to control or ameliorate specific nondissociative symptoms, such as depression, that may interfere with psychotherapy. A psychiatrist can make periodic assessments of the efficacy of medication. Moreover, although outpatient treatment is preferred, the psychiatrist can be a valuable resource if brief hospitalization is necessary.

CASE EXAMPLE

C was 35 years old, married, and the mother of four children. She was participating in a sexual abuse survivors' group as a result of flashbacks of sexual abuse by her mother. In the first group session she revealed graphic details of this abuse but in later sessions seemed unaware of what she had revealed. Her group therapist referred her to me in January 1988 with the goal of uncovering suspected traumatic material through hypnosis.

Prior to being in the survivors' group, C had undergone treatment intermittently since 1978 with at least six different therapists. She had been hospitalized twice for depression and had been treated with antidepressants. During the first session, her presentation fit the typical "host" personality pattern, namely, depressed, blunted affect, anxiety and phobias, and panic attacks. When asked what she wanted out of therapy, she listed work on the above symptoms. However, her first stated goal was to become more "cohesive," in reference to her feeling of being scattered inside.

Several months before I met C, she wrote in her journal,

> I needed to be covered to hide my own self from all that truly scared me because I couldn't face all the fears because there was no way to face them without admitting how badly I was really hurting and if I acknowledged the hurt there would be no way to get through it without admitting all the rest and if I admitted that then I would undo my own self.

She was aware of much but not all the physical abuse she had been subjected to. However, she had no clear memory of sexual abuse, only vague images of "hands" and "eyes." Confusing and conflicting memories and reports are often given by clients with multiple personality disorder.

Despite her stated desire for "cohesiveness," multiple personality disorder was not considered for at least two months in that the author was not familiar enough at that time with the indicators of multiple personality disorder. It wasn't until she had an abreaction after looking at a picture, brought in at my request, of herself at approximately three or four years old that I began to suspect the possibility of multiple personality disorder. At that time, she requested that we work on her fear of bees. I performed a simple hypnotic induction (multiple personality disorder clients are often hypnotized easily) by suggesting she take a deep breath, close her eyes, and "go inside" to find that part of herself that knows more about the bees. Again she had an abreaction, describing a scene in which she had a cage over her head. Her mother wielded an axe, saying she was going to cut C's head off. She also remembered another scene but she couldn't describe it. I asked her to draw it, and she drew a childlike picture of a baby in a crib, a woman with various implements, later discovered to be a shoe horn and a button hook. C was quite disturbed when drawing this but did not recall the scene upon awakening.

In another session, using the same techniques, C described a rape by a stranger when she was 13 years of age as well as mistreatment by her mother and grandmother. She began journaling at my request; multiple personality disorder was further suggested by the widely variant handwriting in her journals.

Upon referral to a psychiatrist, antidepressants were prescribed. As is often the case with such clients, the medications were not effective. Moreover, the side effects were intolerable so the medication was discontinued.

The diagnosis of multiple personality disorder was made and shared with C. She became quite upset, feeling that she was bad. A week later, a shiver ran through my body as I greeted her in my waiting room. There was something different about her. When we were in my office I said, "You seem different today." When she offered no response, I asked "Who's here?" "I'm Nikki," was the reply. It turned out that Nikki, a male protector personality, had come to "check me out." The session was tense but formed the beginning of an extremely valuable alliance.

I eventually met many other personalities, including five child personalities, three helpers, and a persecutor who later became a helper before finally merging. Other personalities existed whom I didn't meet because they had been "banished" for unacceptable behavior. Each personality served a purpose: one to help untie the ropes that were used to tie her in bed and in the fruit cellar, another to deal with the rape and subsequent sexual experiences, another to "hold onto hope," another to take away the pain, another to deal with the abuse perpetrated by C's father, another to cope with abuses perpetrated by her mother, a "public" personality, the host personality, and others. During the course of therapy, several of these personalities merged, feeling that their issues had been addressed and their work done.

During therapy, boundaries between personalities weaken and blur. Although this is a desired goal, it threatens the system by disallowing customary dissociative means of coping with perceived danger. At this point, the therapeutic alliances and commitment to the goal of wholeness become critical. Not only must a particular personality reexperience the trauma during therapy, but in so doing painful memories "leak" across boundaries into other personalities who had been shielded from the full impact of the abuses. Even the protector personalities begin to experience the pain.

The therapists must let clients know in advance that integration will be a difficult and painful process. Honesty is critical, and the therapist will be challenged throughout the treatment process. The relationship between therapist and client must be a corrective one; that is, it must not be perceived as dishonest and thus repetitive of the client's earlier experience with significant others.

C has often experienced despair during the therapeutic process and has often wished to give up or even die. The alliance established between Nikki and me, begun in that early session, as well as my alliances with other helpers (Tornado and Dreamer) have eased the burden of therapy. In addition, C has continued in the survivors' group, in which she has a warm and meaningful relationship with the group therapist. C has also developed a warm and gentle relationship with the psychiatric consultant. These relationships with loving and trustworthy women have helped her face her fears about women in general and her mother in particular. C's husband has had limited involvement in therapy sessions, per his wish. However, he has been very understanding of and supportive to C throughout this painful process. C's children have not yet been told about C's diagnosis but they are becoming involved in family sessions.

C is a bright and talented woman who has been an underachiever throughout much of her life. Her current goal is to return to college in order to discover what she is capable of doing. Her work is far from done, but everyone involved in the therapeutic process is optimistic that she will eventually free herself from this disorder and be able to build on the strengths she has developed.

REFERENCES

Allison, R. B. (1974). A new treatment approach for multiple personality disorder. *American Journal of Clinical Hypnosis, 17*, 15–32.

American Psychiatric Association. (1980). *Diagnostic and statistical manual of mental disorders* (3rd ed.). Washington, DC: Author.

American Psychiatric Association. (1987). *Diagnostic and statistical manual of mental disorders* (3rd ed., rev.). Washington, DC: Author.

Bernheim. K. J., & Levine, R. R. J. (1979). *Schizophrenia: Symptoms, causes and treatments.* New York: W. W. Norton.

Bliss, E. L. (1980). Multiple personalities: A report of 14 cases with implications for schizophrenia and hysteria. *Archives of General Psychiatry, 37*, 1388–1397.

Braun, B. G. (1986). Issues in the psychotherapy of multiple personality disorder. In B. G. Braun, (Ed.), *Treatment of multiple personality disorder.* Washington, DC: American Psychiatric Press.

Caul, D. (1978, May). *Treatment philosophies in the management of multiple personalities.* Paper presented at the annual meeting of the American Psychiatric Association, Atlanta.

Coons, P. M. (1984). The differential diagnosis of multiple personality disorder: A comprehensive review. *Psychiatric Clinics of North America, 7*, 51–65.

Fagan, J., & McMahon, P. P. (1984). Incipient multiple personality disorder in children: Four cases. *Journal of Nervous and Mental Disease, 172*, 26–36.

Greaves, G. (1980). Multiple personality: 165 years after Mary Reynolds. *Journal of Nervous and Mental Disease, 168*, 577–596.

Hale, E. (1983, April 17). Inside the divided mind. *New York Times Magazine*, pp. 100–106.

Kluft, R. P. (1984a). Aspects of the treatment of multiple personality disorder. *Psychiatric Annals, 14*, 51–55.

Kluft, R. P. (1984b). An introduction to multiple personality disorder. *Psychiatric Annals, 14*, 19–24.

Kluft, R. P. (1984c). Treatment of multiple personality disorder: A study of 33 cases. *Psychiatric Clinics of North America, 7*, 9–29.

Kluft, R. P. (1985). Childhood multiple personality disorder: Predictors, clinical findings, and treatment results. In R. P. Kluft (Ed.), *The childhood antecedents of multiple personality.* Washington, DC: American Psychiatric Press.

Lowenstein, R. J. (1989, June 23–25). *Dissociative spectrum and phenomenology of multiple personality disorder.* Paper presented at the Eastern Regional Conference on Multiple Personality Disorder and Dissociation: Diagnosis and Treatment, Alexandria, VA.

Putnam, F. W. (1984). The psychophysiological investigation of multiple personality disorder: A review. *Psychiatric Clinics of North America, 7*, 31–41.

Putnam, F. W. (1989a). *Diagnosis and treatment of multiple personality disorder.* New York: Guilford Press.

Putnam, F. W. (1989b, June 23–25). *Psychophysiological aspects of multiple personality disorder.* Paper presented at the Eastern Regional Conference on Multiple Personality Disorder and Dissociation: Diagnosis and Treatment, Alexandria, Va.

Putnam, E W., Guroff, J. J., Silberman, E. K., Barban, L., & Post, R. M. (1986). The clinical phenomenology of multiple personality disorder: A review of 100 recent cases. *Journal of Clinical Psychiatry, 47,* 285–293.

Rosenbaum, M. (1980). The role of the term schizophrenia in the decline of multiple personality. *Archives of General Psychiatry, 37,* 1383–1385.

Schreiber, F. R. (1974). *Sybil.* New York: Warner Paperbacks.

Watkins, J. G., & Watkins, H. H. (1984). Hazards to the therapist in the treatment of multiple personalities. *Journal of Clinical Psychiatry, 45,* 172–175.

CHAPTER 41

THE PARANOID CLIENT

Monna Zentner

Considered in its more extreme form, paranoia involves a drastic loss of reality. In many respects it may involve an especially serious deviation from normal functioning. However, it is not necessarily psychotic or even near-psychotic behavior. The influence of suspiciousness on a client's style of functioning, affective experiences, style of thinking, and so on, appears along a scale of severity and is helped or hindered in a great many ways by other factors. If we wish to categorize those who are paranoid, we might group them into clients who appear to be rather open about their suspicions, filled with a sense of their own omnipotence, and often rigidly contemptuous of others, or we might have a group that could fairly be described as being very constricted, fearful, and protectively secretive of their own suspicious attitudes.[1] Generally, however, in one's caseload one finds representatives of a great range of severity and representatives whose character distortions do not fit them neatly into either classification exclusively.

CLASSIFYING PARANOID BEHAVIOR

This article will address itself primarily to those clients who may be described as nonpsychotic, clients who have long-standing and pervasive traits, such as suspiciousness, that are classically associated with paranoia.

Some writers have established frameworks for consideration of style, for example, Sibylle K. Escalona and Grace Heider referred to a general "inherent continuity of behavioral style" in their developmental study; Wilhelm Reich suggested that character forms, the crystallization of functioning modes, gave people their uniqueness; Heinz

---

Reprinted from *Social Casework,* Vol. 61 (1980), pp. 138–145, by permission of the publisher, Families International, Inc.
[1] David Shapiro, *Neurotic Styles* (New York: Basic Books, 1965), p. 54.

Hartmann supplied an angle of focus for character development and modes of functioning; Erik H. Erikson described patterns of direction, of approach, of seeking relationships; David Shapiro supplied a carefully developed groundwork for understanding styles or modes of functioning.[2]

When we identify clients as being paranoid, or when we believe that clients are apprehensive and that reality does not support their lack of trust, we are often referring specifically to the content of their thoughts. We usually note fears that do not seem warranted, a continual expectation of being fooled, or certain ideas that the client may have that suggest that he or she anticipates danger from others. In other words, we generally address ourselves to the content of the concern. But, in practice, paranoia, particularly when it is not a single instance, very aptly describes a process, a way of thinking, and a particular direction of attention.

Paranoid clients are individuals who may have an axe to grind, an idea to be supported, persons whose interest in that idea so seems to consume them that they are not open to data other than those that will support their ideas. Caseworkers have learned, often through bitter experience, that if they attempt to persuade their clients to abandon their paranoia not only is the original idea retained, but often the caseworker becomes a target for suspicion.

Case Example

The following occurred with Jane, a twenty-six-year-old social work graduate student:

JANE: I don't care if Dr. Smith doesn't want to take me. I am going to the office, and he's going to examine me.

WORKER: But his secretary did offer you an appointment for next week. I thought she said that he couldn't see anybody except on an emergency basis for the next few days.

JANE: He just doesn't want to see me because I am a feminist.

WORKER: I don't know if he likes feminists, but you were offered an appointment there. Are you feeling that it's an emergency that you see him?

JANE: It doesn't matter if it is an emergency or not. I know damn well why he doesn't want to see me. You are just defending him because you don't like me being a feminist either.

It becomes apparent through looking at this process that the client does not seem to be able to be attentive to data that do not support her idea; ostensibly, she believes that the physician does not wish to see her because she is a feminist. The fact that she has been offered an appointment, although not at the time she preferred, does not seem to influence her at all. It is important to note that Jane does not deny that the doctor might have been too busy to see her, nor does she insist that it was an emergency and that perhaps he was, therefore, treating her unfairly.

---

[2] Sibylle K. Escalona and Grace Heider, *Prediction and Outcome* (New York: Basic Books, 1959), p. 9; Wilhelm Reich, *Character Analysis* (New York: Orgone Institute Press, 1949); Heinz Hartmann, *Ego Psychology and the Problem of Adaptation* (New York: International Universities Press, 1958); Erik H. Erikson, *Childhood and Society* (New York: W. W. Norton, 1950); and Shapiro, *Neurotic Styles*.

She simply seems to dismiss the facts and to be interested only in any aspect or feature that would lend support to her original idea. Further, when the social worker addresses herself to the data she becomes included as somebody to confirm the original idea of some kind of danger from others.

The above process seems to support the thesis that paranoid clients view information with great bias. They certainly don't ignore any piece of information; indeed, they seem to be acute examiners of it. The problem seems to be that if what they examine does not support their original supposition they simply disregard or dismiss it. This is a fairly typical interaction between a paranoid client and a caseworker. Such clients seem to operate with the belief that that which does not confirm their own idea is really only a sham. They will rationalize conflicting or new information by pointing out that it is simply a superficial aspect, that they want to get to the core of the matter, and that the data do not represent the underlying truth but only an appearance of it. What paranoid clients finally term to be the truth is that which seems to justify their own suspicions.

SYMPTOMS OF INTENSITY AND RIGIDITY

Paranoid people may be difficult to work with because their observations, although frequently biased, contain aspects of reality. In truth, they often make brilliant observations and may have great success in attending to that which bypasses most individuals. Their scanning is not only very intense but also extremely active. Many social workers have had the experience of having a client notice that a pencil case, for example, has been moved from the right side of the desk to the left, when the worker may not have noticed it. Most workers have also had the experience of having certain clients notice something different about their own appearance, to which they themselves may not have been particularly attentive at all. At first glance, one might believe that the passionate scrutiny of the suspicious client is only a time-limited response to threat: that is, from his or her point of view, danger exists, and anybody will be much more careful and much more observant in the face of danger. Of course, the social worker must carefully examine the premise held by the suspicious client that there is a threat of danger. But, even if the person were in some potentially threatening position, not all clients respond by such intense observation and by such intense attention.

In long-term treatment, it becomes clear that careful scrutiny and well-directed attention are not simply occasioned by a specific danger, but seem to be a fundamental part of a *modus operandi*. It is not just a specific suggestion of danger that brings forth such careful observation and scrutiny; even when a paranoid client applies attention to problems in mathematics, statistics, or some kind of language abstraction he or she seems to apply the same kind of intensity. Such clients are ever vigilant, and no matter what the external circumstances they do not seem capable of ever being passive or casual. They always seem to be searching, always intensely attentive, always looking for something, as if they always have a very specific aim and purpose.

Certainly, paranoid thinking is only unrealistic in some ways and in many other ways is sharply perceptive. But, perceptive as it may be, it seems to be so biased and so narrow that it does not serve the client well. Helen Merrell Lynd, in discussing Rorschach, pointed out that "underlying his whole method is the conception that style and organization are more basic than the specific content . . . of experience. He regarded the process of arriving at a particular perception as more significant than the end result." In the same discussion, Lynd mentions Schachtel who "elaborated the view of perception . . . as an expression of the whole personality."[3] In essence, for each of us, at any given time or place, there are myriad stimuli, but we perceive only a relatively small number. We are influenced by what we have perceived in the past, as well as by our fears and desires to perceive certain stimuli.

Distortions of Perspective and Reality

Most of us observe our world with ideas that guide us, with beliefs and values that bias our observations, with preconceived notions of that about which we are ignorant, and, it is hoped, our ideas then become influenced by what we do observe. Others view the world from a much less firm stance, with a vague viewpoint, and may become easily impressed in their observations by whatever dramatic proclamations they happen to hear. But paranoid clients view the world from such a rigid interest, with such a narrow focus, that rather than allow their perspective to be modified by fact, they seem to impose their own convictions on whatever data they may observe.

Paranoid clients seem bent on confirming their anticipations. Because these anticipations are based on an idea that seems to be all inclusive of their interests they operate as if they are inattentive either to contradiction or to new information that does not support their anticipations. The not inconsiderable capacity for intellect and the astuteness of some paranoid clients do not become tools to help them to recognize and adjust to reality, but rather are used to mold reality to fit their own prejudices. It is as if paranoid clients are in a very narrow tunnel, and although they may perceive brilliantly within that tunnel, their perceptions are always open to question because they cannot see past the walls of their own trap. For instance, a paranoid client may be the only person to observe that there is a speck of blue on a red canvas. The difficulty is that this talent for intense and direct observation may lead him or her to contend that the only significant color in the painting is blue.

Attitudes Toward the Unexpected

Often a paranoid client seems to have a particular problem in dealing with the unexpected. In fact, for all of us, dealing with that which has not been anticipated or that which is outside of the normal demands that we tolerate uncertainty. Paranoid clients seem extraordinarily aware of and sensitive to that which is unusual. The appearance of something unanticipated seems immediately to invite their searching and intense scrutiny. It is as if they must bring it under their control, into their own framework. And the unexpected is observed very closely—again, as if the client must actively master the

---

[3] Helen Merrell Lynd, *On Shame and the Search for Identity* (New York: Science Editions, 1961), pp. 138, 139.

phenomenon. It does not seem to be merely that they are afraid that that which is new will be of danger to them, although that may be a concern. But whether that which is new is seen to be a danger or not, it is as if the threat exists not merely by virtue of the particular stimulus but by virtue of its newness, by virtue of the fact that the paranoid client did not expect it. Shapiro concludes that this cognition is characterized "by direct-edness that is maintained in a state of such extreme tension that it resembles a muscle so tense it springs to the touch."[4] In other words, alertness is so finely drawn that a mere touch—from a benign or a dangerous stimulus—causes it to quiver and respond.

We have seen that nonpsychotic, paranoid clients have distortions of reality that are certainly not all encompassing. Further, as reflected above, many of their perceptions may be quite accurate. The difficulty for paranoid clients seems to be that they lose sight of the context of their perceptions, and they have a collection of perceptions attended to and based on biases. Although suspicious clients often observe accurately that which is missed by most people, unfortunately they lose their sense of the factual world. Clients will explain this by saying, in essence, that they disdain the superficial, that they want to get beyond the trivial, inside the core of the problem.

Case Example

Tom hated and feared women. Finally, he told the social worker and defended his argument by saying that most women have a capacity for great rage and anger. He thought this was specifically true for mothers of young children and believed that most of them would secretly like to hit their children at times. From this, he seemed to conclude that there was something dangerous and something to be feared about the mothers of young children.

In fact, some of Tom's perceptions may have been based on truth. Some mothers of young children may, at one time or another, feel like hitting or beating their children. However, most mothers of young children neither give in to such wishes nor feel them in isolation. They may wish to hit their child; at the same time they may be feeling dissatisfied with themselves, and may be feeling tenderness, pity, and guilt and so on toward that child. But Tom, as is the situation with so many paranoid clients, could not see the forest for the trees. When this was pointed out to him he observed that, indeed, mothers may have feelings other than angry ones; he could not, however, attend to this, and seemed only to be able to focus on the potential violence of maternal figures.

Projection

Projection, or the attribution to external objects of feelings, motives, and impulses unacceptable to one's self seems to be characteristic of those who are paranoid. Projection does, of course, occur in many people who would not be characterized as being paranoid. The tendency to see the world with subjective blinders dictated by personal values and natures leads to the use of projection as a mechanism in most of us. It is, however, a particu-

---

[4] Shapiro, *Neurotic Styles,* p. 63.

lar feature of paranoid clients, whereas for most of the rest of the world it is not a basic characteristic.[5] The use of projection by paranoid clients is particularly of interest because they bring such scrupulous attention and intense scrutiny to the object of their projection. And, they seem to come up with observations of that which is really there as well as observations having to do with that which is not there. In other words, they attend to the external world with the conviction that they must understand the hidden intent of that scrutinized object. They are already observing with a bias, one that supports the idea that there is a hidden intent—and that, quite possibly, this hidden intent may be threatening.

Because of the biases that attend the scrutiny of paranoid clients there seems to always be a distortion of the meaning of perception. That which clients are already searching for, some affirmation that their fear of the object of projection is well founded, is, of course, always understood according to their prejudice or expectancy. For example, the paranoid client may closely observe the body posture of the social worker. Should the social worker's body unexpectedly stiffen, the client may interpret that stiffness as a sign that the social worker is expressing anger. The client may not have been consciously aware of looking for such a sign, but the change of body posture by the social worker will affirm and often crystallize the expectancy that the social worker is angry. It is possible that sometimes the paranoid client is quite correct that the social worker's body may stiffen because the social worker is angry at the client. But the stiffening of the body is seized on by the client only because it matches his or her already preconceived expectation. Most of us have enough flexibility to test out a bias, to at least consider alternative explanations for a change in body posture, for instance. But the client who has such a narrow focus and who needs support for his or her anticipation will not be able to entertain alternative explanations for the change in posture.

Case Example

The following process demonstrates this. A young psychiatrist, Bill, who had been in treatment for a few months brought in a letter he had received from his supervisor. The psychiatrist's probationary period at work was almost over, and the supervisor had reminded him in the letter that he had not yet begun the research project he had agreed to do when hired. The supervisor had gone on to suggest that Bill not start treatment with a new group of patients; instead he should devote part of his time to setting up the research project.

BILL: Well, how do you like this? I can recognize a set up when I see one (referring to the letter).
WORKER: Why do you think it's a set up?
BILL: C'mon. What else would it be? He wrote this so I could be fired at my probationary review.
WORKER: Why would he want you to be fired?
BILL: I don't know. Maybe because I don't suck up to him.
WORKER: I thought you had the impression that he likes you.
BILL: Yeah, but obviously he doesn't.

[5] Gordon R. Lowe, *The Growth of Personality* (London: Pelican, 1972), pp. 34–36.

WORKER: Why do you think the letter is a set up?

BILL: Well, now if I don't start the research, he can say he warned me but I didn't listen.

WORKER: But you were hired with the understanding that you would set up the research project.

BILL: Yeah, but maybe he's jealous because I do well with patients.

WORKER: The letter sounds as if he's trying to help you to keep your job.

BILL: I just knew he'd get me. I've wondered all along if he's jealous.

The client was unable to shift focus for a few weeks. Finally, after he set up the research in time to save his job, he was able to explore alternative explanations.

Shapiro posits that it is "tension and threat that are invariably and essentially transferred and externalized in projection; they achieve a substitute form in the experience of the projective object but not necessarily by the reproduction of their contents in the attributes of that object." In his view, "the internal tension achieves externalized form, first by transformation into defensive tension, and then, by projective reconstruction."[6]

CONTROL AND PROBLEMS OF AUTONOMY

It often appears that paranoid clients are in a constant state of anticipation for crisis. That is what is so noticeable in their concentrated observation. Sometimes paranoid people seem to be extremely controlled, sometimes irritable and ready to attack. Very paranoid clients certainly seem to lack spontaneity; they observe themselves as well as others very carefully. It is as if all of their behavior must be under constant control. Even certain social behaviors that are automatic in most people seem to be consciously controlled in suspicious clients. And, of course, most paranoid clients attribute to others the same source of intentionality in their behavior. Paranoid clients are often so guarded, their behavior so purposive, their energy so highly mobilized in the event of a feared attack, that it is no wonder that they often seem fearful of feelings that might soften such vigilance. Feelings of concern or tenderness are regarded by paranoid clients with contempt if they appear in someone else; if the paranoid client feels them internally then they seem to be regarded as a sign of weakness. Sensuality seems to be held in constraint, and perhaps understandably so, for how can one open oneself to pleasure if one must be on guard?

The underlying concern of such a constricted mode of functioning seems to be one in the area of autonomy. All of us are probably capable of the intense and narrowed scrutiny of the paranoid client, but we are also able to accept the unanticipated, to be passive in our attention, and to welcome that for which we had not planned. All of us are able to be purposive and directed like the suspicious client, but we are also capable of spontaneity, of letting go, of being playful. It is as if paranoid clients can guard self-mastery or self-authority only in direct proportion to the rigidity with which they direct themselves, and with which they turn their scrutiny to others.

[6] Shapiro, *Neurotic Styles,* pp. 95–96.

We would assume that a sense of internal mastery allows one to feel some freedom in his or her choice of behavior, and also allows one to feel able or competent to behave in various ways.[7] In contrast, very paranoid clients seem to feel neither able nor free, but rather appear to be arrogant, secretive, and almost always ashamed. They seem to feel a general sense of self-contempt and a particular fear of vulnerability to others, as if their control over themselves and over the events and their environment will disappear at a touch. Lynd points out that "even more than the uncovering of weakness or ineptness, exposure of misplaced confidence can be shameful—happiness, love, anticipation of a response that is not there, something personally momentous received as inconsequential. The greater the expectation, the more acute the shame."[8]

For a person to have a sure sense of self and place vis-à-vis others, both sense of self and sense of the outside world must have "coherence, continuity and dependability." In order for an adult to have a clear and consistent sense of self, he or she would successfully have had to test the world outside for coherence. "Shattering of trust in the dependability of one's immediate world means loss of trust in other persons. . . ."[9] Because the development of a clear sense of self would have to depend on a clear sense of the external world, it is no wonder that the person with a brittle sense of autonomy might use a paranoid mode of functioning, and might be afraid of self-betrayal. If the person has an overwhelming sense of shame, he or she would have learned not only that trust in others is not warranted, but trust in self—a self free with feelings, with yearnings and need for contact—is equally dangerous.

Attitudes Toward Power and Mastery

Paranoid clients seem always concerned with a fear of being subjugated. The person with a sense of self-mastery can act with abandon, behave nonpurposively, and, within certain parameters, relax enough to be able to comply with the wishes or authority of others. This can be achieved without feeling undue stress and without feeling subjugated. In other words, the paranoid client's lack of spontaneity, rigid directiveness, purposefulness of behavior, and fear of being subjugated by others are two sides of the same coin. It is as if the feeling or wish for self-mastery will be attacked internally as well as from the outside world. Paranoid clients often seem preoccupied with their fear that somebody will force them to submit to his or her power, someone will trick them into giving over some part of themselves that should be under their own control, someone will force them to have their freedom limited by use of some regulation.

These clients seem to be extremely cognizant of authority and of power: who has the higher rank, who is under whom and who is over whom, who is the chief and who is the lackey, who has the most power to endanger others. When they are with others, part of their narrow focus seems to be on the sense of authority or the position of authority that the other person is in. Their attitude toward authority and power may be one of great anger and resentment, but that is not the important issue: it is most important to recognize their often deep-seated feeling that the one with power, no matter

[7] Erik H. Erikson, *Identity: Youth and Crisis* (New York: W. W. Norton, 1968).
[8] Lynd, *Shame and Identity*, pp. 43, 44.
[9] Ibid., p. 45–47.

how resented he or she is, is to be understood as a person of more value than paranoid clients can attribute to themselves.[10]

Paranoid clients are extremely fearful of any kind of rejection from those in power. In fact, it often occurs that the simple process of having the social worker attentive to the client may awaken in him or her a sense of humiliation, "a sense of being visible and not yet ready to be visible."[11] One great difficulty for suspicious clients is an internal sense of vulnerability. The sense that they have made themselves vulnerable often results in more rigidly sustained suspiciousness.

Case Examples

Mrs. S had experienced very intense negative feelings toward her caseworker for several months. She spent most of her sessions complaining bitterly that the caseworker was ruining her life, hated her, and was against her. Despite this, she couldn't help but note that life in general seemed to be improving. During one session she was able to tell the caseworker very hesitantly that perhaps the caseworker was being of some positive use to her and, even more daring for Mrs. S, that she was beginning to have some positive feelings toward the caseworker.

Soon after she was able to express these positive feelings, her obsessive worry about what the caseworker "really thought" of her became intensified; accompanying that worry was her fear that now that she had "opened" herself to the caseworker, the caseworker would take advantage of her "weakness." Although she continued to do well outside the therapy hours, the next several sessions after her declaration of positive feelings were marked by a tunnel vision that focused only on whether the caseworker was rejecting her, making fun of her, or trying to hurt her in some way.

Apparently, Mrs. S experienced her affection for the caseworker and her declaration of it as a probable self-destructive act, an exposure to shame, and an invitation to invade and hurt. It is as if she were giving up a certain amount of autonomy or inviting the social worker to step in for her.

A nurse, who had always been concerned that taking orders from her superiors might put her in a humiliating position, had a new supervisor whom she admired. The new supervisor was well thought of in hospital circles, and the nurse wished to impress her. She was very careful to make clear to the supervisor that she would follow her orders, simply because she liked her and she wanted to, rather than as an "underling."

Although the supervisor seemed to have positive feelings for the nurse, she obviously did not single her out over anyone else; despite the nurse's wishes, it was clear that she was not a special favorite. At this point, the nurse began to get very

[10] Shapiro, *Neurotic Styles,* pp. 82–86.
[11] Erikson, *Identity,* p. 110.

concerned that perhaps the supervisor might be taking advantage of what she considered her "complacency" in following orders. She not only began to look for signs that the supervisor was taking advantage of her and did not care for her, but began to anticipate such symbols.

Within a relatively short time the client changed from simply longing for the supervisor's approval into being suspicious of her. The nurse became angrier and angrier. Instead of complying with routine assignments, she began to refuse them, feeling that she now had proof that the supervisor was trying to "reduce" her in some way. In a relatively short time the supervisor had gone from a person to be admired and a person from whom one would seek approval to a potential enemy.

As the once-admired person becomes the dangerous person, the behavior of the client may evoke such negative responses that the original suspiciousness, arising from a sense of vulnerability that seemed to have no base in reality, will now be sustained by repercussions from negative behavior toward the suspected enemy. In the beginning of the process described above, the nurse had responded to her own affection for the supervisor in a somewhat paranoid manner, as if a positive feeling for someone would weaken the nurse, might be a sign that her self-mastery was less under control than it should be, or might be a sign that the nurse had something weak or soft inside of her.

The process example reflects how the same concern is now externalized. The nurse examines and has the same intense scrutiny toward the supervisor she once had toward herself, but it is now the supervisor who is the enemy and not some part of the self that might open one to other people in a dangerous way. It is not just that the supervisor is now seen as potentially dangerous, a person who will take advantage of those who comply with her wishes, she is seen as personally, directly, and specifically dangerous to the nurse. In other words, it is not just a specific content that may be attributed to the superior, but a specific process or style—the superior is seen or suspected as bent on the destruction and humiliation of the nurse.

These case examples simply dramatize a constant subjective experience for the paranoid client. For the most part they are continually alert, as if they must never let down their guard. It is as if they may never stop taking precautions for, if they relax, what defenses will they have against an anticipated threat? It has been mentioned that change or surprise is very difficult for the paranoid person. Thus, their ever-ready state of being on guard protects them from being taken unaware by danger, protects them from feeling surprised by the unexpected, and prepares them to be ready for action rather than passivity in response to the unexpected.[12] It is as if they are always open to the possibility of threat.

To express positive feelings for someone, as in the example of the client who expressed affection for the social worker or the nurse who admired her superior, is subjectively experienced as a dangerous letting down of the guard. The subsequent feeling of vulnerability is then critically and negatively evaluated: to like the caseworker is to give in to the caseworker; to admire the supervisor is to be infantile and passive.

[12] Shapiro, *Neurotic Styles,* pp. 54–108, 176–201.

SUMMARY

In summary, paranoid clients might be said to interpret certain subjective feelings—tenderness, admiration, and so on—as a threat to their sense of autonomy. They seem to question themselves and examine their own motivations and feelings with close scrutiny, as if the feelings were in some way a dangerous betrayal of self-mastery. They may then become more paranoid, and with their particular tunnel vision search for proof that their original suspicious ideas are correct and can be confirmed. Paranoid clients tend to ignore the content that most people see and dismiss it as superficial or not the real thing. In other words, that which is substantially real is disdained. Generally, the narrow scrutiny persists until the suspiciousness that seems to have as its origin a fear of the loss of autonomy is confirmed. Even when there is no particular threat to paranoid clients they live in a state of guardedness, ever ready to defend against the unexpected.

This particular angle of vision suggests further areas of exploration for our understanding beyond the scope of this article. The concept of narcissism reviewed by Sophie Loewenstein[13] should be examined with specific focus on difficulties involving autonomy, vulnerability, and suspiciousness. Otto Kernberg's contributions in this field, particularly his theorizations based on experiences with nonpsychotic clients, offer a firm foundation on which to build. Erich Fromm adds valuable perceptions, but a more thorough investigation of the relationship between narcissism and paranoid styles promises to be quite useful.[14] In addition, a more thorough understanding of the development of trust and autonomy as related to paranoid modes of functioning, with their correlates of hope and omnipotence, would appear to greatly bolster an understanding of suspicious clients. Most important, from these studies must emerge a clearly delineated treatment framework for paranoid clients.

---

[13] Sophie Loewenstein, "An Overview of the Concept of Narcissism," *Social Casework* 58 (March 1977): 136–42.

[14] See Otto Kernberg, *Borderline Conditions and Pathological Narcissism* (New York: Jason Aronson, 1975); and Erich Fromm, *The Anatomy of Human Destructiveness* (New York: Holt, Rinehart and Winston, 1973).

CHAPTER 42

DIAGNOSTIC AND TREATMENT CONSIDERATIONS WITH PHOBIC SYMPTOMED CLIENTS

William P. Gilmore

INTRODUCTION

It seems to me that we, from family service and community mental health agencies, who deal with maturational and emotional problems in individuals and families, need to take another look at the way we think about and sometimes deal with phobic symptomed clients.

Phobias and phobic symptoms need to be regarded as ways of dealing with anxiety, rather than as independent pathological processes per se. We have no less an authority than Dr. Sigmund Freud for this.[1]

Phobic symptoms, which I at one time associated with genital (neurotic) functioning are to the best of my understanding, much more commonly found today in people functioning on pregenital levels of development. One can deduce from this that the phobic symptoms we see in these clients are not operating so much to handle genital (neurotic) level feelings but rather to handle earlier, pregenital (character disordered) level feelings.

This paper is a reflection of my own struggle to adapt the psychoanalytic theory I

Reprinted from *Smith College Studies in Social Work,* Vol. 41 (1971), pp. 93–102, by permission of the publisher.
[1] James Strachey and Anna Freud (1909). *Standard Edition of the Complete Psychological Works of Sigmund Freud.* Vol. X, 115 . . . in his discussion of the "Little Hans" case Freud states: "In the classificatory system of the neuroses no definite position has hitherto been assigned to 'phobias.' It seems certain that they should only be regarded as syndromes which may form part of various neuroses and that we not rank them as an independent pathological process."

learned in school, through agency in-service training and consultation, and through my own reading, to the differential diagnosis and treatment of clients with phobic symptoms. For the past ten years, I have been interested in phobic symptoms and the people who suffer from these intriguing, but nonetheless painful and restricting psychic entities. This paper is likewise a further attempt to share with other practitioners some of the helpful insights I have gained from consultations with Dr. Murray Goldstone, one of our agency consultants on adult problems.[2] I am also indebted to the work of Dr. Eduardo Weiss on agoraphobia which has served as a stimulus for this paper.[3,4]

The learning of technical psychiatric theory and its application in practice is a difficult, time and energy consuming process for social work practitioners. This learning makes heavy demands on our cognitive and emotional faculties as the material itself is highly technical and heavily laced with emotional content. As in all learning and as in all application of theory to practice, it comes unevenly in fits and starts, as the learner is able to accept it and make it a part of himself. Such an integration of theory by the worker must come before he can really make it a part of his practice. Another complication arises from the fact that our traditional psychoanalytic theory of human growth and development is based on the theory of neurosis. In our current practice (as mentioned above) we see fewer and fewer people functioning on the neurotic level. We do see more and more people functioning on character disordered levels, hence the need to broaden and adapt our traditional psychoanalytic theory to the differential diagnosis and treatment of people functioning on these pregenital levels of development. This is why we are so indebted to the growing number of casework and psychiatric writers who have been able to adapt psychoanalytic knowledge in an understandable, step by step, practical way to the needs of the clients we serve—a preponderantly large number of clients functioning on pregenital levels of development—and to the needs of the practitioners who serve them.[5,6,7]

DEFINITION OF TERMS

Character disordered people are "those persons fixated at pregenital levels of development and who express their conflicts primarily by behavioral manifestations that are based on characteristics associated with the oral, anal, and phallic-urethral levels of development. . . . They are constantly threatened by the anxiety stemming from an unresolved depression. Much of their activity is designed to ward off the anxiety. They attempt to deal with it "behaviorally" or by developing physical symptoms."[8]

---

[2] William P. Gilmore, *Notes from Consultation with Dr. Goldstone (8–2–68).* Family Service Association of Cleveland—12/4/68 (Mimeographed).

[3] Eduardo Weiss, M.D. "The Psychodynamic Formulation of Agoraphobia," in *Psychoanalytic Forum,* Vol. II, Winter 1966, 378–398.

[4] Eduardo Weiss, M.D. *Agoraphobia in the Light of Ego Psychology* (New York and London: Grune and Stratton, 1964).

[5] Effie Warren, "Treatment of Marriage Partners with Character Disorders," *Journal of Social Casework,* Vol. XXXVIII, No. 3 (1957), 118–125

[6] Beatrice Simcox Reiner and Irving Kaufman, M.D. (1959) *Character Disorders in Parents of Delinquents.* (New York: Family Service Association of America, 1959).

[7] Irving Kaufman, "Helping People who Cannot Manage their Lives," *Children,* Vol. 13, No. 3, (May–June, 1966).

[8] Reiner and Kaufman, *loc. cit.* 7–8.

Phobia or phobic reaction. "The anxiety of these patients becomes detached from a specific idea, object, or situation in daily life and is displaced to some symbolic idea or situation in the form of a specific neurotic fear . . . the patient attempts to control his anxiety by avoiding the phobic object or situation."[9]

Agoraphobia. In psychiatric literature the term agoraphobia was extended from its original meaning of fear of open places, or fear of crossing open places, to designate "all anxiety reactions to abandoning a fixed point of support, e.g., the anxiety reaction to venturing some distance from home."[10]

In this paper the term *phobic symptom* is used to designate both phobic and agoraphobic type thoughts, feelings and resulting behavior.

DIAGNOSTIC AND TREATMENT CONSIDERATIONS

A great many of the phobic symptomed clients now seen, in addition to their phobic symptoms, show depression and often somatic complaints which point to oral, early pregenital problems in ego development and functioning. The similarity of phobic symptoms in these character disordered people and their neurotic level brothers and sisters can be misleading. Needless to say, if we attempt to treat a client with phobic symptoms operating on a character disordered level of development, we and the client are in trouble. It would be similar to an orthopedic specialist treating a patient for leg bruises when in fact he is suffering from a broken leg.

There are, however, certain differences in the phobic *object* and *content* which can be helpful in differential diagnosis and treatment. As we know, the phobic symptom in a neurotic level client is a displacement of feelings from the person to whom the feelings originally were directed onto another object, person. This phobia is usually an *object* phobia i.e., relating to a person or thing (animal). A classic example is Freud's "Little Hans" case. The phobic symptom in a character disordered client is likewise a displacement but on a lower level of differentiation of the self. In this instance, the feelings are related to the *self* in a *situation*. This type of phobia is called *agoraphobia* or situation phobia, e.g., a person is afraid to leave the house, or is fearful of open places, crowds, etc.

The differences in *content* of the phobic thought are also generally an indication of the nature and level of anxiety the client experiences and hence can be an important clue as to the predominant level of development at which the individual is functioning. Object phobias, having to do with specific people or things (such as animals) are a representation of the predominantly sexual anxiety the genital (neurotic) client is struggling with. The danger as perceived by the neurotic client has to do with *external* dangers impinging on the "I" (the ego). Agoraphobic type phobias, dealing as they do with situations, circumstances, environmental factors the client feels incapable of handling adequately, point up the anxiety around early separation and loss of the inconsistent mother figure the client has experienced. His feelings of inadequacy stem from

---

[9] "Diagnostic and Statistical Manual of Mental Disorders," (Washington, D.C.: American Psychiatric Association, 1952), 33.
[10] Weiss, *The Psychodynamic Formulation of Agoraphobia,* 378.

within the self (the ego) in a situation, not from a differentiated object (person, thing) outside the self.[11]

The anxiety with which the character disordered client is struggling is predominantly around handling his own and others' aggression. In the character disordered client the unsatisfactory, primary relationship with mother has, in effect, conditioned subsequent ways of relating to others in a more severely incapacitating manner than in the neurotic client. The frustration, deprivation, primitive anger and discomfort in the primary relationship has left the character disordered individuals terribly vulnerable to their own anger and to the anger, slights, rejections of others. Hence they experience very great and pervasive problems in human relationships, lacking ego strengths and inner resources to sublimate their own basic drives and to cope with the demands of others and their environment.

In treating a neurotic client we would hope to help primarily with the struggle around *sexuality* (related to oedipal, castration anxiety). In treating a character disordered client we would hope to help primarily with the struggle around *aggression, anger* (related to early mother object loss—early separation anxiety).

We all recognize that, just as there is a mixture and/or overlapping in levels of maturity and levels of functioning in human beings, so too we find a mixture, an overlapping of phobic symptoms (like all other symptoms) in people functioning on different levels of development. We do at times find agoraphobic (situation) phobias which have genital (neurotic) aspects to them. Also, although less often perhaps, we find object phobias which have pregenital aspects to them. We at times see, in the common night phobias and irrational daytime fears of young children admixtures of early separation anxiety, phallic symbols and elements of oedipal, castration (neurotic) anxiety. Much of this is age related and dependent on the amount of ego involved in manufacturing the symptoms. Anna Freud explains that the archaic fears of very young children which appear phobic-like are not true phobias, since they are not based on regression, conflict or displacement as are actual phobias.[12]

---

[11] *Ibid.,* 379. Dr. Weiss delineates agoraphobia thus: "All cases which should be called agoraphobia are characterized by two factors: a) an anxiety reaction to a danger which is consciously sensed as an internal one; b) the situation from which it ensues, namely by the patients leaving home and venturing some distance from it. This feeling of insecurity can, of course, also be experienced in other situations, but it is always provoked by the patients leaving a place of support and venturing some distance from it. All types of real agoraphobia are characterized by such a depletion of ego energy and/or the confidence in the ability to function in an adequate manner."

  To further differentiate simple phobia from agoraphobia he states "Patients who have a phobic fear of dogs, of being struck by lightning, or of being run over, fear an *external* danger in an exaggerated and irrational degree whereas agoraphobic patients are actually exposed to a danger which is consciously perceived as an *internal* one. They fear to be trapped by a feeling of ill being which incapacitates them from functioning in a rational and integrated manner."

[12] Anna Freud (1965) *Normality and Pathology in Childhood,* 161. "Before children develop the anxieties which are coordinate with the increasing structuralization of their personality, they pass through an earlier phase of anxiety which is distressing not only to them but also to the onlooker, due to its intensity. These anxieties are often called 'archaic' since their origin cannot be traced to any previous frightening experience but seems to be included in the innate disposition. Descriptively, they are fears of darkness, of loneliness, of strangers, of new and unaccustomed sights and situations, of thunder, sometimes of the wind, etc. Metapsychologically, they are not phobias since, unlike the phobias of the phallic phase, they are not based on regression or conflict or displacement. Instead they seem to express the immature ego's weakness and panic-like disorientation when faced with unknown impressions which cannot be mastered and assimilated. The archaic fears disappear in proportion to the developmental increase in the various ego functions such as memory, reality testing, secondary process functioning, intelligence, logic, etc., and especially with the decrease of projection and magical thinking."

CASE EXAMPLES

Three examples of casework treatment of agoraphobic (character disordered) clients follow:

Mrs. Lamb, a widowed 34-year-old mother of two latency-age children came to the agency several years ago. She was afraid to venture from her own home for fear of "losing control of myself." This lady had been chronically depressed since the death of her husband from cancer several years before. She suffered from what her physician described as spastic colitis. She experienced severe stomach cramps and frequent loose bowel movements, particularly in the morning when thinking of what life demands might be expected from her that day. Mrs. Lamb shared her parents' home with her alcoholic father and depressed, victimized mother, with whom Mrs. Lamb had a very dependent relationship. She was not able to tolerate the mother's leaving her to go to work and required mother to accompany her to agency appointments.

Mrs. Lamb complained of having "no self-confidence whatsoever." She was propelled into casework treatment by her morbid fears of "losing control" and doing harm to her children, plus the realization that when her children became of age and social security benefits stopped, she would have to leave home and work to support herself.

Mrs. Lamb at first could not admit to having negative feelings toward anyone except herself. Slowly she developed a trusting relationship to me, began to talk of irritations with others, feelings of slights and rejections from others, and later the feeling of not being wanted or loved by her parents as a child. Slowly in treatment, as she dealt with her angry feelings and her current everyday life, she began to venture out into the neighborhood, then further from home. She bought another home, although her parents continued to live with her; she also established firm friendships with several neighbor women, and finally took a part-time clerical job. Subsequently she accepted full-time employment, where she often worked in the office alone. Mrs. Lamb even bought her own car, took driving lessons and admitted that she was "beginning to have a little self-confidence." She became much less dependent on her mother. In fact, her relatives began to turn to Mrs. Lamb in times of trouble. She could allow her two children to grow up more independently and lead their own lives. What apparently helped Mrs. Lamb most in counseling was the working on her angry feelings in current day-to-day living. At one time this lady's dream was to "have a trailer and travel where I can take my home along wherever I go." She has settled for a more conventional way of life, using her abilities to support herself and get more gratification from her life with a marked diminution of her agoraphobic anxieties; she became almost free of physical symptoms, was much less depressed, and looked to the future with hope.

Mr. and Mrs. Taylor, parents of four latency- and adolescent-age children, in their early forties, were referred to the agency by a private psychiatrist as he believed that theirs was a family problem rather than a psychiatric problem. In addition, they realistically could not afford private treatment. When first seen they could admit to "no problems between us, no anger, we get along just fine." They said that all of their trouble was around management of their eldest, 17-year-old daughter who had a serious identity problem and severe school phobia. However, the anger in their voices when speaking with, and of each other, the bitter tone and caustic comments they accepted as common conversation, demonstrated longstanding, unresolved conflict.

Mrs. Taylor had had several psychiatric hospitalizations for "depressive reaction." She had numerous psychosomatic complaints, chiefly hypertension and bronchial trouble. In the initial stage of treatment I saw the total family for six interviews at which point Mrs. Taylor became very anxious, had trouble getting to the office and her long-standing fears under stress of leaving the house, anxiety attacks when attending church, fears about mixing with friends and relatives came to the fore.

I switched from family interviews to joint interviews with the parents and focused on their reciprocal anger, disappointments and hurt with each other. Mrs. Taylor later admitted she got upset with the family interviews because she believed that her husband and children would soon be getting around to talking about her, telling about how "sick and complaining I am." Prior to this the children and Mrs. Taylor had all focused their complaints on the rigid, anally-oriented father who inconsistently provided whatever limits and controls the family had.

Mr. and Mrs. Taylor were able to talk with each other about deeply ingrained, ambivalent feelings they had toward each other prior to marriage. They also concluded that Mrs. Taylor's pregnancy with their "problem child" when they married may have something to do with their difficulties in managing this adolescent.

Now whenever Mrs. Taylor has a recurrence of her agoraphobic fears we talk about *what she has been angry about and with whom currently*. This way of dealing with her current anger at the resurgence of her fears invariably diminishes the agoraphobic anxiety and allows Mrs. Taylor and her husband to continue working on their feelings and considering how better to manage themselves and their children.

Mrs. Ford, a 39-year-old mother of four children ages 6 through 18, came to the agency with her husband because of their concern over 7-year-old daughter's trouble in getting to school. This couple readily admitted both had similar trouble in leaving home for school as children. After several joint appointments, Mr. Ford bowed out of counseling on the pretext of his job commitments. I believed that he simply could not tolerate looking at or working on problems in his children or in himself. Since he was functioning better in getting to work than he had at times in the past, I decided to accept this arrangement.

Mrs. Ford then brought the problemed 7-year-old and a middle adolescent daughter in with her for several appointments. After several of these partial family interviews, the communication problems quickly improved between mother and these two children. Mrs. Ford realized that she did not have to have all the answers for everything her children might bring to her. Previously, out of her anxiety she would say, "don't worry," or attempt to answer their questions, some of which were simply unanswerable. She realized that the children did not so much want answers, but rather wanted their mother's understanding and acceptance of their feelings and concerns as individuals.

As Mrs. Ford talked about her long-term depression which started before the 7-year-old was conceived, as she revealed her tremendously ambivalent relationship with her alcoholic mother and her feelings of disappointment and anger with husband for his inability to give, subsequently she was able to set more reasonable limits with and convey more realistic expectations toward her husband instead of accepting his utter dependence and lack of responsibility. In the subsequent school year the 7-year-old daughter showed no ambivalence about going to school; the undifferentiated ego tie between this daughter and Mrs. Ford diminished greatly. Mother's anxieties about her own inadequacy, her former isolation at home and retiring to bed with somatic complaints when upset decreased. After a two-month break in casework treatment, Mrs. Ford returned to the agency, and I believe is about to enter a new stage and level in treatment. She now wants to work on her own problems; previously she always presented the problems of others. Mrs. Ford wants to consider how she can deal with "a feeling of unfulfillment, of emptiness within me." Presently, she states a two-fold problem: (a) how I can effect more mature, adult social relationships and share them with my husband; (b) how I can modify a problem of lack of sexual enjoyment which relates in part to resentment toward my husband.

COMMON PITFALLS IN TREATMENT

I would like to mention two common pitfalls in treatment of phobic symptomed clients. These pitfalls are by no means limited to the treatment of only this category of client, but are perhaps more salient because clients with phobic symptoms often appear more genital, better put together than they really are.

1. If the worker mistakenly treats these clients as operating on the neurotic level of development, he may be tempted to move too quickly into areas of great anxiety. The worker may move precipitously into the matter of their angry feelings or their conflicts about sexuality. The result of this commonly is that the clients break contact. They simply do not possess the ego strengths to deal with such material and their related feelings until a strong, viable relationship with the worker has been established and considerable ego strengthening has already taken place.

2. Some clients, sensing that the worker wants to hear about certain aspects of their lives, e.g., genital problems, will "play the psychiatry game." In other words, the clients will talk endlessly of their difficulties, not really working in a manner to modify or resolve these conflicts but rather to give the worker what they think he wants to hear, to please the worker and keep the relationship with the worker. This so-called "treatment" plays into the dependency needs of the client and is of little value to the client for improving his life.

SUMMARY

To the extent that we can adapt our psychoanalytic knowledge of human growth and development to accurate, differential diagnosis and treatment of pregenital (character disordered) clients, we will meet one of the greatest challenges we face today—the effective treatment of character disordered individuals and families. On the basis of my experience at the Cleveland Family Service, a number of such clients present agoraphobic symptoms. In spite of the neurotic flavor of their symptoms, these clients for the most part are functioning on pregenital (character disordered) levels rather than on a genital (neurotic) level of development. I believe that the phobic *object* and *content,* considered in the context of the clients' overall functioning, can provide very helpful clues as to the level of their problem and hence can offer direction for the focus, level, techniques, and goals of their casework treatment.

CHAPTER 43

POSTTRAUMATIC STRESS DISORDER
AND THE TREATMENT
OF SEXUAL ABUSE

Sylvia B. Patten, Yvonne K. Gatz, Berlin Jones, and Deborah L. Thomas

When a mental health treatment center in a southern city began to offer treatment to sexually abused children in 1984, the social work clinicians assumed that the center would receive about three referrals each month. In the first month, the center received 15 referrals, and by the sixth month sexual abuse accounted for 40 percent of the caseload. The treating clinicians had difficulty determining diagnoses because of the perplexing variety of symptomatology presented by their young patients. Presenting in one session as withdrawn, subdued, and mute, in a following session a patient might be overreactive, overresponsive, and hyperactive. Sometimes bizarre behaviors or patterns of behavior had psychotic elements. Scattered, unable to concentrate one week, the next week a patient might be able to engage in activity with forcefulness and attention to purpose. Anxiety reactions, phobias, and depression all were present over time, interspersed with symptom-free periods during which the child presented normally. More and more often the staff began to identify posttraumatic stress disorder as the most appropriate diagnosis to account for this range of symptomatology.

Reprinted from *Social Work,* Vol. 34, No. 3 (May 1989), pp. 197–203, by permission of NASW Press. Copyright 1989, National Association of Social Workers, Inc., *Social Work.*

An earlier version of this article was presented at the 1987 Annual Conference of the National Association of Social Workers, New Orleans, Louisiana, September 1987.

HISTORICAL OVERVIEW

The hypothesis of sexual trauma as a precursor or causative factor in mental illness has had a long battle for acceptance. When Freud postulated sexual abuse as the cause of hysteria in 1896, the Vienna Psychoanalytical Society refused to publish a summary of the presentation (Masson, 1984; Strachey, 1953). Freud eventually turned to the Oedipal theory, which postulated that such sexual experiences and desires on the part of the child are fantasy. When Freud's friend and colleague, Ferenczi, asserted in 1932 that similar trauma was the result of sexual abuse, his work was dismissed as the ravings of a failing scientific mind (Masson, 1984). Ferenczi's (1949) work remains one of the most eloquent statements about sexual abuse. He recognized such dynamics as the validity of the trauma, the introjection of guilt by the child, the projection of guilt by parent on the child, the pseudomaturity and early maturity of the victim, multiple personality as an outcome, and the child's loss of senses because of an inability to accept the truth. When Masson (1984) reviewed these events, he promptly was dismissed from his position as provisional projects director at the Freud Archives (Crewdson, 1988; Malcolm, 1985).

The concept of posttraumatic stress disorder seems to have formed in the midnineteenth century when Charles Dickens wrote of his experience and slow emotional recovery after a railway accident (Forster, 1969). Nervous disorders attributed to spinal shock from such accidents became an important issue when compensation for injury laws were introduced in Prussia in 1871 (Trimble, 1985). Psychological trauma was recognized again when World War I veterans were classified as suffering from "war neuroses" with underlying predisposing personality defects (Kardiner, 1941). World War II veterans were said to suffer from "exhaustion," and by the Korean War, veterans officially were diagnosed as having "gross stress reactions" by the newly published *Diagnostic and Statistical Manual* (DSM-I) of the American Psychiatric Association (APA) (1952). DSM-II (APA, 1968) recognized only the more general "adult adjustment reaction." After the Vietnam War and persistence by therapists such as Figley (1985b), who recognized the effects of catastrophe and trauma, the psychiatric community again categorized posttraumatic stress disorder specifically in DSM-III (APA, 1980) and DSM-III-R (APA, 1987).

Despite the availability of the diagnosis, current medical thinking often leans toward broader diagnostic categories. Posttraumatic stress disorder symptoms sometimes are diagnosed as adjustment disorder, major depression, or closed head injury (Lyons, 1987). The extensive use of the diagnosis of borderline personality is interesting in the light of estimates of as many as 35 percent of borderline patients who have experienced incestuous sexual abuse (Herman, 1988; Nielsen, 1983; van der Kolk, 1986; Wilson, 1988). Coons (1986) found that patients who suffered from multiple personality disorder almost invariably had been physically or sexually abused. A study of female inpatients in a psychiatric setting found a 75-percent rate of physical or sexual abuse, and the researchers recommended a posttraumatic stress disorder diagnosis as an initial approach to treatment (Bryer, Nelson, Miller, & Krol, 1987). Indeed, Ellenson (1986) found that perceptual disturbances, sometimes dismissed as psychotic, may serve as diagnostic indicators of posttraumatic stress disorder and hidden histories of sexual abuse.

PROCESS OF RECOVERY FROM SEXUAL TRAUMA

The process of recovery from sexual trauma is similar to recovery from other psychological stress. Horowitz (1976) advocated trauma as a primary cause of severe malfunctioning and developed a cognitive model based on the Freudian "urge to completion" concept. Freud advised that "hysterics suffer mainly from reminiscences" (Horowitz, 1976, p. 83), which Horowitz (1976) attributed to the fact that they "cannot remember and they cannot 'not' remember" (p. 83). Horowitz categorized as denial such symptoms of inability to remember as emotional constriction, numbness, inability to evaluate stimuli, forgetting, and selective amnesia. Symptoms of "cannot not remember" are categorized as intrusion and include such symptoms as flashbacks, hypervigilance, nightfears, and inability to concentrate. Horowitz labeled the initial period after shock as "outcry" and said that the victim alternates between denial and intrusion until, through cognitive completion, the event is resolved as part of conscious experience.

Horowitz also categorized symptoms of both denial and intrusion under each bodily system and made treatment recommendations. If a client experiences numbness as a symptom of denial in the emotional system, treatment recommendations include encouraging catharsis, supplying appropriate objects, and encouraging emotional relationships. If an individual experiences intrusion symptoms in the emotional system—such as attacks or "pangs" of fear, rage, shame, or sorrow—treatment recommendations include support; suppression (for example, with medication); desensitization; and biofeedback. Horowitz asserted that both intrusion and denial phases help individuals to function until the trauma is resolved.

The models of the posttraumatic stress disorder process developed by Figley (1985a) and others recognize a more comprehensive approach to the experience. Recovery from trauma occurs when a victim is transformed into a survivor who is able to integrate the catastrophe into his or her life history and use it as a source of strength. Figley divided the process into five stages: (1) the catastrophe, which lasts until the victim feels safe; (2) relief and confusion; (3) avoidance, which reduces anxiety and is used as needed by the victim; (4) reconsideration, which involves an ability to confront the trauma; and (5) adjustment. These models recognize such personality factors as coping styles, life assumptions, and previous traumas or emotional problems.

Factors of the trauma itself influence recovery—such as the length of the trauma, exposure to the grotesque, and the passive or active role of the victim (Green, Wilson, & Lindy, 1985). Age of the sexually assaulted victim also would be a factor. Much of the research on sexual assault and its treatment can be subsumed into these models (Burgess, Groth, Holmstrom, & Sgroi, 1978; Burgess & Holstrom, 1974). The nature and role of the environment can be a positive or negative factor in the recovery process. A model developed by Anderson (1987) expands the scope of the process by recognizing institutionalized presocialization factors (such as the principle of "honor thy parents" as it affects incest situations) and by recommending such nonclinical interventions in the process as political action, public education, and community organization.

Additional clinical data need to be gathered about the time lapse between the abuse and the development of symptoms; such data would help to identify differences between chronic and acute posttraumatic stress disorder. Terr (1983) found differences in early and late symptoms of the kidnapped children of Chowchilla, who all experienced some degree of posttraumatic stress disorder. Previous vulnerability and posttrauma family problems were found to affect the severity of the symptoms.

TRAUMATIC EFFECTS OF SEXUAL ABUSE

As the recovery process takes place, certain traumatic effects often emerge. Finkelhor and Browne (1986) best integrated the themes and content of therapy of the sexually abused individual. Developed to apply to child sexual abuse, the model appears to address adult treatment issues as well. Finkelhor and Browne identified the dynamics, psychological impact, and behavioral manifestations of each of the categories to assist clinicians in moderating symptoms by addressing the underlying area of concern. Traumatic effects of sexual abuse are divided into four categories: (1) traumatic sexualization, (2) stigmatization, (3) betrayal, and (4) powerlessness.

Traumatic Sexualization

Traumatic sexualization refers to a process in which an individual's sexuality, including both sexual feelings and attitudes, is shaped in a developmentally inappropriate and interpersonally dysfunctional fashion. This process can result in a premature eroticization of the abused child, who then relates to others in a flagrantly erotic manner. Conversely, traumatic sexualization can result in the persistent intertwining of sexuality and arousal with the sense of shame and guilt often associated with the traumatic event. In the adult, such sexual dysfunctions as sexual avoidance syndromes and anorgasmia can be found. Problems can range from negatively charged sexuality to inappropriately compulsive eroticism. A related concept is Ochberg's negative intimacy, a component of posttraumatic stress that the victim must confront therapeutically to resolve feelings of disgust and degradation (Frank, 1988). *Negative intimacy* is the intrusion of the undesired sexual experience, which invades personal space and provokes associations of disgust and even self-loathing. What normally should be desirable (intimacy) becomes repulsive.

Stigmatization

Stigmatization refers to the negative connotations (badness, shame, guilt) that are communicated to the abused individual and often are subsequently incorporated into his or her self-image. Sgroi (1982) calls this category the "damaged goods" syndrome.

Betrayal

Betrayal for abused children refers to the dynamics in which the children discover that someone on whom they are dependent has harmed them or failed to protect them. For adults, betrayal issues tend to relate to a sense of a "just world," wherein victimization does not come to people who do not "deserve" it. Such victims often blame themselves and see their environment as having betrayed them. Janoff-Bulman (1985) found that this issue affects victims' belief in personal invulnerability, perception of the world as meaningful, and perception of self as positive.

Powerlessness

Powerlessness is the feeling engendered when a victim's will, desires, and sense of efficacy have been overcome or are contravened continually. Issues of powerlessness are particularly crucial for adolescents, who normally are struggling developmentally with issues of dependency and identity, and for children, who are vulnerable in any case. In incest situations, abusers often emphasize the victim's helplessness as a control technique. For male victims, powerlessness often is the crucial issue because their victim status undermines male identity as strong and aggressive.

AFFECTIVE STAGES OF THE RECOVERY PROCESS

As the individual goes through the posttraumatic stress disorder resolution process and deals with the traumatic effects, predictable affective responses usually occur. Agosta and McHughes (1987) have labeled these responses as denial, catharsis, guilt, loss of control, anger and rage, and integration and acceptance. Clinicians who work with sexually abused victims should be prepared to recognize these stages and be supportive as clients deal with such feelings. Clients' feelings of being overwhelmed with each new emotion may trigger periods of denial. Clinician acceptance and facilitation of these affective states can speed the resolution process.

INTEGRATIVE MODEL OF SEXUAL TRAUMA RECOVERY PROCESS

A synthesis of process, therapy content, and affective stages provides a working view of recovery from sexual trauma. In evaluating the client, clinicians should recognize the individual's personality, coping mechanisms, past experiences, past victimizations, and perception of the event. The nature of the trauma also must be understood—including the type of assault (such as date rape, incest, and so on); the nature of the assault (for example, length of time and resulting physical injuries); and the passive or resisting role of the victim. The client's environment includes the support system, institutional interventions, family and peer reactions, and the like. The victim of the sexual trauma must deal with issues of traumatic sexualization, stigmatization, betrayal, and powerlessness within his or her environment and with his or her characteristics. The client accomplishes this resolution by alternating between an intrusive–repetitive state and a denial–numbing state while experiencing a succession of emotional responses.

The intrusive and denial stages have both negative and positive aspects. Too much intrusive–repetitive phenomena is overwhelming, but controlled and limited intrusion leads to the positive necessary processing of the trauma. The denial–numbing of complete avoidance can lead to blocking and an inability to progress through recovery, but periodic respites from processing are a necessary part of the resolution cycle. Need for respite after the outcry experience is a culturally accepted response to trauma. Soothing and reassurance are normal human responses to an individual in such a situation. The authors propose relabeling the intrusive and denial stages of Horowitz by calling this positive resolution an experience of processing and respite.

Assessment of each client's pace in the sexual trauma recovery process is crucial to successful treatment. The occurrence of trigger symptoms (such as flashbacks or nightmares) usually indicates that more processing is necessary. Other examples of ongoing processing include cognitive reframing of the event, ventilation of feelings, and growing ability to discuss the trauma. A client who is avoiding processing should be evaluated to see if he or she is experiencing a needed respite period. If the social worker believes that respite is becoming denial, the social worker then should assist the client in returning to the processing mode. Also important is determining which symptoms of intrusion–processing or denial–respite relate to which issues of treatment. An intrusive nightmare might relate to a betrayal issue such as parental protection or to another content area. A treatment chart can be used to analyze the treatment needs of each client (Figure 43–1). The plan of therapy is to move from symptomatology of each category to the treatment goals within that category. The treatment planning chart can help clinicians to organize and formulate goals for each client. The following case material illustrates this methodology.

Figure 43–1
Sample Treatment Chart for Sexual Trauma Recovery

Stages	Treatment Issues			
	Traumatic Sexualization	Stigmatization	Betrayal	Powerlessness
Processing (intrusive–repetitive)	From symptomatology To treatment goals:	From symptomatology To treatment goals:	From symptomatology To treatment goals:	From symptomatology To treatment goals:
Respite (denial–numbing)	From symptomatology To treatment goals:	From symptomatology To treatment goals:	From symptomatology To treatment goals:	From symptomatology To treatment goals:

Susan

Susan was a 4-year-old girl who was kidnapped from her home in the middle of the
night by an unknown assailant, sexually assaulted, and left abandoned by the side of a
road. The assailant entered the home easily because the doors had been left unlocked,
and the parents and 7-year-old brother did not awaken during the kidnapping. After
the assault and abandonment, the child was found weeping under some bushes beside a
house in a residential neighborhood. Police were called, the parents were located, and
the child was returned to her home.

Various intrusive–processing symptoms were identified by the social worker as needing intervention. In the area of traumatic sexualization, the child was overwhelmed by
images and memories of the attack and was prone to impulsive verbalization about the
event, often at inappropriate times and places. One treatment goal was for the parents
to provide Susan with opportunity for ventilation without inappropriately suppressing
the child's need to process the event. The social worker and the parents also identified
important caretakers who needed to understand the process to handle the child's verbalization appropriately. For example, Susan's nursery school teacher was given information concerning the event so that she would not dismiss Susan's experiences as
fantasy. A second intervention in this area was play therapy to give Susan an opportunity to act out the attack to diminish her anxiety.

In the area of stigmatization, the social worker was concerned that Susan's parents
and others might feel that the child was "damaged goods." Both parents were given
much opportunity to ventilate their feelings in this area. In addition, the social worker
assisted the parents in identifying appropriate family members to advise of the event. A
treatment goal was to identify family members who would be of assistance to Susan's
recovery rather than who would undermine the process or who would demand nurturing by the already overwhelmed parents. An emotionally dependent grandmother
therefore was not advised of the event because she would have required much emotional support from the parents, who were not able to give it.

Susan clearly demonstrated that she felt betrayal over her parents' inability to protect
her. When she was returned home, she demanded of her mother, "Why didn't you come
when I called you?" She did not meet her parents' outstretched arms with a loving reaction because she was angered by her parents' inability to be available when she needed
their protection. Her previous life experience had been one of adequate parental protection and aid in times of trouble. In the next few weeks and months, the mother noted
Susan's increased testing of well-established rules regarding structure and play activities.
The social worker saw this testing as a projection of underlying feelings of anger and hostility that Susan directed toward her parents for letting her down. Three treatment goals
were established in this area. First, the child needed continued reassurance of her parents'
love and reestablished protection. Second, the parents addressed their guilt regarding
their failure to secure the home. The social worker provided support for the parents' past
and future adequacies and strengths. Third, the parents needed to continue appropriate
limit-setting with Susan, as they had before the traumatic incident. The social worker encouraged the parents to avoid letting guilt undermine their performing a necessary
parental role for their child. The social worker also helped the parents to understand that
because of Susan's age, she might find it difficult to express her anger directly.

In the area of powerlessness, the family felt helpless when the police were unable to apprehend the perpetrator. The social worker supported a ritualized checking of the house each night as a method of symbolically regaining control of the environment. As each door and window was locked, Susan felt some empowerment to control her own environment, and the parents could symbolize their renewed protection of her.

This case is an example of the benefit of early therapeutic involvement to prevent lasting trauma. The family's ability to assist the child through intrusive–processing stages was immediate, and Susan exhibited few examples of denial–respite. In this instance, the influence of the social worker on the child's family to facilitate a helping and nurturing environment greatly contributed to an early resolution of the child's trauma.

MARGARET

An inpatient in psychiatric treatment, Margaret was 11 years old and had been sexually abused during her latency years. Her mother appeared to have condoned sexual abuse of the daughter by the landlord because she often was in the residence when the abuse took place. A state investigation resulted in criminal charges against the abuser, and Margaret was placed with her father. She became increasingly unmanageable and was placed in shelter homes from which she also ran away. Inpatient admission was sought because she was dangerous to herself on these occasions.

In the area of traumatic sexualization, Margaret demonstrated intrusive symptomatology such as sexual acting-out and risking sexual assault during episodes of running away. A treatment goal was to turn this intrusive behavior into processing by decreasing the anxiety that led to her run-away behavior, helping her choose age-appropriate sexuality, and validating her experiences as being traumatic. Margaret's denial symptomatology in this area was her inability to discuss her abuse and the pseudomaturity she demonstrated over sexual matters. Treatment goals were to give her control over the rate of disclosure and to reinforce her appropriate behavior as it appeared.

In the area of stigmatization, Margaret demonstrated intrusive symptoms of self-blame. She believed that she was a bad person and at fault for her abuse. Treatment goals included helping her move from blaming herself as "bad" to viewing her behavior as inappropriate because such a view would provide her with a cognitive defense. Current research in victimology indicates a beneficial effect in the persistent tendency of victims to find reasons to blame their behavior at the time of the trauma (Davis & Smith, 1987, Janoff-Bulman 1985). If a victim believes that his or her behavior is partially at fault, modifications of behavior can lead to a sense of protection and of regaining control over the environment. Margaret verbalized anger over her previous inability to seek help, help that she now saw as having been available had she only asked earlier. Margaret needed assistance to see that her previous isolation, lack of information about the availability of assistance and fear of her abuser had been valid obstacles that prevented her from helping herself. New knowledge, however, could protect her from further abuse. Denial symptoms in this area included Margaret's sense of isolation from other children and the emotional limitations she forced on herself. Treatment goals were to build her self-esteem and to work on recovering appropriate family and peer relationships. Unfortunately, control of all aspects of the recovery environment is not possible, and Margaret returned to the hospital from one visit home with an analogy from her father of herself as the "bad apple" spoiling the barrel.

Betrayal issues figured largely in the intrusive model. Margaret had nightmares, including one in which she was sleeping in her bed when her mattress would disappear and she would fall on knives. Providing a secure hospital environment was a short-term treatment goal, and the rebuilding of trust was a long-term goal for this maternally betrayed child. Denial symptoms included Margaret's inability to express anger toward her mother on a conscious level and her denial of needing others. A major treatment goal was to assist Margaret to recognize her own needs without assuming that no one would be available to meet them.

Powerlessness also was a major intrusive pattern for Margaret. Some staff members saw her running away behavior as attempts to control her environment, in contrast to times in the past when she was physically powerless and assaulted. Fight–flight responses that Margaret previously could not act on she now used intrusively when she became anxious. The social worker began a process of empowerment to assist Margaret in gaining control over her behavior (Taubman, 1984). New abilities and coping mechanisms were emphasized to help Margaret realize her ability to make better decisions about her behavior (Adams-Tucker, 1985). However, Margaret's continued denial in this area was leading to apathy on her part and to repeated victimization as she let herself continue at risk. She continued to be at high risk for self-harm (Sanford, 1987).

ROLE OF THE SOCIAL WORKER

In utilizing the recovery model to treat posttraumatic stress disorder, social workers should begin by identifying symptoms as in either the processing or respite category and by identifying the appropriate treatment issue to which the symptoms relate. Social workers can outline symptoms as they appear at intake or as they manifest during the course of treatment. In working with young children, social workers often will need to include family members' symptoms as they relate to symptoms of the patient. Likewise, treatment goals of young patients likely will incorporate parent or caregiver input and support (Figley, 1988). Social workers' role will be to move the patient from intrusion into processing and from denial into respite when such facilitation appears needed. Facilitating the alternation between processing and respite is the function of therapy. Social workers should model the appropriate environment by validating the trauma as real, accepting the emotional stages of the resolution process, and providing the necessary therapeutic supports while the patient works out his or her recovery.

Evaluating the Recovery Process

Social workers can evaluate from a posttraumatic stress disorder perspective the clinical progress of sexually abused clients through several approaches. Because anxiety can be the predominant emotional response during intrusive phases, periodic assessments of client perception of the degree of anxiety experienced will be helpful. The Clinician's Guide to Assessing Generalized Anxiety Disorder Symptomatology or the Clinical Anxiety Score (Thyer, 1987) and the Cognitive–Somatic Anxiety Questionnaire (Schwartz, Davidson, & Goleman, 1987) are suggested instruments. The Generalized Contentment Scale (Hudson, 1982) is helpful in determining the levels of depression often seen during the denial stage.

Because subsequent sexual dysfunction often is a symptom of sexual trauma, another scale of assistance is the Index of Sexual Satisfaction (Corcoran & Fischer, 1987; Hudson, 1982). The Waring Intimacy Questionnaire can be helpful if marital intimacy issues are a factor, particularly in evaluating sexuality, identity, and affection (Fredman & Sherman, 1987).

Horowitz, Wilber, and Alvarez (1979) has developed an instrument (Impact of Event Scale) that specifically assesses the effect of traumatic events and that recognizes both intrusion and avoidance stages. The instrument is sensitive to change and is recommended for monitoring client progress in treatment (Corcoran & Fischer, 1987). Several clinical measurement instruments have been tested specifically with rape victims and have norms for this population (Beck, Ward, Mendelsohn, Mock, & Erbaugh, 1961; Spielberger, Gorsuch, & Lushene, 1968; Veronen & Kilpatrick, 1980).

Related instruments for children in therapy include the Birleson (1981) Depression Self-Rating Scale for Children; the Kazdin, French, Unis, Esveldt-Dawson, and Sherick (1983) Hopelessness Scale for Children; and the Lipsitt (1958) Self-Concept Scale for Children, in which low self-concept scores correlate with high anxiety in the Children's Manifest Anxiety Scale (Corcoran & Fischer, 1987).

The self-evaluation aspect is one of the assets of the treatment chart's use in treatment. Once the client is aware of recurring treatment themes and the alteration of the processing–respite stages, self-assessment can be ongoing. Periodic updates of the chart can be made with the client's identifying continued areas of difficulty and areas in which treatment goals have been reached.

CONCLUSION

The sexual trauma recovery process model provides a way to view patients with histories of sexual trauma. Posttraumatic stress disorder literature enriches understanding of these cases and expands treatment options. The recovery process model emphasizes that recovery from sexual abuse is a normal and valuable aspect of human resiliency. The treatment chart provides a tool to organize symptoms and treatment goals so that social workers and clinicians can facilitate recovery for clients who have been victims of sexual trauma.

REFERENCES

Adams-Tucker, C. (1985). Defense mechanisms used by sexually abused children. *Children Today, 14,* 9–34.

Agosta, C. A., & McHughes, M. L. (1987). Sexual assault victims: The trauma and the healing. In T. Williams (Ed.), *Posttraumatic stress disorders: A handbook for clinicians* (pp. 239–251). Cincinnati, OH: Disabled American Veterans.

American Psychiatric Association. (1952). *Diagnostic and statistical manual of mental disorders.* Washington, DC: Author.

American Psychiatric Association. (1968). *Diagnostic and statistical manual of mental disorders, Second edition.* Washington, DC: Author.

American Psychiatric Association. (1980). *Diagnostic and statistical manual of mental disorders, Third edition.* Washington, DC: Author.

American Psychiatric Association. (1987). *Diagnostic and statistical manual of mental disorders, Third edition, Revised.* Washington, DC: Author.

Anderson, W. A. (1987, March). *Posttraumatic stress as a unifying exemplar: Teaching a model of social responsibility.* Paper presented at the Annual Program Meeting of the Council on Social Work Education, St. Louis, MO.

Beck, A., Ward, C., Mendelsohn, M., Mock, J., & Erbaugh, J. (1961). An inventory for measuring depression. *Archives of General Psychiatry, 4,* 561–571.

Birleson, P. (1981). The validity of depression disorders in childhood and the development of a self-rating scale: A research report. *Journal of Child Psychology and Psychiatry, 22,* 73–88.

Bryer, J. B., Nelson, B. A., Miller, J. B., & Krol, P. A. (1987). Childhood sexual and physical abuse as a factor in adult psychiatric illness. *American Journal of Psychiatry, 144,* 1426–1430.

Burgess, A. W. Groth, A. N., Holmstrom, L. L., & Sgroi S. M. (1978). *Sexual assault of children and adolescents.* Lexington, MA: D. C. Heath.

Burgess, A. W., & Holmstrom, L. L. (1974). Rape trauma syndrome. *American Journal of Psychiatry, 131,* 891–896.

Coons, P. M. (1986). Child abuse and multiple personality disorder: Review of the literature and suggestions for treatment. *Child Abuse and Neglect, 10,* 455–462.

Corcoran, K., & Fischer, J. (1987). *Measures for clinical practice: A sourcebook.* New York: Free Press.

Crewdson, J. (1988). *By silence betrayed: Sexual abuse of children in America.* Boston: Little, Brown.

Davis R. C., & Smith, B. (1987). Crosstalk: Let's be careful out there. *Psychology Today, 21,* 10.

Ellenson, G. S. (1986). Disturbances of perception in adult female incest survivors. *Social Casework, 67,* 149–159.

Ferenczi, S. (1949). Confusion of tongues between adults and the child: The language of friendliness and the language of passion. *International Journal of Psycho-Analysis, 30,* 225–230.

Figley, C. R. (1985a). From victim to survivor: Social responsibility in the wake of catastrophe. In C. R. Figley (Ed.), *Trauma and its wake: The study and treatment of posttraumatic stress disorder* (pp. 70–87). New York: Brunner/Mazel.

Figley, C. R. (Ed.). (1985b). *Trauma and its wake: The study and treatment of posttraumatic stress disorder.* New York: Brunner/Mazel.

Figley, C. R. (1988). Post-traumatic family therapy. In F. Ochberg (Ed.), *Posttraumatic therapy and victims of violence* (pp. 83–109). New York Brunner/Mazel.

Finkelhor, D., & Browne, A. (1986). Initial and long-term effects: A conceptual framework. In D. Finkelhor, S. Araji, L. Baron, A. Browne, S. D. Peters, & G. E. Wyatt (Eds.), *A sourcebook on child sexual abuse* (pp. 186–187). Beverly Hills, CA: Sage.

Forster, J. (1969). *The Life of Charles Dickens* (Vol. 2). London, England: J. M. Dent & Sons.

Frank A. (1988). Post-traumatic therapy and victims of violence. In F. Ochberg (Ed.), *Post-traumatic therapy and victims of violence* (pp. 3–19). New York: Brunner/Mazel.

Fredman, N., & Sherman, R. (1987). *Handbook of measurements for marriage and family therapy.* New York: Brunner/Mazel.

Green, B. L., Wilson, J. P., & Lindy, J. D. (1985). Conceptualizing post-traumatic stress disorder: A psychological framework. In C. R. Figley (Ed.), *Trauma and its wake: The study and treatment of post-traumatic stress disorder* (pp. 53–69). New York: Brunner/Mazel.

Herman, J. (1988). Father–daughter incest. In F. Ochberg (Ed.), *Post-traumatic therapy and victims of violence* (pp. 190–191). New York: Brunner/Mazel.

Horowitz, M. J. (1976). *Stress-response syndromes.* New York: Jason Aronson.

Horowitz, M. J., Wilber, N., & Alvarez, W. (1979). Impact of event scale: A measure of subjective stress. *Psychological Medicine, 41,* 209–218.

Hudson, W. W. (1982). *The clinical measurement package: A field manual.* Chicago: Dorsey.

Janoff-Bulman. R. (1985). The aftermath of victimization: Rebuilding shattered assumptions. In C. R. Figley (Ed.), *Trauma and its wake: The study and treatment of post-traumatic stress disorder* (pp. 15–35). New York: Brunner/Mazel.

Kardiner, A. (1941). *The traumatic neuroses of war.* New York: Hoeben.

Kazdin, A., French, N. H., Unis, A. S., Esveldt-Dawson, K., & Sherick, R. B. (1983). Hopelessness, depression, and suicide intent among psychiatrically disturbed children. *Journal of Consulting and Clinical Psychology, 51,* 504–510.

Lipsitt, L. P. (1958). A self-concept scale for children and its relationship to the children's form of the Manifest Anxiety Scale. *Child Development, 29,* 463–472.

Lyons, J. (1987). Post-traumatic stress disorder in children and adolescents: A review of the literature. *Developmental and Behavioral Pediatrics, 8,* 349–356.

Malcolm, J. (1985). *In the Freud archives.* New York: Vintage.

Masson, J. (1984). *The assault on truth: Freud's suppression of the seduction theory.* New York: Farrar, Straus, & Giroux.

Nielsen, G. (1983). *Borderline and acting-out adolescents: A developmental approach.* New York: Human Sciences Press.

Sanford, L. (1987, Summer). Pervasive fears in victims of sexual abuse: A clinician's observations. *Preventing Sexual Abuse, 2,* 1–3.

Schwartz, E., Davidson, R., & Goleman, E. (1987). Cognitive–somatic anxiety questionnaire. In K. Corcoran & J. Fischer (Eds.), *Measures for clinical practice: A sourcebook* (pp. 128–129). New York: Free Press.

Sgroi, S. M. (1982). *Handbook of clinical intervention in child sexual abuse.* Lexington, MA: D. C. Heath.

Spielberger, C., Gorsuch, R., & Lushene, R. (1968). *The state–trait anxiety inventory.* Palo Alto, CA: Consulting Psychologists.

Strachey, J. (Ed.). (1953). The aetiology of hysteria. In *The standard edition of the complete psychological work of Sigmund Freud* (pp. 191–221). London, England: Hogarth and the Institute of Psycho-Analysis.

Taubman, S. (1984). Incest in context. *Social Work, 29,* 35–40.

Terr, L. (1983). Chowchilla revisited: The effects of psychic trauma four years after a school-bus kidnapping. *American Psychiatric Journal, 140,* 1543–1550.

Thyer, B. (1987). *Treating anxiety disorders: A guide for human service professionals.* Newbury Park, CA: Sage.

Trimble, M. (1985). Post-traumatic stress disorder: History of a concept. In C. R. Figley (Ed.), *Trauma and its wake: The study and treatment of post-traumatic stress disorder* (pp. 5–14). New York: Brunner/Mazel.

van der Kolk, B. (1986). *Psychological trauma.* Washington, DC: American Psychiatric Press.

Veronen, L., & Kilpatrick, D. (1980). Self-reported fears of rape victims: A preliminary investigation. *Behavior Modification, 4,* 383–396.

Wilson, J. (1988). Understanding the Vietnam veteran. In F. Ochberg (Ed.), *Post-traumatic therapy and victims of violence* (pp. 246–251). New York: Brunner/Mazel.

POST-TRAUMATIC STRESS DISORDER

CHAPTER 44

POST TRAUMATIC STRESSES ON WOMEN PARTNERS OF VIETNAM VETERANS

Linda Jean Maloney

The Vietnam war had monumental impact on the men and women who fought in Southeast Asia. The severe psychological effects of this unpopular conflict on veterans' families were long ignored. These families have experienced repeated stress and upheaval as a result of living with veterans with diagnoses of Post Traumatic Stress Disorder. The families have often suffered extreme isolation, in part self-imposed by the men as an inherent facet of the syndrome itself, and in part as a result of societal indifference. Abuse of alcohol, family violence, and low self-esteem are some of the many struggles endured by these families.

This study explores the hypothesis that the Vietnam war inflicted severe psychic wounding not only on veterans with diagnoses of Post Traumatic Stress Disorder, but on their women partners as well. The lives and concerns of these women will be portrayed through the stories they tell.

According to Lifton (1973), the men who went to Vietnam, on the average much younger than their counterparts in earlier wars, were not granted a psychosocial moratorium, a crucial period of psychological development in which consolidation of identity normally occurs. Instead, they were plunged into an undeclared war in which they were expected and forced to commit and witness unspeakable atrocities, a war they would inevitably lose. Uncared for anywhere else, they returned home to be healed by their families, an often insurmountable task.

Reprinted from *Smith College Studies in Social Work,* Vol. 58, No. 2 (March 1988), pp. 122–143, by permission of the publisher.

In order to learn more about the lives of wives of veterans diagnosed with Post Traumatic Stress Disorder, open-ended, semistructured interviews were held with a small sample of such women. The women were asked not only about their current and past experiences in their nuclear family, but also about their own as well as their partners' families of origin. A number of issues emerged from these interviews. It was discovered that the women had had conflicted relationships with their mothers and idealized relationships with their fathers, that they consider their children as most important to them, that they see themselves as mothers to their husbands, and that both nuclear and origin families present strong patterns of alcohol and physical abuse. The findings help to explain why these women remain in such difficult relationships and suggest the need for various kinds of therapeutic outreach to ameliorate the effects of Vietnam on these women and their families.

THE CONTEXT: AMERICAN INVOLVEMENT IN VIETNAM

The Vietnam war was never a declared war. Although repeatedly advised against involvement, the United States, obsessed with saving the world from a Communist takeover, slowly and willingly inherited from the defeated French the problem of Vietnam. Involvement built gradually over the course of at least three administrations, none of which was willing to assume responsibility for our growing commitment to the war in Vietnam,

Nearly 3 million Americans fought in Vietnam, 60% of whom were drafted and, as the war escalated, the draft became less and less equitable. Men were taken from poor and working-class backgrounds, disproportionately from black and other minority populations. Starr (cited in Figley, 1978) asserts that "America fought in Vietnam in a technological blizzard and a moral vacuum" (p. 74).

All of our fierce might, combined with our advanced war technology, could not seem to defeat the "enemy" side of this tiny country embroiled in civil war. Figley (1978) maintains that our troops were at a disadvantage in that the military goals of the war were never stated clearly, the military hardware issued was inappropriate for guerrilla warfare, pacification was not working, the enemy was too often invisible or ambiguous, and support at home was divided at best. He adds that military successes were hard to measure and that saturation bombing, instead of intimidating the enemy, only hardened their opposition. Furthermore, the traditional concept and the observable reality of victory were elusive during the Vietnam war.

Our soldiers were on tours in Vietnam, time cycles termed "rotation systems." A soldier expected to fight only for a limited amount of time, usually one year, whereupon he would be sent home and replaced by another soldier. Consequently, the fighting men had no continuity with what came before them in the war and what would occur after they had left. Group cohesiveness, so crucial to maintaining morale during war, was, in large part, torn asunder by the rotation system. Many men believed that it was perilous to get too close to anyone else, that each man was on his own. Consequently, group solidarity tended not to occur strongly enough to heighten morale (Moskos, 1980).

Furthermore, as the war dragged on, as the notion of "winning" became unrealistic, and as wanton atrocities and rampant drug use were exposed, disillusionment at home reached a breaking point (Figley, 1978). Loss of life was high while morale was very low.

Soldiers and Adolescence

Most of the first-time enlistees were very young indeed, 17 to 19 years of age, which placed many of them in the fifth Eriksonian stage of development: Identity vs. Role Diffusion. Lifton (1973) suggests that

> beyond just being young and having been asked to fight a war, these men have a sense of violated personal and social order, of fundamental break in human connection, which they relate to conditions imposed upon them by the war in Vietnam. (p. 36)

The emotional tasks at this point in growing up are to separate from parents, to become involved more deeply and mutually in intimate relationships, and to form a sense of inner cohesiveness. Erikson (1968) suggests that

> where a youth does not accomplish such intimate relationships with others—and I would add, with his own inner resources—in late adolescence or early adulthood, he may settle for highly stereotyped interpersonal relationships and come to retain a deep sense of isolation. (p. 136)

Usually youth are granted a psychological moratorium or "time out" to test, to try on various personae, to become acquainted with strengths and weaknesses within themselves, to try out educational/occupational involvements in an overall attempt to integrate self-perception. Wilson (1980) suggests that ideally youth is cloaked by "some system of beliefs to help guide the direction of identity" (p. 133). This was not the case with the young men fighting in Vietnam. The psychosocial moratorium was brutally disrupted.

According to Blos (1962), late adolescence is a time for formulating a strong enough ego to promote a clear and constant sexual position, a firm sense of self, a growing sense of integrity, and the organization of character structure. When this period of development advances well enough, the young person feels more independent, self-reliant, and clear about preferences and ideological and moral stands. Blos points out that the success or failure of adult love relationships depends in part upon adequate prior formation of position amongst the males in families of origin of both the veterans and their female partners. The women report a history, generationally, of physical and/or psychological abuse, usually involving alcohol.

Rather than fostering the development of personality integration, the war in Vietnam often precipitated a return to earlier psychosocial stages, or to a state of identity diffusion. Peck (1983) suggests that when stress is extreme and chronic we all tend to regress, pointing out that a combat soldier's life consists of chronic stress. He says further that "by the nature of its mission, the military designedly and probably realistically fosters the naturally occurring regressive dependency of individuals within its groups" (p. 224), fostering separation without individuation (Tanay, 1980).

Lifton (1973) further describes the military as an antisexual institution in that the young men, instead of developing closer bonds of intimacy, are taught to view women as less than human: "To be graduated from contemptible un-manliness—to be confirmed as a man-marine sharing the power of the immortal group—one had to absorb an image of women as a lower element" (p. 243).

Morrier (1984) suggests that

> the military uses sex-role related techniques to break down murder prohibition. Part of the procedure is to encourage a loosening of the link between sex and intimacy and to return sex to the anal-sadistic stage by equating sex with aggression. The combination of sex and intimacy is seen as feminine while the anal-sadistic linkage of sex and aggression is presented as manly. (p. 107)

Wikler (1980) comments that returning Vietnam veterans experience considerable difficulties re-establishing intimacy. She attributes this struggle to their having lost friends during the war and to the brutality they experienced during their training. She adds that such brutality and loss occurred during the time in which issues of intimacy would have been most predominant, late adolescence.

Also, it should be pointed out that our fighting men were forced or indoctrinated to commit and to witness acts of unparalleled savagery, the memories and experiences of which lay the groundwork for future symptoms of a very painful Post Traumatic Stress Disorder. Wilson (1980) expresses the panic of this theme: "While all wars have death, atrocities and human degradation, few have placed the soldier in an existential quagmire of such intensity or absurdity so as to render ideological justification nearly impossible short of psychological delusion" (p. 135).

When the Vietnam veteran returned, rarely was there a hero's welcome. Vietnam was a non-win war, and America was very new at losing wars. Lifton (1973) talks of warrior mythology, the hero doing battle against all odds, killing in the name of honor and duty, and thus connecting with history and immortality. A rite of passage for young men, war is an opportunity to take part in the "survivor mission," in which sons fight in their wars to pay debt to their own fathers for their prior contributions. Lifton suggests that the Vietnam warrior had no one to whom he could pass his mantle of war. The psychological chain from father to son, handing the mantle, accepting the debt, was broken with Vietnam.

Figley (1978) stresses that Vietnam veterans were alienated from most of the culture to which they returned. They were often estranged from family and friends, to whom they dared not admit what they had done or seen for fear of rejection or abandonment. They were blamed for the war itself and looked upon as "time-bombs," potentially violent, or "sick." Lifton (1973) adds that these men were sent to fight a "filthy" war and, when they returned, were treated as intruders by the very country which sent them to war (p. 375).

Wilson (1980), in his comprehensive study of over 400 Vietnam veterans, concludes that those men who suffer the most from the war tend to experience psychic numbing, deficits in ego strength, and exhibit regressive behaviors echoing earlier psychosocial levels of development. He adds that the men tend to display excessive mistrust, anxiety, doubt, shame, survivor guilt, inferiority, withdrawal, stagnation, and despair. Wilson says: "They have a deep seated conviction that nothing matters anymore; that they are helpless against the external forces of fate that helped create their outlook of hopelessness and the incapacity to experience life richly, fully and in the gut" (p. 148).

In fact, as one researcher points out, many do not survive civilian life:

Within five years of returning to civilian life, army combat vets who served in Vietnam had an overall death rate 45% higher than a comparison group of vets who served elsewhere in the same period. The suicide rate for the Vietnam combat veterans in the first five years after their separation from the military was 72% higher than that of other veterans of the Vietnam Era who did not serve there. (Franklin, 1987, p. 20)

Figley and Leventman (1980), in their book entitled *Strangers at Home,* point out that not only did the veterans have to struggle with intrapsychic pain but also with the rampant institutional neglect they found waiting in the country which sent them to Vietnam. Screening for drugs and venereal disease were the only public programs offered to the returning veterans. Complicating matters, unemployment had reached high levels during the time in which the veterans were coming home. Our veterans were, in effect, excluded from the more traditional institutions of this society and, consequently, excluded from the hope that, as a group, they could readjust to being back home.

While many veterans do indeed go on with their lives, they experience acute dissonance in their attempts to come to terms with Vietnam and to fit back into American society. Wilson (1980) suggests that the veterans, because of what they have been through, often feel much older than they are chronologically, yet are regressed to earlier psychosocial stages. Having missed the process of Identity vs. Role Diffusion, intimacy, although yearned for, is very difficult to attain (p. 144).

In spite of the fact that America was better prepared than ever before to address individually the psychiatric fall-out of war, Vietnam was a psychologically perverse war. It created a social and psychological context which fostered a delayed, often severe, set of reactions (Bourne, 1970). In April, 1979, the Senate Veterans Affairs Committee passed legislation (S-7) authorizing the Veterans Administration to recognize and treat what had come to be termed "Post Traumatic Stress Disorder." For 7 years the House had blocked its passage. The veterans were given a paltry $9.9 million for 2 years to create storefront treatment centers—91 of them.

In 1983, the Center for Policy Research released its study on Post Traumatic Stress Disorder and concluded that from 500,000 to 800,000 veterans were having trouble adjusting. The American Psychiatric Association recognized Post Traumatic Stress Disorder as a definable disorder, and the Veterans Administration officially connected Post Traumatic stress Disorder with being war related and, thus, began approving claims. According to Kelly (1985), the Veterans Administration agreed that "serious and prolonged readjustment problems have been markedly greater for Vietnam veterans than for other veterans" (p. 9).

The symptoms of Post Traumatic Stress Disorder, as listed by the *Diagnostic and Statistical Manual of Mental Disorders* III, 1981, are as follows:

A. Existence of recognizable stressor that would evoke significant symptoms of distress in almost anyone.
B. Reexperiencing of the trauma as evidenced by at least one of the following:
    1. recurrent and intrusive recollections of the event.
    2. recurrent dreams of the event.
    3. sudden acting or feeling as if the traumatic event were recurring, because of an association with an environmental or ideational stimulus.
C. Numbing of responsiveness to or reduced involvement with the external world, beginning some time after the trauma, as shown by at least one of the following:
    1. markedly diminished interest in one or more significant activities.
    2. feeling of detachment or estrangement from others.
    3. constricted affect.
D. At least two of the following symptoms that were not present before the trauma:
    1. hyperalertness or exaggerated startle response.
    2. sleep disturbance.
    3. guilt about surviving when others have not, or about behavior required for survival.
    4. memory impairment or trouble concentrating.
    5. avoidance of activities that arouse recollection of the traumatic event.
    6. intensification of symptoms by exposure to events that symbolize or resemble the traumatic event. (p. 281)

According to Haley (1985), for normal integration to occur in late adolescence, "two elements are essential: clearly defined societal/familial values, ethics and rules to guide the adolescent and consistent, caring and supportive parents and peer groups" (p. 57). The young men in Vietnam were separated from family, precluded from developing adequate peer support even amongst fellow soldiers, and thrust into a foreign land to fight a civil war in which the enemy was most often indecipherable in appearance from the South Vietnamese army and peasants. They were taught conventional warfare with which to fight a guerrilla war and witnessed atrocities, the memories of which cling to their existence even today. Ethics and rules were cloaked in a twilight zone of insanity and, although it must be noted that most veterans of Vietnam cope quite well, the fact remains that too many of them do not. The reasons are becoming clearer with time.

As one veteran (Caputo, 1977) vividly expressed it:

My mind shot back a decade, to that day we had marched into Vietnam, swaggering, confident, full of idealism. We had believed we were there for a high moral purpose. But somehow our idealism was lost, our morals corrupted, and the purpose forgotten. (p. 345)

Women Partners

Contrary to the existing literature relevant to Vietnam veterans, studies involving female partners of the veterans are few in number. Voso (1981) investigated the influences which lead women to remain in stressful relationships with their Vietnam veteran partners. Similar to the approach used in this study, she interviewed 9 women in relationships with veterans who had received diagnoses of Post Traumatic Stress Disorder, focusing on the question of whether early object relations had influenced the women's adult object choices. Voso's findings indicated that the women tended to idealize their parents' marital relationships despite clear evidence that all was not well, to idealize their fathers, and to form negative identifications with their mothers. The women were primary caretakers within their families of origin, were often the oldest children, and within their adult relationships they continued the roles of caretaking and of assuming major responsibility for their partners. Voso found, too, that the women tended to see their mothers as the family disciplinarians and to view their fathers as "easy-going." They denied angry feelings and dependent needs in childhood in order to feel "good" and continued to do so in their families of procreation.

The author discovered that the women stayed in their abusive relationships for many of the same reasons that battered women cite: dependency upon partner, fear of greater abuse towards them or their children, fear of failure due to the marriage ending, hope for improvement, guilt feelings about and love for the partner, and low self-esteem.

Not only were the women's current relationships stressful, their previous relationships were found to have involved abusiveness and alcohol abuse. Drinking of course affects the ways in which people interact, triggering and reinforcing a cycle of problematic actions and relationships in families (Bepko & Krestan, 1987).

These authors point out that there may be an absence of appropriate hierarchical roles within the family, parental triangling of children, and reversing of traditional positions within the family, the woman becoming the provider and the man dependent. Neither acknowledges the inversion of the traditional roles.

Members of alcoholic families tend to become over- or underfunctional and, furthermore, a child who must over-function in her family of origin will likely seek out the same role as an adult. The over-functioning woman's focus on her partner as the center of her life may be her main way of validating herself and of maintaining pride or illusory specialness (Bepko & Krestan, 1987). Voso finds that veterans' families are often plagued by alcoholism; in the families she interviewed the women assumed most of the responsibilities for their families, while alcohol abuse permeated both past and present relationships.

Williams (1980) finds, as did Voso, that women partners feel guilty for family upheaval, overwhelmed by the assumption of often total family responsibility, suffer from low self-esteem, and, more often than not, are victims of battering. Taking a more societal/feminist view than Voso, she goes on to suggest that the women partners are at a disadvantage in a society which views woman as "passive, non-competitive, dependent, sensitive, subjective, nurturant, unable to risk and emotionally labile" (p. 98).

She talks of the "impassion trap," in which women simply cannot win. If they sacrifice to be "good" wives and mothers they are called "overprotective"; if they tend to their own needs they are called "selfish." Learned helplessness sets in, paralysis takes

over, and the women no longer believe they can effect change, not unlike their husbands' experiences with war trauma. She claims that the double-bind effect leaves
women with low self-esteem, loss of identity, frustrated, sometimes "devastated."

Williams (1980) asserts that female partners do share some common problems:

1. Women report a feeling of isolation and not just from the veteran but also
   from society.
2. They often admit they have no one to talk to, including parents, and that no
   one understands.
3. Most feel responsible for the veteran being unable to readjust well enough.
4. They feel mainly responsible for the financial and emotional well-being of the
   family.
5. They see themselves as being sole child-care givers.
6. Self-concepts are low. They complain of guilt, anger, alienation and mistrust.
7. There is often evidence of physical battering among some of the couples, but
   the women are typically reticent to discuss it. (p. 102)

She discovered that the women also exhibit differences. The traditional women in
the groups tend to retain their marriages, to center their lives around their husbands,
and to lack enough strength to leave and to live alone, whereas nontraditional wives
tend to fight back, at least in the sense that although they choose to continue living with
their husbands they manage to maintain emotional distance and to go on with their
lives. Most women fall in between the traditional and nontraditional positions.

Other investigators (Brown & Levy, 1981) support Voso's and Williams' conclusions that the families of Vietnam veterans have certainly suffered along with their veteran partners. The authors, having talked with members of a women's support group,
point out that the women talk most frequently about their husbands' alcoholism, physical abuse, inabilities to hold jobs, flashbacks and nightmares, rages, and withdrawn silences. The women speak of their own depressions, feelings of impotence, and fears for
their children but are convinced that it is unfair to take the children away from their fathers. They ask for groups for the children and for themselves and they talk about continuing to try harder within their families.

Fagan (1986) finds that physical abuse occurs in almost half the veteran families she
has studied and believes that the "battered woman syndrome" is comparable to abuse
patterns in veterans' families. Like Voso (1981), Fagan questions whether the women
enter their abusive relationships already victims of certain pathologies or whether continued stress within their current relationships has caused their seeming inability to extricate themselves. She wonders further whether the women also suffer from symptoms
of Post Traumatic Stress Disorder.

Summary

In sum, it is clear that Vietnam veterans have suffered and continue to suffer extreme
emotional hardship. They fought an illegal and unpopular war, were not allowed entrance to the inner sanctum of American war heroes, and were neglected institutionally,

emotionally, and politically upon returning home. They and their families have borne the brunt of the war's aftermath and many have been subjected to the effects of Post Traumatic Stress Disorder, violence, alcoholism, drug addiction, and poverty.

METHOD

Because of the paucity of prior research on the female partners of male Vietnam veterans, it was decided to conduct an exploratory study based on in-depth, open-minded interviews with a small sample of women. While an interview guide was used to lend a certain degree of structure and consistency, audiotaped interviews were conducted phenomenologically and flexibly in the sense that interviewees were free to depart from the interviewer's questions, and new questions were provoked by prior narratives. The audiotaped interviews were then subjected to thematic analysis, the analytic effort one of searching for those patterns or concerns which surfaced repeatedly throughout the narratives.

Two of the Vietnam veteran outreach centers in central and northwestern Massachusetts which were contacted offered names of women, married to or living with veterans, who they thought might be interested in talking about their experiences as partners of men who had fought in Vietnam. Two women responded and these women subsequently provided the names of three others, who also agreed to be interviewed. A sixth woman, known to this researcher through a referral to an agency some years ago, also agreed to participate in the study. Since this small sample is one of convenience, no statement can be made as to its representativeness or the generalizability of findings. Nevertheless, it is believed that the stories of these women deepen the portrait of the Vietnam experience, suggest directions for further research, and highlight the need for renewed attention to services for this population.

In each meeting, this interviewer explained a longstanding interest in issues affecting female partners of Vietnam veterans, in part due to her personal experience as a Vietnam War widow and in part due to a recognizable and flagrant neglect in the media and literature of concerns of families of Vietnam veterans. Because of the intense emotional nature of the subject, each was told verbally that referral to therapists who could help them process the awakened or reawakened feelings they might experience could be arranged.

The interviews themselves lasted from one to two hours each and each woman was encouraged to speak freely on topics of her choice; certain questions provided a framework for exploring common themes among the group. Questions were integrated and interwoven into the general conversations at various times as they became appropriate to whatever was currently being discussed.

Such questions were designed to secure family of origin information, current family demographics, and descriptions of interactional patterns and themes in both family of origin and in the marital, family situation. Women's perceptions of their husbands' backgrounds were invited, as well as information relevant to their husbands' participation in Vietnam.

Several questions encouraged their perceptions of how Vietnam had or was affecting their families' lives, and a final section included a request that the interviewees discuss what might have been more helpful to them in coping with the aftermath of the war and their husbands' infirmities. What did they think should still be done for women and children, and who did they think should be activating this? The tapes were subsequently transcribed to facilitate the task of searching for common and idiosyncratic responses.

As each transcript was played many times, certain themes began to surface repeatedly. Once these major themes, five in number, were identified, the transcripts were again carefully studied for further evidence and verification. While the women's voices fell resoundingly within the five basic overriding categories, there also emerged several less obvious but persistent subthemes which deserve mention. In the next section, a portrait of these women and their lives is presented, told as much as possible in their own voices.

The Women: A Portrait

Of the 6 women interviewed, a quite heterogeneous group, 2 were 38 years old, 2 were 35, 1 was 32, and 1 was 31. All of the women were Caucasian and from working-class or middle-class backgrounds. Three identified themselves as Anglo-Saxon Protestant.

Five of the women worked outside of the home, full time, while the sixth worked at home. Four of the husbands did not work at all at present, and 2 worked part time.

Two of the women had been married once and currently remained in those relationships, 2 have been married twice, and 2 have been married three times. All but 1, whose husband committed suicide 5 years ago, were married at present. All of their husbands were also of working-class, middle-class backgrounds, had experienced combat in Vietnam, and carried diagnoses of Post Traumatic Stress Disorder.

All of the women had finished high school. Three had gone on to complete 2 years of college, 2 in business and 1 in human services. Four of the women lived in small hill towns in semirural surroundings, whereas the other 2 women lived within college community towns, one designated a small city, and all in New England. Three of the women lived in apartments, and 3 owned their own homes. One woman had two children, aged 13 and 18, a girl and a boy; 3 of the women had two boys each; 1 woman had a 12-year-old daughter; and 1 woman had five children ranging in age from 3 to 14, three boys and two girls.

Major Themes

Five major themes emerged repeatedly: (1) women's conflicted relationships with their mothers; (2) women's idealized relationships with their fathers; (3) the importance of their children to them; (4) their beliefs that their husbands have not grown past adolescence; and (5) the significant part that alcohol and physical abuse have played in their lives from childhood through their adult years.

Five of 6 women reported that they had experienced as children, teenagers, and young adults very difficult relationships with their mothers. They offered such views as, "She's not really the supportive type," or "She's not one you could talk to." One woman said, "She doesn't have a whole lot of sympathy or understanding for other people." Another woman said: "My mother is the typical tough old bird. She figured a boy can take care of himself but a girl better be careful. So no excuse ever worked. Anything, and she'd go off the deep end."

All but one woman spoke of harsh rejection from their mothers throughout their growing-up years, often feeling they "could do nothing right." These women saw themselves fielding the blame for whatever stress existed within their households. Furthermore, 5 of 6 suggested that their mothers had not been "close" to their own mothers.

Three of the women reported that, as they have gotten older, their mothers have "mellowed" and that they get along much better now and are closer, but two felt there was no hope, ever, that their relationships with their mothers will improve.

Voso (1983), in her study of 9 women partners of Vietnam veterans with diagnoses of Post Traumatic Stress Disorder, found, too, that the women, during their growing-up years, tended to devalue their relationships with their mothers and to idealize their relationships with their fathers. These women saw their mothers as the wielders of discipline, and themselves overly responsible for family chores and the care of siblings.

The same dynamic emerges from the present study. Within their families of origin, informants saw themselves as over-responsible. As children and adults, they tended to feel sorry for their fathers, believing that it was they, not their mothers, who had brought happiness to their fathers. They seem to view their mothers as tough and self-sufficient, their fathers as needy and warm.

Quite a different profile emerges when the women talked of their husbands' roles within their families of origin. In their view, the veterans tended to be "close" or "overly dependent" upon their mothers and conflicted or "distanced" within their relationships with their fathers. Voso's (1983) findings seem to corroborate this dynamic when she suggests that 7 of the 9 veteran partners were reported to have been "close" to their mothers, and as having had poor relationships with their fathers (p. 46).

Unlike their views of their relationships with their mothers, the women seemed to feel warmly toward their fathers, frequently to the point of idealization. One woman said, "I'm very close to my father. He had strong values: fight hard and work hard no matter what." Another said, "My father and I were real close. I've always been Daddy's little girl." A third woman reminisced, "My father was easier to talk to than my mother. My character is a lot like his. It's incredible; it's like we're the same person." Another said, "My father had a bad drinking problem when I was little, but he was always good to me, always."

A fifth woman talked of not having seen her father since she was a small child but that "one day I was very depressed and needed my daddy." She called him and for a while he sent flowers and cards but soon disappeared again. She said, "I don't really need to see him. His life has been hard." A sixth woman said, "My father is very proud but he's stubborn. He's just like me."

The women interviewed tend to form quite negative identifications with their mothers and positive, often idealized, identifications with their fathers. An interesting dichotomy emerges: the women depict their mothers as punitive and omnipotent, their fathers as victimized and needy. Mothers are self-sufficient and independent, fathers in need of protection.

The women interviewed, without exception, talked of their children as more important to them "than anything else in the world." In fact, they all said that their children were the main reason for their not having left their abusive relationships and they either stated overtly or implied that mothers have no right to take children away from their fathers no matter what is going on. One woman said that "little girls need their daddies and little boys need a male role model."

Every one of the women saw her children as "doing well" and when asked how the children have come to terms with either witnessing repeated abuse or being victims themselves, the mothers replied that they think the children, as one woman put it, "understand that their fathers don't hate them but have this sickness they can't control." One said, "It's hard for me to state something strongly without sounding as if I'm belittling what their father thinks." Another woman said, "He's their role model so I have to be careful not to say anything against him." Another woman added, "In some ways, they can't afford to hate him because they'll hate themselves."

One of the mothers said, "No matter what, he's still the father. Nobody can take that away from him, ever! I would never try." Another stated:

I try to talk to the kids about what's going on but you have to be careful. For one thing, I'm a woman so they think I don't really know what's going on anyway. Besides, I'm afraid to take a really strong stand because I've seen kids take off in the opposite direction.

The women seemed, in reference to their children, to be in a terrible bind. They were worried about their children and wished to protect them. Yet if they spoke frankly to their children about their fathers' abusive behavior, they believe they would be tarnishing an image of someone who is a necessary role model for their children. One can speculate that for the mothers, given their own childhood histories, it would be crucial in their minds that children need idealized fathers to emulate. Without such idealized male figures with whom to identify, children would have only their mothers; it has already been proved to these women that mothers are "tough, not supportive." In this sense, the mothers' negative identifications with their own mothers may block their ability to see how much they have been able to do for their own children and inhibit them from using stronger voices in the raising of their own children. The women seemed to feel the inherent frustration but seem, also, not to understand that they were in untenable positions.

All of the 6 women said, in various ways, that their husbands did not grow up, indeed stopped growing at around the age of 18 or 19. One woman said:

It's like he stopped growing. He went to Nam from high school at age 18. He came back and was still an 18-year-old kid who thought his mom would still pay his grocery bill—or that I would.

Another woman added, "I had to be the mother, father, disciplinarian—everything. I had five actual kids and one more who stayed 19 and was very upset." A third woman said, "I grew up and he didn't. It's interesting, too, to see the kids grow up and watch him stay the same age."

As the women discussed their husbands' seeming arrested development, it became clear that they were often irritated, sometimes "fed up" with living in marriages in which they were, in a sense, the sole parents. But when asked if they ever considered leaving their marriages because their husbands had "stopped growing," 5 of 6 said that they could not do that. They all said that they had considered leaving but could not see doing it. One woman said, "But if I left him, I'd be leaving somebody pretty helpless—like leaving a child."

History seems to repeat itself, as once again these women, like their mothers, find themselves in relationships with men who appear very vulnerable and needy. And, as in childhood, they seem to feel that they are responsible for protecting and healing these men. Perhaps to leave husband is also to desert father. In this sense, the women have not separated sufficiently from family of origin. They continue to care for their fathers and, in this way, sustain a pride in mothering, in being good daughters/wives. To leave, perhaps, would be to desert one's obligations and to lose the sense of pride that is crucial to self-esteem.

Interestingly, alcoholism or abuse of alcohol, as reported by the women, seemed limited to male members within the families. Indeed, the women seemed to view abuse of alcohol as a male phenomenon which has a certain inevitability attached to it. Perhaps as children, the women, more often than not, grew up in atmospheres in which misuse of alcohol by men and/or fathers was pervasive, whereas women family members were either abstinent or used alcohol in moderation.

The women, when talking of childhoods spent with alcoholic fathers, seemed very forgiving of their fathers' use of alcohol. They said, "I think he was basically unhappy," or "He was always good to me, though." One woman said, "He's had a very hard life." If the women felt any emotional dissonance in trying to fit their fathers' alcoholism into the idealized portraits they painted of their fathers, it was not apparent in the interviews. One could speculate that they had been able to split off the reality of alcoholism sufficiently enough to retain the untarnished images of their fathers.

That the alcoholism of their fathers might have contributed to strife within the marriages of their parents seemed to be a concept unwelcome in the minds of these women. Perhaps, just as the women seemed to need to sort their fathers into idealized compartments, they needed also to retain negative views of their mothers. Enormous energy is devoted to keeping these two images separate and intact. There is the feeling that the women needed to keep their mothers in positions of blame.

Most of the women spoke of physical abuse from their mothers, using such expressions as "a good slap in the face" or "getting the belt," but tended to think there was either no abuse from their fathers or to view the punishment as fitting the crime. All of the women who had been married at least once prior to their current marriages alluded to some physical abuse and certain psychological abuse. All said that there have been occurrences of both within their current marriages.

One woman said, "He doesn't hit me anymore but if he moves fast, I jump!" Another said, "Sometimes he says he's going to kill me. I don't believe him anymore, but you never know." One woman said that physical abuse began almost 10 years after Vietnam, along with her husband's flashbacks. Her husband committed suicide 5 years ago, a day after beating her severely. All of the women agreed that use of alcohol played a major role in the escalation of abuse. Five of the 6 husbands drink and several took drugs.

Minor Themes

Four subthemes emerged alongside the major ones just discussed: (1) the deleterious effects of Post Traumatic Stress symptoms upon the veterans and their partners; (2) the women's static views of their future 5 to 10 years hence; (3) the women's conflicted feelings about the military; and (4) the military as presenting an intergenerational family legacy for both the veterans and their female partners. Because of space limitations, only the first theme, particularly relevant to the original hypothesis, will be discussed here.

As mentioned earlier, all of the husbands of the interviewed women had diagnoses of Post Traumatic Stress Disorder. The women informants were remarkably well informed on the subject of Post Traumatic Stress Disorder. They knew clearly what the symptoms are as designated by the *Diagnostic and Statistical Manual of Mental Disorders III* (1980, p. 281).

They talked of the isolation imposed by their husbands upon the family. One woman said, "He has to know where we are every minute of the day and he doesn't like any company coming into the house." Another said, "We never go out to a movie or a restaurant because he can't be in crowds." A third woman added, "He's afraid of sudden noises and he always sits with his back to the wall so he's protected. He thinks people are out to get him, so we don't go out."

They spoke of violence and flashbacks. One woman said, "I learned that you wake him up very slowly. I landed in the hospital once because I didn't understand that." Another said, "Well, a helicopter went over and next I knew he was down cellar with a shotgun, pointing it at me and the kids. He thought we were Vietcong." A third added,

He got a billy club and he said in a very calm voice, "You're going to know what it feels like to die. I'm going to kill you now," and he would have, if our son hadn't stopped him. He didn't know who I was.

They spoke of withdrawal. One woman said, "He doesn't talk about Vietnam much at all. Only to his buddies." Another woman said:

I couldn't figure out why he suddenly withdrew from the kids. He's always had good relationships with them. It turned out later that he had either seen children their age killed in Vietnam or he had killed them himself. In any case, the guilt was too much. He felt he didn't have any right to be with his own kids.

Because of the women's acute familiarity with the symptoms of Post Traumatic Stress Disorder, they were asked whether they had ever observed such symptoms in themselves. Every woman interviewed said, most assertively, that she, too, was a victim of Post Traumatic Stress Disorder. When pressed for further information, they talked about flashbacks to incidents of battering, and described how they felt during these times. One woman stared for a minute and then said in a quiet voice:

When the light is just right, maybe the same time of day, and I hear a noise I heard back then, I feel for a few seconds as if I'm back there. Takes a little while for me to get back my reality.

Another woman said: "Well, maybe I'll have my back turned and somebody will say something, and I'll be afraid it's happening again, that I'm going to be hit."

But the women also talked about being affected by some of the same catalysts which seemed to trigger flashback responses in their husbands. They mentioned the sounds of helicopters, sudden noises, gunfire, the smell and sound of spring rain, and the sight of fog, meeting Oriental people, and the smell of thick humidity. They said that they felt panicked for a brief time and transported to some other place. One woman explained her unease about the spring rain by saying, "He gets hospitalized in April or May usually—that's when he goes off."

Sometimes they dream of Vietnam. They see rice fields and jungles, helicopters and crashes. One woman said that she dreams of being drafted but tells them she can't go because she has babies. They dream of Vietnamese babies; images of fire are pervasive in such dreams. One woman dreams that she and her husband are on separate planes headed for Vietnam. His plane is shot down.

The women suggested that someone ought to do a study of what, they are certain, are *their* Post Traumatic Stress symptoms.

SUMMARY AND CONCLUSIONS

The purpose of this study was to identify the issues with which female partners of Vietnam veterans with diagnoses of Post Traumatic Stress Disorder struggle and to gain a psychosocial understanding of how these women live.

This writer has found that, indeed, some partners of Vietnam veterans are trying to cope with an enormous amount of stress, in part due to the effects of the Vietnam War on their male partners and in part due to the neglect and abuse experienced by both partners during their respective childhoods. Their personal and interpersonal issues surface in a sociopolitical context which ignores their stories and their needs.

The women, in consistent defense of their veteran partners, talked about the abuse their men have endured as a result of fighting in Vietnam and coming back to a country where no one wanted to listen to them. They say the men fought a war they could not win and much of the time had to fight at odds with their own country, many of whose people protested the war more vociferously as the years wore on.

The women said that their partners were and still are frozen in adolescence and relate to them as needy children rather than as adults, a situation which is supported by the literature. Taken in late adolescence, the men were denied a psychosocial moratorium, the purpose of which is to create a firmer identity and to promote the ability to establish intimacy within relationships. Instead, these young men were thrust into an unconscionable and undeclared war in which they witnessed and sometimes carried out unspeakable atrocities. They were constantly aware of guerrilla attack and had to maintain hypervigilance in order to survive, a common precursor of Post Traumatic Stress Disorder.

Jolted out of adolescence, they had imposed upon them a violent separation from all they had previously understood to be moral and humane. They were robbed of any sane guidance, any credo which would have led to a firmer and healthier identity, and were instead denied the process of individuation.

The young men were also cast into an antisexual atmosphere in which they were taught to view women as less than human, thereby hampering or sometimes precluding the establishment of intimacy within their relationships with families upon return. The women state clearly that their partners do not trust women, are very jealous, and at the same time are very fearful of getting close. The women add, as has been stressed in the literature, that their men came home as nonheroes, usually alone, typically having had no psychological debriefing and to a country which at worst labeled them "baby-killers" and "time-bombs," and which at best simply ignored them through institutional neglect.

The young men were, upon return, excluded from the traditional organizations of American war heroes because they were thought to have lost the war, and their complaints were viewed as those of "crybabies." There were few welcoming home parades, a reality which sorely concerns the female partners. There was also little opportunity for the soldiers to live out the warrior's rite of passage, the warrior legacy of fighting as part of a chain of wars, as did their fathers and grandfathers. The mantle was not passed from father to son, which seems to sadden the women. Traumatized and ostracized, the Vietnam combat veterans returned to their families for healing.

The 6 women interviewed in this study talked of their partners' need for extreme isolation for themselves and their families, and of enduring physical and psychological abuse over periods of many years. They stressed the abuse of drugs and alcohol by their partners and describe family behaviors which closely simulate the portraits of codependency and projective identification found in alcoholic families. During the interviews it became clear that alcohol abuse has held a very influential position amongst the males in families of origin of both the veterans and their female partners. The women report a history, generationally, of physical and/or psychological abuse, usually involving alcohol.

The women tended to stay in these abusive relationships because they feared being alone, worrying that their veteran partners' conditions would worsen and lead to suicide. They believe that they had no right to take the children away from their fathers, no matter what the atmosphere at home. Prior literature suggests, and this study further confirms, that the women also stay in these relationships because of unmet dependency needs.

The women revealed quite negative identifications with their mothers, quite idealized identifications with their fathers, and exhibited firm resistance to any suggestion threatening this dichotomy. Borderline pathology, the splitting off of self objects, may be pervasive amongst female partners of combat veterans with diagnoses of Post Traumatic Stress Disorder. These women seem similar to the larger population of battered women who also choose to remain and often warrant diagnoses of borderline personality disorder.

The women talked of the abuse and neglect experienced by their husbands during childhood. The men were found to have been estranged from their fathers, sometimes deserted as infants, and as having experienced physical and psychological abuse from their often alcoholic fathers. On the other hand, they say their partners had been too close to their mothers, who tended to "baby" them and "not let them grow up." Thus, it seems likely that both veterans and their female partners enter relationships with unmet dependency needs and then find extrication almost insurmountable.

Sole caretakers in their current families, the women seem aware that the assumption of too much responsibility was also their dominant role in childhood. Often they are the only parent to hold a consistent job, as well as to take on full responsibility for raising the children and running the home.

The women speak of their children as the main focus of their lives and stress that they will do anything for them. They seem to feel that they are mothers first, and it could be speculated that, because of unmet dependency needs, they are in part attempting to raise themselves through identification with their children. The women are, in general, unable to leave their abusive relationships despite obvious dedication to their children, a contradiction which might well simulate the stress they underwent while children themselves.

Not at all surprising is the women's acute knowledge of Post Traumatic Stress Disorder. Unexpected, however, was their certainty and conviction that they, too, suffer from Post Traumatic Stress Disorder. They ask that a study be carried out for them explicitly to ascertain whether they are victims themselves.

Indeed the behaviors and emotional reactions the women describe indicate the probable existence of Post Traumatic Stress Disorder, most likely caused by physical beatings and sadistic psychological abuse. However the women also register symptoms triggered by the same catalysts which bring about flashbacks and psychic stress in their veteran partners, an occurrence which might well indicate that the women identify so strongly with their men that they have authentically internalized their partners' stressor imagery; for example, spring rain, fog, sudden noises, helicopters, airplanes, dreams of Vietnam—its geographical features, its weather, and its people. Seeds for future study are most certainly available here.

In terms of treatment, the women ask that groups be run for them away from Veterans Administration facilities, a form of treatment which echoes repeatedly in the literature as an advisable method of healing. Too often, they claim, they have been brought in only as adjuncts to their partners' therapy and taught to understand Post Traumatic Stress Disorder in order to help their partners, rather than having been treated as people in their own right. However, it must be said that the women partners of Vietnam combat veterans are sometimes resistant to asking for help or accepting help for fear of displeasing their partners. Consistent outreach must be offered to these women who are living very isolated and fearful lives.

In summary, it can definitely be said that at least some female partners of Vietnam combat veterans are suffering in the aftermath of the war in Vietnam, perhaps even to the extent of having Post Traumatic Stress symptoms themselves. Not addressed in this study, however, is the plight of the children of these families. Surely the repeated family upheaval, the effects of alcohol and drug abuse, and the witnessing of physical violence have taken their toll on the children. Future study should be devoted to discovering how these children are coping and how help can be extended to everyone in these families.

The Vietnam War has had far-reaching, deleterious effects upon the people who have been touched by its savagery. In addition to the recent plethora of writings concerning the veterans, a literature must be created not only for the female partners of veterans but for the children within the families, who are likely to inherit and to pass on generationally the emotional scars of war.

REFERENCES

American Psychiatric Association. (1980). *Diagnostic and statistical manual of mental disorders* (3rd ed.). Washington, DC: Author.

Bepko, C.. & Krestan, J. (1985). *The responsibility trap: A blueprint for treating the alcoholic family.* New York: The Free Press.

Blos, P. (1962). *On adolescence. A psychoanalytic interpretation.* New York: The Free Press of Glencoe.

Bourne, P. G. (1970). *Men, stress and Vietnam.* Boston: Little, Brown.

Brown, P., & Levy, L. (1981 November 22). The troubled families of Vietnam warriors. *Newsday,* pp. 14–18.

Caputo, P. (1977). *A rumor of war.* New York: Holt, Rinehart and Winston.

Erikson, E. (1968). *Identity, youth and crisis.* New York: W. W. Norton and Company.

Fagan, K. (1986). Mental health issues of women partners of Vietnam veterans. In *Casework,* pp. 302–335. Storrs, CT: University of Connecticut School of Social Work.

Figley, C. (1978). *Stress disorders among Vietnam veterans.* New York: Brunner/ Mazel.

Figley, C., & Leventman, S. (1980). *Strangers at home: Vietnam veterans since the war.* New York: Praeger Publishers.

Franklin, B. (1987), February 11. Veterans of Vietnam found to have high death rate. *The New York Times,* Special, p. A20.

Haley, S. A. (1985). Some of my best friends are dead: Treatment of the post traumatic stress disordered patient and his family. In W. E. Kelly (Ed.), *Post traumatic stress disorder and the war veteran patient* (pp. 54–72). New York: Brunner/ Mazel Publishers.

Kelly, W. E. (1985). *Post-traumatic stress disorder and the war veteran patient.* New York: Brunner/Mazel.

Lifton, R. J. (1973). *Home from the war.* New York: Simon & Schuster.

Morrier, E. J. (1984). Passivity as a sequel to combat trauma. *Journal of Contemporary Psychotherapy, 14,* 99–111.

Moskos, C. (1980). Surviving the war in Vietnam. In C. R. Figley & S. Leventman (Eds.), *Strangers at home: Vietnam veterans since the war* (pp. 71–84). New York: Praeger Publishers.

Peck, S. M. (1983). *People of the lie.* New York: Simon & Schuster.

Tanay, E. (1985). The Vietnam veterans: Victim of war. In W. E. Kelley (Ed), *Posttraumatic stress disorder and the war veteran patient* (pp. 29–43). New York: Brunner/Mazel Publishers.

Voso, E. (1983). *Female partners of post traumatic stressed Vietnam veterans: Factors influencing a woman's decision to remain in a conflictual relationship.* Master's thesis, Smith College School for Social Work, Northampton, MA.

Wikler, N. (1980). Hidden injuries of war. In C. R. Figley & S. Leventman (Eds.), *Strangers at home: Vietnam veterans since the war* (pp. 87–104). New York: Praeger Publishers.

Williams, C. (1980). The veteran system with a focus on women partners: Theoretical considerations, problems and treatment strategies. In T. Williams (Ed.), *Post-*

traumatic stress disorders of the Vietnam veteran. Cincinnati: Disabled American Veterans.

Wilson, J. P. (1980). Conflict, stress and growth: The effects of war on psychosocial development among Vietnam veterans. In C. R. Figley & S. Leventman (Eds.), *Strangers at home: Vietnam veterans since the war* (pp. 123–165). New York: Praeger Publishers.

CHAPTER 45

LONG-TERM GROUP TREATMENT FOR YOUNG MALE 'SCHIZOPATHS'

Audrey Rosen Ely

Mental health care planners, administrators, and clinicians are currently struggling with the problem of how to treat, manage, and cope with a new generation of chronically disturbed young people who are surfacing at an alarming rate in their communities. The combination of deinstitutionalization and of the results of the "baby boom" seems to be the precipitant of this situation.[1] Researchers have identified this formidable client population as predominantly composed of males between 18 and 35 years of age whose varied psychopathology has precluded their maturation to adulthood.[2] Due to their developmental deficits, their needs are enormous. Unfortunately, their capacity for misuse, abuse, and rejection of caregivers' help is equally substantial. As a result, these young people travel on a self-defeating merry-go-round through a myriad of public service agencies. As Pepper and Kirshner wrote,

> They confound our efforts to treat them by conventional means, they evade yet repeatedly disturb our mental health programs, and they appear again and again in our psychiatric emergency services and police stations.[3]

Community residents are clamoring to remove these disturbed people from their streets but are not willing to pay the price tag of services.

Sheets, Prevost, and Reihman studied the broad spectrum of the adult chronic population and defined three distinct subgroups:

1. Clients who are "concretely attached" to aftercare programs and who seldom venture out from the "social isolation of their homes."

Reprinted from *Social Work,* Vol. 30, No. 1 (January–February 1985), pp. 5–10, by permission of NASW Press. Copyright 1985, National Association of Social Workers, Inc., *Social Work.*

2. Clients characterized by "emotional liability" and "fluctuating functional abilities," which are manifested in "their erratic search for services, security and meaning."
3. Clients who function at a "fairly high level," who seek "control over" their illness but reject being identified as a "mental patient."[4]

Bachrach reported that the research literature regarding the young adult chronic population primarily refers to clients who fall under the umbrella of category two.[5] The clients to be described in this article also fall under this grouping. However, the present author does not believe that these categories are mutually exclusive but, rather, that they often overlap, especially over the lifetime of individual clients.

The author and other clinicians use the term "schizopath" to describe young adults who have been diagnosed as chronic schizophrenics but who, in remission, often present as character-disordered or sociopathic individuals. They regularly abuse drugs and alcohol and generally appear to be wending their way through life via manipulation, deceit, and bravado. However, this unsavory facade is quite fragile. These individuals do not have the emotional backup to sustain such characterological maneuvers. They are empty, sad, vulnerable people who desperately use every shred of ego strength available to them to survive.[6]

For the past six years, the author has coled, with a psychiatrist, a therapy group composed of young men who fall into the schizopath category. The origin of the group, its members, the group process, the cotherapists' role and experience, and the group's political significance in the context of the present mental health care system are discussed in this article.

In 1977, when the group began, deinstitutionalization was gaining momentum, but community resources remained inadequate. The Aftercare Clinic of South Shore Mental Health Center in Quincy, Massachusetts, where the author worked, was scantily staffed and its policy was heavily influenced by the medical model of outpatient care. The majority of aftercare clients were seen in brief individual sessions, predominantly on a monthly basis. The emphasis was on medication, although some supportive treatment was provided. A small but excellent day treatment program was in the vicinity; at that time, it operated out of a church basement and was a valuable resource, but the client had to meet certain entry requirements.

The idea for the group evolved from the author's observation of a small group of aftercare clients and the frustration and chaos that reverberated around them. These clients, all young men, irregularly attended their aftercare appointments but frequently, sometimes daily, sat in the center's waiting room, impatiently waiting for the intake worker. While waiting, they badgered the secretary and bummed cigarettes from other clients. Their presentation could vary from aggressive, demanding behavior to pitiful despair; they were often intoxicated from alcohol or drugs. Occasionally they would be chaperoned by a police officer. They were generally "on the outs" with the clinical staff because of the inept, manipulative, and annoying manner of their attempts to get their needs met.

Medication management for these young men was a controversial subject. The clients were typically given monthly prescriptions, which they invariably "lost" (the prescriptions were actually sold or taken inappropriately). On occasion, a psychiatrist would, properly, refuse to medicate these clients. On-call workers would then be inundated by telephone calls from distressed families, other agencies, and emergency-room staff asking what to do and, naturally, berating the policies of the center. Clients would then return either to look for medication or because they were sufficiently decompensated to require readmission to the local state hospital. Although these young people were clearly quite ill, their streetwise facades and chaotic lifestyles prevented them from receiving the consistent care they needed.

Thus, it was surprising to clinicians at the center when the author suggested that these schizopaths, who were known to be "troublemakers," be funneled into a weekly therapy group. Although everyone agreed that the ongoing cycle of treatment was not helpful to clients (and thus not to the staff's morale either), this suggestion initially was not taken seriously. Reactions ranged from chuckling to calling the suggestion "masochistic." Nevertheless, the author managed to cajole a fellow clinician—an optimistic, flexible, kind male psychiatrist—into being a coleader.

In the hope of avoiding previous frustrations and failures with these clients, the group leaders carefully defined expectations, goals, and rules for the group. The initial goal was to gather these young men together consistently on a weekly basis, get to know them better and help them get to know the leaders, and expand the limited social networks of the group members. To accomplish this, the membership had to be limited, which required that the group leaders regulate the number of emergency and walk-in contacts within the center and within other community agencies.

Potential members were informed that drug and alcohol rehabilitation were not goals of the group but that no one could attend sessions while high or drunk. The group leaders made it clear that they would always be available to meet with family members or significant others. The group was to run as a six-month experiment, with an option to renew. The administrators at the center hoped that the group's centralized treatment approach would be more economical, as well as more effective, than previous treatment procedures.

FORMATION OF THE GROUP

The group began with six members who were between the ages of 21 and 28. All had been diagnosed as schizophrenic and, consequently, took psychotropic medication. The number of previous hospitalizations of the members ranged from two to seven, with an average of four admissions. All were getting disability payments for psychiatric disorders. The members tended to recognize each other from encounters at the state hospital or the local subway station, but surprisingly, they had very little personal knowledge of each other. Their family backgrounds and educational experiences were quite varied, but the extreme social isolation common to them all was quickly apparent. Although half the members lived at home and half in rooming houses, their living situations could fluctuate from one month to the next. Typically, those living at home either had worn out their welcome or were in the process of doing so.

 Common denominators between group members seemed to be the timing and circumstances of their initial psychotic episodes and the course of their illness and resulting lifestyles. Their first decompensations occurred during late adolescence and were precipitated by a developmental stress or loss which was aggravated by drugs, alcohol abuse, or both. Only one member, the youngest of the six, had a clear family history of schizophrenia. All the group members recompensated quickly when hospitalized, were viewed as troublesome patients, and were often discharged precipitously because of a behavioral problem. Back in the community, they would soon regress to a state of partial decompensation.

Alcohol and drug abuse are a major cause of the fluctuating emotional states of these young men. The stress and despair caused by lack of direction, safety, and comfort in their lives tend to be their rationale for this abuse.

CASE HISTORIES

Typical characteristics of the schizopaths at the center are prominent in the following case histories of group members:

The Night Tripper grew up in a small fishing town. A bright, friendly young man, he became the head of his household at age 14 when his father died from lung cancer. He graduated from junior college with an accounting degree, began a new job, and was engaged to be married. All this fell apart when his fiancée broke the engagement. The Night Tripper became despondent and lost interest in his job. He took off for a resort area where he heavily abused drugs, particularly amphetamines and LSD. He became disorganized, paranoid, deluded, and prone to attacks of rage. At age 23, his career as a psychiatric patient began. It included two suicide attempts and seven hospital admissions. Because of his tendency to be absent without authorization from the state hospital, he was admitted to a maximum security institution for several months.

When he was an outpatient in the community, the client either refused or sabotaged treatment. He typically would take drugs, stay up for two to three days, and then go to the center in an acute psychotic state. His mother would call, either fearing assault or demanding that staff do something to cure him. The client bounced back and forth from rooming houses to his mother's apartment. He was referred to day treatment, which he attended sporadically. After threatening to harm a staff member who had attempted to set limits, he was expelled.

Macho Man, the youngest group member, reported experiencing paranoid ideation in early adolescence. His mother, a diagnosed chronic schizophrenic, had been hospitalized many times, beginning when the client was 3 years old. He was the youngest of five and "babied" by his siblings and parents. The father, a severe diabetic and double leg amputee, dominated the client and pushed him toward a boxing career. The client began to rebel against his father and at age 16 dropped out of school. He began taking street drugs and had some run-ins with the law for stealing. He was hospitalized three times, prior to joining the group, for paranoid ideation. On one occasion, this episode was accompanied by a physical attack on his father. Macho Man recompensated quickly on the ward, but he was viewed as a "wise guy" by the hospital staff. As an outpatient, he tended to refuse his medication and miss appointments. He resumed wandering the streets in search of drugs.

The Rambler was the son of a doting mother and a distant father in a suburban working-class Jewish family. He played guitar in a band and graduated from high school with a scholarship to a local junior college. Shortly after starting college, he began taking LSD with his musician friends and rapidly deteriorated, requiring hospitalizations.

He met his schizophrenic, alcoholic wife while both were inpatients, and much of his life since then has revolved around her and their sadomasochistic relationship. He was 26 when the group began, and although he had only recently moved into the center's catchment area, he and his wife were well known to the on-call staff. They usually were homeless, destitute, and drunk. They fought with each other, and were confused as to who took which medication.

The Rambler was usually able to manipulate charitable agencies to get some basic needs met, but he could become unruly and abusive if he felt threatened. Periodically, he and his wife would land back in the state hospital only to begin their tumultuous travails once again when discharged.

The Philosopher, an appealing, bright young man who dealt with pain by immersing himself in Eastern religion and philosophy, was 26 years old when the group began. Although pleasant and polite, he frustrated staff with his noncompliance.

He grew up in a suburban lower-middle-class family and was closer to his mother than to his father, whom he felt neglected him. When his mother left home to seek a new life and career on the West Coast, the Philosopher was devastated. He became confused, paranoid, and spiritually obsessed and took off by foot after her. He was hospitalized in Indiana and then was transferred back East, where he recompensated quickly on medication. Unfortunately, his aftercare attendance was sporadic. The Philosopher constantly refused medication because he felt that it was in conflict with his religious beliefs and his dietary laws. He did partake, however, in hallucinogens, including marijuana, and he described some "mystical" experiences that resulted.

The Philosopher was hospitalized a second time prior to joining the group after he reported that he attempted suicide by eating a poisonous mushroom. Because of his appeal, he was often hired for work (usually janitorial) but was unable to remain on the job because of his paranoid ideation and his fear of interpersonal contact.

WHAT WAS ACCOMPLISHED?

With respect to the goals initially set forth by the group leaders, the group program has been a success. Although the beginning was slow, with frequent absences of members and subsequent time-consuming outreach work, the group had begun to achieve cohesion after six months; therefore, it was continued. The members expressed ambivalence, but they continued to attend. If members appeared when they were not scheduled—as they sometimes did when they wanted more medication—they were routinely told to come back at the scheduled time of the group session. As a result, these unscheduled appearances occurred less frequently. The use and abuse of psychotropic medication were monitored more closely by having only one prescribing physician and regular weekly meetings. And if a group member showed up high or drunk, he was asked to leave the meeting (this has only occurred four or five times in six years). Two of the original members dropped out: one left to work in a full-time sheltered workshop, another was placed in a halfway house. A short time later, two new members joined. The group leaders remained constant, with the exception of two maternity leaves required by the author.

One major factor contributing to the group's longevity has been the leaders' method of dealing with the transience of the members. When a member moves out of the catchment area, the leaders are reluctant to transfer care to another system. As long as the commute is reasonable, group membership is maintained, along with some negotiations for emergency care in the new area. This atypical policy requires persistent lobbying with administration but is fruitful because, in most instances, clients return to local towns. Two years into the group, following a mandate by federal funding agencies, the center was divided in half, along with its catchment area. Needless to say, the group leaders made sure the group remained intact.

Considering the severe psychopathology exhibited by its members, the group has been a relative therapeutic success. By providing a constant meeting place, the group has enabled its members to expand their social networks significantly. Although their capacity for sustained empathy and affect tolerance during individual sessions is limited, they have developed caring relationships with each other. They congregate in the waiting room for hours before group sessions and occasionally socialize afterward. They share cigarettes, food, sometimes money, and tips on who might provide them with a day's work "under the table." They advise each other as to when surplus food is being distributed and where community dinners are being served.

Encouraged by the leaders, the members use the group for problem solving, often on a crisis basis. They spend hours talking about their fears, paranoia, and psychotic experiences and have shared coping mechanisms. Within the constraints of their emotional instability, their trust and understanding of each other has increased considerably.

The following is one example of the members' problem-solving skills and of their support for each other:

> The Philosopher stopped taking his medication because he felt it was "impure" and unhelpful. He came to the group session very depressed. When asked how he was, he began discussing his "evil" qualities and his unwanted power to harm others by shooting "devil's bullets" from his eyes. Group members were supportive; they appealed to his sense of humor and told him frankly that he made much more sense when taking his medication. Although not thoroughly convinced (as he never is), the Philosopher agreed to try medication again. He became less delusional shortly after, although low self-esteem and bottomless depression remained.

WHAT WAS LEARNED

Through the years the group leaders have grown increasingly aware of the extent of the malignancy underlying the mental illness these young men display and the constant up-hill battle they experience in their day-to-day lives in the community. With little family support, the absence of long-term hospitalization, and the lack of appropriate community residences, they are left essentially to fend for themselves. The group members often discuss their feelings of being victimized, as a result of their illnesses, by their families, by mental health workers, and by the community. Some of this is quite realistic, but some is projection. Their overwhelming feelings of neediness and attempts to fend off underlying emptiness distort their judgment of others. As a result, they will impulsively follow anyone who promises to fulfill a need or two; as a result, they are often exploited. For example,

> Outside a shelter for the homeless, the Rambler met a Texan who claimed to be a wealthy entrepreneur. The Texan said he had been mugged in the downtown area. He drove a big old Cadillac and offered to take the Rambler back to Texas, promising a job, food, and shelter. However, he needed to borrow gas money to get them rolling. Group members and leaders were skeptical, but the Rambler was determined to try for the "good life." The Texan had also promised to drive through a southern state where the Rambler's parents had retired. Subsequently, the Texan bolted—without the Rambler and without returning the gas money or assorted belongings of the Rambler. The Rambler, seeing the incident as another defeat, felt frustration and despair.

Typically, after such an experience, these young men review their current situation and their lives, grieve for the life ambitions they had prior to their becoming mental patients, and quickly fall back into the morass of drugs and alcohol that clearly is an attempt to dull the pain. The same wish to avoid the pain and emptiness in their lives, coupled with the inability to delay gratification, gets played out in the arena of medication. These clients tend to view medication either as a potential panacea for all their ills or as a "downer," as something that brings them back to a painful reality. Thus, they either beg and manipulate people to get more medication or they resist taking it altogether.

An interesting phenomenon in this group is that several members discount the effects of the antipsychotic medications (primarily Prolixin) and state that the accompanying anti-Parkinson's disease drugs, such as Cogentin and Artane (given to alleviate side effects of the other drugs), are more beneficial. Repeated explanations by the group leaders have not dispelled this belief. That these latter medications do not require injection (and thus can be administered by the clients themselves), eliminate concrete distress quickly, and (reportedly) provide some mood elevation may account for this situation.[7]

Street drugs—marijuana, LSD, hashish, valium, prescription cough medicines, and so forth—was a popular subject in the early days of the group and occasionally is popular now. The clients discuss the highs but also the destructive aftereffects. They talk about the paranoia, the frightening auditory and visual hallucinations, and the hospital admissions that these drugs have precipitated, but they are not interested in giving them up. The Night Tripper reports that grass throws him out of whack and makes him paranoid, but, he poignantly explains, the short-lived high makes his life a bit more tolerable.

The leaders have also realized that the trait of these young men that has alienated caregivers—the willingness to beg, borrow, or steal to get what they need—is, in essence, the source of their ego strength. It is a coping mechanism for street life and needs to be viewed by professionals within the environmental context from which it arises.

LIMITATIONS

There is little question in the leaders' minds that the group has been meaningful and helpful to the members. However, what disturbs the leaders is the limited impact the intervention has had on the lives of these young people. Although their need for rehospitalization and the number of hospital admissions have been reduced, life in the community remains extremely difficult for them. Outside the center, housing continues to be a major problem. One of the clients, for example, spent the winter sleeping in doorways. Armed with a warm jacket and tarpaulin, he spent his days pushing a grocery cart filled with his belongings around the city.

The apartments and rooms in this area are quite expensive and the idea of a security deposit is alien to group members. Once they do obtain affordable housing (usually a room), additional problems arise. They find living alone difficult, become depressed, and tend to decompensate quickly. Often, their nighttime activity, resulting from erratic sleep patterns, annoys neighbors. And the young men's housing is further jeopardized by their inconsistent ability to manage their funds. This is a complicated problem. When the Rambler and his (now estranged) wife were living on the street, the author consulted the local social security office with regard to sending rent directly to the landlord. The person at the office explained that in the absence of a "payee," this could not be done unless the couple in question had children. This was disturbing to say the least. At present, the leaders are trying to work out a method whereby the Mental Health Center, although reluctant to do so, will take on the payee role.

The therapeutic housing that does exist is saturated by the emptying of state hospital wards and usually excludes any individual with a history of drug abuse, alcohol abuse, or aggressive behavior. Young chronic adults, even though motivated, are eliminated from drug and alcohol residential programs because of their need for maintenance medication with psychotropic drugs. Because of this, the leaders have been frustrated in their attempts to stabilize Macho Man. When his father died two years ago, any existing structure in his life dissipated. He became very despondent, paranoid, and ravenous for drugs. He threatened his mentally ill mother, demanding money from her, which caused her to take out a restraining order against him. He moved around often, missed many meetings, but kept in touch with the group members and leaders. He began taking heroin, became physically ill, and was eventually hospitalized for his psychosis. However, he recompensated quickly and was medically cleared and discharged. At one point, he agreed to go to a residential drug rehabilitation program, but after many phone calls it was discovered that there were no facilities that would admit an individual on psychiatric medication, even if it were given by injection. Over the past two years, Macho Man has been in and out of the hospital and has roamed the streets, often in a paranoid daze. Recently the group leaders forcefully persuaded the state hospital to admit him until an appropriate living situation could be arranged by the center's case management team.

The group leaders' attempts to help members acquire jobs or training have had ups and downs. The Philosopher took a course in air conditioning and refrigeration. He passed but felt incapable of taking on the responsibility and interpersonal pressures of the job. All the members have been referred at some point to the state rehabilitation agency, but because of their impatience, inability to make scheduled appointments, and disinterest in sheltered workshops, they do not qualify as appropriate candidates. They tend to be more successful in work picked up on the street. Situations where they are paid in cash immediately ("under the table") or with valued goods are desirable to them. The Rambler, for example, helps unload a delivery truck and gets a carton of cigarettes in return; in addition, he washes dishes at a local lunch counter in exchange for coffee and a meal. The Night Tripper works at a local pub from 3:00 A.M. to 5:00 A.M., sweeping and setting up for $5 and a few beers.

Even within the center, support services are limited. These clients tend to avoid the formal intake procedures and structured treatment milieu inherent in those programs available to them. In addition, the other branches of the center are not as liberal as the leaders with regard to out-of-catchment clients: these branches automatically exclude some of the group's members from services. And although the group leaders have succeeded in improving treatment at the center, they have not yet been able to reduce the chaos that exists for clients outside of the mental health system.

ROLES FOR GROUP LEADERS

Segal and Baumohl posited that the key to therapeutic success with the adult chronic population is an agency's willingness to become a surrogate for the natural helping networks.[8] Sheets, Prevost, and Reiman suggested that providers of mental health care must reframe their therapeutic perspective and "become more willing to enter life enterprises with these patients."[9] The group leaders agree with this and as a result have accepted the role of surrogate parents for these young men. Along with unconditionally accepting the members' feelings and illness, the leaders have also been disciplinarians and educators for the members and have served as their advocates in the community as well as within the center's health care system.

The group leaders' clinical interventions have been primarily oriented toward problem solving and have been consistently focused on real-life situations. In addition, a major part of the leaders' clinical role has been to assess and monitor the constant changes in mental status displayed by these clients, especially with respect to suicidal tendencies.

Within the community, the leaders' role has been a practical one, including such tasks as making arrangements with local pharmacists to dispense medication on a daily basis and arranging for prepaid meal tickets at local fast-food restaurants. These time-consuming but all-important tasks are now being carried out by a newly created case management team, with whom the leaders work closely.

The leaders' role as advocates within the mental health system has been an experience that has sensitized them to the caste system that exists within delivery circles of mental health care. Rubin and Johnson pointed out, in their study of staff attitudes toward treatment of the chronically disturbed, that there is a pervasive belief among practitioners that the stigma of chronic mental illness tends to rub off on those who treat this disorder, that the status of aftercare services within the mental health care hierarchy remains low, and that organizational supports or rewards for such service provision are few and far between.[10] The group leaders' experience tends to confirm this. Although the coleaders are supported by the aftercare program, they have experienced disappointment and frustration with regard to the health care system at large. They have encountered value judgments from clinicians and administrators about the clients, and many of these judgments have been expressed as jests. The frequent lack of empathy for and understanding of the members of the therapy group led by the author and her colleague among mental health professionals demonstrates the need for more education and training in this area.

The group leaders are often asked by other staff members how they can persist in doing group work with the clients at the center. One answer to this lies in the fact that the leaders are committed to the care of severely disabled individuals. This commitment involves empathy with them and a strong belief that, given the needs of schizopaths, experienced clinicians must be a part of the helping network and must be willing to reciprocate the trust and respect the clients have for the caregivers.

Although administrators do not always deem the coleadership model as being economical, they should be apprised that such a model, particularly with respect to countertransference issues, can be helpful. The dependency needs, despair, and anger expressed by these clients can be difficult for the therapist to bear. In the instance of the group at the center, the close and supportive relationship between the coleaders has been a crucial factor in enabling the leaders to tolerate the group for so long. Also, the fact that both leaders have varied workloads and roles within the center and elsewhere has probably contributed to the longevity of their participation in the group, as it has provided some built-in distance and relief. But most important, the leaders do not entertain omnipotent fantasies about their effect on these clients and, as a result, are able to tolerate more easily the unpredictable rollercoaster course of the clients' lives and treatment issues.

RECOMMENDATIONS

Young adults who suffer from chronic mental illness are appearing frequently and repeatedly on the doorsteps of mental health care facilities in many communities. The policy of deinstitutionalization, together with demographic changes, has resulted in a complex chain reaction of difficulties for both clients and health care professionals. Because of the inadequate development of community resources, such as halfway houses and single room occupancy hotels, clients and families have been left to fend for themselves, sometimes with disheartening results. Mental health care administrators and clinicians have been given the task of devising effective yet economically feasible treatment programs for these enormously needy but often help-rejecting clients. Although these clients are usually diagnosed as chronic schizophrenics, their characterological traits often mask their clinical vulnerability.

The author believes that long-term group therapy has been helpful for these clients, particularly when coordinated with a case management team. It is, however, only one part of the solution, one piece of the puzzle. For many of these clients, life in the community remains disturbingly chaotic and, at times, dangerous. Mental health, public health, and public welfare agencies must stop their struggle over who is financially responsible. Instead, they must collaborate to create a network of services geared toward the concrete daily needs of these clients. New types of residences such as therapeutic hotels must be developed. Administrators of existing programs need to reexamine their current structures and their changing clientele and make appropriate adjustments. Mental health clinicians and administrators in the public sector may also need to reassess their clinical responsibilities and personal priorities if they are to be effective in their respective roles. Graduate schools must revise their curricula to include more education about this growing client population, and the legal and ethical issues regarding long-term care of these individuals in the community need to be raised and explored.

NOTES AND REFERENCES

1. See Leona L. Bachrach, "Young Adult Chronic Patients: An Analytical Review of the Literature," *Hospital and Community Psychiatry,* 33 (March 1982), pp. 189–197.
2. Bert Pepper, Michael C. Kirshner, and Hilary Ryglewicz, "The Young Adult Chronic Patient: Overview of a Population," *Hospital and Community Psychiatry,* 32 (July 1981), p. 463.
3. Ibid, p. 464.
4. John L. Sheets, J. James Prevost, and Jacqueline Reihman, "Young Adult Chronic Patients: Three Hypothesized Subgroups," *Hospital and Community Psychiatry,* 33 (March 1982), pp. 200–201.
5. Bachrach, "Young Adult Chronic Patients," p. 191.
6. See Pepper, Kirshner, and Ryglewicz, "The Young Adult Chronic Patient."
7. "Dependence on Anti-Parkinson Drugs," *International Drug Therapy Newspaper,* 13 (March 1978), pp. 11–12.
8. Steven P. Segal and Jim Baumohl, "Engaging the Disengaged: Proposals on Madness and Vagrancy," *Social Work,* 25 (September 1980), p. 363.
9. Sheets, Prevost, and Reihman, "Young Adult Chronic Patients," p. 200.
10. Allen Rubin and Peter Johnson, "Practitioners' Orientations Toward the Chronically Disabled: Prospects for Policy Implementation," *Administration in Mental Health,* 10 (Fall 1982), pp. 1–12.

SCHIZOPHRENIA

CHAPTER 46

AFTERCARE TREATMENT FOR SCHIZOPHRENICS LIVING AT HOME

Jody D. Iodice and John S. Wodarski

Deinstitutionalization, a result of the Kennedy Administration's 1963 Community Mental Health Centers Act, was intended to spawn greater community management of mental illness in order to reconnect patients with their families and to alleviate custodial warehousing in psychiatric hospitals. At the same time as the deinstitutionalization movement, advances in the development of psychotropic drugs and their use in treatment were well underway. The proponents of deinstitutionalization believed that psychiatric patients, helped by phenothiazine treatment, could be easily managed in community-based settings and by their families. Thus, chronically disabled schizophrenic patients poured by the thousands into the communities and the homes of their unprepared families.

It has been well established in the literature that deinstitutionalization has failed to meet its ideal: to do a better job of integrating psychiatric patients into the mainstream of society and to make their lives more normal. As a result of that failure, community-based programs have struggled to provide adequate outpatient care for this unique population via day-treatment programs in community mental health centers and countless rehabilitation programs in the community.[1] However, such programs have seen only occasional success. This article reviews the means available to help maintain this chronically ill population in their communities and discusses subsequent practice issues

Reprinted from *Social Work,* Vol. 32, No. 2 (March–April 1987), pp. 122–128, by permission of NASW Press. Copyright 1987, National Association of Social Workers, Inc., *Social Work.*

for the profession. The importance of this subject is underscored by the political reality that communities will have to provide the focus for services in the future.

BACKGROUND LITERATURE

Researchers have estimated that more than one million Americans are schizophrenic; moreover, Borus and Hatow noted that those classified as schizophrenic occupy between one-third and one-half of all psychiatric hospital beds.[2] In 1980, Fentress and Friend reported that as a result of the movement to return psychiatric patients from state hospitals to the community, a quarter of a million patients were left without supervision, simply wandering the street aimlessly.[3] Many of these individuals have inadequate support systems and, thus, they have no link to community programs. Moreover, families, a "dumping ground" for these patients, have been unprepared for the trauma of managing a deinstitutionalized chronic schizophrenic relative.[4]

A substantial body of literature supports the idea that schizophrenia is characterized by early onset, chronic longevity, and frequent relapse. Kreisman and Joy noted that more than 60 percent of all admissions to state psychiatric facilities are readmissions.[5] Lamb suggested that the problems of and obstacles to deinstitutionalization have resulted from the failure to acknowledge that there are many different types of long-term patients who vary greatly in their ability to respond to rehabilitation in the community.[6] He noted that many programs in the community are grossly inadequate and serve only the small minority of higher functioning long-term patients.

Lamb realistically acknowledged that perhaps most long-term psychiatric patients may never be able to function in the mainstream of society and that those who cannot be rehabilitated must at least be allowed dignity and comfort in the community if public policy and the courts continue to force deinstitutionalization. Thus, families of schizophrenic patients increasingly will become the primary long-term caregivers and treatment coordinators. Several current lines of investigation suggest that if families, in particular parents, are to take on the role of primary caretakers for their mentally ill adult relatives, they must be provided with adequate emotional and instrumental resources.[7]

There is information throughout the literature that families are emotionally and financially overtaxed in response to the mental illness of an adult child, spouse, or another relative living at home.[8] Existing evidence has suggested that families respond to the challenge of dealing with the patient at home by initially experiencing a global family schism and then either a reconstruction period or possible dissolution of the family.[9] It should also be noted, however, that in spite of families' traumatic reaction, a large percentage welcome the patients back home.[10]

PROFESSIONAL RESPONSE

Since deinstitutionalization began, there has existed a long-standing, poignant, yet unanswered call for help from families and spouses who have chosen willingly—although apprehensively—to take care of their schizophrenic relative at home. Families are expected to become the primary caretakers, yet they lack the information and management skills to handle this awesome responsibility. They plead for support and aid from mental health professionals, yet often are given little, if any.

The schizophrenic has a low threshold for stress as well as a low tolerance for the demands of everyday life.[11] Accordingly, the readmission rate of schizophrenics living at home with relatives is often high.[12] Descriptions noting the influence of family structure, dynamics, and communication on the course of schizophrenia and as possible precursors of the disease are abundant in the literature. It is ironic that relatives serving as primary caretakers and seeking information on how to care for their mentally ill family member may unknowingly contribute to the stress felt by the patient. The responsibility for easing this problem obviously lies in the hands of mental health professionals.

AFTERCARE MILIEUS

There have been numerous accounts in the literature of therapeutic aftercare milieus for schizophrenic outpatients, but few of these have involved family members in the course of treatment. Treatment models range in focus and scope from residential to day-treatment programs offering highly structured rehabilitative activities, with certain programs providing live-in staff.[13] Other models such as foster homes or transitional apartments provide less-structured environments with staff available when called by residents.[14] Various research efforts have confirmed that when patients are part of a small community group within a comprehensive rehabilitative setting, they experience a decrease in overstimulation and stress, an increase in socialization and companionship, elevated self-esteem and productivity, an increase in individuation, and a decrease in the rate of relapse.[15]

Comprehensive transitional living programs with specific structured aftercare goals reported more independent living of residents after discharge than did less-structured aftercare milieus such as halfway houses and boarding homes.[16] For example, Berkley House in Boston, a transitional living program, encourages the expansion of the patient's psychosocial network outside of the house along with ongoing in-house comprehensive programming.[17] Weekly meetings for former residents are offered to help them adjust to problems that may arise in community living. Follow-up of 78 former residents after the first three years of the Berkley House program demonstrated that 91 percent were living independently and 74 percent were working or attending school. On average, exresidents had been hospitalized 15 months prior to their admission to Berkley House and had remained in the program for 7½ months.

Meyerson and Herman reported that day treatment proved to be an effective resource for aftercare and, when combined with adequate maintenance drug treatment, it reduced rates of recidivism and produced a higher quality of life for chronic psychotic patients.[18] van der Kolk and Goldberg reported that outpatient schizophrenics who received rehabilitation services with a single consistent aftercare therapist, steady levels of fluphenazine, and continued social therapy did significantly better than patients who received inconsistent aftercare follow-up.[19] Cheadle, Freeman, and Korer supported the theme of consistent monitoring of aftercare with discharged chronic schizophrenics in reducing relapse and rehospitalization.[20]

Although individual comprehensive aftercare transitional living facilities for the discharged schizophrenic patient have reported success, such facilities are usually few and far between: As Tessler et al. noted, such facilities will continue to be scarce under current administrative policy.[21]

Thus, the majority of discharged patients are left in the charge of community mental health centers and the patients' families. But community mental health services usually lack both the programs and the personnel to meet the unique needs of discharged chronic schizophrenics and seldom provide ongoing supportive services for families.[22]

FAMILY INTERVENTIONS

Out of frustration, families have joined together to seek aid and support through their own efforts. Such groups as the National Schizophrenic Fellowship (Surrey, England) and the Schizophrenic Association of Greater Washington, Inc., and numerous others across the country have developed as a response to the failure of mental health professionals to provide the support for and to meet the needs of schizophrenic individuals and their families. These self-help groups provide support for families experiencing similar difficulties in caring for their schizophrenic relatives at home.

These groups also serve as educational resources by making appropriate literature available to members when the need arises. Most of these groups have regular newsletters that provide current information on conferences and symposia pertaining to the needs of families, on legislative action concerning most aspects of care for the mentally ill, or on residential facilities for chronic schizophrenics.

Forerunners in heeding the call of frustration from families and establishing aftercare treatment interventions for the schizophrenic patient have been Barcai and his therapy work for multiple families at Fountain House in New York; Beels and his work with the Bronx Psychiatric Center and the Family Service Organization; and Speck and Rueveni and their network therapy, which included friends and relatives along with families of schizophrenics.[23] Over the past 20 years, these researchers have recognized the family as a necessary part of the successful adjustment of schizophrenic individuals returning to homes and to the community. They have provided a model to teach patients and family members how to tolerate each other and what to look for in time of crisis. They have all worked via their unique aftercare programs to provide prevention and crisis-intervention models for families and schizophrenics.

Successful aftercare intervention models for parents or spouses of schizophrenic adults living at home aim to help groups led by professionals explore and come to grips with the following issues: to identify separation-individuation issues for the caregivers and their schizophrenic relative; to help the schizophrenic individual become more independent; to explore parental or spousal guilt for the patient's illness and the detrimental effects this guilt can have on the management of the illness; to overcome parental or spousal denial of the patient's illness; to deal with feelings of guilt and loss over the expectations relatives may have had for their schizophrenic family member; to teach management techniques for use while the schizophrenic individual is living at home; to give permission to parents or spouses to meet their own individual needs; and to allow ventilation of negative feelings.[24]

Research has indicated that family groups and psychoeducational family intervention models are successful treatment mechanisms for parents or spouses of schizophrenic individuals, as they provide ongoing support and feedback from peers. These mechanisms also lead to the development of levels of toleration of, acceptance of, and separation from the schizophrenic family member not found in other traditional treatment modalities.

Goldstein et al. found that combined effects of a moderate dose (1 ml) of long-acting fluphenazine for the formerly hospitalized patient in combination with a six-week crisis-oriented family therapy intervention program immediately following discharge was successful in reducing relapse over a six-month period.[25] They noted that 75 percent of the sample of 104 remained in the community and were free of major relapses or rehospitalization while following the regime of drug maintenance and crisis-oriented family therapy; a different group receiving low-dose (0.25 ml) fluphenazine enanthate and no family crisis therapy experienced a relapse rate of 48 percent.

Goldstein et al.'s specific model of family intervention requires that (1) patient and family come to accept the patient's psychosis; (2) they attempt together to identify probable precipitating stresses in the life of the patient that bring on psychosis; (3) they attempt to generalize about future stresses to which the patient and family may be vulnerable; and (4) they plan together to minimize or avoid these future stresses.[26] In the estimation of Goldstein et al., such an organized aftercare program diminishes the "revolving-door syndrome" that brings on a crisis in the lives of schizophrenic individuals and their families. Again, such an approach certainly provides support and relief by professionals to help families adjust to having their schizophrenic relative at home.

Based on these reports, it is evident that optimum treatment includes drug maintenance therapy as well as inclusion of family members in aftercare, either in brief crisis-oriented family therapy or ongoing family groups for psychoeducational intervention. What is most important, parents and spouses must not be left alone in their struggle. They need access to professional expertise to acquire adequate knowledge about their family member's illness and appropriate coping methods.

In the parent or relative group, families feel the support and bond of others experiencing similar stress. They are no longer isolated in their great despair, frustration, and anger. They gain insight and understanding from their peers, and they find through the group experience a source of strength and confidence to cope with their schizophrenic relative.[27] Hatfield noted the global effect on families of having a schizophrenic relative at home. Stress, anxiety, emotional strain, and physical strain are almost unbearable for all family members.[28] She stated that a team approach by families and professionals is desperately needed for the care and rehabilitation of the chronic schizophrenic as well as for the reduction of the burden on families.

CURRENT FAMILY TREATMENT MODALITIES

Professionals are on the verge of acknowledging the families' frustrated call. Numerous researchers support the use of relatives' groups in aiding families with a schizophrenic family member. They propose an educative approach.[29] Aftercare programs that include some form of family therapy or family interaction in the treatment have proven to be beneficial to the rehabilitation of the schizophrenic in the family and in the community.[30] Other efficacious means of treating schizophrenia are ongoing parent or relative groups and time-limited psychoeducational family intervention groups for families of schizophrenics. Research findings have indicated that both approaches demonstrate an increase in compliance with aftercare regimes in schizophrenic family members, impressively reduced recidivism, and cost-effectiveness.[31]

In psychoeducational family intervention models, families are educated by mental health professionals about schizophrenia through the use of concise, nontechnical explanation; are provided accurate prognoses; are helped to develop communication skills, problem-solving techniques, and behavioral strategies; and are provided information on the availability of community resources. Aspects of psychoeducational family groups include their didactic nature, usual inclusion of only the relatives of a schizophrenic, education concerning the need for medication and medication regimes, and other aspects of the care and management of the schizophrenic relative or spouse.

Parent or relative groups, developed by professionals, focus on helping relatives to work through guilt and disappointment and to become more independent of the patient. These groups may or may not have the patient present. The group therapy approach used includes ventilating feelings, connecting with the caregivers emotionally, using peer pressure and confrontation, and providing relief from the strains of caring for the schizophrenic individual.

The work of numerous researchers represents recent efforts to reach out to the needs of families with schizophrenic family members.[32] These researchers provide a psychoeducational family intervention model based on the findings that poor family interaction, inadequate communication patterns, and overstimulating environments tend to exacerbate the course and outcome of schizophrenia. Vaughn and Leff identified characteristic "expressed emotion" (EE) attitudes and response styles that were unique to relatives with high EE scores and were not found in low EE households. Relatives with high EE scores were consistently highly critical and emotionally overinvolved in the schizophrenic patient's every move, whereas relatives with low EE scores allowed the patient social distance and respected his or her privacy. High EE households doubted the genuine illness of patients, who were often blamed for their condition, whereas low EE households viewed patients as suffering from a legitimate illness. Relatives with high EE scores showed less tolerance for the patient's symptoms, behaviors, and low performance; made few allowances for the patient's condition; and exerted pressure on the patient to behave as a normal individual in most day-to-day situations. Relatives with low EE scores demonstrated consistent tolerance of the patient's symptomatic behavior and accepted the deficiencies in the schizophrenic family member.

Results of the work of Brown, Birley, and Wing and Vaughn and Leff revealed that the best single indicator of symptomatic relapse of schizophrenia in the first nine months after hospital discharge is the EE level demonstrated by key relatives with whom the patient lives.[33] Relapse rates of 50 percent occurred in high EE households, compared to 13 percent in low EE households, even when patients were receiving their prescribed maintenance psychotropic medications.[34] When the patient continued to maintain face-to-face contact in high EE households, the relapse rate increased to 60 percent in spite of psychotropic medication regimes; without chemotherapy the relapse rate exceeded 90 percent.

CLINICAL PROCESS

Attention deficits, dysfunction in processing information or stimuli, and dysfunction of the neurotransmitters and neuroendocrine system characterize many schizophrenic patients.[35] Anderson, Hogarty, and Reiss thought that such deficits in stimulus processing are particularly manifested in an overly stimulating environment (for example, one with high EE).[36] The work of Falloon et al. supported this view.[37] If schizophrenic family members react at home to overstimulating environments that escalate their psychophysiological impairment and if their relatives are unaware of such effects on the maintenance or exacerbation of the illness, a vicious cycle is produced. This cycle may include increased symptomatic behavior; likely relapse; family disruption; rehospitalization; and continued parental or spousal frustration, despair, and hopelessness. Anderson, Hogarty, and Reiss and other proponents of the psychoeducational approach to family treatment sought the most effective means to work with families.[38] They acknowledged that these parents or spouses probably interacted with their schizophrenic family member at a high level of EE. Anderson, Hogarty, and Reiss stated that in their model,

> a variety of supportive and educational techniques are used to lower the emotional temperature of the family while maintaining sufficient pressure on patients to avoid the pitfalls of negative symptoms.[39]

Anderson and her colleagues at Western Psychiatric Institute and Clinic, University of Pittsburgh, have developed a long-term, highly structured, supportive psychoeducational series for families with a schizophrenic member (see Table 46–1). Their empirical data are not complete at this time; however, their preliminary impressions have been favorable. They noted that of the 12 parental families involved over a 15-month period, no dropouts or relapses occurred, and it appeared that certain families were indeed receptive to long-term management of schizophrenia via professional support and concrete information.

Phase I begins at the time of the patient's hospital admission and involves the family, but not the patient, in at least two sessions per week throughout hospitalization. Patient and family then meet for one session at the time of discharge. Phase II, occurring early in treatment, is a day-long workshop for multiple families. Phase III includes the patient and begins as soon as the acute phase of the illness has been controlled, which allows the formerly hospitalized patient to participate more fully. The sessions progress from weekly to bi-weekly for at least a six-month period. Phase IV is initiated once the family and professional goals for effective functioning have been accomplished to the most feasible degree possible, taking into consideration the patient's abilities and the current family structure. The family and patient may elect at this time to continue in more intensive weekly family therapy to facilitate family interactions. This might involve more traditional family therapy with increased confrontations; increased responsibility of family members for participating in the therapy session; better ability to deal with unresolved family issues and conflicts; developmental issues; sibling issues; marital discord; and increased differentiation of family roles.

Anderson, Hogarty, and Reiss noted that early in the process, families developed in-

Table 46–1
Psychoeducational Model of Aftercare for Schizophrenic Patients:
Overview of the Process of Treatment

Phases	Goals	Techniques
Phase I Connection	Connecting with the family and enlisting cooperation with program Decreasing guilt, emotionality, negative reactions to the illness Reducing family stress	Joining Establishing treatment contact Discussing crisis history and feeling about the patient and the illness Empathy Specific practical suggestions that mobilize concerns into effective coping mechanisms
Phase II Survival Skills Workshop	Increasing understanding by family of patient's illness and needs Continuing reduction of family stress "De-isolating" and enhancing social networks	Multiple family education and discussion Concrete data on schizophrenia Concrete management suggestions Basic communication skills
Phase III Reentry and Application	Maintaining patient in community Strengthening marital/parental coalition Increasing family tolerance for low-level performance and dysfunctional behaviors Resuming of responsibility of the patient gradually	Reinforcing boundaries (generational and interpersonal) Task assignments Low-key problem solving
Phase IV Maintenance	Reintegrating into normal roles in community systems (work, school) Increasing effectiveness of general family processes	Infrequent maintenance sessions Traditional or exploratory family therapy techniques

Source: Adapted from C. Anderson, G. Hogarty, and D. Reiss, "Family Treatment of Adult Schizophrenic Patients: A Psycho-Educational Approach," *Schizophrenia Bulletin,* 6, No. 3 (1980), p. 495.

creased coping skills through exposure to other parents struggling with similar issues and problems.[40] It appeared to Anderson and her colleagues and to others that the creation of a support network through in-depth contact and interaction with other families in similar situations, along with the intensive interaction with professionals, provided an ongoing source of support, desensitization, and normalization about the issue of schizophrenia in the family. As previous evidence has suggested, families of schizophrenics seek specific, honest information, practical management techniques, and clear information from professionals.[41]

Falloon, Boyd, and McGill conducted psychoeducational groups in the homes of parents of schizophrenics to minimize missed appointments and low attendance and to help patients generalize learning to family situations.[42] Falloon et al., McClean et al., and Zelitch conducted their psychoeducational family intervention in treatment facilities.[43] Success appeared to be equal whether sessions were conducted at home or in a facility. (It should be noted that these formerly hospitalized patients participating in psychoeducational family models of intervention had reached stabilization on their maintenance dosage of phenothiazine.)

McGill et al. conducted a two-year outcome study of aftercare treatment involving 39 patients and their parents, 18 of whom received the family psychoeducational model of intervention and 18 of whom received only individual treatment (three patients dropped out).[44] In the psychoeducational model, parents and patients reported:

1. having a high level of satisfaction with the educative sessions;
2. gaining increased understanding of the schizophrenic patient's behavioral disturbances;
3. educating other family members, friends, and neighbors about the illness as well as dispelling some of the myths and stereotypes;
4. having the opportunity for the first time to learn about the patient's frightening delusions and hallucinations;
5. having patients tend to reveal at home more florid symptoms than reported at the hospital or outpatient clinic; and
6. having patients increase their ability to monitor their levels of stress, which prompted them to ask for an increased dosage of medication from their physicians.

McGill et al. administered a questionnaire designed to measure knowledge about schizophrenia and medication at baseline, immediately after educational intervention, at three months, and at nine months after intervention.[45] Patients and parents in the psychoeducational model showed a significant gain in knowledge between the baseline and follow-up period, whereas those in individual treatment demonstrated no significant changes.

McGill et al. and Boyd, McGill, and Falloon carried out their treatment in weekly sessions for three months, biweekly for six months, and monthly follow-up for 15 months.[46] Zelitch offered a 1½-hour psychoeducational parent intervention for eight weeks.[47] McClean et al. conducted their psychoeducational group for a 12-week period.[48] The outcomes of these various psychoeducational models generally included improved social functioning, increased systems of social support for patients and families, helping parents cope with their reacquired role of primary caretaker, and helping the patient adjust to family life.

The psychoeducational models of Boyd, McGill, and Falloon and of Zelitch were used in semistructured workshop or seminar settings.[49] They presented all aspects of the illness, prognoses, medication regimes, communication skills and behavioral strategies, signs of relapse, role of environmental stress and family stress on the course of the illness, as well as exploration of etiological factors of the illness. Visual aids, informational handouts, and programmed text material were used along with a question-and-answer period.

PSYCHOEDUCATION AND SELF-HELP

With deinstitutionalization, parents and spouses unfortunately often become 24-hour primary caretakers of schizophrenic relatives following discharge. In most instances, they are ill equipped and uninformed by mental health professionals as to how to assume this role. Psychoeducational family intervention appears to be the most compatible aftercare modality to meet their needs effectively. It enhances relatives' sources of information and support, expands their social support system, enhances communication and behavioral tactics and strategies, develops coping skills, increases compliance with aftercare regimes, and what is most important, reduces relapse and rehospitalization rates of the patient. Furthermore, self-help groups conducted by and for parents and spouses of schizophrenics help families adjust to the stress and emotional burden, as well as provide them the relief, support, and encouragement they so desperately need.[50]

If such programs are unavailable, research findings suggest that a day-treatment program at a community health center with a single consistent social therapy program would also prove effective.[51] However, program and personnel limitations often keep mental health centers from providing consistent day-treatment programs for chronic schizophrenic patients and their families. Ideally, a highly structured, comprehensive transitional living program that includes family involvement would be a supportive resource.[52] However, such programs are scarce considering the numbers in need.

Thus, it appears that the fruits of deinstitutionalization are psychiatric patients who have been "dumped" on families and community mental health programs ill-prepared to handle the more than 1.5 million patients discharged each year.[53] Although research demonstrates success in day-treatment programs and highly structured transitional living programs, in the aftermath of the deinstitutionalization movement and current public policy, access to such aftercare programs is severely limited—much to the frustration and despair of affected families. Help for these patients and their families is urgently needed, and the psychoeducational family intervention model appears to be a successful cost-effective response to their needs and the constraints of deinstitutionalization and current public policy. The psychoeducational model is suitable to the orientation of the social work profession because historically social work has been concerned with the intricacies of the family system, group processes, and crisis intervention with individuals and families. The psychoeducational model encompasses these areas and is consonant with the value base and orientation of social work practice.

NOTES AND REFERENCES

1. J. Borus and E. Hatow, "The Patient and the Community," in J. Shershow, ed., *Schizophrenia: Science and Practice* (Cambridge, Mass.: Harvard University Press, 1978), pp. 171–196; H. Goldman, "Mental Illness and Family Burden: A Public Health Perspective," *Hospital and Community Psychiatry,* 33 (July 1982), pp. 557–560; H. Lamb, "What Did We Really Expect from Deinstitutionalization?" *Hospital and Community Psychiatry,* 32 (February 1981), pp. 105–109; and C. McGill et al., "Family Educational Intervention in the Treatment of Schizophrenia," *Hospital and Community Psychiatry,* 34, No. 10 (1983), pp. 934–938.

2. Borus and Hatow, "The Patient and the Community."

3. C. Fentress and D. Friend, "Emptying the Madhouse," *Life,* 4, No. 5 (May 1981), pp. 56–70.

4. Goldman, "Mental Illness and Family Burden"; and K. Minoff, "A Map of Chronic Mental Patients," in J. Talbott, ed. *The Chronic Mental Patient* (Washington, D.C.: American Psychiatric Association, 1978), pp. 11–37.

5. D. Kreisman and V. Joy, "Family Response to the Mental Illness of a Relative: A Review of the Literature," *Schizophrenia Bulletin,* 10 (Fall 1974), pp. 34–57.

6. Lamb, "What Did We Really Expect from Deinstitutionalization?"

7. See for example, C. Beels and W. McFarlane, "Family Treatments of Schizophrenia: Background and State of the Art," *Hospital and Community Psychiatry,* 33 (July 1982), pp. 541–550.

8. M. Vannicelli, B. J. Scheff, and S. Washburn, "Family Attitudes toward Mental Illness: Immutable with Respect to Time, Treatment, Setting, and Outcome," *American Journal of Orthopsychiatry,* 50 (January 1980), pp. 151–155; and M. J. Willis, "The Impact of Schizophrenia on Families: One Mother's Point of View," *Schizophrenia Bulletin,* 8, No. 7 (1982), pp. 617–619.

9. A. Hatfield, "The Family as Partner in the Treatment of Mental Illness," *Hospital and Community Psychiatry,* 30 (May 1979), pp. 330–340; and Hatfield, "Helpseeking Behavior in Families of Schizophrenics," *American Journal of Community Psychology,* 7, No. 5 (1979), pp. 563–569.

10. W. Doll, "Family Coping with the Mentally Ill: An Unanticipated Problem of Deinstitutionalization," *Hospital and Community Psychiatry,* 27 (March 1976), pp. 183–185; and Kreisman and Joy, "Family Response to the Mental Illness of a Relative."

11. B. Dohrenwend and G. Egri, "Recent Stressful Life Events and Episodes of Schizophrenia," *Schizophrenia Bulletin,* 7, No. 1 (1981), pp. 15–21; G. Serban, "Stress in Schizophrenics and Normals," *British Journal of Psychiatry,* 126 (May 1975), pp. 397–407; and B. Spring, "Stress and Schizophrenia," *Schizophrenia Bulletin,* 7, No. 1 (1981), pp. 24–33.

12. M. Herz and C. Melville, "Relapse in Schizophrenia," *American Journal of Psychiatry,* 137 (July 1980), pp. 801–805; Kreisman and Joy, "Family Response to the Mental Illness of a Relative"; E. W. Lambert, V. Therwood, and L. Fitzpatrick, "Predicting Recidivism among First Admissions at Tennessee's State Psychiatric Hospitals," *Hospital and Community Psychiatry,* 34 (October 1983), pp. 951–953;

and C. Vaughn and J. Leff, "Patterns of Emotional Response in Relatives of Schizophrenia Patients," *Schizophrenia Bulletin,* 7, No. 1 (1981), pp. 43–44.

13. C. Beels, "Family and Social Management of Schizophrenia," in P. Guerin, ed., *Family Therapy* (New York: Gardner Press, 1976), pp. 249–283; M. Chaudhry and J. Beard, "Rehabilitation of Schizophrenics—A Collaborative Study between Fountain House, New York, and Fountain House Lahore," *International Journal of Rehabilitation Research,* 2, No. 4 (supplement 2) (1979), pp. 39–43; and L. Mosher and A. Menn, "The Surrogate 'Family' and Alternatives to Hospitalization," in Shershow, ed., *Schizophrenia,* pp. 223–239.

14. A. Burger et al., "Congregate Living for the Mentally Ill: Patients as Tenants," *Hospital and Community Psychiatry,* 29 (September 1978), pp. 590–593; and C. Melick and C. Eysaman, "A Study of Former Patients Placed in Private Proprietary Homes," *Hospital and Community Psychiatry,* 29, No. 9 (1978), pp. 582–589.

15. J. Beard, T. Malamud, and E. Rossman, "Psychiatric Rehabilitation and Rehospitalization Rates: The Findings of Two Research Studies," *Schizophrenia Bulletin,* 4, No. 4 (1978), pp. 622–635; and P. T. Donlon, R. Rada, and S. Knight, "A Therapeutic Aftercare Setting for 'Refractory' Chronic Schizophrenic Patients," *American Journal of Psychiatry,* 130 (June 1973), pp. 682–684.

16. A. Meyerson and G. Herman, "What's New in Aftercare? A Review of the Literature," *Hospital and Community Psychiatry,* 34 (April 1983), pp. 333–342; and Mosher and Menn, "The Surrogate 'Family' and Alternatives to Hospitalization."

17. Meyerson and Herman, "What's New in Aftercare?"

18. Ibid.

19. B. van der Kolk and H. Goldberg, "Aftercare of Schizophrenic Patients: Pharmacotherapy and Consistency of Therapists," *Hospital and Community Psychiatry,* 34 (April 1983), pp. 343–348.

20. A. Cheadle, H. Freeman, and J. Korer, "Chronic Schizophrenic Patients in the Community," *British Journal of Psychiatry,* 132 (March 1978), pp. 221–227.

21. R. Tessler et al., "The Chronically Mentally Ill in Community Support Systems," *Hospital and Community Psychiatry,* 33, No. 3 (1982), pp. 208–211.

22. H. Lamb, "Roots of Neglect of the Long-Term Mentally Ill," *Psychiatry,* 41 (September 1979), pp. 210–217; and R. Stern and K. Minkoff, "Paradoxes in Programming for Chronic Patients in a Community Clinic," *Hospital and Community Psychiatry,* 30 (1979), pp. 613–617.

23. A. Barcai, "An Adventure in Multiple Family Therapy," *Family Process,* 6, No. 2 (1967), pp. 185–192; Beels, "Family and Social Management of Schizophrenia"; and R. Speck and U. Rueveni, "Network Therapy—A Developing Concept," *Family Process,* 8, No. 2 (1969), pp. 182–191.

24. N. Atwood and M. Williams, "Group Support for Families of the Mentally Ill," *Schizophrenia Bulletin,* 4, No. 3 (1978), pp. 415–425; and J. Dincin, V. Selleck, and S. Streicker, "Restructuring Parental Attitudes—Working with Parents of the Adult Mentally Ill," *Schizophrenia Bulletin,* 4, No. 4 (1978), pp. 597–608.

25. M. Goldstein et al., "Drug and Family Therapy in the Aftercare of Acute Schizophrenics," *Archives of General Psychiatry,* 35 (October 1978), pp. 1169–1177.

26. Ibid.

27. R. Thompson and E. Wiley, "Reaching Families of Hospitalized Mental Patients: A Group Approach," *Community Mental Health Journal,* 6, No. 1 (1970), pp. 22–30.

28. Hatfield, "The Family as Partner in the Treatment of Mental Illness"; and Hatfield, "Helpseeking Behavior in Families of Schizophrenics."

29. See, for example, K. Bernheim, "Supportive Family Counseling," *Schizophrenia Bulletin,* 8 (November 1982), pp. 634–641; and E. Plummer et al., "Living with Schizophrenia: A Group Approach with Relatives," *Canada's Mental Health,* 39, No. 1 (1981), pp. 32–33.

30. Beels, "Family and Social Management of Schizophrenia"; Chaudhry and Beard, "Rehabilitation of Schizophrenics"; Hatfield, "The Family as Partner in the Treatment of Mental Illness"; Hatfield, "Helpseeking Behavior in Families of Schizophrenics"; and C. Vaughn and J. Leff, "The Measurement of Expressed Emotion in the Families of Psychiatric Patients," *British Journal of Social and Clinical Psychology,* 15 (June 1976), pp. 157–165.

31. Meyerson and Herman, "What's New in Aftercare?"

32. C. Anderson, G. Hogarty, and D. Reiss, "Family Treatment of Adult Schizophrenic Patients: A Psycho-Educational Approach," *Schizophrenia Bulletin,* 6, No. 3 (1980), pp. 490–505; J. Boyd, C. McGill, and I. Falloon, "Family Participation in the Community Rehabilitation of Schizophrenics," *Hospital and Community Psychiatry,* 32 (September 1981), pp. 590–593; and Falloon et al., "Family Therapy of Schizophrenics with High Risk of Relapse," *Family Process,* 20 (June 1981), pp. 211–221.

33. G. Brown, J. Birley, and J. Wing, "Influence of Family Life in the Course of Schizophrenia Disorders: A Replication," *British Journal of Psychiatry,* 121 (September 1972), pp. 241–258; Vaughn and Leff, "The Measurement of Expressed Emotion in the Families of Psychiatric Patients"; and Vaughn and Leff, "Patterns of Emotional Response."

34. Vaughn and Leff, "The Measurement of Expressed Emotion."

35. E. Merrin, "Schizophrenia and Brain Asymmetry: An Evaluation for Dominant Lobe Dysfunction," *Journal of Nervous and Mental Diseases,* 169, No. 7 (1981), pp. 405–416; and S. Snyder, "Dopamine Receptors, Neuroleptics, and Schizophrenia," *American Journal of Psychiatry,* 138 (April 1981), pp. 460–464.

36. Anderson, Hogarty, and Reiss, "Family Treatment of Adult Schizophrenic Patients."

37. Falloon et al., "Family Therapy of Schizophrenics with High Risk of Relapse."

38. Anderson, Hogarty, and Reiss, "Family Treatment of Adult Schizophrenic Patients"; Boyd, McGill, and Falloon, "Family Participation in the Community Rehabilitation of Schizophrenics"; I. Falloon, J. Boyd, and C. McGill, "Treatment of Schizophrenia—Medication" (Los Angeles: University of Southern California Family Aftercare Program, 1980); McGill et al., "Family Educational Intervention in the Treatment of Schizophrenia"; and S. R. Zelitch, "Helping the Family Cope: Workshops for Families of Schizophrenics," *Health and Social Work,* 5 (November 1980).

39. Anderson, Hogarty, and Reiss, "Family Treatment of Adult Schizophrenic Patients," p. 492.

40. Ibid.
41. Hatfield, "The Family as Partner in the Treatment of Mental Illness"; Hatfield, "Helpseeking Behavior in Families of Schizophrenics"; D. Holden and R. Lewine, "How Families Evaluate Mental Health Professionals, Resources and Effects of Illness," *Schizophrenia Bulletin*, 8, No. 4 (1982), pp. 626–633; and S. Platman, "Family Caretaking and Expressed Emotion: An Evaluation," *Hospital and Community Psychiatry*, 34 (October 1983).
42. I. Falloon, J. Boyd, and C. McGill, "What Is Schizophrenia?" (Los Angeles: University of Southern California, Family Aftercare Program, 1980); McGill et al., "Family Educational Intervention in the Treatment of Schizophrenia"; Boyd, McGill, and Falloon, "Family Participation in the Community Rehabilitation of Schizophrenics"; and Falloon, Boyd, and McGill, "Treatment of Schizophrenia."
43. Falloon et al., "Family Therapy of Schizophrenics with High Risk of Relapse"; C. McLean et al., "Group Treatment for Parents of the Adult Mentally Ill," *Hospital and Community Psychiatry*, 33 (July 1982), pp. 564–568; and Zelitch, "Helping the Family Cope."
44. McGill et al., "Family Educational Intervention."
45. Ibid.
46. Ibid.; and Boyd, McGill, and Falloon, "Family Participation in the Community Rehabilitation of Schizophrenics."
47. Zelitch, "Helping the Family Cope."
48. McLean et al., "Group Treatment for Parents of the Adult Mentally Ill."
49. Boyd, McGill, and Falloon, "Family Participation in the Community Rehabilitation of Schizophrenics"; Falloon, Boyd, and McGill, "Treatment of Schizophrenia"; Falloon, Boyd, and McGill, "What is Schizophrenia?"; Falloon et al., "Family Therapy of Schizophrenics"; and Zelitch, "Helping the Family Cope."
50. Atwood and Williams, "Group Support for Families of the Mentally Ill"; and Dincin, Selleck, and Streicker, "Restructuring Parental Attitudes."
51. Cheadle, Freeman, and Korer, "Chronic Schizophrenic Patients in the Community"; Meyerson and Herman, "What's New in Aftercare?"; and van der Kolk and Goldberg, "Aftercare of Schizophrenic Patients."
52. Atwood and Williams, "Group Support for Families of the Mentally Ill"; Beels, "Family and Social Management of Schizophrenia"; Chaudhry and Beard, "Rehabilitation of Schizophrenics"; and Dincin, Selleck, and Streicker, "Restructuring Parental Attitudes."
53. Goldman, "Mental Illness and Family Burden."

CHAPTER 47

THE ROLE OF SOCIAL NETWORKS IN THE MAINTENANCE OF SCHIZOPHRENIC PATIENTS

R. D. W. Taylor, P. J. Huxley, and D. A. W. Johnson

In recent years increasing attention has been paid to the influence that family members might have on the course of schizophrenia. Initial findings on the role played by the living group to which the long stay schizophrenic patient was discharged revealed that those patients who adjusted most successfully were those who returned to live alone, in lodgings or to distant relatives. Those most likely to relapse and require hospital readmission were those who returned to the close emotional ties of a spouse or parents (Brown, 1959). More careful examination of the families to which schizophrenic patients were discharged focused on the different levels of expressed emotion (EE) which relatives revealed when talking about the patient and it was shown that relatives conveying high levels of expressed emotion (as measured by emotional overinvolvement, hostility and critical comments when talking about the patient) were much more likely to have a patient relapsing in the nine months following his discharge than relatives whose level of expressed emotion was low (Brown *et al.* 1972; Vaughn and Leff, 1976). Additionally, spending less than 35 hours per week in face to face contact with the relative and taking medication were found to reduce the likelihood of relapse for the schizophrenic patient living with a high EE relative. Subsequent work (Leff and Vaughn, 1980) has compared the expressed emotion of the relative and the presence of environmental stress, as rated by life events, in schizophrenic and depressed patients. Episodes of schizophrenia in patients living with high EE relatives were found not to be preceded by an excess of life events whereas those in patients from low EE homes were

Reprinted from *British Journal of Social Work*, Vol. 14, No. 2 (April 1984), pp. 129–140, by permission of Oxford University Press.

preceded by such life events. Consequently an excess of life events and having a high EE relative are both independently associated with the onset or relapse of schizophrenia. Furthermore, the role of expressed emotion was also found to be operating in depressive illnesses. While modifying the attitudes of relatives displaying high levels of expressed emotion has become a significant focus for social work treatment (Kuipers and Priestley, 1979) the contribution made by this factor to the maintenance of schizophrenic patients would seem to be emerging as less specific than it first appeared. One of the major problems with such family studies is that they have paid insufficient attention to the interactions of family members with extended kin, friends, work associates and others. Wynne (1972) considers that it is reasonable to hypothesize that not only expressed emotion but family communications generally are in part a product of the social connections of family members with others outside the family.

An overview of maintenance treatments in schizophrenia suggests that a range of psychosocial treatments influence outcome (Gunderson, 1977) and that what such treatments have in common is their provision of a supportive milieu. This milieu has a restorative effect over life event stresses which have caused disruptions in social networks through factors such as loss, migration and conflict (Beels, 1978). In seeking to identify more precisely those variables which might intervene in the association between life events and higher rates of psychiatric disorder, Mueller (1980) considers that social network factors may be the underlying mechanism. Life events such as bereavement, migration, unemployment and divorce are all events which disrupt social networks and weaken the social support available to the individual.

Hammer et al. (1978), Kapferer (1973) and Boissevain (1974) report a fairly consistent pattern in the immediate social networks of groups of people across rural/urban, working class/middle class and Europe/Africa dimensions. These studies report between six to ten individuals intimately known to the focal person and most of whom also know each other, plus about 30 other individuals who are also seen regularly by the focal person. There are five or six clusters of seven to eight highly connected individuals within each cluster. Networks substantially smaller than this, more unstable or socially dispersed would be unlikely to meet the needs of the individual to the same extent. It is this personal network approach which has been used in studies of psychopathology and social networks (Pattinson et al. 1975; Tolsdorf, 1976; Henderson, 1977; 1980a; Silberfeld, 1978; Sokolovsky et al. 1978; Horowitz, 1978; Sosna, 1979). Members of the primary network are people with whom the individual has a personal relationship, usually kin, friends and neighbours, which involves frequent and regular contact. Henderson (1978) considers that these represent the main affective attachments of the individual and are, therefore, the most significant for study in the area of psychiatry.

There are reviews (Hammer, 1973; 1978; Mueller, 1980) and papers providing anecdotal evidence and case studies (Budson and Jolley, 1978; Beels, 1978) pointing to the significance of social support systems in schizophrenia but only three studies (Pattinson et al. 1975; Tolsdorf, 1976; Sokolovsky et al. 1978) which have measured social network characteristics of samples of schizophrenics. They indicate that the social networks of schizophrenic patients are smaller than those of non-schizophrenics particularly with respect to the number and proportion of non-kin connections. El Islam (1979) reports that schizophrenic patients living in extended families have more favourable outcomes than those living in nuclear families and Brown *et al.* (1972) reported that schizophrenic patients had better outcomes where parents had more social contacts.

RESEARCH AIMS AND METHODS

The aim of the present study is to examine the social networks of the nearest relatives of schizophrenic patients. It is hypothesized that the level of social support found in the social network of the patient's closest associate is linked to that person's capacity to cope with the patient and thereby has an influence on the patient's level of functioning. The study asks:

(a) are different levels of functioning in a sample of schizophrenic patients found in association with differences in the social networks of their nearest relatives, and if so

(b) is the social environment of the relative related to the patient's social functioning *and/or* his clinical state, and if so

(c) are the same or different social network factors operating to influence these two aspects of the patient's maintenance in the community?

The sample consisted of patients attending a university teaching hospital out-patients department, who met the criteria for inclusion in the study. They met diagnostic criteria for schizophrenia (Feigner *et al.* 1972) and had been maintained on depot neuroleptic medication for a minimum of 12 months and were rated by their treating psychiatrist as having borderline or mild symptoms at the time of the study. These criteria produced a sample of 45 schizophrenic patients who had been well maintained on an outpatient basis and represented the least psychiatrically impaired group of schizophrenic patients other than those completely discharged from any treatment.

Permission was sought to interview the nearest relative (informant) defined by the patient as the person he felt closest to. If more than one person was named the one having most face to face contact with the patient was selected for interview. In all cases of married patients the spouse is the informant and in all cases of patients living with parents one or other parent is the informant.

Patient social performance ratings, obtained from the nearest relative, are derived from a modified version of the Social Behaviour Assessment Schedule (SBAS), a semi-structured interview schedule developed by Platt, Weyman and Hirsch at the Department of Psychiatry, Charing Cross Hospital, London. Only those measures of social performance on the SBAS which are independent of social relationship measures are included, to eliminate the possibility of a tautological relationship between network measures and social performance. That is, measures of social performance are made of the performance of household and other tasks[a], rather than of social performance items such as 'going out socially' which could clearly be a function of network size and type. Additional ratings of the amount of encouragement given by the relative to the patient

---

[a] Child care, management of money, hobbies, work performance, self-care, decision making.

are made in order to accommodate the effect of reduced volition in many schizophrenic patients which might contribute to poor social role performance.

The nearest relative is asked about his primary network in terms of how far it serves him as a source of social support. The names of people in this network are elicited in response to questions asking the relative about the number of people in his network who meet six provisions of social relationships (Weiss, 1974). These are social integration, advice and guidance, nurturance, attachment, reassurance of worth and reliable alliance. Questions on loss of attachment figures and conflict are also included. Where appropriate these questions are reciprocal so as to identify those fulfilling relationship needs for the informant and those to whom the informant provides these relationship needs. For example, the reciprocal questions about the support provided by Advice and Guidance are: 'when you are worried or in a difficult situation is there anyone you go to for advice or guidance?' and 'is there anyone who comes to you for advice and guidance when they have a problem or a worry?'

The names elicited in this way from the social network schedule constitute the network members from which measures of size, density[b], directionality[c], frequency of contact and proportions of kith and kin are taken.

The clinical rating used in the study is the Brief Psychiatric Rating Scale (Overall and Gorham, 1962).

RESULTS

The social network measures of the nearest relative which are most closely associated with good social performance in the patient are shown in Table 47–1.

It is evident from Table 47–1 that a straightforward rank order correlation of the network factors with the dependent variable, social performance shows a preponderance of structural (morphological) aspects of the nearest relative's network. A large stable

Table 47–1

Informant Social Network Measures Most Closely Associated with Good Social Performance in the Patient

** Patient not nurtured by informant
** Large number of non-kin
* Large number of friends
* Low mean number of contacts with network members
* Low network density
* Informant having people to rely on
* Large number of people visiting the home
* Informant not lost touch with people important to him
* Large size of network

Probability: ** $P < 0.001$; * $P < 0.01$.

[b] Density is the number of links existing between network members divided by the total number of possible links.
[c] Directionality is a measure of the extent to which network relationships are one way or reciprocal in content area.

network with a higher number of non-relatives and low density, indicating varied and separate groups of associates within the network plus relationships which provide the relative with a sense of reliable alliance and an absence of the patient from the relative's nurturance relationships are the network measures most highly associated with good social performance in the patient.

The relationships between patient social performance and relative's social network measures of size, density and proportion of kin are shown below in Tables 47–2, 47–3 and 47–4. In order to observe how these network measures relate to good levels of social functioning in the patients, those patients scoring maximum points or one point below maximum on the social performance scale are grouped into 'good' ($N = 17$) with lower scores grouped under 'poor' ($N = 28$).

Table 47–2 shows that for good social performance patients the trend among their nearest relatives is towards having larger numbers of people in their social networks whereas the trend is in the reverse direction for those patients performing poorly. The biggest difference between the two groups of patients emerges where relatives name less than eight people as meeting their relationship provisions—46.4% of 'poor' social performance patients and 17.6% of 'good' social performance patients are living with relatives who have fewer than eight primary contacts in their network.

Table 47–3 shows that half the nearest relatives of the 'poor' social performance patients have networks with a density of 85% or more, whereas none of the relatives of 'good' social performance patients have such dense networks. It is only at levels of high network density in the relatives that differences between the two patient groups are found.

Table 47–4 points to the significance of having a small number of non-kin members in the network. Of the 28 patients performing poorly, 13 (46.4%) of their nearest relatives had only one or a complete absence of non-kin members in their networks in contrast to only one (5.8%) of the nearest relatives of 'good' social performance patients. Having two or more kith in the network does not discriminate between 'good' and 'poor' groups. It is the virtual or complete absence of relationships with people outside the family for relatives of 'poor' social performance patients which is responsible for the significance of the result.

The social network measures of the nearest relative which are most closely associated with good clinical ratings in the patient are shown in Table 47–5.

Unlike the relatives' social network variables associated with good social performance in the patient (Table 47–1), those found with good clinical state in the patient are all relationship provisions. No structural network measures are present. The network

Table 47–2

Size of relatives' network	Patient social performance (N = 45)		
	Good	Poor	Good(%)
Less than 8	3	13	18.7
9–14	6	10	37.5
15+	8	5	61.5
			$P<0.01>0.001$

Table 47–3

Density of relatives' network	Patient social performance (N = 42)		
	Good	Poor	Good(%)
0–56%	7	7	50
57–84%	7	7	50
85–100%	0	14	0
			$P<0.01>0.001$

The three cases missing from the above table are excluded because informants were not at all clear about the connections among their network members.

measures above show more dependent relationships from others to the informant with the patient being less involved in attachment and conflict with the relative.

It is worth noting here that since the patient sample was selected on the basis of relatively low levels of symptomatology, the range of scores on the clinical rating are limited and consequently reduce the likelihood of a relationship between clinical state and other variables. However, it is important to ascertain the extent to which the clinical state of the patient might be a major determinant of both the relative's network size and form as well as the patient's social performance, and consequently responsible for any degree of association between them. Partial correlation is undertaken to observe the effect of the clinical variable on the observed relationship between patient social performance and relative's network variables (Guilford, 1965). The clinical variable does not alter the significance levels for any of the items in Table 47–1, and therefore is not, on available evidence, responsible for the association between network and performance.

The amount of encouragement given by the relative to the patient is highly negatively associated with patient social performance ($r = -0.76$, $P<0.001$), that is, where patients are rated as performing well in their social roles, their relatives report giving less encouragement to them to perform these roles. Encouragement is not associated with the patient's clinical status. The relationships between these three factors are shown in Figure 47–1.

The mean number of contacts with network members in the week prior to interview is 30.94 contacts for relatives of 'good' social performance patients and 30.41 contacts

Table 47–4

Number of kith in relatives' network	Patient social performance (N = 45)		
	Good	Poor	Good(%)
0–1	1	13	7.1
2–5	8	8	50
6–15	8	7	53
			$P<0.02>0.01$

Table 47–5

Informant Social Network Measures Most Highly Associated with Good Clinical Ratings (BPRS) in Patient

* Fewer deaths of people close to informant
* Large number of people visiting the home
* Absence of recent conflict with the patient
* Patient not rated by informant as significant attachment figure
* More unidirectional relationships: from others to informant
* Informant having people relying on him

* $P < 0.01$.

for the relatives of 'poor' social performance patients. Clearly the relatives of 'poor' social performance patients are not more socially isolated. Both groups have about the same overall level of social interaction. The mean number of network members for relatives of good social performance patients is 13.47 members, compared with 10.11 for 'poor' social performance patients. Relatives of poor social performance patients have, therefore, fewer network members but they see them more often. Relatives of good social performance patients have a mean of 2.19 contacts per network member in the week, with relatives of poor social performance patients seeing their network members an average of 3.41 occasions in the week. Relatives of good social performance patients have, therefore, less frequent contact with a greater number of people.

DISCUSSION

The criteria adopted in this study for defining network links support Mitchell (1969) in finding significant measures in both morphological and interactional areas. They support also the work of Henderson (1977, 1978, 1980a,b) in showing that the provisions of social relationships are measurable and significant aspects of social network analysis. The results support the need for a valid and reliable instrument in psychiatry with which to express social relationships in terms of both the links between people and the provisions obtained through those links.

In this group of schizophrenic patients good social performance is found when the patient's closest associate has a large diffuse network with low density, a large number of non-kin, people who visit him, and people on whom he can rely. In contrast, the pa-

Figure 47–1
Encouragement and Clinical Status of the Patients.

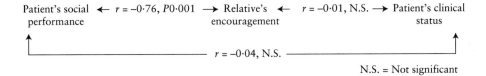

Patient's social   ← $r = -0.76$, $P \cdot 0.001$ → Relative's   ← $r = -0.01$, N.S. → Patient's clinical
performance   encouragement   status

———————————————————— $r = -0.04$, N.S. ————————————————

N.S. = Not significant

tient's clinical performance is related to the interactional aspects of the relative's network. It is those relatives who have other people coming to them for relationship needs, who are not closely involved with the patient either as an attachment figure or through conflict, who are found with patients who are performing well clinically. Whatever the role played by social networks of family members in the functioning of the schizophrenic patient, it is evident that there are different factors at play in the relative's networks for clinical and social performance in the patient.

The significance of these factors must be seen in the context of the sample—a relatively homogeneous and well functioning group of outpatient schizophrenics. It is not unreasonable to assume that among a more representative cross-section of schizophrenic patients the significance of the relatives' social network in differentiating levels of social and clinical performance in the patient might be even greater.

The smaller size of networks found among schizophrenic patients themselves leads Pattinson to conclude that the psychotic patient 'is caught in an exclusive small social matrix that binds him and fails to provide a healthy interpersonal matrix' (Pattinson *et al.* 1975, p. 1249). The results of the present study suggest that it is a less healthy interpersonal matrix among the closest associates of the schizophrenic patient which are associated with poorer levels of social functioning in the patient. This casts doubt on the schizophrenic patient's limited social network functioning being simply a consequence of his illness and the isolation and withdrawal which may accompany it. Since none of the relatives had a diagnosis of schizophrenia or were currently receiving any psychiatric service the patient's pattern of social interaction must be seen in the context of his relative's pattern of social interaction which would appear not to be a direct consequence of a schizophrenic illness.

It is not possible to draw any firm conclusions from this study about how the relative's social network is implicated in the patient's condition. It may be that the relative's network explains the patient's social performance by providing a restricted network which, in addition to the limitations imposed on the patient by his illness, acts to further restrict the patient by reducing the range and quality of opportunity for his social role performance. The comparative isolation of the relative may act to reduce his own expectations of the patient. Against this, is the finding that relatives with poor social performance patients are those showing the highest levels of encouragement to the patient. The results do suggest that it is not a lower over-all level of social contacts among relatives of poor social performance patients but rather that the social contact is with a smaller number of people, seen more often and providing little diversity of membership which is handicapping for the patient. Alternatively, living with a patient who has a poor level of adjustment may make it difficult for the relative to maintain a normal pattern of social interaction. If this is the case, the constraints which the patient puts upon his relative arise from his social performance rather than his clinical functioning since partial analysis indicates that it is not the more clinically disturbed patients who are living with relatives who have poorly integrated social networks.

If we see successful adjustment in schizophrenia as a product of both social and clinical functioning then lesser involvement of the relative with the patient around emotionally charged areas such as conflict and attachment is only one aspect of the problem. It is necessary to facilitate other changes in the pattern of social interaction in the families of schizophrenic patients. Kuipers and Priestley (1979) report on the difficulties of counselling relatives towards lesser involvement of an intrusive nature with the schizophrenic patient, reduced face to face contact and the modification of harmful patterns of family interaction. The present study suggests that an alternative strategy may also be necessary, namely that the schizophrenic's closest associates are encouraged to develop wider patterns of social interaction, particularly with non-kin and with people in varied and unconnected settings.

REFERENCES

Beels, C.C. (1978) 'Social networks, the family and the schizophrenic patient', *Schizophrenia Bulletin,* 4, pp. 512–521.

Boissevain, J. (1974) *Friends of Friends,* Oxford, Blackwell.

Brown, G.W. (1959) 'Experiences of discharged chronic schizophrenic mental hospital patients in various types of living groups', *Millbank Memorial Fund Quarterly,* 37, p. 105.

Brown, G.W., Birley, J.L.T. and Wing, J.K. (1972) 'Influence of family life on the course of schizophrenic disorders: a replication', *British Journal of Psychiatry,* 121, pp. 241–58.

Budson, R.D. and Jolley, R.E. (1978) 'A crucial factor in community program success: the extended psychosocial kinship system', *Schizophrenia Bulletin,* 4, pp. 609–621.

El-Islam, M.F. (1979) 'A better outlook for schizophrenics living in extended families', *British Journal of Psychiatry,* 135, pp. 343–347.

Feighner, J.P., Robins, E. and Guze, S. (1972) 'Diagnostic criteria for use in psychiatric research', *Archives of General Psychiatry,* 26, pp. 57–63.

Guilford, J.P. (1965) *Fundamental Statistics in Psychology and Education,* New York, McGraw Hill.

Gunderson, J.G. (1976) 'Drugs and psychosocial treatment revisited', *Journal of Continuing Education in Psychiatry,* 38, pp. 25–40.

Hammer, M. (1973) 'Psychopathology and the structure of social networks', in Hammer, M., Salzinger, K. and Sutton, S. (eds) *'Psychopathology: contributions from the social, behavioural and biological sciences,'* John Wiley and Sons, New York.

Hammer, M., Makiesky-Barrow, S. and Gutwirth, L. (1978) 'Social networks in schizophrenia', *Schizophrenia Bulletin,* 4, pp. 522–545.

Henderson, A.S. (1977) 'The social network, support and neurosis', *British Journal of Psychiatry,* 131, pp. 185–191.

Henderson, S., Duncan-Jones, P., AcAuley, H. and Ritchie, K. (1978) 'The patients primary group', *British Journal of Psychiatry,* 132, pp. 74–86.

Henderson, S., Byrne, D.G., Duncan-Jones, P., Scott, R. and Adock, S. (1980a) 'Social relationships, adversity and neurosis: A study of associations in a general population sample', *British Journal of Psychiatry,* 136, pp. 574–583.

Henderson, S., Duncan Jones, P., Byrne, D.G., Scott, R. (1980b) 'Measuring social relationships: the Interview Schedule for Social Interaction', *Psychological Medicine,* 10, pp. 723–734.

Horowitz, A. (1978) 'Family, kin and friend networks in psychiatric help-seeking', *Social Science and Medicine,* 12, pp. 297–304.

Kapferer, B. (1973) 'Social network and conjugal role in urban Zambia: A reformulation of the Bott hypothesis', in Boissevain, J. and Mitchell, J.C. (eds) *Network Analysis: studies in human interaction,* The Hague, Mouton.

Kuipers, L. and Priestley, D. (1979) 'Schizophrenia and the family' in Wing, J.K. and Olsen, R. (ed.) *'Community Care for the Mentally Disabled',* Oxford University Press.

Leff, J.P. and Vaughn, C.E. (1980) 'The interaction of life events and relatives expressed emotion in schizophrenia and depressive neurosis', *British Journal of Psychiatry,* 136, pp. 146–153.

Mitchell, J.C. (ed.) (1969) *'Social Networks in Urban Situations'* Manchester, Manchester University Press.

Mueller, D.P. (1980) 'Social networks: a promising direction for research on the relationship of the social environment to psychiatric disorder', *Social Science and Medicine,* 14A. pp. 147–161.

Overall, J.E. and Gorham, D.R. (1962) 'The brief psychiatric rating scale', *Psychological Reports,* 10, pp. 799–812.

Pattinson, E.M., Defrancisco, D., Wood, P., Frazier, H. and Crowder, J. (1975) 'A psychosocial kinship model for family therapy', *American Journal of Psychiatry,* 132, pp. 1246–1251.

Silberfeld, M. (1978) 'Psychological symptoms and social supports', *Social Psychiatry,* 13, pp. 11–17.

Sokolovsky, J., Cohen, C., Berger, D. and Gieger, J. (1978) 'Personal networks of ex-mental patients in a Manhattan SRO hotel', *Human Organisation,* 37, pp. 5–15.

Sosna, U. (1970) *'Empirical Measurement of Social Isolation in Relation to Mental Disorders of the Elderly',* Manheim, W. Germany, Dept. of Epidemiological Psychiatry Zentral Institute fur Seelische Gesundheit.

Tolsdorf, C.C. (1976) 'Social networks, support and coping: an exploratory study', *Family Process,* 15, pp. 407–417.

Vaughn, C.E. and Leff, J.P. (1976) 'The influence of family and social factors on the course of psychiatric illness', *British Journal of Psychiatry,* 129, pp. 125–37.

Weiss, R.S. (1974) 'The provisions of social relationships', in Rubin, Z. (ed.) *'Doing unto Others'* Englewood Cliffs, NJ, Prentice-Hall, pp. 17–26.

Wynne, L.C. (1972) 'Communication disorders and the quest for relatedness in families of schizophrenics' in Cancro, R. (ed.) *'Annual Review of the Schizophrenic Syndrome.'* (vol. 2) New York, Brunner/Mazel, Inc, pp. 395–414.

SCHIZOPHRENIA

CHAPTER 48

TREATMENT ISSUES IN SCHIZOPHRENIA

Judith C. Nelsen

In an earlier article on planning social work treatment for schizophrenia, the writer asserted that to help this client group a social work professional must assess and deal with systems balance over space and time. In this article, core issues in the actual treatment process are discussed. The individuals and families under consideration are primarily those in whom schizophrenic symptoms occur intermittently or in recurring cycles; clinical diagnosis of the identified patient is usually ambulatory schizophrenia or schizophrenia in partial remission. The discussion here is based on material from ego psychology and the systems-communications theorists, as well as on the writer's experience with direct treatment, supervision, and consultation in the area of schizophrenia.

Three major issues will be discussed that are basic to effective treatment and often problematic for social workers. They are the management of relationship factors in individual and group treatment, the dynamic enhancement of ego coping in individual and group treatment, and the reorientation to process factors in family work.

MANAGEMENT OF RELATIONSHIP FACTORS

In individual and group treatment of schizophrenic clients, there is a surfacing of relationship issues which must be handled if treatment is to progress. The initial process of relationship-building is often a painstaking one. Sessions may be characterized by frequent silences which the worker must fill, monosyllabic answers to questions, awkwardness, apparent disinterest in proceeding with treatment, or highly inappropriate discussion. Clients may relate too openly at the outset, spilling innermost thoughts or content apparently straight from the unconscious. Most schizophrenic clients who continue therapy become dependent on the worker, whether or not they can express this emotion.

Reprinted from *Social Casework,* Vol. 56 (1975), pp. 145–152, by permission of the publisher, Families International, Inc.

Almost inevitable problems come with such dependency. Even gentle, supportive workers who are clear about the limitations of their professional role may see clients who show unrealistic expectations about treatment and then flee, via broken appointments or paranoid ideation, with the accusation that the worker has taken over. These typical schizophrenic relationship distortions, or psychotic transference, must be understood and handled.

Theories about early or continuing patterns in the family of orientation can help clarify such distortions. These theories suggest that the parents, for various reasons, have not allowed the schizophrenic offspring to separate from them as he must to establish independent means of dealing with his affects and of evaluating reality. Implicitly, they promise that if he remains with them and represses all negative feelings, they will meet all his needs. Messages about sexuality are conflicting; parents may be subtly seductive while demanding abstinence. Either because the family continues its influence or because the schizophrenic individual has not learned to assess new relationships differently, both positive and negative expectations of parent figures will be transferred onto the treating person.[1]

As the client moves toward the worker emotionally, he will expect the worker to meet all his needs. Inappropriate sexuality and dependency may be made explicit: The client claims that he loves the worker, wants to marry the worker, or wants to go to live as the worker's child. There are sometimes positive expressions about merger; one client told a worker, "We will marry and become one person." Covert signs may include a client's showing up at unscheduled hours with an adoring smile, touching the worker, making overly enthusiastic comments on the benefits of treatment, or showing possessive jealousy in the presence of other group members.

The client usually tries to keep his part of the presumed bargain during this time by repressing or suppressing any negative feelings toward the worker. However, frustration builds because the worker, like the parents, can not meet all his needs. Failures on the worker's part are seen as a lack of concern rather than a limited ability to help, because the worker's omnipotence is taken for granted. At some point, anger will be shown, obviously or subtly, perhaps symbolically by heated complaints about other authority figures. If not handled, increasing levels of rage can cause clients to leave treatment.

Clients who receive no comment from the worker about sexual fantasies which have surfaced in some form may also discontinue treatment because of fears that a sexual relationship will actually take place. The heavy incestual component of their sexual feelings makes this fantasy a terrifying prospect. Clients who express a strong wish for merger are often frightened that the worker will take them over eliminating their very existence as separate human beings.

To deal with these various disturbed relationship elements, a social worker must not send mixed messages related to self-feelings of omnipotence, fear of aggression, or special interest in sexuality. A worker's distress about handling such material may blind

---

[1] Thomas Freeman, John Cameron, and Andrew McGhie, *Studies on Psychosis* (New York: International Universities Press, 1966), pp. 15–37; and Theodore Lidz, Stephen Fleck, and Alice Cornelison, Therapeutic Considerations Arising from the Intense Symbiotic Needs of Schizophrenic Patients, in *Schizophrenia and the Family*, ed. Lidz, Fleck, and Cornelison (New York: International Universities Press, 1965), pp. 61–71.

him or her to the veiled manifestations of relationship distortions that do exist. The writer is convinced that relationship factors must be anticipated, that the worker's stance must be made explicit before or as soon as such issues arise, and that the client's difficulties in accepting such messages must be discussed at times.

Generally, the first factor to arise is the client's belief in the worker's omnipotence. It can be anticipated by the worker's spelling out how he or she will try to help, the limits of such help, and what the client will need to attempt for himself. Many clients will not fully hear these comments. The worker must notice when clients seem to hold unrealistic expectations or to attribute change magically to the worker and must gently expose the realities involved. If the worker's attitude is that misunderstandings do occur in relationships but that it is helpful to look at them, he or she may help clients make their unrealistic expectations a matter for ego awareness and further discussion. A schizophrenic individual can examine and seek to control his conscious ideas about relationships, such as his understandable wish for complete help, without having to consider why he is this way. Finally, prior work in the area of unrealistic hopes will lead to discussion of client disappointments when hopes are not met. Disappointments will be smaller and easier to consider when this groundwork has been laid. The worker must be careful to verbalize disappointments which a client only hints at and to express empathy about them. By means of such discussion, a client may have his first real experience that negative feelings can be expressed and understood in a close relationship.

Wishes for and fears of merger can be handled similarly. The worker may establish himself or herself as a separate individual by some limited revelation of personal material, although this disclosure should not be extensive or it may have the opposite effect of implying that a close personal and, to the client, sexualized relationship will develop. The worker must also empathically examine the client's subtle wishes and fears when they arise and clarify that both worker and client are and will remain separate individuals. Client expressions of love and sexual feelings, especially if made nonverbally by touching, are often difficult for workers to react to because they do not wish to indicate rejection. One may show understanding of the feeling while noting that it can not be appropriately expressed in this relationship. The momentary sense of rejection which the client may feel is preferable to increasingly frightening fantasies or greater feelings of rejection at a later time.

In group treatment, member relationships may dilute the relationship with the worker. However, the above distortions can arise between members as well as between individual members and a group leader. Explicit handling by the worker is necessary in such situations. Although it may be more difficult to notice individual covert reactions in a group, group members often move along together in their expectations, hopes, and fears. Also, in a group, members can learn to help each other find and manage relationship distortions.

There is one other facet of handling relationship material with schizophrenic clients. Frequently, a client will not openly acknowledge feelings that he expresses nonverbally, no matter how nonjudgmentally the worker comments on them. The worker's benign comments are usually received without arousing great anxiety. Sometimes feelings can be acknowledged by a client at a later time; in any case, they do not seem to build up as they do otherwise. It is also true that the worker's clarifications, whether heard or not, do not usually prevent a continuation of some distortions. The difference is that part of the client's ego is now on the side of realistic handling, or at least the client is reassured that the worker will not succumb, for example, to a sexual relationship, even though the client may continue to talk of such a possibility.

DYNAMIC ENHANCEMENT OF EGO COPING

After experiences in which psychoanalytic-style probing led to an increase of symptoms, social workers doing individual or group treatment with schizophrenic clients have often avoided discussion of feelings and have talked only about reality events in clients' lives. Help with reality-testing is important, including the clarification of distortions in client-worker and group member relationships, but a dynamic approach to the enhancement of other ego coping is also necessary.

As a foundation, the worker must gain extensive awareness of each client's coping capacities and personality style from observing him during treatment sessions and in interaction with other people, from hearing how the client is handling life situations, from considering recent historical information, and sometimes from working with collateral persons. Strengths must be found even in situations of considerable pathology. Perhaps the client's intelligence, his physical stamina or ability to discharge stress through physical activities, an appealing manner which makes others more willing to help him, or an extraordinary will to survive his difficulties can be determined. Limitations must be identified, not in the static sense of a symptom picture, but by understanding what causes anxiety or an increase in symptoms.

The worker must determine how the client maintains balance in his life. To whom does he look for positive regard and emotional security? What does he do with affects? If the client does not show anger or sexuality in situations where these would normally be aroused, what defenses are employed to maintain repressions? Workers often must combine knowledge of life happenings and of indirect reactions because clients may be unaware of feelings or their source. How do clients show anxiety or deal with anxiety to avoid showing it? In interviews, decreasing anxiety levels are a sign that current treatment is helpful or inoffensive to the ego; escalating upset indicates that discussion is moving too quickly.

Clients can participate in getting to know themselves, their appearance to others, the areas of functioning that are difficult for them, and their areas of strength. Everyone has personal characteristics, strengths, and limitations; understanding of these factors over a period of time can help an individual anticipate feedback, utilize strengths, and marshal resources to cope with difficulties. For example, a rigid but reliable group member who finds that other members slowly grow to like him can expect something similar to occur in a sheltered workshop situation. Another client may be able to use his intelligence to categorize situations and later devise means of dealing with those that upset him. Awareness of problem areas becomes a strength in itself because clients can help the worker see where assistance is needed. The presumption is that as confidence grows and as mastery and control can be felt in some areas, there is a greater capacity to try to change in other areas.

The most important area with which schizophrenic clients have difficulty is the management of affects. Normal feelings and primitive impulse material are uneasily repressed; they are often clear to the observer in symbolic content. Elaborate ego defenses against frightening affects may be buttressed by unreasonably strong superego prohibitions. Even when conscious feelings are misdirected—for example, when a client fixes on one sibling as the source of all his troubles or shows paranoid anger toward a neighbor—the ego may be defending against an affect, such as rage, which would erupt dangerously if its true object were known. Although social workers know that schizophrenic defenses and inappropriate behavior should not be attacked, they often try unsuccessfully to talk clients out of such incidents. An approach based on dynamic understanding is more likely to facilitate positive change.

The worker must have a sense of when primitive forces are threatening to engulf a client's ego and must actively ally with the ego to maintain repressions at these times. The client who anxiously tells about a hallucination or homosexual feeling does not need implicit encouragement of expression through treatises on the beauty of mind-expanding experiences or the normality of bisexual inclinations. If a client expresses inappropriately directed feelings like paranoid rage, the worker can neither ignore the affects nor in most situations interpret what has actually aroused them. A client usually expresses such content in a safe environment where he knows he will not be condemned and will be helped to regain control. Workers can sometimes listen to inappropriate feelings and then veto their being expressed elsewhere on the grounds that this act can cause trouble for the client. Occasionally, what clients need to discuss regarding such feelings or psychotic material is the fear of losing control.

Additional help may be given by considering with the client how to extricate himself from reality situations which seem to spur the experiences, by talking about medication, by assuring the client that the worker may be telephoned to help with control, and so on. Client strengths in dealing with feelings effectively may be supported—for example, by encouraging the sublimation of aggression through physical activity. The worker who knows his client well may offer another defense to help with a slipping one. Thus, for an intellectualized individual whose envy of a friend is turning into delusional thinking, the social worker may suggest a rationalization about why the friend received what the client did not.

When clients find the worker helpful in repressing primitive material, they are more ready to allow normal affects into consciousness because the worker is sensed as a reinforcement to the ego in case of need. The worker who knows what is going on in clients' lives or in group process can help individuals to identify sources of less primitive feelings and what the feelings are. Even the worker's clarification of what is a normal response can be enlightening. Clients may have been aware of, and concerned about, feelings or they may have been experiencing general distress without knowing why. Discussion of anger toward the bus driver, of jealousy of a friend, or of empathy with other group members may be reassuring. Sometimes normal affects are expressed symbolically. A client whose worker has arrived late may describe with concern how his uncle did not keep a promise to him as a child. In the writer's experience, clients will not be made anxious by a mild inquiry as to whether they are annoyed or by a statement by the worker that any possible annoyance will not upset the worker. Other ego teaching may occur—for example, that talking about feelings with the worker or in a group need not lead to other expression or action unless the individual so chooses. The effort is to help clients experience small amounts of affect in a structured situation where they can be given help. When blanket repression of feelings is no longer necessary some ego energy should be freed for healthier overall functioning.

In eliciting normal feelings, one caution must be noted. Workers should proceed extremely slowly in the area of a client's feelings about family members. Even when such affects are within a normal range, justified, and perhaps volunteered by clients, the worker's encouragement of expression rather than a neutral stance may upset a balance. Possibly, this result occurs because even normal affects toward family members are very close to, if not mingled with, such primitive feelings as rage toward them for not meeting symbiotic needs.

If clients learn to have needs met in less conflicted relationships than are possible with family members, some force of rage owing to unmet needs is reduced and, thus, the pressure on the ego is lessened. A client will be readier to relate to nonrelatives for need satisfaction if and when he can achieve some separation from parental family or feel less helplessly dependent on his spouse. One means of facilitating individuation is through family work. Workers must also help to reduce fears and distortions which could curtail or prohibit outside relationships. Schizophrenic individuals may meet some needs for emotional security, positive regard, and expression of aggression in client-worker and group member relationships, if psychotic transference is kept to a minimum. Continued work on reality-testing and management of normal affects may allow clients to relate more easily to other persons as well. Even if fully mature object relationships are not possible, a capacity for friendships, job functioning, or relative ease in handling day-to-day living can improve clients' need-satisfaction balance.

In all enhancement of ego coping, clients must move at their own pace, whether they are seen individually or in groups. If workers understand clients' dynamic functioning, are willing to teach them much of what they know, and can time their support appropriately, growth can be seen in many situations.

PROCESS FACTORS IN FAMILY WORK

Communications theorists assert that the question in schizophrenia "is not *whether* the members of a patient's family are to be dealt with, but *how.*"[2] The writer's earlier article[3] suggested that work with the parental family is imperative in the treatment of a young schizophrenic client who has never functioned in independent living arrangements. Possibilities for seeing families of procreation were also discussed. The systems-communications literature on treatment techniques with parental families is

---

[2] Don D. Jackson and John H. Weakland, Conjoint Family Therapy: Some Considerations on Theory, Technique, and Results, in *Therapy, Communication, and Change,* ed. Jackson (Palo Alto, Calif.: Science and Behavior Books, 1968), p. 224.
[3] Judith C. Nelsen, Treatment-Planning in Schizophrenia, SOCIAL CASEWORK, 56:67–73 (February 1975).

impressive.[4] However, in the writer's experience, many social workers have difficulty with the necessary reorientation to process factors in family work.

According to systems-communications theorists, schizophrenic behavior of an identified patient living with his parents is in some way appropriate to or required by current family interaction patterns. This assertion may seem similar to the traditional assumption that parents, possibly in interaction with genetic factors, have influenced the individual in childhood toward a pathological development, but the two points of view are divergent in some of their treatment implications. Don D. Jackson, Jay Haley, Murray Bowen, Ivan Boszormenyi-Nagy and others believe that all family members, including the identified patient, are locked into presently dysfunctional family interaction patterns, whatever their original source. All are at some level suffering from the characteristic mixed communication, enforced closeness, and inability to escape the system.[5] If this concept is valid, the family as a whole is truly the client, and all members must equally receive the attention, scrutiny, empathy, and interventive help of the social worker. All persons should be treated, sometimes together, sometimes separately.

Social workers may betray their misunderstanding of this position—thus suffering subsequent difficulties in reorienting to the family as a system—in several ways. These include subtle rejection of parents because of what they have done to the identified patient, expressions of surprise when parents demonstrate disturbed functioning, or interpretations showing parents how they are hurting the identified patient rather than commenting to all on their joint responsibility for family functioning. A more insidious manifestation involves workers' exhorting family members to find outside activities or single parents to date or remarry without realizing that total family fears of separation and individuation must be handled first.

Another difficulty, particularly for those professionals trained in casework, is maintaining an awareness of process as well as of discussion content. In family work, particularly with families with a schizophrenic member where discussion may initially obscure more than it clarifies, close attention to process factors is necessary. They include who is taking over, who is contradicting by bodily movement or facial expression what he is verbalizing, who is assuming responsibility for distracting behavior as someone else is forming a coalition, and so on. It can be productive to view family videotapes with no sound to gain awareness of these matters. How the social worker is entering the dynamic balance must also be considered. A comment can be destructive even if it is accurate and empathically given—for example, if it interprets behavior of

---

[4] See Don D. Jackson, Family Interaction, Family Homeostasis and Some Implications for Conjoint Family Psychotherapy, and idem, Family Therapy in the Family of the Schizophrenic, in *Therapy, Communication, and Change*, ed. Jackson, pp. 185–221; Jackson and Weakland, Conjoint Family Therapy, in *Therapy, Communication, and Change*, ed. Jackson, pp. 222–48; Don D. Jackson and Virginia Satir, A Review of Psychiatric Developments in Family Diagnosis and Family Therapy, in *Therapy, Communication, and Change*, ed. Jackson pp. 249–70; and Ivan Boszormenyi-Nagy and James L. Framo, eds., *Intensive Family Therapy* (New York: Harper & Row, 1965).

[5] See Gregory Bateson et al., Toward a Theory of Schizophrenia, and idem, A Note on the Double Bind—1962, in *Communication, Family, and Marriage*, ed. Don D. Jackson (Palo Alto, Calif.: Science and Behavior Books, 1968), pp. 31–62; Murray Bowen, Family Psychotherapy with Schizophrenia in the Hospital and in Private Practice, in *Intensive Family Therapy*, ed. Boszormenyi-Nagy and Framo, pp. 213–43; and Ivan Boszormenyi-Nagy, A Theory of Relationships: Experience and Transaction, and idem, Intensive Family Therapy as Process, in *Intensive Family Therapy*, ed. Boszormenyi-Nagy and Framo, pp. 33–142.

the identified patient so as to imply that the worker and the parents must align to treat him.

In work with families in which the schizophrenic individual is one of the parents, a systems-communications orientation may seem very unnatural, for the spouse and the children clearly did not cause the schizophrenia. Such thinking suggests failure to grasp the full implications of the theory. No matter how family patterns start, they are assumed to influence the present behavior of all family members. Overt schizophrenic symptomatology may be facilitated or required because family balance both incorporates and perpetuates the pathology. In seeing families of procreation, workers must take care to view identified patient, spouse, and children as fellow sufferers and unwitting co-conspirators of the status quo, not as villains or victims.

Even when parents or spouses are not available for total family work, a systems communications orientation can guide whatever contacts are made with family members. In one situation known to the writer, a schizophrenic client being seen individually developed some delusional thinking about a relative staying in the home on a brief visit. The parents, who were in their seventies and not interested in psychotherapeutic help, had been seen twice by the worker during several years of treatment. However, based on the assumption that the distress shown by the client might exist in other family members, a telephone contact was made. The parents had considered rehospitalizing the client out of their own distress over the relative's visit, on the mistaken assumption that the client was having another breakdown. When the worker offered sympathy and took responsibility for suggesting that they avoid action until the relative left, they agreed. The client's functioning improved and the parents subsequently used telephone help to deal with another emergency.

CONCLUSION

Ego psychology and the systems-communications approaches to understanding schizophrenia can clarify overall treatment-planning and core treatment issues with this client group. Social workers offering service must routinely assess and consider intervention, not only with the identified schizophrenic individual but also with family and impinging social systems. Timing of intervention efforts can be geared to an awareness of cyclical dynamics in chronic schizophrenia. And to treat clients effectively, social workers must deal with schizophrenic relationship distortions, ego functioning especially in the management of affects, and family process.

SUBSTANCE ABUSE

CHAPTER 49

DRUG-FREE TREATMENT SELECTION FOR CHEMICAL ABUSERS

A Diagnostic-Based Model

Carolyn Sandberg, William M. Greenberg, and Joseph C. Birkmann

"I could never work with drug addicts. I'd get too depressed—so few of them make it." "Do drug addicts really recover? It seems to me that they no sooner enter treatment, than they're back out there using again." "Those drug programs don't do a damn bit of good." "He doesn't really want help, this is his third time here. What makes him think it will be any different?"

Any seasoned specialist on chemical abuse (alcohol or other drugs) has heard such sentiments expressed many times, by other mental health professionals as well as by patients' families. Of course, there is more than a grain of truth supporting these attitudes. Chemically abusing patients' motivations for undergoing treatment frequently have less to do with desire for a cure than with a wish to avoid jail by "serving time" in a more desirable setting; with acceding to family's or friends' ultimatums to "get treatment or don't come home"; with a need to "come in from the cold" for "three hots and a cot" and perhaps required medical attention; with a desire to "hide out" from enemies seeking them on the streets; or with a wish to decrease the expense of their habit by decreasing their physical tolerance. Moreover, relapses are common. Although we have by now accustomed ourselves to the sad revolving-door syndrome of individuals afflicted with chronic schizophrenia, we are less likely to excuse the excesses of the recidivist, nonschizophrenic, chemical abuser, feeling angry not only because we perceive their sufferings to be self-inflicted, but because we feel they have the cognitive

Reprinted from *American Journal of Orthopsychiatry,* Vol. 61, No. 3 (1991), pp. 358–371. Copyright 1991 by the American Orthopsychiatric Association, Inc. Reproduced by permission.

capacity to be more responsible for themselves. Such anger, added to our hopelessness, may bring an unpleasant nihilistic atmosphere to what should be a clinical encounter, professional evaluation, and recommendation. Our pessimistic views, abetted by the sampling bias toward recidivists rather than successful "graduates," need correction. Even the stereotypical picture of intravenous heroin use as uncontrolled, continuous, and enduring, is belied by the true diversity of its patterns and outcomes *(Leukefeld & Tims, 1989; Robertson, Bucknall, Skidmore, Roberts, & Smith, 1989)*. It is essential to remember that many individuals *can* achieve and maintain abstinence from the chemicals they abuse, and that patients need knowledgeable counseling about the referrals most likely to work for them.

In past years, the decision-making process for a referral was relatively simple: intoxicated alcoholics without medical or psychiatric complication could go to a "sobering-up station"; those at risk of suicidal or extremely violent behavior would be held in the emergency room for evaluation and, if necessary, admitted to a psychiatric unit; those at risk of dangerous withdrawal complications (barbiturate withdrawal, delirium tremens) would be admitted to a medical unit; those in less acute danger but needing supervised detoxification could be admitted to a detox unit or a longer-stay inpatient alcohol program; those needing outpatient referrals would get an AA (Alcoholics Anonymous) phone number and perhaps a psychiatric referral or an outpatient drug or alcohol program referral (e.g., outpatient alcohol, methadone maintenance). The general clinical wisdom was that physicians could handle the acute medical and psychiatric problems on an inpatient basis, that AA was the most important outpatient referral, that opiate addicts might as well be referred to a methadone maintenance program because nothing else seemed to help, and that there was not much else to offer patients to help them "stop using."

Over the last 10–20 years, several developments have complicated this picture. Serious new problems have emerged, including: *1)* new drugs—both new classes, such as the dissociative hallucinogens (phencyclidine or "angel dust"), and more powerfully addicting substances, such as crack cocaine; *2)* the penetration of drug abuse into all social strata and geographical locations and age groups, abetted by entrepreneurial opportunism and other sociological influences; *3)* the rise in frequency of polysubstance abuse; *4)* more extreme violence within drug subcultures; *5)* the explosion of intravenous route-related serious diseases (initially bacterial endocarditis, hepatitis B and C; now AIDS); and *6)* the dramatic growth of a population with "double trouble"—those presenting with a major psychiatric diagnosis as well as a significant chemical abuse or dependency problem. Alcohol and drug disorders, previously researched and treated separately, now are often diagnosed simultaneously in the same individual. Cocaine users frequently abuse alcohol, and awareness has increased that identified alcoholics very often have drug problems. Mixed substance abuse was apparent in the Epidemiologic Catchment Area (ECA) study, which in the early 1980s interviewed over 18,000 adults in the U.S. Using the *DSM-III*-based Diagnostic Interview Schedule (DIS), this landmark study *(Regier et al., 1988)* found 2.8% of U.S. adults with alcohol abuse or dependence present during a one-month period and a 13.3% lifetime prevalence; a 1.3% one-month and 5.9% lifetime prevalence of drug abuse or dependence; and corresponding one-month and lifetime prevalences of 3.8% and 16.4% for any substance abuse or dependence disorder. Although the lay-administered DIS diagnostic instrument has some weaknesses when used with the "dual-diagnosis" population *(Ford, Hillard, Giesler, Lassen, & Thomas, 1989; Griffin, Weiss, Mirin, Wilson, & Bouchard-Voelk, 1987)*, epidemiologically the ECA remains our strongest study.

The ECA study further found that for lifetime prevalence of abuse or dependence, those with an alcohol diagnosis had an 18% likelihood of also having a drug diagnosis, and 61% of those with a "hard drug" (non-marijuana) diagnosis also had an alcohol diagnosis *(Helzer & Pryzbeck, 1988)*. The significant extent of the co-morbidity of alcohol and drug disorders suggests the wisdom of discussing them together *(Malloy, 1981; Schubert, Wolf, Patterson, Grande, & Pendleton, 1988)*. Moreover, treating both populations together may achieve previously unanticipated clinical benefits *(Heilman, 1982)*.

As well as new problems, new treatment approaches have evolved, with new modalities and settings available. National awareness and concern have resulted in increased research funds, and thus some objective data. We are older, but also a little wiser. This article is intended to help guide the general mental health professional at a crucial juncture, that of evaluating and making a recommendation and referral to the services or agencies that are the most likely to be able to handle the patient's problems once any emergency medical and psychiatric conditions (e.g., acute intoxication states, life-threatening withdrawal states, acute suicidal risk) have been stabilized. To this end, a specific model for selection of drug-free treatment is provided for conceptual clarity. Methadone maintenance programs, although popular, have not proved as successful as had been hoped; their clients frequently still abuse alcohol, cocaine, and heroin itself *(Klein & Miller, 1986)*. Where possible, referral to programs that challenge a self-concept organized around perpetual addiction is recommended. A negative judgment about the value of methadone programs is by no means intended—for otherwise unmanageably addicted patients, they have diminished intravenous drug use with its associated medical risks, unemployment, and crime *(Hubbard et al., 1989; Lahmeyer, 1982)*. However, for the sake of brevity and focus methadone maintenance will not be further discussed, beyond noting its indication for those individuals who clearly cannot or will not successfully discontinue intravenous opiates.

CLINICAL MODEL FOR TREATMENT SELECTION

An immediate goal for most individuals whose chemical abuse is out of control is to achieve abstinence: the patient simply needs to stop getting "high." This may require hospitalization for a supervised detoxification schedule, particularly if there is physical dependence. However, it has been our consistent experience that a significant proportion of the chemically abusing population can stop getting high on an outpatient basis and sustain this accomplishment for at least two weeks, during which time a better diagnostic assessment can be made, together with recommendations for further treatment.

Individuals with chemical abuse and dependency disorders do not comprise a homogeneous population. For professionals who have worked with such patients in multiple treatment settings, the impression is unavoidable that at times treatment failure has resulted from a poor choice of treatment assignment. Too often, the patient is placed in the first program of any sort found to have a bed available. Two vignettes are illustrative:

> Ms. A was an 18-year-old with a three-year history of chronic heroin and alcohol abuse, and an otherwise schizoidal adjustment, who was admitted to a residential therapeutic community. Anxious, timid, and fearful once detoxified, she tried to withdraw from others when she experienced the confrontational style of the community seniors in prolonged encounter sessions. Her inadequate response drew charges of "copping out," as well as more strident criticism, because the community residents were trained in a single treatment model for all, not in recognizing varieties of psychopathology. The escalating pressure led to a paranoid psychotic break, and Ms. A was admitted to an inpatient psychiatric unit.

> Mr. B was a 28-year-old alcohol and cocaine abuser, admitted for the third time in three years to the substance abuse unit of a private psychiatric hospital. He was charming when sober, appeared to adjust quickly and do extremely well on the unit as he had on both previous occasions, and was everyone's model patient. Nonetheless, within two weeks of discharge he was again arrested for driving while intoxicated and without a license. On this occasion he entered a residential therapeutic community. He successfully "graduated," and has stayed on as an effective counselor in the program. His own assessment was: "I needed to get my butt kicked for two years."

The criteria that are clinically relevant to selection of efficacious treatment assignments tend to reside as currently undocumented clinical wisdom in the minds of experienced clinicians, rather than be accessible in the clinical literature. Since the value of a good psychiatric diagnostic assessment as an important part of this decision-making process has not been sufficiently stressed, a diagnostic-based model is presented in an effort to make some of this implicit information explicit, and to do so in a form useful for mental health professionals who do not specialize in treating patients with chemical abuse disorders.

In this model, the patients are divided into three principal categories and a fourth "mixed" clinical category, based on the dominant clinical paradigm that seems to support their chemical abuse/dependence. The division of such a heterogeneous population into only four groups does not, of course, do adequate justice to the individuality of their problems, and some patients cannot neatly fit into any one of these groups, but there is considerable heuristic value in conceptualizing these group descriptions as helpful guides. The groups, together with the treatment programs most suited to each, are outlined in Table 49–1, while the characteristics of the programs are summarized in Table 49–2.

Primary Psychiatric Diagnosis Group

Individuals in the first category are those felt to have a significant *primary* psychiatric diagnosis (excluding uncomplicated antisocial personality disorder) which, if appropriately treated, could leave the chemical problem relatively tractable. This would include

Table 49–1
Treatment Selection Based on Group

Dominant Chemical Abuse Explanation	Treatment Modalities	Psychotherapy Indicated
Group 1: Self-medication of a primary Axis 1 psychiatric disorder	Inpatient psychotherapy (dual dx if available); outpatient psychotherapy; pharmacotherapy; AA/NA meetings[a]	Supportive/exploratory, psychodynamic
Group 2: Addictive disease	14–21-day rehab program; outpatient drug counseling; AA/NA meetings	Cognitive, didactic
Group 3: Manifestation of antisocial behavior or character	Residential TC; outpatient drug counseling; AA/NA meetings[b]	Confrontative, directive, behavioral, social learning
Group 4: Combination of at least 2 paradigms, or severe borderline or narcissistic character	Program for the dually diagnosed	Combination or blend of approaches

[a] Contingent on patient's ability to tolerate group interactions.
[b] Indicated only as an adjunct in early stages of treatment.

those patients who had a primary diagnosis of major depression, bipolar disorder, schizophrenia, other psychotic disorder, and such anxiety disorders as agoraphobia, social phobia, panic disorder, and obsessive-compulsive disorder. The disorder must have *preceded* any significant chemical problem, so that the chemical problem is probably secondary to the primary psychiatric disorder. These are the people who can be viewed as "self-medicating" a significant psychiatric disorder. This conception is supported in the high rates of co-occurrence found for chemical abuse or dependence and psychiatric disorders. For example, odds ratios for a lifetime alcohol diagnosis in the ECA study were 6.2 for those with mania, 4.0 for those with schizophrenia, and 2.4 for those with panic disorder *(Helzer & Pryzbeck, 1988)*. Other studies have also explored the co-occurrence of psychiatric disorders in various populations of chemical abusers, using various diagnostic instruments. Besides the high rates of diagnosis of antisocial personality disorder (usually roughly 50%, when using *DSM-III-R* criteria) and multiple alcohol and drug disorders, most striking are the rates of mood disorders (33% to 74%) and anxiety disorders (16% to 62%)—clearly, many treatable disorders have been overlooked in chemical abusers *(Bowen, Cipywnyk, D'Arcy, & Keegan, 1984; Mullaney & Tripett, 1979; Powell, Penick, Othmer, Bingham, & Rice, 1982; Ross, Glaser, & Germanson, 1988; Rounsaville, Weissman, Kleber, & Wilber, 1982; Weiss & Rosenberg, 1985; Weissman, Myers, & Harding, 1980)*.

It should be noted that Khantzian and his colleagues use the self-medicating paradigm more broadly, denoting all those felt to be using chemicals maladaptively to alter intolerable affect states *(Bell & Khantzian, 1991)*. We limit self-medicating here to

Table 49–2
Treatment Alternatives

Type of Treatment	Primary Focus of Interventions
Inpatient psychiatric	Focus on: *1)* Suicidal/Homicidal behavior; *2)* Detoxification; *3)* Non-chemical abuse primary psychiatric disorder. May include: pharmacotherapy, psychotherapy (individual, group, family), milieu therapy
Outpatient psychotherapy	May have behavior modification, supportive/exploratory psychodynamic, or interpersonal orientation, family therapy
Pharmacotherapy	As indicated for schizophrenic, mood, and anxiety disorders. ECT may also be useful
Inpatient dual diagnosis or MICA unit	Simultaneous focus on treatment of a primary psychiatric disorder and addictive disorder, combining psychopharmacologic, milieu and psychotherapeutic (psychodynamic, behavioral, cognitive, interpersonal), and addiction program
Residential TC (6–24-month model)	Confrontative, directive, behavioral, supportive components in group milieu
Outpatient drug counseling	Directive, cognitive, psychoeducational
Inpatient rehab facility (usually 14–21 days)	Didactic, cognitive, sometimes behavioral
AA/NA meetings	Supportive group—"12 step" model
Methadone maintenance program	Administration of methadone, supportive counseling (not reviewed in this presentation)

refer to those with primary psychiatric disorders and secondary chemical abuse, to link a delineated population with a specific treatment model.

Treatment selection. For this group, the primary psychiatric disorder should be appropriately treated in focused fashion, with psychopharmacological and/or psychotherapeutic interventions, in an inpatient or outpatient setting, as indicated *(Khantzian, 1985)*. Chronological precedence of symptomatology is important. Many short-lived states (e.g., depressed states, lasting only days, or anhedonic states, lasting a few weeks following cocaine withdrawal) are secondary to the drug use *(Gawin & Kleber, 1986)*. Such states may appear indistinguishable from a major depressive episode except for their duration; thus, these patients may need observation for several days to prevent suicide and offer a period of evaluation, but they should not be immediately labeled and treated for a disorder they do not have. On the other hand, some cocaine abusers are self-medicating a major depression or other mood disorder, or an attention deficit disorder *(Gawin & Kleber, 1986)*. Even those who do not have one of these diagnoses may have their symptoms of craving during abstinence diminished by the judicious short-term use of antidepressants such as desipramine *(Gawin & Kleber, 1984; Gawin et al., 1989).*

Opiate addicts frequently suffer from major or minor depressive episodes. One study found that approximately one-fifth had a Research Diagnostic Criteria (RDC) major depression on admission and on six-month follow-up during treatment, but that these groups were largely composed of different individuals. Thus, depressive episodes were very frequent and probably related to life stresses in this group, but were usually remittent, even without pharmacological treatment *(Rounsaville, Weissman, Crits-Christoph, Wilber, & Kleber, 1982).* However, depressed opioid addicts treated with methadone maintenance or drug-free programs appear to be at risk for later increased cocaine abuse *(Kosten, Rounsaville, & Kleber, 1987),* suggesting that special attention is advisable for this group.

Individuals with anxiety disorders often respond well to behavioral therapies and antidepressants. The evaluation of some anxiety disorders may be a challenge, however, as they must be distinguished from withdrawal states, and from manipulative efforts by the patient to receive minor tranquilizers, and also because a life-style of chemical abuse may result in life stresses that contribute to reactive anxiety *(Kushner, Sher, & Beitman, 1990).* In addition, "generalized anxiety disorder," a somewhat controversial residual nosological category, may be difficult to diagnose clearly in a chemically abusing population *(Ross, Glaser, & Germanson, 1988).*

Although chemical abuse or addiction may, in a given individual, have had its roots in self-medication, the chemical problem may persist after adequate treatment of a primary psychiatric disorder. Such cases, in which the abuse or addiction has taken on a life of its own, may need the more sophisticated approaches of a dual-diagnosis program, as with others in our fourth group, below.

Addictive Disease Group

A second group of patients is comprised of those who have developed a significant chemical abuse problem, often with alcohol, in adulthood. Frequently, their fathers also became alcoholic at an older age. This group of individuals may largely overlap Cloninger's "Type 1" alcoholics, who can abstain from alcohol for long periods but lose control once they begin drinking, and are also emotionally dependent, anxious, perfectionistic, and introverted *(Cloninger, 1987).* These individuals have usually navigated age-appropriate accomplishments successfully until the onset of their chemical abuse. When antisocial behavior is present (e.g., the embezzling cocaine-dependent executive), it has typically become significant only after the onset of chemical dependence and in support of its use.

Treatment selection. For these individuals, the "chemical abuse as a disease model" is usually most important in treatment. Environmental factors clearly remain etiologically relevant in the disease model. This can be seen in adoption studies that have found psychiatric disturbance and divorce of adoptive parents to be associated with adoptees' drug abuse *(Cadoret, Troughton, O'Gorman, & Heywood, 1986)* and alcohol abuse in adopted males to be associated with adoptive parental drinking problems *(Cadoret,*

O'Gorman, Troughton, & Heywood, 1985). However, the most dramatic support for the disease concept derives from genetic and physiological evidence of a genetic basis for vulnerability to chemical abuse and dependence. Studies with striking findings include those of alcoholism and drug abuse in cross-fostered early adoptees *(Cadoret et al., 1986; Cloninger, Bohman, & Sigvardsson, 1981),* and altered evoked and event-related brain potentials in high-risk sons of alcoholics *(Begleiter, Porjesz, Bihari, & Kissin, 1984).* The point at which chemical abuse becomes a disease rather than a vice or habit (i.e., a moral or volitional failing) admittedly remains a function of sociocultural context and expectations, and of religious and philosophical views. Jellinek, in a broad review of the disease concept with respect to alcoholism, felt most comfortable applying it to "gamma" alcoholics, who have lost control over their drinking and cannot stop a drinking episode after the first drink, and to "delta" alcoholics, who drink steadily without binges but are unable to abstain for even a day or two *(Jellinek, 1960).*

Most professionals feel that the 12-step self-help programs—Alcoholics Anonymous (AA), Narcotics Anonymous (NA), and the related groups for families (e.g., Al-Anon)—should generally be the linchpins of treatment for these individuals. Chemical abuse can often be halted simply with outpatient support. Inpatient treatment should be limited to detoxification when necessary, or brief hospitalization if significantly dangerous acting-out behavior is present. Outpatient alcohol or drug counseling should generally be offered, especially as aftercare from an inpatient or residential treatment program.

Unfortunately, despite the plethora of persuasive testimonials, the nonprofessional structure and adoption of anonymity that are central features of the 12-step programs have virtually precluded adequately controlled research studies, preventing objective testing of their relative effectiveness *(Bebbington, 1976; Tournier, 1979).* AA or NA involvement certainly does not neatly predict outcome. For example, in one population of 107 individuals who could be evaluated one year after four weeks of treatment in a residential alcohol rehabilitation program, those who did not attend AA after treatment fared best, those who attended regularly did relatively well, and those who attended sporadically had the worst outcome *(McLatchie & Lomp, 1988).* Further understanding of who is most likely to benefit from the 12-step programs would be highly desirable. For example, users early in their alcoholic careers, who believe that they can still control their drinking or that they have not become addicted, might not be able to commit themselves even to the first of the AA steps ("We admitted that we were powerless over alcohol—that our lives had become unmanageable"), while isolated, lonely individuals who have alienated family and friends may connect strongly with the social affiliations that an AA group offers *(Tournier, 1979).*

Some AA and NA groups may have difficulty accepting people who rely on psychotropic medication, but most have become sufficiently enlightened to limit their disapproval to benzodiazepines and related habit-forming medications, and to respect medication regimens prescribed by a physician. The guiding philosophy of these groups is that the "higher power" and "God as we understood him" cited in their 12 steps need not be understood as a specific religious deity and could be individually interpreted, for example, as the group itself *(Anonymous, 1953).* Some groups, however, may alienate atheists and agnostics, although a group can usually be found that is suited to an individual's social background and religious beliefs. Group meetings are open to any chemically abusing individual; serious involvement entails getting a "sponsor" (a helping group member who is a recovering chemical abuser), "doing the steps," and attending group meetings frequently (e.g., attending 90 meetings in 90 days to begin a life of sobriety). Members of AA groups tend to be older than those in NA groups, and they may feel that nonalcohol chemical abuse problems are better understood by NA members. Such factors are sometimes relevant in choosing a 12-step group for a particular patient, although many individuals find their way to these groups without ever being seen by a mental health professional.

Antisocial Behavior Group

A third diagnostic group includes those individuals whose chemical abuse or dependence is complicated by a life-style most significantly characterized by antisocial behavior. Often, the early onset of chemical abuse is complicated by the results of peer support for acting-out behavior, with frequent intoxication, school truancy, unemployment, the sequelae of risk-taking behavior, and lack of age-appropriate accomplishments. Narcissistic and borderline personality traits may be present in such individuals, but should not predominate in the clinical picture over the antisocial behavior disturbance, i.e., these people should not appear extremely fragile or have psychotic decompensations (other than very time-limited drug-induced episodes). Such individuals usually qualify for a *DSM-III-R* diagnosis of "antisocial personality disorder."

One subgroup of these individuals usually has an onset of chemical abuse early in life (usually before age 20), with impulsivity, fighting, criminality, sociopathic behavior not limited to the buying of drugs, and a severe course of chemical abuse. In terms of character, this group may appreciably overlap with Cloninger's "Type 2" novelty-seeking alcoholics *(Cloninger, 1987),* and may have a disturbance in serotonin regulation *(Buydens-Branchey, Branchey, Noumair, & Lieber, 1989).* Although there may be a familial history of alcoholism, the more likely inheritance appears to be an increased risk for development of a sociopathic personality, with alcohol and drug abuse merely complications of the character pathology. This picture is more narrowly in line with the old concept of "sociopathy" or "psychopathy," than with the *DSM-III-R* definition of antisocial personality disorder. The latter diagnosis focuses principally on truant, criminal, and other easily determinable objective behavior, rather than an absence of guilt, anxiety, and loyalty. Thus, antisocial behavior solely in the service of drug-seeking may easily earn this diagnosis, no matter what the individual's behavior in other contexts and times *(Gerstley, Alterman, McLellan, & Woody, 1990).*

Many individuals assembled under this *DSM-III-R* diagnosis are not classic sociopaths. They represent another subgroup, who learned antisocial behavior in the context of a drug-using, truant, and criminal peer group, often potentiated by poverty, broken or abusive families, and lack of perceived better alternatives; they may nevertheless display honesty and loyalty in other contexts. Disadvantaged minority youths may be at particular risk for early exposure to drugs, often being enlisted as "runners" or "spotters" at a very early age in inner cities, and this is clearly related to the development of antisocial behavior and further problems *(Gibbs, 1984).* Included under the umbrella of antisocial personality disorder in *DSM-III* and *DSM-III-R,* such individuals may not be so diagnosed under the more restrictive RDC criteria. Rounsaville found, for example, that 54% of a sample of opiate addicts met *DSM-III* criteria for this diagnosis, but only 27% met the RDC criteria *(Rounsaville, Weissman, Kleber, & Wilber, 1982)*. Studying a population of 48 delinquent female adolescents, Gibbs found evidence that the classically antisocial subgroup abused alcohol and drugs more heavily than did a group of "socialized delinquents." The latter also had healthier peer relationships and appeared to be engaging in delinquent behavior more in affiliation with a peer subculture than because of intrapsychic conflict or classic sociopathy *(Gibbs, 1982)*. Although division of antisocial personalities into true sociopaths and socialized delinquents has appreciable clinical importance (not the least of which is the attitudes brought to the patient in using such labels), the same initial chemical abuse referral is usually to be recommended for both.

Treatment selection. The most desirable treatment for both these groups of antisocial individuals is generally a long-term stay in a residential therapeutic community (TC). Residential TCs, inspired by the inpatient psychiatric unit model *(Jones, 1953)* but significantly modified to treat the chemical abuse and addiction population, are intense programs utilizing encounter group therapy, educational, and vocational components. There are several trained professional staff members, but TCs are run largely by non-professional recovering addicts *(Klein & Miller, 1986)*. Anything less radical is rarely effective in altering what is otherwise a severe course, attended by little motivation for change (usually, most of the antisocial behavior is ego-syntonic).

Therapeutic communities of this sort include Daytop, Phoenix, Renaissance, and Samaritan Houses, to name just a few, and they generally have outpatient programs as an alternative to, or extension of, their residential programs. Constant confrontation and active 24-hour involvement and scrutiny are enforced for a 6–24-month stay in the residential program. The shorter programs focus on chemical abuse and coping skills; the longer "change-oriented" programs are more ambitious, seeking changes in antisocial behavior patterns and personal values, as well. Fragile individuals may not tolerate the confrontation or the enforced separation from family and friends (most TCs do not allow even telephone calls for the first several weeks). TCs try to exclude the very violent or obviously psychotic clients on intake, and will not usually take individuals requiring psychotropic medication. Impressively, ingrained antisocial behavior can be dramatically remittent in such mutative environments, although dropout rates are also high. The process is intense, with street-wise peers challenging attempted deceptions, manipulations, and counterproductive attitudes in what may at times be weekend-long encounter sessions. Residents may be pointedly and repeatedly humiliated before their peers for transgressions of any community rules. The use of a group milieu approach that focuses on limit-setting, confrontation, contracting, "delaying action while clarifying perception," and antiprojective techniques, is necessary to treat the residents' immature defenses (acting out, passive-aggressive behavior, impulsivity, splitting, externalization, and projection), while managing their narcissistic vulnerabilities *(Zarcone, 1982)*.

Meaningful research, although encouraging, has been limited in these settings, and the TCs themselves, in the course of their evolution, have developed distinctive programs *(Bale, 1979)*. Those who graduate the TC program, or at least complete two or three months of it, clearly fare better in terms of subsequent drug use, criminal behavior, employment, and school attendance *(Bale et al., 1980; Bale et al., 1984; Hubbard et al., 1989; Romond, Forrest, & Kleber, 1975)*. Of the TC outcome studies, few have featured meaningful diagnostic assessments. Individuals with greater psychopathology, depression, or polysubstance abuse appear more likely to drop out of these and other programs, but program dropouts also may improve in terms of subsequent drug use, crime, and unemployment *(De Leon & Rosenthal, 1979)*. The national Treatment Outcome Prospective Study (TOPS), which studied over 2800 clients who entered one of 14 residential TCs during 1979–1981, found married or depressed clients less likely to complete these programs, while older individuals and those who had been referred by the criminal justice system were more likely to stay longer. Since outcome variables for clients (not only in the residential TCs, but also in methadone maintenance and outpatient drug-free programs) seem generally to be significantly predicted only by the pretreatment level of the variable (e.g., posttreatment heroin use is predicted by pretreatment heroin use), and positively by the length of stay in the program, interest in the easily-measured length of stay has been understandable *(Hubbard et al., 1989)*. One recent study of 100 consecutive TC admissions found the best predictors of successful program completion to be involuntary admission (pressure from the criminal justice system), family participation in treatment, good social support, and employment when discharged; some psychological testing was performed but apparently was not as predictive *(Siddall & Conway, 1988)*. Other attempts to explore psychological variables as predictors of therapeutic outcome have found little or no value in MMPI or Millon personality tests *(Craig, 1984)*, or have merely found that increased psychopathology predicts a poor prognosis. Evaluation of several new TCs, modified to treat individuals more psychiatrically disturbed (i.e., dual diagnosis patients from our first and fourth groups), may provide more answers about treatment selection *(De Leon, 1989)*.

More to the general issue of treatment selection, there is very little cogent information on whether program drop-outs, or program failures by any other outcome measure, would do better in other treatments, or even on how variables that distinguish programs of the same type may affect outcome for various types of chemically abusing or addicted patients *(Allison & Hubbard, 1985; Baekeland & Lundwall, 1975)*. One group has reported the modest finding that a global rating of "psychiatric severity" predicts poorer outcome in alcoholics and drug addicts *(McLellan, Luborsky, O'Brien, Barr, & Evans, 1986; McLellan, Luborsky, Woody, O'Brien, & Druley, 1983)*, while another found that co-morbidity in alcoholics of *DSM-III*-defined drug abuse, major depression, or antisocial personality disorder predicted a poorer prognosis, except that women with major depression had a better outcome on drinking measures *(Rounsaville, Dolinsky, Babor, & Meyer, 1987)*. The McLellan group did find some interactions relevant to treatment assignment. For example, alcoholics or drug addicts with "middle-level" psychiatric severity (defined as within one standard deviation either side of the population mean) and greater than average employment and/or family problems were found to fare worse with outpatient than with inpatient treatment *(McLellan et al., 1983)*. Other studies have also found unsurprising results supporting commonsense views: that if an individual has a milder chemical abuse or addiction problem, has less criminal involvement, and is married and/or employed, the prognosis is better; and that the best predictor of any particular outcome measure is usually a measure of past functioning in that area *(Rounsaville, Tierney, Crits-Cristoph, Weissman, & Kleber, 1982)*.

Perhaps most provocatively, successful treatment completion in a detoxification program appeared in one study to be most strongly predicted by therapist and staff *unavailability,* and secondarily by the use of methadone *(Craig, Rogalski, & Veltri, 1982).* Almost all studies have been methodologically hampered by over-reliance on client self-reports of drug use and criminal activities, and by lack of any control group, randomization of treatment assignment, or adequate psychological evaluations.

Mixed Group

The last of the four groups, a mixed category, is less well-defined. It includes patients who have both a significant chemical abuse or dependency problem and a more fragile personality disorder. This may be a suicidal or otherwise seriously acting-out individual with a borderline or narcissistic personality disorder, who may psychotically decompensate under stress. Dual diagnosis or mentally ill chemical abusing (MICA) inpatient units have commonly been conceived as principally serving the clientele of our first group, those self-medicating a primary major Axis 1 psychiatric disorder. The patients in this fourth group, who have severe Axis 2 psychopathology, however, would also be best treated in these units, although the program must obviously be designed to meet their specific needs, including a structured approach with behavior modification components. This position receives some support from an outpatient pilot study for 32 dual-diagnosis patients: those with severe (principally borderline) personality disorders appreciably contributed to a high dropout rate of 60% within two months *(Kofoed, Kania, Walsh, & Atkinson, 1986).*

Other patients who might be included in this fourth group, and who might fare better with a combined approach on a dual-diagnosis unit, are those for whom more than one of the above group paradigms appear to be prominently operative (e.g., a patient who is self-medicating a primary psychiatric disorder *and* has an addictive disease). As challenging as the clientele of dual-diagnosis programs may seem, they offer a satisfying opportunity for state-of-the-art attempts to integrate treatment efforts. This can result in a coherent clinical approach to the education of patients about commonalities in the nature of their dual disorders, and even to a fully-developed biopsychosocial integration of individual and family therapy with the specific steps of AA *(Minkoff, 1989; Chatlos, 1989).*

SPECIAL ISSUES

Outpatient programs should offer a variety of modalities and services. Outpatient drug counseling, which can be helpful with many patients from our four groups, generally focuses on issues of self-esteem, on tolerating and coping with unpleasant affect states, on managing wishes for instant gratification, and on avoidance of people, settings, and situations previously associated with chemical abuse. However, as indicated and where available, it can sometimes lead to more involved individual, group, or family therapy, as in inpatient settings. For example, although individuals with diagnosed antisocial personality disorder are usually felt to be poor candidates for individual psychotherapy, when depression accompanies this diagnosis, opiate-dependent patients have been able to use such sessions to make significant gains *(Woody, McLellan, Luborsky, & O'Brien, 1985)*. In group therapy, norms should include mandatory attendance, exclusion of group members who are "high," and consistent confrontation of addict "games" *(Craig, 1982)*. Engagement of addicts' families is often among the most challenging of tasks, but diligent efforts in bringing them into treatment may reap measurable rewards in outcome *(Stanton, 1982)*. Supervised urine screening is a strongly recommended outpatient program component. Educational, vocational, and medical services or referrals should be available.

A necessary counseling component for both outpatients and inpatients is that of addressing medical risks. Previously, this emphasized medical sequelae of alcoholism (ulcers, gastritis, pancreatitis, cirrhosis, withdrawal seizures and delirium tremens, Korsakoff's dementia, etc.), and such intravenous drug-use risks as viral hepatitis and bacterial endocarditis. Now these concerns pale next to the problem of AIDS. An estimated 5% to 33% of the intravenous drug-using population of the U.S. is infected with the HIV virus *(Hahn, Onorato, Jones, & Dougherty, 1989)*. Exploration of past and present intravenous use of drugs and sexual activity should be routine. Particular attention should be paid to confidentiality, to the presence of pathological denial and poor judgment, to lack of information, and to others who could be at risk. HIV testing with pre- and posttest counseling should be offered.

The best treatment on an individual level is prevention; failing that, early recognition and intervention are primary. This particularly applies to preadolescents, adolescents, and their families. Prevention mandates good communication with an adolescent, as well as special attention to school problems, the peer group, "gateway" drugs (alcohol, tobacco, marijuana), and experimentation with any drug. Although children are usually introduced to drugs by peers, families usually introduce them to alcohol; parental drug and alcohol abuse therefore warrant particular concern *(Jalali, Jalali, Crocetti, & Turner, 1981)*. When a pediatrician or other health professional has uncovered a drug or alcohol problem in a child, sensitive involvement of both parents is indicated. Families frequently react to an announcement that their child has a drug problem with shock, denial, anger, guilt, blaming, and protective but enabling behavior. Many of the programs referred to above accept adolescents with significant chemical disorder problems, but there are also programs specifically for adolescents (e.g., Alateen, Families Anonymous, Palmer Drug Abuse Programs, Teen Challenge, Drug Abuse Programs of America). Successful programs should generally be drug-free in orientation, exhibit caring as well as firmness in their attitude, and have strong family and peer treatment components, as well as planned aftercare arrangements *(McDonald, 1989)*.

Special attention, with an active, interventional stance, is particularly required where infants and young children are involved. At least one in ten children in the U.S. is born into a chemically abusing family; 300,000 of them are born each year to women using crack cocaine, and 10,000 to women using opiates. These children suffer prenatal chemical effects such as growth retardation, mental retardation, a variety of birth defects and withdrawal symptoms, and transmission of HIV infection; later they are at tragically high risk for physical and emotional neglect, and physical and sexual abuse *(Bays, 1990)*.

CONCLUSION

Although this presentation has been aimed at the general audience of mental health professionals, those in the chemical abuse field are also at times conceptually unclear about how to select treatments. The division of this patient population into four groups is obviously a simplification, and does not constitute a comprehensive evaluation of a patient's needs by specialists. Treatment success, insofar as it can be evaluated, is also a function of such variables as the presence of legal pressure, degree of family involvement, social support, the willingness of the individual to make a commitment to being drug-free or to a long-term residential program, the perceived reliability of the patient, and the wait for available program beds. Ideally, a system such as New Haven's model (administered jointly by the APT Foundation, Connecticut Mental Health Center and Yale University's Department of Psychiatry) is available. This integrates a comprehensive array of treatment programs which effectively communicate and cooperate with each other, and can effect sophisticated evaluations and treatment plans. Too often, there are fewer options and less sophistication. In the absence of the ideal, a good initial referral is particularly important for a population that does poorly with frustration and often has limited motivation. Despite its simplifications, the model outlined here has served as a useful approach; it is understandable to the general health professional and thus enables more informed initial referrals and more effective consultations, collaborations, and negotiations with other agencies.

Chemical abuse, a leading challenge for the '90s, is epidemic, expensive, and lethal. It destroys young lives, families, and communities. We all need to become fully prepared for its recognition and management with as much sophistication as in our approach to other disorders. Whether chemical abuse or dependency is to be understood as self-medicating, as a disease, as irresponsible behavior, or as something else again is still a matter for debate, with each conceptualization arguing for a different treatment model. Each of these concepts has compelling relevance and heuristic utility, but principally in relatively distinguishable populations. This model is a first step in helping to define these populations. It is to be hoped that it will stimulate more distinct delineations and the much-needed associated research.

REFERENCES

Allison, M., & Hubbard, R.L. (1985). Drug abuse treatment process: A review of the literature. *International Journal of the Addictions, 20,* 1321–1345.

Anonymous. (1953). *Twelve steps and twelve traditions.* New York: Alcoholics Anonymous World Services.

Baekeland, F., & Lundwall, L. (1975). Dropping out of treatment: A critical review. *Psychological Bulletin, 82,* 738–783.

Bale, R.N. (1979). Outcome research in therapeutic communities for drug abusers: A critical review, 1963–1975. *International Journal of the Addictions, 14,* 1053–1074.

Bale, R.N., Van Stone, W.W., Kuldau, J.M., Engelsing, T.M.J., Elashoff, R.M., & Zarcone, V.P., Jr. (1980). Therapeutic communities vs methadone maintenance: A prospective controlled study of narcotic addiction treatment: Design and one-year follow-up. *Archives of General Psychiatry, 37,* 179–193.

Bale, R.N., Zarcone, V.P., Van Stone, W.W., Kuldau, J.M., Engelsing, T.M.J., & Elashoff, R.M. (1984). Three therapeutic communities: A prospective controlled study of narcotic addiction treatment: Process and two-year follow-up results. *Archives of General Psychiatry, 41,* 185–191.

Bays, J. (1990). Substance abuse and child abuse: Impact of addiction on the child. *Pediatric Clinics of North America, 37,* 881–904.

Bebbington, P.E. (1976). The efficacy of Alcoholics Anonymous: The elusiveness of hard data. *British Journal of Psychiatry, 128,* 572–580.

Begleiter, H., Porjesz, B., Bihari, B., & Kissin, B. (1984). Event-related brain potentials in boys at risk for alcoholism. *Science, 225,* 1493–1496.

Bell, C.M., & Khantzian, E.J. (1991). Contemporary psychodynamic perspectives and the disease concept of alcoholism: Complementary or competing models? *Psychiatric Annals, 21,* 273–276, 279–281.

Bowen, R.C., Cipywnyk, D., D'Arcy, C., & Keegan, D. (1984). Alcoholism, anxiety disorders, and agoraphobia. *Alcoholism: Clinical and Experimental Research, 8,* 48–50.

Buydens-Branchey, L., Branchey, M.H., Noumair, D., & Lieber, C.S. (1989). Age of alcoholism onset II: Relationship to susceptibility to serotonin precursor availability. *Archives of General Psychiatry, 46,* 231–236.

Cadoret, R.J., O'Gorman, T.W., Troughton, E., & Heywood, E. (1985). Alcoholism and antisocial personality: Interrelationships, genetic and environmental factors. *Archives of General Psychiatry, 42,* 161–167.

Cadoret, R.J., Troughton, E., O'Gorman, T.W., & Heywood, E. (1986). An adoption study of genetic and environmental factors in drug abuse. *Archives of General Psychiatry, 43,* 1131–1136.

Chatlos, J.C. (1989). Adolescent dual diagnosis: A 12-step transformational model. *Journal of Psychoactive Drugs, 21,* 189–201.

Cloninger, C.R. (1987). Neurogenetic adaptive mechanisms in alcoholism. *Science, 236,* 410–416.

Cloninger, C.R., Bohman, M., & Sigvardsson, S. (1981). Inheritance of alcohol abuse: Cross-fostering analysis of adopted men. *Archives of General Psychiatry, 38,* 861–868.

Craig, R.J. (1982). Group therapy with drug addicts. In R. Craig & S. Baker (Eds.), *Drug dependent patients: Treatment and research* (pp. 127–140). Springfield, IL: Charles C Thomas.

Craig, R.J. (1984). Can personality traits predict treatment dropouts? *International Journal of the Addictions, 19,* 665–674.

Craig, R.J., Rogalski, C., & Veltri, D. (1982). Predicting treatment dropouts from a drug abuse rehabilitation program. *International Journal of the Addictions, 17,* 641–653.

De Leon, G., & Rosenthal, M.S. (1979). Therapeutic communities. In R. Dupont, A. Goldstein, & J. O'Donnell (Eds.), *Handbook on drug abuse* (pp. 39–47). Washington, DC: U.S. Government Printing Office.

De Leon, G. (1989). Psychopathology and substance abuse: What is being learned from research in therapeutic communities. *Journal of Psychoactive Drugs, 21,* 177–188.

Ford, J., Hillard, J.R., Giesler, L.J., Lassen, K.L., & Thomas, H. (1989). Substance abuse/mental illness: Diagnostic issues. *American Journal of Drug and Alcohol Abuse, 15,* 297–307.

Gawin, F.H., & Kleber, H.D. (1984). Cocaine abuse treatment: Open pilot trial with desipramine and lithium carbonate. *Archives of General Psychiatry, 41,* 903–909.

Gawin, F.H., & Kleber, H.D. (1986). Abstinence symptomatology and psychiatric diagnosis in cocaine abusers: Clinical observations. *Archives of General Psychiatry, 43,* 107–113.

Gawin, F.H., Kleber, H.D., Byck, R., Rounsaville, B.J., Kosten, T.R., Jatlow, P.I., & Morgan, C. (1989). Desipramine facilitation of initial cocaine abstinence. *Archives of General Psychiatry, 46,* 117–121.

Gerstley, L.J., Alterman, A.I., McLellan, A.T., & Woody, G.E. (1990). Antisocial personality disorder in patients with substance abuse disorders: A problematic diagnosis? *American Journal of Psychiatry, 147,* 173–178.

Gibbs, J.T. (1982). Psychosocial factors related to substance abuse among delinquent females: Implications for prevention and treatment. *American Journal of Orthopsychiatry, 52,* 261–271.

Gibbs, J.T. (1984). Black adolescents and youth: An endangered species. *American Journal of Orthopsychiatry, 54,* 6–21.

Griffin, M.L., Weiss, R.D., Mirin, S.M., Wilson, H., & Bouchard-Voelk, B. (1987). The use of the Diagnostic Interview Schedule in drug-dependent patients. *American Journal of Drug and Alcohol Abuse, 13,* 281–291.

Hahn, R.A., Onorato, I.M., Jones, T.S., & Dougherty, J. (1989). Prevalence of HIV infection among intravenous drug users in the United States. *Journal of the American Medical Association, 261,* 2677–2684.

Heilman, R. (1982). Combined treatment for alcoholics and addicts. In R. Craig & S. Baker (Eds.), *Drug dependent patients: Treatment and research* (pp. 153–164). Springfield, IL: Charles C Thomas.

Helzer, J.E., & Pryzbeck, T.R. (1988). The co-occurrence of alcoholism with other psychiatric disorders in the general population and its impact on treatment. *Journal of Studies on Alcohol, 49,* 219–224.

Hubbard, R.L., Marsden, M.E., Rachal, J.V., Harwood, H.J., Cavanaugh, E.R., & Ginzburg, H.M. (1989). *Drug abuse treatment: A national study of effectiveness.* Chapel Hill, NC: University of North Carolina Press.

Jalali, B., Jalali, M., Crocetti, G., & Turner, F. (1981). Adolescents and drug use: Toward a more comprehensive approach. *American Journal of Orthopsychiatry, 51,* 120–130.

Jellinek, E.M. (1960). *The disease concept of alcoholism.* New Haven: College and University Press.

Jones, M. (1953). *The therapeutic community.* New York: Basic Books.

Khantzian, E.J. (1985). The self-medication hypothesis of addictive disorders: Focus on heroin and cocaine dependence. *American Journal of Psychiatry, 142,* 1259–1264.

Klein, J.M., & Miller, S.I. (1986). Three approaches to the treatment of drug addiction. *Hospital and Community Psychiatry, 37,* 1083–1085.

Kofoed, L., Kania, J., Walsh, T., & Atkinson, R.M. (1986). Outpatient treatment of patients with substance abuse and coexisting psychiatric disorders. *American Journal of Psychiatry, 143,* 867–872.

Kosten, T.R., Rounsaville, B.J., & Kleber, H.D. (1987). A 2.5 year follow-up of cocaine use among treated opioid addicts: Have our treatments helped? *Archives of General Psychiatry, 44,* 281–284.

Kushner, M.G., Sher, K.J., & Beitman, B.D. (1990). The relation between alcohol problems and the anxiety disorders. *American Journal of Psychiatry, 147,* 685–695.

Lahmeyer, H. (1982). Methadone maintenance. In R. Craig & S. Baker (Eds.), *Drug dependent patients: Treatment and research* (pp. 37–66). Springfield, IL: Charles C Thomas.

Leukefeld, C.G., & Tims, F.M. (1989). Relapse and recovery in drug abuse: Research and practice. *International Journal of the Addictions, 24,* 189–201.

Malloy, T.E. (1981). Toward a generic conception of alcoholism. *American Journal of Orthopsychiatry, 51,* 489–492.

McDonald, D.I. (1989). Diagnosis and treatment of adolescent substance abuse. *Current Problems in Pediatrics, 19,* 394–444.

McLatchie, B.H., & Lomp, K.G.E. (1988). Alcoholics Anonymous affiliation and treatment outcome among a clinical sample of problem drinkers. *American Journal of Drug and Alcohol Abuse, 14,* 309–324.

McLellan, A.T., Luborsky, L., Woody, G.E., O'Brien, C.P., & Druley, K.A. (1983). Predicting response to alcohol and drug abuse treatments: Role of psychiatric severity. *Archives of General Psychiatry, 40,* 620–625.

McLellan, A.T., Luborsky, L., O'Brien, C.P., Barr, H.L., & Evans, F. (1986). Alcohol and drug abuse treatment in three different populations: Is there improvement and is it predictable? *American Journal of Drug and Alcohol Abuse, 12,* 101–120.

Minkoff, K. (1989). An integrated treatment model for dual diagnosis of psychosis and addiction. *Hospital and Community Psychiatry, 40,* 1031–1036.

Mullaney, J.A., & Tripett, C.J. (1979). Alcohol dependence and phobias: Clinical description and relevance. *British Journal of Psychiatry, 135,* 565–573.

Powell, B.J., Penick, E.C., Othmer, E., Bingham, S.F., & Rice, A.S. (1982). Prevalence of additional psychiatric syndromes among male alcoholics. *Journal of Clinical Psychiatry, 43,* 404–407.

Regier, D.A., Boyd, J.H., Burke, J.D., Jr., Rae, D.S., Myers, J.K., Kramer, M., Robins, L.N., George, L.K., Karno, M., & Locke, B.Z. (1988). One-month prevalence of mental disorders in the United States. *Archives of General Psychiatry, 45,* 977–986.

Robertson, J.R., Bucknall, A.B.V., Skidmore, C.A., Roberts, J.J.K., & Smith, J.H. (1989). Remission and relapse in heroin users and implications for management: Treatment control or risk reduction. *International Journal of the Addictions, 24,* 229–246.

Romond, A.M., Forrest, C.K., & Kleber, H.D. (1975). Follow-up of participants in a drug dependence therapeutic community. *Archives of General Psychiatry, 32,* 369–374.

Ross, H.E., Glaser, F.B., & Germanson, T. (1988). The prevalence of psychiatric disorders in patients with alcohol and other drug problems. *Archives of General Psychiatry, 45,* 1023–1031.

Rounsaville, B.J., Weissman, M.M., Crits-Christoph, K., Wilber, C., & Kleber, H. (1982). Diagnosis and symptoms of depression in opiate addicts: Course and relationship to treatment outcome. *Archives of General Psychiatry, 39,* 151–156.

Rounsaville, B.J., Weissman, M.M., Kleber, H., & Wilber, C. (1982). Heterogeneity of psychiatric diagnosis in treated opiate addicts. *Archives of General Psychiatry, 39,* 161–166.

Rounsaville, B.J., Tierney, T., Crits-Christoph, K., Weissman, M.M., & Kleber, H.D. (1982). Predictors of outcome in treatment of opiate addicts: Evidence for the multidimensional nature of addicts' problems. *Comprehensive Psychiatry, 23,* 462–478.

Rounsaville, B.J., Dolinsky, Z.S., Babor, T.F., & Meyer, R.E. (1987). Psychopathology as a predictor of treatment outcome in alcoholics. *Archives of General Psychiatry, 44,* 505–513.

Schubert, D.S.P., Wolf, A.W., Patterson, M.B., Grande, T.P., & Pendleton, L. (1988). A statistical evaluation of the literature regarding the associations among alcoholism, drug abuse, and antisocial personality disorder. *International Journal of the Addictions, 23,* 797–808.

Siddall, J.W., & Conway, G.L. (1988). Interactional variables associated with retention and success in residential drug treatment. *International Journal of the Addictions, 23,* 1241–1254.

Stanton, M.D. (1982). Family therapy of drug dependent veterans. In R. Craig & S. Baker (Eds.), *Drug dependent patients: Treatment and research* (pp. 141–152). Springfield, IL: Charles C Thomas.

Tournier, R.E. (1979). Alcoholics Anonymous as treatment and as ideology. *Journal of Studies on Alcohol, 40,* 230–239.

Weiss, K.J., & Rosenberg, D.J. (1985). Prevalence of anxiety disorder among alcoholics. *Journal of Clinical Psychiatry, 46,* 3–5.

Weissman, M.M., Myers, J.K., & Harding, P.S. (1980). Prevalence and psychiatric heterogeneity of alcoholism in a United States urban community. *Journal of Studies on Alcohol, 41,* 672–681.

Woody, G.E., McLellan, A.T., Luborsky, L., & O'Brien, C.P. (1985). Sociopathy and psychotherapy outcome. *Archives of General Psychiatry, 42,* 1081–1086.

Zarcone, V.P., Jr. (1982). Residential treatment for drug dependence. In R. Craig & S. Baker (Eds.), *Drug dependent patients: Treatment and research* (pp. 67–89). Springfield, IL: Charles C Thomas.

CHAPTER 50

CASE MANAGEMENT IN ALCOHOL AND DRUG TREATMENT

Improving Client Outcomes

William Patrick Sullivan, James L. Wolk, and David J. Hartmann

The importance of considering multimeasures of effectiveness has received increased attention in alcohol and drug treatment programs (Babor, Dolinsky, Rounsaville, & Jaffe, 1988; Cronkite & Moos, 1980; Longabaugh & Beattie, 1985; Lowe & Thomas, 1976; Maisto & O'Farrell, 1985; Schukitt, 1980). Although reduction and/or elimination of substance use is an important, if not primary, concern of these services, it is equally important that treatment result in enhanced employment, life satisfaction, and improved social functioning.

An essential and oft-debated question is how treatment services can most effectively lead to improvement in the overall life functioning of clients served. This article argues that case management is an appropriate complement to traditional alcohol- and drug-treatment services and can make an important contribution to the effort to address multiple outcome areas. Accordingly, factors that appear to affect the postdischarge functioning of clients are discussed and the ways in which case management can bolster treatment effectiveness are demonstrated.

Recent reports estimate that the direct and indirect costs of alcohol and drug abuse in this country approach $115 billion (Rice, Kelman, Miller, & Dunmeyer, 1990). Although nearly one-fourth of these costs can be attributed to the cost of treatment services, 37% of the total outlay is from lost or reduced productivity (morbidity) among the afflicted. Significantly, 96% of the morbidity costs associated with alcohol- and drug-related problems is associated with clients outside institutional care.

Reprinted from *Families in Society*, Vol. 73, No. 4 (April 1992), pp. 195–204, by permission of the publisher, Families International, Inc.

The fact that alcohol and drug abuse results in lost productivity, mortality, and psychological trauma has been recognized for some time (Moskowitz, 1989). Indeed, in the absence of these outcomes, concern about alcohol and drug consumption would reflect purely legal and moral considerations. Because substance abuse has deleterious effects on people and society, treatment services are offered. Ideally, these services counter the negative outcomes of substance abuse, restore individual functioning, and reduce social costs. Traditionally, this help has focused on reducing or eliminating usage by identified clients.

However, the degree to which alcohol and drug use is inextricably related to functioning in various life domains has been the subject of debate. This debate, often couched in terms of unitary vs. multidimensional treatment outcome, reflects the intense interest in unraveling the cause and effects of alcohol and drug use (Babor et al., 1988; McLellan, Luborsky, Woody, O'Brien, & Kron 1981; Vaillant & Milofsky, 1982; Vaillant et al., 1983).

Early studies provided simple correlational analyses, but added little to our understanding of the relationship among personal traits, social influences, and substance abuse (Hall, Havassy, & Wasserman, 1990). In such studies, measures of association are derived, and the inferred results are matched against a dominant model or one that is promulgated by the researcher. Recently, researchers have employed sophisticated techniques such as path analysis, linear structural relations (LISREL), or multiple regression to provide a better understanding of the relationship among substance abuse, measures of individual functioning, and social influences (Gruenwald, Stewart, & Klitzner, 1990; Rhodes & Jason, 1990; Windle & Miller, 1990).

The concern over establishing the relationship between the individual usage patterns and social influences often reflects the clash between contending paradigms. Adherents of the classic disease concept of substance abuse (Jellinek, 1960) state that continued substance abuse results in progressive personal deterioration in important life domains such as employment and family relationships. Individual traits, including psychological health, self-efficacy, and motivation, have also been associated with substance abuse and considered in predicting response to treatment (Brownwell, Marlatt, Lichtenstein, & Wilson, 1986; Burling, Reilly, Moltzen, & Ziff, 1989; Daley, 1987; Longabaugh & Beattie, 1985; Windle & Miller, 1990; Woody, McLellan, & O'Brien, 1990). Others note that social forces such as socioeconomic status, family environment, and marital and employment status inhibit or support usage patterns and that relapse is both directly and indirectly influenced by these variables (Brownwell et al., 1986; Cronkite & Moos, 1980; Daley, 1987; Longabaugh & Beattie, 1985; Miller & Hester, 1986; Rhodes & Jason, 1990).

Thus, it seems reasonable to suggest that research supports the presence of interactions among substance use, individual traits, and social forces that may ultimately result in problematic situations for both individuals and society. Professional and lay debate is concerned with unraveling the relative contribution of each of these factors to the overall problem. This article does not attempt to contribute to or clarify this debate. Instead, it is argued that regardless of the relative contribution of individual and social forces on substance abuse, the appreciation that multiple factors influence individual behavior has clear implications for treatment strategies and for monitoring the effectiveness of interventions.

DETERMINANTS OF CONTINUED SUCCESS

Given the increased pressures to account for expenditures, the general public and elected officials are likely to inquire about the effectiveness of alcohol and drug treatment. Abstinence rate is the most common measure used to assess program effectiveness. But in and of themselves, abstinence rates can be summarily unimpressive. The evaluation literature indicates much variance in reported abstinence rates, which are influenced by the population served and surveyed, whether abstinence is defined in a strict or loose fashion, and the time frames used to gauge results.

Thus, abstinence as an outcome measure for programs and people is unstable. Although older adults may eventually fall into a patterned drinking history, long-term follow-up studies indicate that the drinking patterns of many people fluctuate among the various categories constructed, often alternating between abstinence and heavy drinking (Drummond, 1990; Gruenwald et al., 1990; Emrick, 1982; Polich, 1980; Taylor, Brown, Duckitt, Edwards, Oppenheimer, & Sheehan, 1985). Certainly, this phenomenon can be explained by the grip that alcohol and drugs maintain on people who may desire or are pressured to discontinue usage. Such findings also add credence to the disease concept of substance abuse and may point to certain personality types that are susceptible to drugs and alcohol.

However, some researchers have questioned whether explanatory models of drug and alcohol abuse may have focused too narrowly on individual traits and deficits at the expense of considering the positive or negative influence of the immediate social environment (Longabaugh & Beattie, 1985; Rhodes & Jason, 1990). Current studies indicate that various postdischarge factors influence the resiliency of treatment when alcohol and drug consumption are used as criterion measures. These factors, which reflect levels of social stability (Hartmann, Sullivan, & Wolk, 1991), include marital status and family cohesion (Brownwell et al., 1986; Gruenwald et al., 1990; Longabaugh & Beattie, 1985; Power & Estaugh, 1990; Rychtarik, Foy, Scott, Lokey, & Prue, 1987), residential stability (Brown, 1986; MacKenzie, Funderburk, Allen, & Stefan, 1987; Rychtarik et al., 1987; Longabaugh & Beattie, 1985), and employment (Longabaugh & Beattie, 1985; Miller & Hester, 1986; Power & Estaugh, 1990). The presence or absence of these stabilizing forces is an important mediator when consideration is given to two additional factors frequently mentioned in the literature: interpersonal and environmental stress (Brown, 1986; Cronkite & Moos, 1980; Rhodes & Jason, 1990; Weisner, 1990; Windle & Miller, 1990) and individual competence and problem-solving capacity (Brownwell et al., 1986; Burling et al., 1989; Daley, 1987; Longabaugh & Beattie, 1985).

To summarize, these studies suggest that stressful situations can trigger the desire to return to or continue the use of alcohol and drugs. Stability in important life domains reduces the number of expected stressful life events and modifies the experience of stress, given the availability of needed sources of support. Individual competence reflects the ability of a person to employ positive coping responses to situations in which substance usage might occur.

These findings have important implications for alcohol- and drug-treatment services. Specifically, treatment success will be enhanced if greater attention is placed on the social functioning of clients and environmentally focused interventions are used to address these goals (Cronkite & Moos, 1980; Daley, 1987; Lowe & Thomas, 1976; Longabaugh & Beattie, 1985; Miller & Hester, 1986; Moos, Cronkite, & Finney, 1982). The potential importance of environmentally focused interventions is underscored by the fact that current treatment approaches, even when leading to abstinence, may not necessarily affect important social stability factors (Cronkite & Moos, 1980). McLellan et al. (1981) suggest that reduced substance usage may be a necessary but not sufficient predictor of improved social functioning. Similarly, Polich (1980) suggests that

> it is entirely possible for an alcoholic to solve or improve his [her] alcohol-related problems without improving in other realms of functioning. This observation has been used to attack abstinence as the sole criterion for treatment success, but it applies equally well to non-problem drinking. An important aspect of remission, therefore, is the extent to which alcoholics whose drinking problems have abated may also exhibit modes of social and psychological functioning that are more nearly normal than those of the typical alcoholic at admission to treatment (p. 103).

Obviously, helping clients reduce or eliminate substance use is important. Professionals encounter individuals every day whose lives have been severely damaged by substance abuse. The impact of treatment on social functioning is also difficult to measure. Typical outcome evaluations, by using short follow-up periods, may not capture the long-term impact of interventions. It is probable that improvements in areas such as employment, residential stability, and family functioning may have a longer latency period than do improvements in substance usage (McLellan et al., 1981).

However, the above considerations should not be used as justification for inaction. Peele (1990) suggests that treatment services in the United States have been guided more by traditional and religious considerations than by empirical research. Research clearly indicates that greater focus should be placed on the current and postdischarge functioning of clients in important social domains and, further, that specific interventions should be designed to address these concerns. Perhaps Lowe and Thomas (1976) provide an important agenda for treatment services by suggesting that "a more rational approach is to aim for a reduction of drinking while concentrating on family adjustment, occupational effectiveness and social adequacy" (pp. 886–887).

How can these goals best be accomplished? Although various approaches can be constructed, case management services are well positioned to have a direct impact on the social functioning of clients by enhancing traditional treatment services. Austin (1990) notes that case management is proving to be a popular service delivery mechanism because "it does not significantly alter the relationship and the distribution of resources among providers" (p. 398). However, case management is an incomplete intervention and must be blended with current drug- and alcohol-treatment services to maximize benefits to clients served.

CASE MANAGEMENT: A CONCEPTUAL OVERVIEW

Case management is an important service component in areas such as mental health, aging, children's services, and public welfare. When clients have multiple needs and service delivery systems are fragmented, case management services are being effectively employed (Sanborn, 1983).

Case managers focus services on the individual client or case. Although the client may have entered treatment for a specified problem, he or she may actually have multiple needs. Case-management services are popular in practice arenas in which existing services do not adequately address the full range of client needs. For example, in the mental health professions, many services that were once provided in the state hospital system (such as housing, meals, recreation, treatment, money management, and personal hygiene) must now be met by a host of community providers, and the former psychiatric client may have difficulty meeting these needs due to illness, skill level, and lack of knowledge or resources.

The management function of the case manager's role is equally important. Unfortunately, many psychiatric clients are not monitored adequately after discharge. Many of these clients return to the care of families, to single-room-occupancy hotels, nursing homes, or the streets. To address these concerns, a manager is assigned who must respond to the special needs of the client, link the client to needed services, function as an advocate, and coordinate elements of the overall service delivery system.

The diversity of tasks performed by case managers has led to a multitude of role descriptions. Weil and Karls (1985) define case management as "a set of logical steps and a process of interaction within a service network which assures that a client receives services in a supportive, effective, efficient and cost effective manner" (p. 2). Baker and Weiss (1984) describe the case manager as the human link between needed services to insure necessary support. Perlman, Melnick, and Kentera (1985) suggest that case managers function as advocates, friendly advisers, and interpreters for their clients.

The above definitions suggest the important functions of case management in linking elements of the service delivery system together. However, case managers also provide direct service by maintaining responsibility for designing and implementing a plan of action (Harris & Bergman, 1987; Libassi, 1988; Moore, 1990; Rapp & Chamberlain, 1985; Sullivan, 1990). Given the dual focus on individual and system considerations, case management is here defined as a creative and collaborative process involving skills in assessment, counseling, teaching, modeling, and advocacy that aims to enhance the social functioning of clients.

Austin (1990) states that core case management tasks represent areas that distinguish good professional practice, including attention to comprehensive assessment, continuity of care, and monitoring. In a similar vein, Modrcin, Rapp, and Chamberlain (1985) suggest that case management has been traditionally seen as embodying five core elements: assessment, development of a case plan, procurement of services, monitoring and advocacy, and tracking and evaluation.

Outreach case management, it is argued here, should be considered for adoption by alcohol- and drug-treatment programs. The following sections describe a strengths-based model of case management in relation to the core services provisions detailed above (Kisthardt, 1992; Rapp & Chamberlain, 1985; Sullivan, 1990). In contrast with the conditions that gave rise to the use of case management in mental health, the adoption of such services in alcohol and drug treatment represents an expanded mission rather than an attempt to reconstruct or coordinate a system of care. The above sections suggested the importance of an increased focus on the social functioning of clients, both during treatment and postdischarge. Direct focus on such issues as residential stability, employment, and use of leisure time, in conjunction with the initiation of a specialized professional role to address these concerns, reflects an attempt to find new ways to provide services to clients with drug and/or alcohol problems.

ASSESSMENT

The assessment process attempts to evaluate the nature and scope of an individual's problems. In conjunction with traditional styles of helping in alcohol and drug treatment, assessment focuses on the degree of substance-abusing behavior and the problems that emerge because of this abuse. Inventories such as the Substance Abuse Problem Checklist (Carroll, 1983) are used to identify problematic behaviors and attitudes.

Recognizing the link between problem assessment and treatment strategies, Weick, Rapp, Sullivan, and Kisthardt (1989) suggest that

> if alcoholism is defined as the disease of excessive alcohol consumption, then the therapeutic approach must be centered on abstinence. Getting an alcoholic to stop drinking is the first step in recovery. In this way, alcohol is both the center of the problem and the treatment (p. 351).

Certainly, problem-focused assessments have their place in alcohol and drug treatment, as do interventions that flow naturally from them. However, if case-management services are designed to affect such dimensions as employment, residential stability, and leisure-time use, the assessment process should reflect these goals as well. Data should be collected on clients' present and past involvement in areas such as employment and leisure. It is also important to ascertain clients' interests and aspirations for the future.

In lieu of an agenda for behaviors to be changed, a strengths-oriented assessment process establishes an agenda for desired gains. All present and past activities (from employment to hobbies), available resources, and identified strengths can be employed in an effort to promote social competence (Weick et al., 1989). This assessment process focuses on the uniqueness of the individual, not solely on his or her problematic behavior or commonalities with other substance-abusing clients (Pray, 1991). To be effective, the case manager "assumes at the outset that the client will differ from all others" (Pray, 1991, p. 82).

DEVELOPING A CASE PLAN

If the assessment process is geared toward an identification of the special attributes, resources, strengths, and needs of clients, the case plan that follows will also be individually tailored. From a strengths model, interventions address the needs and aspirations that clients identify. Working in collaboration with the client, the case manager helps establish a series of measurable and observable goals in key outcome areas. Goals are broken into a sequence of steps and necessary behaviors to reflect the complexity of goals and the abilities of clients. This style of working may require some adjustments by practitioners who may find such work difficult, frustrating, and potentially time consuming.

These goals should involve the social functioning of clients and outcome areas identified in the evaluation literature as critical to postdischarge functioning. Ultimately, the individually tailored goals, the plan for meeting such goals, the schedule of contacts, and set of mutual expectations of client and worker should form the basis of a written, signed contract between the parties. The use of formal contracts has been employed successfully with difficult-to-treat and potentially manipulative clients. Miller (1990) provides a list of features that a good contract comprises: a clear statement of purpose; a statement of concrete, achievable goals; description of mutual responsibilities; procedures for modifying the contract; and conditions that will lead to the discontinuance of services.

PROCUREMENT OF SERVICE

Including service procurement as a core function of case management services is consonant with an emphasis on the brokerage function performed by case managers. However, as suggested above, employing case-management services in the field of alcohol and drug treatment should reflect an expanded mission, not simply an attempt to coordinate and concretize existing but fragmented services.

Strengths-based interventions build from the abilities of clients and the resources available in the community. When building interventions from the special needs and goals of clients, access to various external resources is desirable. The list of target resources tapped should not be constrained to services germane to alcohol and drug treatment (such as Alcoholics Anonymous) but should reflect those resources available for everyone (Sullivan, 1992). In practice, this suggests that outreach case managers and clients should be in daily contact with potential employers, landlords, and recreation leaders as well as with Alcoholics Anonymous groups and treatment team staff.

To orchestrate services and to ensure that interventions complement one another, treatment team members must communicate regularly. The case management function is not subservient to core treatment services. Given the importance of postdischarge functioning with regard to treatment resiliency, the case manager should be viewed as an equal member of the treatment team. The community outreach work performed by the case manager is as important to the promotion of sobriety and positive social functioning as are traditional therapeutic and group interventions.

MONITORING AND ADVOCACY

Traditionally, case managers have performed monitoring and advocacy roles. Case managers follow clients as they move through the system (e.g., from hospital to group home to supervised apartment) and make sure that adequate follow-up is provided. As advocates, they assist clients in their attempt to secure the resources they need.

Outreach case managers are in a prime position to provide ongoing monitoring of clients in the community. Drake, Osher, Noordsy, Hurlbut, Teague, and Beaudett (1990) note that case managers have effectively assessed the use of alcohol and drugs by psychiatric clients in the community. Case managers can also provide regular feedback to the client and the agency on current performance in a host of important life domains. Empirical research and professional wisdom indicate that slips and relapses often occur after significant periods of abstinence (Brownwell et al., 1986; Emrick, 1982; Vaillant & Milofsky, 1982; Vaillant et al., 1983). Scheduled posttreatment booster sessions and follow-up have been identified as important in preventing relapse (Brownwell et al., 1986; Vaillant et al., 1983). Vaillant et al. (1983) state that "it is not unusual for a single act of caring such as a follow-up letter or a chance encounter to somehow extend to the patient the power of a therapeutic tool" (pp. 455–456). Research also suggests that individuals may experience multiple hospitalizations and personal difficulties as part of the "natural behavior modification" process before achieving stable abstinence (Vaillant & Milofsky, 1982). Conceivably, ongoing case management services can enhance the natural recovery process and reduce the impact and length of individual relapses.

Clients of alcohol and drug programs and recovering individuals are often misunderstood and suffer from stigma and discrimination. By working with clients in the community, case managers can detect, prevent, and ameliorate the impact of prejudice. Both the intended and unintended consequences of advocacy efforts for the client, case manager, and agency must be considered. Given the possibility for manipulation and negative consequences for all parties, all members of the treatment team should be consulted in order to minimize potential risks.

TRACKING AND EVALUATION

Two important measures can be used to gauge the effectiveness of services. Process measures provide information about program efficiency. Product measures indicate whether desired outcomes have resulted from service delivery.

With computer technology, it is not difficult to track the number of units of service provided both at the individual case and aggregate level. Case managers should also maintain records on the use of community resources, both as a process and product measure. Case managers are thus able to track the progress of clients as they move through the system as well as the units of service consumed.

Simple yet accurate records can be maintained to monitor the goals set/goals achieved ratio. These case goals should be directly related to the desired outcomes of case management, including increased vocational activity, residential stability, and positive leisure-time activities. For example, Rapp and Wintersteen (1989) studied the goal-attainment rate for 12 mental health case-management projects during a six-year period and found a goal-completion rate of nearly 80% among the more than 5,000 goals established across important life domains. Simple computations like these can indicate areas where interventions have made a discernible difference in clients' lives.

The *status method* is another promising evaluation method that can be employed in case management projects (Rapp, Gowdy, Sullivan, & Wintersteen, 1988). Here, status categories are constructed for each outcome area to reflect a continuum from the least desirable (institutional living) to most desirable (independent living) status. Data collected at prescribed intervals detect client movement across status categories. These movement scores are important tools for gauging the relative impact of services on targeted clients.

Such tools are not costly or time consuming but are designed to provide direct information on the impact of services rendered. Case managers can collect such data as a routine part of their work without having to do additional paperwork.

CONCLUSION

Research indicates that treatment resiliency is affected by various postdischarge factors, including employment, residential stability, family environment, and stress. In addition, the degree to which treatment services directly affect these outcome areas has been equivocal. Outreach case management services are specifically designed to address these outcome areas. Furthermore, these services complement existing treatment services that are specifically designed to reduce or eliminate problematic substance use.

Outcomes beyond usage levels can benefit drug- and alcohol-treatment programs, demonstrating that treatment reduces unemployment, legal, and family difficulties. Such goals hold on to the hope that discharged clients will again make an active contribution to society, an outcome that family members, citizens, and elected officials view as critical.

REFERENCES

Austin, C. (1990). Case management: Myths and realities. *Families in Society, 71,* 398–405.

Babor, T., Dolinsky, Z., Rounsaville, B., & Jaffe, J. (1988). Unitary versus multidimensional models of alcohol treatment outcome: An empirical study. *Journal of Studies on Alcohol, 49,* 167–177.

Baker, F., & Weiss, R. (1984). The nature of case manager support. *Hospital and Community Psychiatry, 35,* 925–928.

Brown, S. (1986). Reinforcement expectancies and alcoholism treatment outcome after a one-year follow up. *Journal of Studies on Alcohol, 46,* 304–308.

Brownwell, K., Marlatt, G., Lichtenstein, E., & Wilson, T. (1986). Understanding and preventing relapse. *American Psychologist, 41,* 765–782.

Burling, T., Reilly, P., Moltzen, J., & Ziff, D. (1989). Self-efficacy and relapse among inpatient drug and alcohol abusers: A predictor of outcome. *Journal of Studies on Alcohol, 50,* 354–360.

Carroll, J. (1983). *Substance abuse problem checklist.* Eagleville, PA: Eagleville Hospital.

Cronkite, R., & Moos, R. H. (1980). Determinants of the posttreatment functioning of alcoholic patients: A conceptual framework. *Journal of Consulting and Clinical Psychology, 48,* 305–316.

Daley, D. (1987). Relapse prevention with substance abusers. *Social Work, 32,* 138–142.

Drake, R., Osher, F., Noordsy, D., Hurlbut, S., Teague, G., & Beaudett, M. (1990). Diagnosis of alcohol use disorders in schizophrenia. *Schizophrenia Bulletin, 16*(1), 57–67.

Drummond, D. (1990). The relationship between alcohol dependence and alcohol-related problems in a clinical population. *British Journal of Addiction, 85,* 357–366.

Emrick, C. (1982). Evaluation of alcoholism psychotherapy methods. In E. M. Pattison & E. Kaufman (Eds.), *Encyclopedic handbook of alcoholism* (pp. 1152–1169). New York: Gardner Press.

Gruenwald, P., Stewart, K., & Klitzner, M. (1990). Alcohol use and the appearance of alcohol problems among first offender drunk drivers. *British Journal of Addiction, 85,* 107–117.

Hall, S., Havassy, B., & Wasserman, D. (1990). Commitment to abstinence and acute stress in relapse to alcohol, opiates, and nicotine. *Journal of Consulting and Clinical Psychology, 58,* 175–181.

Harris, M., & Bergman, H. (1987). Case management with the chronically mentally ill: A clinical perspective. *American Journal of Orthopsychiatry, 57,* 296–302.

Hartmann, D., Sullivan, W. P., & Wolk, J. (1991). *A retrospective evaluation of statewide treatment services in Missouri.* Center for Social Research, Southwest Missouri State University.

Jellinek, E. M. (1960). *The disease concept of alcoholism.* New Haven, CT: Hillhouse Press.

Kisthardt, W. (1992). A strengths model of case management: The principles and functioning of helping partnerships with persons with persistent mental illness. In D. Saleebey (Ed.), *The strengths perspective in social work practice.* New York: Longman.

Libassi, M. (1988). The chronically mentally ill: A practice approach. *Social Casework, 69,* 88–96.

Longabaugh, R., & Beattie, M. (1985). Optimizing the cost effectiveness of treatment for alcohol abusers. In B. McCrady, N. Noel, & T. Nirenberg (Eds.), *Future directions in alcohol treatment research* (pp. 104–136). Rockville, MD: U.S. Department of Health and Human Services.

Lowe, W., & Thomas, S. (1976). Assessing alcoholism treatment effectiveness. *Journal of Studies on Alcohol, 37,* 883–889.

MacKenzie, A., Funderburk, F., Allen, R., & Stefan, R. (1987). The characteristics of alcoholics frequently lost to follow-up. *Journal of Studies on Alcohol, 48,* 119–123.

Maisto, S., & O'Farrell, T. (1985). Comment on the validity of Watson et al., "Do alcoholics give valid self-reports?" *Journal of Studies on Alcohol, 46,* 447–450.

McLellan, A., Luborsky, L., Woody, G., O'Brien, C., & Kron, R. (1981). Are the "addiction-related" problems of substance abusers really related? *Journal of Nervous and Mental Disease, 169,* 232–239.

Miller, L. (1990). The formal treatment contract in the inpatient management of borderline personality disorder. *Hospital and Community Psychiatry, 41,* 985–987.

Miller, W., & Hester, R. (1986). Inpatient alcoholism treatment. *American Psychologist, 41,* 749–805.

Modrcin, M., Rapp, C., & Chamberlain, R. (1985). *Case management with psychiatrically disabled individuals: Curriculum and training program.* School of Social Welfare, University of Kansas.

Moore, S. (1990). A social work practice model of case management: The case management grid. *Social Work, 35,* 444–448.

Moos, R. M., Cronkite, R., & Finney, J. (1982). A conceptual framework for alcoholism treatment evaluation. In E. M. Pattison & E. Kaufman (Eds.), *Encyclopedic handbook of alcoholism* (pp. 1120–1139). New York: Gardner Press.

Moskowitz, J. M. (1989). The primary prevention of alcohol problems: A critical review of the research literature. *Journal of Studies on Alcohol, 50,* 54–88.

Peele, S. (1990). Research issues in assessing addiction treatment efficacy: How cost effective are Alcoholics Anonymous and private treatment centers? *Drug and Alcohol Dependence, 25,* 179–182.

Perlman, B., Melnick, G., & Kentera, A. (1985). Assessing the effectiveness of a case management program. *Hospital and Community Psychiatry, 36,* 405–407.

Polich, J. M. (1980). Patterns of remission in alcoholism. In G. Edwards & M. Grant (Eds.), *Alcoholism treatment in transition* (pp. 95–112). Baltimore, MD: University Park Press.

Power, C., & Estaugh, V. (1990). Employment and drinking in early adulthood: A longitudinal perspective. *British Journal of Addiction, 85,* 487–494.

Pray, J. (1991). Respecting the uniqueness of the individual: Social work practice within a reflective mode. *Social Work, 36,* 80–85.

Rapp, C., & Chamberlain, R. (1985). Case management services to the chronically mentally ill. *Social Work, 30,* 417–422.

Rapp, C., Gowdy, E., Sullivan, W. P., & Wintersteen, R. (1988). Client outcome reporting: The status method. *Community Mental Health Journal, 24,* 118–133.

Rapp, C., & Wintersteen, R. (1989). The strengths model of case management: The results from twelve demonstrations. *Psychosocial Rehabilitation Journal, 13*(1), 23–32.

Rhodes, J., & Jason, L. (1990). A social stress model of substance abuse. *Journal of Consulting and Clinical Psychology, 58,* 395–401.

Rice, D., Kelman, S., Miller, L., & Dunmeyer, S. (1990). *The economic costs of alcohol and drug abuse and mental illness: 1985.* San Francisco: Institute for Health and Aging, University of California.

Rychtarik, R., Foy, D., Scott, T., Lokey, L., & Prue, D. (1987). Five–six year follow-up of broad-spectrum behavioral treatment for alcoholism: Effects of controlled drinking skills. *Journal of Consulting and Clinical Psychology, 55,* 106–108.

Sanborn, C. (1983). *Case management in mental health services.* New York: Haworth Press.

Schukitt, M. (1980). Charting what has changed. In G. Edwards & M. Grant (Eds.), *Alcoholism treatment in transition* (pp. 59–78). Baltimore, MD: University Park Press.

Sullivan, W. P. (1990). Becoming a case manager: Implications for social work educators. *Journal of Teaching in Social Work, 4,* 159–172.

Sullivan, W. P. (1992). Reconsidering the environment as a helping resource. In D. Saleebey (Ed.), *The strengths perspective in social work practice.* New York: Longman.

Taylor, C., Brown, D., Duckitt, A., Edwards, G., Oppenheimer, E., & Sheehan, M. (1985). Patterns of outcome: Drinking histories over ten years among a group of alcoholics. *British Journal of Addiction, 80,* 45–50.

Vaillant, G., Clark, W., Cyrus, C., Milofsky, E., Kopp, J., Wulsin, V., & Mogielnicki, N. (1983). Prospective study of alcoholism treatment. *American Journal of Medicine, 75,* 455–463.

Vaillant, G., & Milofsky, E. (1982). Natural history of male alcoholism. *Archives of General Psychiatry, 39,* 127–133.

Weick, A., Rapp, C., Sullivan, W. P., & Kisthardt, W. (1989). A strengths perspective for social work practice. *Social Work, 34,* 350–354.

Weil, M., & Karls, J. (1985). Historical origins and recent developments. In M. Weil & J. Karls (Eds.), *Case management in human service practice* (pp. 1–22). San Francisco: Jossey-Bass.

Weisner, C. (1990). The alcohol treatment-seeking process from a problem perspective: Responses to events. *British Journal of Addiction, 85,* 561–569.

Windle, M., & Miller, B. (1990). Problem drinking and depression among DWI offenders. *Journal of Consulting and Clinical Psychology, 58,* 166–174.

Woody, G., McLellan, T., & O'Brien, C. (1990). Research on psychopathology and addiction treatment implications. *Drug and Alcohol Dependence, 25,* 121–123.

PART IV

PERSONAL ISSUES

"Personal Issues" is a new section in *Differential Diagnosis*. As mentioned in the Preface, throughout the various editions there has been an ongoing challenge as to how to order the articles in a conceptually logical way that reflected practice reality and so ensure the usefulness of the volume for the reader. Over the years we have consistently used as a basis for classification those aspects of cases that social workers are called upon to address in practice, aspects that have some commonalty and that require specific clinical understanding. We have done this with the awareness that all our practice situations are multifaceted and need to be so understood, even though in intervention our strategy may lead us to focus on a specific component of the presenting complexity.

In earlier editions there were fewer sections, since we used a much less sensitive system of dividing the spectrum of articles. This time, rather than attempting to force the articles into a preset structure, we let the articles, as it were, divide themselves.

In this way, in reviewing the literature, we found a grouping of presenting situations that had as a common theme the impact of the particular event on the person. From this perspective we have brought together in this section those articles from the literature that address particular situations from the person's inner perspective; that is, situations in which the stress, for which help is sought, is related to some identifiable aspect of reality that has a direct and immediate impact on the inner person. Thus, in this section those situations are addressed in which the predominating factor is some intense challenge to the person in an existential manner. For example, the excellent article by Donald Krill, which was contained in the previous edition, addresses the question of the highly individualized concept of "anomie" from a specific existential perspective.

Important as it is to understand the specific nature of each of these factors and their idiosyncratic differences, we also need to know the individual person involved, and the differential way in which the problem has impacted or is impacting—again the requirement for accurate diagnosis.

Understandably, topics in this section deal with very fundamental life issues such as death, dying, and suicide but include as well other less fundamental types of situations met with in contemporary society, such as burnout and eating disorders. Still others address situations in which clients find themselves having to make very crucial decisions such as those around abortion, vasectomy, or sterilization. Many of these situations involve the responses of others but remain principally challenges that impact on the ego in a dramatic way.

As mentioned, two of the topics relate to death, that most dramatic of events in our odyssey of life. It is evident that we have finally become sufficiently comfortable with these sensitive topics to understand that, as social workers, we need to be ready to address them as a part of our practice responsibility. This is indeed a step forward from an earlier day when our literature seemed to imply that this was not an area of practice focus, or even that these things did not occur as a part of living.

Of particular import is the extent to which we have recognized the prevalence of suicidal intentions and suicidal thoughts in many of our clients and, of greater importance, the extent to which we can be particularly helpful when we ourselves are prepared to accept their reality. And as this self-comfort develops we begin to understand the tremendous anguish experienced by clients in these situations, anguish that often has to be faced alone, as society continues to deny, or to refuse to hear, the frequent cries for help that are a part of these life events.

One of the crucial challenges of dealing with suicidal clients is the client's own ambivalence, discomfort, and guilt about the feelings, ruminations, and ideation that are a part of this phenomenon and how these can play into our own discomfort and wish to deny their presence and intensity.

This is especially true with young people. Social workers are often the only professionals in contact with adolescents and young adults experiencing these critical decisions and thus are the persons who can be the lifeline for those who, in their many turmoils, unrealistically see suicide as a solution to seemingly hopeless challenges. It is critical that we understand the diverse and veiled ways that this kind of problem is manifested and the extent of our own fear and discomfort when we are confronted with it.

Undoubtedly, in a subsequent edition, we will be able to include articles which address the ever increasing reality where suicide is viewed by some as a rational and carefully thought out decision rather than as an irrational response to an overwhelming and unmanageable reality situation that has been our tradition and of the complex ethical issues that this raises.

We live in a society where there are many individuals who face highly personalized situations in a lonely, frightened manner, persons who desperately need, and can be greatly helped by, clinicians endowed with diagnostic acumen, professional knowledge, skills with empathy, and mature intrapersonal comfort. It is in these situations that, armed with our repertoire of interventions, we can be particularly therapeutically helpful as evidenced in the selection of articles which follow.

ABORTION AND PREGNANCY

CHAPTER 51

SOCIAL WORK SERVICE
TO ABORTION PATIENTS

Alice Ullmann

On July 1, 1970, abortions were legalized in New York State. In the following fifteen months about 200,000 abortions were performed in New York City. Although this demand on services apparently presented no particular problem to the health care facilities in the city, debates about abortion continue among the health professions, religious groups, and the general public. In the face of much public discussion, it is pertinent to ask how the women who are undergoing abortions are affected. What are the psychological implications of having an abortion? Why do women make that decision? Do they need help in coping with their decision?

BACKGROUND

Review of the literature about the implications of abortion does not provide a definitive point of view about psychological conflict regarding abortion or psychological sequelae. Psychologically oriented studies are rare and often deal with the psychiatrist's dilemma in recommending therapeutic abortion. Experience with legal abortion in this country is not yet extensive enough to have produced studies; those from other countries are not always pertinent, in view of cultural differences.

Some years ago, Helene Deutsch wrote of the legal and religious influences in the field of abortion over the centuries and pointed out that it is likely that there have been even deeper psychological motivations against abortion. These motivations, she suggested, are connected with the instinct of self-preservation and the urge to motherhood. She also noted that there must be ambivalence, in that the pregnancy is rejected even

Reprinted from *Social Casework,* Vol. 53 (1972), pp. 481–487, by permission of the publisher, Families International, Inc.

though becoming pregnant represented a wish fulfillment. Abortion, some women feel, destroys something in themselves. Deutsch further reported that, during menopausal depressions, some women who have had abortions express self-accusation—but more recent thinking indicates that this may represent a vehicle for depression rather than its cause. She also described a change in the relationship between the man and the woman after abortion. Since Deutsch's work was published in 1945, it may well reflect the mores of that period.[1]

Mary Calderone has also cautioned about the psychological effect of abortions.[2] Most literature, however, does not support these suggestions. In fact the consensus appears to be that "legal abortion can be performed without fear of severe psychic harm to the woman."[3] Liberalization of abortion laws doubtlessly reflects this opinion, and recent polls of physicians and psychiatrists have shown large majorities in favor of legalizing abortion.[4] It is generally agreed that a woman's reaction to abortion is determined by her general psychological state. However, certain psychological symptoms, it is reported, do appear. One of these is guilt, sometimes as a reaction to the clinical procedure, sometimes as a result of the punitive attitude of those caring for the patient. The guilt may be mild or severe. This guilt and the rarity of severe depression are well described by George S. Walter in his review of the literature.[5] The Kinsey group reported that abortion did not effect subsequent sexual behavior of women.[6]

Edward Senay describes women applying for abortion as a population in crisis.[7] In his clinical experience, there were many instances of insomnia, somatic complaints, anxiety, and suicidal ideation, as well as an intense preoccupation with the problem of ending the unwanted pregnancy. This report reflects experience with psychiatric indications for abortion. One might argue that the women who no longer require psychiatric evaluations, and can obtain legal abortions based on the decision between patient and physician, are not under as much psychological stress. A Scandinavian study shows that the majority of women who have undergone legal abortions do not suffer major psychological sequelae.[8] However, it is not known how many women who ask for abortion have preexisting psychological problems which may be exacerbated by the procedure. Senay speaks of this high-risk group and describes a mourning process that almost invariably takes place and can affect a woman in different ways, depending on preexisting psychological status.[9] He reports, also, that specific questioning of the patients will elicit reports of guilt, depression, and anxiety. *American Journal of Public Health* of March 1971 contains a number of articles about abortion. In one of these,

---

[1] Helene Deutsch, *The Psychology of Women*, vol. 2: *Motherhood* (New York: Grune and Stratton, 1945).

[2] Mary Calderone, ed., *Abortion in the United States* (New York: Harper & Row, 1968).

[3] George S. Walter, Psychologic and Emotional Consequences of Elective Abortion, *Obstetrics and Gynecology*, 36: 482–91 (September 1970).

[4] Eric Pfeiffer, Psychiatric Indications or Psychiatric Justification of Therapeutic Abortion?, *Archives of General Psychiatry*, 23: 402–07 (November 1970).

[5] Walter, Psychologic Consequences of Abortion.

[6] Paul H. Gebhard et al., *Pregnancy, Birth and Abortion* (New York: Harper & Row, 1958).

[7] Edward C. Senay, Therapeutic Abortion—Clinical Aspects, *Archives of General Psychiatry*, 23: 408–15 (November 1970).

[8] Martin Ekblad, Induced Abortion on Psychiatric Grounds: A Follow-up Study of 479 Women, *Acta Psychiatrica et Neurologica Scandinavica*, suppl. 99 (1955), p. 1.

[9] Senay, Therapeutic Abortion.

Henry P. David asks for research in psychosocial factors in abortion.[10] He maintains that more should be known about psychosocial implications now that more and more states are liberalizing their abortion laws.

PLANNING A SERVICE

Prior to 1970 the social workers at New York Hospital—a large voluntary, university hospital in New York City—were involved in obtaining psychiatric recommendations for women seeking abortion. These requests originally came at the rate of about one a week, but in the period immediately before July 1970, there were about five a week. Experience with these patients had shown that they reflected the psychological adjustment of almost any patient group. That is, some women were under greater stress than others, some had histories or evidenced symptoms of varying degrees of psychological disorders, some, although under stress, showed general emotional stability. The problems involved in obtaining an abortion on psychiatric grounds caused all of them some stress.

Supporters of legal abortion claim that the procedure is a simple one and often describe it as less traumatic than a tonsillectomy. Experience of the social work staff in interviewing the patients mentioned above, however, showed that the majority of patients had psychological difficulties in making the decision to have the abortion. This group of patients served to make it clear that the women requesting abortion after July 1970 would be under stress of varying degree and that every effort should be made to provide a social work service.[11]

When the new law came into effect, New York Hospital set aside a thirty-bed clinical ward for private and service abortion patients separating them from obstetrical and gynecological patients. The service patients were seen in the clinic first and admitted to the hospital within a few days. Private patients were not seen in the hospital prior to admission.

The social workers turned their attention to the service patients who could be seen prior to admission. Because of the amount of time involved, individual interviews to find problem situations were not feasible. The decision to see patients in groups, therefore, was a logical means of handling the situation. The group session would provide education about the abortion procedure and family-planning methods and had the added benefit of the interest and support of the nursing staff who eventually became coleaders of the groups.

Further rationale for the establishment of the groups was to allow for the expression of conflict regarding the abortion and to help the patient deal with possible adverse family, religious, and social class attitudes. Group censures may cause feelings of isolation as well as guilt and anxiety in the prospect abortion patient who often has to face the procedure alone. Peer groups would offer the patient the opportunity to share her feelings with others in a similar situation. They might support the patient in the

---

[10] Henry P. David, Abortion: Public Health Concerns and Needed Psychosocial Research, *American Journal of Public Health,* 61: 510–17 (March 1971).

[11] The writer is grateful to the obstetrical and gynecological unit of the Department of Social Work in the New York Hospital for aiding in data collection and providing the patient service, and to Miss Margaret Mushinski for her assistance in preparing the statistical report.

decision-making process. The goal of the groups was therefore threefold: (1) to help the patients share and express feelings of conflict within the group, (2) to help members of the group support each other, and (3) to provide education about abortion and medical procedures and to clear up mistaken ideas about abortion and family planning. It was also hoped that the group process would help to identify those women with significant psychosocial problems or stress so that further help could be offered to those patients.

The Patients

Prospective patients were asked to join the group for a discussion with the social worker, but joining the group was not compulsory. The group meetings took place after every clinic session, and each group met once.

From September 1, 1970, to February 26, 1971, 598 patients were seen in groups, an average of five in each session. This total represented roughly 75 percent of all abortion patients who came to the clinic. Most of those women who did not attend a group session gave as a reason that they wanted to get home. This applied particularly to those coming from out of town. Some who did not wish to join a group explained that they felt they had nothing to discuss, no questions to ask. Each patient coming into a group was asked to complete a small card containing questions of area of residence, age, marital status, race, religion, occupation, source of support, how the patient heard about the service, what birth control methods had been used, and why the patient was seeking an abortion. There were no refusals to fill out the cards although a few patients omitted some items and eighteen patients did not give reasons for seeking the abortion.

As shown in Table 51–1, 60 percent of the patients came from New York City, 5 percent from New York State, and 33 percent from states other than New York. The largest percentage of patients (40 percent) were between the ages of twenty and twenty-four. One-third of the patients were married. Single women comprised 46 percent of the patients, and the remaining 21 percent were divorced, separated, or widowed. The patients were primarily white (68 percent), and the largest percentage of the women were Catholic (47 percent). Almost a third were housewives, a little more than a fifth were employed as clerical or sales personnel, and skilled workers and students were almost equally represented (13 percent and 14 percent, respectively). More than one-half (55 percent) had completed high school, almost a quarter (23 percent) had only an elementary education, and almost a fifth (18 percent) had attended college. The majority of the patients were self-supporting; 21 percent were receiving public assistance.

Table 51–2 shows that one-quarter of the patients had used the pill for birth control, and 46 percent had used no birth control at all. Table 51–3 reflects the reasons given for seeking an abortion; the women were given the opportunity to cite more than one reason. Lack of sufficient money was the reason given by the largest percentage of women (43 percent). Being unmarried was cited by 37 percent, even though actually 46 percent were single. This fact is more significant when *single* is considered to include divorced, separated, and widowed, in which case the percentage of unmarried women is actually 67. It is not clear what was meant by the response, *not ready,* but it was included because earlier experience with abortion patients had shown this to be a reason frequently cited. It appears to include a combination of such reasons as lack of money, desire to space children, and general unpreparedness. The work/school category usually

Table 51–1
Percentage Distribution of Respondents' Characteristics

Characteristics	Percentage of Respondents	Characteristics	Percentage of Respondents
Age		*Marital Status*	
Under 19	15	Single	46
20–24	40	Married	33
25–29	24	Separated	14
30–34	12	Divorced	6
35–39	7	Widowed	1
40+	2	Unknown	a
Race		*Occupation*	
White	68	Housewife	32
Black	26	Clerical, sales	21
Other	5	Student	14
Unknown	1	Skilled	13
Religion		Professional, managers	10
Catholic	47	Unknown	7
Protestant	34	Unskilled	3
Jewish	4	*Area of residence*	
Other	10	New York City	60
None	3	New York State	5
Unknown	2	Other states	33
Education		Unknown	2
Elementary	23	*Means of support*	
High School	55	Self	38
College	16	Husband	26
College+	2	Public assistance	21
Unknown	4	Parents	11
		Other	3
		Unknown	1

a Less than one percent
N = 598

represented school for high school students and work for the older women, although there were some women interested in continuing education.

The Groups

When examining the content of the group discussions, the characteristics of the women should be borne in mind. It is possible that women of different ethnic and educational backgrounds would have other concerns about abortion.

Six social workers participated in the program. A nurse clinician acted as coleader to insure that the educational and clinical aspects of abortion could be handled effectively. One of the leaders usually began the meeting with a statement that being admitted for an abortion has caused many women some degree of social and emotional stress and

Table 51–2
Methods of Contraception

Methods	Percentage of Respondents
None	46
Pill	25
Foam	10
Diaphragm	6
Rhythm	6
Coil	5
Condom	3
Other	2
Jelly	1
Average number of methods per patient[a]	1.1

N = 598
[a] Totals amount to more than 100 percent because there were multiple responses. Percentages were calculated from the number of respondents, not the number of responses.

that hospital personnel wanted them to have the opportunity to discuss their questions and concerns. This comment usually brought out requests for information about the abortion procedures, but it appeared that these questions could not be handled through a purely educational approach. Questions about the procedure included who exactly would do the procedure and what the length of anesthesia would be. The questions also reflected fear of the procedure and its aftereffects. For instance, the question of subsequent sterility came up quite often. For many women this would be their first hospitalization, and they wanted to know what it was like to be in a hospital, whether they

Table 51–3
Reasons for Abortion

Reasons	Percentage of Respondents
Money	43
Not married	37
Not ready	31
Work/school	30
Too many children	20
Other	8
Not husband's child	5
Unknown	3
Average number of reasons per patient[a]	1.8

N = 598
[a] Totals amount to more than 100 percent because there were multiple responses. Percentages were calculated from the number of respondents, not the number of responses.

would be separated from the obstetrical patients, and when they could be visited. They needed education and information, but more than this they were asking for reassurance that the procedure was not harmful.

It was necessary to encourage the group members to express their conflicts on some occasions, but most of the women were very ready to talk about their underlying feelings. The question of guilt came up at every session. It appeared that although abortion had been legalized, it was still felt by many of these patients to be an illegal procedure. Apparently, in this situation, the change in law has come before the change in heart. Religious issues came up very rarely so that the guilt expressed or implied was usually not based on religious conflict. There was discussion about "killing the baby," fear that society would judge them, stress on secrecy, expression of guilt about becoming pregnant and undergoing an unnatural procedure. Often group members tended to appeal to the leaders for alleviation of their guilt. The leaders found that what helped the group most was to receive this reassurance from each other, and they guided the group to talk to each other rather than to the leaders.

It seemed very clear that the majority of women were ambivalent. They described how they suppressed their motherly feelings, which they said they possessed but did not want at this time. They said they did not want to think of the fetus as a baby. There was regret by some that while pregnancy should be a wonderful experience, they could not go through with it now. Many wanted quick admission so that the fetus would not have a chance of becoming "too real."

A frequent topic of discussion was the attitude of the clinic personnel. The women complained they were being talked at, treated like numbers rather than people, and kept waiting too long. They felt the professional staff condemned them. On further discussion it appeared that these reactions had much to do with how the patients felt about themselves; however, the attitude of personnel was a problem at times and certainly bears further exploration. Some patients expressed much anger on such subjects as racism, fathers of the babies, and promiscuous women; again it appeared that some of this feeling was projection of their own anxiety and ambivalence.

Feelings of isolation was also apparent, although the records show that very few patients actually went through planning for the abortion alone. In the groups, however, many patients regretted not being able to discuss their problems with their families. Many out-of-town patients described what it was like to come to New York and to the hospital without family or peer support. Even those who had discussed their plans with families and friends felt that ultimately the decision and experience were personal ones which others could share only to a limited extent.

In some groups, patients talked about their backgrounds and families, their other children, about being or not being married, and about birth control and family-planning. Some blamed birth control device failures, but many admitted to ignorance of birth control methods. This fact is interesting because it was not an educationally deprived group. Knowledge about birth control is apparently not related to education. One might, of course, question the motivation of these women to become pregnant but the group discussions did not deal with this question. The women spoke about their jobs and how to handle job absence. Usually they found someone in the group who had similar experiences and others who had opinions and feelings about these subjects.

Joint leadership was a problem at times. It did provide for nurses and social workers to cooperate in a service to patients and gave them an opportunity to work together. In general, the nurses tended to lean toward more active participation; they taught, guided, and reassured. The social workers tended to encourage the group members to talk to each other and derive help and support from each other. Nurses and social workers met to discuss these differences in approach, but they remained a problem. The nurses were a definite asset in providing information and education about the abortion procedures. However, as the social workers became more familiar with the information, it was not as important to have the nurse handle the educational aspects.

DISCUSSION

No attempt was made at a formal evaluation of the group meetings. A number of patients mentioned during their subsequent hospital stay that they had found the meeting personally helpful and reassuring in relation to staff attitudes. The social work staff felt that the sessions gave patients an opportunity to discuss their questions and concerns with professional staff and with group members having similar experiences. The contact resulted in mutual support and relief of tension. Further evaluation of the group experience would have to be based on study and control groups.

Approximately one patient in every three groups was seen individually subsequent to the group sessions. Some of these patients sought individual service; in other cases the social worker, having identified a disturbed patient during a session, would speak with her afterward, offering help. Service was given most often in relation to ambivalence about the abortion and less frequently in relation to concrete problems such as housing, absence from work, or financial questions. The group sessions were therefore of some help in individual case-finding.

Another area requiring further study and observation is the attitude toward abortion of the professional personnel, who are bound to have some personal conflicts and to be affected both consciously and unconsciously by positive or negative public attitudes. It is quite likely that physicians and nurses—both trained to save lives—find abortion a difficult subject to deal with and have conflict about participating in the procedure. Patients seem to be quickly aware of this feeling. Although social workers are less involved in the actual abortion procedure, they are also likely to have their own conflicts. Another question one might ask is whether men and women have different attitudes about abortion. It would be useful, also, to analyze the contribution of the group leaders and to evaluate the group process in general.

The greatest amount of work, however, needs to be done in the whole area of the nature of emotional conflicts in patients undergoing abortions and the presence or absence of psychological sequelae. For instance, do all women suffer some emotional conflict or ambivalence, and if so, do they all need professional help? Is abortion today a procedure acceptable to most women as a way of limiting family size? Is seeking an abortion symptomatic of other psychological conflict, and does it take place in the presence of other psychological problems? To obtain answers to these questions it would be necessary to conduct personal interviews including follow-up after the abortion.

SUMMARY

This article has examined some of the literature about the psychological aspects of abortion. The 598 patients who came to a large voluntary hospital in New York City and were seen in group-counseling sessions were described, and such subjects as use of birth control and reasons for abortion were considered. The content of the group discussions were examined in an attempt to determine if a need was being met. There was no formal evaluation of the effect of the groups, but it appeared that useful information about abortion was given, that group members expressed their ambivalent feelings, and that they felt that they had derived some benefit from the group experience.

ABORTION AND PREGNANCY

CHAPTER 52

UNPLANNED PREGNANCY IN YOUNG WOMEN

Managing Treatment

Peter Barnett and Deborah W. Balak

Most professional discussion regarding unplanned pregnancies has focused on the special concerns relating to adolescent pregnancy. Because of the high risk to mother and child and the long-term consequences of pregnancy, the sexually active adolescent population has justifiably been the subject of careful scrutiny. However, an extensive search of the social work literature and a computer search of the medical literature of the past five years reveals that the young adult woman who is experiencing an unplanned pregnancy has been virtually ignored in the literature.

The present article describes the population counseled for "problem pregnancy" at Family Services of Tidewater, with special attention focused on young adult women between eighteen and twenty-seven years old. The issues involved for the young adult woman experiencing an unplanned pregnancy and the therapeutic challenges of working with this population are examined.

DIMENSIONS OF THE PROBLEM

Since the majority of women who present for counseling for an unplanned pregnancy are also unmarried, the statistical profile of the birthrate for unmarried women is relevant to

*Reprinted from *Social Casework,* Vol. 67, No. 8 (1986), pp. 484–489, by permission of the publisher, Families International, Inc.
This article was adapted from a paper presented at the Family Service America Biennial Conference, October 24–27, 1985, Indianapolis, Indiana.

illustrate the scope of the problem. Although the overall birthrate in the United States decreased 1 percent from 1981 to 1982, the overall birthrate for unmarried women increased 4 percent in the same period. In fact, the 1982 rate was the highest ever, 30 births per 1,000 unmarried women aged fifteen to forty-four years. For the population described in the present article, the rates were even higher. For eighteen- to nineteen-year-old women, the birthrate was 40.2 births per 1,000, and for twenty- to twenty-four-year-old women, the birthrate was 41.4 births per 1,000. Unmarried women accounted for approximately 20 percent of all births in 1982 (194.3 per 1,000 live births).[1] The number of abortions in this age group is not reflected in these statistics.

Many young women, especially if unmarried, have not finished the developmental tasks of emancipation from family, adult relationships, education, and attaining jobs. Unplanned pregnancy complicates these tasks by forcing young women to make a decision on whether to keep the baby or to place the baby for adoption. The family has a great impact on the decision-making process and may continue to influence the young adult woman after she has established her own home.[2] Even when the influence is subtle, it makes the engagement of these women into a useful therapeutic alliance difficult.

DESCRIPTION OF THE POPULATION

Family Services of Tidewater, Virginia, works primarily with young adult women ranging in age from eighteen to twenty-seven years in its "problem pregnancy" program, although the agency does not exclude younger or older women. From 1983 to 1985, thirty-seven of the problem pregnancy intakes within the age range specified were involved in counseling. Although thirty-seven cases are an admittedly narrow empirical base, the authors' views on therapy have developed from over twenty years of combined experience with problem pregnancy cases in both public and private family service and child welfare agencies. We recognize that some preselection exists in our population, because the pregnant woman may have already made the decision to release her expected baby for adoption or has at least considered such an alternative when she requests an appointment. Thirty-one of the thirty-seven clients graduated from high school and sixteen had additional specialized vocational training or some college education; one obtained a graduate degree. Five were married, seventeen had one or more older children, and twenty-one eventually placed the baby for adoption.

A cluster of characteristics became evident in the women with whom we worked.

1.   The women exhibited a high concentration of effort toward the completion of the developmental tasks of young adulthood. Most began separating from the family of origin by going away to school or setting up their own household. They had graduated from high school and were proceeding with their education or training. Pregnancy demanded a reassessment of plans and expectations about career, life-style, personal status, and relationships.

---

[1] *U.S. Department of Commerce, Statistical Abstract of the U.S.: 1985* (Washington, D.C.: U.S. Government Printing Office, December 1984), p. 61.
[2] Rhoda Abel et al., "Pregnant Adolescents: Cost-Benefit Options," *Social Casework* 63 (May 1982): 286–90.

Other women had been active members of the work force, successfully supporting themselves in a young-adult life-style, learning the skills of personal responsibility, independence, and the enjoyment of new experiences. Pregnancy threatened their freedom and exploration, important aspects of their growth.

Others had already adapted to parenting a child from an adolescent pregnancy. They had established a comfortable family life, either independently or with extended family (usually in the parental home). Family roles that support their continued adult development had been negotiated. Pregnancy renewed the stress of the earlier pregnancy, threatened the current status quo, added pressure to a system already stretched to accommodate the first unplanned child, and undermined self-esteem because a "second mistake" had been allowed to occur.

2.   Despite apparent successes in mastering developmental tasks, these women tended to be emotionally needy, socially immature, and isolated. They had poor decision-making skills.

Pregnancy was frequently the result of an effort to fulfill emotional needs through another person. Their tendency was to become quickly and superficially involved. The crisis arose when the pregnancy was discovered and the expectant mother realized she was more committed to the relationship than the father was.

The young women functioned quite adequately until the stress of the unplanned pregnancy left them adrift without friends, partner, or family with whom they could communicate about serious problems or from whom they could elicit support. Feelings of rejection and confusion about how they got in this predicament were commonplace. The effort required for normal functioning was often monumental for these women.

3.   Clients frequently came from disengaged families in which relationships among members were intense but distant. These families expended great energy in maintaining emotional distance from one another while in physical proximity. This type of family is similar to Salvador Minuchin's description of the disengaged family in which "members of disengaged subsystems or families may function autonomously but have a skewed sense of independence and lack feelings of loyalty and belonging and the capacity for interdependence and for requesting support when needed."[3] Although they may live in the same household and may express a sense of closeness to the family, the relationships are characterized by a tendency to want to "protect" family members from having to deal with emotional or sensitive issues. Even in the event of an illegitimate pregnancy, a problem that can greatly affect the family system, family members either allow the mother to retreat or avoid sharing and make little effort to support her through the crisis.

The expectant mothers may have denied the pregnancy for months to family members, especially their own mothers, and the family members seem to have accepted the obvious secret, never directly questioning whether the woman was, in fact, pregnant or discussing the pregnancy in any way. Frequently, an unspoken agreement existed to avoid talking about any sensitive subject. In the words of one client, "My mother and I are close. We can talk about anything, but I couldn't tell her I was pregnant." The issue in some cases was not discussed even after the mother brought her newborn home.

---

[3] Salvador Minuchin, *Families and Family Therapy* (Cambridge, Mass.: Harvard University Press, 1974), p. 55.

4.   Many clients exhibited an underlying depression that drew on their already taxed emotional reserves. The depression understandably emanated from feelings of rejection by or disappointment in the partner, lack of support, disengagement from family, setbacks in career or education, and the awesome responsibility of parenting alone or "giving up" the child.

5.   Some clients had already terminated a previous pregnancy, and the present pregnancy was related in some way to unresolved feelings about the abortion: "I could never do that again" or "I'm making up for it [the abortion] by having the baby."

TWO CASES
Case 1

T gave birth to her first child when she was eighteen years old. Although life was difficult with a small child and a fixed income, she completed high school and began training as a licensed practical nurse. Two subsequent pregnancies occurred within the next three years. The first she aborted; the second brought her to Family Services to explore the possibilities of placing the expected infant for adoption. She dropped out of school during the last trimester of the third pregnancy and began to evaluate the sacrifice she would have to make in order to parent another child. Her first child did not require as much of her time and energy, and she was once again able to pursue a more active social life and career interests. She and a brother rented an apartment, and for the first time she was living independently of her mother. The prospect of another infant, who would restrict her freedom and demand much of her attention, overwhelmed and depressed her. It became apparent in the weeks before the birth that she would be unable to depend on the father of the baby for emotional or financial support. The expected baby represented another setback in her efforts to achieve independence, career goals, and life-style aspirations. T did not inform her mother of the pregnancy. She expended a lot of energy in arranging counseling appointments at times when her mother would be unlikely to question where she was going, thus deflecting discussion of her lack of preparations for the baby with her mother. She rejected attempts to involve her mother in any counseling sessions, preferring to wait until after the birth and placement of the child before discussing her plans with her mother. She spoke often of how hurt her mother would be to discover her pregnant again; she was determined to protect her mother from this hurt, even at the expense of her own isolation.

Case 2

D, a twenty-six-year-old mother of three children, was living with an aunt at the time of her pregnancy with the fourth child. The pregnancy was unplanned, the result of a short-lived reconciliation with the father of her other children. D was abandoned by her parents at a young age and left to be reared by her grandmother. The grandmother died when D was twelve years old, and D's aunt dropped out of college to raise her. D and the aunt had what D considered a close relationship; they had few other relatives, and they were relatively close in age. D attended college for one year (seeking the same degree that her aunt had sought before dropping out). D became involved with a man who did not meet her aunt's approval. They lived together intermittently for the next few years. D left college, obtained secretarial training, and worked steadily at one job. No one was aware of the pregnancy except the baby's father. D kept the pregnancy secret from her aunt, three children, co-workers, and a babysitter whom she saw daily, and kept up the facade of a jovial, extroverted young woman. Since her relationship with the father was conflictual, she had no one with whom she felt safe to let down her guard and discuss the pregnancy. She believed that her aunt, even if she suspected the pregnancy, would not initiate discussion about it. D made contact with the agency only ten days before the delivery of the baby. The baby was born and placed for adoption, and no mention of the pregnancy was ever made in the family.

TREATMENT PROBLEMS

We worked with this population from a systems perspective. Their problems were similar to those of any client who experiences a crisis. However, we found that we also had to penetrate the defenses of a woman who was fairly unskilled at social relationships and who avoided revealing sensitive, personal information. Her view of the problem focused on the pregnancy, not on the family system or her ability to establish or maintain relationships. She probably came from a family system with rigid boundaries that discouraged her from seeking outside help for personal problems, yet had little experience with resolving problems within the system. Moreover, the presenting problem was time-limited, which further complicated treatment.

Given the characteristics of the population, the pregnancy provided, potentially, an opportunity for the young woman to enter into a therapeutic experience that may broaden her view of life's possibilities. These women were likely to be moderately successful in accomplishing developmental tasks and would probably not be in counseling with mental health professionals if it were not for the added stress of the pregnancy and the attendant need to make far-reaching decisions. The structural organization of the families left these women unprepared to cope with their environment. They invested a lot of energy in maintaining distant, need-denying relationships and in protecting family members at their own expense. These family relationships probably caused the young women to use sexual relationships to satisfy otherwise unmet needs.

The problem pregnancy counselor approached the client with the vision that life could be sustained more efficiently and with more satisfaction. However, the clients did not enter into relationships easily and, in fact, used a great deal of energy to maintain distance. The clients' experience had been that it was not safe to enter into relationships, that closeness was dangerous. Emotionally charged relationships were not part of the client's experience. The client distrusted the therapeutic relationship as well and used all of her defense mechanisms to maintain a comfortable distance. The first treatment challenge was to penetrate this distance to effect or create a therapeutic opportunity.

Often, the family system from which the client originated was extremely rigid. Outsiders were not allowed to enter, which created another treatment challenge for the therapist. The family system surrounded and "protected" the client, thereby excluding the therapist and trapping the client in a homeostatic pattern.

By coming to the counselor with a specific problem, the pregnancy, the client could both request and resist help. She was able to remain symptom-focused, that is, focused on the child and its care while resisting efforts to examine the experience within the greater context of her personal and family patterns. With many concrete details to be concerned about (prenatal care, abortion, adoption, health and nutrition, financial concerns, preparing a home for the child, child care, and so forth) the exploration of "who the client is" and how she characterologically solves problems could be avoided. The therapist was often torn between attending to the concrete concerns and treating the underlying issues.

Social workers depend on language and communication in their work; by withholding personal and emotional information, the client rendered these tools useless. Also, the therapy was under time constraints. When the pregnancy ended, the counseling usually ended as well. Once the client had decided whether to keep, abort, or release the child for adoption, she believed that she had no further need for counseling.

All of these issues contributed to a low energy investment regarding counseling on the part of the client. The client did not share the vision of the counselor. To the client, the request for help seemed simple, was often confined to concrete requests, and was time-limited. Systemic change was alien and frightening. How, then, does the therapist facilitate change in these systems?

TREATMENT TASKS

Facilitating change in the young adult pregnant woman must go beyond simple planning for the pregnancy or baby. The social worker must penetrate the client's defenses and find ways to use the family system as a vehicle for change. In our experience, individual, psychodynamically oriented treatment does not produce lasting change. Moreover, many systems cannot be penetrated by the social worker. However, we have found that treatment that offers a vision of closeness in relationships and direction of energy toward creativity rather than protection is most effective.

During initial meetings with the client, the social worker respected the client's preference for distance in relationships until she invited the therapist closer. A sense of movement toward common goals and mutual respect was developed. Each partner in the therapeutic relationship was an expert in some aspect of the treatment process. The client was the expert on the family system, and the therapist was the expert on methods that the client could use to establish more efficient long-term relationships. Initially, few demands were placed on the client system, and the client's defenses were accepted. The client's description of the problem was discussed with these considerations in mind. Material that was pertinent to the family situation was elicited gradually, at which times the therapist offered the client a more comprehensive view of treatment. As the client shared thoughts and feelings about the family system, the social worker offered his or her vision for change.

The pregnancy and the stress surrounding it provided material for gentle probing during the initial visits. The fact that the client had presented at the agency indicated that the pregnancy was stressful and that the client was asking for help to relieve that stress. In addition to putting stress on practical concerns such as finances and medical treatment, the pregnancy often threatened the delicate equilibrium in the client's life. Her self-esteem, which may have been linked to her ability to manage family, career, and educational tasks, was in jeopardy. The system revealed cracks that could be exploited for change. By first recognizing the impact of the pregnancy on developmental tasks and then on self-esteem, the therapist found an entry whereby treatment could be initiated. In other words, the practical concerns of the pregnancy became the vehicle whereby the systemic insecurities felt by the client could be explored.

If significant others (for example, boyfriend, parents, husband) could be engaged in the treatment when the focus had expanded, the potential for success increased dramatically. The family provided the laboratory in which to demonstrate both the deficits in the system and the potential for change. The caring relationships that existed in the family helped establish an atmosphere amenable to gentle nudges by the client and therapist. Expression of feelings such as "I only want the best for you" or "I want you to be happy" helped open discussion on the changes that were required. As simple needs were expressed, the system changed in order to respond to them. The therapist's task during this stage of treatment was to assure that needs were expressed in ways that would force the system to reorganize itself in new ways.

As soon as the family accepted the restructuring of the problem or the client accepted the expanded definition of the problem, new therapeutic directions could be developed. It was important to connect these forays into new territory with the pregnancy, because clients remained sensitive to the purpose for which they had sought help.

The final stage of treatment was to intervene in the dysfunctional system. By establishing more functional communication patterns, loosening rigid behavior patterns, creating opportunities for nurturance, and teaching methods for setting limits and personal boundaries, the therapist helped clients achieve a more efficient and effective life-style. Although this task was easier if family members attended the treatment sessions, systemic intervention remained the goal even if the client attended the sessions alone.

The following case example illustrates how the participation of family and significant others in the therapeutic process and the commitment of the client to the process may help a client successfully resolve the crisis of an unwanted pregnancy.

CASE STUDY

C, a nineteen-year-old college sophomore, requested problem-pregnancy counseling in the early months of her pregnancy. She and her boyfriend, also a college student, had already made the decision to place the expected baby for adoption. Counseling was viewed as the process for relinquishing parental rights. With support from her mother, both in sessions and at home, C was encouraged to consider a wider focus for counseling.

C presented as a fairly egocentric young woman, extremely concerned about what other people thought about her. Her rigid moral code and self-image did not allow for an unwed pregnancy. She felt very strongly about keeping her pregnancy secret so that she could maintain the image her siblings and peers had of her. Consequently, C dropped out of college for a semester and isolated herself from friends and most of her family for the duration of the pregnancy.

The joining process was initiated around issues directly related to the pregnancy. C used a major portion of the early sessions asking questions about adoption and the procedures to follow and expressing concern about where she would live when her pregnancy became obvious to others. She expressed how unfair she felt it was to become pregnant after her first sexual experience, anger at the interruption in her schooling, and guilt about her "weakness" and disappointing her family. By allowing C to move at her own pace, the therapist established a relationship of trust, which allowed the therapist to probe deeper.

By recognizing that C viewed her pregnancy as an interference in her progress toward completing her education, the therapist was able to begin exploring her definition of self within the context of family of origin and peer relationships. Her self-esteem, which was so closely linked to her image of herself as a "good girl" and model student, served as the focal point for expanding her perception of the problem. The treatment goal was to help her fit the pregnancy and her faults into her self-concept and to help her realize that other people still loved her in spite of her faults. Reassurances offered by her mother and boyfriend during sessions helped reinforce the therapeutic efforts.

The therapist eventually helped C examine herself within the family system. C developed an awareness of the part she played in relationships with others. She began to recognize that her increasing dependence on and insecurity about her boyfriend was causing him to withdraw and creating distance between them. Although her father was not directly involved in counseling sessions, C allowed him to be a part of the treatment process via the pregnancy. She began to ask for an emotional investment from him when she realized that her pattern of relating to him in the past involved protecting him from emotional issues. Her first experience with confronting his avoidance occurred when she expressed her feelings about the baby and adoptive placement.

Through treatment and with the support of her mother and boyfriend, C was able to resolve the discrepancy between her projected self-image and the real C and to recognize her contribution to the interactional patterns with significant others. The success of this case can be attributed in large part to the time commitment made to the treatment by the client. C sought counseling early in the pregnancy, was available for weekly sessions, and did not terminate it when the baby was placed for adoption.

IN CONCLUSION

Our experience in offering services for problem pregnancy shows that unwanted, unplanned, often unwed pregnancy is not a problem unique to adolescents. The adult woman is confronted with problems similar to those of a teenager. Moreover, she must continue to negotiate adult tasks and deal with societal expectations that she "should have known better" at her age and that she should accept her responsibilities (usually to raise the child) because she is an adult. The challenge for the therapist working with this population is to create a treatment framework that will help these women continue to develop as an adult, become more skilled in establishing and maintaining satisfying relationships, and become more effective decision-makers.

CHAPTER 53

EXISTENTIAL PSYCHOTHERAPY AND THE PROBLEM OF ANOMIE

Donald F. Krill

A characteristic of the present age is the increasing freedom of people from traditional ties and associated systems of mores, folkways, and religious disciplines, coupled with the fact that instead of flowering in their newfound freedom a large share have become muddled, confused, highly anxious, and self-driving, and in general resort to ways of "escaping their freedom."[1] Such modern maladies as alcoholism, increased divorce rates, overuse and experimental use of drugs, and the general entertainment and recreation manias have been linked with this desperate flight or search (which one it is depending, perhaps, on the person).

In 1962 Pollak presented several ideas related to this issue:

> Strangely enough, the clients who represent the greatest challenge to social work and a wider community at the present time do not suffer from the scars of submission to the reality principle. They suffer from the ineffectiveness of having retained the pleasure principle as a guide of living. They lead a life of normlessness conceptualized by Merton as anomie. . . . With people who are victims of anomie we have no theory of helping and tradition of success. The culture of social work here is faced with the challenge of becoming a rearing and binding, superego demanding profession rather than of being a liberating one. . . . Here social workers will have to come to terms with a phenomena of normlessness which makes liberating or improving efforts miss the mark.[2]

Reprinted from *Social Work,* Vol. 14, No. 2 (April 1969), pp. 33–49, by permission of the author and the National Association of Social Workers.
[1] Erich Fromm, *Escape from Freedom* (New York: Holt, Rinehart & Winston, 1941).
[2] Otto Pollak, "Social Determinants of Family Behavior." Paper presented at the Mid-Continent Regional Institute, National Association of Social Workers, Kansas City, Mo., April 1962, p. 6.

Many respond to this problem by talking all the more vehemently of the need for increased services in education, welfare, and mental health, but while there is truth in this they miss the central point that is being proclaimed by the existentialists: People have lost contact with many basic human realities that they must accept and understand if they are to have a sense of personal direction or meaning in their lives. One need only look at present-day common behavior patterns and voiced attitudes to see this. With regard to the concept of human love, closeness, and intimacy, it can be seen that marital disappointments are commonly dealt with by divorce, adultery, alcoholism, increased work (the notion that more money or prestige will change the marriage), and individualized social circles that allow two near-strangers to remain together under the same roof "for the sake of the children." The concept of death is often dealt with by avoidance of it as a fact with implicit meaning for present conduct or weak hopes for some scientific "deep-freeze" solution, and of course by the whole ridiculous ritual of the funeral parlors.

EFFORTS OF THE CHURCH

The illusion behind such maneuvers is the widely held belief that one can manipulate and control life in such a way as to bring oneself happiness, security, and freedom from suffering. This idea has been nourished throughout this century by utopian hopes stemming from scientific rationalism. The effort has backfired insofar as men have become increasingly estranged from many realities of the human condition. These attitudes have at the same time considerably weakened the position of the church, which in the past had been the fount for people's sense of direction and meaning and the support for their capacity to endure hardship. Needless to say, the church, especially since the Reformation, has had its part in nurturing the very hopes in scientific rationalism that have weakened its influence. Now the church itself is struggling for a new language and new means with which to express its fundamental ideas, knowing that people have been alienated and disillusioned and have come to feel indifferent toward traditional presentations of beliefs and truths.[3]

The church, as mentioned, has always concerned itself with the conflicts, ideas, feelings, and behavior that make up the state of mind called anomie. Presumably, the church should have important contributions to make to the psychiatric and social work professions in their efforts to cope with this problem. An interesting development in society has been furthered by those serious students of or searchers after a religion that refuses to return to Sunday school fantasies, hopes, rituals, and platitudes. The new religious vitality is one that seeks a sense of direction and unity in the intimacy of direct experience with this world of tasks, suffering, and possibilities. The forerunners of this surge were such religious existentialist thinkers as Dostoevsky, Kierkegaard, Berdyaev, Bergson, Jaspers, Marcel, Maritain, Tillich, Niebuhr, Barth, and Buber. This is the true

---

[3] This is the basic conflict in the "Honest to God" debate. *See* John A. T. Robinson, *Honest to God* (Philadelphia: Westminster Press, 1963); and David L. Edwards, *The Honest to God Debate* (Philadelphia: Westminster Press, 1963).

religious revival and has nothing to do with increased church attendance, faith healing, and the renewed interest in Gospel singing. A profound movement toward unity among the world's religions is in progress and this includes a strong effort toward a unity between religion and science as well.

A similar movement has occurred apart from the church, yet seems related to the same precipitating conditions and personal needs. This has expressed itself in the arts and literature and theoretically in the avid interest of many in existential philosophy and Zen Buddhism—two areas of modern thought representing West and East that are remarkably similar in their concern for the discovery of meaning in the direct, immediate experience of life as one lives it.

The existentialist movement in the fields of psychiatry and psychology may well provide a body of knowledge that is highly valuable and useful in our quest for some answers to the problem of anomie. Existentialism is a philosophy derived from man's immediate experience of the world in which he lives—a confrontation with the realities of the human condition and the establishment of a personalized meaning from them. As a philosophy of daily experience it should be capable of speaking meaningfully about ideas that can be grasped by the unsophisticated, much as a novel does.

Pollak's words (". . . becoming a rearing and binding, superego demanding profession") are provocative to the ears of social workers who have identified their goals, along psychoanalytic lines, to be in marked contrast with his suggestion. There is the ring here of paternalism, authoritarianism, and a judgmental attitude. But let us look at what the church has attempted to accomplish over its many centuries of existence and what this may have to say to us through the modern views of existentialism.

The church has always attempted to deal with the sufferings of people by providing them with a sense of meaning that transcends their own self-derived, suffering-based feelings of futility about life. Religious people have found courage to endure through acceptance of what is considered to be divine revelation. The fundamental services of religion to an individual are the provision of guidance in his way of living and the experience of union with an ultimate reality that relates him to others and all that exists through the transcendent power in which he believes. Religious dogmas, orders, sects, rituals, sermons, discussion groups, sacraments, social action, study, prayer, and meditation are some of the varied efforts to accomplish these two basic services. This variety of approaches reflects the church's efforts to serve people of varying capacities and levels of motivation and understanding. The mental health movement faces a similar problem.

Psychiatry cannot be equated with religion, for the sphere of divine revelation and speculation on the mystery of transcendence is beyond the scope and capacity of scientific methods. But the human need for guidance in the management of one's life and the experience of unity through relatedness to others outside oneself are certainly within its realm. It is here that the existentialist movement has attempted to relate a philosophy of life to mankind's problems by focusing, as the church has done, on guidance and relatedness. This is why the existentialist movement is most commonly characterized as stressing meaning in life and authenticity in relationships.

EXISTENTIALISM VERSUS ANOMIE

Elsewhere the writer defined the concern of existentialism as "meaningful living through self-encounter in the situation at hand despite a world of apparent futility."[4] Essentially, this means that one derives or helps another derive an attitude and direction toward life by becoming increasingly aware of life as he lives it and what this living entails. It is for this reason that the problem of anomie—of aimless, futile, normless lives—can be constructively related to by existentialist thought.

The process of growth in existentialism emphasizes the following reality concepts: increasing awareness of self-deceptions that attempt to define the self as fixed and secure; confrontation with the knowledge of personal freedom and its accompanying responsibilities; discovery of meaning in one's sufferings that actually helps establish a direction in life; realization of the necessity of dialogue or intimacy that nurtures change, courage, and self-assertion; and finally a decision for continued commitment that prizes freedom above attachment to childhood strivings and self-deceptions. This commitment is characterized by responsive action in the world of tasks, duties, and possibilities, in contrast to narcissism and self-pity.[5]

Let us contrast this with patterns of thought and behavior implicit in the state of mind labeled anomie. The characteristic of normlessness mentioned by Pollak is a result of several attitudes about oneself and also oneself in relation to others and the world in general. These attitudes are anti-existential in content because of the nature of the implicit beliefs and assumptions about freedom, responsibility, suffering, authenticity, love, and commitment. The sources of these attitudes are many and have been ably described by such social critics as Erich Fromm, Allen Wheelis, Colin Wilson, David Riesman, and William Whyte.

Anomie is derived from a Greek word meaning "lack of law." As a sociological concept it describes the breakdown or failure of those forces (standards, sanctions, norms, rules, values) that ordinarily bind people together in some organized social whole. This social whole is characterized by a sense of duty and obligation of people toward one another that preserves organization. There are different degrees of anomie and it may take several forms, outlined by Cohen as "confrontation by a situation for which there are no relevant rules, vagueness or ambiguity of the relevant rules, or lack of consensus on which rules are relevant and in the interpretation of rules."[6]

Tiryakian states:

To liberate the individual from all social constraint, adds Durkheim, is to abandon him to his unlimited wants, to demoralize him and to lead him to despair. What the individual should feel, more acutely than ever before, is the need for moral rules.[7]

---

[4] Donald F. Krill, "Existentialism: A Philosophy for Our Current Revolutions," *Social Service Review,* Vol. 40, No. 3 (September 1966), p. 291.

[5] *Ibid.* This entire article is a development of these ideas.

[6] Albert K. Cohen, "The Study of Social Disorganization and Deviant Behavior," in Robert K. Merton, Leonard Brown, and Leonard S. Cottrell, Jr., eds., *Sociology Today: Problems and Prospects* (New York: Basic Books, 1959), p. 481.

[7] Edward A. Tiryakian, *Sociologism and Existentialism* (Englewood Cliffs, N.J.: Prentice-Hall, 1962), p. 31.

He suggests that what is latent in the writings of Durkheim that differentiates the notions of solidarity and anomie are societal analogues of what the existentialist terms an individual's "authentic" and "unauthentic" existence.

ANOMIC MAN

The existentialists have enriched our understanding of "anomic man" in both fictional and philosophical descriptions of the "unauthentic man," the man of "bad faith," and "alienated man." These assessments demonstrate that the anomic state of mind and attitude are not to be limited to delinquent, sociopathic, multiply deprived individuals but apply to an ever increasing number of people at all levels of present-day society. Attitudes typical of anomic man will now be examined.

There is a sense of aimless drifting, or at times being helplessly driven, both of which relate to one's sense of impotence and personal insignificance. One considers oneself as being fixed in place either by tradition, heredity, social position, or psychological and social determinism. One has been formed, or perhaps victimized, by the powers that be or by those that were before.

Paradoxically, along with this sense of missing personal freedom and hence diminished responsibility there is an increased expectation that one's surrounding environment should change in such a way as to bring one increased comfort, protection, and happiness. The experience of suffering is therefore often felt to be unfair, and bitterness as well as envy arises toward others in more fortunate circumstances. Quick and easy solutions are sought to manipulate the environment in order to reduce any personal pain and bring about a state of pleasure or comfort. The variety of efforts is vast and extends from pills and television to infidelity and alcoholism.

A Mexican-American leader recently defended his people, who are accused of filling the jails and reformatories of the Southwest, with this interesting observation:

> When a Mexican kid is brought before the judge he is usually honest in admitting he committed the crime and ready to accept whatever consequences come—leaving his future to God. When an Anglo is in the same situation, he'll do anything possible to avoid a charge of guilty to get out of being punished.[8]

One's sense of self as a feeling, thinking, changing person is replaced by a notion of self as dependent on support from outside. One plays roles or "markets oneself" in such a way as to manipulate others to view one in a specific way that meets one's needs. Relationships are characterized by superficiality, calculation, and "game-playing." Other props used are the identification of self with groups, such as religious, political, or professional, or with slogans and characteristics of models found in society and given acceptance or even acclaim, such as "the good Joe, the hustler, the smart opera-

[8] Rudolph Gonzales, lecture-discussion given to the Child Psychiatry Department of the University of Colorado Medical Center, Denver, November 1966.

tor, the playboy, the status seeker. . . ."[9] When such supports are challenged or threatened, one is prepared to fight righteously and defend his self-identity to the bitter end.

What is apparent in this entire description is that one hides one's inner self both from others and from one's own sensitive judgment. There is an ongoing effort to gratify needs by actions and manipulations and a fleeing from being alone with oneself. Such exercises as meditation and self-examination become foreign, or if adopted are used with magical, naïve expectations that usually end in disappointment. Intuition and spontaneity tend to be lost or warped.[10] The simple joys to be found in the beauty and mystery of life and responsive participation in the ongoing order of things are rare. One feels alienated from other people, the world, and oneself, yet hides this fundamental panic beneath desperate efforts to grasp, contain, and fortify a sense of identity, false as it is.

ADVANTAGES OF EXISTENTIAL PSYCHOTHERAPY

This description of attitudes and behavior is not a presentation of symptoms, but rather a way of life—an anti-existentialist way of living—that has developed to significant proportions in our age. Because anomie can be considered to be an attitude toward life, existential psychotherapy has a unique advantage over many other forms of psychotherapy. The outstanding difference does not lie in techniques or methods, for the existential approach may occur with insight, crisis-oriented, family, group, or supportive therapies. It may be directive, nondirective, or analytical. The uniqueness of existential psychotherapy is that it attempts a philosophical reorientation through the use of therapy content and behavior. There is a process of challenge, re-education, and reconstruction of the patient's basic way of viewing himself, his relation to others, and the world at large.

The mental health professional performing the therapy (hereafter called the therapist) holds to a number of existential philosophical premises based on his perception and understanding of reality. The experiences that are lived through in therapy are utilized to demonstrate and highlight the philosophical implications of those realities apparent in these experiences. Soon experiences take on new meanings for patients, who are helped to rethink and redevelop their own outlook on life in a fresh manner.

It is true that the patient takes on certain values and philosophical attitudes of the therapist. This occurs in any form of psychotherapy to a certain degree. What is important here is that the therapist knowingly permits this. He has in mind certain existential realities within his philosophical frame of reference that he wants the patient to see, understand, and accept if he is to overcome his problems. The goal in this approach is not insight into early traumas, reassurance, catharsis, or enabling the patient to grow in a nondirective atmosphere. It may include any or all of these, but the goal itself is a philosophical re-education through direct experience.

---

[9] A comprehensive elaboration of these "models" is found in Henry Winthrop, "American National Character and the Existentialist Posture," *Journal of Existentialism,* Vol. 6, No. 24 (Summer 1966), pp. 405–419.
[10] This theme is fully developed in Franz E. Winkler, MD, *Man, The Bridge Between Two Worlds* (New York: Harper & Bros., 1960).

The relation between anomie and emotional illness must also be understood. Each can exist without the presence of the other; however, in our present society both occur simultaneously and are interrelated in a vast and growing number of cases. The attitudes of anomie actually predispose the person to emotional illness.

The general view among existentialists of the development of emotional disorders stresses the following factors. Two human needs are considered most fundamental: (1) to be loved and to experience a sense of unity with what is other than oneself and (2) to grow through ongoing creative and responsive change. These are interrelated inasmuch as the mature person, at the moment he is authentically creative by responding to the tasks and opportunities of the world about him, is also experiencing a sense of unity by feeling needed or being a vital and unique part of his own specific area of the world (life space).

A child needs the trust and confidence of his parents to develop as a loving and creative person. As he discovers certain creative or loving expressions to be unacceptable to his parents, he experiences the threat of loss of love. With this goes the fear of a disintegration of his sense of self, for one's early identity is dependent on approval and acceptance by one's parents. This fear of parental rejection is equal to the adult fear of death, for the meanings are precisely the same. To live, to preserve some sense of self, a person willingly gives up or hides those aspects of personality that would produce rejection and adapts himself to what he believes his parents want from him, thus making himself acceptable and of worth. This pattern of self-conformity to a necessitated image in childhood continues into adulthood; one relates to others as if it were still necessary to uphold the same image in order to be acceptable and loved.

What is apparent here are the elements of calculated choice of behavior initially and ongoing manipulative efforts to maintain for others a set image of oneself. Trouble results from the fact that manipulative behavior fosters distance rather than love and intimacy in relationships, and also the clinging effort to maintain and express only specific aspects of the self results in frustration of free and creative growth. The two fundamental needs become endangered and the result is symptoms that cry out distress and a need for help. Guilt and anxiety are often seen to be reality based. Anxiety may be experienced when a person realizes that he could act in a spontaneous and creative way that would express his true, responsive self in a situation, yet to do so would endanger the image he feels he must preserve to be acceptable to others and himself. Guilt may occur when he chooses behavior that preserves his own childhood-based image at the expense of a growth possibility. Genuine open communication and sincere efforts of self-examination actually threaten the image that one wishes to maintain and are thus avoided.

TREATMENT GOALS

Anomie encourages a pattern that leads to emotional disturbance insofar as it emphasizes a helpless, weak, predetermined notion of oneself as lacking freedom and responsibility; a manipulative view of human relationships that nourishes superficiality, deceit, and distance; and an avoidance of pain as one tries with various self-deceptions to resist the meaning of guilt and anxiety in order to hide from what is real within oneself. The causes of anomie are sociological and historical, but the existence of anomie is itself an important contribution to mental illness. When anomie is a part of the emotional problem, it should be dealt with and the issue of treatment then becomes partly philosophical in nature.

The specific treatment goals for existential psychotherapy are essentially philosophical achievements in terms of a patient's coming to grips with those aspects of reality that will produce a significant change in his view of life and his relation to it. The five goals that would appear most important are these:

1. Aiding the process of disillusionment
2. Confronting freedom
3. Discovering meaning in suffering
4. Realizing the necessity of dialogue
5. Accepting the way of commitment

Therapeutic techniques familiarize the patient with these goals, or realities, both by educational guidance and direct experience, much as the church directed its people toward spiritual growth. The balance of this paper will present methods by which these goals may be achieved. Emphasis will not be on an analytical or long-term insight-oriented psychotherapy from the existential framework, but rather on techniques useful for casework, group work, and reality-oriented psychotherapy.[11]

The description of therapy may seem somewhat disjointed, since the author's intention is to develop an over-all sense of direction for therapy rather than a complete system applicable to all clients. There is, of course, the question of which people would most benefit from this approach.

This same question must now honestly be asked about psychoanalytic psychotherapy. Studies of its results with many clients who seemed appropriate middle-class candidates for therapy as well as of persons in low-income groups have clearly indicated its gross ineffectiveness. It has had its successes too, but such studies raise radical questions about whether it is the most useful approach for our age. The entire community psychiatry movement is a vivid response to doubts about traditional methods and efforts toward new, creative approaches.

To what group of clients does Pollak refer when he speaks of "victims of anomie?"[12] Is there a difference between this group and those people who manifest anomic symptoms as a result of depressive conflict? Existential psychotherapy is not being suggested here as a cure-all, nor is it possible to say with assurance exactly what sorts of persons will benefit from it, any more than psychoanalytic practitioners can comfortably state this. May and Frankl have both expressed the view that the existential approach is more attuned to the problems of our age.[13] Fromm, sharing many of the existential concerns about the plight of modern man, has challenged the psychoanalytic approach

[11] Two books illustrating the existential-analytical view are Avery D. Weisman, MD, *The Existential Core of Psychoanalysis* (Boston: Little, Brown & Co., 1965); and J. F. T. Bugental, *The Search for Authenticity* (New York: Holt, Rinehart & Winston, 1965).

[12] *Op. cit.*

[13] Rollo May, ed., *Existential Psychology* (New York: Random House, 1961), p. 21. Viktor Frankl, *The Doctor and the Soul* (New York: Alfred A. Knopf, 1955), pp. 3–26.

on this same basis.[14] The reality-oriented psychotherapists (including Glasser, Ellis, Mowrer, and O'Connell) utilize techniques that are closely aligned with the existential treatment goals mentioned, and have worked successfully with neurotics, psychotics, and sociopaths. As early as 1933 Jung made the following relevant comments:

> A psycho-neurosis must be understood as the suffering of a human being who has not discovered what life means to him. . . . Among all my patients in the second half of life—that is to say, over thirty-five—there has not been one whose problem in the last resort was not that of finding a religious outlook on life. . . . This of course has nothing whatever to do with a particular creed or membership of a church. . . . Today this eruption of destructive forces has already taken place, and man suffers from it in spirit. . . . That is why we psychotherapists must occupy ourselves with problems which, strictly speaking, belong to the theologian. But we cannot leave these questions for theology to answer; the urgent, psychic needs of suffering people confront us with them day after day.[15]

AIDING THE PROCESS OF DISILLUSIONMENT

The major task with this goal is gradually to reveal to the patient the reality that the very way he goes about thinking of himself and relating to other people defeats his purpose. His efforts at self-assurance and manipulation of those to whom he wishes to be close are marked with inconsistencies and self-deceptions that result in alienation and the limited expression of his potentialities. Habit patterns are revealed to him that consistently distort reality in his daily living. This process is anxiety provoking, of course, and requires the accompanying nurture of the therapeutic relationship.

The therapist must be well trained and experienced in the knowledge and operation of self-deception. Perhaps his most direct acquaintance with this is to have undergone psychoanalysis or psychotherapy himself. A corresponding discipline occurs in those religious orders that require intense self-examination by priests, monks, and the like in a search for personal truth. It is perhaps unfortunate that modern Protestant seminaries have for the most part replaced such personal struggle and discipline with rational teaching of history and theory.

A therapist aims initially at understanding the specific, unique patterns his client uses in viewing and relating to his world of tasks and relationships and his sense of self-adequacy. It is often important to develop some historical picture of the client to identify the presence of early patterns that still carry over into his present life adjustment. The existence of these patterns is also identified in the way the patient relates to the therapist. Because of the therapist's ability to maintain himself as a free, authentic person in the therapeutic relationship, he fails to be manipulated by the client's habitual efforts, although his interest and understanding remain solid and intact. As a free person, the therapist has no egotistical investment in curing or failing to cure the client. He of-

---

[14] Erich Fromm, D. T. Suzuki, and Richard Demartino, *Zen Buddhism and Psychoanalysis* (New York: Evergreen Publishing Co., 1963), pp. 135–136.

[15] C. G. Jung, *Modern Man in Search of a Soul* (New York: Harcourt, Brace & Co., 1933), pp. 225, 229, and 241.

fers reality, with himself as a therapeutic agent, but the client must always realize that the choice between change and growth on the one hand and flight toward the security of habitual patterns on the other is his own.

This process of challenging a person's manner of viewing his problem (as well as his general life conduct) can be illustrated in part by the techniques used with an open-ended therapy group for alcoholics conducted by the author. An alcoholic who wishes to join the group is told quite directly at the beginning how his problem will be viewed. This is done in a brief individual orientation session with the therapist. The prospective group member is told that alcoholics usually drink for a specific reason and that reason has to do with feelings that are difficult to bear without the aid of alcohol. Such feelings result from the way he sees himself and also the manner in which he relates to those with whom he wishes to have a close relationship. To benefit from therapy he must abstain from alcohol so that he can experience the feelings behind his drinking and talk about them in the group. By being as open and honest as possible, the group can help him come to an understanding of his problems and change them, so that the suffering caused by inner feelings can be managed better or diminished. It is emphasized that alcoholics can be helped in different ways, but if the client wants group therapy he must accept this notion of the helping process.

In the course of therapy he will usually find opposition to his personal view of his problems. Such ideas as the alcoholic's being born this way, having an incurable disease, or being inherently weak or hopelessly dependent are simply not accepted by the group. What is stressed instead is that the alcoholic never learned appropriate and workable means of expressing and meeting his needs. The manipulative ritual with his spouse is a good example. The cycle of drinking, fighting, threatening separation, confessing failure and appealing for another chance during the hangover period, and the final acceptance by the martyred wife provide several elements of closeness. There is an exchange of feelings, including anger, hurt, despair, contrition, forgiveness, and refound hope. But the closeness is short lived and must be repeated because it fails to deal with the genuine daily relationship struggles between the marital partners.

During therapy it becomes increasingly apparent to the alcoholic that his efforts to control interactions with other group members are related to the specific view he has of himself as a person, which he feels obliged to maintain. Yet this image and his strivings to maintain it are the sources of both his failure at intimacy and his inability to satisfy his needs, as well as an infringement on his ability to think and express himself in new ways.

The following Zen story illustrates how a monk's view of others stemmed from his own self-image. A perceptive friend disillusions his self-complacency.

Following a heavy rain, two Zen monks were walking together along a muddy road. They came upon a dismayed young maiden in a quandary about how she might cross the road without soiling her low-hanging silk kimono. "Come on, girl," said one monk as he lifted her in his arms and carried her across. The two monks resumed their journey without a word to each other. Finally, at a temple at which they were lodging that evening the second monk could no longer restrain himself: "We monks don't go near females, especially not young and lovely ones.

It is dangerous. Why did you do that?" The first monk whimsically replied, "I left the girl there. Are you still carrying her?"[16]

CONFRONTING FREEDOM

In therapy the process of disillusionment dwells on the negative side of personality wherein values, attitudes, judgments, and behavior are revealed to be colored by childhood assumptions. This view of self is counterbalanced by an increasing awareness of the adult part of oneself, which is characterized by the freedom and responsibility available to a person in his daily functioning. Some basic ideas about the nature of the self and its capacity for freedom are stressed.

The self is never a fixed, closed, totally predetermined form; it is only a person's own fears and self-deceptions that make him think this is the case. Everyone is considered to be responsible in accordance with his age. Each is also a completely unique person unlike anyone who ever was or ever will be. His adult self is in a constant process of change and growth. The process of growth requires the ongoing assertion of freedom—the capacity to transcend what one has been before. A person chooses his future direction and utilizes his past knowledge and experiences as he relates to the present, deciding what is to emerge in him. He alone is responsible for his aspirations and whether he strives to fulfill them.

The person comes to see that while he is possessed by childhood strivings that seem to inhibit and interfere with his desired growth, this need not be accepted fatalistically. He chose these patterns as a child because of circumstances that at that time seemed to necessitate them. But as an adult he possesses the same freedom to choose differently and, because he is an adult, the circumstances are no longer the same. It is only his fear that seems to make them so. He can manage new reality-based judgments of situations and how he will respond to them. A certain detachment from identified childhood strivings will be required, and the resulting sense of uncertainty will be painful, yet as a human being he does possess the freedom to accomplish change. His sense of direction will arise entirely from his own unique assessment of the duties, responsibilities, and inner promptings in his daily life. A responsive relatedness to what is going on about him helps him respond to the adult needs and potential within him.

Therapy is partly the teaching of a basic skill: how one may choose a response that is different from the one prompted by identified childhood strivings and their accompanying feelings. It encourages a developing sensitivity to meaning and reality in the confronting therapeutic situation. The client is repeatedly faced with the fact that he does have some choice in the matter at hand, and many of his rationalizations to the contrary are based on his fear and need to maintain old props for security. Therapy, then, does not emphasize the nature of his early bondage that must be relived and changed through the handling of transference manifestations, nor is it viewed as a complete remaking of a person's basic character. Instead, it helps the client to identify actual reality-based choices in the present situation and find satisfaction by asserting himself

[16] Paul Reps, *Zen Flesh, Zen Bones* (Garden City, N.Y.: Anchor Books, Doubleday & Co., 1961), p. 18.

as a free being.[17] Consistent with the emphasis on the client's capacity to choose freely and decide his own direction from what lies within himself is the therapist's willingness to allow him to accept or reject therapeutic interpretations or suggestions. The therapist is not an authority on the specific manner in which a client is to choose and live his life, although he is an authority on the basic elements of the human condition and what this means with regard to the development of emotional disorders and the way toward growth and change.

A client's direct experience of his freedom to rise above the powerful negative driving forces in his daily life is a crucial therapeutic happening. Helping him to recognize choices he had hidden from himself is one way of accomplishing this. There may be many other ways that to date have not been explored and attempted in a sufficiently significant fashion.[18]

The logotherapy of Frankl includes a number of such examples. He sometimes utilizes humor and exaggeration of notions based on a client's neurotic assumptions about his own helpless condition. His aim is always to enable the client to acquire a new perspective on his symptoms and his own nature so that he does not continue to identify his total self with his neurotic symptoms, compulsions, or feelings. He also may suggest that a patient imagine himself to be twenty years older and review his present situation from that vantage point. The patient is able to identify instances in which more desirable choices might have been made by him "back then," and by so doing grasps the importance of the unique opportunity facing him at the present moment.[19]

Kondo, writing on "Zen in Psychotherapy," suggests as an adjunct to therapy the use of sitting meditation, which provides the patient with an experience of "single-mindedness"—an intuitive sense of the unity of body and mind that can enable him to detach himself from old childhood strivings bidding for present control.[20] The exercises of Gestalt psychology are aimed at a similar accomplishment.[21]

Another unique approach is Japan's *Morita* therapy. This is a therapy for hospitalized patients that is related to the philosophy of Zen Buddhism, which itself has many similarities to existentialism. Upon being hospitalized, a patient is placed in solitary confinement for the first several days, with only himself and his thoughts for company. He is asked to maintain a diary from the day of admission. Gradually he is permitted simple work activities and limited contact with a therapist. His range of contacts and tasks is slowly broadened and he begins to experience a sense of satisfaction in performing minor functions and relating to something other than himself. The nature of his problem is interpreted to him by the therapist, who has studied his diary. This interpretation has nothing to do with early trauma or deep insight into childhood relationships. Rather, it is aimed at emphasizing the foolishness and futility of the self-preoccupied existence the patient maintained until his hospitalization. It is further directed at arousing a sense of humility and genuine acceptance of his daily life circumstances as being not only bearable but an intrinsic vehicle for meaning and satisfaction,

---

[17] A detailed description of this technique is found in Richard L. Sutherland, "Choosing—As Therapeutic Aim, Method and Philosophy," *Journal of Existential Psychiatry,* Vol. 2, No. 8 (Spring 1962), pp. 371–392.

[18] One method utilizing casework techniques was described in Gerald K. Rubin, "Helping a Clinic Patient Modify Self-destructive Thinking," *Social Work,* Vol. 7, No. 1 (January 1962), pp. 76–80.

[19] Viktor Frankl, *The Doctor and the Soul* (New York: Alfred A. Knopf, 1957).

[20] Akihisa Kondo, "Zen in Psychotherapy: The Virtue of Sitting," *Chicago Review,* Vol. 12, No. 2 (Summer 1958).

[21] See Frederick S. Perls, Ralph F. Hefferline, and Paul Goodman, *Gestalt Therapy* (New York: Julian Press, 1951).

if he would only perform the tasks required of him instead of brooding over his unhappy lot in life. This treatment approach is continued until the patient is discharged from the hospital in anywhere from one to two months.

What is important in these approaches is the patient's developing awareness of a different aspect of himself—that part of him is beyond the control of childhood striving and compulsive feelings. This aspect of self can manage a perspective over his total self and situation and thereby direct his choices in new ways. This part of him is also adult, creative, and—most important—real. There are lessons to be learned here from the novelists and film-makers who depict men and women discovering new and critical perspectives of their lives. Dickens' *A Christmas Carol* is a classic example, as is Dostoevsky's *Crime and Punishment*. The same theme occurs in Bergman's film *Wild Strawberries* and Fellini's *8½*. In *La Strada* Fellini presents a delightful vignette in which the feeble-minded heroine of the film is confronted by the clown–high-wire artist in a moment of utter despair. He laughs at her troubled face and tells her how foolish it is to feel her life is completely meaningless. He picks up a pebble and tells her that even this serves some purpose—that if it did not, then there would be no purpose in the entire star-strewn heavens. This statement at this particular time resulted in a profound change in the young woman.

The root of one's hope and sense of dignity lies within the preservation of belief in one's freedom, as well as its assertion over and against the forces that seem determined to defeat one. This is quite apparent in the thinking of many alcoholics involved in the therapy group mentioned earlier. The commitment to abstinence from alcohol emphasized by Alcoholics Anonymous reflects the same idea. One alcoholic who has been "dry" for five years put it this way: "My choice is to drink again and face complete hopelessness or else to refuse alcohol and stand at least a fighting chance for happiness sometime." Here is commitment that accepts suffering and frustration without a guarantee of bliss. What is rewarding is the free and ongoing act of refusing to use alcohol as an escape.

As mentioned, in group therapy the notions about the alcoholic being some predetermined, unchangeable kind of being are challenged. It is important that group members sense the personal belief of the therapist in their capacity for freedom. The therapist must always go beyond the role of a sympathetic nursemaid to the "hopelessly sick and downtrodden."

A technique similar to some of Frankl's ideas was used effectively with this group. It had to do with handling the frustrations of one member as his assertive efforts at communication in the group continually failed. He could state his ideas openly until someone disagreed and requested that he clarify something. Then he experienced a blocking of thought that resulted in his having to back down. Next he would withdraw emotionally from the group and feel increasingly depressed at being overpowered by his own anxiety. It was pointed out that he had identified an important pattern within himself. While it was true that he could not control the rising feelings of anxiety and subsequent blocking, he did have control over how he reacted to this. On the one hand, he could give himself up to the notion that he was impotent and helpless and withdraw from any further efforts. On the other hand, he could strive to maintain attention to the continuing group discussion, so that when his anxiety subsided somewhat he could again assert any ideas he might have on some aspect of the discussion. When he was later able to do this, it was emphasized that he was not allowing the feelings to control him, but could find satisfaction in remaining the assertive kind of person he wanted to be in the group.

Repeated assertion that two parts of an individual can be identified—that which strives for new ways of thought, expression, and action and that which is fearful of this because of certain false assumptions about self and others based on childhood experiences—has been found to be quite meaningful to the group. The question that follows is: "Which of these two parts rules in you?"

DISCOVERING MEANING IN SUFFERING

The central theme in the writings of Dostoevsky and Kazantzakis is that suffering is an inherent part of life and one's growth as a person is dependent on acceptance of and being willing to grapple with this suffering. This same thesis must form a crucial part of psychotherapy. The therapeutic stance is that one can learn from one's suffering, but to do so one must bring it out into the open where it can be faced.

A client will seldom be thrown by the frightening and guilt-ridden aspect of himself if the therapist is not. The therapist must be willing to share the client's sufferings by simply being there, as Rogers emphasizes.[22] His acceptance and deep understanding of this suffering can be conveyed by avoidance of reassurance or easy solutions. He may occasionally reveal examples of his own or another's personal struggles, to emphasize that suffering is a shared human condition.[23] Therapeutic techniques are often used to help a person endure his suffering instead of becoming embittered by it or clinging to weak notions of how it may someday be replaced by pleasure and comfort.

In the group of alcoholics described, an important part of the discussion content is learning to read the underlying meanings in what a person presents. These may be expressions or descriptions of guilt, anxiety, anger, depression, somatic illnesses, or acting-out behavior. Essentially, it is some feeling or behavior that has troubled a person about himself. The group's effort, then, is to examine the factors surrounding the occurrence in order to discover its meaning. Perhaps the person's response was not only natural, but could be considered mature. On the other hand, it may reveal an important aspect of a person's problematic life pattern. Guilt may reveal the inhibition of growth potential in a situation or behavior that is seen as being in conflict with what the person feels he could or should be doing Anxiety may indicate that he has the potential to behave in a significantly different way but fears the consequences of so doing. Anger is often seen to be a way of blaming others for what are really one's own shortcomings. These concepts of common meanings associated with varying kinds of feelings soon become useful tools for group members to apply to themselves as well as to one another in subsequent meetings.

For example, a relatively new member of the group, 37 years old, commented that he

---

[22] Carl Rogers, "Becoming a Person," in Simon Doniger, ed., *Healing: Human and Divine* (New York: Association Press, 1957), p. 61.

[23] This openness by the therapist is described in Sidney M. Jourard, *The Transparent Self* (Princeton, N.J.: D, Van Nostrand Co., 1964), pp. 39–65. O. Hobart Mowrer also emphasizes such openness in his integrity therapy. A critique of his over-all approach is made by Donald F. Krill in "Psychoanalysis, Mowrer and the Existentialists," *Pastoral Psychology*, Vol. 16 (October 1965), pp. 27–36.

was operating at "low gear" and could see no reason for this other than what he had once been told by a psychiatrist—that he must constantly punish himself because his parents had always been critical of him. Another group member inquired when the depression had become more apparent to him. The onset was pinned down to the previous Saturday night when he had wanted to go to a movie with his wife, who had encouraged him to go alone since she wanted to do her hair that evening. He had accepted this and gone alone. Further questioning by the group led him to see his disappointment and annoyance and his failure to let his wife know what he was feeling. Because he was afraid to show his own needs to her he had avoided any effort either toward changing her decision or attaining a closer understanding with her. The result was loneliness, resentment, and guilt over his own passivity. This incident revealed a pattern in their marital relationship related to his own fear of being hurt if he exposed a dependency need.

Then there is the type of suffering that either must be endured for a long time—perhaps for life—or else evaded by drinking: loneliness and a sense of emptiness, often accompanied by bitterness and envy. The person may have no friends or spouse, or a spouse who resists all efforts at a more intimate relationship. Perhaps the alcoholic, despite his efforts, finds himself unable to be more open and direct even within the therapy group. Here the only creative effort possible may be the continued endurance of suffering. It is natural to envy those whose upbringing, capacities, and circumstances have resulted in a far easier adaptation to life. Yet to endure suffering can still be meaningful. For some it will be a gesture of faith that relates them to a divine force or power. For others it will be a way of remaining true to the human condition—refusing false havens. For still others it will be a means of relating to the fraternity of alcoholics, who often find courage and hope in the continued sobriety of their brothers.

Suffering is a human reality not to be seen as a meaningless, chaotic disruption of a person's life. There is no pleasure principle norm that says to suffer is to be out of kilter with life. The opposite is the case—to live is to accept suffering. Its acceptance depends on some understanding of its hidden meaning—often seeing it as a guide toward potential growth. Suffering gives direction to one's freedom.

REALIZING THE NECESSITY OF DIALOGUE

All that has been said with regard to disillusionment, freedom, and suffering would be no more than empty thoughts without the nourishment of dialogue. Creative growth and change are seldom intellectual decisions activated by willpower alone. The supportive sense of intimacy and relatedness involved here does not apply only to the therapeutic relationship. As mentioned, it may be an experience of unity with a deity, with fellow alcoholics, or with the human condition.

What must take place in the dialogue of therapy is revelation by the client of what is unique within himself, to which the therapist responds with interest, concern, acceptance, and validation of the client's feelings about himself. This does not, of course, mean continuing approval, but the willingness of the therapist to grasp and understand what is being revealed, even in the throes of disagreement. Increasing directness and openness of communication are therefore necessary. Also required is the lessening of manipulative efforts to control the relationship. There is a risk in allowing another person to respond to one freely. When a person ceases his efforts to control another's image of him, he often experiences a feeling of extreme panic, for his sense of self seems to be at the mercy of another's unknown response. Yet true dialogue requires this, and one of the most significant accomplishments in therapy is for two persons to be authentic and free in relation to one another. This, of course, requires that the therapist reveal himself as a human being with feelings, thoughts, and spontaneity.[24] The client must come to see himself as co-equal with the therapist by virtue of his humanity, and the therapist, to encourage this, must be adept at avoiding the client's efforts to control him.

The capacities both to trust and verbalize are inseparable from such dialogue. Clients will therefore vary in their ability to relate in the way described, and the therapist must carefully assess the modifiability of the client. For some people an effort to change meaningful relationships will be the goal sought. For others a more open dialogue with the therapist alone will be the only effort to implement this necessary aspect of the human condition.[25]

Group and family therapy are excellent proving grounds for examining methods of communication and the reason for failures of dialogue. In the group of alcoholics again, from time to time the specific ingredients of dialogue are structured. There is the initiator and the listener. Courage is often required to initiate a problem, for the response of others is uncertain. Courage is again needed by the listener in his attempt to develop the picture the initiator has begun through sincere curiosity. Responses such as advice-giving, early intellectual interpretations, and silence are frequently identified as defenses against a closer involvement with the initiator's problem. Genuine interest and an effort to understand more deeply may lead the listener to disagree with or challenge the initiator, with the accompanying threat of conflict. It may also lead the initiator to expect to receive a satisfactory solution to his problem from the listener, which the listener is fearful he may not be able to produce. On the other hand, the initiator may feel obliged to accept a listener's advice—even though he is doubtful of its applicability—and be silent in an effort to avoid conflict and the risk of displeasing others in their efforts to be of help.

The fears mentioned in efforts at dialogue can often be clarified in such a way that an individual will see and experience the fact that his very maneuvers to preserve a specific self-image negate the possibility of closeness. To become aware of this is also to realize the self-destructive aspects of one's manipulation of others. One may be more secure through feeling one has control of another person, but for genuine love and closeness to occur, the other must be allowed freedom of response. A gesture of love from another whom one feels one has successfully manipulated can be little more than emotional masturbation. One's own growth and knowledge of oneself is also dependent on the free assessment of others whose view is naturally different in some respects from one's own. To resist another's free opinion is to close off an opportunity for personal growth.

---

[24] The concept of therapeutic openness and authenticity is well developed in Helen E. Durkin, *The Group in Depth* (New York: International Universities Press, 1964), sect. 2, pp. 249–276.

[25] A differentiation of therapy goals in accord with categories of client modifiability is described in Donald F. Krill, "A Framework for Determining Client Modifiability," *Social Casework*, Vol. 49, No. 10 (December 1968), pp. 602–611.

ACCEPTING THE WAY OF COMMITMENT

The way of commitment refers to a loyalty to those realities of the human condition one has discovered to be true and meaningful for oneself. The basis for a new philosophy is found in the realization of the nature and pattern of certain childhood strivings and a disillusionment with some previous way of achieving self-security; recognition that there is a part of oneself that is adult, free, and spontaneous; the finding of ongoing direction and a sense of meaning in one's sufferings; and finally through experiencing some possibility of genuine, sincere intimacy with another. As members of the described group of alcoholics stay on in therapy, these reality factors often become part of their lives as is manifested in the framework within which they use therapy sessions and relate to one another's problems. Gradually they have integrated elements of a new lifestyle.

It is helpful to think in terms of a model of the committed and authentic person as representing the ideal result of an acceptance of the existential realities described in this paper. While such a model would not be an expectation for all patients, it does add clarity and direction to our thinking. The characteristics are the opposite of those describing the state of anomie. One's sense of self is not seen as fixed, determined, or able to be constructed and secured by some set of achievements that prove one adequate because others finally recognize and applaud one. Rather, one's sense of self, as a narcissistic ego, is laughed at for its foolish and self-defeating strivings. Humor—as the capacity to laugh at oneself—is a natural characteristic. The self is seen now as having an ongoing relation to the world, constantly changing as new situations arise, forever being tapped by new possibilities, suspicious of the self-satisfaction that can lead to rigidity. The self as the center of attention and fortification increasingly is lost and replaced by a more avid interest in others, the tasks of one's daily life, and the beauty and wonder of the world about us. As the young English friend of Zorba the Greek said of him, "Zorba sees everything every day as if for the first time."[26] As one disciplines oneself away from self-clinging and delusional attachments to childhood strivings, a creative spontaneity unfolds that is invested in many aspects of one's life—not focused in one isolated area of achievement.

This new state of self is similar to the mindlessness and nothingness in Zen Buddhism, meaning that the mind operates freely without attachment. The inflow of intuitive response with this state of mindlessness is illustrated in a Zen tale of a young man who wanted to learn the art of swordsmanship and apprenticed himself to a master swordsman. He was, however, disappointed when he was refused permission even to hold a sword, but instead had to prepare his master's meals and perform various chores. As the student went about these chores he was periodically assaulted by his master, who would suddenly appear and hit him with a stick. The student was told to defend himself, but every time he prepared for an assault from one direction, it would come from another. Finally, in utter confusion and helplessness, he gave up his hyper-alertness. It was only then that he could intuitively sense the direction of the next attack and defend himself adequately. This is a practice of discipline in certain forms of personal combat in Japan even today.

---

[26] Nikos Kazantzakis, *Zorba the Greek* (New York: Simon & Schuster, 1959), p. 51.

This turnabout way of viewing the self is also the essence of true religious conversion. In religious terms, the self becomes detached from the idols of past devotion and is related now to the will of God, viewing the tasks and relationships of daily life as calling forth a response from oneself that in turn accomplishes a sense of divine unity in the act of free, open, and giving relatedness.

Buber describes this turnabout experience as a change from a reacting "I-it" relation to the world to a responding "I-Thou" relation. Instead of using people in one's environment as objects to support and gratify a self-image, one "enters into relation with the other," whatever form this might take, and such a contact is characterized by awe, respect, care, and creative response.[27] Tillich speaks of this experience as discovering the "courage to be" as a result of experiencing oneself as "being grasped by the power of Being itself." As one feels that one's most ego-gratifying strivings are illusory and false, one also has a sense of being affirmed as worthy and acceptable in spite of the fact that such acceptance has not been earned by the energy expended in these false strivings. The acceptance of this affirmative experience allows one to carry out one's daily tasks with a lessened need for the old security striving. One's "acceptance of being accepted" is seen to be a reunion with the transcendent power of Being that gives meaning to life.[28]

A nonreligious discussion of this same theme is found in Frankl's logotherapy, which is designed to arouse an awareness of the "task character of life." This concept is developed by using the realities of the patient's everyday life. Considering such factors as family background, the nature of time, awareness of death, ever changing circumstances, and ever changing personality, the therapist emphasizes that every person is singular, is unique. Not only will there never be another like him but even the exact circumstances of a momentary situation will never again be precisely the same, so that each decision possesses uniqueness. He is free to respond to the moment at hand, and when he grasps the tremendous sense of responsibility that goes with his uniqueness (which he bears sole responsibility for shaping), then his daily tasks take on a special meaning never before experienced. When he has truly reached this stage, he loses his self-preoccupation in a new sense of responsible relatedness to daily happenings. This might be labeled a new form of self-concern, but the essential difference is that the direction is outward—giving, doing, creating, and enduring—rather than inwardly striving, securing, protecting, and possessing.

A significant portion of Frankl's logotherapeutic technique is designed to enlighten a patient about the kinds of values or possibilities that seem to await realization or actualization in his concrete life circumstance. Values are seen to be creative, experiential, and attitudinal in nature and vary, of course, with the patient. Creative values may refer to work tasks or even to those that may be artistic or athletic. Experiential values have to do with enjoyment of the world about one and this includes the closeness of an interaction in personal relationships. Attitudinal values are those that can be realized as one accepts and endures suffering that is unavoidable or unchangeable. From this per-

---

[27] The best critique of Buber's thought is found in Maurice S. Friedman, *Martin Buber: The Life of Dialogue* (New York: Harper & Bros. 1959).

[28] Paul Tillich, *The Courage To Be* (New Haven: Yale University Press, 1952).

spective, it is apparent that some values can be identified as real and meaningful for any patient, regardless of the nature of his limits and circumstances.[29]

Mowrer and Glasser state that the key factor in therapy is helping a patient identify for himself clearly how he believes he ought to behave—what values seem important to him personally. He can then identify how his actual decisions and behavior are at odds with the way he wants to be. The necessity of changed behavior is stressed, regardless of the feelings involved, in order to bring about the person's increased acceptance of himself as worthy and hence as acceptable to others. Self-pity and self-preoccupation are replaced by identification of one's value and by commitment.[30]

CONCLUSION

The problem of anomie should be seen as a way of life in itself that must be countered by philosophical efforts that become meaningful through the process of psychotherapy. Existentialism is an especially useful philosophical base because it draws its central themes from man's immediate experience of his life. Its emphases on disillusionment, freedom, suffering, authentic relationships, and commitment deal directly with their opposites, which are characteristics of anomie. Existentialism should not be considered a completed philosophical system, but rather a series of emphasized realities that can be adapted to other forms of philosophy and religious belief, depending on the background and thought of the individual therapist.

A danger in the misuse of psychoanalytic thought is the reduction of man to primitive animal drives. Notions of chaos and determinism prevail in this attitude about man's nature, and the resulting pleasure principle goal for people is simply insufficient for those experiencing anomie. The process, common among many psychoanalytically oriented therapists, of classifying and categorizing symptoms and behavioral expressions according to a system based on the primacy of animal drives accentuates this very problem. This process is viewed as "scientific" because it is wholly materialistic, but it is not scientific at all. The belief in the primacy of animal drives is as much a faith as the assumptions espoused in existentialism and other humanistic psychologies.

For the existentialists, man's biological drives are important and must be understood, but they do not fully explain man's nature. As a matter of fact, emphasis on the primacy of instinctual drives is a way of viewing human beings at their minimum level of functioning rather than their maximum level. At this maximum level man has freedom, the power to transcend his egotistical strivings, courage to venture, and a capacity to endure. The spirit is available to men, but they must sometimes seek it out to become aware of its existence. Kazantzakis, in *The Last Temptation of Christ,* expressed the nature of this spirit by proclaiming man as the being who gives wings to matter.

Freud was reported to have said to Binswanger, the existentialist psychoanalyst: "Yes, the spirit is everything. . . . Mankind has always known that it possesses spirit; I had to show it that there are also instincts."[31] Freud's contribution has been immense

---

[29] Frankl, *op. cit.*
[30] O. Hobart Mowrer, *The Crisis in Psychiatry and Religion* (Princeton, N.J.: D. Van Nostrand Co., 1961); William Glasser, *Reality Therapy: A New Approach to Psychiatry* (New York: Harper & Row, 1965).
[31] Ludwig Binswanger, *Sigmund Freud: Reminiscences of a Friendship* (New York: Grune & Stratton, 1957), p. 81.

and he responded honestly and courageously to what he viewed as the problems of his society. But the repression of sexuality, with its resulting neuroses, is not the most common problem in our modern society of *Playboy,* the Hollywood love goddesses, and birth control. To reestablish meaning and direction in people's lives there is a need in the psychotherapeutic method for philosophical guidance and value education. By leaving this up to the church a therapist is being blind to the essential function of therapy for anomic man. This presents an identity problem for many therapists who have long been fond of criticizing and belittling the church, for now, as therapists, they are called on to serve patients in the very way in which for centuries the church has attempted to serve them.

BURNOUT

CHAPTER 54

CONCEPTUALIZING AND PREVENTING BURN-OUT

Charles Zastrow

Ron Pakenham is ten days behind in his paperwork. He has been a juvenile probation and parole officer for the past three and a half years. Both the agency director and the juvenile judge are putting pressure on him to do his paperwork. Mr. Pakenham is also having problems at home. His mother has emphysema, and he and his wife are going through a divorce. While working on his paperwork he receives a call from a houseparent at a group home for adolescent youths, inquiring when high school is starting in the fall. (Mr. Pakenham is supervising two teenage boys at this home.) Mr. Pakenham replies "Hey, I don't know. You'll have to call the school system. I'm not your errand boy. Don't you know I have more important things to do than hunt for information for you." After hanging up the phone, Mr. Pakenham considers his aggressive response. He also thinks about his family problems, and about being behind in his work. Mr. Pakenham realizes he is nearing burn-out.

DEFINITIONS AND SYMPTOMS OF BURN-OUT

Burnout is increasingly recognized as a serious problem, one which affects many people, particularly professionals employed in human services. Pines and Aronson define burn-out as being:

> . . . a state of mind . . . accompanied by an array of symptoms that include a general malaise: emotional, physical, and psychological fatigue; feelings of helpless-

From *The Social Worker,* Vol. 52, No. 2 (Summer 1984), pp. 57–61. Reprinted here with the permission of *The Social Worker/Le Travailleur social.*

ness, hopelessness, and a lack of enthusiasm about work and even about life in general.[1]

Maslach and Pines have studied burn-out among the following professional groups: social workers, psychiatrists, psychologists, prison personnel, psychiatric nurses, legal aid attorneys, physicians, child care workers, teachers, ministers, and counselors. Maslach and Pines define burn-out and summarize a number of symptoms:

> Burn-out involves the loss of concern for the people with whom one is working. In addition to physical exhaustion (and sometimes even illness), burn-out is characterized by an emotional exhaustion in which the professional no longer has any positive feelings, sympathy, or respect for clients or patients. A very cynical and dehumanized perception of these people often develops, in which they are labeled in derogatory ways and treated accordingly. As a result of this dehumanizing process, these people are viewed as somehow deserving of their problems and are blamed for their own victimization,[2] and thus there is a deterioration in the quality of care or service that they receive. The professional who burns out is unable to deal successfully with the overwhelming emotional stresses of the job, and this failure to cope can be manifested in a number of ways, ranging from impaired performance and absenteeism to various types of personal problems (such as alcohol and drug abuse, marital conflict, and mental illness). People who burn out often quit their jobs or even change professions, while some seek psychiatric treatment for what they believe to be their personal failings.[3]

Freudenberger describes the symptoms of burn-out:

> Briefly described, burn-out includes such symptoms as cynicism and negativism and a tendency to be inflexible and almost rigid in thinking, which often leads to a closed mind about change or innovation. The worker may begin to discuss the client in intellectual and jargon terms and thereby distance himself from any emotional involvement. Along with this, a form of paranoia may set in whereby the worker feels that his peers and administration are out to make life more difficult.[4]

BURN-OUT AS A REACTION TO HIGH STRESS

The term "burn-out" has been applied to many different situations. A student who has been writing a term paper for three hours may feel "burned-out" with writing but have

---

[1] Ayala M. Pines and Elliot Aronson, *Burnout: From Tedium to Personal Growth,* New York, The Free Press, 1981, p. 3.
[2] W. Ryan, *Blaming The Victim,* New York, Pantheon Books, 1971, pp. 2–27.
[3] Christina Maslach and Ayala Pines, "The Burn-Out Syndrome in the Day Care Setting," *Child Care Quarterly,* Vol. 6, 1977, pp. 100–101.
[4] Herbert Freudenberger, "Burn-Out: Occupational Hazard of the Child Care Worker," *Child Care Quarterly,* Vol. 6, 1977, pp. 90–91.

plenty of energy to do something else. Individuals who abuse their spouse or children may attempt to explain their actions by claiming that they are under considerable stress and "just burned-out." People who become apathetic and cynical about a frustrating job may claim they are "burned-out." Some sport coaches claim the pressure to win is so great that after several seasons they feel "burned-out." A person in an unhappy romantic relationship may feel "burned-out."

The term "burned-out" is closely related to, and has not been adequately differentiated from, the following terms: alienation, indifference, apathy, cynicism, discouragement, and mental or physical exhaustion.

In order to better understand the nature of burn-out, it is useful to conceptualize it as one reaction to high levels of stress. The advantage to this conceptualization is that it suggests that stress management strategies can be used to prevent burn-out, or to treat burn-out if it does occur.

Stress is a contributing causal factor in most illnesses, including heart attacks, migraine headaches, diabetes, allergies, colds, cancer, arthritis, insomnia, emphysema, hypertension and alcoholism.[5] Stress is also a contributing factor in numerous emotional and behavioral difficulties, including depression, anxiety, suicide attempts, spouse abuse, child abuse, physical assaults, irritability and stuttering.[6] Becoming skillful in reducing stress is now recognized as an effective way to prevent emotional and physical disorders, and as an effective adjunct to the treatment of existing disorders.[7]

Stress can be defined as the emotional and physiological reaction to stressors. A stressor is a demand, situation or circumstance which upsets a person's equilibrium and causes the stress response. There is an infinite number of possible stressors: crowding, noise, death of a friend, excessive cold, loss of a job, toxic substances, arguments, and so on.

Hans Selye, one of the foremost authorities on stress, has found that the body has a three-stage reaction to stress; a) the alarm stage; b) the resistance stage; and c) the exhaustion stage.[8] Selye called this three-stage response the General Adaptation Syndrome.

In the alarm stage the body recognizes the stressor, an argument, for example. The body reacts to the stressor by preparing for fight or flight. The body's reactions are complex and numerous, and are only briefly summarized here.[9] The body sends message from the brain (hypothalmus) to the pituitary gland and instructs it to release its hormones. These hormones cause the adrenal glands to release adrenaline. Adrenaline increases the rate of breathing and heartbeat, increases perspiration, raises blood sugar level, dilates the pupils, and slows digestion. This process results in a huge burst of energy, better hearing and vision and greater muscular strength—all reactions that increase a person's capability to fight or flee.

In the second stage of resistance the body seeks to return to normal. During this stage the body repairs any damage caused during the alarm stage. Most stressors result

---

[5] Walter McQuade and Ann Aikman, *Stress,* New York, Bantam Books, 1974, pp. 27–93.
[6] Herbert M. Greenberg, *Coping with Job Stress,* Englewood Cliffs, New Jersey, Spectrum, 1980, pp. 39–49.
[7] Kenneth R. Pelletier, *Mind as Healer, Mind as Slayer,* New York, Dell Publishing Co., 1977, pp. 12–34.
[8] Hans Selye, *The Stress of Life,* New York, McGraw-Hill, 1956.
[9] For an extended discussion of the physiological reactions involved in the stress reaction see Walter McQuade and Ann Aikman, *Stress, op. cit.*

in the body going through the stages of alarm and repair only. During a lifetime, a person goes through these two stages thousands of times. Much stress is beneficial. Stress increases concentration and the ability to accomplish physical tasks. A life without stress would be boring; in fact, since even dreaming produces some stress, a life without stress is impossible.

The type of stress which causes long-term damage results when the body remains in a state of high stress for an extended period of time. When this happens, the body is unable to repair itself, and the third stage—exhaustion—occurs. If exhaustion persists, individuals are apt to develop one or more diseases of stress, such as ulcers, hypertension, or arthritis.

A number of authorities have noted that stressors have two components: a) events or experiences which happen to a person, and b) that person's thoughts and perceptions about these events and experiences.[10] Table 54–1 presents a conceptualization of stressors, stress, and stress-related illnesses.

This conceptualization views burn-out as one of a number of possible reactions to high levels of continued stress. As suggested in above Table, *burn-out is caused primarily by what people tell themselves about events or experiences.*

Table 54–1
Burn-Out as a Reaction to High Stress

Stressors		
Events or Experiences:	for example, extensive paperwork, or considerable turmoil in family life	
Certain kinds of stressful thinking which lead to:		
Burn-out:	"This is overwhelming. I've had it. Just leave me alone. This is more than I can take."	
Stress		
Emotions:	The emotions identified with burn-out—anxiety, frustration, anger, apathy and so on.	
Physiological Reactions:	The alarm and exhaustion stages of the General Adaptation Syndrome.	These emotions, reactions, and actions constitute BURN-OUT
Actions:	The actions characteristic of burn-out: lack of respect for others; cynicism toward life; decreased attention to work and family life; absenteeism, change of jobs, and so on.	

[10] Donald A. Tubesing, *Kicking Your Stress Habits,* Duluth, Minnesota, Whole Persons Associates, 1981.

STRUCTURAL CAUSES OF STRESS WHICH MAY LEAD TO BURN-OUT

As indicated, burn-out is one of the possible reactions to or consequences of high stress. It follows that events which contribute to high stress levels may also contribute to burn-out.

Edelwich has identified a number of structural factors associated with work which contribute to stress and may lead to burn-out.[11]

- too many work hours
- career dead-end
- too much paperwork
- not sufficiently trained for job
- not appreciated by clients
- not appreciated by supervisor
- not paid enough money
- no support for important decisions
- powerlessness
- system not responsive to clients' needs
- bad office politics
- sexism
- too much travel
- isolation from peers
- no social life

Edelwich adds that people who seek a career in the helping professions are particularly vulnerable to burn-out since many enter these professions with unrealistic expectations. They may expect, for example, that: a) the services they provide will decisively improve the lives of almost all their clients; b) they will be highly appreciated by their employing agency and almost all their clients; c) they will be able to substantially change bureaucracies and make them more responsive to clients' needs; and d) there will be many opportunities for rapid advancement and high status. The frustrations experienced at work, and the gradual recognition that many of their expectations are unrealistic, contribute to stress and burn-out.

Maslach has found high case loads in the helping professions are a major cause of stress and burnout:

> Burn-out often becomes inevitable when the professional is forced to provide care for too many people. As the ratio increases, the result is higher and higher emotional overload until, like a wire that has too much electricity flowing through it, the worker just burns out and emotionally disconnects.[12]

Approved time-outs at work may help reduce stress and prevent burn-out. Time-outs are not merely short coffee breaks from work, but opportunities for professionals

[11] Jerry Edelwich, *Burn-Out,* New York, Human Sciences Press, 1980, pp. 27–54.
[12] Christina Maslach, "Burned-Out," *Human Behavior,* September, 1976, p. 19.

having a stressful day to switch to less stressful tasks. Time-outs are possible in large agencies that have shared-work responsibilities.

Additional causes of burn-out include poor time management, inability to work effectively with other people, undefined goals or lack of purpose in life, and an inability to handle emergencies.[13]

Clients may also be a factor in staff burn-out.[14] Certain clients are more apt to cause high levels of stress, particularly those whose problems are depressing or emotionally draining: for example, terminally ill clients, belligerent clients, suicidal clients, obnoxious clients, and clients presenting problems related to incest or abuse. Working with "chronic" clients who show no improvement (such as an alcoholic family in which the problem drinker denies a drinking problem) is also more apt to lead to staff frustration and stress. Dealing with clients who remind workers of their own difficulties is also emotionally draining: e.g., workers having marital problems of their own may find it difficult to provide marriage counseling.

Another factor contributing to high stress and burn-out at work is excessive family responsibility (taking care of a terminally ill parent, for example). Extensive responsibilities at home can exhaust a worker and lead to burn-out both at home and at work.

In the helping professions, stress can be caused by taking on "ownership" of a client's problems. When a client tells a worker his or her secrets and problems, the worker tends to want to rescue and save that client. Helping professionals, especially in their first years of practice, are apt to fall victim to the rescue or savior fantasy. This fantasy leads the professional to believe he or she has the power to make clients' lives better. When this does not happen, the worker is apt to feel emotionally drained and "burned out."

APPROACHES TO MANAGING STRESS AND PREVENTING BURN-OUT

The following is a brief description of approaches useful in reducing stress and preventing burn-out. A wide variety (a "smorgasbord") of approaches is reviewed. It is up to the individual to select the ones he or she believes are most appropriate and attractive. These approaches are similar to healthy diet plans—they *will* work for those who make an effort to make them work.

Goal Setting and Time Management: It is distressing to lack certainty about what one wants from life. Many people muddle through without ever setting goals, but feel unfulfilled, frustrated, bored, or dissatisfied. Realistic goal-setting leads to increased self-confidence, improved decision-making, and a greater sense of purpose and security.

Considerable stress comes from a feeling of having "too much to do in too little time." Time is life: to waste time is to waste life.

Time management encourages people to set goals and use their time effectively in reaching short-term and lifetime objectives.[15] (Though the process of setting goals is

[13] Ayala Pines and Elliot Aronson, *Burnout: From Tedium to Personal Growth, op. cit.,* pp. 63–81.
[14] Christina Maslach, "The Client Role in Staff Burnout," *Journal of Social Issues,* 1978, Vol. 34, pp. 111–124.
[15] Alan Lakein, *How to Get Control of Your Time and Your Life,* New York, Signet, 1973.

often lengthy, failure to set goals almost guarantees dissatisfaction and a lack of fulfill-ment.) For high priority short-term and lifetime goals, subjects are often asked to list tasks designed to accomplish these goals. These tasks are then prioritized according to importance; subjects are instructed to do the high priority tasks first and are urged to ignore the low priority (low payoff) tasks. Low priority tasks can bog one down and in-terfere with high priority tasks.

Positive Thinking: Everyone has a choice between a negative view of events and a pos-itive view. People prone to burn-out tend to take the negative view and to tell them-selves: "I've had it. I'm no longer going to try. I'm just going to go through the motions. I'm giving in." With such an attitude, they become cynical, apathetic, uncaring and un-productive.

The philosophy of positive thinking asserts that a positive view and positive action will lead to: being liked by others, being appreciated, feeling worthwhile, liking oneself, being productive and creative, having a pleasant disposition, and having good things happen.[16]

Closely related to positive thinking is a philosophy of life which allows one to travel through life at a relaxed speed, to remain calm during crises and emergencies, to ap-proach work thoughtfully and creatively, to enjoy leisure, and to develop more fully as a person.

Rational therapy has demonstrated that the primary cause of our emotions and ac-tions is what we tell ourselves about our experiences.[17] Although often we cannot change the situations we encounter, we have the power to think rationally and posi-tively and to change *all* our unwanted emotions and unproductive actions, including the emotions and actions associated with burn-out.[18] For example, thoughts which pro-duce burn-out can be challenged and changed by telling ourselves: "I'm not going to give up. To give up will only hurt me and other people. I've handled challenges in the past and I can and will be able to handle this. Instead of thinking negatively, I've got to work on things constructively, one step at a time. When the going gets tough, I get going."

Relaxation Techniques: People who burn out tend to remain at high levels of stress for prolonged periods. They have not learned to relax. There are a number of relaxation techniques which induce the relaxation response: deep breathing relaxation, imagery relaxation, progressive muscle relaxation, meditation, self-hypnosis, and biofeed-back.[19] This article will examine just one of these techniques, meditation.

Numerous meditative techniques are practiced today. Herbert Benson has identified four elements common to meditative approaches which induce the relaxation re-sponse.[20] The first element is "a quiet environment" free of external distractions. The

---

[16] Robert Ringer, *Looking Out for #1,* New York, Fawcett Crest, 1977; and Robert Schuller, *Move Ahead with Possibility Thinking,* Moonachie, New Jersey, Pyramid Publications, 1973.
[17] Albert Ellis and Robert Harper, *A New Guide to Rational Living,* North Hollywood, California, Wilshire Book Co., 1977.
[18] For examples demonstrating how to change negative and irrational thinking see Charles Zastrow, *Talk to Your-self,* Englewood Cliffs, New Jersey, Prentice-Hall, 1979.
[19] All of these relaxation techniques are described in Charles Zastrow, *Talk to Yourself, op. cit.*
[20] Herbert Benson, *The Relaxation Response,* New York, Avon Books, 1975.

second element is "a comfortable position." The third element is "an object to dwell on," a word, phrase, chant, sound, image from an exquisite painting, etc. Since any neutral word or phrase will work, Benson suggests repeating silently the word "ONE." The fourth element is a passive attitude in which one stops thinking about day-to-day concerns. Benson states that achieving a passive attitude appears to be the key element in prompting the relaxation response. Meditation seems to induce the relaxation response by stopping us from thinking about day-to-day concerns.

Exercise: Regular exercise also helps reduce stress and prevent burn-out. An enjoyable exercise program assists in a variety of ways. It helps keep us fit—which makes us feel good about ourselves—and also gives us increased energy for meeting crises and emergencies. It helps take our minds off negative aspects of job and home life and directly reduces stress. As mentioned earlier, under stress the body prepares to engage in large muscle activity; through exercising we use up fuel in the blood, reduce heart rate and blood pressure, and set off other physiological reactions which reduce stress and induce the relaxation response.[21]

There are several other things involved in taking care of our physical selves: a nutritious diet, sufficient sleep, and appropriate medical care. Being in good physical condition helps us to handle stresses and emergencies, and thereby decreases the chances of burn-out.

Special Interests and Activities: Hobbies and entertainment also get our thinking off the negative aspects of work and homelife and encourage positive thoughts, thus reducing stress and helping to prevent burn-out. In this connection it is interesting to note that research indicates that "stress reduces stress"; that is, an appropriate amount of stress in one area (in a hobby, for example) helps reduce excessive stress in others.[22]

Pleasurable Goodies: Goodies make us feel good, change our pace, relieve stress, and are "personal therapies." They add spice to life, and serve as reminders that we have value. Different people want different goodies. Goodies may be traveling, listening to music, laughing, being hugged, shopping, sitting in a tub of warm water, or having an exotic drink. Goodies help to "recharge our batteries."

Goodies can be used to reward ourselves. Most of us would not hesitate to compliment others for jobs done well; similarly, we should not hesitate to reward ourselves for successfully accomplishing tasks.

Taking a mental health day is a goody that should not be overlooked. When under extended stress, take a day off and do only the things you want to do. (Some agencies now allow employees to take a certain number of mental health days with pay). Mental health days help people suffering from high stress to relax and recover their balance.

Social Support Systems: Developing trusting and caring relationships at work will result in a "life-line" support system. Maslach notes:

---

[21] Herbert M. Greenberg, *Coping with Job Stress, op. cit.,* pp. 22–47.
[22] Walt Schafer, *Stress, Distress and Growth,* Davis, California, International Dialogue Press, 1978.

Our findings show that burnout rates are lower for those professionals who actively express, analyze and share their personal feelings with their colleagues. Not only do they consciously get things off their chest, but they have an opportunity to receive constructive feedback from other people and to develop new perspectives of their relationship with patients/clients. This process is greatly enhanced if the institution sets up some social outlets such as support groups, special staff meetings or workshops.[23]

Social support groups (at work or outside work) allow people to let their hair down, "kid around," share their lives, keep in touch, and have a source of security and help when crises arise. There are a variety of possible support groups: co-workers, sport or hobby groups, family, church groups, and community organizations such as Parents Without Partners. In the successful support group: a) the group meets regularly; b) the same people attend; c) a feeling of closeness develops; and d) there is opportunity for spontaneity and informality.[24]

Variety at Work: Doing the same thing, such as paperwork, for long periods of time is exhausting. It is particularly important to recognize that work which is emotionally draining (suicide counseling or hospice work, for example) can only be done for a limited time; if limits aren't set, burn-out will occur. Therefore it is important to structure a job in such a way that it includes a variety of tasks each week. "Variety is the spice of life." A useful way of adding variety and helping staff grow is to promote workshops, conferences, continuing education courses, and in-service training programs.

Humor: Humor relaxes us, makes work more enjoyable, and takes the edge off intense emotional situations. Recognizing and using humor at work and home relieves stress and helps prevent burn-out.

Changing or Adapting to Distressing Events: There is an infinite number of distressing "events": an unfulfilling job, the death of someone close, the end of a romantic relationship, unresolved religious questions, an unwanted pregnancy, and so on. When these events occur, it is important to confront them head on and improve the situation.

For example, if you feel you are beginning to burn out at work, it is important to identify the causes and to develop special ways of handling these things. One staff member may find working with incest cases particularly exhausting, while another may find working with the terminally ill to be most difficult; perhaps they can exchange cases.

If a worker is frustrated because program objectives and job expectations are unclear, these need to be discussed with the worker's supervisor and efforts made to clarify objectives and expectations. While most distressing situations can be changed, some cannot be. For example, you may not be able to change certain distasteful aspects of

---

23 Christina Maslach, "Burned-Out", *op. cit.,* p. 22.
24 Herbert M. Greenberg, "Support Groups" in *Coping with Job Stress, op. cit.,* pp. 142–145.

your job. If this is the case, the only constructive alternative is to accept them. There is no point in getting upset and complaining about a situation you cannot change.

SUMMARY

Burn-out is a major problem among professionals, especially human service workers. People who burn out have a high incidence of emotional and physical problems. Agencies and clients are shortchanged by professionals who burn out.

The causes of burn-out are high stress levels, high case loads, lack of approved time-outs, long working hours, poor time management, interpersonal problems, undefined goals and a lack of purpose in life, the rescue or savior fantasy, inability to handle stresses and emergencies, personal problems at home, and working with clients whose problems are depressing or emotionally draining.

Burn-out is one reaction to high stress. Burn-out appears to be caused primarily by what people tell themselves about events or situations. People facing the same events or situations will or will not show a tendency to burn-out depending on their positive or negative attitude to stress. Since burn-out is one reaction to high stress, it follows that strategies to reduce stress will help to prevent and treat burn-out.

Strategies to prevent and treat burn-out include goal setting, time management, positive thinking, changing the thoughts which produce burn-out, relaxation techniques, exercise, hobbies and special interests, pleasurable goodies, mental health days, social support systems, variety at work, humor, and changing or adapting to distressing events. It is up to each person to choose from this "smorgasbord" the strategies he or she finds most appropriate and attractive.

REFERENCES

Benson, Herbert, *The Relaxation Response*, New York, Avon Books, 1975.

Edelwich, Jerry, *Burn-Out*, New York, Human Sciences Press, 1980.

Ellis, Albert and Robert Harper, *A New Guide to Rational Living*, North Hollywood, California, Wilshire Book Co., 1977.

Freudenberger, Herbert, *Burn-Out*, Garden City, New York, Anchor Press, 1980.

Freudenberger, Herbert, "Burn-Out, Occupational Hazard of the Child Care Worker," *Child Care Quarterly*, Vol. 6, 1977, pp. 90–91.

Greenberg, Herbert M., *Coping with Job Stress*, Englewood Cliffs, New Jersey, Prentice-Hall, Inc., 1980.

Lakein, Alan, *How to Get Control of Your Time and Your Life*, New York, Signet, 1973.

Maslach, Christina, "Burned-Out," *Human Behavior*, September, 1976, pp. 16–18.

Maslach, Christina, *Burnout—The Cost of Caring*, Englewood Cliffs, New Jersey, Spectrum, 1982.

Maslach, Christina, "The Client Role in Staff Burn-Out," *Journal of Social Issues*, 1978, Vol. 34, pp. 111–124.

Maslach, Christina and Ayala Pines, "The Burn-Out Syndrome in the Day Care Setting," *Child Care Quarterly*, 1977, Vol. 6, pp. 100–113.

McQuade, Walter and Ann Aikman, *Stress,* New York, Bantam Books, 1974.

Pelletier, Kenneth R., *Mind as Healer, Mind as Slayer,* New York, Dell Publishing Co., 1977.

Pines, Ayala and Elliot Aronson, *Burnout,* New York, The Free Press, 1981.

Ringer, Robert, *Looking Out for #1,* New York, Fawcett Crest, 1977.

Ryan, W., *Blaming the Victim,* New York, Pantheon books, 1971.

Schafer, Walt, *Stress, Distress and Growth,* Davis, California, International Dialogue Press, 1978.

Schuller, Robert, *Move Ahead with Possibility Thinking,* Moonachie, New Jersey, Pyramid Publications, 1973.

Selye, Hans, *The Stress of Life,* New York, McGraw-Hill, 1956.

Tubesing, Donald A., *Kicking Your Stress Habits,* Duluth, Minnesota, Whole Person Associates, 1981.

Zastrow, Charles, *Talk to Yourself,* Englewood Cliffs, New Jersey, Prentice-Hall, Inc., 1979.

CRISIS

CHAPTER 55

SCHOOL-BASED ASSESSMENT AND CRISIS INTERVENTION WITH KINDERGARTEN CHILDREN FOLLOWING THE NEW YORK WORLD TRADE CENTER BOMBING

Nancy Boyd Webb

Children, like adults, experience crises in the normal course of their lives. Contrary to the myth of the magic years of childhood as a period of guileless innocence and carefree play, the reality of the preteen years, like that of later life, includes stressful experiences that provoke anger, jealousy, fear, and grief as well as joy and pleasure. (Webb, 1991, p. 3)

When 17 kindergarten children were trapped in a dark elevator for five hours following a bomb blast at the New York World Trade Center in Manhattan, on February 28, 1993, they certainly all experienced stress. Whether this stress produced a **state of crisis** in specific children, however, depended on each child's unique personal history, and on the nature of the responses of each child's family, school and community network in the aftermath of the disaster. The terms "crisis" and "state of crisis" in this article conform to the definition of Gilliland and James and others as a

Reprinted from *Crisis Intervention and Time-Limited Treatment,* Vol. 1, No. 1 (1994), pp. 47–59, by permission of Harwood Academic Publishers GmbH, Gordon & Breach Publishing Group.

perception of an event or situation as an intolerable difficulty that exceeds the resources and coping mechanisms of the person (Gilliland and James, 1993, p. 3; Roberts, 1990, contains a complete glossary of terms related to the topic of crisis intervention).

We know that it is not the traumatic event itself that provokes a crisis state in individuals, but rather the idiosyncratic **meaning** ascribed to the event by the individual (A. Freud, 1965; Green, Wilson and Lindy, 1985). Therefore, people who undergo the same distressing experience may react very differently. The kindergarten child, for example, who harbors a long-standing fear of the dark may suffer intense anxiety in a situation of an enforced blackout. Similarly, the child who has just recently acquired control of night-time bedwetting may feel shame and humiliation about wetting his pants during the extended period without access to a bathroom. Both of these hypothetical cases describe children whose personal histories would make them especially vulnerable to the stress generated from being trapped in a dark elevator for a long period of time. Their reactions would contrast sharply with those of another child who might feel intrigued and excited by the "adventure" of spending several hours with his classmates and teacher singing songs and reciting the rosary in the intermittent flickering light of a cigarette lighter. Each child's precrisis adjustment and coping style shape the impact and meaning of crisis events in personal terms, determining whether the experience proves to be traumatic for specific individuals.

This article outlines and discusses the interactive components that comprise the assessments of the young child following a traumatic event such as the disaster of the New York World Trade Center bombing. In addition, a recommended crisis intervention plan that is appropriate for use with children, their families and their schools in the aftermath of a manmade or natural disaster is presented.

TYPICAL RESPONSES OF CHILDREN TO DISASTERS

A review of the literature of the past 35 years on the effects of disaster on children documents the following key findings:

(1) After a tornado in 1953, Bloch, Silber and Perry (1956) reported symptoms in 185 children of increased dependency, clinging, remaining close to home, asking to sleep with parents, night terrors, regressive behavior such as enuresis, tornado games, irritability, sensitivity to noise, and phobias. The children in this study ranged in age from 2 to 15 years with the majority between 6 and 10 years old.

(2) After an earthquake, Blaufarb and Levine (1972) reported that the most common problem for 3- to 12-year-old children was a fear of going to sleep in their own rooms.

(3) Farberow and Gordon (1981), summarizing the responses of children in major disasters, emphasized the separation anxiety that threatens young children when frightened and separated from the nurturing person(s) to whom they are attached. During such a time of actual or feared separation children may be very afraid of being alone and of being in the dark, Farberow and Gordon explain.

(4)   NIMH (Lystad, 1985) presented an overview of stress reactions of individuals of various ages after experiencing a disaster. Responses identified for the preschool and latency-age child include (but are not limited to) the following: crying, thumb-sucking, loss of bowel/bladder control, fear of being left alone and of strangers, irritability, confusion, immobility, headaches and other physical complaints, depression, inability to concentrate, fighting and withdrawal from peers.

(5)   In contrast, Terr (1990), who interviewed 29 children from Chowchilla, California who were kidnapped in their school bus, documented the children's controlled, quiet behavior during and immediately following their ordeal. None of them vomited, defecated, shrieked or became mute or paralyzed. Nonetheless, despite the *external* appearance of control among the children, Terr concluded that they were seriously traumatized by the overwhelming experience of helplessness, fear of separation from loved ones and fear of other, more terrible events yet to come. Terr interviewed the children at two different times—5 months and 4 to 5 years after the traumatic kidnapping.

Reactions of Children in the New York World Trade Center Bombing

It is not clear the extent to which any or all of these findings apply to the children who were trapped in the elevator following the New York World Trade Center bombing. The author of this article has spoken to school personnel and to several crisis team members who provided services to the children in the aftermath of the disaster. Accounts in newspapers, magazines and a television dramatization about this event have offered different perspectives about the bombing and its impact on the child survivors. However, because of the need to respect the confidentiality of those involved, some of whom are currently receiving mental health services, this article presents a *general* model for assessing children in crisis situations, rather than analyzing the responses of specific children in this specific disaster. Similarly, the sources of information given to the author by school personnel are not attributed to specific individuals but, rather, are cited in a general form as P.S. #95.

In any crisis situation the reactions of the involved individuals may appear quite different immediately following the crisis event and several months or years later. Therefore, first the reactions of the children during the immediacy of the elevator entrapment are focused on, and then an overview of responses of the survivors three months later is presented. Long-term evaluation remains for future research.

On February 28, 1993, two kindergarten classes from P.S. #95 in Brooklyn, New York, were concluding their visit to the second tallest building in the world. They had enjoyed the view from the observation deck, on the 107th floor, had finished their lunch and had gone to the bathroom. The two groups separated because the elevator was too full to accommodate both classes. Two other classes of *older* children from another school were already on the elevator. All happily counted the floors as the elevator descended; then it abruptly stopped between 36th and 35th floors. The lights went out, and the emergency back-up system failed to provide any illumination or ventilation. The teacher told the children that there had been "some kind of computer glitch" and that they would just have to wait until it was fixed. A television dramatization of the disaster portrayed the children as lying or sitting down on their coats on the elevator floor as they waited. Some children complained of the heat and the dark, and others cried out for their mothers. The teacher and other adults in the elevator managed to re-assure the children, and calmed them by singing songs and reciting the rosary. Some children actually fell asleep. Two vomited, but none of them lost control of bladder or bowel functions. One of the chaperones became panicky and verbalized fear of fire, re-lated to the odor of smoke that pervaded the air. It is important to note that the occu-pants of the stalled elevator did *not* know about the bombing until *after* they were rescued. This clearly distinguishes this event from one in which there is a very evident life threat, such as a kidnapping, a tornado or an earthquake. The crisis for the children in this situation seemed primarily related to being confined for a long period in the dark, and to not knowing how soon they would be free to resume their trip home and reunite with their families.

When the children finally were rescued and returned to Brooklyn, the crisis interven-tion team boarded the bus with balloons; at the same time, "hysterical" parents greeted their children, and hordes of reporters and television newspeople asked questions and tried to interview all survivors. Many of the families scattered to the safety of their own homes, while others accepted the invitation of the crisis team to meet in a group and discuss their experience. One of the participants described this meeting as an opportu-nity for the parents to ventilate their tears and their fears. This debriefing session was attended by only a few families.

The bombing occurred on a Friday, and the crisis team was present in the school on the following Monday when the children returned to class. The team remained for only half of the day because they saw no indications that the children required more exten-sive intervention. During their visit, the team engaged the children in drawing and play activities, using blocks to reenact the damaged, exploding building, which many of the children had viewed on television over the weekend. The team also encouraged the chil-dren to draw pictures of their experiences. The tendency to minimize the emotional aftermath of this crisis on the children was pervasive, and was reflected in an article in the *New York Times* four days after the bombing, titled "Blast Trauma Lingers, but Mostly for Parents" (Tabor, 1993a).

Three months after the bombing, the children rarely refer to their experience, ac-cording to school personnel, except when there are distinct reminders such as a tele-vised movie event. Several children, nonetheless, are receiving mental health counseling, and a number of the children are reported to be reluctant to go on elevators. Some have spontaneously drawn pictures of monsters and of burning buildings. The crisis team has not remained involved with the children, but the regular school-based support team, consisting of a psychologist, a social worker and a guidance counselor, has been working with some children on an individual basis. A meeting for parents to discuss their children's responses three months after the crisis revealed that a number of chil-dren were experiencing sleep problems, fear of the dark, regression to bedwetting and fear of elevators.

THE TRIPARTITE CRISIS ASSESSMENT

In a previous publication (Webb, 1991), I presented a conceptualization of the assessment of the individual in crisis as composed of three interacting sets of factors: (1) the nature of the crisis situation, (2) the idiosyncratic characteristics of the individual and (3) the strengths and weaknesses of the individual's support system. Figure 55–1 illus-

Figure 55–1
Interactive Components of a Crisis Assessment

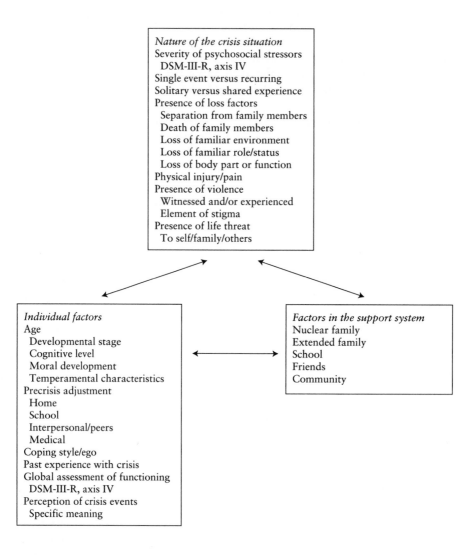

(Note: *From* N. B. Webb (Ed.) (1991). *Play Therapy with Children in Crisis: A Casebook for Practitioners.* New York: The Guilford Press, Copyright 1991 by the Guilford Press, p. 6. Reprinted by permission of the publishers.)

trates the components of the tripartite crisis assessment and suggests how the impact of factors in one set of variables may be balanced and offset *or* magnified by interacting influences among the other two sets of components. A complete review of **all** the factors comprising the Tripartite Crisis Assessment is available elsewhere (Webb, 1991) and therefore is not repeated here. Instead, the following discussion highlights some of the key factors that apply especially to kindergarten children in the traumatic situation that is the focus of this article.

The Nature of the Crisis Situation

Two factors seem particularly relevant in evaluating the impact of this particular crisis situation on the children involved. First, is the severity of psychosocial stressors (American Psychiatric Association, 1987); second, is the presence of loss factors in this crisis. A rating of the *severity of the stress* generated from being trapped in a dark elevator for an extended period of time requires that the evaluator assess

> the stress an "average" person in similar circumstances and with similar sociocultural values would experience from this particular psychosocial stressor(s). This judgment involves a consideration of . . . the amount of change in the person's life caused by the stressor, the degree to which the event is desired and under the person's control, and the number of stressors. (American Psychiatric Association, 1987, p. 19).

Obviously, the assessment of severity of psychosocial stressors in this situation varies with the characteristics of each child's personal history. Most five-year-olds are uncomfortable in the dark, so we can assume that being forced to remain in the dark for an indefinite period was stressful to almost all of the kindergartners. However, because the range of responses varied between children who were secure (or tired) enough to fall asleep and those whose anxiety caused them to cry out for their mothers, or to vomit, it is evident that a ranking of the severity of the stressor will differ according to the *meaning* of the crisis circumstances to each child. My "objective" ranking of the severity of this stress for the "average" five- or six-year-old child would put it between (3) moderate and (4) severe.

The second relevant factor in assessing the crisis situation is an evaluation of *loss factors*. The most upsetting element in this crisis for the adults, and probably also for the children, was the loss of control implicit in the situation. No one knew if and when the elevator would begin to function normally, and therefore all imprisoned in the elevator must have felt a sense of helplessness. They also may have feared that the elevator would plunge to the basement thereby hurting or killing them. Of course, young children are accustomed to depending on adults to guide their activities, so their loss of autonomy in this situation may not have been as stressful as it was for the adults who knew that their personal control regarding the outcome of the crisis was in other hands. The adults probably also had a clearer idea of the possible danger. Both adults and children in this situation experienced a loss of predictability in their lives and, to varying degrees, a loss of their sense of security about the workings of the world.

Individual Factors in the Assessment

In evaluating individual factors in assessing the impact of a crisis on children, the child's developmental stage and level of cognitive understanding is critical. Other important factors relevant to the individuals in *this* crisis are the child's medical history and past experience with crisis.

Reports of the responses of the children trapped in the elevator indicated that the older children (third and fifth graders) were more upset than were the kindergarten children (Tesoriero, 1993). It is likely that the older children understood the potential danger of their situation, whereas the younger ones were able to believe and take comfort in the reassurance (and denial) of their teacher, who told them that there was no smoke in the elevator and that they would "be down in no time." Since five- and six-year-olds are present-oriented and do not have the ability to project very far into the future or a mature understanding about death (Piaget, 1955), their immaturity served to protect them from the stress experienced by the older children. A solid knowledge about child development is essential in assessing the impact of crisis events on children at different developmental stages.

Another individual factor that proved important in assessing the impact of this crisis on the individual child was the child's language proficiency. Since four of the children were not native English speakers, it was difficult for the teacher to effectively reassure them. Fortunately, this circumstance was rectified in the assignment of bilingual speakers to these children in the postcrisis counseling.

The fact that several children in the group of 17 kindergartners were asthmatic also added to the concerns of the teacher, who worried about the effects of the smoke on these children. She made a point of calling out the names of all the children at intervals, as a way of maintaining contact and to ascertain that the asthmatic children were breathing satisfactorily. There were no medical emergencies reported concerning the asthmatic children, but this example points to the possible unique vulnerability of children with preexisting medical conditions in crisis situations.

Knowledge about the child's past experience with crisis contributes to our understanding of the impact of the current crisis situation on the child. For example, a boy whose grandfather and uncle had died recently was fearful that some of his friends had died in the bomb and ensuing blaze (Tabor, 1993a). He had learned to "expect disaster" and was reported to be weeping in school. Past losses and unresolved and/or recent experiences of bereavement certainly can deplete the energy levels of the individual, whether child or adult, and make him or her particularly vulnerable to a new crisis experience.

Factors in the Support System

The third main component in the Tripartite Crisis Assessment considers the strengths and weaknesses of the individual support system, including in this category the nuclear and extended family, the school, friends and the community network. The reactions of family members with respect to the crisis experience of these children varied from the "hysterical" version reported in the news accounts to that of rage because their children were "stuck" in an elevator without a flashlight or viable communication system. Of course the parents were relieved that their children were not harmed in this potentially dangerous situation, but this relief does not exclude feelings of anger that it happened. When dealing with children, the reactions of the people surrounding them must be considered. If the parents are, indeed, "hysterical" and enraged, how can the child remain unaffected or accepting about their experience? McFarlane states emphatically that "parents' ability to contain the anxiety generated by an extreme threat may be the major factor influencing their children's responses" (McFarlane, 1987, p. 764).

Because this disaster received such extensive media coverage, the children immediately perceived that something *very* important had happened to them. During the weekend following the bombing, they all watched the television news reports showing survivors with soot-stained faces being rescued in the building where *their* elevator had stalled! In addition, many families of the kindergarten children were visited at home by reporters seeking exclusive interviews. On Monday the school was literally "flooded" with the news media, to the extent that the ability of the crisis intervention team to hold group debriefing sessions with the kindergarten class was delayed.

As time went on, the children and teachers were given citations of heroism, trips to the circus and special rewards such as watches and T-shirts for bravery. The reaction of the community to the fact that the children "survived" and were "brave heroes" did not permit any hint of residual anxiety on the part of the "heroic" five- and six-year-olds. How very confused some of them must have felt by having their experience of fear so quickly transformed and relabeled as bravery! Children who are traumatized do not feel brave, although their reactions of quiet acquiescence may deceive the untrained eye. Because one of the characteristics of post-traumatic stress disorder involves avoidance of thoughts or feelings associated with the trauma, it is understandable how the supportive actions of family and community following this disaster could reinforce and collude with the individual child's own wish to forget and avoid any recollections of the event that had such frightening overtones.

The section that follows discusses the symptoms of post-traumatic stress disorder as they *might* relate to *some* of the kindergarten children trapped in the elevator following the New York World Trade Center bombing. The author has had no professional involvement with *any* of these children. However, in a situation of evident crisis such as this disaster, it is appropriate to consider the possibility of symptom development among some of the survivors.

Post-Traumatic Stress Disorder

According to the DSM-III-R (American Psychiatric Association, 1987) the symptoms of post-traumatic stress disorder (PTSD) can occur after a person has experienced an unusual event that almost anyone would consider "markedly distressing." When symptoms in three general categories persist for at least one month the diagnosis of PTSD is appropriate. The three categories of symptoms include:

(1) Reexperiencing (dreams, play and physical distress reactions related to the trauma).
(2) Avoidance responses ("forgetting" the event, feeling detached or disinterested, regression and restricted affect).

(3) Increased arousal (sleep disturbances, irritability, difficulty concentrating, exaggerated startle reaction, and so forth.

See the DSM-III-R for a complete description of the associated symptoms.

McFarlane (1990) indicates that "even after extreme trauma, . . . only approximately 40% of an exposed population develop PTSD. . . The available evidence suggests that the degree of distress caused by an event is the major factor determining the probability of the onset of psychiatric disorder" (pp. 70–74). Therefore, in attempting to identify children who might be most "at-risk" for development of PTSD, the crisis team needs to know which children appeared to have been most upset and anxious during the crisis. These children should have individual evaluations, in addition to the group meeting held with all of the children. In addition, children whose parents were extremely anxious need to be followed closely, as do the parents themselves. In this instance 8 parents of the 17 kindergarten children received counseling (Tabor, 1993a).

Another point of logical intervention occurred three months after the crisis when some parents in a group meeting referred to their children's continuing anxiety responses of fear of the dark, sleep problems and regression to enuresis. Referral to mental health specialists needed to be implemented for symptomatic children who were not already receiving services. The section that follows discusses an "ideal" crisis intervention plan recommended for use in schools in the aftermath of a disaster such as this bombing or other crisis events.

SCHOOL-BASED CRISIS INTERVENTION FOLLOWING A DISASTER

Because of the very unpredictable occurrence of either man-made or natural disasters, it is essential that every school have in place written guidelines about procedures to be adapted and implemented in the event of any sudden crisis event. "A time of crisis is not conducive to improvisation, and prior preparation and orientation of staff members regarding management of . . . crisis will greatly assist those expected to assume leadership and take action at the time of need" (Webb, 1986, p. 476).

Many school districts have such plans in place sparked by the necessity of dealing with multiple student suicide crises, and additional life-threatening situations such as natural disasters and emergencies of violence. Crisis response teams serve a very important function at a time of tragedy and emotional turmoil. (See Shulman, 1990 for a description of mental health consultation to a high school following two tragedies.)

Usually composed of school counselors, school psychologists, school social workers, administrators and mental health workers with training in crisis intervention, such a team can be called into action by the Director of Pupil Personnel Services to deal with any emergency that disrupts the usual school routine and proves emotionally challenging and upsetting to staff and students (Sorenson, 1989). When parents and teachers know ahead of time that a crisis response team is prepared and ready to deal with emergencies, they will be better able to utilize these services when the need arises (Kalafat, 1991; Nelson and Slaikeu, 1990).

The functions of the team demand their skillful attention dealing with the multiple components of the emergency situation, such as (1) the crisis event; (2) the emotional reactions of the students, faculty and staff; (3) the identification of populations-at-risk; (4) involvement of parents; and (5) immediate and long-term crisis intervention strategies (Sorenson, 1989, p. 426). How these functions apply to the crisis situation of the kindergarten children trapped in the elevator following the New York World Trade Center bombing is now considered.

The Crisis Team's Response to the Crisis Event

This crisis event occurred outside of the school building while the students were on a field trip. The leader of the team must judge where to focus the efforts of the team, namely, whether some members of the team will travel to the scene of the crisis event and provide immediate help to the students involved, or whether all team members will remain in the school building, available to provide support to parents, the children, staff and community citizens who were very anxious and eager for information about the children's fate.

In this situation, the second option was selected. A television monitor was set up in the school auditorium where parents and others congregated to await the eventual return of the school bus with the kindergartners and their teachers and chaperones. In addition to the parents and members of the school community, scores of media reporters looking for stories invaded the school environs and auditorium. Many of the school personnel report that they felt "overwhelmed" by the media who evidently "were allowed to stick microphones into everyone's faces" (P.S. #95). The tone in which this was conveyed clearly indicated that the media were experienced as adding stress in an already very stressful situation. This matter deserves attention in regard to school policy about media access to individuals in crisis. Shulman (1990) suggests that the principal acts as a liaison between the school and the press.

The Crisis Team's Response to the Emotions of Students, Faculty and Staff

Clearly this is a very important function of the crisis team. In most crisis situations the direct "victims" receive prime attention. This was certainly true in this crisis. The team boarded the bus as soon as it arrived at the school, evidently having decided to assume a celebratory spirit emphasizing the positive outcome of the children's ordeal. Each child received a balloon as a token of the happiness of the occasion.

However, the teachers, parents and other chaperones who were trapped with the children in the elevator and who probably realized the possible life threat of their situation also deserved special recognition. The teacher, as the natural leader, maintaining calm and heroically controlling her own fears and reassuring the children that everything would be all right merited special intervention by someone on the crisis team. The timing of such intervention logically follows a good night's rest in a safe environment. It is likely that the "responsible" adults (teachers and other adults) would feel a tremendous "let-down" once their adrenaline returned to precrisis level and the enormity of what they experienced became apparent. These adults would benefit greatly from a group "debriefing" experience with a specialist in post-traumatic counseling techniques the day after the crisis.

The emotional reactions of the students require attention at several points in time.

The immediate aftermath of the crisis presents one set of circumstances. Several days later, the reality of the experience takes shape based not only on personal recollections, but also on the responses of family and media. This changing scenario requires that the crisis team maintain contact with all involved in the crisis over a period of time.

Initial group "debriefing" of young children ideally includes both verbal and nonverbal approaches. Since kindergarten children do not have sophisticated verbal skills, art techniques can help release the feelings they feel but cannot articulate.

Typical debriefing sessions with children in schools begin by asking some leading questions about the crisis event. Children who are able, describe the details of their experience, emphasizing the involvement of all senses in response to specific questions by the team member: that is, what did you see, smell, hear, do, feel? (Alameda County, 1990). When the children have verbally described their recollections, they then are invited to draw what they experienced. Often the graphic memories have a special poignancy and power not evident in the verbal accounts.

Identification of Populations-at-Risk

The term "populations-at-risk" refers to groups of people who may be especially affected by the added stress of the crisis situation. I have already referred to the child in this situation who had difficulty dealing with the stress of this crisis because of his previous, recent bereavement experiences. Individuals who are most at risk in any crisis are those who were functioning marginally *before* the crisis. They cannot tolerate the extra expenditures of energy demanded to survive the crisis situation.

Typically, the crisis team becomes aware of the individuals who are having difficulty dealing with the stress of the present crisis during the group debriefing sessions. The individual may say something to raise concern, may remain uninvolved or may draw something that indicates intense anxiety. The skillful crisis team member finds a way to suggest an individual meeting with such a person to explore matters further, in the process of completing an assessment of the child or adult. It is important for the crisis worker to convey to all "survivors" that extreme reactions to crises, while disturbing to the individual, do *not* indicate the presence of a mental health disturbance. There should be no stigma associated with receiving crisis intervention services.

Involvement of Parents

Whenever children's health and welfare are threatened, parents **must** be included both as adjuncts to helping their own children, and as "indirect" victims, also deeply affected by the crisis on a personal level. When the children are five and six years of age, the involvement of parents is both appropriate and necessary. I have already referred to the impact of the parents' anxieties on their children (McFarlane, 1987). Since the influence of parents on children is so pervasive, the crisis team must include them to the fullest extent possible.

Group meetings are useful to provide the same information to all at the same time and a natural means for a mutual aid, supportive system to emerge from the group. All the members of the group have experienced similar stress and they potentially can help one another. In addition to focusing on the immediacy of the situation, it is helpful to give parents some basic information about possible *future* responses of their children, based on knowledge about other children who have experienced disasters in the past. Because individuals in crisis may not be able to concentrate on future concerns, it is advisable to give this information in a *written* format for the parents' future reference. The federal government and other organizations that work with children have a wide variety of publications on the topic of helping children after a disaster, including lists and discussion about typical reactions of children (Cooperative Child Care, 1985; FEMA, 1991a, 1991b). Every crisis response team should have copies of these documents in their files, with appropriate handouts for parents ready to be duplicated as needed.

Just as with the children, contacts with the parents must occur at several intervals of time. The immediate need is obvious, but periodic follow-up at monthly intervals is important even when there may appear to be no pressing need or request for services. Because of the tendency to avoid experiences that will stir up anxious memories of the stressful crisis, the individuals involved often minimize aftereffects. The crisis response team has the obligation to continue to monitor the emotional well-being of children, parents and staff who were affected by the crisis, even when reports convey the message that "everything is fine."

Immediate and Long-Term Crisis Intervention Strategies

The previous discussion has emphasized that an effective crisis intervention plan includes both *immediate* and *follow-up* components. The immediate tasks of the team are usually clearer than the follow-up tasks. Professional judgment must inform decisions about the spacing and format of follow-up efforts. Periodic, once-a-month "checking in" with the class of kindergarten children might seem adequate, but when media attention such as television dramatization occurs, the children will have reactions to this, and should receive another group debriefing. Even as I am completing this article, over three months after the bombing, an update about the kindergarten class has just appeared in the *New York Times,* with pictures of the children rehearsing for a show (Tabor, 1993b). In this show, many of the children will sing the same songs that they sang in the elevator, and those children will inevitably make associations to the crisis event during their upcoming performance. Therefore, even though the show is a happy experience, it carries overtones of memories that would merit further exploration by the crisis response team.

Program Evaluation

In order for the crisis team or the school administration to evaluate the effectiveness of the interventions that were implemented, a program evaluation needs to be conducted. Smith (1990) points out the implications of such an evaluation in order to learn about the benefits and shortcomings of services that were provided.

Probably an *ex post facto* survey design would be most appropriate in evaluating the interventions implemented in this situation. A questionnaire to parents and teachers would yield data that might suggest differences in outcomes for children who received *immediate* intervention compared with those who received services later, or not at all.

It also might provide information regarding the effectiveness of different types of intervention.

Obviously, in any such study there are numerous intervening variables. However, learning about the program's level of success or failure from the point of view of the consumers of the services merits serious consideration for future service planning.

SUMMARY

Assessment is an ongoing process, especially in crisis situations, because symptoms may emerge weeks and months after a disaster and may not even be recognized as connected to it. Because of the possibility of delayed onset of symptoms of PTSD, crisis intervention response teams must provide periodic follow-up to monitor disaster victims, their families and the network of people involved with the victims. Some individuals require and benefit from individual counseling; for many others, group debriefing sessions help them cope adequately with the stress caused by the crisis. All can be assisted by access to psychoeducational information that documents typical responses of disaster victims. Crises can and do occur to anybody. We know a great deal about how to help, and when the "victim-survivors" are kindergarten children, the preventive work of crisis intervention is a long-term investment in mental health.

REFERENCES

Alameda County (1990). *How to Help Children After a Disaster*. Santa Cruz, CA: Alameda County Mental Health Services.

American Psychiatric Association (1987). *Diagnostic and Statistical Manual of Mental Disorders:* DSM-III-R. (Revised 3rd ed.) Washington, DC: American Psychiatric Association.

Blaufarb, H. and Levine, J. (1972). Crisis intervention in an earthquake. *Social Work,* 17, 16–19.

Bloch, D., Silber, E. and Perry, S. (1956). Some factors in the emotional reaction of children to disaster. *American Journal of Psychiatry*, 113, 416–422.

Cooperative Disaster Child Care (1985). Some tips for parents and caregivers following a disaster. New Windsor, MD: Cooperative Disaster Child Care.

Farberow, N. and Gordon, N. (1981). *Manual for child health workers in major disasters*. DHHS Publication No. (ADM) 81–1070. Washington, DC: Government Printing Office.

FEMA (1991a). School intervention following a critical incident: Project Cope. Document No. 220. Washington, DC: Federal Emergency Management Agency.

FEMA (1991b). How to help children after a disaster: A guidebook for teachers. Document No. 219. Washington, DC: Federal Emergency Management Agency.

Freud, A. (1965). *Normality and Pathology in Childhood*. New York: International Universities Press.

Gilliland, B. E. and James, B. E. (1993). *Crisis Intervention Strategies*. 2nd ed. Pacific Grove, CA: Brooks/Cole.

Green, B. L., Wilson, J. P. and Lindy, J. D. (1985). Conceptualizing post-traumatic stress disorder: A psychosocial framework. In C. R. Figley (Ed.), *Trauma and Its Wake: The Study and Treatment of Post-Traumatic Stress Disorder*. New York: Brunner/Mazel, pp. 53–69.

Kalafat, J. (1991). Suicide intervention in schools. In A. R. Roberts (Ed.), *Contemporary Perspectives on Crisis Intervention and Prevention*. Englewood Cliffs, NJ: Prentice Hall, pp. 218–239.

Lystad, M. (1985). *Innovations in mental health services to disaster victims*. Washington, DC: US Government Printing Office.

McFarlane, A. C. (1987). Posttraumatic phenomena in a longitudinal study of children following a natural disaster. *Journal of the American Academy of Child and Adolescent Psychiatry*, 26(5), 764–769.

McFarlane, A. C. (1990). Post traumatic stress syndrome revisited. In H. J. Parad and L. G. Parad (Eds.), *Crisis Intervention Book 2: The Practitioner's Sourcebook for Brief Therapy*. Milwaukee, WI: Family Service America, pp. 69–92.

Nelson, E. R. and Slaikeu, K. A. (1990). Crisis intervention in the schools. In K. A. Slaikeu (Ed.), *Crisis Intervention: A Handbook for Practice and Research*. 2nd ed. Boston: Allyn and Bacon, pp. 329–347.

P.S. 95 (1993). Personal communications with teachers, crisis team and guidance staff. Brooklyn, New York.

Piaget, J. (1955). *The Child's Construction of Reality*. New York: Basic Books.

Roberts, A. R. (Ed.) (1990). *Crisis Intervention Handbook: Assessment, Treatment and Research*. Belmont, CA: Wadsworth.

Shulman, N. M. (1990). Crisis intervention in a high school: Lessons from the Concord High School experiences. In A. R. Roberts (Ed.), *Crisis Intervention Handbook: Assessment, Treatment and Research*. Belmont, CA: Wadsworth, pp. 63–77.

Smith, M. J. (Ed.) (1990). *Program Evaluation in the Human Services*. New York: Springer.

Sorenson, J. R. (1989). Responding to student or teacher death: Preparing crisis intervention. *Journal of Counseling and Development*, 67, 426–427.

Tabor, M. B. W. (1993a). Blast trauma lingers, but mostly for parents. *New York Times*, March 2, 1993, Al.

Tabor, M. B. W. (1993b). Kindergarten's 111th story ends happily. *New York Times*, June 6, 1993, p. 42.

Terr, L. (1990). *Too Scared to Cry: Psychic Trauma in Childhood*. New York: Harper and Row.

Tesoriero, A. (1993). Trapped in the towers. *Ladies' Home Journal*, June 1993, pp. 148–151.

Webb, N. B. (1986). Before and after suicide: A preventive outreach program for colleges. *Suicide & Life-Threatening Behavior*, 16(4), 469–480.

Webb, N. B. (Ed.) (1991). *Play Therapy with Children in Crisis: A Case Book for Practitioners*. New York: Guilford Press.

DEATH AND DYING

CHAPTER 56

COUNSELING BEREAVED CHILDREN

Stages in the Process

Mary Elizabeth Taylor Warmbrōd

Most of the scarce literature on the bereaved child addresses the child's reactions to a death. Information is basically missing about what the counselor with the bereaved child could be doing and the special preparation needed. Thus this article will concentrate on the counselor in such a situation with the goal of introducing some guidelines for grief work with children. After the context in which the guidelines apply is discussed, the rationale for conjoint sessions with the bereaved child's family is provided, followed by an identification of the personal qualities of and the knowledge base needed to be a counselor with a bereaved child.

The conceptualization of the process of counseling with those in grief, as organized into three more or less distinct stages, has been developed and refined over the course of the author's work with children in grief. A different aspect of the family's life is the focus in each of the three stages. A therapeutic assessment of the bereaved, proposed by Beverley Raphael,[1] although not focused on children, covers these stages in the same order, confirming the importance for bereaved children and their remaining parent to consider in order those three aspects of their life together.

Examples as to what the counselor might say and do to facilitate the child's sharing the experience are given. A sense of direction and of the areas yet to be covered is provided for the counselor who knows these stages, the kinds of questions appropriate for each stage, and frequent responses of the parent and child at each point.

Reprinted from *Social Casework,* Vol. 67, No. 6 (1986), pp. 351–358 by permission of the publisher, Families International, Inc.
[1] Beverley Raphael, *The Anatomy of Bereavement* (New York: Basic Books, 1983).

THE CONTEXT

Obviously the settings in which a counselor is called on to deal with children in grief vary in many ways. Some of the ways situations vary are the length of time after the death, who died, the type of death, the extent of the counselor's previous contact with the family, and who requested counseling. Therefore each counselor will have to adapt the guidelines to fit a particular environment whether it be a hospital, school, clinic, welfare agency, or religious institution.

The most typical situation the author has encountered involves a parent seeking counseling for the family a few months after the death of the other parent. There had been no previous contact with the family. Therefore the guidelines are directed toward counseling when the arrangement is a remaining parent with children. The situation in which a child dies presents somewhat different challenges and a modification of the guidelines. Also there is no attempt to directly address work with a child who has no active parents or relatives as the result of a death. This type of situation complicates the grief work.

The guidelines are intended as a framework within which a counselor can address the unique features of each family's situation. The focus is on relatively uncomplicated grieving. If the grieving is abnormal, or if additional problems reveal themselves, the counselor can assess whether referral or renegotiation of the counseling contract is necessary.

FAMILY INVOLVEMENT IN SESSIONS

Given that the parent-child relationship is central for a child, the counselor must consider what the effect of the grief counseling is on that relationship. The ability of the mother to cope with the death of her husband in wartime was central in determining how well her child was functioning even a few years later,[2] which indicates that helping the remaining parent is one way of helping the child. Having the child talk and grieve only with the counselor may leave the child still unable to share with the parent, and the parent is left feeling more isolated from the child. Diane Becker and Faith Margolin[3] noted that the remaining parent frequently does not talk with the child about the deceased or about his or her emotions relating to the death. Thus if the child meets only with the counselor, the child has no opportunities to hear how the parent is coping and how the child might be of some assistance, appropriate to the child's age.

Having the parent and children attend sessions together has considerable value and is recommended. The parent can directly answer a child's questions about what caused the death, whether the child might die from the same thing, and whether the remaining parent will now die. The parent can be provided with books about children's under-

---

[2] Esther Elizur and Mordecai Kaffman, "Factors Influencing the Severity of Childhood Bereavement Reactions," *American Journal of Orthopsychiatry* 53 (October 1983):668–76.

[3] Diane Becker and Faith Margolin, "How Surviving Parents Handled Their Young Children's Adaptation to the Crisis of Loss," *American Journal of Orthopsychiatry* 37 (July 1967):753–57.

standing of death and books to read to children.[4] It is often advisable to include such relatives as grandparents, aunts, and uncles if they are involved with the children. The most important benefit of seeing the whole family is that it supports their existence as a family, despite a death, and encourages members to turn to other family members.

The counseling is modified when the parent and children are seen together. If the parent is uncomfortable talking about the subject with the children present, the beginning can be slow. A child may also stop expressing certain feelings when he or she sees that the parent is reacting negatively. Yet it is important to learn how family members are reacting, negatively and positively, to each other in their grief. The counselor can be patient but should not hesitate to raise painful topics again. A valuable contribution to the parent-child relationship is provided by the counselor's modeling for the parent another way of talking and listening to children about death and grief. The modeling will have an effect both during the crisis and on the future of the parent-child relationship. Preventing criticism of each child's way of grieving, which may differ from that of the parent or a sibling, is another role of the counselor in meeting with the remaining family.

Certainly the parent and children had very different relationships with the person who died. Thus groups for bereaved spouses and groups for bereaved children, which allow them to talk with others who share the same position relative to a deceased loved one, are beneficial. Unfortunately such groups are not always available.

Adolescents are in a stage when their life with the family is becoming less important in some ways, but they still live in the family and use it as a base from which to explore. Thus it is particularly appropriate to have individual sessions with an adolescent to recognize his or her growing independence. Group and individual sessions should be in addition to the family sessions.

PREPARATION OF THE COUNSELOR

Counseling the bereaved child requires preparation on the part of the counselor. That preparation will involve two major components, self-knowledge and topic knowledge. Both contribute to the counselor's effectiveness.

Self-knowledge

All counseling necessitates a degree of counselor self-examination and awareness. Grief counseling with children differs from most counseling and intensifies that need for self-knowledge by a counselor.

First, although all counseling is an attempt to help someone with a problem, the types of problems will differ. The counselor who favors a problem-solving orientation and wishes to have the client learn some new skill or make some life improvement may

---

[4] Audrey K. Gordon and Dennis Klass, *They Need to Know: How to Teach Children About Death* (Englewood Cliffs, NJ: Prentice-Hall, 1979); Earl A. Grollman, *Talking About Death* (Boston: Beacon Press, 1976); Jill Krementz, *How It Feels When a Parent Dies* (New York: Knopf, 1981); Eda LeShan, *Learning to Say Good-bye* (New York: Avon, 1976); Marguerita Rudolph, *Should the Children Know? Encounters with Death in the Lives of Children* (New York: Schocken Books, 1978); and Gerald Schneiderman, *Coping with Death in the Family* (Toronto, Ontario: Chimo Publishing, 1979).

find grief counseling difficult because it makes such different demands; the death of a loved one is an unchangeable fact. The counselor is confronted by the inability of the child and the family to reverse the death. The counselor is helpless to change the fact that the deceased person will no longer be a part of the child's life. The general need of children for adults to care for them, which emphasizes their weakness, is impressed on a counselor meeting with a bereaved child.

Second, given the irreversibility of death, it is not surprising that a child and family have such intense emotions over the death of their loved one. Although the expression of emotion may take many forms, such as sorrow or rage, the depth of feeling is apparent. To the extent that children have not learned to inhibit their expression of feeling, they can seem consumed by the pain of the loss. This means that the counselor must be accepting of and attentive to strongly expressed feelings. Counselors who have major commitments to be strong and protect children from pain may feel that they have failed and thus find grief counseling personally distressing. Being with a grieving child is more similar to comforting a teething baby than to keeping a child from a hot stove. Indeed the core of what the grief counselor offers is to listen while pain about an unchangeable situation is expressed and those involved learn to live in a different world.

Third, unlike many clients who come to a counselor with problems the counselor will never face, bereaved clients remind the counselor that everyone, including himself or herself, has loved ones who will die. Furthermore the counselor's own mortality and the fact that others would be affected by it confront one in grief counseling. Young children especially ask such central questions as Why do people die? Thus one is forced ultimately to examine one's basis for living, since everyone dies. For their own sake, counselors who work with the grieving need to find a personal rationale for living despite the realities of helplessness, pain, suffering, and death.

Given those realities of grief counseling, it is incumbent that the counselor review his or her attitudes toward death, experiences with deaths and resultant grieving, beliefs about children and childhood, and degree of comfort with emotion. Failure to do so will leave the counselor at the mercy of his or her feelings aroused by the bereaved child and family. Rather than helping the bereaved child, the counselor may exhibit behaviors that block grieving by the child, with undesirable consequences.

Therefore the counselor cannot substitute knowledge about children, about counseling, and about the grieving of others for self-awareness. There are aids for that self-exploration. J. William Worden[5] has provided a list of questions referring to death and grief that a counselor should answer personally as part of the preparation to work with those who are grieving. Exercises that have been used in training counselors of the dying and grieving are often appropriate.[6]

An exercise developed in the author's work is particularly relevant to assisting the counselor of bereaved children. In a style a six-year-old child could understand, the counselor writes a true story about an incident in his or her childhood that involved a death. The death could be of a pet or a person. The counselor also illustrates the story and shares it with friends and children. The counselor can write a story for each event in which he or she suffered a loss, even for major losses that were not physical deaths

---

[5] J. William Worden, *Grief Counseling and Grief Therapy* (New York: Springer, 1982).
[6] Valerie Young, *Working with the Dying and Grieving* (Davis, CA: International Dialogue Press, 1984).

as, say, losing a treasured toy or moving from a particular place. If desired, a story can later be shared in grief counseling, as appropriate.

Several features of this exercise contribute to its impact and beneficial effect. The counselor is dealing with a particular personal loss experience, not vague generalities about his or her grieving style. The effort to write for a child helps the counselor think from a child's perspective and think back to being a child. The drawing of pictures in the exercise enhances recall of the context of the loss and the feeling states at the time of the loss. Drawing involves the counselor in a form of expression children frequently use. Intertwined in the review of the experiences with deaths will be a wealth of feelings with which the counselor must be comfortable in order to do grief counseling. Finally, sharing the story provides the experience of describing a difficult time for himself or herself and thus an empathy with the bereaved child in counseling.

Topic Knowledge

In addition to self-knowledge, the counselor also needs knowledge in several areas. These include knowledge about children and their means of expression, their understandings of death, and their ways of grieving. Further areas are general principles for counseling children, the bereaved, and bereaved children.

Fundamental for any counselor working with children is information on the developmental stages from birth to adulthood, including the physical, emotional, social, linguistic, and intellectual changes. A particular concern is the extent to which a child's understanding of the concept of death varies with the child's age. Of the published material on these matters,[7] an article, "Children's Concepts of Death," by Barbara Kane, is particularly helpful.[8] Children under two years old appear to have no concept of death, although they do react to the absence of a significant individual and the feelings of those around them. Children from two to five years old usually see death as a special state like sleeping but with no expectation of the permanence of the state. Five-year-old children have some sense of the permanence of death, although the fact that everyone dies, including children, is not understood. An understanding of the finality, irreversibility, and universality of death is reached at approximately nine years of age.

Death as a concept involves several abstract features. It is also often terribly hard for adults to explain. The counselor needs to be aware of the types of explanations of death that children of different ages can understand. Obviously the language needs to be simplified and related to the child's world. Noting what a dead person can*not* do helps many children. One four-year-old child focused on "She can't do laundry now." It is also valuable to explain the absence of pain in the dead by referring to the absence of pain in the child's hair and nails.

Certain explanations of death are to be avoided because of their potential to be mis-

[7] Sylvia Anthony, *The Discovery of Death in Childhood and After* (New York: Basic Books, 1972); Perry Childers and Mary Wimmer, "The Concept of Death in Early Childhood," *Child Development* 42 (October 1971):1299–301; Morley D. Glicken, "The Child's View of Death," *Journal of Marriage and Family Counseling* 4 (April 1978):75–81; Gerald P. Koocher, "Childhood, Death and Cognitive Development," *Developmental Psychology* 9 (November 1973):369–75; Maria Nagy, "The Child's Theories Concerning Death," *Journal of Genetic Psychology* 73 (September 1948):3–27; and Edward White et al., "Children's Conceptions of Death," *Child Development* 49 (June 1978):307–10.
[8] Barbana Kane, "Children's Concepts of Death," *Journal of Genetic Psychology* 134 (March 1979):141–53.

understood and to create problems. Describing death as like sleep is dangerous for its probable effect on the child's sleep. Even religious explanations should be introduced with caution. Religious concepts about what has happened to the dead person and about why the person died are frequently too abstract for children, especially young children. It is likely that "Heaven" or "God took him" will be taken literally. Rather than the specifics of religious ideas, the comfort that believers receive from them is probably more important for the child and will be sensed.

Given children's inventiveness, there are many descriptions that can be misunderstood and thus be harmful. A help in avoiding misunderstandings is to ask the child to explain death with whatever expression is most comfortable, for example, words, drawings, or play acting. By learning how a particular child is trying to make sense of death, the counselor can correct the child's concept if necessary. Gerald P. Koocher and Earl A. Grollman[9] have written helpfully on talking with children about death. It can be expected that a young child will better understand a particular death as he or she grows older.

As part of the basic knowledge necessary for working with children, the counselor must appreciate and make means available for the child's methods of expression. Robert M. Segal[10] developed a rationale and guidelines to help grieving children communicate symbolically. To that end, a variety of play and art materials should be provided. Puppets blocks, paper and crayon, and Plasticene modeling clay would be a minimum supply. Such materials are essential to have for the child under eight years old and may even help older children and adolescents. Play with clay particularly seems to relax children, adolescents, and adults. More than with crayons, work with clay allows expression through talk and the hands simultaneously. Work with clay also eliminates the need for a surface. The drawings, clay products, and play can be very eloquent responses to what is being discussed and attention to them by the counselor is essential. This might involve inviting the child to tell about a drawing or clay product or joining him or her in play with puppets.

It is instructive for the parent in a session to see that a child has some means of expression for feelings, whether or not words are used. The parent can invite that expression in other places. Finally the parent can join the child in drawing or play expression.

In addition to understanding the child's concept of death and means of expression, a focus on the grieving process is necessary. The counselor needs to know about grieving in general, and specifically by children, as well as grief counseling for adults. Worden's excellent book[11] reviews the wide variety of possible grief responses by adults and identifies four tasks of mourning. It also provides guidelines for assisting the mourning process with counseling.

John Bowlby[12] suggested that the three stages of grief a child goes through are protest and denial, despair and disorganization, and reorganization. Although this is a helpful outline, it does not indicate the variety of children's reactions to a death. The

---

[9] Gerald P Koocher, "Talking with Children About Death," *American Journal of Orthopsychiatry* 44 (July 1974):404–11; and Grollman, *Talking About Death*.

[10] Robert M. Segal, "Helping Children Express Grief Through Symbolic Communication," *Social Casework* 65 (December 1984):590–99.

[11] Worden, *Grief Counseling and Grief Therapy*.

[12] John Bowlby, *Attachment and Loss, Vol. III: Loss, Sadness and Depression* (Markham, Ontario: Penguin Books Canada Ltd., 1980).

issue of how children grieve is complicated by their general cognitive level, understanding of death, previous experience with death, the particular manner of the death, and the support the family and child receive after the death. All this means that the counselor must be willing to deal with each individual child, since it often happens that one child may be incredibly angry, while another is exceedingly quiet and withdrawn.

Whatever the level of understanding of death, it helps to keep in mind that a death inevitably involves a separation. Thus the counselor would be wise to become acquainted with Bowlby's books[13] on attachment, separation, and loss. In addition there is the theoretical literature on how children grieve at different ages and descriptions of children in grief to which the counselor can turn.[14] Familiarity with the various possible responses, which are somewhat tied to age, is valuable for the counselor.

A few descriptions of what has commonly been done in grief counseling with families and children are available. Most of them are quite recent, reflecting the increased attention to children's needs.[15] The focus is very strongly on the child, not the counselor.

THREE STAGES IN COUNSELING

In each of the three stages, the focus is on a different aspect of the family's life. First there is the focus on the death and the funeral of the loved one with its accompanying responses. The second stage considers what the dead person was like, what the family did together, and, naturally, what about the dead person is missed. That leads to the third stage, in which the discussion turns to the present with reference to when the person is missed, adjustments finished and forthcoming, and sources of comfort. It can be considered that the first stage is the recent past and major event, with the second stage moving back further in time so that, in the third stage, the family members can recognize what they have in the present as they move forward into the future without denying the past.

---

[13] John Bowlby, *Attachment and Loss, Vol. I: Attachment* (1969), *Attachment and Loss, Vol. II: Separation, Anxiety and Anger,* (1973), and *Attachment and Loss, Vol. III: Loss, Sadness and Depression* (Markham, Ontario: Penguin Books Canada Ltd.).

[14] C. M. Binger et al., "Childhood Leukemia: Emotional Impact on Patient and Family," *New England Journal of Medicine* 280 (February 1969):414–18; Elizur and Kaffman, "Factors Influencing the Severity of Childhood Bereavement Reactions"; Robert A. Furman, "The Child's Reaction to Death in the Family," in *Loss and Grief: Psychological Management in Medical Practice,* ed. Bernard Schoenberg et al. (New York: Columbia University Press, 1970), pp. 70–86; Sidney H. Grossberg and Louise Crandall, "Father Loss and Father Absence in Preschool Children," *Clinical Social Work Journal* 6 (Summer 1978):123–34; Donald Ottenstein et al., "Some Observations on Major Loss in Families," *American Journal of Orthopsychiatry* 32 (April 1962):299–300; Joseph Palombo, "Parent Loss and Childhood Bereavement: Some Theoretical Considerations," *Clinical Social Work Journal* 9 (Spring 1981):3–33; and Helen Rosen and Harriette L. Cohen, "Children's Reactions to Sibling Loss," *Clinical Social Work Journal* 9 (Fall 1981):211–19.

[15] Richard G. Bruehl, "Mourning, Family Dynamics and Pastoral Care," in *Death and Ministry,* ed. J. Donald Bane et al. (New York: Seabury, 1975), pp. 92–101; Lois I. Greenberg, "Therapeutic Grief Work with Children," *Social Casework* 56 (July 1975):396–403; Jeffrey A. Kisner, "A Family Systems Approach to Grief," *Pastoral Psychology* 28 (Summer 1980):265–76; Perihan Rosenthal, "Short-term Family Therapy and Pathological Grief Resolution with Children and Adolescents," *Family Process* 19 (June 1980):151–59; Susan A. Salladay and Margit E. Royal, "Children and Death: Guidelines for Grief," *Child Psychiatry and Human Development* 11 (Summer 1981): 203–12; and Raphael, *The Anatomy of Bereavement.*

The Beginning: The Death and Funeral

Ideally the first session is arranged with the remaining parent for that parent and the children. Appropriate play materials would be out for the children to select what they want. After greetings to learn names and ages, it is time to get to know them in the first stage of the counseling. It may seem very abrupt to begin with the death and funeral without a long period of just getting acquainted. Yet everyone knows that a death has occurred and that this is the primary reason for the upset in their lives and their presence at a counseling session. To postpone talking about the death can increase tension as everyone waits to see who will mention it first. By choosing many other topics to talk about, the counselor may convey nervousness in talking about the death.

It is good to start by calmly asking strictly factual questions: When did the person die? Of what? How were you told that he or she was going to die? What was the person sick with? What was it like going to the hospital? Did death come suddenly? Where was everyone at the time of death? By imagining oneself in the situation, the counselor can find areas of confusion, which lead to more questions about what happened.

More is accomplished by noting the way in which the above questions are answered, and by matching the tone in statements to the children and parent, than by asking a bland question about feelings. This can be done tentatively: It is painful to recall. Sometimes it is hard to talk about. Boy, you're angry about that. Sounds like it was really scary. The examples do not exhaust the questions and statements that are appropriate, which must be chosen to match each parent and each child.

Since death leads to a funeral or a memorial service, questions about it naturally follow: Who came to the funeral? Where was it held? What did you think of the funeral or memorial service? Where is the person buried? Have you been to the gravesite? Was the body cremated? More specific questions can be asked if the family is not talkative.

Young children, of course, are likely to answer the questions in play or artwork. One child drew the marsh in which her father drowned and was able to tell about the picture. Another crashed cars together and fell down as he acted out his father's death in a car accident. It is important for the counselor to appreciate fully what the family and each member went through and to convey that appreciation back to the family and each member.

Depending on the family, circumstances of the death, and comfort with emotion, the first stage may take one to five sessions. Obviously memories of and emotion about the death and funeral will arise occasionally. The counselor can listen again, knowing that such a major and complex event takes time to become integrated. Having reviewed the death and funeral once with the family, the counselor will be better able to understand the connections when portions of the experience are brought up again.

The Middle: The Past and Memories

The second stage takes the parent and children back to the time before the death and introduces the counselor to the person who died. It is important to hear from each child what his or her memories are. Also it is important to recognize that each person has different memories. Questions about appearance are easy to begin with: What did the person look like? Did the person have (blue eyes, curly hair) like you (one of the children)? Do you have pictures to show me? How are you like the person in your personality? What was his or her job? What did you enjoy doing with the person? What was special about him or her for you? What things did the person do that you did not like?

With that last question, the counselor must be prepared for the answer "Nothing," at least in the beginning. A simple, quiet reply about no one being perfect is appropriate. It can set the stage for a time when the family members can admit that there were things about the person who died that they did not like. That is an important step for the parent and children, to allow the dead person to be a human being, not an angel. If (in an occasional family) the dead person has been made into an ogre, the process is reversed, and the counselor must wait for positive statements about the deceased.

Emotions can be intense in this stage, too. However there is a small change in tone from sadness to joy at what was, with some occasional irritation at what was not. The counselor's interest in the deceased can give the children an opportunity to reflect on the parent's life as well as death. The children can be invited to share photographs of the deceased and to draw pictures of happy times. Hobbies begun with the deceased may be shared. The counselor can also make remarks that tie the deceased person to those still living and thus emphasize that the person's influence continues despite the death. Remarks that are appropriate include: Boy, so he (or she) could be silly. That sounds neat. So you learned how to _____ from him (or her). Yeah, I guess that bothered you.

Drawing a family tree on a big piece of paper is helpful as the second stage begins or during it. Once drawn, it can be put up for each session. In drawing it, very specific questions must be asked about ages, marriages, divorces, other deaths, where people live, who came to the funeral, and who has helped. People who are dead are placed on the family tree but have an X over their name or a check beside it, with the date of death noted. This is a physical reminder of the fact of death. Each generation is organized on a different level, older generations being higher. Thus the family tree also serves as a reminder of the continuance of life.

The family tree helps the counselor learn more about the various people in the children's background and present life, while also helping the children. Children often have trouble sorting out various relatives who are just talked about. By visually organizing the information, the children have the opportunity to see all the different relatives they may have contact with or have heard about while learning more about their history. This exercise also draws the parent and children's attention to possible resources in the extended family.

Sometimes drawing the family tree is appropriate in the first session, when the family members are responding unemotionally to the issue of the death and the funeral. Parent and children are generally comfortable with the specific questions. Talking about members of the extended family can bring up issues, sometimes old ones, that they can be emotional about before they can express feelings about the death or that may be interfering with the grieving.

The family tree also can begin to provide information about conflicts in the larger family, which either existed before the death or which have been aggravated by the death. While drawing the family tree, the counselor can obtain clues about the possible need for therapy to resolve such conflicts. Stories about behavior at the funeral by various members can provide important information for the third stage.

The End: The Present and Future

The third stage primarily involves attention to the present and plans for the future. Certainly the counselor will have noted what the parent and the children are doing in their grief with respect to each other. It is very important to check on these relationships because family members are important resources that are often overlooked. This stage gives the counselor a closer look at possible problems in expressing and sharing grief. The kinds of questions to ask are: When do you miss him (or her) the most, in the morning or evening? Who do you talk to when you think of him (or her)? Where do you cry? What do you do when you see someone else cry? What would you like to be done for you when you start crying? How is it in school? Do your classmates and teachers know?

When the parent and children are uncertain about comforting each other, the counselor can look for ways they might do so. Some want to be able to talk, others to have someone sit beside them. Another may want to be alone briefly or to be involved in a particular activity. At appropriate points, the counselor might prompt behavior in the session on the part of one family member toward another.

Comments from the counselor about how they may think or feel when they are trying to relate to family and friends can help family members feel understood and more normal. Examples are: Sometimes it is hard to tell others. You don't always want to let others in class know you are sad. It is difficult to think about schoolwork when something so important in your life has changed. You may not always feel like playing with your friends, and they may not understand.

The process of checking on how family members are grieving with each other as they recall the dead person continues through several sessions.

Interwoven with the focus on support in grieving is concern over plans for the future of the parent and the children. The counselor should check with the parent on the financial situation, employment, and child care arrangements when the children are present. Children do worry about finances and it is better for them to know the facts rather than to create terrifying fantasies. The children may also have opinions about the arrangements. Questions to ask are: Are there savings? Are you receiving money from relatives? Do you want to stay where you are? Do you need to work? What job skills do you have? How are the children being cared for when the remaining parent is working? Who has been designated as the guardian in the event the remaining parent dies? This last question may seem cruel, but children do have worries about being left without any parents, and the remaining parent can often use help in attending to some very real issues. Children are reassured when they know that the remaining parent has thought of their future. If the remaining parent needs help in attending to such matters, then the counselor can arrange it.

Over the course of the sessions, the pain can subside and a wealth of emotions can be expressed. What ideally results is a satisfaction with having known the deceased, a willingness to think of him or her at special times, and the confidence to continue living while choosing which values of the deceased to express. It is unlikely that the parent or children can talk in these terms. Yet the counselor will begin to notice comments, tone, and postures of the family members that convey the change.

Eventually it will be time for the counselor to discuss ending the sessions. This will involve acknowledging the benefits of the counseling situation for all parties, including the counselor. Discussion of the impending loss of the counseling relationship is particularly appropriate. A recognition that difficult times are still ahead can be coupled with the knowledge that the family members can help each other and seek help from others, including the counselor, as needed.

DEATH AND DYING

CHAPTER 57

ILLNESS AND LOSS

Helping Couples Cope

Susan Krausz

Loss has been defined by Peretz (1970) as "a state of being deprived of or being without something one has had or valued". Grief can be defined as intense emotional suffering set off by a loss. Elisabeth Kübler-Ross's (1969) work "On Death and Dying" and Lindemann's (1944) pioneering work on grief have helped professionals to open up these areas for further exploration. Numerous contributions from the analytic literature (Bowlby, 1961; Freud, 1917) have enriched our understanding of loss and grief and its relationship to unconscious processes and the attendant dynamics.

Clinicians have come to recognize that incomplete or unresolved grief may lead to a wide variety of physical as well as psychological problems. Lieber et al. (1976) found that a significant percentage of cancer patients and their spouses reported a deterioration in their communication as a result of the illness. Worden & Weisman (1980) found that profound denial is associated with a higher risk of psychiatric dysfunction and that as denial increases and communication becomes more limited, psychiatric symptoms are more likely to appear. In keeping with these findings, Lewis & Beavers (1977) found that those families who are able to discuss the threat of death tend to have fewer psychological problems.

Simos (1977) suggests that the clinician know what experience constitutes a loss in order to help the patient recognize and cope with it. While it is usual for the illness or disability of a spouse to constitute a serious loss, the intensity, duration, and expression of the loss is quite difficult if not impossible to predict. In some ways, the illness and disability of a spouse may be experienced unconsciously in much the same way as an impending death. Yet, the chronicity of the problem and the continued existence of the relationship pose additional dilemmas for the family.

Reprinted from *Clinical Social Work Journal,* Vol. 16, No. 1 (Spring 1988), pp. 52–65, by permission of Human Sciences Press, Inc.

Grief work with couples following the diagnosis of severe illness or disability is similar to work with the bereaved in that the therapist's goal is gradually to facilitate the expression of feeling set off by the loss. Integration of loss requires that each individual come to terms with (1) the fact that one's survival and positive feeling states are being threatened, (2) the objective meaning of the loss, and (3) the subjective meaning of the loss (i.e. inner apprehension, fear or anger posed by the new or exaggerated burden of illness). In order for the grief process to be adequately completed, ties to the lost object are gradually withdrawn and energy is reconstituted for the establishment of new ties. Yet, how do couples faced with chronic illness or disability continue to maintain satisfying relationships if indeed they have in many ways mourned the loss of the relationship?

CONCEPTUAL UNDERPINNINGS

Kohut's (1971) theory of the self offers a conceptualization, within a normative development context, which may provide further insight into the experience of loss. He proposes that the infant, with a cohesive yet archaic sense of self, requires an environment in which it feels complemented in order to survive. The adult provides this complementarity by becoming a selfobject for the child, and the child experiences this merger with the selfobject as providing a sense of cohesion and wholeness. The selfobject, by responding with approval to the child's grandiose fantasies, acts as a tension regulator, thereby relieving feelings of helplessness in the child. Growth occurs as the child experiences mother as warm and loving during the process of separation and the child continues to see approval and acceptance in his or her parents' eyes while moving toward individuality and strength (Eisenhuth, 1981). The functions provided by the selfobject are gradually internalized, and the child develops a capacity to tolerate victory and defeat as well as acceptance and rejection. Nonetheless, Kohut points out that the need for selfobjects continues throughout life and that they are required for psychological survival. Kohut's theory suggests that the illness of a spouse may be understood in the context of "normal narcissistic" development and that the crisis of illness may pose a threat to the marital relationship when it impedes each spouse's ability to meet his/her partner's selfobject needs.

Palombo (1981), in discussing the loss of a love object through death, describes the process as characterized by initial shock, disbelief (especially if the death is unexpected) and denial. Eventually the defense of denial gives way to a gradual acceptance of reality wherein the painful feelings associated with the anticipation of lost attachment are expressed through the grieving process. According to Palombo the work of mourning involves decathexis of the object representation and gradual identification with aspects of the dead person. Self-representations are modified and partially reshaped in the image of the object. Once the ambivalent memories are worked through, the object representation is transformed into a set of memories, the investment is withdrawn, and libidinal energy becomes available for reattachment. If however, the identifications are defended against because the person finds it too painful to tolerate this process, the object representation may remain unmodified, the unconscious fantasy may exist that the object was never lost, and energy is not available for further reinvestment.

This conceptualization can be applied to the marital couple faced with the illness or disability of a spouse. If both spouses go through a process wherein they identify and mourn those aspects of the relationship which are lost, the representation of the lost aspects of the relationship may be transformed into a set of memories. Once the investment is withdrawn from those aspects of the relationship which have died, the couple is freer to invest in the relationship as it exists in the present. Reinvestment in the post-illness relationship is particularly difficult for the well spouse who is overly reliant on the partner to serve as a selfobject. For the person whose sense of self-esteem is not adequately internalized but rather derived from the relationship, the reinvestment in a partner with a severe disability or life threatening illness may be experienced as too threatening to one's own survival. Under these circumstances the reinvestment can take place if the well spouse can move to a more autonomous position, gradually internalizing the functions performed by the selfobject, thereby disinvesting the object of its need satisfying qualities so that it can be valued for its true self.

Pearlin's (1980) research on marital stress suggests that it is the durable strains encountered in everyday relationships which exert the greatest stress on couples. He identified three types of marital problems and conflict highly associated with marital distress including: lack of reciprocity in give and take relationship between husband and wife; failure of one spouse to fulfill a variety of role expectations such as affection, sexual partnership, and provider and homemaker duties; and lack of recognition and acceptance by one's spouse of one's real quintessential self. The losses imposed by the illness or disability of a spouse may exert an impact on all three of these areas. It is therefore not difficult to appreciate Pearlin's conclusion that couples under stress in these three areas often find it psychologically less disturbing to have the relationship terminated than to live out the relationship under these conditions. Pearlin's conclusion derives support from research findings which point to the fact that couples faced with the serious illness of one of them are at high risk for divorce, particularly if the marriage is young at the onset of illness.

A threat to the health or functioning of a spouse may be experienced as a major threat to survival and can lead to disruption in family functioning. Herz (1980) suggests that the degree of disruption is affected by (1) timing of the death or illness in the life cycle, (2) nature of the death or illness, (3) the family position of the seriously ill member, and (4) the openness of the family system. While the timing, the nature of the illness and the family position of the ill member cannot be altered, the openness of the family system is amenable to therapeutic intervention. Bowen (1976) defines openness as the ability of each family member to be "nonreactive to the emotional intensity in the system" and to communicate her/his thoughts and feelings to others without expecting others to act upon them.

While openness is affected by the individual's level of differentiation (the degree of fusion between emotional and intellectual functioning) and the level and duration of family stress, social and cultural norms support the lack of straightforwardness and openness in dealing with issues related to illness. Although there has been an increasing tendency on the part of physicians, mental health professionals and laymen to confront illness more directly, in many instances patients are faced with complex diagnoses and a limited appreciation of prognosis. The presence of psychological denial coupled with the focus on technical diagnostic data rather than prognostic indications (i.e. changes in life expectancy, capacity to continue to maintain existing work, family, and community roles) may at times tend to obfuscate the inroads we have made in this area. We have often been taught that we can protect others by sharing medical information selectively and by sparing those close to us the depth of our feelings.

The work of Kohut and Palombo, discussed earlier in the paper, contribute a profound appreciation of how past relationships and experiences affect the present marital relationship. On the one hand, the core emotional dynamics of each spouse emerge and dominate the marital patterns of interaction, reflecting conflicts deriving from earlier object relationships (Meissner, 1978). On the other hand, family systems theory suggests that institutionalized patterns and rules of the marital system may be greater than the sum of the characteristics of each of the spouses (Sluzki, 1978). It is the author's belief that these two approaches can be utilized concurrently with one another. However, for the purpose of this paper, the author will focus primarily on the emotional dynamics as they are reflected in the couple's interactional patterns. Basic struggles experienced by the couple, adaptations which promote optimal functioning and interventions which promote the openness of the family system at various points in the process will be addressed.

The remainder of this paper presents a developmental framework which addresses some of the unique processes in which couples engage in coping with chronic illness and disability. It is based on the author's experience as a social worker on a hospital rehabilitation unit and in her own private practice, her supervision of social work students in hospital based practice, as well as her own experience coping with the chronic illness and death of her spouse. While the paper attempts to identify a sequential pattern for the couple coping with these issues, the stages of adjustment may not follow in this order. The process will be affected by the nature of the preexisting marital relationship, the nature of family and environmental supports (Mailick, 1977) the premorbid level of personality functioning (Anthony, 1970) and the ramifications of the realities the couple must face. Although some couples may have a history of severe or chronic marital problems, this model addresses itself primarily to couples who have made a positive adaptation to marriage and considered themselves to have basically satisfying marital relationships prior to diagnosis.

STAGE I

Couples faced with the impact of illness or disability begin to deal with the crisis of illness and its implications at the time of diagnosis. It is useful to ascertain specifically how they discovered the problem, under what circumstances they were informed of the diagnosis and prognosis, who learned about it first, and how both members of the couple arrived at their present understanding of the illness. This introduction provides valuable information regarding the illness, the individuals involved, and the nature of the relationship prior to the crisis. Couples who share all diagnostic information with one another will function differently from those in which one member of the family acts as the gatekeeper of information.

During the initial period couples are most often in a state of crisis, during which time they attempt to cope with the diagnosis and immediate medical realities. In partial shock, the couple's efforts are directed to finding ways of coping with external stresses and demands imposed by diagnosis and illness. The two join to combat the threat to their survival, mobilizing resources and supports within the family and the larger environment.

Couples at this stage are preoccupied with confirming the diagnosis and discovering what medical alternatives exist. This process can be extraordinarily time consuming as well as physically and emotionally exhausting. Little time is left to deal with the emotional ramifications of the experience and couple interaction is usually supportive as they arrive at mutually agreed upon decisions regarding treatment options and procedures. This experience allows the couple to defend against the overwhelming threat to their lives, while at the same time mobilizing their positive coping efforts as well as their commitment to their relationship in this time of crisis. This often promotes a Hansel and Gretel like relationship in which all positive feelings and security are represented in the relationship, while all fears and assaults are seen as external. Given the real external threat to the relationship which is posed by the diagnosis, the pair attempts to keep the relationship as safe and nonthreatening as possible.

The couple's level of interaction is generally high, although affective communication is limited. Spouses may sympathize with one another and occasionally share their pain. However, the primary task of this stage is to cope and manage the current realities. This period is characterized by the avoidance of conflict. Both husband and wife are faced with a new situation in which they are uncertain of the spouse's reactions, and each is fearful of the other's responses. Fears related to the loss of the spouse, abandonment, dependency, or loss of previous forms of gratification are appropriate and common concerns rarely shared by the couple at this time. In order to maintain ongoing communication and allow for some expression without overtaxing the system, couples may engage in parallel conversation. One or both spouses may discuss a particular concern in front of their partner without eliciting or expecting the other's involvement. In moderation, this avoidance behavior may be quite adaptive. However, if it continues for a long period of time, couples run the risk of becoming increasingly isolated from one another.

Role of the Therapist

Working with couples shortly after diagnosis or following a serious medical regression requires support and appreciation of the realistic burdens and problems which confront them. Primary attention should be paid to reinforcing adaptive functioning and supporting the existing defensive structure. While the ultimate goal is to help couples deal successfully with the overwhelming realities and the affective issues related to illness and loss, timing is crucial. The therapist's role at this point is to control the pace and the amount of material which is revealed. Premature expression may prove maladaptive if defenses cannot be maintained during this particularly stressful time. If one spouse begins to deal with the affective issues before the other has had a chance to get over the initial shock, open discussion at this point might cause the other spouse to pull back. In this case, the concerns of the more expressive spouse need to be addressed individually. At the same time, attempts should be made to maintain the involvement of the less expressive spouse, until such time as s/he is available to deal with the affective concerns raised by the mate.

Ego supportive interventions aimed at reinforcing defenses and strengthening positive coping patterns facilitate the couple's reconstitution to a precrisis level of functioning. An attitude of acceptance and respect can be conveyed by the therapist's desire to understand the problems related to medical care and the concrete life changes that have occurred since diagnosis. Active involvement in providing concrete help is highly valued by the client and may be particularly important when family energy and resources are limited. The therapist's sensitivity to the specific problems and needs of the couple at this critical time often lay the groundwork for the development of a strong therapeutic alliance which later facilitates the sharing of other areas of difficulty (Krausz, 1983).

The couple faced with the diagnosis of a catastrophic or disabling illness is in a state of crisis and disorganization in which each spouse is trying to make sense out of what has happened while at the same time trying to regain paradise lost (pre-illness state of being). In an attempt to restore equilibrium, couples may consider making major changes in their living situations or further plans. Therapeutic interventions focus on delaying all major family decisions and postponing gratification until they are in a postcrisis state and have had more time to fully consider the implications of their actions. During this time, psychoeducational material addressing common problems faced by couples experiencing a medical crisis may also prove helpful in allaying future anxiety when new issues or problems emerge. The reassurance that they are not dysfunctional, crazy, or incompetent in the face of such tremendous stress is particularly comforting. In light of this it is often useful to develop small groups or support networks for couples facing similar difficulties. Within this context couples can share their experiences and engage in joint problem solving efforts related to the initiation and maintenance of medical treatment. Often couples who have successfully gone through one stage of a medical regimen may prove an invaluable resource for those who have not yet done so. Acceptance and support from peers as well as professionals help facilitate the couple's movement to the next stage of the process in which they address affective responses to the illness and their implications for the marital relationship.

STAGE II

Once the couple have done all they could to secure the best medical care available to them and are capable of handling the present stresses in their daily routine, a new balance is established. The partners are no longer as defended and are increasingly aware of the many biological, psychological, and social changes which have occurred, and the differential impact the illness/disability may have on each. Differences in style, personality, philosophy and ways of coping begin to surface. The fear that these differences may lead to rejection and or abandonment by the spouse leads to the emergence of a second affective crisis in the relationship.

An approach-avoidance conflict ensues. The need for closeness and support and the desire to maintain the positive aspects of the relationship encourage each spouse to risk approach and to address these affective issues with the partner. On the other hand, the fear of rejection, anger, and conflict support the avoidance of these issues. Trust is a prerequisite for the resolution of this dilemma. To the extent that each spouse trusts the other both can be relatively confident that the expression of their feelings or concerns will not be met with harm, punishment (pulling back), or rejection. This trust is usually based on an earlier resolution of differences in their marital relationship and in their families of origin. Otherwise it is unlikely that they will have sufficient resources to cope directly with this new threat to the relationship. Without trust, the expression of hostility and difference will result in alienation, thereby maintaining distance for the couple and avoiding fears of separation or death evoked by the illness.

Spouses are often frightened by the disintegration of the images they held of themselves (i.e. wife as the all-giving nurturer; husband as the competent provider) and of their mates. Given the realities of the illness, the maintenance of the idealized image of self and other is often impossible. The daily routines, schedule changes, medical regimens, economic changes, and role changes are often a source of tension and stress. The person who is ill may feel guilty or fearful of complaining or acknowledging dissatisfaction with behavior of the caretaking partner. The well spouse may feel angry and annoyed at being overburdened, unable to pursue personal and/or professional interests, yet feel uncomfortable or guilty about burdening the spouse with these reactions. Partners who were previously able to discuss and negotiate issues often do not feel free to do the same when one of them is ill. Unable to acknowledge frustration or irritation over differences, couples may avoid the issues or engage in repetitive spats over concrete matters rather than focus on underlying concerns. The strength and depth of the relationship are often a function of the couple's capacity to risk expression of fears and concerns and to allow the spouse equally full expression. The avoidance of affective issues often results in the perpetuation of a form of pseudointimacy. While this serves to minimize conflict, it may lead to escalation of the problem or to isolation from one another at a time when they need each other's love and support.

Couples that begin to share, accept, and empathize with each other's concerns despite feelings of disappointment and dissatisfaction, reinforce their affective bonds and facilitate further growth and intimacy in the relationship. Fears of helplessness, vulnerability, punishment, rejection, abandonment, physical pain or loss are commonly expressed by both partners. For the "identified patient," fears regarding the assertion of independence are often quite frightening, given the fact that she/he may be in many ways quite dependent physically on her/his spouse. For the "well" spouse, fears of overwhelming responsibility may be experienced when the patient expresses dependent longings. However, as both spouses discover that such intimate feelings can be shared without a sacrifice of autonomy or identity, they can continue to move towards each other despite their fears. Inherent in the issues discussed is the reality that, as a result of the present illness or disability, each has and will continue to suffer serious losses both individually and as a couple. Once these issues are shared, the feelings of loss and the concomitant grief can be addressed.

Role of the Therapist

Once the emotional issues between the two partners surface, the therapist's role is to encourage the expression of feelings, and to support the couple's need to communicate with each other. Since societal values often support shielding those we love, it is particularly important that the therapist present and model norms for coping which encourage open communication. This often involves helping each partner to hear the concerns and fears of the other without feeling the need to respond with concrete suggestions or advice to make it better. If young children or adolescents are still in the home, their involvement in the process should be facilitated (Adams-Greenley & Moynihan, 1983). The goal is to surface common underlying feelings and concerns, so as to establish and reinforce a base of shared values, empathy, and support. At this point couples may engage in diversionary tactics or escalate into arguments about other issues. The defensive interaction can be framed as their continued protection of one another, and the therapist can explore with both the feelings or fears associated with hearing the other's concerns. At the same time, both spouses can be helped to accept that they are not expected to, nor will they ever be able to meet the other's needs all the time. Nevertheless, the expression of the need is still valid.

The first obstacle in this process is reducing fear and guilt sufficiently for partners to maintain affective contact with each other. By slowly sharing limited concerns, the partners get feedback from one another and can begin to find out if their worst fears are true. Once problem areas have become partialized, fears of rejection and retaliation are reduced considerably. If indeed a spouse does respond in a rejecting or inappropriate manner, the therapist's support and validation are critical. Under such circumstances the therapist may need to express or reframe an idea or concern in a less threatening way, emphasizing the sharing of mutual concern and feeling, rather than the need to act. However, if the current realities require immediate action, attempts are made to mediate the conflict between the couple, supporting decisions which take into consideration the needs of the family unit and the maintenance of appropriate boundaries. Once the couple realizes that conflict during this critical time does not constitute disloyalty or rejection, but rather a normative response to this situation, each successive conflict becomes progressively easier to resolve.

This emotional crisis is most difficult and its resolution is often reflective of the couple's capacity for intimacy prior to the illness. The two could not possibly resolve all intimacy conflicts during this initial struggle, and they are successful if they can establish beginning norms regarding the expression of and responses to each other's emotional reactions to the current loss.

Feelings of sorrow and loss which emerge during this process are addressed by the therapist either in individual or in couples therapy. The duration and severity of the illness, the uniqueness of the couple and their capacity for intimacy should be considered when choosing the medium for this aspect of treatment. It is preferable to see the couple together so that interactional patterns of coping can be addressed directly. Emphasis is placed on dealing with current transactions and patterns of communication. If there is a recurrent problematic theme, an effort is made to help the couple enact their argument in the room so that the work can focus on the underlying affective issues as well as role shifts and other structural problems.

STAGE III

For those couples who reach this stage, a new or reclaimed feeling of comfort and inclusion pervades the relationship. While previously, autonomy was suppressed in favor of overt agreement and similarity, differences are now tolerable given the foundation of shared empathy. Roles are less rigidly prescribed, and both partners experience greater comfort in giving of themselves, saying no to their spouse, and in asking or accepting help from others. Each spouse develops the capacity to tolerate her/his own ambivalence and uncertainty as well as that of her/his partner. Disagreement and conflict without fear of rejection enhance the couple's sense of security, as well as feelings of individual self worth. Fears of rejection for certain behaviors or feelings are always present to some extent. However, following the couple's successful struggle with these issues, the experience of relief and the consequent bonding provide a continued base of support allowing the couple to appropriately mourn their losses and to move ahead together within a new structure (postillness). Couples who have not adequately resolved the affective crisis of Stage II invariably are deprived of an opportunity to engage in the mourning process together and to integrate the meaning of their shared loss

Couples in this stage are seen most often when they are faced with a new crisis, particularly a relapse or worsening of the medical situation. The new threat to the couple and each individual is frightening, and the maintenance of intimacy is difficult when the fear of loss is overwhelming. The expression of grief within the context of the relationship is the primary task at this point in the process.

Role of the Therapist

At this stage, the therapist continues to facilitate the mutual helping process, lending further knowledge and insight when necessary. Here and now focus on those issues of concern to the couple are addressed on an as needed basis. At this time, temporary emotional distancing may be necessary in order to allow each person to regroup. Therapeutic intervention is focused on helping the couple eventually to reconnect, if possible. Painful feelings of sorrow and loss which emerge during this process can be recognized and validated by the therapist. If the couple is able to go through this necessary mourning process, while at the same time maintaining strong affective bonds with each other, they are better able to maintain a sense of hopefulness and positive expectation regarding the relationship despite the limitations imposed by the illness. Individuals who mourn the changes in the relationship and the potential losses without maintaining a strong affective bond often find themselves decathecting prematurely from the spouse and limiting the potential for continued support, intimacy, and satisfaction which might still be available. In cases where the losses imposed by the illness are so overwhelming that little satisfaction can be provided within the relationship, the mourning process can assist the "surviving spouse" in gradually decathecting from her/his partner, and slowly investing in other areas of life. The continued affective bond is valuable, especially if death or severe loss which precludes mutual intimacy is imminent. An affective connection can be maintained, focusing on the need to eventually move apart, separate, or accept the pain of losing the other. Each individual mourns the losses and gradually lets go of the connection to the loved one. The shared pain, love, and grief allow each member to move away, neither feeling self as abandoned or as abandoned by the other.

CASE EXAMPLE

Sherry and Joseph, who had been married for 25 years, had difficulty renewing their sexual relationship following the amputation of Joseph's right leg as a result of diabetes. In brief couples therapy Sherry acknowledged her fear that Joseph would be unable to perform sexually and Joseph indicated that while he was physically capable, he was afraid that the amputation would make him unattractive to his wife. The therapist questioned how he himself reacted to the stump, and he cried while talking about how repulsive it was and that he wished to spare his wife by not asking any more of her. Exploration revealed that Joseph avoided showing his wife the stump or allowing her to directly care for it following surgery. Sherry's reactions were elicited and she shared her anxiety as well as her desire to get used to it. Prior to focusing on their sexual relationship the couple were encouraged to spend some time getting used to the stump, how it looked, how it felt, etc. They were then encouraged to talk about their feelings and both acknowledged that the stump symbolized a continued threat to their life together. Upon resuming their sexual relationship, both experienced greater intimacy as well as increased fear that they would lose each other. Sherry's grief was quite overwhelming; she feared the possible death of her husband, and was frightened that she would not be able to manage on her own. Her husband, who initially felt quite helpless and dependent, welcomed the opportunity to comfort and provide support to his wife (moving back into his preillness role). This shift brought about major changes in the relationship, with Sherry experiencing Joseph as still able to take care of her and both beginning to appreciate the help they could provide one another despite the losses and changes they had experienced. Joseph's experience of himself as again strong in the relationship enabled him to take greater risks in other areas, and he returned to expand the social network which they had retreated from over the previous year. At her request, Sherry was seen individually for five sessions and this time was used to enable her to recognize her strengths and anticipate how she could handle living if she were without Joseph. She was encouraged by her husband and children to expand her interests and she did rekindle two strong friendships. The worker focused largely on the existing supports within their marriage and other significant systems. At the time of termination, the couple had returned to their preamputation lifestyle, with Joseph feeling increasingly competent as a man and a husband, and Sherry feeling supported and less frightened of being on her own. Both were aware of the continued threat to Joseph's life, but were able to move ahead and focus on the present rather than the past or the future.

CONCLUSIONS

The author presents a developmental model which identifies three stages of adjustment experienced by couples coping with the illness of a spouse and proposes differential interventive strategies at each stage. Stage I is characterized by denial, focus on concrete medical realities, and on the joining of the couple in their efforts to combat the threat to their survival as a unit. Stage II is characterized by the emergence of the affective crisis associated with the bio-psycho-social changes which have altered the couple's relationship, and Stage III focuses on grief and mourning within the context of the relationship. While the illness of a spouse brings with it profound losses for each partner, once fears and issues of loss are openly discussed, couples are better able to rely on each other for emotional support and to maintain their ongoing investment in the relationship despite the continued threat posed by illness.

REFERENCES

Adams-Greenley, M. & Moynihan, R. (1983). Helping the children of fatally ill parents. *American Journal of Orthopsychiatry 53*(2).

Anthony, E.J. (1970). The mutative impact of serious mental and physical illness of a parent on family life. In E.J. Anthony & C. Koupernik (Eds.), *The child in his family*. New York: Wiley-Interscience.

Bowen, M. (1976). Family reaction to death. In P. Guerin (Ed.), *Family therapy: Theory and practice*. New York: Gardner Press.

Bowlby, J. (1961). Process of mourning. *International Journal of Psychoanalysis, 42*, 317–340.

Eisenhuth, E. (1981). The theories of Heinz Kohut and clinical social work practice. *Clinical Social Work Journal, 9*(2), 80–90.

Freud, S. (1917). Mourning and melancholia. In J. Riviere (Ed.), *Collected Papers, Volume IV*. London: Hogarth Press, 1950.

Herz, F. (1980). The impact of death and serious illness on the family life cycle. In Carter & McGoldrick (Eds.), *The family life cycle: A framework for family therapy*. New York: Gardner Press.

Kohut, H. (1971). *The analysis of the self*. New York: International Universities Press.

Krausz, S. (1983). Short-term group therapy for newly blinded men. In M. Rosenbaum (Ed.), *Handbook of short-term therapy groups*. New York: McGraw Hill.

Kübler-Ross, E. (1969). *On death and dying*. New York: Macmillan.

Lewis, J.M. & Beavers, W.R. (1977). The family of the patient. In G. Usdin (Ed.), *Psychiatric medicine*. New York: Brunner-Mazel.

Lieber, L., Plumb, M., Gerstenzang, M.L., & Holland, J. (1976). The communication of affection between cancer patients and their spouses. *Psychosomatic Medicine, 38*, 379–389.

Lindemann, E. (1944). Symptomatology and management of acute grief. *American Journal of Psychiatry, 101*, 141–148.

Mailick, M. (1979). The impact of severe illness on the individual and family: an overview. *Social Work in Health Care, 5*(2).

Meissner, W. (1978). The conceptualization of marriage and family dynamics from a psychoanalytic perspective. In T. Paolino & B. McCrady (Eds.), *Marriage and marital therapy*. New York: Brunner-Mazel

Palombo, J. (1981). Parent loss and childhood bereavement: Some theoretical considerations. *Clinical Social Work Journal, 9*(1), 3–33.

Pearlin, L. (1980). Life strains and psychological distress among adults. In N. Smelser, & E. Erikson, (Eds.), *Themes of work and love in adulthood.* Cambridge: Harvard University Press.

Peretz, D. (1970). Development, object relationships, and loss. In B. Shoenberg et al. (Eds.), *Loss and grief: Psychological management in medical practice.* New York: Columbia University Press.

Sluzki, C. (1978). Marital therapy from a systems therapy perspective. In T. Paolino & B. McCrady (Eds.), *Marriage and marital therapy.* New York: Brunner-Mazel.

Simos, B. (1977). Grief therapy to facilitate healthy restitution. *Social Casework, 58.*

Worden, W.J. & Weisman, A.D. (1980). Do cancer patients really want counseling? *General Hospital Psychiatry, 2,* 100–103.

CHAPTER 58

ADOLESCENTS' EXPERIENCE WITH DEATH

Practice Implications

Susan A. Cho, Edith M. Freeman, and Shirley L. Patterson

The real experience of death among adolescents has been hidden or obscured by elements in American culture which have suppressed a straightforward appreciation of the fact of death. For example, it is only primarily within the past decade that death, dying, and grief have been openly dealt with by diverse populations of all ages. Kübler-Ross's groundbreaking work in 1969 served as a catalyst for a plethora of empirical and applied death-related research.[1] Much of the current literature emphasizes the conspiracy of silence which has surrounded death and the dying process.

It is difficult, if not impossible, to calculate the impact of massive cultural denial of death on the members of this society. However, the denial process has affected and continues to affect both attitudes and behavior of children, young people, and adults. Death, augmented by cultural bias, has been viewed with dread as a deplorable evil,[2] a fearful and unnatural event. These negative associations make it nearly impossible for human beings to conceive of the cessation of life.[3] The denial process remains intact.

In Rachel Rustow Aubrey's view, the topic of death is taboo, particularly for middle-aged and older Western-educated adults.[4] Other authors, however, assume that indi-

---

Reprinted from *Social Casework,* Vol. 63, No. 2 (1982), pp. 88–94, by permission of the publisher, Families International, Inc.

[1] Elisabeth Kübler-Ross, *On Death and Dying* (New York: Macmillan, 1970).

[2] Avery D. Weisman, "Common Fallacies about Dying Patients," in *Death: Current Perspectives,* ed. Edwin S. Shneidman (Palo Alto, Calif.: Mayfield Publishing, 1976), p. 438.

[3] Kübler-Ross, *On Death and Dying,* p. 2.

[4] Rachel Rustow Aubrey, "Adolescents and Death," in *Social Work with the Dying Patient and the Family,* ed. Elizabeth R. Prichard, et al. (New York: Columbia University Press, 1977), 132–33.

viduals are more vulnerable and less able to cope with the impact of any crisis at certain crucial stages of their psychosocial development.[5] Adolescence is one such stage, when an individual's mental health is especially susceptible to both personal and environmental stresses. The major tasks of adolescents having to cope with identity crises and physical changes in their bodies, in addition to society's expectations that they move into the adult role, are examples of such stresses.[6] Robert J. Kastenbaum argues that adolescents are particularly vulnerable to the dominant cultural attitudes of evasion and encapsulation on the subject of death.[7] When confronted with a death, the adolescent may uneasily mimic such parental coping mechanisms as denial, despair, and avoidance, rather than following through on an initial impulse to deal openly with the situation.[8] In the recent past it is likely that cultural influences have effectively masked adolescents' experience with death (people dying in institutions rather than at home). However, the undesirable isolation of young people from the process of death and dying has not only arisen as a result of lack of knowledge. Negative cultural views of death, which solidify pervasive denial, have also been powerful suppressants to dealing with death.

Additionally, fantasies of adolescents about death have been associated frequently with romantic notions of dying.[9] It is not uncommon for them to fantasize a heroic death in the service of a cause, friendship, or love, although the Vietnam War and more recent cataclysmic events may have modified these fantasies. Both adolescents and adults have viewed the age of youth as the golden years, a time of vitality, energy, and even immortality; surely one who is so young and bursting with life will not be visited by death.[10] This societal theme has served to sustain fantasies of youthful immortality, as opposed to the reality of death at any age.

Assuming the experience of death to be a crisis for adolescents, Erich Lindemann applied crisis theory to grief reactions which follow the death of a loved one.[11] He concluded that an individual had to make an adjustment to the crisis that is precipitated by such a death. He noted that grief reactions to death, like crisis reactions in general, follow a predictable pattern and have specific identifiable stages. These stages are somewhat similar to those that have been suggested by authors whose focus is specifically on grief reactions to dying.[12]

In most of these conceptualizations, the implicit assumption is that it is crucial for individuals to experience all of the identifiable stages in order to cope adequately with the precipitating situation. Experiencing them provides the individual with a different per-

---

[5] Richard A. Pasewark and Dale A. Albers, "Crisis Intervention: Theory in Search of a Program," *Social Work* 17 (March 1972): 70–77.

[6] Erik H. Erikson, *Childhood and Society,* 2d ed. (New York: W. W. Norton, 1963).

[7] Robert J. Kastenbaum, "Time and Death in Adolescence," in *The Meaning of Death,* ed. Herman Feifel (New York: McGraw-Hill, 1959), pp. 111–12.

[8] Aubrey, "Adolescents and Death," p. 133.

[9] E. Mansell Pattison, "Death Throughout the Life Cycle," in *The Experience of Dying,* ed. E. Mansell Pattison (Englewood Cliffs, N.J.: Prentice-Hall, 1977), p. 23.

[10] Robert J. Kastenbaum, *Death, Society and Human Experience* (St. Louis, Mo.: C. V. Mosby, 1977), pp. 141–42. See also Morton Puner, *To the Good Long Life: What We Know about Growing Old* (New York: Universe Books, 1974), p. 230.

[11] Erich Lindemann, "Symptomatology and Management of Acute Grief," *American Journal of Psychiatry* 101 (September 1944): 141–48.

[12] See, for example, Kübler-Ross, *On Death and Dying.*

spective about death. Both crisis theory and cognitive behavioral theory provide a compatible and functional framework for viewing adolescents' grief reactions to the death of significant others. The framework emphasizes that crisis is not pathological, and equips the individual with appropriate behavioral coping skills that permit a relabeling of the problem situation from unmanageable to manageable.[13]

Currently, society is in the midst of a social change—moving from denial of death to acceptance of death as a normal part of the life cycle. Research indicates that adolescents are capable of discarding the mask of denial and dealing openly and realistically with mortality. As one investigator pointed out: "It is difficult to defend the proposition that children are unacquainted with death. More tenable is the proposition that often we are not sufficiently acquainted with our children's thoughts and experiences."[14]

ONE RESEARCH STUDY

According to Patricia L. Ewalt and Lola Perkins, "the degree of young people's isolation from the reality of death may . . . have been greatly exaggerated."[15] In a recent study, Ewalt and Perkins sought to determine the extent to which juniors and seniors in two high schools had had real experiences with death and dying. [16]

The Study Sample and Questionnaire

A six-item questionnaire was given by Ewalt and Perkins to all juniors and seniors in two metropolitan Kansas City schools during a two-day period in September 1978. A response rate of 76 percent was received from both schools. One school had primarily a middle-class population (73 percent white; 27 percent minority), while the other school's students were representative of working-class families (66 percent white; 34 percent minority).

Findings

There were similar findings for both schools: Almost 90 percent of students at both schools (1,303) reported seeing a dead person and losing a grandparent, aunt, uncle, sibling, or someone else they cared about through death. Approximately 20 percent (283) of the students indicated they had been present when a person died. Another 40 percent (591) had experienced the death of a close friend of their own age. Experience with death was more frequent for seniors than for juniors. The investigators observed that by the time students reached their senior year, 11 percent (twice the national estimates) had lost at least one parent through death.[17]

---

[13] Pasework and Albers, "Crisis Intervention: Theory in Search of a Program." See also Michael J. Mahoney and Carl E. Thoresen, *Self Control: Power to the Person* (Monterey, Calif.: Brooks/Cole, 1974).

[14] Kastenbaum, *Death, Society and Human Experience*, p. 123.

[15] See Patricia L. Ewalt and Lola L. Perkins, "The Real Experience of Death Among Adolescents," *Social Casework: The Journal of Contemporary Social Work* 60 (November 1979): 547–51.

[16] Ibid.

[17] Ibid., pp. 548–49.

Assuming that these findings may be generalized to other adolescent populations, it appears that experience with death among adolescents may be quite high. On the basis of this study, Ewalt and Perkins conclude that for the vast majority of teenagers from working and middle-class homes, death may be encountered more frequently than previously thought.[18] The implications of these findings pose a substantial challenge to all who serve adolescent populations.

THE PRACTICE IMPLICATIONS

Social workers often are in strategic positions to intervene with troubled teenagers, and need to be aware of the high possibility of reactions to significant loss. However, to work effectively with the bereaved and dying and those who surround them, practitioners initially must pursue personal mastery of their own fear of death, and temper any of their own professional views which are incompatible with this kind of work. The change must begin with personal insight. Practitioners need to address how they have coped with personal loss, what their family beliefs and values are, and what their vision of their own personal living and dying is. Professionals can use supervision and the support of colleagues to look at case situations and practice dilemmas which stir their own discomfort. They can recognize their individual ways of denying their own inevitable end.

Courses on death and dying are now being offered as continuing education for experienced practitioners. The need for taking such courses often is recognized after working with a difficult case situation. Practitioners should avail themselves of this opportunity to renew their emotional set and social work frame of reference, and to pursue acceptance of their own death.

Only by first facing themselves, can practitioners begin to have an impact on the many barriers to expression of grief among their clients. Whether they function in a one-to-one or a group clinical setting, community consultation practice, or school social work practice, the emotional availability of the practitioner to discuss and work with this volatile issue is the essential seed for change.

Because of the inaccessibility of such learning in the natural life process, more and more professional schools are including courses on death and dying in their curricula. These remedial courses are needed and should be encouraged. Eda Goldstein,[19] a social worker who teaches such a course, discusses the importance of a class process which balances the intellectual and emotional approaches to the subject. She sees this balance as enabling students to use their anxiety about death to promote learning rather than denial.

[18] Ibid., p. 549.
[19] Eda G. Goldstein, "Teaching a Social Work Perspective on the Dying Patient and His Family," in *Social Work with the Dying Patient and the Family*, ed. Elizabeth R. Prichard et al., (New York: Columbia University Press, 1977), pp. 304–05, 311.

The Social Worker in School Settings

School social workers, because of their proximity to adolescents in trouble and their goal of intervening in areas that affect student's academic and social functioning, are in a key practice position to address dysfunctional coping with grief. It is important for school social workers to be trained in child development and depression reactions in order to recognize changes in adolescents who experience death and dying of significant others.

In relation to this diagnostic skill, the social worker should:

1. Be able to identify (as early as possible) students who need help in dealing with grief reactions. The assistance of other school personnel is crucial in this identification process. If the social worker has the reputation for dealing with grief reactions (and not denying them), teachers and other school personnel are more likely to make referrals.
2. Educate other school personnel to recognize symptoms of grief reactions in students. This step may be difficult because other problem behaviors may mask the symptoms.
3. Mediate between the student and his or her environment when the student is dealing with grief.
4. Recognize that the normal identity crisis of the adolescent may be exacerbated when coupled with grief reactions. Special attention will need to be given to problem solving.

Identifying as early as possible students who are experiencing grief reactions may be the most crucial of these four steps in terms of the role of the school social worker. It can be accomplished by increasing the awareness of others in the school environment about grief reactions, which will not only increase the rate of appropriate referrals from teachers and other school personnel, but also from students themselves.

In one example Jean, a high school senior, "dropped in" on the school social worker, ostensibly to discuss her career plans. In the process, she mentioned that recently she had experienced cardiac arrest during kidney transplant surgery. She described a sensation of feeling as though she was outside of her body observing her own death, and moving away from herself toward a bright light. She was frustrated when her doctor and family encouraged her to "forget it." Her relief in discussing this experience with the social worker was evident. Several other sessions were scheduled to allow Jean to confront her fears and the related grief response.

The ability to mediate pressures in both the home and school environment is another important step for focusing school social work interventions. Often, students are unable or unwilling to share information about a loss experience, or to identify easily in what way these pressures are affecting their functioning.

For example, another school social worker got a referral on Terri, a fourteen-year-old student whose above-average marks had gradually changed to failing grades. In addition to Terri, the social worker began to work with Terri's mother and two younger siblings. She learned that a number of family and school problems stemmed from the family's difficulty in dealing with their mother's terminal illness. Interventions included locating a support person in the school for Terri, and helping the mother to locate a community resource for in-home care, so that Terri could participate in age-appropriate recreation with peers.

Many other practice examples within school settings lend support to the need for a systematic approach to dealing with students' loss and grief reactions. Interventions based on such an approach should be focused on the four steps outlined and on other critical points at various levels of the school and family system.

The Social Worker in Mental Health Settings

Social workers in mental health or social service settings can have an impact on situations where adolescents are suffering grief. A key to their effectiveness is how thoroughly they look for and recognize the adolescents who are grieving in silence. Aubrey, in a review of cases in a student psychiatric service, noted that very few students cited loss as a presenting problem. However, a high incidence of cases revealed earlier significant loss.[20] If professional helpers have prepared themselves to be able to consider the reality of significant loss, they should be able to uncover important incidents in their clients' lives. They should have a sharpened intuitive sense to note feelings not commensurate to the presenting situation, and be able to probe further to find earlier or current incidents which may be influencing the present reaction. The ability of practitioners to help identify issues of grief is enhanced by the depth and breadth of their sensitivity to another's plight, their skill in facilitating the exposure of repressed information, and their openness to encountering the uniqueness of their clients.

Frequently, mental health practitioners are engaged as consultants to community agencies and institutions. Their expressed task is to impart information about human behavior and problems so that the consultee can more effectively promote emotional well-being.[21] One author has proposed that there be "outreach" efforts by professionals on university campuses when a student dies or commits suicide. She suggested that the professional informally stop by student gathering places to talk about the incident. He or she can thereby encourage the immediate ventilation of pain, grief, and rage, in order to counter the stiff-upper-lip coping technique.[22]

In another setting, a social worker in a public welfare department describes a program where adolescents who have lost a parent through death offer friendship to other youngsters in similar circumstances. The program's success is attributed to the open, direct sharing of common feelings and experiences.[23] Still another author cites how practitioners need to give direct and persuasive permission for clients to express anger and grief in a one-to-one or group session.[24]

Another means to ameliorate the stringent taboos surrounding death and dying is educating parents to understand their children's needs and, indirectly, their own. This

---

[20] Aubrey, "Adolescents and Death," p. 133.
[21] Raymond M. Glasscote et al., *Children and Mental Health Centers—Programs, Problems, Prospects* (Washington, D.C.: American Psychiatric Association, 1972), p. 36.
[22] Aubrey, "Adolescents and Death," p. 136.
[23] See James A. Cardarell, "A Group for Children of Deceased Parents," *Social Work* 29 (July 1975); 328.
[24] Gary A. Lloyd, "The Expression of Grief as Deviant Behavior in American Culture," in *Social Work with the Dying Patient and the Family,* ed. Elizabeth R. Prichard et al., (New York: Columbia University Press, 1977), p. 15.

training can be provided on a family-by-family basis, in a clinical setting, or through family life education classes. Community education programs on death and bereavement also fight the battle against silence and denial. These are often sponsored by local mental health associations or colleges. It should be noted that a study of what students want and need in a death education class identified the importance of including affective and therapeutic components to help them cope with their confusions and fears.[25]

A MULTILEVEL INTERVENTION MODEL

Whether the social worker practices in a school or a mental health setting, the process of helping must involve a relabeling of grief from unmanageable, fearful, and hopeless. Adolescents need to be helped to see that, while they cannot change the fact of death, they can change their responses to it. Some of the coping skills that are essential to changing the response to death include modification of talk that labels the dying situation as unmanageable, meditation techniques for management of stress, self-monitoring of dysfunctional responses, self-reinforcement for appropriate responses, and completing tasks that allow expression of feelings and remove fears.[26]

The content of sessions with the adolescents must include the following:

1. The opportunity for the teenagers to share thoughts and fears about death with peers, and to come to terms with the particular death experience with which they are involved.[27]
2. Some teaching of the stages of grief and the importance of expression of feelings, with the adolescents receiving help from the social worker and peers in identifying feelings and stages of grief which they are experiencing.
3. Provision of facts about death by the social worker or medical personnel, including physical and psychological changes.
4. Help for the adolescents to identify their fears concerning unusual family responsibilities, changes in their own bodies, and the risks of investing in relationships.
5. The use of humor as a vehicle to express feelings. Humor can help adolescents cope with the awesomeness of the predicament. One author quotes an example: "Humor relieved the tension" and "My sister used to say, 'Don't touch me, you'll give me cancer.' I know it's a joke, it's something that isn't real good, but you joke about it to make you feel better."[28]
6. The use of the vernacular, metaphor, and candor to help establish intimacy. The practitioner needs to remember that teenagers need reassurance that the helper can deal with death, and that he or she need not be protected. A sim-

[25] Charles R. O'Brien et al., "Death Education: What Students Want and Need!" *Adolescence* 13 (Winter 1978): 732–33.
[26] Mahoney and Thoresen, *Self Control: Power to the Person,* p. 270.
[27] Ewalt and Perkins, "The Real Experience of Death Among Adolescents," p. 549.
[28] Myron Karon, "The Physician and the Adolescent with Cancer," *Pediatric Clinics of North America* 20 (November 1973): 967.

ple, "It's all right, I have been there," can go a long way to strengthen a working bond.[29]

For optimal results with grieving adolescents, intervention must occur on several levels to facilitate the relabeling process. This process is depicted in Figure 58–1.

The intervention model includes the following components:

The Adolescent: individual or group counseling that focuses on activities or tasks that link past, present, and future for the adolescent; that give permission to break the ban on talking about death; and that teach stress management. The outcomes are skill development in coping and resolution of grief.

Significant Others: sibling therapy or family counseling when family members are affected by the death in question. The responses of family members, but in particular those of siblings, can affect the primary client's progress in coping with and managing grief. This counseling can also be helpful in providing feedback on the progress of all siblings. It can take the form of placing the siblings in different groups, seeing them individually, or seeing them together. The outcomes are mediation of family stress reactions and spillover effects.

Support Networks: peer supports for social outlets and for reality testing. The social worker can help the adolescent identify and utilize such support. These sources can be recreational, educational, or religious, depending on the interests and needs. This kind of support is important because adolescence is a phase when young people see themselves as being different and alone, and this feeling of being different is exacerbated by the grief reaction and fears about death. Support should involve contact with peers who

Figure 58–1
A Multilevel Intervention Model for Relabeling Death and Grief Reactions

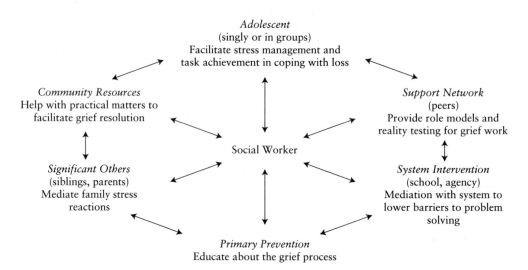

[29] Lloyd, "The Expression of Grief as Deviant Behavior in American Culture," p. 15.

have also experienced a loss. The outcomes are reduced social isolation and the fostering of mutual support systems.

Community Resources: referral for the adolescent and his or her family, especially when the family is also experiencing a grief reaction. The referral might involve financial resources, custody of children, insurance matters, or natural support systems. The outcomes are identification of community and natural helping resources, professional services, and completion of tasks that help with saying "goodbye."

System Intervention: mediation in settings where the adolescent is not being understood or accepted, or where resolution of grief is being blocked by the system. The outcome is removal or modification of barriers, that is, outreach to the adolescent from agency or institutional personnel.

Primary Prevention: education efforts with adolescents singly or in groups. The outcomes are demystification of death, knowledge of grief and grieving, and acceptance of death as the natural completion of the life process.

The value of a multilevel practice approach for dealing with loss and grief is that it can enhance emotional growth and social functioning in adolescents, their peers, families, and persons within their environment. In addition, it promotes a role for social work in the important areas of prevention and problem solving, as well as requiring collaboration between agencies and an integration of clinical and community skills.

AN EDUCATIONAL EFFORT

Social work literature indicates that adolescents tend to deny death rather than accepting it as part of the life cycle. An educational effort, reflected in the writings of Kübler-Ross, has begun to address this denial. It does so by encouraging a recognition of grieving as a natural and necessary process for the continuation of the living. Research reported in this article indicates that death and dying can have significant impact on the teenager—who is already in a developmental crisis. Helping professionals in close proximity to adolescents have the opportunity to provide education about death and dying, and to help grieving adolescents relabel their reactions to this experience. A key to how useful such practitioners will be is the creativity they use to engage themselves with clients and their environments. When constructive work with these adolescents is done, the effects can permanently influence the quality of their lives.

EATING DISORDERS

CHAPTER 59

TREATMENT ALTERNATIVES FOR BULIMIA PATIENTS

Barbara V. Bulow and Neal De Chillo

Bulimia, a psychiatric symptom rarely mentioned a decade ago, has received increasing attention in both the professional and popular literature. Social workers in various settings, from community agencies to private practice, encounter individuals with bulimia. Therefore, they must be able to recognize and properly diagnose the illness as well as to recommend appropriate treatment based on the client's unique psychodynamics and social system. A recent article addressed the assessment of the bulimic client.[1] The present article reviews proposed treatment strategies and suggests treatment alternatives based on the range of manifestations of this disorder.

There is some confusion in the literature pertaining to eating disorders, because American and British researchers use different diagnostic terms with slightly different meanings. The term "bulimia," which is used in the third edition of the American Psychiatric Association's *Diagnostic and Statistical Manual of Mental Disorders* (DSM III), is most commonly, but not exclusively, used in the United States. The diagnostic criteria for bulimia include "recurrent episodes of binge eating accompanied by an awareness that the eating pattern is abnormal, fear of not being able to stop eating voluntarily, and depressed mood and self-depreciating thoughts following the eating binges."[2] A diagnosis of bulimia according to DSM III does not, therefore, necessitate vomiting or purging behavior and does not require preoccupation with body shape and weight.

In contrast, the term "bulimia nervosa," commonly used in Great Britain, requires

Reprinted from *Social Casework*, Vol. 8, No. 8 (1987), pp. 477–484, by permission of the publisher, Families International, Inc.

[1] William J. Swift, "Assessment of the Bulimia Patient," *American Journal of Orthopsychiatry* 55 (July 1985): 384–96.

[2] American Psychiatric Association, *Diagnostic and Statistical Manual of Mental Disorders,* 3rd ed. (Washington, D.C.: American Psychiatric Association, 1980), pp. 69–71.

the existence of vomiting or purging behavior and stresses the fear of fat.[3] As Christopher Fairburn points out, ". . . although the relationship between these syndromes (the bulimic syndromes) has not been formally studied, clinical experience suggests that bulimia nervosa may be regarded as a subtype of bulimia in which binge-eating is accompanied by self-induced vomiting or purgative abuse."[4]

It should be recognized that bulimia, described above as a specific illness, may also be one symptom within a larger constellation of symptoms or may occur concomitantly with other illnesses in a single patient. The most common example is a depressed patient with an eating disorder that is one of many symptoms, such as sleep disturbance, depressed mood, anhedonia, or loss of concentration. For such an individual, treatment that addresses only the symptom of bulimia would be inappropriate. Another example is a patient who is bulimic only when intoxicated with alcohol or other drugs. In such a case, the substance abuse should be treated first and the bulimia treated only if it does not subside with cessation of the substance abuse.

REVIEW OF THE LITERATURE

Many publications in recent years have attempted to document the incidence of bulimia and to describe the course and symptoms of this disorder.[5] The incidence of bulimia in the community has been reported to be as high as 13 percent.[6] Table 59–1 reviews the salient findings of five major studies concerning bulimic individuals.[7] The studies of Craig Johnson and coworkers and Richard Pyle and colleagues used the DSM III criteria for bulimia, whereas the other studies done in Great Britain used the criteria for bulimia nervosa.

As indicated in Table 59–1, the average age of onset of the illness is between eighteen and twenty years; the subjects of the studies suffered with the illness for four to five years before seeking treatment. About half of the individuals represented in these studies binge daily. Although vomiting or purging behavior is not a necessary criterion for a diagnosis in the American studies,[8] more than 80 percent of respondents engaged in

---

[3] Christopher G. Fairburn, "Bulimia: Its Epidemiology and Management," in *Eating and Its Disorders,* ed. Albert Stunkard and Eliot Stellar (New York: Raven Press, 1984); and Gerald Russell, "Bulimia Nervosa: An Ominous Variant of Anorexia Nervosa," *Psychological Medicine* 9 (September 1979): 429–48.

[4] Fairburn, "Bulimia: Its Epidemiology and Management," p. 235.

[5] Katherine A. Halmi, James R. Falk, and Estelle Schwartz, "Binge-Eating and Vomiting: A Survey of a College Population," *Psychological Medicine* 11 (November 1981): 697–706; and Christopher G. Fairburn and Peter J. Cooper, "Self-Induced Vomiting and Bulimia Nervosa: An Undetected Problem." *British Medical Journal* 284 (April l982): 1153–55.

[6] Halmi, Falk, and Schwartz, "Binge-Eating and Vomiting: A Survey of a College Population."

[7] Fairburn and Cooper, "Self-Induced Vomiting and Bulimia Nervosa: An Undetected Problem"; Christopher G. Fairburn and Peter J. Cooper, "The Clinical Features of Bulimia Nervosa," *British Journal of Psychiatry* 144 (February 1984): 238–46; Craig L. Johnson et al., "Bulimia: A Descriptive Survey of 316 Cases," *International Journal of Eating Disorders* 2 (Fall 1982): 3–16; Richard L. Pyle, James E. Mitchell, and Elke D. Eckert, "Bulimia: A Report of 34 Cases," *Journal of Clinical Psychiatry* 42 (February 1981): 60–64; and Russell, "Bulimia Nervosa: An Ominous Variant of Anorexia Nervosa."

[8] Johnson et al., "Bulimia: A Descriptive Survey of 316 Cases"; and Pyle, Mitchell, and Eckert, "Bulimia: A Report of 34 Cases."

Table 59–1
Summary of Studies on Bulimia

	Johnson et al. (316 bulimia subjects)	Pyle et al. (34 bulimia patients)	Russell (30 bulimia nervosa patients)	Fairburn and Cooper (499 bulimia nervosa subjects)	Fairburn and Cooper (35 bulimia nervosa subjects)
Duration before treatment/survey	5.4 years	4 years	4 years	Not mentioned	3.8 years
Average age at onset	18 years	18 years	18.8 years, eating disorder 21.2 years, purging	18.4 years	19.7 years
Binge frequency	51% daily 93% weekly	56% daily 100% weekly	100% daily	27% daily 33% weekly	49% daily 17% twice a day
Vomiting/purging	81% vomited (48% daily) 63% laxatives (15% daily)	88% vomited (47% daily) 53% laxatives	90% vomited 63% laxatives	100% vomited (56% daily) 19% purgatives	100% vomited (74% daily) 31% purgatives
History of anorexia	6%	15% to 30%	57% definite 27% cryptic	Excluded from sample	26%
Weight (Metropolitan Life Insurance tables)	62% normal (± 10%) 21% under weight (75%–89% norm)	35% < minimum acceptable weight 65% ≥ minimum acceptable weight	Not mentioned	83% normal (± 15% matched population mean weight)	88.6% normal (± 15% matched population mean weight)
Menstrual irregularities	51% menstrual irregularities 20% amenorrhea	76% had at least one episode of amenorrhea lasting ≥ 3 months	14% oral contraceptive; of remaining, 46% amenorrhea	38% menstrual irregularities 7% amenorrhea	46% oral contraceptive; xof remaining, 37% irregular menses, 21% amenorrhea
Substance abuse	Not mentioned	24% previous treatment for chemical abuse	Not mentioned	Not mentioned	No evidence
Depression	Not mentioned	Most reported depression	43% severe 43% moderate	Not mentioned	Similar to patients with major affective disorder
Suicide plans/acts	Not mentioned	Not mentioned	37% attempted	Not mentioned	17% planned or acted
Other psychiatric symptomatology	Patients showed small but significant elevations on indices of depression and interpersonal sensitivity (HSLC)	Elevated MMPI: impulsivity, depression, anxiety, alienation	Not mentioned	68% had high scores indicating psychiatric disorder, high depression, and anxiety	Not mentioned
Previous treatment	56% had no previous treatment for eating disorder	50% had no previous treatment for eating disorder	Not mentioned	30% never treated 2.5% currently receiving treatment	60% had no previous treatment for eating disorder

such behavior. Six percent[9] to 57 percent[10] had a history of anorexia nervosa, and menstrual irregularities occurred in one-third to one-half of the bulimic women studied. Although varying standards for acceptable weight were utilized in the different studies, the majority of respondents (65 percent to 87 percent) had an acceptable weight for their height. The incidence of previous substance abuse was not reported in all studies; however, Pyle and coworkers reported that 24 percent of their sample had previously been treated for chemical abuse, whereas Christopher Fairburn and Peter Cooper found no evidence of vulnerability to alcohol or drug dependence.[11] Although most authors noted the presence of depressive symptomatology in the majority of bulimic patients, they did not use formal diagnostic instruments or specific diagnostic criteria for the assessment of depression. Perhaps even more striking than the reported high incidence of depression among these patients is Gerald Russell's report that 37 percent of his sample had made at least one suicide attempt and Fairburn and Cooper's statement that 17 percent of their sample reported suicidal plans or acts. Also of note are the high levels of anxiety, interpersonal sensitivity, and impulsivity reported by the authors as measured by general personality inventories such as the Minnesota Multiphasic Personality Inventory (MMPI) or the General Health Questionnaire (GHQ) in Great Britain.

The studies that discussed the reason for the onset of the bulimic behavior reported that onset occurred after voluntary restrictive dieting or following a period of emotional upset.[12] Reports of family history data are scant; however, half of Pyle and coworkers' subjects reported alcoholism in the family and 68 percent reported obesity in one or more first-degree relatives. Similarly, Fairburn and Cooper report that 29 percent of their subjects reported that a first-degree relative received treatment from a psychiatrist, usually for a depressive disorder, and that more than half the patients (59 percent) had a first-degree relative who had been advised by a physician to lose weight.[13] Pyle and colleagues report that 65 percent of their patients engaged in stealing behavior; most of them began stealing shortly after the onset of the eating disorder.

TREATMENT ALTERNATIVES

Bulimic women rival their anorexic counterparts in being difficult to treat. First, the illness is considered by its sufferers to be a "secret sin" and merely acknowledging the problem is an enormously difficult task. Second, bulimics frequently want "instant cures" and have unrealistic expectations about being able to stop the bingeing and purging cycle in a short time. Finally, it is difficult to determine how patients will respond to specific treatment modes. Many publications have presented various treatment methods; however, the only controlled treatment studies published to date have been medication studies. Most reports fail to include specific inclusion and exclusion criteria that would facilitate comparisons. Despite these limitations, this review of

---

[9] Johnson et al., "Bulimia: A Descriptive Survey of 316 Cases."

[10] Gerald Russell, who is a well-known authority on anorexia nervosa, may have been referred a disproportionate number of cases with a history of the condition.

[11] Fairburn and Cooper, "The Clinical Features of Bulimia Nervosa."

[12] Johnson et al., "Bulimia: A Descriptive Survey of 316 Cases"; and Pyle, Mitchell, and Eckert, "Bulimia: A Report of 34 Cases."

[13] Fairburn and Cooper, "The Clinical Features of Bulimia Nervosa."

treatment approaches provides an understanding of the methods that are advocated and most frequently utilized and, it is hoped, will lead to better treatment dispositions.

The most frequently recommended treatment for bulimia is individual psychotherapy, which ranges from psychoanalysis to psychoanalytic psychotherapy to cognitive and behavioral approaches. The dynamic approach is useful in dealing with underlying conflicts that affect self-image and object relations. Cognitive methods facilitate increased awareness of internal states. Behavioral techniques usually include self-monitoring and self-control strategies. Fairburn reported on a cognitive-behavioral approach in which treatment was divided into three phases and generally extended from four to six months.[14] He emphasized increased self-control with the use of eating diaries, specific strategies to avoid overeating, and the development of an understanding of events that led to the bulimic episode. In contrast to a cognitive-behavioral approach, C. Philip Wilson and co-workers advocate psychoanalytically oriented treatment that focuses on the underlying conflicts rather than the overt symptoms, with emphasis on the patient's understanding of internalized object representations and, ultimately, on the analysis of the triadic oedipal conflict.[15] Eugene Lowenkopf used supportive psychotherapy or exploratory therapy or a combination of supportive therapy with psychotropic medication, depending on the severity of bulimic episodes.[16]

Several psychotherapists have utilized group techniques for treating bulimic patients. The groups that are described in the literature consist exclusively of bulimic patients as opposed to a mixed diagnostic group. An experiential behavior-treatment program was used by Marlene Boskind-White and William White because they assumed bulimia to be a learned behavior that could be unlearned.[17] Elaine Stevens and Jill Salisbury designed a group approach that extended over several months that combined behavioral methods with psychodynamic understanding[18] in a format similar to Fairburn's individual treatment. Craig Johnson and colleagues developed a short-term group for bulimic clients similar to Stevens and Salisbury's except that the emphasis was more behavioral and less psychodynamic.[19] Finally, Peter Roy-Byrne and colleagues described a group format with behavioral/cognitive and psychodynamic components.[20] Their group utilized co-therapists and lasted for one year.

It is difficult to compare and contrast these reports of group therapy since they differ in so many significant aspects. For example, Johnson and co-workers, Stevens, and Roy-Byrne and colleagues' group members were diagnosed as having bulimia, whereas Boskind-White and White's group members were diagnosed as having bulimarexia. Bu-

[14] Christopher G. Fairburn, "A Cognitive Behavioral Approach to the Treatment of Bulimia," *Psychological Medicine* 11 (November 1981): 707–11.

[15] C. Philip Wilson, Charles C. Hogan, and Ira L. Mintz, *Fear of Being Fat* (New York: Jason Aronson, 1983).

[16] Eugene L. Lowenkopf, "Bulimia: Concept and Therapy," *Comprehensive Psychiatry* 24 (November–December 1983): 546–54.

[17] Marlene Boskind-White and William C. White, *Bulimarexia* (Garden City, N.Y.: Doubleday, 1983); William C. White and Marlene Boskind-White, "An Experiential-Behavioral Approach to the Treatment of Bulimarexia," *Psychotherapy: Theory, Research and Practice* 18 (Winter 1981): 501–507.

[18] Elaine V. Stevens and Jill D. Salisbury. "Group Therapy for Bulimic Adults," *American Journal of Orthopsychiatry* 54 (January 1984): 156–61.

[19] Craig Johnson, Mary Connors, and Marilyn Stuckey, "Short-Term Group Treatment of Bulimia," *International Journal of Eating Disorders* 2 (Summer 1983): 199–208.

[20] Peter Roy-Byrne, Karen Lee-Benner, and Joel Yager, "Group Therapy for Bulimia," *International Journal of Eating Disorders* 3 (Winter 1984): 97–116.

limarexia is defined by Boskind-White and White as a cyclical eating disorder characterized by binge/purge episodes and abnormally low self-esteem.[21] It is not clear from the reports how, or if, the patients who were diagnosed with bulimia differed from those who were diagnosed with bulimarexia. In addition, treatment varied in length and frequency of sessions from five hours a day for five days[22] to twelve two-hour sessions over nine weeks[23] to once a week for one year.[24]

Some therapists have combined group or family therapy with individual treatment utilizing cognitive, behavioral, or dynamic methods. J. Hubert Lacey described a treatment method that combined a ninety-minute group session with a thirty-minute individual session on a weekly basis for ten weeks.[25] This treatment method initially used behavioral techniques before moving to more insight-oriented psychotherapy. A cognitive-behavioral sixteen-week program comprised of both individual and group sessions was described by Ronna Saunders.[26] The focus of the program was on developing reasonable eating patterns, understanding feelings associated with eating, and learning alternative coping methods. Nancy Mintz reported that she treated her patients with individual psychodynamic therapy and conjoint family sessions as needed.[27] In her opinion, a combination of individual therapy and group therapy is ideal although the latter was not available for her clients.

Various treatment methods are advocated by Elaine Yudkovitz, who suggests combining dynamic, behavioral, cognitive, and ecological methods in either an individual or group modality.[28] In addition to the methods described above, Yudkovitz theorizes that the ecological perspective aids the therapist in evaluating how the patient's family and environment have affected him or her in the past and the present and how the bulimic symptoms distort and interfere with current object relations and environmental interactions.

A growing body of evidence suggests that bulimia may be closely linked to affective disorders. The prominence of depressive symptomatology in bulimic patients and the prevalence of family histories of affective disorder encouraged some clinicians to treat these patients with antidepressant medication.[29] Several studies have reported successful treatment with antidepressants. However, two published studies that used placebo-controlled, double-blind research methods reported opposite results.[30] Harrison Pope and coworkers' study of imipramine demonstrated a statistically significant improvement in the medication group compared with the control group, whereas E. J. Sabine

---

[21] Boskind-White and White, *Bulimarexia.*

[22] Ibid.

[23] Johnson, Connors, and Stuckey, "Short-Term Group Treatment of Bulimia."

[24] Roy-Byrne, Lee-Benner, and Yager, "Group Therapy for Bulimia."

[25] J. Hubert Lacey, "An Outpatient Treatment Program for Bulimia Nervosa," *International Journal of Eating Disorders* 2 (Summer 1983): 209–14.

[26] Ronna Saunders, "Bulimia, An Expanded Definition," *Social Casework* 66 (December 1985): 603–10.

[27] Nancy E. Mintz. "Bulimia: A New Perspective," *Clinical Social Work Journal* 10 (Winter 1982): 289–302.

[28] Elaine Yudkovitz, "Bulimia: Growing Awareness of an Eating Disorder," *Social Work* 28 (November–December 1983): 472–78.

[29] Craig Johnson, Marilyn Stuckey and James Mitchell, "Psychopharmacological Treatment of Anorexia Nervosa and Bulimia," *Journal of Nervous and Mental Disease* 171 (September 1983): 524–34.

[30] William J. Swift, Donna Andrews, and Nancy E. Barklage, "The Relationship Between Affective Disorder and Eating Disorders: A Review of the Literature," *American Journal of Psychiatry* 143 (March 1986): 290–99.

and colleagues' study of mianserin demonstrated no significant difference between the two groups.[31]

Therapists disagree about the value of hospitalization for bulimic patients. Many therapists agree with Ira Mintz that hospitalization should be reserved for patients who are in danger of dying, becoming severely medically ill, or who are suicidal or psychotic.[32] In contrast, using the British criteria for bulimia nervosa, Russell recommends hospital admission for most patients to interrupt the vicious cycle of overeating, self-induced vomiting (or purging), and weight loss.[33] Hospital treatment includes skilled nursing care, antidepressant medication when the patient is severely depressed, psychotherapeutic treatment, and often behavioral therapy that includes eating diaries.

All the studies cited above report some positive treatment response. However, it is difficult to compare results, because most of the reports do not clearly define the patients who are being treated; that is, although many use the DSM III criteria, most do not clarify the level of social interaction and object relations, the degree of affective instability or substance abuse, the length of time and extent of bulimia, or previous treatment of anorexia. With the exception of the studies that compare medication vs. placebo use, no published, controlled studies compare different types of treatment.

CHOOSING THE APPROPRIATE TREATMENT

A comprehensive initial evaluation is essential for the treatment of bulimic clients. Clinicians must not only evaluate DSM III criteria for bulimia, but must also assess current functioning, family pathology, object relations, the degree of depression, the "fit" between the patient and environment, and the need for medical or psychiatric assessment. As noted above, many forms of treatment have been recommended for individuals with bulimia. The clinician is left with the difficult decision as to which type of treatment best suits the client. A few case examples of patients with DSM III diagnosis of "bulimia" illustrate client characteristics that suggest the use of one modality over another. None of these patients had a concurrent substance-abuse diagnosis, although several had depressive disorders.

Group Therapy

H is a twenty-nine-year-old vice-president of a public relations firm who is quite intelligent, articulate, and personable. Both of her parents function well, although both are "closet" alcoholics. H has been bulimic since her freshman year in college. At first, she would binge eat and vomit four to five times a week. In recent years, she has been able to decrease these episodes of bulimia to approximately one episode per week. However, she has never gone more than two weeks without an episode. H's relationships with others are good, even though, to her regret,

---

[31] Harrison G. Pope, Jr., et al., "Bulimia Treated with Imipramine: A Placebo-Controlled, Double-Blind Study." *American Journal of Psychiatry* 140 (May 1983): 554–58; E. J. Sabine et al., "Bulimia Nervosa, a Placebo-Controlled Double-Blind Trial of Mianserin," *British Journal of Clinical Pharmacology* 15 [Suppl., 1983] 195s–202s.

[32] Ira L. Mintz, "An Analytic Approach to Hospital and Nursing Care," in *Fear of Being Fat,* p. 315.

[33] Russell, "Bulimia Nervosa: An Ominous Variant of Anorexia Nervosa," p. 446.

she has never married. She showed no evidence of depression either by history or mental-status examination.

Group treatment would be the treatment of choice for a client such as H. She successfully functions at work and has meaningful interpersonal relationships. Her bulimic behavior has not adversely affected other areas of her functioning. In addition, she has demonstrated some control over the illness by decreasing the frequency of bulimic episodes. Another consideration is the generally lower cost of group treatment, which can be an important factor in a client's cooperation with a treatment plan. Individual therapy would be considered subsequent to group therapy if alleviation of bulimia revealed intrapsychic and interpersonal difficulties that were masked by bulimic symptoms and that had interfered with a sustained relationship with a man.

Individual Psychotherapy

M is a forty-eight-year-old divorced woman who is the noncustodial parent of a thirteen-year-old son. Her psychiatric history includes abuse of pills and cocaine and two psychiatric hospitalizations for severe depressions with suicidal ideation. After the second hospitalization, seven years ago, she stopped abusing drugs; however, she became bulimic. M divorced her husband prior to her second hospitalization, and she has not had a sustained love relationship since then. She has some friendships with other women; however, generally she is quite isolated. M's bulimia is the "relationship" to which she comes home; every evening she gorges herself and then forces herself to vomit. On the weekends, when she has her son, she does not binge or purge. M is not currently depressed or suicidal. She functions well in her job as a computer programmer.

Patients such as M, who have low self-esteem and problems with interpersonal relationships, often respond best to individual therapy. Other patients, such as very impulsive acting-out individuals with borderline personalities, require the sustained nurturing relationships provided in individual therapy. Older patients may not do well in group therapy, because the majority of bulimic groups are typically composed of younger persons and the age discrepancy may be humiliating. Individual therapy was chosen for M for several reasons. Most important, her degree of social isolation raised concerns that she would flee group therapy because of the fear of revealing herself in such a format. Second, her history of depression and potential for depression and suicide required constant evaluation. Such evaluation is difficult, although not impossible, in group therapy. Finally, M was considerably older than were the group members in the available group. M's need for group therapy concomitant with individual treatment will be reassessed periodically.

Antidepressant Medication

A is a twenty-eight-year-old accountant. She is reportedly the most intelligent of three siblings born to a lower-middle-class family. Her father was very interested in her entering a profession. Although academically quite successful, A always felt like a failure. She binged and vomited several times a day, and her inability to control this behavior augmented her low self-esteem. She suffered from depression, with typical sleep disturbance and depressed mood. Despite her depression, A had both female friends and a boyfriend. However, the latter relationship was strained because of her symptoms.

Bulimic patients, such as A, who fit DSM III criteria for depression and have no medical contraindications should be treated with antidepressants. The choice of medication should be made by a physician, although dietary restrictions that accompany the use of certain medications (such as monoamine oxidase inhibitors) often make them a poor choice for some bulimic patients whose impulsive craving for certain foods could lead to life-endangering binges. In some cases, medications alone can lead to alleviation of symptoms. However, medication is generally most effective when accompanied by individual therapy, group therapy, or both. A attended group therapy in addition to receiving antidepressant medication. Individual therapy was not considered necessary because she functioned relatively well both socially and professionally.

COMBINATION THERAPY

P, age thirty-one years, is the older of two daughters born to an upwardly mobile middle-class family. The client's mother was overinvolved with her daughters and wanted them both to enter the performing arts. After an early abortive attempt at a dancing career, P became an actress and a model and is moderately successful. However, she never enjoyed this career and continually felt that she was not successful enough to please her demanding mother. She is not sure whether she wants to continue in this profession and is considering moving to a different city. Although her relationships with women are stable and deep, she demonstrated difficulty developing a sustained relationship with a man. At the time of the initial evaluation, she demonstrated a depressed mood but no other symptoms of a major depression. At the age of eighteen years, she learned vomiting as a weight-control measure from a fellow dance student. Subsequently, she utilized binge eating followed by vomiting as an emotional release of tension.

A combination of therapeutic approaches often works best for some patients. Patients such as P have sufficient interpersonal skills to utilize the group to discuss the details of their bulimic behavior. With the group's support, they are able to gain some control over their eating behavior. However, their problems of low self-esteem and deeper pathology often cannot be adequately revealed or addressed in the group; therefore, the addition of individual treatment may be necessary. Some patients require antidepressant medication in addition to group and individual psychotherapy to be able to have the emotional strength to overcome the bulimic symptoms. As P progresses in both her individual and group therapies, her need for medication will be reassessed as she struggles with inner conflicts and life stresses. Although family difficulties are present, family therapy was not recommended because of P's age and degree of emancipation from her family.

Hospitalization

S, age twenty-seven years, resides with her parents, who are an upwardly striving Jewish couple. She is the youngest of three children; both her older sister and brother are doing well. S was a bright, precocious child who was athletic and popular with her peers. Despite this popularity, she recalls feeling "alone" as a young adolescent. During high school, she achieved mostly superior grades with "little effort." During college, she began smoking marijuana and abusing cocaine. Her abuse of these substances increased after she left college. Recently, however, her drug abuse has almost stopped and her bulimic episodes have greatly increased. During late adolescence and college, her relationship with her father intensified. He frequently "rescued" her from her interpersonal or occupational difficulties by completely taking over or by providing her with material goods. The patient never developed a sense of adult responsibility or control over her life. S has never been able to hold a job for longer than a couple of months and has no stable object relationship except for her family. She suffered from mood deregulation with angry outbursts and increased episodes of binge eating followed by vomiting. Her bulimic pattern became out of control when her parents went on vacation. She developed increasing suicidal ideation, superficially cut her wrists, and was hospitalized.

S was hospitalized because of the severity of her symptoms, including a suicide gesture. Hospitalization should be reserved for extreme cases of bulimia in which medical management is required or the patient becomes suicidal. Hospitalization usually includes individual therapy three to four times per week, family treatment, and medication when indicated. Medical management includes the monitoring of adequate food intake, the prevention of vomiting and laxative/diuretic abuse, and consultation with a nutritionist and an internist when necessary. When S is discharged from the hospital, an intensive program will be indicated that probably includes individual treatment and supportive group therapy as well as consideration of medication and family therapy.

CONCLUSION

It is important for social workers to understand that all patients who have symptoms of bulimia are not the same and that these patients may require different treatment interventions. Social workers should assess the bulimic client's symptom constellation as well as current and past functioning in interpersonal relationships and employment. Other factors to be considered are client's financial resources with regard to the cost of different treatment options and the availability of various modalities. A self-help group such as Overeaters Anonymous in addition to therapy may be useful.

A complete evaluation leads to more appropriate treatment choices with better outcome. These choices should be continuously reassessed over time and the treatment modified or augmented according to the patient's needs. Until controlled studies compare different treatment modalities for bulimic patients, clinicians must rely on a comprehensive diagnostic evaluation as well as the experience of other clinicians to determine appropriate treatment.

CHAPTER 60

THE CONDITIONING TREATMENT OF CHILDHOOD ENURESIS

R. T. T. Morgan and G. C. Young

Enuresis, or bedwetting, is one of the most widespread disorders of childhood, and is a problem frequently encountered by most social workers. It is a source of embarrassment to the sufferer, often invoking punishment, and can place an intolerable burden upon intrafamilial relationships—especially in those large families living in overcrowded conditions, where several children may wet the bed. For the majority of enuretics, to be a bedwetter carries adverse emotional consequences, and many exhibit some degree of reactive disturbance. Even where this is not apparently the case, enuresis imposes a limit on the child's choice of activities; few enuretics can happily go camping or to stay with friends. In residential establishments, the daily wash of bed-linen is unpleasant and onerous. Because of its widespread, offensive, embarrassing and potentially disturbing nature, the problem of the management and cure of enuresis should be of concern to any caseworker or residential worker involved with an enuretic child; all too often both natural parents and houseparents are forced into a fatalistic acceptance of, and accommodation to, enuresis as an inevitable correlate of child upbringing. It is the purpose of the present paper to suggest that this need not be so, and to describe a rational and well-validated approach to the cure of enuresis, which deserves careful consideration for the benefit of the child sufferer.

Much confusion and many theories exist regarding the aetiology and treatment of enuresis; the literature is extensive and the folk-lore rich. Confusion is enlarged by the use of enuresis as a paradigmatic battleground between conflicting schools of psychological opinion which present mutually exclusive interpretations of this particular disorder. What is urgently required by the social worker confronted with an enuretic child

Reprinted from *British Journal of Social Work,* Vol. 72 (1972), pp. 503–509, by permission of the publisher.

is a relatively simple and well-substantiated form of treatment which offers a high probability of permanent cure without producing harmful side effects.

Consideration of enuresis in terms of a learning deficiency has led to the development of conditioning techniques as a treatment of enuresis. Learning theory postulates that bladder control may be regarded as learned behavior, and enuresis as a failure to acquire or maintain appropriate learned responses. According to the Yerkes-Dodson principle (Eysenck, 1960), the efficiency of learning is affected by drive level, very low or very high levels of drive leading to less effective learning as opposed to some intermediate level which is optimal. This optimal intermediate level of drive varies according to task complexity, and is lower for more complex learning tasks. Application of this principle to the learning of urinary continence suggests three major variables affecting the ability to any particular child to acquire bladder control; (1) the optimal level of drive for a task of a given complexity, (2) the degree of complexity represented to the child by the task of acquiring bladder control, and (3) the level of drive induced by the environment. There are individual differences in the ease with which children acquire control of bladder function, as there are in learning to swim or riding a bicycle, and environmental stresses, whether general or specifically related to toilet training, may affect one child more than another. During the third year of life there seems to exist a 'sensitive period' for the learning of continence, during which the child's sensitivity to appropriate learning situations is most acute. Stresses and anxieties during this period may produce over-optimal levels of drive which act to the detriment of learning and render the child enuretic (Young, 1965b; 1969; MacKeith, 1968; 1972). In the case of the 'secondary' enuretic, who loses bladder control after an appreciable period of normal continence, the learned pattern of control is disrupted by the intrusion of some new anxiety-provoking stimulus, such as disturbances in the family or problems at school. Because appropriate learning is less likely to take place outside the sensitive period, transient stress during the third year of life may produce the lifelong, or 'primary' enuretic, and secondary enuresis may persist even when its provoking stress has disappeared.

Conditioning treatment is based on the assumption that whatever influences may have led to a failure or breakdown of learning, appropriate learning may best be effected by maximizing the impact of the learning situation. The simplification of the learning situation also serves to reduce the decremental effects of whatever over-optimal drive may still be present, by reducing task complexity and thus raising the optimal level of drive according to the Yerkes-Dodson principle.

Treatment itself involves the use at home of a simple commercially produced 'enuresis alarm' (Young, 1965a; Turner, Young and Rachman, 1970).*

The alarm provides a powerful auditory stimulus in the form of a loud buzzer which is activated as urine makes electrical contact between a pair of gauze mats beneath the sleeping child. The alarm, when triggered, is switched off by the child, who then completes urination in the toilet. The alarm thus conditions in the child the two separate responses of awakening and of the inhibition of micturition, both in competition with the

---

* Such as the 'Eastleigh', manufactured and supplied by N. H. Eastwood & Son, Ltd., 48 Eversley Park Road, London, N.21.

response of reflex urination to the stimulus of a full bladder. These responses, repeatedly evoked, eventually supercede that of reflex urination, the learned inhibitory effect of bladder stimulation tending to raise the general tone of the bladder muscle (the detrusor) so that the child not only awakes to urinate, but can eventually sleep for the entire night without either wetting or waking.

It is essential that the alarm is used properly and consistently, and that its use is adequately demonstrated. A high level of interest and involvement on the part of a social worker or houseparent is vital to the success of the treatment. It is necessary to maintain a simple record of wet and dry nights throughout treatment. Some children are punished for wet beds and some parents express the opinion that the child is 'lazy'—it is necessary to counter attitudes likely to increase the child's stress in a situation in which over-optimal drive may already be present. Furthermore, certain management practices such as fluid restriction and 'lifting', which are detrimental to conditioning treatment, should be discouraged. Indeed, it is quite likely that regularly lifting a child may train him to need to urinate at a certain time of night.

The success of conditioning treatment in practice has been well demonstrated. Young (1969) lists 19 clinical studies of such treatment in which the percentage success rate ranged from 63% to 100%. Two carefully conducted studies have found conditioning to be significantly superior to psychotherapy in the treatment of enuresis (Werry and Cohrssen, 1965; De Leon and Mandell, 1966).

The conditioning treatment described above is not new, the first suggestion of such treatment occurring in a paper written by Nye in 1830 (Glicklich, 1951). The therapeutic effects of a signal used to alert nurses to wet beds were accidentally discovered by Pfaundler in 1904, and have been continuously studied ever since. However, the use of conditioning treatment for enuresis has yet to find wide acceptance among social workers and those entrusted with the residential care of children.

Until very recently, it was justifiable to question the efficacy of treating enuresis in the manner described, on the grounds that regardless of patient or treatment variables, approximately one in three children could be expected to relapse to wetting once again following initial cure (Young and Morgan, 1972a). Although not affecting the initial success of conditioning in arresting enuresis, such a relapse rate posed a serious question regarding the long-term usefulness of the treatment. Recently, however, a technique has been developed capable of producing dramatic reduction in relapse by strengthening the pattern of relevant learned responses beyond the level necessary to effect initial arrest of wetting. Known as 'overlearning', the technique requires the child to continue to use an enuresis alarm while drinking up to two pints of fluid in the last hour before retiring, once an initial success criterion of fourteen consecutive dry nights has been achieved (Young and Morgan, 1972b).

Perhaps one of the major reasons for the presently limited acceptance of conditioning treatment by social workers is that, not conversant with such conceptualizations of enuresis, many have permitted certain common and popular assumptions to escape rigorous question. The concept of enuresis as a somatic expression of emotional disturbance is thus traditionally accepted without question. Indeed it is often assumed that the coexistence of enuresis and disturbed behavior in the same child demonstrates a causal relation between the two. Such inference is in contradiction of the research findings of Tapia *et al.* (1960), who found that disturbed children are not especially prone to enuresis, nor enuretics particularly prone to disturbance, and of Baker (1969), who found neither projective personality tests nor assessment of adjustment by psychologists to distinguish enuretics from non-enuretics. The finding that the *persistence* of enuresis relates to familial inadequacies and family disruption, the problem persisting longest where family pathology is most severe (Stein and Susser, 1967), tends to support the view that environmental stresses rather than innate personality disorders are responsible for interference with the normal process of acquisition of bladder control. It is logical to assume that in such circumstances, emotional disturbance and enuresis may coexist, but as quite separate responses to the same external environmental influences. It is thus also logical to give treatment for enuresis as a separate entity, even where it occurs in a context of multiple problems.

A frequent objection to the direct, or 'symptomatic', treatment of enuresis by conditioning techniques is that the elimination of enuresis by these methods may lead to harmful consequences for the child's emotional adjustment. The specific predictions made by opponents of conditioning techniques are that, since a disturbed child is assumed to require an expressive symptom, a substitute symptom will emerge following the removal of enuresis; and that by removing enuresis, disturbance will be increased. Investigation of these predictions has found them to be unsupported. Baker (1969), investigating the 'symptom substitution' prediction, found no supporting evidence in his study of conditioning treatment and its consequences. Most clinicians testify to *improvement* in emotional adjustment following relief from enuresis (Yates, 1970; Young, 1965a). There need, therefore, be little concern that conditioning treatment may do harm to any child.

The above predictions derive from the common assumption that enuresis is a symptomatic expression of deep emotional disturbance, rather than a learning deficit, and that the child thus 'needs' and must not be deprived of his bedwetting. Therapy is directed instead at the inferred disturbance. The behavioral view, however, asserts that enuresis is a useless and troublesome habit from which appropriate training can provide relief. It is unnecessary to assume that because a child cannot control his bladder function, he must 'need' to be unable to do so, and to proceed to 'interpret' the feelings he is presumed to be expressing in somatic form.

Various forms of interpretation of a child's inability to control the act of micturition in the accepted manner have provided a wide variety of possible 'meanings'. One of the most common is the theory of regression, which states that enuresis, being similar to infantile incontinence, represents the attempted return of the older child undergoing stress to the presumed security of infancy. The enuretic may thus be saying, by wetting the bed, 'I will take the privileges of a baby, which you deny me' (Fenichel, 1946). A second range of interpretation is based upon the assertion that urination is equivalent to a sexual act. Fenichel thus regards enuresis as frequently a masturbation-equivalent; although the expected replacement of enuresis by mature forms of sexual gratification at puberty is not found in the age/incidence curves for enuresis (Jones, 1960). As a conversion symptom (i.e. a somatic expression of inner conflict or disorder), enuresis may, writes Fenichel, often be regarded as a 'discharge instrument of the Oedipus impulses'. Such theorists frequently interpret enuresis as an aggressive act—or, where this seems inappropriate, an act of passive submission. Thus enuresis in girls is seen as an active assumption of the male sexual role through fear of males as destructive aggressors—

while in boys it is considered to represent assumption of a passive female role through fear of destruction by women consequent upon playing a male sexual role (Gerard, 1937; Fenichel, 1946). Ferenczi (1925) actually produced enuresis in a number of normally continent persons, by suggesting retention of urine to test a professed potency in the inhibition of micturition and thus apparently 'exhausting' the urinary musclature. This procedure was explained as serving to 'unmask a tendency to enuresis with which the patient had been quite unfamiliar and which threw light on important parts of his early infantile history' (Ferenczi, 1925).

It is maintained that when such interpretations of enuresis are rejected as unnecessary elaborations of a learning failure, the removal of enuresis (by conditioning techniques) is superficial; and cannot represent 'real' cure. However, no more elaborate criterion for the cure of enuresis seems necessary, than that bedwetting should be eliminated without harmful side effects; it is difficult to imagine what further 'cure' is required when a formerly wet child is no longer enuretic, and is better adjusted than before. It is questionable to withhold from any child the chance of relief from wet beds, unless conditioning treatment were proven to be either ineffective or harmful. The infant learns bladder control, and learning failure can be countered by the more effective training afforded by an enuresis alarm.

Apart from lack of information and attitudes of reserve, many are deterred from the use of conditioning treatment by the practical problems involved. When an alarm is used in the home situation, parental cooperation is vital, and may well require a high level of supervision by a caseworker. Parents, siblings (and even patients) who sabotage treatment to avoid disturbed nights will not achieve success; cooperation must be secured before treatment is introduced and should be maintained throughout its duration. The presence of overcrowding and multiple occupation present additional problems, and it may be necessary to arrange for a separate bed in cases where an enuretic shares a bed with another member of the family.

It should prove possible in residential establishments to arrange medical screening for possible organic pathology, and the appropriate supervision of treatment could be undertaken by the staff. Older children can assume virtually full responsibility for the conduct of treatment. Young children and those slow to awaken to the alarm will require a staff member to assist, to ensure that the child awakes and to change the wet sheets before resetting the apparatus. Treatment naturally places a burden upon childcare staff, just as it does upon parents, but treatment forms an essential part of caring for an enuretic child.

Conditioning treatment of enuresis, when properly and consistently carried out and followed by a period of overlearning therapy, thus carries great promise of effective and stable cure without harmful side effects. As such it demands careful consideration by all having professional contact with enuretic children.

REFERENCES

Baker, B. L. (1969) "Symptom Treatment and Symptom Substitution in Enuresis," *J. Abnorm. Psychol., 74,* 42–49.

De Leon, G., and Mandell, W. (1966) A Comparison of Conditioning and Psychotherapy in the Treatment of Functional Enuresis," *J. Clin. Psychol.*, 22, 326–30.

Eysenck, H. J. (1960) *Handbook of Abnormal Psychology*, Pitman, London.

Fenichel, O. (1946) *The Psychoanalytic Theory of Neurosis*, Routledge & Kegan Paul, London.

Ferenczi, S. (1925) "Psycho-analysis of Sexual Habits," *Int. J. Psychoanal.*, 6, 372–404.

Gerard, M. W. (1937) "Child Analysis as a Technique in the Investigation of Mental Mechanisms: Illustrated by a Study of Enuresis," *Am. J. Psychiat.*, 94, 653–68.

Glicklich, L. B. (1951) "An Historical Account of Enuresis," Pediatrics, 8, 859–76.

Jones, H. G. (1960) "The Behavioral Treatment of Enuresis Nocturna," in *Behavior Therapy and the Neuroses* (Ed. H. J. Eysenck), pp. 377–403, Pergamon, Oxford.

MacKeith, R. C. (1968) "A Frequent Factor in the Origins of Primary Nocturnal Enuresis: Anxiety in the Third Year of Life," *Develop. Med. Child Neurol., 10,* 465–70.

MacKeith, R. C. (1972) "Is Maturation Delay a Frequent Factor in the Origins of Primary Nocturnal Enuresis?" *Develop. Med. Child Neurol., 14,* 217–23.

Stein, Z. A. and Susser, M. (1967) "The Social Dimensions of a Symptom. A Sociomedical Study of Enuresis," *Soc. Sci. & Med. 1,* 183–201.

Tapia, F., Jekel, J., and Domke, H. R. (1960) "Enuresis: An Emotional Symptom?" *J. Nerv. Ment. Dis., 130,* 61–6.

Turner, R. K., Young G. C. and Rachman, S. (1970) "Treatment of Nocturnal Enuresis by Conditioning Techniques," *Behav. Res. & Therapy, 8,* 367–81.

Werry, J. S. and Cohrssen, J. (1965) "Enuresis—an Etiologic and Therapeutic Study," *J. Pediat. 67,* 423–31.

Yates, A. J. (1970) *Behavior Therapy,* John Wiley, New York, Ch. 5.

Young, G. C. (1956a) "Conditioning Treatment of Enuresis," *Dev. Med. Child Neurol., 7,* 557–62.

Young, G. C. (1956b) "The Aetiology of Enuresis in Terms of Learning Theory," *Med. Offr., 113,* 19–22.

Young, G. C. (1969) "The Problem of Enuresis," *Br. J. Hosp. Med., 2,* 628–32.

Young, G. C. and Morgan, R. T. T. (1972a) *Analysis of Factors Associated with the Extinction of a Conditioned Response. Behav. Res. & Therapy.* In press.

Young, G. C. and Morgan, R. T. T. (1972b) "Overlearning in the Conditioning Treatment of Enuresis," *Behav. Res. & Therapy, 10,* 147–51.

CHAPTER 61

SUICIDE

Answering the Cry for Help

David J. Klugman, Robert E. Litman, and Carl I. Wold

S uicide, which accounts for at least 20,000 deaths per year in the United States, ranks among the first ten causes of adult deaths in this country.[1] In addition to completed suicides, there are numerous suicide attempts and threats. It has been estimated that each year in the United States about half a million people are affected by a range of suicidal crises, making it a major public health problem.[2]

The purpose of this paper is to examine some characteristics of suicidal individuals and to discuss evaluation and treatment approaches and the need for consultation when suicidal crises arise. The professional activity described took place at the Los Angeles Suicide Prevention Center.[3]

REACTION TO CRISIS

A striking aspect of suicidal people is that they do not form a homogeneous group. They come from a broad spectrum of different life situations and are not seen as similar in personality. Some are stable people with roots in family and community life, while

Reprinted from *Social Work,* Vol. 10, No. 4 (1965), pp. 43–50, by permission of NASW Press. Copyright 1989, National Association of Social Workers, Inc., *Social Work.*

[1] Sam M. Heilig and David J. Klugman, "The Social Worker in a Suicide Prevention Center," *Social Work Practice, 1963* (New York: Columbia University Press, 1963).

[2] Normal L. Farberow and Edwin S. Schneidman, eds., *The Cry For Help* (New York: McGraw-Hill Book Co., 1961). See also Louis I. Dublin, *Suicide: A Sociological and Statistical Study* (New York: Ronald Press, 1963).

[3] Robert E. Litman, MD, Edwin S. Schneidman, and Norman L. Farberow, "Los Angeles Suicide Prevention Center," *American Journal of Psychiatry,* Vol. 117, No. 12 (June 1961), pp. 1083–1087. The Suicide Prevention Center has been supported by grants from the National Institute of Mental Health, administered through the University of Southern California School of Medicine.

others lead unstable lives, riddled with failure in all their interpersonal dealings. All these people, however, share in common the condition of being in a serious life crisis. They are no longer able to sweep their feelings under the rug of indifference and denial. They must face their feelings of hopelessness, helplessness, and dependency. Most commonly their symptoms are those of a severe depressive syndrome—sleep disorder, appetite loss, and psychomotor retardation. Often there are disorganized activity states with exaggerated tension, perturbation, and pan-anxiety.

The crisis may or may not be related to specific life stresses. Such events as a divorce or the death of a loved one, financial loss, or sudden legal involvements may trigger suicidal concerns. In a number of suicidal people, however, there is no discernible precipitating stress. Rather, there seems to have been a slow, steady loss of the ability to function adaptively. With these people there is an erosion process under way such that their roots in life are gradually pulled loose. Relatives, friends, lawyers, helping people, and agencies become alienated and unable to help.

In a suicidal crisis there is a radical change in the person's view of himself and his relationships with others. This often shows itself as an increase in stereotyped perceptions, i.e., it is difficult for people in a suicidal crisis to generate new ideas, feelings, or plans without help from others. A suicidal person is often severely constricted in thinking about his problems. He has so little perspective that the past seems forgotten and the future is unimaginable. His view of the present is rigidly confined to a small number of alternative behaviors of which suicide is one. The following case illustrates this point.

Mr. A, a 38-year-old married man, was referred to the center because of suicidal threats. He had been employed as an aircraft mechanic on the same job for twelve years and had led a quiet, stable life until his wife of ten years had left him in order to be free to see other men. They were not divorced and neither of them wanted to effect a complete separation. Periodically Mrs. A returned to him, contrite about having left, and each time he welcomed her return. However, his disgust with himself and unconscious anger toward her grew as the returns and separations continued. It was noted that he was acutely agitated and depressed, had lost weight, slept very little, and had suffered acute psychological distress. He was about to give up his job, which in the past had provided major satisfactions for him. His conception of his situation was that he could not continue to live with his wife on the present basis but he could not give her up. He loved her and she loved him, but she was now confused and hurting him unintentionally. He hoped that, magically, the situation would prove to be a bizarre mistake, a sort of nightmare. Yet, because of his unbearable anxiety, he could no longer wait for this resolution. He was aware of wanting to kill Mrs. A and he was acutely aware of wanting to kill himself.

Mr. A had lost his ability to see himself clearly. The crisis he had entered distorted his view of who he was, where he had been, and what might happen in the future. Nothing satisfied him anymore, nor could he achieve satisfactions. He admitted to feeling helpless and without hope, powerless to change—killing himself seemed the only solution. The center's staff openly disagreed with his conclusion of hopelessness, and he was told that because of his depression his view of himself and his situation was distorted in such a way that realistic alternatives were not available to him. Staff expressed concern about him, pointed up his need for help, and advised him that there was a good chance that with professional aid he could regain healthy perspectives. The offer of help was accepted eagerly and he began working on a plan for his recovery. He was seen briefly each day for a few days, until he entered regular outpatient psychotherapy at another agency.

AMBIVALENCE ABOUT DYING

This case raises another important characteristic of suicidal people. They are intensely ambivalent about dying.[4] If someone really intended to die, would he tell others about it who would try to prevent his death? Such communications may cast doubts on the sincerity of the suicidal person. Combined with one's own anxieties about helping a suicidal person, these attitudes impede the helping process. The result is that some suicidal people are not taken seriously, which can tip the balance dangerously toward suicide.

An appreciation of the ambivalent state of the suicidal person helps to make sense of behavior that otherwise appears insincere. During such a crisis, there is an admixture of conflicting feelings. In nearly all cases, regardless of obvious attempts to manipulate other people or dramatic bids for emotional response from others, there are genuine wishes to die and to be rid of tension, pain, or confusion. These death-seeking feelings range from well-thought-out plans to impulsive, erratic outbursts that would be lethal only through a combination of adverse chance factors.

Often the mixed motives include rescue fantasies as well as wishes to die. The suicidal person is looking for a rescuer to serve as an alter ego at a time when his own ego functions are severely impaired. Some of these rescue wishes are realistic, but many are magical in character; both types influence the demands made on the rescue person. Thus Mr. A recognized realistically that he was unable to resolve his dilemma without help, that he was weakened, and that his suicidal feelings served to communicate this to the center's staff. Unrealistically and magically, he hoped the center would make a sudden change in the present relationship between him and his wife. He wished only for his wife to love and care for him by meeting all his needs. He saw the helping person as an all-powerful figure who entered his life to make sweeping changes for the better.

Finally, to appreciate better the ambivalence associated with suicide the rescuer should guard against basing his feelings and actions primarily on the content of the suicidal person's communications. He may hear: "Leave me alone; I don't want your help," from a person crying out loudly for help. Someone who desperately wants to go to a hospital and be taken care of will say: "I'd rather die before going to the hospital." These statements demonstrate vividly the ambivalence about being helped. This ambivalence is especially acute in the case of suicidal men. Approximately twice as many men as women kill themselves. Although a man may feel emotionally incapacitated, he cannot bear to know that others may recognize this.

---

[4] Edwin S. Schneidman and Norman L. Farberow, eds., *Clues to Suicide* (New York: McGraw Hill Book Co., 1957), chap. 11; and Robert E. Litman, MD, "Emergency Response to Potential Suicide," *Journal of the Michigan State Medical Society,* Vol. 62, No. 1 (January 1963), pp. 68–72.

HELPFUL TECHNIQUES

Just as there are differences in the personality characteristics of suicidal persons, so are there differences in the degree of suicidal risk, which usually falls into one of three broad categories: mild, moderate, or high. An important part of the work at the Los Angeles Suicide Prevention Center has been to evaluate the degree of suicidal risk of patients referred and then to recommend appropriate treatment modalities. Generally, mild-risk patients can be treated optimally at social work or family service agencies, moderate-risk patients at outpatient psychiatric clinics, and high-risk patients in psychiatric hospitals. The purpose of this section is to describe some helpful evaluative and treatment techniques developed at the center.

Telephone Contacts

Ninety-five percent of initial patient contacts begin on the telephone; the rest are walk-ins. These calls range from emergencies to situations of little or no suicidal risk; regardless of initial impression, however, every call is treated seriously. As a defensive or testing maneuver the caller will often begin in a joking or hostile way. Unless this is accepted and understood for what it is (a defense against feelings of inadequacy), the caller may not go on to reveal his real suicidal feelings and an important therapeutic opportunity may be lost.

The initial telephone call is regarded as extremely important.[5] Sometimes it is the center's only contact. Great care is therefore accorded to it. Usually from twenty to forty minutes are spent carefully evaluating the situation, trying to form a positive relationship by moving into the situation rather than away from it. Staff want the caller to learn quickly that they are interested, they wish to help him, and improvement is possible regardless of how desperate he feels. Above all, staff try to instill a feeling of hope, pointing out, for example, that the center has helped many people with similar problems or that together some new alternative way of dealing with his problem may be found.

Specifically, the job on the telephone is to get information, to evaluate the situation—especially the suicidal potential—and to recommend a course of action. This is all done concomitantly and questions are woven in whenever possible at appropriate moments. The aim is to give the caller a therapeutic experience; staff avoid asking for information in a formal, routine way. They do ask for identifying information and request the caller to discuss any current stress he is under. Further, they ask if there is any past suicidal behavior and any history of medical or psychiatric treatment. If there is a "significant other" in the patient's life, his name and telephone number, which can be of crucial importance in an emergency, are requested. Staff talk about suicidal feelings and thoughts openly, having learned that this relieves some of the anxiety the patient feels. Evasiveness or secretiveness about suicidal feelings increase his anxiety and the danger of a suicidal act.

---

[5] Robert E. Litman, MD, Norman L. Farberow, Edwin S. Schneidman, Sam M. Heilig, and Jan A. Kramer, "Suicide-Prevention Telephone Service," *Journal of the American Medical Association,* Vol. 192, No. 1 (April 5, 1965), pp. 21–25.

Office Interviews

In the office staff are able to do a more intensive evaluation of a patient's suicidal potentiality. The following are taken into account: the amount of stress he is under, the symptoms that disturb him, suicidal plan or feelings (in detail), his financial and interpersonal resources, and, finally, his character—that is, whether he had a history of stability or of chronic disorganization and instability. This is usually done in one interview but may be extended to two or more office visits. Staff's attitude throughout is one of interest, encouragement, hope for the patient, and optimism about the eventual outcome. At the conclusion of the interview the patient is asked to complete a shortened form of the Minnesota Multiphasic Personality Inventory, a psychological test consisting of a series of 479 true or false questions, which usually takes about an hour to complete. Selected patients are asked additionally to fill out a social history form or other research materials. An important aspect of the psychological testing and completion of forms is that it forces the patient to think of himself—past, present, and future—which helps to re-establish his identity in his own mind, a valuable therapeutic assist to anyone in a suicidal crisis.

If there is a spouse or a significant other in the patient's life, that person is asked to come in with him. Often this person is the patient's most valuable resource and it is therefore desirable for him to participate in helping the patient to get through the critical period and then to follow up with recommendations made by the center. The following is an example of work in the office with a middle-aged depressed man.

Mr. R, a 50-year-old married man, was referred by his physician because of severe depression and overt threats of suicide. His son, a 27-year-old police officer, had committed suicide two weeks previously by shooting himself in the temple with his service revolver. He left no note and the motives for his death remained a mystery. Mr. R, who had been depressed before this incident, now felt anxious, tense, unable to concentrate, and nearing exhaustion. He thought of death frequently and expressed a desire to follow in his son's footsteps by shooting himself.

Mr. R. was employed as an equipment maintenance worker, and had been with the same company for twenty-one years. He was a steady worker but he had no hobbies or social life. He and his wife had been married for thirty years, had raised a family, and Mrs. R was now working in order to help with expenses. She was a thin, tense individual who strove to be a good wife but had become more of a mother to her husband. She was sexually frigid.

Mr. R was the sixth of a family of ten children. His father was an alcoholic who abused the family. Because of the difficult times, Mr. R quit school after the eighth grade. He became a sporadic alcoholic and at such times was ugly and abusive; he was beaten up on several occasions. He continued to drink after his marriage, but stopped thirteen years ago and has not had a drink since. Mrs. R reported that during the years he drank he was able to shout and express his hostility, but after he stopped he apparently had no satisfactory way of expressing his angry feelings and had become more and more depressed.

Mr. R was treated at the center with psychotherapy and antidepressant medication, and his wife was asked to come in for supportive therapy. His depression and suicidal thinking did not abate, and it was concluded that hospitalization would be necessary. When Mr. R was told, he refused to submit to this and threatened to do away with himself first. After careful evaluation of the risk involved, staff decided to continue to see him as an outpatient, but with a focus on the need for hospitalization. After two more weeks of concentrated effort with him, the center enabled Mr. R to accept its recommendation and enter a psychiatric hospital. In the hospital he responded well to a series of electroshock treatments, dropped his suicidal ideation, and was then able to return to work.

Mr. R was rated a high suicide risk based on his age and sex, high stress, depression, and suicidal preoccupation. The center's decision to try to treat him at first as an outpatient was based in part on the stability of his work and married life and the fact that he had never had a previous try at outpatient psychiatric treatment.

Mr. R is representative of many suicidal persons seen at the center. Under the brunt of some overwhelming life stress, they begin to experience distressing physical or mental symptoms that sharply heighten their discomfort. If in addition they happen to be emotionally constricted or immobilized with respect to some potentially constructive relief-bringing action, they may develop a severe depression, fears of becoming mentally ill, or extreme tension and anxiety. Under these conditions of near-intolerable affect, they begin to consider suicide as a relief or escape from their tensions and confusions or as a final resolution of their problems. This is a most critical time for these patients, a time when they are likely to request help. With help available and with someone responding appropriately, the suicidal risk usually subsides within a short period of time.

SUICIDAL CRISIS CONSULTATIONS

One of the special features of emergency psychotherapy at the Los Angeles Suicide Prevention Center is the emphasis placed by the staff on frequent consultations. These are informal case discussions conducted in a spirit of rapid communication, mutual support, and teamwork, often leading to continuous collaboration by several therapists. The purpose of this section is to describe this type of consultation as a specific therapeutic device for counteracting certain serious technical problems often associated with suicidal crises. Among these are the prevailing sense of urgency and responsibility, the required personal and emotional involvement by the therapist, and the contagious quality of the patient's panic and pessimism.

The stresses may induce problem reactions in the therapist. Among these are overwhelming affects such as anxiety, anger, or hopelessness, constriction of thought, impulsive actions, or complete immobilization. Frequent informal consultations tend to prevent panic and build up the therapist's self-confidence. Fears of overlooking vital points are allayed. Consultations encourage imaginative solutions to problems and help the therapists preserve their feelings of personal identity and sense of humor even though they participate sympathetically in many frustrating interpersonal transactions.

Reasons for Consultations

Cases that are unusual, associated with legal complications, bring the clinic into conflict with other community agencies, or involve a high suicide risk should have consultations. In evaluating high suicide danger for the patient, probably the best single indicator is the therapist's awareness of his own anxiety. Therapists feel some anxiety at some point with nearly every case. Failure to experience anxiety while interacting with a suicidal person, whether owing to poor imagination or excessively strong defenses against anxiety, disqualifies a therapist for work in the center. Therapists learn various strategies and techniques for dealing with suicidal persons and, by taking appropriate actions, keep their anxiety at levels suitable for effective work.

The consultation is probably the most usual device for constructively handling anxiety in the therapist, who should be alert enough to recognize when he needs help. For instance, when a therapeutic interaction has such impact on the therapist that his reactions spill over into his private life he needs a consultation quickly.

The therapist's anxiety may be focused in one or more of several possible areas. He may be having difficulty in understanding, evaluating, or diagnosing the personality or reactions of the patient and his relatives. "Do these symptoms mean schizophrenia?" "He says he still enjoys sexual relations. Does this contradict the possibility of suicide?" "Do you think his wife can be trusted to keep an eye on him over the weekend?"

Many problems involve decisions about direct action. "Must he go to the hospital immediately or can hospitalization wait a day or two?" "How can I get her to come to the clinic?" "To which psychiatric agency should this patient be referred?"

Sometimes the therapist feels he is in over his depth. "Whenever I talk to this patient she seems to get worse!" "I'm afraid to let her leave the office because she might hurt her baby!" "Have you ever heard of someone who liked to kill stray cats?" "This man hired a woman to tie him up and choke him into unconsciousness!"

Spirit

The spirit of the consultation, which has been derived historically from the original approach of the center's staff to patients, is probably more important than the content. In the first phase of the center, patients were selected one at a time and studied carefully by a team consisting of a psychiatrist, psychologist, and psychiatric social worker. The patient was nominally the responsibility of the psychiatrist but, in practice, whichever member of the team came to have the longest and most intense relationship with the patient took over the practical responsibility for the therapeutic contact and was referred to as the therapist of record. In later years, as the case load increased, the practice of team collaboration on each case could not be maintained nor was it necessary. Consultations continue the spirit of collaboration. Both the therapist and consultant are members of a team and are responsible for the patient's welfare.

There is a great difference between supervision and consultation. The act of supervising is essentially the direction and critical evaluation of instruction as, for instance, in a school or teaching clinic. To supervise is to inspect with authority. To consult is to confer together, to take counsel, to interact and consider, and to give advice leading to action.

The formal case conference is designed to stimulate the entire staff, to formulate research problems, and to continue the education of all, but often adds extra problems, extra speculations, and extra possibilities for the therapist to consider. By contrast, the informal consultation aims to clarify the problem, reach a decision, and motivate toward action.

The center feels strongly that the consultant must share in the responsibility for the outcome of the case and must feel personally involved in the consultation as the therapist must feel personally involved with the patient. One of the most important functions of the consultant is to point out situations when it is time for the therapist to let the patient go. Sometimes correct tactics require the consultant to take the patient over from the original therapist and become the patient's new therapist.

The consultation should start with a statement by the therapist of the reasons he feels anxious and his idea of the goal of the consultation. For example:

> The problem is that this girl is 17 and a minor, so I don't see how we can keep on seeing her here, without consent from her parents. But she won't tell us her family name or address, and she says she will break off with us and commit suicide if we try to find out.

> I'm afraid this man will not follow our recommendations for more psychotherapy. How can we keep him motivated for treatment now that he has come out of his depression?

> Here is a 50-year-old man, pretty much alone and friendless. The only thing that keeps him going is work, but he is very depressed now and I have to decide whether to insist that he go immediately to the hospital.

The therapist should then give a brief case report. The consultant listens to make sure that nothing vital has been omitted and tries to visualize the circumstances of the problem and imagine possible solutions. Finally, a course of action is determined. In the first example, it was decided that the adolescent patient would be seen for a few more interviews and that her parents would be involved as staff's relationship with her strengthened and she could better accept this necessity. In the second example, it was decided to bring the patient's wife to the clinic, acquaint her with the problem of insufficient motivation in her husband, and try to use her to increase his motivation. In the last example, it was decided to see the patient daily as an outpatient for a while in the hope that he would improve. If he did not improve, he would be sent to the hospital.

Emergency consultations are characterized by a lack of formal structure. They may take place in offices, halls, or at lunch. They may involve two or more staff people of the same or different disciplines. For example, the psychiatrist asked a psychiatric social worker where to refer a patient who only spoke Hungarian (the International Institute, a casework agency for foreign-speaking, was suggested). A clinical psychologist asked a social worker to call a patient's brother to check on additional information about the husband who had left her. In relating the case history, he realized that several important aspects were still unclear to him. A social worker talked for an hour with a discouraged starlet who was going to take an overdose of pills. Next morning he received a letter of gratitude and a nude picture, as well as a promise to come in for an interview. Naturally, he requested some consultation with his colleagues before proceeding with the therapy. The following case was presented by a social worker to the chief psychiatrist for consultation.

> Mr. C, a 32-year-old steel worker, was threatening to commit suicide in reaction to a divorce action by his wife. The referral was initiated by the wife's employer and she joined him on the telephone. No one knew of Mr. C's present whereabouts but he had been trying to reach his wife at her place of work for the past two days, threatening suicide. The wife was afraid of him because of his previous violence and did not want to see him. She and her employer wondered if they could get him to contact the center by some sort of trick. The social worker expressed great concern about Mr. C, who sounded to him like the kind of person who was capable of acting on his impulses and of committing suicide in this context.
>
> The consultant felt the situation was serious and suggested that an appointment be given the wife. Mrs. C was advised that the next time Mr. C called her place of employment he should be told she was going to the center and should be given the center's number to call. Mr. C did call, was referred to the center, and after a long conversation came into the office. The social worker interviewed him and then asked the consultant to talk with him also.
>
> Mr. C was a muscular ex-fighter, former captain of his high school football team, who had always earned a good living as a steel worker but had had bad luck with his two marriages. He was not an alcoholic or chronically unstable, but one received the impression that he was impulsive and had perhaps too many fights—there may have been a trace of brain damage. It was known that he had taken a large overdose of sleeping tablets two weeks before, for which he had been hospitalized, but he had demanded his release from the hospital. He found it hard to put things into words and could not explain exactly why he felt compelled to commit suicide. He felt that he would have to do something if he did not get to see his wife; that something would be to kill himself.
>
> Two things were picked up by the social worker and the consultant: (1) The patient felt warmly toward his mother and father in another city and was concerned about the effect of his suicide on them. (2) His suicide threat represented a need for some sort of action. The possibility of substitute action was emphasized with him. After consultation and discussion, it was decided that Mr. C would return to his home town. A long-distance telephone call was made to his parents and his father took a plane to come and meet him.

It can be seen from this case that at each point where doubt existed the consultation helped resolve the indecision so that the participants could move toward further action and resolution of the problem.

SUMMARY

In order to facilitate recognition of suicidal persons the following common characteristics are noted: (1) an objective and/or subjective breakdown in coping abilities accompanied by feelings of collapse and helplessness, (2) severely constricted perceptions of themselves and their difficulties, (3) acute ambivalence about dying and living and receiving help. Various techniques have been developed at the Los Angeles Suicide Prevention Center for evaluating suicide risk and recommending appropriate action. These techniques have the effect of interrupting death thoughts and suggesting action directed toward continued living. Therapists work under special stress owing to the prevailing sense of urgency and great responsibility, the required personal involvement, and the contagious quality of the patient's panic and pessimism. Frequent informal consultations are mandatory as a technical device to maintain the therapists' morale and keep anxiety at an optimal level. These informal case discussions are conducted in a spirit of rapid communication, mutual support, and collaborative teamwork.

SUICIDE

CHAPTER 62

CLINICAL WORK WITH SUICIDAL ADOLESCENTS AND THEIR FAMILIES

Dean H. Hepworth, O. William Farley, and J. Kent Griffiths

Suicide among adolescents and young adults has tripled over the past thirty years, despite the fact that suicide rates in general have remained remarkably stable.[1] According to the latest available data, half a million young people between the ages of fifteen and twenty-four years attempt suicide each year; tragically 5,000 succeed.[2] These data tell only part of the story. Suicide often leaves untold distress for survivors and friends, who suffer acute grief and may be tormented by lifelong feelings of guilt.

Because of the prevalence and gravity of adolescent suicide, it is vital that social workers be well-informed about critical aspects of the problem. The present article discusses psychosocial risk indicators; assessment of suicide potential, including use of an instrument recently developed for that purpose; and implications for clinical interventions with suicidal adolescents and their families. Special focus is accorded to integrating individual treatment with family therapy or group therapy.

PSYCHOSOCIAL RISK INDICATORS

Based on clinical research findings on adolescent suicide attempts, Joseph Teicher has described a three-stage process leading to a suicide attempt.[3] The first stage, predispos-

Reprinted from *Social Casework,* Vol. 69, No. 4 (1988), pp. 195–203, by permission of the publisher, Families International, Inc.

[1] Howard S. Sudak, Amasa B. Ford, and Norman B. Rushforth, "Adolescent Suicide: An Overview," *American Journal of Psychotherapy* 38 (July 1984): 350–63.

[2] National Institute of Mental Health, *Useful Information on Suicide* (Rockville, Md.: U.S. Department of Health and Human Services, Publication No. ADM 86-1489, 1986), p. 3.

[3] Joseph D. Teicher, "Suicide and Suicide Attempts," in *Basic Handbook of Child Psychiatry,* vol. 2 of *Disturbances of Development,* ed. Joseph D. Noshpitz (New York: Basic Books, 1979).

ing factors, consists of a long-standing history of problems from childhood to adolescence. The second stage is a period of escalation of problems related to adolescence. The final stage occurs during a period of weeks or days that immediately precede the suicide attempt. Common precipitating events of this phase include a rapid breakdown of the adolescent's social supports, including contacts and associations with peers, friends, and family.

Predisposing Factors

Traumatic losses or child abuse. Loss of parents through death or divorce predisposes children to later psychopathology, particularly to depression, which typically is associated with suicide attempts. This relationship has been studied extensively, but when all research problems are considered, little evidence documents that loss of a parent is the primary cause of a child's vulnerability to later depression. Rather, adverse psychological effects are more accurately attributed to poor parenting by the person who replaced the absent parent or to defective parenting by the earlier parent. Nevertheless, loss of a parent increases vulnerability to depression when the adolescent is faced with stress later in life.[4]

Physical abuse by parents also predisposes children to suicide in adolescence. In a study of 207 high school seniors and 901 college students, Loyd Wright found that adolescents who reported suicidal thoughts were significantly more likely than were their classmates to have been physically abused during childhood by a parent and had many conflicts with parents. Based on a comparison of his findings with previous results, Wright also concluded that adolescents who consider suicide have much in common with those who actually attempt suicide.[5]

Family climate. Long-standing family difficulties are typically associated with suicide in adolescents. Families of adolescents who attempt suicide have been described as lacking warmth and failing to provide emotional security for family members. Research further indicates a relationship between suicide attempts and disorganized, unstable nuclear families with high levels of hostility and conflict.[6] Young persons in such families may receive subtle messages that they are unwanted and expendable.[7]

Parents of adolescents who attempt suicide appear also to be troubled. One study comparing these parents with parents of adolescents who did not attempt suicide revealed that fathers of adolescents who attempt suicide were more depressed, had lower self-esteem, and consumed more alcohol than did their counterparts. Mothers of adolescents who attempted suicide were more anxious, had greater suicidal ideation, and

---

[4] Gerald L. Klerman et al., *Interpersonal Psychotherapy of Depression* (New York: Basic Books. 1984), p. 54.

[5] Loyd S. Wright, "Suicidal Thoughts and Their Relationships to Family Stress and Personal Problems among High School Seniors and College Undergraduates," *Adolescence* 20 (Fall 1985): 575–80.

[6] C. Williams and C. M. Lyons. "Family Interaction and Adolescent Suicidal Behavior: A Preliminary Investigation," *Australian and New Zealand Journal of Psychiatry* 10 (September 1976): 243–52; J. W. McCullock and A. E. Phillip. "Social Variables in Attempted Suicide," *ACTA Psychiatrica Scandanavica* 43 (1967): 341–46.

[7] Joseph C. Sabbath. "The Suicidal Adolescent—The Expendable Child," *Journal of the American Academy of Child Psychiatry* 8 (April 1969): 272–85.

also consumed more alcohol than did the comparison group mothers.[8] Thus these parents are more troubled, less stable, and less emotionally available than are other parents; they are weak models for their children.

Clearly, family climates such as those described above can have an adverse effect on the developing personalities of children. The critical ego qualities of self-esteem, impulse control, ability to cope, and interpersonal skills are particularly vulnerable to damage or to stunted development. Several researchers have documented that many adolescents who attempt suicide have long-standing personality disturbances. Richard Friedman and co-workers found that more than 50 percent of adolescent patients hospitalized for affective disorders (primarily depression) manifested personality disorders.[9] Other researchers concluded that psychiatric disorder was a necessary precondition for attempted suicide in the young people they studied.[10]

Behavioral indicators. The findings of one of the few prospective longitudinal studies on this population show that certain behavioral indicators observable as early as first grade are predictive of adolescent behaviors that correlate with suicide attempts.[11] For example, underachievement in first grade, as rated by teachers, is a strong and specific predictor of teenage depression in male children. Similarly, low ratings of psychological well-being by mothers and by clinicians of females in the first grade were predictive of teenage depression. Aggressive behavior without shyness is a strong predictor of teenage substance abuse for male first graders. Both depression and substance abuse are implicated in a high percentage of suicide attempts by adolescents.

Escalation in Adolescence

Factors cited in the preceding section predispose young persons to be ill equipped to cope with the turbulence and vicissitudes of adolescence. Moreover, low self-esteem, defective interpersonal skills, and dysfunctional behavioral patterns handicap youth in mastering the developmental tasks of adolescence, most notable of which are achieving a stable and healthy identity and developing adequate social relationships. These and other tasks are challenging even for healthy youth, but when compounded by accumulated personality deficits and by continuing lack of emotional support or escalating conflicts with family members, the consequent stresses may be insuperable. Troubled youth may thus resort to or increase dysfunctional coping behaviors that offer brief

---

[8] Carl L. Tishler, Patricia C. McKenry, and Karen C. Morgan, "Adolescent Suicide Attempts: Some Significant Factors," *Suicide and Life Threatening Behavior* 11 (Spring 1981): 86–92.

[9] Richard C. Friedman et al., "The Seriously Suicidal Adolescent: Affective and Character Pathology," in *Suicide in the Young,* ed. Howard H. Sudak, Amasa B. Ford, and Norman B. Rushforth (Littleton, Mass.: Wright PSG, 1984).

[10] Richard W. Hudgens, "Suicide Communications and Attempts," in *Psychiatric Disorders in Adolescents* (Baltimore: Williams and Wilkins, 1975): Frank E. Crumley, "The Adolescent Suicide Attempt: A Cardinal Symptom of a Serious Psychiatric Disorder," *American Journal of Psychotherapy* 36 (April 1982): 158–65; Daniel Offer, "Affects of Their Vicissitudes," in *The Psychological World of the Teenager* (New York: Basic Books, 1969): Stuart M. Finch and E. O. Posnanski, *Adolescent Suicide* (Springfield, Ill.: Charles C Thomas, 1971).

[11] Sheppard G. Kellam and C. Hendricks Brown, "Social Adaptational and Psychological Antecedents in the First Grade of Adolescent Psychopathology Ten Years Later," in *Suicide and Depression among Adolescents and Young Adults,* ed. Gerald L. Klerman (Washington, D.C.: American Psychiatric Press, 1986), pp. 149–83.

respite from pressures but intensify their problems in the long run. The following sections identify behaviors and circumstances of adolescence that are correlates of suicide attempts. As such they signal to practitioners that unless pressures are relieved, the adolescent, following a stressful precipitating event, may attempt suicide to escape what he or she perceives as an unsolvable problem situation.

School-related behavioral patterns. Dysfunctional behavioral patterns that escalate during adolescence are often manifested at school. Thus early academic underachievement can escalate into academic failure and truancy. Moreover, early problems with peers can escalate either into avoidance behavior in social situations or open peer conflicts. Impulsive behavior may also escalate in frequency and intensity. Research indicates that all of the aforementioned factors contribute to suicide potential.[12]

Academic underachievement, however, is by no means the only precursor of school-related difficulties that contribute to suicide potential. A recent survey of high-achieving teenagers (listed in *Who's Who Among High School Students*) found that of the sample of 5,000 students, 31 percent had contemplated suicide and 4 percent had attempted suicide. The four factors these teenagers identified as contributing most to suicide were feelings of personal worthlessness (86 percent), feelings of isolation and loneliness (81 percent), pressure to achieve (72 percent), and fear of failure (61 percent).[13] From this information, it appears that academic overachievers may struggle with troubling feelings that are similar to those of teenagers who are underachievers: doubts of personal worth, loneliness, and fear of failing. Apparently, overachievers make heroic efforts to measure up to high expectations of themselves and others; however, the consequent pressures and fears of not measuring up may become unbearable. This phenomenon may be even more prevalent in Japan, where suicides by children and teenagers soared by 44 percent between 1985 and 1986. Parental pressure to succeed in school is blamed for more than 25 percent of the deaths.[14]

Substance abuse. Research findings clearly indicate that increased substance abuse over the past twenty-five years has been a major contributor to the increased suicide rates among the young. Based on data from several large cities, Jacqueline Greuling and Richard Deblassie reported that at least 50 percent of the adolescents who committed suicide were involved in moderate to heavy drinking, drug abuse, or both.[15] Data from a recent study of suicides in San Diego indicated that drug disorders were implicated in two-thirds of the suicides of young people and that 53 percent abused drugs or alcohol.[16]

Teenagers who abuse drugs and alcohol often do so to escape pressures and troubling feelings. Drugs and alcohol also create emotional highs and a counterfeit sense of well-being that temporarily supplant painful feelings of worthlessness and loneliness. Of course, other factors may also be implicated in substance abuse, including peer pressure, rebelliousness, and imitation of parents who abuse substances.

[12] Jerry Jacobs, *Adolescent Suicide* (New York: John Wiley, 1971).
[13] UPI news release, *Deseret News* (Salt Lake City), 14 September 1986.
[14] UPI news release, *Deseret News* (Salt Lake City). 12 January 1987.
[15] Jacqueline W. Greuling and Richard R. Deblassie, "Adolescent Suicide," *Adolescence* 15 (Fall 1980): 589–601.
[16] Richard C. Fowler, Charles L. Rich. and Deborah Young, "San Diego Suicide Study, II: Substance Abuse in Young Cases," *Archives of General Psychiatry* 43 (October 1986): 962–65.

Communication deficits. Deficiencies in communication skills have also been cited as a factor in many adolescent suicides.[17] Such a deficiency may predispose a depressed adolescent who feels desperate, hopeless, and powerless to act out with self-destructive behavior. This view was supported in a study that compared delinquent adolescents in a correctional facility who had attempted suicide with adolescents in the same facility who had not attempted suicide. Results indicated that those who attempted suicide had learned from their parents to use action rather than words to express troubling feelings and to cope with conflicts.[18]

Family relationships. Cohesiveness between parents and children is typically low in families of suicidal adolescents. As adolescents strive for autonomy, however, the positive emotional connections between adolescents and their parents tend to erode even further in these families. Thus communication between suicidal adolescents and their parents is generally poor and conflict is high. In a study of adolescents who had overdosed on drugs, researchers found that about one-half of the group reported that they felt unable to discuss problems with their mothers, and 89 percent felt the same about communicating with their fathers. In fact, one-half of adolescents reported that their relationship with their father was constantly difficult, with severe disputes commonly occurring more than once a week.[19] Although conflicts between adolescents and their parents or siblings frequently precipitate a suicide attempt, such conflicts generally occur in the context of long-standing strained relationships.[20] Moreover, adolescents' feelings of being unwanted may escalate during adolescence, and subtle messages from relatives may foster suicide attempts. Based on work with families of suicidal adolescents, Joseph Richman reported that family members may express "death wishes" for unwanted members.[21]

Precipitating Events

Stressful events may occur that temporarily overwhelm an adolescent and produce feelings of depression and desperation. Because such events may trigger a suicide attempt, practitioners must be alert to possible suicidal ideation in these adolescents.

The major precipitant for suicidal behavior is separation or threatened separation from loved persons. The suicidal adolescent overreacts to the threatened or actual separation, its perceived finality, and subsequent association with death.[22] Suicide attempts commonly follow quarrels with parents, siblings, or sweethearts that threaten the status of such relationships.[23] Adolescents who have lost a parent of the opposite sex through death are particularly vulnerable to severe emotional reactions when a romantic relationship is terminated; the romantic relationship may have compensated for the

---

[17] William C. Fish and Edith Waldhart-Letzel, "Suicide and Children," *Death Education* 5 (Fall 1981): 215–22.

[18] Michael L. Miller, John A. Chiles, and Valerie E. Barnes, "Suicide Attempters within a Delinquent Population," *Journal of Consulting and Clinical Psychology* 50 (August 1982): 491–98.

[19] Keith Hawton et al., "Classification of Adolescents Who Take Overdoses," *British Journal of Psychiatry* 140 (February 1982): 124–41.

[20] Richard H. Seiden, "Studies of Adolescent Suicidal Behavior: Etiology," in *Perspectives in Abnormal Behavior*, ed. Richard J. Morris (New York: Pergamon Press, 1974), pp. 117–43.

[21] Joseph Richman, *Family Therapy for Suicidal People* (New York: Springer, 1986).

[22] Ibid.

original loss.[24] Similarly, adolescents who are alienated from their parents may overinvest themselves in peer relationships or romantic involvements and may be vulnerable to suicide following losses of such relationships. Such losses may leave adolescents isolated from significant support systems, which is perilous because alienation and isolation are major correlates of adolescent suicide. Frederick Wenz studied adolescent alienation and found that the three factors that were most highly correlated with alienation (in descending order) were lack of social contact with peers in the neighborhood, conflict with parents, and broken romances.[25] In another study of 108 adolescents who attempted suicide Carl Tishler and co-workers found that the reasons cited as precipitating factors for suicide attempts (in descending order) were problems with parents (52 percent), problems with the opposite sex (30 percent), school problems (30 percent), problems with siblings (16 percent), and problems with peers (15 percent).[26]

A recent suicide by a relative or friend can also act as a precipitating factor. Tishler and coworkers reported that 22 percent of the adolescents who attempted suicide had experienced recent suicidal behavior in family members and 20 percent had experienced a recent death of a friend or relative preceding their attempt.[27] More startling, however, are reports of two carefully designed studies that state that the rate of adolescent suicide increases after television news stories about suicide[28] and television movies that depict suicide.[29] Suicide attempts following exposure to suicide of others apparently involve imitative behavior by adolescents, a phenomenon of sufficient magnitude that researchers have expressed a sense of urgency about developing "a research strategy to identify the components of broadcasts that diminish suicidal behavior, if there are any, and those that encourage it."[30]

ASSESSING SUICIDAL RISK

When the worker recognizes several risk indicators associated with suicide, especially depression, during initial contacts with an adolescent and his or her family, he or she should assess whether the adolescent is at risk for suicide. Information should be obtained from the following sources: (1) parents and significant others (for example, teachers, employers, and friends), (2) interviews with the adolescent, (3) instruments devised to assess depression and suicidal risk, and (4) clinical observations.

Parents and significant others who have ongoing interaction with a young person can provide essential information about the person's behavior and possible depression. Suicidal youth often come to the attention of practitioners when parents seek help for

---

[23] W. L. Walker, "Intentional Self-Injury of School Aged Children," *Journal of Adolescence* 3 (September 1980): 217–28; H. C. White, "Self-Poisoning in Adolescence," *British Journal of Psychiatry* 124 (January 1974): 24–35.

[24] Jeri Hepworth, Robert G. Ryder, and Albert S. Dreyer, "The Effects of Parental Loss on the Formation of Intimate Relationships," *Journal of Marital and Family Therapy* 10 (January 1984): 73–82.

[25] Frederick V. Wenz, "Sociological Correlates of Alienation among Adolescent Suicide Attempts," *Adolescence* 14 (Spring 1979): 19–30.

[26] Tishler, McKenry, and Morgan, "Adolescent Suicide Attempts: Some Significant Findings," pp. 89–90.

[27] Ibid.

[28] David P. Phillips and Lundie L. Carstensen. "Clustering of Teenage Suicides after Television News Stories about Suicide." *New England Journal of Medicine* 315 (11 September 1986): 685–89.

[29] Madelyn S. Gould and David Shaffer, "The Impact of Suicide in Television Movies: Evidence of Imitation," *New England Journal of Medicine* 315 (11 September 1986): 690–94.

[30] Ibid., p. 693.

their child for behaviors other than depression. Many distressed adolescents are not aware that they are depressed and guard against disclosing their thoughts and feelings. Moreover, parents may not realize that their child is depressed. Consequently, practitioners must be familiar with typical manifestations of adolescent depression and must alert parents to the significance of these manifestations.

- Deterioration in personal habits (personal appearance, dirty clothes, messy room)
- Decline in school achievement
- Lack of interest in activities that were previously pleasurable
- Increase in sadness, moodiness, and sudden tearful reactions
- Changes in sleep patterns (too much or too little sleep, fitful sleep or arising too early)
- Loss of appetite
- Use of alcohol or drugs
- Talk of death or dying—even in a "joking" manner
- Sudden withdrawal from friends and family, moping about the house[31]

Given the mood swings and tempestuousness typical of adolescence, these warning signs should be regarded as indications of possible serious depression only when they persist for ten days or longer.

Using interviews. Although adolescents tend to guard against disclosing highly personal information, sensitive and skillful interviewing may yield sufficient information to assess suicidal risk. Skillful interviewing should explore risk factors using the following criteria: sense of self-worth, school adjustment, peer relations, family relationships (past and present), communication with parents, use of drugs or alcohol, emotional and behavioral patterns (particularly recent separations or threatened separations from parents, key peers, or sweethearts). It is also important to explore whether other family members or relatives have manifested serious depression or suicidal episodes.

Possible suicidal ideation should also be explored. When young people acknowledge that they believe that they would be better off dead than alive, clinicians should explore the extent of suicidal preoccupation, possible thoughts about how they might commit suicide, whether they have formulated plans (including a specific time), and whether they possess the means by which they could commit the act. Affirmative responses to all of these inquiries indicate a high degree of risk. It is also important to assess possible deterrents to suicidal actions such as religious prohibitions that clients espouse, strong desires to accomplish certain goals, reluctance to cause anguish for significant others, and unwillingness to give up.

In addition to assessing the suicidal intent of the adolescent, it is important to evaluate the potential destructive impact of the family. This can be best accomplished in conjoint family sessions. Clinicians should be especially alert to expressions of death wishes toward the adolescent. Overt messages that place sole blame on the adolescent for family difficulties or for causing unbearable distress for the parents, such as "Our family would get along fine if it weren't for _____" or "I just don't know how much

---

[31] Mark Gold, as quoted by Earl Ubell, "Is That Child Bad or Depressed?" *Parade Magazine* 2 November 1986, p. 10.

longer I can bear the pain _____ is causing" indicate that the family, either knowingly or unwittingly, is encouraging suicidal behavior. More subtle nonverbal messages include ignoring or responding with indifference to an adolescent's expression of despair or desperate plea for understanding and emotional support.

Use of psychological instruments. Certain diagnostic instruments can help confirm clinical judgments or assess risk when young adults reveal little information about themselves. *The Clinical Measurement Package* assesses depression, self-esteem, parent-child relationships, family relationships, and peer relationships.[32] *The Scale for Suicide Ideation* is an excellent tool for assessing suicidal intention.[33] A new instrument, *Adolescent Stress Inventory* (ASI), also assesses suicidal risk.[34] It consists of four indices: (1) problem events, (2) problem behaviors, (3) intrapersonal conflict, and (4) interpersonal conflict. Each index consists of between fourteen and twenty-five items (seventy-two items total) based on a careful review of the literature dealing with correlates of adolescent suicide. The instrument was tested in three groups; each group consisted of forty-five adolescents between twelve and eighteen years old: (1) suicidal adolescents who were interviewed and administered the ASI two to four days after being released from emergency room treatment; (2) adolescents who had not attempted suicide but who were being treated in outpatient psychological counseling; and (3) adolescents who were hospitalized for medical problems. Analysis of the resultant scores indicated that all four indices clearly differentiated the suicidal and counseling groups from the "medical" group, which served as a "quasi-normal" comparison group. Although both the suicidal and counseling groups scored relatively high on all four indices, compared with the "quasi-normal" group, the suicidal group scored significantly higher than did the counseling group on the intrapersonal conflict index of the ASI. This index differentiates suicidal adolescents from other troubled adolescents. Using discriminant analysis procedures, it was determined that nine of the twenty-five items of this scale differentiated the suicidal group from the counseling group:

1. Feeling hopeless about the future
2. Feeling I can't be helped
3. Having thoughts about harming myself
4. Feeling others are to blame for my problems
5. Feeling unsure of my own self-worth
6. Being unable to express my feelings well
7. Having a negative attitude toward life
8. Being fearful
9. Having thoughts about sex that bother me

Adolescents who agree with all or most of these items should be regarded as high risks for suicide.

---

[32] Walter W. Hudson, *The Clinical Measurement Package* (Chicago: Dorsey Press, 1982).
[33] Aaron T. Beck, Maria Kovacs, and Arlene Weissman, "Assessment of Suicidal Intention: The Scale for Suicide Ideation," *Journal of Consulting and Clinical Psychology* 47 (April 1979): 343–52.
[34] J. Kent Griffiths, O. William Farley, and Mark Fraser, "Indices of Adolescent Suicide," *Journal of Independent Social Work Practice* 1 (Fall 1986): 49–63.

Items from the problem behaviors index of the ASI that differentiated the suicidal group from the counseling group included the following:

1. Truancy from school
2. Getting into drugs
3. Getting into alcohol

Items from the problem events index of the ASI were not sensitive to differences between the suicidal and counseling groups, but persons in the suicidal group scored significantly higher on the following two items from the ASI interpersonal conflict index:

1. Problems with amount of love or harmony in our home
2. Problems communicating with my father

Clinicians can refine their suicide assessment skills by adapting and incorporating these items into interviews.

TREATMENT IMPLICATIONS

When assessment reveals that a young person is suicidal, crisis intervention should be used during the early phase of treatment. After the situation has stabilized and the risk diminished, other interventions may be used.

Antidepressant Medication and Medical Backup

Clinicians are advised to seek psychiatric consultation for a client when suicidal risk appears high. A social worker is obligated ethically to safeguard the life of a suicidal client by seeking medical opinion and intervention, if they appear needed. Social workers who fail to take such precautionary measures are vulnerable to prosecution for negligence and malpractice should suicide occur. Moreover, antidepressant medication and hospitalization, both of which require medical management, may be indicated. Consultation also helps ease the burden of responsibility when evaluating suicidal risk. Because of the hazard of under- or overreaction to such risk, the opinion of an emotionally uninvolved professional can greatly enhance objectivity and provide needed reassurance.

When chemical dependency is implicated in the problems of a suicidal youth, treatment for the chemical dependency should be arranged. Inpatient care in concert with family therapy is often indicated; in such instances collaboration with physicians is essential.

Individual Therapy

Because suicidal adolescents generally have long-standing mental disturbances, individual treatment, combined with family therapy or group therapy, is usually indicated. Individual treatment affords adolescents the opportunity to express troubling feelings they may be unable to verbalize in a family or group context. Moreover, the therapist can monitor clients' reactions to experiences in family or group therapy and assess suicidal risk on an ongoing basis. Because many suicidal adolescents manifest borderline personalities, practitioners should expect vicissitudes in the helping relationship.

Typical areas of therapeutic focus include assisting clients to gain awareness of and to manage painful emotions they have previously coped with by acting out, to search for more effective ways of coping with stressors, and to develop new skills in communicating and negotiating with peers and family members. Because these clients typically have difficulty expressing feelings and needs, therapists must be particularly sensitive to nonverbal cues that signal tensions and troubling emotions.

Therapists should be aware that suicidal youth may temporarily consider the therapist as their primary support system. Frequent sessions may be needed during the initial period of crisis. Flexibility is important, and shorter sessions should be used for adolescents who find it difficult to tolerate longer sessions. Therapists should give their telephone numbers to adolescents and encourage them to call if they experience suicidal impulses. It is important, of course, not to permit manipulative clients to exploit the therapist's good will by calling excessively.

Enhancing self-esteem is another major treatment focus. By discussing a client's score on the Index of Self-Esteem,[35] the client can begin to learn that a major part of his or her problem stems from his or her low sense of self-worth. The worker should help the client become aware of patterns of self-derogation and help the client negotiate a goal to monitor and curtail devaluating self-statements. Moreover, therapists should identify clients' strengths and positive attributes and provide positive feedback to clients who respond favorably to such feedback.

With high-achieving adolescents whose self-esteem is tenuous, it is important to explore mistaken beliefs that underlie their self-doubts. Typical beliefs include: "Excelling in school (or any other endeavor) is the only way I can be a worthwhile person" or "If I do not meet my parents' expectations I am a failure and they will not love me." The worker should help the adolescent understand the unrealistic nature of these beliefs as well as their destructive impact, relinquish them in favor of more realistic beliefs, and develop satisfying activities and relationships.

Family Therapy

The choice between using family therapy or group therapy in conjunction with individual therapy depends on which mode will provide the greatest emotional support to the suicidal youth. Generally, family therapy is preferred because of the potential ongoing availability of family members as a support system and the greater emotional significance of bonds with parents and siblings compared with group members. Moreover, family therapy is an effective means of engaging parents and young persons in efforts directed toward fostering constructive communication and reducing the frequency and intensity of conflicts.

Before meeting with the entire family, it is desirable to see the parents separately to assess their communication patterns. The worker should help prepare parents for later sessions by (1) clarifying the need to create a climate conducive to open communica-

---

[35] Walter W. Hudson, *The Clinical Measurement Package.*

tion, (2) coaching them to adopt a listening stance, and (3) emphasizing the need for them to convey willingness to focus on and to change their own dysfunctional behaviors. Although it is vital to establish rapport with parents by empathizing with their distress over the adolescent's behavior, it is equally important to construe their child's behavior as indicative of broader problems within the family. The objective, of course, is to reduce the pressure on the adolescent by countering the parents' tendency to cast him or her in the role of patient.

In sessions with the entire family, the therapist should actively confront dysfunctional interactions, especially when members attack, blame, and criticize one another. The therapist must translate negative messages into personalized statements of needs and feelings that do not elicit defensiveness and recriminations. It is also essential that the worker teach family members the importance of responding supportively and with positive feedback to one another. Positive communication strengthens family bonds, expands emotional support, and enhances self-esteem of family members.

Adolescents who experience intense parental pressure to excel should be helped to verbalize these feelings. Their parents may need help in reducing the pressures they place on their child and should be taught to provide acceptance and support not conditional upon excelling in school, music, athletics, or other activities.

Because breakdown in communication and conflict with parents are critical problems in suicidal youth, optimal benefits may be achieved by working flexibly with the parent-youth subsystem as well as with the entire family. Concentrating on dyadic interaction facilitates the dissolution of communication barriers and enhances relationships that have deteriorated because of chronic misunderstanding and conflict. Negotiating agreements between parent and youth to participate mutually in constructive activities (for example, attending athletic or cultural events, making household or auto repairs, planning meals, shopping, or hiking) encourages positive interaction and reciprocal positive feelings. Working separately with the parents to teach them parenting skills is also effective in enhancing family interaction (a group approach can also be employed).

Activities that involve all family members foster family cohesiveness. For example, Florence Kaslow and Jack Friedman reported that family photos and movies help family members reexperience the past together.[36] Laughing and reminiscing about shared events and circumstances from happier times reactivate positive connections among family members, especially if parents are coached to focus on the positive aspects of such experiences. Clinicians should also challenge parents to initiate family rituals that foster positive interaction such as planned sharing of daily experiences at the dinner table; family games; celebration of birthdays, achievements, and developmental milestones; family attendance at school, church, and athletic events; and family picnics, hikes, and camping trips.

Despite its desirability, family therapy is sometimes contraindicated or unfeasible. One or both parents may refuse to participate or the adolescent may feel so estranged from the family that reconciliation is not realistic. Moreover, in extreme instances, the

---

[36] Florence W. Kaslow and Jack Friedman, "Utilization of Family Photos and Movies in Family Therapy," *Journal of Marriage and Family Counseling* 3 (January 1977): 19–25.

family climate may be so suicidogenic and malevolent, and family patterns so deeply entrenched, that family therapy is unlikely to be beneficial.

Group Therapy and Other Support

When an adolescent's family is not a viable social support system, group therapy can be a promising alternative. Participating in a group with others provides a reference group and counters the adolescent's sense of isolation. Engaging in problem solving with others who have similar problems also counters the hopelessness and powerlessness that typify suicidal adolescents. The effectiveness of group therapy with suicidal adolescents has been documented by Charlotte Ross and Jerome Motto, who found no suicide attempts in their two-year follow-up study of seventeen suicidal youth treated by individual and group therapy.[37]

Contracting with group members to focus on strengths and positive qualities increases participants' self-esteem. Similarly, assisting members to adopt and to adhere to a guideline that members will personalize and "own" their feelings helps members learn to talk about feelings, which in turn decreases the adolescent's tendency to act out destructively. Goals that are particularly relevant for suicidal adolescents include mastering social skills and learning effective approaches to problem solving. Ross and Motto provide an excellent discussion of group therapy with suicidal adolescents.[38]

Because of the importance of peer relationships, efforts to tap or to mobilize peer support systems can produce highly therapeutic benefits. Alarmed by the incidence of adolescent suicides and suicide attempts by students, some schools and youth leaders have organized hotlines and support networks for troubled adolescents. After meeting with students and faculties following suicidal incidents, William Hill believes that the school is an ideal place to initiate preventive and postcrisis efforts.[39]

For adolescents or families who participate in religious organizations, members of the pastoral staff or clergy in local churches and synagogues may be an excellent resource. These individuals may be willing to mobilize efforts to extend help to alienated adolescents. Leaders of other youth or volunteer organizations may also respond to the needs of suicidal adolescents. When such resources do not exist, clinicians may need to spearhead efforts to organize these types of social support systems.

---

[37] Charlotte P. Ross and Jerome A. Motto, "Group Counseling for Suicidal Adolescents," in *Suicide in the Young.*
[38] Ibid.
[39] William H. Hill, "Mobilizing Schools for Suicide Prevention," in *Suicide in the Young.*

CHAPTER 63

IMPLICATIONS OF VASECTOMY FOR SOCIAL WORK PRACTICE

Sarah F. Hafemann and Catherine S. Chilman

It has been estimated that over three million living Americans have had a vasectomy,[1] and the popularity of this procedure as a method of contraception has been growing in recent years. It is important that social workers become well informed on this subject so that they may more effectively carry out their various roles as counselors, educators, and social planners. However, little information has appeared in the professional social work journals about vasectomy and its effects. This article presents an overview of medical, social, and psychological research. Popular attitudes as reflected in the popular press are also surveyed, and some implications for social work practice are suggested.

MEDICAL ASPECTS OF VASECTOMY

Vasectomy is a simple, safe surgical procedure performed to sterilize the male. It consists of cutting or blocking the tube (vas or vas deferens) through which sperm pass to the penis. As a method of male sterilization, vasectomy has been widely performed since the 1930s;[2] and today throughout the world it is the most commonly performed operation on the adult male.[3]

Physicians vary widely in the qualifications they demand of patients requesting a va-

Reprinted from *Social Casework*, Vol. 55 (1974), pp. 343–351, by permission of the publisher, Families International, Inc.

[1] Gilbert Kasirsky, *Vasectomy, Manhood and Sex* (New York: Springer, 1972), p. 17.
[2] W. S. Haynes, Vasectomy, *Medical Journal of Australia,* 20: 1045–48 (May 1967).
[3] Stanwood S. Schmidt, Vasectomy: Indications, Technic, and Reversibility, *Fertility and Sterility,* 19: 192–96 (March–April 1968).

sectomy for sterilization. Some doctors perform the operation with no evaluation of the patient's life situation or personality. Others may require a stable family unit, minimum ages for husband and wife, at least two children including at least one son, a personal interview, the consent of both husband and wife, a psychiatric evaluation, and a consultation with another physician.[4]

There may or may not be a physician-required waiting period before the actual operation. Most vasectomies are performed in the doctor's office under local anesthetic. The patient prepares himself at home by bathing and shaving the scrotal area. Then, in the office, the area is cleansed with antiseptic and the doctor manipulates the vas to separate it from other tissues so that it is positioned immediately under the skin. Local anesthetic is then injected into the skin and around the vas. The manipulation and injection are the only parts of the procedure that may be uncomfortable. After the anesthetic has taken effect, an incision of three-quarters to one inch is made on one side of the scrotum and a segment of the vas is lifted out.

Early methods involved cutting the vas and tying it to itself with the two ends pointing in opposite directions.[5] A more recent development includes the use of small tantalum clips to close off the vas.[6] There has been considerable criticism of the earlier method because it seems to lead to a greater chance of the formation of sperm granuloma (small nodules appearing around the cut end of the vas where sperm cells may be escaping) and eventual recanalization (forming of a new channel between the closed ends of the vas).[7] After the vas has been closed off, only a few stitches are required to close the incision in the scrotum. After one side has been completed, the procedure is performed on the other. Some physicians prescribe a sedative or tranquilizer for the patient to take before the operation. Any pain after the anesthetic wears off can usually be managed by aspirin and codeine.

After the operation, the patient should wear a scrotal supporter to prevent strain on the wound. Most men can go back to work the day after the operation, and many vasectomies are scheduled for Friday mornings so the patient will have a weekend in which to recuperate. Intercourse may be resumed one to ten days after the operation.

It is crucial to realize that sterility does not result immediately. Even though no new spermatozoa will be released, there will be mature sperm remaining in the male's reproductive tract. For this reason, sperm counts must be made before other contraceptive measures can be safely abandoned. Samples are obtained either by masturbation or the use of a condom during intercourse. There has been continuing debate whether the samples should be requested after a certain amount of time or after a certain number of ejaculations. Research has shown that approximately 68 percent of any remaining

---

[4] Harold Lear, Vasectomy—A Note of Concern, *Journal of the American Medical Association,* 219: 1206–07 (February 28, 1972); and D. M. Potts and G. I. M. Swyer, Effectiveness and Risks of Birth-control Methods, *British Medical Bulletin,* 26: 26–32 (January 1970).

[5] Kasirsky, *Vasectomy, Manhood and Sex,* p. 52.

[6] William M. Moss, A Sutureless Technic for Bilateral Partial Vasectomy, *Fertility and Sterility,* 23: 33–37 (January 1972).

[7] Stanwood S. Schmidt, Vasectomy, *Journal of the American Medical Association,* 206: 522 (April 19, 1971); and Donald J. Dodds, Reanastomosis of the Vas Deferens, *Journal of the American Medical Association,* 220: 1498 (June 12, 1972).

[8] Matthew Freund et al., Disappearance Rate of Spermatozoa from the Ejaculate Following Vasectomy, *Fertility and Sterility,* 20: 163–70 (January–February 1969).

sperm is ejaculated at each emission.[8] The suggestion has been made that the first sperm count be made after ten ejaculations instead of waiting twelve to sixteen weeks after the operation.[9]

The operation is considered to be extremely safe in terms of mortality and is also the most effective method of birth control, with a failure rate of .15 pregnancies per year per 100 couples; this rate is slightly lower than that for tubal ligation and considerably lower than for any other contraceptive method.[10]

As far as morbidity rates for vasectomy are concerned, there is great variation depending on interpretation by the patient or the doctor.[11] The most common immediate complications of vasectomy are infection, bruising, and pain. All three can be kept to a minimum by careful surgical technique.[12] Study has shown that these problems are bothersome to only a small proportion of vasectomy patients. At present, the most significant long-range complication appears to be formation of spermatic granulomas which may occur in the epididymus or at the cut end of the vas any time after vasectomy. These may become painful and require surgical removal.

Perhaps the most disconcerting complication of vasectomy is spontaneous recanalization of the vas, with the possibility of a resultant impregnation. The risk of this happening is about one-half to one percent.[13] Some doctors feel that what actually may happen is simple failure to maintain other contraceptive measures until sterility is finally achieved, but others disagree with this viewpoint.[14]

Possible long-term effects of vasectomy on the hormonal balance have also been investigated. Of major importance is the fact that the production of sperm is not affected by vasectomy.[15] Not only do sperm continue to be produced, but also testosterone, the male sex hormone.[16]

There is a sizable body of medical literature available on the subject of reanastomosis (the surgical reversal of sterility due to vasectomy). This operation is extremely difficult to perform and the success rate tends to be low.[17]

With restoration of fertility so difficult, it has been proposed that men could protect themselves against the need to have the operation reversed by freezing some of their sperm and placing it in a sperm bank in case another child were wanted at a later date. Although the techniques of sperm banking have been developed, there has been little research on patient demand for this service.

Medical opinion has given greater acceptance to vasectomy in recent years. In 1968, the American Medical Association examined the reasons doctors cited for not performing vasectomies—legal or religious considerations and concern for psychiatric trauma.

---

[9] Schmidt, Vasectomy, p. 522.

[10] Joseph E. Davis, Vasectomy, *American Journal of Nursing,* 72: 509–13 (March 1972).

[11] Davis, Vasectomy, p. 509.

[12] Stanwood S. Schmidt, Technics and Complications of Elective Vasectomy: The Role of Spermatic Granuloma in Spontaneous Recanalization, *Fertility and Sterility,* 17: 467–81 (July–August 1966).

[13] Davis, Vasectomy, p. 511.

[14] C. D. Muller, Consideration of Sterilization Vasectomy, *Northwest Medicine,* 54: 1,427–30 (December 1955).

[15] R. S. Grewal and M. S. Sachan, Changes in Testicle After Vasectomy: An Experimental Study, *International Surgery,* 49: 460–62 (May 1968).

[16] Raymond G. Bunge, Plasma Testosterone Levels in Man Before and After Vasectomy, *Investigative Urology,* 10:9 (July 1972).

[17] David Rosenbloom, Reversal of Sterility Due to Vasectomy, *Fertility and Sterility,* 7: 540–45 (November–December 1956).

This editorial concluded that vasectomy for reason of contraception alone should be available to couples who did not display psychiatric contraindications.[18]

PSYCHOLOGICAL ASPECTS OF VASECTOMY

Any couple's experience with vasectomy is complex, with many factors influencing their response to this method of birth control. The research on the psychological aspects of vasectomy reflects the difficulty of studying such subjective phenomena. Much of the work has been colored by the individual bias of the investigator. The relative lack of valid and reliable studies in this area has been a serious omission in the literature of medicine and the behavioral sciences. Work already done can start to answer some of the questions related to vasectomy but a great deal more research is needed.

The medical literature includes several studies reported by doctors who have done vasectomies in their private practices. For the most part, the studies show overwhelming approval of the operation on the part of the patients. These studies, however, have many shortcomings. Usually only surface questions are asked, such as "How would you rate your enjoyment of sexual intercourse since the operation?" and "Would you have the operation if you had it to do all over again?"[19] Characteristically, these studies are conducted over a short period of time, usually six months to a year after the operation. Often the questionnaires do not include open-ended questions but only a checklist for the respondent to complete. It is further reported that many men do not go to their regular family physician for this operation and therefore are not as likely to return to the doctor who performed the actual surgery if difficulties arise.[20]

The studies undertaken by psychiatrists and psychologists specifically to investigate psychosexual results of vasectomy also tend to be unsatisfactory. One of the difficulties is the bias introduced by Freudian theory. Freud's teachings regarding the Oedipal complex and castration anxiety predispose many researchers to expect pathology to result from vasectomy and thus to direct their investigations toward possible pathological outcomes. Many of these studies are further weakened by the use of very small samples, with the heightened possibility of sampling error. Adequate control groups were not set up in a number of investigations. As with the doctors' studies discussed above, many of these studies have not been conducted over a sufficient length of time.

In addition to the methodological difficulties with much of the published research, a new problem has been introduced in our understanding of this aspect of vasectomy. The rapid increase in the number of men undergoing this surgery and the seeming acceptance of this method of birth control may drastically alter many psychological and social effects of male sterilization. As vasectomy becomes increasingly accepted throughout society, the lessened negative cultural sanctions may make the vasectomized male feel less deviant or defensive. Earlier studies that revealed temporary adverse social-psychological effects for some males might yield fewer negative findings if they were carried out today.

[18] Voluntary Male Sterility, *Journal of the American Medical Association,* 204: 821–22 (May 27, 1968).
[19] Pauline Jackson et al., A Male Sterilization Clinic, *British Medical Journal,* 4: 295–97 (October 31, 1970).
[20] Elzena Barnes and Glenna B. Johnson, Effects of Vasectomy on Marriage Relationships: A Descriptive Analysis of 26 Cases Seen in Marriage Counseling by Family Service-Travelers Aid, Des Moines, Iowa, 1964 (unpublished).

The best-known and most careful research in this area was undertaken by David A. Rodgers and Frederick J. Ziegler. Their first article reports on a group of forty-eight California males who underwent vasectomy. Preoperative tests showed that this sample was "much more representative of the stable, productive, successful group in the culture than either the emotionally disturbed or the economically and socially improvident group" and they appeared to be "motivated primarily by rational considerations and were relatively free of neurotic concerns about the consequences of the operation."[21] A follow-up study of thirty-five of these men between one and two years postoperatively found that although they expressed almost unanimous satisfaction with the operation, the Minnesota Multiphasic Personality Inventory (MMPI) scores indicated evidence of increased psychological disturbance for some of them. The authors suggested that preoperative hypochondriasis or concern over masculinity may be predictive of difficulties following vasectomy.[22]

Rodgers and Ziegler continued their work with a larger study involving forty-two couples who chose vasectomy and thirty-nine couples who chose ovulation suppression pills as their method of birth control. Two subgroups of twenty-two couples each—closely matched in terms of age, early sexual history, education, and income—were also studied. Initial testing and interviews were conducted, and follow-up testing and psychiatric interviews were conducted, two years later. When the vasectomy group was compared to the pill group, the first was found to do more poorly, on the average, in the areas of sexual and psychiatric adjustment and marital satisfaction. Some of the vasectomized men emphasized masculine role behavior which called for modifications in their wife's behavior and in the marriage itself. "We thus infer that the vasectomy husbands are more vulnerable to the threats of the typical husband-wife rivalries than they were preoperatively."[23] In a later discussion of these findings, the authors suggest that the vasectomized men tended to avoid behavior that might call into question either their manliness or the appropriateness of the operation. In so doing they showed an increase in culturally approved masculine behavior, along with a decrease in the kind of behavioral flexibility that would be most conducive to a happy personal life and comfortable marriage.[24]

Despite research evidence of poorer average psychological functioning, the vasectomy group expressed satisfaction with the operation and tended to blame other events for changes in their personal or marital lives. The study further reported that the vasectomy couples felt that the preoperative interview was quite useful in reducing or eliminating confusion about the operation. The postoperative interview was also reported by some to have improved understanding and communication between husband and wife. The authors suggest that such discussion may attenuate the potential traumatic impact of vasectomy.

---

[21] David A. Rodgers et al., Sociopsychological Characteristics of Patients Obtaining Vasectomies from urologists, *Marriage and Family Living,* 25: 335 (August 1963).

[22] David A. Rodgers et al., A Longitudinal Study of the Psycho-Social Effects of Vasectomy, *Journal of Marriage and the Family,* 27: 59–64 (February 1965).

[23] Frederick J. Ziegler, David A Rodgers, and Sali Ann Kriegsman, Effect of Vasectomy on Psychological Functioning, *Psychosomatic Medicine,* 28: 62 (January–February 1966).

[24] David A. Rodgers, Frederick J. Ziegler, and Nissim Levy, Prevaling Cultural Attitudes About Vasectomy: A Possible Explanation of Postoperative Psychological Response, *Psychosomatic Medicine,* 29: 367–75 (July–August 1967).

In attempting to identity the causes of the poorer adjustment of the vasectomy group, a study of prevailing cultural attitudes about vasectomy was undertaken in the mid-1960s. Projective tests were given to a group of seventeen couples of a Protestant church group and 127 undergraduate psychology students to determine their attitudes toward couples using oral contraceptives or vasectomy. The couple using vasectomy was seen in a less favorable light by both groups, but there was no consistent characteristic ascribed to the vasectomy couple. According to the authors, a major problem about this form of contraception for the vasectomized male is the nonspecificity of the negative cultural judgment. Thus, the judgment "could never be completely disconfirmed [sic]."[25]

In a follow-up study, the researchers noted a return to virtual similarity between the oral contraceptive and vasectomy groups over four years' time. Differences in scores on the MMPI and the California Psychological Inventory decreased for both groups of husbands and wives. The investigators expressed some surprise that, in light of some of the earlier studies, they did not find more sizable long-range changes in the psychological functioning of the vasectomy couples. Although the sample was too small to develop predictive capability adequately, it appears that the earlier impression that hypochondriacal men or men insecure about their masculinity are unsuited to vasectomy was not validated four years postoperatively. The investigators also stressed that the extensive contact with the study team which provided opportunities to ventilate and discuss areas of concern may have prevented some adverse reactions.[26] It should be recalled, however, that Ziegler and his colleagues studied only a small group of couples, that these people were generally middle class and economically secure, and that extensive counseling may well have been a factor in mitigating possible negative after-effects. So far as we now know, the ultimate effects of vasectomy on personal and marital adjustments are not likely to be different from those associated with use of oral contraceptives.

The task of investigating the psychological ramifications of vasectomy is not yet complete, but several old wives' tales may have been disproved. Research findings show that, in all likelihood, vasectomy does not cure sexual problems. Although release from the fear of an unwanted pregnancy may increase a couple's pleasure in lovemaking, a vasectomy apparently does not cure frigidity, impotence, or premature ejaculation. Vasectomy seems not to increase or decrease infidelity, divorce, or separation.[27] It also does not appear that men are pressured to have vasectomies by overbearing wives.

CHANGING PUBLIC ATTITUDES

It has been suggested that cultural attitudes influence men's adjustment after vasectomy. An examination of the popular press, from 1960 to the present, provides ample evidence of a shift in public opinion about sterilization.

[25] Ibid., p. 373.

[26] Frederick J. Ziegler, David A. Rodgers, and Robert J. Prentiss, Psychological Response to Vasectomy, *Archives of General Psychiatry,* 21: 46–54 (July 1969).

[27] D. A. Rodgers and Frederick J. Ziegler, Changes in Sexual Behavior Consequent to Use of Noncoital Procedures of Contraception, *Psychosomatic Medicine,* 30: 495–505 (September–October 1968).

Throughout the early 1960s, vasectomy gained in popularity. In the five-year period of 1959–1964, the incidence of vasectomy doubled. Attitudes changed slowly, however; even in the mid-1960s "to most Americans there [was] something peculiarly disturbing about the words 'abortion' and 'sterilization.' They [were] uncomfortable words, not exactly obscene but not polite either."[28] Advocates of voluntary sterilization did not propagandize so much as they simply attempted to break down prejudices.

The spectacular increase in vasectomy began in 1967 with the first warnings from British doctors of the possibility of blood clots forming as a result of taking birth control pills. The number of vasectomies has doubled every year since then. Several other factors were also responsible: the 1965 Supreme Court ruling in *Griswold* v. *Connecticut* which expanded the right of privacy to include birth control; the 1968 decision by Planned Parenthood–World Population to include voluntary sterilization in its program; and the decisions of the United States Department of Health, Education, and Welfare and the Blue Cross-Blue Shield to approve payments for voluntary sterilization. The decline of American puritanism and the growing concern about the problems of overpopulation also influenced the rising popular acceptance of sterilization. A crucial step in the changing of public opinion was the gradual conversion of the medical profession. In 1968, an editorial in the *Journal of the American Medical Association* declared vasectomy to be "safe, quick, effective and legal" and took doctors to task for not performing the operation in the absence of certain contraindications.[29]

The 1970 Senate hearing on the safety of the birth control pill stimulated a further surge of interest in vasectomy. Articles describing vasectomy and discussing its tremendous gain in popularity appeared in numerous popular magazines. The information contained in these articles appeared to be medically accurate; it was stressed that vasectomy is not castration and does not alter sex drive or performance. Husbands who had had vasectomies were portrayed as intelligent, considerate, and assured of their manhood.

The 1970 National Fertility Studies reported:

> By 1970 sterilization was the first choice of contracepting [sic] couples where the wife was 30–44 years old (25 percent, as against 21 percent for the pill); and among couples of all ages intending no more children, sterilization was second only to the pill.[30]

These data reflect practices antedating the Senate hearings on possible adverse side effects of the birth control pill. Statistics obtained today would probably show an even higher use of sterilization.

Female sterilization is more prevalent among blacks than whites and is used by 21 percent of the fertile black couples who desire no more children versus 18 percent for whites. However, vasectomy is nine times more prevalent among whites than blacks. Blacks and low-income people may be reluctant to seek vasectomies because of misin-

---

[28] Walter Goodman, Abortion and Sterilization: The Search for Answers, *Redbook*, October 1965, pp. 70–71.
[29] Voluntary Male Sterility, p. 822.
[30] Harriet B. Presser and Larry L. Bumpass, The Acceptability of Contraceptive Sterilization. Among U.S. Couples: 1970, *Family Planning Perspectives*, 6: 18–26 (October 1972).

formation about the consequences of the operation. Vasectomy, as opposed to tubal ligation, is most acceptable to low-parity white couples with above-average education and income. Fears of genocide are frequently expressed by some black males. In general, cultural innovations tend to be picked up first by urban people at higher socioeconomic levels.

The pendulum has now begun to swing away from a wholesale endorsement of vasectomy. Concern has been expressed that vasectomy may become a fad. William A. Nolen has urged that couples consider in advance all aspects of vasectomy, including fears regarding the operation, its near-irreversibility, the possibility of divorce or death of spouse or of children, and assumptions that the operation would, of itself, solve marital problems.[31] The issue of formation of sperm antibodies in the vasectomized male has signaled the beginning of a reappraisal of the safety of the operation. Additional medical research addressed to this problem has not yet made its way into the popular press.

At present there are still many couples who have completed their families or have chosen to forego parenthood completely but have not chosen a permanent method of birth control. The incidence of vasectomy is likely to increase as more of these couples learn what vasectomy involves, talk to friends or relatives who have had the operation, and become concerned about the possible deficiencies of other birth control methods.

IMPLICATIONS FOR SOCIAL WORK PRACTICE

Although not exhaustive, the social and psychological research on vasectomy can provide important leads for social workers. The implications of the available research touch on the areas of prevasectomy screening and postoperative follow-up, marital discord after vasectomy, pregnancy after vasectomy, and the desire for reversal of sterilization.

These implications might well apply to social workers in such activities as program-planning and program development, education, and counseling. They may also apply to social workers in a variety of settings: medical, family service, marriage counseling, family life education, and so on. As literature reviewed in this article suggests, vasectomy involves more than a medical procedure. Social workers, as well as physicians and other human service professionals, have important contributions to make. The social worker involved in such a team approach will require additional training beyond the basic understanding of human sexuality and birth control that all social workers should possess. The training necessary for social workers who frequently work with couples and individuals who may be considering vasectomy should include advanced understanding of vasectomy and alternative contraceptive methods and techniques, including the experience of observing a vasectomy operation; effective counseling and therapy skills; and, finally, a clear and continuing awareness of one's bias and values and those of any sponsoring agency. Implications for counseling and education include consideration of factors related to both prevasectomy decision-making and postoperative adjustments.

[31] William A. Nolen, Vasectomy: A Cautionary Note, *McCall's*, June 1972, p. 60.

Social and psychological prevasectomy screening should probably be conducted in a joint interview with both partners, preferably by a male-female interview team unless special circumstances indicate other approaches. To rule out possible undue influence of one spouse by the other, each should also be interviewed separately. The counselor should explore the reasons both the male and his spouse have for seeking a vasectomy as well as their related attitudes, feelings, and understandings. Before the vasectomy, the couple should be encouraged to consider how their decision might be affected by divorce or death of a spouse or the illness or death of their children, if they have any. Alternatives of adoption and sperm-banking should be explained realistically. (At present, frozen sperm does not seem to last indefinitely, and adoptable children are becoming less available.) Couples should be discouraged from thinking of the surgical reversal of vasectomy as a possibility, since the chance of restoration of fertility is so low. The final decision should be left until the couple have been fully informed, have achieved a clear understanding of the possible complications, and have examined their feelings regarding future changes in their life situation. The social worker should be clear that the couple also have thorough knowledge of alternative birth control measures.

No scale has yet been devised to predict which couples may regret vasectomy or have related social or psychological problems. Contraindications to vasectomy include such factors as impulsiveness, high levels of related anxiety on the part of either partner, hopes that a vasectomy will improve the marital relationship, or a decision based on an overzealous commitment to population control or women's liberation ideology. Social workers should not be too quick, however, to reject couples who manifest some degree of anxiety, insecurity, or difficulty in their relationship, because (1) any surgery is likely to be accompanied by some anxiety; (2) no intimate relationship is completely free of problems; and (3) no individual is completely free of sex-role confusion or insecurity.

In their contributions to the formulation of administrative policy, as well as in their handling of screening interviews, social workers will need to be aware of their own biases about vasectomies for certain couples, for example, very young or childless couples. A possible result of a too-rigid policy regarding acceptance or exclusion is that many couples would seek the operation from physicians who have no screening procedures at all and no provision for follow-up. Policies can be flexible if the couple are provided the opportunity to discuss fully their expectations and anxieties, if the couple have adequate knowledge of vasectomy and of alternative methods of contraception, and if they appear to be comfortable and firm in their decision.

Ideally, every couple who choose vasectomy as a method of birth control should be encouraged to come in for a postoperative interview at the time of the second sperm count. This interview would allow for discussion and clarification of any anxieties or problems that have arisen or may be foreseen. If pre- and postoperative interviews with a knowledgeable and skilled counselor like a social worker become common, it is possible that the rate of postoperative complications might decline.

According to the available research evidence, these postoperative problems involve sexual dysfunction, pregnancy, and a desire for reanastomosis. Sexual dysfunction after vasectomy is usually of psychological origin. For example, if the fear of pregnancy is used by a couple to restrict their sexual activities, a vasectomy eliminates their rationale. With this limit removed, they may find that one or both of them may not wish to engage in more frequent intercourse for a variety of reasons. Skilled marriage counseling may help the couple resolve problems in this area.

According to available evidence, the likelihood of pregnancy following vasectomy is very small. Spontaneous reanastomosis occurs rarely. If the male has received laboratory confirmation of his sterility, the chance of viable sperm remaining in his reproductive tract is also minimal. In the rare case that pregnancy does occur after vasectomy, it may be accompanied by suspicion of the wife's infidelity or the wife's fear that she is suspect. Skilled social workers may be helpful in these cases.

Ill-advised physicians have frequently let the couple work such problems out by themselves; social workers should not ignore such problems and can perform a useful function. A first step is a repeat sperm count to assess the possibility of a reanastomosis. The question of abortion may also be raised. Social pressure on the couple may be great if family and friends have been informed that a vasectomy had been obtained. Some couples may not wish to have a sperm count and will assume that the pregnancy resulted from spontaneous reanastomosis, rather than confront directly the question of infidelity.

Inevitably, some couples will change their minds about vasectomy and will request reanastomosis. The social worker should not hold out bright promise to these people. Vasectomy must be considered as permanent. Because possibility of surgical correction of vasectomy is so slight and because the surgery is so much more complex than the original vasectomy, it may be more fruitful to explore the significance of the reemergent desire for children and the acceptability of substituting other goals or satisfactions. In the case of the death of a child, the desire for another child may be a manifestation of grief and a sense of loss which, with help, can be accepted without the need to restore fertility. In cases of remarriage after divorce or the death of a spouse, the desire to cement the marriage may be expressed by other means than conceiving a child. If a couple's economic or emotional situation has changed and they feel themselves able to care for additional children, adoption or foster care may be suggested.

Most social workers will see problems related to vasectomy in the context of problems within the marriage and family. Ziegler and fellow researchers have suggested that vasectomy may produce changes in the husband's and wife's behavior that may increase marital tension.[32] These changes reflect a polarization of male and female behavior as a result of the male's trying to prove that his masculinity is not impaired. Recent changes in public opinion that give greater social approval to vasectomy may have reduced the likelihood of this possible effect. Social workers should check for increased sex-role rigidity in couples who experience increased marital tension after vasectomy. Techniques useful in marital and family counseling are apt to be appropriate here.

Within the society as a whole and in their roles as program planners and educators, social workers can contribute to policies that provide freedom of individual decision-making regarding vasectomies and access to high-quality related services for people at all income levels. Recent court cases have affirmed the right of a woman to be sterilized

---

[32] Ziegler, Rodgers, and Kriegsman, Effect of Vasectomy on Psychological Functioning, p. 62.

at her own request.[33] There has not been a comparable decision on vasectomy. It is desirable that freedom and rights in this area be scrupulously maintained.

As in many other areas, it is important that social workers not project their own values or bias on their clients. Properly informed, they can join with other professionals in educating the public about vasectomy and in assuring that adequate related services, including counseling, are made available to all persons who desire them.

[33] Vivian Cadden, Very Private Decision, *Good Housekeeping,* May 1972, p. 85.

PART V

INTERPERSONAL ISSUES

In contrast with those in the prior section, which addressed intrapersonal issues, the articles in this section deal with situations where the problem area, as perceived by the client, emerges from some aspect of a relationship with someone else.

Max Siporin once referred to social work practice as boundary work, that is, of helping persons negotiate aspects of their lives that involve interactions between themselves and others with whom they interface. Undoubtedly, much of practice does focus on such boundary or interrelationship issues. This is particularly so in those situations of great stress in which the boundaries involved relate to some of the most essential in the human experience, such as abuse by parents of their children or of their own elderly parents, or the breaking up of marriages. Indeed, as we reviewed the articles that were finally selected for this section, it was evident that the majority of them revolved around the intimate life relationships of family, marriage, adoption, and sexuality and the complex and deep-seated relationship problems that can emerge from them when things do not go well.

There is nothing new about social work's involvement in this area. Indeed, for the clinical stream of the profession, these situations are, and always have been, the heart of practice. Many of the services that have developed over the decades have as their prime focus situations related to these critical human relationships. Some of our most powerful strategies of intervention have developed in such areas as work with children, with foster care, with couples, and with families, and with problems in these systems involving relationships. One of the major contributions of the profession of this century has been its leadership role in the development and implementation of family therapy. Important as has been our initial contribution, along with that of colleagues in other helping professions, to this complex yet highly effective form of therapy, in recent years we have made a further contribution. This involves the expansion of the concept of family to include more than the traditional two-gender couple and their biological children, around which much of family therapy theory and practice first developed.

A particular form of family structure that is very common in contemporary practice is the single-parent situation. Here there is required a deep understanding of the societal, role, legal, and resource issues, as well as the highly complex psychodynamic and interpersonal challenges, of this type of family. It is evident from the literature that we are still learning how to adapt our knowledge of single-unit family situations to the ever-increasing numbers of multifamily situations. These include blended families, adopting families, foster families, and any number of societal interpersonal units that properly can be viewed as family situations and thus appropriately addressed from the knowledge base of family therapy. As well, there are other family situations that we meet with, such as the single-sex union.

Each of these variations has many of the characteristics of all families and thus is amenable to the skills and understanding of family-focused intervention. But as well, each of its own idiosyncratic challenges requiring specific understanding of the societal phenomenon, as well as the ever-present responsibility to individualize the persons involved.

Included, of course, in interpersonal situations is the intriguing and complex area of human sexuality, which frequently can give rise to problems. Social work took a long time to become comfortable with heterosexual issues and accept and understand the problems that can occur and the interventions that can be helpful. Since the last edition, a further development has taken place. We now seek to become more comfortable than we have been in the past with the reality, and the complexity, of homosexual relationships and how these too can be growth-producing or problem-laden. This is a step forward from an earlier time when homosexuality and heterosexuality were seen as opposite ends of a health continuum.

We are now able to understand that what is important is not which life-style is the norm, but how one adjusts and functions. Thus, as clinicians we need be aware that problems can exist in each of these two forms of sexual relations.

At the other end of the spectrum in interpersonal situations are those that involve interactions of a highly personal nature between persons who frequently are total strangers. Thus we have included articles related to personal assaults such as rape. Complex as the immediate impacts on the victim of these terrible societal occurrences are, we know that the assault and its sequellae, often lasting for many years, require skilled understanding and therapeutic intervention. Again, it is often our profession that carries an important and ongoing role in helping persons come to terms with and reorder their sense of self in order to move on in life.

Included in the articles on interpersonal violence is the new reality found in an increasing number of practice situations of clients who act in violent and indeed dangerous ways towards ourselves. Again, this is not a totally new situation for the profession, but for the most part it has been viewed as rarely occurring and only in particular areas of practice. What is new is the possibility of having to deal with violence in virtually all settings and situations. Thus, this is a topic that all practitioners need at least think about from time to time.

One of the intriguing components of interpersonal practice situations, as addressed in this section, is the powerful potential of the helping relationship. Since the problems being addressed here are those stemming from a problem-laden interpersonal situation it is imperative that clinicians understand the complexities of these relationships and of their possible influence on the helping relationship. Although transference is not stressed nearly as much as in an earlier day it remains essential in these types of situations to insure that the power of the therapeutic relationship is fully tapped.

Obviously, an important component of such relationships is self-understanding, so that as we become involved in the complexities of helping with problems we avoid the risk of our own weak spots interfering with the process.

Social work has always seen itself as having a particular competence in addressing the interpersonal problems of our clients. This has not changed. What has changed is the range and complexity of these very human situations and of the need for skilled diagnosis and carefully formulated strategies of therapeutic intervention.

ABUSE OF CHILDREN

CHAPTER 64

PROGRESS IN TREATING THE SEXUAL ABUSE OF CHILDREN

Jon R. Conte

Although professional interest in the sexual abuse of children has long existed, it is only recently that this interest has become widespread. Sexual abuse of children is simultaneously a crime and a mental health, medical, and social problem involving professionals in medicine, law enforcement, mental health, education, and social services. Social workers, because of their involvement with both the children and the adults who share and influence children's lives, come into contact with cases of sexual abuse of children in nearly every field of practice. Indeed, there has been an increasing emphasis on such abuse in the social work literature, which reflects, in part, the interest social workers have in this problem.[1]

This article assesses progress to date in the professional understanding of and work with cases of sexual abuse of children. Such an assessment is inherently subjective and is offered in the hope of stimulating discussion more than as a final report on professional progress in working with these cases. The article briefly discusses several conceptual obstacles to working effectively with cases of sexual abuse of children and reviews progress in professional interventions.

CONCEPTUAL OBSTACLES

Although estimates vary widely and a true picture of the incidence is difficult to obtain, professionals are coming to recognize that sexual abuse affects large numbers of chil-

Reprinted from *Social Work,* Vol. 29, No. 3 (May-June, 1984), pp. 258–263, by permission of NASW Press. Copyright 1984, National Association of Social Workers, Inc., *Social Work.*

dren. A recent and methodologically rigorous estimate was based on a random survey of 900 homes in San Francisco.[2] Of the adult women interviewed in this random sample of homes, 38 percent reported that they had been sexually abused (that is, had been subjected to body-on-body contact) before reaching the age of 18.

Although percentages vary slightly with the particular sample being described, adults who sexually abuse children are strangers to the children in only 8 to 10 percent of the cases.[3] Forty-seven percent of the offenders are members of the children's own families, and more than 40 percent are known by the children but are not family members. Eighty percent of the victims are female, although it is expected that abuse of male children is underreported. Sixty percent of the victims are under 12 years of age, and victims appear in all socioeconomic conditions.

In the author's assessment, professionals appear to view child sexual abuse primarily in two ways—as incest and as pedophilia. The overwhelming bulk of professional attention and public funds has gone to treatment of cases involving father or stepfather and daughter or stepdaughter abuse. Although the literature has scattered references to mother-son, sibling, and extended family abuse, there is not enough professional work in these areas to summarize current trends.[4] A separate professional community and literature concern the pedophile—the adult who has a strong sexual interest in children.[5] In almost all parts of the country there is virtually no communication among professionals working with incestuous offenders and those working with pedophiles, nor is there much integration among the two literatures.

A core set of beliefs about incest appears, in part, to be the cause of this separation between professionals who deal with incestuous or pedophilic abuse of children. A major belief is that when a father or stepfather sexually abuses one of his own children he is giving sexual expression to nonsexual needs.[6] Although the nature of these nonsexual needs varies with the particular clinical theory that is held, this assumption suggests that incest is not a sexual problem and that incestuous fathers and stepfathers do not abuse children outside their own homes.

There are a number of difficulties with such assumptions. First, virtually all sex includes the sexual expression of nonsexual needs, such as the need for closeness, comfort, security, or expression of anger or aggression. In addition. although evidence is just beginning to emerge, it appears that the pattern of sexual contacts of incestuous offenders is complex. Although some men have exclusive sexual contact with their daughters or sons, on the whole there is great variation in whether men have exclusive or multiple sexual relationships with their daughters, with children outside their homes, and with adult women.[7]

There is, in fact, increasing evidence that incestuous and nonincestuous child molesters have much in common. A number of studies have described men who commit sexual offenses against children as dependent, inadequate individuals with early histories of conflict, disruption, abandonment, abuse, and exploitation.[8] Other information about adults who sexually abuse children is varied and the subject can provoke heated disagreement. It appears that some offenders never develop adult sexual orientations whereas others have sexual orientations toward adults and children simultaneously.[9] Although early life experiences and stress are thought to contribute to the development of a propensity to abuse children sexually, little is known about the etiology of erotic desires and sexual behavior. To date, there is insufficient evidence to make a decision about whether adults who abuse only their own children, those who abuse only nonrelated children, or those who abuse both reflect a real difference in pathology or happenstance.

It appears premature to have determined that incest reflects a different clinical phenomenon than other types of sexual abuse of children. In addition, because classic incest represents only about 30 percent of the cases, the excessive attention to this type of abuse—to the virtual exclusion of the 70 percent of other cases—has not only retarded the development of professional understanding but has also failed to help the largest number of victims.[10]

This argument does not ignore the reality that some classic incest cases appear in clinical populations, nor that sexual abuse committed by a parent or stepparent can be among the most complicated types of cases to treat.[11] The point to be made, however, is that clinical beliefs about sexual abuse and families rest on weak empirical grounds. Conte argues that family variables may be important in understanding the development of adults' sexual interest in children, although much research is necessary before the relationship between particular patterns of family interaction and child sexual abuse is understood.[12]

ONLY A MENTAL HEALTH PROBLEM?

Related to the belief that incest is different from other types of child sexual abuse has been the tendency of medical, mental health, and social service professionals to view sexual abuse as solely a mental health problem. Although theories about the etiology of sexual abuse of children vary from those that view it as a problem originating in individual personalities to those that view it as originating in the family system, too few professionals look for causal factors beyond the narrow clinical dimension of intrapersonal or interpersonal functioning.

Rather, it may be helpful to look increasingly to a range of variables that in combination may help to create the psychological and social conditions contributing to child sexual abuse. Illustrative of this larger or systemic perspective are the following brief examples.

A great many liberal professionals believe that pornography is a harmless indulgence that should be protected under the Constitution. Increasingly, therapists who work with adults who sexually abuse children are finding that their clients are deeply involved in the excessive use of pornographic materials. Indeed, there is some suspicion that "kiddie porn" may act as a cognitive disinhibitor, that is, after repeated imagined sexual abuse of children, real abuse becomes easier.[13] If this reasoning turns out to be correct, the toleration of child pornography should be questioned, both because of the abuse of those children employed in it as actors and because, for some adults, it may be part of a chain of events that leads to actual sexual abuse of children.

The preceding discussion directs attention to the ways in which social policies, such as the toleration of pornography, may help to contribute to the sexual abuse of children. Another example of a possible contributing factor concerns a consistent finding about adults who sexually abuse children: the commonality of their early life experiences in which abandonment, discord, and victimization have played significant roles. It appears that these early life experiences set the stage for the development of a propensity to commit sexual abuse. One should note, however, that it appears that these factors set the stage for abuse but do not cause it: At this point, it is not clear what causes adults to abuse children sexually. At any rate, if these family and social variables are associated as preconditions with sexual and perhaps other kinds of interpersonal violence, then social workers have yet another reason to be directly concerned with the life experiences of the many children currently living lives in which abandonment, discord, and victimization are everyday realities.

Social and economic conditions also appear to have an important role in the sexual abuse of children. To the extent that these conditions deprive adults who care for children of the material and personal resources necessary to protect and nurture children adequately, they set the stage for victimization in two ways. First, children who grow up in harsh, violent environments appear at risk for becoming the kind of adult personalities who victimize others. Second and of more immediate concern, these children are placed in a vulnerable position. Indeed, Finkelhor identified eight social variables associated with significant increases in the risk of a child's being sexually abused: living in a family with a stepfather, having lived at some time without the mother, not being close to the mother, having a mother who never finished high school, having had a sexually punitive mother, having no physical affection from the father, living in a family with an income of less than $10,000 per year, and having two friends or fewer.[14]

Finally, as long as professionals continue to view sexual abuse as only a mental health problem of "sick" individuals or families, they will be unable to see it as a fundamental, albeit negative, aspect of a society in which cultural values allow and support the abuse.[15] Because the victims lack the obvious physical wounds of battered children or because they have been repeatedly abused by the same offenders without having asked for help, many social workers believe that violence is not a part of the victimization of these children. Perhaps our culturally bound definition of violence is too narrow and sexually biased in favor of men: It does not take into account the psychological violence and force men use against women and children. Although data are available that document the presence of violence in a number of cases, even these data confuse the issue: Coercion, manipulation, force, and violation are inherent any time an adult sexually abuses a child.[16] To regard the weak, inadequate men who abuse children as nonviolent is to fail to see these offenders as their victims see them—as big and powerful adults.

Abuse is about power and betrayal. Excessive physical force is rarely necessary because most adults who sexually abuse children do so in the context of an ongoing, and often otherwise positive, relationship with the victim. To minimize what has happened to a child who has been abused by suggesting that there has been no violence done is to tolerate the abuse of power and the use of force.

STAGES OF PROFESSIONAL INTERVENTION

There are several distinct stages to the development of professional intervention with cases of sexual abuse of children. These stages are discussed in the sections that follow.

Identification

The first real stage has to do with professional efforts to recognize that the problem exists. Although most professionals working with children have been likely to come into contact with sexually abused children, it was not until the crisis intervention movement for rape began to address the problem of rape of children that professionals began to recognize how many sexually abused children there really are. Professionals have to overcome a number of personal and professional handicaps before this recognition is possible. An understandable disbelief that so many otherwise normal-seeming adults could be sexually involved with children—and clinical ideas that children fantasize sexual contact with adults—are two of the kinds of attitudes that have stood in the way. Although there are some professional groups or specific professionals who are reluctant to recognize the problem, substantial gains in identification have been made.

Along with recognition of the problem, a part of intervention has to do with whether professionals report the abuse to child protection or law enforcement agencies. The question of the nature and degree of involvement with civil and criminal justice agencies is hotly debated across the country. This issue, perhaps more than any other, divides professionals working with these cases and has been the subject of much writing that is readily available.[17]

System-Induced Trauma

The next stage of professional intervention has to do with preventing system-induced trauma.[18] Because medical, legal, mental health, and social service groups have to deal with the abused child and the adults around the child, professionals have become aware of the possibility of creating system-induced trauma. System-induced trauma is the result of insensitive handling of victims by professionals who lack an understanding of the dynamics of sexual abuse and who lack the skills to interact effectively and sensitively with the victims. The trauma may also be the result of inherent aspects of the procedures peculiar to various systems dealing with the victim. For example, the medical practice to ensure that a sexual abuse victim is free of injury and disease as well as to collect evidence, when appropriate, requires a gynecological exam. Preparation of cases for trial requires taking a victim's statement in accordance with specific legal and investigatory procedures. Each of these practices, although understandable and necessary, can in certain circumstances add to the victim's trauma.

There have been substantial efforts by medical, legal, and social service personnel to lessen the possibility of system-induced trauma. Personnel have been trained in the dynamics of child sexual abuse and to be sensitive in interviewing children. Medical protocols, legal procedures, and investigative practices have been developed that work to accomplish the necessary purpose of each system's involvement in the case without traumatizing the victim. Although some cases are poorly handled, this is not because policies, procedures, and training to protect the victim have not been developed.[19]

Although the debate continues nationally about the appropriate role of the various medical, legal, and social service agencies in responding to the problem of sexual abuse of children, the established policies and procedures allow each agency to fulfill its function with a minimum of additional trauma to the victim. However, until rigorous evaluative data confirm this supposition, the debate will continue. The risks to victims of system-induced trauma are too great not to require the presence of evaluative data to put to end the debate.

The concept of system-induced trauma is helpful, and professionals should continue to apply it to ensure that interventions do not further harm victims and their families. Although the concept has generally been applied to law enforcement or justice system interventions, it should also be applied to the full range of mental health, medical, and social service interventions. For example, the medical practice of routinely anesthetizing children during a vaginal exam would seem to communicate to the children that something is terribly wrong with them. The children who are anesthetized are unable to hear from their doctors that they are, in fact, not permanently damaged or changed.

In the mental health area, the desire of some therapists to be involved in a current topic of interest places pressure on them to locate clients who have been sexual abuse victims. As these therapists probe for feelings of victimization, especially in children and adults who were abused in the past, the clients may be pushed to relive experiences that, in fact, have been adequately dealt with previously. It seems important for the therapist to be open to the idea that the client may have resolved the experience and be ready to live life as an individual—not as a member of a class of mental health "victims." The unwillingness of a clinician to believe that a client has resolved the experience of being victimized and the continued pressure to deal with feelings no longer meaningful in the client's life may produce therapy-induced trauma.

One final example of possible system-induced trauma in mental health has to do with the tendency of some therapists never to deal directly with the sexual abuse. These therapists, who believe that sexual abuse is a symptom of some more important mental health problem, such as the offender's bad marital relationship or his feelings of inadequacy with adult women, are content to see the client over an extended period of time without dealing with the problem of sexual abuse. This approach would seem to say that what has happened to the victim is not significant or worth talking about. If the client is the offender, it fails to help the client with the problem.

Clinical Innovations

The next stage of professional intervention should be in the area of greater innovation in psychotherapy. Although each of the previous stages of professional intervention has been important, it is in the area of therapy that much has yet to be accomplished. Ultimately, resolution of the problem of sexual abuse of children can only be accomplished through psychotherapeutic interventions with the victims, the offenders, and the other adults and children living with them.

Traditional Therapy.　To date, there have been two major approaches to clinical interventions with sexual abuse cases. The first may be termed traditional therapy. This approach consists of the direct application of traditional forms of psychotherapy to child sexual abuse. Although a large number of theories of treatment are used traditionally, these approaches have in common the therapist's lack of specialized training in dealing with sexual abuse victims and offenders and the tendency to view sexual abuse as being like other mental health problems.

Various difficulties may result from the application of traditional psychotherapeutic approaches to cases of sexual abuse. As mentioned previously, many therapists without specialized training tend to view sexual abuse as a symptom of a more serious problem. Some theories locate this problem in an individual (usually the mother or the victim but occasionally the offender), and others locate the real problem in the family system.[20] Therapists who hold these beliefs are likely not to deal specifically with the abuse but rather with the presumed "real" cause, such as the mothers' unresolved hostility toward their own mothers, which they act out by subjecting their mother-substitutes (their daughters) to sexual abuse by their husbands. Other therapists treating the offenders will explain their refusal to deal specifically with the sexual behavior because such topics are too anxiety-producing for the weak ego of the offenders and would be likely to threaten the therapeutic process. Other traditional therapists believe that incest is not a sexual problem or that incestuous fathers only abuse their own children.

These kinds of views raise several problems, most of which originate in the lack of special training or the use of untested theory. Basically, professional knowledge has not identified why adults sexually abuse children. Other than the common life experiences described earlier, no theory supported by empirical evidence has adequately described the cause of sexual abuse of children. Nor is there a single thread of evidence to suggest that dealing with some presumed underlying cause—a cause that has never been empirically identified—is likely to be an effective change-producing intervention. Nor are treatment approaches that locate responsibility for the behavior outside the offender or that make it psychologically easy for the offender to deny the sexual behavior likely to be successful. Adults who sexually abuse children develop major denial systems in which they deny or rationalize their behavior. Therapeutic systems that support this denial by not dealing with the sexual behavior support the offender in not accepting responsibility for the behavior.

Specialized Programs. The second major approach to treatment is the increasing number of specialized programs.[21] These programs, which exist throughout the nation, differ along a number of dimensions: attitudes of program personnel toward cooperation with the justice system, whether personnel tend to view the problem as an individual or a family one, the particular theory of treatment personnel use, and the relative importance given to various treatment goals such as protecting the child or keeping the family together. Most programs offer a range of individual, dyad (couple or parent and child), and group therapies. Virtually none of these specialized programs has presented rigorous outcome data indicating the effectiveness of its clinical interventions. Although one may expect that the early stages of program development make it difficult to implement program evaluation efforts, the time is approaching when personnel should be expected to generate outcome data supporting the ability of their programs to produce change. If nothing else, one should expect information describing what happens to clients served by the program: for example, data on how many children are sexually abused during treatment and how many families are reunited. In this regard, it is encouraging that one of the oldest specialized programs in the country has recently reported some evaluative data indicating that, in treating more than four thousand families, 90 percent of the children have returned home and there has been a recidivism rate of less than 1 percent.[22] However, the lack of rigorous evaluative methodology makes these success claims suspect.

The general absence of program evaluation data would suggest that it is far too early in the development of these programs to select one model over another. The relative infancy of many of these programs only partially explains the absence of program evaluation data. Public policy and professional adherence to various program models in the not too distant future should be based, in part, on data describing the outcomes of various program and therapeutic models.

Although a clinical intervention literature is developing much of this literature, with a few notable exceptions,[23] either deals with clinical issues resulting from the crisis intervention phase of initial disclosure or is superficial in describing the long-term treatment of children and adults involved in sexual abuse. With the exception of descriptions of a behavioral therapy approach and the Santa Clara County (California) humanistic program, rarely are clinical techniques described in enough detail to allow for replication.[24]

Initially, single-subject design reports of clinical interventions with single or small samples of victims or families would be particularly helpful in describing the treatment process and special issues involved in treatment of these cases. What is most important, such designs could be quite helpful in beginning the evaluation of effects of various interventions.[25]

Professionals should not forget that treatment of these cases involves, as it does with so many social work clients, active use of social services as well as therapy. In cases involving abuse by fathers or stepfathers, temporary shelter for the victims or offenders may be necessary. Income support, housing, and job training may be needed to help mothers take those actions necessary to protect their daughters from further abuse. There is virtually no literature describing the use of these social services in cases of child sexual abuse.

SUMMARY

This article suggests that some professional thinking about the problem of adult sexual abuse of children is based on weak empirical grounds and is often too narrowly conceptualized. The author urges professionals to view sexual abuse in a larger context in which cultural values, social and political ideals, and economic conditions are seen as linked to the problem. Some ways in which mental health interventions might be more helpful to sexually abused children have been suggested. Nonetheless, professionals have reason to feel a sense of accomplishment in many of the innovations that they have developed in interventions.

Social work—because of its contact with cases involving the sexual abuse of children and because of its expertise in viewing problems as based in the person and in the environment—is in an ideal position to contribute to professional understanding of sexual abuse and of how best to resolve its aftermath. Early efforts by social workers indicate that the profession is fulfilling this special opportunity.

NOTES AND REFERENCES

1. Jon R. Conte and David Shore, eds., *Journal of Social Work and Human Sexuality,* theme issue, "Social Work and Child Sexual Abuse," 1 (Fall–Winter 1982); Conte and Lucy Berliner, "Sexual Abuse of Children: Implications for Practice," *Social Casework,* 62 (November 1981). pp. 601-606; Tamar Cohen, "The Incestuous Family Revisited," *Social Casework,* 64 (March 1983), pp. 154-161. Mary Ellen Elwell, "Sexually Assaulted Children and Their Families," *Social Casework,* 60 (April 1979), pp. 227-235; Christine Dietz and John Craft, "Family Dynamics of Incest: A New Perspective," *Social Casework,* 10 (December 1980), pp. 602-609; Kevin McIntyre, "Role of Mothers in Father-Daughter Incest: A Feminist Analysis," *Social Work,* 26 (November 1981), pp. 462-466; and Jerilyn A Shamroy, "A Perspective on Childhood Sexual Abuse," *Social Work,* 25 (March 1980), pp. 128–131.
2. Diana E. H. Russell, "The Incidence and Prevalence of Intrafamilial and Extrafamilial Sexual Abuse of Female Children," *Child Abuse and Neglect* (to appear in a forthcoming issue).
3. Conte and Berliner, "Sexual Abuse of Children."
4. See, for example, Katharine Dixon, Eugene Arnold, and Kenney Calestro, "Father-Son Incest: Underreported Psychiatric Problem?" *American Journal of Psychiatry,* 135 (July 1978), pp. 835–838; Jean Goodwin and Peter DiVasto, "Mother-Daughter Incest," *Child Abuse and Neglect,* 3 (1979), pp. 935–957; T. C. N. Gibbens, K. L. Soothill, and C. K. Way, "Sibling and Parent-Child Incest Offenders," *British Journal of Criminology,* 18 (January 1978), pp. 40–52.
5. J. W. Mohr, R. E. Turner, and M. B. Jerry, *Pedophilia and Exhibitionism* (Toronto, Ont., Canada: University of Toronto Press, 1964); Benjamin Karpman, *The Sexual Offender and His Offenses* (New York: Julian Press, 1959); and Mark Cook and Kevin Howells, eds., *Adult Sexual Interest in Children* (New York: Academic Press, 1981).
6. See, for example, Hector Cavallin, "Incestuous Fathers: A Clinical Report," *American Journal of Psychiatry,* 122 (April 1966), pp. 1132–1138; and Thomas Gutheil and Nicholas Avery, "Multiple Overt Incest as a Family Defense Against Loss," *Family Process,* 2 (March 1977), pp. 105–116.
7. Richard Josiassen, John Fantuzzo, and Alexander Rosen, "Treatment of Pedophilia Using Multistage Aversion Therapy with Social Skills Training," *Journal of Behavior Therapy and Experimental Psychiatry,* 11 (March 1980), pp. 55–61.
8. See, for example, A. Nicholas Groth, William Hobson, and Gary Thomas, "The Child Molester: Clinical Observations," *Journal of Social Work and Human Sexuality,* 1 (Fall–Winter 1982), pp. 129–144; David Swanson, "Adult Sexual Abuse of Children," *Diseases of the Nervous System,* 29 (October 1968), pp. 677–683; and James S. Panton, "MMPI Profiles Configurations Associated with Incestuous and Nonincestuous Child Molesters," *Psychological Reports,* 45 (August 1979), pp. 335–338.
9. A. Nicholas Groth and H. Jean Birnbaum, *Men Who Rape* (New York: Plenum Publishing Corp., 1979).
10. Conte and Berliner, "Sexual Abuse of Children."

11. See, for example, Kate Rist, "Incest: Theoretical and Clinical Views," *American Journal of Orthopsychiatry,* 49 (October 1979), pp. 630–691.

12. Jon R. Conte, "Sexual Abuse and the Family: A Critical Analysis" (Chicago: School of Social Service Administration, University of Chicago, 1984). (Photocopied by author.)

13. Personal communication from Steven Wolf, Codirector, Northwest Treatment Associates, Seattle, Wash., January 1981.

14. David Finkelhor, "Risk Factors in the Sexual Victimization of Children," *Child Abuse and Neglect,* 4 (1980), pp. 265–273.

15. Judith Lewish Herman and Lisa Hirschman, *Father-Daughter Incest* (Cambridge, Mass.: Harvard University Press, 1981); and Sandra Butler, "Incest: Whose Reality, Whose Theory," *Aegis* (Summer–Autumn 1980), pp. 48–55.

16. Conte and Berliner, "Sexual Abuse of Children"; Russell, "The Incidence and Prevalence of Intrafamilial and Extrafamilial Sexual Abuse of Female Children"; and Carl Rogers and Joyce Thomas, "Sexual Victimization of Children in the U.S.A.: Patterns and Trends," paper presented at Fourth International Congress on Child Abuse and Neglect, Paris, France, September 1982.

17. For discussion of this issue, see Ann Wolbert Burgess et al., *Sexual Assault of Children and Adolescents* (Lexington, Mass.: Lexington Books, 1978); Josephine Bulkley, ed., *Innovations in the Prosecution of Child Sexual Abuse Cases* (Washington, D.C.: American Bar Association, 1981); Bulkley, ed., *Child Sexual Abuse and the Law* (Washington, D.C.: American Bar Association, 1981); Kee MacFarlane, "Sexual Abuse of Children," in Jane Roberts Chapman and Margaret Getes, eds., *The Victimization of Women* (Beverly Hills, Calif.: Sage Publications, 1978), pp. 81–109; David Libai, "The Protection of the Child Victim of a Sexual Offense in the Criminal Justice System," *Wayne Law Review,* 15 (Summer 1969), pp. 977–1032; Elizabeth Kennedy Hartley, "American State Intervention in the Parent-Child Legal Relationship," *Child Abuse and Neglect,* 5 (1981), pp. 141–145; and Jon R. Conte, "The Role of the Justice System in Child Sexual Abuse" (Chicago: School of Social Service Administration, University of Chicago, 1984) (photocopied by author).

18. MacFarlane, "Sexual Abuse of Children."

19. See, for example, Doris Stevens and Lucy Berliner, "Special Techniques for Child Witnesses," in LeRoy Schultz, ed., *Sexual Victimology of Youth* (Springfield, Ill.: Charles C. Thomas, Publisher, 1980), pp. 246–256; Shirley Cook Anderson and Stevens, "Evaluation of the Sexual Assault Patient in the Health Care System: A Medical Training Manual" (Seattle: University of Washington, 1982) (photocopied by authors); Evelyn Brown, Berliner, and Richmond Raymond, "Child Sexual Abuse Investigation: A Curriculum for Training Law Enforcement Officers" (Seattle, Wash.: Sexual Assault Center, Harborview Medical Center); and Bulkley, ed., *Innovations in the Prosecution of Child Sexual Abuse Cases.*

20. Conte, "Sexual Abuse and the Family."

21. See, for example, Henry Giarretto, "A Comprehensive Child Sexual Abuse Treatment Program, *Child Abuse and Neglect,* 6 (1982), pp. 263–278.

22. Ibid.

23. See, for example, Jean Goodwin, *Sexual Abuse Incest Victims and Their Families*

(Boston: John Wright, 1982); Suzanne Sgroi, *Handbook of Clinical Interventions in Child Sexual Abuse* (Lexington, Mass.: Lexington Books, 1982); and Henry Giarretto, *Integrated Treatment of Child Sexual Abuse* (Palo Alto, Calif.: Science & Behavior Books, 1982). For excellent material on disclosure issues, see Ann Wolbert Burgess, Lynda Lytle Nolmstrom, and Maureen McCausland, "Child Sexual Assault by a Family Member: Decisions Following Disclosure," *Victimology*, 11 (Summer 1977), pp. 236–250; Loretta M. McCarty, "Investigation of Incest: Opportunity to Motivate Families to Seek Help," *Child Welfare*, 60 (December 1981), pp. 679–689; David Mrazek, "The Child Psychiatric Examination of the Sexually Abused Child," *Child Abuse and Neglect*, 4 (1980), pp. 275–284; and Burgess et al., *Sexual Assault of Children and Adolescents.*.

24.   For a behavioral therapy approach, see Judith V. Becker, Linda J. Skinner, and Gene G. Abel, "Treatment of a 4-year-old Victim of Incest," *American Journal of Family Therapy*, 10 (Winter 1982), pp. 41–46. For a description of the Santa Clara County, California, humanistic program, see Giarretto, *Integrated Treatment of Child Sexual Abuse.*

25.   Betty Shewon and Jon R. Conte, "Cognitive Behavioral Treatment of a Phobic Sexual Abuse Victim," in Conte and Scott Briar, eds., *A Casebook for Empirically Based Practice* (New York: Columbia University Press, forthcoming).

ABUSE OF CHILDREN

CHAPTER 65

GROUP TREATMENT FOR SEXUALLY ABUSED GIRLS

Catherine K. Gagliano

In 1981 a group was organized for the treatment of sexually abused girls at Family and Children's Service of Tulsa, Oklahoma. A request for therapy was received for two approximately eight-year-old cousins who had been sexually abused by their grandfather. An eight-year-old girl who had been molested by her stepfather was also included in this nascent group of children who had been sexually abused by family members.

At that time, little literature existed on the subject of treatment and therapy of young sexual-abuse victims. The available literature had not indicated an acute need for victim therapy. It was generally believed that after disclosure, treatment should focus primarily on the perpetrator's pathology. The fallacy of this approach became apparent to staff counselors when they perceived the magnitude and scope of traumas that still affected adult clients who, as children, had been victims of sexual abuse.

Currently, it is widely recognized that incest and other forms of child abuse can leave emotional or psychological scars that remain long after any physical effects of the abuse have healed.[1] Family and Children's Service, and particularly the members of the Family Sexual Abuse Treatment Project, counsels children of all ages who are victims of sexual abuse. In our experience, group counseling is the most effective method of therapy for sexually abused adolescents. Group therapy lessens the victims' isolation, pain, and guilt by allowing children to share their experiences with other children who have been similarly traumatized. The children, although innocent, initially assume total responsibility for the acts of the adult abusers. They are led by the abusers to believe that

Reprinted from *Social Casework,* Vol. 68, No. 2 (1987), pp. 102–108, by permission of the publisher, Families International, Inc.

[1] David Finkelhor, *Sexually Victimized Children* (New York: The Free Press, 1979).

they are bad, seductive, and responsible for the adult's sexual behavior. The child assumes the guilt for the acts of the offender. With group participation, however, victims begin to realize that others in the group are worthwhile and honorable individuals who, like themselves, have been emotionally or physically coerced into a nonconsenting relationship by a pathological or antisocial adult.[2]

The Family Sexual Abuse Treatment Project has developed a comprehensive treatment plan for incestuous families. Before incest was recognized as a national problem, this program was a difficult concept to sell to a conservative midwestern community. Currently, the program consists of groups for preteens, teenagers, perpetrators, nonoffending mothers, incestuous parents, and adults who were victimized as children. Individual play–therapy sessions are provided for very young children to help them express their feelings, and individual, marital, and family sessions are available for all.

In the course of providing treatment to hundreds of victims and their families since 1980, we have learned much about the effects of family sexual abuse on innocent young victims as well as about treatment methods designed to alleviate the pain and trauma of incestuous families—perhaps the most dysfunctional of all family systems. Although sexual abuse and incest may occur in any combination of male and female children with male or female adults, most incest occurs between fathers or stepfathers and daughters. Therefore, for the purpose of this article, the term "father" covers all adult offenders.

INCEST VICTIM

Suzanne Sgroi states that all victims of sexual abuse suffer serious consequences as a result of the abuse. Child victims invariably show signs of considerable guilt: for the act itself, for their participation with their fathers in the act, for the concealment of the act, and for the conspiracy that by its very nature causes estrangement between them and their mothers and siblings. Another consequence of sexual abuse is the child's belief that she is inferior or "damaged goods."[3] The child is particularly angry and resentful that she was robbed of her virginity in a nonconsensual and distasteful relationship. She may believe that her body is contaminated and soiled and may feel undesirable as a female. The girl may also believe that the incestuous acts have caused permanent damage to her sexual organs and that if she should marry and become pregnant, her own health and that of the child may be at risk.

Victims may have many other accompanying fears. Some fear the dark and strangers; others may distrust all male adults in their environment. Some develop displacement phobias. They may fear abandonment or banishment by their mothers and by society in general. Due to low self-esteem and feelings of helplessness, some are suicidal. The therapist may observe a pattern of substance abuse, truancy, and running away. Failing grades in school and the desire to avoid peer interaction may also identify victims. Sometimes the young victim may attempt to excel in school because she feels

---

[2] Suzanne M. Sgroi, *Handbook of Clinical Intervention in Child Sexual Abuse* (Lexington, Mass.: D. C. Heath, 1982).

[3] Sgroi, *Handbook of Clinical Intervention,* pp. 112–15.

that school is the sole area wherein she has control of the outcome of her actions. Success in an academic setting may also help to ameliorate her diminished self-esteem.

The youthful victim of sexual abuse may suffer from an impaired ability to trust or believe in the motivations or sincerity of other people because she has been betrayed and deceived by a trusted family member. Typically, roles and boundaries in the child's home are blurred and confused; the child's role alternates between being her father's sweetheart, wife, and mistress and being father's child who is expected to treat him with respect and deference.[4] Abused children frequently lack the conviction that they are competent and can control and manage their own lives in the future since they have consistently failed to receive permission from the abusing parent to own and govern their own bodies. Instead of achieving an internal locus of control, they may unduly rely on others in their environment to structure and control their actions and behavior. They may misinterpret and misconstrue social cues in interpersonal relationships as a result of receiving double messages and covert communication in their early relationships with the offender.

Due to the incestuous experiences, which may have gone on for several years, many of these children fail to accomplish the normal developmental tasks of childhood and adolescence. They are forced to assume adult duties and responsibilities that are overwhelming for their tender years. Often, pleasures of play and recreation have been denied them and they become pseudo-adults.

Children need to feel loved, protected, and respected if they are to develop trust in their caretakers. They need a stable home environment with appropriate limits and boundaries in order to feel safe and secure. They need a mother and a father who are united in marriage and in parenting and who will render protection from the adverse stimulation of physical and sexual abuse. During childhood and adolescence, the trust and security that are gained in the home help the child eventually to tolerate the stresses and frustrations of adult life. A child must be able to read cues from the environment and interpret them correctly, an ability that is impossible to develop in homes in which the child must perform the diverse roles of wife, parent, and child to her own father.

One of the developmental stages of childhood and adolescence involves the gradual lessening of symbiotic ties with both parents. In this way, the child becomes autonomous and able to make decisions in her own best interest without inflicting injustices on others. Childhood tasks include the development of socialization skills with peers and the ability to exchange ideas and laughter. Another task of childhood is learning respect for authority and for parents, teachers, and adults who, by reason of their age, training, or expertise, are advisers to a child. A child from an incestuous family finds it difficult to respect authority because of her distrust of and loss of esteem for the most significant persons in her life. Her father has broken the basic law of honoring mother and child.

In addition, an incestuous relationship prohibits the development of assertiveness and self-sufficiency in the child. A young person is unable to disobey the parent who orders her to join him in pathological behavior. A child cannot learn assertiveness if she is forced to accede to demands for sex under threat of bodily harm, denial of privileges, or loss of affection as a consequence of her refusal.

---

[4] George Thorman, *Incestuous Families* (Springfield, Ill.: Charles C. Thomas, 1983).

Many victims are extremely angry; often this anger at their fathers is displaced to others in their environment. Without therapy, they remain aggressive individuals who, in turn, abuse others.

GROUP TREATMENT
Introductory Sessions

In groups conducted for children who have experienced sexual abuse, it is desirable to limit the number of members to seven so that each girl may have ample time to contribute to the group discussion. A closed group consisting of twelve ninety-minute sessions, with a focused agenda for each session, is preferable. In our program, each group session includes a ten-minute break for refreshments provided by the group leader.

The first session of the group is generally used to get acquainted. Reasonable rules of conduct are established: no running or yelling on the premises, promptness in arriving and departing, and commitment to attend at least five group sessions. It is requested that members not socialize with one another outside the group. After the group has been terminated, those children who wish to phone or visit with others in the group may do so. If outside socialization occurs while the group is in process, members may form dyads that exclude other members, and open communication and sharing of experiences might be inhibited. Also self-revelations occur more safely when leaders are present to protect and interpret the child's emotions.

In the first session the children share information about hobbies, schools they attend, their friends, and their accomplishments. They also discuss current living conditions and recent experiences that have occurred as a result of the disclosure of the abuse. Some of the children may be in a shelter or in foster-care placement because protection from the perpetrator is warranted. Others continue to live with their mothers and siblings because the perpetrator has left the home, either by his own choice or as a result of pressure from the mother or Protective Services. Some mothers, due to fear of poverty or their own personal inadequacies, permit the perpetrator to remain in the home and give temporary custody of the child to the state. Other mothers, in order to protect their own self-esteem and marital status, choose to believe that the child has lied about the abuse.[5] The most crucial goal of therapy is to obliterate the child's guilt and shame. Her guilt stems from many sources: participation in forbidden activities, concealment from the mother, and disclosure of the secret. Therefore, the child's reactions to family confusion, betrayal, or possible abandonment must be recognized.

As part of the introductory session, the children are asked to select an animal they would like to resemble and to mention the reasons for their choices. From each girl's selection, it is possible to interpret her covert need to be loved and valued or her need to control the environment for her safety and protection. An angry child may choose to be a tiger, whereas a helpless child might choose to be a puppy. Most of the girls select animals that have mobility, birds or horses, for example, and that are free from restrictions and control. Some choose animals that play freely yet are protected, such as kittens and puppies. Animals with power, such as lions or tigers, protect body space

---

[5] Ann W. Burgess et al., *Sexual Assault of Children and Adolescents* (Lexington, Mass.: D. C. Heath, 1978).

from others. The therapist should be willing to share information about his or her own animal choice.

In the second session, another get-acquainted period helps lessen anxiety. Discussion then focuses on the group's purpose and function. The group leader acknowledges that all members have shared a common experience of intrafamilial sexual abuse. It is explained that sexual abuse consists of degrees of inappropriate sexual activity between a child and a mature individual. Inappropriate sexual behavior is defined as fondling of breasts or genital areas, insertion of the adult's finger into vaginal areas, coercive masturbation, oral sex, dry intercourse (in which ejaculation occurs outside the female's body), and vaginal or anal intercourse. It is acknowledged that sexual abuse may occur between male and female, female and female, and male and male. Many of the children do not understand what the term incest means even though they have heard it numerous times. Therefore, they are told that sexual abuse is defined as incest when the sexual acts occur between people so closely related that they are forbidden by law to marry and that incest generally occurs between a child and an adult who is in a position of trust and authority. The incestuous relationship is not one of mutual consent and agreement; rather, it is a relationship wherein influence and power are used against a powerless victim.[6]

Sex Education

The third and fourth sessions are devoted to sexual education. Male and female anatomy is taught with the help of illustrations. Various methods of contraception are explained, and the birth process is discussed. The girls usually have many questions concerning stillbirths, miscarriages, causes of brain damage, and physical impairments in newborns. It is always explained to them that pregnancy in mothers who are physically immature increases the risks to the mother as well as to the child.

Since some subject matter may extend through several sessions, it is never possible to maintain a rigid sequence of presentations. The physiology and psychology of boys are discussed in a later session. The comfort and pride that boys derive from their penile organs are discussed lightly and sometimes with a great deal of humor. The girls learn that boys find the penis to be a source of pleasure and curiosity from the time they are very young. The phase of adolescence that girls experience with the development of breasts and the beginning of menses is likened to that of adolescent boys who begin to experience ejaculation or wet dreams during sleep. Many of the teenagers are under the misapprehension that the male's wet dreams represent romantic thoughts about females; this myth is dispelled. The girls learn that boys have pride in their muscular development and that this pride extends to the size and development of their genitals. They learn that the penis is an important measure of masculinity to a male; this is equated with the female's breasts as an indicator of femininity.

Adolescent girls often fantasize about motherhood; adolescent boys fantasize about the effectiveness of their penis and its ability to impregnate females. The penis for boys often represents an instrument of power and control. An example of this is the act of

---

[6] Blair Justice and Rita Justice, *The Broken Taboo—Sex in the Family* (New York: Human Sciences Press, 1979).

rape wherein the penis is used to degrade a victim. Girls are informed that nonconsenting sex represents aggression and hostility on the part of the male and that the male's anger is often unrelated to the victim. Indeed, aggression may be aroused by a male's frustration with a job, spouse, or unmet dependency needs of the past and present. The girls learn that male sexual desire is often not an expression of love, but simply a physical need that requires cathexis.

Discussion of Incest

The girls are taught that the incest taboo is one of the strongest and oldest taboos in all civilization. It is condemned by all societies and cultures and is generally considered a criminal act because of the danger it represents to the family structure and especially to the child. The children are informed that incest, like alcoholism, is not limited to any socioeconomic or ethnic group. At the beginning of treatment most girls express the belief that incest occurs in 90 percent to 95 percent of homes. They are stunned to learn that incest does not take place in most families and that estimates of incest range from one case in one thousand families to as many as one case in ten families.

The girls are asked to describe the very earliest phases of sexual abuse they can recall. They are told that usually a progression of intimate acts occurs, beginning with a "show and tell" or "feel and touch" phase. Because of their age and their love and trust of the adult, the children have no reason to suspect that their father's transgressions are anything other than normal affection. Many girls state that they viewed the initial sexual acts as harmless play or demonstrations of love but that as they matured and the incestuous acts escalated from fondling and masturbation to penile activity, they became increasingly dismayed and fearful. In many cases, the father's requests for secrecy and his caution in approaching her when no one else was present made her aware that he was doing something wrong. However, many girls hoped that they had misinterpreted their fathers' actions. This conflict often caused unjustifiable guilt for suspecting their own fathers of wrongdoing.

Victims blame themselves only after they have failed (for reasons that can easily be imagined) to resist or to report the first abusive acts. They frequently feel that some action of their own has triggered a sexual reaction from their fathers; their sense of shame, combined with guilt for keeping silent, makes them reluctant to discuss the matter in the group. This guilt is most effectively dealt with if each girl tells of her own experiences and has her credibility affirmed by the group leaders and other victims.

The girls in the group acknowledge that they had a desire for appropriate affection and approval from their fathers. They also recognize that their need for acceptance and affection did not encompass a desire for a sexual relationship. They are reassured that all children attempt to please and gain acceptance from parental figures and that it is normal for children not to want to disobey or offend their fathers. Girls are reassured that only compliant or "good girls" are victimized and that "bad girls" frequently reform errant fathers because they choose to disobey their father's commands. When one father demanded oral sex from his "disobedient" daughter, she bit down long and hard. Her father instantly reformed.

Several sessions may be devoted to discussing why the secret was kept and the reasons for its eventual disclosure. Fathers have used various methods to silence daughters:

girls may have been warned that revelation would cause the father to be arrested and jailed; they may have been told that the family would starve and be homeless without the father; some sadistic males may even threaten to kill the child's mother and the child if disclosure occurs. Some fathers threaten to have sex with younger sisters if the victim does not cooperate.

Most of the children in group therapy agree that their primary motivation for keeping the secret was to protect their mothers and to prevent family disintegration. They did not want to hurt or offend their mothers, and they feared their mothers' anger. They were also afraid of being sent away or locked up in an institution as a consequence of their involvement with the perpetrator. Some children say that they kept the secret in order to ensure that their parents would not divorce, although they were repulsed by their father's behavior. Some recall times when their fathers were kind and desirable members of their families, whereas others recall only a single positive experience—for example, when their fathers may have treated them to candy or ice cream.

Alleviating Guilt

The most important function of the group is to relieve the child's shame and guilt. She may feel guilty for having been in an ostensibly preferred position and for small privileges she has received in comparison with other siblings in the home, despite the fact that she has been deprived of many benefits because of her illicit relationship with her father. Her siblings generally recognize that she is Dad's favorite. Even though they do not know the reason for this, they may resent her and exclude her from their activities.

The child may also experience guilt for any pleasure she may have received from the relationship with the perpetrator. Girls must be made to understand that physical contact is frequently pleasurable and that the body may respond positively to many kinds of touching and closeness, regardless of the circumstances. The child may have experienced physical gratification from the close intimate contact with the father because affection was unavailable to her in normal circumstances. Any guilt concerning this pleasure should be eradicated.

Some girls are very compliant and repress their anger at the abuser; others are vindictive. It is important that they be permitted to ventilate this anger fully, even if it appears sadistic or vengeful. Some children express a great need to testify in court in order to publicly denounce the offender. Other girls are extremely intimidated by the possibility of a court appearance and the need to face the abuser. Children require guidance and preparation for court appearances.

Sessions also deal with the feelings of the child when the incestuous relationship is disclosed to others. Disclosure often occurs by accident; for example, the victim may unburden herself to a friend who later tells someone in authority. Most of the children initially experience a considerable feeling of relief and gratitude that the secret is exposed. Later, however, they begin to experience feelings of guilt for having betrayed the father. Some victims have ambivalent feelings of both love and hate for the perpetrator. Many of the girls are extremely depressed because no one believed them. The father may have denied the accusations, and the mother may be unwilling to believe that her husband could do such things to the child. Some girls fear that brothers and sisters will place the entire blame on them, both for the acts and for the consequences thereof.

The girl may have a tremendous dread of family poverty. She may fear her father's anger and possible reprisal. She may feel even more victimized by the legal system, which claims to protect her while sending her to a doctor for a humiliating physical examination and to a shelter where she is lonely, confused, and frightened. Her school life may have been disrupted, and she feels embarrassed to answer questions asked by her friends. She may blame herself for the divorce that may subsequently occur and for the breakup of the family. She may even blame herself for revealing the secret.

She must be reassured again and again that the anguish caused to herself and to the family is not the result of her behavior, but rather the result of her father's failure to control his impulses. The girl must be reassured that her mother and father's marriage was already in serious trouble before the father turned to her for sexual favors. It is also important that the girl understand that the father and perhaps the mother have many unresolved conflicts and traumas from their own childhood that have impeded their adult functioning.

Parental Roles and Types

In one session, the roles of mothers in the home are discussed. Frequently, the child may state that the mother was always busy with outside employment or that she was overwhelmed with the responsibilities of other children. She might add that her mother and father were more or less emotionally distant. Some children explain that the mother was general manager of the home and the finances, whereas the father appeared to be the dependent child. In the group, a girl may role play the interaction that occurred in the home between herself and her parents. Success of therapy depends to a great extent upon the mother's exoneration of the child's culpability in the relationship with the father. With the mother's support and loyalty directed primarily to the child, the child is spared further betrayal and loss of trust in caretakers.

The role of fathers in the home is dealt with in another session. A discussion of the types of fathers involved in incest is very important to victims. They need to understand the motivations for the father's or stepfather's behavior.

Children are generally able to identify different types of fathers. The dictator and tyrant is one type. This person wants total control over others. He issues orders to all the females in the home, and the females are expected to comply. In these homes, wives as well as children may be abused. Sometimes this person pretends to be an educator whose duty is to instruct his daughter in the ways of sex in order to "prepare" her for marriage This individual may have already convinced his wife that he is superior to her intellectually; thus she defers to his wishes to educate their daughter.

Another type of father is the "little boy" or "Mr. Poor-Me" father. This person is dependent upon everyone, generally incompetent, and socially unskilled. He cannot tolerate stress and frequently uses alcohol or drugs to relieve his anxieties about normal daily functioning. His theme in life is "take care of me, don't leave me" or "you're the only one who understands me." He is an extremely immature loner who has never been able to cope with an adult male–female relationship. He attempts to transform his child into a mother figure who will give him unconditional love and a sweetheart who will fulfill his adult sexual needs. He longs for intimacy and acceptance but fears rejection. He turns to his daughter for solace.

Another easily recognized father type is the sexually fixated male. Sexuality encompasses his total experience and answers his needs for pleasure, relaxation, and reduction of stress. He is generally obsessed with sexual fantasies in which he is powerful, charming, and irresistible to females. It is important to help girls understand that this type of father is often childish and immature, despite his age and appearance.

The children also identify father types who display sociopathic behaviors. This father is generally aggressive, sadistic, and physically abusive and may have a history of problems with the law. The children rightly believe this individual should be jailed or institutionalized, because he is a real threat to themselves and to others.

From two to as many as four sessions may be spent discussing fathers and their styles of manipulation or intimidation. The creation of the typologies serves several therapeutic purposes; it promotes insight and understanding, provides opportunities for humor, and perhaps most important helps the girls gain some perspective regarding the abuser. Classification of the fathers' behavior also adds to group cohesiveness since many children can identify similar traits in their abuser's behavior. Exaggeration of the personal characteristics of these men often generates laughter, which is an excellent antidote for the anxieties aroused by memories of trauma.

Effort is made to explore the life histories and childhood traumas of parents that might have contributed to the sexual abuse of their daughters. Often, the children feel empathy and sorrow for the perpetrator when they realize that their fathers, as children, were themselves victims of deprivation and abuse. Although some fathers continue to deny the sexual abuse and are therefore not suitable for therapy, many fathers admit to their actions in order to be forgiven and to return home. These fathers may have been nurturing and caring in nonsexual interactions with the child. The girl's faith and confidence in her father's promises not to offend again are reinforced by his apologies to her and other family members and his assumption of total responsibility for his behavior. The family's belief in the father's sincere desire to change is also reinforced by his willingness to attend long-term individual and group therapy for perpetrators. Family therapy is the final phase of treatment, wherein a family-systems model rather than a victim-advocacy model is used. It is hoped that the child will gain a new respect for herself and other family members during family therapy. Boundaries and rules for effective and satisfying family functioning are established.

IN CONCLUSION

The results of group treatment have been extremely favorable. Girls become more assertive because they practice assertiveness within and outside of the group. Girls who formerly chose isolation and withdrawal as a method of coping with incest become considerably more outgoing and sociable. Some girls who were extremely hostile are able to temper their reaction to frustration in a much more rational manner.

A beautiful fourteen-year-old adolescent was referred to the agency by the school system. The child was a loner and was totally mute in school. She would hang her head, her long hair covering her face, and not respond to any communication. Her grades were straight A. Although the child slowly and painfully revealed to her therapist that she was a victim of family sexual abuse, only in group sessions did she begin to open up and discuss her problem. She felt comfortable with other victims who understood her dilemma of feeling both love and hate for her father, the abuser. A year after group treatment, this young lady was a cheerleader in junior high school and the winner of a local beauty pageant. Her career plans include helping other incest victims battle the humiliation and trauma of incest.

Group treatment successfully neutralizes the excessive feelings of blame or guilt that incest victims experience and lessens or eliminates the consequent depression during adulthood.

CHAPTER 66

GROUP THERAPY WITH SEXUALLY ABUSED BOYS

Notes Toward Managing Behavior

Wayne Scott

Many writers have documented the effectiveness of group therapy for alleviating some of the traumatic effects of sexual abuse on child victims (Delson and Clark, 1981; Knittle and Tuana, 1980; Mandell and Damon, 1989; Sirles et al., 1988; Steward et al., 1986; Sturkie, 1983). While these writers suggest useful interventions, few of them explore how gender differences affect the process of group therapy with child victims. Because the majority of articles on this topic apply to girls and female adolescents, little is known about young male victims in group therapy. Preliminary clinical findings suggest, however, that the process and management of these groups is dramatically different (Friedrich et al., 1988; Schacht et al., 1990).

Although our awareness of their particular needs has grown in the last five years, research on young male victims of sexual abuse is still relatively sparse (Bolton et al., 1989; Briere et al., 1988; Dimock, 1988; Hunter, 1990; Porter, 1986). The lack of empirical research leaves crucial gaps in our understanding of the recovery of sexually abused boys. As clinicians await more empirical data to support their interventions, preliminary observations and interventions with sexually abused boys serve several important functions: encouraging clinicians to work with this challenging and needy population, highlighting the issues these clients bring to therapy, and providing the groundwork for future clinical research.

Reprinted from *Clinical Social Work Journal,* Vol. 20, No. 4 (1992), pp. 395–409, by permission of Human Sciences Press, Inc.

INTEGRATING ACTING OUT BEHAVIOR INTO THE GROUP PROCESS

The literature on group therapy with sexually abused boys suggests two divergent perspectives. While some writers acknowledge the importance of group therapy to recovery, they do not elaborate on any behavioral challenges specific to boys in group therapy (Porter, 1986). Other writers describe a nearly unmanageable level of acting out that calls into question the effectiveness of group therapy for this population (Friedrich et al., 1988; Schacht et al., 1990).[1]

This article considers the special behavioral challenges of group therapy with sexually abused boys. It assumes that group therapy is an effective means for boys to address the impact of past sexual abuse on their current functioning, based on findings with other populations of survivors of sexual abuse (Berliner and Ernst, 1984; Damon and Waterman, 1986; Hazzard, King and Webb, 1986; Knittle and Tuana, 1980; Schacht et al., 1990; Sturkie, 1983). But this article also asserts that the influence of male socialization dramatically alters the content, process, and management of those groups.

Taking the experiences of Friedrich and Schacht as a starting point, the interventions suggested in this article focus only on managing the boys' acting out behavior in group therapy. This article will not consider more general curriculum issues, as a number of articles have supplied ideas in this area (Celano, 1990; Damon and Waterman, 1986; Delson and Clark, 1981; Knittle and Tuana, 1980; Mandell and Damon, 1989; Sirles et al., 1988; Steward et al., 1986; Sturkie, 1983). Because these acting out behaviors interfere with the maintenance of a safe group environment, drastically impeding the group's progress toward its goals, their management demands specific attention. Acting out behaviors are examined in light of gender-specific defense mechanisms connected to the boys' experience of sexual abuse. The interventions suggested in this article attempt to integrate the management of acting out as a vital part of the group's process and learning.

DESCRIPTION OF PROGRAM

Boys are selected from the total caseload at Midwest Family Resource Associates, Ltd., a family systems oriented agency specializing in treating intrafamilial child sexual abuse. The agency utilizes a model for treating abusive family systems that encourages child victims and parents to participate in groups during the course of an overall treatment program that includes family, marital, individual, and sibling sessions (Barrett, Sykes, and Byrnes, 1986; Trepper and Barrett, 1989). A primary therapist refers each boy to group therapy, as an addition to working with him in individual and/or family therapy. Group therapy is viewed as an important addition to the child's recovery from the sexual abuse.

This article focuses on the agency's work with sexually abused boys between the ages of six and thirteen years old. The majority of the clients' sexual abuse can be characterized as intrafamilial, whether the abusive experience involves natural parents, adolescent brothers, mothers' paramours or adoptive parents. Children are grouped

---

[1] Notably, Friedrich's impressions derive from a brief diagnostic group format (four sessions) without interventions designed to address the gender-specific defence mechanisms that boys bring into group therapy. Schacht's open-ended group was conducted on an inpatient psychiatric unit.

according to their social and developmental levels. Therapy groups are closed and time-limited, with younger groups (5–7 years old, 8–10 years old) running approximately 20 sessions and older groups (11–13 years old) running as long as 40 sessions, due to the particular challenges of managing the older boys' anxiety and addressing the group's curriculum at the same time. Groups are closely supervised by senior staff at the agency who have years of experience in leading groups for sexually abused children.

For children, generally, participation in group therapy has several important goals, including: reducing the client's sense of isolation and shame, providing a safe place for clients to experiment with different behaviors, and intensifying their awareness of the issues connected with their abuse. The group also provides clients with a group other than their family in which to have their emotional needs expressed and met by others. This alternative particularly challenges the reclusiveness of incestuous families and encourages children to interact as peers with other children (Trepper and Barrett, 1989).

For boys, specifically, participation in group therapy provides an opportunity to develop trusting, supportive relationships with other boys and the male therapist. The barriers to closeness experienced by most males are intensified for boys who have been sexually abused. The stigmas associated with incest, homosexuality, and male vulnerability are broken down through group therapy, laying the groundwork for participants relating and identifying with other males and developing a comfortable, healthy relationship to their own masculinity. The presence of other boys makes creating a relationship with a male group therapist less frightening than if a boy works individually with a man, which often recalls memories of the original abuse (Porter, 1986).[2]

CHARACTERISTICS OF YOUNG MALE VICTIMS

Before discussing behavioral interventions in group therapy, it is necessary to describe the characteristics of young male victims. Finkelhor has conceived a useful model for understanding sexually abused children. This model, which he calls traumagenic dynamics, breaks down defense mechanisms into four major categories: traumatic sexualization, betrayal, powerlessness, and stigmatization (Finkelhor, 1986). Using these categories as a framework, the salient characteristics of young male victims will be explored, with particular attention to their manifestation in group therapy and the influence of male socialization.

Traumatic sensualization. Finkelhor describes traumatic sexualization as "a process in which a child's sexuality (including both sexual feelings and sexual attitudes) is shaped in a developmentally inappropriate and interpersonally dysfunctional fashion as a result of the sexual abuse" (Finkelhor, 1986). Traumatic sexualization encompasses a wide range of behaviors that emerge with particular intensity in peer groups, including boundary disturbances, sexualized behavior, and confusion about sexual identity.

Larson and Maddock provide an excellent understanding of the interpersonal boundary disturbances that result from intrafamily child abuse. Describing incestuous

---

[2] Dimock, significantly, advocated the use of an exclusively male treatment approach for sexually abused males, in the belief that "underlying conflicts about masculinity must be ultimately solved through the development of close, trusting relationships with other men" who "help affirm masculinity, respect vulnerability, and react with real emotions to the sexual abuse experience" (Dimock, 1988).

families and their interactions, they write, "Personal boundaries become diffuse; interaction produces symbiotic relationship patterns in which each member feels that his/her survival is dependent upon the emotional and psychosocial status of the other members" (Larson and Maddock, 1986). This familial style of interaction replicates itself in the chaotic, confusing interaction of sexually abused boys in group therapy.

Most conflicts in group therapy can be reduced to this central difficulty: each participant's inability to perceive himself as separate and unaffected by the objects in his environment. His personal boundaries have been violated so deeply by the trauma of the abuse, the psychological membrane between himself and the environment has become fragile and permeable, predisposing him to experience most stimuli as intrusive.

This lack of boundaries has both a receptive and an offensive form. Receptively, hypersensitive to each other's fearfulness and rage, young male victims are highly reactive to stimuli, blame each other for their own anxiety, and feel victimized by each others' acting out. They are unable to shut out even relatively innocuous stimuli.

Offensively, young male victims externalize their anxiety. Boys differ significantly from girls primarily by externalizing their responses to the sexual abuse (Friedrich, 1986; Porter, 1986; Schacht, 1990). This acting out behavior can emerge as sexual and physical aggressiveness, a heightened preoccupation with sexual activity, and a high level of sexual and physical intrusiveness with adults and peers. The intrusiveness can take very subtle forms, such as provoking others by making gangs signs behind the group therapist's back.

A third characteristic of traumatic sexualization can be described as profound confusion over issues of sexual identity (Porter, 1986). This dynamic emerges in group therapy in the context of two prevalent norms: a generalized attitude of hypermasculinity, which sanctions and encourages physically aggressive behavior, explosions of temper, and disregard for the feelings of others, at the same time discouraging expressions of hurt and vulnerability; and extreme vigilance to and fear of homosexuality. Homophobia—the fear of homosexuals, homosexual contact, or of being perceived as a homosexual—underlies many problematic interactions in these groups. Homophobia produces a fear of closeness with other boys and heightens group participants' fear and revulsion at any behavior that does not conform to a rigid standard of machismo. Frequently, participants confused homosexuality as an inseparable part of sexual abuse.

Betrayal. One of the traumatic consequences of the sexual abuse is an ensuing inability to form stable, trusting relationships with men and women. In particular, the experience of sexual abuse generates defense mechanisms precluding trusting, supportive relationships with other boys and men. Statistically, the perpetrator for most boys who are sexually abused tends to be a male who is known to them (Dimock, 1988; Finkelhor, 1984; Porter, 1986; Reinhart, 1987). These defense mechanisms inhibited the boys' capacity to create meaningful identifications with men and to develop healthy, flexible attitudes toward their own masculinity.

This characteristic of the experience of sexually abused boys presents one of the most difficult obstacles in group therapy. Not only do boys have difficulty trusting the male group therapist, but the prospect is intensely frightening and recalls their experience of abuse at the hands of a trusted caretaker. While the presence of other boys can alleviate some fears of the male group therapist, more often participants, who themselves act out in sexually and physically aggressive ways, represent potential abusers to each other. Feeling safe within a room of other victim/offenders is a particular struggle for the boys in these groups.

Stigmatization. Boys who suffer sexual abuse at the hands of a male perpetrator face additional complication of social proscriptions against homosexuality. When the perpetrator is a family member, the incest taboo compounds the cultural imperative of silence and shame, leading to withdrawn, isolative behavior and depression. Young male victims wonder how the sexual abuse will affect their sexual preference and whether the sexual abuse means that they are homosexual. They avoid close relationships in order to shield their doubts from others and to protect the secret of the abuse.

Much of the aggressive acting out observed in group therapy, then, serves a distancing function; participants attempt to alienate their peers and the group leader, to defend against the possibility of closeness and a greater awareness of their own vulnerability (feelings of inadequacy and "badness"). Aggressive acting out of this kind can be used as a barometer of participants' need for distance, both physical and emotional, and a need to control the pace at which they become closer to each other. For some participants, however, involvement in physically and verbally abusive struggles with their peers emerges as their only avenue for feeling close to others.

Perhaps the greatest advantage of group therapy is that it offers boys the chance to meet other boys who experienced sexual abuse, to compare survival strategies, and to feel accepted and "normal" in their reactions to the sexual abuse. For some of our clients, merely sitting in the same waiting room with other young male victims had a dramatic impact on their sense of self-esteem. This advantage breaks down the stigmas against homosexuality, incest, and child abuse that boys feel so keenly.

Powerlessness. Like all victims of sexual abuse, young male victims experience an overwhelming sense of powerlessness by being sexually traumatized. Cultural standards of masculinity, however, drastically circumscribe the range of feelings boys can express about their abuse. In addition to the cultural taboos against homosexuality and incest, young male victims experience an entrenched sociocultural prohibition against males being vulnerable, weak, or helpless. Dimock, writing of men sexually abused as boys, comments that

> Most males have been socialized from early childhood to hide physical and emotional vulnerability. Such a stereotype opposes the image of the vulnerable child victim and presents a conflict for many men who were sexually abused as children. In order to acknowledge the sexual abuse, they must also confront the vulnerability prohibition (Dimock, 1988).

Externalizing this sense of powerlessness, young male victims in group therapy act out in aggressive and destructive ways. By hurting others, destroying property, and constantly undermining the group's sense of safety, they experience their own powerlessness vicariously, making their peers and the group leader feel powerless in their midst (Schacht, 1990). Underlying this offending behavior is an unbounded, unremitting anger, characterized by several boys as "being angry all the time," intensified by their inability to contain or control the overwhelming feeling.

The sense of being victimized emerges in more innocuous, though no less consistent manner, through other interactions. Participants are vigilant to the small ways in which other participants and the group leader slight them or treat them unfairly. These "slights" are followed by accusations, demands for fairness, and a constant harkening to the group therapist's authority to eradicate the injustice.

For the purpose of behavioral management, it is useful to conceive of the simultaneous existence of offending and victimized responses to environmental stimuli as *victim/offender patterns* (Porter, 1986). The notion of victim/offender patterns recognizes the concomitant presence of both characteristics in the interactions of any young male victim. It reframes the relationship between the two characteristics as circular and causal: a boy's pervasive feeling of being victimized leads to an externalized response (offending), that protects him from being revictimized. At the same time, his offending behavior creates and maintains the presence of victims within the group, often leading others to revictimize him. Victim/offender patterns explain much of the participants' aggressive interaction with each other, without unfairly designating certain participants as offenders and others as victims, exclusively. The characteristics feed off each other, both interpersonally and intrapersonally.

GROUP INTERVENTIONS WITH YOUNG MALE VICTIMS

The management of young male victims in group therapy demands interventions geared to address problematic behaviors specific to this population. Without those interventions, the group process degenerates into chaos and confusion, impeding the group's structure and goals, making participants feel unsafe, and creating a panic in participants that further escalates and maintains the chaos.

The interventions used in group therapy with sexually abused boys can be conceptualized broadly in three interrelated categories: creating safety, boundary-making, and interrupting victim-offender patterns. These categories of interventions recognize that, while the group activity or topic may change for each meeting, the need to control problematic behavior is continuous throughout the life of the group. The advantage of these interventions is their ability to integrate the management of problematic behaviors as a vital part of the group's process and learning, continuously connecting these behaviors to the traumatic effects of the sexual abuse.

CREATING SAFETY

Group norms. Creating a safe environment is a challenge for the group therapist working with sexually abused boys. While safety in the group room is the priority for all therapists working with abuse survivors, boys externalize and act out their pain and anxiety, creating exceptionally unsafe environments. The beginning of group therapy, in particular, can be characterized by constant provocativeness, threats and aggression (both verbal and physical), hyperactivity, and a pervasive fear of revictimization.

Friedrich and Schacht's experience in group therapy with sexually abused boys confirms the impression that, however chaotic and unmanageable this behavior appears to the therapist, it is a normal, predictable response of boys to being in a room with other young male victims and a male therapist (Friedrich et al., 1988; Schacht et al., 1990). With that in mind, the therapist can adjust his expectations about what the group achieves initially, work to modulate his own anxiety during sessions, and concentrate on the *quid pro non* of work with this difficult population: the basic tasks of creating safety.

Group rules. These basic tasks involve creating and adhering to group rules and continually reminding boys about safe behavior. Boys are asked to create rules to govern group behavior and to insure safety, as in any other children's group therapy (Porter, 1986; Seipker and Kandaras, 1985). The difference in group therapy with sexually abused boys is the amount of repetition they need to enforce these rules and maintain safety. During the first few months of group, the group therapist constantly emphasizes the need for safety, repeating "this doesn't feel safe to me" until participants begin to repeat it to each other. For many participants, the imperative distinction between safe and unsafe behavior is a foreign concept that eludes their understanding.

For the group therapist, it is important to realize that the task of the group during initial sessions may be simply to tolerate being in the same room with each other, at a reasonable level of safety. In the beginning, group may end earlier than the time allotted, if participants' anxiety reaches an unmanageable intensity. The snack may be introduced before the end of group, producing a soothing effect on participants, often enabling the therapist to address behavior problems while participants' hands and mouths are full.

Point system. In order to create an environment where participants constantly monitor their level of safety, the group therapist can introduce a point system to reward positive adherence to group rules and the expectation for safety. The point system exists throughout the life of the group. A chart is posted with each participants' name at the head of a column. Generally, points—in the form of rubber stamps— are awarded to the participants not involved in unsafe behavior, but no one is penalized and points once granted cannot be removed. Once the group reaches a collective number of points, the group as a whole receives a special snack (e.g. pizza).

The point system positively utilizes the intense competitiveness that exists between boys, at the same time it encourages teamwork toward a collective end. Boys become acutely conscious of their performance in relation to the others. At the same time, boys whose total of points lags behind the others receive feedback from the group for "freeloading." A tendency to give out points liberally not only provides incentives to maintain safety, but recognizes basic behaviors like listening and sitting, which, in the beginning of group therapy, are milestones on the road to a productive group.

Telling their stories. While all of the boys are told of the common nature of their abuse—through intake interviews and the first group session—they are assured in the first session that there will be no pressure for them to discuss what happened to them. "You are all here because someone touched you in your private parts in a way that made you feel bad and uncomfortable. But we are not going to talk about that for a long time." In fact, in the first sessions, they are not allowed to discuss the abuse and the group therapist stops those boys who begin to tell their stories. This assurance enables participants to perceive the group experience as different from the often brusque encounters with police, doctors, and caseworkers they encountered when they initially told their stories. This caveat also prevents participants from feeling exposed before they have developed a closer, more trusting relationship with their peers. Some boys, for example, will be anxious to blurt out their stories and "keep a stiff upper lip" in the process. Waiting to tell their stories allows the group to build up enough trust for participants to explore with each other their feelings and reactions to the abuse.

BOUNDARY-MAKING

Boundary-making. In order to address the pervasive intrusiveness and receptivity to stimuli that characterizes young male victims, the following intervention was devised. Using large cardboard boxes, scissors and tape, participants were instructed to construct boundaries around themselves. "Make a boundary between yourself and the rest of the group, so that we know what you need to feel safe." The boys were encouraged to be creative and to decorate their boundaries, because they would be expected to talk about them to the group. Generally, the more disturbed children strive to create impenetrably seamless fortresses, while less traumatized children make more open constructions, with windows and doors to the outside world. Children have made replicas of their homes, castles, fences, and one even constructed a "therapist" to live inside.

After the boundaries were built, participants were asked to describe how their boundaries made them feel safe. They were then asked to study their boundaries and to make a picture of them inside their minds. Although the physical boundaries needed to be removed eventually, they were told, participants were encouraged to devise ways of preserving the safety they insured, by later remembering the boundaries or pretending the boundaries had reappeared. They were encouraged to discuss the behaviors that enabled them to maintain their boundaries.

Subsequent sessions began by the distribution of masking tape, which participants used to mark out the space occupied by their boundaries. This activity underlined the importance of boundaries in making a safe group space. It enabled participants to remind themselves to shut out stimuli as well as to contain their own feelings and to verbalize them unobtrusively. At later points in the group, when behavior began to disintegrate, tape would be redistributed for boundary-making as a reminder.

Boundary-making can be encouraged in other ways as well. Boys can keep their coats with them during sessions and hide under them if they feel the need. Blankets can be supplied. A number of successful groups were conducted with all boys lying on their stomachs under their chairs, peeking out between the legs of the chair (literally, "grounded"). During an exercise where boys constructed clay replicas of the abuser to introduce to the group, they were told to work on their models within the confines of a shoe box. Later, when allowed to "strike back" with plastic utensils at their abusers, they were informed that they could do anything they wished to the abuser as long as it remained within the confines of the box. This provided the safety and structure to allow the full intensity of rage to emerge, without feeling like it could become hurtful to others or overwhelming to themselves.

In addition to providing concrete, metaphoric reminders of interpersonal boundaries, the group therapist connects the physical process of boundary-making to interpersonal skills that allow participants to maintain a sense of their own boundaries. These include confronting intrusive behaviors, ignoring provocativeness and other stimuli, and utilizing the group therapist as a control over other children's unsafe behavior. The last option needs to be used judiciously, however, as young male victims tend to resort to being tattle-tales first, maintaining their own sense of powerlessness in situations they can realistically confront themselves. Assertiveness training presents a particular obstacle to participants, because frequently the distinction between assertive and abusive confrontation eludes them. Here the group therapist's capacity for patient confrontation and limit-setting serves as an important role model.

It is also useful to incorporate these skills—confronting, ignoring, asking for help— into the point system that recognizes positive, safe behavior in the group setting.

Separate space. With younger males (the 6–8 years old group) a game called "Separate Space" was used to illustrate some of the same ideas as boundary-making. When participants' behavior became overly intrusive with each other, the group leader prescribes the group to act out in disorderly, intrusive ways for thirty seconds (or less, depending on the group). "OK, I want everyone to act out and get into each other's space for thirty seconds." After thirty seconds, he calls out "separate space!" and participants have to the count of three to arrange themselves on the floor, with enough room between them for the group therapist to walk slowly in circles around everyone, praising their ability to make separate space, keep boundaries, and recognize the difference between separate space and intrusive behavior.

Father May I? Similarly, with latency aged boys, the traditional game "Father May I?" provides rich opportunities for mastery over the concept of boundary making and makes a fun ending for sessions. One person, the "father," stands at the end of the room opposite the other boys. Boys ask for permission to advance toward him a certain number of steps (usually using another creature as an analogue, e.g. "four baby steps," "three frog leaps," "one rabbit hop"). The father has the leverage to say yes or no, but ultimately, within a time limit, he must allow someone to tap his shoulder and become the next father. While the boys play and inevitably experience fears and conflicts around closeness, limit-setting and being in control, the group leader can initiate discussion about ways to make the game a tolerable and fun experience for everyone.

INTERRUPTING VICTIM-OFFENDER PATTERNS

Interrupting victim/offender patterns in group therapy demands tremendous patience and repetition, lasting, to some degree, for the duration of the group. Often, simple limit-setting on unsafe behavior and reminders to follow the rules (creating safety) fail to produce any lasting capacity for self-regulation and control. The challenge facing the group therapist becomes helping young male victims to understand how the victim/ offender patterns impede the group's progress. While conceptualizing victim/offender patterns requires some sophistication, the following model does provide the vocabulary for boys to discuss and monitor the pattern as it emerges.

The Internalized Parts Model of Intervention is a useful tool for enabling clients to examine different characteristics of themselves without feeling reduced to a single category of behavior. In this model, clients isolate and name behaviors and characteristics ("parts") contributing to their whole personality, e.g., "my critic part," "my offender part," or "my child part." This process enables clients to view themselves as possessing many parts and characteristics that help or harm them in life situations. It also suggests to clients their capacity to choose which parts help them best. The Internalized Parts

Model is particularly useful in working with sexually abusive families, enabling family members to examine their "bad parts" without feeling reduced and categorized by them, thereby enabling them to maintain a sense of self-esteem (Schwartz, 1987; Trepper and Barrett, 1989).

The Internalized Parts Model, then, becomes an effective tool for helping boys to understand the victim/offender patterns that interfere with group safety. The group therapist observes, "We are all made up of different parts. Each of us has an offender part, a victim part, and an assertive part." The assertive part corresponds to the "centered self" that Schwartz describes in his model (Schwartz, 1987). The group leader elicits characteristics of these different parts from participants as well as describing his own perception of the parts. He then describes different situations typical for children in this age group and asks participants to guess how the different parts handle those situations. An example follows:

> George is the new kid in town. He wants to play football with a group of rough guys on the playground, but he is a little smaller than most of them. When George approaches the rough guys, they tell him to leave and they threaten to hurt him if he stays. Discuss how the different parts of George might handle this situation.

Typically, participants provide a good understanding of how the offender and victim parts of George handle this encounter. The offender part gets angry and reacts to the rough boys by threatening, teasing, lashing out at them, or attempting to disrupt their game (externalized, intrusive behavior). The victim part keeps testing the situation, whines and cries about his exclusion, and waits to get beaten up. He complains to others and tattles to his teachers. He may return to the same group over the course of several days and set himself up for more rejection and beatings (passive, helpless behavior).

Boys tend to hesitate in describing how George's assertive part handles this encounter. This hesitation, again, springs from a confusion about the difference between abusive and assertive behavior, rooted in the hypermasculine norms of the group. The group leader can provide information about the assertive part. The assertive part of George takes a moment to examine the situation. He is able to stand up for himself without hurting any of the other boys. He asserts his needs in a nonthreatening way and, if the rough guys still respond with hostility, he withdraws, chooses to ignore them and finds a different set of friends. If he really wants to be with the rough guys, he may seek out one or two of them individually and attempt to get to know them away from the group, in the hope that the new friends can provide an entry for him into the group.

In presenting these "parts" to participants, the group therapist needs to recognize several caveats. First, the offender part is a functional defense mechanism for boys growing up in inner city communities and in dysfunctional, abusive families. This mode of conceptualizing victim/offender patterns does not seek to eliminate the offender part as much as it attempts to help participants recognize a range of alternatives in their response to life situations. The exercise underscores the difference between, for example, a school playground with inadequate adult supervision and the small, protected environment of the group therapy setting. The offender part has no use in the latter setting.

Examining the offender part is also a useful way to confront the denial many boys exhibit that they will ever behave like the person who abused them, without leading them to think that this is an inevitable outcome of the abuse.

Second, it is vitally important, in talking about the victim part, not to invalidate or deny the feelings of helplessness and vulnerability that boys have about the sexual abuse. Talking about the victim part does, however, help alleviate the pervasive feeling of being victimized and powerless in response to all life stresses. Again, it enables participants to recognize the difference between the experience of abuse and the group therapy setting, where assertive behavior is supported and nurtured.

CONCLUSION

This article provides concrete interventions to manage the acting out behavior of sexually abused boys in group therapy. Because of the particular intensity of the young male victims' anxiety and the chaos it can create in group therapy, their acting out demands specific attention and management. By themselves, traditional forms of behavioral management (limit-setting, time-outs, etc.) failed to produce a reasonable level of safety and order, nor any capacity for self-regulation. Using the interventions labelled creating safety, boundary-making, and interrupting victim/offender patterns, the management of acting out behavior is tailored specifically to address the gender-specific defense mechanisms of young male victims of sexual abuse.

The success of a children's group therapy is often measured anecdotally (Seipker and Kandaras, 1985). The interventions described here do, patiently applied over time, produce a safe group setting. They enable participants to discuss the sexual abuse and to explore a range of angry, vulnerable and sad feelings in response to perpetrators, non-offending parents, and other authorities they encountered. These interventions also, importantly, enable the group therapist to understand the boys' anxiety and to address the specific meanings of their behavior, without feeling overwhelmed, helpless or out of control himself. Many of the participants remain in individual or family therapy at the agency after their group ends. Some of these boys, it has been observed, continue to use the language they learned through creating safety, boundary-making and interrupting victim/offender patterns, applying it to other areas of conflict in their lives. Still another set of boys, starting again in group therapy at a different agency, requested some of the interventions used here or described to the new therapist how to organize them.

REFERENCES

Barrett, M. J., Sykes, C. and Byrnes, W. (1986). A systemic model for the treatment of intrafamily child sexual abuse. In: *Treating incest: A multiple systems perspective,* eds. M.J. Barrett and T. Trepper. New York: Haworth Press.

Berliner, L. and Ernst, E. (1984). Group work with preadolescent sexual assault victims. In: *Victims of sexual aggression: Treatment of children, women, and men,* eds. I. R. Stuart and J. G. Greer. New York: Van Nostrand Reinhold.

Bolton, F. (1989). *Males at risk: the other side of child sexual abuse.* Newbury Park, California: Sage Publications.

Briere, J., Evans, D., Runtz, M., and Wall, T. (1988). Symptomatology in men who were molested as children: A comparison study. *American Journal of Orthopsychiatry, 58*(3), 457–461.

Celano, M. (1990). Activities and games for group psychotherapy with sexually abused children. *International Journal of Group Psychotherapy, 40*(4), 419–429.

Damon, L. and Waterman, J. (1986). Parallel group treatment of children and their mothers. In: *Sexual abuse of young children: Evaluation and treatment,* eds. K. McFarlane and J. Waterman. New York: Guilford Press.

Delson, N. and Clark, M. (1981) Group therapy with sexually molested children. *Child Welfare, 60*(3), 175–182.

Dimock, P. (1988). Adult males sexually abused as children: Characteristics and implications for treatment. *Journal of Interpersonal Violence, 3*(2), 203–221.

Finkelhor, D. (1986). *A sourcebook on child sexual abuse.* Beverly Hills, California: Sage Publications.

Friedrich, W., Beilke, R., and Urquiza, A. (1988). Behavior problems in young sexually abused boys. *Journal of Interpersonal Violence, 3*(1), 21–28.

Friedrich, W. Berliner, L., Urquiza, A. and Beilke, R. (1988) Brief diagnostic group treatment of sexually abused boys. *Journal of Interpersonal Violence, 3*(3), 331–343.

Hazzard, A., King, H., and Webb, C. (1986). Group therapy with sexually abused girls. *American Journal of Psychotherapy, 40,* 213–223.

Hunter, Mic. (1990). *Abused boys: the neglected victims of sexual abuse.* Lexington, Massachusetts: Lexington Books.

Knittle, B. and Tuana, S. (1980). Group therapy as primary treatment for adolescent victims of intrafamily sexual abuse. *Clinical Social Work Journal, 8*(4), 236–242.

Larson, N. and Maddock, J. (1986). Structural and functional variables in incest family systems: Implications for assessment and treatment. In: *Treating incest: A multiple systems perspective,* eds. M.J. Barrett and T. Trepper. New York: Hayworth Press.

Mandell, J. and Damon, L. (1989). *Group treatment for sexually abused children.* New York: The Guilford Press.

Porter, E. (1986). *Treating the young male victim of sexual assault: Issues and strategies for intervention.* Syracuse, New York: Safer Society Press.

Reinhart, M. (1987). Sexually abused boys. *Child Abuse and Neglect, 11,* 229–235.

Schacht, A., Kerlinsky, D., and Carlson, C. (1990) Group therapy with sexually abused boys: Leadership, projective identification and countertransference issues. *International Journal of Group Psychotherapy, 40*(4), 401–417.

Schwartz, R. (1987). Our multiple selves. *Family Therapy Networker, 11,* 25–31.

Seipker, B. and Kandaras, C. (1985). *Group therapy with children and adolescents: A treatment manual.* New York: Human Sciences Press, Inc.

Sirles, E., Walsma, J., Lytle-Barnaby, R., and Lander, L. (1988). Group therapy techniques for work with child sexual abuse victims. *Social Work in Groups, 11*(3), 67–78.

Steward, M., Farquhar, L., Dicharry, D., Glick, D. Martin, P. (1986). Group therapy: A treatment of choice for young victims of child abuse. *International Journal of Group Psychotherapy, 36*(2), 261–277.

Sturkie, K. (1983). Structured group treatment for sexually abused children. *Health and Social Work,* 8, 299–308.

Trepper, T. and Barrett, M.J. (1989). *The systemic treatment of incest: A therapeutic handbook.* New York: Brunner Mazel, Publishers.

ABUSE OF CHILDREN

CHAPTER 67

TREATING FEMALE ADULT SURVIVORS OF CHILDHOOD INCEST

Geraldine Faria and Nancy Belohlavek

Because of the strong taboo against it, only in recent years have members of the helping professions begun to take a serious look at incest. The result is a growing body of literature devoted to issues relevant to incestuous behavior, including its nature and extent, the damage to its victims, the family dynamics involved, the specific characteristics of its participants, and the various approaches to treatment. Understandably, much of this literature pertains to children and adolescents. There are comparatively few references to adult women who experienced incest as children or adolescents, and even fewer references to the specific clinical issues involved in the treatment of these women.

Based on figures from five different surveys, David Finkelhor suggests that there are approximately one million American women who have been involved in incestuous relations with their fathers.[1] This figure is viewed as a conservative estimate: the real incidence of father-daughter incest is suspected to be much higher. In addition, this figure does not take other forms of incest into account. If the cases involving grandfathers, uncles, stepfathers, siblings, and mothers were added, the incidence would be higher still.

While the incidence of incest itself suggests that more attention be paid to adults who are victims of childhood incest, there is another reason why this population should not be ignored, namely, that the experience of incest is not innocuous. Several studies indicate that the immediate reaction of the incest victim is usually a negative one involving such responses as depression, anxiety, acting-out behavior, and serious personality dis-

Reprinted from *Social Casework,* Vol. 65, No. 8 (1984), pp. 465–471, by permission of the publisher, Families International, Inc.
[1] David Finkelhor, *Sexually Victimized Children* (New York: The Free Press, 1979), p. 88.

turbances.[2] Perhaps more importantly, there is evidence that incest also has long-term effects. Among adult victims, sexual problems such as indiscriminate sexual activity, prostitution, orgasmic dysfunction, and confusion about sexual preference have been cited in the literature.[3] Additional problems include guilt, negative self-image, depression, and difficulties in interpersonal relationships.[4]

Given the increased visibility of the problem of incest, the incidence of the problem among female adults, and the long-term effects, it is expected that more and more women will seek out mental health clinicians for assistance. In turn, the clinicians must be prepared to deal knowledgeably and effectively with the problems presented by these women. Since a gap exists in the literature regarding the specific clinical issues involved in the treatment of adult incest victims, this article proposes to fill that gap.

IDENTIFYING ADULT VICTIMS

Before treatment can be provided, adult incest victims must be identified. The first step toward identification is to have in mind a working definition of incest which goes beyond the narrower legalistic notions. For the purposes of this article, incest is defined as intimate sexual activity—including fondling, fellatio, cunnilingus, sodomy, and intercourse—between individuals in the same socialization unit (excluding that between husband and wife, or the cultural equivalent) or between individuals who are close blood relatives, such as aunts, uncles, grandparents, or first cousins.[5] Included as incestuous behavior are sexual activities with surrogate relatives such as stepparents and foster parents. This definition is intended to be inclusive as possible because, whatever the relational tie between the violator and the victim, an incestuous psychological impact may be detected.[6]

Female adult victims of incest can be classified into two major groups: those who seek treatment and those who do not. In the latter group, some women may find that the incest experience poses no problems. Others may be reluctant to obtain help because of feelings of shame or the belief that their experience is a singular one. The women who do seek treatment appear to fall into one of three subgroups. The first, and probably the smallest, consists of women who seek help specifically because of their incest experience. The second, and most likely the largest, is comprised of women who enter therapy for other problems but who are aware of their past incest experiences. These women typically do not disclose the incest until several months of treatment have elapsed. Some may not discuss it at all unless the therapist inquires about it. In the third group are those women who seek help for other problems but who are unaware that they have been victims of incest because they have repressed the experience. Because of their conscious or unconscious resistance to disclosing the incest, these victims are diffi-

---

[2] Karin C. Meiselman, *Incest: A Psychological Study of Causes and Effects with Treatment Recommendations* (San Francisco: Jossey-Bass, 1979), pp. 185–93.

[3] Ibid., pp. 221–61.

[4] Mavis Tsai and Nathaniel N. Wagner, "Therapy Groups for Women Sexually Molested as Children," *Archives of Sexual Behavior* 7 (1978): 421–25.

[5] The authors are indebted to Richard Donner, director of Holistic Adolescent Residential Treatment Services, Topeka, KS, for this definition.

[6] Christine A. Courtois and L. Watts, "Counseling Adult Women Who Experienced Incest in Childhood or Adolescence," *The Personnel and Guidance Journal* 60 (January 1982): 275.

cult to identify. The problem may be completely overlooked unless the therapist is alert to signs which suggest a previous incest experience and is willing to raise the issue with the client. There are several indicators in the client's current situation which point to the possibility that she is a victim. Some of these indicators have been noted in the literature; others have been derived from clinical experience. Although there is as yet no research to support it, the authors' clinical experiences suggest that the greater the number of indicators, the greater the probability that the client has been a victim of incest.

Although an adult victim may present a wide variety of problems, she characteristically suffers from low self-esteem and depression, which may be severe enough to lead to suicide attempts.[7] Another prominent indicator is self-destructive behavior which, in addition to suicide attempts, may include alcoholism, drug abuse, or prostitution. In one drug treatment center in New York City, for example, 44 percent of all female addicts in the program had been victims of incest. A Minneapolis study of women working as prostitutes showed that 75 percent had been incestuously assaulted.[8] In another study of 200 prostitutes, the preliminary data analysis indicated that 59 percent of the first 100 subjects had experienced incest in their homes.[9]

Sexual problems may also indicate that a client has been a victim of incest. It is not uncommon for these women to be nonorgasmic or to report that sexual relations are not enjoyable. Some women are able to have satisfactory sexual relations only if they are in control, that is, they initiate sex and take an active role.[10] It should be noted that the need to take control may not be limited to a woman's sexual relations but may extend to other aspects of her social relationships. Some victims indiscriminately engage in sexual activities with a succession of male partners. They may be inappropriately seductive, and they may have difficulty separating sex from affection. While the majority of adult incest victims are heterosexual, there is evidence that some women who are either lesbians or who have experimented with lesbian relationships have been incestuously assaulted as children.[11] It should be stressed that in assessing sexuality issues, the focus, at this point, should not be on the appropriateness or inappropriateness of the woman's behavior. Because the primary goal is to ascertain whether the client has been a victim of incest, the focus should be on exploring the historical issues, experiences, and conditions which prompted the sexual problems or behaviors. It is not unusual for incest victims to be rather vague or even draw a complete blank when asked about past sexuality issues.

A variety of physical complaints have been noted in adult victims. Most commonly, the women suffer from headaches. But they may also report stomach ailments, skin disorders, backaches, and other psychosomatic pains.[12] Relationship problems are also fairly common, particularly with spouses or male partners, in-laws, parents, and chil-

---

[7] Susan Forward and Craig Buck, *Betrayal of Innocence: Incest and Its Devastation* (New York: Penguin Books, 1978), pp. 22–23.
[8] Sandra Butler, *Conspiracy of Silence: The Trauma of Incest* (San Francisco: New Glide Publications, 1978), p. 16.
[9] "Bay Area Prostitutes: Middle Class, 'Good Background,' Sexually Abused," *Behavior Today,* The Professionals' Newsletter, 11 (August 25, 1980): 1.
[10] Tsai and Wagner, "Therapy Groups for Women," p. 423.
[11] Judith Lewis Herman, with Lisa Hirschman, *Father-Daughter Incest* (Cambridge, MA: Harvard University Press, 1981), p. 104.

dren.[13] A general sense of isolation from others is often a complaint. Adult victims may be overly protective of their children, or they may report having difficulty in showing affection toward them. Occasionally, adult victims may resort to helplessness and infantile behavior in order to obtain affection from others. Sometimes the helplessness is not limited to seeking affection. It may become generalized to the point where a victim responds with helplessness to most situations in her daily life. Some women report feeling trapped in a relationship; others feel they have extraordinary sexual powers over men or destructive powers over both men and women.[14] Dreams or nightmares, especially of a sexual nature, provided clues in a few cases that clients had had incest experiences. In at least two cases, an exaggerated fear response to sexual harassment on the job was an additional sign of prior incestuous assault.

Although these indicators are useful in identifying adult victims of incest, they are not infallible. Nevertheless, even if a therapist is only mildly suspicious that a client has been a victim of incest, she or he should raise the issue with the woman. It is better to risk being wrong than to fail to identify what could be a major mental health problem for the client.

FRAME OF REFERENCE

In dealing with incest, a therapist should proceed from a special frame of reference if therapy is to be effective. It consists of certain basic precepts which serve to guide the therapist's actions and undergird the course of treatment.

First of all, incest must be desexualized. In most incest cases it should be seen as a form of child abuse. It is often the violator's only way of expressing a need for affection and love. Second, the therapist should believe the woman's account of the incestuous incident. Women have often made numerous attempts at sharing their secrets with others, only to find themselves disbelieved, discounted, or blamed. Third, revealing that the incest occurred should not be treated as a crisis, since the incident happened years before. Fourth, it is critical for the development of an effective process that the therapist respond to the disclosure with sensitivity and empathy. The fifth guideline is for the therapist to learn the necessary details of the incident, its duration and frequency, the client's age at the time, the identity of the violator, age at the time, the identity of the violator, whether the incest was disclosed or covert, consensual or non-consensual and the amount of force used.[15] Questions eliciting this information do not need to be answered all at once, since pacing is important. Finally, the therapist must be aware of and find outlets for her or his emotions because of the intensity of the client's emotions and the subject matter.

[12] Forward and Buck, *Betrayal of Innocence,* pp. 22–23.
[13] Courtois and Watts, "Counseling Adult Women," p. 276.
[14] Herman, *Father-Daughter Incest,* p. 98.
[15] Courtois and Watts, "Counseling Adult Women," pp. 276–77.

BEGINNINGS

As with anyone entering treatment, the incest victim contributes her own coping skills, personality, ego strengths, and defense mechanisms to the process. Concomitantly, she brings to the situation diverse levels of knowledge, understanding, and integration of the incest, ranging from complete denial to full acceptance. And, as mentioned previously, incest is often not the major reason for her decision to enter therapy.

Depression, self-destructive and self-defeating behavior and an inability to form meaningful relationships are likely to be the identified reason for entering therapy. A victim often denies any connection between these problems and the incestuous experience. One of the most frequent presenting complaints of a victim is a sense of being different and distant from ordinary people. This sense of isolation and inability to make contact may be expressed in many different ways. Victims often do not trust others. They fear that they are dangerously powerful and that others will judge them and not help protect them in times of great distress or be able to deal with their intense anger. Because of this, a therapist often experiences difficulty in forming a relationship with a victim, which then confirms the woman's own self-assessment. Given these circumstances, a therapist should begin working with a victim at whatever point she is regarding the incest and for whatever reasons she may presently be seeking treatment.

Many adult incest victims may have been previously involved in therapy, and the incest may or may not have been discussed or dealt with in any meaningful manner. Therefore, as an additional task in beginning work with a victim, any previous therapy needs to be explored in order to identify the depth to which the incest was worked through.

THERAPEUTIC GOALS

The first goal of treatment is for the therapist to establish a commitment with the client for involvement in the therapeutic process. A second goal is to identify old patterns by which the client flees from relationships. These patterns may surface again, because the victim has such a difficult time being vulnerable and trusting someone else, including the therapist. Thus, a key component of treatment is to engage the woman immediately in an active role in the therapy process. Third, the process of developing a mutual working relationship will aid the woman in becoming aware of her own internal strengths and skills and enable her to regain control while letting go of learned helplessness. Therapy with the incest victim cannot be complete until she is able to trust the therapist (and other significant persons) and give up the "victim behavior" in order to adopt a self-management approach to her life.

Fourth, the therapist must build the client's self-esteem about survival. This is accomplished by: (1) assuring the victim that she is a valuable person and has strength, which is evident in the fact that she has survived until this point; (2) alleviating shame about her experience; and (3) accepting and supporting the victim's intense feelings, especially her anger.

A fifth goal is the constructive expression of anger. The victim must be able to express her rage at the violator and those in a position of protector. This could be either or both parents, depending on who the violator was. Only after being able to express the anger appropriately toward those individuals will the victim be able to express her anger freely toward the therapist without fear of driving her/him away. The ability to do this in therapy will then enable the victim to express anger proportionate to a given situation rather than polluting it with past rage.

In regard to anger, it has been the authors' experience that incest victims fall somewhere between either being unable to externalize their anger—and thereby becoming more suicidal and self-mutilating, or inappropriately dumping their anger. Dumping commonly takes the form of verbal and physical abuse, often inflicted by people on individuals closest to them. Anger and rage require immediate attention. Setting limits and offering suggestions for the appropriate handling of anger during the therapy session give the victim permission to express anger in a safe environment. It allows her to test alternative methods of emotional expression, provides an outlet, and assures her that the therapist is not afraid of her anger and rage. The focus of therapy can then be directed to developing expression of these feelings in ways that will not be harmful to herself or others.

The sixth, and perhaps foremost, goal is to help the client identify and gain control over her self-destructive and self-defeating behavior. It is to be expected that discontinuing such behavior will take time and may not be accomplished until other therapeutic goals are reached. However, if self-destructive behavior such as suicide attempts, self-mutilation, uncontrollable rage, or substance abuse are present, they will need to be addressed immediately. If the behavior is life threatening, it becomes the number one priority in the therapeutic process. The victim needs to understand that treatment cannot proceed until the life threatening behavior is under control.

Networking with other support systems and developing other meaningful relationships is the seventh goal. In this regard, referrals to self-help groups such as Alcoholics Anonymous or Narcotics Anonymous can be a valuable adjunct to therapy. They can assist in addressing the self-destructive behavior, encourage interaction with others, foster the development of support systems, and help remove the myth that the victim is the only person experiencing such intense problems. More importantly, they can assist the woman in changing her self-perception from that of incest victim to incest survivor.

As the issue of anger becomes focused and balanced, the victim releases the rage and can begin to explore feelings of guilt, shame, and fear. It is open at this point that the victim is able to face the incest and unburden herself of the responsibility, placing it where it belongs, on the violator. With the release of guilt, attention can then be focused on the eighth goal—increasing her self-esteem through improving her body image and understanding human sexual response. Because the body has been used and abused, time must be spent on integrating it as a part of the total person. Aiding the client in knowing her body through exercise, diet, and self-pleasure is the beginning of the process in which she assumes responsibility for and regains control of her body. Education in sexuality and physiological response can assist her in relieving the guilt she may have because of past responses to sexual stimulation from the violator. As the woman accepts control over her body, issues such as sexual dysfunction, sexual preference, intimacy, and the separating of sex from affection and love can then become a therapeutic focus.

Throughout the therapy process, it is of vital importance to assist the woman in gaining the courage to reveal the incest, relieving her of the terrible secret often kept for years. It is essential to encourage her to work through painful experiences and the accompanying guilt and shame, so that conflicts can be revealed, understood, and resolved.

TECHNIQUES AND TOOLS

There are a variety of tools and techniques from which to choose in treating an adult victim of childhood incest. The selection process will no doubt, reflect the theoretical orientation of her therapist. However, two fundamental rules should be kept in mind: (1) the specific tool or technique should be modified to fit the particular needs of the client; and (2) the tools and techniques together should reflect a comprehensive approach which takes into account the cognitive, emotional, physical and social problems of the individual.

Tools

Two commonly used treatment tools are journal keeping and letter writing. A journal is useful to a client for keeping track of her thoughts and feelings between therapy sessions. It also provides an alternative medium of expression for those clients who have difficulty communicating orally. Depending on the needs of a client and the degree of comfort she has in disclosing painful material, all or part of the journal may or may not be shared with her therapist. Writing letters provides a client with an opportunity to convey on paper whatever it is she needs to express to the violator or other family members about the incest. Such letters are rarely mailed. But if a client does want to mail a letter, her therapist should carefully assess the ramifications. Sending this type of letter may be equivalent to stirring up a hornet's nest and may ultimately do much more harm than good.

Books and other reading materials which provide basic information on sexuality are helpful resources for a client, especially when she has little knowledge of how her body works and the ways in which it responds physiologically to sexual stimulation. The use of reading material that describes the experiences of other adult survivors is also helpful in reducing a client's feelings of loneliness and isolation. Such material is particularly useful when there are no available therapy groups or self-help groups directed toward the issue of incest.

Because of the problems of low self-esteem, lack of control, and distorted body image displayed by many of these clients, diet and exercise should be included in the treatment plan; they contribute to improving a client's self-image and restoring control over her body.

Techniques

Principles from cognitive therapy are useful in correcting the distortions in thinking commonly seen in incest victims. Techniques from gestalt therapy and psychodrama are particularly valuable for uncovering feelings, working with dreams, and integrating the incest experience. Viewing old photographs depicting family members and childhood events can jar a client's memory of the incest experience, especially when she has only vague recollections of the past. In some cases, old photographs can help make the incest experience less dreamlike and more real. Hypnosis may also be an alternative for uncovering repressed material related to the incest experience. A valuable adjunct to individual psychotherapy is the self-help group, which provides support and reduces an incest victim's isolation. Such groups may be particularly beneficial when her own social network is nonsupportive or nonexistent. Therapy groups designed for incest victims have similar advantages, with the added benefit of treatment.

CHOOSING MODE AND THERAPIST

The question of whether a woman should be referred for group or individual therapy or some combination of the two will depend, in part, on the availability of a suitable therapy group, as well as the particular needs of a client. Another question is whether the therapist should be a man or a woman. On the one hand, a male therapist might be more appropriate because the development of transference would be facilitated and a client would have an opportunity to experience a more positive relationship with a male—assuming that the violator was a male. On the other hand, a female therapist can serve as an important role model for a client, and it may be easier, at least initially, for a client to discuss the incest with another woman. In lieu of any research on the subject, the authors' admittedly biased preference is for a female therapist, primarily because of the role modeling she can provide, including the modeling of more appropriate seduction behaviors and displays of affection. This does not preclude the use of a male therapist. Rather, if a male therapist does work with a client, a female therapist should be involved in the treatment in some way, either as cotherapist or, if the individual therapist is male, as leader of a therapy group in which the client should also be enrolled.

THE CASE OF J

J is a twenty-five-year-old woman with a fifteen-year known history of psychiatric problems and numerous treatment interventions. She related a history of extensive childhood abuse but presented no acknowledgment of sexual abuse. She described herself as the child her mother never liked, the one who was in charge at home, since her mother was often unable to manage the responsibilities. In order to remove herself from the home, she attempted suicide, was hospitalized, and finally, at fifteen years of age, was placed in a group home. At this time she started drinking and using both prescribed and illegal drugs as a way of escaping the emotional pain she felt. She became involved in indiscriminate sexual encounters, but was unable to form any meaningful relationships.

At the time J entered treatment, her coping skills were no longer effective. She was unable to keep a job because of continuous substance abuse, and suicidal ideations and attempts which resulted in frequent hospitalizations. J had no positive relationships with males or females and continued her pattern of casual and superficial sexual relationships with men.

Initially, J was able to reveal extensive physical abuse by her mother. She described her mother as withdrawn and isolated from everyone except her own mother. She actively abused alcohol and drugs, had been married three times, and was involved in numerous relationships with men she met in bars. J described her father in an idealized manner. He was a military man and therefore gone from home often. J waited for him to come and rescue her from a very chaotic situation. When she was questioned about what in fact did happen, her memory was poor, revealing only that she was aware that her parents would drink to intoxication and fight, forcing her father to leave.

Eighteen months into the therapy process and while hospitalized, J was able, through hypnosis, to reveal the incest which started at eighteen months of age and continued with her biological father for four years. J was also able to recapitulate the incest involving her paternal grandfather.

Early therapeutic intervention was to establish a trusting relationship and actively diminish the self-destructive behavior. Because J found verbalizing her feelings extremely difficult, a variety of techniques—story writing, journal keeping, use of blackboard during therapy sessions, and role playing—were used to enhance communication between therapist and client. Another component of having J become an active participant in the therapy process was jointly to establish time-limited contractual agreements focusing on alternative methods of handling self-destructive feelings. After J became an active participant in the therapy process, she was able to become involved in Alcoholics Anonymous and start establishing accomplishable goals for herself.

J's first accomplishment was to gain some control over her drinking and drug abuse, at which time she was able to stop her indiscriminate sexual behavior. Doing this allowed her to experience repressed feelings of anger toward her mother. It was during this time that hypnosis was chosen as an assistive tool to uncover blocked memories of anger. The incest, over a period of time, was disclosed. Then she began the slow process of recapturing her memories, understanding and gaining knowledge about incest, and expressing anger appropriately.

The therapeutic process has had to be a balance of accomplishments: learning coping mechanisms for self-destructive and self-defeating feelings, gaining knowledge about body awareness and sexuality, and developing meaningful long-term relationships. The intensity one experienced as part of the process has lessened; however, the incest still surfaces as self-exploration continues. At those times the feelings of self-destruction and self-defeat return. The awareness of the incest has allowed J to understand the source of those feelings and has allowed her to control her behavior. She is now able to view herself as an incest survivor, no longer needing to continue the victim role. Interacting with and gaining support from other survivors has been extremely important to the therapy process. She will live with the knowledge that the incest occurred but she is aware that it no longer needs to control her life.

UNANSWERED QUESTIONS

Although an attempt has been made to address some of the clinical issues involved in the treatment of female adult victims of childhood incest, there is still much about such women that is not known. For example, is there more severe and long-term psychological damage to a woman if the incest resulted in pregnancy or an inability to have children? Because the incest experience poses no apparent problems for some women, what factors contribute to positive or negative coping responses? Can these factors help predict who will eventually require psychiatric intervention? Is short-term therapy appropriate for some clients? What about a woman who continues the incestuous relationship into adulthood? Although such cases may be rare, it would seem too simplistic to dismiss the victim as merely being severely disturbed. These and other issues await further research. But the task is made easier because of the increasing willingness of the victims to share their experiences. Let us not disappoint them.

ABUSE OF CHILDREN

CHAPTER 68

TREATMENT FOR ADULT MALE VICTIMS OF CHILDHOOD SEXUAL ABUSE

Debra F. Bruckner and Peter E. Johnson

Research over the past decade has verified that women who were sexually abused as children can experience residual trauma as adults. The long-term results of childhood sexual assault on women include poor self-concept, difficulties in sexual functioning, substance abuse, depression, suicidal tendencies, and eating disorders.[1] However, little research on this topic has been extended to adult men or even to male incest victims in general.[2]

The Badgley Commission on Sexual Offences Against Children and Adolescents established by the federal government of Canada reported that 50 percent of women and 33 percent of men are sexually victimized at some point in their lives. The majority (75 percent) of these assaults occurred to persons younger than seventeen years; one third of the assaults against females and one fourth of the assaults against males were considered to be serious offenses covered by the Canadian Criminal Code.[3]

Since 1982 the Calgary Sexual Assault Centre (CSAC) has experienced a major in-

Reprinted from *Social Casework,* Vol. 68, No. 2 (1987), pp. 81–87, by permission of the publisher, Families International, Inc.

[1] Joan Deighton and Phil McPeek, "Group Treatment: Adult Victims of Sexual Abuse," *Social Casework* 66 (September 1985): 403–10; Henry Giaretto, "A Comprehensive Child Sexual Abuse Treatment Program," *Child Abuse and Neglect* 6 (1, 1982): 263–78; Derek Jehu, Marjorie Gazan, and Carole Klassen, "A Treatment Program for Women Who Were Sexually Abused in Their Childhood" (Paper delivered at the Fifth International Congress on Sexual Abuse and Neglect, Montreal, Quebec, September 12, 1984); and Mavis Tsai and Nathaniel Wagner, "Therapy Groups for Women Sexually Molested as Children," *Archives of Sexual Behavior* 7 (September 1978): 417–27.

[2] Maria Nasjleti, "Suffering in Silence: The Male Incest Victim," *Child Welfare* 59 (May 1980): 269–75; and Carl M. Roger and Terry Tremaine, "Clinical Interventions with Boy Victims of Sexual Abuse," in *Victims of Sexual Aggression: Treatment of Children, Women, and Men,* ed. Irving R. Stuart and James G. Greer (New York: Van Nostrand Reinhold, 1984), pp. 91–104.

[3] Robin F. Badgley et al., *Sexual Offences in Canada: A Summary,* Report of the Committee on Sexual Offences Against Children and Youths (Ottawa, Ontario: Supply and Services, 1984), pp. 1–2.

crease in the number of adult males requesting assistance in dealing with their childhood sexual-abuse experiences. In the late 1970s, a similar demand by adult women who had been victimized as children led to the formation of a support-group program.[4] Because the support-group approach was quite effective with women victims, a pilot program consisting of two groups of male victims was implemented.[5] The present article describes this pilot program in an effort to create better understanding of male childhood victims. An attempt is made to contrast men's with women's support groups. Male incest survivors and the feasibility of group formats for treating this population should be further studied.

RATIONALE FOR GROUP TREATMENT

The men who approached the CSAC for counseling exhibited many common problems. These men found it difficult to deal with anger; had poor self-concept, flashbacks, sexuality problems; experienced depression; had problems with substance abuse; and had difficulty establishing and maintaining relationships.

The need to broaden the counseling experience of this population from one-on-one counseling to a group format was reinforced by coworkers at the Calgary Sexual Assault Centre. Male clients who were referred to the group had reached an impasse in their individual therapy. They continued to perceive sexual abuse as an experience unique to themselves. They viewed themselves as societal oddities, which in turn reinforced their guilt. Group counseling was initiated as an alternative and complementary approach to individual therapy.

A major reason for pursuing group treatment was the perceived and expressed isolation of male survivors. The literature has documented the reluctance of sexual-abuse survivors to disclose their experience and has noted feelings of self-blame and alienation.[6] Traditionally, the ideal man is viewed as being strong, silent and in control of his emotions. However, such gender scripts increase the alienation of male survivors of sexual abuse, who rarely disclose their experience to anyone, particularly another man. During individual counseling sessions, these men often expressed a lack of identification with their own gender and an unfulfilled desire for comradery and support. Consequently, further counseling with other male survivors was seen as a natural extension of individual therapy.

THE GROUP-COUNSELING APPROACH

The present article is based on our experience with two groups of sexual-abuse survivors—six men and five men respectively. Six sessions, lasting for two and one-half hours each were held on a weekly basis. All members completed a Tennessee Self-

---

[4] Peter E. Johnson, "Support Groups as a Method of Treatment for Residual Trauma Resulting from Childhood Sexual Abuse" (Master's thesis, University of Calgary, Alberta, 1979).

[5] Peter E. Johnson, Lee C. Handy, and Debra F. Bruckner, "Support Groups for Adult Women Who Were Victims of Child Sexual Abuse: A Continuation" (Unpublished paper, Calgary Sexual Assault Centre, Calgary, Alberta, 1986).

[6] Anne W. Burgess, Nicholas A. Groth, Lynda L. Holmstrom, and Suzanne Sgroi, *Sexual Assault of Children and Adolescents* (Lexington, Mass.: D.C. Heath, 1978); and Tsai and Wagner, "Therapy Groups."

Concept Scale prior to the first session and upon completion of session six.[7] Following termination, a debriefing meeting was held with individual participants and the leaders, which included discussion of the individual's goals, future counseling options, and self-concept scale results.

The goals of the group process were to reduce isolation, to improve levels of self-esteem through normalizing the group members' reactions, and to provide the opportunity to reevaluate their experience in the context of a supportive, safe environment.

All prospective members were interviewed in order to discuss the purpose and general format of the group and to ascertain whether the individual's social functioning and communication skills were at an appropriate level. No referrals were rejected. The groups were closed, so no new members were admitted after the first session. One member in one group terminated early.

A mixed-gender counseling team was used to alleviate anxiety that some group members may have felt. Group members were able to rehearse disclosure with both "threatening" and "safe" persons. Members were also able to experience acceptance from representatives of both sexes as well as be exposed to male–female interaction.

Based on earlier reports of women's group participants, a minority of women found it very difficult to disclose and reveal their feelings openly when a male facilitator was present. Many reported that they overcame this feeling and felt an increased sense of comfort with males as a result of the group experience. Before the group program for men was initiated, male survivors in individual counseling reported feeling anxious about disclosure in the presence of other males. We encountered no childhood victims, even those who had been assaulted by a woman, who expressed concerns about disclosure with a female counselor present.

CHARACTERISTICS OF SURVIVORS

All participants were in their twenties or early thirties; three men were unemployed—one due to a temporary physical disability. Two group members were students, and the remaining seven were white-collar professionals. Five members had children, and five had live-in relationships.

The majority of the participants were initially treated on an individual basis for residual trauma and were later referred to the group by the therapist. The number of individual counseling sessions varied from three to eight sessions. The three members who had not received individual counseling at the CSAC were referred by a mental-health professional within the community. Five of the eleven participants had been abused by a male family member—grandfather, stepfather, uncle, or older brother. Three men reported that they were sexually abused by their mothers. The abuse usually started at a very young age (six to ten years old) when a family member was involved. In nonfamily relationships, the child was usually older (eight to thirteen years old). In three cases, the abuse occurred "a few times"; in the majority of cases, however, the abuse lasted from three months to three years. Ongoing sexual abuse longer than three

[7] William H. Fitts, *Preliminary Manual, Tennessee Department of Mental Health Self-Concept Scale* (Nashville, Tenn.: Nashville Department of Health, 1955).

years occurred in one case. Five of the eleven group members reported that multiple offenders assaulted them; the other members were abused by a single offender.

Specifics regarding the actual sexually abusive behavior (for example, fondling on a weekly basis) are not reported here. As with female groups, the nature of the sexual behavior appeared to have little effect on the degree of the trauma experienced or therapeutic intervention required by individual clients.

Many of the group members had only recently disclosed the abuse for the first time. Disclosure often occurred with a CSAC counselor or a referring counselor. One member had first disclosed the abuse while under sodium pentothal and psychiatric care; he was subsequently referred to the Centre. The hesitancy to disclose and, initially, to participate in treatment was similar to that of women survivors of sexual abuse. Many of the participants were struggling with substance abuse, predominantly alcohol. Five participants acknowledged that they had problems in this area and that they had been actively treated at one time. Seven of the eleven participants had been physically abused in their families of origin by both sexually abusive and nonoffending significant adults. Three of the eleven survivors identified themselves as "gay," and six participants indicated that they had only heterosexual activities and interests as adults. The remaining two participants expressed mixed and confused feelings about their sexual orientation, though their activities were predominantly heterosexual.

SESSION THEMES

Group treatment focused on several themes arising from a combination of the stated individual goals of the members and the leader's previous experience with both women's groups and individual counseling. Although the major issues emerged in some form or another in each session, themes generally progressed in the following order: disclosure, dealing with feelings of anger, sexuality education, the victim as offender, and intimacy and trust. A sequential outline of session themes was not used, because we have found that, with both male and female groups, a flexible format that responds to the varying needs of the groups on a week-by-week basis is more effective.

Disclosure

The first session elicited specific details regarding the nature of the sexual molestation experience. The participants' feelings as a result of disclosure were discussed, as were previous disclosure experiences, both positive and negative. This discussion and resulting ventilation of feelings facilitated a high level of trust within the group. Confronting this difficult issue at the onset of the group sessions also reduced any residual anxiety with regard to revealing such a private and traumatic experience. Disclosure tended to be a continuing process wherein members added details and expanded upon their original descriptions. This openness resulted from an increased level of comfort in the group and better recall.

Anger

The second session focused on the childhood and adult repercussions of the molestation experience. Introductions to this and following sessions began with a review of feelings and concerns that had arisen since the previous meeting. It was anticipated that men would express more anger than women did. Even with this expectation, however, the leaders were surprised by the intensity of anger that was displayed. The anger focused on various issues, including family, the offender, the victim's sense of isolation, and his lack of power. The anger was manifested in fantasies about acts of retribution, concrete plans for taking such action, and in some cases, actual implementation of plans. The victims' intent was to "get back" at family members or to prove themselves. These discussions were particularly dynamic and included descriptions of actual physical assaults on the offender years after the sexual abuse had occurred. This content made the groups more volatile than was anticipated. One member who followed through on his fantasy of retribution wrote a letter to a penitentiary where his offender was incarcerated for an unrelated offense describing the offender's sexual habits with young boys. The intention was to identify the inmate as a "skinner" so that he would suffer abuse by fellow inmates. This incident alarmed the leaders, who consequently became more aware of the possible implications of group discussions.

Sex Education

As sessions progressed, the participants gradually changed the focus of discussion from childhood to early adult relationships and then to current concerns. The majority of participants expressed concerns about the impact of the early sexual abuse on later sexual behavior. To enhance discussion and to establish permission for such disclosure, all members were assigned readings from Bernie Zilbergeld and John Ullman's *Male Sexuality.*[8]

It became evident that many of the participants had avoided self-education regarding sexuality. This avoidance was attributed to the participants self-consciousness or insecurity about their own sexuality. As a result of the readings and being given permission to discuss these matters, numerous open and explicit discussions ensued. Members often remarked that they had never discussed personal sexual issues before and that they were exhilarated by the validation and confirmation of the experience.

Many of the participants reported what might be best described as a history of compensatory behavior. These behaviors tended to be manifested as either an avoidance of sexual activity or an attempt to prove one's worth and adequacy strictly through sexual activity. In the former, participants had either refrained from or experienced considerable guilt from any form of sexual behavior, and in the latter, participants had sex without intimacy and felt that they repeatedly, albeit unsuccessfully, used their partners to confirm their masculinity.

---

[8] Bernie Zilbergeld and John Ullman, *Male Sexuality: A Guide to Sexual Fulfillment* (Boston: Little, Brown, 1978).

Victims as Offenders

All group members evidenced concern about the possibility of other children being sexually abused. This concern was demonstrated by the participants' concern for the vulnerability of children, fear of their own behavior with children, and guilt for having had sexual experiences with children when they were adolescents. No participant indicated that he had sexually abused a child as an adult.

The concern for children and their vulnerability as assault victims was most evident in those who were parents or in a child-care role. Their overconcern may have led to extreme cognitive protectiveness and an avoidance of intimacy with children, possibly because they projected the victim's fear of becoming the perpetrator with others.

In a few cases, participants courageously revealed their own adolescent sexual activities with children. Despite their guilt and fear about relating these events, they disclosed, usually for the first time, their adoption of the aggressor role while they were adolescents. Although members appropriately condemned the act, they expressed compassion for the evident trauma and guilt that was experienced by the speaker. Disclosure of adolescent sexual behavior was a natural extension of the open dialogue about sexual issues. In order to comprehend the unacceptable behavior of some members, each participant sought corresponding examples in his own experience. Participants gained insight into their own needs and behaviors when they were forced to confront the victim/offender dichotomy within themselves, that is, when a fellow victim was suddenly perceived as an offender.

To some degree, all participants acknowledged that they exploited others to gain personal power. Members admitted to being sexually aggressive with adult partners, to physical assault of partners, and to general manipulation of relationships.

The group process helped normalize participants' fears with regard to sexual behavior with children. Concrete discussion of these issues reassured and relieved them that they were not sexual offenders. By not confronting these issues in their adult years, their fears had grown, unchecked by objective appraisal.

Intimacy and Trust

As in any group-therapy experience, intimacy and trust are major issues. The men in these two groups had little experience verbalizing their feelings; their discomfort was increased by the sensitive nature of the subject matter.

The men all described the traditional yet pervasive expectation that they should be strong, able to protect themselves, and in control of their emotions. Since being sexually abused may be viewed as a failure to physically and sexually defend one's self, the men questioned their independence and masculinity. Expressing one's feelings is difficult enough without having to admit to this perceived failure. Because most of the offenders were male, the men's already strong inhibition against disclosing sexual abuse was further complicated by gender myths and concern about sexual orientation. Moreover, the men were even more hesitant to disclose their feelings to other men. All participants stated that they felt more comfortable expressing their emotions to women than they did to men and that they generally avoided such intimacy with other men.

During the first group session, the men admitted that they did not trust the other members in the group. They indicated that they disclosed the details of their sexual abuse because doing so was a group requirement. Although disclosure created a level of intimacy in both groups and helped promote free and open discussion, certain boundaries were maintained. Intimacy did not extend to friendships or socializing outside group sessions.

All group members stated that they had difficulty with intimate relationships. The same issues that had inhibited disclosure also retarded the development of intimate relationships. Because their masculine identity had been threatened they attempted to create particular images of themselves within their relationships or avoided personal relationships. They considered sharing feelings and openness with others as evidence of their weakness and vulnerability. Thus the group environment allowed the men to see other men whom they respected express emotions and be vulnerable. Although one can only speculate on the impact of this experience on their personal lives, three of the men noted that they were more open and intimate with their partners and friends.

TECHNIQUES USED TO FACILITATE THE GROUP PROCESS

At first the group leaders tended to direct the group by establishing the focus of discussion and the need for disclosure. However, as the sessions progressed, members became more active and assertive and the group leaders less directive.

To facilitate disclosure and discussion, the members were asked in the third or fourth session to construct an image of their family and their position in the family by arranging rocks. Although the men were surprised and amused at first, they quickly and enthusiastically performed the task. The placement of rocks was then used to illustrate the roles of individual family members after which the focus moved to the abusive experience and how it affected participants' feelings toward family members. This technique facilitated vivid recollections of experiences, which in some cases had been forgotten. The result was an intense emotional outpouring and a positive cathartic effect.

Bibliotherapy was another technique that was used during group sessions. Our experience with individual counseling emphasized the importance of ensuring that these men had a common, basic understanding of male sexuality. Portions of the book *Male Sexuality* were required reading for all participants.[9] This text provided a good knowledge base that in turn reduced the discomfort of the men during discussions of sexual matters. Thus the men who had limited knowledge were not embarrassed by their lack of knowledge, and the group was given implicit permission to discuss personal sexual concerns.

The Tennessee Self-Concept Scale was administered prior to the first group session and at the conclusion of the last session. When the sessions terminated, each participant was seen individually by a co-facilitator and the results of the participant's pre and post test measures and recommendations for further action or counseling, if necessary, were discussed. The increases in the self-concept scale, which occurred in the majority of

---

[9] Ibid.

men, were often interpreted by the men as a "good report card." If only little gain was noted, the results were used to focus on directions for future development.

Group discussion often exposed many irrational notions and ideas. Sexual abuse is a sensational topic that carries many deeply entrenched myths. Although group members had many of the same myths as the rest of society, they were also burdened with feeling responsible for the assault and fear that the abuse guaranteed that they would either have sexual problems or become a sexual offender later in life. Those attitudes were dealt with by cognitive restructuring and by challenging the beliefs and self-statements of the members as well as their memories of the abuse.

CONCLUSIONS

From the two male groups that were observed, it was concluded that the counseling needs of men who were sexually abused as children are similar to those of their female counterparts. They need a forum where they can disclose their secret in order to be free of their isolation as victims.

The major differences between the men's and women's groups were in the ways that their traumas were expressed. The women tended to internalize their emotions, whereas the men were more outwardly aggressive. In contrast to the women, they displayed more anger than depression or guilt.

Another difference between the men's and women's groups was the manner in which disclosure occurred. Even though the men had less experience relating their abuse backgrounds than did the women and were just as reluctant as the women were to attend a group, the men were more matter-of-fact about disclosure than the women were. It was as if disclosure were part of their commitment to the group, which left no question about their participation or cooperation. Conversely the women delayed disclosure and increased their anxiety by anticipating the event. Even after the disclosure hold occurred, they continued to be anxious about the memory of disclosure.

The men were also more action-oriented than the women were and carried out their plans when they were made. For example, confrontation of the perpetrator or other family members with the facts of the assault was a common topic of discussion. One of the men mentioned that he wanted to talk to his mother, who lived on the other side of the country. Between sessions he traveled to his hometown and confronted her. It was common for female participants, on the other hand, to take eight weeks simply to construct a letter of confrontation without any intention of mailing it. However, one must not assume that a particular form of action is more helpful or desirable than the other is.

Men also showed a willingness, even a desire, to make their childhood abuse and its impact public. Although their initial dread of disclosure was similar to that of the women, the men were more eager to educate others. Perhaps the men were more accustomed than were women to assuming control of their lives. Because the childhood abuse had to some degree controlled their lives, the men now took assertive steps to reverse the dynamics of their situation and retake control of their lives.

The men tended not to associate with each other outside the group, whereas the female participants frequently formed relationships. Although the leaders had anticipated that men would be more reluctant than women to become involved in group activities, after an initial hesitancy the men were as easy to engage in such exercises as the women were.

RECOMMENDATIONS

The exploratory nature of the present article and the small sample size of the population points out the need for further research into the area of adult men who were molested as children and the benefits of the support-group process. Follow-up studies would ascertain the long-term impact of the support-group program. Many questions on the effect of the group experience on self-concept and relationships outside the group remain unanswered.

Therapists should pay special attention to anger management. The action orientation of the men should be monitored, particularly in relation to confrontation of offenders and significant others. Channels and strategies should be established for the expression of such feelings. Role play and imagery homework exercises might be valuable alternatives.

Sex education is important in these groups. Men require a certain level of information about sexual needs, myths, physical responses, and communication. After a knowledge base has been established, open and meaningful dialogue can occur.

Therapists should also experiment with structured, catharsis-producing exercises in order to facilitate deeper levels of disclosure and expression of feelings.

We found it difficult to choose the makeup of the co-facilitator team. From our work with women's support groups, we felt that two facilitators or a mixed-gender team would be more effective. Based on participants' reports, a minority of women's group participants found it very difficult to disclose and reveal their feelings openly with a male facilitator present. No male participants reported heightened discomfort with a female present. However, they expressed interest in the female therapist's reaction to discussion about current sexual behaviors. They seemed to need her acceptance and permission. Based on our work with male groups, we feel that a female co-facilitator helps reduce discomfort while allowing participants to practice disclosure with both sexes.

Traditional gender role scripts and expectations should be considered when working with male and female sexual-abuse survivors. To reduce the long-term trauma following abuse, mandatory reporting, sensitive intervention, and follow-up counseling are recommended for all cases of child sexual abuse. Attention should be focused on male survivors and the establishment of long-term counseling resources for adult survivors.

CHAPTER 69

STRUCTURED CONJOINT THERAPY FOR SPOUSE ABUSE CASES

John W. Taylor

The members of many abusive relationships wish to try to remain together and eliminate the abuse. If we accept this concept and the idea that such couples can be effectively treated, then conjoint therapy can become a logical and effective treatment scheme.

This article describes a conjoint treatment program for couples involved in domestic violence. The scheme is based on the learned aggression model of relationship violence. It demonstrates methods to interrupt the anger escalation sequence through identification of primary stresses, modification of aggressive communication patterns, and establishment of realistic role behavior expectations. Particular attention is given to the development of effective stress management, control through positive self-dialogue, and assertive positive expression of anger. The conjoint treatment scheme is meant for use with couples who wish to explore nonviolent interaction as an alternative to separation, but it does not advocate or require couples to remain together.

This conjoint treatment scheme has been used for the last three years by the author with fifty couples. The couples were all screened prior to admittance into conjoint treatment for alcoholism, drug abuse, child abusiveness, severe mental disorder, and severity of abuse. Only couples with mild to moderate level abuse by physical degree and frequency were considered appropriate and safe for conjoint treatment. The couples were followed up at the three-month and six-month post-treatment marks. The couples were 55 percent court referred and 45 percent voluntary referrals. The author worked on a three-month core program and experienced a 15 percent drop out rate before the twelfth session. Sixty-five percent of the couples reported no new violent incidents at

Reprinted from *Social Casework,* Vol. 65, No. 1 (1984), pp. 11–18, by permission of the publisher, Families International, Inc.

the six-month mark, and 50 percent of those reporting incidents voluntarily reentered treatment.

The learning theory of domestic violence proposes that the raw expression of anger and frustration is often the foundation for later violent marital interaction. The research of Albert Bandura and others shows strong correlation between witnessed aggression and the escalation of aggressive and violent behavior.[1] Learning theory further proposes the existence of reciprocal learning within the marital unit whereby the continued use of coercive and abusive interactions by one spouse stimulates the parallel growth of victim behavior and occasionally equally coercive and abusive responses on the part of the other spouse.[2]

The conjoint treatment approach described in this article advocates the replacement of abusive expression of anger within the relationship with positive expression of anger in the form of assertion and problem solving. The author believes negative learned expressions of anger—rather than the presence of the anger itself—are detrimental to the relationship.

FOUNDATION PRINCIPLES

This model of conjoint treatment of spouse abuse is based on a core of five fundamental concepts. The success of conjoint treatment of abuse rests upon the understanding and acceptance of these concepts by the couple.

1. Abusive anger expressions are learned behavior rather than personal or moral defects.[3] A therapist must establish and explain the learned nature of anger expression as opposed to the mental illness concept often held. Only as the abuser accepts this concept will he or she begin to claim responsibility for anger expressions. The author accomplishes this task by pointing out both the originating learned anger patterns in each individual's early life and the ongoing learned anger patterns in a couple's relationship. Since abusiveness is learned, it can be replaced with new constructive anger expressions. This concept at once reinforces the personal owning of anger patterns and at the same time creates a realistic hopefulness necessary for change.

2. Abusive behavior stems solely from the abuser but over time develops into an abusive system. Within this system, the abusing partner continues to learn and refine the abusive roles and behaviors; the other partner continues to learn the victim role which is similar to an exogenous depression.[4] This learned victimization results in certain affective, cognitive, and behavioral changes.[5]

---

[1] Albert Bandura, *Aggression: A Social Learning Analysis* (Englewood Cliffs, NJ: Prentice-Hall, 1973); Suzanne K. Steinmetz, "Violence Between Family Members," *Marriage and Family Review* 1 (March 1978): 1–16; Maria Roy, *Battered Women: A Psychological Study of Domestic Violence* (New York: Van Nostrand Reinhold, 1977).

[2] Gayla Margolin, "Conjoint Marital Therapy to Enhance Anger Management and Reduce Spouse Abuse," *American Journal of Family Therapy* 7 (May 1979), pp. 11–20.

[3] Suzanne K. Steinmetz, *The Cycle of Violence: Assertive, Aggressive and Abusive Family Interaction* (New York: Praeger, 1977).

[4] Richard J. Gelles, *The Violent Home: A Study of Physical Aggression Between Husbands and Wives* (Beverly Hills, CA: Sage Publications, 1972).

[5] Lenore L. Walker, "Battered Women and Helplessness," *Victimology* (February 1977): 525–34.

Both the lay public and many professionals tend to rigidly label the members of abusive relationships as abuser and victim. Such labeling accurately describes the abuse but, if presented in all-encompassing form, can increase aggressor and victim behavior by reinforcing the generalized cause and effect scheme that the abuser often uses as a justification for behavior. The victim can also be negatively affected by such labeling in that he or she may further sink into depression or become defensive of self, the abuser and the relationship. The author, therefore, presents to the abuser and the victim (if involved in treatment) the concept of the abuser's having an anger control disorder that is dangerous to both partners. The author additionally explains that a system of uncontrolled anger has developed within the relationship and that, while many parts of the relationship are no doubt healthy and good, the uncontrolled anger must be eliminated if the relationship is to endure.

The author makes use of anger inventories and careful study of the individual's anger patterns within and outside the relationship. Quite often, an escalation pattern emerges wherein one spouse is verbally abusive and the other is physically abusive.[6] Button-pushing patterns also tend to emerge, through which mutual feelings of frustration, pain, and resentment are increased within the marital system.

3. Abusive anger release is intensified by stress and by internal abusive self-dialogue.[7] A comprehensive approach to anger control must include an awareness by the abuser and the couple of their stress levels and the stress management techniques they employ. The primary internal anger intensifier and stressor is the abusive, combative set of self-statements that the abuser often employs in fight situations and the victim self-statements that the partner has learned.

For the purpose of awareness and effective change in stress management skills and self-talk script, the author uses a daily diary sheet which includes stressors, stress levels (0 to 10), anger levels (0 to 10), self-dialogue statements, and behavior expression categories. As the man and woman become aware of their patterns and the interrelationship of stress, anger, self-talk, and behavior, the author teaches general and specific counterinterventions. Through this process, the abuser and the couple are able to confront the chain reaction nature of abusive anger behavior and the need to modify behavior patterns outside the relationship, inside the relationship, and inside themselves.

4. Abusive behavior is related to and precipitates feelings of low self-esteem and powerlessness. Both the abuser and the victim often have personal histories exhibiting low self-esteem and corollary feelings of powerlessness, which can act as predisposing factors to anger expression disorders. As the couple continues abusive interaction, both members are subject to increasing feelings of powerlessness and lowered self-esteem, which create a stressful, depressive, highly negative atmosphere within the relationship. This negative aura is directly related to the likelihood of occurrence of abuse and to the intensity of the abuse.

---

[6] John N. Gottman, Howard Markham, and Carl Notarius, "The Topography of Marital Conflict: A Sequential Analysis of Verbal and Non Verbal Behavior," *Journal of Marriage and The Family* 39 (April 1977): 461–77.

[7] Raymond W. Novaco, *Anger Control: The Development and Evaluation of an Experimental Technique* (Lexington, MA: D.C. Heath, 1975).

Abusiveness is then often an attempt to overcome personal feelings of powerlessness that lead to lowered self-image, guilt, and increased feelings of powerlessness.[8]

The author uses this information to promote increased understanding by the couple of the dynamics of abuse and then to begin the process of changing the atmosphere of the relationship. Much of the resistance encountered in conjoint therapy with an abusive couple arises from the depressive and powerless feelings the man and woman have as individuals and as a couple. The author deals directly with this resistance by using their historical and current relationship patterns of powerlessness and negativity to focus the problem and to generate directions and methods of personal and relationship change.

5. Abusiveness arises from and is sustained and increased by inadequate problem solving. Abusive behavior can be seen as an extreme attempt to effect change within the relationship and often within the life patterns of the individuals.[9] It is essential that the couple learn new positive and effective problem-solving procedures for use inside and outside their relationship. Abusive and coercive behaviors are the primary source of the sadness and negativity within the relationship but are also stimulated by and paralleled by feelings of frustration, powerlessness, and depression arising from the couple's lack of positive, highly satisfying problem-solving experiences.[10]

SELECTION FOR CONJOINT TREATMENT

Believing that many different treatment modalities can be employed effectively with abusers, the author uses individual, group, and conjoint treatment modalities. The choice among these three formats is of extreme therapeutic and victim safety importance. The choice between individual or group treatment is given to the abuser with input from the author. The choice between conjoint treatment and abuser-only treatment is suggested by the author with final choice being given to the victim.

Initial screening of all court cases and voluntary cases should be considered as a crucial first step to effective and safe treatment. The author chooses to screen for alcohol abuse, drug abuse, child abuse, prior criminal record for assault, psychosis, and degree and frequency of abuse. Conjoint treatment should only be considered for mild to moderate abusers when the other before-mentioned screened factors are *not* present. The victim should make the final informed choice regarding conjoint treatment with the understanding that the abuser is the primary source of the anger problem and that only he or she has the responsibility and power to change.

The author does not exclude substance abusers, child abusers, severe abusers or criminal repeaters from treatment but rather treats these cases individually or in groups for a period of at least six months before considering conjoint treatment, regardless of

---

[8] John W. Taylor, "Theoretical Considerations for a Male Anxiety Crisis as a Cause of Episodic Family Violence," in *The Many Dimensions of Family Practice* (New York: Family Service Association of America, 1980).

[9] Neil S. Jacobson, "Problem Solving and Contingency Contracting in the Treatment of Marital Discord," *Journal of Consulting and Clinical Psychology* 45 (June 1977): 92–100.

[10] Neil S. Jacobson and Gayla Margolin, *Marital Therapy: Strategies Based on Social Learning and Behavior Principles* (New York: Brunner/Mazel, 1979).

the possible wishes for early conjoint treatment by the victim or the abuser. The author additionally requires substance abusers to be involved either simultaneously or beforehand in substance abuse treatment before admittance to treatment for abuse. The author similarly requires abusers seeking treatment who are either child abusers or psychotic to be in treatment simultaneously or beforehand for those disorders before admittance into anger control treatment.

So structured, the conjoint method of early intervention treatment for mild or moderate level abuse can be an additional effective tool for the therapist working with spouse abuse.

TREATMENT STAGES AND STRATEGIES

First Stage Treatment: The setting of ground rules for behavior within and outside the sessions is extremely important and cannot be assumed. Whether through faulty assumption or fear, many therapists are hesitant to clearly outline, verbally and in writing, their expectations for the couple's work within the therapy setting and the prohibition against further abuse. This should happen in the first session. The consequences of additional abuse should be clear and direct. With involuntary probation cases, the logical effective consequence is notification of the incident to the probation officer for appropriate action. With voluntary clients, the only effective consequence can be the termination of conjoint treatment. The author has found both of these consequences to be effective in setting the prohibition against further abuse. In thirty cases in the last two years, only twice has the author had to take such action.

In the second session, expectations for the couple's therapeutic efforts should be outlined both verbally and in writing. The weekly completion of the anger diary, "daily talk time," problem-solving procedures, and time-out controls, are among the most important expectations in conjoint treatment. The author, by employing such structure, is able to use the couple's compulsiveness and rigidity for positive change, rather than battling against these tendencies.

Second Stage Treatment: Each partner's expressions of stress and anger should be identified. The first step of treatment is stress and anger self-awareness. Each partner must become aware and begin to gain control of his or her own personal anger or stress escalation and expression patterns. This task is begun by and carried forward throughout the course of treatment by use of the anger/stress diary. The object of this stage is (1) to promote personal responsibility for anger and stress expressions; (2) to show the connection between stress build-up and volatile anger levels; (3) to point out and begin to change the mutual anger and frustration escalation behavior patterns between partners; and (4) to use rising anger and stress levels as warning signals by which one can control and redirect anger expressions.

This rational, emotive style of deprogramming the abuser and the couple regarding the nature of anger and anger expression is a priority for the first three sessions and must often be reemployed throughout the course of therapy.

Case Example

Alice and Richard had been married seven years at the time of their entrance into conjoint therapy. Both agreed that uncontrolled anger was their primary problem but disagreed greatly in their assessment of the frequency and intensity of the abuse. Both also tended to blame the other and to rationalize his or her own behavior.

The therapist, from previous case experience, recognized how often they fought about their fights and perceived that these secondary fights constituted a very grave danger both to treatment and to Alice's physical well-being. The therapist therefore directly confronted them with the circular pattern of their arguments. The confrontation began with the explanation of typical couple's anger patterns and the historical foundation of these patterns in the family origin of each of the adults in the relationship. Working first from the general, the therapist moved to a specific analysis of Alice and Richard's fight patterns and the habitual nature of these patterns.

In the course of the next two sessions, the nature of learned anger responses was slowly and thoroughly explained with the use of examples and simple but thorough written handouts. Alice and Richard were asked about their personal early anger experiences. Their personal histories were then tentatively associated with their current behavior. With the therapist's continued explanation, Alice and Richard began to see anger expression as a learned behavior rather than as a definition of personality; they also started to understand that being responsible for changing those learned patterns was different than arguing about the guilt. Only when Alice and Richard let go of the need to blame were they able to reach beyond the superficial categorizing of their anger problems and to deal with the more complex personal and interactional cause and effect that lay beneath their fights.

Third Stage Treatment: The objective is to develop a positive feedback system regarding anger recognition. Spouses, due to their intimate experience with one another, can help in "buddy system" fashion to aid in anger build-up awareness. Additionally, button pushing and misinterpretation of anger can *only* be corrected with couple feedback. Since the dominant mood within abusive relationships is highly negative and critical, the couple must be taught to use positive feedback rather than strife-increasing criticism.

The author first discusses the need for feedback in changing interactional patterns and then explains the difference between positive criticism and feedback and negative, destructive criticism. The author then outlines verbally the exact style of both verbal and nonverbal communication to be used. The couple is given written instructions regarding making complaints, criticisms, and awareness statements. These new verbal behaviors are then further reinforced with in-session role playing.

Fourth Stage Treatment: Negative interaction by both spouses in the form of button pushing, devaluing, and ignoring of anger warning cues must be worked on during the first five sessions. Only as the anger escalation cycle is interrupted can further work with communication and problem solving begin.[11] The author uses three mechanisms to identify buttons and negative reinforcers. Both spouses are asked to list their buttons and those of their spouses. These lists are then compared and discussed within the ses-

---

[11] Jacobson, "Problem Solving and Contingency Contracting Treatment of Marital Discord," pp. 92–100.

sion. The author, using canned arguments, has the couple use button pushing and road-blocking to gain further awareness. The couple is then asked to replay the scenes using responsive listening and "I" messages.

Negative reinforcement behavior such as devaluing and ignoring of anger build-up cues are approached in similar fashion, first with mutual identification and then role-playing exercises. Each spouse is given written material covering these behaviors and is asked to report on him- or herself in a "relationship communication" diary on a weekly basis.

Case Example

Jan and Peter, in their mid-thirties, had been married for twelve years. Jan, the more verbal of the two, had for years verbally pushed Peter in District Attorney fashion (Peter's strongest button) and failed to acknowledge his anger buildup signals of stuttering and physical shaking. With the aid of button identification exercises, Jan became aware of Peter's buttons and his anger build-up signals. She was then able to replace her negative cueing with positive acknowledgement of Peter's need for quiet communication and occasional distance.

Jan's efforts helped Peter to take greater responsibility for control of his anger by giving him a positive ally rather than an adversary. He was also able to reduce his need to avoid problem discussion and to eliminate his use of the "silent treatment," which pushed Jan's buttons and spawned feelings of devaluation and isolation for her.

In the case of Jan and Peter, their individual anger buttons were interrelated and were a key element in their anger escalation sequence.

Fifth Stage Treatment: The goal is to create positive control and expression through assertive communication. Anger is an extremely powerful and often effective means of exerting control. This control-through-anger sequence cannot simply be extinguished but must instead be replaced. The author begins the extinction/replacement process by teaching the couple to use a control balance sheet on which they compare power gains with the short- and long-range emotional, physical, marital, and legal costs of any given power strategy. Couples can quickly understand that anger and abuse are very high cost control strategies, so high as to eventually lead to the possible loss of the relationship.

Power and the need to exert control within a relationship are undeniable realities which must be channeled into positive and constructive behaviors. The author uses the control balance sheet to demonstrate the low cost, high gain potential of assertive communication, "I" messages, and logical consequence communication behavior. The man and woman are given extensive role-playing experience in the use of these communication behaviors. Once again, written material is provided to each member. Finally, practice in mutual positive reinforcement (not related to need agreement, which may or may not result from any given request communication) is given to the couple.

For many couples like Jan and Peter, the rational, logical replacement of anger as a control device was accomplished through role playing and practice. It became habitual as a result of the successful low cost of alternate communication devices and through the positive mutual reinforcement each gave the other. Both Jan and Peter began the process by learning to accept their need to exert control over each other and yet allow for independence. The therapist was able to help Peter to accept "no" answers from Jan by teaching him to use positive self-dialogue and reframing. With considerable role-playing practice and positive reinforcement, Peter was able to deal with a "no" response as a specific answer to a request rather than as a negative rejection of him, his role, or the relationship.

Sixth Stage Treatment: Now the objective is to teach strategies for interrupting and redirecting the anger cycle. The abuser can begin to control and redirect anger in direct proportion to his or her understanding of it as an emotion and its particular expression within the relationship. The author begins with a general explanation of human emotions and anger. Anger is presented as a normal—even positive—emotion when it is expressed in a constructive manner. The abuser is allowed to feel and express anger. He or she is taught how to discriminate between emotions for which anger is often inappropriately substituted and, when properly recognized, how to express it in a low cost, powerful, and constructive manner.

ANGER CYCLE INTERVENTIONS

First Level Interventions: The first type of intervention strategy that the author teaches is "space/time distancing." This control technique is quite easy to learn. It can be applied immediately and should remain indefinitely as a fail-safe mechanism in a couple's coping repertoire. Space/time distancing is expressed in three forms: physical time-out, problem/discussion shelving, and emotional/interaction time-out. Each member of the couple is responsible for monitoring his or her own stress/anger levels and for helping monitor the partner's levels. If either member of the couple feels his or her level is building or perceives that the partner is losing control, that person is responsible for tabling the discussion. If tabling does not work, then taking an announced time-out—either by giving emotional space, reducing interaction, or giving physical space by temporary physical distancing—is called for. After thorough explanation, the man and woman are given practice in the therapy session in the use of space/time distancing. They are asked to contract with one another for its use as a safety mechanism rather than as a "put-off" device or as a power play.

Second Level Interventions: The second level of intervention employed by the author consists of a self-recognition and self-monitoring system. This intervention strategy is meant first to heighten anger build-up awareness—and thus lead to early danger warning and protective distancing—and second, to function as a control mechanism in itself. Both members of the couple, building on an awareness of physical tension increase and "angry self-talk" are taught preventive and remedial deescalation procedures. The major preventive procedures include basic dietary balance, daily noncompetitive exercise, and task scheduling. The remedial interventions to be used when the couple find themselves enmeshed in the anger escalation cycle are "positive control self-talk," relaxation exercises, assertive "I" messages, time/space distancing, reframing, and depersonalization of stressors.[12]

---

[12] Navaco, *Anger Control.*

Case Example

Sharon and Bill, in their mid-twenties, had had a stormy three-year marriage, punctuated recently by abusive incidents. It was difficult for Bill to accept and effectively use time-outs. Bill considered Sharon's time-outs to be cop-outs and tended to call time-outs himself after having thrown the last verbal punch.

Rather than using hard confrontation, which often creates defensiveness, the therapist praised Bill's mastery of physical exercise and relaxation when time-outs were called. The therapist used the remaining thirty minutes of the session for Bill and Sharon to practice "active" time-outs. At the end of the session, both Sharon and Bill said active time-outs seemed less frustrating to them and more like a productive part of the solution.

Bill's business background and his conservative, classic male childhood contributed to his tendency to view time-outs as unproductive problem avoidance. The therapist was able to use Bill's strengths as a solution to the couple's time-out problem because of Bill's need for positive praise and active problem solving.

Third Level Interventions: The last set of anger-escalation-cycle interruption techniques used by the author are positive, nonaggressive, direct communications. The man and woman are taught to deal positively and effectively with road blocking by using the nonaggressive counterstrategies of acknowledgement, repetition, "I" statements, and solution-centeredness. When sending or receiving communications, they are taught to describe clearly and completely, to express their feelings, to emphasize the importance of the communication by stating the consequences in a nonthreatening manner.[13]

Seventh Stage Treatment. The goal is to teach successful solution-oriented problem-solving skills. The culmination of conjoint therapy is a nonviolent coexistence and a peaceful relationship that must contain efficient, positive problem solving. The author uses a simple four-step problem-solving scheme as a foundation: (1) prepare by recognizing problems in advance when possible, use positive self-talk to build and maintain control, relax, and begin to weigh alternatives; (2) confront the problem realistically, continue to stay calm, look for the positives, and stay solution-oriented; (3) deal with provocations and pressures, remember to check your body for tension buildup, stay relaxed, consider alternative solutions, maintain positive self-talk, and take a time-out or shelve the problem if necessary; (4) analyze and reward self-control, areas of agreement, and successful resolutions, and use only positive motivating criticisms when dealing with mistakes.[14]

On this four-step foundation, couples can build a structure of basic positive problem-solving skills. They are taught clear, direct problem statement; discussion time selection; responsive listening; staying on the subject; compromise development; brainstorming; problem dissection; shelving; the use of trial periods; and rewarding.

[13] Jacobson and Margolin, *Marital Therapy.*
[14] Navaco, *Anger Control.*

Case Example

For most angry couples in conjoint therapy, positive solving is the most difficult but often the most exciting section of therapy. Ray and Janice, married twenty years, were able to break their long-term disruptive problem-solving habits by using a tape recorder to monitor themselves. They, like many of the other couples with whom the therapist has worked, discovered that many of their long-term problems stemmed from the continual proffering of vested interest solutions. Once Janice and Ray let loose of their pat solutions and allowed themselves to use creative solutions, they were able to find answers for many of their longstanding problems.

They were able to let loose of their vested interest solutions when they were shown the emotional, physical, and material costs of maintaining their problems. They learned to ask themselves three questions: What will happen to us if we solve the problem? How much does this problem cost to maintain? What are the other possible solutions? Ray and Janice had little difficulty scheduling, sticking to one issue, or even dividing the labor once they learned that a solution was not only less costly but also more practical than "the solution" each had formerly been fighting for.

Eighth Stage Treatment: The final treatment strategy embodies the author's philosophy regarding successful conjoint treatment of abusive couples: the development and nurturing of a positive high quality of relationship feeling. The goal toward which couples strive and the major sustaining force in nonviolent living is the improved quality of their lives together. The successful implementation of this strategy begins and ends with a relentless emphasis on mutual positive reinforcement, positive "talk time," positive intimate interaction, positive individual and couple socialization, and positive goal setting.[15]

An integral part of this change in attitude is a pragmatic testing of values, beliefs, opinions, and sexual stereotypes, and a controlling of jealousy. To this end, the author guides the man and woman through an analysis of their belief systems, with special attention to their relationship and role expectations. They use a four-point test system to evaluate their expectation system: time, logic, reality, and cost. Creating flexibility in the couple allows each member to hold his or her core beliefs but to compromise, update, or modify lesser beliefs and resulting expectations. The reduction in rigidity that can come from flexibility within oneself and toward one's partner creates a positive atmosphere of acceptance without control and compliance based upon desire rather than demand.

Jealousy can be found in both realistic and unrealistic or pathological forms in many relationships. Many abusive couples are frequently drawn into disruptive anger situations as a result of both types of jealousy.[16] The author teaches such couples to reality test their jealousy and either to problem-solve "real" jealousy issues or to deal with the power and insecurity issues that underlie most "unrealistic" jealousy issues.

---

[15] Albert Ellis, "Technique of Handling Anger in Marriage," *Journal of Marriage and Family Counseling* (October 1976): 305–15.

[16] Barbara Star, "Psychological Aspects of Wife Battering" (Paper presented at the American Orthopsychiatry Association Annual Meeting, San Francisco, CA, October, 1978).

Case Example

Louis and Anne, married eleven years, were able to master the skills of anger control and problem solving with relative ease. However, they were still experiencing a "gloominess," in Anne's words, at the time of the eleventh session. During the course of the next two sessions, in which goals, expectations, and roles were discussed, Louis began to speak of their "habit of gloominess." Louis and Anne had, as an abusive, argumentative couple, become accustomed to feeling unhappy and gloomy and had in fact "walked through" the numerous positive interaction exercises of the previous weeks without becoming involved. Both began to realize that without a change in the climate of their relationship, habit, boredom, or frustration would ultimately pull them back into their abusive pattern. For Anne and Louis, the most difficult task was changing the abusive atmosphere rather than their individual abusive behavior.

Once Louis and Anne acknowledged their habit of gloominess, the therapist engaged them in a relationship enrichment contract. This contract, drawn from Masters and Johnson's pleasuring contracts, required that Louis and Anne plan and execute a weekend away from their home. The weekend was meant to be a new beginning in that the primary goal was to be positive—positive in their communication, their activities, their affection, and their responses. The therapist added to this contract a rating system for Louis and Anne to use for themselves, each other, and the weekend. In this system, partial success in any of the categories was to be considered good; successful actions taking place in more than one category were to be considered exceptional; predominating success in any category was to be considered superior; and predominating success in more than one category to be excellent.

Louis and Anne quickly realized that they literally could not fail unless they attempted consciously to fail. They therefore were both free to and motivated to succeed. Their exceptional rating for themselves and the weekend did in fact comprise a new beginning for Louis and Anne. The increase in positive interaction that they achieved was, as it is for most abusive couples, the key to both sustained peaceful interaction and balance for normal disagreement.

FIVE TARGETS

The author's use of conjoint treatment of spouse abuse is based upon five theoretic assumptions: (1) that abusive behavior is learned behavior; (2) that a violent relationship becomes a violent system; (3) that the abuser role and the victim role are not all-encompassing roles but do grow in power and intensity over time; (4) that stress and anger are closely interrelated within violent systems and that such stress/anger cycles can be interrupted; and (5) that abusive systems create and are sustained by negative interactions and attitudes.

The author targets five major areas in the course of conjoint treatment; (1) stress and anger management; (2) positive expression of anger through assertion; (3) problem solving; (4) positive interaction and relationship climate; and, (5) values, expectations, and jealousy. Control and development of the couple's system are thus a function of anger awareness and control, improved communication and problem solving, and the the development of positive pleasurable feelings and less restrictive expectations.

CHAPTER 70

GROUP INTERVENTION STRATEGIES WITH DOMESTIC ABUSERS

Caroline E. Sakai

Spousal abuse is a national problem (Finn, 1985; Gondolf, 1985), as is abuse among couples living together (Bern & Bern, 1984) and in other domestic relationships. In this article, the term "domestic abusers" will be used to reflect this broad range of relationships.

Eisikovits and Edleson (1989) pointed out the need to address the interaction of multiple variables, ranging from the individual to the societal level, involved in domestic abuse. The prevailing treatment approaches for domestic abusers include feminist, cognitive-behavioral, family systems, and integrative approaches (Caesar & Hamberger, 1989). Particular approaches appear to be more germane and effective at different stages of treatment. Initially, the violence must be stopped through coordinated and integrated community service responses that hold abusers accountable and responsible for their violence. The appearance of collusion (Pence, 1989) or the insinuation of tolerance must be avoided. Anger-management interventions, which are predominantly behavioral and cognitive-behavioral approaches, provide abusers with skills to counter their self-escalating negative arousal processes as well as with positive alternative strategies for coping with stress and anger (Novaco, 1978, 1985; Ellis, 1977; Goldstein & Rosenbaum, 1982; Saunders, 1989; Saunders & Hanusa, 1986; Sonkin & Durphy, 1989). Feminist approaches challenge gender-based assumptions regarding rights of dominance and raise abusers' and victims' awareness of oppression and hierarchical control. Dobash and Dobash (1979) discussed domestic abusers' need to control challenges to their authority or to deter future challenges or failures to meet their expectations. These underlying presumptions need to be reversed before communication skills and assertiveness training can be initiated. If these preliminary issues are not resolved, skills can be misused for more sophisticated psychological control and abuse. Marital

Reprinted from *Families in Society,* vol. 72, No. 9 (November, 1991), pp. 536–542, by permission of the publisher, Families International, Inc.

and family counseling is beneficial after couples have made a genuine commitment to nonviolence, anger management has been adequately demonstrated, and attitudes regarding power and control have been positively changed. Positive changes in power and control attitudes are reflected in one's taking responsibility for his or her own behaviors, awareness of non-win cycles in controlling behavior patterns, and desire to foster a sense of mutual benefit and satisfaction. Premature conjoint therapy may result in collusion with the couple's denial of the seriousness of the problem of violence.

The Developing Options to Violence program at Child and Family Service, Honolulu, Hawaii, follows such a sequentially integrative approach. Initially, domestic abusers are assessed individually. They must agree to agency contacts with their partners and commit themselves to terminating their violent behavior. As Sonkin, Martin, and Walker (1985) noted, telephone contacts with the victims of abuse are critical in determining whether further offenses have been committed and whether the abusers are progressing in behavioral changes. Those in need of other services, such as substance abuse treatment or psychiatric interventions, are referred to those services.

The domestic abusers then undergo a four-week orientation that focuses heavily on violence prevention, with emphasis on "time outs" and other physiological arousal dampeners and anger-management alternatives. Physiological–behavioral–cognitive approaches are also included for abusers who are more kinesthetically driven, with greater focus on early awareness of physical cues of tension and anger, together with alternative behavioral strategies. Arousal and/or anger-control training and monitoring through arousal/anger logs, self-reports, and periodic partner telephone contacts continues into the next segment of 18 sessions.

Treatment groups consist generally of 12 to 18 men with two co-therapists (either male-female team or two males). Whereas the more experienced therapists appear to be comfortable in covering all critical areas using a semi-structured approach, less experienced therapists work better within a structured format.

Treatment groups challenge the rights of dominance, power, and control with the help of Pence and Paymar's (1986) curriculum, which begins with an ecological perspective. Carlson (1984) developed an ecological analysis of the causes and maintenance of domestic violence that serves as a helpful framework at this juncture. Pence and Paymar's curriculum utilizes video vignettes of different control tactics to deepen participants' awareness and to open group discussions.

Cognitive–behavioral approaches predominate in the latter segments. Progress is assessed through partner reports, self-reports, pre- and posttest assessments, as well as direct observations of role play and attitudes elicited in group discussions. For those who successfully complete the group program with external indications of progress and whose partners are interested in marital and/or family counseling, referrals are made to the family counseling unit of Child and Family Service. The present article focuses on specific intervention strategies that have been found helpful in group treatment.

GROUP TREATMENT

In treating domestic abusers, group interventions seem to work more effectively than does individual counseling (Scher & Stevens, 1987). Group work reduces participants' sense of isolation and provides an atmosphere that facilitates sharing of inner secrets with persons who can relate to and understand them. Also, because the primary goal is to change the abusers' attitude, peer acceptance, support, and validation of changing attitudes are crucial to the treatment process.

Pence and Paymar (1986) noted that abusive men in treatment groups often talk about their violence as a response to being victimized themselves. The men see themselves as victims of a violent childhood, of a society that makes them hide their feelings, of a culture that tells them to be in control, and of women who "won't make it all better." Many men who have been victims in the past now feel victimized by their partners when, in fact, they are victimizing their partners. Before these men can stop being the victimizers, they must change their views of their relationships. The paradigm that follows helps domestic abusers clarify their need for control and power in their relationships and the negative consequences of such attitudes. More positive and satisfying alternatives are offered.

POWER AND CONTROL CYCLES

A cognitive history of the victim–victimizer polarity can be seen in Ellis's (1977) irrational anger thought generation: (1) How terrible for you to have treated me so unfairly, (2) I can't stand you treating me in such an irresponsible and unjust manner, (3) You should not and must not behave that way toward me, (4) Because you have acted in that manner toward me, I find you a terrible person who deserves nothing good in life and who should be punished for treating me this way. The use of anger as a weapon and justification in the power and control process is apparent in this schema.

Pence and Paymar's (1986) educational curriculum provides a powerful methodology to help domestic abusers understand their behaviors as a means to get or keep what they want, allowing the abuser to explore the connection between his values/beliefs and behaviors. The power and control cycles depicted in Figure 70–1 expand Pence's power and control wheel, allowing therapists to delineate the chain of reactions created by domestic abuse and clarifying how victimization operates and is maintained.

The power and control cycles (paper fasteners are used for each of the wheels) begins with Pence's power and control wheel—the first large wheel. Control tactics include male privilege, emotional abuse, sexual abuse, economic abuse, intimidation, threats, use of children as messengers or pawns for obtaining power and control, and isolation; such tactics are reinforced by physical abuse or the potential of it. These control patterns are fostered and reinforced historically by the cultural, social, and political structures of the larger community, which are represented by the outer ring of the wheel.

As seen in Figure 70–1, the power and control wheel may generate movement in the fear of change wheel, which describes coping with survival behavior patterns in women. Such behaviors include denial of the seriousness of the abusive situations and their consequences; rationalization that extenuating circumstances or precipitating stressors are responsible; self-blaming wherein the abusers' problems are excused and their responsibility absorbed; detachment in terms of emotional distancing and numbing; wariness with regard to hypervigilance and constant defensiveness; clinging in terms of increased dependency, insecurity, and uncertainty and need for reassurance and support; outward compliance to keep the peace; and depression ranging from lethargy and despair to suicidal thoughts or episodes.

Figure 70–1
Power and control cycles.

The power and control wheel may activate the fear and resentment wheel, which also brings out survival issues in victims. Survival tactics include nagging, bargaining, physical avoidance, withdrawal, emotional outbursts, anger outbursts, seeking outside support, and seeking legal protection.

The fear and resentment wheel in turn sets off the fear of loss wheel, wherein the domestic abusers shift tactics to maintain control. This is depicted as the second large wheel. When physical abuse is avoided, emotional abuse, threats, intimidation, and other nonphysical means of control escalate. Prior physical abuse or sexual abuse serves as a threat of potential recurrence, which in itself is intimidating. Hanging-onto-control tactics include the abusers' denial of controlling, abusive behaviors and minimization of the women's suffering; rationalization that the abusers themselves are being victimized, that the victim is provoking them, and that their behaviors are justified or expected of them; blaming the victim for being unreasonable, intolerable, provocative, wrong, bad, worthless, incompetent, dependent, or incessant nags; intimidation by means of rage, shouting, pounding, punching, throwing objects, or menacing looks; emotional abuse by means of put-downs, name calling, mind games, and demeaning and demoralizing verbal attacks; threats to harm or destroy the women or what they treasure or threats to take the children or commit suicide; economic control by withholding financial support, interfering with efforts by the women to become more financially independent, creating economic crises; using children to stir up feelings of guilt, to relay messages, to harass the partner in order to regain control and domination; feeling sorry for oneself with "poor me" looks, behaviors, and stories that play on the sympathies of the partner or influence others who may join them; depression ranging from feeling low to suicidal expressions.

These wheels depict the futile and destructive cycles generated by power and control tactics. Alternative patterns of interaction and behavior need to be engendered by exploring the negative consequences upon the abusers, their partners, and families. To change controlling behavior, the abuser must first take responsibility for his behavior and acknowledge his past and present controlling behavior patterns.

STORYTELLING

Denial, minimization, and blaming are typical defensive postures of domestic abusers. An effective method to move through defensiveness is to tell a story that the abuser can relate to without stimulating his defensiveness. Most domestic abusers have experienced or witnessed abuse as children (Roy, 1982; Hotaling & Sugarman, 1986). Issues of unresolved anger, identification with the aggressor of his youth, and other patterns need to be elicited and resolved before the generational cycle of abuse can be halted. A story about conflict between two brothers has proved effective in bridging abusers' adult perspectives with their own experiences as children. Group participants are instructed to imagine themselves as the father of the two boys.

> Fifteen-year-old Brah a muscular athletic teenager, becomes regularly irritated with the bratty behavior of his pesky five-year-old brother Gigo. On one occasion Brah broke Gigo's arm in a confrontation. Gigo persistently pleads with Brah, who has just returned home from football practice, to play ball with him, as Brah

had promised earlier. Brah threatens, intimidates, and calls Gigo names. As the threats escalate, Brah makes a menacing gesture, which reminds Gigo of the time Brah broke his arm. The father of the boys walks into the room at this moment.

At this point, the group leader asks participants to give their opinion of the situation from the perspective of the father. Participants invariably point out the unfairness of the situation because of the size and strength differential between Brah and Gigo. Although Gigo is being a pest, Brah has no right to use physical force. Participants feel that as fathers they would intervene to ensure that the smaller child was not hurt. They state that they would try to help the boys work out their disagreements in more constructive ways. They discuss the fact that neither boy can always have his way and would need to learn this lesson.

After a lively discussion the group leader shifts the discussion to the parallels between Brah and Gigo and the abuser and the victim. The men usually conclude that the police or courts act as father figures in protecting victims. They acknowledge the strength differential between men and women and recognize the parallels between Brah and Gigo and themselves and their partners.

This activity provides an effective way to allay denial, minimization, and blaming. Participants find it less threatening to focus on the story, after which the group leader can help participants address power and control issues as illustrated in the power and control cycles. The two brothers are brought back in later sessions when issues surrounding acknowledgment of past violence and the question of safety are dealt with.

In the follow-up story, Brah and Gigo's parents have been invited to an important wedding and they don't have a sitter for the boys. The parents wonder whether it is safe to leave Brah and Gigo home alone. In the first scenario, Brah brushes off his father's concerns by saying he doesn't want to hear about the past, whereby participants express alarm about Gigo's safety. In considering what would assure them of Gigo's safety, they generally state that they would feel more comfortable if Brah fully acknowledged his behavior by discussing this issue with Gigo and his parents and by ensuring them that violence would not occur again. Participants generally feel that leaving the boys alone for short trial periods and with the parents readily available would be beneficial. Participants often mention that Brah's increased self-control might be indicated by his dealing nonviolently with Gigo's persistent pestering behaviors. Discussions focus on acknowledgment of the consequences of past violence, forgiving oneself, and moving past shame and guilt to responsibility, change, and growth. Participants are encouraged to get in touch with their potential for violence and to redefine their images of masculinity and femininity (see Scher & Stevens, 1987). This journey involves recognizing their hurt, reframing their anger, learning new behavior patterns, realizing the cost and impact of their anger on others, releasing their need to dominate and control, and forgiving themselves and others. Participants need to accept and respect the decisions of their partners, who may not be interested in reconciliation.

CHANGING PARENTING STYLES

The parenting perspective is used to shift partners to facilitate healthier parenting of their children or prospective children and reparenting themselves. Weisinger (1985) notes that the most intense and damaging conflicts between parents and children center on the parents' need to control their child and the child's need to achieve a measure of independence without losing parental support. Parents' primary responsibility is to raise their children to become independent adults. However, as children become more independent, parents may feel angry, hurt, and depressed. Parents, in turn, may exert increased control over their children, which creates resentment and damages the self-esteem of children. Ironically, parents may then feel angry and frustrated at their childrens' incompetence, which creates even more resentment in the children. A typical interaction might progress as follows:

> Parent: "You're making a mistake. Listen to me and learn from what I've been through." Child: "Don't tell me what to do." Parent: "Well, do what you want, but don't come crying to me later."

The more the children resist, the more these parents attempt to control them either directly or indirectly by withdrawing love and support.

In group work, the participants are encouraged to remember what it was like when they were children. If their parents attempted to dominate and control them, they may begin to relate to their own children's feelings of rebellion and insecurity. Moreover, they may begin to empathize with their partner's experience of being controlled and dominated. The participants may see how they put themselves in parental roles in relation to their partners by withholding approval, especially in conjunction with routine verbal and physical punishment. Adams (1989) noted that by focusing all of their attention on anger and disapproval, domestic abusers validate or invalidate the partner and maintain the authority to give or retrieve permission for the partner's actions.

ACKNOWLEDGING ABUSIVE BEHAVIOR

A major barrier to acknowledging past abusive behavior is fear of losing the partner. Abusers often try to prevent the partner from leaving by becoming even more controlling, which is the primary reason the abused partner wants to leave. The domestic abuser needs to understand that when most people say that they are feeling angry, they do not mean something else. Abusers need to learn to listen to anger without reacting angrily and defensively.

Having participants complete the sentence "When you tell me you are angry at me, you really mean _____" is a useful way to facilitate discussion about how abusers think and how they anticipate what another person means when she says, "I'm angry." Another exercise that facilitates self-awareness is completing the sentence "When someone says something critical or negative to me, I feel _____." This exercise is particularly helpful in work with abusers who blame their partner for their own negative feelings. Challenging participants cognitively and reframing their responses helps to clarify for the group negative thought patterns, anger arousal, rationalization of that anger, and ensuing controlling behaviors. Asking an abuser to role play a conflict by moving from one chair to another chair while expressing the feelings and reactions of both the abuser and the victim until a resolution to the conflict is attained can help participants become more deeply aware of the feelings and needs of others. This exercise can also be role played with another group member.

Abusers are encouraged to work on the types of situations that tend to set them off. Role play, with pauses to process and practice alternative coping behaviors, is helpful. This exercise also helps create a bridge between the group process and the outside world. Group members who are not involved directly in the role play benefit vicariously by moving through the situations according to their own reactions, sensations, cognitions, and coping strategies. Experiences and insights can be shared with the group. The exercise also allows participants to incorporate their own personality and behavioral style into coping strategies.

As the men listen to one another's anger, disagreeing with and confronting one another and group facilitators, they learn that they can accept another person's anger when it is expressed in a respectful manner without controlling and dominating behaviors. They learn that when people are not fearful or resentful, problems can be solved creatively and effectively. Changing their attitude, perspective, and frame of reference in turn changes their experience and expression of anger.

NEW PERSPECTIVES

Relationships based on love and respect are reinforced and solidified by trust and positive communication, as is illustrated in the perimeter of the wheel in Figure 70–2. To

Figure 70–2
Love and respect wheel.

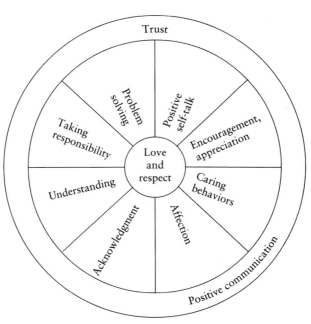

support this wheel, spokes are needed: positive self-talk, encouragement and appreciation, caring behaviors (Stuart, 1980), affection, acknowledgment of past mistakes, understanding, taking responsibility, and problem solving.

Stuart's (1980) model divides decision-making authority into decisions that might be made separately by each spouse, those that might be made by each spouse after consultation with the partner, and those that require joint efforts. Participants are receptive to the idea that the person who is responsible for carrying out the actions of a particular decision should have more weight in the decision-making process. They are also receptive to the notion that in certain situations in which a decision does not affect the partner, decisions can be made independently.

Many domestic abusers must accept and deal with their partners' leaving them permanently. Abusers must understand that their primary goal is to change themselves, regardless whether their partner leaves or stays. As abusers initiate and sustain new behaviors, they begin to see the wide-ranging impact and implications of their behavior on all of their relationships—family, friends, work, and community.

REFERENCES

Adams, D. (1989). Feminist-based interventions for battering men. In P. L. Caesar & L. K. Hamberger (Eds.), *Treating men who batter: Theory, practice, and programs.* New York: Springer Publishing.

Bern, E. H., & Bern, L. L. (1984). A group program for men who commit violence towards their wives. *Social Work with Groups, 7*(1), 63–77.

Caesar, P. L., & Hamberger, L. K. (1989). *Treating men who batter: Theory, practice, and programs.* New York: Springer Publishing.

Carlson, B. E. (1984). Causes and maintenance of domestic violence: An ecological analysis. *Social Service Review, 58,* 569–587.

Dobash, R., & Dobash, R. (1979). *Violence against wives.* New York: Free Press.

Edleson, J. L. (1984). Working with men who batter. *Social Work, 29,* 237–242.

Eisikovits, Z. C., & Edleson, J. L. (1989). Intervening with men who batter: A critical review of the literature. *Social Service Reviews 63,* 384–414.

Ellis, A. (1977). *Anger: How to live with and without it.* Secaucus, NJ: Citadel Press.

Finn, J. (1985) Men's domestic violence treatment groups: A statewide survey. *Social Work with Groups, 8*(3), 81–94.

Goldstein, A. P., & Rosenbaum, A. (1982). *Aggress less: How to turn anger and aggression into positive action.* Englewood Cliffs, NJ: Prentice-Hall.

Gondolf, E. W. (1985). Fighting for control: A clinical assessment of men who batter. *Social Casework, 66,* 48–54.

Hotaling, G. T., & Sugarman, D. B. (1986). An analysis of risk markers in husband to wife violence: The current state of knowledge. *Violence and Victims, 1,* 101–124.

Novaco, R. W. (1978). Anger and coping with stress: Cognitive behavior interventions. In J. P. Foreyt & D. P. Rathjen (Eds.), *Cognitive behavior therapy: Research and applications.* New York: Plenum Press.

Novaco, R. W. (1985). Anger and its therapeutic regulation. In M. A. Chesney & R. H. Rosenman (Eds.), *Anger and hostility in cardiovascular and behavior disorders.* New York: Hemisphere Publishing.

Pence, E. (1989). Batterer programs: Shifting from community collusion to community confrontation. In P. L. Caesar & L. K. Hamberger (Eds.), *Treating men who batter: Theory, practice, and programs.* New York: Springer Publishing.

Pence, E., & Paymar, M. (1986). *Power and control: Tactics of men who batter.* Duluth, MN: Minnesota Program Development, Inc.

Roy, M. (1982). *The abusive partner.* New York: Van Nostrand Reinhold.

Saunders, D. G. (1989). Cognitive and behavioral interventions with men who batter: Application and outcome. In P. L. Caesar & L. K. Hamberger (Eds.), *Treating men who batter: Theory, practice, and programs.* New York: Springer Publishing.

Saunders, D. G., & Hanusa, D. (1986). Cognitive-behavioral treatment of men who batter: The short-term effects of group therapy. *Journal of Family Violence, 1,* 357–372.

Scher, M., & Stevens, M. (1987). Men and violence. *Journal of Counseling and Development, 65,* 351–355.

Sonkin, D. J., & Durphy, M. (1989). *Learning to live without violence: A handbook for men.* Volcano, CA: Volcano Press.

Sonkin, D. J. Martin, D., & Walker, L. E. A. (1985). *The male batterer: A treatment approach.* New York: Springer Publishing.

Stuart, R. B. (1980). *Helping couples change.* New York: Guilford Press.

Weisinger, H. (1985). *Dr. Weisinger's anger work-out book.* New York: Quill.

ABUSE OF WOMEN

CHAPTER 71

WORKING WITH MEN WHO BATTER

Jeffrey L. Edleson

T he number of women who are beaten by their spouses each year has been estimated to be 1.8 million. In addition, an extreme form of domestic violence, a spouse killing a spouse, accounts for 15 to 25 percent of all homicides committed in the United States.[1]

In response to this situation, a network of battered women's shelters has been established during recent years to protect women and their children in times of family crisis. These shelters address an urgent need: the immediate protection of the family members and support of the women during a time of crisis.

A great majority of women, however, return to their spouses following a short stay in the shelter. At present, few postshelter services exist for aiding these families and, especially, for helping the battering male to change. A recent survey, for example, found that fewer than a hundred programs in the entire United States offer such services to men.[2]

New programs for men who batter are being established each year, and many existing ones are being expanded. As the number of men being served expands, it becomes increasingly important to consider both the content and efficacy of such interventions.

Several possibilities exist in the design of programs for men who batter. These include interventions based on psychodynamic, family system, and cognitive-behavioral views of human development and problem resolution. Programs derived from a cognitive-behavioral perspective have, in the past, provided the content for group programs aimed at helping abusive fathers and other aggressive and inappropriately angry males.[3] Similarly designed programs may be effective in helping violent men learn to observe and change both their overt and their covert behavior. The components that are described in this article include both those that have been successfully applied with many kinds of client problems and those that are being widely used in the rapidly growing network of services for the treatment of men who batter women.

Reprinted from *Social Work,* Vol. 29, No. 3 (May–June, 1984), pp. 237–242, by permission of NASW Press. Copyright 1984, National Association of Social Workers, Inc., *Social Work.*

Gelles and Straus have defined battering operationally as any act "carried out with the intention of, or perceived as having the intention of, physically hurting another person."[4] Battering also, however, includes the additional aspect of psychological abuse.

The first aspect—the one focused on in the Gelles and Straus definition—may be defined as physical battering. The operational definition used here for physical battering is the use of a person's hands, feet, or other body parts to inflict physical damage or pain on another person. This aspect of battering also includes sexual abuse.

The second, and often less apparent, aspect of battering is psychological. Psychological battering may be defined as verbal or nonverbal threats of violence against another person or against that person's belongings. Purdy and Nickle have described emotional and environmental elements of psychological battering as including repeated humiliation and degradation, punching walls or throwing nearby objects, threatening suicide, and destroying pets.[5] In this article, both physical and psychological abuse will be implied when discussing a male's battering of his female partner.

Psychological battering is considered important because the continuing possibility that violence may be used creates a constant atmosphere of terror in a woman's (and in a family's) life. This resulting terror is often so difficult to cope with that some women go to extremes such as hiding for hours in order to avoid their male partners. In some cases, women have reported that they asked to be beaten in order to end the unbearable tension and uncertainty.

A GROUP PROGRAM FOR MEN

Designing a group program for men who batter women calls for the inclusion of several intervention procedures that are commonly found in similar cognitive-behavioral programs. These include (1) self-observation of behavior chains (which include cognitions) that precede, occur with, and follow violent events, (2) cognitive restructuring of irrational belief systems and faulty thinking styles, (3) skills training in alternatives to violence (for example, conflict resolution), (4) training in relaxation, and (5) establishing a small-group environment in which the intervention procedures are delivered.

Self-observation

A common remark by many men who come for counseling is, "All of the sudden I find myself in a blind rage." For these men, the events that lead up to a violent incident are open unclear. They seldom connect prior events with the eventual lashing out at a partner. For example, a man's thought patterns, beginning with self-statements that depreciate his role as a breadwinner, a husband, or a boyfriend, may generate doubtful estimates of his relationship's strength, which in turn may generate thoughts of jealousy. Patterns like these may increase the man's anxiety and combine regularly with other events that, in the end, lead to the use of violence.

In addition, many batterers fail to connect their use of violence and threats of violence to the long-term consequences of such actions. A useful term, "time horizons," has been coined by Kunkel to describe the period of time that a person projects into the future when evaluating the existing consequences of actions and the possible occurrence of other consequences.[6] Although the short-term consequences of aggression may be quite reinforcing, the long-term consequences of using violence or threats of violence will often greatly outweigh the initial gains achieved through their use. For example, a man may gain the compliance of his partner by using violence but also may be increasing the likelihood that the woman will eventually seek refuge in a shelter and eventually initiate divorce proceedings.

In order to clarify the connection between antecedents, present behavior, and future consequences, a man's skill in observing himself, the behavior of others, and the events with which he is confronted needs to be improved. Training in self-monitoring is often the first step of treatment in cognitive and behavioral interventions. Clarifying behavioral chains and being able to identify precursors of violence when they occur are seen as prerequisites for attempting to alter those chains in such a way as to preclude the use or threats of violence.

Self-observation has been used extensively. One common method of facilitating self-observation is the use of a diary-style record. When using a diary, an individual records specific situations and several aspects of each situation, including physiological behavioral and, cognitive components of his or her responses.

Diaries have been used extensively in assertion training and weight control programs.[7] The use of diaries has also been reported in programs for helping men who batter women. For example, Sonkin and Durphy have developed an "anger log." This is a method by which a man records the situations in which he became angry; the physical, behavioral, and cognitive cues to his anger; the intensity of the anger; the use of alcohol or drugs around the time of his anger; and how he responded in the situation.[8] Ganley and Purdy and Nickle have reported using nearly identical anger logs that include five steps: (1) a description of the anger-provoking situation, (2) a record of negative self-talk, (3) a description of feelings aroused by recalling the situation, (4) an identification of myths that support justification of abusive responses, and (5) a record of positive self-talk.[9]

Self-observation may, in itself, contribute to a decrease in targeted behavior.[10] It is, however, most often used in an effort to identify overt, cognitive, and physiological behavior in need of change, as well as to monitor changes as they occur.

Cognitive Restructuring

The term "cognitive restructuring" has been used by many to describe a variety of somewhat similar interventions. In general, cognitive restructuring is a process in which individuals are led to analyze thinking patterns and then to change the premises, assumptions, and attitudes that underlie those thinking patterns.[11]

One common precursor to a man's violence is a rigid set of beliefs about how he and his female partner should behave in a relationship. In developing rational-emotive therapy (RET), Ellis has enumerated a list of irrational beliefs that are at the root of many such difficulties.[12] Three of these are directly relevant to working with battering males: (1) one must have certain and perfect control over things, (2) one has little control over emotions and cannot help feeling certain things, and (3) human misery is forced on one by outside people and events.

The above irrational beliefs seem to have a great effect on many battering males. On the one hand, many of these men, as the "man of the house," see it as their role to have certain and perfect control over a partner's behavior. Although this is seldom the reality of a situation, such a belief leads to confrontations over a variety of issues from finances to child care, from sex to the woman's choice of friends. Thus, the use of violence is often justified in the pursuit of certain and perfect control.

Ironically, the second irrational belief mentioned represents almost the opposite of the first. Many battering males justify their violent behavior by attributing it to their temper. One often hears statements, for instance, such as this: "I have a temper. My father had one. She's got to live with it. My mom did." This belief combines with the first in such a way as to justify both the man's expectation of compliance from his female partner and his use of violence. A double standard is created whereby perfect compliance is expected of the woman, but abusive behavior by the man is justified.

The third belief, that "human misery is externally caused and forced on one by outside people and events," works to justify battering behavior. One often hears the batterer say that if the female partner would only stop doing this or that he wouldn't have to hit her—in other words, "She caused me to hit her." Similarly, men often blame alcohol for their violent behavior.

Other cognitive therapists focus on the style of a person's thinking patterns. Beck. for example, has outlined several faulty styles of thinking, including arbitrary inference, magnification, cognitive deficiency, dichotomous reasoning, and overgeneralization.[13] Each of these thinking patterns may, at some point, contribute to a man's use of violence. For instance, arbitrary inference—drawing a conclusion when evidence is lacking or to the contrary—is often evident when jealous thoughts are aroused. In such cases, a female partner's actual behavior, if it provides no justification for jealousy, may be completely ignored. Or an incident may be magnified beyond reality—for example, if a spouse talks to a male neighbor, this may lead to the belief that she is having an affair with that neighbor.

In addition, dichotomous reasoning—an oversimplified perception of events as good or bad, right or wrong—plays an important role in a man's thinking about his partner's behavior and how he thinks she should behave. Conflicts over the possibility that a woman might work outside the home often represent a confrontation with a man's dichotomous reasoning about what a wife should or should not do.

The above examples of irrational beliefs and faulty thinking styles are not the exclusive reasons for battering, but they do represent central themes that produce internal dialogues that can often culminate in violence. Increasing the ability of a man who batters to identify and refute such beliefs and thinking styles is the goal of cognitive restructuring. Cognitive therapies achieve these goals through the teaching of self-monitoring, which challenges the man's irrational beliefs and faulty thinking styles, teaching him to challenge them on his own and to combat them with appropriate internal dialogues.

Many of those who work with violent men have discussed the importance of confronting rigid belief systems, faulty thinking styles, and destructive self-talk (that is, internal dialogue).[14] This is no doubt why, in the few reported programs for men who batter, a great deal of time is spent working in these areas.

Purdy and Nickle have characterized the components of denial by the following five types of behavior: (1) blaming the victim, (2) justifying violence, (3) distorting and minimizing, (4) externalizing, and (5) omitting and lying.[15] These overlap strikingly with the faulty thinking styles as categorized by Beck, as well as with some of the irrational beliefs noted by Ellis.[16] Similarly, these authors all promote a cognitive-restructuring approach to changing internal dialogues.

Interpersonal Skills Training

Cognitive responses are but one link in a chain of events that contributes to the onset of violence. It seems that many battering men possess extremely limited skills when it comes to resolving conflict with others. As a result, coercion and violence are two frequently used modes of resolving conflict by these men in stressful situations. Thus, one component of a program for batterers should involve teaching the men new interpersonal skills in resolving conflicts and in defusing stressful situations without resorting to the use of any type of battering.

Training in specific skills has been reported for a wide range of populations and problems of clients. These include couple communication, parenting skills, and peer conflict resolution.[17]

Interpersonal skills training is most often conducted using set procedures in a specific sequence. These particular procedures have been proven effective in a series of studies carried out by Bandura, McFall, and others.[18]

Such training begins by identifying specific interpersonal situations in which a person has experienced difficulties. These situations are then analyzed in terms of what is called the "critical moment." A critical moment is the point in an interaction with one or more others when a person may have acted differently in order to alter the outcome of the interaction. After the critical moment has been identified, various ways of achieving a more positive outcome in that interaction and at that moment are discussed.

Sifting through the possible courses of action, the one that is most likely to increase the chances of a positive outcome is chosen. This alternative is then modeled by others more skilled than the person who is experiencing the difficulties. After observing the modeled use of new skills, the person having difficulties rehearses the new skills in a role play, with others acting as the significant persons in the situation. Feedback is then offered on the person's performance, and he or she may optionally rehearse the new skills a second time to incorporate the feedback given. The skills training process culminates with an agreement by the person to use the new skills in an upcoming situation and report back on the effect.

Applying skills training procedures in work with battering men requires that a specific set of skills be identified and then taught to the men, using situations that are personally relevant to them. The question is, What are the overt behaviors (skills, in this case) that these men must learn to be able to resolve conflict peaceably and to defuse potentially violent situations? This is an area that requires further research, but there are certain skills that, at face value, seem central to nonviolent conflict resolution.

Included are such skills as the following: the ability of the man who batters to identify and state clearly the parameters of a problem situation, the ability to identify and express his own feelings about what is happening, the ability to be able to identify and state his partner's point of view, the ability to offer solutions from which both he and his partner may benefit, and the ability to negotiate a final compromise. In addition to these skills, the ability to temporarily extricate himself by taking "time-out" from highly stressful situations, so as to break an increasingly tense chain of events, would also seem to be an important skill for a man who batters to learn.

Use of the skills training model to teach behaviors similar to those above has been reported by a number of authors.[19] Others have reported teaching some of the above behaviors to men who batter. In particular, teaching men to take time-out from a tense situation has been reported by almost all of those programs described in the literature to date. Heavy emphasis has also been placed on teaching men to express feelings.[20]

Relaxation Training

Overt behaviors and cognitions are not the only links in a chain of events that may be changed by a man who batters. Physiological components may be identified and systematically altered as well.

A major link in the chain of events leading to violent outbursts is the increasing of body tension. The ability to identify and relax such tension is, therefore, a major component in a program for men who batter.

Most current systematic relaxation procedures are based upon Jacobson's progressive relaxation method.[21] Progressive relaxation, also called systematic relaxation, teaches a person to relax by alternately tensing and relaxing muscles in various parts of his or her body. By contrasting tension with a relaxed state, a person learns to identify tension in different parts of the body and to dissolve that tension quickly.

Systematic relaxation training developed prominence as desensitization procedures became more widely accepted. Early on, Wolpe incorporated progressive relaxation training as a step in desensitizing phobic clients.[22] As such, a relaxed state is viewed as incompatible with anxiety and, when a relaxed state can be achieved at will, it allows a client to perform more easily in stress-inducing situations. In the same sense, a relaxed state may be viewed as incompatible with the highly agitated state that many men experience prior to a violent event. If an abusive man can, at times of stress, learn to relax body tension, then one more link in the chain of events leading to a violent outburst will have been broken.

Relaxation training is a common component in several recently reported programs for men who batter.[23] Most of these authors draw their specific relaxation training techniques from one of several manuals.[24] Many have drawn on the work of Novaco, who has combined relaxation training with a variant of cognitive restructuring, namely, self-instructional training.[25] In a program to aid chronically angry clients, Novaco has found that training in cognitive-change procedures, combined with relaxation training, is more effective than either alone.

It is important to note that all of the program components thus far described may function independently of each other but, as Novaco found with two of the components, they are probably more effective when used in combination.

Small Group Format

The format in which all of the components that have been described are best delivered is the small group. The choice of format through which an intervention is delivered is extremely important, given the population being served. One reason for this is that, although many men who batter express regret about their behavior, they are given mixed messages at the same time by those around them. For instance, the father-in-law of one man responded to hearing that his daughter was being beaten with the following comment: "Well, you got to keep them in line sometimes." This same man's brother-in-law was beating his (the brother-in-law's) wife. He came to the first group meeting and said, "While I feel terrible about it, I look around and see everyone saying, 'It's O.K.'"

For this man and many others, the importance of having other men in the same situation saying, "I don't like what I am doing and I want to stop," is both a powerful model and counterconditioning to what he is commonly reinforced to think. Other men attempting to make similar changes in their behavior may be one of the most powerful reinforcers available during intervention. For this reason, the small group format is a key element in a cognitive-behavioral program for battering men.

The group format is beneficial in that it offers a variety of models and sources of feedback for men learning to self-observe, change cognitions, and interact differently.[26] The participation of other men in every facet of the program and of women role-playing the part of antagonists in behavior rehearsals also more nearly simulates situations in the natural environment and, thus, increases the probability of generalization.[27] In addition, groups offer the possibility of member-to-member interaction, greater activity, and more varied activity patterns on the part of the men involved. All of these aspects of group participation are thought to increase the likelihood of the improvement of individual members of the group.[28]

A twelve-session group program incorporating the components described earlier is currently being offered by the Men's Coalition Against Battering (M-CAB). M-CAB offers group counseling and other services to men who batter women. It is located in New York's Capital District, which includes a population of approximately 700,000 people in urban and suburban Albany, Troy, Schenectady, and Saratoga Springs.

Each session is approximately two hours in length and begins with a check-in period, during which the men report on the events of the previous week. The groups consist of from four to ten men and are led by two male coleaders. A female staff member may be included in later sessions to provide a realistic antagonist in role plays.

Early sessions are devoted to analyzing violent situations in terms of chains of events, such as overt behaviors, cognitions, and physiological responses, that lead up to, occur simultaneously with, and follow battering. Self-observation via anger log assignments is used to supply the content for exercises and discussions. In addition, time-out as a method of breaking an increasingly stressful chain of events is taught.

Middle sessions are devoted to teaching progressive relaxation and cognitive restructuring procedures. Relaxation training is introduced, and taped instructions are distributed for home use in the third session. Each subsequent session ends with a short period of relaxation to dissolve any tension created in group meetings and to strengthen earlier learning.

Cognitive restructuring procedures are introduced over a number of sessions. Describing internal dialogues starts this process. Once the group members can consistently observe and report self-talk, the underlying beliefs and thinking styles are analyzed and changes are proposed. Training and practice in changing self-talk are extensively given in middle group sessions.

Later group sessions are devoted to skills training around specific situations supplied by the men. The interpersonal skills training model described earlier is applied here. Over a number of the later sessions, each man identifies particularly problem-filled situations and, with the group's help, practices new behavior in the sheltered environment of the group. This new behavior is then attempted between sessions, and the results are reported back to the group.[29]

The initial reports of men who have completed M-CAB's program are favorable. They indicate a dramatic drop in violent incidents and psychological battering as well as an increase in the expression of feelings, negotiation of conflict, and other pro-social behavior. In general, the men have greatly increased the degree to which they are identifying problems and dealing with them early in a chain of events, thereby short-circuiting situations that in the past may have resulted in battering. Future studies, with greater experimental controls, are needed in order to draw strong conclusions from early successes of M-CAB and similar groups around the country.

It is an important task of social workers to bring the intervention procedures described in this article, which have been found to be effective, to bear on the problem of men who batter. If abusive men's skills in coping with stress in their daily lives can be strengthened, they can learn to resolve conflicts nonviolently.

NOTES AND REFERENCES

1. Murray A. Straus, "Wife Beating: How Common and Why?" *Victimology,* 2 (Fall 1977–Winter 1978), pp. 443–458; James Boudouris, "Homicide and the Family," *Journal of Marriage and the Family,* 33 (November 1971), pp. 667–676; and Martha H. Field and Henry F. Field, "Marital Violence and the Criminal Process: neither Justice nor Peace," *Social Service Review,*" 47 (June 1973), pp. 221–240.

2. Albert R. Roberts, "A National Service for Batterers," In Maria Roy, ed., *The Abusive Partner* (New York: Van Nostrand, 1982).

3. Jill Crozier and Roger C. Katz, "Social Learning Treatment of Child Abuse," *Journal of Behavior Therapy and Experimental Psychiatry,* 10 (September 1979), pp. 213–220; Peter A. Fehrenbach and Mark H. Thelen, "Assertive-Skills Training for Inappropriately Aggressive College Males: Effects on Assertive and Aggressive Behaviors," *Journal of Behavior Therapy and Experimental Psychiatry,* 12 (September 1981), pp. 213–217; Raymond W. Novaco, *Anger Control* (Lexington, Mass.: Lexington Books, 1975); Raymond W. Novaco, "Anger and Coping with Stress: Cognitive Behavioral Interventions," in John P. Foreyt and Diana P. Rathjen, eds., *Cognitive Behavior Therapy: Research and Applications* (New York: Plenum Press, 1978); Sara Rahaim, Craig Lefebvre, and Jack O. Jenkins, "The Effects of Social Skills Training on Behavioral and Cognitive Components of Anger Management," *Journal of Behavior Therapy and Experimental Psychiatry,* 11 (March 1980), pp. 3–8; and David C. Rimm et al., "Group-Assertive Training in Treatment of Expression of Inappropriate Anger," *Psychological Reports,* 34 (June 1974), pp. 791–798.

4. Richard J. Gelles and Murray A. Straus., "Determinants of Violence in the Family: Toward a Theoretical Integration," In Wesley R. Burr et al., eds., *Contemporary Theories about the Family* (New York: Free Press, 1979), p. 554.

5. Frances Purdy and Norm Nickle, "Practice Principles for Working with Groups of Men Who Batter," *Social Work with Groups,* 4 (1981), pp. 111–122.

6. John H. Kunkel, *Behavior Social Problems and Change* (Englewood Cliffs, N.J.: Prentice-Hall, 1975).

7. Robert E. Alberti, ed., *Assertiveness: Innovations, Applications, Issues* (San Luis Obispo, Calif.: Impact Press, 1977); James A. Hall and Sheldon D. Rose, "Assertion Training in a Group," in Sheldon D. Rose, ed., *A Casebook in Group Therapy: A Behavioral-Cognitive Approach* (Englewood Cliffs, N.J.: Prentice-Hall, 1980); William G. Johnson and Peter M. Stalonas, *Weight No Longer* (Gretna, La.: Pelican, 1981); and Richard B. Stuart and Barbara Davis, *Slim Chance in a Fat World* (Champaign, Ill.: Research Press, 1972).

8. Daniel J. Sonkin and Michael Durphy, *Learning to Live Without Violence: A Book for Men* (San Francisco: Volcano Press, 1981).

9. Anne L. Ganley, *Court Mandated Counseling for Men Who Batter: A Three-Day Workshop for Mental Health Professionals* (Washington, D.C.: Center for Women Policy Studies, 1981); and Purdy and Nickle, "Practice Principles for Working with Groups of Men Who Batter."

10. Alan E. Kazdin, "Self-monitoring and Behavior Change," in Michael J. Mahoney and Carl E. Thoresen, eds., *Self-Control: Power to the Person* (Monterey, Calif.: Brooks/Cole Publishing Co., 1974).

11. Donald Meichenbaum, *Cognitive-Behavior Modification* (New York: Plenum Press, 1977).

12. Albert Ellis, *The Essence of Rational Psychotherapy: A Comprehensive Approach to Treatment* (New York: Institute for Rational Living, 1970); Albert Ellis, "The Basic Clinical Theory of Rational-Emotive Therapy," in Albert Ellis and Russell Grieger, eds., *Handbook of Rational-Emotive Therapy* (New York: Springer, 1977).

13. Aaron T. Beck, *Cognitive Therapy and The Emotional Disorders* (New York: International Universities Press, 1976).

14. David Adams and Isidore Penn, "Men in Groups: the Socialization and Resocialization of Men Who Batter," paper presented at the annual meeting of the American Orthopsychiatric Association, April 1981; Norman Brisson, "Helping Men Who Batter Women," *Public Welfare,* 40 (Spring 1982), pp. 29–34; Ganley, *Court Mandated Counseling for Men Who Batter;* Purdy and Nickle, "Practice Principles for Working with Groups of Men Who Batter"; and Sonkin and Durphy, "Learning to Live Without Violence."

15. Purdy and Nickle, "Practice Principles for Working with Groups of Men Who Batter."

16. Beck, *Cognitive Therapy and The Emotional Disorders;* and Ellis, "The Basic Clinical Theory of Rational Emotive Therapy."

17. Jeffrey L. Edleson, "Teaching Children to Resolve Conflict: A Group Approach," *Social Work,* 26 (November 1981), pp. 488–493; John Gottman et al., *A Couple's Guide to Communication* (Champaign, Ill.: Research Press, 1976); and John R. Moreland et al., "Parents as Therapists: A Review of the Behavior Therapy Parent Training Literature: 1975 to 1981," *Behavior Modification,* 6 (April 1982), pp. 250–276.

18. Albert Bandura, Edward B. Blanchard, and Brunhilde Ritter, "The Relative Efficacy of Desensitization and Modeling Approaches for Inducing Behavioral, Affective, and Attitudinal Changes, *Journal of Personality and Social Psychology,* 13 (November 1969), pp. 173–199; Richard M. McFall and Craig T. Twentyman, "Four Experiments on the Relative Contribution of Rehearsal, Modeling, and Coaching to Assertion Training," *Journal of Abnormal Psychology,* 81 (1973), pp. 199–218; and Robert D. O'Connor, "Modification of Social Withdrawal through Symbolic Modeling," *Journal of Applied Behavior Analysis,* 2 (Spring 1969), pp. 15–22.

19. Edleson, "Teaching Children to Resolve Conflict: A Small Group Approach"; Marvin R. Goldfried, "Psychotherapy as Coping Skills Training," in Michael J. Mahoney, ed., *Psychotherapy Process* (New York: Plenum Press, 1980); and Arthur L. Robin. "A Controlled Evaluation of Problem-Solving Communication Training with Parent-Adolescent Conflict," *Behavior Therapy,* 12 (November 1981), pp. 593–609

20. Ganley, *Court Mandated Counseling for Men Who Batter;* and Sonkin and Durphy, *Learning to Live Without Violence.*

21. Edmund Jacobson, *Progressive Relaxation* (2d ed.; Chicago: University of Chicago Press, 1938).

22. Joseph Wolpe, *Psychotherapy by Reciprocal Inhibition* (Stanford, Calif.: Stanford University Press, 1958); and Joseph Wolpe, *The Practice of Behavior Therapy* (New York: Pergamon, 1973).

23. Ganley, *Court Mandated Counseling for Men Who Batter;* Purdy and Nickle, "Practice Principles for Working with Groups of Men Who Batter"; and Sonkin and Durphy, *Learning to Live Without Violence.*

24. Douglas A. Bernstein and Thomas D. Borkovec, *Progressive Relaxation Training* (Champaign, Ill.: Research Press, 1973); Joseph R. Cautela and June Groden, *Relaxation* (Champaign, Ill.: Research Press, 1978); and Gerald M. Rosen, *The Relaxation Book: An Illustrated Self-Help Program* (Englewood Cliffs, N.J.: Prentice-Hall, 1977).

25. Novaco, *Anger Control.*

26. Sheldon D. Rose, *Group Therapy: A Behavioral Approach* (Englewood Cliffs, N.J.: Prentice-Hall, 1977).

27. Arnold P. Goldstein, K. Keller, and L. B. Sechrest, *Psychotherapy and the Psychology of Behavior Change* (New York: Wiley, 1966); and Trevor F. Stokes and Donald M. Baer, "An Implicit Technology of Generalization," *Journal of Applied Behavior Analysis,* 10 (Summer 1977), pp. 349–367.

28. John V. Flowers, "Behavioral Analysis of Group Therapy and a Model for Behavioral Group Therapy," in Dennis Upper and Steven M. Ross, eds., *Behavioral Group Therapy, 1979* (Champaign, Ill.: Research Press, 1979).

29. This program is described in greater detail in Jeffrey L. Edleson, David M. Miller, and Gene W. Stone, *Counseling Men Who Batter: Group Leader's Handbook* (Albany, N.Y.: Men's Coalition Against Battering, 1983).

ABUSE OF THE ELDERLY

CHAPTER 72

ELDER ABUSE

Issues for the Practitioner

Deborah Bookin and Ruth E. Dunkle

A buse of the elderly by family members is receiving increasing attention as evidence of its prevalence and severity has become more readily available than it was in the past. Existing data now suggest that elder abuse occurs with a rate and frequency only slightly less than child abuse.[1]

Like other types of family violence, abuse of the elderly is not limited to a single act or behavior. It incorporates a wide range of phenomena, including the infliction of physical injury and pain, mental trauma, anguish and isolation, withholding basic necessities of life—such as food, shelter, and medical and personal care—and financial exploitation.

Efforts to deal with elder abuse on a community level have been hampered by a number of factors. The lack of a universally accepted definition of the problem has divided professionals and laymen alike in their efforts to agree upon the nature and parameters of the problem. Because both government and the general public have been slow to recognize the significance of the problem, legal tools and support of community-based services appropriate to meet the needs of this population (such as protective services, respite, day care, and the like) have remained limited in many communities. Even where such services and legal tools are available, the lack of public awareness of the problem and societal taboos about invading the privacy of the family have hampered efforts to deal with it.

Lack of adequate community supports has placed a heavy burden upon practitioners who are assigned to cases of elder abuse. For the individual practitioner, intervention in

Reprinted from *Social Casework,* Vol. 66, No. 1 (1985), pp. 3–12, by permission of the publisher, Families International, Inc.

[1] U.S. Congress, House Select Committee on Aging, *Elder Abuse: An Examination of a Hidden Problem.* Hearing, 97th Congress, 1st Session, 3 April 1981 (Washington, DC: Government Printing Office, 1981).

cases of elder abuse presents significant problems and challenges for which the limited knowledge base on elder abuse provides few answers. Although the present knowledge base relies heavily on data supplied by human services professionals, it has thus far failed to address the unique problems and dilemmas faced by those who must intervene in such situations. Workers assigned to cases of elder abuse experience significant difficulties related not only to the nature of the problem but also to their own personal feelings, biases, and attitudes about violence and the aging family.

This article examines the problems which those workers frequently experience and suggests appropriate strategies for dealing with them.

STAGE I: IDENTIFICATION PROBLEM

In the initial stages of intervention, problems related to identification of abuse may occur. These problems result not only from the worker's lack of awareness or knowledge about elder abuse, but also his or her personal and cultural biases.

At this time, the abuser of the elderly person is believed to be most probably a family member living with the elder and providing some care. The abuser is also likely to be a person under stress and may be abusing a harmful substance, such as drugs or alcohol.[2] The victim of elder abuse is believed to be most probably over the age of seventy-five years, to have a physical or mental impairment, and to live with his or her abuser. Unfortunately, studies of elder abuse thus far have focused on the elderly population in private residences rather than in a cross-section of settings, including nursing homes, boarding homes, and the like, thus introducing a potential bias.

Compounding the problem of identifying the abused elder is the general lack of consensus on a definition of elder abuse and the ambiguity of many definitions used by professionals. The potential for variation in such definitions is significant. Definitions used by states having protective service laws are necessarily broad in order to be applicable to a variety of situations but can fail to give practitioners clear-cut guidelines regarding what degree of maltreatment constitutes abuse. Such broad definitions can leave the practitioner with serious questions as to whether a particular behavior or outcome is of a degree which constitutes abuse.

An unintentional result of such broad definitions is the confusion and misunderstanding of some workers who do not comprehend the boundaries of the legal definition and fail to report suspected abuse because they do not believe that a case fits the definition. Practitioners' personal definitions of elder abuse are largely determined by their own individual experiences, cultural images, and other influences. One survey of physicians at Harborview Medical Center in Seattle found that the group sampled failed to agree unanimously on even one element to be included in the definition of elder abuse. Some family violence experts have used intentionality, effect, evaluation, and standards as the primary determinants of classification as abuse.[3] Of these four

---

[2] Ann Langley, "Abuse of the Elderly," *Human Services Monograph Series,* Department of Health and Human Services (Washington, DC: U.S. Government Printing Office, 1981).

[3] Susan K. Tomita et al., "Detection of Elder Abuse and Neglect in a Medical Setting" (Paper presented at the First National Conference on Abuse of Older Persons, San Francisco, CA, 1–3 April 1981); James Garbarino and Gwen Gilliam, *Understanding Abusive Families* (Lexington, MA: D. H. Heath and Company, 1980).

elements intentionality is probably the most controversial issue, as practitioners have argued that abuse must also include unintentional neglect which results in serious harm.[4]

At present no single factor has been identified as the cause of elder abuse. Researchers believe that a variety of factors relate to the development of abuse of an older person. Most agree, however, that the family in which elder abuse is occurring is likely to be experiencing stress.[5] The genesis of such stress may result from factors lying either within the family's own sphere, the community or society at large, or a combination of sources (see Table 72–1). Researchers in the area have proposed a variety of explanations: developmental dysfunction;[6] pathological problems;[7] stress;[8] ageism and violence as a way of life;[9] cohort changes such as increased longevity, fewer family ties, and greater demand on family resources;[10] and family conflict.[11]

Differential Access/Experience

In general, the abused older person is relatively invisible to professional human services workers in the community. Many practitioners in the community are either unaware that elder abuse exists or have had such limited exposure to cases that they fail to recognize symptoms when confronted with them. Unlike the abused child, who comes into contact with a wider circle of people and helping networks daily through school and other activities, the elderly person is generally more restricted in his or her social contacts outside the home.[12] Impairment and decreased mobility may further limit the elder's contact with others in the community. Family members, seeking to conceal or deny the abuse, also help to keep the abuse hidden from community view.

Human services professionals may experience difficulty in identifying abuse because the nature of their work provides them with differential access and experience with victims of different types of abuse. A study conducted by Richard L. Douglass, Tom Hickey, and Catherine Noel suggested that elder abuse is within the "typical experience" of workers in a variety of human service professions serving the elderly.[13] However, some workers in some professions were found to have varying degrees of experience with different types of abuse and neglect.[14] Differential exposure to different forms of elder abuse can make some professionals more expert at recognizing some

---

[4] Garbarino and Gilliam, *Understanding Abusive Families.*

[5] Langley, "Abuse of the Elderly."

[6] Ibid.

[7] Langley, "Abuse of the Elderly"; Tom Hickey, "Neglect and Abuse of the Elderly: Implications of a Developmental Model for Research and Intervention," (unpublished paper).

[8] Langley, "Abuse of the Elderly."

[9] Helen O'Malley et al., *Elder Abuse in Massachusetts: A Survey of Professionals and Paraprofessionals* (Boston MA: Legal Research and Services for the Elderly, 1979).

[10] Langley, "Abuse of the Elderly."

[11] O'Malley et al., *Elder Abuse in Massachusetts.*

[12] Georgia J. Anetzberger, "Elder Abuse" (Paper presented at the Fifth Annual Ohio Conference on Aging, Cincinnati, OH, 4 March 1981).

[13] Richard L. Douglass, Tom Hickey, and Catherine Noel, *A Study of Maltreatment of the Elderly and Other Vulnerable Adults* (Ann Arbor: Institute of Gerontology, University of Michigan, 1980).

[14] Tom Hickey and Richard L. Douglass, "Neglect and Abuse of Older Family Members: Professionals' Perspectives and Case Experiences," *The Gerontologist* 21 (April 1981): 171–176.

Table 72–1.
Variables Relevant to Causation of Abuse

	Relevant Avenues of Investigation During Assessment
Vulnerability/Dependency of Elder/Ageism	*Family Value System* What is family's attitude toward the elder? What is family's attitude concerning the elder's dependency? Is there evidence of financial exploitation/violation of rights?
Learned Patterns of Violence/Unresolved Family Conflict	*Family's Past History of Coping with Problems* How has family dealt with problems in past? How do members generally resolve conflict? Is there evidence of long-standing, unresolved family conflict? *Environment of Home* Could it support use of force or violence? What are the present sources of stress affecting family? *Developmental Stage of Family* Is family able to accommodate needs and demands of family members? To what extent? Is excessive stress generated in process? How does family system respond to stress?
Stress of Caregiving	*Care Needs of Elder* Are they extensive? Is a great deal of stress generated as a result?
Lack of Family Supports	*State of Family Supports* If these are lacking, is this a short-term or long-term situation? Do other family members live within reasonable proximity but are not involved? Is there or has there been present or previous service from other social service agencies?
Pathological Symptoms	*Pathological Symptoms* Is there evidence of pathological behavior of a family member, such as mental illness, alcoholism, or drug abuse?

symptoms and forms of elder abuse than others. By focusing on a narrower range of symptoms, practitioners from different disciplines come to look for different indicators of abuse and to disregard others.

Differential access of various professions to the elderly victim over the course of the abuse may also account for some of the problems workers experience in detecting maltreatment. It is possible that some human service professionals—such as caseworkers or community mental health workers—are more likely to come into contact with a victim of abuse when the abuse is in its early stages and symptoms are much more subtle or easily concealed. Other professionals—such as physicians and nurses—may be more likely to see victims of elder abuse after the maltreatment has progressed and symptoms of abuse are much more visible. Elizabeth Lau and Jordan Kosberg found that a majority of abused elderly in their study were identified by health professionals because of a health-related problem.[15]

Differential access can cause practitioners in different disciplines to develop their own personal "profile" of the abused elder. The heterogeneity of the population, however, makes such limited profiles inadequate. Elder abuse is believed to cross all racial, ethnic, socioeconomic, and educational strata.[16] Although pioneering research studies have supported efforts to develop profiles of the abused elder and his or her abuser,[17] the heterogeneity of this population limits the utility of such profiles.

Impact of Cultural Biases

The practitioner's ability to identify abuse is not solely determined by the availability of formalized definitions or his or her professional knowledge and skill. The norms, values, and cultural influences of all those involved in the identification process—the abused elder, his or her family, the worker, and significant others—come into play at the time when investigation of possible maltreatment begins.

In the identification process, the worker is no less influenced by his or her own cultural biases and environmental influences than others involved in this situation. Like them, his or her values and attitudes are shaped by the norms, values, and cultural influences operant in society at large and in his or her own family system.

Violence is a very common feature of life in the American family. Within general society, there is a high baseline tolerance of violence. Only a brief review of current literature and the media is necessary to ascertain the extent to which violence has become accepted as a normal part of existence. Murray Straus, Richard J. Gelles, and Suzanne K. Steinmetz proposed that the norms of American society as a whole legitimize and support the use of violence in the family as a means of punishment, control, and resolution of conflict.[18] Through the family, individuals form attitudes about violence and the use of force. Sally Ann Holmes expressed the belief that violence in many instances is a learned behavior that is transmitted from one generation to another and nurtured by

---

[15] Elizabeth Lau and Jordan Kosberg, "Abuse of the Elderly by Informal Care Providers: Practice and Research Issues" (Paper presented at the 31st Annual Meeting of the Gerontological Society, Dallas, TX, 21 November 1978).

[16] Langley, "Abuse of the Elderly."

[17] Marilyn Block and Jan Sinnott, eds., *The Battered Elder Syndrome* (College Park, MD: University of Maryland Center on Aging, 1979); Douglass, Hickey, and Noel, "Maltreatment of the Elderly"; Lau and Kosberg, "Abuse of the Elderly"; O'Malley et al., *Elder Abuse in Massachusetts.*

[18] Murray Straus, Richard J. Gelles, and Suzanne K. Steinmetz, *Behind Closed Doors: Violence in the American Family* (Garden City, NY: Anchor Press-Doubleday, 1980).

[19] Sally Ann Holmes, "A Holistic Approach to the Treatment of Violent Families," *Social Casework* 62 (December 1981): 594–600.

cultural norms and social institutions as well as by laws and religious teachings.[19] Apparently, the dynamics of violence in families are similar, whether the victim is a child, parent, sibling, or spouse.[20] This may be the reason that elder abuse is believed to exist with a frequency and rate only slightly less than that of child abuse.[21]

According to Straus, ". . . most violence in families reflects a combination of normal process and situations." Among the factors cited by Straus are:

- The learned association between love and violence which is established from infancy on through the use of physical punishment;
- The moral rightness of family members using physical force when another person does wrong and persists in it: the "I deserved it" pattern;
- The belief in families that force is both legitimate and expected;
- The socially structured antagonism between the sexes and between generations;
- The assignment of family responsibilities on the basis of age and sex rather than competence and interest;
- The lack of alternatives and ability to escape from a violent family.[22]

While not all families accept violence and the use of force in either the same manner or degree, the important ramification is that all individuals, through socialization in the family, adopt some attitudes about the appropriateness and legitimacy of violence and control. Such attitudes in turn affect the individual's perceptions about the phenomena he or she will later experience or observe. A case example illustrates this:

> *The A Family.* Caseworker S was assigned to the case of the A family, a multigenerational family residing in the same dwelling. Worker S observed symptoms that suggested that Grandmother A was being physically abused. Her repeated efforts to discuss this with the elderly woman's children were unsuccessful. No matter how great her efforts, she could not get them to see that physical punishment was inappropriate as a way of interacting with Grandmother A. The caseworker could not understand why the family could not understand her concern over the elderly woman's treatment. The worker decided to gather more detailed data about the family system and the interactional patterns between other family members. She discovered that violent patterns of interaction (something she had not been able to observe previously) were operative in all four generations of the family.

Thus the worker attempting to intervene in a case of elder abuse is confronted with a situation in which perceptions of the maltreatment by all relevant parties may vary significantly. From the initial identification of abuse, the worker can experience difficulties

[20] Lucile Cantoni, "Clinical Issues in Domestic Violence," *Social Casework* 62 (January 1981): 3–12.

[21] Suzanne K. Steinmetz, "Prepared Statement, *Elder Abuse: The Hidden Problem.*" Briefing by the Select Committee on Aging, U. S. House of Representatives, Boston, 23 June 1979 (Washington, DC, 1980), pp. 7–12.

[22] Murray A. Straus, "A Sociological Perspective on the Causes of Family Violence" (Paper presented at the American Association for the Advancement of Science, Houston, TX, 6 January 1979), p. 22.

in attempting to work with the family and significant others if he or she is either unaware that such differences in perception exist or is unable to bridge these differences
somehow and help those involved to alter their perceptions and reach common ground.

Impact of Other Biases

Attitudes about violence and the use of force are not the only attitudes which influence
the process by which elder abuse is identified and defined. An exploratory study conducted by Deborah Bookin found that some caseworkers and abusive families providing care to their elder differed significantly in their perceptions of the role stress played
in the functioning of the family.[23] Caseworkers sampled tended to perceive more family
caregivers as experiencing a high level of stress than did the caregivers themselves. Such
a discrepancy can impede a practitioner's efforts to intervene by focusing attention on
the wrong issue.

A case example illustrates this point:

> *The D Family.* Worker B was extremely concerned about the D family, an elderly
> woman and her widowed daughter's family. The D family was one in which there
> were multiple demands. Mrs. D was frail and required extensive care in all daily
> living tasks. Mrs. D's daughter was responsible for her care as well as for the rest
> of the family. Mrs. D's other children, who lived in close proximity, provided no
> assistance and frequently seemed to create additional tensions and problems. The
> daughter's children also seemed to contribute to the genesis of these tensions and
> problems. Mrs. D's daughter often complained that her mother's care was too
> much for her and that she couldn't handle it. The house seemed to be in a con-
> stant state of tension. The worker suspected that Mrs. D was being both psycho-
> logically and physically abused. She offered the D family numerous supportive
> services, believing that if the stress of caregiving was reduced, the level of stress in
> the house would diminish to a more tolerable level. To her surprise, the family re-
> fused most of the services offered and sabotaged those which they accepted.
> Worker B began to perceive that although Mrs D's daughter complained about
> the stress of caregiving, it served a purpose not recognized by the worker.

At times, agency personnel do not agree on what constitutes abuse. In another situation, a worker and her supervisor disagreed about whether a case assigned to the
worker was actually one of elder abuse. Although the two discussed the case at great
length on several occasions, the worker still refused to agree with her supervisor that
the situation (a caregiver hitting her elder with a hairbrush whenever the elder became
unmanageable during personal caregiving) was one of abuse. A short time later at the
agency's annual picnic, the supervisor observed the worker physically punishing her
child in public. It was then that the supervisor realized that she and the worker apparently had very different perceptions and attitudes about the use of force.

[23] Deborah Bookin, "Elder Abuse: Family and Community Support Antecedents" (Submitted in partial fulfillment
of student fellowship, Case Western Reserve University, School of Medicine, Office of Geriatric Medicine, July
1981).

STAGE II: INTERVENTION

There are dilemmas of intervention that occur with all violent families. Beverly B. Nichols stated: ". . . Caseworkers rarely pick abusiveness as the focus of intervention—rather, they tend to ignore the symptom."[24] This fact is the result of certain characteristics of the worker as well as the result of problems posed by the violent or abusive family.

Family Context of Elder Abuse

Elder abuse generally occurs within the context of a family system. The worker, therefore, is dealing not only with the problems of the elderly client but also those of the family in which such behavior occurs.

Because most old people remain connected to their kinship network, the needs of the older person have been shouldered by the family. As Lillian Troll et al. stated: ". . . Older people in our population, with the possible exception of orphans, are isolated from families only if they want to be or only when they are so deteriorated that they are no longer functioning social individuals."[25] Care-giving and support of older family members are not always provided by an affectionate family member or one with whom the elder has had a good relationship. Arnold Brown, for instance, found that children visited their parents just as frequently whether they had a satisfying relationship or not.[26] In the same vein, a study of care-giving by Rosemary Kulys and Sheldon Tobin that included friends as well as family, found that only 40 percent of the older care recipients said that the persons responsible for their care made them feel secure, and 37 percent said that this was the person who made them feel the most accepted.[27]

Even when families want to provide care for their elder it is likely to become more difficult with the demographic changes that are occurring. Judith Treas identified a demographic shift toward older people; care-giving children are more likely to be old themselves; they are struggling with declining resources of health, money, and energy; and the changing roles of women in the culture now include employment, thus limiting their care-giving role.[28] Tobin and Kulys also noted the increased likelihood that parent caring will conflict with post-parental freedoms that grown children have begun to enjoy.[29] Family resources are being strained for a variety of reasons, resulting in abuse that makes it more difficult for the family to continue providing care to older relatives.[30]

The stresses on the older family in the care-giving relationship are different than for those providing of care to a child or young person. Difficulties in intervention in situa-

[24] Beverly B. Nichols, "The Abused Wife Problem," *Social Casework* 57 (January 1976): 27–32.

[25] Lillian Troll, Sheila J. Miller, and Robert C. Atchley, *Families in Later Life* (Belmont, CA: Wadsworth, 1979).

[26] Arnold Brown, "Satisfying Relationships for the Elderly and Their Patterns of Disengagement," *The Gerontologist* (14 June 1974): 258–62.

[27] Rosemary Kulys and Sheldon Tobin, "Older People and Their Responsible Others," *Social Work* 25 (March 1980): 138–145.

[28] Judith Treas, "Family Support Systems for the Aged," *The Gerontologist* 17 (December 1977): 486–91.

[29] Kulys and Tobin, "Older People and Their Responsible Others."

[30] Elaine Brody and Stanley Brody, *New Directions in Health and Social Supports for the Aging* (Paper presented at the Anglo-American Conference, Fordham University, New York, 1980).

tions of elder abuse seem even more hampered than with abuse in younger age groups. For example, the care giver is frequently female, with numerous competing demands on her time, energy, and care-giving resources. Many times the care giver is elderly herself. With the older family, it has not been uncommon to find a double-directed violence: the middle-aged child is violent toward the older parent and vice versa.[31]

Bertha Simos[32] has identified emotional problems that adult children have in caring for an elderly parent who attempts to compensate for losses. James Grad and Peter Sainsbury also note instrumental problems, such as providing nursing care and additional personal attention which result in restriction of employment opportunities as well as financial activities.[33] The level of stress, though, is not related to level of disability or needed care. As Joanna Mellar and George Getzel stated: "The care-givers viewing the care-giving role as most burdensome tended to be those care-givers who received minimal support from family or friends in performing the care-giving duties."[34]

Other problems which may be encountered are created by old family patterns. Mary Gwynne Schmidt noted a few: inability of children to accept their parent's decline, sibling rivalry, and lack of independence in the child, as well as child's resentment or dismay when the less favorite or even the younger parent survives.[35]

The family context in which elder abuse occurs presents the worker with a complex system of relationships and issues, of which care-giving may be only a small part. Not all cases of elder abuse relates to the stress of care-giving, and not all families feel overburdened by the responsibilities attendant on assisting an older family member. The care-giving role of the family, however, can generate additional problems and stresses which can contribute to the abuse of an older person and should therefore be carefully assessed by the worker.

PROBLEMS IN INTERVENTION

Powerlessness can be part of the problem of intervention for the worker and the client.

> Worker S was assigned to the case of Mr. and Mrs. L, an elderly couple living in the community. In her case recordings, Worker S suggested that Mrs. L might be physically abused. Yet, she never brought this to the attention of her supervisor, nor incorporated the problem into her treatment plan for the case. When queried about this, Worker S explained, "I'm not equipped to deal with the problem—there's nothing I can do—so I haven't acknowledged it."

Sometimes access to the abused older person is difficult for the worker because the abuser blocks intervention efforts.[36] At other times the elder, believing that little can be

[31] Steinmetz, "Prepared Statement."
[32] Bertha Simos, "Adult Children and Their Aging Parents," *Social Work* 18 (1973): 78–85.
[33] James Grad and Peter Sainsbury, "Mental Illness and the Family," *Lancet* 1 (1963): 544–547.
[34] Joanna Mellar and George Getzel, "Stress and Services Needs of Those Who Care for the Aged" (Paper presented at Gerontological Society Meeting, San Diego, CA, 1980), p. 10.
[35] Mary Gwynne Schmidt, "Failing Parents, Aging Children," *Journal of Gerontological Social Work* 2 (Spring 1980): 259–369.
[36] Langley, "Abuse of the Elder."

done to improve his or her situation, or fearing placement in a nursing home, will not cooperate with the worker.

Frequently the abused older person reacts to abuse with denial, resignation, withdrawal, fear, or depression.[37] These reactions can subsequently result in feelings of guilt, shame, helplessness, and worthlessness.[38] Ann Langley, as well as Kosberg and Lau, acknowledged that the older abuse victim rarely reports abuse.[39] Sometimes this is due to the elder's dependence on the abuser for basic survival needs as well as the additional stigma of having raised an abusive child, if it is the child who is the abuser.[40]

Working with abusive situations can be especially hard when the client is the product of a violent family, culture, and society.[41] Intervention is particularly difficult with an abuser who has had poor socialization and lacks the ability to trust the worker.[42] As the worker attempts to build a relationship with the client, the intensity of the worker's expectations can be very threatening to the client and particularly difficult in family situations where the roles have been reversed for several generations.

Some workers, as the result of feelings of powerlessness and inadequacy, tend to lower their expectations and set less ambitious treatment goals for cases of elder abuse—especially in cases involving long-standing abuse patterns in the family. While it is true that long-standing abuse treated at the end of the life cycle may have a limited prognosis for change, the fact that the worker has a bias from previous experience may cause him or her to believe that helping a family with such a problem may prove not only limiting but deleterious to successful intervention. In a limited sample of workers assigned to cases of abuse, the majority of workers assigned to cases involving long-standing abuse advocated complete separation or nursing home placement as the "ideal" intervention in the case.[43]

Another problem experienced by some workers is the tendency of the worker to focus on care-giving rather than abuse—even though stress of care-giving is clearly not the only potential cause of the abuse. Because some workers feel inadequate to deal with violence and abuse but want to do something to help their client, they tend to offer supports which are clearly not related to the underlying cause of the abuse. This inappropriate help from social service professionals may be the reason George S. Getzel found that social service professionals were seldom used by the care givers.[44] Although there are numerous reasons for this under-utilization, it cannot be denied that one reason has been the ineffectiveness of social work. It is only recently that social work professionals have begun to understand the increase in size of the older cohort as well as their subsequent needs. The temptation has been to try to transfer skills used with younger persons to those who need help but are older. This has been largely ineffective. Social work professionals, as well as other professionals, must acquire new knowledge

---

[37] Lau and Kosberg, "Abuse of the Elderly by Informal Care Providers."
[38] Ibid.
[39] Langley, "Abuse of the Elderly."
[40] Steinmetz, "Prepared Statement."
[41] Holmes, "A Holistic Approach."
[42] Cantoni, "Clinical Issues in Domestic Violence."
[43] Bookin, "Elder Abuse."
[44] George S. Getzel, "Social Work with Family Care-givers to the Aged," *Social Casework* 62 (April 1981): 201–209.

and skills to meet the needs of the older persons who require help with multiple chronic impairments.[45]

Practice Implications

Not surprisingly many workers in the human services express feelings of powerlessness in dealing with elder abuse. Abuse of the elderly is a highly complex, emotionally charged subject which elicits powerful responses and defenses from everyone involved. Couched in fear, denial, and secrecy, it is protected and maintained by societal norms which support the sanctity and privacy of the family, as well as the use of violence as an acceptable response to a variety of situations. Ageism and attitudes about dependence also play an important role in the development and maintenance of the problem.

Many institutional supports which undergird these societal norms lie outside the boundaries of the family system and outside the direct influence of the worker, making it difficult for him or her to impact dysfunctional attitudes and behaviors within the family. Because of this, abuse which is the result of transgenerational patterns of violence within the family seems particularly resistant to direct worker intervention.

Workers frequently feel frustrated by such barriers, not only because of their scope but also because their role in the genesis and maintenance of abusive patterns is not fully understood by most workers. Such influences, however, are not totally insurmountable. As with other, similar problems such as child and spouse abuse, amelioration of elder abuse requires intervention on both a micro and a macro level.

On a macro level, attitudes which result in the maltreatment of the elderly can be influenced through increased efforts in the area of community education. Greater awareness of the problem by both laymen and professionals alike can result in the successful reshaping of attitudes which negatively affect treatment of the elderly. More accurate identification of elderly victims of abuse can lead to the development of new knowledge about abuse and services specifically targeted to serve the victims. Increased dialogue between professionals in the various human services will advance the study of elder abuse significantly and resolve many problems in the identification process which are the result of differential access and experience. Social workers, who of all the helping professions are present in the widest range of settings serving the elderly, are in a unique position to assume leadership in this effort.

The lack of a clear and comprehensive definition of elder abuse is a major roadblock preventing increased community action around this issue. The lack of such a definition has made it difficult for both practitioners and laymen to bridge the varying perceptions and experiences of all those in the community who may be involved. In lieu of such a definition at the present time, two major criteria may present the most acceptable guidelines available: effect and standards.[46]

Defining elder abuse in terms of its effect upon the elder, rather than simply in terms of behavior, puts the focus of intervention on the harm done to the elder and away from any cultural biases about the appropriateness of specific behaviors occurring within the family. This criterion also addresses the problem of defining maltreatment

[45] Ibid.
[46] Garbarino and Gilliam, "Understanding Abusive Families."

both in terms of its nature and its intensity or degree. Two types of standards can be used to define abuse: community standards and professional knowledge. Community standards incorporate those standards held by the community regarding what constitutes appropriate treatment of the elderly. Professional knowledge—medical, psychological, and gerontological—also helps to delineate what conditions are nurturing and what are alternatively harmful or inappropriate for the elderly.

While some personal interpretation will always be inherent in any definition of elder abuse, only continued exploration into the area of abuse will facilitate a more accurate definition and minimize problems rooted in the differential access and experience of practitioners, as well as the cultural biases of those in the helping professions.

On a micro level, successful intervention in cases of elder abuse requires that the worker possess knowledge in these areas: knowledge of self, knowledge of the dynamics of aging and of abuse within the family system, cultural and societal influences, and appropriate helping skills. In cases of elder abuse, the worker's own attitudes and perceptions about violence, aging, and dependency play an especially significant role in the detection and treatment of the problem. The worker who does not have a keen awareness of her or his own feelings and how they may affect perceptions can experience significant difficulty in making an accurate assessment of a case and in bridging divergent perceptions between her- or himself and the client's family system or significant others involved. The worker who views the abusive situation only from his or her own perspective will miss important cues. As with other problems, the worker must begin where the client "is."

Intervention in cases of elder abuse requires the worker to possess a well-rounded view of the societal and cultural influences which affect the family, particularly during the last stage of the family life span. Although the relative importance of these influences in each family varies with the family's unique history, the worker must be able to assess those factors which are relevant and must be dealt with or whose influence must at least be acknowledged during intervention. In order to intervene effectively, the worker must have an accurate perception of what can and cannot be changed through his or her intervention. Failure to make such distinctions between critical variables can result not only in ineffective service but in feelings of powerlessness on the part of the worker.

The specific knowledge base which workers may draw upon in the treatment of elder abuse is limited at the present time but does offer important information which should be used to maximum benefit. The utility of this data is greatest during the assessment process, when the worker must identify all variables relevant to the etiology of the abuse. Using data obtained from studies of elder abuse, it is possible to construct an index of significant variables which can assist the worker in the identification process and the development of a case plan. Table 72–1 presents a selected overview of important variables and related avenues of investigation which can facilitate accurate diagnosis and treatment of the problem.

Successful intervention in the area of elder abuse will also require the development of new helping techniques, rather than the simple transference of skills used in working with other client populations or elderly clients with other types of problems. The elderly, frequently left out of case plans utilizing family therapy, should be considered as an integral part in treatment.

ADOPTION

CHAPTER 73

ASSESSING ADOPTIONS IN DIFFICULTY

David Howe

The suspicion that adopted children and their families are more likely to run into difficulties receives only modest support from the research literature. On the whole, adopted children fare well in their new families and only a few display problems serious enough to bring them to the attention of clinicians and therapists. Estimates have varied over the decades, but recent work suggests that adopted children are approximately twice as likely to be referred for psychiatric help compared to all non-adopted children (for example, Howe and Hinings, 1987). Although the referral rates for adopted children are comparatively high, in absolute terms they remain low. Most adopted children are not referred for psychiatric help.

In spite of their modest numbers, adopted children who do appear in the clinical setting have long held a fascination for both the practitioner and the researcher. As well as being of interest in their own right, they seem to throw light on the mechanisms that drive the more usual arrangements of family life. Yet in spite of this interest, progress in understanding the needs that are peculiar to the adopted child and his or her family has been slow. To the extent that the adoptive dimension is ignored when a child is referred for help, the family is more likely to judge that help unsatisfactory (Howe, 1990b). In an attempt to respond to the particular needs of adopted people and their families, a number of specialist agencies have emerged. One such pioneering agency is the Post-adoption Centre, London.

Among the many people to whom the Centre offers help are adopters and their families. During its first three years (ending July, 1989), the Centre received 261 referrals from families who were finding the behaviour of their adopted child a worry. The range of problems that worried parents varied, but included most of those referred to psychiatric clinics and are typical of adolescents thought to be difficult or troublesome: theft of money from parents, problems at school, eating disorders, self-abuse, aggressiveness, lying and disobedience. Indeed, sixty per cent of the adoptive families had been in-

Reprinted from *British Journal of Social Work*, Vol. 22, No. 1 (1992), pp. 1–15, by permission of Oxford University Press.

volved with either a child guidance clinic or a social work agency before visiting the Centre. Parents would commonly feel that they had failed their child or had been let down by him or her in some way. The problem was usually long standing and the request for help came after the parents felt that they could no longer cope. 'We're at the end of our tether' were typical of the first words any parent was likely to say when he or she contacted the Centre. Of the 261 children reported to be difficult, 53 per cent were boys and 47 per cent were girls. 48 per cent of the children were aged between 13 and 16 at the time of referral (see Howe, 1990*a*).

During the Centre's third year of operation, the opportunity arose to study the assessments made by counsellors of families who were experiencing difficulties with an adopted son or daughter. The research was exploratory. The intention was to analyse the counsellors' assessments and extract common themes and identify the diagnostic concepts that were being used to understand the family, the child and the problem. Counsellors typically saw all members of the family. Assessments would be made over several sessions. Thirty cases were randomly selected for study. Counsellors were interviewed at length about their work with the family, particular attention being paid to the assessment made. Interview transcripts were content-analysed. All quoted extracts use the counselors' own words.

THE TWO DIMENSIONS OF ASSESSMENT

Two dimensions defined the counsellors' assessments. One was developmental in perspective and was derived from the recent work of adoption theorists. The other was interactional and was a product of the counsellors' own diagnostic experiences with families.

The *developmental perspective* owes much to the work of Brodzinsky (1987; 1990). The adopted child has the same developmental tasks to complete as the non-adopted child, but in addition he or she has to handle several more that are peculiar to the adopted condition. In order to negotiate these tasks, the child needs a sympathetic and responsive environment in which parents provide a secure, accepting, flexible climate. Brodzinsky has pioneered a model in which the special psychological tasks of the adopted child are mapped out. Adopted children have to work out what adoption means to them and other people in order to work out who they are, both to themselves and to others. Brodzinsky believes that there is a 'psychological risk factor' in being adopted. This does not mean that all adopted children will have problems but they do face extra developmental hurdles. To explain the situation of the adopted child and their family, he generates a 'model of adoption adjustment' which itself is an adaptation of Erikson's (1963) model of psychosocial development. 'The basic thesis of the model', explains Brodzinsky (1987, p. 30), 'is that the experience of adoption exposes parents and children to a unique set of psychosocial tasks that interact with and complicate the more universal developmental tasks of family life . . . it is assumed that the degree to which adoptive parents and their children acknowledge the unique challenges in their life, and the way in which they attempt to cope with them, largely determines their pattern of adjustment'.

So, for example, all members of the family have to mourn the loss of another (the birth mother, the child that the parents could not have), parents have to 'tell' the child that he or she is adopted, and both parents and child have to integrate feelings of love and hate. The coping strategies used by children shift with age from those which are 'problem-focused' (trying to change the problem which is causing the distress) to those which are 'emotion-focused' (seeking to regulate one's own emotional response to the problem) (Brodzinsky, 1990, pp. 22-3). Although older children still adopt a problem-focused response there is a gradual increase in emotion-focused coping with the use of denial, avoidance, and cognitive re-appraisal when faced with adoption-related stress.

The *interactional perspective* emphasizes the quality of the relationship that exists between parents and child at different stages of the child's life. Loss is endemic to the family life of those who adopt and those who are adopted—the loss of biological parents, reproductive ability, the first few months of the adopted child's life. Small (1987) goes so far as to say that the central focus of all therapeutic work with adoptive families is to help them understand that adoptive family life is 'structured out of loss'. Brinich (1990) is quite clear that before children can re-establish a benign internal representation of themselves and their parents, they need to mourn that which has been lost. In order to do this, children need the help of their adoptive parents who in turn need to have mourned the loss of that which they have lost (Brinich, 1990, p. 13). The normal adjustment problems associated with profound experiences of loss leave people emotionally vulnerable to future stress with the consequent prospect of old emotional feelings of loss and anger resurfacing. The general wisdom is that if either the parents or the child are sufficiently robust, these areas of vulnerability will hold and eventually heal without serious fracture. The success of the majority of adoptions is testimony to the mutually rewarding relationships that most adoptive families achieve.

However, in a minority of cases, areas of emotional sensitivity may re-surface. The unconditional love and responsive parenting that is so important in meeting the needs of the adopted child can be upset by the emotional demands of the child, the parents, or both. These demands are present in the psychological make-up of the child or parents and result from previous, usually difficult, not to say traumatic experiences. In this way, very deprived or disturbed children may expose and then exploit even minor areas of emotional vulnerability in the parents. Equally, emotional problems in the parents may arouse dormant anxieties and insecurities even in children with relatively stable pre-adoption backgrounds. When there are anxieties and unresolved conflicts in both the parents and the child, feelings of doubt and uncertainty are first amplified and then compounded. A vicious circle forms in which the parents are absorbed by their own concerns, leaving them with less emotional energy with which to respond to the needs of their child who, as a result, begins to feel less secure. The Centre receives families in which the ability to provide adequately responsive parenting is failing, either because the parents are increasingly unable to handle their own anxieties and conflicts or because the child's needs place such a huge stress on the resources and emotional coherence of the parents. Even parents who are well-adjusted to their losses find that old, unresolved feelings of loss and anger may be revived.

THE RELATIONSHIP BETWEEN PARENT AND CHILD

There is a clear relationship between different coping strategies and the psychological adjustment of the adopted child. Although the counsellors valued the model of psychosocial adjustment, in this paper I want to emphasize the attention they gave to the effect of stress, brought about by the child attempting to negotiate his or her developmental concerns, on the emotional integrity of the parents. In making this emphasis, counsellors were particularly alert to the two way nature of the parent–child relationship. The behaviour and needs of the adopted child will change the pattern of a family's life. The needs of adopted children are calculated to put a strain on the very quality they most need in their adopters—emotional stability as they handle the demands of a child whose only reason for being with them is because of their own loss. A close, demanding relationship with an adopted child will force parents to face aspects of themselves that may have been long buried, and this makes the union of child and parents potentially problematic.

When the developmental and interactional perspectives are combined, five assessment themes emerge in which the two way character of the psychological stresses associated with adoption are identified:

1. Issues of trust
2. Rejection of difference
3. Insistence on difference
4. Identity
5. Separation and 'how to leave'.

1. *Issues of Trust*

Infants need to develop a basic sense of trust. When parents are warm and relaxed in their role and hold realistic expectations concerning their child's behaviour and development, the baby has a secure base from which to pursue and explore relationships and the environment. Most adopters offer such an experience but there are added emotional demands that occasionally interfere with their ability to provide the child with a basic sense of trust. These pressures include (i) unresolved feelings associated with infertility, (ii) bad starts leading to poor attachment, and (iii) poor social development of older children placed for adoption.

(I) Infertility Those who are infertile need to mourn the loss of their own child. If infertile adopters fail to resolve their own feelings of loss they will not be able to help their adopted child cope with his or her own feelings of loss. Brebner *et al.* (1985) report that the diagnosis of infertility was a traumatic event in the lives of the twenty couples whom they interviewed. Learning of infertility requires a drastic revision of an individual's personal identity. The person has to adjust to the loss of the family he or she imagined that he or she would have had. The method which they chose to resolve their need to become parents was to adopt. However, the study showed that in 'the immediate post-placement period there were dynamic forces from the blow of infertility still at work in some of the adoptive parents which could lead to future problems in their rela-

tionship with their adopted child' (p. 11). The authors recommend that the grief surrounding infertility ought to be resolved before placement of the first child. Two inappropriate reasons for adopting were found amongst some of the couples: the hope that adoption would cure infertility, and the wish to please a marriage partner. Such reasons affected the commitment of the adopters to the child.

Brebner *et al.* remind us that in certain psychological respects adoptive parenthood is different from biological parenthood. Adopters get babies only after they have been assessed, both medically and socially. They do not experience pregnancy and birth. They have to become attached to someone else's baby and make the child psychologically their own. Adoptive parents are responsible for explaining to the child that he or she is adopted. The scrutiny to which adopters are subjected contributes to unconscious and conscious feelings of inadequacy, anger, and guilt. Such feelings, believes Brinich (1990, p. 8), all too easily interfere with the early settling-in of adoptive parents with their newly adopted child. The resentment which such scrutiny provokes often remains hidden as the parents feel that they should be grateful to those who allowed them to adopt. The strong feelings evoked by the adoption process are suppressed, though they are liable to surface if the promised rewards and expectations of adoption are threatened by any severe demands made by the child as he or she expresses his or her needs.

Adopters whose marriage subsequently becomes troubled may project their feelings of hostility on to the child. The fertile parent may blame the other for not being able to have their own child. The adopted child becomes an expression of the parent's sense of failure and may be the recipient of some very damaging emotions from one or both parents. In later years, when the child becomes sexually mature, painful feelings surrounding infertility may be reawakened. This can become even more acute if, say, a daughter becomes pregnant or has an abortion. For example, Sarah's mother, who was infertile, reacted to her daughter's sexuality with anger and rejection, accusing Sarah of being 'wanton, just like her natural mother'.

(II) Bad Starts One of the commonest themes met in adoptions which had run into difficulty was the parents' feeling that the placement had got off to a bad start. Typically the adoptive mother would find the newly arrived child, not infrequently a baby, unresponsive, remote, not even likeable. In turn she would become mechanical and routine in her handling of the child. The difficulty of making a warm, social, playful, and reciprocal relationship with her child inhibited the baby's ability to become attached to the mother. Whereas securely attached children feel confident and self-reliant, the less securely attached child is prone to feelings of anxiety and insecurity. Although parents can tolerate a child's reluctance to respond for a while, eventually they expect the reward of a loving exchange. Barth and Berry (1988, p. 174) note that the development of reciprocity is an indicator to the family that the adoption is working and this provides a resource upon which the family can draw in times of inevitable difficulty. The love and affection provided by the child gives the parents enough reassurance to live through the more stressful times. Without that reassurance, setbacks can soon undermine the relationship's thin base.

Many years later a mother might report that she had never felt close to her baby. In reporting their early experiences, some adoptive parents describe their child as so difficult that they could not relax or relate to him or her. Others described how they themselves were not emotionally able to respond to their child. The long-term effect in both cases was to produce uncertainty in the mind of the child about whether he or she really belonged to the family. Early insecurities continued to echo, leaving the adopted child susceptible and vulnerable to subsequent losses and set-backs. The child could not allow himself or herself to take any relationship for granted. The arrival of younger children or failure in the adoptive parents' marriage was likely to produce particularly difficult behaviour in the child. Many years later not a few parents continued to report feelings of ambivalence about the wisdom of the adoption. Ambivalence and occasionally outright dislike of the child often involved feelings of guilt too.

(III) Late Adoptions Children adopted at older ages have usually experienced a number of losses prior to placement. The evidence is generally strong that the older a child is when placed, the more likely is that placement to be disrupted. Disturbed and distorted relationships with birth parents or multiple changes of caretaker can mean that there was little consistent, affectionate or responsive care prior to placement. This leaves the child inept at social relationships and social behaviour. Children who fail to develop secure, stable attachments arrive in adoptive homes disturbed, mistrustful, or casual about social relationships. The child's initial shallowness of response, and lack of trust or sense of commitment, may disappoint the adopters and undermine their determination to do well by the child. The child's past efforts at handling difficulty and stress will inform the way they approach the new demands of the adoptive home. Neglected children may never have learned to cope with stress by seeking comfort, support and warm conversation. The failure to produce 'positive interactions' may upset the adopters as the child revives old feelings of inadequacy and ineffectiveness. Successful adopters realize that they can expect only slow returns on high emotional investments. Parents who feel that they were not warned about what to expect of the older child or who held unrealistic, inflexible expectations are most likely to have problems. The following example illustrates some of these themes:

> Placed at the age of one, James was two at the time of referral. Mrs Hart said she had not bonded with him and maybe she didn't even like the child. . . . After many years of infertility testing and adoption assessment, James was placed and remains their only child. They said they were made to feel that they were lucky to have him, that beggars can't be choosers and so they found it impossible to admit to social workers or health professionals that they were finding him a difficult child. Throughout it appears as if Mr and Mrs Hart did not have any clear ideas about how a young child of James's age should behave. When they took him home, they thought he seemed backward. Not long after his arrival he cried and cried for six weeks, on top of which he was said to have eating problems. They said he would only eat ham sandwiches. Other aspects of his behaviour were felt to be undisciplined and his adopters blamed his foster-mother and his genetic background for this. His mother was a young Irish girl and Mr and Mrs Hart believed that the Irish blood in him accounted for his wild behaviour and his temper tantrums. At the point of referral, his parents concluded that they didn't really like the boy. They were both disappointed and angry about a number of things including the intrusiveness of the infertility testing and adoption assessment as well

as feeling ill-prepared for the rigours of looking after a one year old child. They felt that James had both dominated and degraded them, that he controlled them and overwhelmed them. Mr and Mrs Hart felt disillusioned; James was not the perfect baby. He had come with a history and a mother. They had been through some unpleasant hoops to get him and then all he did was cry. They had invested so much in the adoption and had felt so few gains and so many losses.

2. Rejection of Difference

Couples who decide to adopt have to handle a number of difficulties. They have to approach outsiders to acquire their child, they are not certain about the status of the parent in adoption, and they are unclear about the nature and status of the prospective child (Kirk, 1964; 1981). These experiences become a handicap in the performance of their role as parents. Adopters are confronted by conflicting obligations. The first requires the adopters to *integrate* the child fully into their family. The second is to tell the child that they are adopted and help them understand what this means, to help them recognize that in basic ways they are *'different'*. Adoption demands that both parents and child resolve the tension between integration and differentiation. The child, too, has to realize that he or she was both chosen (by the adopters) *and* given up (by the birth parents).

This issue becomes most acute during the second half of childhood when the need to explain adoption comes into conflict with the adopters' desire for full and exclusive parenthood. This parental role handicap is bound to affect the quality of interaction between the parent and child. Kirk believes that adopters cope with this conflict in one of two ways. There are those who deny that their situation as parents is any different from that of biological parents. This he calls 'rejection of difference'. And there are those who recognize that aspects of adoptive family life are different to biologically based family life. This he calls 'acknowledgement of difference' and this is seen as the preferred strategy. Denial and the rejection of difference may help assuage the pain of loss and infertility but in the long run it undermines the child's integration into the family. This is the paradox of adoption.

The rejection of difference is likely to become problematic in adolescence when any child begins his or her search for identity. It is clearly difficult for adolescents who are not allowed, or not supported when they examine their origins, to feel secure enough to differ from their adoptive parents and for this difference not to be perceived as threatening. It is possible that many adopted children who do not cause problems simply deny their difference. For many adopted children there lurks the fear of a second rejection which impairs not only their ability to relate in an open way with their adopters but also frustrates the achievement of an independent identity. Only if the parents are able to recognize that the child has to handle some basic issues about who he or she is will that child feel understood. Moreover we discover that parents who can acknowledge difference are free to engage in a more accurate and sensitive relationship with their child (Kirk, 1981, pp. 46-7).

Thus, acknowledging difference facilitates empathy and communication which in turn promotes attachment and security. What at first sight appears paradoxical, that acknowledging difference promotes integration, can be explained in terms of the good quality of interaction that the acknowledgement encourages. Denial of difference frustrates and suppresses interaction on matters which loom large in the emotional experience of both adopters and child. It is also sometimes the case that the adopters feel that to be different is to be deficient. Difference receives a negative connotation and so may be denied, disowned or even interpreted by the child as a deviant condition that no-one is able to talk about openly. Brinich (1990, p. 7), in his clinical experience, found that adoptive parents commonly accepted certain aspects of their child while rejecting others. The bits of the child which they did not like were said to be genetically inherited—'he doesn't get that from us'. To acknowledge difference is not to give it a negative evaluation; it is simply to accept that it is present. Ironically the insistence that the adopted child is no different to a biological child forbids any discussion of an important topic. For example:

> Since the age of eleven, Sue had become increasingly difficult. She had stolen from home and her friends. She lied. Twice she had become pregnant and both her babies were adopted. Family life was tense and stressful. . . . They adopted Sue when the younger of their two birth children was five. Sue was of mixed race and was placed as a baby. It was Mrs Jay's idea to adopt. She wanted to give an unwanted black baby a good family life. But having put themselves forward as a couple fit to adopt, they were now finding it very hard to cope with failure. Although her behaviour is beyond the pale, they feel too guilty to throw her out. . . .

> Sue said she never felt like the rest of her family; she did not behave like a Jay. They tended to agree. For her part she did not feel she was a Jay. There appeared to be some obligation on Sue to be like the family as this would demonstrate her gratitude for having been 'rescued' as a black baby. But the Jays could not express their anger at Sue's failure to behave like them because this would undermine their self-image as altruistic adopters. The whole ethos contaminated the way the family related to her. Spontaneity and authenticity were lost. Whatever Sue did to assert her difference was denied; it seemed to have little outward impact on the family. Therefore Sue seemed driven to greater extremes of independent 'un-Jay' like behaviour. The parents absorbed, and on the surface accepted, her escalating levels of misbehaviour. The more she did wrong, the more they rescued her. They denied that she is responsible and took control of the consequences. They paid her fines; they reimbursed monies stolen from friends. Mrs Jay decided on the adoption of the babies and took charge of all the arrangements. Sue has only a negative understanding of herself; that she is not like a Jay. She has no method of finding herself and understanding herself within the family as it denies her difference.

3. Insistence on Difference

Brodzinsky (1987) develops Kirk's views on the way difference is handled. Although there is a healthy route to be found by acknowledging difference, it can be taken too far and used in evidence against the child. This 'insistence-on-difference' is a helpful notion and is seen as an adverse coping strategy amongst many adopters who seek help. Brodzinsky covers the main features of the idea in these words:

> the differences are often seen as explanations for family disconnectedness and disharmony. Parents may have difficulty seeing their adopted child as an integral part of their family; they may identify the child with the biological parents and resort to 'bad blood' or genetic explanations for the child's behavioural and emotional problems. Children too sometimes adopt this coping style. They may see themselves as so different from their parents and siblings that they feel totally alien within the family; they may be unable to find anything within the adoptive parents with which to identify; they may feel psychologically rejected and abandoned in the midst of their own family (p. 42).

An example is provided by a white adoptive mother who was knowledgeable and alert to the issues of being black in a white family, in a white society. She insisted on helping her thirteen year old son become aware of his blackness at almost every opportunity:

> I felt that the mother's sensitivity to the black issue both distorted and exaggerated matters for the boy. It seemed to get in the way of her being able to see other positive aspects of his character. The boy's behaviour became increasingly difficult. He ran away from home, he stole from his mother's purse and he wasn't doing well at school . . . but mum interpreted his behaviour as his rejecting her.

4. Identity

Understanding what it means to be adopted is something which adopted children have to consider at different stages throughout their childhood. Who am I? Where did I come from? To whom do I belong? All children have to face this psychosocial task but for the adopted child there are additional complications. Often there is a lack of information about birth parents and the reasons why they were relinquished for adoption. Many adopted children do not wish to hurt the feelings of their adoptive parents and so suppress their curiosity and the subject of their origins. Adopters, too, have to consider these questions and generate answers for both the child and themselves. However, the parents generally work through these questions very early on in the adoption often when the child is quite young. The topic of adoption is introduced to the child and thenceforth the parents either behave matter-of-factly about it or never mention it again, believing that they have 'told' the child all about it. But the child can only begin to grasp what it means to be adopted as he or she grows older. The matter only takes on its full meaning when the child reaches early adolescence. That is when he or she is ready to consider and discuss adoption. In some families, therefore, there is a serious mismatch between the outlook of the parents and their adopted child. Emotionally, parents and child are out of phase. To the child it may seem as if his or her parents are avoiding the subject:

At the age of 16, Diane received a letter via the adoption agency from her birth mother. She became very curious about her background though remained uncertain about meeting her birth mother. The letter precipitated a crisis in the adoptive household, raising the whole issue of adoption which had hardly been discussed over the years. The adopters were very wary, threatened and hurt about the sudden appearance of the birth mother. Diane's adoptive mother wanted to supervise and control all contact and correspondence between the birth mother and her daughter. Understandably but regretfully, she was more absorbed by her own fears and anxieties about losing her daughter than trying to understand things from Diane's point of view.

Hodges (1988) has identified two fundamental questions which adopted children have to confront in their development: 'Who were my first parents and what were they like?' and 'Why did they give me up?' We can also turn these questions around so that the child asks 'Who am I?' and 'Who am I in relation to my second parents?' These are not easy questions to ask but useful answers can be given which help the child cope with this special aspect of their development. However, the questions do not always feel comfortable for adopters. In this case the child either learns not to ask such questions (and therefore is unable to answer them) or asks them and precipitates feelings of anxiety, fear, and anger on the part of his or her adoptive parents.

Adopters who are not comfortable with their child's search for identity leave their child to choose one of two strategies. Some conform, meet their parents' expectations, do not revive difficult feelings about origins, and become 'good adoptees'. Others rebel, struggle to assert an independent identity, and become 'bad adoptees'. 'The "good adoptee" appears to conform as a defence against a deeply felt fear of further abandonment, while the "bad adoptee" is motivated by the need to act out the feeling that he or she must have been "no good" to have been given away' (Winkler *et al.*, 1988, p. 90).

5. Separation and 'How to Leave'

Although attachment to parents may remain strong, the adolescent begins to develop ties to other people, particularly peers but other adults too. Becoming independent, establishing one's own identity and leaving home are not always easy tasks for children or parents. However, for adopted children and their parents there is a potential overlay of emotional symbolism that can complicate matters. When the biological child separates, it is less likely to feel like a rejection; a biological tie remains if nothing else. But when the adopted child leaves, there is the fear, by both parent and child, that there is nothing left to connect them. Separation can be interpreted as an act of disloyalty. Matters are particularly difficult when the adopted child was placed at an older age. All adoptive families have the twin tasks of promoting attachment and helping the child separate and achieve independence. 'While conventional families move from complete attachment toward separation and individuation of the children, the adoptive family of older children is striving for attachment to the child at the same time that they must support the development of independence and self-sufficiency' (Barth and Berry, 1988, p. 62).

Separation can be a difficult and fraught time. Some children find it difficult to separate, fearing that they will hurt their parents. Others leave and return, often repeatedly and in an exaggerated fashion. And yet others can separate only in a dramatic and disruptive way, suggesting that the only way to break free of the family is to head for independence and complete detachment. The feeling is that the child separates violently or not at all. For adopters who feel that they have put a lot into a difficult child, his or her eventual departure may feel particularly painful; all their efforts have simply led to the loss of the child in whom they had invested so much:

> Amy was placed as a baby at very short notice with Mr and Mrs Simmons, a childless couple, affording them little time for preparation. . . . Her adoptive mother said she was not an easy baby, eye contact was avoided during feeding and she cried a lot. Her adopted brother, Alan, was placed a year later and in contrast he was said to have been a most rewarding infant. Alan was always the favoured child . . . Amy did not know how to please her mother and felt that love for her was conditional; she had to be like her mother wanted her to be otherwise she was not acceptable. However, as she was not like her mother wanted her to be she was rejected. For her part, Mrs Simmons could not give her love unconditionally and all the effort she felt that she had poured into her daughter did not seem to have been appreciated . . . Mrs Simmons felt extremely ambivalent about Amy. She could neither accept her nor let her go hoping that her investment might yet come good. By the age of sixteen Amy was testing her parents' commitment by stealing money from them. 'If you love me you'll allow me the money; if you don't allow me the money this shows you don't love me'. Amy had grave doubts about her parents wanting her and was driven to test their commitment by resorting to increasingly exasperating behaviour. This merely exposed mother's profoundly ambivalent feelings.

QUESTIONS OF BELONGING

The result of adding together the two diagnostic dimensions is to define a set of experiences that revolve around feelings of belonging, being wanted and loved. The extent to which a child feels he or she belongs to a family is gauged by the answers which both parents and children give to the following questions:

> Do I want you? Are you mine?
> Do you want me? Am I yours?

Of course, the questions need not be asked explicitly, although sometimes they are. More usually, they remain implicitly posed in the situations in which parents and children find themselves. 'When adopted children learn of their adoption,' writes Brinich (1990, p. 12), 'they lose the fantasy that they are lovable no matter what. They also lose the fantasy that parents remain parents no matter what.' In the families referred to the Centre, at least one member was answering at least one of these questions of belonging in the negative. The negative answers reflected the difficulties the family were having in one or more of the psychosocial tasks associated with adoption. Counsellors were therefore aware not only of the two way nature of relationships and behaviour in adoptive families, but also of the patterns and developments that emerged over time. Mapping the family's emotional history in this way allows the counsellors to see the complex interplay of need and counter-need and the manner in which the emotional demands of one family member can trigger and revive old unresolved feelings in another.

REFERENCES

Barth, R. P. and Berry, M. (1988) *Adoption and Disruption*, New York, Aldine de Gruyter.

Brebner, C. M., Sharp. J. D. and Stone, F. H. (1985) *The Role of Infertility in Adoption*, No. 7, London, BAAF.

Brinich, P. M. (1980), 'Some potential effects of adoption upon self and object representations', *Psychoanalytic Study of the Child*, 35, pp. 107–33.

Brinich, P. (1990) 'Adoption, ambivalence and mourning, clinical and theoretical interrelationships', *Adoption and Fostering*, 14, 1, pp. 6–15.

Brodzinsky, D. M. (1987) 'Adjustment to adoption: a psychosocial perspective', *Clinical Psychology Review*, 7, pp. 25–47.

Brodzinsky, D. M. (1990) 'A stress and coping model of adoption adjustment,' in Brodzinsky, D. M. and Schechter. M. D. (eds.) *The Psychology of Adoption*, Oxford, Oxford University Press.

Brodzinsky, D. M. and Schechter, M. D. (eds.) (1990), *The Psychology of Adoption*, Oxford, Oxford University Press.

Erikson, E. (1963) *Childhood and Society* (2nd edn.), New York, W. W. Norton.

Hodges, J. (1988) 'Aspects of the relation to self and objects in early maternal deprivation and adoption', paper given at the Conference on Psychoanalytic Insights into Problems of Adoption, University College, London, 15 and 16 July.

Howe, D. (1990a) 'The Post-adoption Centre: the first three years', *Adoption and Fostering*, 14, 1, pp. 27–31.

Howe, D. (1990b) 'The consumers' view of the Post-adoption Centre', *Adoption and Fostering*, 14, 2, pp. 32–6.

Howe, D. and Hinings, D. (1987) 'Adopted children referred to a child and family centre', *Adoption and Fostering*, 11, 3, pp. 44–7.

Kirk, H. D. (1964) *Shared Fate; a theory of adoption and mental health*, New York, Free Press.

Kirk, H. D. (1981) *Adoptive Kinship*, Toronto, Butterworth.

Small, J. W. (1987) 'Working with adoptive families', *Public Welfare*, Summer, pp. 41–8.

Winkler, R. C., Brown, D. W., van Keppel, M. and Blanchard, A. (1988) *Clinical Practice in Adoption*, Oxford, Pergamon Press.

CHAPTER 74

ADOPTED ADULTS' PERCEPTION OF THEIR NEED TO SEARCH

Implications for Clinical Practice

Doris Bertocci and Marshall D. Schechter

INTRODUCTION

The adopted person's search for birth relatives has been the subject of much controversy in the adoption field (Jones, 1976; Zeilinger, 1979) and much fascination in social science research (Sobol & Cardiff, 1983; Sorosky, Baran & Pannor, 1978). The controversy has to do with the perceived challenge which the search represents to traditional adoption assumptions and practices, at least in English-speaking cultures. The fascination has to do in part with the age-old interest in the determinants of human personality and behavior, i.e., the nature vs. nurture debate (Bohman, 1981; Cadoret, 1978; Grotevant, Scarr & Weinberg, 1977; Munsinger, 1975). In particular, the social sciences of the 20th century have attempted more fully to understand the vicissitudes of human sexuality; attachment, separation, and loss; identity and the evolution of the sense of self; vulnerability to stress and disease. The experience of the adopted person has much to teach us about these matters.

In distinction from the other mental health professions, clinical social work comes to the issues of adoption from a unique perspective, straddling on the one hand the traditions of child and social welfare and, on the other, a rich variety of psychodynamic understandings of personality and human development. This has import not only for how the social work field comprehends adoption and search issues, but for how poten-

Reprinted from *Smith College Studies in Social Work,* Vol. 61, No. 2 (March, 1991), pp. 179–196, by permission of the publisher.

tially it can work toward therapeutic and social changes which reflect that comprehension.

In various attempts to account for the adoptee's need to search, and for the timing of it developmentally, emphasis has tended to be on external precipitating factors such as having children or losing an adoptive parent. It was from our perspective as psychodynamically-oriented clinicians, having had varied exposure to searching and nonsearching adoptees, that we sought to add to the reported findings by further examining the *intrapsychic meanings* of search ideation and behavior. Following a literature review, including some findings from our own survey of adoptees (Bertocci & Schechter, 1987), we discuss the implications for understanding certain common themes in the psychology of adoptees.

STUDIES OF SEARCH PHENOMENA

Until recently the social science literature treated "search" as a symbolic or fantasied phenomenon which was presumed to express internal conflict relating to difficulties with the adoptive family (Frisk, 1964; Goldstein, Freud & Solnit, 1973). For example, Toussieng viewed "wandering" behavior in disturbed adolescent adoptees as representing a symbolic search for the birthfamily (1962). The how-they-fared follow-up studies of adult adoptees (non-patients) also focussed on the subjects' experiences within the adoptive family and minimally, if at all, addressed issues relating to the birthparents (Jaffee & Fanshel, 1979; McWhinnie, 1967; Raynor, 1980).

Literal or activated search—that is, the evolution of internally-perceived need for access to the birthfamily into active attempts to satisfy that need—was addressed only in autobiographical and journalistic accounts in the literature (Allen, 1983; Erlich, 1977; Fisher, 1973; Leitch, 1984; Lifton, 1975, 1979; Marcus, 1981; Maxtone-Graham, 1983; McKuen, 1976; Paton, 1954, 1960, 1968). It was probably in response to the proliferation of these accounts in the 1970s and 1980s that social scientists and adoption workers sought to address more fully the topic of adoptees' fantasies and concerns about the birthparents. Even so, it was with a certain uneasiness as authors proffered reassurance that wishes to search did not seem to be particularly prevalent (Raynor, 1980; Stein & Hoopes, 1985).

Careful inquiry into the subjective experiences of adopted people, in both patient and non-patient groups, reveals that the phenomenon of search behavior falls within a continuum; and that this continuum ranges from unconscious-only associations and fantasies, through conscious-level ideation, to activated search aimed at literal reunion with the biological parent(s). Inquiry also shows that in between both ends of the spectrum fall a variety of consciously-articulated subjective experiences: "thinking or wondering about" the birthparents with no reported fantasies, with vague fantasies, or with specific fixed fantasies (e.g., family romance); "wishing to know about" the birthparents (desire for information, general or specific); desiring direct access to the birthparents but with undefined goals; and wishing to experience a face-to-face reunion (Day & Leeding, 1980; Sorosky et al., 1978; Triseliotis, 1973; Webber, Thompson & Stoneman, 1980). However, even clinically knowledgeable researchers have tended to gravitate back to the concept of "curiosity," as though search rested on a relatively simplistic cognitive process.

Twelve studies focus specifically on activated search and/or reunion, come from primarily English-speaking countries, and vary greatly as to methodology, scope and variables analyzed (Bertocci & Schechter, 1987; Day & Leeding, 1980; Depp, 1982; Kowal & Schilling, 1985; Lion, 1976; Simpson, Timm, and McCubbin, 1981; Slaytor, 1986; Sobol & Cardiff, 1983; Sorosky et al., 1978; Thompson, Stoneman, Webber & Harrison, 1978; Triseliotis, 1973; Webber et al., 1980). A detailed review of these studies can be found elsewhere (Schechter & Bertocci, 1990). It should be borne in mind that the representativeness of any sample in the area of adoption research has always been open to question. This is both because of the paucity of formal research,[1] particularly involving substantial samples, and because no statistics in the United States of even the most basic data, such as numbers of legalized adoptions, have been compiled since 1971 (Sambrano, 1987).

A consistent finding of the 12 studies was that a majority of searchers were white, middle-class females in young adulthood. There was also some consistency in respondents' dissatisfaction with the way communication about adoption-related issues was handled in their families. This has been widely misinterpreted as dissatisfaction with the adoptive parents themselves, which has fueled notions that activated search is a response to this alleged dissatisfaction with their parents.

In the studies that asked why search (activated) was delayed or avoided, respondents to whom this issue was relevant referred almost universally to fears of hurting, alienating, or losing the adoptive parents (Bertocci & Schechter, 1987; Sorosky et al., 1978). A consensus of the studies reporting reunion data was that a completed search usually resulted in significantly improved psychological changes as subjectively experienced by the adoptees; and that the relationships between the adoptee and the adoptive parents was often believed to have improved as a result (Bertocci & Schechter, 1987; Depp, 1982; Lion, 1976; Slaytor, 1986; Sorosky et al., 1978).

There were many differences in the subject populations studied with respect to such factors as the subjects' age when adoptive status was disclosed and as to whether the subjects had siblings. Two main areas of inconsistency in the studies' findings had to do with the respondents' evaluations of their experience within the adoptive family, and the nature of the respondents' fantasies about their birthparents. For instance, the respondents in the Great Britain studies were predominantly negative on both issues (Day & Leeding, 1980; Triseliotis, 1973), whereas the largest groups in the North American studies were more likely to give positive or mixed responses on these issues (Bertocci & Schechter, 1987; Kowal & Schilling, 1985; Simpson et al., 1981; Sorosky et al., 1978; Thompson et al., 1978).

The Bertocci & Schechter (1987) questionnaire study solicited information that was only cursorily, at most, addressed in the other studies. The main issues explored more explicitly were (1) the adoptee's age at placement and history of pre-placement arrangements; (2) the adoptee's history of childhood physical or emotional problems; (3) the degree of preoccupation with adoptive status through their development into adulthood; (4) any physical or mental health problems in the adoptive parents; (5) the signif-

---

[1] It has been observed that "Adoption research remains largely in the world of product-testing, with the primary aim of boosting consumer confidence. The consumers in this context are adoptive parents—children not so much consumers as consumed" (Shaw, 1984, p. 120).

icance of perceived physical similarities with the adoptive family; (6) emotional changes desired pre-search, and experienced post-search.

The Bertocci & Schechter (1987) study found that (1) most respondents had been placed early (77%) and without multiple pre-placement separations (66%); (2) just under half (48%) cited childhood problems, primarily emotional, which clustered into generalized states of anxiety and confusion, followed by behavior problems, depression, and learning difficulties; (3) there was a definite and consistent increment in conscious or preconscious ideation with respect to their own adoptive status from childhood, through the teens, into adulthood, with the desire for specific information about birth relatives (i.e., activation into literal search) not occurring until adulthood; (4) a slight majority (56%) cited significant health problems, primarily emotional, in at least one adoptive parent, just under a third appearing to have been of traumatic significance to the adoptee (e.g., alcoholism, debilitation from chronic medical or mental illness); (5) a majority (60%) regarded the lack of perceived physical similarities to the adoptive family as a significant issue, emphasizing frustration and embarrassment, confusion, envy, and loneliness; (6) regardless of how positively or negatively the adoptive family was evaluated, common themes were of feeling lost, disconnected, unwhole, and pervasively anxious, with post-search internal changes clustering consistently around improved self-esteem, body-image, interpersonal relationships, and lessened vulnerability to anxiety states.

Demographic data from the questionnaire enabled a focus on sex differences which were noted on several discrete variables: as compared with females, males were more likely to have been placed later, to have de-emphasized the importance of physical similarities with adoptive relatives, to have mentioned more frequently positive reactions to adoptive status, and to have seen little connection between adoptive status and any physical or emotional problems. Males were also more likely to have activated the search at a later age.

None of the studies of search ideation and behavior, including our own, had access to information about such important factors as subjects' psychological-mindedness and overall personality and defensive constellations and coping styles. Further inquiry of this kind might shed some light on whether and how activated searchers might be a self-selected population. For instance, it is not understood why a disproportionate number of searchers, at least those who respond to inquiry,[2] are female; but it is also not known whether non-responding searchers or non-searchers are disproportionately male. As discussed elsewhere (Schechter & Bertocci, 1990), a number of psychological and sociocultural explanations are brought to the speculation, such as differences in how connectedness (e.g., family ties) is conceptualized and valued (Feigelman & Silverman, 1983; Gilligan, 1982). It does appear that the gender gap in search behavior is reduced in countries where records are open, i.e., where access to birth records is easier (Day & Leeding, 1980; Triseliotis, 1973).

But quite beyond gender differences in search behavior, further study is needed, not from the more familiar model of "pathogenicity" (Aumend & Barrett, 1984), but according to an adaptational model of personality that takes into account individual vari-

---

[2] As noted even in some forms of research generically, a disproportionate number of respondents is often female; with adoptee-subjects this will include *non-searchers* (Sobol & Cardiff, 1983).

ations in vulnerabilities and resiliences (Anthony & Cohler, 1987). For instance, there may be differences between searchers and non-searchers in the tolerance of ambiguity and of intrapsychic conflict (e.g., in the method and degree of reliance on certain defenses such as externalization, displacement, denial, and sublimation). In any event, the psychology and adaptation of non-searching adoptees are not likely to be well understood because of the relative inaccessibility of this group as subjects.

It has been noted that "Success in the psychotherapeutic treatment of the personality disorders has been the result of extensive clinical experience, not refinements in research design" (Masterson & Klein, 1989, p. 3). The same might be said about evaluating the treatment of any diagnostic entity or client group. With this in mind, we shift to theoretical and clinical considerations for treating the adopted person which are based, in an admittedly rudimentary way, on findings from studies of adoptees who have contemplated or engaged in search.

SEARCH PHENOMENA AND CLINICAL PRACTICE

Regardless of whether an adopted client expresses search fantasies, either directly or in disguised form—or seemingly not at all—the clinician may recognize a number of common themes that reflect the adoptee's attempts to reconcile various confounding elements in his or her life. On the basis of what we have distilled from the twelve studies mentioned above, and noting a direct parallel in comments of our adopted patients in clinical practice, we have identified several universal issues which we believe may come to have multiple psychological complications for the adopted person. Arbitrarily addressed separately, we offer them as thematic "markers" which the clinician might bear in mind in treating any adopted client. These issues are briefly illustrated with vignettes of adoptee-patients and with direct quotes from respondents in our own study (Bertocci & Schechter, 1987), followed by comments on special considerations in the diagnosis and treatment of adoptees.

Loss and Reparation

Loss is a central theme in all discussions of search ideation and behavior (Small, 1979; Sorosky et al., 1978; Winkler, Brown, Van Keppel, & Blanchard, 1988), with implications of pathological mourning as it has come to be understood in the clinical literature (Bowlby, 1961, 1980; Freud, 1917/1957; Lindemann, 1944). In denying the fact of death, it is postulated, the mourner is unable to dis-attach from the lost object, in the process sacrificing potentially healthier attachments to other objects and experiences. However, for the adoptee since the loss is by sociolegal protocols rather than by death, the loss is potentially reversible. Thus the striving to recover the lost object can take a literal, activated form as the adoptee attempts to repair the rupture, as it is subjectively experienced in his or her sense of wholeness.

Adoptees in both the patient and nonpatient population typically refer to spaces within themselves, which represent a painful and distracting vacuum, and to space outside themselves which represents their subjective state of suspension in time and place. The adoptee's experience of mourning cannot, on the face of it, be conceived of as pathological in the traditional sense since the reality of the object's (birthparent's) existence is consciously acknowledged (rather than the object's absence being unconsciously denied). Rather, adoptees experience varying degrees of emotional vulnerability to other losses and rejections in their life experience. Differences should be noted, as well as similarities, from those whose lives have been dismantled and restructured as a result of losses through death or divorce (Brodzinsky, 1990).

> *Patients:* Adele, a member of an adoptee support group, related her consistent sense of emptiness to "not belonging." She had been treated for depression with marginal success. On meeting her birth father, three full siblings, and assorted other birth relatives, Adele reported feeling "whole" for the first time in her life.
>   Prior to a tentative attempt to inquire into his birth history, Mark commented "I'm tired of not knowing who I really am."

> *Respondents:* "Interpersonal relationships never last because I don't trust people, I assume they want me to get lost so I leave."
>   "I don't handle loss well—I can't seem to let go."

Therapeutic considerations. Therapists should be aware that loss-related depression may lie behind a number of physical and emotional symptoms presented by the adopted person. Since the adoptee's initial (primary) loss of the birthfamily is the paradigm of all subsequent interpersonal separations and losses, reparation requires that, at some juncture in the treatment, the adoptee's early history involving relinquishment for adoption must become a central therapeutic focus. The therapist can explore search as an option for the client to consider in activated form. It should be noted, however, that exploring activated search does not necessarily imply recommending it, which would remain at the therapist's discretion. Information-giving (e.g., search support groups) and empathic acknowledgment of the fright and frustration inherent in search might become an integral part of the treatment, depending on the client's reactions to the therapist's exploration.

It should be no surprise to the therapist, when dealing with an adopted person of any age, that the client imagines with varying degrees of conviction that the therapist is actually a long-lost relative. Aside from other meanings that may be found in the client's "curiosity" about the therapist, the fantasy can be seen as an attempt at repairing the original loss, and at finding relief from its associated secrets.

Envy and Jealous Possessiveness

The psychology of envy emphasizes not loss per se, but loss (envy) or threatened loss (jealous possessiveness) of an advantage deemed essential to the individual's physical or psychological well-being (Anderson, 1987). In the experience of envy there is always an implicit or explicit comparison with objects perceived as possessing what the individual perceives to be lacking in self. Saturated with cultural emphases on physical similarities, medical histories, and blood and cultural ties, and complex elaborations on those themes, the adoptee's subjective experience is that of "missing out" compared with the experiences of others. It is considered a fundamental aspect of identity to take both pleasure and comfort in being like, as well as in being distinct and different (Abend, in press). The adoptee's experience of likeness, however, is continually diluted, i. e., any coincidental similarities (especially physically) may have an inauthentic, "as if" quality. Often the experience of "being like" is thwarted altogether. Through completing a search the adoptee attempts to acquire the envied experiences in order to restore (or, actually, achieve) greater psychological homeostatic equilibrium.

Patient: Beth, a registered nurse, consistently presented herself as depressed and unfulfilled. At 26, Beth negatively compared her circumstances in life with all her peers. Unmarried, she idealized her friends' husbands and denigrated the single men who seemed interested in her. Physically Beth was a strikingly beautiful woman who could never recognize her attractiveness. It was this sense of being "Cinderella," unable to attain "the goodies" of life, that contributed to her being dour in her social relationships, driving potential friends away. Beth felt she would never be successful because everyone else had advantages to which she couldn't aspire. She anticipated that, if she ever came close to getting something she wanted, it would be taken away from her.

Respondents: "I felt different from my friends, rather 'unconnected,' envying people who had biological families."
"From seeing people who look like me, I'm much more able to see myself."

Therapeutic considerations. The adoptee's major symptoms and apparent ego functions may indeed have borderline qualities, but the therapist should be cautioned against adhering too rigidly to borderline diagnostic criteria and to the therapeutic limits that may be generally associated with disorders in this area. Just as "paranoid" may not be an entirely appropriate concept where the psychosocial history includes a protractedly abusive environment, the adopted client may "look like" a borderline but not necessarily utilize borderline-level defenses, because of the accumulated adoptee-specific defenses and coping styles. For example, splitting needs to be differentiated from attempts to reconcile dichotomies, dissonances, and contradictions that are inherent in the adoptive experience. If clients appear to be scattered or vague in giving anamnestic material, their presentation may actually reflect certain reality-based lacunae and disjunctions in their life experience. Adoption-specific issues need to be pursued directly and specifically, with attending nuances explored in detail. Similarly, the impersonal stance and anonymity customary in some analytically-oriented therapy may interfere with the adoptee's ability to engage in treatment, or may foster a therapeutic impasse. In this regard there appears to be a certain parallel in treatment parameters recommended for incest survivors.

Body Image and Sexuality

The adoptee's body is his or her only link with the birthparents, which intensifies the meanings which he or she ascribes to physiological texture, coloring, and body type. The unconscious attempt to match likenesses undoubtedly has its infantile origins in experiencing the self as undifferentiated from, and then an integral part of, the primary object (Stern, 1985). This serves as a metaphorical exercise in reinforcing belonging, that fertile medium out of which developmental sequences unfold most favorably. Any attempt in the clinical setting to address the adoptee's body image (e.g., favored and devalued features) is likely eventually to uncover an intense conscious or subconscious craving to encounter the physical image of biological relatives. This transcends mere perception of similarities and differences, but, rather, engages many different dimensions of cognition, affect, and identity.

With respect to sexual identity, one side of sexuality is its potential hazardousness, whether one identifies with the fertile or the infertile, for it is associated with loss, punishment, rivalry, and—perhaps especially for the male—rejection. For the female the capacity to reproduce is particularly fraught with mystery, anxiety, and awe, and the need to differentiate from the flawed mother (adoptive) can be a common and pervasive struggle. Reproductive capacity, and its associations more generally with sexuality, is a particularly poignant milieu within which the adoptive mother's envious resentment (unconscious if not conscious), and the adopted female's jealous possession, may unwittingly foment.

Inherent in the adoptee's confusion is the dissonance created by being told, as is often the case, that he or she was given up because the birthmother loved him or her so much. It is a no-win situation. If you are loved, you are relinquished. If you aren't loved, you are "bad" and sent away. Attachments may be problematic, sometimes leaving the adoptee to question marriage or having children, which could stimulate too much anxiety about being vulnerable. The psychological solution for some adoptees has been the safety of relationships with same-sexed partners.

Patients: Wilhelmina, nicknamed "Willie," never felt comfortable in female garb, and her interests and body language earned her the label of "tomboy." She walked with a swagger and played football with the boys. Reinforced by familial and cultural themes having to do with male prerogatives, her fantasy was that if she had been born a male, she wouldn't have been given up for adoption at birth.

Eric, a graduate student, sought counseling because of a pattern in his dating relationships that was increasingly troubling him: he was attracted only to women who had been abused (i.e., whose capacities for intimacy were more troubled than his own), and their physical coloring had to be very different from his, which would reassure him that he was not dating someone to whom he might be related. At a characteristic juncture in a dating relationship he would abruptly break it off (abandon first) and then become preoccupied with fantasies about his birthmother.

Respondents: "I hated the way people made a big deal of figuring out who I resembled because I desperately wanted to really look like someone in my family—I was constantly searching for someone whom I looked like in any way.

"I had no concept of what I would look like (in the future) and I had no one to share concerns unique to my physical self."

Treatment considerations. The issues of body image and sexuality—and of loss and rejection as well—are inextricably interrelated. However, there may be a difference in the explicitness with which clients identify these as problem areas. Our clinical experience with adoptees has taught us that with them it is especially important to solicit, actively and consistently, the client's fantasies and fears related to her or his body, including associations to *both* sets of parents. For example, one could expect dichotomous fantasies of being reproductively sterile like an adoptive parent, or sexually fecund (often confused with potency) or impulsive, as the birthparent may be imagined. Inherent in the adoptee's attempts at understanding reasons for relinquishment may be thoughts of being "bad" in some fashion. A number of adoptees in treatment have equated "bad" with "defective," like Willie, who was defective in being the "wrong" sex. The sense that they have been "bad" may color many thoughts and activities for which they expect repeated punishments (e.g., rejections), or may cause them to devalue specific physical or psychological traits in themselves, especially if they carry the onus of "different." If these highly charged issues are not directly addressed in the treatment process, undoubtedly they will be left to be acted out, in myriad ways, outside the treatment.

Locus of Control

Locus of control (Friedman, Goodrich, & Fullerton, 1985/86; Rotter, 1975; Strickland, 1989) has come to be used as a measure of the individual's perception of whether the power to control events resides primarily outside the self (externalized) or within (internalized). The decision to activate a search represents a dramatic shift in the adoptee's self-perception as a potentially active agent of change. The adoptee begins to challenge a sense of being indebted, unentitled, and/or powerless, in whatever forms and contexts they may be experienced. In the human development field it would appear that an internalized locus of control, particularly in relation to potentially positive outcomes, can be an important criterion of consolidated identity, in short, of healthy personality development. A parallel concept in the tradition of social work has been self-determination (Freedberg, 1989), its fostering in clients being a primary goal of social work practice, especially with vulnerable populations. A prominent complaint of our respondents, and of adoptee searchers described in other studies, is that "the system" has thwarted their attempts to play an active role in addressing and meeting their needs (i.e., to internalize the locus of control), which they believe has interfered significantly with their development as persons.

> *Patients:* Faced with confusing dilemmas, Fred believed he had no say in how his life progressed. Social workers had selected him for his parents, and his parents had made no secret of how they wanted him to excel. From age seven onward, Fred couldn't understand why his birthmother wanted to let him go to another family because "she loved him so much." He couldn't believe that if he was loved so, why she couldn't get money from somebody to keep him. Even as an adult, Fred presented as passive and dependent, always relying on others to make his decisions. Even when the decisions made intellectual sense to him, Fred emotionally questioned whether any of his actions would be advantageous. His indecisiveness mounted to obsessive-compulsive levels as he considered every facet of every problem so he wouldn't be taken by surprise. It was only when, in therapy, con-

nections were made between the "capricious fate" of his early history and his perpetuating his expectation of helplessness that Fred began to be able to take some control of his life.

Stephanie recalled a painful incident as a child when she was admonished for "stealing" a neighbor's kitten and hiding it in her room. She could not understand why this was such an offense when, to her, it was so exciting and reassuring to know the kitten's first home, and then to be the one (active agent) in control of bringing it into a new home. No one had "disappeared" after all. The sense of shame associated with this memory was lifted when, through treatment, she came to understand that she had actually been busy, in a self-protective way, trying to figure out what happens when someone is "adopted."

Respondents (post-search): "I'm daydreaming less, mixing better socially, have a better self-image—I'm finally growing up and loving it."

"I have better ability to work and love adequately—my life has been stabilized—I've kept a job, stopped getting involved with men who treated me badly."

Treatment considerations. Therapeutically this task of helping the patient experience and internalize personal controls is a major goal. Again, impressionistically, some adopted people have been noted to be particularly passive, tending to allow others to take charge. Having never participated in their relinquishment or adoptive placement, by extension those adoptees may assume that the source of their life's choices and direction lies outside themselves. This characterological passivity, which at times appears to involve some paralysis of ego functions (e.g., in the ability to recognize and process cause and effect, and to conceptualize one's future), is one of the most difficult aspects of treatment. And yet it is the nub of much of what creates the patient's symptoms and dissatisfactions— and of what contributes to therapeutic stalemates.

The Internal Sense of Human Connectedness

The adoptee's struggle with loss, envy, lacunae in body image, sexuality, and locus of control all relate to a particular anguish that is unique to persons permanently severed from their family of birth. Other authors have referred to this anguish as "genealogical bewilderment" (Sants, 1964), "need for human continuity" (Pannor, Sorosky, & Baran, 1974), and "threatened sense of biological identity" (Winkler & Midford, 1986). In an attempt to engage the affective, as well as cognitive, components of the experience, the authors conceptualize instead the adoptee's profound difficulty acquiring an internal sense of human connectedness. We define this as:

> The subjective experience of the self as fully, literally, and genuinely human with an attending capacity to conceptualize one's own personal evolution from past through the present and into the future, physically, temperamentally, psychologically, and intellectually. (Schechter & Bertocci, 1990, p. 64)

Adoptees attempting to explain their need to search make frequent references in their language to variations on the theme of disconnectedness and suspension. This difficulty tends to be reinforced by empathic deficits in the adoptee's social environment which has been unable to identify with this form of psychological amputation.

Patient: When Anne went to a new physician who asked her family medical history, eventually she felt forced to admit that little of what she knew about her adoptive family was in any way relevant to the questions which the doctor was asking. She had no way of knowing in what areas she might have some physiological vulnerabilities, which made her feel more vulnerable than ever. She could not imagine how her body—even if she were to remain healthy—might change and mature over time. Anne only knew herself in the present.

Respondents: "The similarities gave me a feeling of continuity, of strength, of excitement that I really inherited something, I really was born."

"There is much more similarity (with birth relatives) than among any members of my adoptive family. It told me I wasn't a freak—gave me validation for being who I am."

Treatment considerations. Within the treatment setting, the adopted person frequently reminds the therapist of the patient's tenuous connection with other people, however subtly it may be revealed. This may be especially true of the adoptee before the decision to search has helped the adoptee to gain a clearer sense of personal intactness, competence, and inner controls. Elements of distrust, coped with by distancing and detachment, become repeated themes for some adoptees. They may threaten the therapeutic process through acting out in a variety of ways, including discontinuing treatment entirely. Therapeutically the "abscess" which needs gradual excision is the defensive structure(s) erected against engulfment and rejection. Overwhelming dependency may represent an attempt at finally belonging, but is so frequently experienced by the client as crushing that even announcing the end of a session, or the therapist's vacation, brings tears and recriminations of not being likeable or wanted. The struggle around attachment and separation has as one of its underpinnings the intense yearning to experience biological relatedness, i.e., to be in some *concrete* form part of a family-of-birth with all that attends to it in the past, present, and future (e.g., feeling connected to one's human (genetic) forebears and memorialized by one's descendants). The therapist's empathic recognition and exploration of this struggle—unknown with all other clients—sometimes facilitates a quantum leap in the therapeutic engagement.

OTHER TREATMENT ISSUES

The above comments on treatment considerations highlight a number of modifications in diagnostic assessment and treatment approaches that may assist the clinician in treating the adopted person. Generically-trained clinicians already bring to their work with the adopted patient considerable perspective and skill in treating other more or less discrete patient-groups, skills which may, in selected ways, be transferred and applied to the treatment of adoptees. We offer the following observations.

Adoptees who eventually activate the search typically experience the withholding of their birth information as a sadistic violation of their physical and emotional intactness.

For some adoptees, in their sense of powerlessness and of bodily and sexual vulnerability, and in their inclination to self-blame, there is a certain parallel with the psychology of rape survivors. In their deferentiality, compliance, need to please and/or take care of others, and in their hypersensitivity to rejection, they may resemble adult children of alcoholics (Small, 1987). In their preoccupation with themes of betrayal and "guilty secrets," and/or in the confusion some adoptees may present to both themselves and to their therapists when clinical phenomena cannot satisfactorily be accounted for, there is a certain parallel with the psychology of incest survivors.

There is no implication here that adoptive status per se is pathogenic. However, toxic conditions may develop, for a range of reasons, including genetic/constitutional predispositions in character structure, empathic capacities of the adoptive parents, untoward events in life experience, and complex factors in the sociopolitical structure of the culture. Not the least of these is the role of legal and welfare establishments, such as in the United States and Canada, that are based on the concept of adults' ownership of children (Derdeyn, 1979)[3]; and an archaic adoption system that has been based on a simplistic, static, and untested psychology of families and individuals. The clinically-trained social worker is in a unique position to bring to work with adoptees all that he or she has come to understand about the complex interrelationship between personality and culture.

SUMMARY AND CONCLUSION

Various studies of adoptees who have searched for birth relatives find that many adopted people express considerable sensitivity, anxiety, and confusion around a number of universal issues which raise particular complications for them. Through extrapolating and condensing respondents' comments reported in these studies, the authors highlight the issues of loss and attachment, envious resentment, body image and sexuality, internal controls and empowerment, and the acquisition of a sense of human connectedness. More extensive and methodologically rigorous studies need to be conducted in order to validate our preliminary impressions and conceptualizations. These would necessarily include a comparison of different subgroups of adoptees, including nonsearchers, as well as control groups of non-adoptees. As noted earlier, of equal importance is the pressing need for more extensive discussion and dialogue in the clinical literature on the psychology of the adopted person.

To whatever extent our observations may have some validity and pertinence, there are implications for special considerations that may need to be given to diagnosis and treatment of adopted clients. This is necessary in order to facilitate the client's engagement and to define and achieve treatment goals with greater precision and effectiveness. Because of the treatment parameters that may at times have to be considered, the methods and traditions of clinical social work are especially well-suited to clinical work with adopted people.

---

[3] Even the social work profession has embraced the notion of "entitlement to possession" of a child as a criterion of effective parenting (Jaffee & Fanshel, 1970). This serves as an example of social work following the sociolegal assumptions and traditions of its culture rather than leading reconceptualizations which emphasize values other than power through ownership.

REFERENCES

Abend, S. M. (in press). Identity. In B. Moore & B. Fine (Eds.), *Psychoanalysis: The major concepts*. New Haven: Yale University Press.

Alter, E. C. (1983). *Mother, can you hear me?* New York: Dodd, Mead.

Anderson, R. E. (1987). Envy and jealousy. *Journal of College Student Psychotherapy, 1,* 49–81.

Anthony, E. J., & Cohler, B. J. (Eds.). (1987). *The invulnerable child*. New York & London: The Guilford Press.

Aumend, S., & Barrett, M. (1984). Self-concept and attitudes toward adoption: A comparison of searching and non-searching adult adoptees. *Child Welfare, 63,* 251–259.

Bertocci, D., & Schechter, M. D. (1987) *Adopted adults' perception of their need to search: An informal survey*. Unpublished study.

Bohman, M. (1981). The interaction of heredity and childhood environment: Some adoption studies. *Journal of Child Psychology & Psychiatry, 22,* 195–200.

Bowlby, J. (1961). Childhood mourning and its implications for psychiatry. *American Journal of Psychiatry, 118,* 481–498.

Bowlby, J. (1980). *Attachment and loss: Vol. 3 Loss: Sadness and depression*. New York: Basic Books.

Brodzinsky, D. M. (1990). A stress and coping model of adoption adjustment. In D. M. Brodzinsky & M. D. Schechter (Eds.), *The psychology of adoption*. New York: Oxford University Press.

Cadoret, R. J. (1978). Psychopathology in adopted-away offspring of biological parents with antisocial behavior. *Archives of General Psychiatry 35,* 176–184.

Day, C. & Leeding, A. (1980). *Access to birth records: The impact of section 26 of the children act 1975*. London: The Association of British Adoption and Fostering Agencies.

Depp, C. H. (1982). After reunion: Perceptions of adult adoptees, adoptive parents, and birth parents. *Child Welfare, 61,* 115–119.

Derdeyn, A. P. (1979). Adoption and the ownership of children. *Child Psychiatry and Human Development, 9,* 215–226.

Erlich, H. (1977). *A time to search*. New York and London: Paddington Press.

Feigelman, W., & Silverman, A. R. (1983). *Chosen children* . New York: Praeger.

Fisher, F. (1973). *The search for Anna Fisher*. New York: Arthur Fields.

Freedberg, S. (1989). Self-determination: Historical perspectives and effects on current practice. *Social Work 34*(1), 33–38.

Freud, S. (1957). Mourning and melancholia. In J. Strachey (Ed. and Trans.), *The standard edition of the complete psychological works of Sigmund Freud* (Vol. 14) London: Hogarth Press. (Original work published in 1917).

Friedman, R., Goodrich, W., & Fullerton, D. C. (1985/86). Locus of control and severity of illness in the residential treatment of adolescents. *Current Issues in Psychoanalytic Practice 3*(2), 3–13.

Frisk, M. (1964). Identity problems and confused conceptions of the genetic ego in adopted children during adolescence. *Acta Paedo Psychiatrica, 31,* 6–12.

Gilligan, C. (1982). *In a different voice*. Cambridge, Mass.: Harvard University Press.

Goldstein, J., Freud, A., & Solnit, A. (1973). *Beyond the best interests of the child.* London: Free Press.

Grotevant, H. D., Scarr, S., & Weinberg, R. A. (1977). Patterns of interest similarity in adoptive and biological families. *Journal of Personality and Social Psychology, 35,* 667–676.

Jaffee, B., & Fanshel, D. (1970). *How they fared in adoption.* New York: Child Welfare League of America.

Jones, M. S. (1976). *The sealed adoption record controversy: Report of a survey of agency policy, practice, and opinions.* New York: Child Welfare League of America.

Kowal, K. & Schilling, K. M. (1985). Adoption through the eyes of adult adoptees. *American Journal of Orthopsychiatry 55*(3), 354–362.

Leitch, D. (1984). *Family secrets: A writer's search for his parents and his past.* New York: Delacorte Press.

Lifton, B. J. (1975). *Twice born: Memoirs of an adopted daughter.* New York: McGraw Hill.

Lifton, B. J. (1979). *Lost and found: The adoption experience.* New York: Dial Press.

Lindemann, E. (1944). Symptomatology and management of acute grief. *American Journal of Psychiatry, 101,* 141–148.

Lion, A. (1976). *A survey of 50 adult adoptees who used the right of the Israeli 'open file' adoption law.* Paper presented at the annual meeting of the International Forum on Adolescence, Jerusalem, Israel.

Marcus, C. (1981). *Who is my mother?* Toronto: Macmillan.

Masterson, J. F., & Klein, R. (Eds.). (1989). *Psychotherapy of the disorders of the self: The Masterson approach.* New York: Brunner Mazel.

Maxtone-Graham, K. (1983). *An adopted woman.* New York: Remi Books.

McKuen, R. (1976). *Finding my father: One man's search for identity.* Los Angeles: Cheval Books/ Coward, McCann & Geoghegan.

McWhinnie, A. M. (1967). *Adopted children and how they grow up.* London: Routledge & Kegan Paul.

Munsinger, H. (1975). Children's resemblance to their biological and adopting parents in two ethnic groups. *Behavior Genetics 5*(3), 239–254.

Pannor, R., Sorosky, A., & Baran, A. (1974). Opening the sealed record in adoption— the human need for continuity. *Journal of Jewish Communal Service, 51,* 188–196.

Paton, J. M. (1954). *The adopted break silence.* Acton, Calif.: Life History Center.

Paton, J. M. (1960). *Three trips home.* Acton, Calif.: Life History Center.

Paton, J. M. (1968). *Orphan voyage.* New York: Vintage.

Raynor, L (1980). *The adopted child comes of age.* London: George Allen & Unwin.

Rotter, J. B. (1975). Some problems and misconceptions related to the construct of internal vs. external control of reinforcement. *Journal of Consulting and Clinical Psychology, 48,* 56–57.

Sambrano, S. (1987). Social science researcher, Department of Health and Human Services, Washington, D.C. Personal communication.

Sants, H. J. (1964). Genealogical bewilderment in children with substitute parents. *British Journal of Medical Psychology, 37,* 133–141.

Schechter, M. D., & Bertocci, D. (1990). The meaning of the search. In D. M. Brodzinsky & M. D. Schechter (Eds.), *The psychology of adoption.* New York: Oxford University.

Shaw, M. (1984). Growing up adopted. In P. Bean (Ed.), *Adoption Essays in social policy, law, and sociology*. London & New York: Tavistock Pubs.

Simpson, M., Timm, H., & McCubbin, H. (1981). Adopters in search of their past: Policy induced strain on adoptive families and birth parents. *Family Relations, 30,* 427–434.

Slaytor, P. (1986). Reunion and resolution: The adoption triangle. *Australian Social Work, 39*(2), 15–20.

Small, J. (1979). Discrimination against the adoptee. *Public Welfare 37,* 38–43.

Small, J. (1987). Working with adoptive families. *Public Welfare, 45,* 33–41.

Sobol, M., & Cardiff, J. (1983). A sociopsychological investigation of adult adoptees' search for birth parents. *Family Relations, 32, 477–183.*

Sorosky, A., Baran, A., & Pannor, R. (1978). *The adoption triangle.* New York: Anchor Press/Doubleday.

Stein, L. M., & Hoopes, J. L (1985). *Identity formation in the adopted adolescent.* New York: Child Welfare League of America.

Stern, D. N. (1985). *The interpersonal world of the infant: A view from psychoanalysis and developmental psychology.* New York: Basic Books.

Strickland, B. (1989). Internal-external control of expectancies: From contingency to creativity. *American Psychologist, 44*(1), 1–12.

Thompson, J., Stoneman, L, Webber, J., & Harrison, D. (1978). *The adoption rectangle: A study of adult adoptees' search for birth family history and implications for adoption service.* Project Report of the Children's Aid Society of Metropolitan Toronto (unpub.).

Toussieng, P. W. (1962). Thoughts regarding the etiology of psychological difficulties in adopted children. *Child Welfare, 41, 59–65.*

Triseliotis, J. (1973). *In search of origins: the experience of adopted persons.* London: Routledge & Kegan Paul, Ltd.

Webber, J., Thompson, J., & Stoneman, L. (1980). *Adoption reunion: A struggle in uncharted relationships.* Unpublished study for the Children's Aid Society of Metropolitan Canada.

Winkler, R. C., Brown, D. W., Van Keppel, M. & Blanchard, A. (1988). *Clinical practice in adoption.* New York and Oxford: Pergamon Press.

Winkler, R. C., & Midford, S. (1986). Biological identity in adoption, artificial insemination by donor (A.I.D.) and the new birth technologies. *Australian Journal of Early Childhood, 11,* 43–48.

Zeilinger, R. (1979). The need vs. the right to know. *Public Welfare, 37*(3), 44–47.

DIVORCE

CHAPTER 75

DIVORCE

Problems, Goals, and Growth Facilitation

Dory Krongelb Beatrice

The rapidly increasing divorce rate in the United States indicates that divorce is a phenomenon widespread enough to affect most individuals either directly or indirectly. Accordingly, people going through divorce are increasingly represented in social work caseloads. This article will first present what divorcing persons are saying about their complex situations and the many problems they face. A framework for significant goals in divorce work will follow. Divorce groups, which attempt to develop support systems and to facilitate movement toward significant goals in the divorce process, will then be discussed as a way to resolve some of these problems.

PROBLEMS OF DIVORCING PERSONS

One of the most difficult problems faced by divorcing persons is that of identity crisis.[1] They often feel that the entire structure of their lives has fallen apart, leaving them empty, worthless, and with nothing to offer. Loneliness can be overwhelming, as can loss of a sense of purpose. This may be especially true of the long-married wife and mother whose identity revolved completely around her marriage, family, and her role and status as a homemaker. With that gone, she wonders, "Who am I?"

Economics is another major problem area. Vocational identity may be part of this, especially for the homemaker who feels a financial and/or emotional need to work outside the home after a divorce.[2] In such a case, "marketability," or the development of

Reprinted from *Social Casework*, Vol. 60 (1979), pp. 157–165, by permission of the publisher, Families International, Inc.

[1] Reva S. Wiseman, "Crisis Theory and the Process of Divorce," *Social Casework* 56 (April 1975): 205–12.
[2] Ibid., p. 210.

needed work skills, needs to be assessed.[3] This process may be blocked by inexperience, low self-esteem, reality issues such as child care, guilt over children's' emotional needs, and so on. E. E. LeMasters found that, although households headed by women make up only about 10 percent of all United States households, they constitute about 25 percent of families in the poverty group in American society.[4] Another study of divorce and poverty found that "a family headed by a female is more than twice as likely to be poor and stay poor as one led by a male—28 percent versus 12 percent. . . . Divorced women who are heads of families are worse off financially than any other family leaders and much more likely to live below the poverty line."[5]

In addition to the realistic problems of dividing up the economic assets of a two-parent household, property battles become overloaded by the emotions involved, in which the objects of the battle serve as symbols of the emotional pain the contestants are feeling. This is also true in the case of custody battles. As the divorcing couple becomes involved with lawyers, the legal ramifications of their decision may become an additional source of confusion and bewilderment. Much has been written in the way of critique of the way the legal profession currently interacts with divorce clients: lawyers are trained to defend their clients' interests and attack those of the spouse; they are not trained in family and marital dynamics, and so on.[6] The result is that lawyers often unwittingly contribute to escalating the marital conflict, rather than to aiding in its resolution.

Role Conflicts

Another area of difficulty and confusion for the single parent may be in dealing with role conflicts and role shifts. The single parent wonders, "Should I try to be both mother and father to my children?" In many cases the responsibilities of the now-absent spouse's role falls upon the remaining present parent to absorb. When this is so, conflicting parent roles may be overwhelming to the present parent. For example, parents may need to work and be away from their children because of financial necessity; yet they feel this is a time when their children's needs for them is especially great. The parent feels overwhelmed by the many demands on him or her and may feel totally helpless and inadequate to meet them.[7] There may be strong feelings of needing to compensate to the children for the divorce, with guilt then adding to the demands of the situation. A related problem is how, in the face of so many real demands from others, can they get something emotionally for themselves; where is the single parent's emotional replenishment going to come from?

An encouraging development in the area of overwhelming single-parent responsibilities is that "an increasing number of men who have been separated or divorced from their wives . . . have consciously chosen to remain fully involved in their children's up-

---

[3] Kenneth Kressel and Morton Deutsch, "Divorce Therapy: An In-Depth Survey of Therapists' Views," *Family Process* 16 (December 1977): 413–43.

[4] E. E. LeMasters, *Parents in Modern America* (Homewood, Ill.: Dorsey Press, 1970).

[5] "A Surprising Profile of America's Poor," *U.S. News and World Report*, 8 (November 1976), pp. 57–58.

[6] Kressel and Deutsch, "Divorce Therapy," p. 425.

[7] Kay Tooley, "Antisocial Behavior and Social Alienation Post Divorce: The 'Man of the House' and His Mother," *American Journal of Orthopsychiatry* 46 (January 1976): 33–42.

bringing and to assume increased responsibility for taking care of them."[8] There is also a trend among family therapists to work with the entire family after a divorce in order to ensure continuing constructive involvement of both parents in the child's life.[9]

While single parents try to juggle shifting roles, they must also deal with the reactions and attitudes of others. Many divorcing people have had the experience of suddenly finding themselves dropped from past friendships and relationships, just at a time when they feel most in need of others. In spite of the increasing acceptance of divorce in our society, many vestiges of stigma remain which label divorced people as deviants, misfits, failures, or threats to intact marriages. Consequently, divorced people may internalize these perceptions and see themselves the same way.

Effects on the Children

The sense of failure may be especially intense in relation to one's children. Divorcing parents wonder if they are doing irrevocable damage to their children's development by ending their marriage, and they have many questions about how best to handle and help their children through this difficult period. Sometimes the trauma to the parent is such that it is difficult to have enough energy left over to deal effectively with the children. Many dysfunctional parent-child patterns may appear during this period. In a study of young boys and their mothers, Kay Tooley found that "women raising children alone after divorce often find their new sociopsychological world frightening and unmanageable. Perceiving this, their young sons may undertake a counterphobic defense of themselves and their mothers, manifested as antisocial behavior."[10]

Another common problem is acting out by the parents of all their unfinished feelings about their ex-spouses through the children. Parents may unwittingly use the children as weapons against the ex-spouse: "Conflicts leading to divorce persist afterward and the child can remain a pawn in parental maneuvers after the divorce as well as before.[11] Joan B. Kelly and Judith S. Wallerstein found that strong wishes for the parents' reconciliation persisted in a third of their sample of early latency age boys, and that these fantasies were "either being kept alive by the openly expressed wishes of a parent, or the parent-child relationship had deteriorated to such an extent that the child perceived reconciliation as his only hope."[12]

Loyalty conflicts are often exacerbated by parental interaction.[13] Many single parents engage in role reversal and look to the child as a substitute spouse, searching for the love, companionship, and protection that are lacking in their lives. Very distraught

---

[8] Harry Finkelstein Keshet and Kristine M. Rosenthal, "Fathering After Marital Separation," *Social Work* 23 (January 1978): 11–18.

[9] David Weisfeld and Martin S. Laser, "Divorced Parents in Family Therapy in a Residential Treatment Setting," *Family Process* 16 (June 1977): 229–36; and Janice Goldman and James Coane, "Family Therapy After the Divorce: Developing a Strategy," *Family Process* 16 (September 1977): 357–62.

[10] Tooley, "Antisocial Behavior," p. 33.

[11] Jack C. Westman, "Effect of Divorce on a Child's Personality Development," *Medical Aspects of Human Sexuality* 6 (January 1972): 38–55.

[12] Joan B. Kelly and Judith S. Wallerstein, "The Effects of Parental Divorce: Experiences of the Child in Early Latency," *American Journal of Orthopsychiatry* 46 (January 1976): 20–32.

[13] Ibid., p. 29.

parents may imply that the divorce is the children's fault, thus adding to the feelings of responsibility, guilt, and rejection that the children may already have. Or they may inappropriately displace all of their anger, frustration, fear, and helplessness onto the children.

Effects on Absent Parents

Whereas custodial parents may at times feel resentful and overwhelmed by all the responsibilities of their new situation, absent parents have another set of problems. They may be kept away from the children by an extremely hostile situation surrounding attempts to see them. The roles of the former spouses who continue relationships with their children are often plagued by ambiguity and confusion on all sides. The new relationships with the children lack a clear-cut definition. A tremendous sense of loss at the separation from the children is experienced. No longer in the house, the absent spouse (usually the father) is, in effect, stripped of most of his former authority; he feels doomed to frustration as he tries to influence and shape the children's lives the way he had hoped. Guilt and anxiety are intense: "The anxiety they experienced was made up of many components and involved fear of losing their relationship with their children, of losing their status within the family as a source of self-definition, of being criticized by their ex-spouse, of being rejected by their children, and of losing their roots and the structure and continuity of family life."[14] Fear of inadequacy as a single parent is also strong.

New Relationships

Another major problem area for newly single people develops as they venture out into the world of the opposite sex. The central conflict here is likely to be independence versus intimacy. They may long for the closeness, companionship, sex, and shared responsibilities of an intimate relationship, yet they are enjoying their newfound freedom and have many fears of vulnerability based on the dissolution of the marriage. In the areas of dating and sexuality, new singles often experience a resurgence of unresolved adolescent conflicts, and this self-perceived regression can be quite demoralizing. Low self-esteem is likely to add to one's fears of new relationships. Yet, "there is a real need to explore further interpersonal and sexual potentials . . . `the need to experiment sexually at this time is of vital importance to many divorcing persons."[15] New relationships may also create unexpected reactions in the children than can bewilder the parents.

SIGNIFICANT GOALS IN DIVORCE WORK

In the course of working with divorcing people, it is necessary to erect a general framework of significant goals. Reaching these objectives, in addition to clients' individual goals, are critical if one is going to successfully negotiate the divorce experience and be able to grow through it.

[14] Keshet and Rosenthal, "Fathering After Marital Separation," p. 12.
[15] Wiseman, "Crisis Theory and Divorce," p. 210.

GRIEF WORK: DEALING WITH LOSS

One of the most crucial aspects of finding autonomy and growth out of this crisis situation is the person's ability to fully accept and mourn the loss of the mate, to say good-bye to the spouse, the marriage, and whatever other losses are experienced. The absent parent is dealing not only with the loss of spouse, but of the children, too.

Grieving must be done, yet is often blocked, both from within and from sources outside the individual. Society has no ceremony for mourning the loss of a spouse through divorce, in contrast to the funeral and rituals surrounding death. This leaves the divorced person very much alone in a labyrinth of confusion, anger, despair, sadness, and fear. In addition, intense ambivalence is often a feature of this time. "Grief work must be done with great thoroughness or there will remain the danger of constantly living in the presence of the open casket of a dead marriage."[16] Newly single people often need to say good-bye not only to their former spouse, but to an entire past. When people are able to deal with divorce in a "growthful" way, they will be faced with the prospect of change in lifestyle, responsibilities, freedoms, relationships, in their children and themselves. In order to become ready for these pervasive changes, they must be able to come to terms with, and let go of, the past.

It is important to communicate to clients an atmosphere that is permissive to feelings so that they will internalize this permission and allow themselves to grieve. Therapists need to be familiar with the grief process[17] and how it relates to divorce, so that they can facilitate mourning and help bring it to completion.[18] They need to help clients allow their anger, depression, confusion, fear, and sadness, and help this develop into eventual acceptance of the loss, with reintegration and growth. Therapists need to help clients express their pain and their hopes, their resentments and appreciations of their former mate, what they miss, and what they enjoy in their new life. Therapists need to help remove the blocks and let all this happen.

For example, when Mr. and Mrs. Y sought marriage counseling, Mrs. Y stated that she wanted a divorce after twenty-one years of marriage. Exploration revealed that she felt strongly about ending the marriage, but had agreed to marriage counseling in the hope that it would soften the impact on her husband, who had initially talked about suicide if she left him. He entered counseling in the hope that they could heal the marriage. As it became more and more clear that Mrs. Y did not want to invest any more in the marriage, Mr. Y continued to insist that things were improving, and to deny the ending of the marriage. Mrs. Y, feeling more and more frustrated at her inability to get through to Mr. Y, resorted to the passive-aggressive means of having him find her in bed with another man. This speedily brought the marriage to an end. Mr. Y soon entered a divorce group (Mrs. Y left the state) and spent several sessions ventilating his anger at his wife's lover. The group and leaders confronted him on his wife's responsibility for the situation also. As he gradually began to allow himself to feel anger toward her, he was able to break through his denial and move through grieving. He was soon

---

[16] Ibid., p. 206.
[17] Elisabeth Kübler-Ross, *On Death and Dying* (New York: Macmillan Co., 1969).
[18] Wiseman, "Crisis Theory and Divorce," pp. 205–12.

able to let go of the marriage and reinvest his energies in other relationships, which offered him more than his marriage had for a long time. Eventually, he even became grateful for the divorce. He found more vitality in his own life and in more satisfying relationships.

Development of Support Systems

One of the critical needs during and after a divorce is for an authentic and workable support system. Loneliness and isolation are often intense problems for the divorcing individual, and the development of meaningful relationships is important to combat these.

This can be a fruitful time to help clients reassess their relationships in general and what they want to give to and get from them in the future. It can be a time to discover that independence and intimacy are not mutually exclusive, but that one can build a relationship on one's own terms. It can be a time to choose new friends who are nurturant and reject those who are toxic. For example, in working with women who took a submissive role in their marriages, it was discovered in the course of divorce work that they also reproduced this role in many of their relationships. As they began to place a higher priority on their own needs, to increase their self-esteem, and to become more assertive, they were able to either change some of those relationships or leave them for healthier ones.

This is a time to encourage clients to broaden the range of their relationships with others, to find satisfaction in the company of several or many people rather than channel all of their companionship needs into marriage. Close friends become important and same-sex relationships deepen. This can be a time to explore one's sexuality and, perhaps, nonsexual intimacy with the opposite sex.

The other aspect of developing a support system is that of developing *self*-support. This often seems nearly unattainable to the person emerging from the marriage with crushed self-esteem, yet it can be developed. The self-supporting person will convert loneliness into solitude, taking pleasure in a certain amount of aloneness. Therapists can help clients discover how to activate their own capabilities and resources and take responsibility for their own fulfillment in order to experience growth out of pain and loss. Therapists also need to help clients work through their feelings of failure and inadequacy, which may be intense. Without resolution of these feelings, self-esteem will be greatly damaged. The issue of self-support is closely related to the third task, that of developing autonomy.

Development of Autonomy

Successful divorce work also involves developing a sense of autonomy and new self-identity as a whole—in divorcing persons, the ability to see themselves as growing human beings in their own right. This can be most difficult for people who married before developing their own identity in the first place, perhaps having sought to find themselves through their spouse or their marriage. "Divorce forces the individual to take up the work of individuation once more without the illusory support of the marriage."[19] Suddenly finding oneself alone in the search for identity can be a frightening and lonely experience, but it also offers tremendous potential for growth. The search involves separating one's identity from familiar roles as wife and mother, breadwinner and father, and sorting out one's own uniqueness as an individual. Therapists need to help clients ask themselves what *their* feelings, needs, resentments, capacities, limitations, thoughts are. They need to help clients get in touch with and accept undiscovered or suppressed aspects of themselves, thus becoming more whole.

This is a particularly potent time to reevaluate one's male or female identity, and to develop qualities that will round out and enrich the overall personality. For example, Harry Finkelstein Keshet and Kristine M. Rosenthal found than single fathers had a very difficult time relating to their children's emotionality at first. However, "to maintain the emotional attachment between himself and his children, a father must develop a sensitivity to them." He must face their dependency, their feelings of powerlessness, their emotions, and their irrationality, as well "as elements that he himself had to suppress during his own childhood as he acquired the veneer of masculinity. . . . As an adult he has an opportunity to resolve them for himself in new and better ways."[20] The female has this opportunity to develop her stereotypically "masculine" traits—aggressiveness, strength, competence, and independence, as well as her career interests. Reva S. Wiseman has delineated four areas of identity—personal, vocational, social, and sexual—that can be reworked during this time.[21] In general, therapists also need to help clients take responsibility for their own lives, based on their sense of individuality, autonomy, self-support, and relatedness to the world.

Reevaluation of the Marital Relationship

Another important component of divorce work is reevaluation of the marriage. Therapists need to help clients sort out what happened in the marriage. How did it come to be dissolved? What were the strengths and weaknesses of the relationship? What was each partner's contribution to the problems? What led them to choose this person as a mate originally? What vestiges of their relationships with their parents were brought into the marriage; how did these affect the marriage? What have they learned from this experience? What will they do differently in the future? It is important for divorcing persons to gain some insight into the unconscious conflicts and distortions that led to the choice of mate, and to gain an appreciation of their contribution to the dysfunctional patterns in the old marriage. "A one-sided view of the marital breakdown was taken as *prima facie* evidence that something far short of an optimal divorce had been achieved."[22] Therapists are all familiar with the person who leaves an unhappy marriage, only to quickly enter another relationship with similar dysfunctional patterns. Those with long-standing patterns of pathological mate-selection will need the most help here.

An example of following a dysfunctional pattern is Mrs. S, who sought therapy after

---

[19] Goldman and Coane, "Family Therapy After the Divorce," p. 362.
[20] Keshet and Rosenthal, "Fathering After Marital Separation," p. 18.
[21] Wiseman, "Crisis Theory and Divorce," pp. 209–10.
[22] Kressel and Deutsch, "Divorce Therapy," p. 422.

the break-up of a second marriage. In both her first and second marriages she had become a battered wife, yet had wanted both marriages to continue, and blamed herself completely for their dissolution. Her history revealed, predictably, a childhood in which she had been frequently beaten by her father. She grew up assuming that she must have done *something* to deserve this treatment, and that it was all her fault. She also had learned to associate affection and attention with abuse. Thus, she sought the same type of relationship in her marriages, highly motivated by crippling guilt and a need for punishment. When one husband left her, she again felt it was her fault and she proceeded, unconsciously, to seek and find exactly the same situation in a second marriage.

The reevaluation process is designed to break up this sort of pattern, and to get people moving in a more satisfying direction. Ms. H, who sought therapy during a separation from her husband, is someone who may be able to break past patterns. She was ambivalent about divorce, feeling the marital relationship had grown empty, but fearing another poor choice of mate. As her original choice of her husband was explored, some understanding of some of the unconscious reasons for it were gained. She had been extremely angry at her mother and had chosen the only boyfriend that her mother disapproved of as a passive-aggressive maneuver. Also, she had seen her father as a weak man who submitted to her mother's domination. Ms. H. had tended at first to choose men who were also submissive so that she could dominate them as her mother did her father; but the man she chose to marry was quite domineering himself and filled the more assertive role she had wanted her father to fill.

Because Ms. H's therapy is currently at this stage, the outcome cannot be presented here. However, it is quite likely that, as Ms. H gains these insights, she will be able to make a freer and healthier choice of men in the future.

Coping with Reality Demands

As always, therapists need to start where the client is, and some clients may be too overwhelmed with reality problems to have any energy available for grief work, reevaluation, or identity development. To make peace with the demands of reality, such as employment, money, housing, child care, child management, and so on is crucial. If not peace, at least peaceful coexistence can be hoped for. In their fascination with the intrapsychic and interpersonal dynamics of clients, therapists should not underestimate the force with which these practical problems impinge on clients, especially bearing in mind the facts and statistics cited earlier regarding divorce and poverty. Social workers, by virtue of orientation and training, should be especially sensitive to these problems, know the community resources well, and make appropriate referrals. This is where the utilization of other agencies such as social services, legal aid facilities, vocational counseling, and so on may be appropriate.

Therapists can help solve some of these reality problems, teaching problem-solving techniques in the process. They can assist clients with tackling one thing at a time, building successes bit by bit, so that their self-esteem, independence, and capacity to cope and grow are increased in the process. What will emerge from these processes are people who are coping with the demands of reality, have reevaluated the marriage and assimilated the divorce, have developed a clearer evolving positive sense of themselves as unique individuals, and are developing caring and authentic relationships with others.

THE DIVORCE GROUP

Increasingly, the divorce group is being used as a vehicle to assist those who are in the process of divorce with their many problems, some of which have been outlined above. Such groups are usually time-limited (optimally about twelve to sixteen weeks), designed that way to communicate the idea that what most of the members are experiencing is an adjustment reaction, with improvement likely over a relatively short period of time. Those who are dealing with more chronic emotional difficulties in addition to divorce may benefit from such a group, but will often need to go on for further individual or group therapy. In the divorce group that is described here, membership is closed after the first or second meeting so that relationships can develop and deepen.

Format and Materials

The group is loosely structured in format, with some structured materials being used at the beginning to facilitate interaction and help members discover common areas of concern. Examples of materials used include brief, relevant magazine articles, and a sentence completion questionnaire developed for the group with open-ended statements such as: "Some of my strongest needs now are for . . ."; "When I'm feeling lonely, I . . ."; and "Since my marriage broke up, my children . . ." Pregroup interviews are used with all members, and individual goals are established.

One of the original assumptions in starting this type of group was that a variety of group members, at different stages of dealing with a common core of difficulties, would have a lot to offer each other, and this has proved to be true. The people who have solved some of the problems of divorce provide tangible evidence to the others that it can be done, that one can grow through the crisis. This approach affirms their growing sense of independence and competence as they discover that they can help themselves and each other, rather than feeding into a sense of dependence on professional experts. A sense of "normalcy" of an adjustment reaction to divorce also develops, as opposed to people believing they are "going crazy" because they feel depressed, angry, confused, and so on.

Avoiding Sexual Stereotypes

It is extremely important to recruit and include both men and women for the group. Many people emerged from their marriage with inaccurate stereotypes of the opposite sex based on their former spouses; developing emotional intimacy through the group with other members of the opposite sex who are different from their ex-spouse is an important corrective process. For example, in one session several women began expressing anger about their ex-spouse's neglect of the children and failure to send child support payments. This soon grew into a general expression that "Men are no good." However, the input of the male members of the group about *their* feelings about their children, which was quite different from what the women had experienced, had a corrective impact and helped the women put their feelings back onto a personal rather than global plane.

As was previously mentioned, one of the major goals of divorce work is to develop a workable and authentic support system. The value of simple support in a client population that is experiencing loss, isolation, and loneliness should not be underestimated. "The companionship of other formerly marrieds of the same and opposite sex becomes an important form of support to the divorcing person and is a positive force in helping to work through the divorce process."[23] Members experience universality in discovering that they share the same problems, fears, and worries as many others in their situation. They find understanding, acceptance, and validation of their emerging identities; thus feelings of the stigma of divorce are also lessened. Members value the honesty, emotional intimacy, and self-disclosure possible in this setting as compared to other social situations. A lasting support network may grow from the group and should be encouraged by the leader. Supportive confrontation usually develops, with a tone of "I recognize what you're doing because I've done it myself."

FACILITATING GROWTH THROUGH ACCEPTANCE AND GROUP SUPPORT

Self-esteem increases with support, validation, and acceptance, but is also aided by the discovery of the capacity to help others through their pain. Many found the emotional replenishment lacking in their lives coming from the group.

Some of these effects are illustrated by the example of Mr. J, who was having a very difficult time preparing to divorce his wife of twenty-one years. He joined the divorce group for support, and for preparation to face the difficulties and pleasures that might await him. He was highly ambivalent and fearful about the divorce. He was especially concerned about how others, especially his children, would react to him, and about his isolation in a world of married friends. He also expressed a strong sense of emptiness and loss—the disillusionment of feeling that the goals he had struggled with for years had come to nought. He had never felt satisfied.

He entered the group with great anxiety. He listened to others share their problems and their successes, and he expressed his fears. He gradually began to feel that it was up to him to grow from the divorce. He began to tell others about the divorce, and found acceptance and support among his (grown) children and friends. Self-esteem began to increase. The divorce became final, and he felt relief. He found he could talk things over with his wife as they never could before, but both felt increasingly certain they had made the right decision. They began to evaluate what had gone wrong, to learn from it, and to move off in different directions. This freed him to experiment with different aspects of his personality, and to strengthen his sense of identity and autonomy. Through supportive confrontation in the group, he learned how he had tried to control others, and he began giving that up. In its stead, he discovered more control over his *own* life. He also began, with the help of the group, to examine his overly strong superego and to

[23] Wiseman, "Crisis Theory and Divorce," p. 211.

allow more of his own wishes and needs to surface. He began appearing more relaxed and gave up taking tranquilizers. He stopped feeling overly responsible for and the need to control others, and became more responsible for his own wants and needs. He was able to discover an inner sense of direction. Finally he reported, "I feel more satisfied than I ever have before."

FEELING WHOLE AGAIN

In another example, discussion focused on how people had dealt with a common reaction to divorce, that of feeling like half a person with nothing much to offer others. Several people had found help by getting out with others, meeting people, and getting involved in satisfying activities. But Ms. E raised the question of whether such things could emotionally replace the marital relationship, or if this remained an empty place in people. There were varied reactions, with several members saying that such activities helped them feel better about themselves and made them less lonely, but did not fill the gap. Others said they struggled with this by focusing on their own growth and fulfillment rather than looking for others to fill them up.

The central theme that tends to develop (with leader facilitation) is that of the two sides of the divorce coin—pain coupled with growth. Many feel tremendous losses and deprivations, but are gradually able to discover new freedoms and opportunities. Although it is, of course, important for the leader to be accepting of the pain and trauma involved for divorcing persons, it is also crucial that he or she explore and support the tremendous growth potential of this crisis.

SUMMARY

This article has sought to share the author's findings and observations from working with divorcing individuals. The central issues faced in divorce are seen as problems of identity crisis, loneliness, economics, vocational identity, legal issues, role conflicts and shifts, need for emotional replenishment, loss of support system, sense of failure, parenting (both of the present and absent parent), intimacy, and sexuality.

An understanding of the problems of divorce leads to a formulation of the principal goals in divorce work: movement through grief work, development of support systems, development of autonomy and identity, reevaluation of the marriage, and coping with the demands of reality.

The use of groups of divorcing individuals has been very helpful in developing support systems and in facilitating movement toward the other significant goals in the divorce process. Clients are able to utilize such groups to maximize the growth potential of the crisis of divorce.

MARRIAGE

CHAPTER 76

A FOCAL CONFLICT MODEL
OF MARITAL DISORDERS

Marquis Earl Wallace

Marital disorders are common and their consequences grave. For people in disordered marriages, the available options are continued misery, spontaneous solutions, divorce, or some kind of professional help. Divorce frequently leads to more misery and to a variety of social ills as well—financial difficulties, mental illness, problems with children such as delinquency, and so forth.

Frequently, social workers attempt to help a troubled marriage, either because of a direct request from a member of the couple or indirectly in response to requests for some other service. However, social workers encounter difficulties in working with troubled marriages and many divorces occur even among those couples that seek professional help. These difficulties may indicate a weakness in the social provisions for dealing with marital problems, but also indicate problems in understanding what causes them and how to help. The purpose of this article is to improve the level of theory used by social workers who work directly with disordered marriages.

APPROACHES TO PRACTICE WITH DISORDERED MARRIAGES

Approaches used by social workers in practice with couples in disordered marriages have been of two basic types: the first is work with the individual, either in a one-to-one setting or as a member of a group; the other is work with the marital unit, the husband and wife together, sometimes including other family members as well. There are, of course, many variations of these two basic approaches. Some of the variations are indi-

Reprinted from *Social Casework*, Vol. 60, No. 7 (1979), pp. 423–429, by permission of the publisher, Families International, Inc.

vidual work with both partners separately by the same worker, a mixture of individual interviews with conjoint ones, couples' groups, and the use of multiple workers, either in groups or with the marital pair, as in the treatment of sexual dysfunction.

These two basic approaches to practice come from contrasting behavioral science orientations regarding the causes of marital disorder. Work with the individual is based on the idea that the cause of marital disorder is located primarily within the individual(s) in the marriage. The logic here is that each individual's personality constitutes a separate independent variable for which marital disorder is a dependent variable. Work with the individual helps to sort out the extent to which the marital disturbance fills irrational needs, or if indeed the marital choice was primarily determined by irrational forces.

The approach in which the couple is worked with as a unit actually includes a variety of theoretical approaches, which currently are associated with the "family movement." Family theory differs so radically from the individually oriented approach that its adherents believe their approach constitutes a new orientation to behavior.[1] One of the crucial ways in which family therapy differs from the individual approach is in the belief that marital disorder and even psychopathology result from certain kinds of relationship interactions. Although differences in "personality" are acknowledged by family theorists, their influence on marital disorder is rejected, because some individuals who are quite clearly disturbed nonetheless have happy marriages, and some individuals who seem to be functioning quite well as individuals nonetheless have marital disasters. The family-oriented approach then totally reverses the individualistic paradigm: the relationship interaction is the independent variable while personality functioning and marital unhappiness are the dependent variables.

For those who believe that practice should be based on theory and that theory should be internally consistent, this contradiction—disordered personalities cause disordered marital interactions versus marital interactions cause marital and personality disorder—merits further attention. Resolving such contradictions provides opportunities for new theoretical integrations. These can pave the way for improved approaches to practice and greater help for clients. Ignoring such contradictions leaves their implications up to the art of practice rather than the science and therefore to the practitioner. When the practitioner attempts to integrate different conceptual approaches in practice, inconsistent and even haphazard activities with clients may occur unnecessarily and may be detrimental to treatment.

A FOCAL CONFLICT MODEL OF MARITAL DISORDERS

The purpose of this article is to integrate the psychoanalytic and family systems perspectives in relation to marital disorders. The concepts of focal conflict theory, a psychosocial approach taken from psychology, will be used in the integration.

The argument follows this format: a description of a point at which psychoanalytic and family systems theory intersect (agree), a description of the elements of focal con-

---

[1] Group for the Advancement of Psychiatry, *The Field of Family Therapy,* vol. 7, no. 78 (March 1970): 581–93.

flict theory, recent extensions of focal conflict theory to groups, and a description of the focal conflict theory as applied to marriage as a small group. Then, using the focal conflict model, a classification of marital disorders by content and form will be presented. The description of form (interactional type) will be shown to be related to intrapsychic operations and the interpersonal consequences.

An Intersection of Psychoanalytic and Family Systems Theories

One way to integrate two differing points of view is to examine their areas of agreement. One area of agreement between psychoanalytic and family systems theory concerning marriage is that the marital partners are very similar. Peter Giovacchini defends the traditional approach to marital treatment—that is, treatment of individuals— nonetheless he focuses on their equal need for each other, which he calls symbiosis, and the equivalence of their respective pathologies.[2] The symbiosis may be of a limited type, the "symptom-object relationship" in which there is a need for a specific trait in the other or a "character-object relationship" in which the need is for the whole of the other at many deferent levels. Although Giovacchini never treats both marital partners, his discussions with colleagues who treat the spouses of his patients led him to conclude that, at least in marriages of long duration, the pathology of the partners is equivalent. The fact that marital partners may appear so different can be attributed to different defenses (he emphasizes the use of projective-introjective mechanisms in the couple), and that the pathology of one can serve to hold off the appearance of pathology in the other. Underneath, however, he believes that the points of fixation and regression and the kinds of conflicts are the same.

Similarly, Murray Bowen, one of the early family researchers and the originator of "family systems theory," also conceives of a type of union in marriage which he calls the "common self," an aspect of the "undifferentiated family ego mass."[3] Bowen believes that marital partners are equal in their basic levels of pathology and health, their "level of differentiation of self." He accounts for the apparent differences between spouses in this way: People of equal maturity marry. An automatic battle ensues to see who will get the "ego strength" and become the "functional self" and who will give it up and become the "functional nonself." A typical result is that the "functional self" becomes the "overadequate" partner, functioning at a better level than outside the marriage, and the other partner becomes the "underadequate" one, functioning at a lower level than outside the marriage. The resulting "overadequate-underadequate reciprocity" is a relationship disorder that describes the apparent differences in levels of functioning while the view is maintained that they are basically equal.

---

[2] Peter Giovacchini, "Treatment of Marital Disharmonies: The Classical Approach," in *The Psychotherapies of Marital Disharmony,* ed. Bernard L. Green (New York: Free Press, 1965), pp. 39-82; and "Characterological Aspects of Marital Interaction," in *The Psychoanalysis of Character Disorders,* ed. Peter Giovacchini (New York: Jason Aronson, 1975), pp. 253–60.

[3] Murray Bowen, *Family Therapy in Clinical Practice* (New York: Jason Aronson, 1978).

Basic Concepts of Focal Conflict Theory

Thomas French's focal conflict theory is an especially convenient way to examine the integrative function of the ego.[4] Its major elements are these: In response to the environment, an individual may have a wish which for any of a variety of reasons may be unacceptable to the ego. Such an unacceptable wish is called a "disturbing motive." Disturbing motives may proceed from the id, being therefore primarily sexual or aggressive, or may be more distinctly ego wishes, such as a wish for independence, dependence, or mastery. A disturbing motive is disturbing because it elicits other internal fears called "reactive motives." Examples of reactive motives are guilt, fear of being punished, fear of loss of love, shame, fear of being destructive or being destroyed, or the recognition that the wish is unrealistic. The combination of the disturbing and reactive motives constitute the "focal conflict" for the ego. The ego's task is to work out a solution to the focal conflict in relation to and using reality.

Often the focal conflict is beyond the integrative capacity of the ego. The ego may then substitute a problem within its integrative capacity for one beyond it. Hence, a person troubled by a fear of a specific destructive impulse toward a loved one may substitute a worry about whether the car is tuned properly, because getting a tune-up is something that can be coped with much more easily than the feared impulse. This, of course, does not solve the original conflict, but it does facilitate successful ego activity and, therefore, ego integrity.

Substituting one problem for another in this way involves some use of defenses, particularly projection. In projection, a drive, an affect, or a thought from the id, ego, or superego can be experienced as originating in someone else, when in fact it is not. The optimal conditions for projection are twofold: first, a situation in which what is self and what is nonself is not clear, and second, projection is best directed where it can be met halfway by reality. As Otto Fenichel states, even the most disturbed paranoid finds a microbe of reality on which to place his projections.[5]

Focal Conflict Theory and Small Groups

Dorothy Scott Whitaker and Morton A. Lieberman extended French's focal conflict model to formed groups.[6] They believe that the apparent diversity of behavior of members of a group reflects an underlying concern about the here and now situation that can be expressed in focal conflict terminology, that is, consisting of reality, a disturbing motive, a reactive motive, and attempted solutions. They believe that people in groups direct their efforts toward establishing a solution that will reduce their anxiety by alleviating their reactive fears and at the same time satisfy their disturbing wishes as much as possible. Successful solutions are those in which all group members' behavior is con-

---

[4] Thomas M. French, *Psychoanalytic Interpretations* (Chicago: Quadrangle Books, 1970); see also Thomas M. French and Erika Fromm, *Dream Interpretation: A New Approach* (New York: Basic Books, 1964).

[5] Otto Fenichel, *The Psychoanalytic Theory of Neurosis* (New York: W. W. Norton, 1945), pp. 146–47.

[6] Dorothy Scott Whitaker and Morton A. Lieberman, *Psychotherapy Through the Group Process* (New York: Atherton Press, 1964).

sistent with or bound by it. Successful solutions may be restrictive, that is, primarily designed to ward off the reactive motive, or enabling, allowing for greater satisfaction of the disturbing motive.

Focal Conflict and Marital Disorders

The essential elements for developing a focal conflict model of marital disorder presented above will now be applied to marriage and integrated into the model itself.

1. People may respond to reality with conflict: the spouse, marriage itself with its special intensity and structure, and other realities impacting on the marriage can elicit deep conflict.

2. Frequently, a conflict will be beyond the integrative capacity of the ego, and the ego will substitute a problem within its integrative capacity for one beyond it. Although marital disorder causes considerable grief, marital problems may be more desirable from the ego's point of view than experiencing conflict in the self. This may be because somewhat different coping mechanisms can be used in marital trouble—one can blame the other, seek comfort from outsiders, get divorced, and so on.

3. The defense of projection used in such substitute problems works best when the situation of self and nonself is least clear, and when the projection can be met halfway by reality. There is a tendency in marriage toward confusion of self and other (if psychoanalysis and family systems theory are correct) because the partners are so similar and even have identical conflicts. This means projections in the area of conflicts can be met *more* than halfway.

4. Behavior of small groups can be understood as being directed toward the solution of an underlying concern, which can be expressed in focal conflict terms. A marriage is a small group and marital disorder is a part of marital behavior. Marital disorder can, therefore, be understood as directed toward the resolution of an underlying concern, which can be conceptualized in focal conflict terms.

A focal conflict approach to marriage therefore states that *marital disorder can be considered an attempt to solve shared psychological conflict within the context of the marriage.* The shared conflicts are not experienced within the self because they are beyond the integrative capacities of the individual egos. Aspects of the conflicts are instead experienced in the marriage, in the spouse, or in the world as a way to bring them within the integrative capacities of the respective egos. This involves the use of projection, which is made easy by the similarity of the marital partners' conflicts and the confusion of self and other in marriage.

CLASSIFICATION OF MARITAL DISORDERS

Marital disorders can be categorized by their content and their form. The content, what is actually talked about and acted on, is determined by the level and type of the shared conflict as well as, at times, a shared ego dysfunction. The form is determined by how the projections are managed and the response of the recipient.

The Content of Marital Disorders

The variety of different conflicts that a marital disorder may express is limited only by the kinds of conflicts an individual may have. Some typical conflicts and examples of the kinds of resulting marital disorders are described briefly below. Within each pair, these examples are designated as "more restrictive" or "more enabling" of the disturbing motive.

Aggression versus guilt can be seen (1) in a couple who never disagree and are horrified by couples that do (more restrictive of the disturbing motive of aggression), or (2) in a couple who engage in intense arguments, including physical baffles, while accepting mutual verbal and physical abuse (more enabling of the disturbing motive of aggression).

Dependency versus fear of loss of love can be seen (1) in a couple in which one is an alcoholic and the other a nondrinker who threatens divorce (more restrictive of the disturbing motive of dependency), or (2) in a couple who remain on welfare unnecessarily or take drugs, but live in fear of being found out and cut off from welfare (more enabling of disturbing motive of dependency).

Sexual impulses versus fear of punishment can be seen (1) in a couple who refrain from sexual relations (more restrictive of disturbing motive of sexual impulse) or (2) in a couple in which physical abuse is a prelude to sexual relations (more enabling of the disturbing motive of sexual desire).

Ego dysfunctions, either innate or in response to conflict, may also be shared and become part of the content of the marital disorder. A couple who have poor social relations, or are concerned that they do, may fight over who is the socially inadequate one, as if establishing this will make the other more adequate. Or, a couple may have poor judgment, such as a couple always in debt, but may between them attempt to establish one or the other as the cause of this trouble.

Four Forms of Marital Disorder

More important than the content, for the purpose of integrating focal conflict theory with family systems theory, are the forms that marital disorders may take. Four forms (interactional structures) of marital dysfunction can be discovered from a study of family systems theory.[7] These four interactional patterns are the "overadequate-underadequate" relationship, the "conflictual" relationship, the "distant" relationship, and the "united front" relationship. These are gross categorizations of classes of interpersonal behavior, and, of course, in a marriage more than one type of dysfunctional interaction can occur. From a focal conflict point of view, the form is determined by two factors: to whom the projections are directed and whether the recipient introjects, projects back, or avoids.

Overadequate-Underadequate Relationships. Both Bowen and Giovacchini describe

---

[7] Bowen, *Family Therapy in Clinical Practice,* pp. 18–22, 377-79; and Charles Kramer et al., *Beginning Phase of Family Treatment* (Chicago: Family Institute of Chicago, 1968).

the marital situation in which one person appears disturbed.[8] The symptomatic spouse may have problems with sexual dysfunction, drinking, psychosomatic illness, wife or child beating, anxiety, depression, schizophrenia, or a host of other manifest symptoms and disorders. The other spouse appears to have no problems.

It can be argued that in such an overadequate-underadequate relationship, the behavior of one spouse primarily reflects the disturbing motive and the behavior of the other reflects the reactive motive. For example, in a marriage in which one spouse has severe sexual inhibition and the other seems to have no inhibition at all, the person with the inhibition may be expressing the reactive motive through the defense against it and the person with no inhibition, the disturbing motive.

This behavioral outcome appears to result from these intraphysic conditions: The overadequate, or seemingly well-functioning spouse, Spouse A, has a conflict of sex versus guilt that is beyond the integrative capacity of his or her ego. Spouse A defensively assigns (or splits) only the disturbing motive of sexual desire to the self-representation (image of self in ego), while assigning inhibition, a defensive activity associated with guilt, to the object representation (image of spouse in ego), Spouse B. Assignment of the inhibition to the spouse constitutes a projection. Based on this perception, behavior on the part of Spouse A indicates to Spouse B, that Spouse B is inhibited about sex (projective identification). Spouse B, who has the same conflict of sex versus guilt, defensively reciprocates by assigning (splitting) the inhibition to the self-representation and the disturbing motive of sexual desire to the object representation of Spouse A. This constitutes a projection of sexual desire to Spouse A. This perception leads to behavior indicating to Spouse A that he or she has sexual desire and is not inhibited or guilty. Each spouse introjects the perception of the projections of the other spouse (introjective identification).

By assigning part of the conflict to the other spouse, each ego has brought the focal conflict of sex versus guilt within its integrative capacity. Now, instead of dealing with the whole conflict in self, each must only deal with part of the conflict in the self. Instead of having to deal intrapsychically with the other half of the conflict, one contends with it in reality by projecting it onto the other spouse. Spouse B's behavior, sexual inhibition, replaces for Spouse A the function of inhibiting his or her own sexuality as a defense against guilt. Spouse A's sexual approaches replace for Spouse B the function of dealing with his or her own disturbing sexual impulses. The type of behavior that is demonstrated by Spouse B presents the appearance of dysfunction, while Spouse A's behavior does not appear to be disturbed. Yet, this superficial perspective ignores the fact they are performing similar mental and behavioral operations (and therefore are equally dysfunctional). Similarly mutual projections and introjections can lead to one spouse who is alcoholic while the other does not drink, or one who is depressed and the spouse happy-go-lucky, and so forth.

Conflictual Relationships. A conflictual relationship involves similar attempts to assign disturbing or reactive motives to the spouse. Assigning whichever motive is desirable to the self-representation and the other to the object-representation (the spouse) is

---

[8] Bowen, *Family Therapy in Practice,* pp. 77 and 166; and Giovacchini, "Treatment of Marital Disharmonies," pp. 46–50.

followed by behavioral indications to the spouse as to how to validate these in reality. However, in a conflictual marriage each spouse refuses to introject the projections (refuses introjective identification). Instead, conflictual partners will project back and even organize their behavior so as to disprove the spouse's projections (which may mean intrapsychically there has been some temporary introjection).

A spouse may engage in sexual practices to convince the other that he or she is not inhibited, or give up drinking entirely to prove the absence of a drinking problem. Assignment of the desirable motive to the self-representation and the undesirable one to the object-representation becomes difficult under these conditions, because reality fails to confirm the projections, and the ego is saddled with the full conflict. The ego's choices are to maintain the projections and withdraw from reality, to recognize that the self's problems are in the self (beyond integrative capacity), to try to get others to confirm one's projections, or to decide that the "marriage" is bad (not self or other, just a bad "match"; see "united front" below). Individuals in the conflictual situation, therefore, have considerable difficulty managing themselves and their marriage with accurate reality testing. The conflictual situation then differs from the overadequate-underadequate one in that the projections are refused and no stable intrapsychic condition of having to deal with only one motive is achieved.

Distant Relationships. The distant marriage is characterized by an absence of emotional interaction between the spouses and can be seen as a flight from the anxiety present in a conflictual marriage. It may take the form of having only superficial communication, no communication with the spouse at all, or avoiding the person of the spouse entirely (separation or divorce). The purpose of this avoidance is to keep the focal conflict from being elicited. Projections to the spouse are maintained intrapsychically through avoidance of the reality of the other. Facing the reality of the other would undo the projection and expose the ego to both sides of the conflict and therefore elicit anxiety. The distant marriage, unlike the overadequate-underadequate marriage or even the conflictual marriage, does not produce a sense of closeness between spouses. Frequently, significant involvement with others such as affairs or hyperinvestment in work or social activities—sometimes where projections can be better accepted by others—replaces the marital closeness.

United Front Relationships. Closeness can be achieved within the marriage if a third party is willing to accept one part of the conflict, or at least not refute it. This type of marital dysfunction, the united front marriage, often looks to the outsider like a healthy marriage. It involves an absence of dysfunction in either spouse and the illusion of closeness. However, the united front marriage must have something to unite against— we are together against or for "x." The internal arrangements with regard to the focal conflict appear to be these: The self and object representations of both spouses align with respect to one side of the focal conflict while the other motive is projected (through splitting) to a child, someone in the community, an institution, a life problem, or the past or future which will not project back. Behavior directed toward the person that the motive has been projected to frequently results in the third party, for example, a child, confirming the projection by developing a problem (introjective identification).

For example, concerns about dependency by parents can successfully be projected to an unborn child without harm. But, continued projection beyond realistic necessity may be introjected leading to distorted development, such as inability to separate or function in school. Projection of disturbing sexual impulses to an adolescent child, while inhibitions against reactive fears of punishment are assigned to self and object representations of both parents, can result in adolescent promiscuity and severely punitive actions by the parents. Threatening disturbing motives toward independence can likewise be projected to an adolescent, while reactive fears of abandonment are assigned to the self and object representations of both parents, resulting in a runaway child with parents chasing right after.

The projections of the united front couple can be directed outside of the family as well. A couple may manage aggressive impulses through projection to concerns about United States military involvement overseas while retaining fears of being destructive for themselves. Another example may be a couple accepting disturbing dependency impulses for themselves, taking drugs and living useless lives while projecting fear of rejection to society.

SUMMARY

Marital disorder, then, is a part of the ego activity of the marital partners. It is a shared attempt to solve shared conflict and is maintained because it protects the partners from suffering the effects of experiencing anxiety. From a focal conflict point of view, at least three independent variables can be presumed to influence the type of marital disorder: (1) the type and level of the shared psychological conflict, (2) the one to whom the projections are directed, and (3) the response of the recipient of the projections.

The point of view that *shared conflicts* are involved helps clients and workers alike protect themselves against the all too easy tendency to find fault or blame in one of the marital partners. This faultfinding often takes the form of benign labeling of one partner as being "sicker" than the other. That the marital disorder is a *shared attempt* to deal with difficulties emphasizes that both marital partners are involved in a joint effort, albeit a painful one, at precisely those times that they may feel most isolated and cut off from one another, and the social worker can make this point to the couple. The idea that marital disorder is an *attempt to solve* a problem rather than a problem per se opens the possibility of solving the "real" problem in a new way other than marital disorder, an idea that offers hope to the couple being helped. Finally, that the marital dysfunction serves a functional (anxiety reducing) *purpose* should alert the practitioner to the clients' temporary need for the marital problem. In turn, this should help the worker understand in advance that attempts to modify either the psychological level of a marital partner (as is done in individual treatment, for example) or the nature of the marital interactions can have the unintended effect of creating anxiety and other psychological and interpersonal difficulties to both the marital partners and even those in their extended relationship system.

CONCLUSION

Marital disorders are an important problem. A variety of practice approaches, based on two very different behavioral explanations of the causes of marital disorder, are commonly used. The purpose of this article has been to integrate psychoanalytic and family theories by proposing a focal conflict model of marital disorders.

The focal conflict model presented views marital disorder as an attempt by the marital partners to solve shared psychological conflict(s) in the context of the marriage. The content of marital disorder is seen as influenced by the type and level of the shared psychological conflict while the form—here integrated with four relationship disorders from family systems theory—is influenced by where the projections are directed and the response of the recipient. The relationship dysfunction then is a part of a psychosocial steady state in which conflict, problem solving efforts, and interactional elements have a part. This view casts marital disorder in a more favorable form for work with disordered marriages.

CHAPTER 77

EXTRAMARITAL AFFAIRS

Clinical Issues in Therapy

Sonya Rhodes

In a rapidly changing society, traditional social structures are giving way to new interpersonal patterns. A radical departure from traditional monogamous marriage is the tendency for marriages to be increasingly vulnerable to the extramarital affair. Such an affair often precipitates a therapeutic crisis; it is a complex phenomenon that requires skillful therapeutic management.

The various theoretical perspectives in the literature on extramarital affairs were carefully summarized by Robert Taibbi.[1] His distinction within the interactional perspective differentiated between affairs as a distance-maintaining mechanism in marriage, as a way of precipitating a crisis to break a marital impasse, and as a function of life crisis transitions.

This article is concerned with the role and impact of the extramarital affair on the marital relationship. Clinical profiles are described which show how the affair reflects dynamics in the relationship; courses of therapy are predicted, and the relevant therapeutic issues are discussed. Case examples are used to illustrate the basic concepts.

THE AFFAIR AS A CRISIS IN MARRIAGE

This article seeks to conceptualize the extramarital affair as a dynamic of the couple's relationship. Placing the extramarital affair in the context of the marital system obviates several hazards and results in several therapeutic advantages.

Reprinted from *Social Casework*, Vol. 65, No. 9 (1984), pp. 541–546, by permission of the publisher, Families International, Inc.
[1] Robert Taibbi, "Handling Extramarital Affairs in Clinical Treatment." *Social Casework* 64 (April 1983): 200–04.

If the extramarital affair is viewed as part of an interpersonal pattern, this therapeutic lens is still broad enough to include the intrapsychic conflicts and defensive maneuvers of each partner which dictate the underlying individual motivation for the affair. But if the extramarital affair is viewed solely from the traditional psychodynamic perspective as the acting out of unconscious conflicts,[2] the affair is constructed as a negative event, a regressive pull, rather than as part of the process of relationship negotiation. The unfolding of marital conflicts and crisis as a function of change and growth places the emphasis on rebuilding viable marital structures that meet the changing needs of the couple.

Creating viable, dynamic relationships which overcome the immediate crisis of the affair is the general goal of couple's therapy. However, whether couples work out the conflicts that surface as part of the process of dealing with the extramarital affair or whether they seal over the crisis by reverting to the precrisis relationship depends on many factors, including therapeutic management of the crisis.

The disclosure or discovery of an affair usually precipitates a crisis in marriage. Three stages to the "affair as crisis" sequence are broadly sketched below. The dynamics of each stage relate to the meaning of the affair to the couple, the flaws and strengths of their relationship, and their style of recovery.

1. *Grief Reactions.*[3] The impact of the affair usually produces profound feelings of anger and loss in the "victim": loss of self-esteem, loss of the "marriage that existed prior to the affair," loss of confidence, and a loss of trust (accompanied by feelings of betrayal). Fantasies of retaliation are common. The partner who had the affair often reacts with feelings of relief or guilt and shame.

If the impact of the affair has shaken the foundations of the marriage and the marriage is seriously threatened, a planned separation can be proposed as part of the recovery process. Planned separations provide psychological as well as physical distance between the couple and are an effective counterpart to projection and blame. Furthermore, separation often boosts self-respect, reinforces individual boundaries, and raises the couple's consciousness to issues of voluntary commitment in a relationship.

The grief reaction can last from several weeks to several months. If grief, as the predominant motif, persists longer than six months, the therapist should consider more carefully what secondary gains each person is getting out of his or her respective role of victim, betrayer, or placator (for example, power, retribution, control, self-flagellation).[4] These roles are usually exaggerations of the interpersonal games the couple is accustomed to playing.

2. *Evaluation.* The couple who move into the second stage begins to consider "how we got here." An attitude of concern and curiosity about the marriage *without* overtones of accusation signals a readiness to examine the relationship. The affair has receded into the background. Individual and joint disappointments, fears, and needs take precedence. Developmental shifts reflecting changing personal and interpersonal needs are shared and explored. During this stage, a profound shift can occur in the couple's

---

[2] Herbert Strean, "The Extramarital Affair: A Psychoanalytic View," *Psychoanalytic Review* 63 (Spring 1976): 101–13.

[3] Taibbi, *Handling Extramarital Affairs,* p. 200.

[4] Ibid., p. 203.

appreciation of each other as whole objects. One man was shocked by his wife's disclosure of her masturbatory activity and her sexual fantasies which had made her ripe for an affair. Heretofore, he had regarded her as a nonsexual "homey" type and had no idea that she was "so sexual a person." By keeping her sexuality a secret, she protected both of them from their sexual inhibitions.

During this stage the rules of the relationship are examined with special emphasis on the flaws in the relationship. They are viewed by the therapist and the couple as contributing to the crisis.

3. *Restructuring.* The third stage begins when clients express the desire to modify and rebuild their relationship. This is the guts of the marital therapy and usually takes from six months to two years.

While the three-stage sequence gives a broad theoretical stroke, few clinical situations correspond precisely to theoretical constructs. Therefore, these stages should be thought of as theoretical footings or anchors. Clinical situations usually are more complex and less precise, causing intense reactions in clients and countertransference in therapists. The following situations describe some of the complexities and ways of handling extramarital affairs in clinical practice.

THE AFFAIR AS A RELATIONSHIP STABILIZER

In this category are couples whose relationships have been characterized by a series of affairs involving one or both of the partners—or one partner's long-term affair—which has not threatened the stability of the marriage. The occurrence of extramarital involvements as part of couple's history is usually a reliable indicator that the affairs serve an important regulatory function in the relationship. In other words, the affairs maintain a relatively stable triangle to regulate distance between the couple. These relationships are usually very resistant to change as they have a built-in homeostatic mechanism that siphons off tension as it builds up in the system. Thus negotiation and problem solving are short-circuited, and the relationship, while stable, tends to be static and unchanging.

These couples present for treatment when the homeostatic cycle has been disrupted by an escalation or intensification of the extramarital activity. The source of the stress is an increase in distance between the couple or a shift in the distribution of power between them that destabilizes the relationship. The "discovery" of the affair can be dramatized as the presenting issue, but a quick shift in focus to the current stress is necessary to capitalize on the crisis and produce some modest change in the system.

For example, Sharon's application for counseling was prompted by the discovery that her husband of fifteen years had had a brief sexual encounter. She found out about it because she contracted a venereal disease and her husband, when confronted, acknowledged casual sexual contact with someone else. She requested individual therapy to evaluate whether she should leave the marriage. In relation to her husband's sexual activity, she was distraught and felt betrayed, but focused extensively on her belief that she could not tolerate a marriage which was not based on an explicit contract of monogamy.

Since a client's construction of the meaning of an affair shapes therapeutic intervention, the therapist listened to her focus on the affair as a precipitant to her leaving the marriage. However, when asked about the marriage, she described it as stable and satisfying, formed by the blending of his two children by a former marriage and her child by a former marriage into a unit which placed his business responsibilities and her child care responsibilities at the center. His business required a great deal of social entertaining which she executed with flair and graciousness. In general, she described a marriage that was marred only by her husband's fatal indiscretion.

Continuing to assess the rules of the relationship, the therapist focused on those governing communication and the extent of openness and directness. Careful inquiry elicited the fact that she and her husband had been collusive in keeping his past affairs a secret. She had contracted venereal disease several times without seeking the source of infection. That her husband had most likely infected her went unacknowledged in spite of the fact that medical attention was necessary.

Since infidelity was unacknowledged but permissible within the implicit rules of the relationship, the next area of clinical assessment concerned precipitants, with special attention to developmental stresses. It was significant to note that the last of their children—his youngest—had recently left home. As a result, Sharon's arena of responsibility was diminished. Thus, the imbalance in roles, in combination with the couple crisis triggered by the last child's leaving home, produced stress and tension which destabilized the marital system.[5]

After assessing the strengths and weaknesses of the marriage, gathering the history of extramarital activity, which was known but unacknowledged, and evaluting the source and extent of current stress on the marital pair, the therapist constructed the hypothesis that Sharon was seizing on the "discovery" of a current affair to justify a marital split at a time when she felt her power in the relationship was diminished. The most recent affair took on special significance because it represented the inequities of power as experienced by Sharon.[6] It is only a slight exaggeration to create the imagery of his domain as a harem of lovers and hers as an abandoned cottage hearth.

The therapeutic task addressed to vital concerns of this couple involved a rebalancing of power and closeness as they went through the transition of adjusting to their childless marital state. Helping Sharon validate herself and rebuild her power base through worthwhile occupational pursuits (she was a weaver) obviated the need for her to establish a power base by seeking divorce. A short-term treatment contract including several joint marital sessions was successfully completed. The contract concerning extramarital affairs was restated in terms of "how they are going to show they need each other" without any basic change in the rules of the relationship.

---

[5] Sonya Rhodes, "A Developmental Approach to the Life Cycle of the Family," *Social Casework* 58 (May 1977): 301–10.

[6] A variation on this theme is presented by Elaine Walster, Jane Trampmann, and G. William Walster, "Equity and Extramarital Sexuality," *Archives of Sexual Behavior* 7 (March 1978): 127–42. The authors propose that extramarital sex be viewed as an "equity restoration mechanism" to rebalance power in a relationship.

THE AFFAIR AS AN IMPASSE TO MARITAL THERAPY

If one partner is involved in an extramarital affair which continues after the couple's therapy is initiated or in progress, therapeutic vigilance is essential. Most couples who present this clinical picture have long-standing marital dissatisfactions which have been collusively avoided and overlooked. The affair brings the couple into therapy because it provides an unavoidable obstacle to maintaining the myth that the marriage is viable.

The affair is perceived by the couple to be a threat, and in fact it is, because it is invested with more energy and vitality than the marriage. The affair poses a real threat to the marriage because it siphons off what little energy is left in the system. Often the "victimized" partner sees the extent of the problem simplistically as "he (or she) must give up the affair," which is the equivalent of reinstating the previous status quo. Moreover, if the marriage is "on empty," the partner having the affair is reluctant to give it up, and, under these conditions, has often invested a great deal of fantasy into idealizing the romance.

A slight variation on this clinical picture is a situation in which, during the beginning phase of marital treatment, the partner who did not initiate the therapy requests an individual interview. A therapist should always be aware of the timing of such a request and anticipate an important area of resistance to therapeutic progress. If the partner discloses an ongoing affair to the therapist as a secret, beware! The client's motivation for sharing this information must be explored, and his or her desire for a collusive relationship with the therapist must be confronted. The client may be asking for permission to end the marriage or for permission from the therapist to continue the affair. The therapist implicitly grants this permission if he or she does not claim the right to use the new information as he or she feels is therapeutically indicated. Regardless of what unconsciously motivates the client, the therapist is in danger of being manipulated and, more specifically, of being incorporated into the marital system of secretiveness and deception.

Clinical management of the situation is tricky. As a general rule, the goals of marital therapy cannot be accomplished if one partner is continuing an affair. Continuing an affair while marital therapy proceeds dilutes and distorts the process of joint therapy and reinforces the schism in the relationship that the couple has cultivated over the years. The therapist should continually stress that the wife and husband need all their energy to evaluate their relationship and can't afford to siphon off any energy to other relationships. In this way, the therapist is setting limits, dealing with resistances to therapy, and establishing the conditions for a contract for the therapy.

If the affair continues to the therapist's knowledge, she or he should focus on the affair as an impasse to further marital treatment and pose this as a dilemma to the clients. If they want to continue "working on the marriage" while the partner makes up his or her mind about the affair, the therapist may express astonishment at the lengths to which they will go to deceive themselves. The approach usually forces a decision, breaking the therapeutic impasse, and often leads to more appropriate therapeutic goals such as planned separation, individual treatment, or divorce therapy.

THE AFFAIR AS A HARMLESS DALLIANCE

An extramarital affair should never be regarded as a harmless dalliance. The initiation or escalation of an extramarital affair always represents an attempt to solve a problem in the marriage; it should be viewed by the therapist as a warning signal.

The client in individual therapy who discusses extramarital activity presents special therapeutic problems. To what extent does this require a shift in focus as well as modality to include the spouse to give the relationship priority as the main focus of treatment?

As a therapist, the author has struggled with this problem over the years, trying to develop a therapeutic strategy that did not neglect either psychodynamic or systems formulations. For a while, she thought she could help the client examine the extramarital affair as a reflection of personal conflicts. Most often this has failed; a crisis eventually develops in the marriage for which the therapist had handicapped herself by being a "co-conspirator" in the affair. After reviewing these cases carefully and giving much thought to individual and marital dynamics, the author has found that a clear therapeutic stance is necessary. The client in individual therapy who discusses extramarital activity is bringing her or his relationship into the treatment. Extramarital involvement reflects a breakdown in the couple's problem-solving activity. A relationship problem can no longer be ignored or denied. The partner involved in the extramarital affair is clearly frustrated by the marital impasse. His or her extramarital activity will be incorporated into the marital system as a misplaced problem-solving device. With this approach, the therapist is able to focus on the relationship problems. The nature of the impasse, the extent of erosion of the marital relationship, and relevant precipitants and imbalances in the relationship can be addressed to gain therapeutic leverage. A shift in modality to couple's therapy is most often the result.

Case Example

Fred, thirty-five years old and married for one year, sought individual therapy for himself. He described a major life crisis with respect to his masculine identity and sexuality. Because of a rather sheltered adolescence and early commitment to the woman who later became his wife, his sexual experimentation and curiosity were curtailed. Now, he was obsessed with sexual curiosity and fantasies. He had begun to withdraw sexually from his wife, with whom sex had become bland and boring.

Related to his heightened sexual excitement was the fact that he was becoming more frequently involved in extramarital affairs. His initial attitude toward his affairs was that they were harmless dalliances which therapy would help him control so that they would not endanger his relationship with his wife. Though the extramarital activity violated the explicit marital contract, the affairs were consistent with the implicit marital contract that he could do whatever he wanted as long as his wife didn't find out. The "forbidden," secretive nature of his extramarital activities heightened the intense excitement he felt about them.

As his treatment progressed, Fred began to express more concern about the intensity of his need for sexual liaisons. Much of his behavior seemed reactive to his fear that marriage placed too many restrictions on his freedom. His early history clearly reflected his vulnerability to feeling engulfed by a woman and his lifelong characterological defense of compulsive, intense, and sometimes rebellious "outside" activities to protect his independence. The "forbidden" rebelliousness of extramarital activity heightened both excitement and guilt. This became a theme of his treatment.

In spite of the individual focus, the therapist began to wonder how his perception of marriage as an entrapment matched with the interpersonal rules of his relationship. His relationship with Helen, his wife, was a deep, long-term attachment begun thirteen years before, when they were college students. Due to a joint reluctance and shared fear of marriage, they had deferred marriage until the year before, although they had been living together up to that time. It is significant that his extramarital activity as a distancing maneuver escalated immediately after they formalized their relationship in marriage.

The therapeutic dilemma, which the therapist hedged on for several months, was whether to involve Helen. Fred did not want her involved, as he preferred to see the problems as a personal struggle which individual therapy would help him resolve. Finally, as he withdrew more and more from the marriage, the therapist took the position that, although his current problems reflected individual issues, they were also embedded in a serious deterioration in his marriage which could no longer be ignored. The therapist encouraged him to confront Helen with his feelings about the marriage. At this point, the therapist knew that Helen had been collusive with him about his affairs; they had been blatant and obvious but had gone unacknowledged. Immediately upon his confrontation with Helen, the marital crisis exploded. As anticipated, Helen saw the therapist as a co-conspirator. While focusing on the displacement of her anger, the therapist also acknowledged the part that was real. Although Helen was initially reluctant to continue with the therapist in couple therapy, she later decided to go ahead. A planned separation produced a great deal of pain and loss for both partners. The couple's therapy sessions continued throughout the separation.

While it is not relevant to describe the following year's course of marital therapy, it is important to point out that Fred's internal representation of marriage corresponded to a relationship which, in spite of the outward appearance of a contemporary couple, was based on rigid rules of control and management. The roles of hearth keeper, impulse manager, and rule maker were carried by Helen; Fred depended on her but at the same time resented her and needed to rebel. Their relationship, destabilized by Fred's personal crisis, led to a profound and productive search for the flaws that contributed to the marital crisis. Fortunately, this couple was able to build a new and better relationship based on this experience.

THE AFFAIR: ARGUMENT AGAINST 'CONFESSIONS'

In contrast to Fred and Helen's case, where disclosure became pivotal to treatment, some affairs are more trivial than others, and not all affairs need to be brought to the attention of the unsuspecting spouse. The confession of an incidental affair is not encouraged, especially since it is often motivated by unconscious hostility or the wish to create instant closeness. Revealing an extramarital affair in a burst of intimacy is, at best, unwise, and at worst, sadistic. The timing of the impulse to disclose a past affair is significant. Timing may relate to a client's unconscious hostility and disappointment, a client's fears about taking a risk in the marriage, a client's wish to sabotage a relationship which is improving. Or it may be a genuine quest for greater openness and intimacy. Anticipating the consequences of disclosure, as well as exploring motivation, is always helpful.

MARRIAGE

CHAPTER 78

THE NEED FOR CRISIS INTERVENTION DURING MARITAL SEPARATION

Robert M. Counts and Anita Sacks

Holmes and Rahe, in their study of stressful life events, ranked the relative impact of 43 commonly experienced events.[1] (See Table 78–1.) The death of one's spouse was first, with a mean value of 100; divorce was second, with a mean value of 73; and marital separation was third, with a mean value of 65. The present authors' experience has been that marital separation is often much more disruptive, both immediately and in the long term, than losing one's spouse. The authors discuss why marital separation should be viewed as a stressor of the first magnitude. Factors likely to result in disruption will be considered and a framework for judging the extent to which this common experience is likely to be stressful will be presented.

In this article, the authors have chosen to use the phrase "marital separation" to describe the overall process characterizing the end of a marriage. This is a dynamic phrase for a complicated long-term process. "Divorce" and "legal separation" are legal terms; the latter has little to do with many separations, which may be only temporary. Both terms are static and imply that a relationship has been ended forever when the new court-sanctioned reciprocal responsibilities and entitlements that constitute a divorce or legal separation exist.

Much has been written about marital separation. Prior to 1965, however, there were no comprehensive studies that followed a large population over a long period. Most of these articles dealt with just a few cases, were anecdotal, and were largely based on the biases of the respective authors. Recent studies have a larger number of cases and follow the cases for several years after the initial disruption. Wallerstein and Kelly; Robert Weiss; Bloom, White, and Asher, and others have made valuable contributions to the professions knowledge.[2] They suggest that marital separation is a very stressful event

Reprinted from *Social Work,* Vol. 30, No. 2 (March–April, 1985), pp. 146–150, by permission of NASW Press. Copyright 1985, National Association of Social Workers, Inc., *Social Work.*

Table 78–1
Social Readjustment Rating Scale[a]

Rank	Life Event	Mean Value
1	Death of spouse	100
2	Divorce	73
3	Marital separation	65
4	Jail term	63
5	Death of close family member	63
6	Personal injury or illness	53
7	Marriage	50
8	Fired at work	47
9	Marital reconciliation	45
10	Retirement	45
11	Change in health of family member	44
12	Pregnancy	40
13	Sex difficulties	39
14	Gain of new family member	39
15	Business readjustment	39
16	Change in financial state	38
17	Death of close friend	37
18	Change to different line of work	36
19	Change in number of arguments with spouse	35
20	Mortgage over $10,000	31
21	Foreclosure of mortgage or loan	30
22	Change in responsibilities at work	29
23	Son or daughter leaving home	29
24	Trouble with in-laws	29
25	Outstanding personal achievement	28
26	Wife begin or stop work	26
27	Begin or end school	26
28	Change in living conditions	25
29	Revision of personal habits	24
30	Trouble with boss	23
31	Change in work hours or conditions	20
32	Change in residence	20
33	Change in schools	20
34	Change in recreation	19
35	Change in church activities	19
36	Change in social activities	18
37	Mortgage or loan less than $10,000	17
38	Change in sleeping habits	16
39	Change in number of family get-togethers	15
40	Change in eating habits	15
41	Vacation	13
42	Christmas	12
43	Minor violations of the law	11

[a]See notes and references, no. 1.

with serious immediate and long-term consequences; they also have emphasized that the recovery period is prolonged (four to five years).

A broad, cross cultural population sample was selected for Holmes and Rahe's study. The respondents were instructed to rate the readjustment consequent to a stressful event, using marriage as a frame of reference for comparison. The scale was found to be both consistent and statistically reliable. For example, Holmes and Masuda found it to be useful in predicting the likelihood of physical and psychiatric illness.[3] They scored stress in Life Change Units (LCUs); the larger the score, the more the person was at risk for stress-related health problems. If a person experienced events that led to a score of between 150 and 199 LCUs in a year's time, for example, that person was considered to be in a mild life crisis. The incidence of negative health changes for this group was 37 percent. With a score indicating a moderate life crisis—200 to 299 LCUs—the incidence was 51 percent. For a major life crisis score—300 or more LCUs— the rate was 79 percent. Couples with children who separate are likely to score in excess of 300 LCUs. This is true even when the couple is in agreement on most, if not all, issues and their separation is accomplished without the fireworks so commonly associated with the end of a marriage. If the process *is* complicated by battling and rancor, the scores are likely to be high indeed.

Using Holmes and Rahe as a point of departure the authors became interested in developing a frame of reference for considering the special stresses of marital separation.

STRESS FACTORS

Factors that influence how stressful separation will ultimately be for an individual fall into three broad overlapping categories, namely, (1) the circumstances surrounding the separation, (2) intrapsychic status, and (3) events that activate the memory of earlier attachments and relationships and thus have the potential to interfere with stability in the patterns and fabric of life after separation. If the circumstances existing at the time of the initial separation are considered, it is apparent that a host of factors contribute to whether the process will be more or less stressful. These factors can include how the couple have come to pick the alternative of separation and whether or not it is a mutual decision. Weiss, for example, pointed out that when one person surprises the other, having unilaterally reached the conclusion that he or she wished to end the marriage, the other is usually much more upset than when the element of surprise is absent.[4] (This is consistent with an observation made by Bowlby.[5]) Anticipation of the death of a spouse, as in cases of prolonged illness, makes it easier for the surviving person to adjust to the loss. Similarly, when a decision to separate comes after efforts to resolve differences, both members of the couple are usually less upset. In addition, when the partners of the marriage retain some measure of respect and affection for one another despite the presence of tension and conflict, parting is less traumatic and they can usually find a way to end the marriage that does not result in an emotional bloodbath.

Many other elements that are part of the immediate circumstances influence the extent to which the process will be stressful for those concerned. (In this article, only the stress on the marital partners will be considered. However, in line with the findings of Wallerstein and Kelly, the present authors believe that most marital separations are far more stressful for the children than for the adults.[6]) Stress is likely to be increased when the couple have been married for a number of years, have children, have problems with one or more of their children (birth defects, mental retardation, and so forth that may have contributed to the marital discord and unhappiness and also pose special problems in the event of marital separation), have had fights over money, or have been incited by lawyers or others to battle with each other.

These examples (which, of course, do not exhaust the possibilities) can, depending on circumstances, increase the stress and pain manyfold. An ameliorating factor, as Wallerstein and Kelly pointed out, is that the continued involvement of both parents with the children helps to limit psychological crippling.[7] The present authors concur and have found that consideration and concern both for one's children and for one's former mate contribute to a quicker and more complete recovery from marital separation.

Intrapsychic factors influence how skillfully a person involved in marital separation is likely to manage the event. Two aspects of intrapsychic functioning are (1) the overall personality structure of the person, and (2) specific vulnerabilities the person may demonstrate. The first of these, the role of personality structure, seems obvious: The greater one's adaptational abilities and ego strengths, the more likely one will be able to manage this event with competence. With regard to the second, the question is, What specific personality configurations or early life experiences result in one person's being more vulnerable than another? The capacity to consciously tolerate the variety of painful effects involved in a marital separation is a crucial requirement for an optimal recovery.

Considering the number of losses usually involved in a marital separation, mourning and expressions of grief should be present. An inability to grieve can be disastrous and is likely to prolong the recovery process. Similarly, those who have had difficulty in separating from their families of origin may find the fears aroused by being on one's own after a separation very threatening.

Mourning is the appropriate reaction to loss whether the loss involves a person, a place, an ideal, hopes, or expectations—regardless of whether it is due to death, marital separation, desertion, or other vicissitudes of life. Mourning is adaptational and in its absence, or when it is insufficient, the person is very much at risk. It is as necessary to grieve the end of a marriage and all that this entails as it is to grieve the death of a loved one. Therefore, the two "disordered variants of mourning" described by Bowlby are of special interest. These variants are "chronic mourning" and the "more or less prolonged absence of conscious grieving."[8]

Bowlby noted that three types of personalities are especially vulnerable to disordered mourning: personalities who exhibit anxious and ambivalent attachments, personalities who are prone to compulsive caregiving, and personalities who "insist on their independence of all affectional ties."[9] He found that certain childhood experiences often precede these personality configurations. Furthermore, Bowlby suggested that those who form anxious and ambivalent attachments are "likely to have experienced discontinuities in parenting and/or often have been rejected by their parents," and that in such cases "the rejection is more likely to have been intermittent and partial than complete. As a result, the children, still hoping for love and care yet deeply anxious lest they be neglected or deserted, increase their need for attention and affection, refuse to be left alone and protest more or less angrily when they are."[10]

Those prone to compulsive caregiving usually reported either experiencing intermittent or inadequate mothering or that they had been expected to take care of a physically ill or a very emotionally troubled parent. This expectation was often reinforced by the inference that the child was responsible for the parents' difficulties.

Individuals who avoid or are chary of all affectional ties report two rather different types of childhood experience. Some had lost a parent during childhood. This loss may have been the result of the death of a parent or separation of the parents. In some instances, the "loss" was the result of a parent's being depressed for a significant period. According to Bowlby, the other commonly reported experience with this type of disordered grieving is "the unsympathetic and critical attitude that a parent may take towards her child's natural desires for love, attention, and support."[11] Sometimes this attitude occurs when the child attempts to separate and be autonomous. The presence of this parental attitude has been noted in the histories of adult borderline patients. Masterson believes that the borderline disorder is a consequence of the emotional unavailability of the mother, for whatever reason, during the rapprochement phase of separation-individuation.[12] This unavailability results in separation anxiety, abandonment depression, and mobilization of defenses to manage these painful affects. Patients who are borderline or who lost a parent during childhood are at higher risk than others when exposed to the unique stresses of marital breakdown.

Other examples of behavior that may result in an adult's vulnerability when exposed to marital separation are marital partners with a history of school phobia, difficulties in staying overnight with friends during latency and adolescence, refusing to go away to camp or college, or prolonged homesickness. The origins of separation problems and of the borderline personality disorder may have similar roots in the separation-individuation process.

Events that occur years after any separation may have profound, even devastating, impact. Feelings of grief, guilt, and resentment that, although dormant, remain alive, may be reawakened and leave one heir to trouble and heartache. Most individuals who have gone through the end of a marriage have within them seeds of further trouble. Life is often a compromise—thus, many of the feelings aroused by an event are often only partially resolved, so that the grieving process is never completed. As a result, when events conspire against people, persisting and unresolved grief may be reactivated when it is least expected, and may be a surprise, in any case, because of a belief that the issues and feelings had been sufficiently dealt with and long ago put to rest. A few of the events that are likely to stir up pain and cause stress are (1) the former mate remarries or has another child, (2) the former mate becomes seriously ill or dies, (3) one of the children develops physical or emotional difficulties, (4) one of the children refuses to accept either a new mate or the birth of a half sibling, (5) a former mate reopens or challenges the existing legal agreement, and (6) one of the couple's children fails to find his or her place in life (with regard to career, marriage, and so forth).

Most people who choose to separate are unprepared for what follows unless they have been through it before. Often, the consequences turn out to be much worse than anticipated. Many end up feeling they went from bad to worse. (In the authors' experience, children of separated couples most often believe things are *much* worse after marital separation than before.)

Professionals need to keep in mind the overall picture and to anticipate mounting risk to the individual. Holmes and Masuda noted that with increases of stress, illness was more likely to occur.[13] They also noted, however, that "on the average, associated health changes followed a life crisis by about a year."[14] If professionals do not intervene until after the illness has become manifest, they are a year late. Intervention efforts should occur during the crisis, not months later.

A TYPICAL SEPARATION

As an example, the circumstances of the following case can be considered typical: Mr. and Mrs. W had been married for 15 years. They had three children, aged 13, 9, and 3. They parted amicably by mutual agreement, although they blamed one another for the failure of their marriage, and there was some ill feeling between them. The wife (who had been quite attached to her in-laws) planned to move back to her parental home, which was 800 miles from suburban New York City (where the couple had resided). Her parents blamed the husband, because they believed he was more interested in his career than in the family. The couple expected to sell their home at the end of the school year. The husband then planned to move to an efficiency apartment in Manhattan. The children realized the contact with their father would be quite limited.

Although there was, perhaps, less rancor than with most, this was not an unusual separation. The decisions had been carefully thought out and would, no doubt, be carefully implemented. How much stress would the family be likely to experience? To determine the degree of stress in the case of Mr. and Mrs. W, the authors will use Holmes and Rahe's scale, although it is not a perfect fit.

The couple would have to contend with a change of residence; loss of some of their close friends and of their respective in-laws; changes in opportunities for sex, recreation, social activities, and family get-togethers; changes in eating habits; and a major change in financial status. The husband, in addition, would be faced with the loss of daily contact with his children. Each member of the family would experience a major life crisis, with LCUs in the range of 450 to 500.

What if a separation is complicated by circumstances common during partings that are less amicable than that of Mr. and Mrs W? For example, what if there is a battle for custody of the children; if families or lawyers are inciting the couple to do battle; if the former mates are playing the children off against one another; or if disgrace, humiliation, or criminality are part of the picture? These complications can indeed be stressful, although it may be difficult to quantify them accurately in terms of Holmes and Rahe's 43 life events.

INTERVENTION STRATEGIES

The authors do not wish to extensively review techniques of intervention but, rather, to discuss the special problems associated with these patients. Few people caught up in the process of separation are equipped to deal effectively with the considerable and unique stresses that have been discussed. This is especially true of children and adolescents. Thus, intervention is important and should be the rule, not the exception.

The authors prefer to work with the entire nuclear family. The aim is to prevent the vicious circles that often result in mounting stress for all. Parting couples, for instance, often orchestrate events so that the separation, the move from the family home, a change of schools for the children, and the loss of their support systems will occur at the same time. It is to be hoped that an intervention will encourage a couple to take things gradually, one step at a time. A slow, deliberate approach allows each member more time to adjust to the many changes that will occur.

Each of the family members needs to be evaluated—specific vulnerabilities, especially those mentioned earlier, should be kept in mind and addressed when present. With separation, grief is often masked by other more obvious emotions. Thus, the grieving process is likely to be far more complex and treacherous than with a death. The fact that the family members have continuing and often highly conflicted contacts with one another may also result in the adaptational process being exceedingly complex. Resolution of the attachments and affects may be most difficult. The presence of young children is more likely to be a stressful factor in marital separation than it is in the death of a spouse.

The destructive acting out that is so common between parting couples needs to be controlled by firm but sympathetic interventions. Steinberg has described an approach that is useful. In working with such couples, he stresses just how destructive their battling may be, especially when children are involved.[15] He points out that their failure to resolve differences may result in decisions being taken out of their hands and transferred to the control of the court, where individuals who have little personal interest in the outcome may end up making important decisions that relate to the welfare and the future of the couple's children. The authors have been impressed by the extent of leverage that can be exerted by professionals in such interventions.

The authors actively encourage the working out of joint custody agreements and of parents living near one another after the separation so that the children are able to enjoy two easily accessible households and daily contact with both parents. Other arrangements that emphasize parental cooperation and friendship are encouraged. This is as much for the welfare of the former mates as for the children.

There is ample evidence that even under the best of circumstances, marital separation is enormously stressful for couples. The lay public, teachers, guidance counselors, and those who are part of the legal system need to be apprised of this fact and must learn ways to effectively mobilize such couples to seek the help they so desperately need.

CONCLUSIONS

Marital separation is usually a stressor of the first magnitude. It is often far more stressful—both immediately and, especially, in the long term—than the loss of one's mate through death. Circumstances that surround the event, intrapsychic factors, and what happens during the years that follow, will determine both the extent to which this interruption in the family life cycle will be stressful and how long the recovery process will take.

Those prone to disordered grieving, those with a history of problems in separating from their families of origin, and those with borderline personality disorders are especially vulnerable to the stress of marital separation. They are likely to recover more slowly and less fully.

The amount of stress that will be involved in marital separation can be anticipated using the Social Readjustment Scale, although many aspects of marital separation do not fit neatly into the 43 items on the list. The scale, however, is a beginning point for estimating stress. Most people who go through marital separation score far higher on the number of LCUs—300—that indicate the presence of a major life crisis. Holmes and Masuda found a high incidence of negative health changes, 79 percent, among those who experienced a crisis of that magnitude. The present authors have found that the stress and its consequences that are generated by separation are consistent with these findings. Health changes following stress may be delayed for a year or longer. Because of this delay, the authors believe that crisis intervention should be initiated early in the separation process.

The goal of professional intervention should be (1) to reduce rancor and friction, (2) to help the couple devise a lifestyle that facilitates continuing but constructive involvement with one another, especially when they have children, (3) to encourage grieving and the recognition and expression of the emotions that are an inevitable consequence of separation, and (4) to address those intrapsychic problems that are interfering with the person's adjusting to the pain and losses involved.

NOTES AND REFERENCES

1. F. H. Holmes and R. H. Rahe, "The Social Readjustment Scale," *Journal of Psychosomatic Research,* 11 (1967) pp. 213–218. Reprinted with permission of the authors and Pergamon Press.
2. J. S. Wallerstein and J. B. Kelly, *Surviving the Breakup: How Children and Parents Cope with Divorce* (New York: Basic Books, 1980); Robert Weiss, *Marital Separation* (New York: Basic Books, 1975); and B. L. Bloom, S. W. White, and S. J. Asher, "Marital Disruption as a Stressful Life Event," in G. Levinger and O. C. Moles, eds., *Divorce and Separation: Context, Causes, and Consequences* (New York: Basic Books, 1979), pp. 184–200.
3. F. N. Holmes and M. Masuda, "Life Changes and Illness Susceptibility," in Barbara Snell Dohrenwend and Bruce R Dohrenwend, eds., *Stressful Life Events: Their Nature and Effects* (New York: John Wiley & Sons, 1974), pp. 45–72.
4. Weiss, *Marital Separation.*
5. John Bowlby, *Loss: Sadness and Depression,* "Attachment and Loss Series," Vol. 3 (New York: Basic Books, 1980).
6. Wallerstein and Kelly, *Surviving the Breakup.*
7. Ibid.
8. Bowlby, *Loss,* p. 138.
9. Ibid., p. 211.
10. Ibid., p. 219.
11. Ibid., p. 224.
12. J. F. Masterson, *The Narcissistic and Borderline Disorders: An Integrated Developmental Approach* (New York: Brunner/Mazel, 1981).

13. Holmes and Masuda, "Life Changes and Illness Susceptibility to Stressful Life Events."
14. Ibid., p 61.
15. J. L. Steinberg, "Towards an Interdisciplinary Commitment: A Divorce Lawyer Proposes Attorney-Therapist Marriages or, at the Least, an Affair," *Journal of Marital and Family Therapy,* 6 (July 1980), pp. 259–268.

CHAPTER 79

A THERAPEUTIC GROUP
EXPERIENCE FOR FATHERS

Richard R. Raubolt and Arnold W. Rachman

Psychoanalytic theory has traditionally emphasized the position of the mother in child and adolescent development, while the father is viewed as a secondary agent. With the exception of the development and resolution of oedipal conflicts and struggles, fathers are rarely mentioned. Yet the crucial role of the father becomes apparent to any therapist involved in the treatment of adolescent males. There is a need to delineate the role of the father in adolescent development and to develop treatment procedures that recognize, encourage, and support active fathering.

Rachman (1970), recognizing the importance of fathering with delinquent adolescent males, noted four crucial functions in fostering ego identity formation: (1) final emotional separation from mother and full emotional communion with father; (2) the prime model for masculine identity; (3) emotional support for judicious role experimentation in the areas of sexuality, assertiveness, authority relations, independence, decision-making, social responsibility; (4) encouragement to pursue independent behavior in education, career, recreation, etc. The significant point here is that the father must be available and involved, serving as a bridge from the family to the outside world. Through such involvement the son is assisted in developing a firm sense of masculine identity and independence. The father must be willing to engage his son, to share his beliefs, goals, and ideals, in short, to serve as an ego identity role model.

Fathers often, however, are not available to their sons due to their own developmental "mid-life transitions" (Lionells and Mann, 1974). In fact, Levi et al. (1972) propose an interlocking crisis of integrity and identity between fathers and sons. Describing the father's integrity crisis, they have written,

Reprinted from *International Journal of Psychotherapy,* Vol. 30, No. 2 (1980), pp. 229–239, by permission of the publisher.

With increasing awareness of declining physical and sexual power and of the imminence of death, the middle-aged father pauses to evaluate both his work and his personal relationships, especially his marriage. He goes through a normative crisis in which he will likely doubt the value of his work efforts and the meaning of his marriage. If the resolution is successful, he will achieve a state of more solid self-esteem basic to integrity. He will perhaps see more clearly the limitations of his marriage and of his work. He must grieve for longtime aspirations, now clearly beyond reach, and reassess the meaning of what seemed success. His ego ideal undergoes a major remodeling toward what is both realistically attainable and relevant in a changed society. Where the man fails to grieve his unattained goals or find value in his achievements, he may indeed strike out on a new course, either in work or in marriage. In our observations of the families of troubled adolescents, however, fathers were unable either to grieve successfully or to find a satisfying new course of action. . . . If the father cannot do this, he may envy and disparage his son or, alternatively, overidentify with his son in trying to relive through him what he feels he has missed [p. 49].

Lesse (1969), approaching the absence of fathering from a different position, has emphasized the effects of our current economic structure.

A large number of adolescents and young adults seen in psychotherapy today have not had fathers with whom they could develop a strong, positive identification. This appears to be particularly so in families in which fathers work for large organizations, whether it is a large industrial company, the government, or as a member of a large union. This type of father typically comes home and talks in terms of "we" in which he is an integral part of the organization. Too often the child, particularly the male offspring, is unable to identify with a father figure whose feeling of identity is primarily based upon a positive conception of personal worth [p. 381].

FORMING THE GROUP: GOALS AND STRUCTURE

An opportunity to translate theoretical concepts into clinical practice was presented when one of the authors (R. R.) became a psychological consultant to an affluent suburban school system. In four adolescent psychotherapy groups, a striking number of father/son conflicts became evident. These conflicts ranged from struggles over academic work, use of drugs and/or alcohol, to use of the family car and hours out in the evening. The connecting theme was that of authority and discipline. This theme was complicated, however, by the fact that the fathers of these boys were seldom home. They worked long hours and their professional positions required a great deal of travel. To all intents and purposes they were "absent fathers."

It became clear that the most meaningful way to help these youngsters was to actively engage their fathers. It was decided to offer, with the support of the school system, a group for fathers. The concept of an "educational group seminar" was developed to suit the needs of the fathers and encourage maximum participation. The rationale for this format included the following considerations:

1. An educational focus would be perceived as more helpful and less threatening than a therapeutic focus.
2. A time-limited format of ten sessions would relate to their busy schedules and frequent need to be out of town.
3. A seminar designation was a familiar, acceptable training experience for both business and professional men.
4. A group conducted in a school setting for the community seemed appropriately advertised as an educational experience.

A news release was sent to the community to announce the availability of an educational group seminar for fathers who wished to improve relationships with their sons. Written invitations and telephone calls were also employed to develop a population of fathers from which to form the group.

The group was initially structured to conform to the prototype of a seminar that business men and professionals had experienced in their work lives. The setting was the guidance suite at the high school. Members were gathered around a small round table. Coffee was served at each meeting. It was expected that as the group coalesced and special techniques were introduced, this table would be removed and a more traditional group format would be adopted.

GROUP PROCESS AND FOCUS

A group of six fathers was formed as a result of the news release and written invitation. Those who were approached directly by letter were fathers of sons who were seen by the pupil personnel team as having academic problems (defined as truancy, class failures) and social problems (defiant, disruptive behavior, or in one case socially isolated). All six fathers were professional men in their late 40's and early 50's. Five of the six fathers came because they had trouble talking to or understanding their sons. One felt he had a good relationship with his son but wanted to improve it.

These fathers were selected on the basis of interest and time availability. Four fathers were screened out because they could not make a ten-week time commitment and one because his son was pre-adolescent. One also dropped out just prior to the first session, feeling family therapy was more appropriate.

Three of the fathers had sons who were being seen in groups. The problems, as defined by the fathers, varied but centered on two conflicting areas: lack of academic success and poor communication between father and son.

In the first session, after a go-round of introductions and individual expectations, the group was described in the following manner:

> "Since I [R.R.] have been in the position of initiating and organizing this seminar, let me build on our stated goals and share the three basic ways I would like to proceed to realize our goals. I conceive this seminar as (1) information-giving, imparting to you some basic information. I have prepared a packet on adolescent development and common problems between boys and their fathers. (2) A second method will be getting in touch emotionally with the problems of adolescents and the problems of being a father. In order to reach our emotional goal, I will ask you to share, as best

you can, feelings about yourself and your adolescent youngster, the kinds of joys and hopes and the kinds of conflicts and angers that you have. The more we share, the more comfortable we are going to feel together in recognizing the typical difficulties of adolescent growth. As a special part I would like you to consider sharing what your adolescence was like with your father. This will serve to give a perspective on how your interaction with your father has influenced your son's perspective of you. (3) Once we have discussed the information and shared the experience of being an adolescent and a father, we will have a unique experience here to translate into some direct action. This experience can be created by role-playing. We are going to set up role-playing situations with everyone taking a turn being an adolescent and a father in a basic shared father/son conflict."

We then proceeded over the next few sessions to explore excerpts from Erikson (1968), Josselyn (1952) and Rachman (1970, 1975) on normal adolescent development and the role of fathering. As the group began to talk about the concept of identity conflicts in adolescence, the topic of values became more and more prominent. As the discussion centered on identity questions of: Who am I? What do I believe? and Where am I going? the fathers began to vacillate between being very dogmatic and being unsure about their own values and beliefs.

Initially, the exploration revealed the fathers' need to have their sons adopt their own strict code of values. This code of hard work, academic success, and "pleasure in moderation" (i.e., relaxation, drinking, sports) was initially presented as an unyielding, nonnegotiable demand. Any violation of this code by their sons was to be dealt with harshly. Physical punishment was seen as necessary but as the last resort.

In order to highlight this clash in value codes, a role-playing experience was developed. In this way the group was able to examine the specific flavor of father/son interactions. It soon became apparent that the fathers themselves were often unsure of what to believe in because of their own developmental crises. These professional men were all highly successful in their companies/businesses or in the schools they administrated, but, while they maintained the respect of those above and below them in their professions, they had reached the peak of their careers and did not expect to progress much further. It was a time in their lives when they began to realize that most of their financial dreams had been achieved (oftentimes exceeded). They realized they had success. The question was: now what? This life crisis (and it is important to note these feelings were shared by five of six members) was heightened by their sons' disregard for the code the fathers had lived by all of their professional lives. Since they themselves were unsure of what might lie ahead and did not want to force the "limits of their success" (as one father put it), they reacted severely to their sons' enthusiasm and testing.

This factor became particularly evident in the third session during the following role-play situation: "Your son came home really drunk last night and your wife has been telling you all morning, 'Go talk to him.' When you come down for brunch he is alone in the kitchen. What are you going to say and/or do?" One of the fathers played the son and another the father. The exchange lasted for about twenty minutes, with the father calmly trying to talk to and reason with his son about drinking and the son not giving an inch, answering all questions with a simple "no." Finally, the father, in desperation, stated to his "15-year-old son" . . . "It's not that I expect you to be a teetotaler, but you have to moderate your drinking." When the role-play ended the other fathers were adamant in their disapproval of this statement. The theme of their responses was, "You were too calm. I would have laid the law down," and "Who is he [the son] to argue with you? It wasn't like that when I grew up. I respected my father, what he said went, there was no discussion about it." In the ensuing discussion, it became evident that the group viewed punishment as necessary to maintain respect and that the trait they could tolerate least from their sons was insolence.

In order to achieve greater clarity and understanding of the issues involved here, we began to focus on Erikson's concepts of "free role experimentation and psychosocial play." The intent of the discussion was on developing an awareness for the fathers of the difference between positive and negative experimentation. Positive examples cited included interest in ecology, civil rights, Eastern thought, and structured risk-taking activities, such as racing and athletics. Negative examples cited included drug abuse, vandalism, and violence. These distinctions became necessary as the fathers, in an attempt to maintain their authority and control, had lost sight of the need for positive guidance. Discipline became synonymous with punishment rather than as a means of providing guidance and direction.

To provide another experience that might assist them in understanding this conceptualization and also to develop a new level of participation and intensity, a meditative experience was suggested. In terms of group process, it had become apparent that the role-playing experience had introduced a more emotional quality to the group that the fathers found helpful. It now became clear that the group format could be restructured along more psychotherapeutic lines. The group interaction was expanded to include a balance between the original cognitive format and a sharing of life experiences.

FATHERS RE-EXPERIENCE THEIR ADOLESCENCE

Using the technique of clinical meditation in groups (Rachman, 1976), the following experience was presented.

> I would like to suggest a positive, meditative experience to help you remember your adolescence. I am going to turn off all but three lights over the bookshelves to reduce all outside stimulation so we can concentrate. I would like all of you to close your eyes and get comfortable in your chairs, relax. I would like you to let your imagination go back to the time when you were fifteen.
>
> Picture in your mind how you looked as a fifteen-year-old. You are getting dressed to go out and meet your friends on the corner. You are putting on your favorite outfit. What does it look like? What kind of shoes are you wearing? What is your hair style? Now you are fully dressed and on your way to meet the guys.
>
> Picture yourself saying "Hi." Picture your group of friends. How are they dressed? What do you talk about? After standing on the corner for five or ten minutes, someone says, "Hey, why don't we . . ." Fill in the blank. It's the kind of crazy notion that excites everyone and you begin planning. Get in touch with what you do to make this happen. Now fully concentrate for a moment on this "crazy experience" so that when we finish you can share it in detail. Take a minute.

Okay, now I'd like everyone to open his eyes and keep alive the experience you had as a fifteen-year-old. Okay, now I'd like to discuss what you have just fantasized. Go around and each person describe to the group how you looked at fifteen, what your group of friends looked like, and what was the crazy experience and who thought of it.

The results of this experience were dramatic. The group shared in an open, direct manner many of the exciting "risky" pranks of their own adolescence. These included stealing from a local fruit stand, staying out all night playing cards and shooting pool when they were thought to be attending a religious retreat, and trying to "gang bang" a girl known for her sexual activity only to "chicken out" when she really showed up. The tone of the group at this point was active, loud, and exciting as the fathers began spontaneously to mention other events of their adolescence.

Before long a most significant theme began to emerge. Many of the group members recalled a very distant relationship with their own fathers. They were all sons of immigrants who were trying to establish businesses and better themselves economically. Consequently, there was little father/son interaction. As one of the fathers noted at the time, "We had to learn how to be fathers by ourselves, trial and error. We had to develop a role we had never experienced for ourselves."

THE LOVING FIGHT: LEVELS OF DIALOGUE AND ACCEPTANCE BETWEEN FATHERS AND SONS

When the fathers became aware of the discrepancies between their value code and their sons' and its relationship to their own adolescence, they were freer to explore alternative, less conflictive modes of responding to their sons. We then focused on improving father/son communications skills.

In order to assist the group in developing fathering skills, we developed seven necessary communication skills for fathers. They included:

1. *Talking it out:* becoming involved, being present with your son, i.e., "I want to talk with you." "Let's talk this out." "I won't run from you, don't you run from me."
2. *Creating an open dialogue:* allowing your son to say what he feels and thinks; encouraging your son to say anything he wishes, whether you like it or not; being free to say what you feel about him
3. *Developing emotional communion:* identifying true feelings, owning your own feelings, being aware of and taking responsibility for feelings of anger, frustration, fear, inadequacy, failure as well as tenderness, compassion, vulnerability; being emotionally responsive; allowing yourself to be known to your son
4. *Confrontation:* being able to say you don't agree; the art of the loving fight, i.e., "Hey look, you want to do this, but let me tell you how I see it"; giving your son something to bounce off of; taking a stand

5. *Sharing:* being known to your son, i.e., what you believe in and that you hold true to your beliefs, philosophy of life, your values, your identity
6. *Compromising:* being able to give in, i.e., "Well, I really don't agree. I wish you would do it my way, but you have your own life, and I'll just have to sweat it out."
7. *Maintaining the relationship:* giving your son room to breathe, staying with him, i.e., "I will be here with you and for you. I will not excommunicate you; I will stand by you as you go your own way. I will not give up on you. Even though we don't agree, I am still connected to you."

This guide created a great deal of discussion, particularly point seven. The idea of *never* giving up on their sons was a hard notion for them to accept.

In order to provide a structure where they might try out these skills we presented a series of videotapes done by the high school drama class. In these videotapes an adolescent boy spoke directly to the camera and expressed rage, confusion, and sadness. The fathers took turns responding to the filmed vignettes. Interaction was greatly enhanced after each response, and the fathers were actively involved in trying out the new skills.

RESULTS AND EVALUATIONS

Upon termination of the group, the leader noted a number of significant changes occurring in the sons of the fathers involved. There was a dramatic decrease in school absences, with only one unexcused absence coming to the school's attention during the time the group was meeting. There were also fewer reported incidents of disruptive classroom behavior. Teachers noticed a bettering of academic performance; more work was being turned in with fewer failing grades.

To substantiate these clinical impressions, evaluation measures were developed. A fourteen-point questionnaire was constructed and given to the fathers to elicit their reactions to the group experience. Those questions that measured the father/son relationship before and after the group included:

1. With what problem(s) or concern(s) in your relationship with your son did you want help when you joined the group?
2. Have you changed any of your attitudes, feelings, or behaviors toward your son as a result of this group experience?
3. Did your relationship with your son improve? If so, please cite specific examples of improvement in your relationship with him.
4. Did your son show any changes in his behavior or attitudes, for example, with the school, in his relationships with other family members, or with his friends?
5. Did you find yourself reevaluating any of your beliefs, values, feelings, or ideas as a result of this group experience?

A majority of the fathers (five of six) indicated they joined the group because of communication problems with their sons and a desire for help in this area. According to the results of the questionnaire, this goal was accomplished as all six indicated improved relationships with their sons, with more activities engaged in together, less fighting, and greater academic success cited as examples. In response to the question on perceived changes in the son's behavior, five of the fathers noted there was a change in their attitudes toward the family, with more consideration and friendliness.

All six fathers mentioned that the group encouraged them to reexamine their values and beliefs. This reexamination centered on "life goals and priorities." Three of the fathers felt that they had shortchanged their families and realized now the importance of their involvement. All the fathers, in one way or another, said they now saw the need for greater communicating, sharing, and understanding between father and son.

For all of us concerned, the personal meaning of this group may perhaps be best summed up by the following letter received two months after the completion of the group: "I am sorry I could not get back to you sooner. I have had a chance to reflect on the impact that the sessions had on me and I feel I ought to let you know. When I started I had basically given up. Matt was on his way toward excommunication. I was at the end of my wits. I can say that I have gained a better perspective, and therefore hope. I think I can do something about the situation because I have learned to be more patient and more tolerant. P.S. Matt naturally did not submit his term paper on time, but he did get it in a week late. I hope and pray the English teacher will accept it."

REFERENCES

Erikson, E. (1968), *Identity, Youth and Crisis.* New York: Norton.

Josselyn, L. (1952), *The Adolescent and His World.* New York: Family Service Association.

Lesse, S. (1969), Obsolescence in Psychotherapy: A Psychological View. *Psychotherapy,* 23:381–398.

Levi, S., Stierlin, H., and Savard, R. (1972), Fathers and Sons: The Interlocking Crisis of Integrity and Identity. *Psychiatry,* 35:48–56.

Lionells, M., and Mann, C. (1974), *Patterns of Mid-Life in Transition.* New York: William Alanson White Institute.

Rachman, A. (1970), Role of the Father in Child Development. Paper delivered at Emanuel Midtown Y.M.C.A. Parents-Teachers Association, New York.

———(1974), The Role of "Fathering" in Group Psychotherapy with Adolescent Delinquent Males. *J. Corrective & Soc. Psychiat.,* 20:11–22.

———(1975), *Identity Group Psychotherapy with Adolescents.* Springfield, Ill.: Charles C Thomas.

———(1976), Clinical Meditation in Groups. (Unpublished paper.)

PARENTHOOD

CHAPTER 80

MOTHERHOOD, MOTHERING, AND CASEWORK

Beverly B. Nichols

The redefining and reordering of roles in American family life do not accurately reflect the reality of family life in America. New ideas envision what may come, not what *is*. Role shifts, which may reflect personal dissatisfactions, institutional trepidation, a restructuring or breakdown of the social system, are first tried in *avant-garde* circles. But only very slowly are the resulting processes assimilated by those in the mainstream of society. Change is an ongoing and often painful process, reflecting gaps between ideals and realities, the polarizing and realigning of feelings and attitudes of many divergent individuals and groups.

Motherhood is one of those processes about which there is question and confusion. Motherhood is intrinsic, but the feelings, attitudes, and values regarding it are changing. Most experts in child development agree that the mother provides a crucial first relationship for the infant; that the quality and reciprocity developed in that relationship contribute significantly to the child's achieving his or her optimal potential. That there is conflict between awareness and acceptance of this view with the effort and time necessary to carry it out is evidenced by the numbers of parents who seek help with problems involving parenting their children.

Parent-child relationships comprise one of the major categories of presenting problems in family agencies; marital conflicts affect children; individual problems, focusing on identity issues, self awareness, personal development, and role conflicts, may affect family members; social issues such as child abuse, abortion, day care, and population control remind us constantly that, for many, motherhood is not synonymous with an idealized state of joy and fulfillment.

Reprinted from *Social Casework,* Vol. 58 (1977), pp. 29–35, by permission of the publisher, Families International, Inc.

The social worker is often confronted with questions relating aspects of mothering to specific problems. Experiences of being a mother and of being mothered are inexorably woven together. Understanding the mothering factors and fitting them into a social context facilitates process, contributes to the development of a meaningful exchange, and promotes treatment goals. When the worker is also a mother, an added dimension in terms of identification and empathy exists.

This article will examine some of the theoretical material connecting motherhood and mothering with current casework problems; discuss mothering as a factor in casework treatment relationships; and present some ways in which a knowledge of the mother-child relationship can be used in preventive work.

THEORETICAL FRAMEWORK

According to Helen Deutsch, a woman's psyche contains a factor that is lacking in that of the masculine sex—the psychologic world of motherhood. She says that as a result, the human female displays varied behavior and greater complication with regard to the polarity between life and death.[1]

The experience of motherhood is one that is passed from generation to generation, never really beginning, never really ending, described by a "world of events within itself . . . psychologic processes . . . the operation of biologic laws of heredity and adjustment, rational processes and seemingly absurd processes, historical and individual psychic elements."[2]

Deutsch distinguishes between the concepts of motherhood and motherliness. She describes motherhood as the relationship of mother to child as a sociologic, physiologic, and emotional entity. By motherliness, she refers to a "definite quality of character that stamps the woman's whole personality and the emotional phenomena that seems to be related to the child's helplessness and need for care."[3]

The quality of motherliness in an individual woman is determined by many factors: religious commitments to procreate; social and economic motives; cultural elements; and personal experience. Beyond these influences, motherhood seems to envelop a mystique of feelings, needs, and destinies, with both positive and negative elements.

Deutsch's Freudian-based concepts of motherhood and mothering have been challenged, particularly by representatives of the Women's Movement. The increased importance of cultural factors; Masters and Johnson's studies on human sexuality and new research in endocrinology have relevance to the newer theories. Roles for both sexes are generally described in less rigid terms today. The trying-out of new roles and the increasing opportunities for choice are evident in many segments of society.[4]

---

[1] Helene Deutsch, *The Psychology of Women: Motherhood,* vol. 2: (New York: Grune & Statton, 1945), p. 21.
[2] Ibid., p. 16.
[3] Ibid., p. 17.
[4] Elizabeth Janeway, *Between Myth and Morning: Women Awakening* (New York: William Morrow & Co., 1974), pp. 84–92.

PROBLEMS SURROUNDING PARENTING

The expanding role options for women have had the effect of allowing negative feelings to surface. These feelings, which previously were usually hidden, are being verbalized more than ever before. Young women question the personal sacrifices necessitated by motherhood.[5] Some women are unsure and apprehensive of their competency to become mothers or of their spouse's maturity regarding parenting. Others find relief, often mixed with guilt, at having the option to reject motherhood. Most women have concerns for the uncertain future. Older mothers, still feeling maternal emotion for grown offspring who no longer need them, question the efforts they have made while waiting in vain for grandchildren. When newspaper columnist Ann Landers conducted a poll of her readers on "Parenthood: If you had a choice, would you do it again?," 70 percent of the respondents said "no."[6] And groups such as the National Organization for Non-Parents support couples who do not plan to have children at all.[7]

Parenting—or sharing the emotional and physical aspects of the total experience of bearing and rearing children—is readily sought after by some young couples. But those who have made a conscious decision to share parenting responsibilities, do not find the process easy. Deutsch says that "the most intuitive and introspective women shy away from observing their own psychic processes during pregnancy,"[8] thus making sharing difficult.

Despite goodwill, expectant fathers often feel isolated and left out. One man expressed his frustration by saying, "I have tried to share her feelings but she is either on cloud nine or she is down in the dumps. I never know whether I am helping or hurting."

Expectant parents face many decisions relative to their lifestyles: If the mother-to-be has been working, should she continue to work after the baby is born? If so, who will care for the infant? Couples wonder how they will be able to adjust to the demands of a baby. Problems of space and money are not uncommon. The sex and name of the baby often become major issues.

In fact, parenting proves a more useful concept when children are older. It is still rare that the father participates extensively in the caretaking and primary relationship aspects of the infant's life. In this connection, a father may claim the more rewarding tasks of parenting, leaving the less pleasant ones—changing diapers, formula-making, laundry, and so forth—for the mother. This lack of participation may generate strong feelings of resentment in the mother, while exacerbating her guilt at being critical of the father's efforts.

Because parenting involves redefining and readjusting roles, it is a process which may activate identity problems, stimulate power struggles, and threaten the stability of the marriage itself. Social trends have influenced the size and character of the American family, but rearing even one child is an awesome undertaking.

Of late, more fathers are participating in the actual experience of birth. Increasing interest in natural childbirth and birth in the home are slowly infiltrating our customs. The vast majority of births, however, still occur in a hospital without the father present.

---

[5] Jessie Bernard, *The Future of Motherhood* (New York: Dial Press, 1974), p. 21.
[6] See Albert Rosenfeld's article, Who Says We're a Child-Centered Society?, *Saturday Review*, August 7, 1976, p. 8.
[7] Information on local level non-parent support groups may usually be obtained from Planned Parenthood.
[8] Deutsch, *The Psychology of Women: Motherhood*, p. 105.

Following delivery, many women experience postnatal depression. Difficulties in breast feeding may occur. And soon after the baby is born, the responsibility of caretaking imposes restrictions on the parents' freedom. Most young mothers and their babies quickly find themselves in a relatively isolated social milieu—alone together.

Other concerns regarding motherhood include: a failure to conceive, which becomes an emotionally laden issue—women who experience difficulties in becoming pregnant suffer and so do their husbands; and problems in carrying to term which cause women to know the pain of failing at an experience close to the very heart of femininity.

These concerns continue to emerge despite freer choices, less rigid roles, and more opportunity for personal development. Making the choice to have children is a soul-searching and value-laden process. Such decision-making may endanger a relationship; preclude a going-back; change a person's life; or destroy a dream.

MOTHERING AND THE DEVELOPING CHILD

Ego psychologists are credited with recognizing and describing the central importance of the mother's role in child development. Briefly, ego growth permits differentiation of instinctual drives, the development of object relations, and the acquisition of speech.[9] "Indicators" that such development is proceeding depend on the presence of "a good enough mother."[10]

As an outcome of adequate mothering, the infant develops an ability to distinguish between self and others and eventually gains the ability to deal with another person on a reciprocal basis. The libidinal availability of the mother is essential for the optimal development of ego functions; it serves to coordinate maturation and development so that both can coincide.[11]

According to John Bowlby, interruptions and other difficulties in the mother-child dyad are relevant to the development of adult pathology. He reviews the importance of the mother-infant relationship, stating firmly that the warmth, intimacy, continuousness, and reciprocity of that relationship are essential for mental health.[12]

Bowlby believes that adults are often still responding to the trauma of early separations from the mother,[13] expressing their pathology by being demanding and angry, by experiencing chronic anxiety. He considers many pathological situations, tracing their origins directly to anxiety brought on by interruptions in the mother-child relationship which are then carried over in some form to adult life.

The adult client seeks therapy because of some dysfunction in the interpersonal part of his or her life. Dysfunction may range from the mildly disturbing to psychotic behavior. The therapist treats the client according to the dictums of the theoretical framework he embraces. He is limited by agency purpose, practices, time, and also by other

---

[9] Rubin and Gertrude Blanck, *Marriage and Personal Development* (New York: Columbia University Press, 1968).
[10] Ibid., p. 15.
[11] John Bowlby, Preface, *Attachment and Loss,* vol. 2 (New York: Basic Books, 1973).
[12] Ibid.
[13] Ibid.

factors including those brought by the client, but the individual caseworker influences all other variables. Whether the worker is old, young, experienced, male, or female, will affect the developing relationship in relevant ways.

Mothering attitudes, for example, that are a part of the older female social worker's image will affect treatment regardless of whether they are consciously employed. The motherly qualities of the social worker, openly exhibited, hidden, or unrealistically anticipated by the client color the relationship and, to some degree, set its tone.

MOTHERING AS A TREATMENT TECHNIQUE

Mothering, as a treatment technique, is defined as a process by which the caseworker consciously undertakes a nurturing role designed to support, encourage, and gratify the client, while, at the same time, conveying, through the medium of the relationship, an appropriate expectation of growth. The female caseworker who is willing to utilize her mothering skills can often provide an atmosphere which will enable the client to share feelings, to ventilate, to discuss options, and to become therapeutically involved. The following case illustrations from a family agency's records, provide examples of when it is helpful to employ mothering as a technique.

Mrs. C. is a middle-aged, former career woman who had married late and has three children. She is temperamentally ill-equipped to manage a young family. Mr. C's busy career excludes her. Older than the other mothers in her neighborhood, she is isolated from them. She comes to the agency because of a secret drinking problem.

Mrs. C responded to a "mothering" caseworker immediately, sharing her concerns about failing her family, her disappointment with homemaking, the neighborhood's unfriendliness. She expresses a wish for someone to value her as an individual. It is not that being mothered solves Mrs. C's problems simplistically. Rather, it is that the motherly response, with its components of tenderness and understanding, provide space for the client to renew herself.

Mrs. T has suffered from asthma since childhood. She has had the problems that years of chronic but intermittent dependency bring, along with the passive hostility her constant care evokes in others. Mr. T is weary of her demands. Her children are reacting to her absences. She is depressed.

This client ventilates her hostilities and manipulates in an effort to evoke the rejection which she unconsciously anticipates. The caseworker, aware of the issues, begins by mothering the client. She acknowledges the feelings uncritically and identifies realistic problems. The client's right to her emotionality is accepted. The worker's hopeful outlook, sustained by practical help for Mrs. T, encourages a constructive channeling of energy.

Men, too, are often responsive to mothering techniques:

Mr. M is thirty-two. He has lived away from his parents since entering the service at age seventeen. Married now for ten years, he and his wife became involved in marriage counseling. Later, he continued in therapy for problems involving chronic irritability, temper tantrums and feelings of isolation.

That Mr. M had requested an "older woman" as a caseworker is indicative of his need to have a "motherly" person with whom to relate. A positive transference was developed through counseling which motivated Mr. M's growth. His wife was enabled to give up her mothering of Mr. M which had been a source of discord.

Mrs. D was referred because of abusing both of her children. She is very young, separated from her husband. Her history includes having lost her own mother when she was five; subsequently, poor relations with her father and siblings were constant and there is evidence of much deprivation.

Mrs. D recognized and commented upon her daughterly response to her worker. As the relationship deepened, she began to ask for advice, to offer confidences, and to test the worker's approval of various actions.

If the presenting problem concerns the parent-child relationship, usually the mother is experiencing feelings of responsibility and guilt, even if the problem involves the father-child relationship. These feelings are engendered by the mother's awareness of her importance to the child and complicated by her resentment and anger at being in this role.

Such ambivalence relates to the demands of motherhood pitted against the need for self-expression of a different kind. Fathers rarely experience this phenomenon. They are protected by the social system which grants them greater freedom and does not demand from them the intensity of commitment in the form of service to the young. There are, of course, class differences between families in terms of the father's involvement in child care but when the father is involved, it is always a freer choice for him.

As Deutsch says:

We find in it, [motherhood], a world of polarities—ego instincts and service to the species, the mother's tendency to preserve her unity with the child and the child's drive to freedom, love, and hostility and a large number of personal, frequently neurotic, conflicts.[14]

When social workers see mothers who present mothering as a problem, the recognition of conflict, latent or active, in the mother is necessary. In today's society, social workers cannot assume that the mother's wish to be a "better" mother supersedes all her other wishes.

---

[14] Deutsch, *The Psychology of Women: Motherhood,* p. 330.

TRANSFERENCE AND COUNTERTRANSFERENCE

Unconscious feelings about mothering and being mothered are present in the therapeutic relationship through the process of transference. Transference is defined as the client's unconscious displacement of attitudes, wishes, conceptions, impulses, and ideas from important figures in the past onto the person of the therapist, independent of the objective situation, including the therapist's personality.[15]

Generally, important figures from the past refer to the mother and father. Grandparents, older siblings, or other influential persons may contribute to or reinforce patterns of responses which derive from the infant's experiences in having early needs met.

According to psychoanalytic theory, negative and erotic feelings are repressed from consciousness although they retain potency in behavior motivated by the unconscious. Because they are so absolutely incorporated into the basic personality of the individual, there is no awareness of them. Margaret Ferard sums up the importance of transference when she states:

> Relationships an individual establishes with those who had the care of him in his early days are among the most important influences that have shaped his life because they are the pattern or prototype of all subsequent relationships.[16]

Repetitiously, and often inappropriately, in adult life, the individual transfers these early learned responses to persons who are meaningful to him or her. A client can transfer maternal responses to a male therapist or paternal responses to a female therapist. Identifying with a female worker who "reminds me of my mother" is not transference, *per se*. But this kind of identification may enhance or influence transference, perhaps making it more readily accessible in treatment.

In the casework relationship, an understanding of transference provides diagnostic clues to an individual's characteristic patterns of behavior. This understanding can be used in treatment to further psychological growth through correcting unhealthy attitudes and limitations.

Transference is revealed in interview content through associations, timing of material shared, tone, and so forth, and by the affect shown. The relationship itself contains clues to both positive and negative effects of transference.

Because transference reactions are rooted in the unconscious, they are not readily available to discussion, at least not until a strong relationship has been developed. The worker may demonstrate that a difference between the therapist and the parent does indeed exist. Feelings may be examined and connected to behavior, past and present.

Florence Hollis describes this process as a "corrective relationship" which makes use of the transference. She writes:

> By allowing a relationship to develop in which the client regards the worker as a mother figure, it may be possible to counteract the earlier bad mother-daughter

---

15 Definition given by A. F. Valenstein in a course lecture on "Psycho-therapeutic Principles in Casework, " Boston University School of Social Work, 1955–1956, taken from author's notes.
16 Margaret L. Ferard and Noel K. Hunnybun, *The Caseworker's Use of Relationship* (London: Tavistock Publishers, 1962), p. 13.

experience by enabling the client to see that the characteristics of her own mother which caused her unhappiness are peculiar to her mother and not generally characteristic of all women.[17]

The "corrective relationship" can result in many therapeutic changes for clients, not the least of which is an improved self-image. It is important too for social workers to be aware of countertransference. Motherly feelings toward clients may be inappropriate, overzealous, or sentimental. Deutsch indicates that "excessive motherly feelings can empty real motherliness of its emotional components."[18] Helen Harris Perlman defines countertransference feelings as "impulsive sympathies, impatiences, protectiveness, angers—any of the emotions that certain situations or certain people evoke in us."[19]

Countertransference responses stem from our own early experiences. We seek to recognize and control them; to minimize their influences by the development of self-awareness and through supervision and consultation.

The following is an illustration of some aspects of both transference and counter-transference:

A thirty-five-year-old policeman, hospitalized for alcoholism, broke his hand in an impulsive rage. It was known that he had been a favorite of his mother; that she had indulged him and overprotected him. The client was married, had five children and was separated from his wife. He had been seeing the social worker with whom he was manipulative and evasive.

An interview was focused on helping Mr. S talk about the angry feelings which had led to his rage. During this session, he played the role of a sheepish little boy, inappropriately playing down the behavior, joking, and flirting with the worker. (He did not see her as a professional person, indeed, he cannot see any female in an important role.) Interacting with him, the worker's sympathetic and protective stance was not unlike his mother's habitual way of relating to him. It validated his refusal to accept responsibility for his behavior. The social worker, in fact, unconsciously accepted the client's assumption that she was unable to help him; he does not need help and if he did, a woman would not provide it. This reaction is an example of what Annette Garrett means when she says the client "intuits our response" and thus "directs our treatment."[20]

In this context, it is important for women to feel both confidence and competence in therapeutic situations. Experiences relative to the functioning and authority of mothers need to be examined. Because mothers have traditionally functioned as family peace-makers and go-betweens, they are often inappropriately assigned to, or assume, this role which offers minimal satisfaction and lacks vitality.

As a professional group, social workers have not dealt with the changing status of

---

[17] Florence Hollis, *Casework: A Psychosocial Theory* (New York: Random House, 1965), p. 26.

[18] Deutsch, *The Psychology of Women: Motherhood*, p. 21.

[19] Helen Harris Perlman, *Social Casework* (Chicago: University of Chicago Press, 1964), p. 82.

[20] Annette Garrett, The Worker Client Relationship, in *Ego Psychology and Dynamic Casework,* ed. Howard J. Parad (New York: Family Service Association of America, 1958), pp. 53–94.

women. As individual caseworkers, many are confused and unsure. Because many social workers are mothers too, they need to examine the ways in which their personal beliefs influence their work with families.[21]

MOTHERING AND PREVENTIVE ASPECTS OF CASEWORK

The preventive aspects of social work are difficult to measure but they are often confirmed by individual clients, by members of groups, and by those for whom the profession has provided consultation and collaboration. In this area, however, social workers have also been subjected to criticism. For example, Burton White says:

> Social workers become intimately involved in the problems of large numbers of families; as such, the opportunity is there to respond to a request for help by young parents . . . it is unfortunate that none of the professions (social workers, visiting nurses, homemakers, child study association people) provide very high-caliber training in parent education.[22]

White also criticizes professional training in the early educational development of children, and suggests that *experienced* mothers are better able to help parents than a professional person. He writes:

> I would even suggest that you are lucky enough to know a wise woman who has raised three or four or more children, and if you are on good enough terms with that person to be able to get the benefit of her advice, you will more often than not find that she will be better able to help you deal with educational concerns in the first years of your child's life than a professional can.[23]

While social workers, as a professional group, can and should challenge this critical view, perhaps those who are mothers too, share a special responsibility to use their experience in helping as wide an audience as possible.

Through Family Life Education programs, originally developed and fostered by family agencies, many parents can be reached. Focusing on the newer theories of child development presents a challenge that infuses parent groups with interest and vitality.[24]

Educational groups can focus on discussions of social change and how families learn to adapt; how the members feel about adaptation; and what they have lost or gained in this process. Such groups have positive effects in reducing the polarization common to families in conflict. They encourage movement toward the kinds of compromises necessary in today's complex family settings.

---

[21] Sanford B. Sherman, The Therapist and Changing Sex Roles, *Social Casework,* 57:93–96 (February 1976).
[22] Dr. Burton L. White, *The First Three Years of Life* (Englewood Cliffs, N.J.: Prentice-Hall, 1975), p. 247.
[23] Ibid., p. 248.
[24] See, for example, Henry W. Maier, *Three Theories of Child Development* (New York: Harper & Row, 1965).

SUMMARY

The subject and experience of motherhood has increasingly become the focus of negative thinking. The resulting concerns and questions influence the kinds of problems people have. Social workers, many of whom are mothers themselves, can be helpful in identifying issues and presenting options. Their own feelings and biases, however, must be recognized and handled.

Mothering is important to healthy child development. Inadequate mothering, particularly at an early stage of life, is related to pathology. The appropriate use of mothering, as a technique in casework, can stimulate therapeutic progress. The female social worker clearly has a special and unique opportunity to use her capacity for motherliness constructively.

All therapists can be certain that both they and their clients will unconsciously relate to aspects of mothering, real or imagined. Through self-awareness and understanding, these feelings, and the messages conveyed by them, can be used in effective therapeutic intervention.

CHAPTER 81

RAPE TRAUMA SYNDROME

Ann Wolbert Burgess and Lynda Lytle Holmstrom

Rape affects the lives of thousands of women each year. The Uniform Crime Reports from the Federal Bureau of Investigation indicated a 121-percent increase in reported cases of rape between 1960 and 1970. In 1970, over 37,000 cases were reported in the United States (1). A District of Columbia task force studying the problem in the capital area stated that rape was the fastest growing crime of violence there (2).

The literature on sexual offenses, including rape, is voluminous (3-5), but it has overlooked the victim. There is little information on the physical and psychological effects of rape, the therapeutic management of the victim, and the provisions for protection of the victim from further psychological insult (6-9).

In response to the problem of rape in the greater Boston area, the Victim Counseling Program was designed as a collaborative effort between Boston College School of Nursing and Boston City Hospital to provide 24-hour crisis intervention to rape victims and to study the problems the victim experiences as a result of being sexually assaulted.

The purpose of this paper is to report the immediate and long-term effects of rape as described by the victim.

METHOD
Study Population

The study population consisted of all persons who entered the emergency ward of Boston City Hospital during the one-year period July 20, 1972, through July 19, 1973, with the complaint of having been raped. The resulting sample was made up of 146 patients: 109 adult women, 34 female children, and 3 male children.

We divided these 146 patients into three main categories: (1) victims of forcible rape (either completed or attempted rape, usually the former); (2) victims in situations to

Reprinted from *American Journal of Psychiatry,* Vol. 131 (1974), pp. 981–986, by permission of the publisher.

which they were an accessory due to their inability to consent; and (3) victims of sexually stressful situations—sexual encounters to which they had initially consented but that went beyond their expectations and ability to control.

The rape trauma syndrome delineated in this paper was derived from an analysis of the symptoms of the 92 adult women in our sample who were victims of forcible rape. Future reports will analyze the problems of the other victims. Although not directly included in this paper, supplementary data were also gathered from 14 patients referred to the Victim Counseling Program by other agencies and from consultation calls from other clinicians working with rape victims.

A major research advantage in the location of the project at Boston City Hospital was the fact that it provided a heterogeneous sample of victims. Disparate social classes were included in the victim population. Ethnic groups included fairly equal numbers of black and white women, plus a smaller number of Oriental, Indian, and Spanish-speaking women. In regard to work status, the victims were career women, housewives, college students, and women on welfare. The age span was 17 to 73 years; the group included single, married, divorced, separated, and widowed women as well as women living with men by consensual agreement (see Table 81-1). A variety of occupations were represented, such as schoolteacher, business manager, researcher, assembly line worker, secretary, housekeeper, cocktail waitress, and health worker. There were victims with no children, women pregnant up to the eighth month, postpartum mothers, and women with anywhere from 1 to 10 children. The women ranged in physical attractiveness from very pretty to very plain; they were dressed in styles ranging from high fashion to hippie clothes.

INTERVIEW METHOD

The counselors (the coauthors of this paper) were telephoned when a rape victim was admitted to the emergency department of Boston City Hospital; we arrived at the hospital within 30 minutes. We interviewed all the victims admitted during the one-year period regardless of time of day or night. Follow-up was conducted by use of telephone counseling or home visits. This method of study provided an 85-percent rate of direct follow-up. An additional 5 percent of the victims were followed indirectly through their families or reports by the police or other service agencies who knew them. Detailed notes of the interviews, telephone calls, and visits were then analyzed in terms of the

Table 81–1
Distribution of Marital Status by Age (N = 92)

Marital Status	Age (in Years)				
	17–20	21–29	30–39	40–49	50–73
Single	29	25	0	2	1
Married	2	1	2	2	0
Divorced, separated, or widowed	2	6	7	2	2
Living with a man by consensual agreement	4	5	0	0	0

symptoms reported as well as changes in thoughts, feelings, and behavior. We accompanied those victims who pressed charges to court and took detailed notes of all court proceedings and recorded the victims' reactions to this process (10, 11). Contact with the families and other members of the victims' social network was part of the assessment and follow-up procedure.

MANIFESTATIONS OF RAPE TRAUMA SYNDROME

Rape trauma syndrome is the acute phase and long-term reorganization process that occurs as a result of forcible rape or attempted forcible rape. This syndrome of behavioral, somatic, and psychological reactions is an acute stress reaction to a life-threatening situation.

Forcible rape is defined in this paper as the carnal knowledge of a woman by an assailant by force and against her will. The important point is that rape is not primarily a sexual act. On the contrary, our data and those of researchers studying rapists suggest that rape is primarily an act of violence with sex as the weapon (5). Thus it is not surprising than the victim experiences a syndrome with specific symptomatology as a result of the attack made upon her.

The syndrome is usually a two-phase reaction. The first is the acute phase. This is the period in which there is a great deal of disorganization in the woman's lifestyle as a result of the rape. Physical symptoms are especially noticeable, and one prominent feeling noted is fear. The second phase begins when the woman begins to reorganize her lifestyle. Although the time of onset varies from victim to victim, the second phase often begins about two to three weeks after the attack. Motor activity changes and nightmares and phobias are especially likely during this phase.

The medical regimen for the rape victim involves the prescription of antipregnancy and antivenereal disease medication after the physical and gynecological examination. The procedure usually includes prescribing 25 to 50 mg. of diethylstilbestrol a day for five days to protect against pregnancy and 4.8 million units of aqueous procaine penicillin intramuscularly to protect against venereal disease. Symptoms reported by the patient need to be distinguished as either side effects of the medication or conditions resulting from the sexual assault.

THE ACUTE PHASE DISORGANIZATION
Impact Reactions

In the immediate hours following the rape, the woman may experience an extremely wide range of emotions. The impact of the rape may be so severe that feelings of shock or disbelief are expressed. When interviewed within a few hours of the rape, the women in this study mainly showed two emotional styles (12): the expressed style, in which feelings of fear, anger, and anxiety were shown through such behavior as crying, sobbing, smiling, restlessness, and tenseness; and the controlled style, in which feelings were masked or hidden and a calm, composed, or subdued affect was seen. A fairly equal number of women showed each style.

Somatic Reactions

During the first several weeks following a rape many of the acute somatic manifestations described below were evident.

1. *Physical Trauma*. This included general soreness and bruising from the physical attack in various parts of the body such as the throat, neck, breasts, thighs, legs, and arms. Irritation and trauma to the throat were especially a problem for those women forced to have oral sex.

2. *Skeletal Muscle Tension*. Tension headaches and fatigue, as well as sleep pattern disturbances, were common symptoms. Women were either not able to sleep or would fall asleep only to wake and not be able to go back to sleep. Women who had been suddenly awakened from sleep by the assailant frequently found that they would wake each night at the time the attack had occurred. The victim might cry or scream out in her sleep. Victims also described experiencing a startle reaction—they become edgy and jumpy over minor incidents.

3. *Gastrointestinal Irritability*. Women might complain of stomach pains. The appetite might be affected, and the victim might state that she did not eat, food had no taste, or she felt nauseated from the antipregnancy medication. Victims described feeling nauseated just thinking of the rape.

4. *Genitourinary Disturbance*. Gynecological symptoms such as vaginal discharge, itching, a burning sensation on urination, and generalized pain were common. A number of women developed chronic vaginal infections following the rape. Rectal bleeding and pain were reported by women who had been forced to have anal sex.

Emotional Reactions

Victims expressed a wide gamut of feelings as they began to deal with the aftereffects of the rape. These feelings ranged from fear, humiliation, and embarrassment to anger, revenge, and self-blame. Fear of physical violence and death was the primary feeling described. Victims stated that it was not the rape that was so upsetting as much as the feeling that they would be killed as a result of the assault. One woman stated: "I am really mad. My life is disrupted; every part of it upset. And I have to be grateful I wasn't killed. I thought he would murder me."

Self-blame was another reaction women described—partly because of their socialization to the attitude of "blame the victim." For example, one young woman had entered her apartment building one afternoon after shopping. As she stopped to take her keys from her purse, she was assaulted in the hallway by a man who then forced his way into her apartment. She fought against him to the point of taking his knife and using it against him and in the process was quite severely beaten, bruised, and raped. Later she said:

> I keep wondering maybe if I had done something different when I first saw him that it wouldn't have happened—neither he nor I would be in trouble. Maybe it was my fault. See, that's where I get when I think about it. My father always said that whatever a man did to a woman, she provoked it.

THE LONG-TERM PROCESS: REORGANIZATION

All victims in our sample experienced disorganization in their life-style following the rape; their presence at the emergency ward of the hospital was testimony to that fact. Various factors affected their coping behavior regarding the trauma, i.e., ego strength, social network support, and the way people treated them as victims. This coping and reorganization process began at different times for the individual victims.

Victims did not all experience the same symptoms in the same sequence. What was consistent was that they did experience an acute phase of disorganization; many also experienced mild to moderate symptoms in the reorganization process, as Table 81–2 indicates. Very few victims reported no symptoms. The number of victims over age 30 was small, but the data at least suggest that they might have been more prone to compounded reactions than the younger age groups.

Motor Activity

The long-term effects of the rape generally consisted of an increase in motor activity, especially through changing residence. The move, in order to ensure safety and to facilitate the victim's ability to function in a normal style, was very common. Forty-four of the 92 victims changed residences within a relatively short period of time after the rape. There was also a strong need to get away, and some women took trips to other states or countries.

Table 81–2
Severity of Symptoms During Reorganization Process by Age (N = 92)*

Severity of Symptoms	Age (in Years)				
	17–20	21–29	30–39	40–49	50–73
No symptoms: no symptoms reported and symptoms denied when asked about a specific area	7	4	2	0	0
Mild symptoms: minor discomfort with the symptom reported: ability to talk about discomfort and feeling of control over symptom present	12	16	0	2	1
Moderate to severe symptoms: distressing symptoms such as phobic reactions described: ability to function but disturbance in lifestyle present	12	5	1	1	2
Compounded symptoms: symptoms directly related to the rape plus reactivation of symptoms connected with a previously existing condition such as heaving drinking or drug use	7	5	3	3	0
No data available	0	5	4	0	0

*At time of telephone follow-up.

Changing one's telephone number was a common reaction. It was often changed to an unlisted number. The woman might do this as a precautionary measure or as the result of threatening or obscene telephone calls. The victim was haunted by the fear that the assailant knew where she was and would come back for her.

Another common response was to turn for support to family members not normally seen daily. Forty-eight women made special trips home, which often meant traveling to another city. In most cases, the victim told her parents what had happened, but occasionally the victim contacted her parents for support and did not explain why she was suddenly interested in talking with them or being with them. Twenty-five women turned to close friends for support. Thus 73 of the 92 women had some social network support to which they turned.

Nightmares

Dreams and nightmares could be very upsetting. Twenty-nine of the victims spontaneously described frightening dreams, as illustrated in the following statement.

> I had a terrifying nightmare and shook for two days. I was at work and there was this maniac killer in the store. He killed two of the salesgirls by slitting their throats. I'd gone to set the time clock and when I came back the two girls were dead. I thought I was next. I had to go home. On the way I ran into two girls I knew. We were walking along and we ran into the maniac killer and he was the man who attacked me—he looked like the man. One of the girls held back and said, "No—I'm staying here." I said I knew him and was going to fight him. At this point I woke with the terrible fear of impending doom and fright. I knew the knife part was real because it was the same knife the man held to my throat.

Women reported two types of dreams. One is similar to the above example where the victim wishes to do something but then wakes before acting. As time progressed, the second type occurred: the dream material changed somewhat, and frequently the victim reported mastery in the dream—being able to fight off the assailant. A young woman reported the following dream one month following her rape.

> I had a knife and I was with the guy and I went to stab him and the knife bent. I did it again and he started bleeding and he died. Then I walked away laughing with the knife in my hand.

This dream woke the victim up; she was crying so hard that her mother came in to see what was wrong. The girl stated that in her waking hours she never cries.

Traumatophobia

Sandor Rado coined the term "traumatophobia" to define the phobic reaction to a traumatic situation (13). We saw this phenomenon, which Rado described in war victims, in the rape victim. The phobia develops as a defensive reaction to the circumstances of the rape. The following were the most common phobic reactions among our sample.

Fear of Indoors. This occurred in women who had been attacked while sleeping in their beds. As one victim stated, "I feel better outside, I can see what is coming. I feel trapped inside. My fear is being inside, not outside."

Fear of Outdoors. This occurred in women who had been attacked outside of their homes. These women felt safe inside but would walk outside only with the protection of another person or only when necessary. As one victim stated, "It is sheer terror for every step I take. I can't wait to get to the safety of my own place."

Fear of Being Alone. Almost an victims reported fears of being alone after the rape. Often the victim had been attacked while alone, when no one could come to her rescue. One victim said: "I can't stand being alone. I hear every little noise—the windows creaking. I am a bundle of nerves."

Fear of Crowds. Many victims were quite apprehensive when they had to be in crowds or ride on public transportation. One 41-year-old victim said:

> I'm still nervous from this, when people come too close—like when I have to go through the trolley station and the crowds are bad. When I am in crowds I get the bad thoughts. I will look over at a guy and if he looks really weird, I will hope something bad will happen to him.

Fear of People Behind Them. Some victims reported being fearful of people walking behind them. This was often common if the woman had been approached suddenly from behind. One victim said:

> I can't stand to have someone behind me. When I feel someone is behind me, my heart starts pounding. Last week I turned on a guy that was walking in back of me and waited till he walked by. I just couldn't stand it.

Sexual Fears. Many women experienced a crisis in their sexual life as a result of the rape. Their normal sexual style had been disrupted. For the women who had had no prior sexual activity, the incident was especially upsetting. For the victims who were sexually active, the fear increased when they were confronted by their husband or boyfriend with resuming sexual relations. One victim said:

> My boyfriend thought it [the rape] might give me a negative feeling to sex and he wanted to be sure it didn't. That night as soon as we were back to the apartment he wanted to make love. I didn't want sex, especially that night. . . . He also admitted he wanted to know if he could make love to me or if he would be repulsed by me and unable to.

This victim and her boyfriend had considerable difficulty resuming many aspects of their relationship besides the sexual part. Many women were unable to resume a normal sexual style during the acute phase and persisted with the difficulty. One victim reported, five months after the assault, "There are times I get hysterical with my boyfriend. I don't want him near me; I get panicked. Sex is OK, but I still feel like screaming."

CLINICAL IMPLICATIONS
Management of Rape Trauma Syndrome

There are several basic assumptions underlying the model of crisis intervention that we used in counseling the rape victim.

1. The rape represented a crisis in that the woman's style of life was disrupted.
2. The victim was regarded as a "normal" woman who had been functioning adequately prior to the crisis situation.
3. Crisis counseling was the treatment model of choice to return the woman to her previous level of functioning as quickly as possible. The crisis counseling was issue-oriented treatment. Previous problems were not a priority for discussion; in no way was the counseling considered psychotherapy. When other issues of major concern that indicated another treatment model were identified by the victim, referrals were offered if the woman so requested.
4. We took an active role in initiating therapeutic contact as opposed to more traditional methods where the patient is expected to be the initiator. We went to the hospital to see the victim and then contacted her later by telephone.

Management of Compounded Reaction

There were some victims who had either a past or current history of physical, psychiatric, or social difficulties along with the rape trauma syndrome. A minority of the women in our sample were representative of this group. It became quite clear that these women needed more than crisis counseling. For this group, who were known to other therapists, physicians, or agencies, we assumed a secondary position. Support was provided for the rape incident, especially if the woman pressed charges against the assailant, but the counselor worked closely with the other agencies. It was noted that this group developed additional symptoms such as depression, psychotic behavior, psychosomatic disorders, suicidal behavior, and acting-out behavior associated with alcoholism, drug use, and sexual activity.

Management of Silent Rape Reaction

Since a significant proportion of women still do not report a rape, clinicians should be alert to a syndrome that we call the silent reaction to rape. This reaction occurs in the victim who has not told anyone of the rape, who has not settled her feelings and reactions on the issue, and who is carrying a tremendous psychological burden.

Evidence of such a syndrome became apparent to us as a result of life history data. A number of the women in our sample stated that they had been raped or molested at a previous time, often when they were children or adolescents. Often these women had not told anyone of the rape and had just kept the burden within themselves. The current rape reactivated their reaction to the prior experience. It became clear that because they had not talked about the previous rape, the syndrome had continued to develop, and these women had carried unresolved issues with them for years. They would talk as much of the previous rape as they did of the current situation.

A diagnosis of this syndrome should be considered when the clinician observes any of the following symptoms during an evaluation interview.

1. Increasing signs of anxiety as the interview progresses, such as long periods of silence, blocking of associations, minor stuttering, and physical distress.
2. The patient reports sudden marked irritability or actual avoidance of relationships with men or marked change in sexual behavior.
3. History of sudden onset of phobic reactions and fear of being alone, going outside, or being inside alone.
4. Persistent loss of self-confidence and self-esteem, an attitude of self-blame, paranoid feelings, or dreams of violence and/or nightmares.

Clinicians who suspect that the patient was raped in the past should be sure to include questions relevant to the woman's sexual behavior in the evaluation interview and to ask if anyone has ever attempted to assault her. Such questions may release considerable pent-up material relevant to forced sexual activity.

DISCUSSION

The crisis that results when a woman has been sexually assaulted is in the service of self-preservation. The victims in our sample felt that living was better than dying and that was the choice which had to be made. The victims' reactions to the impending threat to their lives is the nucleus around which an adaptive pattern may be noted.

The coping behavior of individuals to life-threatening situations has been documented in the work of such writers as Grinker and Spiegel (14), Lindemann (15), Kübler-Ross (16), and Hamburg (17). Kübler-Ross wrote of the process patients go through to come to terms with the fact of dying. Hamburg wrote of the resourcefulness of patients in facing catastrophic news and discussed a variety of implicit strategies by which patients face threats to life. This broad sequence of the acute phase, group support, and the long-run resolution described by these authors is compatible with the psychological work rape victims must do over time.

The majority of our rape victims were able to reorganize their lifestyle after the acute symptom phase, stay alert to possible threats to their lifestyle, and focus upon protecting themselves from further insult. This latter action was difficult because the world was perceived as a traumatic environment after the assault. As one victim said, "On the exterior I am OK, but inside [I feel] every man is the rapist."

The rape victim was able to maintain a certain equilibrium. In no case did the victim show ego disintegration, bizarre behavior, or self-destructive behavior during the acute phase. As indicated, there were a few victims who did regress to a previous level of impaired functioning four to six weeks following the assault.

With the increasing reports of rape, this is not a private syndrome. It should be a societal concern, and its treatment should be a public charge. Professionals will be called upon increasingly to assist the rape victim in the acute and long-term reorganization processes.

REFERENCES

1 Federal Bureau of Investigation: *Uniform Crime Reports for the United States.* Washington, D.C., U.S. Department of Justice, 1970.

2 *Report of District of Columbia Task Force on Rape.* Washington, D.C., District of Columbia City Council, 1973, p. 7 (processed).

3 Amir, M. *Patterns of Forcible Rape.* Chicago, University of Chicago Press, 1971.

4 Macdonald, J., *Rape: Offenders and their Victims.* Springfield, Ill., Charles C. Thomas, 1971.

5 Cohen, M., Garofalo, R., Boucher, R. et al. "The Psychology of Rapists." *Seminars in Psychiatry* 3:307–327, 1971.

6 Sutherland, S., Scherl, D. "Patterns of Response Among Victims of Rape." *Am. J. Orthopsychiatry* 40:503–511, 1970.

7 Hayman, C., Lanza, C. "Sexual Assault on Women and Girls." *Am. J. Obstet. Gynecol.* 109:408–486, 1971.

8 Halleck, S. "The Physician's Role in Management of Victims of Sex Offenders." *J.A.M.A.* 180:273–278, 1962.

9 Factor, M. "A Woman's Psychological Reaction to Attempted Rape." *Psychoanal. Q.* 23:243–244, 1954.

10 Holmstrom, L. L., Burgess, A. W. "Rape: the Victim Goes on Trial." Read at the 68th annual meeting of the American Sociological Association, New York, N.Y., Aug. 27–30, 1973.

11 Holmstrom, L. L., Burgess, A. W. "Rape: the Victim and the Criminal Justice System." Read at the First International Symposium on Victimology, Jerusalem, Sept. 2–6, 1973.

12 Burgess, A. W., Holmstrom, L. L. "The Rape Victim in the Emergency Ward." *Am. J. Nursing* 73:1741–1745, 1973.

13 Rado, S. "Pathodynamics and Treatment of Traumatic War Neurosis (Traumatophobia)." *Psychosom. Med.* 4:362–368, 1948.

14 Grinker, R. R., Spiegel, J. P. *Men Under Stress.* Philadelphia, Blakiston, 1945.

15 Lindemann, E. "Symptomatology and Management of Acute Grief." *Am. J. Psychiatry* 101:141–148, 1944.

16 Kübler-Ross, E. "On Death and Dying." *J.A.M.A.* 221:174–179, 1972.

17 Hamburg, D. "A Perspective on Coping Behavior." *Arch. Gen. Psychiatry* 17:277–284, 1967.

RECONSTITUTED FAMILIES

CHAPTER 82

BRIEF THERAPY
FOR RECONSTITUTED FAMILIES

Marthe Panneton

Many parents who consult child psychiatry clinics seek help for their child's problems in adjusting to life in a reconstituted family. Such families constitute a new form of social unit that has no clearly defined model in society.

To more adequately assist this type of family, whose functioning is extremely complex, I have used a new social work approach called "brief therapy". This therapy is part of the existing group of strategic or systemic approaches. It consists generally of individual therapy with the complainant and comprises, among other things, a limited number of interviews focused on solving problems by exploring the previous solutions attempted by the family.

The method of intervention is based on the philosophy that human problems can be perceived and resolved in a different way. The approach differs from other short-term treatment methods developed in social work since the 1960s. Paul Watzlawick, Richard Fisch, J. H. Weakland and L. Segal, who work together, are the main architects of brief therapy.

Very little has been written about the treatment of reconstituted families. The structure and rules of functioning of these families are different from those of nuclear families. Therein lie the main problems. The persons concerned transpose their vision of the nuclear family to the reconstituted family, and they resort to inadequate solutions that only perpetuate the problems. The goal of brief therapy is to modify these repetitive models by taking concrete action that is related to one's behavior, thus creating new rules of functioning.

From *The Social Worker*, Vol. 61, No. 2 (Summer 1993), pp. 53–58. Reprinted here with the permission of *The Social Worker/Le Travailleur social*.

THEORETICAL ASPECTS OF BRIEF THERAPY
Historical Overview

Brief therapy was introduced in 1959 by Don Jackson at the Mental Research Institute (MRI) in Palo Alto, California. Jackson treats the family as a system with a set of rules whose balance is maintained through positive and negative feedback. According to Jackson, who bases himself on cybernetics, if one member of the family presents symptoms, the whole family should be treated and not only this member. Problems are seen as resulting from faults in the family system. Brief therapy seeks to change the system through appropriate action in order to solve the patient's problems.

Paul Watzlawick has analyzed the intuitive therapeutic techniques of Don Jackson and Milton Erickson, and has developed with his colleagues, Richard Fisch and John Weakland, the frame of reference of brief therapy. This has led them to clearly explain the concepts of "family homeostasis, treatment of symptoms and paradoxes."

The Palo Alto School has acquired an international reputation, and was introduced in Europe in 1970. The brilliant Italian psychiatrist, Mara Selvini Palazzoli, based herself essentially on the work of the Palo Alto team to spread family systems therapy across Europe.

During the 1980s, Steve de Shazer became director of the Brief Therapy Center in Milwaukee. He focused primarily on developing the main components of effective therapy.

At about the same time, a brief psychotherapy center was established in the province of Quebec. This center provides intensive training sessions, as well as consultation and supervision services, with the assistance of Richard Fisch and Paul Watzlawick of the Brief Therapy Center.

Interest in brief therapy has been growing. Public agencies, such as local community service centers and social service centers in Quebec, have shown increasing interest in this approach which appears to meet the criteria of effective and quality services.

Basic Principles

Paul Watzlawick, J. Weakland and R. Fisch have seriously examined the concepts of permanence and change. They based themselves on the theory of groups and the theory of logical types to clarify their understanding of these concepts. Their analysis was more an illustration by analogy than a rigorous examination of these phenomena.

The theory of groups can help to explain the concept of permanence, i.e., a change within a group is invariable, thus the well-known expression "the more things change, the more they remain the same." The theory of logical types reveals that a transformation occurs only if there is a change in level from inside to outside the system.

Watzlawick concludes that change entails movement from a logical level to an immediately higher level, thereby producing modifications in the rules that govern structures and internal order.

Watzlawick applies the systemic model. He uses this model to explain the conditions required for change, based on the two principles of open systems: negative feedback (minimizes a phenomenon and reestablishes stability) and positive feedback (emphasizes a phenomenon and results in transformation).

Clients[1] often attempt to solve a persistent problem by repeating the same behavior each time. This causes negative feedback, since "the more things change, the more they remain the same." In order to produce change, one must induce fluctuations and introduce new and surprising elements that completely or partially transform existing structures. This results in positive feedback even though the approach may appear to be illogically and paradoxically discontinuous. What actually occurs is that one moves from a logical level to a higher level, and from a degree of abstraction to another.

This conceptual framework helps to better understand where problems originate and how they can be solved. In fact, the Palo Alto group considers above all that "the problem itself is nothing other than the solution."

Understanding Problems

One must define change from a cybernetic or systemic point of view in order to understand problems. Emphasis is placed on the observable behavior of persons and their interaction. The purpose of any intervention is to identify and successfully modify the repetitive model that perpetuates problems. In other words, the therapist seeks to block the negative feedback (stability) in order to induce positive feedback (transformation).

> The types of problems that psychotherapists encounter persist only if these problems are maintained by the current, continuous behavior of the patient and those with whom he interacts. Consequently, if this type of behavior is adequately changed or eliminated, the problem will disappear or be solved, whatever its nature, origin or duration.[2]

In other words, Watzlawick and Weakland consider problems as poorly "managed" or "negotiated" difficulties, not because people act illogically but because their fundamental reasoning is flawed. They keep repeating "more of the same", which only exacerbates the problem.

The proponents of brief therapy maintain that a different solution must be attempted if something has already been tried unsuccessfully twice.

Observing what works and what does not work should prevail over what might seem to be true or logical solutions.

The Palo Alto team considers that the problems for which people seek help are often related to poor adjustment to life's normal stages of transition like birth or marriage. People are so biased that they expect all of the normal phases of life, except death, to be happy events. This overly optimistic view contributes to certain problems. This is particularly true in the case of reconstituted families whose hopes and expectations are unrealistically high.

The approach used in brief therapy is fundamentally pragmatic. Its concepts and intervention strategies are based exclusively on direct observation.

Therapeutic Process

In brief therapy, solving the problem is the main criterion of success. The therapist must be skilled in defining the problem as well as being flexible and creative. He must draw upon his own experience and skills, and use interventions that have worked previously.

He is able to assist a client effectively by using both familiar and innovative techniques.

Generally speaking, the therapist works with the "complainant," who often is not the "identified client," because the former is more motivated and more likely to commit to change. The therapist may still meet the whole family together for purposes of evaluation. However, he should preferably meet family members individually to obtain information, understand their personality and empathize with them to obtain their cooperation. By doing so, the therapist avoids the never-ending aggressive behavior that leads nowhere. He can become familiar with their language and use it appropriately to intervene effectively.

The clear choice in brief therapy is to treat the symptom presented by the client at the first session. The therapist must therefore define the problem in terms of concrete behavior, set minimal treatment objectives, and explore in depth the previous solutions attempted.

Since brief therapy considers that problems persist because people repeat the same inappropriate behavior ("more of the same thing"), it is important to understand the common dynamics that underlie each attempt at solving problems. This is not an easy thing to do. Nonetheless, consider the following simple example: you try absolutely everything to fall asleep, you go to bed late to make sure you are tired, you avoid stimulating activities before going to bed, etc. You are literally confined to repeating the same behavior: you "are trying hard to fall asleep."

Once the therapist identifies this redundant behavior, he can plan his interventions. The first step consists in locating the "minefield"[3]: this precaution enables the therapist to avoid provoking the client's resistance or aggravating the symptom. As soon as the first defensive reactions appear, the therapist must change his attitude and relate to the client's language and view of the world.

Secondly, the client expects change when a specific objective is set. He will therefore be more inclined to attempt new ways of solving the problem. The therapist should establish a minimal objective by asking the following question: "What would you consider an important change that would make you think you had made satisfactory progress?"

When the repetitive model that maintains the problem is clearly identified, and the objective is set, the therapist chooses an intervention strategy that is very often the complete opposite (or "180°") of the solutions already attempted. He will also ask the client to behave in bizarre and surprising ways which do not make common sense. He may also induce change by simple and direct interventions. What really matters is that a well-thought-out strategy can break the vicious circle that perpetuates the problem.

Treatment ends when the objectives directly related to the client's complaint are met. The results of this approach are measured by changes in the client's behavior, in the solutions attempted, or in the way he defines his problem.

Usual Brief Therapy Techniques

Reframing is the most generally used technique in brief therapy. In fact, it is often a prior condition for the client to agree to a new task or behavior.

Paul Watzlawick defines this technique as follows:

Reframing means to modify the conceptual and/or emotional context of a given situation, or how the latter is experienced, by placing it in another framework that accords with the facts of this concrete situation whose meaning subsequently changes completely.[4]

The purpose of reframing is to change the rigid symptomatic framework to reveal new possibilities and bring about a neutral or positive perception. Here are a few simple illustrations: aggressiveness would be redefined as being potential energy, uncertainty as prudence, etc. These reframings, though not cure-alls, help to modify the emotional context. Therefore, reframing a situation to obtain a different response will bring a client to consider things in another way, and to review other causal factors.

Paradoxical Instructions

Watzlawick believes there are only two ways of giving instructions: the first consists in persuading the client to change (he usually fails because he cannot control his symptom). The other method consists in encouraging him to act as he normally does. This paradoxical instruction produces a behavior that can no longer be spontaneous. It forces the client to change his behavior because he finds himself in an unbearable situation. Consequently, he begins to control his symptom since he cannot continue to say: "I can't help it." By rebelling, he has fewer symptomatic reactions and achieves the objective set in therapy. It is clear that paradoxical instructions promote therapeutic progress. However, they must not be used intuitively but only objectively and prudently. Any use of paradoxical instructions must be preceded by an in-depth evaluation of the persons concerned and the dynamics of the problem situation.

Other types of paradoxical interventions are used more generally in brief therapy, e.g. recommending that the person "slow down" when improvements begin to appear. This intervention reduces the client's anxiety and sense of urgency which, in some cases, lead him to repeatedly attempt to solve the problem by "trying harder."

In using this approach, it is much better for the therapist to adopt a position of inferiority. For example, telling a client that "there are no more solutions" is often a very effective strategy. This produces a surge of energy which brings the client to solve the problem himself.

The proponents of brief therapy (Fisch et al.) have stated that the fundamentals of their approach were not definitive, and could be perfected. Thus, other techniques can be developed as the result of a therapist's creativity. The primary objective above all is to find a solution to the problem.

RECONSTITUTED FAMILIES AND THEIR PROBLEMS
Major Problems Encountered in Reconstituted Families

The terms "reconstituted family," "blended family" and "mixed family" are used to designate a family in which one of the spouses (or both) has one or more children from a previous relationship.

The reconstituted family is a new form of family unit whose arrangement is unique and distinct from that found in traditional families. Though similar in many respects, the reconstituted family is a much more complex unit.

In every culture, the family plays a predominant role in the life of its members. It meets two essential but contradictory needs that Salvador Minuchin has defined as the sense of belonging (to a family group) and the sense of separation and individuation resulting from involvement in various familial or extra-familial subsystems.

According to Salvador Minuchin, "in every culture, the family imparts to its members their identity.[5] It restructures itself at different stages and adapts to change in order to survive and encourage the growth of its members. Minuchin maintains that the boundaries of the system must be clear to ensure the family's proper functioning.

In the nuclear family, the members belong to a single family system in which the rules, expectations, purposes and duties are well defined. These respect the generational boundaries and the established sexual mores. What lies within the family is clearly delimited from what lies outside.

However, in the reconstituted family, belonging to the family system can be interpreted differently. A few members belong in principle to both families, but are related in fact to only one or none at all. These new social units have flexible boundaries and are influenced by previous spouses, grandparents and agencies that have had a major impact on their operation and survival. In the case of these families, the rules, expectations, purposes and duties are poorly defined by society. Each reconstituted family must define its own model: it will seek to develop a sense of belonging despite the existence of more numerous problems than in the family that is intact.

Visher and Visher consider that this type of family must ensure the healthy growth of its members through a strong relationship between the spouses. This kind of relationship is of prime importance in a nuclear family, but even more so in a reconstituted family where there is much less interpersonal cohesion than in an intact family due to the integration of new members.

In addition, couples with a strong relationship must show flexibility in their roles and accept that certain aspects of the family unit may be challenged by other members. Such a flexible structure[6] benefits both the adults and the children: the former are happier in their spousal relationship, and the latter have greater freedom. It seems preferable, therefore, to promote a sense of autonomy rather than belonging among the reconstituted families.

According to Visher and Visher, more individual freedom and less intimate interpersonal relationships would seem to be essential for reconstituted families to function properly.

The existence of family bonds between parents and their respective children before a new family unit is formed produces a number of problems: this is truly a characteristic of the mixed family. Relations with ex-spouses create most problems for the majority of couples, in part because of the confusion that ensues. It has been shown that cooperation between natural parents allows each child to relate more freely to different parents. This may, however, strain the relationship of the new couple and produce spousal arguments. The ideal situation would be close cooperation between the spouses without disturbing the newly formed relationship. This would require having fully dealt with the emotional separation from one's ex-spouse.

One of the most difficult tasks facing natural parents is to redefine the co-parental relationship so as to pursue harmoniously the children's education and assume all related responsibilities. This paradoxical process is at the heart of the reorganization of the divorced and remarried family.

Children often fantasize and try to divide and destabilize their new parents, so as to get their natural parents together again. New spouses must understand the children's intense feelings, and show a great deal of caring. This will help to eliminate the children's attempts to break up the new marriage.

Anxiety, stress and painful interactions among family members are the daily lot of reconstituted families. The spouses who head these families may form gratifying relationships if they can handle stormy situations and solve crises. Their relationships become neither monotonous nor uncaring since they never take each other for granted. Their bonds are strong and deep.

Men's Excessive Expectations

What is expected of men in a remarriage is different from what is expected of women. They are generally less involved in the children's education. Consequently, there are fewer myths about their role.

The stepfather may feel sometimes that he has no role to play since the latter is so poorly defined. In society, the natural father assumes the educational and financial responsibilities, while the stepfather has only partial obligations regarding the socialization of children.

The stepfather of a reconstituted family is unfortunately not very realistic, and expects from the outset that he is an integral part of the family. However, he must find his place progressively in a functional group. The problem results from the fact that the stepfather tries to set limits for the children without having had a close relationship with them over a period of time.

The stepfather, who moves slowly and attempts to make a friend of the child before moving to control him, has a better chance of having his discipline integrated into the sentimental order of the family.[7]

Women's Excessive Expectations

Women usually have unrealistic expectations about their role in a reconstituted family. They hope to make everyone happy, and to compensate for the suffering of the children whose original family has broken up. They assume responsibility for the family's emotional balance, but they are unable to undo the pain that family members have experienced in the past. They can seek to understand and accept this suffering, which provides some measure of support to family members, but they cannot erase the pain.

The role of stepmother is extremely difficult since relations between family members are complex and conflicting emotions are intense. There is also the myth of the "bad" stepmother as portrayed in the Cinderella story. The stepmother requires in fact a great deal of support to restore her self-esteem and function better in the reconstituted family.

Children

In nuclear families, children can be loyal to one or the other parent, as the case may be. They must deal, however, with their contradictory feelings of love and hate towards the "good" and the "bad" parent. They may also manipulate parents to deal with sibling rivalry and to form their identity. They may, therefore, experience emotional pain and feel rejected.

These difficulties are amplified in reconstituted families where there is increased competition because there are more people and more complex family structures. Children feel a greater degree of insecurity and lack of identity.

They have also experienced the universal feelings of grief and sorrow (denial, guilt, aggressiveness and despair) associated with the process of separation and divorce over which they had no control. At the end of these various stages of grief, they may accept the situation and reorganize their life.

Children inevitably experience conflicts of loyalty since they are partially separated from one of their parents. When the spouses come to an amicable agreement about their separation or divorce, the children are less divided in their loyalty since they may not have to choose one parent over the other.

Though part of a reconstituted family, children keep hoping for a long time that their natural parents will become once again reunited. It is important that parents answer all their questions and remind the children of their new family reality so that they do not live in a world of fantasy.

It would seem that a child born in a remarriage—in itself a sign of the spouses' love—may be beneficial for both children and adults in a reconstituted family. The adults must draw, however, on their own psychological strengths to create a new model of family cohesion, with normal and appropriate rules of conduct that are different from those of the nuclear family. This new conceptual model, with a distinct theoretical base, constitutes a system. When there are dysfunctional problems in this system, a systems-based therapy such as brief therapy may be used successfully in many cases.

PROBLEM-SOLVING IN RECONSTITUTED FAMILIES

As stated previously, Salvador Minuchin defines the family as a system undergoing transformation that restructures itself at different stages, and that adapts to change in order to survive and ensure the growth of its members. The family becomes dysfunctional in periods of stress such as the addition of a new member or the merger of two families.

The reconstituted family experiences, above all else, problems in adapting to a period of transition in life. This entails a remodeling of interpersonal relationships, which is difficult in view of the absence of any existing model. The therapist must focus initially on helping the family members to cope with their various developmental tasks in order to restructure the family system.

The therapist seeks in a sense to break the vicious circle. His intervention consists in identifying the ineffective interactions of the family, and proposing more appropriate behavior. Family members can thus experience different modes of interaction instead of continuing to repeat the same behavior.

The proponents of brief therapy set treatment objectives in relation to how the members define the family's problems. It is taken for granted that any change will lead to other changes that may be even more important.

I will now present the first case where I used this conceptual framework. The results convinced me that this approach with reconstituted families was effective.

The case of Mr. Émile Édoin[8] demonstrates how discipline problems prevented the formation of the new family unit. It also shows the loyalty conflicts experienced by most members of the reconstituted family. The family sought help following a crisis involving Élise, a fifteen-year-old adolescent, who apparently lost contact with reality. She had a fixed and unusual gaze, and did strange things like rocking her brother and making coffee at the most unusual times. She had become extremely aggressive towards Émile, her stepfather.

According to the mother, Élizabeth, this disturbing episode was the result of a lengthy conflict between Élise and Émile. Throughout this conflict, the adolescent girl had displayed constant rudeness and hatred for her stepfather, who had been very hard on his stepdaughter. He is the father of two children, a seventeen-year-old daughter and a thirteen-year-old son, who are not in his custody. His own childhood had been very difficult: he was very young when his father died and his mother, who cared for him, emphasized hard work and financial success.

I identified the following dynamics in the evaluation of this case. Most of the difficulties seemed related to loyalty towards the absent family members: Élise and her brother Étienne were loyal to their father, and Émile was loyal to his own children. I made certain assumptions to explain Élise's behavior: she projected onto Émile the aggressiveness she felt towards her father who had abandoned her and made her suffer. The intransigence of her stepfather exacerbated this feeling which generally led to violent behavior.

Élise also protected Élizabeth from her spouse by coming between them and exposing the injustices which she, her mother and her brother suffered at the hands of Émile. She also prevented them from communicating and dealing with their problems.

By being loyal to his own children, the stepfather applied the same rules as in the former family, but he reserved any privileges for his children only. A more flexible attitude on his part would have indicated that he questioned the way he educated his own children.

Moreover, the mother's poor ability to set rules and have them followed reinforced her partner's rigidity.

There were, however, certain strengths in the marital relationship. The spouses clearly identified the love bonds between them. Élizabeth was conciliatory, diplomatic and understanding: she was a perfect companion for Émile. They both wanted to live together and were receptive to change.

I was concerned about Élise's condition because of the violent episodes and her excessive aggressiveness. I suspected that she had serious personal problems in relation to how she perceived her father.

She was evaluated by a child psychiatrist who diagnosed dissociative reactions related to a family conflict.

My first intervention was to place Élise in a foster home for one month to help control her aggressiveness, and to allow the spouses to communicate with one another.

Étienne remained with the family but did not come between the couple nor did he serve as a scapegoat. Émile and Élizabeth were asked to set rules to which they would adhere and which family members would follow.

Élise had been the family's spokesperson who denounced Émile's excessive control. My goal was to reestablish the family roles by reinforcing the couple's relationship and preventing Élise from interfering in this relationship.

Foster care was very difficult. Élise had trouble with the rules and lost her temper very quickly. Following my interventions, the foster parents agreed to make some changes in how they dealt with Élise.

Despite the difficulties, the experience allowed Élise to better appreciate her family. Élizabeth and Émile came to realize that their conflicts were serious since they had never agreed on how to educate their children.

My intervention was simple up to that point. After identifying the problems and their dynamics, I worked on family structures and achieved positive results.

However, the sessions with the family were so full of animosity that all of my colleagues noticed what was going on! Émile and Élise were incapable of communicating with one another and everyone got into the act. Therapy with the entire family became impossible. However, since I had established a good relationship with each family member in previous contacts, I decided to intervene strategically. I met each person separately, and each one tried to prove that no agreement was possible. I repeated their own words as best I could and told them individually that, after careful thought, I had no solution to help them live together. In fact, I intentionally amplified the problems.

A few of the immediate reactions were disturbing. Élise told me in a very cavalier manner: "Finally, you've understood!" Over a period of time, however, the results were very satisfactory since each family member would come up with a solution and discuss it with the mother, the family's key person. My role was to state that it was impossible for them to live together: they had convinced me. This paradoxical approach was effective for the following reasons: Émile and Élise, who are contrary persons, wanted to prove me wrong; everyone in the family tried to find more realistic solutions to the problem situation.

I can also assume that the fact of adopting a weak position and admitting my inability to help them actually enhanced their self-esteem, and freed them from their feelings of guilt at not finding a solution. This seemingly different attitude from what they usually encountered was the total opposite (180°) of what they had known previously. There was a change of levels and the ensuing positive feedback led to modifications in the system.

As time went on, Élise rapidly improved in individual therapy. She even developed a harmonious relationship with Émile. Following discussions with her mother, she became aware that she and her brother would some day leave home, and that her mother needed a partner. She became more tolerant.

The mother continued to follow therapy sessions with me in order to deal with all the changes that occurred. She decided to continue her relationship with Émile, and to adapt to his rigid personality. When she terminated treatment, she recognized that she was now able to cope with difficulties.

At the outset of my intervention, I was somewhat perplexed by the complexity of the problem situation: the adolescent girl's severe behavior problem; the stepfather's rigid personality; and the whole dynamic of the reconstituted family. I was quite worried and uncertain about my interventions and the ultimate results.

The use of brief therapy greatly simplified the situation and empowered me as a therapist. The initial sessions with family members helped to establish my credibility and create alliances. My strategic interventions were well received, and helped each person to adopt a more appropriate behavior. The mother was given the necessary support to cope with the changes.

The results were positive, though unpredictable at the outset. They clearly demonstrated that the brief therapy approach is effective with reconstituted families. I do not claim that this is the only effective approach, but it does provide a new way to solve problems.

NOTES

1. The masculine gender was used throughout this text to make it easier for the reader. This must not be interpreted as discriminating against women.
2. P. Watzlawick and J. Weakland, *Sur l'interaction* (Paris: Éditions du Seuil, s.d.), ex. pp. 361.
3. "Minefield" is an accepted term in brief therapy: it means "any subject that activates the client's defenses."
4. P. Watzlawick, J. Weakland and R. Fisch, *Changements, paradoxes et psychothérapie* (Paris: Éd. du Seuil, 1975), 192 pp., ex. p. 116.
5. Salvador Minuchin, *Familles en thérapie* (Éd. France-Amérique, 1979), 365 pp., ex. p. 63.
6. Structure: "The family structure is the invisible network of functional demands that organize the way family members interact." Salvador Minuchin, *Familles en thérapie* (Éd. France-Amerique, 1979), 365 pp., ex. p. 67.
7. P. N. Stern, *Stepfather Families Integration Around Child Discipline* (S. I. Issues in Mental Health Nursing, 1978), ex. p. 50.
8. The real names of clients have been replaced by fictitious names.

REFERENCES

de Shazer, Steve. *Keys to Solution in Brief Therapy*. New York: W. W. Norton, 1985, 190 p.

Duberman, Lucille. *The Reconstituted Family*. Chicago: Nelson-Hall, 1975, 181 p.

Fisch, R., J. H. Weakland, and L. Segal. *Tactiques du changement. Thérapie et temps court*. Paris: Éd. du Seuil, 1986, 385 p.

Messinger, Lillian, and James Hansen. *Therapy and Remarriage Families*. Rockland, Md: Aspen, 1982, 206 p.

Minuchin, Salvador. *Familles en thérapie*. Montréal: Éd. France-Amerique, 1979, 285 p.

Sager, Clifford, Hollis S. Brown, Helen Crohn, Tamara Engel, Evelyn Rod Libby Walker. *Treating the Remarried Family*. New York: Brunner Mazel, 1983, 388 p.

Visher, Emily, and John S. Visher. *Stepfamilies. A Guide to Working with Stepparents and Stepchildren.* New York: Brunner Mazel, 1979, 280 p.

Watzlawick, Paul, J. Beavin-Helnick, and D. Jackson. *Une logique de la communication.* Paris: Éd. du Seuil, 1972, 288 p.

Watzlawick, P., and J. Weakland. *Sur l'interaction.* Paris: Éd. du Seuil, 1981, 389 p.

Watzlawick, P., J. Weakland, and R. Fisch. *Changements, paradoxes et psychothérapie.* Paris: Éd. du Seuil, 1975, 192 p.

SEXUALITY

CHAPTER 83

FAMILY THERAPY FOR LESBIAN AND GAY CLIENTS

Michael J. Shernoff

With growing frequency, social workers find themselves making clinical assessments of families whose members' affectional or sexual orientation cannot be ignored. Social workers, therefore, would be well advised to develop a professional approach that includes the treatment of lesbian and gay clients within the context of the family. Family therapy is such an approach; applied to the treatment of homosexuals, it focuses on the family systems and the family dynamics of this special client group.

The social worker as family therapist recognizes that although many lesbians and gays are estranged from their families of origin, roles acquired in these families reemerge in other social relationships and that those roles need examining. Many adult homosexuals marry and produce offspring, thereby creating families of their own. The family therapist must investigate these newly created family systems. A large number of family households as well include homosexual adolescents who, as minors, are under the care of their parents.[1] Here, the family therapist must explore the dynamics between parents and their children. Furthermore, it is safe to assume that social workers have homosexual clients and are not aware of this fact, perhaps because such clients are married and have children, thus providing the appearance of heterosexuality. If the family therapist is to be able to decipher family secrets and alliances, thereby helping client families receive the services they seek, it is crucial that the sexual orientation of family members be addressed and that family work be advanced with homosexual clients.

Despite the critical nature of such work, to date there has been a general lack of

Reprinted from *Social Work*, Vol. 29, No. 4 (July–August, 1984), pp. 393–396, by permission of NASW Press. Copyright 1984, National Association of Social Workers, Inc., *Social Work*.

[1] See Alan P. Bell, Martin S. Weinberg, and Susan Kiefer-Hammersmith, *Sexual Preference: Its Development in Men and Women* (Bloomington, Ind.: Indiana University Press, 1981); and A. C. Kinsey, W. B. Pomeroy, and C. E. Martin, *Sexual Behavior in the Human Male* (Philadelphia: W. B. Saunders, 1948).

training for social workers who provide clinical family services for this client population. Schools of social work typically teach little or nothing about family therapy with
homosexuals or about their families and support systems. Moreover there is very little
in the professional literature addressing either the treatment of lesbian and gay clients
through family therapy or the attitudes toward homosexuality held by therapists who
work with these clients. Hall's work stands out as a pioneering effort.[2] She argued for
practitioners who work with lesbian families to examine their own attitudes toward
members of this minority group prior to attempting intervention in the family systems
of their clients.

Clearly, family therapy with homosexuals and their families, a new phenomenon in
social work practice, warrants exploration. To this end, the author explores issues and
presents practice methods based on his observations as a clinical social worker in a suburban community's mental health center and as a private practitioner in a large city. By
expanding the traditional meaning of "family" to include the important others in the
lives of lesbian and gay clients, the author hopes this article will provide the beginnings
of an ongoing discussion of the practice of family treatment with the homosexual
client. Such a beginning may also help to convince social work educators and supervisors of the need for training in this area, from a nonhomophobic perspective. Here,
homophobia is defined as fear of homosexuality and is commonly associated with prejudice toward and discrimination against homosexuals.[3]

SELF-DISCLOSURE IN FAMILY OF ORIGIN

Family work with homosexual clients poses unique problems not found with other client
groups. The most significant is self-disclosure—"coming out"—to the important others
in the client's life. The client may be hesitant for or not wish the family to know about
his or her sexual orientation. This hesitation must be respected, but also explored. The
therapist may choose to investigate with the client whether the decision not to disclose
his or her sexual orientation is based on a perceived need to save "unnecessary pain" or
on persistent self-hatred. For the family therapist, an exploration of this question can
be a diagnostic probe into how the client views the workings of his or her family.

One approach might be to initiate a discussion of the motives and timing for such a
disclosure. Having worked with angry clients during the initial stage of treatment, often
the author has observed their coming out to parents, spouse, or children as a vehicle for
hostile acting out. When such behavior seems likely to occur, ordinarily, the client is
counseled to use restraint until this information can be used as a bridge to increase family intimacy. If such disclosure serves as a way to improve communication, rather than
as a weapon, it is advisable. Otherwise, the client's sexual orientation is better left
undisclosed, at least on a short-term basis.

Very often the self-identified homosexual client blames his or her sexual orientation
as being the "cause" of a current dilemma. In such a case, the nonhomophobic, skilled

[2] Marny Hall, "Lesbian Families: Cultural and Clinical Issues," *Social Work,* 23 (September 1978), pp. 380–385.
[3] See George Weinberg, *Society and the Healthy Homosexual* (New York: Doubleday & Co., 1973).

family therapist points out this dynamic for what it is: the client's internalized homophobia: it is merely a defense and must be labeled as such by the therapist. Often a partial projection is in operation in such cases: what is usually fostering the client's feelings of discomfort is society's negative response to the homosexual parent, child, or individual. Thus the homosexual adolescent or the divorced homosexual becomes the family's symptom bearer in ways very similar to those of a person with a psychiatric or emotional disability. Instead of looking clearly at all the multiple stresses currently affecting their family system and involving themselves in completing the required tasks of restructuring, homosexual clients often allow their homosexuality to assume all the responsibility for family homeostasis.

Legal Issues

Some people marry and have children long before they discover or accept their homosexuality. The emotional and psychological strain on the entire family system that is created by the necessity of a homosexual parent having to decide how "out" to be because of the fear of losing his or her children through court decisions cannot be underestimated. Decisions such as whether to live with one's lover, whether to tell the children about one's sexual orientation, whether to fight to retain custody or win joint custody, and whether to fight for alimony or child support are some of the issues that homosexual parents face, and with which family therapists must be familiar.

These issues must be seriously considered because it may not be in the best interest of a lesbian or gay client to come out to his or her spouse and family. The courts routinely rule, solely on the grounds of sex preference, that natural parents are unfit to have partial custody or even unsupervised visitation rights. (In 1980, in Kentucky, a judge cited an article published in *Social Work* in support of his decision to deny custody to a lesbian mother following her divorce.[4]) Therefore, the family therapist must be aware of the need for caution about self-disclosure if there is *any likelihood* of a custody battle for the children, and the homosexual parent wishes to have custody or visitation rights. If such a battle appears probable, the client must be helped to see that his or her long-range need for self-protection must come before the immediate need for self-disclosure, which commonly accompanies the euphoria associated with accepting one's sexual orientation.

When working with homosexuals who are parents and, as such, members of a minority group, the social worker must be prepared to have his or her own values and assumptions about sex roles and stereotypes challenged. There is an increasing number of gay fathers who are seeking, at a minimum, joint custody of their children. Correspondingly, there are lesbian mothers who choose to relinquish rights of custody and visitation after coming out and ending marriages. In the author's practice, for example, a lesbian client spent seven years working through feelings of guilt, anger, and depression, as well as relief, resulting from her voluntarily relinquishing custody and all visitation access to her two daughters.

[4] S. v S., Ky. App. 608 S.W. 2d 64.

Parents' 'Coming Out' to Their Children

A therapist would be doing the client a disservice not to ready him or her for possible rejection by loved ones. In the case of homosexual parents, the possibility of rejection by their children increases with the age of the offspring. The younger the children, the more accepting they are about mom or dad's "being different." A useful analogy is to a child of interracial parentage, who learns early in life the price one pays for being different, for being a person of color in a racist society. This child also grows rich in the rewards of being the offspring of people from two different cultures. The ugly reality of racism—that some people loathe one simply because of who one's parents are and who they have dared to love—becomes a fact of life.

The child of a homosexual parent, just as the child of interracial parents, can learn at an early age to be more tolerant about difference and can grow stronger as a result of being different.[5] The child may be forced to contend with harassment from other children, particularly if residing with a custodial parent and that parent's same-sex lover. For instance, other children may taunt the child with, "Your dad's a 'fag'!" or "Your mom's a 'dyke'!" Despite such experiences, the child who grows up weathering the abuse of other children and who is secure in being loved will likely emerge as a healthy and resilient adult.[6]

Lesbian and gay parents often seek counseling for help in telling their children that they are homosexual. Family work in such cases usually focuses on the parents' ability to communicate clearly their reasons for agreeing to or initiating the dissolution of their marriage if, in fact, either decision has been made. Both parents and children usually require help in understanding one another's reactions and in expressing their love directly. Sometimes, behaving in typically preadolescent or adolescent ways, the children attempt to make use of this newly disclosed information by either acting out or attempting to manipulate in some way. For instance, the author's work includes that with families in which the children focus on the parents' homosexuality in an attempt to divert attention from behavioral problems that predate their parents' coming out. In such instances, the skilled family therapist helps the family to view the behavior as manipulative and to separate the content of the parents' sexuality from the real issues to be resolved.

The case that follows highlights a parent's feelings about coming out to his children, the children's response, and the role of the family therapist.

A gay father in his mid-50s, who had been estranged from his two adult daughters for 15 years, sought professional help to facilitate a family reconciliation following the death of his ex-wife. Treatment was very brief. Sessions focused on having current communications clear up misconceptions the three people had been holding about one another for years The father's guilt about his sexual orientation had prevented him from ever speaking to his daughters directly about his reasons for having left the family home. These family sessions were the first time he had the opportunity to ventilate his feelings of sadness, loss, and guilt. For his daughters,

---

[5] See Bernice Goodman, "Some Mothers Are Lesbians," and especially pp. 55–57, in Elaine Norman and Arlene Mancuso, eds., *Women's Issues and Social Work Practice* (Itasca, Ill.: F. E. Peacock Publishers, 1980).
[6] Gail Karen Lewis, "Children of Lesbians: Their Point of View," *Social Work*, 25 (May 1980), pp. 198–203.

the sessions provided a safe arena to talk about their feelings of abandonment by him, ensuing financial difficulties, and resulting rage toward and emotional distance from their father.

In this case, the father used his sexual orientation as scapegoat. His guilt about being gay prevented him from dealing with himself or his children and their feelings about his having left the marriage and them.

For therapy with reconstituted families, an important factor is to include members who comprise the entire family system at certain therapy sessions. The live-in lover of the custodial parent needs to be included as well as the noncustodial parent and his or her new partner.

'Coming Out' to Parents

The family therapist must prepare the client for a number of possible reactions from his or her family to the disclosure of sexual orientation. For instance, on being told of his homosexuality, the family members of a Jewish client sat *shiva* for him and have not seen or spoken to him since. (*Shiva* is the traditional week of mourning for Jews following the burial of a family member.) Though an extreme response, this example is, unfortunately, not singular.

Another task for the social worker who is helping a client decide when to come out to his or her family is a thorough exploration of the client's expectations of the parents' response in particular. The client may be in an emotionally needy time, for instance, following the breakup of a long-term love relationship, and he or she may hope that the disclosure will bring about nurturing from the parents. The client may need help to see this as a highly improbable outcome of self-disclosure.

A common case in the author's clinical experience is that of an adolescent who already self-identifies as gay or lesbian. This young person may have labeled him- or herself this way despite never having actually engaged in sexual activity with a same-sex partner. The fact that the adolescent considers himself gay or herself lesbian may be discovered by the parents by reading a letter or discovering a gay or lesbian book in the child's room. Overwrought by the discovery, the parents often will seek help for their child. Ordinarily, what they mean by "help" is for the therapist to "fix" their child by making him or her "straight," or heterosexual.

At the outset, this situation is usually one of crisis intervention. Treatment can be short term, geared to assuaging the parents' feelings of responsibility for and guilt about the sexual orientation of their child. Bibliotherapy plays an important part in helping parents learn that being gay or lesbian is not the worst thing that could have happened to their child. Books, such as *A Family Matter: A Parent's Guide to Homosexuality* and *Now That You Know: What Every Parent Should Know About Homosexuality,* help the parents adjust to this disruption in *their* expectations of their offspring.[7] Referring parents of lesbians and gays to the self-help group Parents of Gays is often

---

[7] Charles Silverstein, *A Family Matter: A Parent's Guide to Homosexuality* (New York: McGraw-Hill Book Co., 1978); and Betty Fairchild and Nancy Hayward, *Now That You Know: What Every Parent Should Know About Homosexuality* (New York: Harcourt Brace Jovanovich, 1979).

beneficial for parents who need peer support in working through their shock, anger, or denial.

Working with the adolescent client who is a self-identified homosexual almost always involves the therapist's assumption of the parental role on a temporary basis. Often the parents themselves are so needy for emotional support that they are frequently unable to parent their homosexual offspring properly, at least initially. For many parents, therefore, the time immediately following the confirmation that their child is homosexual is when they require the greatest amount of nurturance and support from both their child and the therapist.

FRIENDSHIP NETWORK: 'FAMILY OF CREATION'

It is generally accepted by family theorists that behavioral dynamics and roles acquired in families of origin reemerge throughout peoples lives, and that these patterns reemerge especially in families of creation.[8] This process is no less true for lesbians and gays, or even for those instances in which homosexuals do not form traditional family units. A pervasive aspect of the lesbian and gay communities, and one that has been overlooked in the professional literature, is how chosen friendship networks and support systems become, in effect, new families of creation.

Indeed, when working individually with lesbian and gay clients, the author finds it helpful to complete genograms and sociograms. A genogram, on the one hand, is a history of the client's social network: it includes the client's current as well as past networks of lovers and friendships. A sociogram, on the other hand, is actually a diagram or map of where the individual places him- or herself in relation to all the interlocking systems within which he or she functions. Included in this diagram would be the client's affiliation with professional, social, familial, religious, and political organizations and his or her sexual liaisons. Used in addition to the traditional genogram, a sociogram is one way of both gathering the necessary history and charting a dynamic formulation.

Charting a sociogram helps illustrate many of the presenting issues that cause the client difficulty. At the same time, it clarifies for the therapist data that originally were reported in inconsistent or contradictory ways by the client. Furthermore, when reviewed with the client, the diagrams and maps help generate therapeutic discussion in which the client compares current positions in the various systems with positions he or she would like to hold, and investigates the means by which these dynamics have changed over the years. The technique provides insight-oriented psychotherapy as well, by enabling the client to evaluate the roles important others currently play in his or her life and to recognize the ways in which these roles are similar to and patterned after those in the family of origin.

[8] See, for example, Alan S. Gurman and David P. Kniskern, *Handbook of Family Therapy* (New York: Brunner/Mazel 1981).

'FAMILY SCULPTING' IN DRUG TREATMENT

For clients who are self-identified as lesbian or gay and are severely depressed, suicidal, or undergoing detoxification from drugs or alcohol, the author finds treatment planning with members of the existing friendship network to be an effective treatment strategy. At times, merely having the client's existing social resources mobilized has a positive therapeutic effect in the recovery from psychiatric disability.

When members of a family of origin or family of creation (friendship network) are brought into a session "family sculpting" proves to be a valuable tool. Family sculpting is the physical positioning of the members of the client's family (of origin or creation) in ways that show the client's perceptions of the emotional ties between each member. The technique helps family members to clarify their perceptions of the dynamics that are present in the various family subsystems. This process has been effective in helping everyone—the client and the client's friends or family members—to find alternative ways of dealing with their problems.

Recent research suggests that in an enmeshed family system the addict or alcoholic is often the primary system bearer for family homeostasis.[9] Whereas traditional outpatient, drug-free, insight-oriented psychotherapy has not proved successful in rehabilitating addicts or alcoholics, family sculpting is an especially useful tool for working with such chemically dependent individuals. When members of the primary family system or friendship system of a substance-abusing client are included in treatment, they become actively engaged in changing the patterns that perpetuate the drug-abusing behavior. Through their active participation, the client's self-destructive behavior should cease.[10]

The following case illustrates the application of theories and techniques of family therapy in the author's work with a lesbian, identified as a substance abuser.

> Susan is a 24-year-old lesbian from a middle-class suburban family, and Ruth is her 40-year-old lover of three years. Ruth initiated therapy, seeking help for her "friend's" problem of taking nonprescribed codeine. Ruth prompted Susan to seek help for her drug problem by threatening to end their relationship if she did not begin treatment.
>
> During the course of treatment they were seen exclusively as a couple. The drug taking seemed to be a symptom of Susan's unexpressed needs to be taken care of. Therapy is teaching Susan how to ask directly for what she needs and wants from Ruth, and to do so in ways that are not self-destructive.

CONCLUSION

The application of family therapy to lesbian and gay clients is limited only by the skill and creativity of the therapist. It is a method of psychotherapy for people who identify

---

[9] See Duncan M. Stanton, *Family Therapy of Drug Abuse and Addiction* (New York: Guilford Press, 1982).

[10] See Peter Steinglass, "Family Therapy with Alcoholics: A Review," pp. 147–186, and Edward Kaufman, "The Application of the Basic Principles of Family Therapy to the Treatment of Drug and Alcohol Abusers," pp. 255–272, in Kaufman and Pauline N. Kaufmann, *Family Therapy of Drug and Alcohol Abusers* (New York: Halsted Press, 1979).

themselves as homosexual that will certainly grow in importance as lesbians and gays build more support systems that function as families. Family therapy will also prove important when social workers learn to recognize the changing definitions of "family" in contemporary America.

By such recognition, workers can provide a great deal of support, guidance, and good clinical work to the families of lesbians and gays. This support may be both emotional and practical in nature. In order to do this work effectively, however, social workers must first recognize their own homophobia and then seek to work through possible prejudice toward homosexuals, as well as preexisting heterosexual bias.

SEXUAL DISORDERS

CHAPTER 84

INTERVIEW TECHNIQUES TO ASSESS SEXUAL DISORDERS

J. Paul Fedoroff

During the past century, the clinical assessment and treatment of sexual problems have undergone a dramatic transition. One hundred years ago, the only data available to researchers were anecdotal reports of unusual sexual problems often obtained through the criminal-justice system. Biased sampling methods and inadequate data collection contributed to the development of incorrect theories about sexuality. For example, so little was known about normal sexual behavior that Krafft-Ebing, who primarily interviewed individuals involved in forensic cases, proposed that masturbation caused mental illness (Krafft-Ebing, 1899). Since then, more careful epidemiologic surveys (e.g., Kinsey, Pomeroy, & Martin, 1948) have gradually increased our knowledge about the prevalence of normal and abnormal sexual behaviors. This growing knowledge has been accompanied by increasing awareness of the importance of sexuality in the general population (Shiavi, Schreiner-Engel, Mandeli, Schanzer, & Cohen, 1990) and in clinical populations (Swett, Surrey, & Cohen, 1990).

Evaluation and treatment of sexual problems have become more sophisticated; many sex clinics routinely use standardized psychometric tests (Derogatis & Melisaratos, 1978), sex hormone assays (Spark, White, & Connolly, 1980), nocturnal penile tumescence testing (Karacan et al., 1977), and penile plethysmography (Freund & Blanchard, 1989). Berlin's (1983) finding that a large percentage of hospitalized sex offenders have physical and mental abnormalities supports the hypothesis that, in selected cases, karyotyping, electroencephalography, and computerized tomography may be indicated as part of the assessment of sex problems. Treatments have also become more sophisticated and may now involve various forms of individual (Crown & Lucas

Reprinted from *Families in Society*, Vol. 72, No. 3 (1991), pp. 140–146, by permission of the publisher, Families International, Inc.

1976), couple (Masters & Johnson, 1970), and group therapy (Leiblum, Rosen, & Piere, 1976) as well as pharmacotherapy (Berlin & Meinecke, 1981) and even surgery (Schmidt & Schorsch, 1981).

In addition, sex clinics themselves have tended to specialize on the basis of the types of problems they evaluate: sexual dysfunctions, paraphilias, gender-identity problems, or consequences of sexual abuse. According to current diagnostic criteria, sexual dysfunctions are defined as disorders characterized by problems of decreased sexual desire or by psychophysiologic changes that characterize the sexual response cycle (American Psychiatric Association, 1987). Gender-identity problems are characterized as involving persistent discomfort regarding one's gender. Paraphilias are sexual disorders characterized by arousal in response to stimuli that are not normally considered sexually exciting and that may interfere with a person's capacity for reciprocal, affectionate activity (American Psychiatric Association, 1987). Sex-victim clinics serve the needs of children, adolescents, and adults who have been sexually abused. Although the trend toward increasingly sophisticated and specialized sex clinics has increased awareness about the importance of sexual problems, general clinicians still tend to ignore sexual problems. This is particularly worrisome because many people first present their sex problems to their general clinician.

Given the increased sophistication of assessment procedures and the increased specialization of evaluation centers, why do general clinicians need to be able to conduct an interview about sexual behaviors and problems? There are at least four reasons.

First, sexual problems often influence nonsexual behavior. For example, a common side effect of some medications is change in sexual functioning (Barnes, Bambor, & Watson, 1979). However, because people tend to be uncomfortable talking about sexual problems, they frequently prefer to stop taking their medication rather than ask about their sexual difficulties. Thus sexual problems are one of the chief causes of noncompliance with medication. For example a man precipitated a myocardial infarction by stopping his antihypertensive medication when he realized (correctly) that it was interfering with his ability to have sex. Had someone taken the time to discuss this common side effect, the man's heart attack might have been prevented. It is always a mistake to assume that sexual functioning is a trivial concern. Unfortunately, however, even experienced clinicians sometimes forget this, especially when treating elderly, developmentally disabled, or handicapped people.

A second reason for conducting an interview about sexual behaviors and problems is that society expects clinicians to be knowledgeable about sexual problems. Sexual behaviors, which used to be the concern of specialists, are now everyone's concern. Many legislatures now require clinicians to report to state authorities people under their care whom they suspect to be sexual abusers (Jellinek, Murphy, Bishop, Poitrost, & Quinn, 1990).

A third reason is that, in the final analysis and despite many advances in assessment procedures, the clinical interview is still the "gold standard" against which all other assessment techniques are measured. If the clinician does not consider sexual problems and is unable to conduct an interview concerning them, or the person is unwilling to discuss such issues, many problems are likely to remain undiscovered and therefore go untreated.

Finally, attending to sexual concerns and difficulties is simply part of caring for people who seek our help. Consider the following case example:

A 65-year-old woman presented with depression. During the initial interview, I learned that she had had a colostomy for 10 years following a successful operation for cancer of the bowel. Since then she had become increasingly withdrawn and anxious that her husband would leave her. She had not responded to antidepressant medication. When asked whether she or her husband had experienced any sexual problems since her operation, she looked at me in shock—not because I had asked her about sex but because she had thought that sex was not possible with a colostomy. She had assumed that it was forbidden. Both she and her husband were unhappy with this situation but were too embarrassed to seek help or advice. As a consequence, she and her husband had moved into separate bedrooms and had not had sexual intercourse for 10 years.

The remainder of the interview focused on reassuring this woman that sexual activity was possible and quite safe following a colostomy operation. The next week I learned that following our conversation she had gone home and told her husband that sex was not prohibited. That night they checked into a local motel and had sex for the first time in 10 years. On her next visit, all symptoms of depression had vanished. She also brought her husband with her who shook my hand vigorously and said, "My wife and I have needed help for 10 years. In all that time no one ever asked us about sex. Why has it taken so long?"

Conducting an interview includes asking questions about sexual functioning, concerns, and problems. This article discusses ways to make this important task easier.

TYPES OF INTERVIEW

Not all sex interviews are the same. A common mistake is to assume that the nature of an interview is determined by its topic. However, clinical sexual and nonsexual interviews are more alike than are clinical and research interviews that both deal with sexual issues. Thus therapists who would like to conduct clinical sexual interviews should be reassured that their clinical experience is directly applicable to conducting such interviews.

Table 84–1 lists several types of interviews, together with the chief purpose and typ-

Table 84–1
Types of Interviews

Style	Purpose	Characteristic
Talk show	Entertainment	Superficial, leading questions
Survey	Population-based	Extensive, menu-type
Forensic	Court report	Nonspeculative, multiple informants
Therapeutic	Alleviation of problem	Feelings more important than facts
Diagnostic	Individual assessment	Problem-oriented

ical characteristics of the interview. Each type of interview could involve sexual topics, yet each would be very different. For example, late-night television talk-show hosts frequently discuss sex with their guests, but the purpose of their interview is entertainment. Talk-show hosts rarely ask questions to which they do not already know the answer. When the conversation becomes too intimate, the host or guest will frequently resort to humor in order to increase the entertainment value of the show (and decrease his or her own anxiety). Clearly, the interview style of a talk-show host is a poor example for clinicians to follow. People enter treatment to be helped, not to provide entertainment. Therefore, before the interview begins, the clinician should always let the interviewee know how the information will be recorded, who will have access to it, and what will be done with it.

Clinicians should always be honest about the purpose of the interview. Is the interview part of ongoing psychotherapy? Will it be used to generate a court report? Is it part of a research project? Because the purpose of the interview affects how the interview will be conducted, the interviewee needs to know why the interview is being conducted, especially when the interview may be used for more than one purpose. Freud's work provides an example of the sort of problems that can occur when this principle is not followed. Many of his interviews were conducted for the purpose of psychotherapeutic treatment. As part of this process, he trained his patients to speak their thoughts without censoring themselves. However, when the purpose of his interviews changed from psychotherapy to data collection in support of his developing theory of personality, Freud found it difficult to interpret what he learned. For example, during psychotherapy sessions, many of his patients reported having had sexual relations with their parents, but one could not be sure whether these reports represented fantasy or reality (Masson, 1984).

OPENING THE INTERVIEW

After explaining the purpose of the interview, the clinician should be sure that the interviewee agrees to be interviewed and knows why he or she is being interviewed. Sexual problems are extremely difficult for couples to discuss. Commonly, the person with the problem remains quiet and lets the partner do the talking. It is not unusual to discover that the man who is referred for treatment because he shows too little interest in sex has never heard this complaint directly from his wife and is surprised to discover that this is the purpose of his appointment with the therapist.

ESTABLISHING RAPPORT

After opening the interview, some level of mutual understanding should be achieved. This process is facilitated if the interviewee feels he or she is understood and will not be judged prematurely. The clinician should clarify all terminology, especially terms such as "making love," "sexual problems," or other euphemisms. Technical terms without mutually agreed upon definitions can also be misleading. For example, a man who says he has "premature ejaculation" may actually have inhibited sexual desire, erectile dysfunction, retarded ejaculation, retrograde ejaculation, or anorgasmia. In fact, assumptions of any type are dangerous. For example, one couple went to a sexual dysfunction clinic with the complaint that the male partner ejaculated after two minutes of sexual intercourse. The clinician interviewing the man began by explaining that he would be asking some questions about premature ejaculation. Fortunately, the man quickly interrupted to say that his wife disliked sex and complained that he took too long! Thus the clinician had made an incorrect assumption about what this couple thought their problem was based on the clinician's preconceived ideas of normal sexual behavior.

Rapport tends to increase when people feel that they are in control. In a clinical interview, it helps to tell people that they do not have to answer every question and that they can stop the interview if they feel uncomfortable. They should be encouraged to ask for clarification if they don't understand a question. People who are at ease will generally provide more information about themselves. Rapport is also facilitated if the interviewee is convinced that the *clinician* will not lose control. Clinicians frequently underestimate the degree to which clients try to protect them. A person with a shocking secret is unlikely to reveal the secret to a clinician who becomes easily flustered. Talking about sexual matters may be a new experience for some people. Some may not have achieved this level of intimacy even with their own sexual partners. The clinician should be especially alert to transference or countertransference feelings.

IDENTIFICATION OF PROBLEMS

During this stage the clinician should focus on the main purpose of the interview, that is, identifying specific problems that the clinician can help resolve. People tend to be embarrassed by or ashamed of sexual problems and prefer that the clinician "discover" the problem. People tend to be unsure about what "normal" sexuality is and often attempt to find out what the interviewer thinks is normal before committing themselves. Thus the clinician should beware of answering questions about "normal" sexual behavior.

At this point in the interview, the clinician should discourage the client from offering explanations for his or her behavior. Try to "stick with facts." As in other areas of life, people who have one sexual problem often have several. Usually people will start the interview by stating the problem that they consider to be the least abnormal or least distressing. The clinician should not settle for the first sexual problem mentioned or discovered. The clinician should try to convey the impression that he or she is knowledgeable about sexuality and is unlikely to be overwhelmed by the person's current problem. Closed-ended questions, to which replies of "yes" or "no" can be made, should be avoided by the clinician. Finally, the practitioner should not jump to conclusions in diagnosing a problem. Sexual problems are extremely complex and usually involve at least two people. If only one of the parties is interviewed, the clinician knows only half the story at most.

BACKGROUND INFORMATION

The first part of the interview can be used to establish what the presenting problems are, after which the therapist should obtain some background information about the person and the problem. It is helpful to ask the person his or her opinion of the problem. In my experience, these theories are usually wrong but always informative. For example, it is helpful to know early in treatment that the married man with erectile dysfunction has had an affair and believes his problem is an early symptom of syphilis.

This section of the interview can often be less structured. However, it helps to proceed in a chronological direction—either from the present backward or from the past forward. People generally provide more complete information if they are able to place it in the context of other important life events. Frequently, in the process of tracing the exact course of a problem new insights into possible causes emerge. For example, a man who presents with the complaint of premature ejaculation "all his life" may be asked whether he had this problem before he was married, before he left home, before he graduated from school, and so forth.

COMPLETING THE INTERVIEW

When is the interview over? Most interviewers agree that a single interview of more than 90 minutes is too long. Usually, it is better to have several shorter interviews. It may help to say how much time is available at the start of the interview. If people know they have only one hour, they may get to the crux of the problem faster. Other important interview topics include what the person thinks will happen if he or she doesn't get treatment. Does the person think he or she will ever get better? What type of therapy, if any, does the person think he or she needs?

At this point, the clinician should do a mental check of items to be covered. What is the primary problem? What does the person think the problem is? What does the partner think the problem is? Is the chronology clear? Does the story have any gaps? Why did the person seek help at this time? Leave the door open for further elaboration, as people are rarely able to tell their whole story in a single interview. They may hold back vital pieces of information until after they evaluate the interviewer. The clinician should double check to be sure the interview hasn't focused on the wrong issues. A comment such as the following may help: "I've asked you a lot of questions, but every person is different. What other things that we haven't discussed today have you wondered about?"

CLOSING THE INTERVIEW

During the last few minutes of the interview, the clinician should briefly summarize what he or she has learned. The clinician should state what will happen next: schedule another appointment? an interview with the partner? referral to a specialist? A simple statement such as the following may be reassuring:

> People frequently have concerns like yours about their sexual behavior and I am glad you have trusted me enough to tell me about them. We've covered a lot of ground today and you are likely to have other thoughts about what we have talked about. If you think of anything or have any concerns, you can reach me at _____.

The point here is to reassure the person that he or she has made the right decision to seek help and to leave the door open for further dialogue. Finally, the clinician should always give the person a chance to ask questions.

HELPFUL TECHNIQUES

Much of the advice discussed in the foregoing sections of this article applies equally well to nonsexual clinical interviews. Several techniques, however, are especially helpful in taking sex histories. With experience, most clinicians develop their own strategies and techniques. The following techniques may be useful to clinicians with little experience in this area (Money, 1986).

Sportscaster Technique

As mentioned earlier, it is often a mistake to invite the interviewee to spend too much time speculating on his or her behavior or problem. The "sportscaster technique" can help avoid this pitfall. Ask the person to describe an event as though he or she were a sportscaster and the event was happening right now. Typically, the person will begin talking in the past tense or start offering explanations or justifications about his or her behavior. However, after being interrupted and reminded to tell the story as if it were actually occurring, people will often begin describing important details that would have been left out otherwise. The effect can be enhanced by asking for details: for example, "What do you hear?" This technique helps the clinician learn how the event was experienced.

Topics in the Public Domain

Discussing sexual behavior with a stranger provokes anxiety in most people. However, people are often less anxious about discussing the sexual problems of others. In some cases, clinicians can encourage people to talk about sexual problems by introducing the topic through a reference to a recent news story or event. For example, attitudes toward homosexuality can be elicited by bringing up the topic of AIDS. Sexual abuse can be investigated by mentioning recent cases in the news.

Alternative Names, Hypothetical Situations

Sometimes it helps to ask the interviewee to imagine particular situations. Transsexual interests and attitudes toward the opposite sex can be assessed by asking whether the person has ever had a dream (or nightmare) about being the opposite sex. Has the person ever imagined he or she had a different name? Sometimes it's easier for people to talk about sensitive issues if they don't have to admit to their own participation. For this reason, people often find it easier to discuss sensitive topics in the subjunctive mood: What would happen if . . . ?

Sexual Fantasy Letters

As many know, some popular sex magazines regularly publish letters describing the sexual adventures of their readers. Even if clients have never read such a letter, it is often possible to convince them to compose the sort of letter they would write to such a magazine if they were to describe their "most unusual sexual experience," "best sexual experience," or the like. People who are embarrassed to talk about sex often find it easier to write about it. Asking what a person's most unusual sexual experience is elicits information about what the person *thinks* is unusual as well as about actual behavior. Asking about fantasies is especially important when evaluating paraphilic sexual disorders because responses may provide clues about the nature of the disorder. For example, a man who presents with a complaint of exhibitionism and who describes fantasies of being seen by children should be carefully evaluated for pedophilia.

Projection

It is always useful to know what the client thinks will happen in the future. By asking the person what the future will be like with and without treatment, the clinician can estimate the person's commitment to treatment. This technique also provides an index of how hopeful or hopeless the person is feeling.

CONCLUSION

Assessing sexual functioning requires the same kinds of skills used in assessing other aspects of people's lives. However, assessing sexual functioning is complicated by the reluctance of clinicians and clients to talk about sex due to embarrassment, shyness, or lack of knowledge. Probably the best advice on how to conduct a good sex interview can be found in Freud's papers on how to conduct psychoanalytic interviews. The principles that he advocated included avoiding clinician self-disclosure, encouraging the patient to speak freely about anything that comes to mind without censorship, and attention to dreams and fantasies (Freud, 1958).

Of the thousands of interviews that I have conducted, I have never had a patient become upset or angry because I have asked a question about sex. Some say they would rather not discuss that area of their lives and we move on to another topic. However, many more people have thanked me for giving them a chance to talk about their sexual difficulties or concerns. Sexual interviewing certainly becomes easier with practice. In the final analysis, the clinical history should be tailored to the skills of the clinician and the needs of the individual seeking help. If it is done correctly, the person is left with the impression that he or she can talk about any aspect of his or her life with an understanding, competent professional who sincerely wishes to help.

REFERENCES

American Psychiatric Association. (1987). *Diagnostic and statistical manual of mental disorders* (3rd ed., rev.). Washington, DC: Author.

Barnes, T. R. E., Bambor, R. W. K., & Watson, J. P. (1979). Psychotropic drugs and sexual behaviour. *British Journal of Hospital Medicine, 21,* 327–340.

Berlin, F., & Meinecke, C. (1981). Treatment of sex offenders with antiandrogenic medication, conceptualization review of treatment modalities and preliminary findings. *American Journal of Psychiatry, 138,* 601–607.

Berlin, F. S. (1983). Sex offenders: A biomedical perspective and a status report on biomedical treatment. In J. G. Greer & I. R. Stuart (Eds.), *The sexual aggressor: Current perspectives and treatment.* New York: Van Nostrand Reinhold.

Crown, S., & Lucas, C. J. (1976). Individual psychotherapy. In S. Crown (Ed.), *Psychosexual problems.* London: Academic Press.

Derogatis, L. R., & Melisaratos, N. (1979). The DSFI: A multidimensional measure of sexual functioning. *Journal of Sex and Marital Therapy, 5,* 244–281.

Freud, S. (1958). On beginning the treatment (Further recommendations on the technique of psychoanalysis). In J. Stackey, A. Freud, A. Strachey, & A. Tyson (Eds.), *The standard edition of the complete psychological works of Sigmund Freud.* London: The Hogarth Press.

Freund, K., & Blanchard, R. (1989). Phallometric diagnosis of pedophilia. *Journal of Consulting and Clinical Psychology, 57,* 100–105.

Jellinek, M. S., Murphy, J. M., Bishop, S., Poitrost, E, & Quinn, D. (1990). Protecting severely abused and neglected children—An unkept promise. *New England Journal of Medicine, 323,* 1628–1630.

Karacan, I., Scott, B., Salis, P., Attia, S., Ware, C., Altinel, A. & Williams, R. (1977). Nocturnal erections, differential diagnosis of impotence and diabetes. *Biological Psychiatry 12,* 373–380.

Kinsey, A. G., Pomeroy, W. B., & Martin. C. E. (1948). *Sexual behavior in the human male.* Philadelphia: Saunders.

Krafft-Ebing, R. (1899). *Psychopathia sexualis with special reference to antipathic sexual instinct: A medicoforensic study.* London: Rebman Limited.

Leiblum, S. R., Rosen, R. C., & Piere, D. (1976). Group treatment format: Mixed sexual dysfunctions. *Archives of Sexual Behavior, 5,* 313–322.

Masson, J. M. (1984). *The assault on truth: Freud's suppression of the seduction theory.* New York: Farrar, Straus and Giroux.

Masters, W. H., & Johnston, V. E. (1970). *Human sexual inadequacy.* Boston: Little, Brown.

Money, I. (1986). Longitudinal studies in clinical psychoendocrinology: Methodology. *Journal of Developmental and Behavioral Pediatrics, 7,* 31–34.

Schmidt, G., & Schorsch, E. (1981). Psychosurgery of sexually deviant patients: Review and analysis of new empirical finding. *Archives of Sexual Behavior, 10,* 301–323.

Shiavi, R. C., Schreiner-Engel, P., Mandeli, J., Schanzer, H., & Cohen, E. (1990). Healthy aging and male sexual function. *American Journal of Psychiatry, 147,* 766–771.

Spark, R., White, R., & Connolly, P. (1980). Impotence is not always psychogenic. *Journal of the American Medical Association, 243,* 750–755.

Swett, C., Surrey, J., & Cohen, C. (1990). Sexual and physical abuse histories and psychiatric symptoms among male psychiatric outpatients. *American Journal of Psychiatry, 147,* 632–636.

SINGLE-PARENT FAMILIES

CHAPTER 85

SINGLE MOTHERS AND SUPERMYTHS

Rosemary Kiely

. . . Certain factors strike the attention of the welfare theorist because they are culturally abnormal or disapproved. The welfare worker tends to regard as determinants of illegitimacy those events which, like illegitimacy itself, are considered unfortunate and in need of remedy. Being in the habit of focusing attention upon things that require remedial work anyway, it is natural that he should fall into a species of the like-causes-like fallacy—in this case the theory that evil causes evil.[1]

When single motherhood was surrounded by shame and secrecy, it suited a moralistic public imagination to think of single mothers in terms of exaggerated stereotypes—as scarlet women, or as the tragic victims of rape or seduction.

The growing public acceptance of single mothers that has accompanied the liberalization of sex mores and the growing independence of women in modern industrialized societies has made these older myths harder to sustain. But more subtle forms have risen to replace them. These later myths have originated in the impressions of some less enlightened members of the helping professions to whose doors the least fortunate single mothers have been driven by their lack of personal and family resources. Such people have a vested interest in reducing the welfare tax burden which, as members of the affluent middle class, they have to bear, while their employment depends on the existence of a pool of underprivileged families to be their clientele, and to supply babies for their adoption market.

Much of the early research performed by overseas social workers, psychologists and medicos upon their captive clients assumed that there must have been something wrong in the mothers' backgrounds to make them commit such anti-social folly, and they set out to find out what it was. The causes identified varied over the years with the changing fashions in social theory.[2] In the early twentieth century, reflecting evolutionary the-

Reprinted from *Australian Journal of Social Issues*, Vol. 17, No. 2 (May, 1982), pp. 155–161, by permission of the publisher.

ories of the time, single mothers were seen as victims of inherited tendencies to immorality or mental retardation.

In the thirties, the search shifted to environmental conditions: broken homes, poverty and social instability. Later in the thirties and forties, ex-nuptial pregnancy came to be seen as a subcultural phenomenon. The prevailing professional view of the psychologically oriented fifties and sixties was that single mothers were victims of an unconscious masochistic drive for ex-nuptial pregnancy which originated in abnormal family patterns. Their neuroses made them unfit to rear their babies.[3]

While it is possible that all of these theories explained why some women became single mothers, the upsurge in ex-nuptial births to women of all childbearing ages and social classes that accompanied the liberalization of attitudes to sex in the affluence of the post Second World War years showed that none of these stereotypes had any general application.

As the methodology of social research improved most of these interpretations were discredited. The myth of psychodynamic causation was dealt its most effective blow by an American researcher, Pauker, who used data from a statewide survey of adolescents in Minnesota to compare those who subsequently became pregnant with those who did not.[4] Pauker was unable to find any evidence that the schoolgirls who subsequently became pregnant were more disturbed than the other schoolgirls, but when he compared them with a group of pregnant girls in a Minnesota maternity home he found a higher level of personality disturbance among the latter. This suggested that personality disturbance was a result of the experience of pre-marital pregnancy in a maternity home, rather than a cause.

Nevertheless the notion that single mothers are generally disturbed adolescents in the grip of fantasies which make them unfit mothers has never quite lost its appeal.

Its latest manifestation is the 'Superdoll Syndrome'. According to this theory, as outlined by social and charity workers interviewed in the press in recent years, 'to a certain type of immature girl who has had a rotten homelife, a baby has become a kind of superior walkie-talkie doll', and 'the number of young teenage girls from unhappy homes who are deliberately setting out to become pregnant so that they will have "something to love" is swelling alarmingly'.[5] This 'new phenomenon' only reached these frightening proportions after the Supporting Mother's Benefit began. This 'well-defined and depressing trend' is associated with the assertion that 'a lot of older girls are electing to keep their babies and when they find it is more than they can cope with, the baby is offered for adoption at two or three years'. A variant of this theory contends that many schoolgirls are choosing single motherhood as 'a way out of the dole queue'.

Like the older mythology, this new formulation is likely to erode public support for single mothers keeping their children, to anaesthetize the sympathies of those professionally engaged in helping them, and to provide a rationale for adoption oriented case work. The Superdoll Syndrome appears to be as mythical as its predecessors, for none of its components is supported by the facts about single mothers from survey and statistical evidence.

Firstly, available survey evidence indicates that only a small proportion of single mothers become pregnant deliberately. Out of a sample of 93 single mothers studied by this writer in 1973-4, only a quarter said they had planned or wanted to be pregnant.[6] They tended to be older than the other single mothers, and their pregnancies were asso-

ciated with what the mothers apparently hoped would be continuing, loving relationships with the fathers of their babies, or with bereavement after the loss of an earlier
child through adoption, abortion or death.

On the other hand, the main reason why teenagers had become pregnant was lack of
knowledge of contraception. They were less educated, had lower status occupations
and came from less cohesive families than those who had been older when they became
pregnant. The teenage single mothers had found single motherhood more of a battle
and less satisfying than other single mothers, but more of them had either married since
the birth or were confident they would marry. What this adds up to is that teenagers
were a disadvantaged minority among single mothers, but they generally had not chosen their course, and they were less likely than other mothers to remain single.

Second, there is the claim that the introduction of Supporting Mother's Benefit in
1973 has led to an increase in the number of women (particularly teenagers) having and
keeping ex-nuptial children. The introduction of this Benefit did not lead to an increase
in ex-nuptial births to teenagers. Ex-nuptial confinements in Australia declined from
1972 to 1976, and the proportion of ex-nuptial births to teenagers has continued to decline from 41.8% in 1972 to 36.2% in 1979. This means that more than 60% of ex-
nuptial births are to mothers aged 20 or more. The average age of single mothers (at the
time of birth) in Victoria has risen from 22.8 years in 1972 to 23.3 in 1979,[8] a fact
which seems to have been overlooked by those who were vociferous in their alarm
when single mothers were getting younger, as well as by the Superdoll theorists. This
rise is probably due to the increasing availability of contraception and abortion to
teenagers, and to the increase in the number of children born to older women in cohab-
iting unions. A British analysis of different outcomes of ex-nuptial pregnancy to women
of different ages found that of the different categories (termination, marriage during
pregnancy, birth registered by the father, and birth registered by the mother), the only
one which increased between 1964 and 1976 was births to women over 25, registered
by the fathers.[9] This, when taken alongside the current decline in the Australian first
marriage rate, indicates that the increase in ex-nuptial births since 1976 is probably due
to an increase in the number of couples who live and rear children together without
legal marriage.

The statistics also contradict what Montague described in her research as a general
impression that rising unemployment had led to an epidemic of teenage single parenthood.[10] The teenage ex-nuptial birth rate rose in the late sixties and early seventies
when unemployment rates were steady, and began to decline as unemployment rates
started to climb after 1973.

Apart from the increasing age and declining numbers of women giving birth ex-nup-
tially, the other major trend affecting single mothers in the seventies has been the declining proportion who give up their babies for adoption. This trend is common to all
Australian States and to Britain.[11] It is reasonable to suggest that the introduction of
government welfare payments has allowed more single mothers to keep their babies,
particularly in Victoria where until 1969 there was no social welfare payment for a single mother who kept her child, unless she was sick, unemployed (and looking for work)
or breastfeeding.

But it is not a satisfactory or complete explanation for the trend in other states,
where Supporting Parent's Benefit has merely replaced state benefits for single mothers,

or in Britain, where the rising proportion of single mothers keeping their babies was not accompanied by any change in welfare provisions. Instead we must look to the fundamental changes in mores in western industrialized nations, to explain why fewer single mothers now feel compelled to place their babies for adoption.

There has always been a moral conflict for single mothers deciding about adoption. On one hand, mothers are supposed to stand by their young and defend them against all odds. On the other hand, when the institution of marriage was regarded as the only morally defensible environment for rearing children, there was strong pressure to conform to the marriage norm by relinquishing children for adoption by a married couple.

Changes in marriage mores over the past two decades have reduced pressures of the second kind on single mothers. Pre-marital sex is no longer widely regarded as immoral, and many children of married couples are brought up today in one-parent families due to the dissolution of marriages.

A new emphasis on human relationships rather than material standards encourages single mothers to believe that if they love and want their children they should keep them, despite material problems.

As we learn of the experience of adopted people through organizations such as Jigsaw, their explicit loyalty and gratitude to their adoptive parents fail to conceal evident distress for many at their separation from their natural parents. This, and the long term bereavement suffered by natural mothers who have placed children for adoption, means that adoption has not been the tidy solution it seemed at the time of the mass adoption of the ex-nuptial babies of the post-war baby boom. In retrospect, it seems that adoption was an attempt to promote the norm of marriage and the values of affluence and materialism at the expense of personal ties and inner feelings.

The decline in the adoption traffic has left adoption agencies free to devote more resources to the placement of children with special needs. Children left homeless at an older age or in sibling groups because of death or misfortune, or whose physical or mental handicaps made them unadoptable when new babies were in plentiful supply, and who would then have spent their childhoods in institutions, and now being adopted and the institutional children's homes are being emptied. Now that more single mothers are keeping their babies there has been a dramatic increase in the adoptions by 'natural parent and spouse' in Victoria from 226 in 1972-3 to 540 in 1978-9.[12] Studies have found that after a few years the overwhelming majority of single mothers rear their children either in nuclear families with the father or step-father or in extended families with relatives or non-relatives. In my study, the mothers who lived on their own with their children managed as well or better than those in larger households.

A third misleading implication of the Superdoll label is that single mothers will discard their babies when they have tired of them. This is an old saw, dating from before the payment of benefits to single mothers in Victoria. Johns, in a follow up study of 90 ex-nuptial children born in 1968, found it 'most worthy of note' that at the end of three years only six children who had been kept at birth by natural mothers were known to be living outside their care.[13] She said, 'This would seem to contradict a belief popularly held in this country that a considerable proportion of single mothers return their children for adoption before the age of three years'. The proportion of single mothers placing their children for adoption when they are past infancy in Victoria has declined since the introduction of Family Assistance payments for single mothers in 1969 and of Supporting Mother's Benefit in 1973.[14] In 1966-7 the number of children placed for adoption over the age of one represented 3.6% of all children kept by single mothers in the previous year. By 1978-9 this proportion was down to 1.6%, despite the new directions in adoption which probably meant that an increasing proportion of these children were the 'unadoptables' of previous years.

The Superdoll Syndrome is no new phenomenon, but rather a rehash of several old myths which, insofar as they represent a tendency to see single mothers in terms of derogatory stereotypes, are probably a reincarnated form of moral prejudice.

In the climate of moral and social reaction ushered in by the recession of the late seventies, it is quite likely that single mother bashing will become a popular practice for the affluent middle classes, for whom the tax and welfare cuts of supply side economics offer a means of hanging on to what they managed to get in the earlier boom years, and of making the most of any resource led recovery.

But if there is a new revolution of technological and social styles, based perhaps on a fusion breakthrough, then all this will be forgotten. Moral and social choices will once again expand, as they did in the fifties and sixties, the single parent family will increase in numbers and viability until we reach a 'natural' proportion of women in society who will choose to rear their children without the trammelling assistance of a resident male, and there will be more wringing of hands by doctrinaire moralists who will remember the golden seventies and early eighties.

REFERENCES

1. Davis, K., Illegitimacy and the Social Structure, *American Journal of Sociology,* 1939, 45, 217–8.

2. See reviews of the literature in Kronick, J., An Assessment of Research Knowledge Concerning the Unmarried Mother, in Roberts, R. W. (ed.), *The Unwed Mother,* New York: Harper & Row, 1966; Vincent, C., *Unmarried Mothers,* New York: Free Press, 1961.

3. For example, Young, L., *Out of Wedlock,* New York: McGraw-Hill, 1954; Clothier, F., Psychological Implications of Unmarried Parenthood. *American Journal of Orthopsychiatry,* 1943, 13, 531–549.

4. Pauker, J., Girls Pregnant out of Wedlock, in Wrieden, J., et al., *The Double Jeopardy: The Triple Crisis—Illegitimacy Today,* New York: National Council on Illegitimacy, 1969.

5. The Superdoll Phenomenon, *National Times,* 27 October 1979; Motherhood . . . the Alternative, *The Age,* 27 February 1980.

6. Kiely, R., Single Mothers in Society, unpublished MA thesis, University of Melbourne, 1979, pp. 154–172, 215–218, 305.

7. Calculated from figures supplied by the Australian Bureau of Statistics.

8. *Demography: Summary Statement—Victoria, 1977–1981,* Melbourne: Australian Bureau of Statistics, 1981.

9. *Social Trends, London,* No. 9, London: Central Statistical Office, 1979.

10. Montague, M. *Labour Force or Labour Ward; Is This a Choice Young Women are Making?* Research Report, Melbourne: Brotherhood of St Laurence, 1981.

11. Victorian Social Welfare Department, *Annual Reports,* 1971–1979; National

Council for One-Parent Families, *Annual Report* 1977–8, p. 40; and figures supplied by the Australian Bureau of Statistics.

12. Victorian Community Welfare Service Department, *Annual Report,* 1978–9, and figures supplied by the department in 1974.

13. Johns, N., *The Health of Babies Kept by their Single Mothers: a Study of the First Years of Life of a Melbourne Sample.* Unpublished DM thesis, University of Melbourne, 1974.

14. Calculated from figures supplied by the Australian Bureau of Statistics, Victorian Office, and in Victorian Community Welfare Services Department, *Annual Reports,* 1967–1979.

CHAPTER 86

LONE FATHERS IN THE UNITED STATES

An Overview and Practice Implications

Geoffrey L. Greif

For almost twenty years, fathers raising their children alone following a marital separation or the death of the mother have been a source of interest to researchers in Great Britain. George and Wilding's (1972) classic work on 588 fathers drawn from the caseloads of health, education and social services departments throughout the country was the first of a number of projects that were published in the next few years (see, for example Ferri, 1973; Murch, 1973; Ferri and Robinson, 1976). A wave of research in the United States followed and, since the late 1970s, the US has been the source of a number of other studies of this population. This article will provide an overview of the research in the United States on the lone father. It will then discuss some of the implications for social work that flow from this review and from the author's work with this population. Because of the potential similarities between the two cultures it is hoped that this information will aid social work practice with lone fathers in Great Britain and foster the future exchange of information.

Fathers with custody (usually defined as having primary responsibility for the children a majority of the time) have become an increasingly important family form to study as their numbers have grown. In 1970 there were 393,000 male head of households in the US raising alone at least one child under the age of eighteen. By 1990, the number had more than tripled to 1,351,000. The number of mothers raising children alone in 1990 was 8,398,000 (US Department of Commerce, 1990). In that twenty-year period the number of fathers raising children alone as a percentage of total single parent families increased by about one-third to 14 percent, while the percentage of mothers dropped to 86 per cent (US Department of Commerce, 1990). Similarly, the

Reprinted from *British Journal of Social Work*, Vol. 22, No. 5 (1992), pp. 565–574, by permission of Oxford University Press.

number of children being raised alone by fathers almost tripled to 1,993,000 between 1970 and 1990. The number of children being raised by mothers nearly doubled to 13,874,000 (US Department of Commerce, 1991).

A range of reasons has been given for the growing numbers of lone fathers. Chief among them is the trend toward equalization of the sexes and the growing use of gender-free laws in deciding custody arrangements (Keshet and Rosenthal, 1976; Mendes, 1976; Bartz and Witcher, 1978; DeFrain and Eirick, 1981). This has made it easier for men to gain custody in the US. Fathers also seem to be displaying a greater interest in fathering, in their own relationship with their father, and their role as a man, as evidenced by recent journal articles related to men's issues (see, for example, Napier, 1991). Women, in turn, are finding more options for how they wish to define themselves and may no longer feel as compelled to retain custody to avoid public censure as they did in the past (Greif and Pabst, 1988).

Lone fathers pose new challenges to social workers. Social workers, like the rest of US society, often hold stereotypical views about the role of the mother and the father in the family which can impede work with them. When fathers move into the traditionally female role of primary parent, until recently, there have been few models available to guide work with them. Normative data have been lacking. These fathers need help in terms of their relations with school personnel, health care professionals, and the court system, where many of the custody arrangements that in the past went almost automatically to the mother are now being adjudicated or mediated. As a profession concerned with the fit between families and societal institutions, social workers play an important role in helping these fathers and their children adapt.

EARLY STUDIES OF LONE FATHERS

Unlike George and Wilding's systematic attempt to gain a sample from a wealth of counties, the early US studies used convenience samples usually gained from one region of the country. Respondents were drawn largely from snowball sampling, advertisements, attorneys, contacts with local agencies where fathers might seek help, and outreach to self-help groups. Occasionally widowers and divorced fathers were combined in samples. These early studies, almost all of which were undertaken during the 1970s, used small samples (the nine cited here had an average n of 33) and were drawn primarily from middle-class white respondents. They were descriptive in nature, acknowledged the difficulties facing fathers in this new role, and were generally upbeat in their findings (Gasser and Taylor, 1976; Keshet and Rosenthal, 1976; Mendes, 1976a; Orthner et al., 1976; Bartz and Witcher, 1978; Gersick, 1979; DeFrain and Eirick, 1981; Hanson, 1981; Smith and Smith, 1981).

The potential problem areas identified in the research included: handling children's emotional needs (Bartz and Witcher, 1978; Keshet and Rosenthal, 1976; DeFrain and Eirick, 1981); feeling the necessity to prove themselves as being capable, caring parents (Mendes, 1976a; DeFrain and Eirick, 1981); dealing with loneliness and the loss of companionship of the wife (DeFrain and Eirick, 1981); experiencing some potential discomfort in raising daughters (Orthner et al., 1976; Bartz and Witcher, 1978); not having enough time for and being bored with house chores (Gasser and Taylor, 1976;

Bartz and Witcher, 1978); finding adequate day care while at work (Mendes, 1976a; Bartz and Witcher, 1978; Keshet and Rosenthal, 1976); being torn between the children and work (Orthner et al., l976); dating (Gasser and Taylor, 1976); and being forced to raise the children alone when a shared or no custody arrangement had been preferred (Mendes, 1976b; Hanson, 1981).

Occasionally, comparison samples were employed in the research. DeFrain and Eirick (1981), using a like sized sample of lone mothers, found few differences between the parent groups with the exceptions that fathers had more income, experienced more residential stability, and were more likely to encourage their children to side with them against the mother, a behaviour rarely admitted to by the mothers. Gersick (1979) compared custodial and noncustodial fathers and found that the more angry the father felt at the ex-wife, the more apt he was to seek custody. Lone fathers were reported to have been closer to their mothers and more distant from their fathers when growing up than were fathers living away from their children. Rosenthal and Keshet (1981) also compared lone fathers with those living away from their children and found the first group to have more residential stability, less contact with the children's mother, and to be less likely to have chosen this custody arrangement. Gasser and Taylor (1976), in looking at a third possible basis for comparison, divorced lone fathers and widowers, found the former to be better adjusted than the latter.

Most of the early research concluded that fathers are capable of raising children alone and that their relationships with their children improve with this arrangement. The need for more education and support for the fathers was a common recommendation, as was making day care more readily available.

STUDIES FROM THE 1980s

In the 1980s, interest in US lone fathers grew. Chang and Deinard (1982), drawing the biggest US sample to that point in time (n=80), supported earlier claims of the satisfaction experienced by fathers. Finding time to spend with the children and battling against depression proved to be the most serious hurdles. The children's adaptation became a focus of some research. In one study, lone fathers reported greater satisfaction with their children's behaviour and greater expression of appreciation by their children towards them than did lone mothers (Ambert, 1982). Santrock and Warshak (1979) had earlier found that children may do better when raised by the same sex parent.

By the mid 1980s, larger and more nationally derived samples were being gathered which allowed for better statistical tests of relationships. Working in 1982 in conjunction with the largest self-help group for single parents in the US, Parents Without Partners (affiliated with Ginger in Great Britain), Greif compiled a sample of 1,137 lone fathers from 48 different states and Canada (Greif, 1985a–d). In a second survey undertaken in 1987–8, using the same method and gaining a similarly sized sample, Greif and DeMaris (1989; 1990; and Greif, 1990) confirmed some of the previous research and looked at a new set of issues. In both research efforts the tasks facing lone fathers were divided into six areas: housekeeping and child care; father–child relations; the father's relations with his ex-wife; dating; working while childrearing; and contact with the court system. Using the theory of role ambiguity, fathers were viewed as being potentially at a loss how to fulfil a role for which there were competing demands and for which no models existed. Nearly 40 per cent of the fathers reported that arriving at a custody decision was stressful for them (Greif, 1985a). Fathers felt they were treated dichotomously—perceived on the one hand to be wonderful parents because they were a male parenting alone, yet seen as being incompetent on the other (Greif, 1985b). Despite this stress, like previous fathers studied, they were generally pleased with their parenting situation.

In specific areas it was found that housekeeping was troublesome at the beginning but did not pose a continual obstacle to well-being (Greif, 1985b; 1985d). Fathers turned more to daughters than sons for help with the daily chores (Greif, 1985c). Fathers were often dissatisfied with child care, with half of them leaving children under 18 alone after school for some period of time. This appeared to be a particularly acute problem for fathers with children in the 5- to 11-year-old range, one-fifth of whom left the children on their own (Greif, 1985b).

Father–child relations were characterized as good. When examining the father's relationship with the children and controlling for age and sex, pre-adolescent daughters were the most satisfactory for the fathers to raise (Greif, 1990). Fathers raising girls, though, were also more apt to have had to battle for them in court than fathers raising boys (Greif and DeMaris, 1989). Relations between the father and the ex-wife tended to vary greatly. No significant trends were found in these relationships other than that fathers reported more satisfaction with their own parenting if there was frequent contact with the ex-wife.

Establishing a satisfactory social life and trying to balance child rearing with working were the two most difficult areas for the fathers. Even though fathers maintained fairly active social lives, with half dating once a week, most fathers were not especially satisfied socially. They reported waiting approximately three years before having a significant relationship (Greif, 1990). Social satisfaction was perceived as declining over time. More than two-thirds found it hard to work and raise children, with almost three-quarters having to undergo some adjustment related to their work (Greif, 1985b; 1990). Finally, the court system proved unpredictable to the fathers (even though they won custody) and often expensive. Most custody cases that went to the father (80 per cent) were decided without significant court involvement, with the remaining 20 per cent involving either a short or a protracted battle (Greif and DeMaris, 1989).

The situations of the lone fathers and lone mothers were compared. While it was not determined that either group was worse off, mothers were noted to struggle with the lack of social support and more financial instability, while fathers struggled with the lack of role models (Greif, 1985b). Fathers in joint or shared custody arrangements were described as being better educated, higher wage earners, and as having a more positive view of the ex-spouse than lone fathers (Greif, 1990). Despite lone fathers becoming more prevalent between the 1982 and 1988 studies, lone fathering has not become noticeably easier. Balancing the competing demands of work and parenting and establishing a social life appear increasingly difficult for the more recent group. One possible interpretation is that more exceptional men, those who knew they were pioneers in parenting, were seeking custody at the time of the first study. Since then, as it has become easier for fathers to gain custody, the pool of fathers by definition becomes more typical of all fathers and thus more difficulties arise. The fathers identified as being the most uncomfortable as parents were those who had had custody for a short period of time, were unhappy with their social life, were affiliated with a religion, were not increasing their income, and gave themselves a low rating as a parent. Poor relations with their children and having an unsettled visiting arrangement were also related (Greif and DeMaris, 1990).

Other recent research focuses both narrowly (Risman, 1986; 1987; Stewart *et al.*, 1986; Giles-Sims and Urwin, 1989; Facchino and Aron, 1990) and broadly (Nieto, 1990) on lone fathers. Risman (1986; 1987), basing her findings on a sample of 141 fathers, applied microstructural theory to test the hypothesis that 'single fathers will adopt parental behavior that more closely resembles that of women who mother than that of married fathers' (1987, p. 6). Microstructural theory refers to behaviour that is shaped not by biology and early socialization experiences but rather by opportunities and access to social networks. Her analysis supports the hypothesis.

Stewart *et al.* (1986) compared lone fathers on a variety of standardized measures with fathers without custody and married fathers (twenty respondents in each group). Lone fathers were similar to married fathers in their level of depression and anxiety, with both groups exhibiting less than fathers living away from their children. The presence of children after a marital breakup is seen as a key variable in adjustment.

Giles-Sims and Urwin (1989) examined changes that led from maternal to paternal custody among fourteen single and remarried fathers. The main reasons for a shift of custody to the father were based on mothers being overstressed and relinquishing it, on mother–child relationship problems, and on the child's seeking a closer relationship with the father. Facchino and Aron (1990), using a sample of fifty-six, also examined the method of fathers obtaining custody. No differences were found between fathers who obtained custody through mediation, litigation, and by mutual agreement with the ex-wife.

Nieto (1990), basing his findings on a sample of 213, states that slightly more than a quarter saw their living situation as deviant and that a nearly similar number were uncomfortable in the role. The typical father perceived positive regard from others, believed he performed his role well, and was not interested in remarriage at the time of the interview.

Finally, Greif (1987) re-examined fathers three years after they had participated in a previous study. Twenty-eight fathers who remained single had not changed significantly on a variety of measures. Twenty-two fathers who had remarried reported a higher level of participation in housework in their new marriage than in their previous marriage, implying some changes in their view of men's and women's roles. The level of contact the noncustodial mother had with the children had not changed significantly with the remarriage.

IMPLICATIONS FOR SOCIAL WORK PRACTICE

From the review of the literature, it would appear that many fathers report adjusting adequately to their situation. For fathers who are experiencing difficulty, the ones most likely to seek social work services, seven broad areas would appear to need addressing. The first is the general category of handling the children's emotional needs, particularly those of daughters. Fathers in the US have often been excluded and have excluded themselves from many of the daily chores of child rearing, even when both parents work (Blumstein and Schwartz, 1983). Dealing with the daily concerns of childhood, like establishing friendships, completing school work, buying clothing, going through puberty, and so on leave many fathers bewildered. They often have little knowledge about the range of behaviours that children may display. Social work interventions that focus on providing developmental data can be helpful in normalizing the parenting experience for the father. This can be especially true for the father raising a daughter. He may feel that asking for help from another woman may be an indication that he is not capable of raising his daughter alone, a common fear. The father may need permission from the social worker to involve other adult women in the daughter's life where appropriate.

The second area, experiencing loneliness, may be approached by the social worker by directly asking about it and by identifying it for the father as a common reaction. Some men deny feelings and will need help in admitting any weaknesses. Referral to support groups for single parents can be helpful with this and other child rearing problems.

Concerns about keeping the house clean may best be handled by discussing with the father realistic expectations for the home. Some fathers feel they have to maintain the house as well as it was kept when two adults lived there. Fathers need to guard against overburdening children or relieving them too easily of responsibilities (Greif, 1985c). Parentifying children, i.e. putting them in charge of younger children to an excessive degree, should be discouraged (Minuchin, 1974). The appropriate level of assistance from the children will vary with the children's ages, their capabilities, and the family's schedules.

The fourth area, balancing work and child rearing, is one of the more difficult. Fathers often judge their success as men by their success at work. Many who become lone fathers will not be able to maintain the same commitment to work as before. When a father cannot pursue a job as he could have when his wife was in the home, his self-esteem may suffer (Greif, 1990). Again, helping the father to gain a realistic appraisal of his capabilities given his changed family situation is important. A redefining of masculinity to include child care responsibilities may need to be explored.

Learning to cope with the presence or absence of the ex-spouse, the fifth area, is a necessary rite of passage for any divorced parent. Normalizing feelings of anger, hurt, rejection, or indifference can help the father to move past them. The key here is to help the father separate his role as parent from his role as ex-spouse. Clear boundaries have to be drawn so the children are not 'triangulated' between the parents if there are conflicts (Weltner, 1982).

The sixth area involves navigating the court system. Not all fathers have on-going court battles but many worry, because of the historically precarious nature of fathers in custody disputes, that they will lose custody in the future. Referral to lawyers or clinics with father-custody experience can lessen anxiety. The social worker should have some knowledge of the issues involved in custody so that appropriate expectations for any impending court proceedings can be set. The social worker should also be aware that he or she may have to testify as a witness at some future date. Careful notes of treatment plans, contact with the children, and contact with the ex-wife should be kept so as to best assist the family and the court.

Finally, the father may need help with dating. To many fathers, socializing will mean they are beginning to adapt to the divorce and life as a single person. The father who is uneasy about dating may benefit from hearing that it may take months before he will feel comfortable dating or having sexual relations. He should be advised that sexual dysfunction may be a common occurrence. The father will also have to discuss dating with his children. They may object to the fact of his dating (because it dashes their fantasy that their parents will reunite) or his choice of dates (Greif, 1990). Encouraging the father to talk to the children in advance of dating is advised so that they are not taken by surprise. In addition, the father may need help in clarifying his expectations for the person he is dating—for example, will this person be a friend, a sexual partner, or a replacement for the children's mother? These fathers tend to place greater importance on their relationship with their children than with their dates. For the dates, 'coming second' is often unsettling and adds to the difficulty around dating.

CONCLUSIONS

It can be seen that the single father has been the centre of intense interest during the last fifteen years, and particularly the last ten. He is described as adjusting well to a situation that would seem, given the demands of parenting alone and the non-traditional role he is fulfilling in the family, to be fraught with difficulties. Despite these vicissitudes, lone fatherhood is found to have a positive impact on his life and to be a wholly viable custody arrangement.

The western world is witnessing a change in the involvement of fathers and mothers in the family. Fathers are spending more time with child care responsibilities while more mothers are working outside the home. This shift has profound importance for the increase in lone fathering, the structuring of the family, and the provision of social services. Policy changes that will support fathers, as well as mothers, in having more flexibility at work, more understanding in the workplace, and more community services can go a long way towards helping these families adapt.

REFERENCES

Ambert, A.-M. (1982) 'Differences in children's behavior towards custodial mothers and custodial fathers', *Journal of Marriage and the Family*, 44, pp. 73–86.

Bartz, K. W. and Witcher, W. C. (1978) 'When father gets custody', *Children Today*, 7(5), pp. 2–6, 35.

Blumstein, P. and Schwartz, P. (1983) *American Couples*, New York, Morrow.

Chang, P. and Deinard, A. S. (1982) 'Single-father caretakers: demographic characteristics and adjustment processes', *American Journal of Orthopsychiatry*, 52, pp. 236–42.

DeFrain, J. and Eirick, R. (1981) 'Coping as divorced single parents: a comparative study of fathers and mothers', *Family Relations*, 30, pp. 265–73.

Facchino, D. and Aron, A. (1990) 'Divorced fathers with custody: method of obtaining custody and divorce adjustment', *Journal of Divorce*, 13, pp. 45–56.

Ferri, E. (1973) 'Characteristics of motherless families', *British Journal of Social Work*, 3, pp. 91–100.

Ferri, E. and Robinson, H. (1976) *Coping Alone*, London, NFER Publishing.

Gasser, R. D. and Taylor, C. M. (1976) 'Role adjustment of single parent fathers with dependent children', *The Family Coordinator*, 25, pp. 397–401.

George, V. and Wilding, P. (1972) *Motherless Families*, London, Routledge and Kegan Paul.

Gersick, K. (1979) 'Fathers by choice: divorced men who receive custody of their children', in G. Levinger and O. C. Moles (eds.) *Divorce and Separation*, New York, Basic Books, pp. 307–23.

Giles-Sims, J. and Urwin, C. (1989) 'Paternal custody and remarriage', *Journal of Divorce*, 13, pp. 65–79.

Greif, G. L. (1985*a*) 'Single fathers rearing children', *Journal of Marriage and the Family*, 47, pp. 185–91.

Grief, G. L. (1985*b*) *Single Fathers*, New York, Lexington Books. Free Press.

Greif, G. L. (1985*c*) 'Children and housework in the single father family', *Family Relations*, 34, pp. 353–7.

Greif, G. L. (1985d) 'Practice with single fathers', *Social Work in Education*, 7, pp. 231–43.

Greif, G. L. (1987) 'A longitudinal examination of single custodial fathers: implications for treatment', *American Journal of Family Therapy*, 15, pp. 253–60.

Greif, G. L. (1990) *The Daddy Track and the Single Father*, New York, Lexington Books. Free Press.

Greif. G. L. and DeMaris, A. (1989) 'Single custodial fathers in contested custody suits', *The Journal of Psychiatry and the Law*, 17, pp. 223–38.

Greif, G. L. and DeMaris, A. (1990) 'Single fathers with custody', *Families in Society*, 71, pp. 259–66.

Greif, G. L. and Pabst, M. S. (1988) *Mothers without Custody*, New York, Lexington Books. Free Press.

Hanson, S. (1981) 'Single custodial fathers and the parent–child relationship', *Nursing Research*, 30, pp. 202–4.

Keshet, H. F. and Rosenthal, K. M. (1976) 'Single parent families: a new study', *Children Today*, 7(3), pp. 13–17.

Mendes, H. A. (1976*a*) 'Single fathers', *The Family Coordinator*, 25, pp. 439–44.

Mendes, H. A. (1976*b*) 'Single fatherhood', *Social Work*, 21, pp. 308–12.

Minuchin, S. (1974) *Families and Family Therapy*, Cambridge, Harvard University Press.

Murch, M. (1973) 'Motherless families project', *British Journal of Social Work*, 3, pp. 365–76.

Napier, A. (1991) 'Heroism, men, and marriage', *Journal of Marital and Family Therapy*, 17, pp. 9–16.

Nieto, D. S. (1990) 'The custodial single father: Who does he think he is?'; *Journal of Divorce*, 13, pp. 27–43.

Orthner, D. K., Brown, T. and Ferguson, D. (1976) 'Single parent fatherhood: an emerging lifestyle', *The Family Coordinator*, 25, pp. 429–37.

Risman, B. J. (1986) 'Can men "mother"? Life as a single father', *Family Relations*, 35, pp. 95–102.

Risman, B. J. (1987) 'Intimate relationships from a microstructural perspective: men who mother', *Gender and Society*, 1, pp. 6–32.

Rosenthal, K. M. and Keshet, H. F. (1981) *Fathers without Partners*, Totowa, NJ, Rowman and Littlefield.

Santrock, J. W. and Warshak, R. A. (1979) 'Father custody and social development in boys and girls', *Journal of Social issues*, 35, pp. 112–25.

Smith, R. M. and Smith. C. W. (1981) 'Child-rearing and single parent fathers', *Family Relations*, 30, pp. 411–17.

Stewart, J. R., Schwebel, A. I. and Fine, M. A. (1986) 'The impact of custodial arrangement on the adjustment of recently divorced fathers', *Journal of Divorce*, 9, pp. 55–65.

US Department of Commerce, Bureau of the Census (1990) *Household and Family Characteristics; March 1990 and 1989* (Series P-20, No. 447), Washington, DC, US Government Printing Office.

US Department of Commerce, Bureau of the Census (1991) *Marital Status and Living Arrangements: March 1990* (Series P-20, No. 450), Washington, DC, US Government Printing Office.

Weltner, J. S. (1982) 'A structural approach to the single-parent family', *Family Process*, 21, pp. 203–10.

CHAPTER 87

PREVENTIVE INTERVENTION WITH STEPFAMILIES

Greta W. Stanton

A stepfamily is one in which children live some, most, or all of the time with two married adults, one of whom is not a biological parent. Researchers may call this family "blended," or "reconstituted," or "remarried," or "multiparent"—indeed, according to Wald, "a survey of the literature uncovered seventeen names to describe this family."[1] However, some authors and practitioners prefer the term "stepfamily"; these individuals offer help with the pejorative aspects associated with steprelationships.

There is little empirical research on remarriage and on stepparenting. A review of the research and literature listed only nine empirical studies on stepparenting since 1956 and noted that the empirical literature of the last decade is based on the responses of no more than 550 stepfamilies.[2] Articles in social work journals concerning stepfamilies have appeared more recently, as have chapters in books addressing divorce, single parents, and general family problems. Wald's comprehensive book on remarriage is, to the present author's knowledge, the first work with a complete social work perspective.[3]

Social workers need to recognize that the complexity of stepfamilies warrants our professional attention. As one of the largest groups of professionals to whom these families turn—usually with a teenager or a younger child as the presenting problem—we must define the differences between the nuclear family and the stepfamily. Stepfamilies are "healthy" (that is, socially functional) but often lack the skills to cope with new family roles. Defining the needs of these families brings us into the arena of primary prevention—a form of treatment often neglected by social workers—and leads us to

Reprinted from *Social Work*, Vol. 31, No. 3 (May–June, 1986), pp. 201–206, by permission of NASW Press. Copyright 1986, National Association of Social Workers, Inc., *Social Work*.

begin developing and evaluating different models of intervention. A mandate arises as well to update the structure of agency services and to offer new educational service models to this emerging client population, which can be temporarily vulnerable as it passes through transitional life stages.

UNIQUE PROBLEMS

Current research efforts suggest that the problems associated with stepfamilies are unique to the multiparent family system. Such research lists interpersonal stress as the major problem in all steprelationships. Stress is manifested in parent-child, sibling, and marital relationships and in relationships among extended family members. The following are among the causes of stress identified: (1) discontinuities in children's socialization experiences and in parent-child bonding processes; (2) conflicting lifestyles of biological families and stepfamilies; (3) power and authority issues; (4) distribution of material and emotional resources; (5) different phases of family members' life cycles; and (6) changes in children's ordinal position in the family. In addition, incongruity of expectations and ambiguity regarding appropriate behavior for steprelationships seem to be underlying themes of troubled stepfamilies. Some clients liken the situation of the stepfamily to that of an immigrant in a strange land. Bewilderment about new family roles is noted not only by family members, but frequently by professionals who work with them.

As with other families, stepfamilies vary greatly in life experiences and in how they manage those experiences. In addition, all stepfamilies have experienced a couple's separation, precipitated by death or divorce, and subsequently, have dealt with decisions about children's caretakers or custody and with issues brought on by the remarriage of at least one partner. These experiences have an impact on the functioning of all family members. It is probable that sociocultural, legal, and developmental complexities create crises that challenge even the most adaptive and the healthiest families. Empirical work is necessary to clarify which, if any, of these problems, are generalizable to all multiparent family structures and which appear primarily associated with those families applying for help to health, mental health, and social agencies. Wald's "problem-process profile" is an excellent beginning effort at developing differential diagnostic assessment which leads to more systematic problem classification. It is of particular importance that Wald's analysis, in the tradition of the social work discipline, considered both the outer reality of the environment (e.g., cultural and legal influences) and the intrapersonal and interpersonal reverberations of that outer reality.[4] In this regard, Espinoza and Newman, in a review of the literature, identified the following 12 areas that are of concern to stepfamilies: "discipline, money, relatives, myths, guilt, ghosts (from the past), adoption, law, incest, name, visitation, and territory."[5]

Three Myths

To understand the tremendous influence of cultural mores and formal (legal) and informal (community) interpretations of these mores, we must examine three myths having a major impact on stepfamilies.

Myth #1: The stepfamily is a nuclear family. This myth rests on the assumption that two parents and two children constitute the "normal" family. This idealized image obstructs our value judgment as clinicians because, in fact, only 37 percent of all families in the United States live in nuclear family units. Professionals have just recently (and, in this author's opinion, fortunately) begun to realize and act on the premise that perhaps the one-parent family is not an "abnormal" family. Nor is the stepfamily a deviant family. Previous clinical definitions of differences in family structures as deviant or sick have caused many problems for professionals. It should be emphasized strongly that "different" does not necessarily mean "abnormal." (In this regard, Wald emphasized the wrong idea of steprelationships as less than blood relationships.) On the other hand, "different" family structures may suggest that members require professional help for adaptational, usually brief, periods of transitions. One goal of professional help is to enable all stepfamily members to feel comfortable with the difference between their family and the so-called average nuclear family, which actually, is increasingly less prevalent.

Myth #2: Instant love. The expectation of instant love, both parental and filial, haunts the family, the community, and even professionals. The myth of instant love produces massive guilt and forces genuine feelings to be concealed and pushed underground. It is indeed possible for stepfamily members to develop true love and attachment for one another. Such a bonding pattern, however, grows out of an affective experience that is cumulative, requiring time and the investment of oneself.

Myth #3: Cinderella. The myth of Cinderella is an example of the exaggeration of power issues in the stepfamily. The splitting off of the parent into "good" and "bad" parent is present in all children's fantasies and in many fairy tales. This splitting off has been immortalized in the literature and has been institutionalized in the community's value system. Both Simon and Wald have traced the development of the stepmother myth in fairy tales, of which Cinderella is the most prominent.[6] The Cinderella myth is reflected in community sentiment, which engenders widespread empathy for the children and contributes to the stepmother's no-win status.

Plight of Children

The plight of children in stepfamilies is examined by focusing on (1) potential problems in the development of the children's self-concepts and (2) interventions that attempt to strengthen the self-concept of children by improving their families' interrelationships. Children have the least power to influence the family system and may manifest the most obvious reactions to the structural changes experienced by stepfamilies. Wallerstein and Kelly noted in their study of divorced families that "astonishingly little professional attention was being paid to the children in these families."[7] There is increasing evidence that all children in stepfamilies struggle with issues of loss, separation-individuation, allegiance, and self-worth. An exacerbation of these struggles, especially in adolescence, often leads to problems in functioning which are likely to be expressed by depression, alcohol abuse, and drug abuse. The family's earlier need for help in forming a new family—a need that is frequently unnoticed—may have contributed significantly to these problems. Wald offered considerable evidence for professionals to consider the remarried family at risk.[8] Many clinicians may interpret this finding as a reference only to familiar problems traditionally associated with children and families, and therefore, these clinicians may neglect issues that are of key importance to stepfamilies. For example, clinicians may neglect to help socialize the children of stepfamilies into unaccustomed roles required of them because one of their biological parents is absent from the household, or because they are weekend or summer children, or because they have new siblings, new extended families, new peer groups, and so on.

The conflicts surrounding these changes are often masked by acting-out behaviors of children. Conceivably, the change in family structure itself may be the dynamic factor that accounts for or seriously contributes to the presenting problems of children in such families. Therefore, influencing the manner in which families deal with these changes may result in a reduction of problematic behaviors for many children. Wallerstein and Kelly noted the ameliorative impact of and the continuing positive quality of their relationship, as clinicians, with children during the research study they conducted.[9]

Loss and Self-Identity

A stepfamily is a family born out of the losses endured by each family member: The child has lost a parent, at least one parent has lost a partner, and even a previously unmarried stepparent has lost the dream of a nuclear family. However, on the remarriage of one parent, custodial or not, the loss is greatest to the child. The parent has or at least hopes to have a positive new life experience. For the child, however, not only does the remarriage put an end to the dream of parental reunion (in the case of divorce), but it is also supposed to be an occasion for joy for the child, as well as for the re-wed parent. Not much time or energy goes into looking at the situation from the child's perspective. This unmet need, that is, the emotional preparation of the child prior to the remarriage, is particularly urgent. It is essential for the child to be reassured that there will be continuity with the remarried parent—whether resident or nonresident in the child's new household—as well as with the other biological parent.[10] Moreover, the myth of instant love between the stepchild and stepparent, even with the best of motives, is not a good omen, because the stepchild and stepparent suffer guilt and frustration at their inability to comply with this unrealistic expectation, which is similar to the development of relationships in foster homes and institutions. The realization that one must wait to develop a relationship with a child slowly over time and through the process of resolving daily living issues is extremely important, although frequently absent.

Another significant loss that occurs many times at the point of remarriage is the loss to the children of important relatives who have frequently played prominent roles, especially during transitional periods. Relatives of the nonresident spouse, and often even of the resident or custodial spouse, withdraw partially or wholly, are excluded, or gradually vanish from the scene. The withdrawal of important support systems, of significant others at the point of crisis, represents a serious loss for children. In addition to this loss, some children experience the losses of peers, neighborhoods, and economic stability. Wallerstein and Kelly commented on the greater vulnerability of children in middle-class white families based on the assumption that a greater "sense of extended family and community exists in other socio-economic and ethnic groups."[11] A study of both formal and informal support systems in these other groups may well point to the strengths that enhance feelings of self and of identity.[12]

Bohannan's research on divorce, Wiseman's work with the divorced, Kübler-Ross's examination of death and dying, Bowlby's research of the bereavement process, and Tessman's work in child therapy clearly indicate various stages of the grief process. According to these researchers, the stages of grief involve protest and denial, despair and disorganization, and reorganization on a new level, all of which are essential to master successfully serious life crises and to cope with traumatic experiences.[13]

In the author's view, remarriage represents a constructive effort at reorganization. Although many children ostensibly adjust well to parental divorce or death, they have problems that surface with greater intensity at the point of or after remarriage of one or both of their biological parents. Perhaps it is reasonable to answer the "why now" question of crisis theorists in the affirmative, and recognize the need to provide a mini-corrective emotional experience at this time for the purpose of taking care of the unfinished business of the child's separation from the other biological parent and from relatives. As indicated, Wallerstein and Kelly's comments on the efficacy of their short-term efforts and Wald's important contribution of clinical examples show practitioners of the need for different emphases, which depend on a sophisticated differential assessment.[14] Practitioners must assess whether the corrective emotional experience for the children would be aided by individual, or peer-group, or family treatment. Practitioners have an array of short-term tasks from which to choose in working with the different members of stepfamilies to enhance the growth of the families' children.

CHILDREN'S NEEDS

Establishing a wholesome new family occurs in two ways: (1) by allowing family members to grieve over both old and new losses and (2) by permitting and encouraging families to continue interacting with significant others in order to strengthen the children's sense of identity and belonging. This advice involves complex interactions. The Vishers pointed out that nuclear families contain 28 dyads and 247 possible interactions, whereas the remarriage of both marital partners in a nuclear family with two children yields 253 pairs and 8,388,584 possible interactions.[15] Certainly, we, as professional caregivers, are not concerned with the quantity of interactions but with encouraging stepfamilies to preserve or reestablish the quality of these interactions. Above all, it is suggested that professionals refuse to enter a conspiracy of silence about previous relationships, because through such collusion they would deprive stepchildren of their roots and of their right to a past.

Despite widespread evidence of family and marital problems, it is reasonable to assume that people will continue to remarry in considerable numbers. The complexity of the stepfamily constellation, especially as this complex constellation is acted out by children and by adults with respect to children, makes remarriage a good entry point for professional helping efforts; it is the point at which the proverbial "stitch in time saves nine." Golan commented on the need for treatment in transitional situations as a "new coming-to-awareness of what some of us have been engaged in for years."[16] For the children in these families it is important to clarify key issues with which they are struggling, such as their unresolved grief, and especially their sadness and anger. The major tasks that many family members must complete in order to cope effectively are related to the grief process and to the process of defining new relationships with both biological parents and stepparents, as well as with blood relatives. It is important for professionals to remember that there is no timetable for the mending of a discontinued relationship or for coping with loss, and therefore, that the crisis of the new family-in-formation presents a challenge to all participants in the treatment process. The keynote of treatment involves creating a climate for opening up these issues which, prior to this time, have been glossed over, or handled as family secrets, or taken for granted.

LESSONS FROM FOSTER CARE

According to Colon, "[a] person's identity is profoundly related to and affected by his sense of connection to his family of origin."[17] In Colon's reminiscings of his own experiences as a foster child and of his subsequent reconnection with his biological family, he stressed the "primacy of the child's experience of biological-familial continuity in establishing his sense of self and personal significance."[18] Because work with newly remarried families deals with parenting and with child-development issues, practice methods used in foster care can be applied to define and operationalize the tasks of helping stepchildren with identity problems and of helping stepparents and biological parents with separation experiences. The important therapeutic task of differentiating marriage and divorce issues from parenting issues is frequently mentioned or at least inferred in the literature on divorce and remarriage. The practice wisdom of some MSW-trained child welfare workers can provide a model for clinicians who work with remarried families. Practitioners in foster care spend a considerable amount of time helping children to understand and to connect with their biological identity. For example, babies and infants are taught to call foster mothers "Auntie," and teenagers are taken to visit mentally ill parents. Moreover, foster care workers promote and arrange for family visits, sibling visits, and the discovery of extended family members.[19] Such professional activities are founded on a conviction in the primacy of children's need to develop a sense of self by knowing and understanding their origins. Before the advent of Erikson and before the recent upsurge of people's interest in searching for their beginnings, the literature rarely addressed the significance of a child's family of origin to his or her development of identity

Children's Self-Image

Over 25 years ago, Weinstein examined the self-image of foster children in relation to variables such as natural parents, foster parents, and agency.[20] Weinstein's findings showed an unexpected, strong correlation between the children's sense of self and the existence of contact with their natural family, even in cases in which the children had been placed in quasiadoptive or absorptive homes. In 1962, Meier's study showed that former foster children functioned in adulthood on a par socially with the study's control group, but among the former foster children "an impairment of the sense of well-being was more frequently found than was a lack of social effectiveness."[21] These two early studies provide some evidence for the correlation between a person's connectedness with his or her roots and sense of well-being. Although more recently researchers such as Fanshel and Shinn have corroborated and expanded earlier data, they have also noted their uncertainty about whether their procedures completely captured the potential for pain and impaired self-image created by lack of permanence in foster care living.[22]

Some of the research on stepfamilies appears to show findings similar to those conducted on children in foster care. For instance, analogies to the foster child's struggle can be found in Wald's formulation of the stepchild's experience, in which she broadened the concept of the steprelationship to include four basic aspects of the human experience: "bereavement, replacement, negative connotations, and the lack of institutionalization of this family in the constellation of families."[23] As described by Wald, the contemporary struggle "between the parents' self-actualization and needs for a companionate marriage and the socialization needs of their children"[24] leads stepchildren, like foster children, to perceive themselves and their families as stigmatized. Because many segments of the American community continue to view divorce and remarriage with no less bias than they view foster care, the perception of stigmatization results in children asking, "What did I do?" and "Why didn't my parents want me?" Community stigma seriously affects the children's sense of self. Therefore, the professional must work with *both* biological and "substitute" families toward achieving greater self-acceptance and social sanction for the new family's validity, despite its difference from the nuclear family.

Some theorists of family therapy believe that clients can achieve a better sense of self and identity by gaining an enhanced understanding of intergenerational patterns. Practitioners can help children enhance their sense of identity by providing the children with a scrapbook, in which they note important occurrences or "nodal events," and in which they include stories about significant figures and role models. It is strongly suggested that workers understand the analogy being made between foster children and stepchildren so that what has been learned from the foster children of yesterday can be offered to the stepchildren of today. Pragmatic experiences of child care practitioners in the past and of medical social workers in the present have shown that, in dealing with clients in crisis situations—such as life-threatening illness, separation, and death—even serious trauma can be mastered. Clients can achieve such mastery by working through the trauma—by opening up and viewing the trauma in all its painful human aspects, by reacting to the emotions it arouses, and, finally, by putting it to rest.

NEW PERSPECTIVE ON FAMILY TREATMENT

McGoldrick and Carter provided a developmental outline of the remarried family, in which six of nine developmental issues dealt with children. One recommendation supports the view that stepfamilies should "work on openness" in the new relationship and should "avoid pseudomutuality."[25] The term "pseudomutuality" originated in the earlier writings of family therapists, and in the stepfamily situation, refers to the "as if" status of stepfamily members—that is, the tendency on the part of the family, the community, and the social agency and its workers to behave as if the stepfamily and the nuclear family are the same, thereby denying the differences between the stepfamily and the traditional nuclear family. As discussed earlier, denial blocks children's access to their biological heritage and past and prevents them from working through the pain of adjusting and reacting to their present life situation.

Stepfamily members who expect instant love or who build relationships based on silence regarding the past or on denial of the past are unlikely to develop true love, caring, and intimacy. Practitioners can help stepfamilies to develop intimacy by encouraging or permitting members to have contact with biological relatives and with extended family or, at the least, by working with symbolic representations, such as pictures, reminiscences, and so on. For example, one program with remarried families found that members were able to define the areas they wished to work on when treatment began with family interviews that included significant persons who had been previously shut out of the child's life and when genograms and sculpting were used to legitimize both the actual existence of and the emotional associations regarding biological relatives and significant others.[26] Wallerstein and Kelly corroborated findings showing that most children made room in their lives for more than two major parental figures quite successfully, although the children's feelings for biological parents and stepparent were not the same. Adults' inability to accommodate wider relationships tended to cause or to contribute to the children's conflict. In this regard, the authors noted that "[n]either divorce nor remarriage appeared to change substantially the importance or the emotional centrality of both biological parents for the growing child."[27]

THE 'PSYCHOLOGICAL PARENT'

The concept of the "psychological parent" is of particular significance to stepfamilies.[28] Goldstein, Freud, and Solnit either coined the expression or they reinforced its use within the professional establishment. Although the concept has been constructive in modifying the rigidity of the court system, it also has been destructive in leading to recommendations that allow for the psychological parent to acquire almost sole rights over the child, which ignores the child's emotional attachment to the other parent. Wallerstein and Kelly indicated that their findings and recommendations were "greatly at variance" to the concept of the psychological parent in spite of the "common psychodynamic framework" that they shared with Goldstein, Freud, and Solnit. They recommended flexibility as "a symbol of society's recognition of the child's continuing need for both parents."[29] Models newer than these authors' traditional psychoanalytic model (for example, crisis intervention and family systems) add knowledge and skills to the clinical armamentarium. These newer models can help deepen rather than inhibit the child's relationship to his or her psychological parent—whether that parent is the foster parent, or adoptive parent, or stepparent—without denying the facts and biological connections in the child's life. Self-help and advocacy organizations, such as ALMA Society (Adoptees' Liberty Movement Association) in New York City, or Stepfamily Association of America in Palo Alto, California, remind us of our responsibilities as professionals and encourage us to make better use of our knowledge and skills. Furthermore, unless we update practice knowledge and skills and fill Wald's "information gap,"[30] we, as professionals, are only slightly ahead of the lay public.

FAMILY-FOCUSED APPROACH

It should be emphasized that during transitions in the life cycle, for example, at times of divorce, death of a spouse, and subsequent remarriage, marital partners have different needs as adults and as parents. Moreover, needs of parents differ from children's needs and growth processes during the life cycle, and practitioners must acknowledge these differences.

Differential Assessment

It is unfortunate that, traditionally, social agencies have neglected to include parental figures in children's treatment programs, based on the mistaken assumption that treatment of children—through play therapy or through institutional placement—would "cure" the children and thus make them more sell-sufficient in adulthood. Yet we know by now that, for children, biological parents—whether actually known to them or fantasized about—do not disappear from children's emotional lives and that children's yearning for roots does not stop, even in adoptive situations. For this reason, the treatment focus of the 1980s has concentrated not on children but on the family's function as a socializer. We have learned from experience of the personal and professional costs of denying the importance of early family figures to children's lives. Consequently, the author suggests a family-systems focus to treatment, which includes other treatment perspectives. In this way, treatment that is focused on children, depending on their developmental level, can involve interventions: (1) with individual children or with groups of children, concentrating on age-appropriate issues, such as identity confusion and relationships with the parent absent from the household and with extended family members and (2) with parents and children, simultaneously, focusing on parenting issues, such as separation and problems of identity.

Wald offered social workers guidance in making differential assessments by providing data on the early problems of families at risk and on the motivations of at-risk families to deal with these problems. Moreover, Wald set forth the problem-process profile, which presents a scheme for making differential diagnosis.[31] For successful interventions, social workers must focus on the current situation, its effects on family members' adjustment to the remarried family, and the children's troublesome relationship with family members not included in the new household's social interactions. The treatment goal is to identify and enhance the strengths and coping skills of the family participants; enabling them to solve current problems and preventing acting-out behavior in the future. The suggested goal is preventive in orientation and assumes that both "new" and "old" relationships between parental figures and children are enhanced by a strategy that places emphasis on family continuity— in actual or in symbolic ways—and on its members' healthy functioning and coping capacity rather than on pathology.

EARLY INTERVENTION

The social worker's role in preventive efforts has been receiving renewed attention.[32] It is believed that early intervention may alleviate the remnants and possible adverse effects of earlier experiences of separation and, eventually, may develop positive aspects of relationships and bonding among steprelatives. Families undergoing role crises have been found to be more amenable to interventive efforts that apply crisis theory to alleviate the distress and disequilibrium experienced by family members at particular phases of remarriage. In addition, programs that provide services to single and multiple family groups, parents' groups, couples' groups, and children's groups enhance the functioning and the psychological well-being of remarried families. Strategies for intervention also can include ex-spouses and other extended family members who have an impact on remarried family members. These strategies are based on multiple family therapy, on crisis intervention techniques, and on family life education approaches.

Intervention goals for children involve preventing further development of dysfunctional behaviors and of internal stresses related to issues of separation, such as loss and strained relationships with parents, which are reactivated at the point of remarriage. Intervention goals also include assisting children to achieve a realistic understanding of life situations and helping them to adjust to different lifestyles, new forms of parenting, and multiple models of identification.

Intervention goals for parents focus on developing new structures in almost all aspects of living, developing ways of communicating more openly and more clearly with spouses and children, creating new ways of relating to former spouses about parenting issues, and completing the process of emotional separation from former spouses. Parents' success in completing these tasks permits children to have more autonomy about their feelings vis-à-vis biological kin and steprelatives.

Intervention goals for the total family include opening communication among members through the workers' understanding and objectivity and altering old family patterns that may be dysfunctional. These goals also involve the workers' helping family members to redefine family roles in order to allow for the development of new alliances and identifications without denigrating old ones.

Community Education

Based on site visits to 13 programs, experts on the stepfamily identified as useful the following three models of intervention: the family counseling model, the educational model, and the self-help model.[33] The models are multifocused and offer professional help with life problems. However, the present author's personal communications with professionals who have attempted to apply the models in clinics in New York, New Jersey, and California indicated that even strong clinical efforts at community education were not particularly successful in reaching stepfamilies. Part of the failure to reach stepfamilies is, without doubt, related to the time it takes to develop community acceptance of innovative approaches and related to curtailments of funds and programs in social service agencies in recent years. Nevertheless, part of the failure is also attributable to the social work profession. In the author's view, the dichotomy within the profession of "clinical work" and "other," which appears to overemphasize intrapsychic and interpersonal features of professional interventions, works to the detriment of our efforts to reach stepfamilies. It is therefore dysfunctional in reaching out to these families to hold on to the separation of counseling and educational efforts. Traditionally, social work is well-equipped to engage in both efforts. Wald stated: "A problem that begins as a cultural problem may ultimately be experienced as an intra-personal problem of low self-esteem or negative identity."[34] The "schema for study" that Wald developed also encompassed a two-pronged perspective by focusing on the stepfamily's "broad historical, cultural, social, and legal context" and by contrasting the stepfamily with the nuclear family along the same dimensions in the here and now.[35] Clients and practitioners "must clarify and narrow the gap between the objective reality and the subjective views of the family situation."[36] Isn't this recommendation at the core of social work practice? Isn't this "new-old" social work?[37]

"NEW-OLD" SOCIAL WORK

Children's problems always involve, at the core, issues of separation, identity, and bonding, although these are often obscured by a variety of presenting problems. In the lives of stepchildren, there are continuing ecological complexities—such as legal constraints of alimony, visiting rights, gifts; and participation in holidays and in other ceremonies—which provide the arena for dealing with these core issues. Reconnecting estranged relatives is reminiscent of the tasks of traditional child placement workers who intervened with at least two, and usually more, families in behalf of children. Workers, therefore, resemble stage directors or conductors, because they orchestrate children's growth and performance through the life cycle, despite many conflicting demands. Workers must bring into harmony competing adults who have their own emotional needs, in order to help children grow up soundly.

There is no evidence that children can relate only to two biological adults called parents. The social work professionals who work with stepfamilies have joined sociologists and anthropologists in acknowledging the significance of and the supportive role of the traditional extended family. Social workers also have suggested that with some help in working out unfinished adult issues, feuding parents, grandparents, aunts, uncles, and so on could remain or become identification figures for children, thereby significantly contributing to the healthy growth of the children across generations. In fact, more permeable boundaries would permit stepparents and relatives to enrich children's lives as significant others, just as extended family members did for "prenuclear" families.

As family therapists often demonstrate, those families in which parents relate well to each other are the families that have well-defined boundaries for parents and siblings and that allow freedom for the children to grow. In contrast, in those families in which generational boundaries are rigid or weak, children experience problems. The encouragement of boundary permeability and of continuity of biological ties (original family) and ties-in-formation (stepfamily) can be growth producing.

In practicing the "new-old" social work we, as professionals, must seriously consider the repackaging of our agency service structures and, even more important, the way in which we use our expertise. Industry, the school system, and the legal system provide possible opportunities for collaboration and for access to families at stress points in normal living. Reaching out from our customary workplaces and reconnecting ourselves and our agencies to our communities should give us new opportunities to reach families for prevention, perhaps beginning rather than ending with self-help groups and family life education. From that beginning, we might then make use of our skills of assessment in order to determine the need for continuing interventions with selected stepfamily members.

NOTES AND REFERENCES

1. E. Wald, *The Remarried Family: Challenge and Promise* (New York: Family Service Association of America, 1981), p. 32.

2. R. Espinoza and Y. Newman, *Stepparenting*, Publication No. 78-579, Center for Studies of Child and Family Mental Health, U.S. Department of Health, Education and Welfare (Rockville, Md.: Alcohol, Drug Abuse, and Mental Health Administration, 1979), pp. 3–5.

3. Wald, *The Remarried Family*. For recent articles on social work interventions with stepfamilies, see J. E. Hunter and N. Schuman, "Chronic Reconstitution as a Family Style," *Social Work*, 25 November 1980), pp. 446–451; D. S. Jacobson, "Stepfamilies: Myths and Realities," *Social Work*, 24 (May 1979), pp. 202–207; H. C. Johnson, "Working with Stepfamilies: Principles of Practice," *Social Work*, 25 (July 1980), pp. 304–308; M. O. Kent, "Remarriage: A Family Systems Approach, *Social Casework: The Journal of Contemporary Social Work*, 61 (March 1980), pp. 146–153; and J. W. Ransom, S. Schlesinger, and A. P. Derdeyn, "A Stepfamily in Formation," *American Journal of Orthopsychiatry* 49 (January 1979), pp. 36–43.

4. Wald, *The Remarried Family*, especially pp. 177–189.

5. Espinoza and Newman, *Stepparenting*, especially pp. 23–36.

6. Wald, *The Remarried Family*, pp. 45–65; and A. W. Simon, *Stepchild in the Family* (New York: Odyssey Press, 1964), pp. 23–34.

7. J. S. Wallerstein and J. B. Kelly, *Surviving the Breakup* (New York: Basic Books, 1980), p. 6.

8. Wald, *The Remarried Family*, p. 31.

9. Wallerstein and Kelly, *Surviving the Breakup*, especially pp. 5–9.

10. L. Messinger, "Remarriage between Divorced People with Children from Previous Marriages: A Proposal for Preparation for Remarriage," *Journal of Marriage and Family Counseling*, 2, No. 2 (1976), pp. 193–200.

11. Wallerstein and Kelly, *Surviving the Breakup*, p. 309.

12. Traditionally, social problems were defined relative to poor people and psychological problems were defined relative to middle-class people. In examining secular trends and data on children and families, such as, lower school achievement and rising rates of child homicide, suicide, child abuse, and so forth, Bronfenbrenner noted that the general trend is confined no longer to the urban poor. Indeed, recent reports of the experiences of middle-class families resemble those of low-income families in the mid-1960s. U. Bronfenbrenner, "Encounters of the Third Kind: Ecological Perspectives on Social Work." Paper presented at Lucille Austin Visiting Fellow Lecture, Columbia University School of Social Work, New York, April 20, 1981.

13. See P. Bohannan, ed., *Divorce and After: An Analysis of the Emotional and Social Problems of Divorce* (New York: Anchor Books, 1971); R. S. Wiseman, "Crisis Theory and the Process of Divorce," *Social Casework,* 56 (April 1975), pp. 205–212; E. Kübler-Ross, *On Death and Dying* (New York: Macmillan Publishing Co., 1969); J. Bowlby, *Loss: Sadness and Depression,* Vol. 3, "Attachment and Loss Series" (New York: Basic Books, 1980); and L. H. Tessman, *Children of*

Parting Parents (Northvale, N.J.: Jason Aronson Publishers, 1978).

14. Wallerstein and Kelly, *Surviving the Breakup*, pp. 5–9; and Wald, *The Remarried Family*, p. 40.

15. E. B. Visher and J. S. Visher, *Stepfamilies, A Guide to Working with Stepparents and Stepchildren* (New York: Brunner/Mazel, 1979), pp. 25–27.

16. N. Golan, *Passing Through Transitions: A Guide for Practitioners* (New York: Free Press, 1981), p. xix.

17. F. Colon, "In Search of One's Past: An Identity Trip," *Family Process,* 12 (December 1973), p. 429.

18. F. Colon, "Family Ties and Child Placement," *Family Process,* 17 (September 1978), p. 289.

19. The author's experience in the private sector of foster care in New York City from 1947 to 1954 is the model for these practice examples.

20. E. A. Weinstein, *The Self-Image of the Foster Child* (New York: Russell Sage Foundation, 1960).

21. E. G. Meier, "Foster Children as Adults," p. 46. Unpublished Ph.D. dissertation, Columbia University School of Social Work, 1962.

22. D. Fanshel and E. Shinn, *Children in Foster Care: A Longitudinal Investigation* (New York: Columbia University Press, 1978).

23. Wald, *The Remarried Family*, 47.

24. Ibid., p. 51.

25. M. McGoldrick and E. Carter, "Forming a Remarried Family," in Carter and McGoldrick, eds., *The Family Life Cycle: A Framework for Family Therapy* (New York: Gardner Press, 1980), p. 272.

26. See C. J. Sager et al., *Treating the Remarried Family* (New York: Brunner/Mazel, 1983), p. 241.

27. Wallerstein and Kelly, *Surviving the Breakup*, pp. 292–294.

28. J. Goldstein, A. Freud, and A. J. Solnit, *Beyond the Best Interests of the Child* (New York: Free Press, 1973).

29. Wallerstein and Kelly, *Surviving the Breakup*, p. 311.

30. Wald, *The Remarried Family*, pp. 2–4.

31. Ibid., p. 9 and pp. 177–185.

32. For some programmatic suggestions, see M. Roskin, "Integration of Primary Prevention into Social Work Practice," *Social Work,* 25 (May 1980), pp. 192–196; and D. S. Simon, "A Systematic Approach to Family Life Education," *Social Casework,* 57 (October 1976), pp. 511–516.

33. American Institutes for Research, Office of Human Development Services, Administration for Children, Youth, and Families, *Helping Youth and Families of Separation, Divorce, and Remarriage: A Program Manual,* Publication No. 80-32010 (Washington, D.C.: U.S. Department of Health and Human Services, 1980), pp. 41–42.

34. Wald, *The Remarried Family*, p. 178.

35. Ibid.

36. Ibid.

37. M. Siporin, "Social Treatment: A New-Old Helping Method," *Social Work,* 15 (July 1970), pp. 13–25.

CHAPTER 88

WHOSE CHILD IS THIS?

Assessment and Treatment of Children in Foster Care

Wendy Glockner Kates, Rebecca L. Johnson,
Mary W. Rader, Frederick H. Strieder

The assessment and treatment of a child in foster care presents a unique dilemma to mental health professionals. A child often arrives in foster care from a neglectful, abusive, or chaotic family in which the parent-child relationship is distorted and dysfunctional. Within such an environment, the child's resolution of early developmental tasks (*Erikson, 1964; Mahler, Pine, & Bergman, 1975*) has been tenuous at best (*Horner, 1984*). The child's compromised developmental adaptation is threatened further by the traumatic separation from and loss of the primary caregiver entailed by foster placement. For children who enter foster care with an impaired sense of trust and autonomy, issues of separation involve not merely the mourning of losses (*Bowlby, 1973*), but an actual threat to their survival.

The intrapsychic needs of a foster child, therefore, represent a developmental emergency that often requires immediate psychotherapeutic intervention (*Kempe, 1982*). The clinician who focuses on the child's intrapsychic needs, however, rapidly discovers that therapeutic interventions are constrained by a complex and confusing interpersonal and systemic network in which the foster child lives. This network includes the biological family, foster family, child welfare worker, attorney, and school. The therapist of a child in foster care must continually balance the pressing developmental needs of the child with the roles and expectations of the caregivers within the child's entire interpersonal network.

The therapist's dilemma is further complicated by the discrepancy between the network's and the child's perceptions of the experience of foster care placement. Whereas children in foster care experience *placement* as a threat to survival, child welfare workers, foster caregivers, and clinicians naturally view the abusive or chaotic conditions that precipitated placement as the primary threat to the child's survival. In the face of such a threat, the myriad caregivers and professionals who comprise the child's interpersonal network tend to direct their efforts toward "rescuing" the child. Parents are removed from their executive role in the family. Children are placed in single or successive foster homes in a short period, and they are expected to relate successfully to several caregivers. Multiple agencies (including child welfare, the courts, and hospital evaluation units) become involved with the children, the foster parents, and the biological parents.

The responsibilities of individuals and agencies within the child's network become splintered and confused. Role boundaries between agencies blur to the point at which no one knows who is responsible for the child. In the face of the confusing and expansive network in which the child must interact, the major therapeutic focus for the child becomes, "Whose child am I?" To be maximally effective, however, therapeutic interventions must incorporate the child's entire interpersonal network, as well as the network of professionals and agencies that influence the life of the child. The clinician's task is to clarify whose child this is not only for the child, but for all those who interact with the child. The authors' premise is that a therapist must not intervene solely from the perspective of the child as an individual, but must become active in the child's entire network, clarifying the roles of each participant and framing a structure that can make the identification, "This is our child."

This article addresses both the individual question of "Whose child am I?" and the systemic question of "Whose child is this?" It describes, from both an individual and a systemic framework, the experience of a child in foster care that renders these therapeutic issues so central. It outlines strategies for addressing the questions at the levels of evaluation, psychotherapeutic treatment, and advocacy. In doing so, it draws from the authors' experiences as therapists and advocates for foster children and their families in an outpatient clinic of an urban hospital.

CHILD ASSESSMENT

Foster children respond both to perceived threats to their survival and to boundary confusion within their interpersonal networks with a wide range of symptoms. Their longing for the lost attachment figure is often accompanied by intense generalized hostility (*Horner, 1984*). Crying, tantrums, verbal aggression, and school difficulties are behavioral manifestations of the depression and anxiety that may result from the unresolved mourning of separations. The destruction of property, physical violence, and threats of suicide are at the more extreme end of the behavioral spectrum that we have observed.

Child welfare workers generally respond to the onset of symptomatic behavior in foster children with a referral for a psychological evaluation. The psychodiagnostic process for children in foster care, however, is constrained by the children's experiences in the foster care system The trauma of separation and loss that are inherent in foster care color the children's approach to a psychological evaluation and constrain the interpretation of the psychodiagnostic data that are obtained. Placement in foster care undermines the children's interpersonal trust, sense of mastery, and control over events within the environment. Consequently, their motivation to establish a cooperative, productive relationship with an examiner and to perform optimally is significantly compromised.

Furthermore, a psychological evaluation that is completed before a child's adjustment to a foster care placement stabilizes can reveal significant yet transitory pathology that may be resolved once the child has restored psychological equilibrium. Many referral questions, therefore, cannot be answered validly by a psychological evaluation that is completed at the point of a child's entry into foster care or at the point at which the child's placement is changed.

In addition, the multiple interpersonal contexts to which a foster child must adapt greatly constrain the inferences that can be made from psychological test data alone. Traditional assessment tools often do not provide information that is sufficiently specific to answer the questions posed about a child in foster care. Although projective tools certainly provide information about the quality of the emotional relationship between the child and his or her caretakers, the multiplicity of caretakers for a child in foster care confuses both the content of the data obtained and the inferences we attempt to draw from the data. For example, a child may depict maternal figures as emotionally unavailable. Without extensive collateral information and observation of parent-child interactions, we cannot make inferences about those aspects of the child's experience that may be serving as the reference to his or her perceptions of maternal figures. Nor can we describe the extent to which the child differentiates between multiple maternal caretakers in his or her perceptions of and interactions with each.

The inclusion of the child's foster family and biological family, through family interviews and parent-child observations, serves a systemic function as well. Psychological evaluations can inform us about a child's current emotional vulnerabilities and strengths. Because psychodiagnostic data cannot provide specific information about the child's experience in multiple interpersonal contexts, a psychological evaluation cannot fully address the question that is unique to a foster child: "Whose child am I?" It is essential to integrate information about the multiple interpersonal contexts in which the child lives in order to make recommendations that will both support the child's adaptation to care and facilitate (when appropriate) the reintegration of the biological family.

Ecological Assessment

Such information must be obtained through an accompanying ecological assessment of the child and his or her interpersonal network (despite the extensive administrative coordination and clinical time this assessment necessitates). An ecological assessment that addresses the question, "Whose child am I," should focus on the following issues:

1. What is the quality of the child's attachment to the biological parents? To what extent does the child perceive those parents as people who can be counted on and for whom he or she feels affection?
2. How does the child express and gain mastery over the grief, anger, and anxiety engendered by parental separation and loss? In the face of intense emo-

tional turmoil over parental separation, how does the child cope with the impending interpersonal closeness with the foster family (*Katz, 1987*)?

3. What is the child's perception of the way in which issues of interpersonal trust, autonomy, and parent-child boundaries are negotiated within the family? To what extent is that perception based on the child's experience in the biological family? How does that experience differ from that in the foster family? Are rules and expectations for family functioning and interaction sufficiently different to create conflict or confusion in the child?

4. What is the child's perception of his or her integration within the foster family? To what extent does the child feel accepted, nurtured, and secure? To what extent does the child's uncertainty within the foster home parallel that within the biological family? How does the child cope with the uncertainty and fear of abandonment and rejection that may be engendered by separation from and loss of the biological parents?

By describing the child's self-experience in foster care, we can offer recommendations for treatment that focuses upon facilitating the child's optimal adaptation to foster care. Further, by differentiating between the child's experiences in foster care and the biological family, we can describe some of the challenges that will be posed by the eventual attempt to reintegrate and empower the biological family.

THERAPEUTIC APPROACHES
Child Therapy

The questions "Whose child am I?" and, more basically, "Who am I?" which foster children bring to individual treatment stem from the following prominent issues that accompany the children into foster care: 1) the tendency of children to split the maternal image into "good" and "bad," 2) their shattered sense of "belonging" and of familial identification, and 3) their inability or reluctance to form attachments to substitute caregivers. These are the issues on which the clinician must focus in child therapy with foster children.

These children have difficulty distinguishing the real characteristics of biological parents from those of serial foster caregivers. Actually having two or more "mothers" reinforces the splitting of the maternal image into good and bad. Implicit in the children's removal from biological parents and placement with foster parents is the message that the biological parent or the child is a failure, or bad, while the rescuers are good. When problem behavior results in the removal of children from the foster home, the children's view of themselves as bad is reinforced. The "good" foster parent is transformed into another rejecting adult who has failed to parent the child.

After serial placements, children may be confused about the appropriate application of the terms *mother, father,* and *parents.* Presented with models that repeatedly fail, the children face a dilemma concerning with whom to identify, and in addition to struggling with loyalty must also struggle with multiple identities. They may identify with glorified images they have created to meet their needs (*Goldstein, 1985*) or with the actual or imagined characteristics of incompetent parents or foster parents. If foster parents actually are "good," the children are torn between rejecting the biological parent or parents and being "good," or rejecting the foster caregiver and being "bad." Because of their attachment to their biological parents or denial of the negative characteristics of those parents and their fear or mistrust of other persons, foster children may choose to be "bad."

A series of brief aborted attachments may predispose the children to establishing only transient shallow relationships (*Horner, 1986*). Because the children expect any relationship to be followed by loss, there is an unwillingness to attach to a significant "object" (*Mullan, 1987*). "I'll reject you first" becomes the children's approach to relationships. Rejecting before being rejected gives illusory control over feeling worthless (*Kendrich & Wieder, 1975*), but insecurity and conflicts tend to become more pronounced with every change of homes.

In the face of these issues, the therapist's primary tasks in individual treatment must include: *1*) mobilizing the child's ego resources to help the child both integrate conflicting images and experiences in relation to biological and foster parents and regulate self-esteem; *2*) assisting the child to rework early stages of development in which the capacity for engagement and attachment have been seriously undermined; *3*) assisting the child to build a stable sense of self and to construct a sense of familial identification in which to address the issue, "Whose child am I?"

The clinician who focuses on the intrapsychic needs of the child will also find his or her therapeutic interventions constrained by the ambiguous interpersonal network in which the child lives The blurring of role boundaries among individuals and among agencies results in a vacuum, in which no one accepts responsibility for the child. Psychotherapeutic work, therefore, must continually balance attempts to support the ego development of the child with efforts to define clearly the roles of both the biological family and the foster family. The inclusion of *all* family members within the therapeutic focus clarifies the answer to the question, "Whose child is this?" In addition, the inclusion of the child's interpersonal network within therapy mitigates, to some extent, the child's experience of separation and loss. By integrating the principles of family therapy with the principles of individual treatment outlined earlier, a clinician can move beyond the limitations that are posed by individual child therapy with children in foster care.

Family Therapy

The model that we propose for incorporating the child's interpersonal and systemic network into treatment draws on both our experience and Minuchin and Elizur's (1990) work with foster families in New York City. Minuchin and Elizur argued that foster care should be oriented toward providing services to whole families, rather than solely to children. They suggested that the well-intentioned efforts of professionals in the welfare system are sometimes misdirected in that professionals work to save the child at the child's expense. Biological parents are often cast as sinful, bad, incompetent, or destructive; this results in a splitting between foster parents and biological parents that is not in the children's best interests. Minuchin and Elizur suggested that foster parents be considered part of an extended kinship network of the child so that they and the biological parents will be seen as part of one large family unit to be addressed by professionals.

This view implies that the therapist must develop a therapeutic approach toward working with children in foster care that incorporates the entire network of individuals who interact with the child. We will outline the components involved in broadening the therapeutic focus of work with foster children to include the issues "Whose child is this?"

The biological family. Placement in foster care frequently cuts children off from their biological families. Often, they are taken from their parents to protect them from harm. While professionals and society cannot condone any form of mistreatment of children, the belief that they need to be "rescued" from their families may be counterproductive. The rescue myth not only deprives the children of their natural place in their families, it also encourages the disengagement of their parents.

As the system is usually currently defined, rescuing children from neglectful or abusive parents is the child welfare worker's raison d'être. This myth underestimates the children's separation trauma, ignores the risks of foster care itself, and engenders an attitude of repugnance and pessimism toward the biological parents. The parents respond by becoming intimidated or alienated by the social service system; furthermore, if they are unable to maintain meaningful contact with their child, they respond to their emotional devastation by beginning to detach. Their ensuing noncooperation or even abandonment can only be considered iatrogenic. It is the clinician's job to help the child welfare worker replace the belief in the rescue myth with a conviction of the value of protecting the entire family, so that these iatrogenic problems are minimized.

The engagement of the biological parents further depends upon a shift in the prevailing attitudes toward parents who utilize foster care. Child welfare workers and foster caregivers must be encouraged to punctuate the biological parents' positive attributes and strengths. The goal is to create the unified parental unit that is the hallmark of the healthy family (*Colapinto, 1982; Minuchin, 1974; Minuchin & Fishman, 1981*).

From the moment a child is placed outside the home, it is necessary to continue to involve the biological parents in the child's daily life. (We are not suggesting that clinicians be "blind advocates" for biological parents. We are suggesting that, regardless of the appropriateness of reunification, the clinician must work to ensure the best possible relationship between the biological parents and their children.) Biological and foster parents would need to collaborate in helping to make decisions about the child's care, which obviously means that the biological parents are as intimately involved with the foster parents as is the child. Thus, foster parents need training to work directly with the child's biological parents to accept the help that the latter have to offer while maintaining the executive role in their own home. Professionals also need a practice model that would promote parental involvement and direct interaction within foster homes. Again, such a model would support the appropriate parental behavior of the biological parents and unify the executive role system of the foster parents and biological parents.

Essentially, the therapist must help the child's interpersonal network to focus on protecting the family, not just the child. Thus, the network must maintain the biological parents' position as authorities and experts on their child. This network must resolve not to overfunction and thus usurp the parents' role, and to capitalize on the biological parents' strengths rather than focus on their weaknesses.

The foster family. The role of foster parent has no direct precedent in our society. Its paradoxes and ambiguities exemplify the term *role confusion.* Yet, unless the foster parents' role is clearly defined, uncertainty can lead to troubled relationships with their foster children and damage to the children's relationships with their biological parents. Both exacerbate the foster child's trauma of separation and loss.

Common areas of ambiguity include these: How shall the foster parents view and relate to the biological parents? What is the foster parents' level of physical commitment to their foster child—is the child in their home conditionally or unconditionally? What emotional role will the foster parents take with respect to the child—do they convey love or that they will merely care well for the child? What, if any, permanent relationship will they establish with their foster child? What is the level of the foster parents' authority-responsibility-power over decisions concerning the foster child? Foster parents' stances on these and other issues will significantly influence their foster parenting.

Our experience is consistent with Minuchin's and others' who have proposed that the experience of foster care may be least traumatizing for the child and family if the foster parents adopt the role of extended family members, viewing themselves as offering (as an aunt or grandmother might) respite for a parent who is temporarily incapacitated. In this model, the parents' ultimate bond with and authority over their child is respected. The foster parents view themselves as helpers of the biological parents, not as antagonists or replacements. The foster parents maintain a relationship with both the child and the biological parents that persists after formal foster care has ended. This model has the advantages of having a natural precedent in society, of reducing parental alienation and noncooperation, of minimizing the disruption of parent-child bonds, and of not subjecting the child to another catastrophic loss when foster care ends.

Many foster parents, however, choose to limit their relationship to the foster child alone, and then only while that child is in their care. Foster parents, as well as child welfare workers, easily fall prey to the rescue myth, and it is particularly critical that these more traditional foster parents understand the importance to children of their biological parents. The child who cannot resolve separation trauma and adjust to the foster household is especially susceptible to being labeled "bad" or "disturbed." Foster parents must be helped to understand the importance of the biological parent–child relationship and to view themselves as supporters of that relationship. That is, they must make the child as available as possible for visits; they must provide the child with a supportive but nonpartisan forum in which both positive and negative feelings about the biological parents can be expressed; and they must refrain from open conflict with the biological parents or from making negative comments. Perhaps the best model for these foster parents is that of the custodial parent in a divorced family, who recognizes the importance of the child's relationship with the noncustodial parent and facilitates it accordingly.

Thus, foster parents must see themselves as active rather than passive agents in the process that helps families change and move toward healthy functioning. This shift in orientation may necessitate the training and funding of foster parents at a level that is currently maintained by specialized foster care programs.

The child's interpersonal network. Application of the proposed model to working with families who are involved in foster care is made more complex by the multiplicity of other persons and agencies involved. These open include several (and often shifting) child welfare workers, other social service workers (who arrange for financial aid, housing, health care, and so forth), several attorneys, medical personnel, and school personnel, all of whom must be coordinated and focused in handling the situation.

It is as important for the family's network to think and function according to the proposed model as it is for the therapist and foster family to do so. The therapist's job is to facilitate this way of thinking and functioning among the network members. In addition, because of the complexity of efforts in such a network, it is essential that its functioning be well-organized. That is, the roles of the network members must be clearly defined, and there must be a clear system of communication and decision making. Most important, adequate organization of the network requires a clearly assigned coordinator who will receive and maintain all relevant information and integrate discussions. As the system is currently construed, the organization of services is weak, and the roles of the various professionals evolve independently of each other.

The child welfare worker is generally the most suitable person to be the network coordinator. He or she is the agent who represents society's power to decide the placement of the family's children. Because of this decision-making power, the worker must have all relevant information and must coordinate others' involvement with the family. Because the worker may not automatically assume the role of coordinator, however, and because the functioning of other professionals tends to evolve independently if it is not well coordinated, it is important that the clinician facilitate and make clear this role assignment. In short, the therapist must recognize the central role that competent case management plays in the effective treatment of families who are involved in foster care, and must facilitate and support the child welfare worker's efforts to fulfill that unjustifiably maligned role.

The family therapist's success in clarifying "whose child this is" for the foster child and the biological and foster parents depends on a shift in orientation from protecting the child to protecting the family. In addition, it implies the provision of services to children and families that engage, rather than disengage, children, foster parents, biological parents, child welfare workers, and all other pertinent professionals. The therapeutic approach is thus broadened to include the child's entire network, in order to empower its members to help the child and the family.

CONCLUSIONS

The statement that the child protection system must redefine itself as a *family* protection system is easily made but has wide implications. For the reasons outlined above, however, the actions of the system will be constructive, not destructive, to the child *only* if it is redefined thus.

Protection of the family implies a movement away from the use of foster care toward an emphasis on services that maintain the parent-child relationship and keep families together. Intensive, comprehensive services are needed to help families who are at risk of foster care placement while the child is still in the biological home (*Schorr, 1988*). At the same time, the continued development of local family support programs (*Weissbourd & Kagan, 1989*), in which families could receive these services or just play, talk, and get to know each other, would help to provide the peer support and modeling that extended family members are often no longer available to provide.

When foster care is unavoidable, every effort must be made to minimize the experience of separation and loss for the child. Foster parents should be trained to understand and follow the tenets of the model presented here. In our experience, they also require training on a number of other issues that may not commonly be discussed during their preparation. Among these issues are the importance of unconditional commitment to the child in their home so as to facilitate a secure attachment between them and the child. Children of families whose circumstances make foster care unavoidable may have been so traumatized as to display in the foster home various kinds of maladaptive behavior that are often emotionally upsetting to foster parents and behaviorally difficult for them to manage. However, the message given by foster parents to children should not be, "Shape up or ship out," but "I'll help you shape up." Foster parents need the training in child development and behavioral management that makes such a commitment possible.

The extent of the training, as well as the necessity for continued involvement with family and network, would suggest that foster parents be regarded as professionals, with all the concomitant responsibilities and remuneration thus implied. Although foster parents are sometimes given such a role when they serve as "specialized" foster-caregivers, we are suggesting that all foster care—to be helpful and not hurtful—should be viewed as specialized foster care.

Clinicians who work with families involved in foster care, in the "child protection" system as it is presently construed, must realize the painful dilemma involved in such work. In telling the child protection system that they will work with the individuals and families caught up in it, therapists are supporting the system by implying that it is possible to be effective within it as it is currently defined. In doing so, they may only stave off the crisis that is necessary in such systems (as in families) to bring about real change. They may help perpetuate the havoc that such well-intentioned but actually destructive systems wreak upon families and their children. Clinicians who are involved in foster care work must always function with this dilemma in mind, to minimize (although not eliminate) its dangers. Inevitably, such considerations will lead them to become involved in efforts to change the system.

REFERENCES

Bowlby, J. (1973). *Attachment and loss, Vol. 2: Separation*. New York: Basic Books.

Colapinto, J. (1982). Structural family therapy. In A. M. Horne & M. M. Ohlsen (Eds.), *Family counseling and therapy*. Itsca, IL: F. E. Peacock.

Erikson, E. H. (1964). *Childhood and society*. New York: Norton.

Goldstein, W. (1985). *An introduction to the borderline conditions*. Northvale, NJ: Jason Aronson.

Horner, A. J. (1984). *Object relations and the developing ego in therapy*. Northvale, NJ: Jason Aronson.

Horner, A. J. (1986). *Being and loving: How to achieve intimacy with another person and retain one's own identity.* Northvale, NJ: Jason Aronson.

Katz, L. (1987). An overview of current clinical issues in separation and placement. *Child and Adolescent Social Work, 4*(3 & 4), 61–77.

Kempe, C. H. (1982). Changing approaches to treatment of child abuse and neglect. *Child Abuse and Neglect, 6,* 491–493.

Kendrich, C., & Wieder, H. (1974). *Panel on foster children and adopted children, Long Island Psychoanalysis Society.* Unpublished.

Mahler, M. S., Pine, F., & Bergman, A. (1975). *The psychological birth of the human infant.* New York: Basic Books.

Minuchin, S. (1974). *Families and family therapy.* Cambridge, MA: Harvard University Press.

Minuchin, S., & Elizur, J. (1900, January–February). The foster care crisis. *Family Therapy Networker,* 44–51.

Minuchin, S., & Fishman, C. H. (1981). *Family therapy techniques.* Cambridge, MA: Harvard University Press.

Mullan, B. (1987). *Are mothers really necessary?* New York: Weidenfield & Nicholson.

Schorr, L. (1988). *Within our reach.* New York: Doubleday.

Weissbourd, B., & Kagan, S. (1989). Family support programs: Catalysts for change. *American Journal of Orthopsychiatry, 59,* 20–31.

THE FAMILY

CHAPTER 89

PRACTICE STRATEGIES FOR ENGAGING CHRONIC MULTIPROBLEM FAMILIES

Shirley B. Schlosberg and Richard M. Kagan

Families who are referred to child welfare agencies are often fearful, angry, distrustful, and expecting to be blamed. Most of these families have a history of involvement with agencies, courts, hospitals, and child protective services. They view mental health professionals as intimidating parental figures who are insensitive to the family's primary needs.

Families with severe problems such as recurrent incidents of abuse, neglect, family violence, and delinquent behavior are often referred to agencies. These families typically have not sought help on their own. Thus they feel victimized by interventions from family courts, educators, and social service agency staff[1] and may resist intervention as an intrusion into the family. Moreover, services of limited duration (for example, less than four months) may have little long-term impact on members of chronically troubled families.[2] These chronically dysfunctional families are generally unresponsive to traditional family or individual therapies.[3] The most striking thing about them is their resistance to change, despite the orders, pleas, exhortations, and combined efforts of multiple community agencies.

Working with families who have long histories of severe problems can be over-

Reprinted from *Social Casework,* Vol. 58 (1977), pp. 29–35, by permission of the publisher, Families International, Inc.

[1] Lisa Kaplan, *Working with Multi-Problem Families* (Lexington, Mass.: D. C. Heath, 1986).
[2] Helen M. Land, "Child Abuse: Differential Diagnosis, Differential Treatment," *Child Welfare* 5 (January–February 1986); 33–34; and Beulah Compton, "The Family Centered Project Revisited," (School of Social Work, University of Minnesota, May 1979, photocopy).
[3] Jack Weitzman, "Engaging the Severely Dysfunctional Family in Treatment: Basic Considerations," *Family Process* 24 (December 1985): 473–85; and Frank Riessman, "New Approaches to Mental Health Treatment for Low-Income People," in *Interpersonal Helping: Emerging Approaches for Social Work Practice,* ed. Joel Fischer (Springfield, Ill.: Charles C. Thomas, 1973), pp. 529–44.

whelming. Therapists experience hostility and rejection from these families and often become frustrated and feel the same despair experienced by their clients. The helplessness, depression, and repetition of serious problem situations can exhaust the most energetic practitioner.

The present article examines family resistance to change in an effort to identify underlying dynamics, engage families, and develop effective strategies for intervention. A model of home-based family work is proposed, which is based on more than nine years of experience working with more than 800 families with children at high risk of imminent institutional placement. In the past four years, use of this model has prevented placement of children in 88 percent of families served.[4]

DEDICATION TO THE FAMILY

Families are often trapped between the need for change and the need to protect their current patterns, roles, and organization.[5] Severely disturbed families are often able to protect their ongoing dysfunctional patterns when a child is institutionalized as unmanageable, delinquent, or psychotic. Similarly, families often maintain their dysfunctional patterns with an adult incarcerated as a criminal or institutionalized as an alcoholic or mentally ill patient.

Resistance, from this perspective, is part of the interactional process of families, therapists, and other community agents.[6] Resistance protects the family against dangers that are feared much more than are the decisions of judges or the warnings of social service workers. Family disintegration, abandonment, exposure of sexual abuse, and so forth are often major concerns in these families. Loyalty to the family[7] and maintaining the family's precarious balance become more important than the personal development or well-being of individuals. Change may risk loss of individual family members' identity, accusations of betrayal, collapse of the family, and isolation from other family members. Consequently, resistance is viewed as a positive statement of dedication and loyalty to the family.

WORKING HYPOTHESES

The challenge for practitioners is to utilize resistance to change in ways that allow them to understand family-therapist interactions and to develop strategies for building positive relationships with families. Resistance cannot simply be labeled as "bad"; it must be used to gain insight and leverage in working with difficult families. The following working hypotheses provide a foundation for this work:

---

[4] This figure does not include surrendered children, wherein the goal of placement was to develop reattachments to an adoptive family. Total *N* for this study was 288.

[5] John Elderkin Bell, "A Theoretical Position for Family Group Therapy," *Family Process* 2 (1, 1963): 1–14.

[6] See Carol M. Anderson and Susan Stuart, *Mastering Resistance: A Practical Guide to Family Therapy* (New York: Guilford Press, 1983); and Michael Nichols, *Family Therapy Concepts and Methods* (New York: Gardner Press, 1984).

[7] Ivan Boszormenyi-Nagy and Geraldine M. Spark, *Invisible Loyalties* (New York: Brunner/Mazel, 1984).

1. *The therapist must begin where the family is.* Services must be relevant to the needs and wishes of clients.[8] This basic principle is often overlooked because of the dangers and risks perceived and accepted by professionals working with these families: continued physical or sexual abuse of children, neglect and risk of injury, violence to family members and the community, threats to helpers, self-destructive behavior, and eviction or abandonment of a family member. Community agencies and practitioners often feel a greater urgency for change than do the families themselves. This pressure for change can easily lead an otherwise sensitive practitioner to expend a lot of energy probing into a family's background in a desperate search for causal factors or old wounds. The family's concerns, however, may be very different. The family may want to focus on issues such as dealing with the shame of being in therapy, the dread of an upcoming court hearing for a neglect petition or custody settlement, or getting child protective services "off their backs." Ignoring these issues can make a family feel unheard and resentful.

2. *Resistance often reflects unresolved issues with extended family that are acted out with community agencies, therapists, and others.* Conflicts that cannot be managed within a family are often acted out with police, teachers, or therapists. Practitioners need to know the context of a family's behavior in order to understand its meaning.[9] Many families who are referred to prevention or placement programs have experienced abuse, losses, abandonment, and chronic problems from one generation to the next.

3. *A family's level of resistance to counseling corresponds to both the pressure experienced for change and the pain inherent in confronting the family's dilemma.* It can be assumed that families who have worked with multiple agencies over many years without progress have extremely difficult problems that allow for little flexibility and change. Therapeutic responses must address the family's perceived dilemma. For example, a family may be concerned that the mother not return to prison and may resist a practitioner's efforts to discuss the children's behavioral problems and imminent risk of placement. The family's avoidance of painful issues of loss and grief may increase as pressure for change is experienced from professionals.

4. *The type of resistance fits the emotional stage of individuals in the family and serves to maintain the family system at its current stage of development.* Families go through stages of development just as individuals do,[10] and family problems may serve to protect a family from difficult transitions.[11] Family histories often reveal that the grandparents, parents, and children have experienced severe losses, abandonment, or abuse. Repetition of abuse from generation to generation has been reported in many

---

[8] Anthony Maluccio, *Learning from Clients* (New York: Free Press, 1979), p. 186; Kaplan, *Working with Multi-Problem Families;* and Geraldine McKinney, "Adapting Family Therapy to Multideficit Families," *Social Casework* 51 (June 1970): 327–33.

[9] Anita Morawetz and Gillian Walker, *Brief Therapy with Single-Parent Families* (New York: Brunner/Mazel, 1984), p. 76.

[10] Monica McGoldrick and Elizabeth A. Carter, "The Family Life Cycle," in *Normal Family Process,* ed. Froma Walsh (New York: Guilford Press, 1982).

[11] Paul Watzlawick, John H. Weakland, and Richard Fisch, *Change: Principles of Problem Formation and Problem Resolution* (New York: Norton, 1974).

studies.[12] The emotional development of family members is often stymied by acting-out behavior typical of an earlier stage of emotional development. From this perspective, a parent's frequent moves, for example, from city to city or from home to institution, correspond to a child's running away and the physical abuse or temper of a parent is similar to the tantrums of a child.

5. *Resistance tests the usefulness of the therapist–family relationship.* From this perspective, resistance provides families with a valuable screening technique to determine whether it is safe for them to establish a relationship with the therapist and whether they are able to make potentially risky and painful changes. For example, can the therapist handle their pain, their secrets; their misery, and the awful things they have done, such as incest, abuse, or neglect of an infant? Will they be able to talk about their primary fears: feelings of panic over feared abandonment, fear of being alone, a yearning for their mother despite years of abuse, and so forth? Can the therapist help them while understanding how frightening change can be? Can they trust this person after working with so many professionals who have left them after short periods? Will the therapist reject them as so many have apparently done before? From the family's experience of generations of abandonment and rejection, developing a positive relationship with a therapist is a major accomplishment.

BASIC STRATEGIES TO ENGAGE FAMILIES AND PROMOTE CHANGE

Work with resistant families involves careful navigation through seemingly endless roadblocks that test a therapist's persistence and sensitivity to a family's dilemma. The following strategies are useful in avoiding major pitfalls in work with troubled families.

Coordination with Referral Sources And Other Service Providers

Involvement of all systems—schools, other therapists, probation departments, child protective services, and so forth—is essential. Services must be coordinated or the professionals who are involved will tend to reflect the conflicts within the family and change will not occur.[13] Service providers should meet and develop an integrated plan based on a shared understanding of the family's problems, strengths, and goals. The family therapist should be introduced to the family by the referral source whenever possible, and respective roles should be clearly delineated. Intake conferences and quarterly review conferences are ideal times for coordinating efforts to achieve goals and for further defining the roles of service providers. Conferences also allow the therapist

---

[12] See Eva Frommer, "Preventive Work in Vulnerable Families with Young Children," *Child Abuse and Neglect* 3 (March 1979), p. 778; John Spinetta and David Rigler, "The Child Abusing Parent, a Psychological Review," *Psychological Bulletin* 67 (April 1972): 296–304; and Jack Oliver, "Some Studies of Families in Which Children Suffer Maltreatment," in *Challenge of Child Abuse,* ed. Alfred Franklin (New York: Grune and Stratton, 1977), pp. 16–37.

[13] Beulah Compton, "The Family-Centered Project" (Paper presented at the annual meeting of the Children's Aid Society of Winnipeg, April 25, 1962, Winnipeg, Manitoba).

to see how the family interacts with the other agencies and professionals who are involved.

Outreach

For extremely closed and chronic family systems such as those involving incest, child abuse or neglect, and family court referrals, home visits help engage family members by allowing the therapist to communicate his or her concern and to establish personal contact with individual members.[14] A therapist often picks up vital clues during home visits. A house with tightly drawn shades often reflects depression. A light shining on the mother's medications may indicate her feelings of disability and extreme dependence on drugs for support. The lack of a bed for a child currently in placement may reflect a family's reluctance to take the child home. An empty liquor bottle on the mantle may suggest a family's struggle with alcohol.

Maintaining Respect and Validating the System

Family systems approaches have described problems as creative solutions to underlying dilemmas.[15] From this perspective, it is possible to respect a family's efforts, to respect the efforts of other professionals, and to identify the positive aspects of an individual's behavior. When respect is lacking, family members tend to be defiant and involvement of the family in a working relationship is impossible to achieve.

It is essential to identify the dilemmas of all members of the system, including those who are absent, while being empathic to their needs and recognizing their contributions to the family. Past treatment efforts and family helpers should be acknowledged by finding out the family's perception of their value and asking for past assessments by other professionals. It is also important to identify cultural values, negative and positive networks, and connections with friends, relatives, and religious organizations. These families are often isolated; support networks with friends, relatives, other professionals, and neighbors need to be developed and nurtured to facilitate and maintain change.

Avoid Symmetrical Power Struggles[16]

It is important that the therapist not take over for families and that he or she promote the family's efforts to make choices. The family's options should be stressed at the time of referral, for example, to work with another clinic or to return to court to try to change an order for counseling. Often therapists increase pressure on a family to make

---

[14] See Marvin Bryce, "Family Support Program for Trouble Juveniles," (Chicago: School of Social Services Administration, University of Chicago, September 1981); Kaplan, "Working with Multi-Problem Families"; and Salvador Minuchin, "The Plight of the Poverty-Stricken Family in the United States," *Child Welfare* 49 (March 1970): 124–30.

[15] See Peggy Papp, *The Process of Change* (New York: Guilford Press, 1983); Morawetz and Walker, *Brief Therapy with Single-Parent Families;* Richard Fisch, John H. Weakland, and Lynn Segal, *The Tactics of Change: Doing Brief Therapy* (New York: Jossey-Bass, 1982); Frank S. Pittman, "Wet Cocker Spaniel Therapy: An Essay on Technique in Family Therapy," *Family Process* 23 (March 1984): 1–9; and Joel Bergman, *Fishing for Barracuda* (New York: Norton, 1985).

[16] Guy Ausloos, personal communication, March 1985.

changes in response to that family's resistance. In such cases, an adversarial relationship develops that prohibits change. In the end, the family will reassert the importance of protecting their own integrity over compliance with outside demands.

It is important for therapists to remain sensitive to the family's need for stability.[17] Encouraging restraint in changes and urging the family to consider carefully the advantages and disadvantages of change are useful techniques.[18] The family must feel that the therapist appreciates the functional value of their problems.[19]

Circular Questioning to Expand Perspectives

The circular questioning process developed by Mara Palazzoli and associates is a very helpful approach for expanding a family's perspectives and options.[20] The therapist can ask a family member how his or her mother, father, grandmother, and so forth have handled a problem. Who was the most upset? How did different family members perceive the problem? What will happen if the problem continues for ten years? Who will still be in the family? Questions such as these help clarify differences in behavior and perceptions that reflect the interactional process in the family. Questions and redefinitions that connect current problems to a time perspective (past to the future) and to relationships with extended family can introduce new information to the family.

MAINTAINING PRESENCE WHILE ADDRESSING PAINFUL DILEMMAS

Therapists must demonstrate genuine concern, persistence, and a belief in their work. The therapist must use him- or herself fully as a therapist by using his or her feelings to assess the family system and by employing humor, warmth, "I" messages, and flexibility to engage a family. Therapists need support from supervisors, consultants, and colleagues in order to maintain objectivity and potency. Use of teams and working within a training-research model provide the context needed for staff to work with resistance and painful dilemmas as well as to test and refine approaches.[21]

FRAMEWORK FOR ASSESSMENT AND TREATMENT PLANNING

Specific strategies to engage and promote change within families must be based on hypotheses about how the process of resistance protects families from their primary fears and tests the family-therapist relationship. Table 89–1 outlines a process for identifying typical patterns of resistance encountered in family work. A therapist begins to utilize resistance by identifying his or her own reactions and feelings when a stern-looking

[17] Weitzman, "Engaging the Severely Dysfunctional Family in Treatment."
[18] Fisch, Weakland, and Segal, *The Tactics of Change*.
[19] Weitzman, "Engaging the Severely Dysfunctional Family in Treatment."
[20] Maura Selvini Palazzoli et al., "Hypothesizing Circularity-Neutrality: Three Guidelines for the Conduction of Sessions," *Family Process* 19 (March 1980): 3–12.
[21] See Peggy Papp, *The Process of Change;* Miranda Breit, Won-Gi Im, and R. Stephanie Wilner, "Strategic Approaches with Resistant Families," *American Journal of Family Therapy* 11 (1, 1983): 51–58; and Bergman, *Fishing for Barracuda*.

Table 89–1.
Working with resistance: A framework for assessment and treatment planning.

Primary resistance patterns (examples)

Denial ("No problem.")
Blaming ("It's all_____'s fault.")
Labeling ("He's been diagnosed as _____.")
Fragility ("Don't push too hard.")
Driven parent ("If I don't do everything, nobody will.")
Induction ("We like you. You're part of our family.")
Avoidance ("He couldn't be here.")
Crises ("We're in terrible trouble.")
Discounting ("It hasn't helped. You're no good.")
Helplessness ("What's the use?")
Environmental hurdles/dangers ("Cockroaches, lice . . . it's the pits.")
Therapist's resistance ("I can't, I shouldn't, I must . . .")

Identification of feelings

Therapist's reaction/feelings toward resistance
Family feelings/beliefs, what they fear most

Development of strategies to engage family and promote change

Hypothesis on the function of resistance in therapist-family interaction
Specific strategies

family member sits stiffly with arms crossed or when a therapist enters a family's dwelling and is greeted by large barking dogs, strange odors, and a blaring television. The therapist's gut feelings provide clues to pressures and unstated messages in work with families; these reactions can be used as indicators of the family's feelings and fears. A hypothesis can be formulated that addresses how the pattern of behavior of resistance makes sense in terms of the family's dilemma (see Table 89–1) This hypothesis can then serve as the foundation for creative interventions to engage the family,[22] to build on family strengths, and to begin the process of change, that is, "to get a family past its snag point."[23]

CASE EXAMPLE: THE CRAZY ODOR

The P family was referred by a child protective services worker who stated that the oldest daughter, E, had not attended school for two years. E, who was fifteen years old, had been hospitalized and diagnosed for childhood schizophrenia approximately one

---

[22] Specific strategies for engaging families, based on each pattern of resistance identified in Table 89–1, can be obtained by writing to the authors.
[23] Pittman, "Wet Cocker Spaniel Therapy."

year prior to the referral. At the time of the referral, the family had exhausted the staff of three other agencies. In one instance, E had smashed a one-way mirror at a mental health clinic, telling one and all that no one should observe the family.

E's mother, father, and four other children lived in a three-bedroom, somewhat run-down home. The family owned two dogs (one rather large), five cats, twenty-seven white mice, and a fish tank of piranhas. The home was smelly and dark.

E was at imminent risk of placement either in a residential treatment facility or hospital, and the family was being taken to court by the department of social services for educational neglect. It was apparent that the family members would not seek help on their own.

The therapist's first role was to coordinate the efforts of the child protective service worker, the school, and the court. The process of placement had to be delayed in order to give the therapist a chance to intervene and work with the family. Because the family was such a closed system, it was necessary to contact the family by letter and to set up a home visit. They distrusted professionals and had isolated themselves from the community. To engage the family, a "don't trust" message was incorporated in a letter, which had the paradoxical effect of allowing staff of the prevention program to make an initial home visit.

Dear _____:

I would like to begin by asking you *not* to trust me. I know you have had many caseworkers before me, and because I am just another caseworker and a stranger to you, there is *no* reason why you should trust me.

Please allow me to introduce myself as both your and your daughter's new caseworker. I realize, Mrs. P, that it has been a while since you have been involved with a caseworker from Parsons Child and Family Center, as you never got the chance to actually meet _____ in person, and it can be pretty hard having to talk with a stranger. What I really need, Mrs. P, is your help in planning for your daughter's future so that we can work together in making permanent plans for her.

Again, Mrs. P, I know it can be scary having to talk with someone you do not know, especially when you do not have the option of choosing that person yourself, but I would like very much to have the opportunity to meet you. Would you be so kind as to contact me at 555-2222, so that we may arrange a convenient time either here in the office or at your home, whichever you prefer. Thanks so much for your anticipated cooperation.

I am looking forward to meeting you.

On the first visit, the therapist had to deal with the following types of resistance (see Table 1):

1. *Environmental resistance*—Terrible smells that permeated the home, dogs barking and snapping.
2. *Denial of the problem*—"She's not crazy." "They called her schizophrenic, but she's my right hand." "We can't be without her help."

3. *Little trust in helpers*—The shades were drawn, the windows and doors were locked.

4. *The driven parent*—"We have tried everything for her and our other kids, but no one seems to be able to help."

5. *Helplessness*—"And we don't think anything will change. Look at my husband and myself—we have been sleeping on the couch and a chair in the living room for over seven years."

6. *Blaming*—Everyone in the family stated that it was the outside world that was to blame. "If it weren't for the school" or "if it weren't for child protective services and the neighbors," they would be all right.

7. *Fragility*—The family seemed frightened, constantly on guard, and fearful that E would do something dangerous. (Prior to hospitalization, she had tried to stab her father.)

8. *Induction*—The family attempted to get the therapist to agree with their views about the outside world and to identify with and become a part of the family. Disagreement caused them to feel that the therapist would betray the family and that they might have to evict the therapist from the home.

9. *Crisis*—The family feared E's removal from the home and the disintegration of their closed system.

All these resistances in the family masked the family's greatest fears—the death of a family member and the permanent dissolution of the family. No one would voice these fears. However, the therapist, who was frightened and on guard, began to anticipate an unpredictable and scary crisis.

To engage the family, it was necessary to deal with the many resistances used to fend off the outside world. The family was again instructed during the initial visit "not to trust me." The therapist put herself in a "one down" position by stating that she was no better than previous helpers and perhaps worse. The therapist could try to work with them, but only if they wanted some help, not because they were referred or ordered to have help. The "don't trust me" message and the placing of the therapist in a "one down" position precluded the family's efforts to discount the therapist while giving members an opportunity to recognize the truth.[24]

Denial, labeling, and the environmental obstacles of this family were approached by using dramatic statements and gestures. The therapist coughed and said that the smell was making her choke. The therapist began to use the word "crazy" as a descriptive adjective in order to redefine E's (and the family's) label as crazy and to diffuse its potency. Whenever possible, the therapist asked about "that crazy smell" in the house or talked about "those crazy drivers" and how "it's pretty crazy to sleep sitting in a chair for seven years." The word "crazy" was used in a humorous, nonconfrontational manner. The continued visits of the therapist helped the family realize that outsiders could enter their home without posing a threat.

The fragility of the family was also addressed. The therapist felt anxious with each intervention and recognized her own concerns about someone getting hurt. She trans-

---

[24] Margaret Griffel, personal communication, May 1980.

ferred these feelings to the family by talking in general terms about how everyone feared that someone could get hurt—especially by the outside world. The family was told that all work would proceed very slowly and carefully in order to deal with their fear that the therapist, as a representative of the outside world, might also hurt them. This message of restraint helped the family feel that they had some control over the pace of work, which was especially important for a family that was so fearful of losing control. Family members were also given the opportunity to set their own goals and were not pressured to make dramatic changes. For example, the parents making a decision as to what goals they wanted to work on was accepted as a goal in itself. In this family, significant decisions had not been made in more than fourteen years. Paradoxically, the messages given by the therapist, especially those of restraining change and setting simple goals, helped the family react a little faster to needed changes.

The fragility and fear of induction of the therapist was addressed by informing the family that the therapist would be bringing the team consultant to their home. It was explained that the consultant was for the therapist's use only in an effort to enhance her work with such a mind-boggling family. The therapist also addressed her own fear of E's unpredictable behavior, such as throwing books and other objects down the stairs or running unexpectedly into the room, by openly stating how startled and scared she was when this behavior occurred. The therapist's fears opened discussion about the family's fears.

The crisis issue was addressed by exploring the family's views of their current situation. The details of their current crisis as well as their initial crisis trust got them involved with the psychiatric, social services, and legal community were explored. These discussions helped the family begin to develop an awareness of the dysfunctional patterns operating in the family and of how each member's acting-out behavior contributed to these patterns. The therapist was thus given the means by which to predict future crises and help the family anticipate and change patterns of behavior.

Using these interventions, this resistant, isolated family worked with the therapist on a weekly basis. The drawn shades were opened. The "crazy smell" drifted out the open windows, and many of the animals, including all twenty-seven mice and the two dogs, were given away. By giving the parents permission to work slowly on developing a single goal, the family was able to begin looking for a new home with adequate sleeping space for everyone.

As the parents' behavior became less "crazy," they were able to perceive that E was not the only problem. In turn, E began to understand that she no longer had to sacrifice herself to keep the family safe from the outside world. Despite strenuous effort on her part to maintain her "sacrificial" role, she eventually ceded power to her parents and began to explore training programs in an adult education center.

With the help of the therapist, the family slowly began to negotiate successfully with the outside world. Further work began as long-term problems and family cut-offs surfaced.

CONCLUSION

The case example shows how working with resistance based on a therapist's self-knowledge and openness to his or her own feelings can facilitate change in severely dysfunctional families. Home-based family work often requires a therapist to experience a family's tension, turmoil, and fears without becoming defensive or aggressive. The therapist must be persistent enough to establish and maintain a relationship that allows the development of sufficient trust so that the family can begin to make changes in patterns of behavior and roles. By tracing the patterns of resistance encountered and by identifying the therapist's and family's feelings, a therapist can develop a hypothesis about the function of resistance in the therapist–family interaction. This hypothesis can then be used to help the therapist understand the family's experience and to engage the family.

THE FAMILY

CHAPTER 90

HOME-BASED FAMILY THERAPY

Leonard J. Woods

Treatment of families in the home setting is not a novel idea: the practice dates back to the roots of social work in the early twentieth century.[1] In the beginning, the technique of reaching out with "friendly visitors" was the modus operandi of social work.[2] The status of the home visit and the emphasis on clients' social environments have lost ground as the social work field was influenced by psychoanalysis and individual pathology theory. In the areas of social work that traditionally have used the least trained personnel, home visits continued to be relied on, but in other areas of social work, especially psychiatric social work, home visiting began to be seen as unprofessional and even as an invasion of clients' privacy.[3] As psychiatry became entrenched in social service institutions, the locus of treatment became the office or hospital setting. Home visits were reported to be valuable to the psychiatric clinician as a diagnostic and a therapeutic tool.[4] In practice, however, few therapists actually made home visits, particularly not those who worked for large psychiatric clinics.

Additionally, as psychiatry became more institutionalized it became less involved in and concerned with matters outside of the inner sanctum of the office, and its domain became the inner world of id, ego, and super ego. This focus created a separation between the realm of psychiatry and individuals' social environments. St. Elizabeths Hospital in Washington, D.C., sought to use home visits with schizophrenics to initiate therapy at the hospital. Behrens noted that when social workers accompanied therapists on home visits, their presence was valued because of their experience dealing with reality situations.[5]

Therapists' unfamiliarity and discomfort with reality situations of clients result from psychiatry's segregation of people from their day-to day social reality. Social work willingly joined psychiatry and sought refuge within its institutional walls, leav-

Reprinted from *Social Work*, Vol. 33, No. 3 (May–June, 1988), pp. 211–214, by permission of NASW Press. Copyright 1988, National Association of Social Workers, Inc., *Social Work*.

ing its clients and their realities outside. With the emergence of family therapy and the focus on individuals as part of a larger set of family and social interactions rather than in isolation, a renewed effort to deal with the family in its own social context might have been expected. Despite its historical roots, and its periodic resurgence, therapy in the home has not received the amount of direct application and close scrutiny it deserves.[6] Minuchin argues that "the importance of the individual's context is recognized, but there has been a curious dearth of therapeutic attempts to modify that context. . . ."[7] Instead of renewed attempts to modify the context, family therapy has followed the way of psychiatry and become institutionalized. Simon noted that although there are hundreds of family therapy institutions around the world that have trained thousands of people, the institutions that serve people themselves have remained unchanged.[8]

The author has worked predominantly with lower-income multiproblem families, and is concerned with developing models to increase the level of effective service to this population. Traditional family therapy models primarily have produced poor results with this population (except certain aspects of structural family therapy). Family therapists have abandoned this population because of shrinking resources allocated to this population and because of their legitimate desire to better their own living situations. Simon stated recently that

> Few of family therapy's leaders work regularly with low income groups; and journal and conference programs are hardly overflowing with reports of innovative projects with the poor. Faced with economic necessities in their own lives, most family therapists today treat a middle class clientele.[9]

In-home family therapy should not be espoused to the exclusion of therapy done in other settings. On the contrary, the merits of in-home family therapy should be explored to raise it to the same level of respectability as other forms of family therapy, and therefore expand rather than restrict the field. Haley points out the importance of variety in the field of family therapy:

> Experienced family therapists also recognize that family therapy is an orientation to a problem and not a method of treatment so that different approaches sometimes have different advantages.[10]

Social work's aims to expand the range of possible options within a family, and thus it is appropriate that social workers strive for a similar goal within the therapy system itself.

Family therapy can be used in different ways (for example, various settings, lengths of therapy, different members present during the sessions), and each form of therapy deserves attention. The exclusion of certain family therapy formats is premature, particularly because so little currently is known about what makes family therapy effective.[11] In-home family therapy has some unique qualities and potential advantages that merit exploration.

STRUCTURING TO MEET FAMILIES' NEEDS

Although family therapists accommodate families' needs by having office hours that include evenings and Saturdays, this is insufficient to accommodate the pressures certain segments of the population (such as single parents, lower-income families, and underorganized families) face. For example, one family the author worked with consisted of a mother and five children ages 3 to 13.[12] They had to take two buses to get to the therapy appointments, and the mother decided that they were going to stop coming to therapy. Bus tickets were offered, but there were other factors even more important than the expense in her decision to stop therapy: the time and energy needed to prepare dinner, feed and dress five children, and take two buses and a transfer stop were enormous. However, the major factor in her decision was the return trip, because it took place in dangerous neighborhoods after dark. For families whose resources are taxed already, if getting help for themselves requires traveling to an office, that itself can be another overwhelming factor working against any potential benefit of therapy for the family. When these issues are not addressed, agencies that espouse the beliefs of a family system approach disregard the context of the family and only treat the family as an isolated unit. Social work agencies thus replicate the mistakes of the medical psychiatric model, except individuals separated from their social realities are now replaced by families separated from their social realities.

DIRECT OBSERVATION

Direct observation of a family in the natural environment of their home can bring into focus more quickly the significant dynamics in the family and can help guide the treatment. A family's home setting can remove the facade of adjustment a family presents in a therapist's office and can increase the possibility of dealing directly as with a family's real problems. Although alert therapists can discern many family patterns in any context, observing them occurring directly and spontaneously in a family's most familiar setting creates an especially vivid picture.[13]

For example, during three office therapy sessions the father in one family spoke glowingly about the family's improved financial status as a result of his efforts to budget the family's money. During a fourth session held in the home a thunderstorm left the family and the therapist sitting in the living room barely able to see each other because the electric service had been shut off. This led to the revelation that the gas and phone service also had been disconnected. The children confronted their father with their concern and fears about the discrepancies between what he says and what he does about budgeting. Talking about the discrepancies between the goals of managing the house and his lack of concrete efforts was a natural way to address the family's tendency not to follow through or back up with actions the intentions they verbalize.

Physical characteristics of a family's home (how it is cleaned, arranged, and furnished) also can tell a therapist a lot about how a family views itself. The home not only reflects certain qualities of a family but also may maintain patterns it was created to exemplify. One family who lived in a low-income housing project boarded up the windows to prevent break-ins. They were physically and psychologically closed in and isolated from the rest of the community. Discussions with the family often centered on their worry about the "people in this project" stealing from them. Their boarded-up house indicated their desire to separate themselves from what they perceived to be the "undesirable" community.

Every family home is full of symbolism to family members, and each family manifests the symbolism in different ways. It may be manifested in the arrangement of family pictures on the wall, where pictures are displayed, or whose picture is missing. Most families have a "special chair" in the living room that has significance. Heirlooms of every kind possess tremendous importance to families, and for many families their entire house serves as an heirloom. Heirlooms can provide powerful "anchors" to families.[14] Therapists can understand a family by being in the home and being exposed to these anchors. Statements such as "this is still Grandma's house," "no one can sit in Dad's seat," "excuse the hole in the wall, but we've never been able to get around to fixing up all the damage done by my ex- . . . ," are spoken spontaneously in the home. The information provided by these anchors might never be revealed in a therapist's office.

Seeing a family in their home also allows for a more natural and less resistant avenue to confront family patterns. One family owned eight extremely active poodles, who were put in the basement during sessions because they yelped at strangers. In one session the therapist pressed the father to assert himself as an authority figure in the family. He became anxious and opened the basement door freeing the poodles and creating such a disturbance that for 20 minutes the session was disrupted. The avoidance and resistance behavior was so obvious that not even the father could resist addressing the matter. This incident was critical because the father's role in perpetuating the family problems was uncovered and because the drama allowed for a more lighthearted and less threatening discussion in following sessions. To conduct in-home family therapy effectively, therapists must be flexible and creative enough to recognize and stimulate such chance occurrences. They also must be able to stay out of family patterns and allow a family to enact behaviors before actively intervening to bring about behavior change.

HEIGHTENED REALITY CONTEXT

The therapy process is altered when it is moved into the home setting, because the therapy occurs in a heightened reality context that includes the possible participant--observer role of the therapist, more active involvement of family members, and the opportunity for immediate analysis of family members' actual behavior.[15] In the home setting, the family is in its natural habitat and the therapist is the intruder. Much understanding of human relationships can be gained when roles are reversed. When a family comes to a professional's office, they often dress in their "Sunday best" and treat the therapist with deference. The therapist often assigns seats and roles, and much of the family's normal spontaneity is cut off by the artificial setting of the office. At home, the family is more apt to play their everyday roles; if anyone has to undergo an unnatural role shift, it is most likely the therapist.[16] One client observed about a home session that "This was good for us. When we come to your office I am aware of minding my p's and q's and being on my best behavior. It's hard to relax and just be myself."

Most therapists agree that first-hand knowledge of a family's interaction and environmental influences is necessary to make an accurate diagnosis and treatment plan for the family.[17] In-home reenactments of behaviors or incidents offer a therapist the opportunity not only to see the problem behavior or situation as it could never be described in words, but also to use interventions to alter it as it occurs.

Family seating arrangements reveal information about family interaction patterns. In the home, the seating arrangements usually are well established. It can produce powerful change to, for example, have a father shift some of his actions and responsibilities in an office setting; it can be even more potent to orchestrate such family pattern shifts immediately in the family's home. The author worked at home with a family consisting of a husband, wife, and 15-year-old son; at one session the mother sat on a couch and the son on a love seat, while the father sat in the recliner. The mother and son shared their feelings for 30 minutes while the father sat in withdrawn silence. When asked why the father did not get to speak about his feelings, the mother and son offered various explanations, apologies, and criticisms, and the father remained silent. When the father was asked to change seats and did so, he began to speak of his silence as an attempt not to interfere with the mother–son relationship. Feelings then surfaced that brought the whole family close to tears. The developments were not anticipated by the therapist before the seating rearrangement, but were used as they occurred.

The in-home family therapist places value in arranging the family's home so that it becomes maximally functional for the family. All the power instilled in the home environment is acknowledged and developed so that established dysfunctional behavior patterns give way to more functional patterns.

IMPLEMENTATION OF NEW BEHAVIORS

The heightened reality context of family therapy in the home alters the therapy process. Friedman observed that:

> The transfer value of therapy conducted "in vivo" in the real milieu of the family and home, is greater than that of psychotherapy done in the socially isolated context of office or hospital. In conventional therapy the patient has to transfer what he has learned in his therapy, secondarily, over to the relationships with the members of his family.[18]

In-home family therapy allows the family to implement immediately the new behaviors right in the home. New behaviors can he applied directly, not practiced in an artificial setting. Some behavior therapists use in-home sessions to role play and monitor performance of certain skills.[19] The therapist's ability to coach new behaviors on the spot helps to minimize clients' failures, however, it does increase the therapist's risks because the therapist will be present if the technique fails and thus will have to own, along with the family, any lack of progress.

In-home family therapy allows the therapist to use the home itself to maintain therapeutic gains even after sessions have concluded. It is possible to build into the home setting anchors that the family can use to maintain or extend the progress made in therapy.

For example, one family functioned constantly in competition with a television set on high volume every waking moment. When the therapist requested the television be off during sessions, an unbelieving silence ensued. One of the youngsters turned the volume off and left the picture on; the picture served as a security blanket for the family. Two sessions later the therapist requested the television be turned off because the family needed to listen and talk to each other without distraction. As the picture faded, the anxiety level rose dramatically, and the youngest child began to cry. The child was fearful that the silence might mean the divorce of the parents because other times the television had been off the parents had fought or been silent. Further discussion without the television allowed the family to experience interactions that were fearful, painful, touching, and joyful and that eventually decreased the fear of what silence might bring. The mother in this family now says that "When I enter the room and turn the volume off on the television, the family hears and respects every word I say. When I turn the television off completely everyone prepares for a family discussion. It's amazing that I don't have to fight to get them to hear me anymore."

ACCESS TO FAMILY SYSTEM

In-home therapy provides access to all of the relevant members in a family system. The family may include any number of related members, boyfriends and girlfriends, neighbors, friends, and other individuals. Any individual who lives in the home is relevant to the functioning of the family; the therapist's presence in the home opens up a way to involve them in the process of therapy naturally.

In-home therapy increases the likelihood of access to family members who find it difficult or impossible to attend an office appointment. Family therapy must be available to employed family members and those who are handicapped, young children, or aged, or its effectiveness is diminished.[20] In one case the first session allowed unanticipated access to three generations. The case involved a 15-year-old girl who had problems in school and episodes of running away, drug and alcohol abuse, and sexual promiscuity. During the first session a maternal aunt happened to stop by and shortly thereafter the maternal grandmother called and asked to stop by. Once everyone was assembled, the room contained the therapist, the 15-year-old girl, her 18-year old sister, the mother, the maternal aunt, a 9-year-old niece, and the 83-year-old grandmother. An interesting change took place in the girl as these people arrived at her house. The conversation became more and more focused on the helplessness of the adult women to "figure out the child" and to gain control of this dangerous situation. They pointed out how each had tried to reach her through kindness and gentleness. The girl changed from presenting herself as a pleasant, intelligent, resourceful young woman into someone who was vulgar, abusive, and callous. When the therapist remarked that her behavior resembled that of an abusive husband, the youngest child broke into tears.

A major issue for the family was the multigenerational influence of abusive alcoholic men. As the abusive figure left each generation, the next generation produced someone to replace him. Not surprisingly, this girl's personality change occurred shortly after her father's death from drug- and alcohol-related causes. All of the family members were struggling with this issue and were together helping this girl fill the void of the abusive male. It would have been impossible to work with this group in an office setting and the potency of the multigenerational factor would have been untouched, and therefore able to counteract any change attempted between family members.

Another important advantage of in-home therapy is the ability to more easily and naturally involve children of all ages. Very young children, in particular, can more easily be accommodated in the home because the environment allows them to enter and exit the process with limited adult interaction. Speck wrote on the input from young children to enhance therapy:

> In an ordinary office setting, it is usually a difficult to work with family members under the age of eight. In the home, however, children as young as one year can be present for shorter or longer periods during the family therapy session. Young children in the five to 10 age group frequently make significant contributions to the therapy, often by way of softly spoken, seemingly innocuous remarks. It has repeatedly been found that disturbed psychotic adults or relatively normal young children have been the most direct and cogent in their expression of some of the on-going family problems.[21]

ENTERING THE FAMILY'S REALITY

One of the most common sentiments people in therapy express, particularly those whose cultural, ethnic, or financial status and values are not reflected in the agency or therapist, is that professional helpers do not really understand and appreciate the difficulty of the client's situation. Whether true or not, perceptions of misunderstanding must be resolved if therapy is to be successful.

When a therapist works in the client's home, he or she sends a message to the family that they are willing to step into the family's world. The pressures and concerns a family faces come into the open and the family can see if the therapist can appreciate and understand their problems. Therapists are put in the same vulnerable position that they routinely ask clients to occupy. The family evaluates their therapist and makes judgments based on how he or she reacts to their reality. This process becomes even more important if the class, race, gender, or cultural gap between family and therapist is wide. When a therapist is in the clients' home, the potential exists for a very strong rapport to develop between the therapist and the family. Clients often feel their therapist understands them because the therapist has seen how things really are in the family.

One parent had seen two previous therapists who had given her suggestions to implement at home with her children. The suggestions were not found ineffective and discarded, but never were used because the mother became overwhelmed by a sense of hopelessness about the child's behavior problems. The mother felt that the third therapist understood the extreme nature of the problem because he was present during a temper outburst and she felt that she had support at home; thus she was able to attempt to implement one of the alternatives suggested. Erickson explained:

> Merely to make a correct diagnosis of the illness and to know the correct method of treatment is not enough. Fully as important is that the patient be receptive of

the therapy and cooperative in regard to it. Without the patient's full cooperativeness, therapeutic results are delayed, distorted, limited or even prevented.[22]

Acknowledging the need to continue their functions of family life with minimal interruptions is a tremendous message of respect to a family. Actions such as going to their home and accommodating the family's schedule not only minimize disruption but also help establish a strong sense of rapport with a family.

PRACTICE CHANGES USEFUL

In-home family therapy is feasible and successful for both diagnostic and therapeutic purposes. Regardless of whether the home is used only for the initial meeting, to break an occasional impasse, or for the duration of therapy, each in-home session allows an opportunity for a therapist to experience the unique aspects of each family. Fisch states:

> Continuing work with families will demonstrate that without having visited the home at least once, the therapist loses considerable information about timing, pacing, who waits for whom, who tends to set the tempo of family life, and how this is agreed upon. . . .[23]

Haley spoke of the need for "new ways" in therapy:

> What family therapists mostly have in common they also share with a number of behavioral scientists in the world today: There is an increasing awareness that psychiatric problems are social problems which involve the total ecological system. There is a concern with, and an attempt to change what happens with the family, its interlocking systems, and the social institutions in which it is embedded. The fragmentation of the individual or the family into parts is being abandoned. There is a growing consensus that a new ecological framework defines problems in new ways, and calls for new ways in therapy.[24]

Using the home as the locus of family therapy is just one possible new way. In-home family therapy does not guarantee success, but it does enhance the chance for success. Because the tenets of family therapy and the experience of those who practice it all support the efficacy of therapy done in the home or natural context, the focus should not be the locus of therapy, but rather the institutions that prevent the use of a therapeutic approach. Sefarbi calls this an "effort to reclaim a legacy," specifically, to draw attention again to the need of therapists to stop spending so much time in their offices working on peoples' heads.[25] Montalvo said:

> The problem is that, because of funding problems and ill-conceived ideas about "cost-effectiveness," agencies no longer can be paid for home visits with families. As a result, the invaluable time a therapist might put in at a school conference or trying to help a family negotiate with a housing authority is no longer reimbursable. I'm afraid the tradition of community outreach work is being lost.[26]

Agencies should apply principles of family systems thinking when examining why new ways are not being used and why a tradition of social services is being lost. Service providers may be failing to include themselves in the formula when they think in terms of systems and service delivery to families.

NOTES AND REFERENCES

1. M. E. Richmond, *Social Diagnosis* (New York: Russell Sage Foundation, 1917).
2. M. L. Bloom, "Usefulness of the Home-visit for Diagnosis and Treatment," *Social Casework*, 54 (February 1973), pp. 67–75.
3. Ibid.
4. M. D. Behrens, "Brief Home Visits by the Clinic Therapist in the Treatment of Lower Class Patients," *American Journal of Psychiatry*, 124 (September 1967), p. 128; and J. M. Chappel and R. S. Daniells, "Home Visiting in a Black Urban Ghetto," *American Journal of Psychiatry*, 126 (April 1970), pp. 1455–1460.
5. Behrens, "Brief Home Visits by the Clinic Therapist in the Treatment of Lower Class Patients," p. 128.
6. N. W. Ackerman, *Treating the Troubled Family* (New York: Basic Books, Inc., 1966).
7. S. L. Minuchin, B. L. Baker, and L. Rosman, "A Conceptual Model of Psychosomatic Illness in Children," *Archives of General Psychiatry*, 32 (August 1974), p. 1032.
8. R. Simon, "Stranger in a Strange Land: An Interview with Salvadore Minuchin," *Family Therapy Networker*, 8 (November–December 1984), p. 30.
9. R. Simon, "Across the Great Divide," *Family Therapy Networker* (January–February 1986), p. 26.
10. J. Haley, "Beginning and Experienced Family Therapists," in A. Ferber, M. Mendelsohn, and A. Napier, eds., *The Book of Family Therapy* (Boston: Houghton Mifflin Co., 1973), pp. 166–167.
11. M. Bryce, *Home Based Services for Children and Families* (Springfield, Ill.: Charles C Thomas, 1979).
12. All case examples and direct quotes not otherwise attributed are from the author's practice experience.
13. R. V. Speck, "Family Therapy in the Home," *Journal of Marriage and Family*, 26 (February 1964), pp. 72–76.
14. M. King, C. Citrenbaum, and L. Novik, *Irresistible Communication* (Philadelphia: W. B. Saunders Co., 1983), p. 104.
15. A. S. Friedman, "Family Therapy as Conducted in the Home," *Family Process*, 1 (March 1962), pp. 132–140.
16. Speck, "Family Therapy in the Home."
17. C. C. Hansen, "An Extended Home Visit with Conjoint Family Therapy," *Family Process*, 7 (April 1968), pp. 67–87.
18. Friedman, "Family Therapy as Conducted in the Home," p. 133.
19. G. R. Patterson, J. B. Reid, and R. E. Conger, *Families and Aggressive Children* (vol. 1; Eugene, Oreg.: Castalia Publishing Co., 1975).

20. H. P. Laqueur, "Multiple Family Therapy," in A. Ferber, M. Mendelsohn, and A. Napier, eds., *The Book of Family Therapy* (Boston: Houghton Mifflin Co., 1973), pp. 618–636; and R. H. Schlacter, "Home Counseling of Adolescents and Parents," *Social Work*, 20 (November 1975), pp. 427–428.

21. Speck, "Family Therapy in the Home," pp. 73–74.

22. M. H. Erickson, "The Use of Symptoms as an Integral Part of Hypnotherapy," *The American Journal of Hypnosis*, 8 (July 1965), p. 57.

23. R. Fisch, "The Home Visit in Private Psychiatric Practice," *Family Process*, 3 (March 1964), p. 116.

24. Haley, "Beginning and Experienced Family Therapists," pp. 166–167.

25. R. Sefarbi, "To Reclaim a Legacy: Social Rehabilitation," *Child and Adolescent Social Work Journal*, 3 (Spring 1986), pp. 38–49.

26. B. Montalvo, "Lessons From the Past," *Family Therapy Networker*, (January–February 1986), p. 39.

VICTIMS

CHAPTER 91

WORKING WITH VICTIMS OF VIOLENT ASSAULT

Judith A. B. Lee and Susan J. Rosenthal

Crimes involving sudden violent assault are a fact of life in American society. Traumatic experiences such as mugging, gunshot wound, and rape are often devastating to the victim and the victim's family, friends, and neighbors. Helping professionals in all agencies and communities need to utilize special knowledge and skills to help clients in this acute situational crisis. Some clients receive psychological help after such an experience, but countless others simply go home after receiving medical care and try to resume their lives, often haunted by unresolved feelings and in need of a range of services. Once the experience is over, many people cope by repressing it and, as a result, may be misdiagnosed when they finally come in contact with mental health professionals. In one case, a client was not able to admit that she had been raped to her mental health worker, who was seeing her for a mild depression, reactive to separation from her husband. The worker viewed the increase in agitation and a host of other fears and fantasies as psychotic symptoms. She discouraged the client from staying with her job and had her evaluated for medication. Further immobilized by medication and staying home, this client continued to deteriorate until she responded to outreach by a worker from an agency that served crime victims. Once she was able to disclose what had happened and share it with her mental health worker, she was able to progress toward resuming life.

In response to such needs, specialized agencies have emerged such as the Victim Services Agency in New York City, which is designed to reach out to victims of violent assault. Building on the knowledge base generic to all helping situations, it has also

Reprinted from *Social Casework*, Vol. 64, No. 10 (1983), pp. 593–599, by permission of the publisher, Families International, Inc.

developed a particular expertise in dealing with victims. One of the authors has been employed at the agency for several years. This article seeks to formulate notions on general patterns of response to violent assault and to evolve principles to guide helping in such situations. In illustrating the patterns and helping principles applicable to three types of assault— mugging, gunshot wound, and rape—the authors seek to determine strategies applicable in a range of situations. It is understood that rape, in a sense, deserves its own space because of the host of issues around sexuality and crisis protocol related to such an assault. Many authors have developed theory in this area.[1] However, violent assault in all of its manifestations produces certain common responses and it is possible to develop common strategies which would enable professionals to serve all assault victims more knowledgeably. The intent of this article is to examine commonalities useful in assessment and intervention with a range of victims of violent assault. Some parallels will also be drawn to the victims of assaultive illnesses.

THEORETICAL FRAMEWORK

Crisis theory as developed by Gerald Caplan, Lydia Rapoport, Howard J. Parad, Naomi Golan and others offers a general theoretical framework useful to practice with assault victims.[2] Specialized agencies and organizations such as Victim Services Agency and New York Women Against Rape have identified the particular themes commonly expressed by victims of rape and other violent crimes.[3] The life model of social work practice developed by Carel B. Germain and Alex Gitterman presents a holistic ecological perspective with which to view the total phenomena as does the theory related to coping and adaptation developed by such ego psychologists as Robert W. White, Heinz Hartmann, and George V. Coelho and associates.[4] These practice orientations seem most applicable to restoring equilibrium in the victims of violent assault.

The life model approach sees stress as arising in three interrelated areas: life transitions involving developmental changes, status and role changes, and crisis events; the unresponsiveness of social and physical environments; and interpersonal difficulties in families and other primary groups.[5] When a problem is presented in one area—such as

---

[1] See, for example, Gail Abarbanel, "Helping Victims of Rape," *Social Work* 21 (November 1976); Ann W. Burgess and Lynda L. Holmstrom, "Rape Trauma Syndrome," *American Journal of Psychiatry* 131 (September 1974): 981–86; Naomi Golan, a*Treatment in Crisis Situations* (New York: The Free Press, 1978), pp. 205–19; Grace Hardgrove, "An Interagency Service Network to Meet Needs of Rape Victims," *Social Casework* 57 (April 1976): 245–53; Sandra Sutherland and Donald J. Scherl, "Patterns of Response Among Victims of Rape," *American Journal of Orthopsychiatry* 40 (April 1970): 503–11; and Sutherland and Scherl, "Crisis Intervention with Victims of Rape," *Social Work* 17 (January 1972): 37–42.

[2] See, for example, Gerald Caplan, *Principles of Preventive Psychiatry* (New York: Basic Books, 1964); Golan, *Treatment in Crisis Situations;* Howard J. Parad, ed., *Crisis Intervention: Selected Readings* (New York: The Family Service Association of America, 1965); and Lydia Rapoport, "The State of Crisis: Some Theoretical Considerations," in *Crisis Intervention,* ed. Parad, pp. 22–31.

[3] The authors are indebted to these organizations for their training in working with victims of violent crime.

[4] Carel B. Germain and Alex Gitterman, *The Life Model of Social Work Practice* (New York: Columbia University Press, 1980); George V. Coelho et al., eds., *Coping and Adaptation* (New York: Basic Books, 1974); Heinz Hartmann, "Comments on the Psychoanalytic Theory of the Ego," in *Psychoanalytic Study of the Child* vol. 5 (New York: International Universities Press, 1950), 74–95; Robert W. White, *Lives in Progress: A Study of the Natural Growth of Personality* (New York: The Dryden Press, 1952); Robert W. White, "Strategies of Adaptation: An Attempt at Systematic Description" in *Coping and Adaptation* ed. Coelho et al. (New York: Basic Books, 1974), pp. 47–68.

[5] Germain and Gitterman, *Life Model,* p. 13.

the situational crisis of assault—it is necessary to assess the total ecological field for contributions to the event, reverberations, and supports available to the client. In a neighborhood riddled by muggings or rape, for example, it is not enough for an agency to take a case-by-case approach. Community involvement and preventive work are needed. Systems of communication among police, hospitals, and other agencies must be developed. Policies may need to emerge. In one instance, fifteen rapes had been committed by a young man with a history of sex crimes who had gone AWOL from a youth facility. The agency should have notified the police of his disappearance but apparently had no policy regarding this. After working with two of this man's victims, the worker decided to discuss the matter with the youth facility and the police. Moving from "private troubles to public issues," as William Schwartz describes it, is characteristic of the worker who uses this practice model.[6] Each case described in this article will illustrate assessment and intervention in the related areas of the life model.

Relationships are inevitably affected by a violent assault on an individual. Assessment is made in terms of the nature of the relationships which historically and currently represent sources of support or problems for the client. Where a client is developmentally and in terms of life transitions is also taken into account in building a quick holistic assessment of his or her adaptive abilities. Such an assessment allows the worker to understand the meaning of this event in the client's life. Clients often seek to make sense of the senseless, attributing meaning to it in terms of other events in their lives. The worker, while being careful to explore this meaning with the client, is aware that earlier struggles are sometimes reawakened and that the crisis represents an opportunity to either work them through or to regress further.

The Crisis State

In its simplest terms, crisis is an "upset in steady state."[7] Since steady states are rare in human life, Ludwig Von Bertalanffy's concept of the "moving steady state" further defines the so-called equilibrium in which the crisis occurs.[8] According to Germain and Gitterman, "Crisis events refer to sudden changes that have an immediacy and enormity. They are experienced as disastrous and overwhelming, and tend to immobilize people. They often represent a situation in which ordinary adaptive patterns are not adequate, so that novel solutions or coping skills are required."[9] This is an excellent description of the experience of the victim of violent assault. When coping fails and disequilibrium sets in, the person is in a state of active crisis.

The crisis may be perceived as a threat, in which case the reaction is anxiety; a loss which is met with depression; or a challenge which is met with mobilized energy.[10] Victims of assault may respond with all of the above reactions. According to Golan, the

6 William Schwartz, "Private Troubles and Public Issues: One Social Work Job or Two?" in *The Practice of Social Work,* ed. Robert W. Klenk and Robert M. Ryan (Belmont, CA: Wadsworth Publishing, 1974), pp. 82–99; Germain and Gitterman, *Life Model,* pp. 297–341.
7 Golan, *Treatment in Crisis Situations,* p. 61.
8 Ludwig Von Bertalanffy, *General Systems Theory* (New York: Braziller, 1968).
9 Germain and Gitterman, *Life Model,* p. 97.
10 Richard Pasewark and Dale Albers, "Crisis Intervention: Theory in Search of a Program," *Social Work* 17 (March 1972): 70–77.

five components of the crisis situation are: the hazardous event; the vulnerable state; the precipitating factor; the state of active crisis; and the stage of reintegration or crisis resolution.[11] Clearly, a mugging, rape, or gunshot wound is such a hazardous event, accurately perceived by the victim as such, and leaving him or her in a vulnerable state. The precipitating factor, defined by Golan as "the straw that breaks the camel's back," brings tension and anxiety to a peak.[12] Such factors may be associated with the hazardous event, such as the loss of one's eyeglasses or identification, being left naked, or the reactions of disgust or anger expressed to the victim by significant others. They may be connected with unresolved core conflicts. When there is such a connection, crisis psychotherapy of an ongoing nature may be recommended.[13]

The Victim's Reactions

In the state of active crisis, the victim may: withdraw and never leave the house; have frightening repetitive dreams, feel numb, violated, humiliated, depressed, disconnected, out of control or even crazy; fear everyone and everything; become suspicious as opposed to cautious; and, be full of rage, shame, and guilt. Victims may have cognitive lapses in which judgment is suspended; they may court danger and literally not know how to think about what has happened They may be consumed with internalized rage and self-reproach or may direct this inappropriately at well-intentioned helpers. The state of active crisis is time-limited—about six weeks—though the effects may linger on if quick and knowledgeable intervention is not given.[14] Phases which characterize active crisis are: impact, recoil, disorganization, recovery, reorganization, and resolution.[15] With help and strength, the person is often able to achieve a positive reintegration and resolution which restores precrisis functioning. Yet, even as victims return to normal living, they may experience a flood of feelings of panic, rage, and depression when events remind them of the trauma. This can go on for quite awhile. More vulnerable victims may be left shattered and unable to return to their precrisis levels of functioning.

In general, the situation calls for work on the effective, cognitive, and operational or task-centered levels. The worker offers empathy, recognition and verbalization of feelings, cognitive restructuring of the event, discussion of the options available, task-oriented problem solving, and the development of new patterns of seeking and using help toward regaining competence.[16] Golan has developed an extensive and excellent model for giving help in crisis situations.[17] Additionally, knowledge of the stages of the grief process are essential in working with assault victims, as there are losses they must mourn.[18]

---

[11] Golan, *Treatment in Crisis Situations*, pp. 63–71.

[12] Ibid., p. 63.

[13] David L. Hoffman and Mary L. Remmel, "Uncovering the Precipitant in Crisis Intervention," *Social Casework* 56 (May 1975): 260.

[14] Rapoport, "The State of Crisis," in *Crisis Intervention*, ed. Parad, p. 26.

[15] Pasewark and Albers, "Crisis Intervention."

[16] Golan, *Treatment in Crisis Situations*; Pasewark and Albers, *Crisis Intervention*; and Naomi Golan, *Promoting Competence in Clients: A New/Old Approach to Social Work Practice*, ed. Anthony N. Maluccio (New York: The Free Press, 1981), pp. 74–100.

[17] Golan, *Treatment in Crisis Situations*.

[18] Erich Lindemann, "Symptomatology and Management of Acute Grief," in *Crisis Intervention*, ed. Parad, pp. 7–21; and Elisabeth Kübler-Ross, *On Death and Dying* (New York: Macmillan, 1969).

THEMES AND RESPONSES IN HELPING

A general frame of reference for viewing and helping victims of violent assault has been established. Major themes and responses particular to this population and practice principles in working with them can be illustrated by case examples. Words seem inadequate to capture the shock and impact of violent assault. Tom P, a tall, husky Polish-American young man, and his cousin, Bill S, were walking home from a late party. They were talking about Tom's marital troubles. Bill heard a loud noise and turned to see Tom doubled over, clutching his midsection. Blood was everywhere. Bill could not think. Tom, struggling to walk, instructed Bill to get him to the hospital which was one block away. Tom remained there for two months and, somewhat miraculously, recovered to return home, a different person.

This actual case example provides an apt analogy for the impact of violent assault. It is a bullet from nowhere—in this case a random, apparently senseless, anonymous attack which left the victim physically and emotionally devastated and fighting for his life. In a split second, his whole world was turned upside down. This situation is most similar to the sudden onset of major life-threatening illness. At least in the case of mugging or rape there is a person to direct the anger toward, even though the victim may not be aware of the assailant's identity. A shot in the night or a sudden illness leave the victim with a feeling of the senselessness and uncontrollable nature of such an event. Why me? Where to direct the anger? How to regain control? How does one deal with the fear that it could happen again? How does one go on with life? These are questions we may all face in some form during life. The answers can be different for each person. It is a particularly awesome combination for the victims of violence to have to deal with such questions, as well as the assaultive event itself, at a time when they are struggling for life.

As a victim seeks to cope with the event, the following themes and patterns of response have been noted and practice principles have evolved:

The client may feel immobilized and constricted in feelings and mobility; this may be combined with numbness or denial of the impact. The worker respects these defenses and starts helping the client regain a sense of control by asking if he or she wants to talk about what happened at present. Many clients have been bombarded by medical and legal authorities and feel a tremendous invasion of privacy that amounts to a secondary victimization. The crisis worker needs to distinguish him or herself by offering to focus on the issues which are of greatest concern to the client. The worker's understanding and appreciation of the overwhelming nature of the event need to be communicated along with an expectancy that the client will feel safe enough to work on what happened as time goes on. Some clients may need to feel that life is "the same as before" quickly and may not wish to enter more than one or two counseling sessions which remind them of the event. The worker needs to accept this time limit while leaving the door open for further work. The degree of help required in negotiating an array of complex systems, including hospitals, medical insurance, courts, police, the workplace, unemployment or financial assistance, family, and friends, is also assessed and mediation offered where needed. Involving the client in making some of these connections may also help him or her feel back in control again. Much of the work on emotional issues is accomplished as the worker and client join in negotiating the system.

The client may feel loss of control in all areas of living. This is combined with a feeling of vulnerability that makes action on one's own behalf tentative and sometimes frightening. In this situation, the worker credits the coping the client has already shown and responds to the need to regain control. The worker helps the client describe feelings. The victim is reassured that the trauma is over; he or she is safe and these feelings are normal, albeit painful and frightening. The client has survived and coped successfully.

This will to survive is a primary strength to credit and build on. The worker can help the client own this strength and partialize ways to regain control by: asking questions and negotiating relevant systems; becoming more cautious; being informed about his or her medical problems and how to handle them: sharing with significant others and asking for support; and, when ready, offering others support through self-help organizations, and retraining or returning to work. A one-step-at-a-time approach is most useful. In some cases a systematic "sensitization" approach, using the behavioral principle of approaching the fear slowly, is helpful.[19] It is crucial that the worker have faith in the client as an active mastery-seeking person and that the worker convey this and share a vision of how the client can get back on his or her feet. The worker, experiencing the process through which the client gradually regains control, becomes more confident in lending this reassurance and in helping the client manage the period of active crisis. The image of self as victim is a passive one which can lead to regression. The client has indeed been victimized but has already shown ability to master under these most trying circumstances.

The client may be struck with the senselessness of the event and seek to make sense of it, to find meaning in what appears to be meaningless. Viktor Frankl, who developed the theory of logotherapy or existential analysis after his experience at the death camp at Auschwitz, spoke of the human need to find meaning in life, even after the most overwhelming experiences violence.[20]

The Search for Meaning

Almost paradoxically, confrontation with death brings about a search for meaning in life. The worker needs to listen for the client's struggle to find meaning in the event; to understand the client's meaning; and to assess with the client whether a constructive or destructive synthesis is being made. For example, Tom P, who had suffered the bullet wound, felt that his life was spared miraculously and that his "coat tails were pulled" so that he would have "a second chance" to get his life in order, to find a career, and to reevaluate his relationship with his wife. He was separated from her; theirs had been a destructive relationship. This meaning attributed to the violence was constructive as it enabled Tom to gather strength to go on living and to progress from the precrisis state In another case, however, a victim responded in a different way. A young woman, who was raped, had been separated from her husband for some time. She attached a meaning to the rape that was laden with guilt. Here. the worker needed to help the client reflect on the self-blame for an event over which she had no control. In each case, the

---

[19] Joel Fischer and Harvey L. Gochros, *Planned Behavior Change: Behavior Modification in Social Work* (New York: The Free Press, 1975).

[20] Viktor Frankl, *Man's Search for Meaning* (New York: Pocket Books, 1963), pp. 183–88.

worker needs to tune in to what Frankl calls the "meta-clinical" level and be aware that this is not pathology but a human being expressing a very human struggle for meaning.[21]

When there is no visible assailant to blame, the client may attach rage and anger to loved ones, to the self, or to various circumstances. This is because of the difficulty of accepting what is apparently an arbitrary event. There is no logical reason to explain what has happened. For example, Tom P wondered if he had wasted too much of his life as a loafer; he secretly blamed his cousin for not helping enough; and he strongly felt that the attack was somehow his wife's fault. He fantasized that his wife's new lover, who had a history of hospitalization for mental illness, was the one who had shot him. His need to attach the event to someone was so strong that he did not share his suspicion with the police. Terry M, an older adolescent rape victim from a traditional European family, expressed the idea that it was her parents' fault for not protecting her, rescuing her, or teaching her how to use better judgment or to defend herself.

These are not particularly pathological responses to such trauma; in fact, they are typical. Attaching feelings to some object is less frightening than dealing with a nameless assailant. The worker needs to accept these feelings and honor their service as a defense while helping the client to separate issues and acknowledge the anger, rage, depression, and fear that the projections represent. For example, the worker conveyed to Tom P her understanding of this need to attach the anger and blame to someone but also asked him to reflect on his feelings about his wife and their relationship separately from the violent incident. It was particularly difficult for Terry M to feel angry at her parents as she also needed them. The worker helped Terry to direct her anger at the rapist while acknowledging her wish to be protected by omnipotent parents. There were legitimate reasons for her to be angry at her parents and these could be worked on.

An Outlet For Anger

In cases of violence, the worker needs to be able to absorb a great deal of the anger and is, in fact, a safe object for it. The more the client is able to share anger and fear with the worker, the freer he or she is to go on with life and deal with significant others around the usual difficulties of living. Dependency issues are particularly pertinent to work on because the client will need help and may have trouble asking for it. Families and friends of victims often need support and help from the worker. This is not only because it is extremely painful to see a loved one go through such experiences but also in order to deal with the feelings the victim has about them and to become more aware of what he or she is going through. In Terry's case, the worker also talked with the parents. In a case where the mother of a large family died of gunshot wounds, all of the family members were seen for grief work and help in planning care for the younger children.

The fear of a violent event happening again is a particularly difficult area for both client and worker to handle. It is obvious to both parties that the awful unexpected happens and false reassurances cannot be helpful. Yet, through the process of regaining

---

[21] Ibid., p. 183.

control, the client has learned to take precautions, which allows for the feeling that she or he is doing everything possible to avoid danger. Faith in the ability to cope with whatever comes is restored because the client has already coped. Moreover, through the process of sorting out feelings, the client may be more at peace with him or herself and significant others. The individual can count on self-support and the support of others if similar events occur. The memories of a violent act do not have to be totally bad; they can remind a person that she or he has had the ability and courage to deal with violence in the past. There is now less fear of the unexpected moment, no matter what it may bring.

Mourning the loss of the old self is usually an important component of working with a victim of violent assault. Where there is physical disability or disfigurement as the result of the attack, the loss is an obvious one. Even for those who bear no obvious scars, there may be profound losses. Clients have expressed the feeling that they "will never be the same again." For some, the loss is their view of the world as a safe, reliable place. For others, it is more symbolic, as in the case of the rape victim, Terry M, who felt that she had been rendered unmarriageable. The worker needs to reach for the sense of loss as the client feels it and help the client mourn in order to go on with life. The client is then able to build self-esteem, which includes a healthy regard for a self that has integrated a truly traumatic experience and continued to grow.

MUGGING—CASE ILLUSTRATIONS

Types of muggings range from a purse snatching with a little roughing up to a severe beating or knifing which can result in serious harm or death. The degree of active crisis may be related to the degree of damage, although even the emotional reaction to a purse snatching can be quite strong, leaving the person in need of professional intervention.

Matilda A, a physically and emotionally healthy West Indian woman of eighty-six years, was mugged on her way to the store. Her purse was roughly pulled from her, causing her to fall and injure her shoulder. She was terrified of the aggression she felt from the mugger and in much pain. She "didn't believe people could be so full of hate" and feared going outside her house. The worker empathized with the horror she felt and helped her to tell the story. As she did this, she cried and showed anger. The worker was moved as Mrs. A tried to understand the mugger and stated, "If he needed money for food, I don't have much, but I would have given it to him." Together they felt the injustice of the act. The worker then asked Mrs. A if she would like to work on going outside again. She suggested that the longer Mrs. A was housebound, the harder it would be. Mrs. A agreed and said she would like to go back to her church and the senior center. Taking it step-by-step, Mrs. A agreed to call her pastor and was happy that a ride could be arranged for her.

At the same time, the worker realized that Mrs. A needed some time for life review to consolidate her feeling that she "always did for herself" and, therefore, could continue to do so. The worker shared Mrs. A's stories of past competence at working and traveling. Matilda A was able to put the mugging into perspective and gain the courage to face the world again. She also attended a lecture given by the Victim Services Agency and the police on senior self-defense. She still felt vulnerable but also felt more aware and able to assess dangerous situations. After four crisis sessions, she was able to resume her self-confidence and high level of functioning.

Differential Assessment Needed

Differential assessment is important. For another elderly woman, a similar mugging brought out strong paranoid feelings. The worker did not assess this as a sign of the need for hospitalization since the woman had functioned well independently—despite a history of mental illness—until this point. The woman was in enough contact with reality to have a new lock put on her door because her keys had been stolen. In fact, one of her delusions was functional. She believed that the police were looking in on her and protecting her through the electrical outlets. She was able to tell the story even though the worker had to decode her messages. For a few months, calling the worker on the phone brought the needed reassurance; after that time, she gave up being preoccupied with police protection. It takes an experienced crisis worker not to panic at the "craziness" and to help the client get back on his or her feet again.

In the case of John R, a large man in his thirties, another type of intervention was needed. Mr. R was jumped from behind, robbed, and left unconscious. The head wounds left him paralyzed with some brain injury. After three months in the hospital, he regained much functioning but walked slowly, with a cane. The worker met him after discharge and found him extremely dependent, frightened at being home and at having to take control of his life again. The hospital had become a haven for him. Initially, he could not recount the event that had hospitalized him, preferring not to "dwell on it." The worker started by having him discuss the hospital stay. As she conveyed understanding of how he felt about losing the hospital's support, he was able to trust her with the story of the mugging. He felt enraged and held back tears, feeling he would "split apart" if he let out his feelings.

As the worker accepted his feelings, giving permission to cry and to need to be taken care of, his tears and rage poured forth. John R had difficulty in thinking about vocational rehabilitation. His goal was to do nothing less than resume his precrisis functioning; this was unrealistic. The worker recognized that to shut him off totally from his career interest would take away his hope. She carefully helped Mr. R to develop long-term and short-term work goals. John R was furious when his vocational counselor said that he could not be retrained in his area of interest. The worker mediated and was able to help him choose training that would be satisfying, although different from what he had been doing. She helped him mourn the loss of mobility, which meant that he could not do all he would wish at present but left him with hope that he could continue to make progress. Mourning the losses was hard for him. At one point, Mr. R brought the worker a picture of himself before the mugging. He tried to convince himself and her that he looked the same. The reality was that he did not but this was a beginning attempt to deal with the changes. In ten sessions, he was able to make enough gains to cope more realistically with himself and his world without losing his optimism about future progress.

GUNSHOT WOUND—A CASE ILLUSTRATION

The case of Tom P, who was the victim of a sniper's bullet, has already been touched upon. Tom's key struggles were to make sense out of the event and to separate it from the issues involving anger at his wife. He also struggled with taking responsibility for maintaining his health. As his medical condition required more treatment he became more furious at his wife and less involved in managing his medical needs. It was quite true that his wife was literally parading her lovers in front of him and continuing to provoke him. But he needed to separate his rage over this from blaming her for the violent event and, therefore, taking no responsibility of his own to get better. As long as he could blame a real object, his fear of violence happening again was controlled. As the worker helped Tom P separate the issues, he decided to "put his foot down" with his wife and to seek counseling about their problems. Further, he realized that he was in touch with feelings of fury at his mother, who had abandoned him in infancy. He was then able to deal with the sniping as a separate terrorizing event and felt more able to go out again and to resume his medical treatment. The need for crisis counseling was over, but the worker encouraged his decision to pursue therapy as he was moving beyond the precrisis state to a higher level of awareness and functioning.

RAPE—A CASE ILLUSTRATION

Rape has been characterized as "the ultimate violation of self short of homicide."[22] In addition to the hostility and violence involved, it is an attempt at humiliation and degradation which often succeeds. Rape combines the double taboos of sex and aggression. In an irrational way, it seems to double the sense of shame for its victims. Self-reproach and self-blame may be what distinguish a rape victim's reactions from those of other victims of violence. The case of eighteen-year-old Terry M, who blamed her parents as well as herself, has been discussed. Terry would literally bang her head against the wall in self-reproach. Much work was done to help Terry with her self-blame and guilt. In her shame and fear, she also isolated herself from friends and feared going out of the house. This played into her family's need to keep her close and further complicated age-appropriate strivings for independence. Prior to the rape, she had adopted a passive stance toward life; the traumatic event of rape reinforced these attitudes. Relatively minor incidents would bring back memories of the rape and she would be full of fear and anger and feel immobilized.

In discussions with the worker, Terry realized that she needed to take an active role in asking for help and that there were other ways of handling situations like hers. She said that she knew she blamed her parents for the rape even though that "didn't make sense." The worker conveyed understanding of her need to be protected and indicated how that need could sometimes be in conflict with wanting to be independent. Terry worked on learning to assert and to protect herself. The worker suggested that their work might involve reaching out to her friends and getting into the world as she was ready. Slowly, Terry was able to do this, as well as to direct her anger more appropriately toward the rapist.

---

[22] Hardgrove, "An Interagency Service Network," p. 264.

Termination of the crisis work was difficult for Terry M. The worker made a special effort to tune in to her feeling of being abandoned by a trusted "protector." She helped Terry to express feelings of loss and sadness, letting her know how hard endings were for everyone, including grown-ups. Terry shared the fact that she had been banging her head on the wall when she thought about ending. The worker had helped her to think better of herself and to go out of the house again—now she was on her own. The worker acknowledged how frightening that was. She shared her own feeling that she would miss Terry, at the same time crediting her progress and ability to manage on her own and to ask for help from her family and friends. They reviewed the work they had done together. Terry had gone out of the house and had reestablished relationships with her friends. She had learned to express her thoughts and feelings and not to pout or bang her head as much. Her fearful dreams had stopped; she talked to her parents more directly. The worker credited Terry for her growth under such trying circumstances. They explored whether Terry wanted a referral to do more work and she accepted one. After twelve weeks of crisis work, Terry felt she had weathered the storm, and in time her precrisis functioning was restored.

CRISIS PRINCIPLES AND ASSAULT CASES

In each case, patterns emerged; both general crisis principles and those particular to working with victims of violent assault were applied. The worker assessed and intervened in the transitional and developmental issues related to the violent assault. After getting help to put the mugging in perspective, Matilda A was able to use life review to consolidate her gains in the direction of ego integrity instead of despair. John R was able to continue to move toward the career goals that are so important to a young adult. Tom P worked on the issue of intimacy versus isolation while he dealt with the resurgence of earlier issues precipitated by the sniping. Terry continued to work on similar concerns as well as the identity, separation, and individuation tasks of older adolescence. In each situation, it was critical to deal with the interpersonal area. Both worker and client negotiated the environment in various ways. Wherever possible, preventive approaches in the community were also taken.

In each case, the worker helped the client to regain control and move back into the world. She attempted to understand the meaning the client ascribed to the event and to separate functional and dysfunctional coping and defenses. She encouraged the expression of a range of feelings, absorbed the anger and blame, and helped the client redirect them. She particularly accepted the client's dependency feelings and struggles and fears of the violent event happening again. She helped the client to mourn losses but also to accept him or herself as having the strength to cope successfully with this most difficult event.

The worker also adhered to the mutually established goal of restoring precrisis functioning. It is tempting in this type of work to want to follow up on the possible long-term work opened up by the trauma. However, to do so could rob the client of the restored equilibrium. It could also prolong dependency at a time when the client can use the momentum to move forward autonomously. When clients want referrals, this is encouraged, of course, although the decision needs to be part of the termination phase of the crisis work. This is the most critical phase, in which the gains can be consolidated or lost.

Worker Self-Awareness

Workers need a large amount of self-awareness in working with victims of violent assault. The sense of panic, fear, and depression can be almost contagious; we are aware that, indeed, assault could happen to us and our loved ones and it becomes self-referential in terms of similar personal experiences or fears. Even the concept—victim—may make a worker less able to view the person as active, mastery-seeking, and capable. The anxiety, anger, and dependency struggles need particular attention in terms of the professional's countertransferential responses. Moreover, the tendency to rush toward solutions without the full expression of feelings and work on them must be checked. It is the combination of working in phase appropriate ways on the affective, cognitive, and task levels that ultimately brings about positive crisis resolution, even in the face of the violent and life-threatening events dealt with here.

The major lesson learned in conceptualizing and doing this work is to respect the strengths of people who have experienced such events. The fact that individuals survive and grow in the face of such onslaughts attests to the resiliency and tremendous strengths of human beings.

CHAPTER 92

CRIME VICTIMS AND OFFENDERS IN MEDIATION

An Emerging Area of Social Work Practice

Mark S. Umbreit

Interest among social workers and others in victim–offender mediation has been growing during the past decade. In 1978, only a handful of mediation programs existed, primarily in the Midwest. Today there are victim–offender mediation programs in nearly 100 jurisdictions throughout the country (Umbreit, 1988a), including major urban areas such as Miami and smaller communities such as Valparaiso, Indiana.

Programs continue to be sponsored primarily by private social services agencies that work closely with the courts. However, a growing number of victim–offender mediation programs are being directly sponsored by probation departments or other public agencies. In this growing network, social workers are becoming active in many roles, including community organizers, program developers, board members, trainers, and staff or volunteer mediators.

The rich heritage of social work practice in the juvenile and criminal justice systems dates back to the turn of the century, when the juvenile court was established. The concept of victim–offender mediation, however, is largely absent from the social work literature. This article begins to build a bridge between social work practice in this emerging field and the social work literature. The article presents the purpose of this practice model and describes the mediation process. A case study of conflict mediation between the victims of a home burglary and the offender is offered. Finally, important issues related to program development and replication are presented.

Reprinted from *Social Work*, Vol. 38, No. 1 (January 1993), pp. 69–73, by permission of NASW Press. Copyright 1993, National Association of Social Workers, Inc., *Social Work*.

PURPOSE

Victim–offender mediation programs provide a conflict resolution process that is meant to be fair to both the victim and the offender (Umbreit, 1985, 1988a). The mediator facilitates this process by allowing the parties first to address informational and emotional needs and then to discuss the victim's losses and to develop a mutually acceptable restitution plan (for example, repayment, working for the victim, working for the victim's choice of charity).

Both crime victims and offenders are placed in a passive position by the criminal justice system, and often neither receives basic assistance or information. Anger and frustration increase as the victim and offender move through the highly depersonalized justice process. Victims often feel powerless and vulnerable. Some even feel twice victimized, first by the offender and then by an uncaring criminal justice system that does not have time for them. Offenders rarely understand or are confronted with the human dimension of their criminal behavior—that victims are real people and not only objects to be abused. Offenders have many rationalizations for their actions against others.

The victim–offender mediation process draws on old-fashioned principles that recognize that crime is fundamentally against people, and not only against the state. Instead of placing the victim in a passive role and reinforcing an adversarial dynamic that often results in little emotional closure for the victim and little, if any, direct accountability by the offender to the victim, the mediation process actively facilitates personal conflict resolution.

MEDIATION PROCESS

There are four phases in the victim–offender mediation process (Umbreit, 1988a): intake, preparation for mediation, mediation, and follow-up.

Intake Phase

The intake phase begins with the court referral of the offender (most often convicted of theft or burglary). Most programs accept referrals after a formal admission of guilt has been entered with the court. Some programs accept cases that are referred before formal admission of guilt as part of a deferred prosecution effort. The case is assigned to a mediator.

Preparation Phase

The preparation phase begins when the mediator meets separately with the offender and victim. During the individual sessions, the mediator listens to the story of each party, explains the program, and encourages each party's participation. Mediators usually meet first with the offender and, if he or she is willing to proceed with mediation, later with the victim.

Encouragement of victim and offender participation in the mediation process must not be confused with coercion. The process is meant to empower victims and offenders by presenting them with choices.

Mediation Phase

Following the separate meetings and if both parties choose to participate, the mediator schedules a joint meeting. The mediation session begins with the mediator explaining his or her role, identifying the agenda, and stating communication ground rules. The first part of the meeting is a discussion of the facts and feelings related to the crime. Victims are given the rare opportunity to express their feelings directly to the person who committed the crime. They can get answers to questions such as "Why me?" "How did you get into our house?" "Were you stalking us and planning to come back?" Victims are often relieved to finally see the offender, who usually bears little resemblance to the frightening character they had envisioned.

The mediation session places offenders in the uncomfortable position of facing the person against whom they committed the crime. They are given the equally rare opportunity to display a more human dimension to their character, even to express remorse personally. Through discussion of their feelings, both victim and offender can deal with each other as people, often from the same neighborhood, rather than as stereotypes and objects.

When the sharing of facts and feelings related to the crime is concluded, the second part of the meeting is directed to discussion of losses and negotiation of a mutually acceptable restitution agreement as a tangible symbol of conflict resolution and a focal point for accountability. Mediators do not impose a restitution settlement. Joint victim–offender meetings usually last about one hour, with some meetings lasting two hours.

Follow-up Phase

The follow-up phase begins when the referral agency approves the restitution agreement and ends with the closure of the case. Tasks to be completed during this phase include making monthly telephone calls to the victim to monitor fulfillment of the restitution agreement; if necessary, contacting the probation officer to secure compliance by the offender; if necessary, scheduling a joint meeting with the victim and the offender; and completing the final paperwork to close the case.

CASE STUDY

Anne and Bob's home was burglarized for the second time. They were furious. Both felt violated, as though they had been personally assaulted. Many questions went through their minds. Why was their house picked? Was it the same criminal who had broken in several months before? Were their movements being watched? Did someone have a vendetta against them?

Jim was arrested within several weeks of the burglary. He was 20 years old and had had several minor brushes with the law as a juvenile but no prior adult convictions. Two months before the burglary, Jim lost his job at a factory. He pleaded guilty to the charge.

During the sentencing hearing in court, as a condition of probation, he was referred to the Center for Victim Offender Mediation in Minneapolis, a program of the Minnesota Citizens Council on Crime and Justice. When first approached about the mediation program, Jim was not enthusiastic. During the individual meeting with Jim, the mediator explained to him that confronting his victim might be helpful for several reasons. First, he could discuss what happened with the victim. Second, he could negotiate a restitution agreement that was considered fair to both parties. Third, by taking direct responsibility for his criminal behavior, he would have input into a portion of his court-ordered punishment.

The mediator explained that although the court preferred his participation in this mediation program, he was not required to do so. If he felt that it was not appropriate for him, he could be referred back to the court to fulfill restitution through the normal procedures. He finally indicated that he would be willing to meet the victim and work out restitution.

After having secured Jim's willingness to try the mediation process, the mediator then met with Bob and Anne at their home. She first listened to their story about what had happened. Both Bob and Anne expressed a great need to talk about how outraged they felt about the burglary. In addition to feeling angry at the criminal who robbed them, both indicated anger at a criminal justice system that seemed to treat them like a piece of evidence.

After the mediator explained the program to Bob and Anne, they initially were not interested. They could not see any value in confronting the offender. The mediator pointed out some possible benefits. They could let the offender know how angry they were and how this crime affected them, and many of the questions that Bob and Anne had asked the mediator could be answered directly by the offender, the only person who really knew the answers. Also, rather than sitting on the sidelines of the justice process like most victims, Bob and Anne could get directly involved and help shape part of the penalty that their offender would be required by the court to pay. Finally, they would have the opportunity to negotiate a restitution agreement that was considered fair to all parties.

After further thought, Bob and Anne agreed to try the mediation process. Both said that they were not certain of the value of such a confrontation, but they certainly wanted to let the "punk" know how angry they were.

Because of the heightened level of anger involved in this case, co-mediators, both of whom were trained social work practitioners, were used. The mediation session was held at a neutral community center.

Several introductory comments were made by the lead mediator. She thanked participants for coming and for trying the process. She clearly identified the purposes of the session: first, to provide time to talk about the burglary and how those involved felt about it, and second, to talk about the losses and the possibility of negotiating a restitution agreement. The role of the mediators was explained. They were not official representatives of the court, nor could they impose any settlement on either party. Rather, their role was to provide an opportunity for both parties to talk about what had happened and to see if a settlement could be reached. Whatever was agreed on, they emphasized, must be perceived as fair to both parties. The parties would first have some uninterrupted time to tell their stories.

The lead mediator asked Bob if he could tell Jim about what had happened from his perspective and how it affected him. The hand movements of the mediator indicated that Bob was to talk directly to Jim. At this point, Bob had both arms rigidly crossed on his chest. He quickly began talking about how he was furious about this kind of "crap." He said he was fed up with kids who violated other people's property. Anne chose not to speak at this point.

Because of the level of anger expressed by Bob, the mediators were about to intervene to prevent any direct verbal attacks on Jim. Just before they intervened, however, something atypical occurred. Jim jumped out of his chair and said, "I'm not taking this crap any longer—I've had it, I'm leaving." At that point, the co-mediator intervened by saying directly to Jim, "I'm sure it has been difficult listening to the anger expressed by Bob, but I know that he is interested in working out a settlement. Could you just give it another 10 minutes? If you can, I think we might be able to work something out tonight. If you want to leave after 10 minutes, it's up to you." Jim paused and then sat down.

The comments of the co-mediator appeared to have validated some of Jim's concern that he was being "dumped on." From this point on, Bob's communication to Jim was far less emotional, and his body language slowly began to loosen up.

When it became evident that Bob and Anne had completed their initial statement, the lead mediator then asked Jim if he could tell them what happened from his perspective. Jim explained that he was out drinking with some friends, and they needed extra money. They were cruising around in the neighborhood and saw what appeared to be an empty house; no lights were on. They knocked on the front door and when no one responded, they walked around the house and broke in through the back door. Once in the house, they took a television, videocassette recorder, stereo, and about $100 in loose cash. Jim explained that they had not initially intended to break into Bob and Anne's home and that when they did break in, he was nervous and anxious to get out of the home as quickly as possible. Jim clearly admitted that he took the items he mentioned.

After Jim completed his explanation, Bob and Anne asked Jim numerous questions. "Why us? Were you watching our movements?" Jim indicated that he had not been watching them. Anne then asked Jim if he knew their daughter Carol. Jim said he did. She mentioned that Carol had been living on the streets for a year after leaving a drug treatment center. Jim said he knew that. Bob asked Jim if, when he saw Carol again, he would mention that her parents loved her and would welcome her home if she was willing to return.

It was clear that the conflict had been reframed; rather than interacting in stereotypic roles of "victim" and "offender," the participants now interacted at a more human level, with concern about issues beyond the criminal event.

Discussion of what happened that evening and how all parties felt about it lasted for nearly one hour. Before the lead mediator suggested discussing restitution, some time silence was allowed to give all parties an opportunity to raise any additional questions.

The lead mediator then stated that it was time to review the losses that Bob and Anne had incurred and to begin negotiating restitution. The mediator turned to Anne and asked her to identify the losses they incurred, including providing any documentation. Anne presented a long list of items. Jim was then asked to review this list and comment.

Jim had a number of questions about several items, particularly their replacement value. After discussing this further with Anne and Bob, he indicated that he now understood the full impact of what he did and was ready to talk about a plan to "make things right."

Bob, Anne, and Jim worked out a restitution plan that required Jim to pay $50 a month over 10 months, beginning the next month. The terms of the restitution were read to both parties before being written up into an agreement. When the agreement was written, both parties signed it, and copies were given to each. A copy was also forwarded to Jim's probation officer.

One of the mediators then stated that "in cases like this when an agreement is reached, we prefer that both parties meet briefly several months from now to check out how the agreement is working. What do you think about doing this?" Jim turned to Bob and Anne and said "I'd really like to do that. Could we have it at my house?" He added, "I would like you to meet my wife and my baby. I'm not a criminal." The meeting was scheduled for two months later at Jim's home, with the mediators present. Jim offered to cook lasagna. Bob and Anne quickly indicated their interest.

Reflections on the Case Study

The initial anger and hostility of the victims and offender were transformed into a human understanding of each other and a specific plan for "making things right." This transformation had little to do with the amount of information and advice provided by the mediators (which was minimal) during the mediation session. Rather, the process of reconciliation had more to do with the safe structure provided by the mediators that allowed the parties to deal directly with each other.

The two mediators talked at most 15 to 20 percent of the time, and the disputants talked 80 to 85 percent of the time. Mediators were more verbally active at three points in the process. First, during the opening statement, the mediators explained their role, identified ground rules and the agenda, and initiated direct victim–offender communication. The mediators then faded into the background. Midway into the session, a clear transition point was required from talking about what happened and how the parties felt to discussing the need for restitution. The mediators again faded into the background. Finally, when efforts were being made to work out a written agreement, the mediators needed to present various options and help the parties structure a workable agreement.

The mediators in this case used an empowering, or nondirective, mediation style (Umbreit, 1988a). Experience in victim–offender mediation has shown that an empowering, rather than controlling, style is often more effective in addressing the emotional needs of the parties and securing workable restitution plans.

The experience of Bob, Anne, and Jim illustrates the purpose of the victim–offender mediation process. Consistent with a growing body of research (Coates & Gehm, 1989; Davis, Tichane, & Grayson, 1980; Marshall & Merry, 1990; Umbreit, 1989, 1990; Wright & Galaway, 1988), Bob, Anne, and Jim felt the mediation process and outcome were fair. All were satisfied with their participation in the program. Rather than playing passive roles in the resolution of the conflict between them, Bob, Anne, and Jim actively participated in "making things right." During a subsequent conversation with Bob, he commented that "this was the first time [after several victimizations] that I ever felt any sense of fairness. The courts always ignored me before. They didn't care about my concerns. And Jim wasn't such a bad kid after all, was he?" Jim also indicated that he felt better after the mediation and was more aware of the impact the burglary had on Bob and Anne.

DEVELOPMENT AND REPLICATION ISSUES

As a growing number of communities consider developing a victim–offender mediation program, a number of important issues should be considered. Building public and system support for the new program is crucial. Experience in many communities has indicated that although some criminal justice officials may be initially skeptical (most notably prosecutors, judges, and victims' advocates), their support usually can be obtained. Once they learn more about the mediation process and how it affects both victims and offenders, officials usually become supportive, or even active, in developing the new program.

The most likely referral sources are judges and probation staff. Prosecutors, defense attorneys, and victims' assistance staff can also be effective sources.

Identifying an appropriate group of victims and offenders to work with is vital. Experience in thousands of mediation cases over the past 10 years has shown that the program is effective with nonviolent property offenses such as vandalism, theft, and burglary. Most offenders are either first- or second-time law violators. Unlike other types of mediation, most (but not all) victims and offenders have no prior relationship.

Many programs also work with assault cases. A few programs are beginning to work with more violent crimes such as armed robbery, sexual assault, and attempted homicide. In fact, victims of violent crime have often been among those who advocate extending the mediation process to more serious cases. However, this does not include domestic assault. The mediation process has been effective in assisting victims of violent crime in regaining a sense of power and control in their lives, as well as the ability to "let go" of the victimization experience (Umbreit, 1988b). However, mediation for a violent crime requires a more intense process and is not recommended for new programs.

Those interested in being mediators need to decide early whether to work with juvenile or adult offenders. Because the juvenile and adult systems are different, working with both requires more initial development time.

Working collaboratively with existing victims' services programs and offender treatment programs is important. Although the victim–offender mediation process offers a number of benefits to both parties, the process also has limitations. Many victims and offenders need more extensive services than can be offered through the mediation process. At best, the mediation process is part of a larger response to the needs facing crime victims and their offenders.

Securing resources to operate a new victim–offender mediation program is critical. In most communities, a small staff that supervises a larger pool of trained volunteer mediators is sufficient. This keeps the program's costs down and, more importantly, empowers citizens to become directly involved in resolving criminal conflict in their communities. The provision of 25 to 30 hours of effective mediation training and continued in-service training is important.

Replication of the victim–offender mediation model requires effective community organizing and program development skills. Most importantly, it requires a deep commitment to restorative principles of justice that empower crime victims and their offenders to resolve their conflict and to let go of the victimization experience.

REFERENCES

Coates, R. B., & Gehm, J. (1989). An empirical assessment. In M. Wright & B. Galaway (Eds.), *Mediation and criminal justice* (pp. 251–263). London: Sage Publications.

Davis, R., Tichane, M., & Grayson, D. (1980). *Mediation and arbitration as alternatives to prosecution in felony arrest cases: An evaluation of the Brooklyn Dispute Resolution Center.* New York: VERA Institute of Justice.

Marshall, T., & Merry, S. (1990). *Crime and accountability: Victim offender mediation in practice.* London: Home Office.

Umbreit, M. S. (1985). *Crime and reconciliation: Creative options for victims and offenders.* Nashville, TN: Abingdon Press.

Umbreit, M. S. (1988a). Mediation of victim offender conflict. *Missouri Journal of Dispute Resolution, 85–105.*

Umbreit, M. S. (1988b). Violent offenders and their victims. In M. Wright & B. Galaway (Eds.), *Mediation and criminal justice* (pp. 99–112). London: Sage Publications.

Umbreit, M. S. (1989). Crime victims seeking fairness, not revenge. *Federal Probation, 93*(3), 52–57.

Umbreit, M. S. (1990). The meaning of fairness to burglary victims. In J. Hudson & B. Galaway (Eds.), *Criminal justice, restitution, and reconciliation* (pp. 47–58). Monsey, NY: Criminal Justice Press.

Wright, M., & Galaway, B. (Eds.). (1988). *Mediation and criminal justice.* London: Sage Publications.

CHAPTER 93

GUIDE-LINES FOR SOCIAL WORKERS IN COPING WITH VIOLENT CLIENTS

Sally Johnson

Any broad-based survey of the responses of individual groups to a common problem may be conducted along the lines of a fishing expedition—throw the line and see what comes up. Yet to be of use the analysis of the survey should offer something to the preparation of future responses to the problem. This analysis was undertaken with that in mind. The common problem is violence towards social workers, and a common response to the problem has been the publication of guide-lines by local authority social services departments. Guide-lines are not, of course, the only way to respond to the problem. For example, some local authorities have taken steps to insure their social workers against the effects of violence. Guide-lines may be, however, the employing local authority's chosen means of telling their employee social workers how to behave in response to the threat of violence.

At the beginning of this study the intention was to explore the nature of local authority social services departments' response to violence against social workers as expressed in guide-lines. It was expected that they would embody some current theories of violence and that identifying these theories would clarify the nature of the response. But the guide-lines revealed more than this. Because they are the employers' recommendations for practice to employees, they also reveal where effective responsibility for the prevention and management of violence is believed to lie. In the end, this offers more useful information about the efficacy of the guide-lines than an understanding of their theoretical backdrop.

In the first part of this paper consideration is given to why so many guide-lines have recently appeared. Current theories of aggression are discussed and analysed as the

Reprinted from *British Journal of Social Work*, Vol. 18, No. 4 (August 1988), pp. 377–390, by permission of Oxford University Press.

sources for the specific practical suggestions about how to avoid violence which are contained in the guide-lines. The second part of the paper identifies some of the attitudes of social services departments about aggression, and who is responsible for controlling it, which the guide-lines reveal. In both cases, content analysis was used. This meant reading the guide-lines in order to draw out hypotheses about underlying issues, framing these as statements and counting how many similar statements occurred throughout the guide-lines. The results are discussed in general terms, but a table of precise findings is included to be read alongside the text. Two of the assumptions of content analysis should be recorded. The manifest content of the text is presumed to hide ideas which systematic analysis can expose, and the frequency of statements is related to the accuracy of the hypothesis.

Local authorities named in *Community Care* or *Social Work Today* as having produced guide-lines were asked to send copies. From the seven social services departments which responded, the guide-lines of Bexley, Hampshire, Birmingham and Dorset were chosen. Since the number of statements is equated with strength of feeling, it was thought important to balance the guide-lines as to length. Bexley and Dorset guide-lines contain five pages: those of Hampshire and Birmingham are longer, twelve and fourteen pages respectively. Bexley and Hampshire guidelines are in their final form, but Birmingham's and Dorset's are drafts. The guide-lines were also selected to provide a balance between authorities where a death has occurred—Hampshire, Birmingham and Bexley; and Dorset, where no one has been killed. Even the selection process prompted a tentative conclusion about Birmingham. The recent death of Frances Bettridge seemed to have inspired a serious attempt to cope with future violence, expressed in comprehensive, comparatively long guide-lines which are nevertheless considered to merit further development.

WHAT THE GUIDE-LINES ARE RESPONDING TO

An inevitable question is: what provoked the recent flurry of guide-lines? It was expected that they were prompted by events and a search through *Community Care* and *Social Work Today* in 1985–6 confirmed this. Four social workers have been killed in ten years: Peter Gray (Hampshire, 1978); Isobel Schwarz (Bexley, 1984); Norma Morris (Harringey, 1985) and Frances Bettridge (Birmingham, 1986). The topic has more often been treated as a news item in the social work press than as an issue. In *Community Care* the subject was raised almost monthly in the section entitled 'News'. This suggests that the guide-lines resulted from the fear of apparently increasing violence. Towards the end of 1986, the subject's value as 'news' subsided as the professional organizations were reported to be studying the problem.

Other reasons for the flurry of guide-lines were considered. There was no evidence of concern about claims against the social services departments as employers for failing to provide safe conditions of work. Only Victor Schwarz (1986) suggests that negligence by officers of the social services department and Health Authority may have led to his daughter's death. Nor was there evidence that pressure from workers' organizations inspired the guide-lines. These organizations seem to have acknowledged a developing consensus that 'something must be done' by forming study groups. There was no clear evidence that the guide-lines took account of the three recent studies on the subject by Rowett (1986), Crane (1986) and Brown *et al.* (1986). There is evidence, however, that the guide-lines borrow from each other, suggesting that the authors of guide-lines sought inspiration from those of other authorities rather than from recent research. Among authorities surveyed in this report, Bexley and Hampshire quote one another once. It is worth mentioning the recent studies, since they present a broader picture of the problem than the news reports.

In Rowett's study, individual social workers in a shire county were asked to report incidents of violent assault against them. The rate they reported was twenty-two times greater than the rate projected from a survey of all social services departments at county level. There is thus a serious problem of under-reporting by individual social workers, and the true incidence of assault is not recognised at county level. Only 44 per cent of local authorities collated information about assaults, although 90 per cent recorded them. In effect, less than half of senior management teams were made aware of the number of recorded incidents in their own departments. Crine (1982) had noted a few years before that because of the failure to collate reports, violence was seen in terms of sporadic, serious incidents rather than as a recurring threat. Rowett's own conclusion was that under-reporting followed from the (erroneously) unflattering picture most social workers hold of those social workers who are assaulted. Clearly, there are obstacles to grasping the implications of reported violence.

Instinct Theories

Instinct theories stress that aggressive responses are innate, a continuing undercurrent. Freud (cited in Megargee and Hokanson, 1970) held that the biological instinct for self-preservation needed to have aggression at its disposal. Yet he also believed that instincts cannot operate in isolation but are modified by opposing instincts. Thus, the instinct for self-preservation is subject to the interplay between aggression (destructive forces) and preservation (creative forces). If the guide-lines showed an acceptance of instinct theories, they should contain statements acknowledging the continuing presence of destructive forces in individuals and society; but none were found.

Social Learning Theories

Led by Albert Bandura, social learning theorists state that aggressive behaviour is a learned response, heavily influenced by particular environmental stimuli (Bandura and Ribes-Inesta, 1976). Dolland and Miller (in Baron, 1977) and Berkowitz (1962) emphasize that aggressive behaviour is always instigated by frustration, although aggression is not its only outcome. Theories of aggression based on frustration hold that aggression will be lower if sources of frustration in the environment are eliminated. The guide-lines were searched for statements acknowledging the translation of frustration into aggression or suggesting that the displacement of frustration would reduce aggression, and all of the guide-lines included statements of this type.

However, Bandura identifies much broader sources of aggressive behaviour than frustration. The breadth and specificity of his theory offers many possibilities for use in practical guide-lines. Bandura felt that individuals learned their repertoires of aggressive behaviour by observing others, particular sources for learning being the family and cultural models. The guide-lines were checked for statements which acknowledge the importance of family or sub-cultural modelling, but only Birmingham explicitly acknowledged this.

Bandura also accepted that not all learned behaviour would be put into practice; anticipation of the likely consequences would be a controlling factor. The positive consequences which reinforce aggressive behaviour may be tangible rewards (such as the acquisition of territory) or intangible rewards (such as improved status). Negative consequences include sanctions against aggressive behaviour. None of the guide-lines anticipated possible rewards for aggressive behaviour but all had statements concerning specific retaliation or deterrence. Birmingham took the unusual step of considering writing to clients officially, warning of legal action, and stated that any person who assaults staff in the course of their duties may be prosecuted. None of the other authorities named prosecution as the clear outcome of assault. Instead, Bexley, Dorset and Hampshire tend to see the police as helping to control a violent situation.

Of particular relevance to social workers confronting aggressive clients are Bandura's insights into the prediction of violence. He felt that predisposing conditions and aversive stimuli were crucial in prompting an individual to put learning into practice. Aversive treatments, such as humiliation or pain, are said to create a general state of arousal which facilitates aggression. Statements were counted concerned with the effects on clients of pre-disposing conditions, provoking events, and aversive stimuli and also statements about avoiding or controlling arousal. Forty statements of this type were found.

Practice Theories: An Alternative?

A final theoretical source of ideas about controlling violence examines what happens during the violent encounter and is concerned with the transaction which occurs between two individuals during it. Although these theories appear to be the less abstract 'practice' theories, they have the advantage of addressing the problem head-on by examining *what* is happening between two individuals during an incident rather than *why*.

One of these practice theories is described by Bailey (1976), who lists four ingredients in a violent encounter: arousal, trigger, weapon and target. Brown et al. (1986) drew the useful conclusion that the absence of one of these factors might prevent a violent incident. Statements about controlling arousal have been mentioned already in relation to social learning theory, but statements concerned with weapons were counted as well, and ten were found.

Kaplan and Wheeler (1983) also analyse the process of the violent encounter, seeing it as a sequence of phases. The triggering phase occurs when the client's behaviour first moves away from its identified baseline. During the escalation phase movement away from baseline behaviour intensifies and responsiveness to intervention diminishes. The crisis phase—which can include threats as well as action—is when an assault occurs. Successful intervention is unlikely. During the recovery phase, there is a gradual return to baseline behaviour, but because adrenalin levels take up to ninety minutes to normalize, the authors warn that incorrect handling of the client may cause a return to the crisis phase. Finally, there is a phase of exhaustion and depression in which the client regresses below baseline behaviour and is most responsive to interventions. The theoretical basis of these practice theories lies in games theory and general systems theory. Small (1985) mentions the work of Kroll and Makensie (1983) in which the relationship between the parties is the essential factor and escalation of the conflict is seen as 'a series of other-directed moves rather than . . . an unfolding of an inner purpose' (Kroll and Makensie cited in Small, 1985, p. 14). The guide-lines were searched for statements showing some idea of the violent encounter as a series of transactions between individuals, but none were found. Instead the guide-lines present an amorphous idea of what happens when violence occurs, identifying (through social learning theory) a number of elements which may be present, but giving no clue to the workers of 'what might happen next', nor any framework in which to order his or her perceptions of the encounter as it develops.

ATTITUDES OF THE LOCAL AUTHORITIES TOWARDS THE PREVENTION OF VIOLENCE

Clearly, the writers of the guide-lines relied most on social learning theories of aggression for practical suggestions about how to control violence. The reason for this may be that the instinct theories identify the basis of aggression without explaining how to handle a violent incident, and the potential contribution of transaction theories has not yet been appreciated. The pressing purpose of the guide-lines was to suggest to employees practical steps for reducing violence, and social learning theories served this purpose well. Effectively, the guide-lines are the social services departments as employers advising their employees. In giving this advice, they express attitudes about whose responsibility it is to contain violence or cope with its aftermath. The advice also reveals the ambivalence of the local authorities towards violence: they do not believe violence is innate, but they expect that it is inevitable.

Although no statements were found acknowledging the continuing presence of destructive forces in individuals and society, each authority nevertheless stated explicitly that violence was inevitable. Bexley and Hampshire, however, modify this by adding that violence must be dealt with, and Bexley puts the emphasis on control: 'Violence is not always preventable, but it is often avoidable.' If violence is inevitable but not innate, then it is learned but not ultimately preventable. If not preventable, then the extent of avoidance and control is questionable. This attitude hinders a proactive response to the problem.

Limits of Management Responsibility

Any approach which starts from the premise that violence is inevitable implies a limit to what can be done to help employees. Yet none of the authorities attempts to identify where that limit lies. The effect of this attitude is to undermine their commitment without specifying the practical limits of help. Such limits should be clarified in defining the responsibilities of management, but the local authorities are ambivalent. Some tasks are attempted; others left for the imprecise future.

On the one hand, none of the authorities denies management responsibility for helping to control violence (except where staff ignore guide-lines or act unreasonably). Dorset makes no statements at all denying management responsibility, and Bexley emphasizes that even if staff should break the guide-lines, they can expect management support provided their actions were reasonable. On the other hand, most authorities recommend, rather than require, training and counselling after a violent incident. There is thus some failure to follow through on the practical steps full responsibility would imply. Birmingham alone mentions provision already made for training. Hampshire recommends training, but Dorset and Bexley are entirely silent on the subject. Similarly, although all the authorities require a report on a violent incident, only Dorset goes so far as to insist upon counselling afterwards. Hampshire and Birmingham recommend it; Bexley is silent.

This failure to ensure counselling is surprising in social services departments. It would seem that the well-established lessons of the life cycle of a crisis have not been absorbed. Golan states that when a personal crisis is triggered by an unanticipated event, 'the key to being able to work (with it) is to become aware of the specific effects that particular stressful events tend to have upon persons *and systems* [emphasis mine] and to be able to forecast the problem-solving tasks that need to be carried out during the different phases of the total situation so that the crisis can be resolved adaptively' (Golan, 1978, p. 188). Rowett noted in his interviews with assaulted staff a strong impression that some were experiencing the classic psychological sequelae of violent assault. He commented upon the need to acknowledge 'that the well-established responses of victims of violent assault are important factors which should be taken into account by social work management when counselling assaulted staff (in order to) facilitate a shorter and more efficient emotional resolution of the incident' (Rowett, 1986, p. 130). Although Dorset, Birmingham and Hampshire guide-lines contain statements showing a recognition of the need to deal with victims' feelings, only Dorset acts upon this by requiring counselling. Bexley simply acknowledges that injuries may give rise to a legal claim.

For an authority to follow through its commitment to help employees handle violence, there should be clarification of where responsibility begins. The guide-lines were searched for statements indicating that management—at Team Leader level or above—is responsible for the control of violence and its effects upon staff. Bexley gives no indication. Hampshire is vague, advising staff members to consult with the line manager 'to help define how potential violence should be managed'. Dorset and Birmingham are explicit in anticipating the specific problem posed by visiting a potentially violent client at home. Dorset guide-lines state that in this case 'It is the duty of the Team Leader to ensure that the worker is accompanied by at least one other person'.

The Problem of Assessing Risk

The most pressing issue of responsibility is who is to be responsible for assessing risk? Perhaps understandably, all the authorities hand this responsibility to their social workers. In practical terms it is difficult to see how it could be otherwise since risk cannot be assessed adequately by someone who is not involved. Although it may be unavoidable, this puts the worker in a vulnerable and somewhat isolated position. Dorset states categorically that 'It is *never* a departmental requirement that any staff member should go alone into a potentially dangerous situation'. Unfortunately, because there may be one worker at a time on duty in area offices, a Dorset worker on after-hours stand-by has to choose when faced with a worrying call. Either s/he takes what-may-not-turn-out-to-be a serious risk after all, or s/he awakens colleagues in the middle of the night, possibly several times over a period of months. Birmingham guide-lines anticipate the worker's dilemma in saying that 'No one should feel foolish or in any sense inadequate if they use the alarm system available or follow these guide-lines, even if the violence does not then occur'. Although this is a dilemma which may be impossible to resolve adequately, the solution so far is always to leave the worker to assess risk and to ask for help. This is the same solution which has already been shown to be inadequate in the sense that it has so far been insufficient protection. A more positive approach might require the worker to discuss possible risks with the Team Leader and to record the decision taken, justifying, for example, why the social worker should not be accompanied by a colleague. Although this approach does not cover every situation, it could at least offer a more positive approach to those situations already known to present risks, such as Mental Health Act admissions and in dealing with clients known to have been violent before.

Although the worker is responsible for assessing risk, nowhere in the guide-lines is either risk or danger defined, despite a willingness to use these terms as if their meaning were understood. Perhaps it is unfair to criticize the local authorities for this failure when many people have wrestled with the same questions—long, hard and unsuccessfully. Yet the lack of awareness on this point again conveys the impression that the question has been dealt with when it has not. Dorset offers no guidance whatever on which sort of situation might constitute a risk. Bexley mentions only that significant behaviour and mood changes may be warning signs. Hampshire guide-lines note the significance of mood or behaviour changes and of explicit threats. They also list risky situations, such as formal admissions under the Mental Health Act. Birmingham, however, makes a determined attempt, if not to define risk itself, at least to list in detail situations which may be risky.

Clearly, the dilemmas of defining and assessing risk have not been resolved. This failure seems positively dangerous when local authorities also seem to believe that their workers, rather than their clients, are responsible for controlling the clients' violence. Two sorts of statements were counted: those suggesting that the worker was responsible for controlling the client's violence (other than by physical means), and those suggesting that clients are responsible for controlling their own violence. Interestingly, Birmingham was equally balanced between the two sorts of statement. In the other authorities statements allocating responsibility to the worker outweighed those giving the client responsibility. Hampshire guide-lines contain no less than twenty-two statements putting responsibility on to the worker as against one suggesting that the client is responsible for his own aggression. The effect of this attitude is to put workers at fault when they become the victims of a client's aggression.

An attitude of 'blame the victim' was also uncovered by Rowett. 'Both assaulted and non-assaulted social workers painted a common picture of the typical assaulted social worker as someone who sought out riskier situations, confronted the client, challenged unnecessarily, was more demanding and less flexible, and less able to detect potentially violent situations and handle them once they had arisen' (Rowett, 1986, p. 121). Yet when he compared the assaulted and non-assaulted on several criteria, such as personal hostility scores, these differences were not substantiated.

The impression emerging is that while the social services departments accept their responsibility as employers to confront the problem of violence in general terms, the assessment of risk and control of the violent encounter falls to the employees. This solution has already been shown to be inadequate. Moreover, preparation for the task through training is not ensured, nor is counselling afterwards. Nor do the authorities seek out the responses of employees to their guide-lines. Apart from Birmingham (which has five statements), no authority's guide-lines contain statements inviting employee or trade union participation or feedback. This is unfortunate. As Ward (1984) noted, violent incidents may be understandable retrospectively and an opportunity to aggregate this knowledge could improve preventive techniques.

The most serious criticism of the guide-lines as a management response to a problem arises when noting the number of statements saying 'steps should be taken', without specifying which steps. The failure to follow through is significant because the statements imply that a problem has been confronted when it has not. One tragedy could expose the inadequacy of some preparations. Even Birmingham, which in many ways has written the most comprehensive guide-lines, offers statements such as 'All appropriate checks must be made with allied agencies to seek information about clients with particular reference to potential risks'. Birmingham's statements of good intent average more than one per page. Does this mean that this authority is simply long on words but short of the action required to put them into effect? Or, does it mean that Birmingham is attempting to deal with a complex situation by stating how things should improve? Considering that in other respects Birmingham's guide-lines are both comprehensive and careful, their statements may reflect seriousness of purpose rather than lack of thoroughness. Nevertheless, it is necessary to be rigorous in analysing the practical implications of statements made in the guide-lines in order to estimate their likely effectiveness.

CONCLUSIONS

It is disheartening to see as a result of this analysis that despite well-intentioned efforts, some of the worst dilemmas have hardly been tackled. The idea of man's innate potential for aggression is rejected, but violence is accepted as inevitable. This might be construed as a denial of the overall problem coupled with a lack of determination to devise effective strategies to control violence. At the least, the attitude is ambivalent and undermines the attempt to create effective guide-lines. Management accepts its general responsibility to assist workers in controlling violence, but there are considered to be limits to what can be done and yet these are not specified.

Another dilemma is that the causes of aggressive behaviour are acknowledged, but the behaviour itself is not analysed, except in noting that changes of mood are a significant precursor. Reflections upon the causes of violence may allow workers to understand why a client felt aggressive without explaining how the incident itself developed. Not surprisingly, therefore, Rowett found that although assaulted workers believed they had learned much from the experience of assault, they had not learned how to avoid it in future. He discovered that there was a 'dearth of response strategies' (Rowett, 1986, p. 131) and little ability to identify the specific behaviour cues which often precede violent assault. While it may be true that we know more about the underlying causes of violence than about how to handle it, this dilemma needs to be confronted rather than avoided.

The guide-lines also show a tendency to reframe old problems as if they were solutions. Birmingham restates the problem of discovering adequate information about a client's potential for violence by requiring 'appropriate checks (to) be made with allied agencies'. This begs several questions: which checks are appropriate; with which agencies; will the information be shared; what can the social services department do if this is not possible; how should the information be recorded; and how is it to be related to the assessment of risk? A brief personal example illustrates the problem: In attempting to assess a client's potential for violence against his wife after a serious incident I discovered the Police would not agree to check their records because no case conference had been called. Like Birmingham, Hampshire merely reframes the problem of deciding how to proceed when violence is anticipated by advising staff to discuss it with the line manager 'to help define how potential violence should be managed'. No suggestions are made as to which alternatives should be considered or how their potential effectiveness might be evaluated in the particular circumstances. Reframing old problems in this way makes it appear that a solution has been found when it has not, and this decreases the effectiveness of the guide-lines.

Since some of the so-called solutions are in fact restatements of the problems, it is not surprising that in relation to the most demanding problems—assessment of risk— the guide-lines do not provide any new answers. As before, the initiative in assessing potential risk and seeking help has to come from the worker. A modification has been added in highlighting the possible assistance of the Team Leader in general terms, but social workers have always been expected to seek advice and help from Team Leaders in troublesome situations. Telling workers to talk things over does not contribute enough to the solution of the problem of risk assessment.

The failure to attempt any comprehensive assessment of risk is a most serious one (although Birmingham includes a long list of potentially risky situations). There is, for example, no attempt at a risk assessment model of the kind suggested by Small (1985). His model, which incorporates factors likely to increase the risk of violence, is linked to a strategy of risk reduction, which itself is tailored to meet the factors identified in the model. By contrast, the guide-lines dealt with risk assessment by giving workers the responsibility for assessing risk and for controlling the client's violence. As a result, there is a tendency to explain a violent incident afterwards in terms of the attributes of the workers rather than to examine situational factors; Rowett found that both assaulted and non-assaulted workers used attributional explanations even though in reflecting upon their own assault, the assaulted workers considered that a violent incident was 60 per cent the result of interaction and 40 per cent the clients own fault.

Schwarz (1987) concluded that social workers like to pretend that violence can be minimized or eliminated by the right sort of response. This view takes insufficient ac-

Table 93–1
Analysis of Statements in Guide-Lines

Statements	Number of statements in the guide-lines			
	Bexley	Dorset	Hampshire	Birmingham
1. Statements acknowledging the continuing presence of destructive forces in individuals and society	0	0	0	0
2. . . . acknowledging the translation of frustration into aggression and/or statements suggesting that elimination of frustration will reduce aggression	1	1	3	5
3. . . . suggesting that the displacement of frustration will reduce aggression	0	1	0	1
4. . . . acknowledging the importance of family or sub-cultural modelling	0	0	0	3
5. . . . concerning specific retaliation or deterrence	1	8	6	15
6. . . . concerned with the effect on clients of predisposing conditions, provoking events or aversive stimuli	1	2	7	6
7. . . . about avoiding or controlling arousal (Bandura) or triggers (Bailey)	4	2	9	9
8. . . . concerned with weapons	4	5	1	0
9. . . . relating to game theory or transactions	0	0	0	0
10. . . . suggesting that violence is inevitable	2	1	2	1
11. . . . denying management responsibility for the control of violence	–	0	1	1
12. . . . requiring training or stating provision already made	0	0	0	1
13. . . . recommending training	0	0	3	2
14. . . . requiring post-incident counselling	0	2	0	0
15. . . . recommending post-incident counselling	0	0	4	1
16. . . . requiring a report on violent incident	2	1	1	1
17. . . . acknowledging victim's feelings	0	2	1	2
18. . . . acknowledging client's feelings	0	1	6	10
19. . . . stating that management at Team Leader level or above has responsibility for the control of violence and its effects upon on workers	0	9	1	32
20. . . . giving workers responsibility for assessing risk	3	15	11	14
21. . . . defining risk or danger	0	0	0	0
22. . . . saying that workers are responsible for controlling clients' violence (other than by physical means)	2	1	22	8
23. . . . saying that clients are responsible for the control of their own violence	0	0	1	3
24. . . . inviting employee/trade union participation or feedback in further development of guide-lines or checking of safeguards	0	0	0	5
25. . . . saying 'steps should be taken' without specifying which steps	3	1	9	16

count of a dedicated aggressor, who would be least likely to respond appropriately. It is effectively a strategy of denial in order to minimize anxiety, and its most serious consequence is to muddle the attempt to assess risk rationally. Rowett also found that social workers tended to play down the harm actually intended. They believed that the most likely types of violence were pushing, holding, kicking and punching; whereas they were actually punching, kicking, use of a weapon and pulling. Floud and Young (1981) note that in any case the sense of personal vulnerability decreases with time and distance from the problem. It is difficult to imagine a serious assault happening to oneself. With similar optimism, local authorities rely on the belief that violent assault does not happen to many of their workers. While violence is accepted as inevitable, it is considered to be so rare that extensive plans for training and counselling are unnecessary. This clearly leaves the worker who is assaulted in an isolated position.

Although the guide-lines show some difficulties in conceptualizing completely the crisis of an assault or aggressive behaviour, and some failure in following through the implications of management assumption of responsibility, they have at least been produced. The danger is that, guide-lines having been produced, the problem will be considered to have been dealt with, when in fact this work has just begun. Only in the Birmingham guide-lines is input from workers invited. None of the guide-lines reveals any arrangements for monitoring their application in practice. No plans are put forward for the collation of reported incidents of violence .

The apparent failure to ensure monitoring of the guide-lines in practice and collation of reported incidents of violence invites the most serious criticism of all. This failure inhibits the flow of information about violent incidents which would assist effective revision of the guide-lines in the future. More efficient monitoring and collation require practical administrative adjustments for which, in social services bureaucracies, the machinery already exists. It is a comment on the nature of these bureaucracies that these pragmatic steps have not been taken (or have not been communicated to employees) despite a willingness to issue guide-lines on how violent situations are to be handled.

ACKNOWLEDGEMENT

I acknowledge with thanks the help of Peter Ford for his suggestions about ways of approaching the topic of violence against social workers and in particular for suggesting the technique of content analysis.

REFERENCES

Bailey, R. (1976) *Violence and Aggression,* Time-Life (Nederland) BV.
Bandura, A. and Ribes-Inesta, E. (1976) *Analysis of Delinquency and Aggression,* Hillsdale, NJ, Lawrence Erlbaum Assoc.
Baron, R. (1977) *Human Aggression,* New York, Plenum Press.
Berkowitz, L. (1962) *Aggression: a Social Psychological Analysis,* New York, McGraw-Hill.
Brown, R., Bute, S., Ford, P. (1986) *Social Workers at Risk,* London, Macmillan.

Crane, D. (1986) *Violence on Social Workers,* Norwich, Social Work Monographs, University of East Anglia.

Crine, A. (1982) 'An Occupational Hazard', *Community Care,* **437,** pp. 16–18.

Floud, J. and Young, W. (1981) *Dangerousness and Criminal Justice,* Cambridge Studies in Criminology, London, Heinemann.

Golan, N. (1978) *Treatment in Crisis Situations,* New York, The Free Press.

Kaplan, S. G. and Wheeler, E. G. (1983) 'Survival Skills for Work with Potentially Violent Clients', *Social Casework,* **4,** pp. 339–71.

Kroll, J. and Makensie, T. B. (1983) 'When Psychiatrists are Liable', *Hospital and Community Psychiatry,* **34,** no. 1.

Megargee, E. and Hokanson, J. (1970) *The Dynamics of Aggression,* New York, Harper & Row.

Rowett, E. (1986) *Violence in Social Work,* Cambridge, Cambridge Institute of Criminology.

Schwarz, V. (1986) 'Don't Settle for Whitewash', *Community Care,* **441,** p. 2.

Schwarz, V. (1987) 'Social Worker, Heal Thyself', *Community Care,* **442,** p. 14–5.

Small, N. (1985) 'Minimising the Risk', *Community Care,* **440,** pp. 14–16.

Ward, L. (1984) 'Keeping it Cool', *Social Work Today,* 17 January, p. 27.

CHAPTER 94

WIFE TO WIDOW TO WOMAN

Naomi Golan

During the past twenty-six years, the phenomenon of early, unanticipated widowhood has become one of the tragic byproducts of Israel's struggle for existence. Since the War of Independence in 1948, some 2,130 women have lost their soldier-husbands.[1] However, until the Six-Day War in 1967, except for the certification and implementation of material benefits, the periodic homage paid to bereaved families in official memorial ceremonies, and the mixed reactions of the rest of the population, little attempt was made to ease the plight of war widows. Since that time, and especially after the 1973 war, there have been numerous efforts undertaken to help these women. And from these efforts much has been learned about the process of widowhood that may be applied to other situations and other countries as well.

Mental health professionals from all disciplines, staffs of social service departments, volunteers from various backgrounds, and interested others have been involved in both organized programs and unorganized efforts. In some situations, a crisis intervention framework, aimed at returning the bereaved family to a precrisis level of equilibrium, has been attempted. In others, bereavement has been assumed to exacerbate previous intrapsychic and interpersonal difficulties and treatment has been geared to a resolution of underlying personality conflicts.

More recently, in response to the publicized cry of widows, "Don't make a case out of me," the extensive use of paraprofessionals and other widows who have successfully passed through the mourning process has been urged, with professionals holding a "watching brief," to use Caplan's term, on the sidelines.[2]

No matter what theoretical approach is used, the professional background of the caregiver and his theoretical frame of reference matter less than his personal involvement during the crucial stages following the husband's death and his willingness to remain in active contact until the various tasks with which the widow and her family are

Reprinted from *Social Work,* Vol. 20, No. 5 (1975), pp. 369–374, by permission of NASW Press. Copyright 1975, National Association of Social Workers, Inc., *Social Work.*

struggling have been resolved. The following framework, a composite of several theoretical stances, is suggested as a workable model to provide direction for helping these women.

BEREAVEMENT

The sudden, violent death of a soldier is a crisis-inducing event because no matter how psychologically geared a woman is to the possibility, it still is unexpected and irreversible and is an occurrence with which most survivors, particularly young ones, have had little prior experience. Such a death sets off a series of ever widening reverberations in and among the soldier's wife, children, parents, and siblings, all of whom function within interacting role networks. These reverberations then spread to the interlocking systems of friends, relatives, work companions, army comrades, neighborhood acquaintances, and the general public. Each person reacts to the event according to the significance the death has for himself, his customary patterns of defense and coping, and the resources available to deal with the crisis.[3]

This article deals with the impact of a soldier's death on one particular person—his wife. Not only must the widow struggle with the crushing emotional and physical loss of her husband, but she also must pass through a complex, two-stage transitional process that may take months and even years. That is, from being a wife, she must become a widow, and then a woman ready to engage in future personal involvement with others, including another man.

A transitional crisis is a period in which a person moves from one state of relative certainty to another. It upsets a person's normal equilibrium and creates a shift in his vital roles. It is normal in that it can happen to anyone in similar circumstances. By its nature, it generates a pressure toward reequilibrium and growth of the ego. Each transitional state has its tempo, specific characteristics, and discernible set of instrumental and affective tasks.

Although each person passes through the transitional period in his own fashion, it is possible to discern some common patterns that can provide guidelines for possible intervention. Lindemann, in his seminal study on bereavement, notes that the duration of a grief reaction seems to depend on the success with which the person carries out his grief work: to emancipate himself from his bondage to the deceased, to readjust to the environment in which the deceased is missing, and to be able to form new relationships.[4]

According to Bowlby, the bereavement process consists of three stages: protest and denial, despair and disorganization, and reorganization.[5] During the first stage, Krupp notes, the person makes a desperate effort to recover the deceased in fantasy, which expresses an unconscious denial of the death. Eventually these feelings merge with the second stage in the form of apathy, depression, and withdrawal.[6] In the third stage, the person reorganizes himself and his surroundings and transfers his love and interest from the deceased to a new person or persons.

Silverman uses the disaster framework to talk of impact, recoil, and recovery. Basing her approach on the findings of an extended research project on widowhood at the Laboratory of Community Psychiatry of the Harvard University Medical School, Cambridge, Massachusetts, she sees mourning as a dynamic, changing phenomenon, with each phase having its own demands and tasks.

The initial phase can take from one day to six months or more:

> The bereaved report experiencing a sense of being lost and not knowing what to do. Their sense of being suspended from life, inability to concentrate, indifference to immediate needs, disbelief that the deceased is really gone, and feeling that life can never be worth living again, hinders their ability to arrange for the funeral and make plans for other ongoing life needs.[7]

The second phase, says Silverman, overlaps the first and cannot always be clearly differentiated from it. It can cover from one month after the death to a year or longer. During this stage,

> . . . the widowed report experiencing the loss most acutely . . . because the numbness has lifted and the ability to feel returns. Some report going through a period of trying to do things exactly as the deceased would have liked, as if trying to recapture him in spirit if not in fact. A need to talk about the deceased and to review the facts of his death can become an obsession, to the annoyance of friends and relatives. Sometimes frighteningly irrational feelings about the tricks life has played can come out with great intensity. . . . This is the time when the widowed person experiences acute periods of loneliness. . . . They also report that they begin to move away from their married friends; they resent their sympathy and begin to feel like a "fifth wheel."[8]

The final recovery phase can occur from three months after the death to two years and marks a time of looking at the future. It involves learning to be alone and to find a meaningful social and emotional life in addition to being the head of the household, breadwinner, and combined father and mother. By this time, some widows become aware of their own estrangement and begin to reach out to others in similar situations. They become more independent of their families and tend to find their own modes of accommodation. For people without an extended family who are unaccustomed to reaching out, recovery is marred by isolation and loneliness.[9]

Widowhood, Silverman concludes, does not just "happen" when a spouse dies; the legal status of widowhood does not always coincide with a woman's social and emotional acceptance of the role. Except in those cultures where the role of widow is clearly defined, the first period after the death of a spouse is anomic: the widow does not know what to do, what the death means, what to expect of and for herself.

Gradually she is confronted with the finality of her loss and the truth that her husband is gone permanently. Only then can the period of recovery begin. As she passes through the grief process, she changes her sense of self, and the very nature of her outer world becomes different. She has to adjust to the fact that her life will never be the same, that the past is history and a prologue to the future.[10]

Parkes notes that although grief has no clear ending, it is common for widows to describe one or several events associated with a major revision of their feelings, attitudes, and behavior that both reflect and engender an abandonment of old modes of thinking and living. These events often occur after a special time, such as an anniversary. A memorial service or visit to the cemetery can thus have the significance of a rite of passage, setting the bereaved person free from the dead and allowing him to undertake new commitments.[11]

THE TRANSITION

If bereavement is to be considered a normal transitional state for the widow, how can she be helped to pass through this period of disequilibrium more fruitfully? Several years ago, in attempting to work out a model for assisting new immigrants to become integrated into a new society, this author and Gruschka tied Studt's formulation of social tasks involved in problems of social functioning to Kaplan's concept of phase-specific psychological tasks in situations of acute stress.[12] They believed that in situations of acute stress an individual and his family have to accomplish a series of tasks along two parallel and complementary dimensions: "material arrangemental" and psychosocial. (The term "material-arrangemental" refers to the provision of financial assistance and the setting up of substantive arrangements such as housing changes, homemaker services, and substitute child care—services generally grouped under the term "environmental modification.") The model developed seems to be applicable to other types of transitional situations.[13]

On the material-arrangemental level, the person in acute stress must carry out the following activities:

1. Explore available solutions, resources, and possible roles
2. Choose an appropriate solution, resource, and/or role and prepare himself for it
3. Apply formally for the solution or resource, take on the new role
4. Begin to use the new solution or resource, function in the new role
5. Go through a period of adaptation and development of increasing competence until performance rises to acceptable norms

Concurrently, the individual must fulfill the following psychosocial tasks:

1. Cope with the threat to his past security and sense of competence
2. Grapple with the anxieties and frustrations in making decisions or choosing the new solution, resources, or role
3. Handle the stress generated in applying for the solution or resource and in taking on the new role
4. Adjust to the new solution, resource, or role with all it implies in terms of position and status in the family and community
5. Develop new standards of well-being, agree to diminished satisfaction, and be able to delay gratification until he is able to function according to acceptable norms

Obviously, any such model suffers from the limitations of oversimplification. Nevertheless, with some bending and overlapping, it can offer guidelines to where in the transitional process the widow finds herself stuck and with what tasks she needs help. It should be kept in mind that some of these tasks can be carried out by the widow herself and some by others on her behalf.

BRIDGING THE PAST

In the initial phase of bereavement, a number of immediate, practical decisions must be made regarding the funeral, burial, financial arrangements, and so forth. The widow may choose to leave such matters in the hands of competent relatives and friends or the physician, clergyman, or funeral director, but she is, at least, usually aware of what is going on. In other areas, she forces herself to take hold: to feed the children, prepare the meals, sign the checks, and carry out all the routine aspects of her other roles as mother, housekeeper, and family manager that serve to give some semblance of normalcy to her shaken world, bring her closer to the present, and act as a bridge to push the transition forward by translating passive grieving into active coping.

In Israel, during and after the Yom Kippur War in 1973, special conditions provided little opportunity for this immediate grappling with the stark reality of death.[14] Because of the difficulties in recovering and identifying bodies, a wife was usually informed of her husband's death several weeks after he had died, was buried, and the survivors dispersed. Sometimes it took weeks and months before a grubby parcel of blood-stained clothing, a burnt-out watch case, or a returned pack of letters marked "died" brought home the first physical encounter with the death. Families were almost unanimous in saying that this lack of certainty, of not knowing and experiencing what had happened, was the hardest aspect of the situation to bear. The tragic situation of the "missing" delayed for many wives even the start of the bereavement process. For some it took a full nine months, until the bodies were reinterred in permanent civilian or military graves in August and September 1974, for death to become a tangible reality.

Ada, 21 years old, widowed after two months of marriage, represents a typical case of the inability to pass through the first stage of bereavement:

> Ada said her husband was first listed as missing and then, when she was finally informed of his death, there were conflicting reports of what had happened. She added that she never believed he was really dead and buried in Sinai. Most of her activities in the first five months were concentrated in trying to verify the facts about his death. Even after the repatriation of the Egyptian prisoners, she clung to the belief that he might still be alive somewhere in Egypt. She closed her apartment and returned to her parents' home, where she is protected from material pressures. She spends much of her time going from office to office and writing letters to army and Ministry of Defense officials.

The primary psychosocial task in the first phase is to loosen the ties with the deceased husband and to take in the fact that he is dead.[15] To do this, the wife must learn to break the thousands of threads of shared experiences with her husband, however poignant this may be, and to transform them into loving memories. This will include such overt acts as learning to use the past tense in talking about him. This phase requires a benign, permissive atmosphere that encourages the overt expression of grief and loss.[16]

Religiously observant widows in Israel found their psychosocial tasks considerably eased in the first phase by the observance of *shi'va*, the week of prescribed ritual mourning.[17] Even though it may have taken place weeks after the actual death occurred, the *shi'va* allowed for an open, shared bereavement; for permitting or even prescribing the recounting of past events in the fallen soldier's life; and for sitting together with childhood friends, fellow soldiers, and relatives, each of whom contributed his share of personal recollections. Through the healing balm of prayers and ordered rituals, the widows gained a measure of comfort and the feeling of continuity.[18]

Women with oriental ethnic backgrounds found relief and comfort by observing the overt mourning rituals and customs sanctioned and followed by their community: tearing their hair and clothes, scratching their cheeks, rocking back and forth rhythmically, and indulging in periodic *crisot* with symptoms of faintness, nausea, and even blackouts. Not only did these rituals serve to demonstrate the intensity of grief, but they enabled the women to slip more easily into their new role of widow. Visits to the cemetery became absorbing and ritualistic in their intensity.

Women from a restrained western background and those who were not religious found it harder to cope with the initial threat to past security. Many reported being given tranquilizers to "ease the pain of suffering" and said it took weeks to take in fully what had happened. In some cases, they confessed they would have liked to weep and wail but felt restricted by well-meaning relatives, who resolutely changed the subject when they tried to talk openly about their husbands or were inhibited by the common *sabra* (native-born Israeli) ethic of denial, stoicism, and inarticulateness.

The widow in the kibbutz, for example, experiences a special problem. In some kibbutzim, although the death of a member is keenly felt and mourned by all members, the absence of meaningful mourning rituals and the tendency to shield the widow from outside contacts or worries usually leaves her roleless and bottled up, unable to find a socially sanctioned way to grieve. She may be relieved of her work and child-caring responsibilities and often spends her time in loneliness or in putting up a facade.

LIVING WITH THE PRESENT

Once the wife has begun to cut herself off from the past, she must pass on to the second phase in which she turns her attention to the realities of her present role as widow. Again, much of her attention is directed toward material-arrangemental tasks: how to support her family, how to be a single parent to her children, how to manage the household alone. Frequently she has to grapple with such unfamiliar matters as mortgage payments, inheritance taxes, and insurance and survivors' benefits; in some cases she has to enter her husband's business to salvage what she can. She may soon have to face the grim need to provide additional income for her family and must reenter, or enter for the first time, the labor market. This may involve finding out what marketable skills she has to offer, taking vocational retraining, and arranging day care for her children. Silverman reported that some women who previously worked found a return to their jobs a source of comfort and continuity.[19]

At this time many widows become increasingly absorbed in their role as single parent. In addition to their motherly tasks, they must take on such fatherly roles as arbiter of disputes, disciplinarian, captain of outings, and reader of stories at bedtime. They must also deal with the young children's stomachaches, tantrums, regressions, fears, and nightmares that are a reaction not only to the loss of the father, but to the changes the death has wrought in the mother. Even older children, absorbed in their own loss, resort to new behavioral patterns with which the mothers find it hard to cope. Some older children, on the other hand, take over part of the father's role, even to the point of nurturing the mother.

The situation of the war widow in Israel is both easier and harder than elsewhere. Financial assistance is adequately and, in some instances, generously established by law. Among the numerous benefits are these: monthly financial payments; assistance with current debts and mortgages; help in purchasing new housing, furniture, household equipment, and a moderately priced car; cancellation or reduction of purchase taxes and customs duties; and partial telephone, medical, and dental payments. In keeping with its prescribed function of rehabilitation, the social service staff of the Defense Ministry makes a special effort to provide advice and assistance with vocational training programs.

Much of social workers' activities are devoted to filling out the necessary application forms and struggling with departmental red tape to establish eligibility and obtain financial benefits for the widow and her family. On the whole, despite difficulties in breaking through bureaucratic patterns, the occasional oversights and errors caused by confusions in the reporting system, and the sometimes exaggerated expectations of family members, most widows report they have little to complain of in this respect.

However, in the more intangible psychosocial tasks of grappling with anxieties and frustrations, making choices and decisions, and handling the stresses imposed by the shift in their roles, many war widows experienced emotional problems and upsets, particularly after friends, relatives, and well-meaning volunteers returned to their own concerns. At this point, the widows were faced with the essential loneliness of their situation, with feelings of inadequacy and lack of emotional support. As one widow, Ronit, aged 25, said:

> During the day I try to keep myself busy. I go on with my studies, take the children to lessons, am active in the parents' committee at school, polish the pots, and rearrange the furniture. But in the evening, after the children are finally in bed and I can no longer lose myself in television, the loneliness sets in and I feel restless and lost.
>
> What do I do? Fortunately, I have a few friends who still have the patience to listen to me, so I pick up the phone—even at midnight—and we just talk about anything, until I feel tired enough to try to go to sleep.

Another widow, Sara, aged 26, said she found it difficult to adjust to being physically alone. She came from a large, close family and, after her marriage, had never left the house after dark without her husband. She never recalled sleeping alone and, after her husband was killed, her younger sister would come over at night to sleep with her. Sara said she feels strange being alone and has the sensation when she walks on the street that "everyone is looking at me as if something is wrong, something is missing."

During this stage, talking with other widows was sometimes the most helpful means of learning to cope. The Northern Office of the Defense Ministry organized, during the spring and summer of 1974, social interest groups of widows, led jointly by a social worker and a widow who had already passed "successfully" through the mourning process. Small groups met, usually biweekly, at each other's homes and talked about their experiences in fitting into the world without their husbands. Discussions often concentrated on their roles as mothers; at other times the women talked frankly about their lack of companionship and their sexual needs and about their feelings of estrangement from and discomfort in their former social circle of married couples.

Women in these groups developed their own language and grim "in" jokes about their progress in adjusting. They would announce proudly, for example, that they had reached the "red outfit" milestone, when they could put aside their subdued clothes, worn uncaringly all those first months, and purchase a defiantly scarlet suit or dress "with all the accessories."

For some widows, having a volunteer babysit for a few hours a week, provided a welcome respite from the constant pressures and reminders and enabled them to mingle with other people. For others, a car, purchased at nominal cost through the Defense Ministry, was their means of release. "When things got too hard to bear, I'd allow myself the luxury of escaping in the car and driving for hours—anywhere, aimlessly—until I felt ready to come home again."

Still others spent these months crystallizing the memory of their husbands, preparing an album of snapshots of their lives together, and collecting letters and poems and arranging to have them published. Some set up memory corners in the living room, with pictures and mementoes, "so the children shouldn't forget their Daddy."

PATHS INTO THE FUTURE

Sometime between the first and the second year, the widow enters the third phase in which she begins to find some measure of adjustment and habituation to her new status. She has learned to function more competently, has become more sure of herself in making decisions, can express herself with great confidence, and feels more adequate in managing the children. At this point she begins to consider her future, not as a widow (although that condition may continue), but as a woman. Observers have noted that a woman at this stage may become more interested in community affairs and active in special interest groups such as Parents Without Partners.[20] Parkes found the turning point often occurs when widows become interested in men and begin to date.[21]

Many of the women widowed during the 1973 Israeli war seem well on their way to adapting to their situation. Some have completed or are in the process of completing retraining courses or obtaining university degrees. Others have become active in parents' groups, joined civil defense units, or begun to press for more rights for themselves and their families.

Because of their youth, remarriage has become a serious issue. In some cases well-meaning friends or relatives have offered to serve as matchmakers. In other cases, the women have taken the initiative in beginning to date and consider a second marriage, often phrased in terms of finding "another father for their children." An interesting complication has arisen in this respect. Because of the benefits obtained, some widows have become more affluent than they were before, and some report that the men they date are interested in their money. One benefit offered by the Defense Ministry is a lump sum of money as a "dowry" to enable the widow to remarry. The monthly allotment, of course, ceases on her remarriage, although child support continues until the last child reaches age 18.

The public nature of the war widows' bereavement, the repeated reminders brought on by the reports in the news media of the return of war prisoners, the search for missing bodies, and the rehashing of the families' reactions to their loss served both to keep emotional wounds open and to help the widows work through their grief reactions. For some women, the continuous chain of memorial services—the Days of Remembrance, the reburial ceremonies, the memorial meetings, the anniversaries of the war, and the religious holidays—was painful. Those who could find comfort in religious services found the *shloshim* (thirty-day service) and *shanah* (first-year memorial) ceremonies marked an end and a beginning.

In other situations, it took well over a year for the widow to begin to come to grips with what had happened and was still happening to her. Some, at this point, began to seek professional help to examine the nature and quality of their relationships with their dead husbands and to consider the maturational effect brought on by their grief. In some cases they were even able to acknowledge that their marriage had not been the idyllic experience they had heretofore maintained it to have been.

The general feeling expressed individually and in the groups is that grieving is not something one "gets over"; one learns to live with it. Perhaps the situation can be summed up in the report of one widow, not from Israel, whose words echo what many widows feel:

"Widow" is a harsh and hurtful word. It comes from the Sanskrit and it means "empty." I have been empty too long. I do not want to be pigeonholed as a widow. I am a woman whose husband died, yes. But not a second-class citizen, not a lonely goose. I am a mother and a working woman . . . and a vital woman. I am a person. I resent what the term widow has come to mean. I am alive. I am part of the world.

Acceptance finally comes. And with it comes peace.

I am stronger, more independent. I have more understanding, more sympathy. A different perspective. I have a quiet love for Martin. I have passionate, poignant memories of him. He will always be a part of me. But—If I were to meet Martin today . . . ? Would I love him?

I ask myself. Startled. What brought the question to my mind? I know. I ask it because I am a different woman.[22]

NOTES AND REFERENCES

1. *Report of the State Controller's Office* (Jerusalem: Israel Government Press, 1974).
2. Gerald Caplan. "Crisis Intervention in Time of War." Paper presented at a workshop at the University of Haifa. Haifa, Israel, February 1974.
3. For a discussion of the nature and phases of crises, *see* Naomi Golan, "Crisis Theory," in Francis J. Turner, ed., *Social Work Treatment: Interlocking Theoretical Approaches* (New York: Free Press, 1974), pp. 421–439.
4. Erich Lindemann, "Symptomatology and Management of Acute Grief," *American Journal of Psychiatry,* 101 (September 1944), pp. 1–11.
5. John Bowlby, "Grief and Mourning in Infancy and Early Childhood," *Psychoanalytic Study of the Child,* 15 (New York: International Universities Press, 1960), pp. 9–52.
6. George Krupp, "Maladaptive Reactions to the Death of a Family Member," *Social Casework*, 53 (July 1972), pp. 425–426.
7. Phyllis R. Silverman, "Services to the Widowed: First Steps in a Program of Preventive Intervention," *Community Mental Health Journal,* 3 (Spring 1967), p. 38.
8. Ibid., p. 40.
9. Ibid., pp. 41-42.
10. Phyllis R. Silverman, "Widowhood and Preventive Intervention," *Family Coordinator* (January 1972), pp. 95–102.
11. Colin Murray Parkes, *Bereavement: Studies of Grief in Adult Life* (New York: International Universities Press, 1972), p. 176.
12. Elliot Studt, *A Conceptual Approach to Teaching Materials* (New York: Council on Social Work Education, 1965), pp. 4–18; and David Kaplan, "Observations on Crisis Theory and Practice," *Social Casework*, 49 (March 1968), pp. 151–155.
13. Naomi Golan and Ruth Gruschka, "Integrating the New Immigrant: A Model for Social Work Practice in Transitional States," *Social Work*, 18 (April 1971), p. 84.
14. The following material is based on the author's experience as a social work consultant for the Rehabilitation Division, Israel Ministry of Defense, Northern District, from November 1973 to June 1974. Illustrations are from case studies.
15. Lorraine D. Siggins, "Mourning: A Critical Review of the Literature," *International Journal of Psychiatry,* 3 (May 1967), p. 423.
16. Stanley B. Goldberg, "Family Tasks and Reactions in the Crisis of Death," *Social Casework*, 54 (July 1973), p. 400.
17. Maurice Lamm, *The Jewish Way in Death and Mourning* (New York: Jonathan David Publishers, 1969), pp. 77–144.
18. For an extensive discussion of the sociocultural aspects of death, see Phyllis Palgi, "Death, Mourning, and Bereavement in Israel," *Israel Annals of Psychiatry and Related Disciplines,* 9 (1973).
19. Silverman, "Widowhood and Preventive Intervention," p. 97.
20. Silverman, "Services to the Widowed," p. 42.
21. Parkes, op. cit., pp. 76-77.
22. Lynn Caine, *Widow (*New York: William Morrow & Co., 1974), pp. 221 and 222.

PART VI

SOCIOPERSONAL FACTORS

In previous editions of this book this section was entitled Sociocultural Issues and focused on those perceived major divisions in society that have traditionally been combined under that general heading. As we reviewed the literature of recent years and sought for groupings of articles this seemed too restrictive. Hence we decided to expand this section by using as the unifying theme aspects of a client's reality that relate to being a member of some particular identifiable group that is viewed by society as having some common properties. These properties are presumed to make its members in some way different, resulting in identifiable societal perceptions or reactions. These identified differences can emerge as the result of birth, history, accident, or choice. In this way we have greatly expanded this section, which had been the smallest, and moved beyond class, ethnicity, race, and culture, which were the principal topics previously addressed.

This was a difficult section to organize, and the articles under the various headings were difficult to select. This for a variety of reasons. One is the lack of precision with which some of these categories are used in the literature and in practice. For example, there is still considerable overlap, and indeed confusion, between such terms as race, ethnicity, and culture. This is true both in common parlance and in professional writing. In prior editions we avoided this challenge by including all three under the general heading of ethnicity. Thus the article by Marsella on Japanese Americans could have been considered under any one of these three important headings. Another term that frequently is used imprecisely is "minority groups," which is also frequently identified with race, ethnicity, and culture. So too with the terms "immigrants" and "refugees."

It is imperative that we continue to seek precision in the use of these terms, not just for the sake of conceptual purity, but more importantly so that we are aware of the critical, albeit at times subtle, factors related to these societal roles that need to be understood both diagnostically and in treatment.

Important as these variables are in practice, they are topics on which a great deal has not been written. I suggest that one of the reasons for this is our very realistic and strong awareness of the dangers of stereotyping that can accompany discussions about ethnic, cultural, and racial factors. This has created a dilemma for us. On the one hand we are increasingly aware of the need to know more about, and be therapeutically responsive to, these differences. Yet on the other hand we are warned about the dangers of over-generalizing and the need to individualize. Of course this is one of the ongoing challenges of much of practice. This area has been particularly sensitive because of the harm that has been done through negative stereotyping.

One term that has become increasingly useful in helping us walk this fine line is "central tendencies." This term helps us find a way between learning about a particular group in society and the patterns of response that are frequently observed within it, and the ever-present need to understand that in each and every case we need to individualize. This readies us to find that a particular client or family is totally different from what has been observed in others of the same group.

This has helped us move away from articles on how to treat clients of a particular ethnic or cultural group to articles on aspects of a particular group that may be present and that may help us work more effectively with a client or family.

Thus, we have noticed two trends in the literature. First, the reduction in over-generalized articles about particular groups and second, the increase in articles that look at a variable such as ethnicity from a more theoretical basis. Examples of this are the article by Solomon on a multicultural perspective on practice and the article by Gelfand and Fandetti on ethnicity in a generic sense.

Socioeconomic class is another area about which we know much but are very sensitive to talk in a formal way. Frequently all that is said, and usually in a pejorative manner, is that social work is a middle-class profession and thus is out of touch with persons from other classes, especially the poor. It is not a topic to which we have given much attention from the perspective of intervention. This is in spite of the evidence that values, problem solving, access to resources, and many other aspects of the therapeutic process appear to be very different when class is used as a variable. Indeed, so little has been written that the articles in the subsection on class are nearly the same as those in the last edition.

Another area of considerable import in practice is that of values and value differences within and between groups of clients. Much work that has been done indicates that our various theoretical approaches to practice have unique value bases that fit some clients much better than others. Yet we do not seem to have done much with this apparently critical finding from the perspective of its application to treatment.

In reviewing the literature of recent years for this section we were encouraged to find that, in addition to the variables discussed above, we have begun to address other societal roles or statuses that we have long believed to have import for treatment. For example, we found material indicating that, when properly understood and addressed, the spiritual lives of our clients can be a powerful positive growth-enhancing agent.

As our society becomes increasingly multicultural, we need once again to address the complex role of immigration and being a refugee. There is much to be learned as we work with persons who chose or were forced to come to our shores. Again, the need to sort out the differential impact of immigrant or refugee status and minority status, and we need to understand the unique aspects of the odysseys and backgrounds of such persons.

Although at first it appeared that the topic of legal offenders was out of place in this section, we finally decided that it was not. This too is a status in society that marks the person as different and that, in turn, provokes stereotypical responses. Although we have long worked with such clients we have not written much about how their being legal offenders can have an important influence on our diagnosis, treatment, and use of resources.

Again, as we expand our knowledge of all societal groupings we can become more effective at building our understanding into therapeutic strategies with which to effectively intervene in the lives of our clients.

CHAPTER 95

BICULTURALISM AND SUBJECTIVE MENTAL HEALTH AMONG CUBAN AMERICANS

Manuel R. Gómez

In clinical social work it is now assumed that to be well adjusted, members of an ethnic group living within a dominant culture must not only assimilate the larger culture but simultaneously maintain their own roots.[1] This duality is commonly referred to as biculturalism. However, this axiom has been accepted only ideologically and has limited empirical validation. Although this twofold burden is increasingly implied in the literature, it is seldom recognized formally.

José Szapocznick and William Kurtines have challenged the traditional view that, for ethnic individuals such as Cuban Americans who live in bicultural communities, acculturation is a linear and unidimensional process. According to the traditional view, an ethnic individual's identification with his or her original culture slowly fades as he or she gradually becomes assimilated into the host culture. These authors suggest that, among Cuban Americans, acculturation should be studied as an accommodation that takes place along two independent dimensions. One dimension involves the acquisition of the host culture, the second dimension involves the retention of the original culture.[2]

Yoel Camayd-Freixas and Hortensia Amaro view biculturalism as a balance in this accommodation.[3] In this study, it was assumed that monoculturalism is represented by either of the two extremes of a continuum of acculturation. At one end of this continuum, monocultural ethnocentrism implies a rejection of the host culture in favor of a

Reprinted from *Social Service Review*, Vol. 64, No. 3 (September 1990), pp. 375–389, by permission of the publisher.

total or almost total identification with the ethnic culture. At the other end of the continuum stands monocultural assimilation, which implies a rejection of the original culture in favor of a total or almost total identification with the host culture. Biculturalism is found at the middle ranges of the continuum.

Most empirical studies that explore the relationship between psychological adjustment and acculturation follow the traditional view of acculturation. An awareness of the personal effect of cultural transition on members of an ethnic group has led these investigators to predict that the better people are able to assimilate, the fewer psychological and interpersonal problems they will experience in their adjustment. The results of these studies have invariably contradicted their expectations; level of acculturation has not been found to be related significantly to psychological adjustment.[4] These contradictions lead to the hypothesis that biculturalism rather than assimilation is positively related to subjective mental health. The term "subjective mental health" is used here to refer to subjects' own evaluations of their experiences in different, but specific, aspects of their lives.[5]

In two studies by John Lang, Ricardo Munoz, Guillermo Bernal, and James Sorensen, and by Szapocznick and Kurtines, it was concluded that biculturalism, not higher levels of acculturation, is significantly related to psychological adjustment.[6] The Lang et al. study was flawed by the failure to screen out subjects with histories of mental health problems, and the Szapocznick and Kurtines study was based on a clinical population. Subjects known to suffer from mental health problems might score at the extremes of acculturation scales because of their mental health, not their acculturation problems. Thus, neither study addressed the overall relationship between acculturation and mental health. The present study was designed to clarify the relationship between biculturalism and subjective mental health within a healthy population.

Among the research questions that have not been asked are, Is the subjective mental health of a healthy ethnic group member related to the degree of identification he or she maintains with his or her own ethnic group? If such a relationship exists, which individuals report better adjustment—those who identify most with their ethnic culture or those who identify most with the dominant culture? Or, as some evidence suggests, is optimal adjustment associated with a dual identification with both cultures? This study was designed to answer these questions.

The study's general hypothesis was that, after controlling for variability due to sex, age, marital status, socioeconomic class, and length of stay in the United States, there would be a positive linear relationship between subjective mental health and one's level of biculturalism. This general hypothesis generated a specific hypothesis for each of the four variables used to measure subjective mental health: psychological well-being, self-esteem, marital adjustment, and job satisfaction. Each of the variables used in this study has been shown to be related significantly to mental health in the past.

These variables were explored using a sample of Cuban Americans who have no history of psychiatric problems, drug abuse, or psychotropic medication use. The Cuban-American community is the third largest Hispanic group in the United States. Cubans were chosen because a body of data exists from other studies that investigated the relationship between level of acculturation and psychological adjustment.[7] These data allow the comparison of results of this study with other studies of the same population that have employed different measures in different locations.

VARIABLES

Overall psychological well-being.—Norman Bradburn has defined overall psychological well-being as the relative combination of positive and negative affect in the same individual. He has shown that a person's psychological well-being is related significantly to an excess of positive affect in an individual's life.[8]

Corrective feedback from members of the dominant culture is essential to becoming bicultural. Diane de Anda has noted that negative feedback generates negative affect, which interferes with the discriminative learning of complex behaviors and concepts. An excess of negative feedback may drive the individual to withdraw from the socialization process and reject the dominant culture. An excess of negative feedback may also lead the individual to reject his or her ethnic background to avoid the punishment experienced for being different from others. Retaining the original ethnic culture while simultaneously acquiring the dominant culture is a difficult and complex task that can be accomplished only when the individual experiences positive affect in the socialization experience.[9] This is why we expect bicultural individuals to report experiencing more positive than negative feelings.

Self-esteem.—Self-esteem is defined as the expression of the ability to perceive oneself and to evaluate these self-perceptions according to a variety of standards.[10] A negative perception of self has been seen traditionally as a sign of emotional problems, as well as a symptom of mental illness. A positive perception of self has been linked to happiness[11] and subjective mental health.[12] The individual acquires from within the context of his or her family the basic criteria from which to evaluate him- or herself. However, the larger social environment in which the family lives also influences the individual. It can complement or contrast with the family's values, supporting or challenging them.

Individuals who have acquired a positive sense of self from within their family context begin to feel strange and devalued when the larger social environment does not support the family's criteria for self-evaluation. Morris Rosenberg's work with individuals raised in Catholic, Jewish, or Protestant homes but who live in communities that do not share their religious values has shown that those individuals have lower self-esteem than those who live in communities in which the majority share their religious views.[13] Harriet McAdoo's work with blacks supports these findings.[14] The implications of these studies suggest that a sense of continuity and belongingness bolsters self-esteem. Support from the family and larger society appear to be necessary sources of self-worth.

Ethnic individuals who live in a society that does not understand their language and often does not support the ethnic values learned at home can be expected to experience feelings of low self-worth. The degree of acculturation they acquire is likely to be related to their level of self-esteem.

Monocultural individuals who reject their original culture acquire a sense of belonging to the host culture, but at the expense of having to devalue the ethnic values learned from their families. These individuals lose a primary source of self-esteem when they break their ties with the culture that originally provided value and worth. Monocultural individuals who reject the influence of the host culture retain a sense of continuity with their original values, but at the expense of never feeling that they belong to the society in which they live and work. These individuals are missing the necessary support from their social environment to retain their self-worth. Bicultural individuals accept the presence and influence of the host culture without devaluing their original ties to the ethnic family. They recognize the differences between the two cultures, but they learn to accept the host culture in spite of the differences. Learning the language, attitudes, and beliefs of the host culture and accepting its values improve their chances of being accepted since they no longer appear so different. They gain a feeling of belonging without ever losing continuity with their ethnic origins. Both sources of self-esteem are maintained, mitigating the negative impact of environmental dissonance on their self-esteem. It is for these reasons that we expect bicultural individuals to have higher self-esteem than monocultural individuals.

Marital adjustment.—Graham Spanier and Charles Cole define marital adjustment as the outcome of several factors, including marital satisfaction, dyadic cohesion, and dyadic consensus.[15] They found these variables to be interrelated dimensions of marital adjustment. Ed Diener notes that marital satisfaction has been found to be the strongest predictor of subjective well-being.[16] The ability for consensus and cohesion are the hallmarks of intimacy and mutuality in a relationship that is possible only between mature and healthy individuals.[17]

Culturally determined gender roles are part of the repertoire of attitudes and behavior that ethnic group members bring with them when they enter the host culture. The literature on Cubans describes the aggressive, dominant, and provider role of the Cuban man and the passive, submissive, and dependent role of the Cuban woman.[18] An ethnic couple could avoid conflict between the traditional gender roles and the more egalitarian values of the U.S. culture by isolating the traditional relationship from the new influence. However, financial need often makes this isolation impossible. The woman is forced to assume the role of coprovider and to be less financially dependent on the man. The inevitable conflict created by this violation of the traditional gender role has led Bernal to predict emotional difficulties and marital disharmony among Cubans.[19] Yet for some the conflict may not be as severe as originally expected. There is evidence that many Cuban women who work have not given up their belief in emotional dependence and male dominance.[20] The violation of gender roles has more severe consequences for the men in social condemnation and psychosocial stress.[21] However, these negative consequences are likely to be minimized under conditions that improve the financial situation of the family while allowing the man to still feel needed by his wife. He could then be expected to be less rigid in his adherence to the traditional gender role, resulting in a reduction of marital conflict and disharmony. Bicultural individuals are more likely to achieve this type of accommodation in their marriages since it involves both the acquisition of behaviors sanctioned and approved by the dominant culture and the retention of the ethnic philosophy that governs relationships between men and women. It is for these reasons that bicultural individuals were expected to be more satisfied with and better adjusted to their marriages.

Job satisfaction.—The meaning of job satisfaction varies according to what each individual values in his or her work. Psychological satisfaction in the job is often defined in terms of the sense of accomplishment the individual derives from his or her labor and the extent to which the job matches the worker's interests and abilities.[22] Job satisfaction is known to be related to overall happiness,[23] and Diener notes that it is a predictor of subjective well-being as well.[24]

Ethnic individuals tend to participate in the economic institutions of a society to the extent that their work ethic is similar to that of the majority group. The discrepancy between the work ethic of the ethnic individual and that of the majority group must not be too big. If it is, then the ethnic individual must be willing to accept the dominant work ethic in order to find and maintain a rewarding job.[25] In the case of Cubans in the United States, this means accepting the North American emphasis on work as an end by itself instead of the Cuban view of work as a necessity.[26]

There are three options for ethnic individuals facing these value conflicts: economic separatism, assimilation, and biculturalism.[27] Monocultural separatism is not a solution for Cubans. They lack the numbers and the resources at a national level to create their own economy. Like others who reject the work ethic of the dominant culture, Cubans are likely to experience cultural dislocation, social alienation, and low job satisfaction.[28] Assimilation is also a poor alternative. Cultural assimilation has not been found to be a predictor of job satisfaction among Cubans.[29] It is for these reasons that bicultural Cubans were expected to report greater job satisfaction.

METHOD
Sample

The sample used in this study consisted of 151 Cuban-American citizens 18 years or older from West New York, New Jersey. The participants had no history of psychiatric treatment or drug abuse and had never used prescribed psychotropic medication. The sample was drawn using a combination of random and accidental sampling procedures based on census tract mappings.

West New York is divided into nine census tracts of different sizes. Three square blocks were selected at random from each tract. Thus, regardless of size, each tract contributed the same number of square blocks (three) to the final selection of the sample. All homes or apartments in each block were visited to determine how many of them were occupied by Cuban Americans. Each tract contributed a different percentage of subjects to the sample. This percentage was the same as the percentage of the population residing in the tract.

Once all subjects were identified, an interviewer went to each address selected and requested an interview of the first person 18 years or older who met the research criteria. If the subject refused the interview, changed her or his mind, or knew the interviewer, the next person available at home was approached. In cases in which no one in the home agreed to be interviewed, no one met the criteria, a member of the family knew the interviewer, or no one was at home, the closest Cuban-American home in that square block was approached. On many occasions the interviewer had to schedule an appointment with a subject to interview her or him at a more convenient time.

In the 207 homes visited, 12 refusals were encountered. In addition, nine people could not be interviewed because they knew the interviewer. While 45 potential subjects did not meet the research criteria, in only 10 of the cases was another person from the same household used. For the other 35 cases, the interviewer proceeded to the next closest home. The total number of interviews completed was 151.

The obtained sample was heterogeneous. The age range was from 18 to 72 years, with a mean age of 41 years. All subjects were employed. Although 17 were officially retired, they continued to work *por la izquierda* (under the table). The sample contained 25 subjects (16.6%) who were single, 109 (72.2%) who were married, and 17 (11.2%) who were separated, divorced, or widowed. There were 86 male (57%) and 65 female (43%) subjects in the sample. Subjects' educational and occupational levels were diverse, with every Hollingshead category from highest to lowest represented. The periods of residence in the United States ranged from 5 to 40 years. The largest percentage of respondents (54%) reported from 20 to 24 years of residence in the United States, representing the first wave of migration from Cuba following the revolution. The second largest (17.2%) reported from 5 to 9 years of residence in the United States, representing the last wave of migration during the Mariel boat lift.

Measurements

Psychological well-being. The Affective Balance Scale (ABS) developed by Bradburn and David Caplovitz has 10 items, five that measure positive affect and five that measure negative affect.[30] The difference between scores on positive and negative affect has been found to be the best predictor of overall well-being.[31] Bradburn has reported a 3-day test-retest reliability coefficient of .90 for the ABS. Validity estimates for the ABS include gamma coefficients between .45 and .51 when the ABS scores are correlated with selected indicators of happiness and life satisfaction.[32]

Self-esteem. A modified version of the Rosenberg Self-Esteem Scale was used in this study.[33] Rosenberg's original scale included items designed for use with adolescents. The items in the modified version can be used with any population. Rosenberg reports a Guttman-scale reproducibility coefficient of .92. Earle Silbert and Jean Tippett reported a 2-week test-retest reliability coefficient of .90.[34]

Marital adjustment. A modified version of a measure of marital adjustment developed by Spanier is used in this study.[35] The Dyadic Adjustment Scale (DAS) was designed to measure marital adjustment, but it is also applicable to unmarried couples living together. The modified DAS is composed of three subscales and a total of 27 Likert-type items. The subscales are Dyadic Consensus, Dyadic Cohesion, and Dyadic Satisfaction. An alpha coefficient of .96 was reported for the DAS. Alpha coefficients reported for the subscales were Dyadic Consensus, .90; Dyadic Cohesion, .86; and Dyadic Satisfaction, .94. The scale discriminates between married and divorced couples.

Job satisfaction. The "Job Satisfaction Blank Number Five" scale (JSB) developed by Robert Hoppoch was used in this study.[36] The JSB is an overall measure of job satisfaction, applicable to any occupation. The instrument is composed of four items, with seven response options for each item. When the scale is adapted to an interview, respondents are asked to say which of the seven possibilities for each item applies to them. Each of the possibilities represents different degrees of satisfaction with the current job. The scale is scored by adding the scale values of respondent's choices. Hoppoch reported a split-half reliability coefficient of .93 for a sample of over 300.

Biculturalism. Biculturalism was measured by using an adaptation of the biculturalism scale of the Latino Bicultural Assessment Questionnaire (LABIA) developed by Camayd-Freixas and Amaro and designed to be used with any Latino population.[37] The scale used in the present study is a 45-item questionnaire using a five-point Likert-scales format. It measures three factors selected from a review of previous studies on acculturation on the basis of their repeated presence in many of those studies. These factors are language use and preference, ethnic identity and cultural contact, and ethnic social interaction.

The scale produces an overall measure of biculturalism in which extreme scores represent monoculturalism (either Latin or North American) and middle scores represent biculturalism. The scoring procedure for the scale is modified for the purpose of the present study. In order to obtain a single interval scale in which higher scale values represent greater biculturalism and lower scale values represent greater monoculturalism, the extreme scores are combined for each item. For example, in items designed to identify language preference, respondents answer by choosing one of the following values: (1) always or almost always Spanish; (2) more Spanish than English; (3) both Spanish and English approximately equally; (4) more English than Spanish; (5) always or almost always English. The two scores 1 and 5 are combined into the single score, 1. The two scores 2 and 4 are combined into the single score, 2. This yields a scale that goes from 1, representing the greatest degree of monoculturalism, to 3, representing the greatest degree of biculturalism. The averaged sum of all item responses provides an overall measure of biculturalism.

Standardized alpha coefficients were calculated for the three factors, based on the study data. These coefficients were .94 for language use and preference, .92 for ethnic identity and cultural contact, and .80 for ethnic social interaction and contact. The validity of the instrument was determined by comparing the scores of a group of self-identified Latinos, a group of North American bilinguals, and a monolingual group. Significant differences were found between the groups on the overall measure of biculturalism.

The control variables used in this study have been identified in the literature as possibly related to the dependent variables alone (i.e., marital status) or both the dependent and independent variables (i.e., age, sex, socioeconomic status, and length of residence in the United States).

Diener has identified marriage as one of the strongest predictors of subjective well-being.[38] In terms of age, younger persons have been found to be happier[39] and to experience higher levels of joy than older persons.[40] Diener notes little difference between the sexes on measures of subjective well-being, but he reports an interaction of sex with age. Younger women appear happier than younger men, and older women appear less happy than older men.[41] There is evidence to show that socioeconomic status[42] and length of residence in the United States have an indirect effect on subjective well-being.[43]

Szapocznick, Mercedes Scopetta, and Kurtines report that the longer a person lives in the United Suites, the more acculturated that person becomes. Younger individuals acculturate faster than older ones, and females acculturate slower than males.[44] Eleanor Rogg and Rosemary Cooney have found that the higher the education and the occupational status, the higher the score of respondents in some measures of assimilation.[45]

RESULTS

Table 95–1 shows the mean, standard deviation, and the matrix of bivariate correlations among the five independent and dependent variables. The table shows that the four dependent variables were substantially intercorrelated. The range of correlations between these four indices of subjective mental health indicate that subjective mental health may in fact be a unitary concept, tapped by affective balance, self-esteem and marital adjustment. Job satisfaction would appear to be a related but distinct, dimension. A principal components analysis showed that one factor accounted for 70 percent of the variability of scores in the four variables. The factor loading for psychological well-being was .93; for self-esteem, .94; for marital adjustment, .84; and for job satisfaction, .46.

To determine whether any of the demographic characteristics measured in the study were related significantly to the dependent measures of subjective mental health, t-tests were performed for the two dichotomous variables, sex and marital status (categorized as married vs. not married).

Pearson product-moment correlations were calculated between the dependent measures and the interval-scale control variables (age, years of residence in the United States, and socioeconomic status). The results of the first set of tests showed no significant differences between men and women on any of the four indices of subjective mental health. Married respondents expressed greater job satisfaction than unmarried respondents ($t = 3.60$, $p < .001$, df = 134). Table 95–2 shows the correlations between the dependent measures and the continuous demographic variables. Weak but significant negative relationships were obtained between age and self-esteem and between age and psychological well-being. This indicates that there was a tendency for older people to experience less positive affect and less self-esteem. Also, a weak but significant posi-

Table 95–1
Means, Standard Deviations, and Intercorrelations of
Independent and Dependent Variables (N = 151)

Variables	Mean	SD	(1)	(2)	(3)	(4)	(5)
1. Biculturalism	5.87	1.46					
2. Psychological well-being	5.73	2.38	.86***				
3. Self-esteem	8.88	2.90	.87***	.86***			
4. Marital adjustment	77.74	32.53	.89***	.87***	.87***		
5. Job satisfaction	20.34	5.88	.38***	.35***	.38***	.27***	

NOTE.—Column numbers correspond to the numbered variables.
*** $p < .001$.

Table 95–2
Intercorrelations between Dependent Measures and Continuous Demographic Variables

Variables	Age	SES	Years in the United States
Psychological well-being:			
r	−.14	−.26***	.05
p	.040	.001	.258
Self-esteem:			
r	−.15*	−.26***	.09
p	.025	.001	.128
Marital adjustment:			
r	−.01	−.19*	.07
p	.460	.025	.232
Job satisfaction:			
r	.19*	−.28***	.19*
p	.016	.001	.013

NOTE.—In the Hollingshead system, lower numerical scores indicate higher socioeconomic status (SES).
* $p < .05$.
*** $p < .001$.

tive relationship was found between age and job satisfaction. This suggests a tendency for older subjects to be more satisfied with their work than younger subjects. Weak but significant relationships were also obtained between socioeconomic status and the four indices of subjective mental health. Since lower numerical scores on the Hollingshead Two-Factor Index signify higher socioeconomic status, the negative signs on these correlation coefficients show a tendency for higher socioeconomic status subjects to have greater job satisfaction, greater psychological well-being, higher self-esteem, and better marital adjustment. Period of residence in the United States was related significantly to only one measure, job satisfaction.

Thus, all of the relationships between indices of subjective mental health and subject's background variables were found to be weak. Because several of the relationships were significant, a multivariate multiple regression analysis (MANOVA) was employed to control for variability attributable to these factors while the effects of biculturality were tested. However, the Statistical Package for the Social Sciences (SPSS-X) MANOVA program used for this analysis excludes all individuals with missing data on any variable. In this study, those respondents who were not living in an intimate relationship or who were unmarried did not have scores on the marital adjustment measure and therefore would have been excluded by the SPSS-X MANOVA program. To avoid this undesirable consequence, marital adjustment was excluded from the analysis so that all subjects could be used; losing 42 unmarried subjects not only would have reduced the sample size considerably but also would have restricted the sample to married individuals.

The results of the multivariate multiple regression analysis are presented in table 95–3. The multivariate Pillais test indicated a highly significant relationship between the predictors and the dependent variables of subjective mental health (F (approx.

Table 95–3
Multiple Regression of Subjective Mental Health Indicators on Biculturalism and Background
Variables: Test for Individual Dependent Variables

| Variables | | Standardized Regression Coefficients | | | | | |
	R^2	Biculturalism	Age	Sex	Marital Status	SES	Years in the United States
Psychological well-being	.72***	.73***	.14	.11	.36*	−.13	.03
Self-esteem	.75***	.74***	.06	−.16	.14	−.24	.31
Job satisfaction	.26***	.51***	.31*	.01	−.12	−.46**	.22

NOTE.—SES = socioeconomic status.
* $p < .05$.
** $p < .01$.
*** $p < .001$.

28,488) = 6.34, $p < .001$). The univariate tests for the significance of each dependent variable on the predictors were all highly significant ($p < .001$). This indicates that the predictor variables explained a significant amount of the variability in each of the three indices of subjective mental health.

The data in table 95–3 indicate that biculturalism explained a highly significant ($p < .001$) portion of the variability of each index of subjective mental health, even after variability due to the other predictors was partialed out. Another finding indicated in table 95–3 is the significant ($p < .01$) relationship between socioeconomic status and job satisfaction. When all other predictors were controlled for, there was a tendency for respondents with higher socioeconomic status to report greater job satisfaction. Age was also related significantly ($\rho < .05$) to job satisfaction. There was a slight tendency for older respondents to report greater job satisfaction. Finally, marital status was found to be related significantly ($p < .05$) to psychological well-being. There was a slight tendency for married respondents to report greater psychological well-being.

DISCUSSION

This study sought to determine whether subjective mental health is related to an ethnic group member's degree of biculturalism. It was expected that biculturalism would be related to overall psychological well-being. The results support this hypothesis. The more bicultural the Cuban-American subjects were, the higher their psychological well-being. These results support those of Lang et al., who found that bicultural Latinos reported greater psychological adjustment when the ABS was used to measure the affective component of their life experience.[46]

A positive relationship was anticipated between biculturalism and level of self-esteem. The results obtained support this hypothesis. The more bicultural the Cuban-American subjects, the higher their self-esteem. These results support those of Judith

Klein, who found self-esteem improved in young affiliated Jewish individuals as they integrated their Americanism with their Jewishness, about which they had previously experienced many negative feelings.[47]

A positive relationship was expected between biculturalism and degree of job satisfaction. The results support this hypothesis. The percentage of variability in job satisfaction explained by biculturalism, however, was relatively small (9%) when compared to psychological well-being (54%) and self-esteem (61%).

The discrepancy between the findings on job satisfaction and those obtained with respect to psychological well-being and self-esteem may be explained by a higher degree of job specialization. It seems quite possible that a craftsman or skilled worker could transfer his or her work from one culture to another and continue to derive satisfaction from this activity, whether or not that worker adopted a substantial portion of the new culture. In contrast, psychological well-being and self-esteem appear to be factors that are tied to a broad range of interactions the individual may have with his or her environment. As such, it is difficult to imagine that these factors could be determined without reference to the influence of the dominant culture.

A positive relationship was expected between biculturalism and level of marital adjustment. Since 42 subjects did not respond to the question on marital adjustment because they were not married or living in an intimate relationship, the marital adjustment measure was excluded from the multivariate analysis. However, the bivariate correlation between biculturalism and marital adjustment presented in table 1 indicates that, among married individuals, marital adjustment was related significantly ($p < .001$) to biculturalism.

The results of this study support the work of Szapocznick and Kurtines with Cubans in Florida and the work of Lang et al. with Latinos in California.[48] Both of these studies suggest that effective acculturation and psychological adjustment entail adaptation to the majority culture and retention of the ethnic culture. Further research is needed, however, to apply this conclusion generally to all Cuban Americans and other culturally similar and dissimilar groups regardless of geographical location and clinical status.

The results of this study can be used to empower the Cuban-American community with the knowledge that a culturally sensitive mental health service that supports the establishment and development of biculturalism is better equipped to help those with mental problems than a service that neglects the bicultural dimension. Mental health planners and administrators need to be aware not only of the differences among the ethnic composition of the community that a program is intended to serve but also of the style of cultural adaptation that the community has chosen.

These results are also particularly relevant for the mental health assessment and treatment components of social work practice. My findings suggest that an assessment of an ethnic group member is not complete without an evaluation of the client's level of biculturalism.

NOTES

1. Monica McGoldrick, John K. Pearce, and Joseph Giordano, eds., *Ethnicity and Family Therapy* (New York: Guilford, 1982), p. 43.

2. José Szapocznick and William Kurtines, "Acculturation, Biculturalism and Adjustment among Cuban Americans," in *Acculturation: Theory, Models and Some New Findings,* ed. Amado Padilla (Boulder, Colo.: Westview, 1980), pp. 139–59.

3. Yoel Camayd-Freixas and Hortensia Amaro, *The Measurement of Hispanic Bilingualism and Biculturality in the Workplace* (Boston: Massachusetts Department of Social Services, Office of Human Resources, 1984).

4. Fernando Ruiz, "Effects of the Interpretation of Acculturation and Generational Membership on the Mental Health of Hispanics" (doctoral diss., California School of Professional Psychology, 1981); John G. Lang, Ricardo F. Munoz, Guillermo Bernal, and James L. Sorensen, "Quality of Life and Psychological Well-Being in a Bicultural Latino Community," *Hispanic Journal of Behavioral Sciences* 4 (1982): 433—50; Eleanor M. Rogg and Rosemary S. Cooney, *Adaptation and Adjustment of Cubans: West New York, New Jersey* (New York: Hunter University, Hispanic Research Center, 1980), p. 59.

5. Joseph Veroff, Richard A. Kulka, and Elizabeth Douvan, *Mental Health in America* (New York: Basic, 1981); Joseph Veroff, Elizabeth Douvan, and Richard A. Kulka, *The Inner American* (New York: Basic, 1981).

6. Lang et al. (n. 4 above); Szapocznick and Kurtines (n. 2 above).

7. Rogg and Cooney (n. 4 above), p. 59; Szaposznick and Kurtines (n. 2 above).

8. Norman M. Bradburn, *The Structure of Psychological Well-Being* (Chicago: Aldine, 1969).

9. Diane de Anda, "Bicultural Socialization: Factors Affecting the Minority Experience," *Social Work* 29 (March–April 1984): 101–7.

10. Charles Zastrow and Karen K. Kirst-Ashman, *Understanding Human Behavior and the Social Environment* (Chicago: Nelson-Hall, 1987), p. 483; Edith Jacobson, *The Self and the Object World* (New York: International University Press, 1980), p. 72; Eleanor E. Maccoby, *Social Development* (New York: Harcourt Brace Jovanovich, 1980), pp. 270–75.

11. Warner Wilson, "Correlates of Avowed Happiness," *Psychological Bulletin* 67 (1967): 294–306, esp. 294.

12. Veroff, Douvan, and Kulka (n. 5 above), pp. 112–14.

13. Morris Rosenberg, *Conceiving the Self* (New York: Basic, 1979), p. 32.

14. Harriet P. McAdoo, "Racial Attitude and Self-Concept of Young Black Children over Time," in *Black Children: Social, Educational and Parental Environments,* ed. Harriet P. McAdoo and John L. McAdoo (Beverly Hills, Calif.: Sage, 1985), pp. 213–42.

15. Graham B. Spanier and Charles L. Cole, "Toward Clarification and Investigation of Marital Adjustment," *International Journal of Sociology of the Family* 6 (Spring 1976): 121–46.

16. Ed Diener, "Subjective Well-Being," *Psychological Bulletin* 95 (1984): 542–75, esp. 556.

17. Jay R. Greenberg and Stephen A. Mitchell, *Object Relations in Psychoanalytic Theory* (Cambridge, Mass.: Harvard University Press, 1983), p. 189.

18. Magaly Queralt, "Understanding Cuban Immigrants: A Cultural Perspective," *Social Work* 29 (March–April 1984): 115–21, esp. 117; Guillermo Bernal, "Cuban Families," in McGoldrick, Pearce, and Giordano (n. 1 above), 193–95.

19. Bernal (n. 18 above), p. 194.

20. Marie L. Richmond, *Immigrant Adaptation and Family Structure among Cubans in Miami, Florida* (New York: Arno, 1980).

21. Joseph H. Pleck, *The Myth of Masculinity* (Cambridge, Mass.: MIT Press, 1981).

22. Herbert G. Morton, "A Look at Factors Affecting the Quality of Working Life," *Monthly Labor Review* 2 (October 1977): 64.

23. Edward Noll, "Adjustment in Major Roles II: Work," in Bradburn (n. 8 above), pp. 202–4.

24. Diener (n. 16 above), p. 555.

25. Genevieve De Hoyos, Arturo De Hoyos, and Christian B. Anderson, "Sociocultural Dislocation: Beyond the Dual Perspective," *Social Work* 31 (January–February 1986): 61–67, esp. 63.

26. Queralt (n. 18 above), p. 118.

27. De Hoyos, De Hoyos, and Anderson (n. 25 above), p. 65.

28. Ibid., p. 64.

29. Rogg and Cooney (n. 4 above), p. 59.

30. Norman M. Bradburn and David Caplovitz, *Report on Happiness: A Pilot Study of Behavior Related to Mental Health* (Chicago: Aldine, 1965).

31. Bradburn (n. 8 above), p. 67.

32. Ibid., p. 69.

33. Morris Rosenberg, *Society and the Adolescent Self-Image* (Princeton, N.J.: Princeton University Press, 1965).

34. Earle Silbert and Jean Tippett, "Self-Esteem: Clinical Assessment and Measurement Validation," *Psychological Reports* 16 (1965): 1017–71.

35. Graham Spanier, "Measuring Dyadic Adjustment: New Scales for Assessing the Quality of Marriage and Similar Dyads," *Journal of Marriage and the Family* 38 (1976): 15–28.

36. Robert Hoppoch, *Job Satisfaction* (New York: Harper, 1935).

37. Camayd-Freixas and Amaro (n. 3 above).

38. Diener (n. 16 above), p. 556.

39. Wilson (n. 11 above).

40. Diener (n. 16 above), p. 554.

41. Ibid., p. 555.

42. Ibid.

43. Thanh Van Tran and Roosevelt Wright, Jr., "Social Support and Subjective Well-being among Vietnamese Refugees," *Social Service Review* 60 (September 1986): 449–59.

44. José Szapocznick, Mercedes A. Scopetta, and William Kurtines, "Theory and Measurement of Acculturation," *Interamerican Journal of Psychology* 12 (1978): 113–30.

45. Rogg and Cooney (n. 4 above), p. 54.
46. Lang et al. (n. 4 above).
47. Judith Klein, *Jewish Identity and Self-Esteem: Healing Wounds through Ethnotherapy* (New York: Institute on Pluralism and Group Identity, 1980).
48. Szapocznick and Kurtines (n. 2 above); Lang et al. (n. 4 above).

ETHNICITY

CHAPTER 96

COUNSELING AND PSYCHOTHERAPY WITH JAPANESE AMERICANS

Cross-Cultural Considerations

Anthony J. Marsella

Counseling and psychotherapy with Japanese Americans pose a complex challenge for Western mental health professionals because of numerous differences between Japanese and Western ethnocultural traditions and practices. These ethnocultural differences influence the entire counseling and psychotherapy experience because they implicate virtually all critical counseling dimensions, including basic values regarding the nature of the person, morality, health, communication patterns and styles, person perception, and therapeutic assumptions and processes.

Japanese Americans have long been a topic of interest to American social scientists and mental health professionals, and there is a considerable body of research and clinical literature on various aspects of Japanese-American culture and behavior. Much of this literature goes back to the period between 1940 and 1970 (*Connor, 1977a; Ogawa & Fujioka, 1975*). However, within the past two decades, the study of Japanese-American culture and behavior has greatly increased, and there is now a sizable body of knowledge that can be used to facilitate understanding. However, much of this information has appeared in a diverse array of scientific, disciplinary, and professional publications, and a summary and synthesis of the implications of this information for both clinical practice and research are lacking.

Reprinted from *American Journal of Orthopsychiatry* Vol. 63, No. 2 (April 1993), pp. 200–208. Copyright 1993 by the American Orthopsychiatric Association, Inc. Reproduced by permission.

RESEARCH AND CLINICAL LITERATURE

Much has been published in the scholarly literature over the past two decades on Japanese-American culture and behavior (*Connor, 1977b; Daniels, 1988; Daniels, Taylor, & Kitano, 1991; Fugita, Ito, Abe, & Takeuchi, 1992; Johnson & Marsella, 1978; Kitano, 1976; Kitano & Daniels, 1988; Ogawa, 1973; Sue & Wagner, 1973; Yamamoto, 1982*). Many publications specifically address counseling and psychotherapy, and mental-health service utilization issues and practices (*Atkinson, Maruyama, & Matsui, 1978; Henkin, 1986; Kalal, 1982; Kinzie & Tseng, 1978; Kitano, 1981, 1989; Leong, 1986; Sue, Fujino, Hu, Takeuchi, & Zane, 1991; Sue & Morishima, 1982; Sue & Sue, 1990; Uomoto & Gorsuch, 1984; Yamamoto, Silva, Chang, & Leong, in press*). Others address Japanese-American mental disorders and psychiatric problems in the past few decades (*Fujii, Fukushima, & Yamamoto, in press; Katz, Sanborn, Lowrey, & Ching, 1978; Kitano, 1973; Marsella, Kinzie, & Gordon, 1973; Marsella, Sanborn, Kameoka, Brennan, & Shizuru, 1975; Marsella, Shizuru, Brennan, & Kameoka, 1981; Nagata, 1990, 1991; Takemoto-Chock, 1985; Yamamoto, 1982; Yanagida & Marsella, 1978*).

The purpose of the present paper is to summarize and systematize some of the growing knowledge on counseling and psychotherapy with Japanese Americans from the perspectives of traditional values and communication sensitivities, and the clinical considerations to which they give rise.

Ethnic Identity

Ethnic identity refers to the extent to which an individual endorses and practices the ethnocultural traditions of a given group. Ethnic identity is important because it indexes the extent to which an individual client may be committed to living within a non-Western cultural tradition. For more than a half century, the topic of ethnic identity among Japanese Americans has been the subject of numerous publications (*Berrien, Arkoff, & Iwahara, 1967; Caudill, 1952; Connor, 1974a, 1974b, 1975, 1976a, 1976b, 1977a, 1977b; Matsumoto, Meredith, & Masuda, 1970; Maykovitch, 1971; Meredith, 1966*).

While some Japanese Americans are highly Westernized, others, even fourth-generation members, continue to endorse traditional Meiji-era (1868–1912) Japanese values (*Johnson, Marsella, Johnson, & Brennan, 1992*). While the philosophies and methods of Western counseling and psychotherapy may be appropriate for Westernized clients, use of the same approaches with those who are not may have pernicious and destructive consequences. The issue is not whether the client is Japanese American, but the degree to which the client embraces, practices, and endorses traditional Japanese ways of life.

Many studies of Japanese Americans have emphasized generational differences among the first (*issue*), second (*nisei*), third (*sansei*), and fourth (*yonsei*) generation members. However, ethnic identity is not a linear and sequential process, but a complex function of historical, political, social, and individual experiences in which ethnic identity may assume a variety of patterns, including biculturality, multiculturality, traditionality, marginality, full acculturation, and varying degrees of alienation. Thus, to establish a therapeutic relationship, the ethnic identification patterns and dynamics of the Japanese-American client must be determined.

The determination of ethnic identity in Japanese Americans can be accomplished through both formal assessment and informal clinical interviews. Among the methods that have been used are self-nominations, multicultural profile scales, attitude scales, and behavior checklists (*Marsella, 1990*). In any case, it is important that the counselor index ethnic identity because of its implications for the therapeutic process. The assumption that a Japanese-American client is acculturated or bicultural simply because of English-language fluency and appearance can result in problems. A thorough assessment must be made of ethnic identity to determine the appropriateness and applicability of different therapeutic styles and approaches.

TRADITIONAL JAPANESE VALUES

The roots of Japanese culture are more than two thousand years old and reflect strong religious (e.g., Buddhism, Shinto), social (Confucian), and political (Tokugawa Shogunate [1615–1868] and Meiji eras) influences. Through the years, this has resulted in a highly homogeneous culture that has a strong sense of pride and identity; for instance, *Yamatodamashi*—a belief in Japanese ascendancy. Even amidst the pressures of contemporary Westernization, Japan has continued to prize and celebrate traditional values and ways of life. Under strong pressures for social conformity and adherence to traditional values and ways of life, there continues to be relatively little deviancy from widespread normative expectations. This has also been true of Japanese Americans, who, despite their obvious allegiance to and pride in the United States of America, have continued to respect and admire their cultural heritage.

Counseling and psychotherapy with Japanese Americans requires an understanding of these fundamental values, and the following dimensions are important considerations in the therapeutic encounter with Japanese Americans who maintain traditional ethnic identification.

Hierarchical status. Traditional Japanese culture maintains a strong hierarchical status orientation that respects and defers to authority. Much of this orientation is derived from hierarchical family structures that sharply distinguish age, gender, and social status markers.

Collective identity. A group or collective identity that gives priority to maintaining a strong social nexus over pursuing individual priorities has long been part of traditional Japanese culture. This results in social interdependence rather than independence. This quality is sometimes referred to as a *sociocentric, unindividuated, collective* self-identity.

Tradition and the past. Respect and regard for tradition and the past are important aspects of Japanese culture. They provide stability across time in the face of rapid change. This, in turn, offers security and predictability to the social and cultural fabric, and is one of the major forces that maintain coherence and order under the pressures of Westernization.

Duty, obligation, and responsibility. An emphasis on duty, obligation, and family over personal comfort, priorities, and preferences is an integral part of the collective social structure and identity in Japanese culture. The willingness to sacrifice individual agendas for familial and group priorities reinforces the collective identity. This helps create a strong social-support network that, in turn, reinforces the collective orientation. From a practical point of view, collectivity is an effective resource for coping with modern day uncertainties. The Japanese word *on*, which refers to reciprocal obligation and responsibility, while short in length, is enormous in its impact on Japanese life.

Endurance. Japanese culture emphasizes tolerance for difficulty, and willingness to sacrifice and endure in the face of adversity. Much of this attitude is probably derived directly from Buddhism, but it is also related to the social values of collectivism and interdependence. It is sometimes mistaken for passivity in the West; however, it is a resource rather than a liability within the context of preserving familial and generational survival.

Quality and process. In Japanese culture, the *do*, defined as "the way," stresses process rather than the product, as is illustrated in the martial arts of *judo, kendo,* and *kyudo.* In many art forms, a person is expected to learn a skill so well that the ego will become absorbed in the actual process, thus creating a new and different experience of consciousness. This leads to a strong commitment to quality for the sake of quality. Much of the emphasis on process rather than product stems from ancient Buddhism and Taoism.

Harmony. Achievement of order through harmony rather than through power and control is a subtle but nevertheless important part of Japanese cultural tradition. Balance, rather than the pursuit of extremes, is valued in the quest for harmony, which is experienced as an integrated physical and mental state of well-being. Harmony requires synthesis across person, community, nature, and spirit. Harmony is considered to be mastery, because in the harmonious state the self is embedded in the larger nexus (the Japanese term *sunao* captures this value).

Cooperation and competition. Despite the culture's strong emphasis on cooperation, the Japanese, like people of many other cultures, value competition. They enjoy winning and being first (indeed, *Yamatodamashi* is a national value, often unspoken because of its nationalistic implications). Competition is reserved, however, for very specific occasions in which it is understood to be acceptable (e.g., sports). Even then, there is a highly ritualized code of conduct for winners to follow so as not to humiliate losers. Cooperation is the norm. Individuals are not expected to stand out but rather to show anonymity. In Japan, it is often said that "the nail that stands out gets hammered down."

Mind–body relationships. The mind–body distinction is not as sharply made or encouraged in the East Asian way of life as it is in the Western world, though it obviously exists. Part of this is a function of the inclination to accept and fuse opposites in ways that defy Western logic and linear rationality; objects are perceived as possessing opposing qualities simultaneously. Separating mind and body runs counter to culturally holistic views of the cosmos that assume continuity across all levels of life. Thus, the mental state and the somatic state are considered to be much more integrally related and continuous than is usually the case in Western culture.

COMMUNICATION IN THERAPY

Communication is the foundation of effective counseling and psychotherapy. However, communication is obviously a function of cultural variables. These variables include a broad spectrum of verbal, paraverbal, and nonverbal factors. In working with the Japanese-American client, it is essential that the counselor attend to all aspects of the communication process. Words alone are not the key.

Nonverbal Factors

Touching and proximity. Physical contact with Japanese-American clients, no matter how sincere and spontaneous, may be perceived negatively by these clients and introduce additional tensions into the relationship. Concern and affection should be expressed through more formal media, especially in the early phases of therapy. Touching and excessive proximity can cause discomfort because they raise issues about the nature of the relationship: the counselor is likely to be perceived as an authority to whom one should defer, and touching can introduce the notion of equality into the relationship, causing confusion about role expectations.

Eye contact and staring. Within traditional Japanese-American culture, eye contact and intense staring are considered rude. In counseling and therapy, it will make clients feel tense, anxious, uncomfortable, and defensive. Occasional visual contact is important to reaffirm relationship, but the intense and concentrated staring that sometimes accompanies a Western counselor's communication of concentration and interest may be misinterpreted by Japanese Americans as disdain and contempt for the client. Minimally, it reflects insensitivity, and should be limited. Among some Japanese Americans, eye contact and staring (*taijin kyofu*) may give rise to profound fear, anxiety, and discomfort.

Personal appearance. First impressions are important and may serve to reinforce stereotypes. In general, conventional and conservative dress find more favorable response by Japanese Americans, largely because expectations are associated with roles rather than with individuals. A counselor or therapist is a "doctor" and should look the part. Japanese-American clients may actually feel embarrassment for a therapist who does not look or act the part properly and may discontinue therapy because they are disappointed in the counselor, regardless of the counselor's actual skills and talents.

Acknowledgment of emotion. It is important to acknowledge and to attend to feelings and emotions in most forms of healing, but care must be taken to avoid making Japanese-American clients feel embarrassed that they are showing their feelings or emotions excessively. In addition, because of variations in expressive patterns, care must be taken to ensure that conclusions about feelings and emotions are accurate. A counselor might, for instance, mistake silence for depression or pain; a tear could mean anger rather than sadness; closed eyes might indicate deep thought, not despair. Reflexive reactions by the therapist, however well-intentioned, could involve misinterpretations; ultimately, such misinterpretations could undermine the therapeutic process because the counselor is perceived as not understanding the client's experience.

Verbal Factors

While verbalization is critical to counseling and psychotherapy, greater acceptance of the positive aspects of silence is necessary in working with Japanese Americans. Within Japanese cultural traditions, a wise person uses silence as well as speech to communicate. Nonverbal communications are as important as verbal ones. The Japanese have a complex nonverbal system that is a potent mediator of interpersonal relationships. Many Japanese sayings show distrust for verbal communication: "The mouth is the source of disaster," for instance, and "By your mouth you will perish" (*Kato, 1962*). This is because of distrust in what is being said versus what is actually intended (*Yoshikawa, 1982*). Japanese culture distinguishes between *tatemae*, the expected, formal, or ceremonial communication, and *honne*, actual communication.

It might be said that the Japanese place a premium on the intuitive understanding of what is being communicated. The emphasis is on feeling what has been communicated rather than logically processing the information. According to Yoshikawa (*1982*), Japanese children are trained from early childhood not to speak too much. He maintained that the negative attitude toward verbalization is a vestige both of the Tokugawa Shogunate period, when people were taught not to share their thoughts because of political dangers, and of the Buddhist heritage, which holds that reality is a ceaseless flow that cannot be described in words but must be experienced and felt (*p. 23*). According to Kato (*1962*), a Japanese person believes that:

> If you don't understand what I am trying to say by now, I don't think you will ever understand, even if I continue talking, and if you really can understand me, you will have understood me already; thus, it is no use talking further. (*p. 98*)

Thus, in counseling or therapy encounters, clients of Japanese ancestry may feel that the therapists should understand their communications, even if they are minimal by Western standards. In contrast, therapists may see such clients as guarded, suspicious, and resisting change. Wagatsuma (*1973*) noted that, for Japanese people, a great deal of guessing goes on in a relationship as people try to infer and understand intuitively what is actually being communicated. Thus, for the Japanese, the way in which something is said is as important as the words that are used (*Wagatsuma, 1973*).

Use of Symbolism

An effective way to open communications and enhance trust and confidence is to use the indirect but powerful method of symbolism. Metaphors, allegories, fables, and myths often have direct sensory parallels and an immediacy that cannot be found in such abstract concepts as personal growth and autonomy. This is more likely to be an issue among older or more traditional Japanese Americans, but it can be an effective method for all groups.

CLINICAL CONSIDERATIONS
Therapeutic Orientation

Counselors and therapists may have to assume a more directive but still accepting and nonjudgmental role (i.e., the role of the *sensei*) with Japanese-American clients than they would with Western ones. Depending on the degree of Westernization, communications should tend to be quietly intense, allegorical and metaphorical, practical rather than abstract, and aimed toward family harmony unless the family situation is highly pathological. Cultural brokers should be called upon, if necessary. A rigidly nondirective approach is likely to lead to discomfort and, perhaps, termination of therapy.

Therapist-Client Relationships

As previously noted, Japanese culture is very hierarchically oriented. While a Japanese-American client may be seeking freedom from blind adherence to authority (e.g., a young Japanese female seeking independence from her family), the sudden and unexpected introduction by the therapist of such freedom (e.g., informality, intimacy, and equality) can be confusing and distressing for the client.

Education of the client about counseling style, expectations, and process variables may first be necessary so that behavior is not misunderstood. In fact, the assumption of equality in the therapeutic relationship may not be the best way to communicate warmth, acceptance, and regard when working with the Japanese-American client. While there is likely to be a certain tolerance for "American" ways, the process could prove uncomfortable, and ultimately unacceptable, for more traditional Japanese Americans. Deference to authority (*joge kankei*) is an accepted practice, as is modesty (*enryo*) in the presence of superiors. The importance of maintaining proper hierarchical relationships extends to all relationship patterns, including those between parents and children (*oyakoko*), employer and employee, senior and junior (*sempai-kohai*), and even male and female.

Client Behavior

As well as traditional Japanese values, ways of life, and variations in communication processes, it is also important to understand certain types of behavior by Japanese Americans within the counseling context.

Emotional expression. Within traditional Japanese culture, emotions are usually understated or expressed indirectly. Thus, severe outbursts by Japanese-American clients are more likely to reflect a serious loss of control and personal decompensation that would be true with clients from cultural groups in which emotional expression is open and direct. In addition, emotions may be communicated obliquely through such modes as substitution. Shame, for instance, is a commonly expressed substitute for depression, anxiety, grief, and trauma. The informed therapist will delay reaching a conclusion about a problem until the underlying feeling can be understood.

Somatic symptoms and distress. As in many non-Western groups, reports of somatic and physical discomfort among Japanese Americans are frequently expressions of psychological and interpersonal disturbance. With careful and sensitive communication, the client may become able to express problems more directly. However, the somatic symptoms should be seen as an index of distress and taken seriously.

Ethnic identity and assimilation. Because of tensions between ethnic consciousness and involvement and the pressures of assimilation and acculturation, ethnic identity may find expression in many forms. Often, "split level" or situational identities are learned and assumed to increase adaptability. Biculturality is often present among the better adjusted. However, in many instances, cultural conflicts lead to marginality, cultural confusion, and, in the case of some youth, to alienation or anomie.

Ritualistic self-denigration. Self-denigration may occur ritualistically and carry no implication of depression, low self-esteem, or guilt. This is because Japanese cultural traditions de-emphasize individual assertiveness and dominance in favor of group primacy. There is a strong tradition of personal modesty, humility, and reserve. Extreme variations from these cultural norms may reflect deviancy or high assimilation.

Stereotypes. Stereotypes on the part of both clients and therapists must be worked through. Trust will not be automatic. Suspicions may take longer to resolve because of strong differences in values and lifestyles, and patience is needed. Therapists will earn trust most surely through quiet sincerity, competence, and a style of presentation that carries a feeling of confidence in their ability to heal.

Taboo and aversive topics. Certain topics will be difficult to discuss because of cultural traditions. These include anger toward parents, spouse, or children; particular types of sexual behavior and dysfunctions; and family matters such as money, mental illness, and alcoholism. Much of this difficulty is a function of family loyalty, pride, obligation, responsibility, and honor. Disclosure to strangers is not encouraged in Japanese culture, and words are not a popular medium for resolving problems.

Endurance and acceptance. The Buddhist tradition has helped socialize values of endurance and acceptance of one's problems. Destiny and *kharma* work against efforts to change one's situation. Among males and females alike there is a tradition of endurance (as, for example, in the saying "eat bitter rice"). Suffering is regarded as a part of life and a reminder of our humanity. There is an emphasis on the acceptance (*shikata ga-nai*) of certain events. It is not so much that misery can never be escaped, but, rather, that certain circumstances may have to be accepted because that is the way things are.

Indeed, in the Meiji era, the idealized woman was expected to have a slightly melancholic air about her, an air of suffering that was indifferent to change.

Metaphors and idioms of distress. Communication among Japanese Americans is often in terms of metaphors and idioms of distress that are unfamiliar to Western people. Clients may speak of hot stomachs, ancestral spirits, sad eyes, and so forth. These should not be taken as indications of delusions or hallucinations. Rather, they reflect the culture's metaphorical construction of illness and human experience. In turn, counselors or therapists will probably find that they can communicate very successfully via use of metaphors. While it may seem indirect, it is a powerful way to show that the client's experience is understood. The indirectness of the metaphor also displays delicacy in communication, in contrast to what Japanese Americans view as the disrupting effect of direct communications.

Verbal behavior. The entire spectrum of verbal behavior is subject to considerable cultural influence. Research has indicated that Japanese Americans continue to follow traditional practices with regard to verbal behavior (*Johnson & Marsella, 1978; Johnson, Marsella, & Johnson, 1974*), and this will evidence itself in the counseling and psychotherapy encounter. It is likely that counselors and psychotherapists will find propriety, verbal cautiousness, delicacy of assertion, and suppression of opinion in their clients' communications. Problems are usually understated, even if they are very serious.

CONCLUSIONS

It is essential that counselors and psychotherapists understand and respect their clients' ethnocultural traditions and heritage in all aspects of clinical practice, including those of standards of normality, diagnosis, and classification; communication styles; psychological and social assessment; and therapeutic styles and procedures. Good intentions are not sufficient in themselves when helping people to resolve problems and to grow and develop. Clients' personal histories, expectations, and aspirations are all influenced by their ethnocultural heritage. Failure to be sensitive to this heritage can result in iatrogenic consequences.

For groups such as the Japanese Americans, the dramatic differences in their ethnocultural heritage require that counselors and therapists adjust their therapeutic goals and methods in ways that may often seem strange and in conflict with their normal course. Failure to do so may result in pernicious consequences for both therapist and client. There are numerous training programs, academic courses, and publications that can assist counselors and therapists in understanding Japanese-American history, culture, and behavior. Mental health professionals whose clientele may include Japanese Americans should pursue knowledge of the Japanese-American experience as a way of enhancing the opportunity for therapeutic success.

REFERENCES

Atkinson, D., Maruyama, M., & Matsui, S. (1978). Effects of counselor race and counseling approach on Asian-Americans' perceptions of counselor credibility and utility. *Journal of Counseling Psychology, 25,* 76–83.

Berrien, F., Arkoff, A., & Iwahara, S. (1967). Generation differences in values: Americans, Japanese-Americans, and Japanese. *Journal of Social Psychology, 71,* 169–175.

Caudill, W. (1952). Japanese-American personality and acculturation. *Genetic Psychology Monographs, 45,* 3–102.

Connor, J. (1974a). Acculturation and changing need patterns in Japanese-American and Caucasian-American college students. *Journal of Social Psychology, 93,* 293–294.

Connor, J. (1974b). Value continuities and change in three generations of Japanese Americans. *Ethos, 2,* 232–264.

Connor, J. (1975). Value changes in third generation Japanese-Americans. *Journal of Personality Assessment, 39,* 597–600.

Connor, J. (1976a). *Joge Kankei:* A key concept for understanding Japanese-American achievement. *Psychiatry, 39,* 266–279.

Connor, J. (1976b). Persistence and change in Japanese-American value orientations. *Ethos, 4,* 1–44.

Connor, J. (1977a). *Japanese culture in the United States of America: An annotated bibliography.* Cross-Cultural Resource Center, California State University, Sacramento.

Connor, J. (1977b). *Tradition and change in three generations of Japanese-Americans.* Chicago: Nelson-Hall.

Daniels, R. (1988). *Asian-America: Chinese and Japanese in the United States since 1850.* Seattle: University of Washington Press.

Daniels, R., Taylor, S., & Kitano, H. (Eds.). (1991). *Japanese-Americans: From relocation to redress.* Seattle: University of Washington Press.

Fugita, S., Ito, K., Abe, J., & Takeuchi, D. (1992). Japanese-Americans. In N. Mokuau (Ed.), *Handbook of social services for Asian Americans and Pacific Islander communities* (pp. 61–77). Hartford, CT: Greenwood Press.

Fujii, J., Fukushima, S., & Yamamoto, J. (in press). Japanese Americans. In A. Gaw (Ed.), *Culture, ethnicity, and mental illness.* Washington, DC: American Psychiatric Association.

Henkin, W. (1986). Toward counseling the Japanese in America: A cross-cultural primer. *Journal of Counseling and Development, 63,* 500–603.

Johnson, F., & Marsella, A.J. (1978). Differential attitudes toward verbal behavior in students of Japanese and European ancestry. *Generic Psychology Monographs, 975,* 43–76.

Johnson, F., Marsella, A.J., & Johnson, C. (1974). Social and psychological aspects of verbal behavior in Japanese-Americans. *American Journal of Psychiatry, 131,* 580–583.

Johnson, F., Marsella, A.J., Johnson, C., & Brennan, J. (1992). *Ethnic identity in fourth generation* (Yonsei) *Japanese Americans.* Unpublished paper, Department of Psychology, University of Hawaii, Honolulu .

Kalal, B. (1982). *Changes in psychiatric admissions at Hawaii State Hospital.* Unpublished master's degree thesis, University of Hawaii, Honolulu.

Kato, H. (1962). *The world of eyes and ears.* Tokyo: Asahi Newspaper Press.

Katz, M., Sanborn, K., Lowrey, H., & Ching, J. (1978). Ethnic studies in Hawaii: On psychopathology and social deviance. In L. Wynne, R. Cromwell, & S. Mathysse (Eds.), *The nature of schizophrenia: New approaches to research and treatment* (pp. 572–585). New York: John Wiley.

Kinzie, D., & Tseng, W. (1978). Cultural aspects of psychiatric clinic utilization: A cross-cultural study in Hawaii. *International Journal of Social Psychiatry, 24,* 177–188.

Kitano, H. (1973). Japanese-American mental illness. In S. Sue & N. Wagner (Eds.), *Asian-Americans: Psychological perspectives* (pp. 54–60). Ben Lomond, CA: Science and Behavior Books.

Kitano, H. (1976). *Japanese-Americans: The evolution of a subculture.* Englewood Cliffs, NJ: Prentice-Hall.

Kitano, H. (1981). Counseling and psychotherapy with Japanese-Americans. In A.J. Marsella & P. Pedersen (Eds.), *Cross-cultural counseling and psychotherapy* (pp. 228–242). Elmsford, NY: Pergamon Press.

Kitano, H. (1989). A model for counseling Asian-Americans. In P. Pedersen, J. Draguns, W. Lonner, & J. Trimble (Eds.), *Counseling across cultures* (pp. 139–152). Honolulu: University Press of Hawaii.

Kitano, H., & Daniels, R. (1988). *Asian-Americans.* Englewood Cliffs, NJ: Prentice-Hall.

Leong, F. (1986). Counseling and psychotherapy with Asian-Americans: Review of the literature. *Journal of Counseling Psychology, 33,* 196–206.

Marsella, A.J. (1990). Ethnic identity: The "new" independent variable for cross-cultural psychology research. *Focus: American Psychological Association Division 45 Newsletter, 5,* 6–7.

Marsella, A.J., Kinzie, D., & Gordon, P. (1973). Ethnocultural variations in the expression of depression. *Journal of Cross-Cultural Psychology, 4,* 435–458.

Marsella, A. J., Sanborn, K., Kameoka, V., Brennan. J., & Shizuru, L. (1975). Cross-validation of self-report measures of depression in different ethno-cultural groups. *Journal of Clinical Psychology, 31,* 281–287.

Marsella. A.J., Shizuru, L., Brennan, J., & Kameoka, V. (1981). Personality correlates of normal depression across ethno-cultural groups: I. Body image. *Journal of Cross-Cultural Psychology, 12,* 360–371.

Matsumoto, G., Meredith. G., & Matsuda, M. (1970). Ethnic identification: Honolulu and Seattle Japanese Americans. *Journal of Cross-Cultural Psychology, 1,* 63–76.

Maykovitch, M. (1971). *Japanese-American identity dilemma.* Tokyo: Waseda University Press.

Meredith, G. (1966). Amae [dependence or interdependence] and acculturation among Japanese-American college students in Hawaii. *Journal of Social Psychology, 70,* 171–180.

Nagata, R. (1990). The Japanese American internment: Exploring the transgenerational consequences of traumatic stress. *Journal of Traumatic Stress, 3,* 47–69.

Nagata, R. (1991). The transgenerational impact of the Japanese American internment: Clinical issues in working with the children of former internees. *Psychotherapy, 28,* 121–128.

Ogawa, D. (1973). *Jan ken po.* Honolulu: Japanese Chamber of Commerce and University Press of Hawaii.

Ogawa, D., & Fujioka, J. (1975). *The Japanese in Hawaii: An annotated bibliography of Japanese-Americans.* Honolulu: Social Science Research Institute, University of Hawaii.

Sue, S., Fujino, D. Hu, L., Takeuchi, D., & Zane, N. (1991). Community mental health services for ethnic minority groups: A test of the cultural responsiveness hypothesis. *Journal of Consulting and Clinical Psychology, 59,* 533–540

Sue. S., & Morishima, J. (1982). *The mental health of Asian-Americans.* San Francisco: Jossey-Bass.

Sue, D.W., & Sue, D. (1990). *Counseling the culturally different: Theory and practice.* New York: John Wiley.

Sue, S., & Wagner, D. (1973). *Asian-Americans: Psychological perspectives.* Ben Lomond, CA: Science and Behavior Books.

Takemoto-Chock, N. (1985). *Ethnocultural variations in psychiatric symptomatology in Hawaii.* Unpublished doctoral dissertation, Department of Psychology, University of Hawaii, Honolulu.

Uomoto, J., & Gorsuch, R. (1984). Japanese American responses to psychological disorder: Referral patterns, attitudes, and subjective norms. *American Journal of Community Psychology, 12,* 537–550.

Wagatsuma, H. (1973). *Japanese and Americans: How we see each other.* Washington, DC: United States–Japan Trade Council.

Yamamoto, J. (1982). Japanese Americans. In A. Gaw (Ed.). *Cross-cultural psychiatry.* Boston: John Wright–PSG, Inc.

Yamamoto, J., Silva. J., Chang, C., & Leong, G. (in press). Cross-cultural psychotherapy. In A. Gaw (Ed.), *Culture, ethnicity, and mental illness.* Washington, DC: American Psychiatric Association Press.

Yanagida, E., & Marsella, A.J. (1978). Self-concept discrepancy and depression in Japanese-American women. *Journal of Clinical Psychology, 34,* 654–659.

Yoshikawa, M. (1982). *Japanese and American modes of communication and implications for managerial and organizational behavior.* Paper presented at the International Conference on Communication Theory: Eastern and Western Perspectives, Yokohama, Japan.

ETHNICITY

CHAPTER 97

PERSPECTIVES OF POST-WAR GERMANS ON THE NAZI PAST OF THEIR FATHERS

Judith Ann Schwartz

This exploratory study focuses on the generation of German children whose parents lived through the rise and fall of the Third Reich. The primary caretakers of this generation had been active Nazis, Nazi sympathizers, or had tried to remain politically uninvolved. The older members of this generation were born during the rise of fascism and the war that followed, while its younger members were born into a period of national defeat and chaos, resulting in widespread deprivation, fear and disillusionment. They grew up in the age of the "economic miracle" of the 1950s, a time of such frantic compulsion and enthusiasm to rebuild that it seemed to seal over the sins of the former Nazi era. Yago-Jung (1980) characterized this period as one "that transformed the wounds [of fascism] into permanent scars." Sought here is understanding of some of the legacy of that Nazi past.

The facts of Nazi genocide are well documented. Not well understood is how the Germans could allow such evil to take place. Some say that the answer lies in the nature of the German personality. Labelling the Germans as a people less moral than the rest of humanity, however, may indicate a defensive attempt to differentiate Germans from the rest of us. It is not my intent in this study to condemn the Germans. I agree with the sociologist Hughes (1964) when he states,

> We can attribute to [the Germans] some special inborn or ingrained race consciousness, combined with a penchant for sadistic cruelty and unquestioning acceptance of whatever is done by those who happen to be in authority. Pushed to its extreme, this answer simply makes us, rather than the Germans, the superior race. It is the Nazi tune, put to words of our own. . . . To say these things could

Reprinted from *Smith College Studies in Social Work,* Vol. 56, No. 3 (June 1986), pp. 184–205, by permission of the publisher.

happen in Germany simply because Germans are different—from us—buttresses their own excuses and lets us off too easily from blame for what happened there and from the question whether it could happen here (25–26).

My interest is in studying the German postwar generation to gain an understanding of how this particular group dealt with the fact of having parents who were branded societal criminals. Their parents were of the generation that bore witness and even participated in "the most colossal and dramatic piece of dirty work the world has ever known (Hughes, 1964, 23)."

How are such harsh judgments accommodated in a child's personal experience of a parent?

PRIOR WORK

While the literature dealing with the children of Holocaust survivors is extensive, little has been written about the postwar German generation. That which is available in the United States is mostly limited to contributions translated from German psychoanalytic writing. Even in Germany itself, the topic has been relatively neglected by the psychological professions. A Congress of German-Speaking Analysts held in Bamberg, West Germany in 1980 addressed the psychological sequelae of the war and Nazism on the second generation of the "perpetrators" in those countries. Entitled "The Return of War and Persecution in Psychoanalyses," this conference of the middle European psychoanalytic societies was the first since the end of World War II that dealt with this issue, and also drew more participants than any of their former conferences (Henseler & Kuchenbuch, 1982).

Prior relevant work is found in the autobiographies of German and Austrian writers since 1966 as well as psychoanalytic material. This literature reveals two major intergenerational issues that have shaped the lives of postwar children: (1) the silence between the generations in regard to Nazi history, and its relation to possible feelings of shame and guilt that reinforce the inclination to remain silent about the past; and (2) changes in the traditional German parent/child relationships as a result of the Nazi period.

Silence

"Nowhere is the silence as abysmal as in German families," writes Wolf (1976/1980, 206) in her autobiography, referring to the lack of discussion between the parents' generation and their postwar children about the Nazi past. All who wrote on postwar Germany agree on this point. There are, however, a number of different interpretations of this phenomenon.

Many authors (Bergmann & Jucovy, 1982; Miller, 1980/1983; Mitscherlich & Mitscherlich, 1967/1975) explain the silence as a form of a collective taboo. Bergmann and Jucovy compare the silence of the Germans with the silence of the concentration camp survivors. They suggest that this silence originated during the Nazi period, when it was dangerous to talk openly. They state, "The conspiracy of silence in survivors, persecutors, and their children has many determinants; but, no doubt, it also has as its source the taboo on telling and the denial instituted by the Nazis themselves and continued to this day by neo-Nazis (162)." The Mitscherlichs suggest this shared taboo serves to bind people together, while those who might disregard the mutual taboo are rejected by the majority.

The Mitscherlichs (1967/1975) then expand upon this theory by defining the silence as a defense mechanism, a manifestation of the denial of the past. Denial prevents mourning and thus wards off the mass melancholia Germans might otherwise suffer. These authors believe that a sense of guilt has been transmitted to the second generation. They maintain that the postwar generation "repudiates any imputation of responsibility for the infamous behavior of their elders (xix)," while at the same time they unconsciously identify with their parents' sense of guilt. The postwar Germans adopted the "striking emotional rigidity" (28) of their parents, which blocked any conscious sense of guilt or empathy with the victims of Nazism. The Mitscherlichs believe that by searching for the truth about the past, the younger generation will be taking "the first step toward freeing themselves from the compulsion to repeat" (Mitscherlich & Mitscherlich, 1967/1975, 110) and thus toward liberation from unfounded guilt.

Miller (1980/1983), in agreement with this theory, also maintains that the taboo of silence would be broken if the German people were to mourn instead of feeling guilt. "Mourning is the opposite of feeling guilty; it is an expression of pain that things happened as they did and that there is no way to change the past (250)." She believes it would help liberate the later generation from the taboo of silence if parents and children could share their pain about Nazi crimes without guilt for feeling that pain, without trying to repress their resentment about history.

Simenauer (1981/1982) and Stierlin (1981) both detect a sophisticated form of denial which defends against guilt, originating in the parents' generation and also operative in the second generation. Germans minimize their country's crimes by comparing them with the wartime actions of enemy forces. Stierlin gives this example:

> [The parents] referred to Germany's great and heroic war, played down the murder of the Jews, and balanced any (grudgingly admitted and understated) German misdeeds with accounts of Allied atrocities—e.g., the cruel expulsion of many Germans from the Eastern provinces, the rapes and murders committed by Russian invaders, the bombardment of Dresden, etc. (381).

Simenauer goes so far as to say that the mechanism of equating "incompatible, unrelated deeds" (170) is indicative of primary process thinking.

Some authors (Hardtmann, 1982; Leyting, 1982; Simenauer, 1978) emphasize the parents' responsibility for this silence. Simenauer, describing the psychological determinants leading to the student rebellion of the sixties, blames the guilt-ridden parents' inability to discuss their own Nazi past frankly as causing their sons and daughters to turn against them. The second generation, he writes, "experienced their parents' guarded evasiveness as a severe deprivation (Simenauer, 1978, 413)." Leyting (1982), whose analytical paper includes autobiographical comments, remembers how the questions she asked about her father's past were met with either inadequate answers or utter silence. (Only later during her adolescence did she learn from an uncle that her father, who died when she was ten, had been in the SS.) Hardtmann (1982) believes the parents' silence (which could be felt even in the occasional cold and reserved responses) lead some of the second generation to experience themselves as the persecuted and hunted; as the "Jews" of their parents' generation.

Others (Schneider, 1981/1984; Westerhagen, 1982) cite the children's role in maintaining the silence between the generations. They observe a reluctance on the part of the postwar generation to even pose questions. Westerhagen, in a psychological essay based on autobiographical material, argues that instead of initiating a dialogue with their parents, the postwar generation totally rejected them. By believing they already knew everything, they could avoid confronting their own past. She notes that she and her peers never took the opportunity to ask specific questions: "For instance, to ask about the reactions to the posters with the warning not to buy from Jews, to ask what they remembered of the Crystal Night, or to ask about what their attitude had been towards the 'Feuhrer' (327)."

The recent appearance of numerous autobiographies of German postwar generation writers (Gauch, 1982; Haertling, 1980; Handke, 1974; Kersten, 1980; Krueger, 1966/1982; Meckel, 1983; Rauter, 1979; Rehmann, 1979; Schwaiger, 1980; Vesper, 1977; Wiesner, 1979; Wolf, 1976/1980) represents an attempt to break that silence. It is noteworthy that most of these authors had to wait until their parents' death to write these works. One common denominator of these autobiographies is the rigid family atmosphere permeated by a terrible silence in which these writers were raised.

Krueger (1966/1982), who was 14 when Hitler rose to power, wrote about his teenage years under Hitler as a way to free himself from his Nazi legacy. The theme of the typical German family, in particular Krueger's parents' home, becomes a metaphor for Germany. He writes:

> I am the typical child of those innocuous Germans who were never Nazis, and without whom the Nazis would never have been able to do their work. That's how it is (14).

Wolf (1976/1980), born 10 years after Krueger, begins her narrative by stating that in order "not to remain speechless (3)," she must write her autobiography. Wolf chooses to write in the third person singular, naming herself "Nelly." The knowledge that, had she been a few years older, she would easily have done almost anything the Nazi authorities commanded, has led to a sense of shame about and alienation from her childhood self. "Because it is unbearable to think the tiny word 'I' in connection with the word 'Auschwitz.' 'I' in the past conditional: I would have. I might have. I could have. Done it. Obeyed orders (230)." This obedience to the authority of parents and state, according to Wolf, is based on an intergenerational reticence to recognize and deal with one's own true feelings, whether they pertain to one's inner life or the external fascist system.

> Moreover, since the unacknowledged feelings, fantasies and thoughts must remain unconscious, Nelly becomes isolated and alone (which in turn she must not acknowledge). She cannot develop distinctions between feelings, fantasies and thoughts, hence acquires no language in which to speak of them. All the way

through her account, the silence in her family is deafening (Mahlendorf, 1982, 32).

Day (1980), born in Austria in 1940, illustrates in her autobiography how her silence grew out of her having taken on her parents' guilt. Her father was an unemployed locksmith who joined the Nazi party in its inception, and was automatically incorporated into the SS after Germany annexed Austria in 1938. She regrets that even as an adult, she never asked him why he joined the Nazis nor found out about her mother's political leanings. Her struggles with the tendency to accuse her parents' generation and blame them for the evils of the past are evident in these passages:

> "It all happened" because my father joined his party and idolized him [Hitler], and because my mother did and felt whatever my father did and felt, and enormous masses of people did and felt as my parents did and felt. . . . Even if they did not "cause it all," even if they did not cause anything, directly, one prefers not to have one's parents lumped with history's worse: Nazis (Day, 1980, 7 & 9).

There is agreement among many authors that the second generation has been assigned the task of making up for their parents' (unmourned) losses and settling the accounts that their parents were unable to settle.

> The postwar generation either took care to accept the suppressions and mystifications put forward by their fathers or preferred, for the sake of their nerves or out of fears of sanctions, not to question their "enigmatic pasts" which hung over the family like the sword of Damocles. And yet, it was this "enigma" which stood like an invisible wall between the generations from the very beginning. The obscured past of the parents was shared subconsciously by the children precisely because of the fact that it could not be discussed. The silence of the parents was glaringly obvious and was partially responsible for the "glass house" atmosphere which characterized most postwar German families (Schneider, 1981/1984, 8).

The covenant of silence between the German generations can be regarded as a means for the children to preserve their "invisible loyalty" toward their parents (Boszormenyi-Nagy & Spark, 1973). A loyal member of any family group has internalized his or her family's system of fairness and obligations. Failure to comply with these expectations leads to guilt feelings, upon which the homeostasis of this loyalty system depends. The loyalty system of an entire family, "the invisible fabric of loyalty (37)," can be maintained by certain myths shared throughout the generations. Loyal adherence to family myths can balance the "intergenerational accounting of merit" and balance the scale for many transgressions on the part of past generations.

The historic anti-Semitism upheld by many generations of Germans, which "justifies" Nazi genocide, is a relevant example of such a "myth."

> Since the problems of fairness, justice, and loyalty can never be fully resolved, all of us must resort at times to defensive avoidance and denial of reciprocity. In some

families, however, these defensive mechanisms become almost exclusive ways of coping with loyalty conflicts (Boszormenyi-Nagy & Spark, 112).

Fathers

The German postwar generation has been called a "fatherless" generation (Mitscherlich, 1963). It has also been called "the generation damaged by its fathers (Schneider, 1981/1984)." In any event, changes took place in the traditional German father/child relationship as a result of World War II. The fact is that most fathers were absent for years fighting on the front, and that many of them were then held captive in prisoner-of-war camps for years after the war ended. Those who did return usually came back home feeling emotionally and physically defeated.

Even those children whose fathers survived the war tended not to learn much about their fathers' active pasts, nor what motivated them to agree with National Socialist politics. Instead, the fathers' information was mostly in the form of stories, "which emphasized their military courage or bore witness to moral courage (their treatment of a prisoner of war or of a persecuted Jew), [and] which aroused suspicion primarily because of the frequency with which they were told (Schneider, 1981/1984)."

Mitscherlich (1963) and Simenauer (1978) emphasize the conflicts of postwar individuals whose "beaten and impotent fathers" (Simenauer, 412) lack ideals their children can comfortably identify with. In this sense they are "fatherless." Simenauer believes that a crisis in the lives of the postwar German students occurred when "their defeated and completely powerless 'hero' fathers returned to the families which until then had been fatherless (412)."

The two authors came to opposing conclusions about how this lack of a paternal role model, discredited by fascism and having lost the war, comes to bear on successive generations. Mitscherlich (1963) maintains that the fathers were not able to exercise lasting influence on the second generation and were thus stripped of their traditional authoritarian power in the family. In this way, the father figure became depreciated, with the resulting negative identification then blocking the healthy development of sexual and social identity. Simenauer (1978), however, suggests that the identification with the internalized father has only been undone in those identifications located in the ego. He believes that the original ego ideal (formed in the superego) is not affected and "has never been relinquished (424)." Thus, as he states in a later paper (1981/1982), "the parents have passed on their views and attitudes to their children (173)." Especially when the father is unconsciously idealized, certain aspects of his past Nazi activities must be ignored or at least distorted. This requires the postwar generation to modify their view of Nazism itself; if their fathers believed in it, and their fathers were admirable men, Nazism could not have been so bad after all. Hence, Nazi ideology is perpetuated in the second generation.

Meckel (1983) dramatizes Mitscherlich's version of a "fatherless" individual in his autobiography, showing how he lacked a positive paternal role model and how that produced an embittered silence between father and son. He describes his own childhood disappointment when a broken man returning from a 3-year absence in the war, proved so different from his imagined hero father. He remembers at age 8 that:

The memories from my early childhood seem to have embellished him. I ran to him with this embellished image. After a few months, his radiance had evaporated. The disenchantment I felt was fundamental—at first it was devastating, and finally it turned a dull gray. The demi-god I had worshipped in my child's heart was a nervous man, a parent who was lacking in authority. . . . As a child, I no longer went to him. No requests and no questions (Meckel, 1983, 74–75).

Gauch's (1983) father, accused by the chief prosecutor at the Eichmann trials of being one of the originators of the plan to annihilate the Jewish race, was personal physician and cultural/political assistant to Heinrich Himmler. In order to deal with a potentially devastating sense of guilt, Gauch finds consolation in discovering and writing in his autobiography about an insecure, cowardly man beneath his father's Nazi facade. He is thus able to feel sympathy for his father, evident in his description of the "pure fear" his father had felt in the trenches during both world wars. He remembers often waking his father from his sleep because the latter had been crying and moaning for help. In Schneider's (1981/1984) opinion, Gauch identified with his father's "latent feelings of guilt (42)." Schneider bases this opinion on the remarkable absence in Gauch's autobiography of "any outbursts of anger or rage against his father as a stubborn, nearly incorrigible representative of an inhuman ideology (42)."

Eckstaedt (1982a) and Rosenkoetter (1981/1982) base their observations of psychic traumatization in postwar German individuals on developmental theories about how ideals are formed in successive generations; how history and individual pathology are interwoven. They agree with Peter Blos (1962), that a child needs to be able to identify with intact parental ego ideals in order to resolve infantile dependencies. Eckstaedt and Rosenkoetter present case summaries of patients born in 1939 who do identify with their fathers, but in a pathological way, by identifying with the tough and murderous elements in their fathers. This identification with the aggressor causes a traumatic intrapsychic conflict: one becomes fearful of being murdered or of committing murder himself. These patients have not been able to develop adequate control against their own aggressive impulses.

Eckstaedt (1982b) and Leyting (1982) both detect a kind of survivor guilt among the mothers and the children feeling they had not suffered as much as other victims of war and persecution; i.e., the men who had to fight and those who perished in concentration camps. Leyting recalls her terrible feeling of shame in latency years, needing to justify the fact that her father was still alive, while most of her schoolmates' fathers had been killed, were missing, or prisoners.

The literature illustrates how the traditional role of the father as an authoritarian figure and creator of conscience has deteriorated as a result of the Nazi past. The postwar generation has been called "fatherless," referring to the Nazi period having seriously interfered with postwar children's ability positively to identify with their fathers and consciously view them as admirable figures, worthy of emulation. This characterization reflects significant depreciation of the father, who is now stripped both of his authority and respect. Conversely, in some cases a defensive idealization of the father has been cited. In these instances attitudes stemming from the National Socialistic period have been transmitted to and adopted by the postwar child, who must then deny or idealize certain aspects of the father's past.

METHODOLOGY

There has been little research done on the unique psychological situation of the German postwar generation and how they have dealt with having parents who are stigmatized by most of the world. This exploratory study was undertaken to learn more about the German postwar generation, in particular those not residing in their native country. The issue of shame and guilt about one's parents having been more or less involved in Nazi activities was given particular attention in an attempt to determine how it affected an individual's relationships with family members and—by extension, to the nation and culture at large.

The convenience sample was drawn from the Boston area of German adults born between 1935 and 1945. The age interval was chosen to insure that the respondents' parents had been adults during the development of National Socialism in Germany and therefore old enough to bear responsibility for their political decisions.

The obtained sample consisted of 13 non-Jewish Germans; 8 females and 5 males. It was drawn from several networks. One respondent was a direct acquaintance and some were friends of friends. Several respondents were drawn from Harvard University's Center for European Studies and the Goethe Institute of Boston. One individual was contacted at the suggestion of a letter from the author of a *New York Times* book review in response to my inquiry. Of the 17 people who were approached as candidates for an interview only four refused, indicating that the topic of conversation was too sensitive or that they were concerned about confidentiality.

The respondents ranged from 40 to 50 years old. The 13 respondents had been living in the United States anywhere from 1 week to 29 years, with an average residence here of 14 years. Only two of the respondents' fathers were still alive, whereas nine of the respondents' mothers were still living. All but one had at least one sibling. Ten respondents were married, two were divorced, and one, widowed. Seven had chosen spouses of German (or Austrian) nationality, two were married to Americans, and two were married to people of other nationalities. Eight respondents had at least one child of their own.

The sample was obtained from an affluent population. In terms of careers, half of the respondents were academicians. In addition, there was a full-time student, a scientist, two journalists, two housewives, and one German official living temporarily in the United States.

As for the background of the respondents' families of origin, represented were six (out of a total of 10) West German states ["Laender"], with one respondent from West Berlin, and others from areas now belonging to East Germany, Czechoslovakia, and Poland. Most of them were from middle-class homes; only four had fathers who had not been professionals. Five of the respondents came from Catholic families, the others were from Protestant homes.

The fathers of eight of the respondents had belonged to the National Socialist party (one of whom had also been in the SS) and two mothers had been party members.

This was a study designed to look at the emotional experiences of having grown up in Germany during and after World War II to assess the feelings these (now adult) children have about their past family life and their parents' participation in Nazism. A semi-structured interview was selected to elicit affective data, and give the interviewees the opportunity to recollect their past. The use of face-to-face interviews made it possible to probe the sentiments that might underlie an expressed opinion.

In most cases an informal discussion of the topic was conducted by phone before a date for an interview was set. In five cases, an informal meeting was held prior to an interview. The interviews all lasted from one to two hours. They were held in locations familiar to the interviewees, in their homes or offices. All were taped except those of two respondents, both males, who did not feel comfortable with having the interviews taped. In these cases I took written notes instead.

It was my belief that the use of a foreign language might offer the respondents an opportunity to defend against certain aspects of their past life in Germany. Greenson (1978) notes that the use of the mother tongue can help break through defenses isolating a newer, more conscious self from an older one. Therefore, I asked each respondent at the onset of the interview whether they would prefer to conduct the interview in their native language. Although I encouraged speaking German, only five of the respondents agreed. I then translated (if necessary) and transcribed all the tapes.

FINDINGS
Silence

All respondents reported that silence about Nazism had prevailed in their families of origin. Thus, none of the 13 actually learned about the Holocaust from their parents. And all but two reported that they were taught virtually nothing about Nazism in school after the war. Thus knowledge about the social and political positions of their parents was strikingly limited and fragmented.

Some respondents indicated that their parents forthrightly ruled out any discussion of the Nazi era. Hildegard, for example, respected her parents' right to remain silent and complied by refraining from any dialogue about her father's strong support of Nazism. When I asked if the topic of Nazism was ever discussed in the family, she said she "sometimes" probed the question with her father during adolescence. However, when pressed during the interview to describe the dialogue they did have, Hildegard became vague and could not remember any actual discussions. Her father's anti-Semitism and "narrow-mindedness" seem to have blocked meaningful discussions.

> I think it was talked about. But—I think it was only really talked about if I asked, I think. And I did ask a few times. I guess I didn't pursue it, because even after the war my father was terribly anti-Semitic and I couldn't reach him there.

In Irmgard's family the topic of Nazism and the Holocaust was never discussed. Neither of her parents talked about the past, nor did she ever ask them any questions. Irmgard rationalized this lack of dialogue by saying that since "the chapter about the Second World War was completely left out of [their] history lessons at school" the subject was simply not on her mind. Indeed, she stated that the whole topic "did not exist" for her until she was 19 when she met Jews for the first time as an au pair girl in France.

Other respondents had apparently been willing collaborators in the "conspiracy of silence." Adelheid, as a child and in her adult life, preferred not to raise any "unpleasant issues" with her parents. She always denied aspects of her family's past that were tainted with Nazi politics. She indicated that she had to protect herself, saying these issues were "too painful" to deal with. Her empathy with their suffering during the war and postwar periods dominated her feelings regarding their former political persuasions.

She recounted the time her mother took the children to stay in a farmhouse in the woods to escape the heavy bombing in the city. The farmer who lived there told them never to go across the river: "We don't know what's there, but that is government stuff. We are not allowed there. That is off limits." Adelheid remembered playing in a sandbox one day and observing the following scene:

> I remember one day, that a train stopped there, and there was a lot of yelling. There were soldiers. And I remember seeing these people. I don't remember faces. I remember just a moving mass of people. . . . And then these people moved up in sort of formation up the hill, into the direction of that government place. My mother came out. She tore me away from there. Lifted me up and ran with me into the house.

That trainload of people had arrived at Buchenwald concentration camp. When I asked if she ever talked with her parents about their family's direct exposure to an extermination camp, Adelheid revealed her own reluctance to deal with the question. There was a defensive tone in her response as she quickly changed the subject, reminding me that her family had suffered enough pain to deserve their silence:

> I don't know. Not really. Not really. Because—not because it is a closed subject— they would talk to me about it. I might do it sometime. . . . We talk about good things. That thing, that, and the war is for my parents and for me difficult, because it was one of the toughest periods in their lives. . . . It's not that I challenge them, or accuse them of not—when they talk about how they tried to make our lives liveable, possible. They had no water. We were totally bombed out.

Helmut and Gisela (whose father was in the SS) did not consider it useful to ask their parents to clarify the horrors of the Nazi period. Their comments reflect defenses of rationalization and dissociation. Helmut felt that there was "no time" to talk, since the needs of the present were so dominant during the postwar period. Gisela argued that, "These things were not touched with a 10-foot pole!" Both respondents mentioned similar reactions upon first reading about Nazi crimes in books after the war; they did not associate this information with their own parents. Helmut said learning about the concentration camps was "like a horror story, but it had no relationship with [his] own self." Gisela said, "I don't remember being horrified. Somehow I could not see my parents participating in that, you know, concentration camps and so on."

Those who eventually confronted their parents on the Nazi issue did so only after they had received a certain external impetus to act. Except for Conrad, none of these respondents attempted to hold a dialogue with their parents until they either began studying at a university or emigrated to the United States.

Conrad violated the code of silence in his family, but in the interview devalued his reason for doing so. He mentioned confronting his parents about Nazism, but said his adolescent phase of questioning what his Nazi father did in a wartime job in the Secret Service was "only a peg to hang on." Conrad felt it was merely an excuse to enter into a power struggle with his father that had little to do with the actual subject matter.

When she was young Elsbeth accepted her parents' silence:

> My father goes for a walk with us one Sunday, and I see a man—I can still picture him today before my eyes—and he has on a brown coat and a star. And I ask my father what he has on his coat. And my father: Be still, I'll tell you later. And then I ask him again and he says: No, I don't want to tell you.

Later in her life, however, breaking her parents' silence became a lasting challenge for Elsbeth. When she was a teenager Elsbeth joined the pacifist movement. Her own political involvement prompted "intense disputes" with her parents. "And we argued vehemently," she recalled, "which was focused around the fact that I was against rearmament, and found it horrendous that there were German soldiers again." Elsbeth explained that the subject of the Jewish extermination was still then of secondary importance to her pacifism. It was when she was 19 and began university that her "eyes were finally opened" to the facts of the Nazi atrocities. She remembered that transition: "I felt that pacifism was no longer the thing I should fight for. I was thrown back into a previous world that I had experienced unconsciously and was not being consciously faced with." But the topic of the Holocaust remained one she could not discuss with her parents "for a long time." The fact that Elsbeth's father "felt the common German anti-Semitism felt by most Germans" made conversation with him almost impossible.

Inge said her parents "refused to talk about it." She cited her mother's defensive reaction to her specific questions:

> Whenever I asked my mother the typical questions that young Germans would ask at that time—How could that happen? How was it possible?—my mother felt attacked and answered "Listen, if you had lived at that time, you would have done the same."

As an adult, Inge rejected her parents totally, breaking off her relationship with them.

Silence appears to be a price for family membership. In all but one case (Elsbeth), this silence has continued into the present. In their interviews for this thesis, certain terms were avoided. The word "Auschwitz" has become a generic term for "concentration camp" in the German language. Yet, only three respondents (all of whom admitted to feeling shame or guilt about their Nazi past) used the word "Auschwitz." Most of the respondents did not feel comfortable using the word "Jew," saying "a Jewish person" instead. Furthermore, despite their own childhood experience, of seven respondents with children of at least adolescent age only three had held meaningful dialogue with them. One respondent used the transcript of this theses interview to relate experiences of her childhood in Nazi Germany to her daughter.

Shame and Guilt

Of the 13 respondents interviewed, six admitted to feelings of shame or guilt while the remaining seven claimed not to have such feelings. While four of the respondents said they did not deserve to bear responsibility for the German atrocities, they felt guilty nevertheless. Their statements all seemed to contain some hidden anger at having been born the children of German war-generation parents.

Monika said, "I believe my generation is the one that carries the most guilt about this whole terrible episode of history. But I don't really understand why. Because I wasn't part of the decision making." She went on to remark that, "I was as much a victim as probably even the Jews, if you want to look at it that way." This corresponded to Hardtmann's (1982) theory that some second generation Germans experience themselves as the persecuted and hunted of their parents' generation.

Inge, one of the two youngest interviewees, said her guilt was induced by her fellow postwar Germans who are not able to face their Nazi past and work out their guilt. She complained about their lack of remorse: "With one exception I do not know of any German who ever said, 'Well, we are guilty and I am sorry for what has happened.'"

Three respondents denied absolutely any feelings of shame or guilt. Two of these individuals, both men, did not want the interviews taped and also committed very little time to the interviews. Both these men, Conrad and Helmut, seemed proud of certain aspects of Nazism. Conrad considered his father's secret service career in occupied Paris an "exciting adventure."

Helmut was proud of his two-year experience in the Hitler Youth group, in which he rose to the first level of leadership. He spoke in detail of the special whistle, leather strap, and knife he had carried while an active "Vorpimpf" [junior member of the Hitler Youth]. Helmut equated the Jewish tragedy with alleged German misfortune: "Besides, the Jews just had bad luck, just like the six million, I mean, two million Germans in Poland who disappeared." This is the sophisticated form of denial noted by Simenauer (1981/1982) and Stierlin (1981).

Gisela demonstrated no difficulty dealing with her father's allegiance for the Nazis; she excused his membership in the SS. First she said his SS membership was a technicality beyond his control and "had nothing to do with the concentration camps." In the next sentence she added that he had really wanted to become part of the Waffen-SS [Hitler's elite combat troops] but that his poor eyesight disqualified him.

> No, I don't [feel guilt]. I don't. Maybe if my father had been a camp commandant, maybe I would feel differently. I don't know. If I knew that he was in any way connected with something like that.

Two others who said they felt no shame or guilt, Reiner and Hildegard, both remarked that their lack of guilt was untypical for their generation. Both seemed to need to justify this alleged unusual lack of guilt by listing several reasons. Reiner explained how his freedom from guilt enabled him to feel positively toward his fellow Germans. Hildegard emphasized her "refusal" to acknowledge shame or guilt, using the seemingly logical rationalization that she herself was too young to have committed any Nazi crimes:

You know how a lot of Germans do feel guilty—certainly a lot of my generation. . . . But I refuse to feel guilty. I just refuse to. There's no point in walking
around the rest of your life with this guilt. I was a very little child. If I had not just
by chance been born in Germany but somewhere else, I wouldn't have to have this
guilt anyway. I mean I didn't do anything myself; I was born to these people.

Adelheid and Annette, two other women, became vague and were unable to answer
the question of whether they felt shame or guilt. I would interpret their inability to respond as an indication of some inner conflict and defensiveness about these feelings.
Annette answered:

I think the question of guilt is not the decisive one. It's hard to say if one feels
guilty or not. It's a question of personal attitude. [And what is your personal attitude?] I think it is a part of our history. . . . It has somehow affected our lives. It
has made us more alert politically, more sensitive to various political opinions.
There is a responsibility not just to talk about things endlessly, but to think about
them. And to prevent something—like that from happening again.

*Fathers**

The fathers of all 13 respondents survived the war. The fathers of 10 respondents were
combatants and eight were also held prisoners. They were absent from their families for
periods ranging from nine months to eight years. Ernst's father was a clergyman at several nearby churches, and Irmgard and Adelheid's fathers worked in local utilities companies. Annette and Irmgard's fathers died soon after the war of causes unrelated to
their army service when they were less than six years old. The impressions that these
two women had of their fathers were quite sketchy and were therefore not included in
this analysis.

Only one subject (Inge) rejected her parents, in particular expressing a good deal of
anger about "this authoritarian machine" that was her father. Her parents had not supported Hitler.

Two respondents seemed to minimize the importance of their fathers in their lives.
These two respondents also claimed to feel no shame or guilt about the past. It is
possible that a general lack of emotions is connected to their having internalized their
fathers' ideals of manliness which may condemn expression of certain emotions— particularly to a stranger such as I was—as a weakness. These respondents may not have
been able to express their possibly disappointed feelings about their fathers or shame
about their fathers' past. These respondents fit the description of the "fatherless" generation cited in previous literature. The majority of subjects showed respect or great admiration for their fathers.

The attitudes shown by five respondents toward their fathers were basically respectful, but critical of their political pasts. In general, these respondents tended to feel some
ambivalence about their relationships with their fathers.

---

* Omitted due to space limitations is material about the mothers of the respondents.

Gisela indicated that she never really got to know her father. She did not know her father had been a member of the SS as well as a Nazi party member until recently. In the interview, she got out an old photograph she had discovered not long before.

> I had always seen my mother's wedding picture, but there existed no wedding picture of my parents, because my father was in uniform on it. The scissors went to work, and you just don't have an existing picture of anybody in uniform. The youngest sister of a grandmother of mine lived out in California, and she died several years ago. When she died, they had a whole box of pictures. And they sent them to me; their kids didn't need them, they were the part of the family that wasn't German. In that bunch of pictures was a wedding picture of my parents! They had no reason to cut it up over here. And that was the only one existing. The interesting part is that he is in SS uniform.

Nonetheless, Gisela did not criticize her father for his political activities. On the contrary, she was sorry she never "had the opportunity" to find out more about it. In reference to her father's support of Nazism, Gisela said, "Unfortunately, I never had a chance to double check with my father about all this." Gisela was 24 when her father died. Like so many authors who had to wait until their parents' death to write their autobiographies, Gisela waited until her father's death to become curious about his past.

Three respondents greatly admired their fathers and claimed to have been closer to them than to any other family members. Adelheid stood out in this group of respondents who admired their fathers. Her praise for her father was abundant: "brilliant"; "[possessing] a lot of self-discipline"; "highly ethical"; and "very moral." There is some sense that as her father was not a member of the National Socialist party, she could "afford" to hold these views. The other highly admired fathers were Nazi supporters.

Hildegard's high regard for her father was maintained beyond early childhood by remaining completely unaware of his past political ties. It was not until 1978, when Hildegard's mother died, that she learned from a friend of her mother's at the funeral that her father had "actually worn a uniform and was actually a real member of the Nazi party." Hildegard said:

> My father was a Nazi. At least in attitude. And of course, to this day—and it's too bad [he] died—I don't really know how much of a Nazi he was.

One way in which several respondents were able as adults to retain positive images of their Nazi-era fathers in spite of their current antifascist perspectives was by separating Hitler's dogma from their wish to protect German culture. In a manner reminiscent of the defense mechanism of splitting, Ernst, Gisela, Hildegard, and Uwe held the opinion that Nazism and patriotism were two different phenomena. Ernst explained:

> During the war, there was this war effort, and you felt as if the whole world had risen up against Germany and you had to fight. . . . [Our family] did not admire party members. But that had to be separated from the war effort. From the basic idea that we felt we were in a just war. Not towards the end, but at the beginning. . . . The emotional effort until the bitter end to hold out, to endure. And

then to be told that this is all for a corrupt government that killed millions of Jews.

Gisela also pointed out the distinction between Nazism and nationalism when talking about her father's SS involvement. She claimed that, contrary to the racist beliefs one would expect to hear from a Nazi, she never heard "one word of prejudice" against anyone during her entire childhood. She maintained:

And my father had very definite opinions, he would not have hidden them. . . . I think [my parents] felt very strong nationalist. That wasn't prejudice against the Jews, or feeling superior, necessarily. But they felt very proud of their German heritage. And that was the aspect, I think, why he felt he wanted to join the Waffen-SS and be really in an elite group.

Hildegard said her parents were both involved in a German cultural group in the 30s with strong patriotic ties. She pointed out:

They would sing German folk songs, and there was a revival of German nationalism in music, in folk tradition. It was totally nonpolitical, I believe, when it started. . . . And since my father was very involved in it, I think for him the Nazi nationalism was sort of a natural extension of this, maybe. . . . And it was something he believed in, you know, we should figure out our own stuff—why should we play somebody else's music when we have this heritage?

Uwe commented that few of his fathers' comrades were really Nazis, but they were "all convinced they were defending Germany." He continued:

Because the myth is still that the German soldier fought for his country and had nothing to do with the Nazis. Because you can't wade around through that mud and blood and be able to say afterwards, "First, I lost the war and; second, I should have lost it sooner. I should not have won it at all."

Respect and admiration seemed to be the dominant feelings of the respondents toward their fathers regardless of party membership. Empathy for their fathers' difficult life circumstances was expressed by most respondents by enumerating one or more of these hardships. Some spoke of their fathers' having fought in World War I and the years of economic misery following that war. Others raised the issue of the dangers of military life their fathers had to undergo in the Second World War. Still others expressed sympathy for their fathers' physical and psychological despair after the war in the 40s.

These findings do not seem to fit the image of the "fatherless" generation as posited by the literature on this generation. Only two of 13 had fathers whose apparent brokenness rendered them emotionally distant from their sons (who then turned to their mothers for care and nurturing). Although several of the fathers of other respondents were also shattered by their war experiences, they were apparently able to develop meaningful relationships with their children.

The attitudes of these 13 respondents do correspond with those in the literature that point out the postwar generation's ability to admire their fathers in spite of their own current anti-Nazi beliefs. This ability to harbor positive views of their fathers seems to result from denial of their fathers' pasts. Rationalizations which support the view that their fathers did not *personally* engage in brutal or murderous acts against Jews or other civilian populations also helped maintain their fatherly loyalty.

CONCLUSIONS

The reports of the subjects studied here are consistent with the prior documentation of silence between the generations about the Nazi era. Neither these children nor their parents could apparently bear the pain of forthright examination of past that has been widely condemned. Both generations have collaborated in avoiding the subject. The burden of the Nazi era included shame and guilt for about half of the respondents. The burden however seemed equally pressing for those subjects who did not acknowledge shame and guilt.

The reports of these subjects differs from the prior documentation of a "fatherless" generation. Perhaps related to the use of an advantaged, non-referred sample, the fathers of all these subjects had survived the war. And, in spite of their war-related absences, most of these fathers had remained significant figures in the lives of these respondents. Almost all subjects expressed basic admiration and respect for their fathers.

The silence and the benign view of the father appeared related. To continue to love and respect their parents, to maintain their ties of loyalty to their families, these postwar respondents had apparently had to turn away from certain realities. They apparently separated out the father of personal experience from the father as agent in a real social world of time and place. And that era for both generations has had to remain outside awareness.

World War II ended more than 40 years ago. Yet the Nazi era remains part of the "unthought known." A marker for events that are placed as occurring before or after the era, it remains unmetabolized.

The warded off past is recurrently reverified by events, such as an American president's visit to the Bitburg Cemetery where former SS soldiers are buried. As our German journalist (Strothmann, 1985) put it, "The old wounds that should have healed have been reopened again." According to a poll taken in February, 1985, 54% of all West Germans were "tired of the Nazi past" and wanted to hear no more (Erlanger, 1985). The legacy era appears destined to extend its influence some further distance into the future.

REFERENCES

Bergmann, M. S. and Jucovy, M. E. (Eds.). 1982. *Generations of the holocaust.* New York: Basic Books.

Blos, P. 1962. *On adolescence: A psychoanalytic interpretation.* New York: Free Press.

Boszormenyi-Nagy, I. and Spark, G. M. 1973. *Invisible loyalties: Reciprocity in inter-generational family therapy.* Hagerstown, Maryland: Harper and Row.

Day, I. 1980. *Ghost Waltz.* New York: The Viking Press.

Eckstaed, A. 1982a. A victim of the other side. In M. S. Bergmann and M. E. Jucovy (Eds.), *Generations of the holocaust* (pp. 197–227). New York: Basic Books.

————. 1982b. Eine klinische studie zum begriff der traumareaktion: Ein kindheits-schicksal aus der kriegszeit [A clinical study towards understanding psychic trauma: A childhood fate during the war period]. In H. Henseler and A. Kuchenbuch (Eds.), *Die wiederkehr von krieg und verfolgung in psychoanalysen: Eine Sammlung der auf der Arbeitstagung der Mitteleuropaeischen Psychoanalytischen Vereinigungen gehaltenen Referate* [The return of war and persecution in psychoanalyses: Proceedings of the Conference of the Middle European Psychoanalytic Societies] (pp. 17–25). West Berlin, Ulm, West Germany: German Psychoanalytic Society.

Erlanger, Steven. 1985, May 8. Germans still must struggle. *The Boston Globe,* 13.

Gauch, S. 1982. *Vaterspuren: Eine erzaehlung* [Traces of father: A story]. Frankfurt/Main: Suhrkamp.

Greenson, R. R. 1978. The mother tongue and the mother. In R. R. Greenson (Ed.), *Explorations in psychoanalysis* (pp. 31–43). New York: International University Press.

Haertling, P. 1980. *Nachgetragene liebe* [Begrudging love]. Darmstadt: Luchterhand.

Handke, P. 1974. *A sorrow beyond dreams: A life story.* (R. Manheim, Trans.). New York: Farrar, Straus, and Giroux. (Original work published 1972).

Hardtmann, G. 1982. The shadows of the past. In M. S. Bergmann and M. E. Jucovy (Eds.), *Generations of the holocaust* (pp. 228–246). New York: Basic Books.

Henseler, H. and Kuchenbuch, A. (Eds.). 1982. *Die wiederkehr von krieg und verfol-gung in psychoanalysen: Eine Sammlung der auf der Arbeitstagung der Mitteleu-ropaeischen Psychoanalytischen Vereinigungen gehaltenen Referate* [The return of war and persecution in psychoanalyses: Proceedings of the Conference of the Middle European Psychoanalytic Societies]. West Berlin, Ulm: German Psychoanalytic Society.

Hughes, E. C. 1964. Good people and dirty work. In H. S. Becker (Ed .), *The other side: Perspectives on deviance* (pp. 23–36). New York: Free Press.

Kersten, P. 1980. *Der alltaegliche tod meines vaters* [The everyday death of my father]. Munich: dtv.

Krueger, H. 1982. *A crack in the wall: Growing up under Hitler.* (R. Hein, Trans.). New York: Fromm International. (Original work published 1966).

Leyting, G. 1982. Kriegserleben: Erfahrungen und ueberlegungen zum betroffensein [To know war: Experiences and reflections on its effect]. In H. Henseler and A. Kuchenbuch (Eds.), *Die widerkehr von krieg und verfolgung in psychoanalysen: Eine Sammlung der auf der Arbeitstagung der Mitteleuropaeischen Psychoanalytis-chen Vereinigungen gehaltenen Referate* [The return of war and persecution in psy-choanalyses: Proceedings of the Conference of the Middle European Psychoanalytic Societies] (pp.39–52). West Berlin, Ulm, West Germany: German Psychoanalytic So-ciety.

Mahlendorf, U. R. 1982. Confronting the fascist past and coming to terms with it. *The American Journal of Social Psychiatry, 2,* 28–34.

Meckel, C. 1983. *Suchbild: Ueber meinen vater* [Wanted: My father's portrait]. Frankfurt/Main: Fischer (Original work published 1980).

Miller, A. 1983. *For your own good: Hidden cruelty in childrearing and the roots of violence.* (H. Hannum and H. Hannum, Trans.). New York: Farrar, Straus, and Giroux (Original work published 1980).

Mitscherlich, A. 1963. *Auf dem weg zur vaterlosen gesellschaft* [On the way to a fatherless society]. Munich: Piper.

Mitscherlich, A., and Mitscherlich, M. 1975. *The inability to mourn: Principles of collective behavior.* (B. R. Placzek, Trans.). New York: Grove Press (Original work published 1967).

Rauter, E. A. 1979. *Brief an meiner erzieher* [A letter to the person who brought me up]. Munich: Wiesmann.

Rehmann, R. 1979. *Der mann auf der kanzel. Fragen an einen vater* [The man in the pulpit. Questions for a father]. Munich: dtv.

Rosenkoetter, L. 1982. The formation of ideals in the succession of generations (J. Jucovy, Trans.). In M. S. Bergmann and M. E. Jucovy (Eds.) *Generations of the holocaust* (pp. 176–182). New York: Basic Books (Original work published 1981).

Schneider, M. 1984. Fathers and sons retrospectively: The damaged relationship between two generations (J. O. Daniel, Trans.). *New German Critique,* 11 (1), 3–51 (Original work published 1981).

Schwaiger, B. 1980. *Lange abwesenheit* [Prolonged absence]. Vienna: Zsolnay.

Simenauer, E. 1978. A double helix: Some determinants of the self-perpetuation of nazism. *Psychoanalytic study of the child,* 33, 411–425.

———, 1982. The return of the persecutor (J. Jucovy, Trans.). In M. S. Bergmann and M. E. Jucovy (Eds.), *Generations of the holocaust* (pp. 167–175). New York: Basic Books (Original work published 1981).

Stierlin, H. 1981. The parent's nazi past and the dialogue between the generations. *Family Process,* 20 (4), 379–390.

Strothmann, D. 1985, May 3. Gesichtsverlust mit Augenzwinkern: Die peinlichkeiten um Reagans besuch belasten Deutsche wie Amerikaner [Loss of face with a twinkle of the eye: The fuss over Reagan's visit burdens Germans and Americans alike]. *Die Zeit,* 1.

Vesper, B. 1977. *Die reise, romanessay* [The trip, a novel/essay]. Frankfurt/Main: Maerz.

Westerhagen, D. von 1982. Der januskopf Ergebnisse einer grabung [The janus head—Results of an excavation]. *Familiendynamik,* 4, 317–330.

Wiesner, H. 1979. *Der riese am tisch* [The giant at the table]. Munich: dtv.

Wolf, C. 1980. *Patterns of childhood* (U. Molinaro and H. Rappolt, Trans.). New York: Farrar, Straus, and Giroux (Original work published 1976).

Yago-Jung, Y. 1980. Growing up in Germany: After the war, after Hitler, "afterwards." *New German Critique,* 7 (2), 71–80.

ETHNICITY

CHAPTER 98

THE EMERGENT NATURE
OF ETHNICITY

Dilemmas in Assessment

Donald E. Gelfand and Donald V. Fandetti

The literature on ethnicity has been expanding in a number of important directions. Wynetta Devore and Elfrieda Schlesinger in their work and Shirley Jenkins in hers concentrate on the role of the worker in interactions with individuals from various ethnic groups as well as the development of agencies oriented to particular ethnic groups.[1] Collections have also focused on the importance of ethnic background in delivering health care as well as family therapy.[2] In all of these volumes, the traditional culture of the ethnic group is the starting point in the intervention. In the case of Asians, Caribbeans, and "white ethnics," the traditional culture is assumed to be the culture brought to the United States by the original immigrant generation.

The wider acceptance of the potential importance of ethnicity is welcomed. We believe, however, that the wide use of an approach based on traditional immigrant cultures is not always warranted and may hamper advancement of our scientific understanding of pluralism in American society, as well as the effectiveness of many interventions.

In the present article, we begin with epistemological concerns and argue that, although calling attention to ethnicity is valuable for clinical practice, the use of tradi-

Reprinted from *Social Casework,* Vol. 67, No. 9 (1986), pp. 542–550, by permission of the publisher, Families International, Inc.

[1] Wynetta Devore and Elfrieda Schlesinger, *Ethnic Sensitive Social Work Practice* (St. Louis: C. V. Mosby, 1981); and Shirley Jenkins, *The Ethnic Dilemma in Social Services* (New York: Free Press, 1981).

[2] Alan Harwood, ed., *Ethnicity and Medical Care* (Cambridge, Mass.: Harvard University Press, 1981), and Monica McGoldrick, John Pearce, and Joseph Giordano, *Ethnicity and Family Therapy* (New York: Guilford Press 1982).

tional models or paradigms of ethnic cultures is fraught with serious problems. The most fundamental problem is that ethnic culture is now being proposed as a variable that is *ipso facto* vital in an individual or family situation, rather than as a concept whose importance must be assessed along with other potentially significant factors. Even when this problem is recognized, the tendency is to slip into reification of ethnic culture, that is, to attribute an independent or real existence to a mental creation.

ANALYSES OF ETHNICITY

Contributors to recent literature have admitted that the picture of ethnic groups they present may be based on a simplification of the values, norms, and beliefs of individual groups. It is also possible, they acknowledge, that characteristics of ethnic cultures may be based on attitudes and behaviors that have changed under the influence of many variables, including modernization, urbanization, and industrialization. McGoldrick and co-workers,[3] however, do not see a danger in using stereotypes. They argue for openness to the use of extensive generalizations about cultural differences in clinical intervention.

Accepting traditional ethnic culture as a given leads to a number of possible analytical errors, including reductionism and unwarranted generalizations. Reductionism occurs when the effects of factors such as class and religion are mistakenly assumed to be the effects of ethnicity. Unwarranted generalizations take many forms, but among the more common are characterizations about ethnic groups that ignore important intra-ethnic group differences. Even a quick sampling of the recent literature on ethnicity reveals a large number of attributions that may be questionable in relation to contemporary ethnic populations in modernized, industrialized societies such as the United States. For example,

> Norwegians have always attributed great importance to the body—its health and diseases—and have neglected the psychological side of life.[4]

> . . . since everyone outside the family is mistrusted until proved otherwise, gaining acceptance as an outsider is the first hurdle in dealing with Italians.[5]

> Feeling inadequate is a core British-American symptom.[6]

Although these generalizations may be accurate in describing the immigrant, their applicability to second-, third-, or fourth-generation descendants of the original immigrant generation is questionable.

Moreover, many generalizations about ethnic groups are based on traditional ethnic cultures that were formed in agrarian societies. With industrialization, the value systems in the native country may also change dramatically. Indeed, many Japanese–Americans find modern Japan baffling and discordant with their impressions of traditional Japanese culture. A recent Japanese immigrant to the United States may therefore

---

[3] McGoldrick, Pearce, and Giordano, *Ethnicity and Family Therapy.*
[4] C. F. Midelfort and H. P. Midelfort, "Norwegian Families," in *Ethnicity and Family Therapy,* p. 445
[5] Marie Rotunno and Monica McGoldrick, "Italian Families," in *Ethnicity and Family Therapy,* p. 352.
[6] David McGill and John Pearce, "British Families," in *Ethnicity and Family Therapy,* p. 470.

have different value orientations from those of the Japanese immigrant who arrived in the United States at the end of the 1880s.

ETHNICITY AND SOCIETAL CHANGE

The economic and social changes that are occurring in European, Asian, and Latin American countries may also alter the reliance on the informal network that is often assumed to be intrinsic to many ethnic groups. This change may be most evident among immigrants from countries with extensive public social services, such as the socialist and communist countries. A recent example can be found in the attitudes of elderly Russian Jews who emigrated to the United States in the 1970s.[7] In a sample of 259 older individuals (mean age sixty-seven years) living in New York, respondents indicated a preference for using social agencies rather than informal support networks for assistance. This preference may arise from the feeling that relatives, primarily children, are unable to provide the assistance needed even if they are willing when called upon. More important, however, is that the use of social agencies appears to be a societal pattern. Soviet citizens are constantly required to deal with governmental agencies in order to meet any of a range of social and economic needs. This pattern of Soviet life has been transplanted to the United States by recent immigrants who have great difficulty understanding that voluntary agencies are not arms of the government.

Thus culture is not only emergent to conditions in the new country but may be changing over time in response to political and social changes in the country of origin. Assuming that culture brought to the United States by recent immigrants is the same as the culture brought by immigrants in the late 1800s is a dangerous mistake for clinicians in contact with ethnic families.

Whatever the culture of the ethnic group, a high degree of intermarriage may be important in altering these values. Indeed, all ethnic groups have viewed intermarriage as a major threat to their continued cultural existence. Richard Alba and Ronald Kessler have reported on the continued growth of intermarriage among all white and nonwhite ethnic groups with the basic exception of Hispanics.[8] As this trend continues, some groups, such as Jews, have begun to fear for their survival, whereas other groups fear that the rate of intermarriage will hinder their continued cultural development. Thus the idea of a "pure" ethnic family or individual becomes more tenuous for the practitioner who attempts to understand the factors that have an impact on individual and family needs and problems.

In order to emphasize the complexity of assessing ethnic culture among contemporary ethnic groups, we must first turn our attention to the social factors that affect the maintenance, or attenuation, of traditional immigrant culture in the United States. Then we must focus on the need to be cognizant of "intraethnic" as opposed to ethnic differences. Finally, rather than adopting a position advocating for or against the utilization of ethnicity as a factor in clinical practice, we attempt to provide the practitioner with some assistance in determining the basis of ethnic family interaction and participation in social institutions.

---

[7] Donald E. Gelfand, "Assistance to the New Russian Elderly," *The Gerontologist* 26 (August 1986): 444–48.
[8] Richard Alba and Ronald Kessler, "Patterns of Interethnic Marriage Among American Catholics," *Social Forces* 57 (November 1979): 1124–40.

A number of factors have been cited as having an effect on the degree of cultural allegiance and ethnic affiliation of the family. These factors include immigration experience, the language spoken at home, race and country of origin, place of residence, socioeconomic status, education, social mobility, emotional processes in the family, and political and religious ties of the ethnic group.[9] Since these factors are detailed in a number of publications, we briefly examine those that are most directly related to maintenance of the culture or change within the ethnic group.

SOCIOECONOMIC STATUS AND ETHNIC CHANGE

Individuals from a low socioeconomic status may maintain strong ethnic values after they arrive in a new country. Their limited economic resources and low educational levels may retard their social mobility by limiting the jobs they can obtain. These lower-class family members may also not feel comfortable with individuals from other ethnic groups because of their limited educational background.

Facing what may seem to be a threatening environment of other ethnic groups, the new lower-class immigrant may seek jobs that were considered "traditional" in the old country. Besides not requiring new skills, these jobs may act as a bulwark against the pressures of adjusting to the new society, even if the jobs offer only limited opportunity for social mobility.

LANGUAGE FLUENCY AND ETHNIC CHANGE

A lack of fluency in the language of the new country affects the new immigrant in much the same way as does low economic status, including an inability to obtain many jobs. Lack of language fluency also makes it difficult to obtain more advanced education to assist in overcoming limited socioeconomic resources. Individuals who speak only the language of the home country are also retarded in their ability to develop primary, personal interaction with members of other ethnic groups. Primary interaction is viewed as the most important step in acculturation, leading eventually to intermarriage among ethnic groups.[10] In a positive sense, as McGoldrick notes, "The language of the country of origin will serve to preserve its culture."[11] This function of language is clearly evident among recent Spanish-speaking and Asian immigrants to the United States. Gillian Stevens recently showed that if only one parent is foreign born, a child is significantly less likely to speak the so-called mother tongue.[12]

RELIGION AND ETHNIC CHANGES

For many ethnic groups, especially Catholics and Jews, religion may also be a bulwark against the pressures of adjusting to a new society. This may be significantly more true

[9] Donald E. Gelfand, *Aging: The Ethnic Factor* (Boston: Little-Brown, 1982); Harwood, *Ethnicity and Medical Care;* and McGoldrick, Pearce, and Giordano, *Ethnicity and Family Therapy.*

[10] Milton Gordon, *Assimilation in American Life* (New York: Oxford University Press, 1964).

[11] Monica McGoldrick, "Ethnicity and Family Therapy: An Overview," in *Ethnicity and Family Therapy.*

[12] Gillian Stevens, "Nativity, Intermarriage and Mother-Tongue Shift," *American Sociological Review* 50 (February 1985): 74–83.

in religious groups that are organized around the specific nationality of the immigrant, a unique feature of American Catholics. As in the case of language, education, and traditional jobs, affiliation and participation in a nationality-based parish has allowed immigrants from Italian, Polish, French, or other backgrounds to continue to associate with individuals from the same background and thus avoid drastic shifts in their values or life-style.

RESIDENTIAL PATTERNS AND ETHNIC CHANGE

One important element in the intergenerational transmission of ethnic values has been the socialization of children into ethnic traditions and values. This socialization process is obviously more easily undertaken when the family is living within a homogeneous ethnic community. In a homogeneous area, the values of the community correspond to those of the nuclear or extended family unit. Living within the ethnic community may thus help to reinforce the traditional cultural values and norms of behavior. At the same time, remaining within the ethnic community as a geographic unit may retard the immigrant's adjustment to a larger society with values discrepant with the ethnic culture. Residence in an ethnic community may limit interaction with members of other groups. If the extended family is also clustered within the same ethnic community, traditional family values, including traditions of dealing with problems, may also be reinforced. The family network may continue to be more important than professional practitioners as a source of assistance.

GENERATIONAL SUCCESSION AND ETHNIC CHANGE

Inability to obtain or lack of interest in more advanced education, failing to gain fluency in the language of the new country, remaining in jobs comparable to those of the old country, and living within a homogeneous ethnic community may enable a first-generation immigrant to retain his or her ethnic identity at a level comparable to that of the "old country." For their children, however, historical evidence does not indicate that this low level of "acculturation" is regarded as satisfactory. Whether as slaves, refugees from political turmoil, or as legal and illegal immigrants seeking better economic opportunities, second-generation ethnic group members usually manifest a great desire for better life conditions than was available to their parents.

This betterment means greater adjustment to the new society. As this adjustment takes place, the ethnic culture subtly and inevitably changes. William Yancey and co-workers note that the dialectical nature of contact between the traditional ethnic culture and the new society produces an ethnic culture that is "emergent" and thus a unique blending of the ethnic subgroup culture and the culture of the larger society.[13] In this emergent ethnic culture, standard descriptions that are based on traditional cultures are suspect and should be considered questions rather than givens. Second-, third-, and even fourth-generation American ethnic groups may also have achieved higher education, be in professional occupations, and live away from the homogeneous ethnic

---

[13] William Yancey, Eugene Ericksen, and Robert Juliani, "Emergent Ethnicity: A Review and Reformulation," *American Sociological Review* 41 (May 1976): 391–403.

community of their forebears. In his classic study of an Italian–American working-class community in Boston, Herbert Gans concluded twenty-five years ago that acculturation had almost completely eroded ethnic cultural patterns among the second generation.[14] Gans went so far as to predict that remaining traces of ethnic group cultural heritage would be erased in the third generation. Moreover, he saw the features of group life among Italian–Americans as associated with working-class life-styles common to many ethnic groups in American society.

The importance of ethnicity as an emotional bond and source of distinctive norms and values may thus be greatly lessened among second-, third-, or fourth-generation individuals of ethnic origins who are professionals and living in heterogeneous neighborhoods. Indeed, appeals to the ethnic background may be resented by these individuals. In a study of professional Italian men living in a heterogeneous suburb of Baltimore, a strong negative reaction was registered to any suggestion that these men might cast a vote for a candidate because he was Italian.[15] For this group, the role of the church, often stressed as a basis for interaction and community networks, may also be lessened. Data from a recent large-scale study in two major cities raises questions about the validity of traditional views of the central role of the clergy in urban ethnic neighborhoods.[16]

ILLUSTRATING ETHNIC COMPLEXITY

It is not difficult to describe how change produces complexity with respect to ethnicity. However, the relevance of change and complexity for the clinician can be best observed by examining specific examples. The following vignettes of four families who reside in a northeastern urban area illustrate intraethnic group variation and the subsequent difficulties in generalizing about ethnic group cultural traits. These vignettes depict families from similar ethnic groups with differing attitudes on attributes such as educational achievement, kin and other social relationships, residential patterns, participation in religious and community associations, and language.

Vignette 1

Mr. V is a forty-year-old Italian–American who is employed as an oil-heater repair man. He is also active in a housing rehabilitation program in the ethnic neighborhood where he resides. Despite his obvious intelligence, he left high school without graduating. His parents are second-generation Italian–Americans, and his father operated a small heating-oil delivery business in the ethnic neighborhood. Mr. V decided to leave high school in the tenth grade, feeling that he was more suited for employment in the heating-oil and furnace repair business. His parents accepted his decision to quit school and raised no concerns about his failure to graduate or pursue a college education. Indeed, his parents made it clear

---

[14] Herbert Gans, *The Urban Villagers* (New York: Free Press, 1958).

[15] Donald V. Fandetti and Donald E. Gelfand, "Care of the Aged: Attitudes of White Ethnic Families," *The Gerontologist* 16 (December 1976): 544–49.

[16] David Biegel and Donald E. Gelfand, "Clergy and the Urban Ethnic Neighborhood," University of Maryland at Baltimore, Baltimore, Maryland.

that they shared his attitudes about higher education, perceiving it as inadequate preparation for dealing with life in the "real world" of the urban ethnic neighborhood.

Despite being involved in business activities in the neighborhood, Mr. V and his parents avoid participation in community associations. They do, however, enjoy speaking Italian with friends and neighbors. The Vs are not active in the local parish and attend church only sporadically. The Vs' life is centered around the city, since all Mr. V's siblings live in the same city in which the ethnic neighborhood is located. Mr. V is very conscious of his ethnic heritage and is very comfortable when relating to fellow Italians. His discussions of political issues and especially of other ethnic groups provide ample evidence that his background as an Italian–American is very important to how he views the world.

Vignette 2

Mrs. D is in her forties and is of Irish–American heritage. She dropped out of high school before graduating, married, and is now a housewife with two children. Mrs. D's only sibling is a high school graduate and a housewife. Mrs. D's parents were born in the United States. For most of his working career, her father was employed in the costume-jewelry manufacturing industry where he worked as a solderer. He was indifferent to the value of higher education, an attitude that was shared by the entire family.

Although Mrs. D's mother attends church occasionally, other members of the family rarely attend. Mrs. D and her sister are very attached to their parents and live close by in the same neighborhood. They have daily contact with one another. The family members also confine their leisure time primarily to socializing with one another and indicate only a very limited interest in news, politics, community-association issues, civic events, or international problems.

Vignette 3

Mr. G is a thirty-five-year-old Italian–American who is employed as a chemist by a large oil corporation. Raised in an ethnic neighborhood, he remained there until graduating from an Ivy League university. Mr. G's parents are both high school graduates, and his father owned a small tobacco wholesale business that supplied markets and corner stores in and around the ethnic neighborhood. Mrs. G has three siblings all of whom attended college. After obtaining a doctoral degree in chemistry, Mr. G married and a few years later moved with his wife and child to another state.

Mr. G's father is an articulate and engaging individual in his social and business relationships. He attends church occasionally, but his wife attends more regularly. She is also considered to be a person of charm and grace. Mr. G's father and mother are the only family members still living in the ethnic neighborhood. Mr. G's siblings reside out-of-state with their families. Neither Mr. G nor his siblings are able to speak Italian.

Vignette 4

Mr. B and his wife are third-generation Irish–Americans. They are both in their mid-forties and are college graduates. Mr. B has completed graduate studies. The Bs have five children. Mr. and Mrs. B and their oldest child are devout Catholics. Their oldest child is very bright and received a merit scholarship to a major north-western university. Mr. B's parents are also college graduates.

Mr. B is very attractive and outgoing. He has raced in a marathon. His wife is also a runner. The Bs are very active in church and participate in the social ministry sponsored by the archdiocese. They regard themselves as liberal in social and political outlook. Mr. B's parents and siblings do not live in the same state and personal contact among family members is infrequent, usually on an annual basis. The Bs live in an upper-middle-class suburban neighborhood. They do not belong to any ethnic association or mention their ethnic background and do not seem intent on passing their heritage on to their children.

Discussion

The Italian family in vignette one resembles the Irish family in vignette two. Neither family is strongly oriented toward high educational achievement. Both are enmeshed with the extended family and tend to avoid participation in community associations. These two families are similar, despite the continuing use of Italian and the sense of ethnic identification in the Italian family.

Similar observations can be made about the two families in vignettes three and four. Again, the Irish and Italian families in these vignettes are more similar to each other than they are to the families sharing their respective ethnic backgrounds. Orientation to high educational achievement is evident in both families, and both families live at a considerable distance from their extended family kin. Rather than confining themselves to members of the family circle, these two families have frequent interaction with non-family members. Social relationships are not oriented to members of the extended family. A positive attitude toward participation in community activities and the church is shared by these families, yet neither exhibits a strong sense of ethnic identity.

The four vignettes highlight the danger in making generalizations based on ethnic groups and the pitfalls involved in assuming that common cultural traits and patterns exist in families by virtue of their membership in a given ethnic group. Indeed, the four families described in these vignettes demonstrate that variation within ethnic groups is often as significant as variation among different ethnic groups. Although the vignettes focus on Euro-Americans, similar processes are at work among nonwhite groups.

ASSESSING THE ETHNIC FAMILY

As the vignettes illustrate, importance of ethnicity for an individual or family should be assessed. To assist in this endeavor, a two-step process is suggested.

Step 1

The questions listed below can be used as the first step. These questions are similar to those developed by Alan Harwood[17] but focus upon general clinical practice rather than the more limited issue of health care. The questions help determine whether cultural differences are a factor in individual and family functioning.

1. What is the generation of immigration of the client (first, second, third, fourth)?
2. Does the client and his or her family live in an ethnically homogeneous neighborhood?
3. Does the client speak only English or is the individual bilingual, and to what extent is the "old" language used (at work, at home regularly, at home occasionally)?
4. To what extent is the client active in the traditional religious group?
5. What is the socioeconomic status of the client (income, educational background, profession)?
6. Is the client self-referred?

Question six is included because self-referral rather than referral by another person tends to occur more among assimilated middle-class families than it does among individuals who are strongly adherent to the ethnic culture. Working-class ethnic families often utilize intermediaries such as older brothers and relatives when requesting services from social agencies; they may assist in overcoming feelings of strangeness and possible lack of confidence in negotiating organizations outside of the family and the ethnic neighborhood.[18]

Evaluating the responses to these questions is not merely an additive process in which a certain number of "yes" responses indicates that strong cultural differences exist. In the same manner, a lack of positive responses to all of these questions does not indicate that ethnic background is unimportant for an individual. In general, however, responses that show the client and his or her family to be third- or fourth-generation immigrants who do not use the old language extensively, who have higher socioeconomic status, and who live outside a homogeneous ethnic community should alert the practitioner to the possibility of an attenuation of cultural differences.

This attenuation may not only be evident in formal patterns of membership in ethnic organizations, but in beliefs and behaviors as well. In a study of mental-health attitudes, second-generation residents in a working-class area of Baltimore indicated a greater preference for professional rather than local helpers than was found among their first-generation counterparts.[19] In another study that compared inner-city Italian Americans with more affluent suburban Italian–Americans who were living in a heterogeneous community, the individuals in the suburbanized sample were more willing to use nursing homes for their bedridden elderly relatives.[20] A significantly smaller pro-

---

[17] Harwood, *Ethnicity and Medical Care.*

[18] Irvine Levine and Judith Herman, "The Life of White Ethics," *Dissent* (Winter 1972): 286–94.

[19] Donald V. Fandetti and Donald E. Gelfand, "Attitudes Toward Symptoms and Services in the Ethnic Family and Neighborhood," *American Journal of Orthopsychiatry* 48 (July 1978): 477–85.

[20] Donald V. Fandelti and Donald E. Gelfand, "Suburban and Urban White Ethnics: Attitudes Toward Care of the Aged," *The Gerontologist* 20 (October 1980): 588–94.

portion of the suburban Italian–Americans wanted to have ambulatory older relatives living in their home.

These differences represent important indications of movement away from very prized traditional values of assistance and care among this ethnic group. Indeed, the concept of emergent ethnicity means that a number of the traditional generalizations commonly made about ethnic groups may not be applicable to present-day individuals and families.

Step 2

The dilemmas of ethnic assessment become clear in this step. We have already argued that the immigrant paradigm among white and nonwhite groups is an increasingly inappropriate baseline for use in ethnic assessment. In addition, the clinician is confronted with the fact that little empirical information is available with respect to the emergent properties associated with many ethnic groups in our society. However, as Braulio Montalvo and Manuel Gutieriez suggest, it is important that practitioners move beyond their limitations in assessing ethnicity toward a full assessment of other social factors that form the basis for interaction within the ethnic family and for ethnic family participation in social institutions of the society.[21]

Figure 98–1 provides a family/institution interaction approach based on the six questions of the first step. The social institutions include workplace, school, social services, health and mental-health services, and the community. The social characteristics related to ethnicity have already been discussed. Generation of immigration has been omitted from Figure 98–1 because characteristics attributable to a specific generation of immigration are reflected in the other items, for example, place of residence.

Ascertaining the interaction between the individual or family and the institutions in Figure 98–1 will help the practitioner shift from a static view of ethnicity to an interactional view of social factors that affect ethnic family interaction and participation in social institutions. For example, finding that the primary language of the individual or family is not English, the practitioner would probe how the use of a foreign language affects the interaction of the individual with the social institutions listed in the figure;

Figure 98–1
Ethnic family/institution interactions

| Social characteristic | Institution | | | | |
	Work	School	Social services	Medical services	Community
Language	_____	_____	_____	_____	_____
Socioeconomic status	_____	_____	_____	_____	_____
Residence	_____	_____	_____	_____	_____
Religion	_____	_____	_____	_____	_____

[21] Braulio Montalvo and Manuel Gutieriez, "The Mask of Culture," *Networker* (July–August 1984): 42–46.

that is, does the primary use of a foreign language make the individual hesitant to join nonethnically related community organizations? This hesitation may limit his or her contacts with individuals from other ethnic groups.

Socioeconomic status can also have an impact across many of these institutions. For example, low educational levels may limit the ability of parents to assist and support their children in school. Educational background may also be a factor in the family's knowledge about a variety of social and medical services or their willingness to use these services. Low income may make it difficult for the family to pay for advanced education or for needed social and medical programs.

Residential location can have numerous implications for assessment of ethnic families. In close-knit, homogeneous neighborhoods where neighborhood attachment and local orientations are strong, support for local parochial schools may be evident, and the schools may be viewed as an extension of the family. Orientation toward the local network of individuals and institutions may predispose residents to use local physicians, priests, and other helping persons. Unfortunately, strong local attachments may also favor the development of "we–they" attitudes toward individuals residing in other neighborhoods.

Among the effects of adherence to traditional religious values may be the development of strong attitudes toward health- and human-services access and utilization.[22] Traditional religious values may thus promote an emphasis on divine intervention as a cause for recovery from illness, and individuals professing these beliefs may use formal health providers only when strongly urged by a family member.[23]

The six questions and framework exemplified in Figure 98–1 will not provide a complete picture of possible differences among ethnic families. However, using these two steps will provide the practitioner with a beginning point for more dynamic clinical assessment of family social functioning.

CONCLUSION

All too frequently, ethnicity is accepted as a given. However, clinical assessment must also consider the "emergent" nature of ethnicity and the dilemmas this emergent nature introduces. As members of ethnic groups and their descendants come into contact with new and changing social environments, change or attenuation of ethnicity inevitably occurs. In a dialectical process, ethnicity is transformed as emergent properties surface. Unfortunately, the tendency has been to underestimate the complexity of ethnicity in contemporary society and to fall back on immigrant culture for an understanding of ethnicity. In so doing, however, families are viewed in terms of cultural models that may be increasingly inaccurate with the passage of time. The need to view ethnicity as an emergent phenomenon is important for blacks, Hispanics, Asians, as well as whites.

In the current situation it is extremely difficult, perhaps impossible, to generalize accurately about ethnicity in clinical practice and to separate the effects of ethnicity from other social factors such as religion and socioeconomic status. The process of ethnic as-

---

[22] Alfred J. Kahn, *Theory and Practice of Social Planning* (New York: Russell Sage Foundation, 1969).

[23] David Biegel and Wendy Sherman, "Neighborhood Capacity Building and Ethnic Aged," in *Ethnicity and Aging: Theory, Research and Policy,* ed. Donald E. Gelfand and Alfred J. Kutzik (New York: Springer Publishing, 1979).

sessment has given rise to a problem that is exceedingly difficult to resolve; that is, as interest in ethnicity increases among professionals, the ability to document core cultural characteristics of many ethnic groups in our society has become less and less possible. The rediscovery of ethnicity in clinical practice has been accompanied by much enthusiasm and many expectations. It is possible, however, that this enthusiasm has resulted in a process of denial and lack of realism about the limits of our knowledge on this topic. Although these limitations are especially evident in regard to many ethnic groups in American society, they are especially evident with white ethnics. We must deal with these limitations and move toward a less static and less stereotypical approach to ethnic assessment.

SOCIOECONOMIC CLASS

CHAPTER 99

FAMILY TREATMENT OF POVERTY LEVEL FAMILIES

Ben A. Orcutt

Poverty is both an objective and subjective phenomenon. Objectively, there is too little income to provide adequately for basic needs. Subjectively, the inability to meet needs and expectations is shrouded with emotion and may be felt differentially, depending on life-style and exposure to affluence. The increase in modern technology, wide availability of goods, and powerful advertising serve to stimulate the desires and expectations of people; however, those who are chronically poor may be so enmeshed in a struggle for survival that hope and expectations become blunted.

Poverty is currently measured by a poverty index centered around the economy food plan developed by the United States Department of Agriculture, and reflected in changes in costs of living. The Bureau of the Census,[1] in 1975, identified as poverty level: an income of $5,038 or less for a family of four for the year 1974. Regardless of how poverty is measured, however, it has a depressing and erosive effect on individuals and families.

It is reported that 25.5 million Americans are living on submarginal incomes.[2] Of those persons sixty-five years old and over, about 4.3 million (22 percent) were below the low income level. In addition, statistics reveal that 12.6 million persons below the poverty level were living in families headed by a male and there were 5.5 million related children under eighteen years of age in these families. Further, 7.8 million persons were living below the poverty level in families with a female head, in which there were 4.8

Reprinted from *Social Casework,* Vol. 58 (1977), pp. 92–100, by permission of the publisher, Families International, Inc.

[1] U.S. Bureau of the Census, *Statistical Abstract of the United States,* 96th (Washington, D.C.: U.S. Government Printing Office, 1975), p. 399.

[2] U.S. Bureau of the Census, Characteristics of the Low Income Population, 1971, *Current Population Reports,* no. 86 (Washington, D.C.: U.S. Government Printing Office, 1972), pp. 4–30.

million related children under eighteen years of age. It is clear from these statistics, that a great number of submarginal families have a male head, which suggests relatively intact, but struggling families.

This article describes the poor family with multiple deficits in relational processes in which socioenvironmental conditions are so impoverished that interaction at the market place is limited. It is important to emphasize that all poor people do not have social, psychological, or relationship problems, but being poor greatly increases one's vulnerability. Florence Hollis warns of the fallacy of lumping together the so-called multiproblem, hard-to-reach and impoverished families.[3] Although there may be overlapping problems, many low-income families are not multiproblem or hard to reach. It seems advantageous to identify poor families who may be poorly functioning in many areas of their lives as those with multiple deficits. It is this author's intent to underscore the need for social work concern with these families, who experience multiple concomitant deficits; problems, of poor and crowded housing, health problems, relationship difficulties, family breakdowns, delinquency, addictions, and so forth. All of these problems mean pain and frustration for the individual, the family, and the larger society.

Helen Harris Perlman writes dramatically of experience with poor people in the Washington Heights and the Harlem areas of New York City, where she learned the lesson

> that a long repeated experience of being dead-poor, disadvantaged, stigmatized, closed off from the common good, a chronic experience of deficits of means, resources, opportunities or social recognition, will cut down the human spirit, constrict its capacities, dwarf or debilitate its drives. I became agonizingly aware of how details of everyday living may add up to a massive, overwhelming sense of defeat, frustration, and anger, and of how, then, to maintain social relationships and carry daily tasks, all the energies of the ego must be used chiefly to cover over, hold back, defend, protect. Yet even in this squalid jungle there were here and there those persons, young or old, whose thrust and ability and determination to beat the devil—to study, to help the kids look forward to a better day, to hold on to a job and "make it"—leaped forth as affirmations of life and hope.[4]

Perlman is cautioning that the conscious strivings and energies of the ego must be reached for in the human being. It is imperative that the family and the environmental strengths be supported for change.

In the multiple deficit families, structural organization may be characteristically loose, inefficient or conflictual, and dependency generationally perpetuated. The parent as the primary agent of socialization may have never learned cognitively or affectively what he needs to teach or to be a parent to children. Inadequate learning and self-image tend to be generationally perpetuated. Ivan Boszormenyi-Nagy and Geraldine Spark emphasize that children can be used as an arena to rebalance the parent's own unfair exploitation; underlying abusive behavior toward their children may be unresolved in-

---

[3] Florence Hollis, Casework and Social Class, in *Differential Diagnosis and Treatment in Social Work*, rev. ed., Francis J. Turner, ed. (New York: The Free Press, 1976), pp. 552–64.

[4] Helen Harris Perlman, *Perspectives in Social Casework* (Philadelphia: Temple University Press, 1971), p. xviii.

dividual and marital conflicts, which derive from negative loyalty ties to the family of origin.[5] Shirley Jenkins' research also notes the pain and despondency of the neglectful parent when his child needs to be placed.[6] Evidence is mounting that direct intervention must be multifaceted in order to serve families undergoing multiple stresses.

All foci of the social work practice system—social policy, planning, organization, and the direct services to individuals, families, and groups—must be utilized to alter poor environmental conditions and to foster the growth potential of these families. This article is focused, however, on four major propositions important to the task of mobilizing direct social services efficiently to aid this target population. First, a major effort must be made by social agency systems to reach the multiple deficit, dysfunctional family in need. Second, intervention must address the transmission of generationally perpetuated problems. Third, intervention strategies must be carried out in combinations to include four foci: the individual, the nuclear family, the family of origin, and the representatives of the interlocking community agencies. This step requires individual and conjoint sessions with a coordinated plan of action identified and participated in by the clients and the interlocking agencies with which they are linked. The final suggestion involves planned follow-up of treatment with accountability for service located with a central agency to provide an open door in the event of future insurmountable stress.

Danuta Mostwin's model of short-term multidimensional family intervention covers many of these aspects in its unique approach to dealing with the stress and magnitude of family difficulties in individual and family sessions that may include the additional participation of other agency workers.[7] This idea can be further expanded through agency commitment, organization of service patterns, a combination of individual and family group strategies, and maintenance of a followup and open-door policy.

OUTREACH TO FAMILIES

In regard to proposition one, a concerted, organized pattern of identifying and reaching vulnerable families that enables and stimulates their mutual participation in a change process will be acceptable to them and is required for any substantial change. The unit of attention must be the family as it transacts with the systems of its environmental space.

Families who are alienated from the larger community and have become locked into a lifestyle fraught with poor tolerance of frustration, weak controls of rage or sexuality, self-defeating relationships, who have parents functioning as siblings, and who are prone to acute crises in their lives, pose special problems for growing children. The White House Conference of 1970 reported that in 1968, approximately 10 percent of the fifty million school age children had moderate to severe emotional problems.[8] This statistic does not imply that all of these children came primarily from families of lower

[5] Ivan Boszormenyi-Nagy and Geraldine Spark, *Invisible Loyalties* (New York: Harper & Row, 1973), p. 300.
[6] Shirley Jenkins, *Filial Deprivation and Foster Care* (New York: Columbia University Press, 1972).
[7] Danuta Mostwin, Social Work Interventions with Families in Crisis of Change, *Social Thought,* 2:81–99, (Winter 1976) and Mostwin, Multidemensional Model of Working with the Family, SOCIAL CASEWORK, 55:209–15 (April 1974).
[8] James K. Whittaker, Causes of Childhood Disorders: New Findings, *Social Work,* 21:91–96 (March 1976).

socioeconomic status, but the magnitude of the problem deserves attention. The family must be viewed systemically, with its transaction to all linking systems assessed, for interventions to enhance the restorative exchanges with the environment for the individual and family.

Virginia Satir points out that it may well be that the family system is the primary means by which individual internal dynamics are developed. From Satir's observations of families where there are symptoms or problems, the rules of the family system do not totally fit the growth needs of its members in relation to survival, intimacy, productivity, and making sense and order, for all of the family members who are parts of the system.[9] Salvador Minuchin and Lynn Hoffman, as well as others, graphically describe the structural dysfunctioning in the family, which may or may not be multiple deficit, of cross-generational coalitions that tend to maintain, detour, or perpetuate marital conflicts, or that prevent normal growth and separation.[10] The emphasis in family intervention is on restructuring boundaries, shifting and delineating role tasks, and dealing with the dynamics of the relationship system that lock in the scapegoated or problem member. Actions are stimulated that will maximize family competence and self-confidence with the expectation that structural and relationship changes, supported by environmental changes, will indeed move the family to a new and more functional equilibrium.

Changes in family functioning are complex, especially when there is a parental life pattern of self-defeating behavior with few positive environmental resources, nurturance, and stimulation. Motivation and hope can be difficult to achieve. Intervention must be massive to unleash family adaptive forces for change. Although social work must serve families from all segments of society, the social worker must emphasize innovative direct services to help the impoverished who suffer multiple deficits, especially in their environment and in their interpersonal relationships. Advocacy and negotiation of environmental resources and services to reduce the frustration and deprivation must be as high on the helping scale as the intrafamilial, interpersonal relationship dimension. The social worker must reach out to link the family with every possible systemic input that can transmit new energy, knowledge, information, and emotional relatedness into the family system.

Attuned to the impact of environmental transactions, Ross V. Speck and Carolyn Attneave, through social network intervention, use the massive, relational environment for nurturing, growth, and healing.[11] They report network intervention in which as many as fifty friends and relatives of a patient may be assembled for intensive sessions of discussion, interaction, and psychodynamic exploration. In these sessions the difficulties experienced by the patient and his family are discussed and dramatized within the larger network, which itself goes through several distinct stages and where successful changes may occur.

[9] Virginia Satir, Symptomatology: A Family Production, in *Theory and Practice of Family Psychiatry,* ed. John G. Howells (New York: Brunner/Mazel, 1971), pp. 663–64.

[10] Salvador Minuchin, *Family and Family Therapy* (Cambridge: Harvard University Press, 1974); and Lynn Hoffman, Enmeshment and the Too Richly Cross-Joined System, *Family Process,* 14:457–68 (December 1975).

[11] Ross V. Speck and Carolyn Attneave, *Family Networks* (New York: Pantheon Press, 1973).

SECOND-GENERATION PROBLEMS

The second proposition concerns the finding that dysfunctional families tend to reflect transmission of problematic behavior and adaptive patterns originating in their families of origin. The relationships over three generations must be assessed and the intervention processes must include the three generations.

Murray Bowen asserts that a certain amount of immaturity can be absorbed by the family system and that large quantities may be bound by serious dysfunction in one family member. The family projection process focuses on a certain child or children and may leave others relatively uninvolved. Bowen notes, however, that there are other families where the quantity of immaturity is so great, that there is maximum marital conflict, severe dysfunction in one spouse, maximum involvement of children, conflict with families of origin, and still free-floating immaturity. The mechanisms that operate outside the nuclear family ego mass are important in determining the course and intensity of the process within the nuclear family. When there is a significant degree of ego fusion, there is also a borrowing and sharing of ego strength between the nuclear family and the family of origin.[12]

Boszormenyi-Nagy and Spark postulate that the major connecting tie between the generations is that of loyalty based on indebtedness and reciprocity.[13] Loyalty ties and the forms of expression may be a functional or a dysfunctional force connecting the generations. The person remains deeply committed to the repayment of benefits received; the struggle for all adults is to balance the old relationship with the new and to continuously integrate the relationships with one's early significant figures with the involvement and commitment to current family relationships.

Of the voluminous literature describing multiple deficit, loosely organized, low-income families, none is so poignant with regard to generational immaturities as the descriptions of Louise Bandler on the North Point Family Project in Boston.[14] The parents' immaturity and inability to exercise even minimal skills in maintenance of daily routines in the home, in care and discipline of children, and in interaction with the outside community were striking. It was common for one-parent mothers to parentify the older child, assume a sibling position, and reflect the deep unmet dependency needs that stemmed from their own parental deprivation. Bandler speaks of the mothers' relationship to and nurturing of their children as being so affected by their own pressing needs that they could not distinguish them from the needs of their children, even when their children's needs were urgent. When the parent's own affective development and learning has been greatly impaired by a depriving social environment and parental failure of dependable, consistent, nurturing objects, it is predictable that immaturity will abound with deep dependency needs, feelings of resentment, anger, inadequacy, and low self-esteem. The needs and loyalties in the conflictual family relationships diminish family strengths for coping and must be addressed.

---

[12] Murray Bowen, The Use of Family Theory in Clinical Practice, in *Changing Families,* ed. Jay Haley (New York: Grune & Stratton, 1971), pp. 177–78.

[13] Boszormenyi-Nagy and Spark, *Invisible Loyalties,* pp. 216–24.

[14] Louise Bandler, Family Functioning: A Psychosocial Perspective, in *The Drifters,* ed. Eleanor Pavenstedt (Boston: Little, Brown and Co., 1967), pp. 225–53.

COMBINATION OF INTERVENTION STRATEGIES

The third proposition, to repeat, states that intervention targeted to the family unit must be a combination of sessions with the individual, conjoint nuclear family and family of origin, and community agencies. These four foci must be balanced in regard to the use of a modality that can address itself to: (1) the parent's and child's individual need for nurturance and growth; (2) the family systems' communication, structural, and role deficits and the scapegoating mechanisms that have become patterned or supportive of myths and collusions within the family; (3) the inclusion of the family of origin to deal with destructive patterns or loyalties that are transmitted and to strengthen whatever positives that can be enlisted for growth; and (4) the conjoint meeting of the linking agencies and family to weave a massive, coordinated effort toward new goals and change. The coordinated agency sessions with the family are of the highest importance, for the family system then becomes more thoroughly integrated in a positive way with linking services and social resource systems. Hypothetically, if the individual and family sessions are agreed upon to be carried primarily by the social worker in the residential treatment center where the child is placed, the child welfare, probation, or related agencies involved would also plan together in family sessions a course of action that supports the major goals. When the child can be returned from residential treatment to the home, new plans for continuation and followup should emerge, depending on the case situation. In this example, the responsibility and accountability would be carried by one agency—the residential treatment center—for the major treatment role with the collaboration and additional service input of linking agencies. As growth and change occur, the collaborating agencies should continue with the family to locate the central responsibility of the helping service.

NEED FOR FOLLOWUP

High risk families require followup at intervals and a central resource for help when stresses become insurmountable. Too often their ties to the agency have not been strong enough to stimulate their reapplying for help in times of stress and they lose the gains they had made. The four steps outlined above should substantially improve the family's social functioning and their capacity to anticipate and deal with stress, reducing the self-generated crises that bring the families to agencies at the time of stress and that allow a dropping out when the crisis subsides.

It has been observed that seriously impaired families do not always use a crisis approach effectively. For example, Naomi Golan suggests that:

While they manifest the overt symptoms of urgency, disordered affect, disorganized behavior, and ineffectual coping, closer examination shows that underneath the superficial appearance, the basic character structure reveals severe and chronic ego depletion and damage. The crisis appearance involved is not a reaction to the original hazardous event, but a maladaptive attempt to ward off underlying personality disturbance or even psychosis. While such persons, often classified as borderline personalities or character disorders, may need help in emergencies, they do not seem to be able to engage in the crisis resolution work involved in learning from earlier experiences and in developing more adaptive patterns.[15]

With coordinated and massive input, learning can occur that will make possible some shifts in the social functioning of immature families.

In such families, a family service agency might well be the central agency among the collaborating agencies which maintains the open door for help and periodic followup, especially when there are growing children. Margarat B. Bailey's findings in the Alcoholism Inter-Agency Training Project conducted by the staff of the Alcoholism Programs of the Community Council of Greater New York reported that regardless of whether the alcoholic was referred to a special agency such as an alcoholism clinic, to a mental health clinic, or to another service, it was imperative for the family agency making the referral to retain the locus of treatment.[16] Otherwise, the sensitive alcoholic tended to fall through the cracks between the services. This situation is quite analogous to the multiple deficit family or a severely impaired family.

With the overburdened staff of social service agencies, including the correctional, mental health and medical facilities, is there sufficient time for the suggested followup, collaboration, and location of central responsibility? In the long run, it would be more economical for resources to be used massively and in a coordinated way during periods of stress. Depending on the needs of the family, substantial improvement in the family system equilibrium could be predicted with this kind of consistent help and strengthening of their coping powers to handle their predicament when threatened.

It has been more than twenty years since the Report of the Family Centered Project of St. Paul, Minnesota.[17] It reported that 6 percent of the city families accounted for 77 percent of its public assistance, 51 percent of its health services, and 56 percent of its adjustment services in mental health, corrections, and casework. The striking fact was that many of these families were known to a range of agencies during chronic periods of crisis, but coordination in agency services and resources was not sufficiently integrated to insure improvement in the family system's equilibrium. Today, families are still divided among agencies without sufficient attention to the transactional processes within the family, the agencies, and the social environment that could be coordinated for change.

ILLUSTRATION OF NEED FOR INTERVENTION

The following case illustration highlights the need for the strategies indicated—focus on a family unit with a growth-inducing individual relationship, conjoint sessions of the nuclear family with the family of origin, and the agency service network. Formed groups could also be used as appropriate. Exemplified in the following is the fact that coordinated efforts with clients can bring change in a family in which there is severe

---

[15] Naomi Golan, Crisis Theory, in *Social Work Treatment,* ed. Francis J. Turner (New York. The Free Press, 1974), p. 442.

[16] Margaret B. Bailey, *Alcoholism and Family Casework* (New York: New York City Affiliate, National Council on Alcoholism, 1974), p. 189.

[17] Alice Overton, Katherine H. Tinker and Associates, *Casework Notebook Family Centered Project* (St. Paul, Minn.: Greater St. Paul Community Chest and Councils, 1957).

psychological damage and where overt rage and child abuse are generationally perpetuated.

James, an eight-year-old, white, Catholic boy of lower socioeconomic advantage was referred for residential placement because his mother was considered emotionally disturbed and unable to handle him.[18] James ran away from home taking his younger brother, Jerry, aged five, with him. James frequently set fires in the home and in the community. He was also enuretic and his school attendance was poor.

Mrs. A, James's mother, was a twenty-eight-year old divorcee who received an Aid to Families with Dependent Children grant. She resided with her younger son, Jerry, in a five-room apartment in the central city. James was born out of wedlock when Mrs. A was seventeen. His father disappeared before his birth and his whereabouts were unknown. Mrs. A's mother would not permit her to keep the child so that she was forced to relinquish James to foster placement, where he spent the first twenty-one months of his life. She later married and while pregnant with her second son, Jerry, she was able to regain possession of James. She was separated from her husband soon after the birth of Jerry and eventually divorced him, because he was serving a sentence in the penitentiary. Since her divorce, she had dated several men and just prior to James's placement in residential care she was jilted in an affair of several months' duration.

James was placed in residential treatment to provide him with a consistent environment of warmth, acceptance, and discipline. Initially, he had great difficulty adjusting to the environment: disrupting his class by manipulating fights between others and running away from school, his cottage, and the treatment center. When his mother and brother visited him, he would go into wild temper tantrums when it was time for them to leave, and the early visits precipitated his running away.

Initially, it was extremely difficult to engage James in regular treatment sessions; he was hostile, resentful, and frightened. His home environment included inconsistent, abusive, and seductive mothering coupled with neglect. His punishment for misbehavior was severe and cruel. For example, following a fire-setting episode, Mrs. A would punish him—first, by holding an extinguished hot match against his hand; second, by burning him with a lighted match, and third, by holding his hands over a lighted stove. One time he was badly injured.

Mrs. A readily admitted that she had tormented James with a knife, urging him to stab himself to prove that he was a man. When he had failed to do so, she dressed him in girls' clothing to make fun of him. This act was a frequent punishment which she had used when James argued or disagreed with her. When questioned, she seemed unable to grasp the potential danger of her act, with its psychological implications.

On another occasion, it was reported that because James forgot to remind her to turn off the gas when cooking and the food burned, she knocked him uncon-

---

[18] The author is grateful to Thomas J. Ciallelo, student at Columbia University School of Social Work, New York, New York, for the case illustration.

scious. When he came to, she did allow him to lie down and rest for several hours. Mrs. A admitted to beating him severely and said that at times she thought she might kill him.

In contrast to her loss of control when enraged, Mrs. A spoke in loving terms of her children and openly demonstrated affection for James on her visits to the treatment center. She said she missed him very much, that he would often sleep with her, and that they were a great comfort to one another. She brought him gifts and books, showed pride in his reading ability, and encouraged his education. She also brought construction toys, which he liked.

The disturbed mother-child relations described here bear close relationship to the mother-grandmother relationship and to the larger family constellation in which Mrs. A was reared and continued to be actively involved. Mrs. E, Mrs. A's mother, also lived in the central city with her fourth husband and two teen-age sons. One of these sons was Mrs. A's natural brother and the one person in the family for whom she felt some closeness. He was a narcotics addict.

Mrs. E's treatment of Mrs. A as a young girl bore similarity to Mrs. A's treatment of James. For example, Mrs. E had disciplined Mrs. A for wearing a short skirt to school by forcing her to strip naked and sit on the steps in the hall outside their tenement apartment for other tenants to observe. In relating this incident, Mrs. A said, "No wonder I started to act like a whore; she made me feel like one."

Mrs. A spoke of having tried suicide several times. She had seen several psychiatrists and was once hospitalized. She had also been seen intermittently at an outpatient psychiatric clinic in the city. Its records indicated that she had been placed in a parochial children's home at age six after stabbing her father and attempting to kill her mother. She had also received psychiatric treatment at age nine, age fifteen through seventeen, and again as a young adult in the city hospital. Mrs. A related details of attacking her husband with a knife for intimating that she behaved like her mother.

Mrs. A and her family of origin have a history of impulsive violent outbursts and fights. However, their ambivalence and distorted loyalties compel them to seek out one another repeatedly. At the time of one of these violent episodes, a family life space session was held on the spot to evaluate the situation. During the session, which was full of arguing and shouting, a pattern emerged of the belittling and scapegoating of Mrs. A by her own family.

From the above material, it can be observed that three generations of disturbed family relationships are characterized by inadequate nurturance and weak control of rage. As communication with Mrs. A's own family was characterized by harsh violence, inconsistency, and ambivalence, so she related to her own children. In the early sessions she appeared to be a rebellious adolescent and at the same time was in strong competition with her mother for possession and control of her own children. Her relationships with men were marked by abandonment, disappointment, and failure. Her role as healthy mother-father for her two children has been distorted and generational boundaries crossed as she alternately seduced and aggressively rejected her son James. However, because she had been the scapegoat in her family of origin, James, who was split off from the family in infancy and represented her bad self, came to serve the same role within the nuclear family.

Over the years, attempts were made by various agencies to help Mrs. A but no consistent change was noted. She reached out by attending a few individual therapy sessions at a local mental health clinic, but then would discontinue. A homemaker was once sent by the bureau of child welfare to assist with care of the home and children, to teach her more consistent methods in child rearing, and to free her to utilize her skills as keypunch operator. She was unable to follow through. The evidence was clear that while the grandmother openly encouraged these interventions on her daughter's behalf, she also undermined their success with interference and criticism. There was no purposeful plan to work with the family of origin. In addition, Mrs. A's caseworker at the bureau of child welfare reported being so overloaded with cases that she could not adequately support and assist her in her efforts.

The worker described Mrs. A clinically as having a severe borderline disorder. Individual interventive sessions, where Jerry was generally present, attempted to strengthen her grasp of reality situations and anticipation of consequences and to increase impulse control through learning and identification in a dependable relationship and through active tasks and limits so as to experience achievement and to relieve stress. It was hoped that order and routine in the home could be accomplished. These sessions were laborious and trying in the beginning as Mrs. A lashed into tirades blaming her mother and step-father for interference in her life and in the care of her children. She condemned the bureau of child welfare worker for failing to maintain contact with her or to assist her with care of Jerry or job placement; she blamed the residential treatment center for giving her double messages and keeping James away from her. At the same time, Jerry would run wildly about the house grabbing food from the table, smashing toys, and hitting at the worker. Mrs. A would attempt to reprimand him verbally, but when this procedure failed she would hit him and threaten him with punishment "by you know what!" without clarifying what she meant. She would seem to restrain herself from harsh discipline during the interview as the worker utilized the situation to discuss dealing with Jerry and his multiple health problems. Mrs. A talked of taking him to the hospital but criticized the doctors for incompetence and lack of action. She blamed the bureau of child welfare worker for not helping her follow through with the out-patient clinic appointments for him. In due course, however, her anger and projections began to subside as she worked in individual sessions with the young male social worker. Gradually she began to accept some responsibility for her own actions.

As the work progressed and the worker checked the validity of her claims against the bureau of child welfare and the mental health clinic, he arranged with Mrs. A to have an interagency meeting for the purpose of clarifying their assistance on her behalf and for Jerry. Problem-solving also included the issue of home visits for James.

The worker helped Mrs. A to expand her understanding of James's needs as they toured together the campus of the center and visited James's teachers, child-care staff, religious instructor, and other involved personnel so that she, as a parent, could get first-hand reports on his adjustment and progress.

On one such occasion, she returned to her individual session and began to speak of her current personal problems with her family of origin. She became very emotional and tearful and began to consider why James had had to be placed; however, in the beginning she was not able to connect the consequences to her own behavior. She could only see James as the problem (running away and setting fires) and being interfered with by her mother.

Confrontation to help her begin to see her own responsibility brought further tears, evasion, and an attack on the worker and the institution for giving her a run-around and keeping her from her son. However, her worker moved to a more supportive approach; he communicated his belief that she sincerely loved James, that James had expressed love for her, but that James was very frightened of her.

She responded thoughtfully that she believed James feared her because at times, when she was in a bad mood or was extremely nervous, she had punished him too severely for not obeying her. She quickly added that she had recently changed her method of punishment from physical beatings to having him kneel on the floor with his arms outstretched, as she had been punished by a teacher in her youth. This discussion was the first time that she could consider alternate methods of punishment and consequences and could begin to use concrete suggestions. Later, she brought out that she thought James's fearfulness was also connected with his witnessing much physical violence between herself and her mother and her ex-husband.

Once Mrs. A had made the above disclosures and shared these insights, she was helped to draw further connections between her severe treatment as a child and her present handling of her own children. Family treatment sessions with Mrs. A, her children, and her family of origin were not held. However, the destructive intergenerational ties, modeling, and scapegoating can be seen. Conjoint sessions could increase their ability to detach and reduce the destructive hostile-dependent indebtedness. Any strengths and family supports could then be more easily mobilized.

Individual sessions were equally important with James. The worker tried to meet James at his emotional level by using play in the treatment sessions and to interact with him at his cottage setting. In play James was initially cautious in inviting the worker to join in his games and creative activities. He enjoyed immersing his hands in globs of brown paint and smearing them over paper. He seemed to look for disapproval. When his paintings began to take form, the worker noticed that he chose bright red, black, and gray. He was intense and aggressive in his painting. Verbalization of such feelings as anger and fear by the worker brought responses associated with blood, monsters, and fires.

Often he enjoyed punching a toy clown in a very aggressive way. He asked whether the clown inside the toy was being hurt when he hit him. He questioned whether a person would be hurt if a picture of someone he disliked were pasted on the toy clown's face and he hit it. He stated he did not really want to hurt anyone, even if he did dislike them. To alleviate this confusion between reality and fantasied thoughts, the worker began to help him separate his fantasies and feelings from actions. In the course of one session when punching the toy clown, James said that he wished that it were his mother and little brother.

This discussion occurred at the time of a heightened controversy over his home visits. He spoke of a recurrent dream which he had had at home and which had reappeared. The dream involved the stabbing and killing of his mother and brother. Observing his fear and disturbance, the worker explained that many people have similar dreams or nightmares and that they usually follow feelings of anger at being punished unjustly that cannot be expressed to people they love or depend upon. He seemed somewhat relieved by the explanation, and it marked the beginning of their talks to straighten out his disturbing fears and feelings. It served to connect these with his experiences at home.

The interagency meetings inspired Mrs. A to obtain further help at the mental health center. She later began to work part time to supplement her Aid to Families with Dependent Children check and took the initiative to arrange for an appropriate sitter and health care for Jerry. She was helped to be more active in age-appropriate activities and to achieve some skill and success toward enhancing her strengths and the ability to regulate and control herself.

Social work practice that is family system oriented and coordinates the treatment among the significant interlocking systems with followup and centralization of responsibility will vastly improve the outcome with the high-risk and vulnerable poor family that has been locked into a generationally perpetuated destructive lifestyle.

CHAPTER 100

FAMILY THERAPY AND THE BLACK MIDDLE CLASS

A Neglected Area of Study

Dennis A. Bagarozzi

When reviewing the family therapy literature, one is struck by the dearth of empirical work which deals specifically with the treatment of Black middle class families. The purpose of this article, therefore, is to focus on some of the factors which the author believes have contributed to the current state of affairs, to offer some conceptual guidelines for working with these families, and to address some unresolved issues concerning the treatment of Black families by White clinicians.

The term Black middle class family is used herein to describe families which are: (a) economically secure, (b) conjugally stable, and (c) upwardly mobile.

In such families, either one or both spouses is steadily employed and household economics fall substantially above the poverty level. These families value stable and enduring conjugal relationships and strive to achieve this ideal. The dominant orientation is one of upward mobility, achievement, and assimilation into the opportunity structure of the larger White society.[1]

WHY A NEGLECTED AREA OF STUDY?

False notions seem to be held by many clinicians and laymen alike that they already possess valid and reliable information concerning Black middle class family structure and functioning. These erroneous beliefs often take the form of stereotypes such as: the

Reprinted from *Journal of Marital and Family Therapy*, Vol. 6, No. 2 (1980), pp. 159–166, by permission of the publisher.

Black matriarchy, the pervasiveness of one-parent households, illegitimacy within the Black community as a whole, and the overall instability of Black marriages. These stereotypes have been perpetuated, in part, by inaccurate generalizations drawn from early works of pioneering researchers who investigated *lower class* Black families (e.g., Moynihan, 1965; Rainwater, 1966). These misconceptions still persist, however, despite the Civil Rights movement of the 60s and the emergence of a larger middle class.

There have been relatively few qualitative investigations of the Black middle class family. Those that are available (e.g., Frazier, 1966; Scanzoni, 1971), however, offer the clinician few insights into the internal dynamics of these families which can be used for clinical intervention. The White therapist, therefore, has little to draw on for assistance in his/her work with such families. If one does not have Black colleagues with whom to confer, or if one's supervisors are White, the therapist might be tempted to apply the little that has been written about treating the lower class Black family to his/her work with the Black middle class.

Since no empirical data are available, the White clinician's main source of guidance derives from therapists' personal accounts and anecdotal reports. For example, Zuk's (1971) clinical experiences with Black lower class families and Jewish middle class families has led him to make the following generalizations: (a) Jewish families are likely to talk more in family therapy and to be more self-disclosing than Black families, (b) Jewish families find the prospect of extended family treatment to be appealing; Black families tend to fear long-term contact, (c) Jewish families are verbally facile; Black families are slow to express themselves in words, are distrustful, and maintain distance from the therapist, (d) Jewish families are easiest to engage in treatment; Black families are the most difficult, and (e) Jewish families are good therapy risks. Blacks are not.

The acceptance of Zuk's (1971) account as if it reported empirical findings rather than as personal experience which may not be generalizable to the Black community as a whole may interfere with the qualitative practice of family therapy in the Black community. Recently, in contrast to Zuk's idea, Sattler (1977) has proposed that family therapy may be particularly relevant for lower class Black clients because it tends to be action-oriented, short-term and to focus on changing concrete behaviors rather than developing insight.

In order to counteract some of the stereotypes and clarify some misconceptions, reference will be made to the latest sociological research concerning the Black middle class. These findings will be discussed in terms of family systems concepts. By doing this, it is hoped that some general guidelines for family intervention can be developed.

A FAMILY SYSTEMS PERSPECTIVE

The systems paradigm (Haley, 1959, 1976; Jackson, 1957) appears to be an appropriate framework for conceptualizing Black family processes because it seems to transcend ethnic, racial, and socioeconomic boundaries and offers specific guidelines for analyzing how a particular family functions. The Black middle class family will be discussed below in terms of a number of central concepts of systems theory.

Systems Goals

Lederev and Jackson (1968) emphasized that humans are goal-directed, and the goals that individuals strive to achieve are strongly influenced by cultural norms. For the majority of Americans, a stable, monogamous marriage is a goal to be attained. In this respect, Black middle class families do not differ from their White counterparts (Billingsley, 1968). Black middle class parents have been found to share similar goals and expectations for their children with White middle class parents (Berger and Simon, 1974). Scanzoni (1971) found that most Black middle class children whom he studied experienced their parents as giving them more than adequate preparation for marriage and family life, had stressed educational attainment to achieve upward mobility, and aided them in achieving these goals through financial and emotional support and modeling.

Barriers to Goal Attainment

While their basic goals do not differ significantly from their White counterparts, Black middle class families find their attainment more difficult because of discrimination and prejudice which is inherent in many social, cultural, and economic institutions in the United States. These barriers to goal attainment contribute to the Black client's reluctance to seek help from White clinicians in private practice, in social agencies, and in mental health facilities which are seen as supportive of the same social system which erected those barriers (McAdoo, 1976). Such attitudes may explain to some extent why Blacks have been found to drop out of therapy earlier and more frequently than Whites do (Raynes & Warren, 1971; Sue, McKinney, Allen & Hall, 1974).

Discrimination also affects the internal dynamics of Black families. Scanzoni (1971) found that the more economic-status rewards a husband supplies to his wife, the more she sees him as meeting her expressive needs, and the less likely she is to resent him. Since middle class Blacks tend to use Whites as reference points for education, income, and job status, inequities in social advancement and financial reward allocation become salient and the resentment which results may cause Black wives to become dissatisfied with their spouses' consumption potential. If the wife reacts to this disappointment with annoyance, there is a good possibility that the hostility will be reciprocated (Patterson and Hops, 1972). Such treatment by the wife will tend to compound the already existing resentment and frustration that the husband experiences because he has been denied access to the opportunity structure. As a result, he may displace his negative feelings on to his wife. The escalating cycle of mutual coercion may work to undermine the types of successful marital exchanges and bargains which are believed to take place in White middle class families. This explanation has been offered as one possible reason for the greater dissolution of marriages among higher status Black families than among comparable White couples (Scanzoni, 1971).

Transactional Patterns and Systems Boundaries

It is impossible to understand Black family functioning unless one views the Black family in the context of the Black community in which it lives and the dominant White society from which it has been excluded. Because the Black community has been set apart from White society, informational barriers have been erected between the two groups. When such barriers exist, coalitions inevitably form between members in each of the segregated groups (Haley, 1976). As a result, many Black families have become intimately involved with subsystem groups within the Black community like church groups and kinship groups. Stack (1974) has described how kinship ties and extended family problems may become an integral part of family life. The Black family system, therefore, is one which is relatively more open to influences outside of the nuclear family than is the White middle class family unit. Adult children, relatives, friends, and children of extended family members often are cared for and periodically may become part of a family unit (Stack, 1974). Such permeability of boundaries makes the family more susceptible to inputs from other systems within the Black community. This continual flow of new information necessitates frequent structural changes and adjustments in family members' role relationships.

Power in the Black Middle Class Family

Sociologists noted that Black middle class spouses tend to share power in a more egalitarian fashion than do White middle class spouses (Jackson, 1973). These findings have important clinical implications. For example, if a spouses's power to influence the conjugal decision-making process is derived from his/her ability to dispense or withhold resources (Scanzoni, 1971), it follows that egalitarian relationships will develop more often in those marriages where both spouses possess approximately equal amounts of reward power. Some clinicians (Bagarozzi & Wodarski, 1977, 1978) suggest that when power is shared equally in this manner, the probability of successful conflict resolution is greater than when large discrepancies exist. It also has been postulated that behavioral contracting will be most effective when resource power is shared equally between spouses (Rappaport & Harrell, 1972).

The Nature of Systems Development: Homeostasis and Morphogenesis

The growth, development, and ultimate viability of any living system depends upon its ability to utilize positive feedback, to change organizational structures and interactional patterns, to meet changing internal demands and external pressures, and to set new and more complex goals. In addition to these morphogenic processes, families also must be able to use negative feedback in order to maintain certain levels of homeostasis which provide order, predictability and stability. Young (1969) has described four possible ways in which Black family systems might function while preparing their children to live in a White controlled society. They might: (a) lack any clear plan except to attempt to meet crises as they arise, (b) physically remove themselves from any stresses caused by the majority groups, (c) willfully maintain externally imposed or self-imposed segregation, or (d) attempt to remove major barriers to assimilation into the opportunity structure.

There is mounting evidence (Scanzoni, 1971) which shows that Black middle class families have elected to function according to the latter principle of removing barriers to assimilation. From my perspective, this course of action probably will prove to be most beneficial for Black middle class family development since it requires the family to function in a manner which closely approximates those systems described as mor-phogenic and viable (Wertheim, 1973). While the first three alternatives might allow the family to maintain the status quo or to continue its existence unhampered, they do not allow for continued growth and development.

DIFFERENCES BETWEEN BLACK AND WHITE MIDDLE CLASS FAMILIES

It is important to recognize that there are a number of differences between Black and White middle class families even though they are similar in a number of ways. For ex-ample:

1. The stages of the family life cycle proposed by some sociologists (Rodgers, 1972) may not be as clearly defined in the Black community as they are be-lieved to be in the White middle class. For example: in the Black community, children (of relatives who cannot care for them, or grandchildren born to a teenage unwed daughter or a divorced son or daughter who is working and not available for parenting) still may be entering the household at what is normatively considered to be the launching phase (Deitrich, 1976). In the White community, this phase usually is concerned with the spouses' attempts to readjust to each other and their new roles after their children's departure.

2. While Black family boundaries may be more open to outside influences (McAdoo, 1976, 1978), they may be more rigidly closed to inputs which come from the White community (Grier & Cobbs, 1979).

3. The more egalitarian power structure among the Black middle class also af-fects husband and wife roles. For example, there are fewer sex-linked roles and tasks among the Black middle class than there are for Whites (Dietrich, 1976). This may stem from the fact that more Black wives are employed than are White wives (Scanzoni, 1971).

BLACK FAMILIES AND WHITE THERAPISTS

While this article was being written, I was unable to locate any empirical work which addressed the issue of racial differences between therapists and family members and the effects these differences might have on the outcome of family therapy. A definitive statement about the interaction of these factors, therefore, cannot be made at this time. Some initial work in the field of individual psychotherapy has been conducted, how-ever, which may shed some light on this issue. A number of individuals have postulated that inherent difficulties arise whenever White therapists encounter Black clients (Phillips, 1961), and that sociocultural and racial biases held by White clinicians make rapport between therapist and client extremely difficult (Vontress, 1972). Some limited support for racial stereotyping has been found (Waite, 1968).

In a comprehensive analysis of empirical studies, Sattler (1977) found that Blacks do prefer same-race therapists over White therapists, but that competent White professionals are preferred to less competent Black professionals. He also found that the therapist's style and technique are more important factors in affecting Black client's choices than is the therapist's race. Preference for therapists was found to be related to the client's temperament, with highly dogmatic Black students preferring same-race practitioners. Middle class Blacks tended to have similar attitudes and expectations toward therapy and its potential outcome as did middle class Whites.

Sattler (1977) found that results from analogue studies and actual therapy sessions point to the same conclusion: Black clients do benefit from therapeutic services offered by White clinicians, but the lack of research on therapy conducted by Black clinicians makes it impossible to evaluate whether Black therapists are more effective with Black clients than are White therapists. Studies of non-clinical interviews have found White interviewers to be as effective with Black clients as Black interviewers (Ewing, 1974). Based upon his review, Sattler (1977) believes that when White therapists are empathic, experienced with Black clients, and use techniques that meet their clients' needs, they are likely to be especially effective with them.

It becomes obvious that a clear statement about the effects of racial differences and outcome in individual psychotherapy cannot be made at this time. Although the findings outlined above are meager, they represent an effort to investigate a sensitive and essential component of the psychotherapeutic process. It is hoped that future investigations will provide some insights into the effects that a therapist's race might have on his/her ability to intervene across racial lines, to cross family systems' boundaries, to establish a therapeutic alliance, to enter into a family's interaction process, and to effect positive changes within family systems. These findings also should alert professionals, educators, and clinical supervisors to aspects of training and therapy which heretofore have been neglected; that is (a) how the therapist's racial attitudes, prejudices, expectations, and perceptions influence his/her work with families of different racial groups, (b) to what extent our contemporary models of family process and family therapy reflect a White middle class ethnocentrism, and (c) whether ignorance of a client's background and differences in language usage and communication style are barriers to rapport between racially different therapists and family members.

CLINICAL IMPLICATIONS

1. While Black middle class Americans are more similar to their White counterparts than they are to lower class Blacks, they still should be considered an ethnic subsociety which is bound together by a common definition and treatment by the dominant White society (Billingsley, 1968). The anger which results from such treatment, therefore, must be dealt with in the therapy process (Halpern, 1970). Helping family members recognize and deal with this anger may prove to be an essential component of treatment, especially when the therapist is White. Once these feelings are confronted, the therapist can begin to help family members use them in more constructive and self-actualizing ways.

One may wonder whether the therapist should become an active agent of social change, or whether he/she should merely support Black clients in their struggle to make better use of their capacities and potentials. The answer seems to rest with the individual therapist. Sattler (1977) has suggested a dual role: (a) to help clients recognize the sources of their difficulties and (b) to restructure society by eliminating those forces which perpetuate discrimination and limit individual achievement. The family therapist has an additional task. He/she must help family members become aware of how anger at societal injustices may be displaced and acted out within the family context. He/she also should help families determine how much of their difficulties stem from the effects of discrimination and how much they result from personal dysfunctional behavioral styles, faulty communications patterns, unverbalized expectations or coercive interpersonal behavior change attempts.

2. The therapist should be aware of the possible influences on family processes of kinship and community groups. McAdoo (1976) has described how interference from extended family members may create marital difficulties when family members are unable to say "no" to unreasonable demands made by their kin and relatives. He suggests that the clinician should help the clients to differentiate from their extended family and to develop healthy boundaries between families. To achieve these goals, he suggests seeing the family member and his/her kin in separate sessions. Once family boundaries have been negotiated, the therapist can work to repair or develop new boundaries within the nuclear family.

The clinician might find it advisable to view Black family systems in terms of the social networks in which they exist (Speck & Attneave, 1973), rather than as isolated nuclear families which are more characteristic of the White middle class. Kinship groups also can be used by the therapist as support systems. For example, grandparents may be used as parental surrogates who can provide nurturance and acceptance for an abused or scapegoated child.

3. Since many Black middle class families have egalitarian family structures, behavioral contracting may prove useful (Patterson & Hops, 1972; Rappaport & Harrell, 1972).

CONCLUSION

Within any family, there exists a dynamic interplay and continual transaction among three cultures: (a) the family culture, with its own rules, myths, and secrets, (b) the culture of the ethnic or racial group of which the family may be part, and (c) the broader culture of the society. Understanding this interplay and how the family may use its subculture and that of the dominant society to maintain a homeostatic balance may be an important part of the assessment and diagnostic process. In order to effect change, the therapist first must be permitted to enter the family system. Understanding the ethnic and social subculture may facilitate this process. Once the therapist has gained admittance, confronting racial and ethnic differences may help the therapist gain acceptance. Eventually, however, attempts will be made by the family to neutralize the therapist's change efforts by making him/her a member of the system who is invested in maintaining the status quo. Perhaps this is when the family will use racial and ethnic differences to resist change. Metacommunicating about this process may be necessary if treatment is to proceed and change is to be brought about. The efficacy of such an approach, however, awaits empirical verification.

In this article, I have attempted to treat a topic which has been neglected in the family therapy literature, to highlight where research might be conducted, and to offer some tentative suggestions for understanding and working with Black middle class families. It is hoped that this article will draw attention to the need for qualitative research in this important area of study.

REFERENCES

Bagarozzi, D. A. & Wodarski, J. S. A social exchange typology of conjugal relationships and conflict development. *Journal of Marriage and Family Counseling*, 1977, *3*, 53–60.

Bagrozzi, D. A. & Wodarski, J. S. Behavioral treatment of marital discord. *Clinical Social Work Journal*, 1978, *6*, 135–154.

Berger, A. & Simon, W. Black families and the Moynihan report: A research evaluation. *Social Problems*, 1974, *22*, 145–161.

Billingsley, A. *Black families in White America*. Englewood Cliffs, N.J.: Prentice-Hall, 1968.

Dietrich, K. T. A critical reaction to sociological research on Black families. Unpublished paper. Texas Agricultural Experiment Station, Texas A&M University, 1976.

Ewing, T. M. Racial similarity of client and counselor and client satisfaction with counseling. *Journal of Counseling Psychology*, 1974, *21*, 446–449.

Frazier, F. F. *The Negro family in the United States*. Chicago, IL: The University of Chicago Press, 1966.

Grier, W. W. & Cobbs, P. M. *Black rage*. New York: Bantam Books, 1969.

Haley, J. *Problem solving therapy*. San Francisco: Jossey-Bass, 1976.

Haley, J. The family of the schizophrenic: A model system. *American Journal of Nervous and Mental Disorders*, 1959, *129*, 357–374.

Halpern, F. Psychotherapy in the rural south. *Journal of Contemporary Psychotherapy*, 1970, *2*, 67–74.

Jackson, D. D. The question of family homeostasis. *Psychiatric Quarterly Supplement*, 1957, *31*, Part 1, 79–90.

Jackson, J. J. Family organization and ideology. In K. S. Miller & R. M. Dreger (Eds.), *Comparative studies of Blacks and Whites in the United States*. New York: Seminar Press, 1973.

Lederev, W. & Jackson, D. D. *The mirages of marriage*. New York: W. W. Norton, 1968.

McAdoo, H. R. The impact of extended family variables upon the upward mobility of Black families. Unpublished paper, Families Research Project, 1978.

McAdoo J. L. Family therapy in the Black community. Unpublished paper presented at the American Orthopsychiatric Association, 1976.

Moynihan, D. P. *The Negro family: The case for national action*. Washington: Department of Labor, 1965.

Patterson, G. R. & Hops, H. Coercion, a game for two: Intervention techniques for marital conflict. In R. C. Ulrich & P. Mountjoy (Eds.), *The experimental analysis of social behavior*. New York: Appleton-Century-Crofts, 1972.

Phillips, W. B. Role of the counselor in the guidance of Negro students. *Harvard Educational Review*, 1961, *31*, 324–326.

Rainwater, L. Crucible of identity: The Negro lower class family. *Deadalus,* 1966, *95,* 172–216.

Rappaport, A. & Harrell, J. A behavioral exchange model for marital counseling. *Family Coordinator,* 1972, *21,* 203–212.

Raynes, A. E. & Warren, G. Some distinguishing features of patients failing to attend a psychiatric clinic after referral. *American Journal of Orthopsychiatry,* 1971, *41,* 581–588.

Rodgers, R. *Family interaction and transaction: The developmental approach.* Englewood Cliffs, N.J.: Prentice-Hall, 1972.

Sattler, J. The effects of therapist-client racial similarity. In A. Gurman (Ed.), *Effective psychotherapy.* Pergamon, 1977.

Scanzoni, J. H. *Opportunity and the family.* New York: The Free Press, 1970.

Scanzoni, J. H. *The Black family in modern society.* Boston: Allyn and Bacon, 1971.

Speck, R. V. & Attneave, C. L. *Family networks.* New York: Pantheon, 1973.

Stack, C. B. *All our kin: Strategies for survival in a Black community.* New York: Harper and Row, 1974.

Stuart R. B. An operant interpersonal program for couples. In D. H. Olson (Ed.), *Treating relationships.* Lake Mills: Graphic Publishing, 1976.

Sue, S., McKinney, H., Allen, D. & Hall, J. Delivery of community mental health services to Black and White clients. *Journal of Consulting and Clinical Psychology,* 1974, *42,* 794–801.

Vontress, E. E. The Black militant as counselor. *Personnel and Guidance Journal,* 1972, *50,* 576–580.

Waite, R. R. The Negro patient and clinical theory. *Journal of Consulting and Clinical Psychology,* 1968, *32,* 427–433.

Wertheim, E. S. Family unit therapy. The science and typology of family systems. *Family Process,* 1973, *12,* 361–376.

Young, D. R. The socialization of minority peoples. In D. A. Goslin (Ed.), *Handbook of socialization theory and research.* Chicago: Rand McNally, 1969.

Zuk, G. H. *Family therapy: A triadic-based approach.* New York: Behavioral Publications, 1971.

NOTE

1. For a fuller and more complete description of the Black middle class family, the reader is referred to J. H. Scanzoni, *The Black family in modern society* (Boston: Allyn and Bacon, 1971).

SOCIOECONOMIC CLASS

CHAPTER 101

SOCIAL WORK WITH THE WEALTHY

Elizabeth Herman McKamy

Social work education and practice equip social workers to deal with people who are primarily disadvantaged by their economic, social or cultural backgrounds, and secondarily disadvantaged by intrapsychic or physical handicaps. Psychosocial studies underline the fact that social workers are trained to consider not only a client's psychopathology, ego strengths, and immediate family situation, but also to evaluate these as assets and liabilities relating to capacity for *minimal* functioning within the community's socioeconomic framework.

Although a substantial number of social workers are recognized as competent psychotherapists and psychoanalysts, the deepest root of their identity is grounded in orientation toward alleviating poor people's distress. Gordon Hamilton, Annette Garrett, Helen Harris Perlman, Charlotte Towle, and others have illustrated the systems and conditions of human suffering of those who lack the basic resources for an equal position in society. Many social workers, along with some of their first clients, moved on: but the generic identity of social workers as helpers of the poor remains.

Oriented as he is toward helping the poor, how does the social worker approach work with the wealthy? Even though most people are adversely affected by a troubled world economy today, a small segment of the population regards money as no obstacle in searching for and obtaining psychiatric care. Characterized not only by affluence, the wealthy patient and his family often have an impressive heritage of achievement. Dysfunction arises frequently from an acute or chronic psychodynamic conflict, rather than from social or economic stress impinging on a weak psychological structure.

In a traditional public or voluntary institution the multiproblem family might manifest social, economic, or educational malfunction in conjunction with psychiatric problems. Conversely, multiproblem families in private settings are usually characterized by

Reprinted from *Social Casework,* Vol. 57 (1976), pp. 254–258, by permission of the publisher, Families International, Inc.

a complexity of psychodynamic breakdowns and few, if any, social, economic, or educational ones. Whatever purity of approach this fact may afford, it nonetheless demands that the social worker reassess some of the basic assumptions of his task.

THE SOCIAL WORKER'S ROLE

As part of his role at The C. F. Menninger Memorial Hospital, the social worker usually functions as liaison between hospital and family. As a member of the patient's treatment team, the social worker is the primary interpreter of the history and current situation of the family for the team. While this information helps the team to better understand the patient, it also facilitates clearer insight into countertransference phenomena as they develop. Based on an overall understanding, the team recommends individual psychotherapy, group psychotherapy, or family therapy as adjuncts to the patient's milieu treatment program. The social worker communicates the team's concept of the problems and its recommendations to the family.

Whether intensive family therapy or planned periodic visits are recommended during the course of hospitalization, the family is encouraged to become involved. Some families are amenable from the beginning to their own active participation in the process; others are resistant.

Affluence and successful management in business and social spheres characterize many of the families with whom the staff work. Such families are accustomed to and adept at controlling their environment. They rarely experience situations where their own resources are not sufficient to solve their problems. In fact, such people seldom find themselves having to ask for help. The social worker, popularly thought of as a helper of the socially and economically distressed, finds himself in an unusual position.

He needs to defend himself and his professional task in an arena which is somewhat alien both to him and to his clients; he is not used to working with people of wealth and power, and his clients are unused to asking for help. Treatment difficulties arise involving families with means because of long-established patterns of resistance to placing themselves in a position seemingly controlled by others. The social worker too may experience conflicts in relating to people whom society may deem more capable and influential than he.

WEALTH AS POWER

"You get what you pay for" is a maxim to which our culture has given credence. Despite progress in social security and public and voluntary health and child-care services, the belief is still espoused that the more an individual pays, the higher the quality of service he gets. Accordingly, one might expect that where direct party payment for service prevails, there is also a greater demand for achievement and performance. The rich are people who do not have to knock on doors, deal with secretaries, or with middlemen of any kind. Indeed, they are people who can put pressure on the hospital administration regarding anything that is done or not done to the designated patient. Such pressure, filtered down to the clinician, can be a stimulus for excellence on the job, or it can be experienced as a constraint.

Although most hospitals support their workers in clinical decisions, whether they meet, or fail to meet, the immediate approval of the patient and his family, there still remains an atmosphere of concern: the call of the board member who attempts to persuade through threat if an acquaintance is not given the treatment that he or his family dictates; the angry removal by a family of its member who is a well-known writer; the elopement of a patient of national renown, as a consequence of disagreement with staff; the threat made to a hospital that a much-needed grant will be withheld if existing policy within, for example, the social work discipline is not altered to accommodate what an individual family feels are its particular needs at a given time.

Powerful, educated, wealthy families are accustomed to direct access and management over what they have bought. They are used to controlling business and, as they see it, payment for private hospitalization is not unlike an investment in a business. In not offering a precise prospectus, however, the psychiatric hospital business often stimulates anxiety in families and the concomitant impulse to want to dictate and control through familiar patterns, for example, demand and litigation. Currently, health services and practitioners are particularly sensitive to suggestions of or hints at litigation. A hospital may be known to support its employees in their clinical decisions, but the concern for legal consequence to the institution and the individual employee still exists. Such concern is a significant influence—for better or worse. Sometimes the accessibility of resources and information to families, coupled with direct party payment for service, facilitates communication and cooperation with the treatment team. At other times, however, the very assets that allow these people to choose "the best" can make delivery of "the best," as clinically determined, a tenuous and difficult task.

Rich or poor, most families defend themselves against the recognition that they, as well as the patient, are part of the problem. Pain, confusion, and fear of change are orchestrated in almost any troubled family into a complexity of defenses that resist intervention. At the time when hospitalization of the patient has become necessary, most families would prefer, consciously or unconsciously, that the problem, namely the patient, be treated and that they, the family, support such treatment but remain essentially outside of it.

Visits, encouragement, and assuming responsibility for things the patient can not do are among the many ways a family can help its sick member while he is in the hospital. Most often, though, when deep understanding and change of personality are the goals of treatment, families have to become more intensively and purposefully involved.

RESISTANCES OF THE WEALTHY

The wealthy sometimes present resistances to more active therapeutic involvement that are different from those of other kinds of families in other kinds of settings. "We're functioning just fine" is often heard from families of the patients treated in our hospital. Frequently, such a statement is difficult to confront.

Father, for example, may be operating at full capacity as a corporation lawyer while at the same time involving himself in a home and social life replete with every sign of success. Mother, with children grown beyond school age, may have returned to her earlier career as a drama reviewer for the city newspaper. She explains that this job has always allowed her a flexibility of hours so that she can maintain her home as the first priority in her responsibilities. The patient's oldest sibling may have just married, while another enters his second year of college. All members of the family, including the designated patient, state that the only problem is the patient's illness.

As the patient, who had seriously attempted suicide shortly after beginning college, gains confidence in his treatment staff, he evidences in his behavior anxieties about separation from the family that showed up initially in psychological testing. He has always feared leaving his parents because he sensed from an early age that there were deep marital problems that might emerge were he to move away from home. Crazy as these fears may be, this seventeen-year-old's suicide attempt might lend sufficient evidence of trouble in the family to induce the treatment team to recommend family therapy along with the hospitalization of the patient.

INVOLVING THE FAMILY IN THE THERAPY

By the time hospitalization is necessary, chronically ill patients and their families are often veterans of years of psychiatric care. A high level of general education and sophistication, coupled with multifaceted and often unsuccessful experience with doctors, psychologists, psychiatrists, and so forth, can form an impressive defensive structure. Some of these families and patients use diagnostic jargon with ease. They are skilled at anticipating interventions and interpretations. Moreover, they can intellectually acknowledge an understanding that they may not truly feel. They can take the therapist's seat literally and figuratively.

A physician father, for example, may insist that continuing to medicate his daughter is his effort to be helpful and expedient in the treatment process. A mother may defend herself against recognizing the family problems that are stirred up by her daily calls to her son. She explains that her psychoanalyst at home is encouraging a closer relationship between herself and her children. An entire family can lucidly explain the dynamics of family life as they relate to the patient's illness. They can even try to convince the social worker that this understanding is more than enough homework for them to think about while the patient is in the hospital.

Splitting away from the central focus of family treatment by intellectualization and bringing in auxiliary supports and other specialists can present formidable resistance to intervention by the social worker. Although putting forth parallel interpretations and offering alternative concrete supports to the family can be useful some of the time, more often the social worker finds that sharing his experience of the family process in action is the most effective means of engaging them in a working alliance.

"We'll support anything you do" is a position taken by some families. Years of struggle and pain with a chronically ill relative have brought them over the threshold of frustration into hopelessness. Such families have come to feel that all they can offer their sick member is protracted financial security in a private hospital. In such a setting they hope that the patient will have the maximum of physical comfort while they themselves find a long-desired peace of mind. These families may experience difficulty in translating their passive despair into a sense of personal purpose in a treatment process.

The unremitting illness of the patient has come to seem like an unremitting affront to the family's ability to cope and care. The very hope that the social worker communicates in his effort to engage the family can easily be taken by them as a further insult to their capacity to be good parents or caring people.

DIFFICULTIES IN ESTABLISHING
A WORKING ALLIANCE WITH THE FAMILY

In a state hospital, the proposition of unlimited financial backing for any treatment approach would be unlikely and fairly extraneous to the administrative system. In a private hospital, however, where the treatment teams feel constrained at times by the presence and power of families, there can be a temptation to collude with a carte blanche proposal that full responsibility for the patient be left in the treatment team's hands, thus excluding the family from the therapeutic task.

The very fact that the family's wish to reject the patient seems so blatant can stimulate in the team a counter wish to reject them; allowing the family to remove itself entirely from the arena of treatment. Yet, when the goal is to help facilitate an integration of the patient's past in a way that will enable him to function autonomously as an adult in the future, it is almost always advisable that the family be accessible to work with the treatment staff. In the ongoing process with such families, the social workers often have to deal with their own frustrations, anger, and temptation to assume a "better" parental role that by its nature might have them reenact the same pathological patterns that the patient and his family experienced among themselves.

In work with less advantaged people, a social worker is usually able to help a family see that there are areas of dysfunction within the overall structure of their lives. Financial difficulties are common concerns, as are frustrations about underachievement in school or community. An asset in establishing a working alliance with socially or economically disadvantaged families is the social worker's often-given position as role model. When the social worker is viewed by the family as someone who has achieved an admirable level of professional, economic, and social success, the family may feel that at least some learning may take place from their contact with him.

With wealthy, successful families whose apparent level of functioning is at the apex of our social structure, it can be more difficult to establish this necessary working alliance. The social worker may find himself relying more on symptomatology revealed in the process of a family meeting than in the factual information shared. There may be fewer nonverbal assets to rely on in his initial work with these people. There is less likelihood of the social worker being taken from the start as a role model in the classical sense. Moreover, with the affluent family comes the additional demand for the social worker to be in touch with his own feelings about assuming an authoritative position with people whose lifestyle connotes a formidable authority in its own right.

COUNTERTRANSFERENCE

Most of those who work in a psychiatric setting—psychiatrists, nurses, psychologists, activities therapists, aides, social workers—are from lower to upper middle-class backgrounds, and have grown up with the injunction that in order to achieve or maintain a comfortable income for themselves they have to work. Most people on the staff of a private hospital do not come from backgrounds of wealth. Therefore, at the risk of being simplistic, one might say that the present achievements of the individual members of a hospital staff are based on individual resourcefulness and effort, and the staff members' future financial and social prospects are, relatively speaking, somewhat limited.

Most social workers bring with them to their jobs a professional image as it was originally hewn out of their predecessors' exclusive work with the poor. Like his colleagues, the individual social worker has to consider countertransference that may be stimulated by his contact with patients. He may envy and resent the wealthy. Furthermore, he may find difficulties in being assertive enough, or difficulties in being too assertive in trying to counter a tendency to appease. In a psychosocial paradigm, prominent patients and their families may well represent parental figures to the social worker. And, similarly, a recovered patient may threaten as yet another powerful figure in the social worker's environment. In fact, enabling the privileged patient to achieve, or regain, his potential level of functioning might well mean helping him to *exceed* the social worker within the socioeconomic framework of society.

Finding ease with the fact that one's patients and their families might, out of the context of their current distress, far outdistance one along the continuum of success that exists in our culture is a sobering thought. Yet this difference in status militates against the social worker's efforts only insofar as he is unaware of its importance.

In working with wealthy patients and their families, the social worker must exert care to maintain a sensitive and strong self-image. He may need to take extra pains to strengthen his professional identity while realistically accepting both his assets and limitations. Armed with such insights into both his personal and professional background, he can formulate realistic goals and keep a sense of perspective. Only then can he effectively manage his job, especially the tasks centering around work with wealthy patients and their families.

The treatment of people of means may be limited by their wealth just as treatment of the poor may be limited by their poverty. Nevertheless, along with the unique difficulties that such caseloads present, there exist some equally unique assets. Wealthy patients and their families can, by and large, afford a treatment program individually determined on the basis of their needs. If indicated, families can travel for scheduled appointments, as many do at The C. F. Menninger Memorial Hospital. Or they can pay for adjunctive treatment at home. Most of the people worked with are verbal and can become motivated toward a goal they think worthwhile. They are resourceful and can focus their energies over an extended period of time if it is necessary. Many of them have generations of security and comfort behind them, and can therefore envision regaining an overall peaceful existence which to less privileged people might be a Utopia unknown.

When these assets can be channeled into a therapeutic alliance, the rewards for all are considerable. Such an alliance, as a prerequisite for meaningful treatment, evolves from a sensitivity to the social worker's personal and professional feelings, awareness of the fears, anxieties, and defenses of the patients, and an acceptance of the unique strengths that each patient and his family, no matter how wealthy, bring to the private hospital setting.

VALUES

CHAPTER 102

EFFECT OF VALUE REEVALUATION ON CURRENT PRACTICE

Francis J. Turner

Over the past two years, the writer has become increasingly aware of a group of clients whose psychosocial stress has originated from two related yet separate phenomena—a personal reevaluation of values and ethics and a recurrence of previously dormant superego concerns. This article examines these two phenomena and offers some knowledge and practice implications of their occurrence. It includes some case illustrations, theoretical comments, implications for learning, and diagnostic and management observations.

It is no surprise that persons in our society are experiencing value and ethical difficulties during a period of rapidly changing value and ethical systems at all levels of society. What is noteworthy is that persons are turning to social work professionals for help in dealing with such problems. This trend is significant in relation to the tradition in which the client's values were considered as a therapeutic no-man's-land and the therapist's values as something to be kept private and rarely shared with the client. Whether social workers adhered to these taboos is, of course, a moot question.

This tradition is now changing. Individuals, groups, and families are turning to us for help with stress in psychosocial functioning directly related to value and ethical conflicts that are sometimes recognized, sometimes not. These clients are diagnostically within the range of normal functioning, yet still in need of skilled help. Such requests require that social work professionals respond in an understanding and helpful way and give this content more consideration.

It should not be surprising that a challenge to one's ethical position or a commitment to change one's value position would have implications for the superego component of personality, especially if the approach to practice is from a developmental base. Each

Reprinted from *Social Casework,* Vol. 56 (1975), pp. 285–291, by permission of the publisher, Families International, Inc.

person brings to new situations his whole developmental history, including superego development. These pasts influence how we are affected by or affect our present. But we also know that this is not a one-way influence; new experiences and perceptions can shift, alter, diminish, or increase the extent to which our pasts influence the present and, in turn, alter the way we will function in the future.

It is because these two phenomena—one society-wide and current and the other individual and past-related—can reciprocally influence each other that their simultaneous occurrence becomes of interest and importance therapeutically. Four types of situations that the writer has observed and which are related to this topic are described in the case illustrations below.

CASE ILLUSTRATIONS

First, there is the client who initially appears in a mild or moderately severe crisis situation resulting from a shift in life view, the effects of which are only partially recognized and understood.

> Mr. M is an intelligent, successful businessman of forty-five, who experienced a mild crisis reaction that he related to a recent upset in his marriage. This upset had resulted in diminished effective functioning in most life areas, including his business. His sales had dropped off drastically, and he was facing the possibility of losing his position. It was soon evident that his stress was more broadly based than the difficulty with his marriage; he was, in fact, in a process of reevaluating his whole view of life, his commitment to his marriage, and his aspirations.
>
> In brief, he was striving to move from a rigid view of life and duty to a more open one in which self-fulfillment was the goal. This upheaval had reactivated some of his earlier ambivalent feelings toward his father, a man who had high standards and expectations of him that he rarely could meet. These feelings became transferred both to his boss and to the therapist and showed in his wanting to please and to hurt. Only after some of this material was clarified and he began to recognize both his present shifting perceptions and commitments and the strings on him from the past was he able to begin to function in his accustomed self-fulfilling, socially responsible manner and to reexamine his commitment to his marriage.

A second type of client in a value dilemma is the individual who recognizes that he has altered his self-concept along with his perception of desirable behavior and responsibility; the problem that moves him to seek help stems from his inability to follow through on the implications of his value shifts.

> Mrs. J is a twenty-five-year-old woman of above-average intelligence, married to a successful, upwardly mobile man whom she met while both were in the armed forces. She had felt abandoned by her husband and unfulfilled in her role as mother of three. To counter these feelings, she began taking university courses at night and became involved in a women's discussion group. She was significantly influenced by the campus climate and the content of some of her courses and de-

cided to pursue a full university career along with her responsibilities as wife and mother. Although her husband concurred with this plan and encouraged her, the decision evoked a wave of anxiety and marked ambivalence that confused her husband and put severe strains on the marriage. In individual and joint interviews with her and her husband, it quickly became apparent that her decision had evoked both the spectre of her dead father—a controlling, demanding man who viewed women as being second-best—and her feelings about her highly critical, dependent mother, who was still alive. Several stormy interviews took place in which some of the components of the unresolved emancipation from parental demands and expectations were worked through and their influence on her present goals clarified. Following this stage, Mrs. J began to follow through on her decisions and resumed effective functioning as wife and mother.

A third form of value-related problems concerns marital situations where support for the altered life view is not present and where the stress comes from the lack of such support. This problem appears to be the situation in an increasing number of marriages in which there have been several years of a reasonably stable, apparently healthy relationship of essentially mature spouses. Nevertheless, under the influence of recent societal trends, conflict emerges as one or both partners begin to change attitudes toward broad life objectives, role perceptions, or moral stances related to sexual conduct within or outside the marriage. Examples are the man who decides to leave a secure job after several years in order to establish his own business or the woman who wishes for a new career outside the home. In these cases, the conflicts that emerge frequently evoke the same superego immaturities identified earlier.[1]

The fourth cluster of problems in this area is similar to some traditional family problems but with a new dimension. These cases involve value and ethical shifts that have taken place differentially in various family subsystems. Customarily, social workers have seen these from the viewpoint of the parent-system and sibling-system dyad, but currently other kinds of subsystem splits seem to be taking place. Usually social workers have viewed them as normal maturational emancipation struggles and have understood the superego components of the child's struggle. What has not been given sufficient attention is the real value-based struggle. The latter situation is considered here: a situation where there has been a value shift in some component of the family that results in new stress. One example involved a changed perception of the acceptability of parents' arranging an abortion for a fifteen-year-old daughter.

Mr. and Mrs. N had long been a stable, socially conscious couple with strong church ties. In recent years, Mrs. N had begun to question some of her long-held moral views, and it was concerning the decision on the daughter's abortion that the couple realized how far apart they had grown in their perceptions of acceptable behavior. This differential perception on the part of the parents created additional conflict for the girl who was struggling with her own emerging system of morality. This issue was never resolved for the family, and the daughter eventu-

---

[1] Elizabeth Bott, Urban Families: The Norms of Conjugal Roles, in *The Psychosocial Interior of the Family*, ed. Gerald Handell (London: George Allen & Unwin, 1968), pp. 141–58.

ally left home following the abortion. Mr. and Mrs. N's marriage suffered a serious blow. After several months, they began to make some progress in reestablishing a functioning system with themselves and their other children.

No doubt there are other clusterings of cases.[2] The four categories above identify some situations in which the persons involved have histories of adequate functioning and mastery of many life situations but have met unmanageable difficulties in psychosocial functioning because they, significant others, or significant institutions have altered or questioned earlier-held positions on values, ethics, or responsibilities. In seeking to resolve these attitudinal changes, they have also found themselves struggling with issues stemming from their own maturational histories. To fully assist these clients, it is necessary to understand both their superego functioning and current social value changes.

BACKGROUND ON THE SUPEREGO

In the 1923 article "The Ego and the Id," Sigmund Freud redescribed the personality structure in a manner that gave proper emphasis to the superego.[3] Important as this reconceptualization was, professionals have tended to direct more emphasis and interest to the censoring, restricting, inhibiting components of the superego than to some of its more positive components. The fact that the process of superego development affects the person's attitudes to himself, his perceived esteem or lack of it, and his attitudes to authority persons, initially parents and parent-like authorities but ultimately all authorities, has been understressed.

The superego goal for the maturing person is the development of a psychic structure that fosters the establishment of norms, attitudes, and identities in a way that is increasingly autonomous. This stance permits an individual throughout life to set his own life rules and attitudes and to select the societal systems by which he will be influenced, rather than be directed with little autonomy.[4]

It has been generally accepted that by early adulthood a person has developed a functioning and generally stable superego and a self-image reasonably well accommodated to the significant others and systems within which he functions. Apart from some gradual maturing and realignment of life views as identified in the last three of Erik H. Erikson's eight stages, professionals have presumed that there would be little change in a person's ethical stance, although it was understood that other components of self-image and self-attitudes would change.[5]

[2] Eric J. Cleveland and William D. Longaker, Neurotic Patterns in the Family, in *The Psychosocial Interior of the Family,* ed. Handell, pp. 159–85.

[3] Sigmund Freud, The Ego and the Id, in *The Standard Edition of the Complete Psychological Works of Sigmund Freud,* ed. James Strachey (London: Hogarth Press, 1961), 9: 19–39.

[4] Eunice F. Allen, Psychoanalytic Theory, in *Social Work Treatment,* ed. Francis J. Turner (New York: The Free Press, 1974), pp. 19–41.

[5] Erik H. Erikson, *Childhood and Society* (New York: W. W. Norton & Co., 1950), pp. 219–34.

VALUES AND ETHICS

We no longer live in a social system where values are stable in individuals, family systems, ethnic groupings, or larger political or religious systems. Both ethical and value systems are in flux for many individuals and groups. By *ethics* is meant those consciously adhered to, explicit or implicit, codes of behavior that govern the lives of individuals and groups. Values are those less obvious and less conscious pragmatically oriented preferential choices, almost automatic in operation, that assist individuals to develop patterns of selection from the vast array of daily decisions and choices. The latter are more accurately called value orientations. Although ethics and values or value orientations are separate but related concepts, they do tend to be combined in the general term *values*.

From the ethical aspect, there are many individuals who have drastically altered their long-held convictions about such things as duties to one's country and to one's neighbors, be they old or young, born or unborn. Questions of when one is or is not a human person, when one is or is not alive or dead, are now clearly topics for dispute.

In the area of value orientations, there are interesting and rapid shifts. From a North American society that probably in Florence R. Kluckhohn's scheme had a predominant first-level orientation to the future, to doing, to individuality, and to man over nature, significant components of society have shifted to a present, being, collateral, man-with-nature orientation.[6] Thus, many persons who had thought their moral and value development had been completed are having to face a new developmental challenge, obviously with differing degrees of success.

Both ethical and value shifts have taken place within the social work profession that must be acknowledged in current practice. Ethically, social workers have had to come to terms with the same questions as society or at least come to terms with their unanswered dilemmas. From a value orientation perspective, there have also been some shifts that are influencing practice styles. The increased interest in present-oriented, here-and-now, short-term therapeutic engagements, the value placed on experiential kinds of therapy, the heavy involvement in groups, and the expanded interest in communities and community action and in environmental and ecological issues all reflect value orientation shifts and reorderings from an individualistic, long-term, future-oriented, insight-based, problem-solving approach.

These comments about value orientations should not be viewed as definitive, but only as indicators of this much-discussed and well-identified social phenomenon. Of more relevance to this article is a brief consideration of what social work has already learned from this development and what implications are emerging for practice.

IMPLICATIONS FOR KNOWLEDGE

One thing we all have learned is that ethical and value systems are not as stable and unchanging as social workers had thought. Whether or not historians or philosophers held this view, practitioners have tended to view moral codes and value systems of

---

[6] Florence R. Kluckhohn and Fred S. Strodtbeck, *Variations in Value Orientations* (Evanston, Ill.: Row Peterson & Co., 1961).

themselves and their clients as generally fixed, once professional and personal maturity was achieved. Many social workers have been surprised at the ability of persons to make dramatic and fundamental shifts in standards and behavior, a further example of the ongoing learning about one's ability to change and mature. People are highly flexible and adaptable.

Social workers have also learned that the ability to adjust to new norms and values is not as age-related as had been thought. Some of the most flexible persons, in regard to values, observed in recent years have been old, and some of the most restricted and value-constricted have been among the young. It is misleading to overstress the positive results because it is also evident that many personal and social problems arise from these identified changes—problems of both a primary and secondary form. The term *primary* refers to the problems of those individuals for whom value changes produce internal stress and uncertainty that can approach or reach crisis situations. The term *secondary problems* covers those situations that emerge as a result of internal value changes—that is, the effects of the changes on significant others in a person's life, such as parents, spouse, or children.

A further component of value-related problems is their frequent connection to a person's developmental history. Many persons, in the process of working through alterations of formerly held standards, experience a resurgence of developmental gaps and painful experiences. As professionals have learned from crisis work, earlier unsolved issues frequently are reawakened under stress, and such reexperiencing presents to the client and the alert therapist an opportunity to work on them. This opportunity is the so-called second-chance aspect of crisis work.

Because value issues and superego development and functioning are closely related, some unfinished components of superego development can be dealt with in these situations. Because of the high possibility of current-based, value-related contents evoking emotions and material from the past, therapists must be sensitive to the effect of such transferred feelings, especially with negative components.

The above material becomes further complicated in working with adolescents and the family. The struggle for the adolescent to face parental standards and to accept, reject, or modify them in making them his own is sufficiently difficult at any time. It becomes even more crisis prone when the parents are in conflict, transition, or confusion in this area. This kind of situation sets up a reciprocating form of influence which puts further stress and confusion on both the parents and the adolescent, thus exacerbating the superego struggle. If, in addition to this parent-sibling value struggle, a therapist is struggling with his own value conflict or dilemma, the potential for therapeutic confusion is vast.

Superego development is closely related to one's psychosexual development and the formation of attitudes toward acceptable or nonacceptable conduct. However, the sphere of sexual attitudes, beliefs, and practices is one of the areas most influenced currently by societal value shifts. Thus, as persons are influenced by changing societal sexual values, they may reexperience earlier superego conflicts that would complicate the resolution of value issues in this area.

DIAGNOSTIC AND MANAGEMENT IMPLICATIONS

From the viewpoint of diagnosis, the above information suggests that it is important for social workers to be alert to the possibility of value dilemmas as a key source of conflict or stress in their clients. At times, these conflicts will be obvious, but this source of stress may not be apparent to the client and can be overlooked or misunderstood by both client and worker. Implied in this description is the necessity to focus more attention than has been common on the value and ethical orientation of clients, particularly when there is a likelihood of these life areas' being in transition, either in the client or in his life space. The worker must also consider the risk of being overenthusiastic about the possibility of value dilemmas and developing a tendency to see them where they do not exist. We do not have sufficient data about the prevalence of this type of situation. However, as a general diagnostic stance, it is better to be aware of the possibility of various presenting situations than to be surprised by their occurrence.

The necessity of anticipating the appearance of revived unfinished developmental material in situations where value shifts are in progress has been described. In such instances, professionals must be interested in developmental history and alert to developmental clues available from current functioning. Indicators of the intensity, consistency, and appropriateness of superego functioning can be derived from such factors as the client's attitudes toward his aggressive and sexual impulses, his attitudes to authority figures, and, most important, his level and profile of self-esteem. When there are concerns of more than a minor nature in these areas accompanying reactions to value matters, the likelihood of intrapsychic, historically based therapeutic complications is high.

From a case management viewpoint, several observations can be suggested. Assuming that both current value stress and earlier-based reactions are present, there are at least three choices open. One would involve focusing only on the present value material, assuming that its resolution would reestablish an adequate level of functioning without having to reexamine earlier material. A second stance would include focusing primarily on developmental material, with the rationale that helping the client resolve unfinished material from the past would free him to deal objectively with the present. The third perspective would involve attempting to find a balance between the two sources of strain and to seek for growth-enabling resolution of both areas. Although the writer's preference is for the latter approach, the decision must be made on the experiences of the individual situation and the theoretical stance of the therapist.

In working with clients in these situations, one of the crucial responsibilities of the therapist is to be aware of his own value dilemmas and value shifts and the extent to which such developments may have reactivated developmental scars that could, in turn, influence his perceptions and reactions to the client-worker relationship. If there is adequate awareness of therapist involvement in the relationship, careful attention must be given to the probable presence of transferred feelings. They will be significant if earlier parent-child conflicts on standards and values are active. Because of the importance of such early experiences, there is the risk of moving too quickly into potentially negative material; the therapist may become the recipient of these negative feelings before the relationship is sufficiently strong to tolerate them. Frequently, discussions of values and moral standards take on a rational, discursive, philosophical format and appear present-oriented, with the result that the affective component and reactions are unperceived or misunderstood.

In situations where the client is struggling to evaluate and to understand, the writer has found it helpful to share personal value concerns and dilemmas. This step seems to help some clients appreciate that the struggle is more widespread than his own and to obtain a more reality-based perception of the worker. It is also useful in helping the client to begin to understand the new demand of current psychosocial functioning—learning to live comfortably with uncertainty and change. Professionals clearly underserve their clients if they convey to them, either overtly or implicitly, certainties in these areas that they do not have or that others do not have. However, when therapists have arrived at value solutions and have found ways of resolving uncertainties, they can be helpful in sharing this success with clients. Clients do expect professionals to share their knowledge and views and the benefits of their experience as a way of answering their own questions. The risks of overusing authority are known, but failure can also result from not sharing knowledge and experience.

When professionals are involved in helping clients explore and struggle with value-related issues, much of the interview content will consist of "reflective thinking," the D material of Florence Hollis's outline.[7] This type of procedure leads the client to reflect upon a range of components of his significant environments and the nature of his responses to them. In these cases, the client should be helped to reflect on both the conceptual and attitudinal component of values and to look at their influence on himself and others. Although the focus will tend to be present-oriented, there will be some reflective consideration of the past and its influence on the present. Support will be needed, especially as the client struggles to risk new ideas or new actions. These are situations in which clients individually and jointly need information, new ideas, and the opportunity to reflect, discuss, and share. Because of this tendency, working with groups of parents, for example, with similar related concerns and value dilemmas can be rewarding to the professionals and helpful to the group members.

Implied in the need for discovery and discourse is the need to look for resources not ordinarily used, such as colleagues from the disciplines of theology and philosophy. Many persons in our society need direct contact with theologians and philosophers in a consultative role to struggle with moral, personal, and familial value dilemmas. Related to the possible need for information as well as an enabling and corrective experience, the possibility of clients' having mistaken or incorrect views and perceptions of significant others and systems in their lives can not be ignored. Of particular concern are persons who believe they have cut themselves off from significant groups—for example, church or family membership—because of their perceived violation of rules or norms. There has been a dramatic reevaluation of some moral and ethical positions in many societal systems that can accommodate a much wider range of viewpoints and practices than in an earlier day. Tremendous relief and comfort can be available to persons from friends, families, and systems when they find acceptance in lieu of expected rejection.

Another component of work with this kind of client is the question of the length of involvement. There are clients in this category for whom the present emphasis on short-

---

[7] Florence Hollis, *Casework: A Psychosocial Therapy* (New York: Random House, 1972), pp. 109–24.

term treatment is both adequate and the treatment of choice. However, factors are emerging to indicate that some identified value-based cases will require a much longer period of treatment, especially in situations where the value issues have revived significant earlier superego material that has to be reassessed. Often, these persons can be helped initially on a short-term basis, especially if a crisis has developed, but they will be underserved if the professionals involved do not offer the opportunity to build on the crisis through some further maturational progress of which they are capable. In this kind of situation, where a form of personal reevaluation and recommitment to the future based on the freedom gained in value shifts is taking place, probably four to six months of contact will be required.

The kinds of situations discussed in this article represent a range of therapeutic opportunities for which several current thought systems offer rich resources. Initially, the developmental and superego concepts are best understood and managed from an ego-psychological framework. Existential thinking is important to fully appreciate the questions of purpose and authenticity that value questions can raise. Crisis theory is necessary to understand the normalcy yet the wide-ranging effects of high-stress situations and their reopening of earlier life episodes. Crisis theory gives some clear indicators of the skills helpful to bring about growth-producing solutions. Finally, role theory is useful both for the therapist and the client to sort out changes in role perceptions and role enactment that result from alterations in ethics and values.

To responsibly understand and aid in such cases, a reexamination and use of social work's traditional knowledge of superego development and functioning, linked to current views on treatment, will provide social work professionals with the necessary knowledge and skill. Some research efforts should be made to clarify the extent and parameters of these cases and to experiment with alternate approaches.

CHAPTER 103

OUR CLIENTS, OURSELVES

The Spiritual Perspective and Social Work Practice

Patricia Sermabeikian

Spirituality in social work practice may be disputed by those who are pragmatic, who may ask about its usefulness in helping clients attain basic human needs such as food and shelter. Clients' use of spirituality as a weapon in their coping arsenal is precisely why spirituality must be acknowledged. Strengthening clients' abilities to develop viable strategies to both meet basic needs and maintain mental health is a social work goal.

Psychologist Carl Gustav Jung (1933, 1958, 1959) postulated that a universal concept of spirituality exists that, when explored, can enable a person to see beyond differences in religious beliefs and philosophical viewpoints. More than any other theorist, Jung integrated spirituality into clinical practice. His perspective can enhance social workers' sensitivity to the spiritual dimension of their clients, which may help the clients face their problems and difficulties.

In the tradition of social work practice, diligent effort has been made to provide a solid foundation of knowledge and skills to practitioners who intervene in human problems. Social workers aid people who are suffering because of myriad issues. Spirituality has found a place in the areas of death and dying and catastrophic illness or life events, but it has not been fully examined for its application in life and living. Spirituality is an important feature of social work practice and ethics and should be considered an area for educational and clinical training.

Reprinted from *Social Work,* Vol. 39, No. 2 (March 1994), pp. 178–183, by permission of NASW Press. Copyright 1994, National Association of Social Workers, Inc., *Social Work.*

IMPORTANCE OF SPIRITUALITY IN CLINICAL PRACTICE

What occurs between the client and the social worker involves not only the traditional interventions, methods, and skills the social worker applies, but also a two-way exchange of ideas, feelings, beliefs, and values that may or may not be directly addressed or acknowledged. Research has suggested that "patient values appear to be the second most powerful predictor of clinical bias; only patient social class is stronger" (Abramowitz & Dokecki, 1977, p. 465). Many value judgments are made in the treatment process, and social workers must continually be aware that nothing is value free. Objectifying approaches and interventions may be useful, but in doing so social workers must be careful not to deny or compartmentalize phenomena experienced in day-to-day practice.

Whether professionals are "believers" in the spiritual dimension is important. "Nonbelievers" may not be fully able to accept clients who consider spirituality and religion to be meaningful and useful within the context of their life experiences (Shafranske & Maloney, 1990). A spiritual bias can be just as harmful as racism or sexism. Goldstein (1987) convincingly argued that "students and seasoned professionals alike are bearers of significant moral, value and spiritual beliefs that are bound to find expression in work with individuals, families, and communities" (p 186).

EXPLORING THE SPIRITUAL PERSPECTIVE

Siporin (1985), in a discussion of clinical practice theory, observed the following:

> An examination of our perspectives requires that we sharpen our minds and eyes so as to see things clearly and fully. We will not, however, look under a nearby bright light for the treasures that we lost elsewhere, but rather we will search where it is dark, or where we can expect the sunlight to come up. There we may discover lost or new treasures or rediscover old gems in a new light. We seek just and beautiful truths for and in social work practice—fair to the evidence, clear, cleanly stated, revelatory, and illuminating. We want such truths so that they may propel us into new pathways of a more effective practice. (p. 198)

To understand the spiritual perspective, we must be willing to reverse our usual way of thinking and looking, which is linear and externally focused. We must look beyond what is easily counted and accounted for and examine what does not fit into our categories and conceptions of the world. There can be no preconceived notions about what may be helpful. The spiritual perspective requires that we look at the meaning of life, that we look beyond the fears and limitations of the immediate problem with the goal of discovering something inspirational and meaningful rather than focusing on the past and on pathology.

Jung sought to prove that the spiritual dimension is the essence of human nature. He was an investigator of the inner world who developed the theory of analytical psychology and a theory of personality that included a dynamic conceptualization of the physical, mental, and spiritual dimensions as striving for unity and wholeness within each person. He undertook a five-year personal journey into the layers and depths of the psyche and produced 18 volumes of work (Brome, 1978).

Among Jung's better-known concepts are the collective unconscious and the archetypes of the psyche, thought to contain the inherited and accumulated experiences of the human and prehuman species evidenced by the symbols, myths, rituals, and cultures of all times. Jung attempted to confirm this hypothesis by documenting and analyzing his own dreams and experiences and the dreams of his patients. He also studied and validated the archetypes as expressed in comparative religion studies and mythology (Brome, 1978; Campbell, 1971).

Mythologist Joseph Campbell (1988) referred to the ancient origins of spiritual practices in an interview with journalist Bill Moyers:

MOYERS: How do we learn to live spiritually?

CAMPBELL: In ancient times, that was the business of the teacher. He was to give you the clues to a spiritual life. That is what the priest was for. Also, that was what ritual was for. A ritual can be defined as an enactment of a myth. By participating in a ritual, you are actually experiencing a mythological life. And it's out of that participation that one can learn to live spiritually. (p. 182)

Among the archetypes is the spirit, which, in Jung's theory, is "universally present in the preconscious makeup of the human psyche" (Jung, 1959, p. 214). His concept of spirit is best exemplified in these passages:

The word "spirit" possesses such a wide range of application that it requires considerable effort to make clear to oneself all the things it can mean. Spirit, we say, is the principle that stands in opposition to matter. By this we understand an immaterial substance or form of existence, which on the highest and most universal level is called God. We imagine this immaterial substance also as the vehicle of psychic phenomena or even of life itself. . . .

Equally common is the view that spirit and psyche are essentially the same and can be separated only arbitrarily. Wundt takes spirit as "the inner being, regardless of any connection with an outer being." Others restrict spirit to certain psychic capacities or functions or qualities, such as the capacity to think and reason in contradistinction to the more "psychic" sentiments. Here spirit means the sum total of all phenomena of rational thought, or of the intellect, including the will, memory, imagination, creative power, and aspirations motivated by the ideals. (Jung, 1958, pp. 62–63)

Jung was considered by Sigmund Freud to be the most brilliant of his students in the "inner circle" of the psychoanalytic school, and he was Freud's chosen successor. But insurmountable differences developed between them that finally resulted in a personal and theoretical divergence. Jung rejected Freud's theory of the pleasure principle and postulated that the human being has a primary driving spirituality that is just as instinctive as sex, aggression, and hunger. He did not deny the presence of the biological drives but stated, "The wheel of history must not be turned back, and man's advance towards a spiritual life, which began with the primitive rites of initiation, must not be denied" (Jung, 1933, p. 123).

It has been suggested that Jung's rejection of Freud's sexual animality was, in part, his reaction to his sexual trauma in early youth. This factor contributed to his interest in spirituality and his striving "to reorient psychology to a higher spiritual plane" (Goldwert, 1986, p. 557). However, rather than simply reacting to his own experience, or being focused on the rejection of Freud's concepts, Jung apparently pursued the understanding of spirituality for its intrinsic value. He wrote, "We moderns are faced with the necessity of rediscovering the life of the spirit. We must experience it in ourselves. It is the only way we can break the spells that bind us to the cycle of biological events. . . . The human psyche from time immemorial has been shot through with religious feelings and ideas" (Jung, 1933, pp. 122–123).

SPIRITUALITY AND RELIGION

Some resistance to the spiritual perspective appears to be due to its being perceived as synonymous with religion. Although spirituality is expressed in religion, as well as philosophy and culture, it transcends ideologies, rituals, dogma, and institutions. As Siporin (1985) clearly explained,

> The spiritual element of the person is the aspect of an individual's psyche, consciousness and unconsciousness, that is also called the human soul. It is in terms of the spiritual dimension that a person strives for transcendental values, meaning, experience and development; for knowledge of an ultimate reality; for belonging and relatedness with the moral universe and community; and for union with the immanent, supernatural powers that guide people and the universe for good and evil. The spiritual aspect of the person is not subsumed or dealt with in psychoanalytic ego theory or in cognitive theory, though it has a place in Jungian and existentialist therapies. (pp. 210–211)

Religious views of spirituality have been contrasted with philosophical views of spirituality. Bergin's (1980, 1990) theistic values are based on Christian religious philosophy. Ellis's (1980) clinical humanistic–atheistic values are based on rational humanistic philosophy. A main element of this controversy concerns the existence and divinity of God. A hypothesis of God as existent or nonexistent, as an entity or a force remains one of the eternal ultimate reality issues in religion and philosophy.

The following commentary by Brome (1978) illustrates Jung's quest for the understanding of the reality of God:

> When Jung was confronted with this question, "Do you believe in God?" . . . Jung still tended to remain evasive. . . . He seems to refer to his Wise Old Man [archetype] as if the whole humanity were in touch with the God-like personification of the collective unconscious. . . . He describes God as the inexplicability of fate and the voice of conscience. . . . "All that I have learned has led me, step by

step, to an unshakable conviction of the existence of God. I do not take his existence on belief. I know that he exists." (p. 255)

The problem of the existence of God is a spiritual issue that each person struggles to resolve through experiences, philosophy, and religion.

SPIRITUALITY AND HUMANISM

Bergin and Jensen (1990) suggested that ideological differences between people may be bridged through the development of the perspective of spiritual humanism. This perspective encompasses the search for more universally accepted concepts that can be integrated into clinical practice.

Elkins, Hedstrom, Hughes, Leaf, and Saunders (1988) developed a humanistic definition of the components of spirituality that was designed to assess agreement or disagreement with statements reflecting their nine dimensions of spirituality: transcendent dimension, meaning and purpose in life, mission in life, sacredness of life, material values, altruism, ideals, awareness of the tragic, and fruits of spirituality. Elkins et al. admitted that what they had done was not "hard science" but felt that their initial steps "will help clarify, define, describe and perhaps even measure spirituality from a humanistic perspective" (p. 15).

The importance of the spiritual dimension is also noted by humanistic and existential theorists such as Frankl (1963), Fromm (1950), and Maslow (1962), who are outside the traditional religious ideologies. Maslow observed that "The human being needs a framework of values, a philosophy of life, a religion or religion-surrogate to live by and understand by, in about the same sense he needs sunlight, calcium, or love"; he believed that all people have a "cognitive need to understand" and to have a "validated, usable system of human values" (p. 206).

SPIRITUALITY AND TRANSFORMATION

Carl Rogers, another humanist, acknowledged, "I do believe that there is some kind of transcendent, organizing influence in the universe which operates in man as well. . . . My present very tentative view [of humans] is that there is an essential person which persists over time, or even through eternity" (cited in Bergin, 1990, p. 394). Jung described the transcendental function within the individual as "the psyche's remarkable capacity for metamorphosis" (cited in Jacobi, 1951, p. 190). People are able to change attitudes, to accomplish transitions, and to achieve the unity of oppositions, and this ability grows as they age.

Jacobi (1951) provided the following example of this transcendental capacity:

The diseased person or the person, too, for whom life has lost its meaning stands before problems with which he vainly struggles. The greatest and most important problems are basically insoluble; they must be so because they express the necessary polarity immanent in every self-regulating system. They cannot be solved, but only transcended. . . . This transcendence of the individual's personal problems reveals itself, however, as a raising of the level of consciousness. A loftier and wider interest comes into view, and through this broadening of the horizon the insoluble problem loses its urgency. It is not logically solved in its own terms but pales before a new and stronger vital direction. It is not repressed and made unconscious but simply appears in a new light and so becomes itself different. (p. 178)

Jung (1933) postulated that life's challenges, conflicts, and problems are necessary for the process of transformation by which a person changes from an instinctual being to a spiritual being. He noted that spiritual symbols and transcendental values such as spirit, faith, hope, surrender, and forgiveness are able to propel a change from one attitude to another. A person can use these human qualities to develop a higher potentiality. Jung believed spiritual and transcendental values can aid the therapeutic process by helping a person resolve suffering or painful issues so that they are able to recover, heal, and grow beyond them. When a person confronts painful issues, he or she may also question the reason, meaning, and purpose of life. For this reason Jung admonishes helping professionals to remember "that certain religious convictions not founded in reason are necessary for life for many people" (p. 193).

SPIRITUALITY AND PRACTICE

The Jungian spiritual perspective has been applied in the treatment of alcohol and substance abusers (Berenson, 1987; Krystal & Zweben, 1989). The recovering alcoholic who accepts a 12-step approach establishes a practical connection to a higher power. It has been found helpful in treatment for the client to create, in visualization, a symbol of his or her personal interpretation of the higher power in a spiritual dimension. The symbol is used to develop internal resources such as courage, strength, and willpower to help the client deal with painful emotions that may arise during the recovery process. Jungian concepts have also been applied in treatment and recovery from trauma and in dealing with issues such as grief, loss, and alienation (Breen, 1985; Klein, 1986).

Spirituality is a human need; it is too important to be misunderstood; avoided; or viewed as regressive, neurotic, or pathological in nature. Social workers must recognize that a person's spiritual beliefs, values, perceptions, feelings, and ideals are intrinsically connected to religious, philosophical, cultural, ethnic, and life experiences. It is important that the practitioner acknowledge that spirituality in a person's life can be a constructive way of facing life's difficulties.

As a human need, spirituality is multidimensional, and as such it can be manifested in healthy and unhealthy ways. Bergin (1990) noted that "spiritual phenomena have equal potential for destructiveness, as in the fundamentalist hate groups" (p. 401). Religious pathology, rigid ideologies, religious fervor associated with mental illness, cult involvement, and the nonconstructive consequences of certain beliefs and practices present additional challenges to professionals.

Acceptance of the spiritual perspective also requires that the client and practitioner develop a greater level of comfort in sharing spirituality. Powell (1988) and Renshaw (1984) recognized spiritual intimacy as one of the six forms of intimacy that operates in relationships: "Spiritual intimacy is created through the shared revelations of faith, beliefs and insights into spiritual matters," which can "help create a common bond, a context of belief in which understanding and trust can be fostered" (Powell, 1988, pp. 158–159).

Our professional knowledge and understanding of spirituality can be enhanced by an examination of traditional and nontraditional religions and of nonreligious human- istic and existential philosophies. Developing practice skill in addressing spirituality be- gins with acceptance of the values, beliefs, and attitudes that are fundamental to the client. When the client chooses to use spiritual perspectives, practitioner empathy and encouragement of client self-determination should follow. Clients may choose to pur- sue self-help group membership, church involvement, prayer, meditation, or commit- ment to a social action or cause. The practitioner should be willing to incorporate goals in treatment that include spiritual values for the accomplishment of tasks. When decid- ing what is in the client's best interests from his or her own perspective, the practitioner should consider spiritual issues.

The development of sensitivity and comfort in discussing the client's spiritual issues will help practitioners facilitate spiritual solutions in keeping with the client's belief sys- tem. A spiritual value or belief may connect to, or be, a powerful resource in the client's life that can be used in problem solving, coping, or the process of recovery or emotional healing. The practitioner who respects the client's spiritual values and beliefs may dis- cover that therapeutic benefits can be accomplished through them.

CONCLUSION

Social work values, beliefs, and ethics are based on certain tenets of faith and convic- tion about what we believe to be moral or good for individuals and society (Compton & Galaway, 1989). Our professional spirituality could be defined as the collective in- spiration derived from the ideal of human compassion or well-being that drives us to advance our cause. Social workers may have individual aspirations and interests, but there is a sense of unity in working toward an ultimate goal, which includes some trans- formation of society.

For social work, Jung's perspective can serve as a frame of reference for a spiritual examination of our profession and of our clients. We must explore the loftier issues of life because they are relevant to daily practice with clients. In the spiritual realm, we face the larger view and the meaning of life itself in a way that is difficult to explain and comprehend. The questions that are shrouded in mystery remain a challenge to our clients and ourselves. We must follow Jung's lead and embark on the journey to dis- cover the answers to questions that are part of the struggle toward human develop- ment.

REFERENCES

Abramowitz, C. V., & Dokecki, P. R. (1977). The politics of clinical judgement: Early empirical returns. *Psychological Bulletin, 84,* 460–476.

Berenson, D. (1987). Alcoholics Anonymous: From surrender to transformation. *Fam- ily Therapy Networker, 11,* 24–31.

Bergin, A. E. (1980). Religious and humanistic values: A reply to Ellis and Walls. *Journal of Consulting and Clinical Psychology, 48*, 642–645.

Bergin, A. E. (1990). Values and religious issues in psychotherapy and mental health. *American Psychologist, 46*, 394–403.

Bergin, A. E., & Jensen, J. P. (1990). Religiosity of psychotherapists: A national survey. *Psychotherapy, 27*, 3–7.

Breen, J. (1985). Children of alcoholics: A subterranean grieving process. *Psychotherapy Patient, 2*, 85–94.

Brome, V. (1978). *Jung, man and myth*. New York: Atheneum.

Campbell, J. (1971). *The portable Jung*. New York: Penguin Books.

Campbell, J. (1988). *The power of myth with Bill Moyers*. New York: Doubleday.

Compton, B. R., & Galaway, B. (1989). *Social work processes*. Belmont, CA: Wadsworth.

Elkins, D. N., Hedstrom, J. L., Hughes, L. L., Leaf, A. J., & Saunders, C. (1988). Toward a humanistic-phenomenological spirituality: Definition, description, and measurement. *Journal of Humanistic Psychology, 28*, 5–18.

Ellis, A. (1980). Psychotherapy and atheistic values: A response to A. E. Bergin's "psychotherapy and religious values." *Journal of Consulting and Clinical Psychology, 48*, 635–638.

Frankl, V. E. (1963). *Man's search for meaning*. New York: Washington Square.

Fromm, E. (1950). *Psychoanalysis and religion*. New Haven, CT: Yale University Press.

Goldstein, H. (1987). The neglected moral link in social work practice. *Social Work, 32*, 181–186.

Goldwert, M. (1986). Childhood seduction and the spiritualization of psychology: The case of Jung and Rank. *Child Abuse and Neglect, 10*, 555–557.

Jacobi, J. (1951). *The psychology of C. G. Jung*. New Haven, CT: Yale University Press.

Jung, C. G. (1933). *Modern man in search of a soul*. New York: Harcourt, Brace & World.

Jung, C. G. (1958). *Psyche and symbol*. Garden City, NY: Doubleday Anchor.

Jung, C. G. (1959). *The archetypes and the collective unconscious*. Princeton, NJ: Princeton University Press.

Klein, B. (1986). A piece of the world: Some thoughts about Ruth. *Women and Therapy, 5*, 33–40.

Krystal, S., & Zweben, J. (1989). The use of visualization as a means of integrating the spiritual dimension into treatment: Part 2. Working with emotions. *Journal of Substance Abuse Treatment, 6*, 223–229.

Maslow, A. H. (1962). *Toward a psychology of being*. Princeton, NJ: Van Nostrand Press.

Powell, W. E. (1988). The "ties that bind": Relationships in life transitions. *Social Casework, 11*, 556–562.

Renshaw, D. C. (1984). Touch hunger—A common marital problem. *Medical Aspects of Human Sexuality, 18*, 63–70.

Shafranske, E. P., & Maloney, H. N. (1990). Clinical psychologists' religious and spiritual orientations and their practice of psychotherapy. *Psychotherapy, 27*, 72–78.

Siporin, M. (1985). Current social work perspectives on clinical practice. *Clinical Social Work Journal, 13*, 198–217.

CHAPTER 104

RELIGIOUS CULTS, THE INDIVIDUAL AND THE FAMILY

Lita Linzer Schwartz and Florence W. Kaslow

In the late 1960's "hippies" and "flower children" ostensibly "dropped out" of a society filled with an unpopular war, poverty, racism, and materialism. In the 1970's, young adults have turned instead to a variety of religious cults that similarly present individuals with the opportunity to separate from their families, renounce the larger society and find a sense of belonging and of purpose in a visible and demarcated subculture. The counter culture of the 1960's featured drugs, sex and radical philosophy (Roszak, 1968); today's cults are drugless, ascetic, asexual, and politically more conservative. Although parents were disturbed and upset when their children became part of the "Haight-Ashbury" scene or drug oriented communes elsewhere, they knew that the choice was deliberate and hopefully only represented a transitional phase. That is often not the situation in the case of membership in today's pseudo-religious, expansion-minded cults.

An additional source of contemporary parental distress is the fact that becoming a cult[1] member involves a religious conversion; and acceptance of the new religion then frequently demands a complete rejection of the family as well as of its values, traditions and sanctions, while perhaps affording the opportunity the young adult seeks to rebel and escape to what *seems like a viable alternative to the family*. It may therefore represent initially a declaration of (personal) independence. The cults offer members a milieu in which to negate the technology, education, science and rationality which are so highly respected, even venerated, by their parents, and to replace these with learning acquired through spiritual devotion and mysticism. (Daner, 1976, p. VI)

Parents whose children embrace the cults have asked, "How could any religion that as its first consideration tries to break the biological and psychological bond between

Reprinted from *Journal of Marital and Family Therapy*, Vol. 5, No. 2 (1979), pp. 15–26, by permission of the publisher.

child and parents be good? How can they pose as Christians, when they reject one of the commandments that underpins the Judeo-Christian philosophy: 'Honor thy father and thy mother.'" (Adler, 1978). Therein lies the lure and strength of the cults' approach—a demand for complete fidelity and allegiance to their mission which provides a sense of meaning in life and a purpose for living for a confused, existentially adrift young person away from the influence of his or her parents which could dilute the intensity of the involvement.

Cult membership thus affects the family and the individual in ways more basic and destructive than earlier modes of withdrawal from the family orbit. Joining a cult is seen as a total and permanent commitment, whereas parents could at least hope that being a "hippie" was a temporary phase for their children. Cult membership becomes inextricably linked with the opportunity to help save the world by assisting "the Messiah" (Singer, 1979, p. 82) and who can defect from such a grandiose mission?

The Cult phenomenon has catapulted onto the national scene in the past decade. One reads with a mystified horror about the Manson gang in California and the mass suicide at Jonestown, Guyana. One sees young sari-wearing, head-shaven members of the Hare Krishna playing pitiful instruments, chanting and peddling literature on city sidewalks, or clean faced, wholesome looking Moonies selling candy or pretzels on corners to "raise money for my Church." Several descriptive and expository books have been written about the cults, but little has appeared in the professional literature which attempts to (1) analyze the dynamics of the families from which cult members come, (2) determine the common factors in the personality profiles of the recruits, (3) look at how the cults accomplish the conversions, (4) assess the impact of the cult experience and of either deprogramming or voluntary exodus from the movement, (5) the treatment interventions that might prove or have proven efficacious with troubled individuals and families who have become entangled with the cults.

Therefore, this article attempts to fill this gap by providing a concise overview of the main premises and features which appear central in one kind of cult, those which recruit from the upper-middle and upper class college student population. (We are speaking mostly about cults similar to the Unification Church [Moonies], Hare Krishna, Church of Scientology, the Jesus Movement and Alamo Christian Foundation). Further, it attempts to delineate and explicate, based on perusal of the existing literature, on clinical observations gleaned in treating ex-cultists, and on semi-structured in-person interviews with former cult members, their relatives, and with therapists and clergymen who have treated them once they have left the cult, some of the key ingredients that led to vulnerability and something about treatment strategies that seem to prove helpful.

This material is intended to provide tentative hypotheses about the young people who have become ensnared by the growing cult phenomenon that appears to entail brain-washing and extreme personality conversions, euphemistically called "snapping" because of the apparent instantaneous quality of the change. (Conway and Siegelman, 1978). It is further intended to stimulate dialogue among family therapists and hard research by clinicians so that we will be better able to comprehend the cults, their appeal and impact—perhaps to prevent some young people from joining and certainly to more knowledgeably and effectively treat those who have re-entered the larger society and their families when they seek our "healing" services.

INDIVIDUAL AND FAMILY DYNAMICS
AS PRECURSORS TO CULT VULNERABILITY

In the United States, adolescence is often a protracted period of personal limbo and turmoil. School, which teenagers often find irrelevant and boring, fills their days. Their relationships with their parents, though possibly under-girded with affection, suffer frequently from mutual misunderstandings tinged with resentment and recriminations of non-appreciation, the expectation of adolescent rebellion, and inter-generational conflict over values and life styles. The search for personal, individual identity and independence ascribed to this life stage (Erikson, 1968) is in conflict with the realities of the psychological and economic dependence they have on their parents and with their need for belonging, affiliation and reciprocal loyalties (Nagy and Spark, 1973). Idealism, with concomitant anger at parental hypocrisy, real or exaggerated, and at the ills and injustices that exist in our society, is a dominant value in the late teens and early twenties. Social disorganization and political chicanery further contribute to feelings of alienation and disillusionment.

One's failure to individuate and achieve a strong sense of separate identity, and at the same time, the inability to reduce the feeling of loneliness, is a serious hazard in a complex society. The resulting unpredictable behavior, rapid mood swings, role confusion and identity diffusion, described so clearly by Erikson (1950), parallels the general profile that appears in the literature about the young people successfully recruited by the cults and proselytization movements. According to published descriptions (JCRC Report, 1976; Daner, 1976) they evidence:

1. Willingness to accept a leader as a major source of authority and arbiter on acceptable behavior to whom they become extremely devoted
2. A disturbed time perspective
3. Use of a group identity to reduce the sense of personal "incompleteness"
4. Acceptance of a rigid belief system that results in clannishness and intolerance of non-believers
5. A confusion of values
6. A search for a prescribed and structured daily routine

The emerging young adult, usually from an upper middle-class background, rejects the obvious materialism surrounding him,[2] and attempts to disassociate himself from the ambition, narcissistic pursuits, and superficial concerns that appear to consume his parents' lives. At the same time, the youth seems to sense a serious deficit within the family, an absence of ethical/moral/spiritual values in actual practice and the lack of a raison d'etre.

There is ample evidence to demonstrate that parents who are leaders in community affairs, ostensible or real subscribers to religious values, and who genuinely try to be "good" parents may also be afflicted with rebellious children, as are non-leaders and negligent parents. A few examples should suffice to make the point. In 19th century Alsace, the brothers Ratisbonne, sons of the lay leader of the Jewish community, not only were converted to Catholicism, but founded a religious order (Congregation of Notre Dame de Sion), the mission of which was to educate and convert Jewish children. (Isser,

1978). In Britain's royal family, Edward VIII was the ultimate rebel in rejecting not only his parents' values, but a kingdom. Closer to home, public officials have children who are arrested in connection with drug sales or possession, and psychotherapists have children who evidence severe "behavior problems" in school. The publicity, sometimes notoriety, that accompanies these events heightens the feelings of guilt, hurt, resentment, shame and anger felt by the parents. These "negative" emotions, which provoke anguish and turmoil, are also in conflict with the affection that parents hold, or claim to, for their errant children.

What kinds of underlying dynamics have been observed in families whose children must yank themselves away from the bonds of family ties so forcefully as to be vulnerable to the pull of a cult? Some patterns we have observed follow. In some cases, seemingly exemplary parents hold out a model of perfection that their children are unable to fulfill; in other situations the closeness much admired by friends is a pseudo-mutual one (Wynne, 1958) or an expression of an overly enmeshed family (Minuchin, 1967).

The extreme dependency evidenced by many of those who accept the recruiter's bait and become embroiled in the cult, further substantiates the supposition that they grew up in quite enmeshed families. Vickers (1977) notes that earlier periods in history were characterized by the high value placed on *responsibility*—to family and community. Such responsibility *to others* is a hallmark of the enmeshed family. Today's culture, however, values personal *autonomy* more than responsibility. Because these two values conflict, children from enmeshed families experience a real bind in trying to survive in an autonomy-valuing world. This may be why they are so susceptible to giving up autonomy in favor of an even more confining/enmeshing group that they can be responsible to for all their behavior. It will tell them exactly what to do, when and how.

Another dynamic which appears clinically is that contradictory communications from "good" parents have been internalized—"we love you tremendously *but* we resent your continuing needs and demands and want time alone—(to follow our own inclinations)—so you must go to camp, boarding school and/or far away to college." All of this is communicated at the meta-level; at the manifest level it is expressed as "camp is the best possible way for you to spend the summer, and therefore, we are sending you away because we love you and want you to have the best." . . . Often few rules of behavior have been incorporated since external structure was missing. Frequently, the father, who is upwardly mobile and determined to become successful, is away from home, working long hours to support his family or for personal aggrandizement, or playing golf to "make contacts" to enhance his career. Thus, the presence and influence of the father as a male authority figure has been minimal. (As might be anticipated, those non-vulnerable young adults we have talked to, taught, or treated, indicated strong, sometimes domineering, fathers whose expectations about acceptable behavior were quite clear. The strength of the father-child relationship appears to be a critical factor in the vulnerability/non-vulnerability of youth to cult recruitment. Those who have had a reasonably satisfying ongoing relationship with a strong father do not need to become part of an organization headed by an omniscient and omnipotent father figure.

In addition to the individuation and rebelliousness of adolescence, and the searching by this group for a strong father-person as a source of guidance and wisdom, other conditions usually are present to increase vulnerability in the young adult. Cult recruiters tend to look for the "loners," the disillusioned or floundering ones and those who are depressed. (Stoner and Park, 1977; Patrick, 1976). Other likely recruits are those who are confused by rapidly changing values, perhaps between keeping virginity and succumbing to peer and libidinal pressures to become involved sexually, and who therefore seek external authoritative answers to resolve their inner conflicts in preference to having to make their own difficult choices. Or, some of the vulnerable are extremely anxious about the responsibilities of adulthood and welcome the cocoon of perennial childhood offered by the cults (Rice, 1976). As indicated earlier, many have been reared in permissive homes and crave more structure and direction.

In the case of converts to the Jesus movement, it has been suggested that many of them (97% in one sample) have simply moved from *drug addiction to a different sort of dependency* (Simmonds, 1977). This last adaptive response is a more voluntary one, however, than most of those being stressed here, and may even be viewed by some parents as less harmful than drug addiction. (JCRC Report, 1976, p. 11) Nevertheless, the possibility is raised that involuntary converts may also be "addictive personalities," highly anxious, low in self-confidence (Peele and Brodsky, 1975), and dependent on external persons or organizations for answers to their personal and existential questions. As noted in the introductory comparison of youth and sub-culture in the 1960's and 1970's, the surface differences do not totally mask the basic similarities of meeting affiliation and dependency needs, providing an alternative family to the one from which the rebellious young person is trying to individuate and/or escape, and a way of asserting one's uniqueness.

Salzman, in an intriguing article on "Types of Religious Conversions" (1966), discusses several cases, principally those he calls "regressive" conversions. In discussing one treatment case involving a Protestant who planned to convert to Catholicism and to become a monk in an ascetic order, he writes:

> Shortly before he began therapy he detailed his plans for conversion in a long letter to his family which was full of both subtle and direct hostility, directed primarily at his father. His family had always been quite antagonistic to the Catholic Church; *thus his plans represented a double blow to them since he proposed both joining the Church they disapproved of, and removing himself forever from contact with them.** (pp. 16–17)

The parallel to those joining the cults should be apparent, although in the case chronicled by Salzman, the proposed conversion is clearly voluntary, whereas in the cults it is not.

RECRUITMENT AND CONVERSION

Cult recruiters are trained to look for the apparently friendless and "lost." They offer a gentle, supportive affection, followed usually by an invitation to join the recruiter for dinner at the latter's home. Here, the friends of the recruiter make the lonely one feel that he is part of their circle—warmly welcomed, the center of their loving attention.

---

* Italics inserted by current authors.

The evening's discussion focuses on the group's efforts to help those who are disadvantaged, to rid society of its ills, and perhaps to save the world from destruction. Religion is rarely mentioned, although it is obvious in the case of the Hare Krishna movement. At the end of the evening, the "recruit," who has been accorded seemingly *unconditional acceptance,* is invited to return for a weekend or longer. If he does so, he is again greeted with warmth and, in addition, is constantly surrounded by his new friends. The activities of singing, listening to lectures, communal eating and work activities, and prayer are again "low-key," but very enticing and gratifying, and verge on the hypnotic. The astute leaders fill every moment so that the newcomer has little time to think about what he is experiencing (Lofland, 1977; Adler, 1978; Stoner and Parke, 1977; Weisen, 1977a).

The technique used is the classic method of thought reform or coercive persuasion. This requires continuous supervision and indoctrination in a fully controlled environment. Such an environment often takes the form of a retreat in a setting isolated from telephones and other normal communication channels; every escape route is blocked. Simultaneously, the victim is *"robbed of the usual social supports of his beliefs and values; . . . he is subjected to a massive pressure to conform to a new, unanimous society . . ."* (Holt, 1964, p. 296). Isolated from the familiar and surrounded with a smothering blanket of "love," based on a well devised strategy called "love bombing" (JCRC Report, 1976), the recruit feels guilty if he rejects the messages being given him. As this "visit" continues, the group focuses on the recruit's weaknesses, assaulting aspects of his previous identity, and applying the principles of behavioral reinforcement systematically. Ties to family members, former associations, and personal standards must be destroyed if resistance to the new ideology is to be overcome. Sincerity and enthusiasm for the movement and *its* ideology must be generated and positively reinforced in order to gain the youth's total commitment. In this process, a new identity is created. The conversion to the cult is complete when the individual himself sets out to proselytize others. (Schwartz and Isser, 1978; Salzman, 1966). As Hacker, a forensic psychiatrist, pointed out in discussing terrorists and crusaders, modern conversion techniques are "novel in that they produce not merely consent but inner conviction" (Hacker, 1976).

Holt's description of the features of the educational phase of the thought reform process, which appears in a chapter entitled, *"Forcible indoctrination and personality change"* (1964, pp. 295–298) is indeed chilling. He indicates that:

1. Thought reform is prolonged;—it goes on for months or years.
2. It is conducted continuously around the clock (also Singer, 1979).
3. It occurs in a completely controlled environment—no contrary information is available.
4. It utilizes social aspects of environmental control: "on the one hand, . . . (he is) robbed of the usual social supports of his beliefs and values; on the other, he is subjected to a massive pressure to conform to a new unanimous society . . ." (p. 296).
5. Thought reform is personalized.
6. There is a lack of privacy.
7. There is an assault upon previous identity.

8. There is systematic application of rewards and punishments.
9. Sincerity and enthusiasm are demanded—"total emotional commitment to the new idea" (p. 297) is mandatory.
10. All sources of resistance to the new ideology are exhausted—fostering "symbolic death of the old personality" (p. 297).
11. "Thought reform demands that its victims be active in reforming others" (p. 297)—proselytizing.
12. Synthesis and reconstruction—birth of a new identity.

It is not surprising that the group of cults under consideration here share in common the following characteristics and that they utilize many techniques elucidated by Holt to indoctrinate and convert.

1. A charismatic leader
2. Demand total submission to an overriding male authority (father-God figure)
3. Engage in conversion to their rigid belief system that perceives all non-believers (non-members) as the enemy
4. Demand complete commitment to the cult group as one's family and a negation of ties to the family of origin
5. A communal life style
6. Restrict communications with non-members—except for—
7. Active recruitment efforts
8. Physiologic deprivation (of food, rest, health care)
9. Fund raising for the leader and cult community, ranging from selling various items to surrender of all of one's assets

We have frequently been asked how these cults differ from close knit, ethnocentric religious groups such as the Mormons, Amish and Orthodox Jews. Despite some resemblances, key fundamental differences include that the family as a whole is encouraged to be active in the church and to be concerned for one another, that deprivation of adequate nutrition, sleep and health care are not sanctioned, one is expected to have personal belongings and a family place of residence, and privacy is accorded to all.

IMPACT ON THE FAMILY

The negative impact on the family of this involvement with the cults is greater than the usual reaction to youthful alienation because of the way in which it occurs. There is a perception of entrapment, of uninformed consent, of cunning recruitment efforts, that is very frightening. There is also the parents' realization that at some deep, unconscious level their offspring has moved very far away from them emotionally, rejecting them and their heritage—and this is extremely painful. The rejection may well have been a two way process. Efforts to reestablish contact may stir up the young person's fears of again becoming overly dependent or attached and the parent's fears of battling anew. Parents also realize it may be extremely difficult to break through to the individual's pre-cult behaviors when he is surrounded constantly by members of his new, potent, replacement "family." Attempts by the family of origin, when contact is re-established, if this is possible, to reason with the youth may only result in driving him "underground" within the cult; that is, the cult may relocate the member and make his whereabouts impossible to trace. Deceptive answers from cult leaders such as "we do not know where your son is" are not uncommon. Apart from efforts to kidnap and "deprogram"[3] the young adult, efforts presently floundering in a legal quagmire, (ACLU, 1977), and which may also prove deleterious to the young person's mental health since they are usually carried out against his wishes (JCRC Report, 1976, pp. 35–36), what happens within the family when one of the young adult children is "lost" in this way?

Any number of emotional reactions occur, depending upon the individual personalities, interrelationships, and undercurrents present in a given family unit. Shock and bewilderment—"How and why did this happen to *us?*"—are initial responses. Following this, parents may be overwhelmed by a sense of failure and guilt, in that they were not supportive of or involved enough with their child, or they were too permissive and overly involved, or did not provide him with sufficient ego-strength and sense of self to resist the beckoning persuasion of the cult. They may be very hostile to the straying child, feeling that the episode is deliberately directed against them by an ungrateful, disloyal, and retaliatory child. They may be furious at the cult and its deceptive recruiting tactics and at the government for allowing such pseudo-religious groups to operate, protecting them under provisions of freedom of religion and granting them tax exempt status. Often they feel devastated, helpless, hopeless, with nowhere to turn. The family's sudden and continuing sense of loss and unresolved grief is sometimes analogous to that felt by families who have experienced the death of a child. They may blame each other for the child's abandonment of all they consider of value, thus precipitating a marital crisis.

Note that throughout, most parents view the individual in question as a child, not *as* an adult, and therefore as not ready to make his own decisions. This may not be totally in error. Holt (1964) and other investigators have indicated that part of the thought reform process involves reducing the individual to child-like dependence. It seems that such regression is essential so that transformation of a person's cognitive processes and personality organization can occur. Conway and Siegelman (1978) label this phenomenon of seemingly sudden, drastic personality change *snapping;* this word encapsulates the moment at which the person takes on a new identity, adheres to the cult's articles of faith totally, believes in the omnipotence of the cult's spiritual leader, is willing to proselytize for the movement and in many cults—sees non-believers as "being with Satan". Also, as to their being children, if they were more mature, autonomous and self-directing—they would not be vulnerable to the seduction of the cults which require submergence, even destruction, of one's uniqueness and independence.

There may also, of course, be physical consequences for parents in the form of a heart attack or severe psychosomatic reactions—uncontrollable crying, self punishment, or irrational outbursts. Younger siblings may be bewildered, frightened, hostile, or extremely anxious. The parents may also become concerned about the possible influence of the cult convert on these younger siblings as cults encourage members to actively recruit their brothers and sisters. Inter-generational conflicts may erupt. In short, the very fabric of the family is threatened (Weisen, 1977b) by a bigger, richer, more powerful, alternative family. Clearly therapeutic intervention is often needed to help family members cope with this crisis in their midst.

THERAPEUTIC INTERVENTION

The mental health professions have been accused of not assuming leadership in attempting to understand the appeal of cults, the myriad problems enmeshment in them evokes for the member and his family, in helping bereaved parents deal with the family crisis, or in treating de-programmed ex-cultists (Conway and Siegelman, 1978). Many therapists have remained remote from the cult scene, not attempting to become knowledgeable about this new phenomenon. Although some groups of therapists have held program meetings on the topic, this has tended to be the exception for professional organizations. Only now are papers and panels on the cults slowly beginning to appear on conference programs. There is a dearth of literature on the topic in the professional journals—which seems to confirm the accusation of non-concern and involvement. Numerous well respected therapists have told us that there is nothing special one needs to know to treat this population since cult membership is only a new manifestation of adolescent rebellion and should be handled as such; thus missing the added dimensions wrought from such a total experience and the accompanying traumatic personality and life style changes.

When parents of a young cultist turn to their churches, communal agencies, or private therapists for help, they rarely find anyone who is conversant with the many facets of this complex problem (Levine and Slater, 1976). In an excellent comprehensive report on "The Challenge of the Cults," a special study committee of the Jewish Community Relations Council of Greater Philadelphia (1976, pp. 47–78), came up with specific recommendations regarding *Help for Parents* which we have paraphrased and expanded considerably with the intent of making them valid for many communities and religious groups. Parents who learn that their child is in a cult need to know where to get information, advice, and aid. They need factually correct data about what cults are and particularly about the specific cult that has indoctrinated their own child (Singer, 1979). They need to know what their options are in terms of responding to this situation, that is, what has worked for other parents who have been confronted with a similar problem and what the legal ramifications of different options are likely to be. The assistance they require will probably include legal, psychological, social, and possibly financial aid. More specifically:

1. There is a need for a central clearinghouse in each community through which parents can make their initial contact with the agencies and/or individuals who may be able to help them. Family Service Agencies and Community Mental Health Centers are good possibilities and may designate several staff members who have (or are willing to acquire) special expertise on the subject.

2. The availability of an agency as a central clearinghouse should be publicized widely. Special mailings might go to clergy, educators, college counselors, therapists, family physicians and others who are likely to have the first contact with a distraught parent so that these people will know where to refer them.

3. Community agencies and religious institutions should develop a cooperative network for the provision of services to parents of cult members so that the factual material accumulated can be disseminated to all helping professionals for use with parents, thus giving them a solid data base upon which to evaluate the options being considered.

4. Provision of *group counseling* for parents of cult members is a sound and desirable practice. They seem to need a special support system of others who are experiencing the same plight, share their consternation, can candidly discuss feelings and together explore ways to cope and actions to take.

5. Many of the family's difficulties that seem to have exacerbated the susceptibility of a young person to the lure of the cults stem from longstanding problems and uncertainties that parents have about their effectiveness as parents. Programs such as standard Parent Effectiveness Training might be appropriate to help group members develop better parenting skills, thereby diminishing the vulnerability of their younger children. Or in a parents' support or therapy group, their self blame and guilt can be a focal point; once this is reduced and the reality of their child's involvement confronted head on, they may be enabled to pick up the threads of their own shattered lives and begin to plan more effectively for next steps regarding the family's missing member specifically and their overall functioning more generally.

6. Therapists who are consulted by parents should be cognizant of the legal issues that surround what is called "kidnapping" one's own child back—at least enough to recommend that the parents contact an attorney knowledgeable about this topic, and about the legal decisions in earlier pertinent cases. They should also be well informed about the pros and cons of deprogramming and the possible long-lasting effects of one's having been a committed cult member—malnutrition, other diseases since medical care is negligible, a sense of loss and isolation when the close-knit cult support group is unavailable if one has been snatched away from it unwillingly, confusion about the two very different realms in which one has lived, residual thought disorders, guilt and shame over their earlier responsiveness to the cult, listlessness and a lack of purpose, and sometimes a frantic zeal to help "save" and deprogram others.

LIFE AFTER THE CULT AND TREATMENT CONSIDERATIONS

Many young people who are involuntarily deprogrammed, and some who voluntarily leave the cults and rejoin their own families, seek professional help during the re-entry and readjustment phase. We believe it is incumbent upon therapists who are called upon to treat this population that they have an understanding of the cult phenomenon and what it means to join one, to live within its habitat and share the cult life style, to leave it and to be reunited with one's nuclear family. Some ex-cult members report they were told that deprogrammers "are of Satan", that if they leave the cults they are "doomed to be invaded by Satan", and that many other horrors will befall them—intimidating and traumatic pronouncements indeed.

The impact of such an experience is staggering on all family members. There is likely to be a mixture of many conflicted feelings—parental joy that their offspring is home, tempered by anger or confusion over the original renunciation of them. The ex-cultist may be partially relieved to be back in the outside world and wondering how he got "hooked", he may be fearful of punishment by the cult for his defection, he may experience periods of "floating" and altered states of consciousness, or he may yearn to return to an "Ashram" or other cult residence and resent his parents' latest interference in his life. Frequently a profound depression is experienced. Because of the complexities of these situations, the fragility of the family relationships, the fears and hurts that have been sustained—each case should be carefully evaluated and the treatment of choice recommended.

We have come to the conclusion that since one's family background and relationships appear to contribute to one's vulnerability to the cult's invitation to join as well as to one's leaving of the cult, family involvement in the treatment is often essential for lasting progress to be made and for family members to attain a better understanding of one another, respect for each other's differences, needs and goals. Thus, all members of the family unit should be involved in treatment. If the intensity of the conflict between parents and ex-cult member is extremely high, it is quite probable that concurrent treatment is more feasible, at least at the beginning, so that the ex-cult member has a caring, "tuned-in" therapist all to himself, who may represent, as the cult did, an authority source and ego ideal outside of the family, but this time one who does not demand total loyalty and renunciation of the parents. In this way, each of the parties can separately receive all the attention and concern and have a private time to ventilate feelings and clarify thoughts. If each voices some desire for a rapprochement, then it is likely they can be seen concurrently by the same therapist. However, if the antagonism is still acute and mistrust rampant, it is advisable that they see different therapists who can collaborate without violating confidentiality. Where, during the initial family evaluation session(s), it appears everyone is interested in working on the problems together, then conjoint family therapy constitutes the most efficacious treatment strategy.

It is important to try to comprehend the function the young adult's joining of the cult served for the family system. Was this already a scapegoated member being extruded, was he diverting attention from an about to erupt parental war in order to save his mother and father's marriage; or was he perhaps designated to lead the family on a quest for spiritual fulfillment? An adequate mapping of the family's genogram and understanding of their equilibrating mechanisms and structure is essential in helping them toward greater awareness of their needs and transactions as they strive toward wholeness and health. The former cult member often suffers something akin to withdrawal symptoms during the period following his exodus, and one of these is the loss of a sense of group belonging and the feeling of identity and mission this provides. Thus, it is often advisable to involve the young person in a therapy group with other ex-cult members who are facing similar dilemmas and with whom he can sympathize, share, identify, and seek solutions. Such an involvement in group therapy can occur during the same time that the person participates in family therapy so that healthy peer group ties are fostered which replace those that may have been abruptly terminated. Often the ex-cult member feels alien to his pre-cult friends and needs to establish new meaningful friendships; the therapy group provides a transitional place to do this. Regardless which treatment modality is selected, it is crucial that the therapist be clear about his own views on the cults, be able to articulate his ideas if asked what he really thinks, and that these are consistent with the ethical values and philosophy that undergird his therapeutic practice. An optimistic outlook is important; to convey pessimism is to exacerbate the despair deep within the patients. They yearn to know if they will ever again function effectively as independent, competent individuals not prone to floating and thought dissociations.

In some instances, the young adult should not move back into his parents' home, yet to live alone would be to heighten the pervasive sense of isolation. Perhaps mental health professionals might be instrumental in collaborating with other public spirited citizens in seeing that attractive, high quality, small group residences are developed in which ex-cult members can reside with a sense of both camaraderie and privacy; of belonging and independence; of mutual concern and individual responsibility; residences that offer group therapy and wholesome group activities and are staffed by "house parents" who can provide necessary, but not intrusive, nurturance and guidance.

Since many of the ex-cult members gravitate into pseudo-religious cults, one can assume some of the attraction is related to a spiritual-religious quest. Thus, the healing process might well need to minister also to the individual's unmet spiritual needs. A communique from Rabbi Gerald Wolpe (1978) speaks cogently to this point:

> I have met enough cultists and former cult members to realize that therapy has to take the religious phenomenon into consideration. It may be a "culte de moi" but these children are speaking in religious and pseudo-religious terms. The vocabulary is quite clear, and in many cases, thoroughly traditional. If that vocabulary is misunderstood or ignored, then therapeutic activity is doomed from the very beginning . . . From time to time, I deal with families of both Jewish and Christian persuasion who have to adjust to a returning former cultist . . . Much of the strain deals with the inability of the family to accept the fact that there is a serious spiritual vacuum in the . . . family values. The cultic member is caught between his sense of love and loyalty to the family to which he wants to return [including the knowledge that he has caused pain to others] and his sense of déjà vu in a spiritually bereft home. Many of the youngsters have said to me after some weeks at home, "nothing has changed; they are the same and they just don't understand that they are hypocrites." In a significant cross identification [transference]*, they will make the same accusation towards their therapist accusing him/her of "secularism", a position that they hold in great disdain. They contrast the definite value position of their former cult setting with the ambivalence of a technique (therapy) that seems to urge a vague adjustment.
>
> In no way is my reaction to be construed as a crusade for using clergymen as therapists; they (most of them) are not trained in that direction . . . However, as it is recommended that clergymen learn therapeutic techniques and values in order to become more conversant with their utilization and to recognize their own limitations, so it is imperative for therapists . . . to recognize the essential key of the spiritual element in this process and problem.

Given the above, any therapist treating ex-cultists and/or their families must have a great depth and breadth of knowledge and skill to draw upon, the flexibility to use an appropriate combination of treatment modalities—individual, group and family, as well as to collaborate with religious leaders and pastoral counselors, to help make special living arrangements, to construct support systems and perhaps to help move the young person back into college or toward a fulfilling job.

---

* Bracketed words inserted by authors.

SUMMARY

In this article we have tried, in bold strokes, to paint a collage regarding those who become cult members and the ramifications of their involvement on their entire family.

Although the cults do not publish membership statistics, they jointly claim millions of members. The Unification Church (Moonies) alone officially claims 30,000 members in the United States (JCRC Report, 1976, p. 15). Thus, since a sizeable number of young people and their families are involved and will continue to be affected by this phenomenon which has traumatic reverberations for those affected, it is incumbent upon therapists to learn about, try to make sense of, and be ready to treat this population and to contribute to the body of literature on this subject. We believe concurrent or conjoint family therapy usually constitutes the treatment of choice and that whenever feasible, group therapy should be used as an adjunct to family therapy for the ex-cult member. This is a fertile field for basic and applied research; one we dare not ignore if we believe in doctrines of free will, personal responsibility, individuality, autonomy, physical and mental health, and self actualization.

REFERENCES

Adler, W. Rescuing David from the Moonies, *Esquire,* (June 6), 1978, *89,* (10), 23–30.

American Civil Liberties Union, *Civil Liberties,* Sept. 1977.

Conway, F. & Siegelman, J. *Snapping: American's Epidemic of Sudden Personality Change,* Philadelphia: J. B. Lippincott, 1978.

Daner, F. J. *The American Children of Krsna,* New York: Holt, Rinehart and Winston, 1976.

Erikson, E. H. *Childhood and Society,* New York: W. W. Norton, 1950.

Erikson, E. H. *Identity: Youth and Crisis,* New York: W. W. Norton, 1968.

Hacker, F. J. *Crusaders, Criminals, Crazies: Terror and Terrorism in our Time,* New York: W. W. Norton, 1976. (particularly chapter on "Rape of the Mind")

Holt, R. R. "Forcible indoctrination and personality change". In P. Worschel and D. Byrne, (Eds.) *Personality Change,* New York: John Wiley, 1964, 289–318.

Isser, N. The Mallet affair: Case study of a scandal. Unpublished manuscript, 1978.

Jewish Community Relations Council of Greater Philadelphia Committee Report, *The Challenge of the Cults,* Philadelphia: JCRC, 1976.

Levine, S. V. and Slater, N. E. Youth and contemporary religious movements: psychosocial findings. *Canadian Psychiatric Association Journal,* 1976, *21,* 211–420.

Lofland, J. *Doomsday Cult,* (enlarged ed.), New York: Irvington Publishers, 1977.

Minuchin, S., Montalvo, Braulio, et al. *Families of the Slums,* New York: Basic Books, 1967.

Nagy, I. B. and Spark, G. *Invisible Loyalties,* New York: Harper and Row, 1973.

Patrick, T. (With T. Dulack), *Let Our Children Go,* New York: E. P. Dutton, 1976.

Peele, S. and Brodsky, A. *Love and Addiction,* New York: Taplinger Publishing, 1975.

Rice, B. Messiah from Korea: Honor thy Father Moon. *Psychology Today,* Jan. 1976, *9,* (8), 36–47.

Roszak, T. *The Making of a Counter Culture,* New York: Anchor Books, 1968.

Salzman, L. Types of religious conversion, *Pastoral Psychology,* 1966, *17,* (8), 8–20; 66.

Schwartz, L. L. Cults and the vulnerability of Jewish youth, *Jewish Education,* 1978, *46,* (2), 23–26; 42.

Schwartz, L. L., and Isser, N. "A note on involuntary techniques". *Jewish Social Studies,* 1979, in press.

Simmonds, R. B. Conversion or addiction. *American Behavioral Scientist,* 1977, *20,* 909–924.

Singer, M. T. Coming out of the cults, *Psychology Today,* Jan. 1979, 72–82.

Stoner, C. and Parke, J. A. *All Gods Children: Salvation or Slavery?* Radnor, Pa.: Chilton Book Co., 1977.

Vickers, G. The weakness of western culture, *Futures,* 1977, *9.*

Wiesen, I. Inside Alamo, *Jewish Press,* Sept. 2, 1977 (a).

Wiesen, I. Mind Control, *Jewish Press,* Sept. 9, 1977 (b).

Wolpe, Rabbi G. Private communication, Nov. 1978.

Wynne, L. C. et al. Pseudomutuality in the family relations of schizophrenics, *Psychiatry,* 1958, *21,* 205–220.

NOTES

1. Cult is used herein to denote a group of people who submit to the authority of a self-proclaimed (and often charismatic) religious leader, and who are united by a rigid set of "sacred" beliefs and attitudes shaped by that leader, and who, as a result, tend to be estranged from reality and their fellow humans (after Salzman, 1966).

2. He is used in the generic, literary sense and not intended to have any sexist, political connotation.

3. Deprogrammers like Ted Patrick employ many of the same "thought reform" techniques as do cult leaders—restricted environment, sleep deprivation, positive reinforcement for desired changes in behavior—but for a more socially acceptable end. One must question here if the ends therefore justify the means. It is also important to note the similarity to Skinnerian behavior modification approaches and to techniques used by est and at marathon sessions at growth centers.

CHAPTER 105

FROM CONSULTATION TO THERAPY IN GROUP WORK WITH PARENTS OF CULTISTS

Arnold Chanon Bloch and Ron Shor

Parents whose children have been involved in destructive cults are a special population. Nonetheless, elements of group treatment of this population have broad applicability to work with families: First, it deals with the effects of an externally imposed traumatic loss upon the family system. Second, it examines how an external system can intrude upon the family system and exacerbate normal problems of separation. Third, it illustrates how a group process can stabilize and empower the family to reach out and assist children in crisis and work toward reunification.

Michael Langone defines a destructive cult as "a highly manipulative group which exploits and sometimes physically and/or psychologically damages members and recruits."[1] In the 1970s and 1980s cult groups became more prevalent and sophisticated. Current estimates indicate that 2,500–3,000 cults exist in the United States and that between two million and three million Americans, mostly between the ages of eighteen and twenty-five years, are involved in cults.[2]

As mental health professionals, the authors do not seek to proclaim one particular religious belief or practice over another, nor do they wish to evaluate the integrity and worth of those who offer instant healing through mass therapies. Rather, the effects of

Reprinted from *Social Casework,* Vol. 70, No. 4 (1989), pp. 231–236, by permission of the publisher, Families International, Inc.

[1] Michael D. Langone, *Destructive Cultism: Questions and Answers* (Weston, Mass.: American Family Foundation, 1982), p. 2.
[2] Louis West and Margaret T. Singer. "Cults, Quacks, and Non-Professional Psychotherapists," in *Comprehensive Textbook of Psychiatry III,* ed. Harold I. Kaplan, Alfred M. Freedman, and Benjamin J. Sadock (Baltimore: Williams and Wilkins, 1980), pp. 32–48.

unorthodox beliefs and practices on the cult member and his or her family are the focus of concern. Most of these beliefs and practices are untested and not subject to any outside system of ethics because of a cult's tendency toward secrecy and isolation. This lack of a system of checks and balances to monitor the activities of radical groups makes participation in such groups risky and potentially dangerous.

Destructive cults are relatively closed systems and are usually set in opposition to the mainstream society and/or family. Their use of manipulative or mind control techniques make it especially difficult and complicated to reach out to the cultist. The cultist's family, therefore, is often the only available resource with which to work. The rationale for working with such families is not only to create a bridge to the cultists, but also to fulfill the family's need for support and advice. Although these families may be supported by relatives and friends, such individuals may not be helpful to these families in discussing problems related to the unfamiliar and stigma-laden cult phenomenon.

A short-term parents' group of ten sessions was conducted at the Cult Clinic of Jewish Family Service of Los Angeles. The participants were recruited from an ongoing parents' support group. The therapy group was co-led by two social workers with different primary therapeutic orientations. One was an expert in cult work who integrated transactional analysis into his work; the other expert integrated the "double-bind" theory into an ecosystems approach.

THEORETICAL CONCEPTS APPLIED TO CULT RECRUITMENT AND INDOCTRINATION

The theoretical concepts applied in the group work related primarily to the effects that the cult has on the cultist and his or her family during and after participation in the cult. Phillip Cushman describes cult indoctrination as an attack on the ego and a subsequent regression to an earlier narcissistic stage, during which the need for mirroring and idealization arises.[3] Flo Conway and Jim Siegelman describe mind control as loss of one's ability to think critically.[4] Typically, persons who have undergone cult indoctrination become very dependent on the leader or group for most of their information about themselves and the world. In addition, cult members often become highly self-punishing. Using transactional analysis concepts of ego states,[5] cult indoctrination involves a diminishing of adult ego-state functioning, with the consequence of severe regression. The individual becomes limited to the most negative aspects of the child ego-state functions (such as extreme dependency and fear), increases his or her critical parent functioning (such as self-criticism), and experiences a corresponding reduction in the nurturing parent functioning (such as the capacity to soothe oneself).

The reduction of adult ego functioning is brought about through the cult's induction and reinforcement of the premise that lack of critical thinking and confusion are desirable states. Any discriminating questions that the recruit may ask in order to gain clari-

---

[3] Phillip Cushman, "The Self Besieged: Recruitment-Indoctrination Processes in Restrictive Groups," *Journal for the Theory of Social Behavior* 16 (March 1986): 1–32.

[4] Flo Conway and Jim Siegelman, *Snapping: America's Epidemic of Sudden Personality Change* (New York: Dell, 1979), p. 170.

[5] Eric Berne, *What Do You Say After You Say Hello* (New York: Barton Books, 1973).

fication or any thoughts expressed that do not conform to the "group-think" are labeled products of the "devil" or the workings of an unenlightened mind. The individual's confusion and self-doubt are validated as "growth."

Regression to the most negative aspects of the child ego state is often accomplished through the use of double-bind mechanisms. Double-bind communication occurs when an individual in an intense relationship is exposed to contradictory messages to which he or she is required to respond, while simultaneously being unable to escape from or comment upon the confusing communication.[6] The cult, as a relatively closed system, creates an environment of intense relationships and activities. Its intense activities and "love bombing" create a milieu in which the cultist is constantly exposed to contradictory messages.[7] For example, on the one hand, the cultist is told that he or she is unconditionally loved by the group or leader and that the cult is the individual's new "family." On the other hand, the cultist is told that he or she is worthless and unlovable unless he or she totally accepts the group doctrine. The cult's closed system, intense relationships, and authoritarian structure prevent the cult member from escaping the double bind, and the member experiences consequent intrapsychic distress.

One way to cope with the double bind is by achieving a state of uncritical receptivity. Many cults use a mechanism that provides the cultist with an outlet for the confusion experienced in the double bind. Various cults' dissociative techniques of intensive meditation, chanting, and glossolalia meet the individual's need to adapt to the double-bind situation. Thus cultists' symptoms, such as their tendency to slip into dissociative states, can be partially explained as an attempt to cope with the cult's milieu by distancing themselves from subjective emotional distress and suppressing egodystonic thoughts.

A major goal in the parents' group was to help the parents understand the implications of the above theories in the hope that this knowledge would help them in their efforts to establish contact with the cultist. An understanding of the double-bind dynamic was essential for the parents. If the parents merely opposed and criticized the cult, the cultist might be exposed to an additional double bind and be further weakened. Also, by providing the parents with an understanding of how cult indoctrination results in a decrease in the recruit's adult ego-state functioning and a regression to the child ego state, parents were empowered to be supportive and nurturing rather than critical and alienating. Parents need to be aware that a critical attitude might increase the cultist's regression. They must try to stimulate the adult ego state of the cultist by helping the cultist think for him- or herself. They must avoid adding to the already overactive critical parent in the cultist by not being judgmental and rejecting. According to these theoretical concepts, group purpose was defined as helping the parents to deal with the family crisis so that their adaptive functions and problem-solving skills were supported and strengthened.

---

[6] Gregory Bateson et al., "Toward a Theory of Schizophrenia," in *Double Bind, The Foundation of the Communicational Approach to the Family,* ed. Carlos E. Sluzki and Donald C. Ransom (New York: Grune and Stratton, 1976), p. 14.

[7] "Love bombing" is a term used in the Unification Church that refers to the strategic use of intense demonstrations of affection to attract the recruit to the cult.

PARENTS' REACTION

Shirley Jenkins and Elaine Norman studied parents' reactions to their children's placement in foster homes and residential treatment, defining the concept "filial deprivation" as the separation experienced by parents when children leave. They found that feelings of sadness were most frequently reported. Parents also reported feelings of emptiness, anger, and bitterness. Relatively few reported a feeling of numbness or a feeling of being paralyzed.[8]

Parents of cultists have similar reactions. Their emotional responses may include:

- *Anxiety, fear, and helplessness:* The cultist's sudden behavioral and cognitive changes are upsetting and frightening. These changes, the mystery surrounding cults, and parents' lack of knowledge about the cult phenomenon are a source of anxiety, fear, and helplessness.
- *Guilt:* Lack of knowledge about a cult's manipulative and mind-control techniques often leads families to assume blame for the changes in the cultist and to develop guilt feelings.[9]
- *Anger:* Often, the cultist's involvement results in alienation from his or her family because many cults maintain control over the cultist's contact with the family. Anger and frustration are natural responses of parents to being abandoned and rejected.[10]
- *Sadness:* Parents experience a sense of sadness about the loss of their son or daughter to the cult and about the loss of the pre-cult child, that is, the personality that existed prior to cult indoctrination.

Parents of cultists experience a grieving process as a result of the loss of hopes and dreams regarding a child. According to Carol Samit and colleagues, grieving parents move through stages of denial or disbelief, shame, guilt, and depression in order to achieve acceptance or resolution.[11] These stages overlap and recur with varying frequency and duration. With increased awareness of their sensitivity and fears, parents can be empowered to respond rather than react to the cult phenomenon.[12]

GROUP PROCESS
Group Consultation

The group discussed in the present article consisted of parents of present and former cult members. These parents had previously attended an open-ended, ongoing, bimonthly support group for families of cultists. As Marsha Addis and colleagues point

---

[8] Shirley Jenkins and Elaine Norman, *Filial Deprivation and Foster Care* (New York: Columbia University Press, 1972), pp. 102–103.

[9] Carol M. Anderson, Douglas J. Reiss, and Gerard E. Hogarty, *Schizophrenia and the Family* (New York: Guilford Press, 1984), pp. 109–10.

[10] Lita L. Schwartz, "Hidden Victims: The Families of Cult Members," Academy of Psychologists in Marital, Sex and Family Therapy, Anaheim, Calif., August 1983, p. 3.

[11] Carol Samit, Kathleen Nash, and Janeen Meyers, "The Parents Group: A Therapeutic Tool," *Social Casework* 61 (April 1980): 215–22.

[12] Michael Langone, "Cult Involvement: Suggestions for Concerned Parents and Professionals," *Cultic Studies Journal: A Journal on Cults and Manipulative Techniques of Social Influence* 2 (Spring–Summer 1985): 148–68.

out, the support group focuses primarily on mutual aid for group members, whereas the short-term group is set up to facilitate greater introspection in addition to the support and advice-giving of the prior group.[13] The parents were given the opportunity to participate in a closed, time-limited therapy group for ten sessions. The group was attended by seven parents: three couples and one single parent.

The group members initially needed and were ready for consultation, not therapy. These parents were faced with a perplexing and unusual problem. Because of the mystery and destructive effects of cults, members needed immediate assistance.[14] Information and advice helped demystify their experience.

Initially, the parents asked for specific information. Their questions varied according to the different stages of their family member's cult involvement. For example,

> the K's only child, D, was an eighteen-year-old involved in a Christian Bible group that communed behind closed doors in a small house. Since his involvement with the group, D had withdrawn from his family and former friends. He would leave his parents' home and disappear for long periods. Upon reappearing, he would refuse to discuss where he had been for the past months. The parents initially asked the group specific questions, such as how to establish contact with their son, how to relate to their son's behavioral changes, and whether to give him money and let him use their car.

The educational component in consultation was more explicit than in most therapy situations.[15] The goal in working with the parents was to help them become more knowledgeable about and skilled in handling cult-related problems. This approach was oriented toward health and resources. By implying that the families were not "sick," the therapist helped them feel qualified to deal with the cultist.

An important step in the group process was to deal with the parents' sense of helplessness. Some of the group members lost sight of their potential to be a positive influence on their child. The despair and anxiety of family members were exacerbated by their fears that they might have contributed to their child's involvement in the cult. During the initial phase of the group process, parents were told that their children were under the influence of an external system, which helped reduce the parents' feelings of responsibility and failure.

A process of normalization helped the parents deal with their feelings of helplessness and isolation.[16] Because involvement in cults is considered abnormal behavior, cultists' parents are often judged by their peers as having somehow failed to raise their children in accordance with the normative expectations of society. The group experience allowed them to share their experiences with others in similar circumstances. Family

---

[13] Marsha Addis, Judith Schulman-Miller, and Meyer Lightman, "The Cult Clinic Helps Families in Crisis," *Social Casework* 65 (November 1984): 515–22.

[14] Margaret T. Singer, "Consultation with Families of Cultists," in *Systems Consultation,* ed. Lyman C. Wynne, Susan H. McDaniel, and Timothy T. Weber (New York: Guilford Press. 1986), p. 277.

[15] Wynne, McDaniel, and Weber, eds., *Systems Consultation,* p. 18.

[16] Marshall D. Roseman and Ira P. Berkman, "Application of the Normalization Principle to Support Groups for Parents with Children in Residential Treatment," *Residential Group Care and Treatment* 3 (Spring 1986): 54–56.

members compared experiences and found that they were not alone in their struggle and that their problems were not unique.

Move toward Group Therapy

The information given to the parents and the increased support provided by the group members reduced the parents' sense of failure and enabled them to become more introspective about the loss they were experiencing. By the middle phase of the group process, the leaders assumed less of a consultant role and more of a therapeutic role by helping parents look at their own and their family's internal processes and reactions to the cult. This phase can be characterized as a move from consultation to therapy.

By the third and fourth sessions, the parents had begun to progress through the stages of the grief process, although not all the parents were at the same stage.

> One father, C, whose twenty-seven-year-old son M, was involved in a Bible cult, had passed through the stages of disbelief and denial and was ready to become more introspective. C was able to try to focus not only on the person whom M was involved with in a cultic relationship, but also on his and his wife's relationship with their son. At this stage, one of the co-leaders presented transactional analysis concepts of ego states. The parents were encouraged to view their transactions as system analysts.
>
> By viewing the cult indoctrination process as an attack on the child ego state of the cult victim and by understanding the resultant narcissistic wounding of the child, C and his wife were able to empathize with the cultist rather than view the cultist as an aggressor or rejector of the parents' values. This empathy was strengthened by the parents' ability to identify and understand their own wounds and fears that existed prior to the intrusion of the cult into the family system as well as those that were induced by the cult crisis.
>
> The parents were able to analyze and understand the transactions occurring among family members in general and among themselves and the cult member in particular. C understood that during his son's childhood, his son often functioned as a parent to him. This unhealthy transaction was a burden for his son, who felt responsible for taking care of his father. C realized that in order to improve relations with his son he needed to assume a stronger parental role. This insight motivated him to change.
>
> The application of the ecosystems view that family difficulties are a result of the interaction between the family dynamic and complex outside forces helped alleviate C's guilt about his son's situation and allowed him to become more introspective. C's readiness to be in therapy was a catalyst for the other group members to move toward group therapy.

The leaders' strategy was to identify with the parents' situation, feelings, and previous efforts at managing the problem by emphasizing that parental strength can facilitate change. The parents' feelings, such as guilt and shame, were channeled into more constructive directions. This strategy is illustrated by the following case:

G's nineteen-year-old daughter, B, had been involved in a highly coercive astro-logical/metaphysical group. B was traumatized by her indoctrination and even-tual rejection by the group. B was unable to understand why the cult had rejected her. Instead of venting her anger at the people in the cult who rejected her, she dis-placed this anger onto her mother and sister. The group process enabled G to stop feeling guilty about her daughter's pain and confusion. G was encouraged to use the "nurturing parent" part of herself to offer consistent love and support, even in the face of her daughter's hostility. In so doing, the mother was able to slowly reestablish a trusting relationship with her daughter that had existed prior to the daughter's indoctrination into the cult.

The leaders emphasized that receptivity and flexibility are important elements in reaching out to an estranged child. These elements are crucial because the cult member is often in a double-bind situation. By encouraging this approach, the co-leaders were able to help the parents avoid their natural tendency to criticize the cult and therefore intensify the double bind experienced by the cultist.

The Ks, whose son, D, was involved in a cultic Bible group, were able to become more receptive and flexible in their approach to D. Their awareness that D was in-volved in a deeply regressive process enabled the Ks to empathize with him rather than threaten him. Consequently, D began to open up and become closer to his parents. The Ks successfully asked D questions regarding his cultic involvement in an effort to stimulate his critical thinking abilities. For example, the Ks asked their son whether the loyalty and friendship group members showed him would continue if he left the group. This question challenged D to think about whether his cult friendships were authentic. Even though D disappeared again after ten days, the Ks were enthusiastic about the quality of their contact with him.

According to the ecosystems perspective, life experience is a model for and primary instrument of change.[17] Therefore, interventions with families that promote natural systems and life experiences that enhance client competence and autonomy were fa-vored. The parents were encouraged to use their natural support network, such as the cult member's siblings, as a way to establish contact with the child. Sometimes a cultist is less resistant to other family members than he or she is to the parents. For example, G, who found it difficult to engage her daughter, was advised to get her other daughter to help her sister become reunited with the family. The parents were also encouraged to notice how family interactions, such as those between parents and other children in the family, affect the cultist.

Toward the end of the group process, the parents were increasingly invited to look at themselves as individuals having normal problems and needs of their own. For exam-ple, the group supported one mother in mourning her father's death. The parents shared information that was not related directly to their childrens' cult involvement.

---

[17] Joan Laird, "Working with the Family in Child Welfare," in *A Handbook of Child Welfare,* ed. Joan Laird and Ann Hartman (New York: Free Press, 1985), p. 373.

They were encouraged to realize that if their own general needs and problems were dealt with, they would become more effective parents.

The possibility that the parents' relationship with their son or daughter might never be the same as it was in the past was a difficult, but significant, realization to deal with. Upon her daughter's return home from the cult, G described her feelings: "I feel sadness, terrible sadness. She has been changed so much." The parents' goal was reunification. The group leaders' task was to maintain a balance between hope and unrealistic optimism.

By the final session of the group, all the group members noted that they felt more empowered in their relationships with their children. They attributed this change to the advice and information that they received and to their increased awareness of their feelings and behaviors. The parents also felt that the group served as a refuge where their cult-related problems were understood.

CONCLUSION

A group for parents of cult victims enables parents to find support and understanding during a crisis in which parents may feel stigmatized and for which they may feel responsible. In the group discussed in the present article, members were faced with an externally imposed traumatic loss due to their children's involvement in a destructive cult. A major difficulty for these parents was their lack of control over contact with their children and the extreme changes they saw occur in their children

The integration of different theoretical perspectives enabled the group leaders to relate in a comprehensive way to the parents' problem. The group experience provided the parents with vital information, emotional support, communication skills, and greater insight regarding themselves and their relationships with their children. The parents moved from feeling helpless and immobilized to feeling positive about their ability to engage actively with their son or daughter in a constructive manner.

CULTURE

CHAPTER 106

CLINICAL DIAGNOSIS AMONG DIVERSE POPULATIONS

A Multicultural Perspective

Alison Solomon

Clinicians often assume that issues of discrimination and the improvement of services to minority clients will be addressed by professionals whose work is policy oriented. It is imperative, however, that clinicians who provide direct service to people of all racial and ethnic backgrounds examine their own practice with minority clients. Much has been written about the treatment of minorities in the psychotherapeutic relationship (Hines & Boyd-Franklin, 1982; Boyd-Franklin, 1989; Bryant, 1980; Canino & Canino, 1982; de Anda, 1984; Jue, 1987; Pinderhughes, 1982). Before clients enter such a relationship, however, they are evaluated and diagnosed. This diagnosis is key to the type of treatment they will subsequently receive. Moreover, once a psychiatric label is attached to a client, it often sticks. Thus, a diagnosis of schizophrenia is not usually changed, even if the person no longer shows symptoms of the illness. The illness is considered in remission, but the person is not considered cured. It is crucial, therefore, that clinicians be aware not only of racial and cultural bias in the *treatment* of minority members but also of biases inherent in present forms of psychiatric *diagnosis*.

This article highlights and discusses differences in psychiatric diagnoses applied to various racial and ethnic groups. The focus is primarily on instances in which the differences are caused by misdiagnosis. Ways to minimize misdiagnosis are suggested.

Reprinted from *Families in Society*, Vol. 73, No. 6 (1992), pp. 371–377, by permission of the publisher, Families International, Inc.

CULTURAL DIFFERENCES IN THE LITERATURE

Researchers have described various diagnoses that appear to be connected to the race, class, cultural background, or gender of the client:

- Blacks and Hispanics are more likely to be diagnosed with affective or personality disorders, whereas whites are more likely to be diagnosed with organic disorders (Hines & Boyd-Franklin, 1982; Jones, Gray, & Parson, 1983).
- Blacks and Hispanics are more likely to be misdiagnosed as schizophrenic when they are, in fact, suffering from bipolar affective disorder (Mukherjee, Shukla, & Woodle, 1983).
- African American children are diagnosed as hyperactive more often than are white children, who are, in turn, diagnosed as hyperactive more often than are Asian American children (Sata, 1990).
- Lower-class children are more frequently described in terms of psychosis and character disorder, whereas middle-class children are described as neurotic and normal (Harrison et al., 1965).
- When diagnosed with psychotic or affective disorders, minority clients are more likely to be labeled as having a chronic syndrome than an acute episode (Sata, 1990).
- Adult white males of all ages have a much lower rate of admission to outpatient psychiatric facilities than do white women and nonwhite men and women (Chesler, 1972).
- Research in the 1960s found a higher rate of schizophrenia among Puerto Ricans than among the general population (Padilla & Padilla, 1977).
- Puerto Ricans on the mainland are more likely to be diagnosed with mental illness than are Puerto Ricans in Puerto Rico. Depression is diagnosed more frequently in Puerto Ricans than among other Hispanic groups, including Cuban Americans and Mexican Americans (Canino, 1990).
- Alcohol abuse is at least four times more prevalent among Puerto Ricans in Puerto Rico than it is among the non-Puerto Rican population in the United States (Canino, 1990).
- Studies often show that Puerto Ricans use mental health resources at a higher rate than do "all other populations" or "non-Puerto Rican populations" (Canino, 1990).

Findings such as these require explanations, which in some cases are readily available. For example, Padilla and Padilla (1977) explain the high rate of schizophrenia among Hispanics by the fact that the Hispanic population is poor and psychotic disorders are more prevalent among the poor. Social conditions, migration, prejudice, and language barriers make Hispanics more vulnerable to psychotic disorders. In a similar vein, Sedgewick (1982) notes that although the factor of racism should not be ignored, labels of psychopathology are social indicators of the stress experienced by populations that lack power; thus, we should expect the oppressed and underprivileged to show more psychopathology.

In addition, behavior that is considered "normal" in one country or ethnic group may be considered pathological or dysfunctional in another country or locale. For example, the consumption of large quantities of alcohol is considered more acceptable in Puerto Rico than it is in the United States. Thus, although alcoholism is a significant problem in Puerto Rico, fewer people are considered "dysfunctional alcoholics" there because Puerto Rican society makes allowances for heavy alcohol use (Canino, 1990).

Although explanations for diagnostic differences are sometimes reasonable, misdiagnosis often occurs. Four basic reasons for misdiagnosis are (1) cultural expression of symptomatology, (2) unreliable research instruments and evaluation inventories, (3) clinician bias and prejudice, and (4) institutional racism.

CULTURAL EXPRESSION OF SYMPTOMATOLOGY

People from different cultures express the same feelings in different ways. Conversely, they also express feelings in ways that may suggest different symptoms in different cultures. For example, in depression one feels unable to cope with daily life; individuals show depression by manifesting symptoms that contradict normal expressivity in a given culture or society. In a culture in which extroversion is valued, depression will be expressed as quiet, introverted behavior. In a culture in which subdued, less expressive behavior is valued, depression is indicated through acting-out behaviors. Moreover, if someone from an "introverted" culture acts out in American culture, he or she is likely to be misdiagnosed with mania or antisocial personality.

In some cultures, the division between psychological and somatic problems is less clearly delineated than it is in American culture. Canino (1988) cites research indicating that Mexicans do not dichotomize or separate emotional illness from somatic diseases. Thus various psychological or emotional disorders that are indicative of grief in Western societies—agitated depression, feelings of helplessness—may be manifested as somatic symptoms among Mexicans (Canino, 1988). Kleinman and Good (1985) note that Asian Indians and Iraqis often present to physicians with somatic complaints rather than affective ones (i.e., "my stomach hurts" rather than "I'm depressed").

In addition, various religions and cultures have quite different ways of expressing grief, including what Westerners might term "hallucinations," "grandiosity," and "hearing voices." Such differences can lead to misdiagnosis. For example,

> S, a Ghanian woman, presented to an outpatient psychiatry service with feelings of apathy, confusion, and depression. S and her husband were in America while he worked on his postdoctoral studies. S had little social life and found caring for her children, which she had previously enjoyed, burdensome. During the mental-status portion of her interview with a psychiatric resident, she was asked if she ever heard voices other people didn't hear or saw things that other people didn't see. She replied that she had vivid visions of her recently deceased mother, who came to S's room and talked to S. She was asked whether she simply envisioned her mother or literally saw her mother standing before her. S replied that the latter was the case. She was then asked if she ever felt as if someone else controlled her thoughts. S replied that her mother's voice was constantly inside her head, telling her what to do. S mentioned that her mother had died four months earlier

but that she and her husband could not afford to go home for the funeral. The attending physician deemed that the sudden and dramatic changes in S's life had triggered a psychotic episode, a form of schizophrenia, and she was started on a course of psychotropic medication.

During this interview, no questions were asked regarding S's spiritual/religious beliefs, nor were cultural aspects of her grieving process examined. Normal grieving in some cultures includes elements that Western culture might view as psychotic (e.g., seeing the dead and communicating with them as they were in life or as transformed into birds, animals, or spirits). Had this aspect of S's reactions been examined, a more appropriate diagnosis of depression or bereavement might have been made.

In discussing cultural variants of depression, Kleinman and Good (1985) provide an excellent argument for the essential importance of considering cultural background in psychiatric diagnosis:

> Because the analytic categories of professional psychiatry so fundamentally share assumptions with popular Western cultures . . . the complaints of patients are viewed as reflecting an underlying pathological phenomenon. From this perspective, culture appears epiphenomenal; cultural differences may exist, but they are not considered essential to the phenomenon itself. However, when culture is treated as a significant variable, for example, when the researcher seriously confronts the world of meaning and experience of members of non-Western societies, many of our assumptions about the nature of emotions and illness are cast in sharp relief (p. 492).

UNRELIABLE RESEARCH INSTRUMENTS
AND EVALUATION INVENTORIES

To recognize symptoms of mental disorder, a normative measure is required. However, whose norm should be employed? As with educational testing, psychiatric testing in America is clearly biased toward the dominant white, male, Western cultural experience and thus is not culturally syntonic for people outside this population. When I was a student doing field practice in an outpatient psychiatric clinic, clients were asked during the mental-status exam if they ever heard things other people didn't hear. In one instance, an educated, middle-class, white male replied, "If you're asking me if I'm schizophrenic, then the answer's no!" In another instance, a 60-year-old working-class African American woman replied, "Well, yes, sometimes when I'm alone in the house, I think I hear voices." Her response led to the question, "And are other people really there?" She said, "No, when I go to look, I never find anyone." Thus, people who are unaware of psychiatric procedures and jargon tend to answer such questions honestly, unaware that they may be setting themselves up for misdiagnosis. People who live in a dangerous neighborhood may indeed hear things other people do not hear. And clients whose grief expression is non-Western may see things other people do not see.

Canino (1990) pointed out that women are more often diagnosed as mentally ill than are men, yet the research instruments measuring mental disorders often do not include items concerning alcohol abuse and antisocial personality ("male" disorders) though they do include anxiety and depression scales ("female" disorders). Canino also pointed out the importance of geography in research on ethnic minorities, noting that studies comparing Hispanics in New York with Cuban Americans in Miami may yield different results because life in New York, especially in the areas where Hispanics typically live, is more difficult than life in Miami. He also pointed out that seeking mental health care is less stigmatizing for Puerto Ricans on the mainland than it is in Puerto Rico, which may explain the higher rate of mental illness among Puerto Ricans here. Moreover, whereas Puerto Ricans may use mental health facilities more, they may use other health facilities less (Canino, 1990). In other words, one must look at their total use of all medical and mental health services offered. Also, the difficulties of intergroup comparisons among persons of the same (or different) ethnic background should not be underestimated. Are immigrant populations compared with nonimmigrant populations? Are people who have come to the United States voluntarily compared with those who were forced to flee their home country?

CLINICIAN BIAS AND PREJUDICE

Misdiagnosis can also be caused by clinician bias. Spurlock (1985) and Gardner (1990) note that many psychiatrists do not perceive African Americans' psyche as being as complex as that of whites. Therefore, the same symptoms that would be labeled emotional or affective disorders among whites are labeled schizophrenic among African Americans. Sata (1990) notes that psychiatry's focus is exclusively on individual pathology and not on social, cultural, and political realities. This focus is inherently racist due to its detrimental effects on clients from the nondominant culture. Gardner (1990) points out that even African American doctors are not immune to such bias—when they don the physician's white coat, they often don its values, too. Language barriers, both obvious and the not so obvious, also exist, complicating the problem of making cross-cultural psychiatric diagnoses. Clearly, immigrants whose English is poor have difficulty making themselves understood. However, even if minority clients speak English well, communication may still be impeded by cultural barriers. For example, Teichner (1981) found that because Puerto Ricans are underrepresented in the mental health professions, professionals' lack of knowledge of Puerto Rican culture is likely to lead to misdiagnosis.

Gardner (1990) takes the problem one step farther, asking whether psychiatrists really want to understand their clients or whether it is easier for most psychiatrists to "blame" clients by labeling them noncompliant or resistant. To examine the meaning behind such labels, one must examine psychiatrists' own values, attitudes, and countertransference issues. Psychiatric training does little to raise awareness of professionals' bias and prejudices. Psychiatric social workers should be aware of this during team diagnosis, and social workers in general should consider the possibility of bias in reports from psychiatric professionals. Most psychiatrists are not aware of their own bias and therefore do not do adequate assessments and history taking.

INSTITUTIONAL RACISM

Institutional racism can also cause misdiagnosis. For example, the *Diagnostic and Statistical Manual of Mental Disorders* (American Psychiatric Association, 1987) claims to be objective and nonpolitical but in fact contains inherent assumptions regarding pathology and mental disease that demonstrate a Western bias. Some of its earlier assumptions have been challenged and changed in later editions—for example, it no longer classifies homosexuality as a mental disorder. However, many diagnostic assumptions that affect women and minorities are less overt and have not been adequately questioned. For example, wife-battering is considered a crime but not a psychiatric disorder. If it were labeled a psychiatric disorder, perpetrators could be hospitalized involuntarily. As another example, schizophrenia is characterized by hostility, suspicion, and paranoia. An African American in today's society may manifest all of these emotions in the course of daily survival.

At the other extreme, Spurlock (1985) notes that in their efforts to avoid cultural bias, mental health care providers often miss pathology when they preidentify it as a cultural trait. Thus, a therapist facing an Asian American who is withdrawn may consider such behavior typical of Asian American peoples instead of recognizing it as a sign of possible depression. Alternatively, if a symptom is dystonic within a particular culture, but not dystonic within the dominant culture, it may not be recognized as pathology. Thus, as noted earlier, Asian American children are often underdiagnosed with hyperactivity because they are measured against the white American cultural norm instead of against their own cultural norm (Sata, 1990).

In a mental-status examination, affect is measured. White Americans may be more open to sharing their feelings than are African Americans, who, although they are very expressive in their mode of communication, may have learned not to share their inner feelings, especially with someone whom they do not know well. Asian Americans learn not to be overtly expressive; thus what appears as blunting of affect to non-Asians may actually represent self-control to Asians. Also, many Asian Americans believe that what is spoken is not as important as that which is left unsaid. Hispanic men verbalize their anger but rarely express fear or anxiety (Jue, 1987). Direct eye contact is viewed as disrespectful in some cultures; thus these clients should not be considered shy or hostile unless these diagnoses are supported by other factors in the interview. Other nonverbal cues, such as the way the client sits, may have less to do with pathology than with cultural dictates. The clinician needs to be familiar with such behaviors if he or she is to interpret them correctly.

TREATMENT ISSUES

Diagnosis may be reached after a single evaluation session or may occur during treatment. Thus, treatment must be evaluated when the possibility of misdiagnosis is considered.

Many authors have discussed the importance of clinician awareness of minority cultures and issues during therapy (Jue, 1987; Hines & Boyd-Franklin, 1982; Boyd-Franklin, 1989; Pinderhughes, 1982; de Anda, 1984). Therapists need to be aware of their own biases and of clients' self-perception and understanding of therapy so that client behaviors can be placed in their proper context. For example, behaviors that help African Americans to survive in the larger society affect their behavior and consequent diagnosis in the therapeutic environment. African Americans may be especially wary of the motives of authority figures and thus may test relationships before allowing themselves to develop a trusting and intimate bond with a therapist. Asian Americans, in contrast, are taught to be cooperative in social relationships and respectful toward authority figures. They may thus maintain a low profile as a survival technique. Hence, in therapy, they may smile and nod in agreement even when they do not agree or understand.

Stereotypes concerning minority clients once permeated the mental health professions and may still influence therapists' behavior in some instances. For example, Hines and Boyd-Franklin (1982) cited various studies indicating that black clients were less likely than were white clients to be in psychotherapy. Black clients were also discharged sooner than were whites. Fewer than one-third of black clients were referred to group or individual therapy, whereas one-half of the white patients were referred to such treatment (Yamamoto, James, & Palley, 1968).

An accusation often leveled against minority clients by clinicians in public health institutions is that they have no respect for time constraints and often are late for or miss appointments (Kupers, 1981). However, therapy appointments are often scheduled to meet the needs of the therapist, not the client. Problems with transportation and babysitting may cause clients to miss appointments. Moreover, poor minority clients' experiences with institutions and services in other areas of their life do not serve as models for responsible behavior. For example, why should a client who typically waits four hours in a welfare line believe that his or her 9:00 A.M. appointment for outpatient psychiatry will be any different?

Depending on cultural background, clients may use Western medicine or psychiatry in conjunction with other forms of healing techniques. Most cultures have spiritual healers—priests, rabbis, shamans, spiritualists—whose advice is sought on mental health issues. In a random sample of Puerto Ricans in New York City, Canino (1990) found that 31% had seen a spiritualist at least once. Canino also found that 73% of a group of outpatients at a New York City mental health clinic reported visiting a spiritualist prior to seeking psychiatric consultation. Clinicians need to be aware that their advice or opinion may conflict with that of the spiritual healer and to respect and integrate differing approaches in the best interests of clients.

RECOMMENDATIONS

How can clinicians ensure that misdiagnosis does not occur when dealing with clients from different cultural backgrounds?

First, clinicians need to examine critically the means used to categorize pathologies and illnesses. Kleinman and Good (1985) recommend that more clinical/descriptive research should be conducted to serve as a basis for evaluating the cross-cultural validity of our current diagnostic categories of mental illness. They also hold that new standards for cross-cultural epidemiological studies should be developed and emphasize that cross-cultural research can help us better understand the relationships among emotions, social influences, causes of illness, cognitions, and somatization. In addition, they believe that serious consideration should be given to adding a cultural axis to the *Diagnostic and Statistical Manual of Mental Disorders* (American Psychiatric Association, 1987).

Perhaps most important, clinicians should focus on the specific personal, familial, and cultural history of the client. Accurate assessment of a client's history includes:

- immigrant-generation status of the client
- level of cultural assimilation—that is, is the client monocultural (e.g., a new immigrant), bicultural (balancing and integrating nondominant culture into the dominant culture), or unicultural (assimilated to the point of no longer identifying with ethnic background)
- level of integration within cultural assimilation (i.e., is the client isolated, marginal, acculturated?)
- religious beliefs
- social class
- child-rearing practices
- school influence

For example, Jones (1985) recommends that clinicians consider the following when assessing the psychological adaptation of African Americans: (1) reactions to racial oppression, (2) influence of the majority culture, (3) influence of African American culture, and (4) individual and family experiences and strengths. The model is interactive; that is, each set of factors has an influence on psychological functioning and an influence on the operation of the other factors. Thus factors such as political activism within the family, personal experience with discrimination, and attendance at a predominantly white or black school and how these factors influence one another would be considered in the assessment.

Some authors have suggested that, depending on the cultural background of the client, one form of therapy may be more culturally syntonic than another. Canino and Canino (1982) recommend goal-oriented, directive, structural family therapy for low-income Hispanic clients. They describe this approach as being appropriate for cultures in which men are expected to assume a dominant role and women and children a passive role. Although clinicians from the dominant culture should not impose their values on those from other cultures, this does not mean that issues of abuse, such as wife-battering or degradation of women, should be overlooked because of different cultural attitudes toward women.

In familiarizing themselves with different cultures, clinicians must note that diversity exists *within* a population as well as between different populations. The term "Middle Eastern" covers peoples from Syria to Algeria to Lebanon. African Americans include Americans whose origins are spread across the whole continent of Africa. Stereotypes of economic class for different populations must also be avoided. Clinicians need to understand the cultural nuances of their clients and remain curious and open to the information that the client presents.

CONCLUSION

Clinical treatment usually follows and is dependent on a given diagnosis. Research has shown that particular racial or ethnic groups are frequently diagnosed as having particular disorders. Although these diagnostic differences are sometimes valid, they can also reflect misunderstandings based on ethnocentric and racist assumptions of the profession.

Cultural background can affect clients' presentation of symptoms. Behaviors that are considered dysfunctional or abnormal in the dominant culture may be considered functional and normal in another culture. Because research instruments and treatment modalities are often based on experiences and needs of the white, male, Western client, they may not reflect the cultural realities of minority clients. Moreover, studies that examine the cultural differences among particular communities often do not take into account factors such as immigrant status, geographical location, and economic status.

Clinician prejudice, bias, and lack of familiarity with different racial and ethnic groups can also result in misdiagnosis. Clinicians need to examine their own potential bias, in that diagnoses are based on deviations from normative measures. If the normative experience of clients from a given cultural background is not considered, diagnosis is likely to reflect the majority culture's bias.

To minimize misdiagnosis, more cross-cultural research is needed. Clinicians must examine their own prejudices and biases so that assessment procedures can better reflect the reality of clients' experience.

REFERENCES

American Psychiatric Association. (1987). *Diagnostic and statistical manual of mental disorders* (3rd ed., rev.). Washington, DC: Author.

Boyd Franklin, N. (1989). *Black families in therapy.* New York: Guilford.

Bryant, C. (1980). Introducing students to the treatment of inner-city families. *Social Casework, 61,* 629–636.

Canino, G., & Canino, I. (1982). Family therapy: A culturally syntonic approach for migrant Puerto Ricans. *Hospital and Community Psychiatry, 33,* 299–303.

Canino, I. (1988). The clinical assessment of the transcultural child. In C. Kestenbaum & D. Williams (Eds.), *Clinical assessment of children and adolescents.* New York: New York University Press.

Canino, I., (1990, April). *Working with persons from Hispanic backgrounds.* Paper presented at the Cross-Cultural Psychotherapy Conference, Hahnemann University, Philadelphia.

Chesler, P. (1972). *Women and madness.* New York: Doubleday.

de Anda, D. (1984). Bicultural socialization: Factors affecting the minority experience. *Social Work, 29,* 101–107.

Gardner, G. (1990, April). *Working with persons from African American backgrounds.* Paper presented at the Cross-Cultural Psychotherapy Conference, Hahnemann University, Philadelphia.

Harrison, S. I., et al. (1965). Social class and mental illness in children: Choice of treatment. *Archives of General Psychiatry, 13,* 411–417.

Hines, P. M., & Boyd-Franklin, N. (1982). Black families. In M. McGoldrick, J. Pearce, & J. Giordano (Eds.), *Ethnicity and family therapy*. New York: Guilford.

Jones, A. (1985). Psychological functioning in black Americans: A conceptual guide for use in psychotherapy. *Psychotherapy, 22,* 363–369.

Jones, B., Gray, B., & Parson, E. (1983). Manic-depressive illness among poor urban Hispanics. *American Journal of Psychiatry, 140,* 1208–1210.

Jue, S. (1987). Identifying and meeting the needs of minority clients with AIDS. In C. Leukenfeld & M. Fimbres (Eds.), *Responding to AIDS*. Washington, DC: National Association of Social Workers.

Kleinman, A., & Good, B. (Eds.). (1985). *Culture and depression*. Los Angeles: University of California Press.

Kupers, T. A. (1981). *Public therapy*. New York: Free Press.

Mukherjee, S., Shukla, S., & Woodle, J. (1983). Misdiagnosis of schizophrenia in bipolar patients: A multiethnic comparison. *American Journal of Psychiatry, 140,* 1571–1574.

Padilla, E., & Padilla, A. (Eds). (1977). *Transcultural psychiatry: An Hispanic perspective*. Los Angeles: Spanish Speaking Mental Health Research Center (UCLA).

Pinderhughes, E. (1982). Afro-American families and the victim system. In M. McGoldrick, J. Pearce, & J. Giordano (Eds.), *Ethnicity and family therapy*. New York: Guilford.

Sata, L. (1990, April). *Working with persons from Asian backgrounds*. Paper presented at the Cross-Cultural Psychotherapy Conference, Hahnemann University, Philadelphia.

Sedgewick, P. (1982). *Psycho politics*. New York: Harper and Row.

Spurlock, J. (1985). Assessment and therapeutic intervention of black children. *Journal of American Academy of Child Psychiatry, 24,* 168–174.

Teichner, V. (1981). The Puerto Rican patient. *Journal of the American Academy of Psychoanalysis. 9,* 277.

Yamamoto, J., James, E., & Palley, N. (1968). Cultural problems in psychiatric therapy. *Archives of General Psychiatry, 19,* 45–49.

RACE

CHAPTER 107

AMERICAN INDIANS

Working with Individuals and Groups

E. Daniel Edwards and Margie E. Edwards

T here are approximately one million American Indians living in the continental United States today.[1] The 1970 census reported that about 80 percent of all American Indians claim to be members of some 250 tribes.[2] In addition, there are an almost equal number of native Alaskan groups located throughout Alaska.[3] Each of these tribes is unique. Many of them continue to maintain their own tribal languages, values, customs, religions, and leadership systems.[4]

THE PLACE OF THE GROUP IN AMERICAN INDIAN CULTURE

Historically, American Indians developed societies with well-defined roles, responsibilities, government and economic systems, recreational and leisure styles, religious rites and ceremonies, and social behavior in which group involvement, support, and consensus played major roles. Their social, economic, and political traditions reflect a strong emphasis on group involvement and decision making.

Group solidarity was achieved in a number of ways. Many "work" assignments were combined with recreational and leisure activities. Elderly American Indians taught the younger people crafts, narrated myths, gave moral talks, and in other ways instructed the young.[5]

Reprinted from *Social Casework,* Vol. 61 (1980), pp. 498–506, by permission of the publisher, Families International, Inc.

[1] Jamake Highwater, *Fodor's Indian America* (New York: David McKay, 1975), p. 61.
[2] Mary Ellen Ayers, "Counseling the American Indian." *Occupational Outlook Quarterly* (Washington, D.C.: U.S. Department of Labor, Spring 1977), p. 24.
[3] Ibid.
[4] Ibid.
[5] Clark Wissler, *Indians of the United States* (New York: Anchor Books, 1966), p. 274.

Some tribes utilized "potlatches" to achieve group solidarity. These gatherings were held to bestow titles or other honors, to conduct family rites, to show mourning, to announce a new chief, to save face, and to demonstrate power and wealth. All members of the family group presenting the potlatch participated in the preparation and actual event, which would last for several days and feature huge amounts of food, dancing and singing, and the giving of many gifts.

Group consensus was valued by most Indian tribes. Many meetings, discussions, and "powwows" were lengthy because American Indians strove for group consensus, not majority rule, in their decision-making processes that would affect the majority of Indian people. Each individual's opinion was heard and weighed in arriving at decisions affecting the group. Although group consensus was highly valued, so was the Indian's appreciation for each person as an individual. Most tribes respected the individual and allowed each person a great deal of freedom and autonomy, particularly in those areas that would have more repercussions for the individual than for the group as a whole. However, Indian values were repeatedly reinforced. The individual was well acquainted with those values and roles that reinforced group closeness. They were also well aware of areas in which individual decision making was allowed.

CULTURAL STRENGTHS AND WEAKNESSES

Culturally, American Indians enjoy many group activities. They are energetic, fun-loving people who enjoy sports, games,[6] music, crafts, participation in ceremonies, and a variety of other small and large group recreational and cultural activities. Hospitality, generosity, good humor, and good sportsmanship are values that have been emphasized in their group activities. Self-discipline, self-control, and self-development were emphasized through play. Feelings of pleasure and enjoyment were shared by participants and spectators.[7]

Since the time of Christopher Columbus, many detrimental cultural changes have been imposed on the American Indian people. In 1890, after the massacre of the Sioux at Wounded Knee, South Dakota, all Indians recognized as such by the federal government were relocated on reservations.[8] This disruption of Indian culture, combined with subsequent attempts at forced assimilation, broken treaties, and unfulfilled promises has contributed greatly to the Indian's distrust of Anglos and subsequent poor relationships. Because of these events, American Indians may require a substantial time commitment before they develop professional relationships with non-Indian social workers.

The diversification of American Indian tribes and individuals may also contribute toward blocking of group cohesion. Historically, some tribal groups have competed against one another, and there are carry-overs of past events to present-day relationships that may negatively affect group involvement. Many different lifestyles and philosophies exist among American Indians today, which sometimes lead to feelings of divisiveness.

---

[6] Stewart Cullen, *Games of the North American Indians* (New York: Dover Publications, 1975).

[7] Brad Steiger, *Medicine Talks: A Guide to Walking in Balance and Surviving on the Earth Mother* (New York: Doubleday, 1975), p. 67.

[8] Sar A. Levitan and William B. Johnston, *Indian Giving: Federal Programs for Native Americans* (Baltimore: Johns Hopkins University, 1975), p. 7.

STEREOTYPES AND MYTHS

A number of stereotypes and myths persist regarding American Indians, many of which are incorrect or short-sighted. Examples of these stereotypes include: Indians are oil-rich, lazy, drunken, unproductive, good with their hands but not with their heads, on the government dole, stoic, long-suffering, warlike, blood-thirsty, debauched, barbaric, unemotional, aloof, and with little hope for the future. Other stereotypes view Indians as proud, controlled, reserved, honest, sharing, and self-sufficient.

American Indians are as individualistic as members of any other group. These stereotypes, however, cannot help but influence their feelings toward themselves as well as their perceptions of the non-Indian's attitude toward the Indian. The National Congress of American Indians felt so strongly about the image of American Indians that they began a national public relations campaign in 1969 to create a "new and true picture" of American Indians that would portray important values and result in an improvement of the Indians' image to Indians and non-Indians alike.[9]

RELATIONSHIPS IN CROSS-RACIAL SITUATIONS
Dealings With Authority

The historical treatment of American Indians provides some basis for their suspiciousness of Anglo people in "authority" roles. On occasion, Indian clients have been "promised" results that were not obtained, or they may have misunderstood the procedures, "promises," or role of the professional person. These misunderstandings may lead to suspiciousness, mistrust, and reluctance to become involved with other professionals.

Social workers should move slowly, identify problems and procedures clearly, make commitments regarding situations in which they have control, follow through consistently, and use client strengths appropriately in order to help develop feelings of trust and establish professional relationships. For example, an eight-year-old girl was returned from foster care to the care of her mother. A month later, the girl ran away. Her mother located her, spoke with her firmly, and told her that she was wanted and needed and was never to run away again. The daughter complied. The social worker praised the mother for the strength she had shown in locating her daughter and setting the limits for her daughter's behavior.

In working with an American Indian client, the social worker should assume an appropriate authoritarian position that permits the client to assume as much responsibility as possible for his or her activities, discussions, and decision making.

Sociocultural Expectations

Indians have been taught to value themselves, their families, clans, and tribes, and to adhere to values that are revered by their various tribal groups. When working with these clients, social workers should consider the values of each specific tribe.

As social workers learn about the specific Indian tribal group with which they are working, they will be more able to discuss tribal matters, cultural customs, and current

[9] Howard M. Bahr, Bruce A. Chadwick, and Robert C. Day, eds., *Native Americans Today: Sociological Perspectives* (New York: Harper and Row, 1972), pp. 48–49, 524.

areas of concern to the group. This understanding will facilitate a more successful intervention.

It is important for social workers to understand that Indian values are interwoven throughout their culture, lifestyle, religion, and daily activities. In many Indian tribal groups tribal values are reinforced through the use of ceremonies. When ceremonies are held, it is important for family members to participate, even if participation requires traveling long distances or giving up other commitments.

Non-Indian social workers should expect that it will take time before they are trusted and accepted by the Indian people with whom they work. The sometimes rapid turnover of social work staff has contributed to the wariness with which American Indians approach relationships with a new social worker. Social workers can expect that it will take three to six months before they are accepted by the people in traditional Indian communities.

In the "not too distant past," all social workers working with American Indians have been non-Indian. In recent years, a number of professional and paraprofessional American Indian people have been employed to work with Indians. Regardless of the ethnic background, Indian clients will individually and collectively assess the expertise and commitment of any helping person before relationships will develop.

Introspection is often difficult for Indians. Self-evaluations may also be difficult for students involved in professional training programs. Indians reared in the traditional ways of their tribes may have difficulty talking about themselves. Indian tradition dictates that Indians do not exaggerate their abilities or use their own name or the word "I" excessively. Traditionally, Indian people are expected to know their strengths but not to exaggerate them; they are to exhibit confidence, but not flaunt their skills. An Indian client may bring another person with them to an interview so that they will have someone there who can speak on their behalf.

American Indians believe that people should be able to understand one another; it is not necessary to explain one's feelings or problems in detail. The Indian client therefore, often expects the professional person to be able to understand without the client having to voice concerns in detail.

Many American Indians have learned to relate to new situations by being passive. The pace of the interview must be geared to motivate clients to respond more as an interview progresses. Social workers should strive to feel comfortable in periods of silence, to listen, hear, understand, and respond as an American Indian would as important considerations are discussed. One technique that is helpful in building a relationship with American Indians is helping clients resolve tangible problems. Economic needs, employment referrals, health care, school-related problems, housing, and other tangible needs often bring clients to a social service agency. Helping an Indian client obtain the services desired facilitates the development of a relationship that may continue in subsequent contacts or allow the client to return for services in the future.

Language Problems

Most American Indians are bilingual; however, some Indians, particularly older ones, may not speak English very well or at all. A social worker must assess the client's communication skills and respond appropriately.

Because the bilingual client's vocabulary in English may be limited, verbal messages may be misinterpreted. It is not uncommon for American Indians to ask how long they "have to come" to see a social worker, when what they are really asking is "will this experience be long enough and important enough for me to risk getting involved?" It is also common for young people to ask repeatedly when groups will be held, will they be allowed to attend, and so on. This constant questioning of others about events is a result of past experiences in which many enjoyable activities were cancelled or discontinued. They fear that this enjoyable experience may also not continue. Social workers need to clarify the purposes for social work intervention and the time commitment, and help clients develop positive therapeutic relationships at an appropriate pace.

Clients may also not understand what is being proposed in the case of a group experience. On one occasion, several group members were participating in a group activity collecting pine cones in the nearby mountains. They also went to the local park to add more to their collection. Several group members then asked if they could also go to the cemetery to find more pine cones. One group member did not know what a "cemetery" was; she came from a very traditional Indian family who had a great deal of respect for dead people. Upon entering the cemetery, she became very frightened. Had the group worker told her the group was planning to go to a "graveyard" instead of a "cemetery," the girl would have understood the terminology used and would have been in a better position to express her feelings about this experience.

With some bilingual clients, it is necessary to explain problems that the English-speaking social worker can express in English with one or two words. In some Indian languages there is not a word that means "retarded" or "developmentally disabled." Some words that are closely related are entirely different. For example, one Indian mother was very frightened when she asked, "You don't mean my child is crazy, do you?" when the social worker had tried to explain that her child had some learning problems and would probably be classified as an educably retarded youngster. It therefore requires a great deal of time to work with bilingual clients where language barriers are present.

USING CULTURE-SPECIFIC TECHNIQUES

Because of the vast number of individual tribal groups, it is important for the individual and cultural values of each American Indian, individually and as a group, to be considered in social work intervention. Efforts should be directed toward helping clients understand the social work intervention process. It is also important to consider modifying procedures when it would be beneficial to the client.

Sometimes Indian clients' problems are related to someone close who has recently died. In the interview process, when a topic directly relates to the deceased, it is wise to use a term such as sister, brother, father, and so on, other than the person's given name because it is a violation of tradition to use the dead person's name. Moreover, if the social worker feels that he or she may not have the expertise to handle the above topic, a suggestion could be made to involve the skills of a medicine man, should the client desire.

When helping clients solve problems, a social worker may use role-playing techniques that reflect the here-and-now within the client's culture. The clan system may be utilized to support or implement change. For example, if a male Indian is having problems with his in-laws, and his culture does not allow him to speak directly to his mother-in-law, role playing the use of other clan members as intermediary sources could be helpful.

Eye contact may sometimes cause uneasiness with an Indian client. The worker should develop a technique of looking elsewhere when interviewing or develop an activity or game where worker and client can talk without constant eye contact.

It is important for workers to understand when Indian clients may be experiencing conflicts related to their cultural values. For example, one young adult Indian male had a difficult time identifying goals for his future. It was very difficult for him to verbalize these frustrations when working with a social worker because he had been taught by a very traditional father that "any Indian 'worth his salt' was to handle all of his problems on his own." It was important for the social worker to verbalize this conflict between the client's own personal frustrations and the expectations of his culture. After discussing these verbally, the young man was able to look at his options and plan for his future. However, at the end of the interview he showed evidence of being embarrassed. During the subsequent interview, he was very quiet. The social worker once again verbalized the conflict and identified for the young man the ways in which he was assuming responsibility for himself; the worker also provided feedback that indicated he saw the young man as a valuable, worthwhile, strong, capable person. This feedback was important to the self-esteem of the client. The client terminated shortly after this interview, but would return for counseling on a limited basis.

The setting in which the social work services are provided is important to the success of the treatment. Some young people who have been reared on Indian reservations will be more verbal and responsive in outdoor settings, where the atmosphere is similar to their home environment. Adults may also prefer to work with the social worker on the porch or in an outdoor patio area.

The use of humor, particularly as it relates to being teased and teasing one another about incidents related to everyday living, can help set a positive atmosphere for the Indian client. Indian people tease and use humor as an indication of acceptance and comfort. If social workers can make fun of themselves and the things they do, Indian people often read this as an indication of the social worker's comfort in the experience also.

It is important for social workers to assess the uniqueness of each client, whether the client is seeing the worker as an individual or as a member of a group. In dealing with the Indian client, however, it is also important to assess the degree of affiliation and identification with traditional Indian culture, the conflicts that exist between minority and majority culture values, the willingness to risk, and the real issues with which the Indian client desires help.

A consistency of appointments with clients should be maintained, and appointments should not be broken, unless absolutely necessary. Sessions should be held regularly, even if some members are missing. Clients should be given time to warm up to the counseling or group situation, time to think through matters being discussed and possible alternatives, and time to unwind in terminating the sessions.

When a client does not keep an appointment, the worker should make an effort to contact the client to let the client know that he or she was missed, then the appointment should be rescheduled. The worker should avoid imposing any feelings of guilt on the client. Clients should understand what they can expect from the social worker and what the social worker will expect from them. Once the relationship has been developed, it is important to identify goals and to partialize the assignments to be accomplished. Short-range goals often help clients see that something of worth is being accomplished.

Relationships with Indian clients take time. Workers must avoid overestimating a relationship initially. Even though a relationship is developing, and the client's goals are being worked on, the Indian person may still desire distance in the relationship.

Social workers must not underestimate the relationship at termination. Many American Indians develop close working relationships with professional people, both individually and in groups, and may wish to continue the relationship, even though it is necessary to terminate. Clients may become physically ill, avoid final sessions, develop other problems, or negate the benefit of the services they have received. They may, however, respond with appreciation and identification of areas of personal growth.

Because of the Indian's belief in the value of individuality, some of them will consider it inappropriate to discuss the problems of other members of their families in meetings with social workers.[10] Social workers can be helpful by expressing an understanding of this value and the conflict it may cause. The value of individuality also dictates to some Indians that they must resolve individual problems on their own. In such situations, social workers should identify their role as a "sounding board" and help Indian clients develop their own plans for working through the conflicts involved.

INTERVENTION STRATEGIES AND SKILLS WITH GROUPS

The value that American Indians place on consensus can readily be used in forming the basis of group work practice.[11] When working with clients in groups, solutions to problems should take into consideration the Indian client's cultural traditions and values. These cultural resources may be seen by the clients as valuable and appropriate resources to use in other times of stress as well.

Working with Indians in task groups may require a long-term investment. Individual citizens and elected or appointed tribal representatives often seek to be involved in decisions that will affect Indian people as a group. Consensus for community activities and programs is still valued by some American Indian tribes.

One of the roles of a professional worker in task groups is to interpret and clarify policies for committees, suggest viable alternatives, help identify leadership and potential leadership among American Indian people, see that programs and policies are enacted at a suitable pace, and support appropriately American Indians who assume leadership roles on policymaking boards and committees. These procedures may be time-consuming, but they will result in more effective policy decisions. For example, one task group assignment on an Indian reservation involved several months of work to establish a boys' home. Members of the Indian community were actively involved in all aspects of this project, from initial planning to implementation. When the home was es-

[10] Ronald G. Lewis and Man Keung Ho, "Social Work with Native Americans," *Social Work* 20 (September 1975): 380–81.

[11] Charles E. Farris and Lorene S. Farris, "Indian Children: The Struggle for Survival," *Social Work* 21 (September 1976): 388.

tablished, it was accomplished with the support, interest, and sanction of the community.

It is important that practitioners working with groups of American Indians become acquainted with resources available in the community. Once relationships are established, referrals for other community services can be a part of the group experience. The interest and support of the worker and other group members may motivate some participants to seek assistance from other agencies.

Groups led by more than one leader have been a successful technique, especially with groups of children, adolescents, married couples, and families. Co-leaders provide support for one another as well as gain greater insight and awareness into the problems and strengths of group members

Providing positive reinforcement for clients is particularly important. In the initial stages of a group's development, it may be more appropriate to provide positive reinforcement on an individual basis. Being praised in front of other group members in the initial stages of a group's development may often be embarrassing and culturally inappropriate in working with groups of American Indians. When group cohesiveness is developed, group members may appropriately provide positive support to one another.

Treatment methods with American Indians experiencing alcoholism problems should be task-centered. Social workers should continue to reach out to Indian clients with understanding and sensitivity. Specific tangible goals should be identified for Indian clients that can realistically be achieved.

Family group sessions with Indian families may involve participation from extended family members, members of the clan, and others. These sessions may need to be informal in nature and require longer periods of time to develop relationships and to achieve desired goals. The work accomplished, however, will be with the knowledge and support of a large number of significant people.

YOUTH GROUPS

The wide diversification of American Indians lends itself to considerable creativity in programming for Indian groups. Activity groups are especially enjoyed by Indian youths. These groups have been helpful in boarding school settings, because they provide group members with an opportunity to discuss mutual interests and concerns, to develop talents and skills, to enjoy experiences in the community, to develop leadership skills, to discuss future goals and plans, and to enjoy the association of one another.

Leadership groups with young Indians have been particularly successful. These groups are designed to help group members practice and develop their leadership skills and share their group experiences with others.

Special interest groups may also be developed to meet specific needs of Indian young people. A group may focus on participation in outdoor activities such as hiking, mountain climbing, hunting, or fishing. Other groups may develop special interests such as American Indian dancing, beading, or making dance costumes. A cooking group, where youths learn to cook traditional Indian foods, could provide an appropriate outlet for young people.

Community or school project groups can be developed for Indian youths to choose their own projects. They may ask to have the local gym remain open one night per week. They may develop a volleyball program at the gymnasium or Indian center. Another project may seek to have the school library open one night per week with special help available to Indian students to help them with homework assignments, school papers, or special projects. For example, one young Indian leadership group planned and decorated a float for their high school's homecoming parade. Other Indian classmates were somewhat apprehensive about participating in building or riding on the float until they saw the finished product, which was so attractive that several young Indian people volunteered to ride on the float.

Groups that help to make Indian young people aware of community resources are helpful. Group members could visit employment centers, job service centers, businesses that hire young people for on-the-job training, technical colleges, junior colleges, and four-year colleges. It is important for young Indian people to talk with older Indians who are actively involved in employment, training, or educational programs as they visit various sites.

Groups which focus on increasing positive feelings about one's "Indianness" could also be helpful. The University of Utah's American Indian Social Work Career Training Program staff recently conducted a group experiment with American Indian girls.[12] Group members participated in a number of discussions and activities that were related to traditional and modern-day American Indian activities, including dancing, singing, beading, crafts, foods, and games. Discussions related to historical, cultural, and present-day concerns of American Indians. Everyone involved perceived this group as a positive experience. The use of experimental groups such as this have been successful with Indian young people, who seem to enjoy participating in innovative group experiences.

Groups for the Elderly

Groups for the elderly have been particularly well received. They enjoy participating in crafts and cultural activities specific to their own cultural group and to other tribes as well as doing modern-day crafts that originate in the dominant culture. Excursions of both long and short duration are motivating group activities. Some Indian aged groups have planned fundraising events to provide financial assistance for such excursions. They enjoy sports activities, including bowling and golf. Dinners and special events where food is served are also very popular among American Indian aged. American Indian elderly have keen senses of humor; they enjoy participating in groups, and enjoy one another's company. They tend to be willing to risk and involve themselves in new activities.

What the Worker Can Do

Groups can be organized around clear purposes and goals. Group members should actively participate in the formulation and modification of these goals. Programming for group sessions should tie in directly and specifically to individual and group goals.

---

[12] E. Daniel Edwards et al., "Enhancing Self-Concept and Identification with 'Indianness' of American Indian Girls," *Social Work with Groups* 1 (Fall 1978): 309–18.

An effective group programming method is that of "unit programming." Group workers and members agree to focus on the attainment of two or three goals over a period of four to ten group sessions. These goals may include self-image improvement, development of communication or problem-solving skills, developing better relationships with peers, understanding racial and cultural differences and similarities, or achieving skills in American Indian activities. The repetition involved in unit programming is reinforcing and facilitates the attainment of goals.

Group members should be encouraged to use their new skills in their relationships with people outside of the group. Assignments should be given to group members to assist them to achieve their goals. Assignments should be discussed at each group session with continued encouragement or modification as necessary.

For example, Sharon, a teenage girl who did not have many friends, was given two tickets to a weekend movie at her boarding school. Sharon agreed that she would take a friend with her. The following week Sharon returned to see the group worker with the two movie tickets. Sharon said that she had wanted to go to the movie, but was reluctant to ask a friend to go with her. The assignment was restated for the coming weekend. The next week the group worker met Sharon and the friend who had gone with her to the movie. This "beginning friendship" was then generalized to others at the boarding school.

A group worker should use the communication patterns that are evident in the group. For example, one group of adolescent girls was particularly artistic. The group worker asked each of the girls to draw a picture of something that was causing them some concern or difficulty either at school, home, or with their friends. Every group member willingly participated in this activity. This exercise helped many of the quieter group members to discuss their concerns more freely.

Group workers should reserve time after each group session for group members who would like to stay and talk individually or in subgroups with the worker. A flexible time period for group sessions also allows group members to bring up areas of concern when they are ready to do so. It is not unusual for Indian group members to bring up problems at the end of a group session; this is most often not an avoidance technique.

For example, a young adult alcoholism group was meeting to reinforce the maintenance of their sobriety. After an involved group discussion, one group member indicated that she had a concern that she wanted to share with the group. She then proceeded to discuss a "dry drunk" incident (an experience where a recovering alcoholic has all the symptoms and reactions commonly associated with heavy drinking, when no drinking has occurred). She was very troubled by this experience. The group helped to identify the incident, shared similar experiences, and offered understanding and possible alternatives for ways of handling future episodes. She was most relieved, and expressed her appreciation to the group.

Group workers have alternative methods to offer as many services as possible to clients, thus allowing them choices. The more choices which can be made available to American Indians, the better the opportunities for success. Social work services may be offered to clients individually, with their friends or acquaintances, in subgroups, small groups, leadership groups, or special project groups.

IMPLICATIONS FOR EDUCATION AND PRACTICE

Social work education should undertake to prepare American Indians and non-Indians to practice with people from both cultures. Students should be prepared to practice social work with individuals, groups, and communities in a generalist approach. Social work techniques that have the most potential for work with Indians should be emphasized in innovative and creative approaches.

Practicum opportunities should be made available for Indians in agencies serving Indians exclusively, agencies serving non-Indians exclusively, and agencies serving both Indians and non-Indians. All students should have opportunities for choice in terms of their practicum placements and an opportunity to work with clients from a variety of ethnic cultures. Practicum instruction should be highly professional. American Indian professional faculty and consultants should be available in both the academic and practicum settings.

Students should be encouraged to invest themselves in an ongoing learning process. This process should encourage students to develop an interest in continuous learning that will better enable them to meet the unique needs of special populations throughout their social work careers.

Students should gain expertise with several group techniques and how they may be combined and integrated to provide the best possible services for American Indians. Students should acquire both activity skills (including American Indian cultural activities) and discussion approaches to meet the needs of each client and group more effectively. Students should also strive for greater self-awareness and understanding of themselves and their professional roles.

Specific American Indian content should be integrated into the curriculum in such a way as to provide a knowledge base to enhance social work practice with Indians. This knowledge base should include historical, cultural, and present-day concerns. Students should understand that minority people participate within two cultures—the majority culture and their own minority culture—and they must understand the concerns and strengths utilized by American Indians as they negotiate relationships within both the majority and their minority cultures.

CHAPTER 108

EMPOWERING TREATMENT SKILLS FOR HELPING BLACK FAMILIES

Donna R. Weaver

"The black family has a history and a future, as well as a present, that are viable, worthwhile, understandable and which serve the peculiar survival needs of a group which continues to suffer discrimination, prejudice, and subtle institutional racism."[1] As the melting-pot view of ethnic minorities in American society is seriously challenged, social workers acknowledge the need to devise treatment modalities that respond to the particular needs of various ethnic groups. Ethnic minorities are those groups of non-white people who are set apart from the American mainstream by their race, culture, or national origin. Social workers are sensitive to the fact that differences among the many ethnic minorities need to be addressed if effective social services are to be implemented. Although the approach presented can be generalized to other ethnic groups, the focus here will be on treating black families.

The purpose of this article is to facilitate the social worker's ability to intervene more effectively in the black family system. Empowerment and the uniqueness of the black culture are important variables for intervention and treatment of black families. Social workers must be sensitized to the impact of cultural differences on the social functioning of black families, and need to use techniques that are culture-sensitive while intervening in black family systems. Four considerations are important in meeting these objectives: (1) the values and the knowledge base of professional social work, and their implications for treatment of black families; (2) the cultural variant perspective of the black family system; (3) survival techniques necessary for black family functioning; and

---

Reprinted from *Social Casework,* Vol. 63, No. 2 (1982), pp. 100–105, by permission of the publisher, Families International, Inc.

[1] Marie F. Peters, "Notes from the Guest Editor," *Journal of Marriage and the Family* 40 (November 1978): 655–58.

(4) treatment skills that can increase a social worker's effectiveness while intervening in the black family system.

PROFESSIONAL KNOWLEDGE BASE

Within any professional orientation there is a knowledge base that includes various theories, concepts, and techniques foundational to skill building. The values that guide social work practice are expressed in the United States Constitution and in the Code of Ethics cited by the National Association of Social Workers. Basically, these values have to do with a belief in the innate worth and dignity of all human beings, the right to self determination, and the rights of the individual to life, liberty, and personal gratification. "The basic value system and principles of the social work profession explicitly and unequivocally affirm human equality, dignity, and the meeting of basic human needs."[2]

The value system of the social work profession emphasizes the need to recognize both the client's unique needs as well as the needs he or she shares with all humanity. Although traditional social work knowledge relating to human social functioning provides a foundation for professional intervention, many people believe that the knowledge base is inadequate for effective intervention in black family systems.[3] Consequently, there is a need for additional concepts that are relevant to the unique needs and values of black families.

Providing treatment to enhance family functioning of black and other ethnic minority families that are economically and socially disadvantaged is difficult. Researchers have suggested that the historical patterns of discrimination and racism found in the United States have caused some ineffectiveness in the social service system, particularly in its treatment of black families.[4] This ineffectiveness can be attributed to a lack of knowledge for servicing people who have been systematically denied assimilation into the American Society. In such populations, the range and content of life experiences are in sharp contrast to those of the middle-class professionals who are usually providing the treatment. Consequently, any attempts to understand the familiar patterns of these groups necessitates a different form of assessment tool. Professional social workers need to know more about the culture and survival techniques of black families.

CULTURAL VARIANT PERSPECTIVE

Before the social worker can begin to provide effective services for the black community, he or she must be knowledgeable about various conceptualizations that are essential to understanding black culture. "Culture is sometimes defined as ways of acting and believing."[5] Attributes of culture are endemic to individuals' sharing similar life experiences, these individuals are usually associated with other people who belong to the

[2] "A Statement of Objectives, American Racism: Implications for Social Work Practice" (Philadelphia: University of Pennsylvania School of Social Work, 1977).

[3] Darielle L. Jones, "African-American Clients: Clinical Practice Issues," *Social Work* 24 (March 1979): 112–17; Alfred Kadushin, "The Racial Factor in the Interview," *Social Work* 17 (May 1972): 88–98; and Barbara E. Shannon, "Implications of White Racism for Social Work Practice," *Social Casework* 51 (May 1970): 270–76.

[4] Kadushin, "The Racial Factor"; and Shannon, "Implications of White Racism."

[5] Robert Staples, "Toward a Sociology of the Black Family: A Theoretical and Methodological Assessment," *Journal of Marriage and the Family* 33 (February 1971): 119.

same cultural group. Clifford J. Sager, Thomas L. Brayboy, and Barbara R. Waxenberg state that, "It is essential that the social worker know and, more importantly, want to know and to understand the living conditions, cultural patterns, and value systems of the people he/she seeks to help. Certain areas of sensitivity require understanding and tact that can come only from intimate knowledge of black people and their culture."[6]

The cultural variant perspective of black family functioning is a concept that is the most useful for perceiving the functioning of black families. This concept recognizes that black and white families exist in different social and cultural environments and consequently differ in both structure and ways of functioning. "This perspective emphasizes the need for 'cultural relativity,' that is, black-white differences are treated as outgrowths of their respective sociocultural contexts."[7] However, it is important to be aware that critical misuses of the cultural variant perspective can evolve. The cultural variant perspective can be used to undermine the need for society to adopt any commitment toward providing services to black families. This misuse can be justified by stating that a black family's dysfunction may be misinterpreted as being relevant to black culture and, therefore, not given any support for treatment. There are strengths and weaknesses in all patterns of family functioning, despite their cultural relevance. Social workers may continue to be confused about black behavior patterns and lifestyle unless they begin to view the black community as a culturally distinct group with a unique set of values and coping mechanisms. With an increased awareness of the black culture, the social worker can increase his or her skill in working with black families.

SURVIVAL TECHNIQUES

Social workers can also better understand black families' functioning by being sensitive to their survival techniques. In order to survive, black families have to adapt to a difficult, humiliating, and hostile environment. This struggle to survive has evoked a variety of adaptive mechanisms and emotional behaviors that are necessary for self-preservation. One behavior necessary for self-preservation is aggression or rage. Rage and aggression are often repressed, internalized, and accumulated; when ventilated, they may seem to be displaced or expressed in an inappropriate manner. However, the seeming inappropriateness of verbal or physical expression of rage is often due to the system's failure to meet the needs of black people. When a black person, especially a black male, deviates from society's mode of behavior, he or she tends to be labeled "aggressive." One example known to the author was that of a black male who had had a career in the military. He was a short, solidly-built man with a strong, deep voice, and a forthright posture. He had a very self-assured and stern personality which a worker labeled as aggressive.

Perhaps this social worker was accustomed only to the dependent and helpless posture that many black people use as a strategy to gain access to a variety of society's resources. Whichever the strategy used, black people have developed their own unique manner of coping. Social workers must be aware of the survival patterns that have en-

---

[6] Clifford J. Sager, Thomas L. Brayboy, Barbara R. Waxenberg, *Black Ghetto Family in Therapy—A Laboratory Experience* (New York: Grove Press, 1970), p. 228.

[7] Walter R. Allen, "Search for Applicable Theories for Black Family Life," *Journal of Marriage and the Family* 40 (February 1978): 117–29.

abled black families to maintain themselves under the extremely difficult position of being black in a humiliating environment.

TREATMENT SKILLS FOR EMPOWERMENT

Many social workers believe that black families are so preoccupied with the struggle for subsistence that they are unable to make use of clinical counseling and treatment services. Other social workers contend, however, that black families need help on a personal and interpersonal level for the purpose of enhancing their ability to cope with present realities. Thus, it is important for social workers to create a climate conducive to conveying a sense of self-determination and control within the family's present reality. If not, the family will feel a greater sense of powerlessness. Powerlessness is the family's inability to control or alter significantly its life situation and the forces impinging upon it. Consequently, the treatment skills used in providing services to black families must deal with the concept of power. Power is defined as: the actual or potential ability to influence behavior of others; or the control of resources that are essential to the functioning or survival of an individual or social system.

Given the power blocks created by oppression and the powerlessness which results in the lives of black clients, empowerment as a goal and process of intervention is of great significance in social work practice with black clients. "Empowerment is defined here as a process whereby the social worker engages in a set of activities with the client system that aim to reduce the powerlessness that has been created by negative valuations based on membership in a stigmatized group."[8]

Empowerment is a necessary goal and process when intervening in the family system of blacks or any other oppressed population. Three skills have potential for being empowering: relationship building; search for strength; transactional process.

Relationship Building

The process of relationship building is a crucial skill, especially when intervening in a black family system. Because of the abundance of stereotyping of blacks in society, the social worker must acknowledge and be extremely sensitive to the fact that there are heterogeneous lifestyles, values, and family structures existing within the black community. There must be a constant effort to understand and experience these differences. "Out of this familiarity with 'where the client is' it is possible to develop a skill in demonstrating your appreciation for those aspects of his life space, lifestyle, or value hierarchy as a means of establishing rapport."[9]

To get to the root of a family's problem, it is important to establish a relationship with not only the family as a unit, but also with each member of that unit. Howard Goldstein refers to a "kind of triple vision." He explains that in this situation there are three components in a relationship with a family unit :"(1) between the practitioner and specific individuals; (2) between other individual members of the unit; and (3) within

[8] Barbara Bryant Solomon, *Black Empowerment—Social Work in Oppressed Communities* (New York: Columbia University Press, 1976), p. 19.
[9] Ibid., p. 321.

the latter relationships as they are influenced by the presence of the practitioner."[10] The social worker has to maintain an accepting environment in order for the client to feel free to participate in the relationship building. The following case example illustrates this skill.

> Mr. and Mrs. P are a common-law couple with four children. Mrs. P brought her teenage son to the agency because she could not handle his violent temper and constant acting-out behavior. The social worker believed that it was extremely important for Mr. P to be involved in the family session. After numerous telephone calls and several letters, the social worker was unable to persuade Mr. P to attend the family sessions. However, she persisted in trying to engage him in counseling despite his extreme resistance. Mrs. P told the social worker that her husband was very suspicious and distrustful of social service agencies. He was a very proud man and did not like outsiders prying into his affairs. He felt that as the man of the family he should be able to handle his family's problems without the help of a social worker. This kind of survival technique is used by many black fathers and husbands who have been made to feel powerless in an oppressive society.
>
> The social worker recognized this attitude as typical of the feelings of many black males. However, she believed that she could help him recognize that he would not lose control of his family by joining them in treatment. By empowering him to feel that she could not fully understand or help resolve the family's problems without his influence and full participation, she was finally able to convince him that he was a viable and significant component of the treatment process. Once involved, Mr. P was very cooperative and actively participated in all of the counseling sessions.

Search for Strength

Search for strength relates to the social worker's emphasis on positive aspects of individuals and family systems. It is crucial to begin with strengths of the family system: families move on strengths, not weaknesses. There are inherent strengths in the design of every family; the social worker must help the family use their own strengths in making choices and decisions that will enable them to achieve their desired goal. This skill, as it relates to the search for and use of strength within the family system, has the potential for being very empowering.

The following is a family record demonstrating the social worker's skill in recognizing and acknowledging a mother's inner strength, and empowering her to use her strength.

> Mrs. M lived with her six children, ages two through seventeen. The husband of Mrs. M and the father of the four oldest children left the family when the youngest child was two months old. As a single parent, Mrs. M cared for and pro-

---

[10] Howard Goldstein, *Social Work Practice: A Unitary Approach* (Columbia: University of South Carolina, 1973), p. 138.

vided for her children. She was also doing very well in giving them the support and guidance they needed. However, when Mr. M fell behind in his child-support payments, it was decided that the four oldest children would move in with him, thereby eliminating the need for support payments to Mrs. M.

After nine months with their father, one by one the children began returning to Mrs. M because of discord and fighting within his home. By the time all of them were back with Mrs. M, one of the daughters was pregnant and all the children had been involved with the juvenile justice system. The children's behavior and attitude had changed so dramatically that Mrs. M was unable to handle them. They had become impudent, disobedient, and constantly stayed out past their curfew. All of this turmoil and conflict caused Mrs. M to feel powerless and incompetent as a parent.

The social worker began by helping Mrs. M recognize the strengths she had as a woman and mother and praising her for not giving up on her children. The worker also complimented her on the strength she had exhibited in coping with all of the things that had happened. The social worker's role in her relationship with Mrs. M was to empower the client to recognize and reclaim her inner strength, self-worth, and her many capabilities. The worker enabled Mrs. M to examine the strengths and capabilities she had demonstrated in the past. Through constant reinforcement and praise, Mrs. M was able to regain her self-confidence, self-esteem, and her effectiveness with her family.

The Transactional Process

"The tendency for powerless people to perceive social workers and other helping professionals as extensions of the powerful institutional forces which negatively value them is unquestionably prejudicial to the development of an effective problem-solving process."[11] Thus, when the client system has a history of being in powerless situations or has strong feelings of powerlessness, as is the situation with many black families, the social worker must maximize every opportunity for the client to be in charge rather than be controlled This empowering activity is based on what Harriet P. Trader refers to as "the transactional teaching-learning process . . . [and] is based on the assumption that both individually and collectively blacks possess unique and varied knowledge and skills. . . . [It] depends on a horizontal rather than a vertical transmission of such knowledge and skills. It implies a shared experience in the teaching-learning process, and it rejects the traditional vertical transmission of knowledge from the expert practitioner to the inexpert client. Rather, the role of the expert is seen as shifting between worker and client."[12]

One of the tasks in facilitating the use of the transactional teaching-learning process is that the sharing of information is planned. The social worker's and the client's areas of expertise are identified and clarified during the beginning of therapy and integrated as an on-going process in all of the sessions.

The transactional process provides a structure for the social worker to test precon-

---

[11] Solomon, *Black Empowerment*, p. 321.
[12] Harriet P. Trader, "Survival Strategies for Oppressed Minorities," *Social Work* 22 (January 1977): 11.

ceived assumptions about the family's structure, functioning, cultural background, and their priority problem. It also enables the family to test out any preconceived ideas they have about the worker and the agency. By carrying this process throughout the length of treatment, the family is less likely to feel a sense of powerlessness. The counseling session does need some leadership in order for change to occur; however, in light of empowerment as a goal, and the sense of powerlessness that most black families feel, the "transactional teaching-learning process" is more effective than the expert-social-worker-to-inexpert-client model when intervening in black family systems.

ENHANCING EFFECTIVENESS

In summary, culture and survival techniques—knowledge of which is necessary when providing services to black families—are related to the dynamics of power, powerlessness, and empowerment The possible consequences of growing up black in America can be better understood by knowing the relationship between all of these concepts.

It follows that the social worker whose purpose of intervention is to enhance family functioning needs to be engaged in change efforts on many levels if intervention is to be effective. This is especially true in providing services to black families where the impact of environmental stresses greatly impinges on day-to-day functioning. Social workers can enhance their effectiveness by not only facilitating change related to the area of the family's dysfunction, but also by changing the dysfunction in other systems that are impinging on the black family system when indicated.

As each social worker assesses the viability of his or her services to black families, the pertinent issues that need to be addressed are the interaction of three major variables: what the social worker brings to the session (cultural background, cultural biases, values, knowledge, professional skill); what the family brings to the session (culture, cultural biases, values, and needs); and the interrelationships of the historical, social, political, and economic environment and their impact on the therapeutic process.

RACE

CHAPTER 109

INSIGHT-ORIENTED PSYCHOTHERAPY AND THE CHINESE PATIENT

May Tung

Insight-oriented psychotherapy" and "Chinese patient" are terms that may appear contradictory to those mental health professionals who are interested in cross-cultural issues concerning the Chinese. They must by now be familiar with the interdependent and situational nature of Chinese life (*Hsu, 1985; Lin & Lin, 1981; Sue & Zane, 1987*). Furthermore, there is a wealth of literature regarding somatization of the Chinese (*Cheung, 1985; Kleinman & Kleinman, 1985; Tseng, 1975*). Lin (*1985*), however, has pointed out that the number of well-trained, psychoanalytically-oriented Chinese psychotherapists is so small that insight-oriented psychotherapy has not been adequately tried with Chinese patients. It may therefore be premature to assume that it does not work with this population. Roland (*1989*) utilized clinical examples to show how, with some modifications, psychoanalytic psychotherapy can be used with at least some Asians.

It seems evident that in considering the application of insight to psychotherapy, the first question must be: "Insight into what?" Some kind of road map, as it were, is necessary to give us an overview of the relevant areas to be explored. This paper is an attempt to chart such a map, exploring the topics of the world of the Chinese "self," and of characteristic Chinese defense and coping mechanisms. Issues raised are illustrated by clinical examples, some from reports in Chinese psychiatric journals, and some from case histories of Chinese-Americans in therapy in this country.

Reprinted from *American Journal of Orthopsychiatry,* Vol. 61, No. 2 (April 1991), pp. 186–194. Copyright 1991 by the American Orthopsychiatric Association, Inc. Reproduced by permission.

THE CHINESE "SELF"

Popular Chinese creation stories named P'an-ku as the creator who, in turn, had come into existence by way of cosmological evolution (*Williams, 1976*). Human beings are depicted as having come either from parasites on P'an-ku's body or from clay figures which he made in large supply (*Eberhard, 1965*). Thus, the Chinese view of the origin of human species is in sharp contrast to that of the Christian West, which views man as made in the image of God, unique and well defined.

The core of the Western definition of self, then, is reflective awareness. The issue of boundary applies to components within a system of the self; conflict is among these components, and is therefore intrapsychic (*Johnson, 1985*). In summarizing the world of a Chinese self, Hsu's (*1985*) concept of psychosocial homeostasis is useful. Instead of stressing personality, which is an individualistic concept, Hsu delineated the affective involvement of individuals with other people, gods, and objects. The Chinese are rooted in their kinship system, called by Hsu "intimate society and culture" (*p. 28*). The people who occupy this region for any individual are stable, and their accessibility is predictable and automatic. In contrast, Westerners are expected to leave this region of origin in order to find their own identity in a self-created world where relationships are voluntary and conditional. Thus, the Eastern definition of intimacy is the extent to which one can depend on the other (*Roland, 1989*). The Western definition is the extent to which one can feel safely undefended regarding one's innermost world.

Implied in the intimate region of the Chinese kinship system is that the structure predates the individual. This system is maintained by the durability of roles and regularity of the social order. A Chinese father-son story illustrates the absolute nature of this social order (and is especially interesting when compared to the story of Oedipus). In the Chinese story, a famous warrior leaves his pregnant wife to conduct a distant campaign for his emperor. He is away for 18 years. On his way home he meets a young man to whom he loses a marksmanship competition. The warrior immediately drives an arrow into the young man's heart, killing him, because no one is supposed to be superior to the warrior. The young man, it transpires, is his son, whom he had never seen before. The warrior justifies his act by asserting that the son had violated his cultural role, first by not recognizing his own father, then by daring to defeat him (*Bond, 1986*). The story implies that, without exception, role distinctions must be adhered to at all times.

During my ten years of practice as a Chinese-American psychotherapist in San Francisco, the differences between Western and Chinese worlds of the self have been broadly reflected in the way of life of my patients. Most of the Caucasian patients are from out of state; they live away from their families, with whom they have only occasional contact. All the Chinese patients, whether American-born or foreign-born, live near their families of origin. Many of them work for their parents, or for relatives or family friends. Some of them live in parental properties, and unmarried adult children frequently live with their parents.

DEFENSE AND COPING MECHANISMS

The characteristic coping and defense mechanisms of a culture are important in this context insofar as they reveal a people's psychological make-up and patterns of pathology. From these can be gleaned directions to be taken in treatment. Hsu (*1983*) pointed out that, while repression is more representative of cultures that emphasize internal control and individual responsibilities, suppression is more applicable to cultures of external control and situation-centered behavior. The contrast between situation and individual centeredness was discussed by Roland (*1989*), who used the terms "universalistic" as more characteristic of the West and "contextual" as characteristic of the East. Johnson (*1985*), characterizing Eastern and Western systems of perception and experience, called them "monotheistic" and "polytheistic," respectively. These terms suggest that, in the West, certain types of behavior are right or wrong under all circumstances; the ideal is a land governed by law. In the East, on the other hand, whether behavior is considered right or wrong depends on the circumstances and people involved; actions are compartmentalized, and there are clear guidelines as to what constitutes appropriate behavior in particular situations or relationships. For example, humor is considered inappropriate in formal settings or in speaking to an elder. One is expected to do what is right in a particular situation regardless of one's feelings (*Hsu, 1985*). The ideal is the endurance and stability of the social order as, in nature, one season forever follows another in certain order. In terms of individual behavior and adjustment, value is attached to rational control, compromise, and patience.

Appreciation of these basic contrasts in emphasis will enable us to understand that a Westerner can be "psychologically hurt" (*Hsu, 1985, p. 121*) by circumstances that would not have the same effect on an Easterner, and vice versa. This understanding will, in turn, affect the clinician's views of what constitutes an appropriate intervention in psychotherapy. An example of clinical work with a Chinese-American may illustrate this point:

> David, an Asian-born professional man in his 40s, sought help for a profound depression of one year's duration. His symptoms included significant weight loss, insomnia, inability to concentrate on his work, and general loss of interest in life. David's own explanation was in terms of guilt feelings toward his wife's death. When she had had to go to the hospital with what proved to be her final illness, David had been too busy at work to take her. Their son did so instead. David's life history showed no indications of childhood trauma or previous psychiatric problems. His marriage had been primarily duty-bound, as were most other aspects of his life. As therapy progressed, the only significant material that emerged was his lifelong wish to be a teacher, a profession not known for its financial rewards. Being the eldest son of a Chinese family he had felt responsible for providing for his parents. He became an engineer, worked diligently and strenuously, and was financially successful. As we were reviewing his life, David reported a dream in which he was in an airplane with colleagues on the way to a construction site. As the plane landed he realized that he was in the middle of Paris, which was bustling with color and gaiety, a far cry from the dusty construction site he had expected. By the time David had this dream, he had already gained enough self-understanding to recognize the message from his unconscious, and we shared a moment of humor. David's therapy lasted only eight sessions. He began to sleep and eat normally, then resigned from his firm and went to Asia. Eight months later, he called to express thanks for the treatment. He had been traveling, doing

free-lance consultations, and writing a text book on his engineering specialty for schools in Asia.

This case of bicultural psychotherapy combined the Chinese value of filial responsibility, doing what is right for one's parents, with the Western value of individual pursuit. The wife's sudden death was like an unexpected stop signal, jolting him into realization of the pointlessness of continuing in the same direction. He was at a loss. Without the cultural knowledge of how essential it is for an eldest Chinese son to be filial, this man's course of action in life could easily be misdiagnosed as neurotic dependency, or even masochism. In China, on the other hand, he might be considered selfish for wanting fulfillment of his own wishes. Of course, if he had lived in China, he might not have experienced such a bicultural conflict in the first place. But even if he wanted such changes, there would be much more social pressure there for him to stay put. Alternatives would be far fewer, and a fling in Paris definitely not an option!

CLINICAL EXAMPLES FROM CHINA

Increasing Asian immigration to North America has brought with it a growth in the Asian patient population in this country. In working with these patients, it is important for the clinician to understand the cultural roots that are firmly planted, even in second and third generation Asian-Americans. On the continuum of individual/situation orientation and affective/cognitive emphasis, case histories from China can exemplify that end of the continuum at which situational and cognitive elements are culturally dominant. By referring to the source, we may acquire some fundamental knowledge.

Psychotherapy is still rare in Chinese psychiatry. In case records of psychotherapy from Chinese psychiatric journals of the 1980s, the most prominent feature is the pivotal role of rational, cognitive, commonsense understanding. Chinese psychotherapy invariably takes the form of the doctor explaining to the patient that the symptoms or preoccupations presented are illogical and abnormal. Common sense, reasoning, and objective reality are cited as "evidence." The treatments prescribed combine medication, specific behavioral homework (e.g., keeping a diary), desensitization exercises, and a few "talk" sessions with the doctor to reinforce the prescription. The goal is symptom removal (*Tan, 1988; Yang, 1983; Zhao, 1987*).

Reflected, but not explicitly stated, in these records is the kindly and supportive, but directive and parent-like position of the doctor, who patiently guides the child-patient to see reason. This impression of the therapeutic relationship is consistent with the family orientation of the Chinese.

A departure from this therapeutic attitude, although more in content than style, is the work of Zhong You-bin,* a Beijing psychiatrist, who is considered to be China's authority on Freud. He had found Freud's emphasis on child experiences a familiar concept to the Chinese, illustrated in Chinese folktales and proverbs. By means of self-analysis ("Just like Freud himself did!"), he concluded that Freud's concepts were applicable in his own practice. The core of his psychotherapy is to explain to his patients

---

* In Chinese names the family name comes first, again consistent with the emphasis of family over the individual. (In the reference list. consequently. the names of Chinese authors from China are without punctuation.)

that their current difficulties are rooted in their childhood and therefore no longer appropriate for an adult. He instructs them to recall childhood trauma, often with the help of family members, and to trace how certain behavioral and thinking patterns were established. He has been successful in treating some severe pathologies in just a few sessions. In essence, the style remains uniquely Chinese, addressed mainly to the cognitive and rational rather than to the affective and unconscious. However, what is new about Zhong's approach is his use of a different content—childhood experiences—and the fact that he requires more participation from the patients and their families in working on recollection and understanding. In other words, his approach is a form of structured and guided insight, reminiscent of the therapeutic process described in Bellak's intensive brief psychotherapy (*1983, p. 39*).

Though Zhong has published many of his successful cases, for our purpose, the following two case examples that he recorded as failures (*Zhong, 1988*) are more relevant as illustrations of how cultural style can be an asset as well as a limitation in any treatment:

> Y was a female high school teacher in her 40s. Her difficulties began when she graduated from high school with superior grades. She was refused college entrance because her father had been classified as an "intellectual" which often meant being regarded as a "reactionary rightist" in China's political climate of the late '50s. Y worked in a factory before becoming a high school teacher, which did not require a college degree in certain parts of China. From depression in her late adolescence, her difficulties escalated to phobic preoccupation with cancer and obsessive-compulsive ritualistic washing of everything in sight. She had 13 sessions with Zhong within one year. She understood and agreed with the doctor's explanations but terminated treatment after only a minimum degree of improvement.

In this case, as in all others from China, nothing was said about affective aspects such as her many losses, great sadness, and other emotional injuries. Unlike other Chinese therapists, however, Zhong acknowledged "more deep seated reasons" for her resistance. In his second failed case:

> Z was a female factory worker in her mid-30s. In her background were an aggressive, intrusive mother and a quiet, passive father. When her father died, she became depressed and gradually developed obsessive-compulsive cleaning and washing behavior. Within a period of nine months she had ten sessions with Zhong. At each session, Z talked incessantly, leaving little opportunity for the doctor to do so.

Zhong correctly identified this form of resistance as "the best defense is offense." He further conceptualized this case in terms of Z's need for these symptoms as a defense against her situational stresses. In other words, the symptoms were the lesser of the two evils. This interpretation, accurate or not, is the only one implying unconscious motivation that I have come across in case histories from China. As in the first case, no mention was made of any intervention on the affective level or of addressing the unconscious. The possibility that Z had adopted with the doctor her mother's strategy of being always on the offensive to avoid being dominated in the way her father had been—a matter of transference—was not discussed. Whether and how transference interpretations should be made in psychotherapy with Chinese patients is another complex issue (addressed later in the paper). In both of Zhong's cases, guidance and explanations were apparently not enough. Chinese people do not openly challenge authority, in this instance personified by the therapist: they just stop coming. Thus, one must be careful not to overstate the effectiveness of the authoritative approach in treating Chinese patients.

These clinical examples from China raise important issues—the role of affective, irrational, and unconscious material, and the nature of the therapeutic relationship—all key concepts in psychodynamic psychotherapy.

CLINICAL EXAMPLES OF CHINESE-AMERICANS

To explore some of these issues, two case histories of Chinese-Americans seen in therapy in San Francisco are illustrative:

Lynn

Lynn was a third generation Chinese-American woman. She was in her mid-20s when she began therapy, and attended sessions once a week, with rare cancellations, for almost six years. Her presenting complaints were mainly in somatic terms: hyperventilation, insomnia, night sweats, severe stomach aches with no organic basis, and general nervousness. She had to be driven everywhere, and displayed agorophobic symptoms in such places as restaurants and supermarkets. In the first session, she reported a recurrent dream of huge spiders and spider webs that she associated with death. She described herself as pessimistic, and believed that she was born that way.

Lynn was the oldest of three children, and the only girl. Her childhood was marked by an elderly father, a paranoid mother, frequent parental fights, and beatings by her mother. Her father was disappointed that his first child was a girl, which is a common Chinese reaction. Lynn's wish to continue her father's work repeatedly met with strong objections from both her father and his contemporaries in the business.

In the initial sessions she dwelled mainly on her many painful memories, although she first had to be given permission to do so and assured that she was not being selfish to think of herself (a typical Chinese attitude), and that her feelings were understandable. She was greatly relieved to be told that her pessimism was learned, rooted in her childhood experiences, and could therefore be unlearned.

Hyperventilation was greatly reduced within a month of starting therapy. After working through her fears of being condemned or criticized by the therapist, she began to deal with her sense of worthlessness and guilt. For example, in the fifth month of therapy, she talked one day about the fact that her father was vague and distant, and that she always felt disapproval from him. Later in the session she mentioned that her worst fear was that "God will come to me before I'm ready" and she would be condemned to "eternal suffering." When the therapist commented on the similarity between her perception of her father and her perception of God, she was able to see that her anxiety about God was related to her experiences with her father. This insight into the fact that her problems were "inside" herself, gave her a degree of freedom. The following week, she reported a dream of being on horseback. She wanted the horse to go in one direction, but "he had a mind of his own," and overtook another horse to gallop across the San Francisco-Oakland Bay Bridge. She felt good: "We won!" This dream of her aspirations and innate power was used repeatedly as a metaphor in the course of her treatment.

In her eighth month of therapy she experienced two episodes of severe stomachache in one week. In the therapy session she was able to associate her symptoms with her pain at her father's unfair treatment of her and to "the way I am," meaning she was "unclean." She recalled how her mother used to tell her that she was "no good" because she was not a boy.

There were continuous indications of increasing self-awareness and more realistic assessment of her life situation, as well as the evolution of skills to bring about changes. Lynn used psychotherapy not only to remove symptoms but also for growth. The fact that she had been deprived of adequate parenting made long-term psychotherapy even more beneficial.

Barry

Barry was a married Chinese man in his late 20s when he began therapy. He saw the therapist once a week, with rare cancellations, for four years and ten months. He was the younger of two sons, born and raised in Asia, and came to the United States to attend college. Depression was his presenting complaint with no somatic component except moderate overweight. The core conflict was his fear of his father, for whom he worked. All his life Barry had been convinced that the father favored the older son, a common Chinese phenomenon. With this conviction as a base, Barry construed detailed "evidence" of slights, deception, and conspiracy against him on the part of his father and brother. His intelligence and his compulsive style lent themselves to "documenting" these conjectures so well that they reached paranoid proportions. While Barry managed the office in San Francisco, his father and brother basically lived in Asia. They were in regular telephone communication several times a week. The three were so close knit that they could have been living and working under the same roof. In his relationship to his wife Barry was rigidly controlling, though extremely dependent on her emotionally. They lived a guarded life and did not take a vacation until his second year of therapy for fear his father would think him irresponsible.

There was no evidence of abuse or neglect in Barry's early life. It appeared that while his father and three siblings were all outgoing and verbal, Barry had always been introverted, awkward, and "out of it." Only after some years of therapy and the experience of fathering a child somewhat like himself did he appreciate the anxiety he had caused his parents. They had kept him under close surveillance as a young child to insure his safety. For instance, they would come into his room to check up on him, even when he had locked the door; they would also look through his belongings while he, on his part, pretended to be asleep. (In Chinese family life, while emotions are considered to be private, property is not, so that searches such as the ones by Barry's parents would not be viewed as extreme.) Since they never explained or even mentioned their actions, Barry grew up assuming that something was wrong with him.

Two other features in Barry's background are relevant. First, he was brought up by his widowed maternal grandmother (a frequent practice in Chinese families) who was herself an unhappy and suspicious person. Second, instability and unrest prevailed in Asia during Barry's childhood; he recalled, for instance, anxiety and fears of kidnapping when his father went on business trips. Thus, suspicion and caution were also endemic in this larger context.

It was understood in the family that Barry and his brother would grow up to work for their father. Despite feeling unnoticed and undervalued, Barry always had a deep love for his father, often fantasizing great achievements that he would dedicate to him. During therapy, he realized that his desire to please his father was, in part, competitive. In working for him, he often felt that his father got all the credit. He felt unable to really "see" himself. As he put it, he wanted a sense of himself as a whole tree (an individualistic goal) and not just as a branch (a Chinese view). Even though he felt suffocated in the family business, however, Barry saw the outside world as a fearsome jungle. For many years, he had a recurrent dream of being literally glued to a spot from which he could not pull himself up.

Ambivalence toward his father coiled through therapy. In the third year of therapy he had enough money to purchase a house on his own. He thought his father would be pleased; instead, his father was cool toward the project. It was obvious that he felt Barry should have honored him by asking his advice. Barry reclaimed his father's interest by skillfully involving him in a financial arrangement. This experience taught Barry how difficult it would be for him to become independent in the Western sense. Purchasing a house independently would have been praiseworthy for a Caucasian-American, but in Chinese culture, fathers must be consulted at all times. For Westerners, to stay with one's parents much beyond adulthood is undesirable. For Chinese, to leave one's parents is a serious offense.

Toward the end of his third year of therapy, Barry went through two months of extreme depression, during which time he played with the idea of resigning from the family business, much like a person preparing to plunge from a great height. The depression lifted just as abruptly as it had started, as if a fever had broken. Retrospectively, Barry felt that it had been his last flirtation with independence before finally committing himself to the family business; after resolving to stay, he looked almost light-hearted and happy—in his own metaphor, he had just come out of incubation.

Equipped with more self-knowledge and awareness of his bicultural life situation, Barry was able to make decisions that gave him a sense of self-worth and freedom.

DISCUSSION

It is clear, then, that Chinese tradition persists, even with vastly different pathologies and lengths of exposure to the West. In this section three key issues regarding insight-oriented psychotherapy and the Chinese patient will be addressed: the "territory" of psychological exploration, the therapeutic relationship, and the role of didactic teaching.

Therapeutic Territory

The main difference between the latter two Chinese-American cases and insight-oriented psychotherapy with middle-class Caucasian-Americans is in terms of the "territory" of exploration. The term "insight" in this context is usually limited to an intrapsychic sense, as in Johnson's (1985) definition of the Western self, the locus of control residing in the individual self. Since the boundary of the Chinese self is vastly different, so must be the application of insight. For most Chinese-Americans, therapeutic explorations are never far from the family sphere. The core conflict is worked out directly with the original cast of characters.

The energy and emotional investment of Chinese-Americans are permanently centered on this original cast. Emotionally, they need not be as mobile as their Caucasian counterparts. Therapy with Caucasians, on the other hand, deals mainly with patterns of transference distortions. Because they have to create their own structures and conditions in each new encounter, these patterns persist from one relationship to the next. Slater (1970), while discussing dependence and independence, described American society as having:

> ... fewer "givens," more ambiguous criteria, less environmental stability, and less social structural support, than any people in history. [Within this fluid culture the] mobile individual must travel light, and internalized controls are portable and transistorized, as it were. (pp. 21, 23)

This is a graphic image of a highly charged, compact, and enclosed bundle of energy. For this group, each new involvement becomes of central importance for that time period. In other words, the territory of psychological significance is directly related to the next issue.

Therapeutic Relationship

When the new involvement of the Caucasian patient is the therapeutic one, then that is the matter of central importance, the present focus of energy for that patient. My own therapeutic work with Chinese-American patients has seemed to lack the intense patient-therapist relationship of my work with Caucasian-American patients. Coming from a psychodynamic background, where transference interpretation is of central importance, I feared having overlooked something, or possible interference from my own countertransference. At the same time, my Chinese patients seemed much less concerned about their dependence on me as the therapist than did many of my Caucasian patients. The Chinese patients as a whole were also less likely to tolerate or benefit from frequent sessions—say, twice a week—or from long-term work. These phenomena may be related, but no literature has discussed them except in terms of frustration and bewilderment at the tendency for Chinese people to be "underserved" in mental health services.

In Hsu's (*1981*) analysis of family structure and emotionality, he observed that a deeper emotional involvement between parents and children obtains in a Western, exclusive, nuclear family because the parents are the sole authority figures in a child's life. In the Chinese extended family, parent-child relationships are "diluted" by frequent exposure to other significant adults, often of equal authority over the children.

Typically, the Chinese patient in therapy continues to be centrally involved in the original extended family; the therapist is of only peripheral importance. Space does not allow a full description of the typical formation of a Chinese support network, but in terms of that network, the professional relationship with the therapist is functional and pragmatic; it does not define or threaten the patient's concept of self-worth.

In comparison, dynamic or psychoanalytic psychotherapy with Caucasians entails hundreds of hours working on issues involving one's family of origin, especially the parents. The very concept of transference is based on the pivotal role of the parents. Perhaps the culturally necessitated separation and independence from them further intensify these earlier ties, leaving little opportunity for resolution. In the absence of real parents who can be dealt with directly, this intensity is transferred onto the therapist. The complexity of this transference is increased by the Westerner's cultural ambivalence toward dependency needs, and the consequent suspicion that therapy may lead to dependence on the therapist. A recent Hawaiian study (*Harvard Mental Health Letter, 1990*) of ethnic differences in marital status and psychiatric symptoms reported that, after correction for age, the correlation between psychiatric symptoms and unmarried state disappeared for Filipino and Japanese Hawaiians, but not for white and native Hawaiians. The authors speculated that the two former groups receive from their extended families support that substitutes for the protection of marriage, while the latter two do not. Thus, it seems appropriate to allocate a secondary role to transference analysis in working with Chinese patients. Emphasis on this aspect of psychotherapy sometimes frustrates these patients, disrupting the flow of their work because it is basically unimportant, even irrelevant, for them. Further detail with regard to Chinese styles of therapeutic relationship can be found in articles by Hsu (*1985*) and Tung (*1984*).

Didactic Teaching

The role of didactic teaching, which applies to cognitive understanding, is of unique importance to the Chinese population. Again, space limits do not allow a more detailed discourse on the relation of Chinese cognition to learning and functioning. Liu (*1986*) spoke of the "respect superiors" rule of Chinese life style. Pillsbury (*1986*) discussed the differences in styles of learning between East and West, representing the former as passive, with the responsibility for initiation being the teacher's. The Chinese typically prefer the teacher to outline the parameters of action. In the case of psychiatric treatment, a rational explanation, direction, and even justification from the therapeutic authority is consistent with the external locus of control of the world of a Chinese self, where situational givens have to be noted alongside subjective reactions.

Although two of the Chinese-American cases, those of Lynn and Barry, used substantially affective and unconscious material, cognitive understanding was necessary to establish a working relationship. Because the therapist occupies a peripheral and functional role in Chinese patients' lives, it is not enough to rely on the transference. It is necessary to help them to see how therapy is relevant in terms they find familiar. Lynn, for example, was "taught" to explore her feelings by being told that her pessimism was learned and could be unlearned; and that, while the Chinese tend to perceive self-analysis as being selfish, it is hard work of eventual benefit to the patient and the family. In Barry's case, much discussion of cultural differences was necessary to clarify his bicultural dilemma and misunderstandings.

It is also extremely valuable to discuss and concede importance to the experience of being uprooted that both the patient and the patient's parents have usually undergone. These experiences often have a direct correspondence to fragmented self-identity.

CONCLUSION

The applicability of insight-oriented psychotherapy for the Chinese patient appears to be twofold. On the specific level of somatic expression of distress among the Chinese, Lynn's case demonstrates that "liberation" of suppressed material is effective in dealing with somatic symptoms, and can lead to better integration and functioning. In this sense psychodynamic insight-oriented psychotherapy should be particularly appropriate for some Chinese patients. More generally, psychodynamic principles are only partially based on knowledge of such human conditions as the power of the emotions and the unconscious. However, a great deal of the approach, at least as it is practiced in the West, is based on cultural values, belief systems, and life styles. With modifications appropriate to the patient's personal world—be it unicultural or bicultural—the basic principles have the potential for broad applications. When the cultural-dynamic dimension is combined with psychodynamics, the approach can only enrich psychotherapy for everyone.

REFERENCES

Bellak, L., & Siegel, H. (1983). *Handbook of intensive brief and emergency psychotherapy.* Larchmont, NY: C.P.S. Inc.

Bond, M., & Hwang, K. (1986). The social psychology of Chinese people. In M. Bond (Ed.), *The psychology of Chinese people* (pp. 213–266). New York: Oxford University Press.

Cheung, F. (1985). An overview of psychopathology in Hong Kong with special reference to somatic presentations. In W.S. Tseng & D. Wu (Eds.), *Chinese culture and mental health* (pp. 287–304). Orlando, FL: Academic Press.

Eberhard, W. (1965). *Folktales of China* (3rd. Rev.). Chicago: University of Chicago Press.

Harvard Mental Health Letter. (1990, December). *Marriage and psychiatric symptoms: Ethnic differences*, p. 7.

Hsu, F.L.K. (1981). *Americans and Chinese: Passage to differences* (3rd. Ed., pp. 76–120). Honolulu: University of Hawaii Press.

Hsu, F.L.K. (1983). Suppression versus repression: A limited psychological interpretation of four cultures. In F.L.K. Hsu (Ed.), *Rugged individualism reconsidered* (pp. 104–129). Knoxville: University of Tennessee Press.

Hsu, F.L.K. (1985). The self in cross-cultural perspective. In A. Marsella, G. DeVos, & F. Hsu (Eds.), *Culture and self* (pp. 24–55). New York: Tavistock Publications.

Hsu, J. (1985). The Chinese family: Relations, problems, and therapy. In W.S. Tseng & D. Wu (Eds.), *Chinese culture and mental health* (pp. 95–112). Orlando, FL: Academic Press.

Johnson, F. (1985). The Western concept of self. In A. Marsella, G. DeVos, & F. Hsu (Eds.), *Culture and self* (pp. 91–138). New York: Tavistock Publications.

Kleinman, A., & Kleinman, (1985). Somatization: The interconnections in Chinese society among culture, depressive experiences, and the meanings of pain. In A. Kleinman & B. Good (Eds.), *Culture and depression* (pp. 429–490). Berkeley: University of California Press.

Lin, T.Y., & Lin, M.C. (1981). Love, denial, and rejection: Responses of Chinese families to mental illness. In A. Kleinman & T.Y. Lin (Eds.), *Normal and abnormal behavior in Chinese behavior* (pp. 387–401). Norwell, MA: D. Reidel.

Lin. T.Y. (1985). Mental disorders and psychiatry in Chinese culture: Characteristic features and major issues. In W.S. Tseng & D. Wu (Eds.), *Chinese culture and mental health,* (pp. 369–393). Orlando, FL: Academic Press.

Liu, I.M. (1986). *Chinese cognition in the psychology of the Chinese people* (pp. 73–105). New York: Oxford University Press.

Pillsbury, B. (1986). *Medical learning in North America: A handbook for Chinese visiting scholars in the United States and Canada.* San Francisco: U.S. China Education Institute.

Roland, A. (1989). *In search of self in India and Japan.* Princeton, NJ: Princeton University Press.

Slater, P. (1970). *The pursuit of loneliness.* Boston: Beacon Press.

Sue, S. & Zane, N. (1987). The role of culture and cultural techniques in psychotherapy. *American Psychologist, 42*(1), 37–45.

Tan, Y.C. (1988). *Notes of a Chinese psychiatrist.* Beijing: Quonzhong Publications. (In Chinese)

Tseng, W.S. (1975). The nature of somatic complaints among psychiatric patients: The Chinese case. *Comprehensive Psychiatry, 16,* 237–245.

Tung, M. (1984). Life values, psychotherapy, and East-West integration. *Psychiatry, 47,* 285–292.

Williams, C.A.S. (1976). *Outline of Chinese symbolism and art motifs.* (3rd ed.) New York: Dover Publications.

Yang, H.Y. (1983). Phobia and its psychological treatment. *Chinese Journal of Nervous and Mental Disease, 9* (2)102–103. (In Chinese)

Zhao, G.Y. (1987). Eight cases of anxiety disorders and obsessive compulsive behavior. *Chinese Mental Health Journal, 1*(5), 236. (In Chinese)

Zhao, G.Y. (1988). Fear of height and "treatment dependency." *Chinese Mental Health Journal, 2*(2), 90. (In Chinese)

Zhong, Y.B. (1988). *Chinese psychoanalysis.* People's Publications of Lian Nin. (In Chinese)

CHAPTER 110

CLINICAL TREATMENT OF BLACK FAMILIES

Issues and Strategies

Jeanne B. Robinson

Black and white mental health professionals and paraprofessionals have been concerned with the possibility that racial differences could affect negatively the treatment of socially or psychologically dysfunctioning black individuals and families. Controversy also has existed regarding the appropriate theoretical approach for considering the relationship between race and psychotherapy. Two major controversies exist: (1) whether the concept of a black personality is itself functional or valid and (2) whether the racial biases of white or black therapists seriously affect the therapeutic process with black clients. Although the biases of black clinicians possibly also may affect therapy with white clients, the author will not focus on that particular configuration. The purpose of this article is to demonstrate how racial biases may affect the treatment process with black clients and to present strategies for alleviating the effects of biases.

The author believes that the initial phase of therapy is the point at which the clinician must assess both the impact of race and racism on the life of the client and the potential influence of racism on the process of therapy. *Racism* is an institutionalized disparity between the two groups defined by this society as the black race and the white race. The proposed model for assessment will enable the clinician to use the therapeutic engagement process to identify and address racially based impediments to treatment. The specific goal is to enhance the ability of the clinician to minimize the potentially negative influence of race on the therapeutic process. With the provided framework,

Reprinted from *Social Work,* Vol. 34, No. 4 (July 1989), pp. 323–329, by permission of NASW Press. Copyright 1989, National Association of Social Workers, Inc., *Social Work.*

clinicians can assess and mitigate the impact of race and intra- and interracial differences on the process of therapy.

Whether overt or covert, racism often is the apparent basis of decisions and actions that will profoundly affect the life of the black individual. Psychological testing and diagnosis, school placement, job or career opportunities, and living conditions are the primary concerns of black consumers of sociopsychological services. The profound and pervasive influence of racism in at least one of these areas has been endemic to the experience of black Americans. Failure to consider this factor may result in the clinician and client having significant unacknowledged differences in their definitions of the problem to be addressed in therapy and in their estimates of the viability of specific solutions (Helms, 1984). For example, the clinician may not know that the client includes race as a relevant factor in the presenting problem. By choosing not to elicit or acknowledge the client's perspective regarding race, the therapist risks disrupting the formation of an alliance that the client experiences as empathic. The degree of empathy experienced by the client is one of the most salient elements in the treatment relationship, and its absence frequently has led to premature withdrawal from individual, family, or group treatment (R. Katz, 1963).

THE BLACK EXPERIENCE

The black experience refers to those interactions between black and white people, and among black people, in which racial identification of the parties is a dominant behavior determinant. The black experience consists of black persons being the objects of overt and covert racism.

Some researchers have focused on racism as an integral part of the American culture, established as a result of the economic and psychological demands of the dominant group and currently maintained through the acquiescence to the values and practices of the larger society (Kovel, 1970; Ryan, 1971). Ogbu (1983) pointed out that an inclusive analysis of the situation confronting black people in this society would focus on the instrumental exploitation, expressive exploitation, and expressive responses. Thus, understanding the conditions under which black people live in American society requires examining the behaviors and statements of white people and the behavioral and verbal responses of black people. Given the complexity of racism and the variability of individual experience, one can assume that removing the overt impediments to clinical treatment (for example, availability of centers, fee schedules, and the like) will only begin to address the constellation of factors related to race that will affect the outcome of the treatment experience. Several scholars have described the necessity for clinicians to address the black experience in the treatment process (Gibbs, 1985; Hays & Banks, 1972; Helms, 1984; White, 1980).

In an effort to delineate specific elements of the experiences of American black people that appear to be common, scholars have tended to focus on overt and covert racism (I. Katz, Wackenhut, & Hass, 1986; Kovel, 1970), or on the efforts of black people to organize their responses in an integrated manner (Chestang, 1972; Hall, Cross, & Freedle, 1972). Other scholars have analyzed the process by which some black people organize their experiences both conceptually and affectively to manage their activities realistically in an essentially hostile environment. For the purposes of this discussion, Chestang's (1972) categorizations of the elements of racism are useful for considering the impact of the black experience on the black personality. These elements are

> social injustice . . . the denial of legal rights; social inconsistence . . . the institutionalized disparity between word and deed; and impotence . . . the feeling of powerlessness to influence the environment. (Chestang, 1972, pp. 3–4)

BLACK PERSONALITY STRUCTURE

Early professional literature regarding a black personality structure appears to reflect a consensus that the mental and emotional development of black people is less sophisticated and less self-accepting than the mental and emotional development of white people. Valentine (1968) reviewed the history of works by black and white scholars that spawned what he referred to as the *pejorative tradition,* which denigrated black members of the lower class, questioned their value system, and predicted poor prospects for change in their circumstances primarily because of the "deficiencies" of the black personality. Valentine is particularly scathing about the research methods and unfounded assumptions underlying the research. Typically, the characterizations in the early literature of black people as deficient or inferior are derived from researchers' observations of black people who were in psychotherapy or indigent, with the findings generalized to all black people as if they were a homogeneous group (Meyers, 1982). To propose that unscientific samples of black people who were clients or were the subsidized poor represented the characteristics of the black population at large was defective reasoning that served to stimulate or encourage negative stereotypic images of black people (McAdoo, 1981; Wilson, 1986).

Some scholars think that low self-esteem is a common characteristic of black individuals and attribute it to experiences with racism and the acceptance of the negative reinforcement received from the environment (Banks, 1985; Taylor, 1976). Other scholars think that much of the behavior that has been attributed to lack of self-esteem should be reclassified as adaptive responses to white expectations and oppressive behaviors (Gibbs, 1985; Hays & Banks, 1972; Jackson, 1980; White, 1980). The latter perspective involves an interactional approach to the study of black and white individuals. The essential concept in this approach is that of *synergism*—that is, the concept that in contexts involving white people, the self-esteem and behavior of black people are related, in part, to the influence of attitudes and behaviors of the white people they encounter. An essential component of therapeutic interventions with black clients is recognizing the variability among black individuals in their experiences of racism and in their responses to those experiences. These differences in experiences are determined partly by the variability of attitudes and behaviors toward black people displayed by white people in different environments and socioeconomic strata (I. Katz et al., 1986; Linville, Salovey, & Fischer, 1986).

In the Chestang (1972) paradigm, the reality of racism is seen as influencing the development of the individual personality or character in a unique manner. Depending on the individual black person's experiences with both the familial (nurturing) and the so-

cietal (sustaining) environments, the person exhibits one of three patterns of social responses: (1) exploitative, (2) transcendent, or (3) unified/integrated. The exploitative
response involves an unabashed effort to extract goods, services, and the like from the
environment while exhibiting a self-deprecating attitude. The transcendent response is
a tendency to endure the practices of racism while maintaining a faith in the essential
humanity of people. The unified/integrated response is the development of an integrated personality that acknowledges racism as a factor in society yet establishes an
identity not influenced significantly by the inherently racist behaviors encountered in
society. The unified/integrated personality surpasses the exploitative and the transcendent positions. The unified/integrated personality is facilitated by the presence of a nurturing family and community and presupposes access to means of economically based
sustenance. This personality is impeded by barriers to social recognition, such as inadequate access to justice, consistency, and power (Chestang 1972).

The Hall, Cross, and Freedle (1972) model of black personality development is congruent with Chestang's. Those authors denoted four developmental stages: (1) pre-
encounter, an awareness that identity is based on "a world view dominated by
Euro-American determinants" (p. 159); (2) encounter, a dislocation of old referents
and an attraction to black referents; (3) immersion–emersion, a temporarily reactionary
perspective of racism that ends with sorting the strengths and weaknesses of blackness;
and (4) internalization, a "resolution between the old and new world views . . . black
[is] the primary reference group and the person moves toward a pluralistic non-racist
perspective, with confidence in one's own personal standards of blackness" (p. 159).
Research by Parham and Helms (1985) has indicated that black people vary in terms of
their development of a racial identity.

Each black person's experiences and interpretation of them influence the attitudes
regarding race that the person brings to the therapeutic environment. Black people
often find that social recognition does not accompany economic success as it does for
their white cohorts (Bass, Acosta, & Evans, 1982). The realization of this fact can affect self-perception negatively:

> Individuals derive important aspects of their self concepts from the social groups
> to which they belong . . . because self evaluation depends in part on their evalua-
> tion of groups to which they belong . . . they are therefore motivated to perceive
> those groups in positive terms. (Hamilton & Trolier, 1986, p. 156)

However, Porter (1971) found that among black children from working- and middle-
class families, acceptance of racial identity correlated negatively with social class. Black
children from working-class families had the most positive racial self-concept of children in any socioeconomic group. In contrast, black children from middle-class families
had low self-esteem that related to their perception of their racial identity. Middle-class
black children tend to be exposed to more racism because they have more contact with
white people than lower class black children. Taylor (1976) reviewed several studies
and concluded that

> the black child's day-to-day interpersonal encounters in the black community are
> largely responsible for determining his [or her] self regard . . . that his [or her]

encounters with the white world are filtered through a black frame of reference, the latter being the context within which his [or her] self-esteem is developed and in large measure protected and maintained. (p. 15)

Gaertner and Dovidio (1986) referred to a

systematized tendency in all people to desire positive self esteem, in terms of both personal and group identity, [and therefore] there is a tendency to see positive distinctions for the ingroup over the outgroup. (p. 61)

In summary, racial self-concept is variable. Therefore, its immediate and potential influence on the treatment process is not readily predictable. The assessment and management of racial issues in clinical practice must be studied and elucidated in the context of this complexity.

RACIAL ISSUES IN CLINICAL PRACTICE

A strong possibility exists that in treatment situations involving black clients, the establishment of a working alliance will be influenced by the race of the therapist, the attitudes of the clinician toward the client, or the attitude of the client toward the clinician based on the beliefs of either party about race and racism or about the role of race and racism in the presenting problem. Research about stereotypes indicates that stereotypes pose a threat to effective therapy (Acosta, Yamamoto, & Evans, 1982; Franklin, 1985; Gardner, 1970; Hollingshead & Redlich, 1958). However, the data do not support the procedure of matching therapists and clients by race. Rather, the potential exists for therapists of any race to be effective or ineffective depending on the extent to which they have unresolved racial prejudices. Considerable evidence exists of the current presence of disparate attitudes and behaviors toward black people in American society. Gaertner and Dovidio (1986) reported that

prejudiced thinking and discrimination still exist, but the contemporary forms are more subtle, more indirect, and less overtly negative than are the more traditional forms. (p. 84)

Similarly, a black client is more or less likely to impede the development of a working therapeutic alliance based on the extent to which the client has evolved a unified personality as defined by Chestang (1972).

Four issues may present significant impediments to achievement of treatment goals: (1) racial congruence of the client, (2) influence of race on the presenting problem, (3) the clinician's racial awareness, and (4) the clinician's strategies. The clinician has specific therapeutic tasks related to each issue. The client's racial congruence is the client's acceptance of group identity. The clinician must clarify the client's relationships with individuals and subgroups of the client's race and the client's own identity as a member of the group. For the issue of influence of race on the presenting problem, the clinician must assess the extent to which race is a factor in the problems presented by the client. The clinician must assess this influence both in the client's own perception and in the clinician's independent contextual understanding of the circumstances. For the therapist's racial awareness, the clinician must address the racial attitudes and beliefs that he or she is bringing to the treatment process professionally and personally. Finally, the clinician must master strategies for addressing the other three issues during the engagement process and in the pursuit of treatment goals.

The questions that follow can aid the clinician in eliciting information regarding race as a factor in the treatment process with black clients. These factors are an addendum to the customary theoretical framework that underlies the process of clinical assessment and treatment. The style and training of the clinician will determine the manner in which the data are collected. For example, a question such as, "What do you think causes you difficulty?" may elicit a direct statement about racial factors or may lead to hesitation, which suggests that the client is reluctant to state an opinion at that particular stage of the interview. The client may respond with a socially acceptable response, which suggests a lack of understanding that the clinician is referring to the possibility that racial factors affect the problem. A relatively common error for the clinician during the early stage of treatment is premature clinical anticipation of the direction or content of the client's response and, further, presentation of a suggestion in that direction. To avoid discomforting exposure of a racially based concern, the client may accept direction implied by the therapist's suggestion all too willingly. Discussion of racial factors thereby may be delayed or eliminated in the treatment process. Any information elicited can be used to indicate the extent to which a particular racial factor relates to the problem and requires direct exploration. The clinician may inquire whether the client perceives a connection between the experiences of racism and the presenting problem or may postulate such a connection after hearing details of the situation. Although all black clients and all therapists (regardless of race) are influenced by the racism prevalent in American society, Helms (1984) noted that many black people enter sociopsychological treatment without major concerns either about racism as a factor in their problems or about the race of the clinician as a potential deterrent to the success of treatment.

RACIAL CONGRUENCE

Racial congruence, perhaps paradoxically, is related to an individual's acknowledgement of personal membership in the black group and of the continuing struggle of the group for a positive interaction with an ambivalent society. The quintessential difference between persons identified as black in American society and persons of any of the other immigrant cultures is the manifestation of unremitting societal ambivalence regarding the matter of assimilation. One result of the ambivalence of white people is that the goal of assimilation is not attainable for members of the black population, as it is for white people. That fact must be incorporated formally into the process of clinical assessment of black clients. Many clients of social and psychological services have experienced serious disruptions in the development of their group or personal identity (Elson, 1986). Clinical exploration of such disruptions tends to focus on intrapsychic, family, or cultural processes. A client's ability to establish an integrated group identity is compromised in varying degrees by encounters with racism and the client's management of those encounters. As with other important aspects of identity, failure to achieve a level of racial congruence generally leads to complications in problems of living and can interfere in the client's efforts to resolve those problems.

A series of questions can clarify the client's relationships with peer group, family, community, and self in racial terms. The questions on congruence are designed to alert the clinician to how a particular black client perceives and responds to his or her identity as a black person and as a member of an oppressed group. The following assessment questions and suggestions for clinicians address those issues:

- Does the client express or exhibit generalized feelings of impotence in discussing biracial circumstances that are a part of the problem? Obtain detailed information about problem interactions.
- How does the client interact with family and black peers, particularly those who either have not achieved or have markedly exceeded the client's level of success? Questions regarding intergenerational family life will provide information regarding socioeconomic status and the client's rationale for involvement or distance from family members.
- Does the history of the client suggest a pattern of avoidance of contact with other black people? With whom does the client associate?
- Does the client demonstrate discomfort with the fact that he or she is identified with two cultures? Is there information that suggests ease or discomfort with cultural duality?
- Is the client overtly or covertly emphasizing or avoiding the inclusion of the topic of race or racism in the discussion? Does the client make allusions to race and subsequently deny their significance or state that race is the only problem?

If the client appears to have achieved a realistic level of racial congruence, it will be demonstrated by an ability to discuss him- or herself in racial terms, and the clinician probably will not need to explore this area further. However, if the client appears to have difficulty in any of the areas of the questions, the clinician must consider the necessity of directly addressing issues of race as they affect the client's identity. Race then would be included among the factors the clinician considers while working with the client toward the development of an integrated identity. A person with an integrated identity can accept all aspects of him- or herself, is aware of the racism and ambivalence in society, is simultaneously aware of his or her capacity for self-definition without reference to the depreciation inherent in societal constructs, and is aware of the pervasive aspects of racism as it affects all black people.

INFLUENCE OF RACE ON PRESENTING PROBLEM

Another series of questions will allow the clinician to assess the extent to which race is a factor in the presenting problem, from the client's perspective and from the clinician's understanding of the context in which the problem occurs. This area is the one most often addressed in the literature regarding race and psychotherapy, possibly because it is the topic most likely to be initiated by the client (Bowles, 1978; Gardner, 1970). At issue is whether the clinician's contextual view of problems includes an acceptance of the fact of racism as an integral part of current social interaction between black people and white people. The questions proposed can organize the clinician's attention regarding the level of importance that racism has in the problems presented by a particular client and can help the clinician in determining appropriate interventions:

- Does the client make any statements that suggest a belief that race contributes significantly to the presenting problem?
- Given the context of the problem, is there evidence or reason to believe that racism places a constraint on the client's power to resolve the difficulty?

These questions require particular attentiveness on the part of the clinician, because the answers are so easily obscured by concrete data, the emotionality surrounding the problem, or the crisis aspect of the situation. The contextual reality of the client influences his or her real and potential power to intervene on his or her own behalf. The attitude of individuals in the client's environment may be masked, ambivalent, ambiguous, or open. Clinicians should be familiar with the social context in which the intervention will occur.

Whether the goals of intervention include change in behavioral patterns, intrapsychic restructuring, environmental change, or change in interpersonal relationships, the presence of racist behaviors may contribute to difficulty in problem resolution. This realization allows the clinician to help the client acknowledge the complexity of the situation and clearly delineate the goals of treatment and the potential impact of planned interventions. Initiating a frontal attack on racist policies or behaviors usually is not appropriate or effective. It is extremely important for the clinician to have some ideas regarding the racial factors influencing a problem and the attendant implications for the alternatives that the clinician considers as interventions. The clinician accrues this knowledge base as a result of an awareness of the community in which he or she practices. The clinician's affirmation of the contextual reality of the client tends to increase the intensity of the treatment alliance and the client's availability to consider his or her own contribution to problem maintenance.

RACIAL AWARENESS OF THERAPIST

The questions that follow address the identification of both the development and modification of racial attitudes and beliefs to which the clinician has been exposed and the management of those attitudes in nontherapeutic situations. Such management is based on the assumption that racial attitudes are included in the collection of introjections that relate to socially acceptable adult behavior. A person's development of adult attitudes occurs primarily as a result of the interpretation of important experiences. A clinician's early negative attitudes may reemerge in the course of treatment with black clients who exhibit certain communication or behavioral styles. The client may evoke the clinician's dormant anxieties, hostilities, aggression, autonomy conflicts, or guilt regarding racism. The questions provide a structure for identifying these factors.

Because clinicians have various levels of maturity, introspection, experience, and expertise, each clinician will have a different capacity to use the questions effectively. The author suggests that all clinicians who work with black clients review the questions as an attitudinal overview. Periodic reviews are recommended whenever a rupture appears in the progression of the treatment relationship. These reviews help to ensure that the influence of the clinician's racial attitude will be considered in the assessment of the treatment alliance. The questions are as follows:

- What is the history of the clinician's experience with black people? Include positive, negative, and neutral events and their outcomes.
- What did the clinician's family of origin teach regarding black people? Apply this question in the following areas: intelligence and intellectual capacity and potential; cleanliness of person and environment; hierarchical status vis-a-vis white people; veracity (truthfulness) versus duplicity (deceitfulness); sexual potency and restraint; sex-role functioning in family interaction; worth (internal quality rendering a person deserving of respect); pugnacity (inclination toward hostility, attacking others, or fighting). How have these teachings been incorporated over time? What influenced the clinician's decisions about which teachings to maintain and which to discard as part of a personal belief system?
- How does working with black people affect the clinician's finances and professional status?
- What is the clinician's personal style for dealing with diversity and conflict?
- How does the clinician exercise authority and relate to the authority of others?
- How does the clinician react in situations in which he or she observes black people being subjected to racist behaviors or ideology?

Undoubtedly, the beliefs of all clinicians evolve over the course of their personal and professional development. Any racist beliefs taught in the family tend to be reinforced during the life course for members of American society. Thus the development of mature attitudes regarding black people often requires either the occurrence of fortuitously positive experiences that are interpreted as meaningful or efforts to learn about the reality of the diversity among black people, which may not receive the active support of those in the clinician's immediate environment. Many families teach attitudes of acceptance and equality, but they may or may not prepare family members for contact with black people in situations as intimate as treatment or for the depreciation of black people that they are likely to observe in daily life. The questions about beliefs provided above were developed by the author from issues that arose in the process of supervision and consultation with clinicians who worked with black clients. The questions are intended to address the prevailing stereotypes regarding black people that appear most frequently as influencing the attitudes of clinicians who treat black people.

Because racial differences between white clinicians and black clients usually are obvious, the need to examine the clinician's racial awareness may seem reasonable and easily accessible. Where the clinician is black, the matter of racial congruence is as important to consider in relation to self as for the client. The black clinician struggling with racial incongruence will have serious difficulty in making an accurate assessment of the racial congruence of clients and of the extent to which racial factors influence the problem.

The decision to treat black clients may be voluntary or involuntary, temporary or long term. Such work may constitute the culmination of a professional ambition, the most viable means of a livelihood for the clinician, a lucrative agency, private practice, or a special research project. Each of these areas of work is associated with a status within a given profession; the hierarchy that exists within and between the helping professions is rather stable. Clinician's behaviors and attitudes reflect their position in that hierarchy, their level of satisfaction with that position, and their goals for achievement within the hierarchy.

In treatment involving racial issues, as with other issues, clinicians' personal styles for management of conflict range from avoidance to confrontation, to flexibility to address issues in whatever manner is deemed most effective. A clinician whose style is one of conflict avoidance risks the possibility of establishing a pattern with certain clients (for example, provocative individuals) that is characterized by appeasement, referral, or chemical treatment. When the clinician's style is predominantly provocative, a risk exists that the establishment of therapeutic alliance will be impeded by challenges to the attitude and belief system of the client and will end with the withdrawal of the client from therapy. The development of an effective clinical style is an intricate and lengthy process and is the expression of the autonomous aspect of the self. The judicious use of self by the clinician depends on his or her ability to understand power and authority as they pertain to the relationship between the client and the clinician. Effective use of concepts of empowerment, as presented by Solomon (1976), is contingent on the clinician's ability to evaluate and adjust his or her own power base in accordance with the needs of the client. The power base of the clinician reflects both the level of ability to accept responsibility for self and society and an understanding of the limits of power as well as the obligations of power and authority. Such an understanding includes an awareness of the relative aspects of power in hierarchies, including the power of the client. A person must not only exercise power over others but also must be subject to the power of others. Enhancing this area of functioning invariably is an implicit or explicit goal of the treatment process. Clients using sociopsychological services frequently need to learn new approaches to the understanding and use of power. The capacity to contribute to the client's understanding in that area is another hallmark of an effective clinician.

Perhaps the most difficult question is that of the clinician's reaction to his or her observations of racist behavior directed against black people in situations that may or may not be related to professional activity. Kovel (1970) in his description of racism, called this reaction *metaracism*. In this form, racism is manifested by discriminative observational habits and behaviors of a person in his or her own environment, regardless of his or her level of cognitive commitment to equality or activity in antiracist groups, organizations, or movements. Kovel cited the ability of many white persons to stand by while racist behaviors are being enacted and to participate in the accoutrements of society that result from or perpetuate racism. Gaertner and Dovidio's (1986) discussion of aversive racism updated Kovel's conceptualization. A realistic perception of black clients as members of American society requires that the clinician become aware of the ambivalent social environment within which black clients function. Clinicians vary in terms of their awareness of racial issues and racist events. Many white Americans feel that blacks have at least reached a state of parity, if not advantage, with respect to opportunity (Gaertner & Dovidio, 1986, p. 69). Such a belief may contribute to a clinician's tendency to overlook racist events in the immediate environment. Each such occurrence is an opportunity for the individual to affirm, challenge, or disregard the depreciating social message. The importance of the clinician's participation in such situations revolves around the extent to which these occurrences contribute to, support, or alter his or her belief system about black people and about him- or herself; how his or her relationship with the client is affected; and whether his or her capacity to conceptualize the client's social system is enhanced.

Among the factors reflecting maturity on the part of a social work professional is the expression of empathy and the ability to take a position that is appropriate for the client and possibly unpopular among colleagues. This is not to suggest that a mature clinician acts on every observed instance of racist behavior. Rather, a mature clinician is aware when racist behaviors occur and makes an informed decision to act or not based on the circumstances, the goals of the client, and the immediate and protracted consequences attendant to that decision. These capacities determine the estimable maturity of the clinician in managing experiences with overt racism.

THERAPEUTIC STRATEGIES

The specific interventions listed in this article are designed to facilitate the discussion of the material necessary for the clinician to make an assessment of the impact of race on the treatment process. The suggested strategies may appear simplistic. However, they are a reflection of sound clinical judgment. These questions are posed by the author in response to queries encountered in numerous clinical consultations. The primary goals of the strategies are to facilitate the identification and respectful maintenance of the boundary between the clinician and the client and the development of a treatment system with clear boundaries that acknowledge contextual realities. To facilitate the ultimate treatment goal of increased client effectiveness, the relational experience developed in treatment must differ significantly from those other experiences the client has experienced in daily living. The uniqueness of the treatment relationship and its meaning for the client results largely from this effort, regardless of the treatment modality. The intervention strategies are designed to maximize this relational aspect of treatment and to include proactive use of the black experience in the pursuit of this goal. Proactive use of the black experience by the clinician involves the intentional introduction of the concept of racism in the factors being considered in the assessment–engagement process. Therefore, whether or not a specific client's experiences with racism are thought to affect his or her difficulties significantly, the possibility is included as part of the clinician's exploration. The following strategies also tend to diminish the possibility that the clinician will assume prematurely that race is not a factor or that a treatment alliance has been established:

- When the clinician is not black and client is black, assume that a racial barrier exists in addition to or as part of the initial anxiety anyone has on entering into the treatment process. If both the clinician and the client are black, assume that the clinician's experiences with racism differ significantly from the experiences of the client.
- Demonstrate respect for the boundary between the clinician and the client and for the hierarchical boundaries within the client's relational systems. Use last names until invited by the client to do otherwise. The racial importance of the use of first

names is exaggerated for the black client because of the historical tradition of calling black people by their first names in situations in which first names would not be permitted if the participants were both white. Support the leadership potential of the client regardless of the level of functioning initially evident. One of the most detrimental client experiences (all too frequent with black clients) is that the clinician assumes profound disturbance and establishes goals accordingly, rather than basing goals on a deferred, careful, and conscious assessment of the client's level of functioning. Premature assessment often consigns the client to the realm of inadequacy and chronic use of service.

- Collect data for the racial congruence questions.
- Explicitly clarify racial concerns expressed by the client, whether they are direct or indirect. These concerns may refer to the problem for which help is sought or to entering into a relationship with the clinician.
- In the process of discussing the uniqueness of the client's situation, recognize differential experiences with and reactions to racism.
- Request immediate and future discussion with the client of the adequacy of the attention directed in treatment toward all issues related to the problem and the process of treatment.

CONCLUSION

This article presents an approach to the identification and management of racially based issues in the treatment process. Therapists should address the related issues explicitly to delineate the client's responsibility in clarifying the parameters of the presenting problem and in developing and maintaining the problem. This approach is an aspect of systems-oriented assessment and intervention, which has waxed and waned in prominence in hypotheses regarding the importance of specific factors that affect the development of therapeutic relationships. With the resurgence of widespread patterns of economic hardship and the anticipated diminution of opportunities of black people (which historically has followed such hardship) it seems timely for clinicians to reexamine these matters and routinely incorporate new techniques in the treatment process.

REFERENCES

Acosta, F., Yamamoto, J., & Evans, L. (1982). *Effective psychotherapy for low income and minority patients.* New York: Plenum.

Banks, J. A. (1985). Racial prejudice and the black self concept. In J. A. Banks & J. D. Grambs (Eds.), *Black self concept* (pp. 5–35). New York: McGraw-Hill.

Bass, B., Acosta, F., & Evans, L. (1982). The black American patient. In F. Acosta, J. Yamamoto, & L. Evans (Eds.), *Effective psychotherapy for low-income and minority patients* (pp. 83–108). New York: Plenum.

Bowles, D. D. (1978). Treatment issues in working with black families. *Smith College Journal for Social Work, 4,* 8–14.

Chestang, L. (1972). *Character development in a hostile environment.* Chicago: University of Chicago Press.

Elson, M. (1986). *Self psychology in clinical social work.* New York: W. W. Norton.

Franklin, D. (1985). Differential assessments: The influence of class and race. *Social Service Review, 59*, 44–61.

Gaertner, S., & Dovidio, J. (1986). The aversive form of racism. In J. Dovidio & S. Gaertner (Eds.), *Prejudice, discrimination and racism* (pp. 61–89). Orlando, FL: Academic Press.

Gardner, L. (1970). Psychotherapy under varying conditions of race. In R. Pugh (Ed.), *Psychology and the black experience* (pp. 37–53). Montgomery, CA: Brooks/Cole.

Gibbs, J. T. (1985). Can we continue to be color-blind and class-bound? *The Counseling Psychologist, 13*, 426–435.

Hamilton, D., & Trolier, T. (1986). Stereotypes and stereotyping: An overview of the cognitive approach. In J. Dovidio & S. Gaertner (Eds.), *Prejudice, discrimination and racism* (pp. 127–163). Orlando, FL: Academic Press.

Hays, W., & Banks, W. (1972). The nigger box or a redefinition of the counselor's role. In R. L. Jones (Ed.), *Black Psychology* (2nd ed., pp. 225–232). New York: Harper & Row.

Helms, J. (1984). Toward a theoretical explanation of the effects of race on counseling: A black and white model. *The Counseling Psychologist, 12*, 153–165.

Hollingshead, A., & Redlich, F. (1958). *Social class and mental illness.* New York: Wiley.

Jackson, G. (1972). The emergence of a black perspective in counseling. In R. L. Jones (Ed.), *Black psychology.* New York: Harper & Row.

Katz, I., Wackenhut J., & Glass, R. (1986). Racial ambivalence, value duality, and behavior. In J. Dovidio & S. Gaertner (Eds.), *Prejudice, discrimination, and racism* (pp. 35–59). Orlando, FL: Academic Press.

Katz, R. (1963). *Empathy: Its nature and uses.* Glencoe, IL: Free Press.

Kovel, J. (1970). *White racism: A psychohistory.* New York: Pantheon.

Linville, P., Salovey, P., & Fischer, G. (1986). Stereotyping and perceived distributions of social characteristics: An application to ingroup-outgroup perceptions. In J. Dovidio & S. Gaertner (Eds.), *Prejudice, discrimination and racism* (pp. 165–208). Orlando, FL: Academic Press.

McAdoo, H. (1981). *Black families.* Beverly Hills, CA: Sage.

McConahay, J. (1986). Modern racism, ambivalence, and the modern racism scale. In J. Dovidio & S. Gaertner (Eds.), *Prejudice, discrimination and racism* (pp. 91–208). Orlando, FL: Academic Press.

Meyers, H. (1982). Stress, ethnicity, and social class: A model for research with black populations. In E. Jones & S. Korchin (Eds.), *Minority mental health* (pp. 118–148). New York: Praeger.

Ogbu, J. (1983). *Crossing cultural boundaries: A comparative perspective on minority education.* Unpublished manuscript, University of Berkeley, CA.

Parham, T., & Helms, J. (1985). Attitudes of racial identity and self esteem of black students: An exploratory investigation. *Journal of College Student Personnel, 26*, 143–146.

Porter, J. (1971). Black child, white child: The development of racial attitudes. Cambridge, MA: Harvard University Press.

Ryan, W. (1971). *Blaming the victim.* New York: Pantheon.

Solomon, B. (1976). *Black empowerment.* New York: Columbia University Press.

Taylor, R. L. (1976). Psychosocial development among black children and youth: A re-examination. *American Journal of Orthopsychiatry, 46,* 4–19.

Valentine, C. A. (1968). *Culture and poverty: Critique and counterproposals.* Chicago: University of Chicago Press.

White, J. L. (1972). Toward a black psychology. In R. L. Jones (Ed.), *Black psychology* (pp. 43–50). New York: Harper & Row.

Wilson, M. (1986). The black extended family: An analytical consideration. *Developmental Psychology, 22,* 246–258.

CHAPTER 111

CASEWORK CONTACTS WITH BLACK–WHITE COUPLES

John A. Brown

The 1980 census revealed that 613,000 interracial couples reside in the United States.[1] This number almost doubles the count of 310,000 interracial couples in the 1970 census. The estimated number of interracial children varies from 600,000 to five million.[2] Social workers have paid little attention to interracial families and their problems, whereas sociologists have paid greater attention to interracial families in American society.[3] In the 1960s and 1970s, considerable attention was placed on race as a factor in the therapeutic relationship. Race as a variable must also be considered in practice with interracial families as they present themselves for social work services. Although many variations of interracial couples reside in the United States, the present article focuses on black–white couples.

Black–white couples, in addition to violating a fundamental social taboo, face the same problems that are faced by any other family. Even though a recent poll suggests that public attitude has changed toward black–white unions,[4] the additional stress caused by black–white unions still exists.

Black–white unions are certainly not a new phenomenon in the United States; they have occurred throughout blacks' history in American society. However, the majority of these relationships involved white men and black women. The suspected or actual involvement of a black man with a white woman in certain parts of the country often

Reprinted from *Social Casework*, Vol. 68, No. 1 (1987), pp. 24–29, by permission of the publisher, Families International, Inc.

[1] Randolph Schmid, "Interracial Couples Increase, U.S. Says," *Oakland Tribune*, Oakland, Calif., 5 July 1984, p. E-2.

[2] Glenn Collins, "International Children Are More Successful Than Myths Suggest," *Oakland Tribune*, Oakland, Calif., 26 June 1984, p. 1.

[3] Gail Fullerton, *Survival in Marriage* (Hinsdale, Ill.: Dryden Press, 1977); and Lloyd Saxton, *The Individual, Marriage and the Family* (Belmont, Calif.: Wadsworth Publishing, 1972).

[4] "National Poll Reveals Startling New Attitudes on Interracial Marriages," *Ebony*, September 1975.

resulted in violence directed at the black man and ostracism of the white woman. Some states had laws that prevented black–white unions. It was not until 1967 that the Supreme Court, in Loving vs. Virginia, held that laws prohibiting black–white unions were unconstitutional and that the right to marry was a fundamental civil right protected by the Constitution.[5] However, laws do not eradicate sentiments, and strong feelings still persist against black–white marriages. Thus, although black–white unions are more visible today, vestiges of racist attitudes remain and may influence the therapeutic relationship.

Lloyd Saxton suggests that the black–white couple are a target for bigotry and a cause for illogical fear.[6] As a target for bigotry, the black–white couple may experience problems with relatives, friends, housing, and employment.

The children of black–white unions may also be affected by society's attitude toward and treatment of them in addition to the problems faced by the black child. As a result of his or her dual heritage, the child may find him- or herself in a marginal position. The child who is the product of a black–white union is always viewed by society as being black—a status that does not always follow children of other mixed unions, such as white–Asian or white–American Indian. Gail Fullerton states

> that a de facto caste line based on race has existed in the United States—and to some degree remains today. It has been maintained in the past by occupational barrier, by the prohibition of interracial marriages and by defining as black all children of mixed white and black ancestry. Even when interracial marriage has been legal, it has not been possible for the white spouse to confer his or her status on the black.[7]

To engage black–white couples effectively, the social worker must possess a knowledge of the black experience; an awareness of how psychological, social, and racial dynamics may present themselves in the problem area, and the capacity to be creative in his or her contacts with them. Even in the most stable of black–white unions, race remains a dynamic. It may present itself in heated arguments between the individuals when one may use a racial slur as a weapon, or it may present itself as a family myth that race has never concerned the couple or presented a problematic area in the family.

The purpose of the present article is to discuss some aspects of casework contacts with black–white couples who are involved in conflict situations. Problems are identified and treatment techniques are discussed. Supervision is emphasized as a primary tool in helping the worker to identify and come to grips with racist attitudes that may creep into the therapeutic relationship. Several case examples are presented to reveal the complexities involved in casework contacts with black–white families.

RACE IN AMERICAN SOCIETY

Of the three types of racism that have been identified in the United States—cultural, institutional, and individual—social workers have been most aware of institutional

---

[5] Fullerton, *Survival in Marriage*.
[6] Saxton, *Individual, Marriage, Family*.
[7] Fullerton, *Survival in Marriage*, p. 550.

racism and may be unaware of or deny the presence of individual racism within their personalities. More often than not, individual racism is involved in the therapeutic relationship when the social worker has myths and stereotypes about minority groups. Individual racism is personal in nature, has similar dynamics to those that are present in a countertransference situation, and is essentially irrational. Irrationality results from the social worker's acceptance of cultural myths about minorities. Since more than 75 percent of interracial marriages involve a black male partner, it is important that social workers be aware of their perceptions of the black male.

The black male has always been heavily stereotyped. He has been depicted as a violent, pleasure-oriented person who is brutal in his relationships with women and desirous of possessing white women. He has been viewed as being superficial in relationships, primitive in his thinking, and incapable of developing insight into his problems. The mass media perpetuate these myths by portraying the black male as an irresponsible person who is aggressive, either a pimp or a stud. If the social worker has accepted these myths, then barriers exist in the helping relationship; these must be addressed if intervention is to be effective.

DYNAMICS OF BLACK–WHITE UNIONS

The dynamics of black–white unions are varied and complex. Although we may believe that the majority of them are motivated by love and shared feelings between the couple, some may have different motivations. Saxton states that "the degree of difficulty which the interracial couple faces in American society varies according to the couple's economic level, their place of residence, and the races of their partners."[8] Because of the history of blacks in the United States, the black–white union faces greater hostility than other mixed unions. Although Saxton suggests that many interracial marriages occur for the simple reason that the couple are in love, he suggests that an interracial couple are aware of the difficulties that their union poses and thus factors in addition to romantic attraction, propinquity, shared interests, and personal compatibility operate in the union.[9]

Robert Staples suggests that "one must always look for ulterior motives" in interracial marriages.[10] Joseph Washington, who is quoted by Staples, states that "the imputation of ulterior motives to interracial marriages says more about the individual making these interpretations and about the society in which we live than about the couple who intermarries."[11] Ernest Porterfield states that interracial marriages are not related to any psychological abnormality on the part of the couple or a desire to make "some sort of statement against racial prejudices."[12]

I believe that the issue of race in black–white unions must be recognized and assessed for its contribution to the tensions faced by a couple in the same way as variables such as communication patterns, sexual relationship, child-rearing patterns, recreational

[8] Saxton, *Individual, Marriage, Family,* p. 275.
[9] Ibid.
[10] Robert Staples, *The Black Woman in America* (Chicago: Nelson-Hall Publishers, 1973), p. 122.
[11] Ibid.
[12] Ernest Porterfield as quoted in Collins, "Interracial Children."

pursuits, decision-making patterns, in-law interferences, and economic pressures are recognized and assessed. If social workers do not consider race as a variable in the problems faced by the black–white family, then they do not consider all of the possible forces that may impact on the family. Staples states that "while the motivation for an interracial marriage may or may not differ from that of an intraracial marriage, certain problems are unique to this type of marriage."[13]

These problems include the public attitude toward the union as well as attitudes of in-laws, friends, fellow workers, and possibly employers. Problems are compounded when personality problems are also present.

Due to their discomfort with black–white unions, some social workers compensate by denying any feelings toward such unions and by approaching them with a very liberal perspective. Workers who possess negative attitudes toward such unions may view the couple's problems as a validation of their beliefs that races should not mix. Others may attempt to minimize their negative attitudes by minimizing the impact of race on the couple's problems or by becoming "color blind." Workers must analyze and understand their feelings toward such unions before they work with black–white couples.

CASE EXAMPLES

Although race is not necessarily a critical dimension in the problems of black–white couples, race as a variable and its possible contribution to problems must be assessed. Because of the high failure rate of interracial marriages, black–white couples must be viewed as an at-risk population. The couple's strength and adaptability are revealed in how they address the issue of race in their social and personal relationships. In the cases presented here, race impacted on the problems that brought the couples to the agency.[14]

Child Abuse

Mrs. H, who was thirty-eight years old and white, was referred to the agency for suspected child abuse and for assistance with her seven-year-old son, M, who had problems in school. Mrs. H revealed a long history of marginal adjustment. Her black ex-husband had deserted her, following a history of considerable abuse in which he had forced her into prostitution. All of Mrs. H's hostility toward her ex-husband in particular and men in general focused on M. She appeared obsessed with the notion that he would turn out to be like his father, who was described as a charming con man. She wondered if such behavior was inherited and felt she could "beat the devil" out of M by physically disciplining him for the slightest reason. She had no supportive group and her family had disowned her when she married Mr. H. Following a couple of appointments, she informed the worker that M had been placed in foster care because she had been accused of child abuse. She saw no further need to continue her contact with the agency.

---

[13] Staples, *The Black Woman*, p. 125.
[14] Case examples were drawn from students, professional workers, and the author's practice.

Foster Care

Mrs. G, who was thirty-three years old and white, was referred to the agency by the juvenile court for an evaluation to determine whether her twelve-year-old daughter who had been placed with a paternal aunt should be returned to her. The child had been made a dependent of the court because of Mrs. G's personality problems and inability to care for her. The child's adjustment with the paternal aunt had been excellent, and the request for reunification had been initiated by the child, who had telephoned and asked the mother if she could return home. Mrs. G had met the child's father, a black militant, during the Civil Rights struggle. He was very active in the movement. Both Mrs. G and her husband had been rejected by their spouse's family on racial grounds. The marriage ended when Mr. G left. She then turned all of her attention to the daughter and began drinking heavily. Her brother-in-law resented her because he felt that she had led his brother astray. He did not approve of mixed racial unions.

However, the daughter was well accepted by the paternal aunt and uncle. The child had been placed due to Mrs. G's inability to care for her and at the time of agency's contact with Mrs. G had been with the paternal relatives for two years. During this time, Mrs. G had made no serious attempts to improve her situation, rarely visited the daughter because she was afraid of the brother-in-law, and talked to her daughter only on the telephone. Mrs. G had met a white male friend and the relationship was becoming serious. She had experienced deprivation and domination at the hands of perfectionistic, cold, aloof parents and had many unresolved problems. At the time of contact, she appeared to be moving toward the white world. Her friends were primarily whites, and she had few contacts with blacks. The daughter presented an obstacle to Mrs. G's return to the white world, however, her inadequacies and feelings of guilt pushed her toward complying with the daughter's wishes. Although Mrs. G loved the child, she recognized ambivalent feelings and frequently stated that her daughter was so happy where she was.

Racial Slur

J, age six years, was brought to the agency for general feelings of sadness and a change of behavior in school. J, the product of a black–white union, was described as a previously happy child. He attended a school where blacks constituted a minority. The apparent reason for J's change of behavior was a racial slur in which a classmate had referred to him as a "white nigger." The parents, who were middle-class, were alarmed that this had happened and had considered changing schools. The social worker helped them to understand that changing schools would not resolve the problem and that J needed to attain skills that would assist him in dealing with such situations.

A Marital Situation

Mr. and Mrs. S came to the agency for assistance with marital problems. Mrs. S was white and Mr. S was black. They had met while they were in the military service; following discharge they had moved to a large industrial city where Mr. S had been raised. They soon had four young children. Mr. S was of little help around the house, and Mrs. S was developing feelings of isolation. Their social contacts had been essentially with blacks. Mrs. S had begun to resist these contacts, as she felt that black women resented her. Mr. S denied this and stated that her reaction was a result of her thinking that she was better than blacks. Mrs. S strongly denied this. In spite of their arguments, the Ss revealed much love for each other and wanted their marriage to work. Racial conflicts were used as shields that prevented them from facing other issues. During casework contacts, the social worker found it difficult to focus on issues without also considering the racial conflicts and how they presented in the Ss' situation. The problem was exacerbated by the fact that the social worker was a white female; Mr. S frequently accused her of siding with his wife and of having racist feelings.

Supervision: A Tool in Worker's Growth

Mrs. T, who was twenty-six years old and white, had recently moved to a city from a small town in the South because her husband was transferred. Mrs. T's parents and her white husband were decidedly racist. She had accepted employment at an agency located in a black area of the city despite her husband's objections. One of her first cases involved a black–Asian union. The couple had been referred to the agency for marital counseling. Mr. F, a black, had a history of abusing his Asian wife. The abuse case aroused considerable anxiety in Mrs. T— to the point that she requested that the case be transferred. The supervisor, a black, rejected her reason for the transfer—her fear of Mr. F—because it was obvious to him that Mrs. T was struggling with her own cultural racism. The feelings did not transfer to the supervisor because in Mrs. T's words, "he was different."

Even though Mrs. T continued with the case, she faced much difficulty in focusing on the case as well as in cloaking her feelings toward Mr. F. However, as she began to collect data and develop an assessment, she began to develop an awareness of Mr. F as an individual and of his behavior. She felt that his behavior was his way of showing his masculinity. The problem that Mrs. T faced with this case was reflected in the supervisory session. The supervisor's objective was to help her focus and apply diagnostic assessment to this case in the same way as she had to other cases. As she collected and analyzed data, she began to individualize Mr. F and see his strengths. He shared interests in poetry and painting with Mrs. T and invited her to visit him and his wife so that he could show her some of his work.

Despite her husband's objections, Mrs. T made the home visit and saw the love and warmth that they shared. She was so impressed with Mr. F's drawings that she encouraged him to inquire into art school. Her acceptance of Mr. F was so great that the supervisor had to remind her that the wife was also part of the problem. After Mrs. T moved beyond her racist feelings toward Mr. F, she was able to engage Mr. and Mrs. F as a couple and to focus on the marital interactions that resulted in abusive behavior.

In a session with her supervisor, Mrs. T admitted that the case represented an important breakthrough for her, that she had always heard blacks spoken of in a derogatory manner and had come to believe what was said about them. This and her relationship with the supervisor allowed her to resolve her initial mistrust of black men, feelings that had been reinforced by a lifetime of hearing blacks being maligned.

DISCUSSION

Personality problems accentuated the racial impact in some of these cases. In the case of Mrs. G, reunification of the family was strongly contraindicated. The daughter had made an excellent adjustment with the black relatives. Because of Mrs. G's own problems, needs, ambivalence, and movement toward the white world, Mrs. G would not be able to sustain these gains. Moreover, her guilt over the black–white union made it difficult for her to impose limits on her daughter because she resented being left with the responsibility of raising the daughter. Reunification of the family at this point would have retarded the progress that Mrs. G had made putting order into her life. The hostility of the paternal relatives toward Mrs. G would also have created stress. The child had found greater acceptance among her black relatives than she would find among her white relatives, who had rejected Mrs. G because of the marriage.

Mrs. H's rejection of her child was connected to her hostility toward men in general and her black ex-husband in particular. Her husband had abused her, forced her into prostitution, and deserted her. She was concerned that her son may have inherited his behavior patterns. Her marriage could also be evaluated as an indication of her "fall from grace" with the white world. She had married outside of her race, and the child was a constant reminder of her transgression. The physical abuse of the child may well have been an indication of her desire to be free of him, which his removal and placement in foster care accomplished.

J, age six years, learned early, despite his parents' attempt to shelter him, that he was black and would be a target of racial slurs. Unprepared for his first encounter with racism, he became depressed, unhappy, and wanted to withdraw from school.

Mr. and Mrs. S used race as a weapon and had not yet developed an understanding of the problems of a black–white couple in American society. The problem was compounded by Mrs. S's isolation, and her attitude toward black women made it difficult for her to build meaningful relationships with them. The couple used race as a weapon, which prevented them from dealing with other issues.

With Mr. and Mrs. F, the social worker had feelings of cultural racism and had accepted racial stereotypes about the black male that interfered with her ability to successfully engage the couple in treatment. Her acceptance of racial myths about black males had to be resolved before she could assist Mr. and Mrs. F with their marital conflicts.

Treatment Techniques

Some of the techniques that were employed in these cases are the same as those that are used in any case—support, advice giving, acceptance, and engagement in problem solving. However, innovative treatment approaches were also used. In the case of J, it was important that he learn the survival skills and coping techniques that are needed by black children. He needed to develop some assertiveness in responding to racial comments of a negative nature. J's father was white and his mother black. J was assigned to a black social worker who assisted him in dealing with such situations by referring to his own experiences and how he had dealt with them. Emphasis was placed on "black is beautiful" and how he must be prepared for people who will say bad things to him because of their own problems. Fullerton describes a black mother in an interracial union who told her child to tell a white child that he smelled his upper lip when the white child made negative comments about "his odor" to him.[15] Preparing the black child to deal with racial slurs will probably become the responsibility of the black parent who by his or her own experiences will have gone through similar situations. I believe that in practice with black children who are products of black–white unions, a black worker is more effective than a white worker is in enhancing the self-image of the child. The parents need assistance in helping the child develop skills that will enable him or her to survive racist behavior. At the same time they must teach the child to value his or her dual heritage.

Mr. and Mrs. S's treatment required innovative techniques to address the issue of race and how the couple was using it in their marital conflicts. Part of the difficulty resulted from Mr. S accusing the worker of siding with his wife and of having no real understanding of black life. To circumvent this problem, a black male was assigned as a co-therapist for this couple. Thus the black social worker was able to address Mr. S's racial accusations since both men shared the same social reality. The co-therapists were also able to model ways to face and address sensitive issues. Two factors initiated the breakthrough in this case: (1) the presence of the parallel social structure of black and white therapists and (2) locating and connecting the couple with other black–white couples.

One may wonder about the gender issue, that is, why a black male was assigned instead of a black female. Some resentment exists among black women about white females marrying black males. The resentment may result from a couple of reasons: (1) the shortage of black men and (2) a general feeling that the races should not mix. Thus Mrs. S's feelings that she was not accepted by black females may have been based on fact. As of 1977, 33 percent of black women were single, which was attributed to the shortage of black men. It has been suggested that as a result of changes in the black community's stance toward certain relationships, the number of interracial and homosexual relationships and intensification of de facto polygamy may increase in the future.[16] Thus a black male co-therapist was more appropriate than a black female.

In conclusion, black–white unions present a challenge to social workers, who must be sensitized to the complex dynamics that present in such cases.

---

[15] Fullerton, *Survival in Marriage.*

[16] Saundra Rice Murray and Daphne Harrison, "Black Women and the Future," *Psychology of Women Quarterly* 6, (Fall 1981): 113-22.

CHAPTER 112

A STAGE-OF-MIGRATION FRAMEWORK FOR SERVICE TO IMMIGRANT POPULATIONS

Diane Drachman

A major wave of migration to the United States has recently occurred. According to the U.S. Bureau of the Census (1970, 1980), the foreign-born population increased by 46 percent between 1970 and 1980. The continued increase in immigrant populations—that is, all foreign migrant populations in the United States—has been highlighted in labor force projections for the 21st century. One report (Johnston & Packer, 1987) stated that immigrants will represent the largest share of the increase in the population and in the work force since World War I.

The newcomers, who are diverse in age, language, country of origin, and culture, have been arriving mainly from Asia, the West Indies, Central America, Africa, and Eastern Europe. Their immigration status varies and includes refugees, immigrants, undocumented aliens, entrants, and parolees. The Immigration and Naturalization Service (INS), the federal agency assigned to carry out immigration law and policy, determines the status of aliens. The different statuses carry different entitlements to services. These newcomers have been seen by service providers in health, mental health, and educational organizations; family and children's service settings; and the workplace.

Although social work historically has been involved in service to immigrant populations, the professional response to the recent wave of migration has been limited. Social workers in the field have reported a paucity of professionally trained personnel capable of understanding the cultures of the newcomers, their migration experiences, and the is-

Reprinted from *Social Work,* Vol. 37, No. 1 (January 1992), pp. 68–72, by permission of NASW Press. Copyright 1992, National Association of Social Workers, Inc., *Social Work.*

sues they face in the process of adjustment to living in the United States (Drachman & Ryan, 1991).

The limited service response is partially the result of the view that population movements typically are isolated temporary historical events rather than recurring phenomena (Stein, 1986). This "temporal perspective" has led to an emergency ad hoc service delivery pattern resulting in a cycle of new programs that surface and end. In addition, it has obscured consideration of commonalities in immigrant and refugee group experiences and behavior as well as lessons learned from past population movements and experiences that could inform current helping approaches and service delivery (Stein, 1986).

This article presents a framework that assumes that migration is a recurring phenomenon and thus mitigates the problems generated by the temporal perspective (Drachman & Ryan, 1991). The framework has both generic and specific usefulness: It can be applied to all immigrant groups and specific groups. It also can be applied to the individual immigrant because it offers a lens for assessing the individual in the particular circumstances of migration. It builds on the work of numerous writers in the field and study of migration who have observed and formulated stages in the migration process (Cox, 1985; Keller, 1975).

STAGES OF MIGRATION

The framework highlights three phases: (1) premigration and departure, (2) transit, and (3) resettlement (Drachman & Ryan, 1991). It is based on the following assumptions:

All immigrants have an experiential past; some experience abrupt departure while others experience a decision-making process and a period of preparation for a move; a physical move is always involved and finally resettlement and some type of adjustment to a new environment occurs. (Cox, 1985, p. 75)

Although the framework is emphasized in this article, it is assumed that age; family composition; socioeconomic, educational, and cultural characteristics; occupation; rural or urban backgrounds; belief systems; and social supports interact with the migration process and influence the individual or group experience in each stage (Table 112–1).

Premigration and Departure

The social, political, and economic factors surrounding the premigration and departure experiences are significant. The experiences in this phase often are evident in the reactions and behaviors of individuals during the later stage of resettlement, when adjustment to the new country is required. Separation from family and friends, the act of leaving a familiar environment, decisions regarding who is left behind, life-threatening circumstances, and loss of significant others are some of the issues individuals face in this stage (Drachman & Ryan, 1991). Despite the differences among migrating groups, the stage-of-migration framework can be applied to various populations, such as the Southeast Asian, Haitian, and Soviet populations.

Table 112–1.
Stage-of-Migration Framework

Stage of Migration	Critical Variables
Premigration and departure	Social, political, and economic factors
	Separation from family and friends
	Decisions regarding who leaves and who is left behind
	Act of leaving a familiar environment
	Life-threatening circumstances
	Experiences of violence
	Loss of significant others
Transit	Perilous or safe journey of short or long duration
	Refugee camp or detention center stay of short or long duration
	Act of awaiting a foreign country's decision regarding final relocation
	Immediate and final relocation or long wait before final relocation
	Loss of significant others
Resettlement	Cultural issues
	Reception from host country
	Opportunity structure of host country
	Discrepancy between expectations and reality
	Degree of cumulative stress throughout migration process

Southeast Asians. Sudden evacuation characterized the departure experiences of many Vietnamese during wartime conflict in Indochina. As a result, close family members often were left behind. Many families never were reunited because members were either lost in Vietnam or died during escape. These experiences have been associated with survivor guilt and depression reflected in some unaccompanied minors and others who migrated to the United States without their families (Kinzie et al., 1982).

Many Chinese Vietnamese immigrants escaped by boats that were attacked by pirates. Some survivors were tortured and repeatedly raped; others witnessed the murder or rape of family members and saw family members taken away. The rape trauma for Southeast Asian women is even more complex because the Indochinese value highly chastity and virginity, and women who have been raped are no longer considered valuable or marriageable. In addition, the family perceives rape as a disgrace to the family. The rape experience, therefore, has been a closely guarded secret to protect the future of the individual and members of her family. To reveal a rape would also break a cultural tradition of emotional restraint. This cultural information is valuable to service providers because it sensitizes social workers to a possible past trauma and offers insight into the cultural meaning attached to the experience. Because methods of helping are influenced by cultural interpretations of an experience, rape counseling for Southeast Asian women often may entail helping approaches different from those used with American women (Drachman & Ryan, 1991).

The premigration and departure experiences of the Cambodians also were traumatic. The Cambodians, who lived in a peaceful agricultural country, witnessed the murder of their family members and nationals during the Pol Pot regime. They saw family members die of disease and starvation. They witnessed torture and executions and experienced forced labor. Many escaped in the midst of fear and crisis, taking with them, when possible, their children, wives, and parents. Many family members died while escaping.

The severity of these premigration experiences also has been associated with the onset of posttraumatic stress disorder, with symptoms including conscious avoidance of remembering the past, panic attacks, startled reactions, uncontrollable intrusive thoughts, thoughts about suicide or killing members of one's own family, recurrent nightmares, insomnia, poor concentration, and emotional numbness (Kinzie, Fredrickson, Ben, Fleck, & Karls, 1984). Practice implications therefore include an understanding of posttraumatic stress disorder, recognition of its symptoms, familiarity with appropriate methods of helping, and consideration of psychiatric referral or consultation.

Haitians. The exodus from Haiti has been due to two major forces: extreme poverty and fear of reprisal resulting from an individual's opposition to the government. The departure experiences of Haitians include a complex process of decision making that revolves around the issue of who in the Haitian family is the most appropriate member to leave. For rural Haitians, departure could involve establishing temporary residence in Port-au-Prince to await the preparation of immigration papers. Departure involves considerable contact with a travel agent or intermediary who assists the client in developing a strategy for visa eligibility (LaGuerre, 1984). Remuneration for these services can absorb the total financial resources of the extended family. Other Haitians arrive clandestinely in boats. A reservation on a boat often costs the individual his or her life savings. Boats sometimes capsize, and survivors have witnessed friends and family die at sea.

Soviets. Until recently, Soviet émigrés experienced a long wait before they could leave their country because of the Soviet government's view that emigration was a betrayal of one's country. Thus, an application to leave involved loss of employment, uncertainty about departure possibilities, and years of waiting while unemployed. In addition, individuals were expelled from the Communist Party and the Communist Fleet, a compulsory organization for citizens ages 14 to 28. Former co-workers and fellow students confronted, humiliated, and vilified the expelled individuals. Consent from both parents for permission to exit also was required regardless of the individual's age or relationship with the parent; in some cases, the biological parent had limited or no contact with the individual. When parents provided consent, they too were viewed as traitors and were harassed. Some parents refused consent because it jeopardized their personal, social, and occupational lives. The issue ruptured relationships in many families.

The negative attention a departure application received in the Soviet Union combined with government attempts to hold onto potential émigrés and with world press attention to the issue fostered unrealistic expectations regarding one's reception and life in the new land. Unrealistic expectations revolved around views that most people in the United States were wealthy, and therefore émigrés would obtain economic gain, and that the wealthy United States would provide all citizens with needed services (medical care, housing, job training). Moreover, at the point of departure and during resettlement, individuals also were concerned that their decision to emigrate would further jeopardize the welfare of relatives left behind (Drachman & Ryan, 1988).

The premigration or departure and transit experiences of individuals from the Soviet Union are changing as a result of political shifts in that country. The receiving countries also are modifying their admissions policies. The framework therefore will be useful in obtaining information about the more recent circumstances and experiences of the new arrivals.

Transit

In the transit phase, experiences may range from a perilous sea journey on a fragile boat or an illegal border crossing to an uncomplicated arrangement for travel on a commercial flight (Cox, 1985). The duration of the transit phase may vary from hours to years. For example, an individual might live in limbo in a refugee camp for years while awaiting a final destination. The transit phase also could involve a long stay in a detention center while awaiting the decision of a receiving country regarding entry or deportation. On the other hand, an individual may leave the country of origin and within hours connect with family or friends in the new country (Drachman & Ryan, 1991).

Southeast Asians. The transit experiences for many Southeast Asians have included life in refugee camps. Thailand, for example, has been a first asylum country for Cambodians, Laotians, Khmer, hill-tribe people, and Vietnamese, many of whom have remained in Thai camps for years. The refugees in the Thai camps arrive as homeless, starved, frightened people, many in poor physical health. Some die shortly after arrival. They arrive in the context of loss—they have left behind family; friends; possessions; community; social, religious, and political organizations; and leaders.

Despite humanitarian efforts, problems in the camps have included clothing shortages, inadequate water supply, and poor housing conditions (Sughandabhirom, 1986). The competition for resources and services between the refugees and local people has led to conflict both in the camps and along the Thai borders. Thus, many refugees have encountered an unfriendly reception. The years of waiting in the camps before resettlement in the United States or another country have been cited as a significant problem; children have grown up in the camps, adolescents have become adults, and middle-aged individuals have grown old in the camps. Thus, a period of trauma has been followed by years of waiting for permission to relocate to begin a new life.

Haitians. The transit experiences of Haitians have been influenced by vacillating federal policy. At times, Haitians have received asylum in the United States as entrants or refugees. At other times, the United States has viewed Haitians as economic migrants and placed them in a detention center following arrival where they await a decision on deportation or entry. Some have been moved from one detention center to another. Their detention center stays have ranged from weeks to more than one year. Thus, after arrival, many Haitians have lived in legal limbo and in isolation from the American community (Drachman & Ryan, 1988).

Soviets. The transit experiences of Soviets generally have been orderly. Individuals have planned their plane or train departures from the Soviet Union. They often have traveled to Vienna, spending one week to two months there before proceeding to

Rome. In Rome, they have been housed in apartments while awaiting their papers to be processed for final relocation.

Resettlement

As individuals resettle in the new country, cultural issues assume prominence. These issues include different views on health, mental health, education, help-seeking behavior, and childrearing practices, as well as the degree of cultural consonance or dissonance between the country of origin and the receiving country. Cultural factors also assume prominence in the interactions between service personnel and their clients The reception offered by the host country, the extent of services available, the degree of cumulative stress experienced by the immigrant, and the discrepancy between the individual's expectations and the actual quality of life in the United States are issues that also surface in resettlement. Depression, suicide ideation and attempts, substance and chemical abuse, parent-child conflict, and spouse and child abuse are commonly reported problems during the resettlement phase (Drachman & Ryan, 1991).

Southeast Asians. Resettlement for many Southeast Asians has been difficult because of significant differences in Eastern and Western ways of life and modes of thinking. These cultural differences have been more extreme for rural or hill-tribe people, because some of these people have had little or no formal education in their home country. In response to the culture shock, some immigrants have limited their contact outside the home.

Service providers have reported that in families in which culture shock occurs, parents may not learn to speak English, creating greater isolation and reducing their sense of control over their environment. Children in these families often develop competency in English, adopt American ways, and are called on by parents to translate for them or perform functions ordinarily accomplished by the parents in their own country. The reversal of roles between parents and children has been reported as a source of family stress because parental roles and authority become weakened. Moreover, parents perceive that their children consider the parents to be less important in the new country than in their home country. This is difficult for most Indochinese parents and elders to accept, because in their native society they were revered and respected, and their opinions were essential for any major family decision. Service providers need to be aware of this situation as a potential problem in the interview session if a child is used as a translator (Drachman & Ryan, 1991).

Spousal role reversal also has been a source of difficulty. Some wives have found employment more easily than their husbands because they tend to accept lower-paying jobs as housekeepers or garment workers. When the wife becomes the wage earner, the husband may stay at home, care for the children, and do the housework—a situation considered intolerable by many Vietnamese and Cambodian men. Many of these men have resorted to alcohol abuse, spouse and child abuse, gambling, and gang activity. Divorce, a rare phenomenon in Southeast Asia, has also begun to occur within this population (Drachman & Ryan, 1988).

Southeast Asian views on mental health differ significantly from Western concepts of mental health. Western-trained service providers often believe in intrapsychic influences on behavior. According to Southeast Asians, mental problems may be caused by organic disorders, genetic vulnerability, supernatural factors, physical or emotional exhaustion, metaphysical factors such as the imbalance between yin and yang, fatalism, and character weakness (Kinzie, 1985; Nidorf, 1985; Sughandabhirom, 1986; Tung, 1980, 1985; Wong, 1985). To resolve a personal or interpersonal problem, the Indochinese in their home countries relied on leaders in the community, elders in the family, religious leaders, and other community support mechanisms. What Americans view as professional interventions many Southeast Asians view as the meddling of an unwelcome stranger. Models of health care also differ. Scientism undergirds the Western model, whereas traditional and folk healing practices are common in Southeast Asia. For more relevant and effective service delivery, providers therefore require knowledge of Southeast Asian views on health, mental health, and help-seeking behavior.

Haitians. According to Haitian service professionals, several factors contribute to this population's difficulty and reluctance in becoming involved in American society. These factors include shifting U.S. policy regarding their entry, fear that Haitians are carriers of acquired immune deficiency syndrome (AIDS), and race. In addition, Americans often mistakenly believe that Haitians are fluent in French whereas many immigrants speak only Creole (DeWind, 1990).

Cultural differences regarding authority over children also have complicated resettlement. Because Haitian schools are ascribed strong authority over children, they have the right to discipline using corporal punishment. In Haiti, parents are rarely consulted about a child's school problem because resolution of such a problem falls within the school's jurisdiction. When U.S. school personnel request consultation with Haitian parents, the parents may not attend because they do not consider management of a school problem to be a parental issue. This cultural difference has resulted in a tendency for U.S. school and service personnel to label Haitian parents as neglectful.

Moreover, DeWind (1990) reported child abuse among the Haitian population as a problem. Cultural factors influence this problem because the stresses of resettlement tend to increase the customary Haitian use of corporal punishment. U.S. service personnel are unfamiliar with the extent of this childrearing custom; thus, informed assistance is diminished. Moreover, Haitians are wary of institutional services and authority because of the years of oppression during the Duvalier regimes. Therefore, they rarely seek or reluctantly accept assistance from service organizations (Drachman & Ryan, 1988).

Soviets. Soviets have encountered unexpected difficulties obtaining work or resuming an occupation for which they have been trained. Many well-educated émigrés have experienced lowered status as they have shifted from, for example, Soviet engineer, teacher, or musician to American street vendor. Some have been unprepared for the multiple choices available to them in U.S. life, and many have been unprepared for the absence of services such as housing, employment, occupational training, and medical and dental care to which citizens in the Soviet Union are entitled. These difficulties have led some immigrants to question or regret their decision to leave. Soviet émigré service professionals have suggested that the difficulties have contributed to parent-child conflicts, depression, and chemical and alcohol abuse—the more commonly reported problems experienced by this group (Drachman & Ryan, 1988).

The problems experienced by the émigrés often are misunderstood by service personnel because of differences in cultural interpretation. For example, citizens in the Soviet Union perceive depression as a biological entity; thus, biochemical treatment is offered. A refugee client experiencing depression therefore expects to be treated with a pill. A service provider who attempts to deal with the depression through a commonly used method of talking therapy is perceived not only as strange but also as incompetent because the client does not receive what he or she thinks is needed. This issue assumes greater complexity given that psychiatry has been used as a form of social control in the Soviet Union; thus, a service provider who initiates a talking therapeutic approach is likely to be received with suspicion (Drachman & Ryan, 1988).

Cultural problems have led to substance and chemical abuse among Soviet adolescents, according to service organizations that have contact with this population (Drachman & Ryan, 1988). Drachman and Ryan suggested that adolescents' vulnerability to drug use is associated with previous problems presented in school that received little parental attention because of the stresses of resettlement and cultural differences that revolve around the function and authority of the educational system. In the Soviet Union, schools assume considerable authority over children. Children attend school six days a week from 9 A.M. to 5 P.M. Schools also assume socialization and recreational functions. Therefore, Soviet parents consider the direction and management of a student's school problem to be primarily within the jurisdiction of the school. The greater role for parental direction and monitoring of children's education in the United States and the greater role of student autonomy confuses Soviet parents and their children. As a result, some children have become lost in the U.S. school system, resulting in truancy, continuation in school but avoidance of classes, and dropout. As these children enter adolescence, many experiment with and later abuse drugs (Drachman & Ryan, 1988).

VEHICLE FOR OBTAINING KNOWLEDGE

Through the use of the framework, social workers may distill the commonalities and differences each group faces in migration. For example, the populations discussed in this article commonly experienced stress, loss, intergenerational conflict, and parent-child difficulties. However, their transit experiences were different, as were the social, political, and economic circumstances surrounding their premigration and departure. Moreover, the different belief systems or values of the groups influenced each group experience in each phase. Thus, each group and individual experience was different.

Overall, the framework is broad enough to consider the changing circumstances surrounding the migration of different populations, including the different cohorts of Haitians and recent Eastern European immigrants. The framework is a vehicle for social workers to obtain knowledge of the needs, experiences, and circumstances of the new immigrant groups as well as future newcomers. It enables practitioners and organizations to examine the relevance of previous immigrant group experiences and attendant service delivery patterns to current experiences and program responses.

REFERENCES

Cox, D. (1985). Welfare services for migrants: Can they be better planned? *International Migration Review, 23*(1), 73–93.

DeWind, J. (1990). Haitian boat people in the United States: Background for social service providers. In D. Drachman (Ed.), *Social services to refugee populations* (pp. 7–56). Washington, DC: National Institute of Mental Health.

Drachman, D., & Ryan, A. S. (1988). Social work practice with refugee populations: Curriculum development in graduate social work education. In *Final Report to National Institute of Mental Health* (pp. 35–42). Washington, DC: U.S. Department of Health and Human Services.

Drachman, D., & Ryan, A. S. (1991). Immigrants and refugees. In A. Gitterman (Ed.), *Handbook of social work practice with vulnerable populations* (pp. 618–646). New York: Columbia University Press.

Johnston, W., & Packer, A. (1987). *Workplace 2000: Work and workers for the 21st century*. Indianapolis: Hudson Institute.

Keller, S. (1975). *Uprooting and social change: The role of refugees in development*. Delhi, India: Manohar Book Service.

Kinzie, J. D. (1985). Overview of the clinical issues in the treatment of Southeast Asian refugees. In T. C. Owan (Ed.), *Southeast Asian mental health: Treatment, prevention, services, training, and research* (pp. 113–135). Washington, DC: U.S. Department of Health and Human Services.

Kinzie, J. D., Fredrickson, R., Ben, J., Fleck, J. & Karls, W. (1984). Posttraumatic stress disorder among survivors of Cambodian concentration camps. *American Journal of Psychiatry 14,* 645–650.

Kinzie, J. D., Manson, S. M., Do, T. V., Nguyen, T. T., Bui, A., & Than, N. P. (1982). Development and validation of a Vietnamese-language depression rating scale. *American Journal of Psychiatry 139,* 1276–1281.

LaGuerre, M. (1984). *American odyssey: Haitians in New York*. New York: Cornell University Press.

Nidorf, J. F. (1985). Mental health and refugee youths: A model for diagnostic training. In T. C. Owan (Ed.), *Southeast Asian mental health: Treatment, prevention, services, training, and research* (pp. 391–430). Washington, DC: U.S. Department of Health and Human Services.

Stein, B. (1986). The experience of being a refugee: Insights from the literature. In C. Williams & J. Westermeyer (Eds.), *Refugee mental health in resettlement countries* (pp. 5–23). Washington, DC: Hemisphere.

Sughandabhirom, B. (1986). Experiences in a first asylum country: Thailand. In C. Williams & J. Westermeyer (Eds.), *Refugee mental health in resettlement countries* (pp. 81–92). Washington, DC: Hemisphere.

Tung T. M. (1980). *Indochinese patients: Cultural aspects of the medical and psychiatric care of Indochinese refugees*. Falls Church, VA: Action for Southeast Asians.

Tung, T. M. (1985). Psychiatric care for Southeast Asians: How different is different? In T. C. Owan (Ed.), *Southeast Asian mental health: Treatment, prevention, services, training, and research* (pp. 5–40). Washington, DC: U.S. Department of Health and Human Services.

U.S. Bureau of Census. (1970). *U.S. census of population 1970* (Final Report PC70(1)-C1). Washington, DC: U.S. Government Printing Office.

U.S. Bureau of Census. (1980). *U.S. census of population 1980* (Final Report PC80(1)-C1). Washington, DC: U.S. Government Printing Office.

Wong H. (1985). Training for mental health service providers to Southeast Asian refugees: Models, strategies and curricula. In T. C. Owan (Ed.), *Southeast Asian mental health: Treatment, prevention, services, training, and research* (pp. 345–390). Washington, DC: U.S. Department of Health and Human Services.

CHAPTER 113

DIFFERENTIAL ACCULTURATION AMONG VIETNAMESE REFUGEES

Jon K. Matsuoka

The concept of differential acculturation is a fruitful approach to understanding age-related adjustment difficulties and intergenerational conflict among Vietnamese refugees in America. Although the Vietnamese and American societies both attempt to produce well-functioning, self-sufficient individuals, the developmental process differs in the two cultures. Adolescent Vietnamese refugees come to this country at a critical period in their development and are much more vulnerable than their adult counterparts to American social pressures. Adults, on the other hand, must cope with role loss and make immediate adjustments to secure employment.

PROBLEMS OF ACCULTURATION

Culture conflict occurs when people migrate from one culture to another or when individuals in pluralistic cultures leave their ethnic communities for a mainstream environment. Exposure to a different framework of implicit rules and expectations predisposes individuals to disruptive emotional states and a perceived loss of personal effectiveness. Chance (1965) suggested that although acculturation can and frequently does encourage positive changes in one or both groups undergoing contact, by far the most common pattern has been cultural conflict. The conditions that predispose individuals to mental health problems following initial contact include conflicts in identity, roles, and values; drastic ecological and demographic shifts; changing levels of aspiration; and the use of coercion by the dominant group to attain its objectives.

Vietnamese refugees settling into American society confront social forces that will

Reprinted from *Social Work*, Vol. 35, No. 4 (July, 1990), pp. 341–345, by permission of NASW Press. Copyright 1990, National Association of Social Workers, Inc., *Social Work*.

shape their development as a community and their identity as an ethnic minority. Earlier Asian arrivals in this country suffered severe racial discrimination and consequently settled in insulated enclaves where they could cultivate traditional ways without fear of persecution. There is substantial evidence that the Vietnamese are repeating the patterns of their Asian forebears (Lin & Masuda, 1983; Skinner & Hendricks, 1979). However, their refugee status implies circumstances different from those of previous Asian immigrant groups. Most Vietnamese refugees left their homelands abruptly, without knowing where they were going or for how long. The trauma of evacuation has had discernible effects on their resettlement and acculturation experiences.

The decision by government officials to disperse Vietnamese refugees throughout the United States precluded the development of ethnic enclaves that would reinforce ethnic values and identification. Policymakers anticipated that dispersing refugees would accelerate the assimilation process. Refugee families and individuals thus have little choice but to accommodate themselves to an alien culture as rapidly as possible.

Although Vietnamese enclaves are forming as refugees migrate to be near each other, there remain countless numbers of isolated families across the United States. Because the refugees lack means of preserving cultural practices outside the family, structural and marital assimilation may occur within the next generation of Vietnamese in America.

On coming to America, family members have socialization experiences that affect the rates at which they acculturate. The age of entry into this country is a significant determinant of how quickly one assumes American behavioral patterns. This phenomenon creates disunity within the family as younger members adhere to new standards and expectations and older ones cling to traditional roles.

FAMILY, AGE, AND GENERATION

Problems of acculturation related to age and generation can be generalized to all Asian American groups. The literature on Chinese Americans (Cheng, 1978; Fong, 1965; Lyman, 1968); Japanese Americans (Ishizuka, 1978; Kiefer, 1974); Filipino Americans (Lapuz, 1972; Lott, 1976); and Vietnamese Americans (Montero, 1979; Yee, 1979) has focused on the difficult issues associated with elderly people, differential acculturation, intergenerational conflict, and identity conflict. Each person reacts somewhat differently depending on age, prior experiences, and the ability to understand situations. The transition seems especially difficult for people at a critical stage of physical and emotional development (Matsuoka, 1979). Because the process of development differs across cultures, a radical cultural shift at a critical stage can disrupt development, inhibiting growth and leading to stage fixation.

In the radical shift from one culture to another, members of many refugee families lose their traditional age-related roles. Ishisaka (1977) described self-image as an aggregate of experiences related to performance in an individual's social roles. This description may be especially appropriate for people in a traditional society in which severe prescriptive and proscriptive norms still define appropriate behaviors. Evacuation and resettlement have displaced many Vietnamese refugees from the social roles they fulfilled in their homeland.

Traditional Family System

The Vietnamese family is not a nuclear family like the norm in the United States. Instead, the family is a superorganism that includes generations past and future. The Vietnamese family is characterized by strong solidarity, mutual helpfulness, and a patriarchal structure. Family themes include filial piety and respect for age and seniority. One's primary duty is to the family lineage. Family interests take precedence over personal interests. For example, a child chooses a particular career because it is the choice of the parents, who see it as most beneficial to the family.

Vietnamese child-rearing practices allow young children considerable freedom in behavior. In later years, this permissive approach to child rearing changes to a far more strict set of expectations regarding conduct. Adolescents are expected to fulfill their responsibilities to family and family lineage. With the onset of adolescence, girls are expected to manifest modesty, obedience, and chastity. Boys are expected to exhibit adult male behavior. Family members are expected to share in household tasks to the extent of their abilities.

Family harmony is an important goal. It is customary to avoid conflicts between child and parent, or between younger and older siblings, through deferential and respectful behavior. Filial relationships with parents and siblings are among the highest priorities within the Vietnamese culture.

Adults

Ishisaka (1977) claimed that the authority pattern implicit in Confucianism and Buddhism emphasizes an individual's position in a structured hierarchy or authority. The individual is expected to defer to the goals of the family and to the head of the household in all matters dealing with family welfare and continuity. The father, as the head of the household, is expected to adequately support his dependents. He is viewed as the full authority on all matters inside the family. The mother is generally responsible for everything inside the house and is expected to be somewhat subservient to her husband.

The rapid movement of Vietnamese families to the United States has sometimes hampered the father's ability to support his dependents. People who are underemployed and working in menial capacities may experience a dramatic loss of self-esteem. Also, a person's type of work has meaning in Asian cultures. There is a clear ranking of work positions, which parallels ancient values regarding occupational status. The loss of occupational status and the attendant financial implications have serious psychological and emotional significance to the individual and the family (Ishisaka, 1977).

Acculturation to American norms shifts the locus of personality development from the family and community to the individual (Kiefer, 1974). The effects of this shift include a decrease in the size of the resident unit; an increased separation among the spheres of basic human activity (for example, work, worship, and education); an increase in geographic mobility; and a shift in responsibility for developmental changes from the family and community to individuals.

Changes in family functioning reduce the supportive value of family involvement. It is difficult, for example, to maintain extended-family living patterns given the cost of living in the United States and the employment difficulties of refugees. Also, in many cases both spouses must work, when employment is available, to support their children. In many such cases, changes in role expectations from traditional patterns to those required for survival produce family conflict and disruption. Absorbed in meeting basic survival needs, parents may leave their children unattended. Left to their own devices, children may gravitate away from family concerns and responsibilities.

Vietnamese refugees entering American society confront new roles for men and women. In Vietnam, the division of labor in these families was generally quite different from that in America. Women, especially mothers, were confined to domestic duties and child care. The situation in America is generally more equitable between men and women. For the first time, Vietnamese women can join the work force to contribute to family income. Other family members then must accommodate this change. Changing standards of socialization and evaluation tend to reduce constraints on the behavior of individuals. This freedom inevitably leads to changes in individuals, which can lead to family problems when some members change before others do—for example, when women acculturate at a faster pace than their husbands do. Vietnamese women generally have more personal growth potential because American society places fewer social restrictions on them. As Vietnamese women adopt American norms and values while sharing wage-earning responsibility with their husbands, they are likely to become more influential within their families. Such changes may not be readily accepted by husbands who adhere to traditional role expectations.

Youths

Youths, especially adolescents, come to this country at a vulnerable period in their development. They face the problems of learning a new language, getting accustomed to new patterns of behavior, and understanding and accepting conflicting values. Along with these adjustment difficulties, they must accomplish a number of developmental tasks brought on by sexual maturity and the flood of new feelings that follow. They must establish effective social and working relationships with peers and begin preparing for a meaningful vocation.

The adolescent's search for a new identity can be seen as persistent attempts to define and redefine himself or herself. Adolescents in Vietnam have had little choice in moral values. Traditionally, culture and society have reinforced the morality taught in the family. However, Vietnamese coming to this country often find that their traditional family values are inconsistent with those in American society. Because American adolescents are more autonomous and self-determining, American ways seem attractive to Vietnamese youth. Traditionally, Vietnamese adolescents have given parents or other adults the major role in determining the situations to which the adolescents were exposed. However, Vietnamese adolescents in America often begin to refuse guidance from parents or enter into situations without parental consent.

To an American adolescent, personal identity is a developmental need that is met through strong identification with age-mates. Vietnamese culture places greater emphasis on achieving one's identity and sense of worth through close relationships with family adults and being a member of an established lineage and extended-family system. However, the disruption and separation of many Vietnamese families, coupled with exposure and socialization in an age-segregated society, increase the importance and influence of peers.

Many factors affect an adolescent's acceptance or rejection by peers. Acceptance may rest on physical appearance and skills, and on membership in the cultural and racial majority or in a particular peer group. Refugee youths who do not conform to styles of dress, social conduct, and idiomatic language may be rejected by their white American age-mates. Such youths either exist in isolation or attempt quickly to acculturate.

Adolescent Vietnamese refugees, like adults, experience a severe disruption in their lives. The former group, however, may be more affected by this disruption because it occurs during a critical juncture in their development. The circumstances associated with refugee status suggest that Vietnamese adolescents must resolve issues associated not only with physical maturity but also with an acute sense of loss—the loss both of significant family members and of culture. Family disruption and cultural discontinuity at this stage impede normal development and predispose individuals to stage fixation. A lack of continuity and meaning within a new social context inhibits growth beyond this point (Newman & Newman, 1984).

AGE-RELATED ISSUES AND INTERGENERATIONAL CONFLICT

The individual's age at the point of transition from one culture to another is critical in determining the degree to which he or she is affected by the new culture. It could be surmised that resettlement has a somewhat different meaning to family members of different ages. Younger people may look forward to a new life in America and a promising future. Older people, on the other hand, may feel that their best years are behind them and place their aspirations in the younger generation.

The concept of differential acculturation can help explain intergenerational conflict. Adults generally have well-defined identities. They are not as open to experiences in the new society that are antithetical to their established beliefs and values. Acquiring new attitudes, values, and behaviors is often difficult.

Younger people have had less time to acquire such patterns and are easily influenced by the new society. School and the mass media—particularly television—are pervasive socialization forces and regulators of behavior, attitudes, and standards. Much of the socialization of Vietnamese youngsters in the United States emphasizes behavior and values alien to the traditional cultural pattern. For example, Vietnamese youths see other children act informally with their elders and assume this is acceptable and normal behavior in the United States. Inconsistencies between family and institutional education generate conflicting sets of moral values.

When efforts to earn an adequate income reduce the time that refugee parents spend with their children, the importance of the youth culture increases. Conflicts with parents about moral values may reflect efforts to establish an independent identity. Many aspects of adolescent life become difficult to share with parents, especially in those areas where such communication traditionally is prescribed. The emotional needs of children are prone to change with acculturation, and refugee parents may be ill prepared to address them, which places refugee youth in a high-risk situation. In other immigrant cultures, the transitional generation is the one most affected by cultural conflict and shows high degrees of delinquency, mental illness, and anomie (Haskell & Yablonsky, 1974).

IMPLICATIONS FOR SOCIAL WORK

The development of ethnic enclaves reflects the desire of Vietnamese refugees to live close to each other. In many cases, refugees who move from their original placements sacrifice the economic security granted to them by resettlement programs for the social and emotional comforts of living near those who share a common linguistic and cultural background. The formation of geographic communities creates an environment where refugees can practice traditional ways and begin to interrelate new and old cultural material. This condition promotes economic development, community organization, and political strength in the larger society. The emergence of churches, temples, and social organizations within the community gives refugees a major source of social and emotional support and possibly compensates for the loss of family members. The establishment of Vietnamese enclaves balances the socialization experiences of youth and reinforces cultural values and mores taught in the family.

Community social service centers could accommodate the special needs of refugee families. Services offered through these centers could include English education programs, job skills training, health services, mental health treatment, and even day care services for families with young children. Bilingual and bicultural caseworkers would assist refugee clients in obtaining social services.

Clinical Considerations

In traditional Vietnamese culture, there is a great deal of stigma attached to behavioral or mental health problems. Social workers are therefore advised to take an indirect approach to assessment. For example, the social worker should address general issues of adjustment before addressing the most obvious family problems. It is crucial to understand that family problems may be highly sensitive topics.

The social worker must first gain the basic trust of the family. This can usually be done by appropriate advocacy, which encourages family members to disclose small problems that carry minimal risk of losing face. Gradually, family members will confide more personal problems. It is extremely important for the social worker to treat these situations in an open and nonjudgmental manner. Workers who do not speak Vietnamese should be more direct about the purpose of the visit when introducing themselves. Yet even in these situations it may prove helpful to spend time talking generally about the family's children, how old they are, what school they attend, and so on. Such comments and questions often reduce initial apprehension by the clients.

Although problems adjusting to a new culture need not be seen as "psychological," the close-knit organization of the Vietnamese family suggests that family therapy techniques may prove useful. In establishing a relationship with a Vietnamese family, the social worker should be aware of the family hierarchy and address initial questions to the head of the household, which in most cases is the father. The social worker should not project a paternalistic attitude. These behaviors are viewed as disrespectful and counterproductive to the process of building a relationship. Establishing mutual respect between the social worker and clients is essential to creating a healthy working relationship.

In cases where the family is in turmoil because of structural realignments, extensive assessment must precede intervention. Problems stemming from the wife working can be addressed in several ways. One is to encourage a more equitable division of household labor so that the wife is not overburdened with responsibilities. In addition, cognitive therapy techniques can be used to help the husband make situational attributions and not internalize his reduced role in economic support and governance of his family. A therapeutic objective is to help the husband realize that many factors in his new environment (for example, finances and employment status) result from cultural changes and not necessarily from his lack of skills. The husband must be helped to see the value of increased child-rearing and household responsibilities.

Techniques described by Beck, Rush, Shaw, and Emery (1979) for depressed clients can be applied to Vietnamese refugees who make excessive internal attributions for failure and set unrealistic standards for success. Further, the social worker can examine the clients' recent life experiences to develop a context from which to set realistic and attainable goals. Such a context would help the clients realistically examine past behaviors and outcomes and make accurate attributions for success and failure.

Applying cognitive therapy responsibly requires a thorough understanding of the Vietnamese worldview, which diverges considerably from the Western sensibility. For example, deeply ingrained superstitions about events beyond the individual's control are highly resistant to cognitive modification techniques.

Family members whose ages keep them out of the labor market are often at risk. Children and grandparents are often neglected by the working members of the family, which may lead to acting out or delinquent behavior by children and withdrawal or depression in the grandparents. In such cases, therapy should aim to reintegrate displaced members in the family system so that they feel as though they contribute to its welfare. The reinstatement of particular family roles should be preceded by a thorough analysis of family structure and dynamics. Data gathering on family history and the use of ecological models are viable tools for assessment.

The ecological approach is well suited for assessing the interplay of elements in an individual's social and psychological sphere (Germain, 1979). It can be used to conceptualize interpersonal problems that affect broader levels of experience. The ecological approach provides a context for understanding traditional family structure, role-related expectations, and change.

The disruption of many families and socialization in an age-segregated society create further schisms between Vietnamese parents and their children. Parents who are bewildered by their children's new priorities and behaviors should be reminded that acculturation is a natural human response to cultural change. Parents who rigidly adhere to traditional child-rearing patterns may provoke rebellion by their children.

Problems stemming from differential acculturation can generally be addressed by encouraging families to keep components of their Vietnamese culture intact until they have adapted to American culture. Maintaining a familiar culture by which to define themselves, at least until the new culture is learned, gives Vietnamese a broader knowledge base by which to interpret new behaviors.

Case Illustration

The case of Phuc, a 15-year-old who arrived in America during a critical point in his development, illustrates a problem arising from differences between traditional Vietnamese culture and American customs. As a student in Vietnam, this young man excelled in mathematics and was encouraged by his parents to pursue a career in engineering. Although an only child, Phuc was part of a close-knit extended family and was often called upon to care for his grandparents and younger cousins. Upon the death of his father, and seeing little future for themselves in Vietnam, Phuc and his mother set out as "boat people" to seek a better life elsewhere. They eventually resettled in America.

After a year, Phuc's mother met and married another Vietnamese refugee, and they moved to a home in a middle-class community without a concentrated population of Vietnamese. Because of the lack of a Vietnamese community, reinforcement for appropriate Vietnamese behavior was unavailable beyond Phuc's family. The loss of reinforcement and role patterns that would ordinarily have given him a strong identity left him confused and depressed. In school, Phuc was having great difficulty understanding the lessons because he could not speak fluent English. Phuc felt inferior because he was doing poorly, and soon he began skipping classes and spending time in the city with other Vietnamese youth who were involved in gang activity. Because he lived so far away, Phuc was regarded as a marginal gang member although he experimented with drugs and participated in some gang-related activity.

The school officials became concerned about his truancy and reported it to his parents. When his stepfather and mother discovered that their son had not been attending school, they became very angry, because back home he was an outstanding scholar. The stepfather felt that Phuc was lazy and disrespectful, so he physically punished him for his truancy at school. As a result, Phuc ran away from home. The police eventually picked him up, and because he refused to return home, he was placed in foster care.

Treatment

Phuc remained in foster care until a bilingual and bicultural social worker was assigned to the case. The social worker became aware of the severity of the family problems and prescribed individual treatment for Phuc and family therapy for the entire family.

The therapist found that the severe consequences of events in Phuc's childhood were exacerbating current developmental issues associated with the ambiguity of adolescence. The untimely death of his natural father in a Vietnamese "reeducation" camp had been extremely traumatic and apparently had triggered a whole series of family disruptions. Phuc had been unable to appropriately terminate any of his family relationships before his clandestine escape from Vietnam. He had left behind cousins, aunts, uncles, and grandparents whom he could never hope to see again. This sense of loss at such a critical period in his development was extremely traumatic.

Much of Phuc's individual therapy was based on reminiscing about the past and analyzing his current feelings associated with those experiences. Phuc's feelings of guilt and depression over lost loved ones needed to be treated before he was able to move ahead to other concerns. He experienced a type of guilt that could be best described as "survivor guilt." He wondered why his life was spared when his relatives in Vietnam were forced to live under such oppressive conditions. The treatment focus was on reliving, analyzing, and working through the events contributing to his feelings of guilt and depression. The therapeutic objective was to help him accept the oppressive conditions of his relatives and to reconceptualize the traumatic events and thus reduce the feelings of self-blame. Next, he was encouraged to move away from the stressful events and the associated thoughts. Reminiscing about his natural father, with the support of his mother, Phuc was able to grieve his death for the first time. The grieving brought a degree of self-awareness and a connection with his past. It also brought him closer to his mother, who was able to support her son and reconcile her own unresolved feelings from the past.

Phuc generally felt neglected by his parents, who were working long hours. This may in part explain his decline in school performance and his acting-out behaviors. Family therapy was aimed at reestablishing a family culture that he would feel part of. The parents were encouraged to take more interest in Phuc's social and academic activities and to take time for family activities, especially those that linked them to the Vietnamese community. Family members were also taught to reward each other for desirable behaviors, which were defined by mutual agreement. Contractual agreements were made to prevent physical punishment from recurring. The social worker also advocated and received a bilingual educator to assist Phuc in his schoolwork.

This case illustrates the type of problems encountered by Vietnamese faced with the arduous task of finding reliable alignments between old and new cultures. The social worker in this case used psychodynamic techniques to enable Phuc to resolve past conflicts, existential techniques to help him examine his past in relation to his current life and develop self-awareness, and cognitive-behavioral techniques to encourage an atmosphere of family support.

REFERENCES

Beck, A., Rush, A. J., Shaw, B., & Emery, G. (1979). *Cognitive therapy for depression.* New York: Guilford Press.

Chance, N. (1965). Acculturation, self-identification, and personality adjustment. *American Anthropologist, 67,* 372–393.

Cheng, E. (1978). *The elder Chinese.* San Diego: Campanile Press, San Diego State University.

Fong, S. M. (1965). Assimilation of Chinese in America: Changes in orientation and social perception. *American Journal of Sociology, 71*(3), 265–273.

Germain, C. (1979). *Social work practice: People and environment. An ecological perspective.* New York: Columbia University Press.

Haskell, M., & Yablonsky, L. (1974). *Juvenile delinquency.* Chicago: Rand McNally.

Ishisaka, H. (1977). Audio-training tapes focused on the mental health of Indochinese refugees. Seattle, WA: DHEW Region X; Asian Counseling and Referral Service.

Ishizuka, K. C. (1978). *The elder Japanese.* San Diego: Campanile Press, San Diego State University.

Kiefer, C. W. (1974). *Changing cultures, changing lives: An ethnographic study of three generations of Japanese Americans.* San Francisco: Jossey-Bass.

Lapuz, L. (1972). A study of psychopathology in a group of Filipino patients. In W. Lebra (Ed.), *Transcultural research in mental health.* Honolulu: University of Hawaii Press.

Lin, K. M., & Masuda, M. (1983). Impact of the refugee experience: Mental health issues of Southeast Asian refugees. In *Bridging cultures: Southeast Asian refugees in America* (pp. 33–52). Los Angeles: Special Services for Groups.

Lott, J. T. (1976). Migration of a mentality: The Filipino community. *Social Casework, 57*(3), 165–172.

Lyman, S. M. (1968). Contrasts in the community organization of Chinese and Japanese in North America. *Canadian Review of Sociology and Anthropology, 5*(2), 51–67.

Matsuoka, J. K. (1979, April). *Differential acculturation among Indochinese refugee adolescents.* Paper presented at the National Association of Interdisciplinary Ethnic Studies Conference, LaCrosse, WI.

Montero, D. (1979). *Vietnamese Americans: Patterns of resettlement and socioeconomic adaptation in the United States.* Boulder CO: Westview Press.

Newman B. M., & Newman, P. R. (1984). *Development through life: A psychosocial approach.* Homewood, IL: Dorsey Press.

Skinner, K., & Hendricks, G. (1979). The shaping of ethnic self-identity among Indochinese refugees. *Journal of Ethnic Studies, 7*(3), 25–41.

Yee, B.W.K. (1979). *A life-span developmental approach to studying the Caucasian, Japanese, and Vietnamese elderly: Cognitive attributions for control over life situations and its relationship to performance on a cognitive task.* Unpublished master's thesis, University of Denver.

CHAPTER 114

CLINICAL ASSESSMENT AND INTERVENTION WITH SHOPLIFTERS

Sanford Schwartz
Herman V. Wood

Shoplifting is a serious social problem with resultant financial losses in excess of $5 billion per year (Kallis & Vanier, 1985). These costs spread; merchants pass along their losses to consumers in the form of higher prices. Recently, community, corporate, and judicial interest in ways of effectively curtailing shoplifting has been heightened as the proliferation of large shopping malls has created increased opportunities for theft-related offenses. For example, retail merchants routinely employ security personnel and use sophisticated detection equipment. Furthermore, it is now common for store managers to prosecute even the most benign shoplifter to send a message to all customers that any theft—no matter how inexpensive the item—will have serious legal consequences.

As many as one in 12 people engage in shoplifting (Baumer & Rosenbaum, 1984). Although some shoplifting incidents go undetected, people who are apprehended and convicted often are placed under court supervision for up to one year with an agreement to expunge their conviction record if they successfully complete probation. This disposition allows the judicial system to censure unacceptable behavior while encouraging the resolution of contributing psychosocial problems. During court supervision, correctional social work staff may conduct presentence social histories, provide counseling services, or refer clients to other community-based social agencies. In each instance, client-derived information must be gathered and synthesized to form an accurate assessment of the client's presenting problem.

Shoplifters can benefit from social workers' professional skills because the offense frequently is a manifestation of personal problems experienced by otherwise law-abiding citizens (Edwards & Roundtree, 1981; Ray, 1987). Shoplifting is a complex and multi-faceted crime that necessitates the differential assessment of motivational patterns underlying client behavior. Harsh punitive sanctions are unnecessary and may be counterproductive if appropriate attention is diverted from clients' psychosocial situations.

A growing body of social work literature explicitly acknowledges the mandated nature of many worker-client relationships (Hutchison, 1988; Palmer, 1983; Rooney, 1988). Ades and Spiro (1985) spoke of social work's unique ability to "strengthen the capacity of the criminal justice system to deliver effective rehabilitation services [by responding] sensitively and intelligently to the needs of the individual offender" (p. 105). By examining unique factors that contribute to a client's legal problems, social workers can formulate differential assessments to help them select appropriate treatment goals.

This article presents a typology to guide social work assessment of and interventions with shoplifters. Material was derived from two different but related contexts: a publicly funded probation office and a private treatment agency used as a referral source by the local court system. In both settings, client participation in individual and group counseling was required by judicial mandate with the expectation that conditions leading to the shoplifting offense would be addressed. The typology is based on over 10 years of clinical observations of clients referred by the judicial system for misdemeanor shoplifting violations. Practice implications also are examined with specific attention on helping strategies for legally mandated clients.

ASSESSMENT ISSUES

The success of any social work intervention is determined substantially by the accuracy of the assessment. Clinical assessment is a challenging task that relies on the client's struggle to identify, define, and communicate his or her level of dysfunctioning. Assessing clients whose presence has been legally mandated is even more complicated; clients who resent being forced to seek help may initially be uncommunicative. Missed appointments, hostility toward the social worker, and the use of denial and projection as defense mechanisms are common reactions to involuntary participation in treatment (Hepworth & Larsen, 1986). A more subtle form of resistance occurs when clients willingly accept a simple legal definition of their problem to avoid closer examination of contributing psychosocial factors. To the extent that social workers permit this to happen, attention will be diverted from any consideration of substantive problems that may have resulted in the client's current legal difficulties. For example, failure to explore the drug-taking behavior of people convicted of property crimes may allow a chemically dependent client to complete court supervision without ever confronting his or her substance abuse.

In addition to obstacles inherent in the mandated client-worker relationship, several other issues weigh against a thorough consideration of factors underlying shoplifting violations. For example, a control- or punishment-oriented agency may discourage professional staff from conducting differential client assessments. Treatment plans are likely to be standardized and to consist of encouraging clients to adhere to conditions of supervision such as maintaining steady employment and regular contact with the social worker and avoiding circumstances similar to those that precipitated the current offense (for example, avoiding a specific department store or shopping mall). Heavy caseloads further increase the pressure on social workers to focus on superficial compliance rather than on more time-consuming clinical assessment and interventions.

Differential assessment also is unlikely to occur if clients are mistakenly stereotyped (Logan, McRoy, & Freeman, 1987). Only recently has the myth of the adult shoplifter as an economically disadvantaged female been challenged (Ray, 1987). Contrary to expectations, "shoplifting appears to be a working- to middle-class phenomenon" (p. 31) with a growing number of offenders coming from upper-income households (Baumer & Rosenbaum, 1984). The social status, respectable appearance, and absence of a prior criminal record of many shoplifters may create a false impression of psychosocial stability and thus divert attention from conducting a thorough clinical assessment. Although some clients may be indigent, routine referral to financial planning seminars is inadequate and inappropriate for many shoplifters. For example, one-half of the subjects assessed by Arboleda-Florez, Durie, and Costello (1977) engaged in shoplifting as a response to stressful personal situations or as a result of serious psychiatric disorders. Cupchik and Atcheson (1983) suggested that most first-time and infrequent offenders shoplift to compensate for recent losses in their lives (for example, of a spouse or health). Approximately one-third of shoplifting teenagers, college students, and young adults, for whom economic pressures may be especially salient, cited reasons other than financial as their primary motivation (Moore, 1984). Other common characteristics noted among shoplifters include low self-esteem and social isolation (Yates, 1986).

MOTIVATIONAL CLASSIFICATIONS AND PRACTITIONER ASSESSMENT SKILLS

Unlike previous attempts at classification, which rely on psychometric variables, the following typology addresses five specific motivational factors—entitlement, addictions, peer pressure, stress, and impulsiveness—and the requisite practitioner skills for conducting accurate client assessments for each factor. People whose primary source of income is derived from shoplifting are omitted. Such professionals often travel in groups to cities outside their home base. If caught, they post bond and move to another jurisdiction, leaving the bond to be forfeited as a routine cost of doing business. If apprehended and successfully prosecuted, professional thieves are likely to be incarcerated. Even if referred for court supervision, they rarely respond to education, treatment, or reason as long as they are making more money than they pay in fines or bonds.

Entitlement

One form of shoplifting results from a perception of being treated unfairly. The shoplifter believes that he or she is being victimized and thus deserves some form of compensation. Such feelings can be directed at a particular retail establishment that refuses to replace a faulty item or that, in the client's opinion, charges too much money for its merchandise. A more generalized phenomenon has been noted among recent college graduates who are unable to attain an income they feel is commensurate with their time and financial investment. Feeling that they have accomplished all of the prerequisites for success, these clients justify shoplifting as an appropriate response to an unjust situation. Similarly, elderly shoplifters view cost increases fueled by inflation as unfair. This type of shoplifting is not motivated by an inability to acquire necessary goods and services. Rather, the client's sense of unfair treatment precipitates the offense, which serves as an emotional outlet for accumulated frustrations (Moore, 1984).

Most entitlement clients readily acknowledge their offense and then explain their justification. However, this type of client presents several dilemmas for the social worker. Shoplifters in this category feel that courts should be reserved for criminals who pose a serious threat to society. Furthermore, the size and apparent profitability of many large retail stores make it difficult for shoplifters to identify with the victim. These factors, coupled with an inability to see beyond their own situation, combine to insulate entitlement clients from experiencing remorse for their behavior.

In such instances, the social worker should educate shoplifters about the financial consequences to the victimized store and to its consumers and about the legal repercussions to themselves. Accountability for one's actions must be heightened by communicating firmly that although negative circumstances may be unavoidable, they are not an acceptable excuse for shoplifting. Finally social workers should remind these shoplifters that any problems that precipitated the offense will not become less real because a client uses them to justify stealing. Social workers should also make efforts to assist clients with personal problems.

Addictions

Addictive disorders are characterized by compulsive behaviors that become the focal point of clients' lives (Wesson & Smith, 1985). Loss of control and a desire to keep one's addiction a secret combine to make shoplifting a potential means of surreptitiously acquiring the substance or item on which one is dependent. For example, data from clinical studies indicate that between one-third and two-thirds of clients seeking treatment for eating disorders engage in some form of shoplifting (Johnson & Connors, 1987; Pyle, Mitchell, & Eckert, 1981).

Examining police reports for the type of merchandise stolen may be important for client assessment. Bulimic people often steal gourmet foods or very rich foods for an eating binge. Anorexic people usually perceive themselves as lacking in physical attributes and shoplift appearance-enhancing items such as jewelry or clothes. People who experience severe drinking problems may steal alcoholic beverages as well as medicines or personal care products with a high alcohol content. They may conceal such items and later consume them on the premises to immediately stave off withdrawal symptoms and to minimize detection by security personnel and their families. Chemically dependent clients may steal and resell expensive merchandise to support their habits. Addicts who must steal costly items frequently visit the exchange counter of department stores. After obtaining sales slips from friends or people in the parking lot, they will take a similar item from a store display directly to the exchange counter for a cash refund.

The assessment of addictive disorders among shoplifters is complicated by the denial that often accompanies the illness. In addition to identifying the particular items stolen, court social workers should carefully assess their clients for clinical symptoms that accompany bulimia (for example, dental hygiene problems), anorexia (for example, anemia), and alcoholism (for example, amnesiac episodes). Such information helps social workers confront clients who may admit stealing but who may be unwilling to acknowledge an eating disorder or substance abuse.

Peer Pressure

A third type of shoplifter is influenced by his or her peer group. These clients are often high school or college-age students who engage in shoplifting as a way of gaining acceptance. Such incidents often occur on the spur of the moment with little forethought about the risks or consequences involved. Because the items taken may not be expensive, offenders frequently are angry at the sanctions imposed by the court system and puzzled about why their offer to make restitution does not result in dismissal of all charges. Mentally retarded people also can be motivated by peer pressure, either to accept a challenge from their friends or to attempt to acquire the same kinds of material possessions that their friends have.

Although youths may shoplift in groups, this category should be differentiated from the professional shoplifting team approach where each group member has a carefully thought-out role (for example, to divert the attention of the salesperson). For youths, the group provides the impetus, moral support, and lure of conditional acceptance. In addition to education about the legal consequences of shoplifting, clinical interventions should focus on enhancing assertiveness and peer refusal skills through cognitive-behavioral training.

Stress

The broadest category in this typology concerns people whose shoplifting is associated with stress resulting from changing role expectations, demands, and status. Yates (1986) speculated that "an accumulation of stressors over time" (pp. 209–210) creates a sense of desperation that results in out-of-character behavior, including stealing items for which the person has no conceivable use. In an attempt to draw attention to themselves, some shoplifters make little or no effort to hide the fact that they are stealing. If they are not caught or if they are apprehended and released without arrest, they often return to the same store and steal again. This pattern is particularly noticeable in people who have been abandoned recently by loved ones as a result of marital, health, or employment problems.

This perspective frames shoplifting as an inappropriate coping response to psychosocial stress rather than as a solely criminal activity. Both clinical research and practice experience support such a position. In approximately one-third of the cases studied by Cupchik and Atcheson (1983), cancer in self or significant other was identified as a precipitating factor in shoplifting. Other health-related stressors have been noted in the literature; clients forced to confront their own mortality undergo enormous stress (Ray, 1987). The anxiety associated with sudden job loss and retirement may create economic pressure to steal (Yates, 1986). The relationship between stress reactions and shoplifting may be further complicated in clients who are under the influence of a prescription drug, who begin a new medication, or who alter the drug dosage (Williams & Dalby, 1986). Finally, as illustrated in the following case study, marital conflicts can play an important role in shoplifting.

Dora, a 22-year-old female, was convicted of petit larceny (shoplifting) and placed under the supervision of a court social worker for six months. Dora had a two-year-old child, had no prior criminal or traffic record, and worked as a waitress. Her husband of two years was sporadically employed as a construction worker. A review of the official police report indicated that, after leaving work one afternoon, Dora stole a can of hair spray and a variety of makeup products from a nearby department store. The total cost of the items was $51.

During the initial intake interview where court expectations were clarified, Dora exhibited considerable resistance toward the social worker. She was sullen, distant and uncommunicative beyond some minimal formalities. Dora voiced resentment about having to complete the 50 hours of community service required by the judge and was also concerned about the time-consuming nature of maintaining weekly contact with the social worker. Dora attempted to minimize the seriousness of her offense and wanted to "put this thing behind me and get on with my life." She acknowledged having sufficient money to pay for the stolen items (although finances were tight) and genuinely seemed unaware of what prompted her actions.

During the third session, Dora was asked to discuss the 24 hours before her arrest and what specific use she had for the stolen items. Her response was emotional, tearful, and revealing. During the previous eight months she had become increasingly suspicious of her husband's marital fidelity. Dora was not feeling pretty or sexually attractive, and in some vague, unspecified way, she hoped that the cosmetics would encourage her husband's affection and attention. Further probing by the social worker revealed that Dora suspected her husband of having an extramarital affair with her sister, with whom he had a previous relationship before marrying Dora.

The remaining months of probation were devoted to a further exploration of Dora's marital relationship and to enhancing her self-esteem. During this time, Dora was cautioned against using her personal problems as an excuse. She was encouraged by the social worker to view her shoplifting as a socially unacceptable and personally counterproductive response to an extremely stressful situation. Ultimately, court supervision was terminated, and Dora participated in a marital support group, reported improved relations with her husband, and volunteered her services to the local food bank where she had completed her community service requirement.

This case illustrates the progress that can result from reformulating a legal problem into a psychosocial problem. Given the financial condition of Dora and her husband, it would have been easy to assess this case as resulting entirely from economic hardship. Furthermore, it is likely that Dora would have concurred with—or at least not objected to—such an assessment in light of her initial resistance to being placed on probation and her inability to articulate the reasons for her seemingly out-of-character behavior. Only with careful and sustained probing of Dora's motivations and family situation was the social worker able to uncover the precipitating circumstances of the shoplifting behavior. Once identified, appropriate clinical interventions could be planned and initiated.

Keefe (1988) referred to responses that cause more stress than they alleviate as "maladaptive coping." As with Dora, stress may gradually accumulate or, as with an unexpected medical problem, may occur suddenly. In either case, arrest and adjudication for shoplifting heightens client stress and vulnerability to the point where a highly emotional reaction to the court social worker can be anticipated. However, if addressed nonjudgmentally, initial resistance often gives way to feelings of embarrassment at being involved in the criminal justice system and to consideration of unacknowledged or unrecognized personal problems. It is not uncommon for some shoplifters experiencing high degrees of stress to engage in self-recriminations that are even harsher than the judicial censure. Clients feel guilty and embarrassed after having violated an established code of conduct to which they previously adhered. Although these feelings may deter future shoplifting offenses, they in no way ensure that contributing stressors will be satisfactorily addressed. Consequently, social workers should allow clients to work through their anger, assist them in examining their coping mechanisms, and offer to help them cope with stressful situations through anticipatory guidance and other problem-solving strategies.

Impulsiveness

Many clients make a conscious but spur-of-the-moment decision to steal while shopping. It is very common for such clients to lack understanding of the reasons underlying their shoplifting. Their inability to articulate any motivation for their behavior is reflected in comments such as "It looked so easy" or "I don't know why I did it. I could've paid for the items." Such responses can be characterized mistakenly by social workers as resistance, unwillingness to accept responsibility, or lack of impulse control. If any of the explanations are accepted as a complete assessment, then efforts to explore contributing psychosocial factors are minimized as social workers attempt to convince clients of the need to exercise more self-control and to resist temptation.

Court social workers must recognize that this assessment category deals more with ignorance than with knowledge of contributing factors to shoplifting. For example, a young man spontaneously stole items on three occasions of no apparent use to him. After considerable probing, the social worker discovered that he was experiencing sexual identity problems and that his shoplifting always occurred immediately after encountering an attractive store worker.

Rare cases of kleptomania do exist. However, the assessment that a shoplifter's behavior was impulsive is usually incomplete because the professional was unable to identify the motivating factor.

PRACTICE IMPLICATIONS

Acquiring needed information for accurate assessments of court-mandated clients is a challenging task for any professional who seeks to establish a basis for an ongoing helping relationship. Gitterman (1989) discussed client and social worker reactions to the involuntary provision of social services in the criminal justice system:

> Clients test professional and organizational authority, boundaries, and limits through such active behaviors as provocation, interruption, seduction, and overt

hostility or such passive behaviors as withdrawal and silence. "Flight" behaviors, such as cancellation of appointments, precipitous termination, and instant recovery, and "avoidance" behaviors, such as changing the subject, minimizing issues, withholding data, denial, and dissembling, also test professional and organizational authority. (p. 165)

General social work guidelines for addressing client resistance have been developed and include clarifying worker roles, agency expectations, reasons for mandated referral, and definitions and consequences of noncompliance. Social workers are advised to explore the clients' perceptions of their problems and their feelings about mandated status and to acknowledge the validity of client reluctance regarding mandated transactions (Gitterman 1989; Hutchison, 1988). The central issue is to establish a professional relationship that acknowledges the connection between psychosocial problems and legal difficulties so that social work's responsibilities to help the client and to protect the community are satisfied.

Social workers must be careful not to allow shoplifters to divert responsibility for their actions by externalizing blame for the offense to problems that have been discussed or uncovered in the course of the professional relationship. Although community corrections can encourage social work interventions for clients and may even acknowledge that one's psychosocial condition helps to explain a criminal offense, the criminal justice system ultimately demands that clients be held accountable for their behavior. Thus, personal problems may explain but never excuse the offense.

This delicate balance between etiology and responsibility is not unique to corrections. It has surfaced repeatedly in alcoholism literature, where the merits of the disease concept and its implications for client motivation to change are the subjects of ongoing debate. A promising strategy for addressing this issue is to hold clients accountable for initiating changes in their future behavior. This involves acknowledging that although prior circumstances beyond either their control or ability to cope have contributed to their present situation, those circumstances need not detract from their intention or ability to change. Accordingly, Dora was not permitted to use her husband's presumed infidelity as an excuse for shoplifting. Instead, she was encouraged to examine her feelings about and reactions to her marital relationship and to develop alternative responses to her stressful situation.

Professional practice with legally mandated clients often requires that social workers seek additional information from ancillary sources. In some instances, the spouse is already aware of the husband or wife's legal status; therefore, attempting to involve them in assessment and treatment does not compromise confidentiality. However, notification of significant others may be problematic for shoplifters when the information jeopardizes an already fragile marital or employment situation.

An important source of readily accessible information about the shoplifter is the official police report. An examination of the items stolen, method of concealment, and client reactions can help social workers determine the appropriate classification of shoplifters. Finally, reactions to being arrested, ranging from defiance and indignation to confusion and acquiescence, can help workers gauge client receptivity to court-initiated interventions.

CONCLUSIONS

Working with shoplifters in community-based corrections is a promising arena for social workers to apply their clinical expertise. The willingness of judges to consider alternatives to incarceration in all but the most extreme cases places a premium on the services of professionals who can assess and resolve contributing psychosocial factors. Such knowledge cannot guarantee a favorable judicial and clinical disposition in every instance. However, failure to conduct individualized assessments of shoplifters' situations and needs deprives people in crisis of an opportunity to receive assistance and support.

REFERENCES

Ades, J., & Spiro, B. (1985). A social service lever for criminal justice sentencing. *Social Service Review, 59,* 95–106.

Arboleda-Florez, J., Durie, H., & Costello, J. (1977). Shoplifters: An ordinary crime? *International Journal of Offender Therapy and Comparative Criminology, 21,* 201–207.

Baumer, T., & Rosenbaum, D. (1984). *Combatting retail theft: Programs and strategies.* Boston: Butterworth.

Cupchik, W., & Atcheson, D. (1983). Shoplifting: An occasional crime of the moral majority. *Bulletin of the American Academy of Psychiatry and the Law, 11,* 343–354.

Edwards, D., & Roundtree, G. (1981). Assessment of short-term treatment groups with adjudicated first offender shoplifters. *Journal of Offender Counseling Services and Rehabilitation, 6,* 89–102.

Gitterman, A. (1989). Testing professional authority and boundaries. *Social Casework, 70,* 165–171.

Hepworth, D., & Larsen, J. (1986). *Direct social work practice: Theory and skills.* Chicago: Dorsey.

Hutchison, E. (1988). Use of authority in direct social work practice with mandated clients. *Social Service Review, 61,* 581–598.

Johnson, C., & Connors, M. (1987). *The etiology and treatment of bulimia nervosa.* New York: Basic Books.

Kallis, J., & Vanier, D. (1985). Consumer shoplifting: Orientations and deterrents. *Journal of Criminal Justice, 13,* 459–473.

Keefe, T. (1988). Stress-coping skills: An ounce of prevention in direct practice. *Social Casework, 67,* 475–482.

Logan, S., McRoy, R., & Freeman, E. (1987). Current practice approaches for treating the alcoholic client. *Health and Social Work, 12,* 178–186.

Moore, R. (1984). Shoplifting in middle America: Patterns and motivational correlates. *International Journal of Offender Therapy and Comparative Criminology, 28,* 53–64.

Palmer, S. (1983). Authority: An essential part of practice. *Social Work, 28,* 120–125.

Pyle, R., Mitchell, J., & Eckert, E. (1981). Bulimia: A report of 34 cases. *Journal of Clinical Psychiatry, 42,* 60–64.

Ray, J. (1987). Every twelfth shopper: Who shoplifts and why. *Social Casework, 68,* 234–239.

Rooney, R. (1988). Socialization strategies for involuntary clients. *Social Casework, 69,* 131–140.

Wesson, D., & Smith, D. (1985). Cocaine: Treatment perspectives. In N. Kozel & E. Adams (Eds.), *Cocaine use in America* (pp. 193–203). Rockville, MD: National Institute on Drug Abuse.

Williams, R., & Dalby, J. (1986). Benzodiazepines and shoplifting. *International Journal of Offender Therapy and Comparative Criminology, 30,* 35–39.

Yates, E. (1986). The influence of psychosocial factors on non-sensical shoplifting. *International Journal of Offender Therapy and Comparative Criminology, 30,* 203–211.

CHAPTER 115

WORKING WITH FEMALE OFFENDERS

Beyond 'Alternatives to Custody'?

Anne Worrall

According to official criminal statistics (Home Office, annually) women are responsible for about fifteen per cent of all recorded crime. In relation to sentencing, they appear to be over-represented on probation orders (about twenty-six per cent of all orders made), under-represented on Community Service orders (about six per cent of all orders made) (Home Office, 1987) and placed on both with fewer previous convictions than men (Home Office, 1986). Each of these facts might be interpreted in a number of ways and each explanation has its own implications for defining the 'moment' and nature of probation intervention in the lives of female offenders.

During the 1980s, the Probation Service has been emerging from what has been termed its 'loss of direction' (Raynor, 1985) in the mid and late 1970s. The banner under which it has recreated its identity and restored its self-confidence has been that of 'Alternatives to Custody'. During the same period, there has been a steadily increasing interest amongst both academics and practitioners in a previously neglected aspect of the criminal justice system—the treatment of female offenders. The separate trajectories of these two concerns have been moving relentlessly closer in recent years and a collision has seemed inevitable. Awareness of gender biases within the criminal justice system has made it increasingly difficult for many probation officers to accept uncritically that their prime task is to find alternative disposals for those offenders who have been defined by the courts as being in danger of imprisonment. This article will examine the particular contradictions in the rhetoric of 'Alternatives to Custody' which have been exposed by recent attempts to demythologize the 'women and crime' issue and will explore the implications of such an examination for policy and practice in the Probation Service. It draws on material obtained from interviews with probation officers

Reprinted from *British Journal of Social Work*, Vol. 19, No. 2 (April 1989), pp. 77–93, by permission of Oxford University Press.

and female offenders and arises from a wider research project which began in Stafford-shire in 1983. This research examined the attitudes and practices of magistrates, solici-tors, psychiatrists and probation officers in relation to those increasing numbers of female offenders who cannot readily be categorized as either warranting imprisonment or as being in need of 'treatment' (Worrall, 1987a; 1989).

TENSIONS IN WORK WITH FEMALE OFFENDERS

Traditional probation work has been forced to accommodate attacks on the 'rehabilita-tive ideal' by critics from both the political right and left. On the one hand, 'treatment' has been dismissed as little more than 'compulsory persuasion' (Raynor, 1978), ampli-fying rather than reducing deviance. On the other, the apparent desire of 'common sense', hailed by the 'new right', requires that offenders are more strictly supervised and called to account. The 'Alternatives to Custody' debate arose from attempts by the Pro-bation Service to resolve the sense of 'dissonance' that resulted from these tensions (Harris, 1980). The emphasis in work with offenders has been laid increasingly on ne-gotiation, responsibility and informed choice (Raynor, 1985). Faith is placed in the compelling logic of rational argument to influence both court and client. Clearly, since offenders are held responsible for their actions, they may have to face the fact that their choices are limited and that the nature of their freedom may have to be negotiated with the court. But within this model, such limitations are compatible with the offer of real-istic help rather than so-called treatment by experts (Bottoms and McWilliams, 1979).

The debate, however, has been pursued in such a way that it both largely ignores and is irrelevant to female offenders. This is not because women are not sent to prison; clearly, they are—and in increasing numbers (Home Office, 1988a). But the current de-bate ignores the complexity of the route that leads them there. On the one hand, it ren-ders the majority of female offenders invisible by interpreting their offences as petty, harmless and 'one-off' matters (Eaton, 1986; Allen, 1987; Worrall, 1987b). On the other, it renders a minority of female offenders highly visible by assuming that their presence in prison demonstrates either their dangerousness or their incorrigibility, rather than demonstrating the inadequacy of the process by which they came to be de-fined as being 'at risk of custody' (Seear and Player, 1986).

Much has now been written about women's experience of the criminal justice system in general and implicit throughout the literature is the existence of a 'gender contract' which routinely offers the female offender the opportunity to neutralize the effects of her lawbreaking activity by permitting her life to be described or represented primarily in terms of its domestic, sexual and pathological dimensions (Carlen and Worrall, 1987). Whilst many female offenders accept this deal and a few reject it outright (see, for example, Carlen *et al.*, 1985), this article argues that there exist many women whose circumstances and attitudes place them at the margins of the categories which are seen to excuse their lawbreaking behaviour. Consequently, they are both neglected by, and elude the controlling influence of, the gender contract in subtle ways which place their liberty in jeopardy, despite the fact that, in strict tariff terms, they do not qualify for 'Alternatives to Custody' intervention.

The research reported here indicates that considerable numbers of female offenders are trapped by an inappropriate judicial need to fit them into stereotyped categories. It shows that many female offenders are not readily classifiable in this simplistic way, but that their 'nondescriptiveness' results in their definitions of their own problems being unheard and their needs remaining unmet. Probation officers, too, are trapped in their work with such women because, whilst they recognize the contradictions of the gender contract, they often experience a sense of powerlessness to challenge it and a frustration which is often exacerbated by the apparently self-destructive contract avoidance behaviour of some women clients. Despite this, it is possible for officers to experience a sense of achievement when, in the absence of any alternative provision, the contradictions of the gender contract are exploited to the benefit of women clients or when some women are empowered to find non-self-destructive solutions to the gender contract for themselves.

IDENTIFYING THE CONTRADICTIONS OF THE GENDER CONTRACT

A male probation officer working in a women's prison was asked whether he agreed with the view of a previously interviewed female probation officer that women evade reality more than men and that prison helps them to face up to the consequences of their behaviour. He replied:

> For some women, reality *is* provision for their families. I have found that women in prison are on the whole more realistic than men . . . and perhaps they suffer more from the fact that they are rooted in relationships.

Most of the probation officers I interviewed recognized that many women who commit crimes do so because they are chronically short of money. But the relationship between poverty and criminal activity is often more complex than that. The extent to which the families in which some women live can be held to be actively responsible for their criminal activity was also recognized. Lack of appreciation, a sense of injustice and having to cope with 'chaos' were all proposed as factors precipitating the commission of crimes by women. One probation officer spoke of a widow who chose to plead guilty to shoplifting 'to get it over with', although the officer felt she might have had a defence to the charge:

> It's the saddest case I've ever come across. Her family meant everything to her but they didn't have the same regard for her.

The subsequent probation order provided an opportunity for the probation officer to undertake 'grief counselling' with the woman—a valuable service but, it might be argued, one which should not have required the catalyst of a criminal conviction to obtain. Another probation officer described a woman whose husband had left her for a younger woman. Ethel was on probation for the apparently inexplicable theft of a chicken valued at £2:

She's a sad little lady who has just had all the spirit knocked out of her. . . . But she's a very upright woman—she thinks it's terrible that her husband should be allowed (to be unfaithful). . . . She got herself into a state . . . and she had to sit there and not be able to defend herself about what he'd done to her. And she put her coat on and went out and thought 'Why should I pay for this chicken?'

Perhaps the most vivid description of the damaging effects of the family came from a probation officer's account of Maureen's chaotic family situation:

Maureen, although she's cast as the non-coper, is the coper, and she copes by committing offences, to try, in her way, to get them out of trouble. But all she manages to do is get herself into trouble. The family do survive while she's away, and they have very little regard for her really. Maureen's been diagnosed over the years as schizophrenic, personality disordered—it's usually been those sorts of labels that have been bandied about—or 'subject to anxiety attacks'. I mean, I don't know what you do with a label when you've got it. . . . The family collude with each other in isolating Maureen as *the* problem. In effect, the problems are family-based, rather than all centred in Maureen.

The demand for the woman in a family to be the one responsible for bringing about change was illustrated by a probation officer who was supervising both a husband and a wife on probation. It was clear that his expectations of what could be achieved in work with the two clients differed greatly. His overall aim in the case was to improve communication between the couple but the focus was primarily on the wife:

I've got her practising telling him specifically where she is going and talking to him about it when she comes back. . . . He is more reporting as a probationer. He comes in and we play a game of pool or something like that.

Eaton (1986) found that when probation officers were preparing social inquiry reports on men, they used home visits to meet and assess significant others (usually women) in the men's lives, whereas such visits in the cases of women were used to see what kind of home they maintained. Probation officers also seem more keen to involve the female partners of men under supervision than the male partners of women. Implicit in this practice is the assumption that it is women who can influence and bring about change in relationships. A probation officer working at a Day Centre, whose clientele (as with all Day Centres) was predominantly male, told me:

We are also attracting wives . . . or girlfriends of men who are clients. Some females here are not clients and are as near to volunteers as possible.

By the term 'volunteers' he was referring to the Service's 'voluntary associates' who befriend clients and assist in other ways without payment. The use of the term in this context, however, seems somewhat ironic, given the level of choice which these women probably had within those relationships. The nature of that relationship was also, however, heavily circumscribed. The 'volunteer' could very easily be reconstructed as the 'whore' if she overstepped the bounds of correct behaviour in this male domain, as the officer continued to explain:

> They may have a boyfriend who is at the centre . . . that boyfriend may change from week to week, but they will tend to relate to a particular man. One or two of the women will tend to relate to a number of men. We've had suspicions, for example about the activities of one of our females . . . about using us as a sort of picking up spot.

When relationships founder, it is again often the woman who is blamed. She is seen as exploiting the relationship for her own ends—as seducing/manipulating the gullible, vulnerable man. One probation officer described one of his female clients thus:

> Much of her life is based on deception . . . and she's certainly one of the most untruthful people I've ever met. And because she is so unreliable in what she says, she doesn't form relationships that last. She tends to abuse friendships. So we keep going round in cycles—she gets a friendship, she abuses it, she loses it, and she's down to rock bottom again.

The 'rooting' of largely unemployed, working-class women in relationships produces a paradoxical 'reality' in which:

1. They are expected to be 'providers' for their families but are denied the material resources with which to provide in a socially and legally approved manner;
2. They are held responsible for any problems within their families and also for bringing about positive change in those families. This means that, whilst they suffer the stigma of being the 'Identified Patient' (or 'Client'), they are not allowed to enjoy the 'benefits' of being ill;
3. Whilst they are expected to be stabilizing influences on their wayward male partners, any attempt to reap satisfaction for themselves from these relationships is interpreted as 'abuse' of the relationship.

Probation officers are not unaware of these paradoxes, but often find themselves powerless to offer alternative definitions of 'reality'. One probation officer summarized the predicament in describing her own attempt to 'make sense' of one woman client:

> The choices are either to see her as a good woman, caring for her family but suffering from psychological disorder which causes lapses into anti-social behaviour, or, bluntly, to see her as a liar and a thief, who attempts to con her way out of difficult situations. The truth is, no doubt, in the grey area between.

It is therefore apparent that the stereotypical assumptions underlying the 'gender contract' are real and still shape the way in which probation officers approach work with female offenders, despite the ostensible rationality and 'offence-focused' nature of the 'Alternatives to Custody' rhetoric. Within the confines of such tensions, probation officers experienced both frustrations and rewards in their attempts to influence the lives of their women clients.

CONTRACT AVOIDANCE—LOSING MODES?

One of the frustrations experienced by probation officers in their work with women was that, in their attempts to avoid the 'gender contract' implicit in supervision, the women also threatened—or seemed unimpressed by—the more overt contract which constitutes the basis of the relationship between probation officers and all their clients. Much of this contract avoidance seemed ultimately self-defeating since it failed to produce any sense of satisfaction or achievement for either the women or those who sought to help them. Probation officers identified such 'defences of the weak' (Mathieson, 1972) as elusiveness, demands, deviousness and refusal.

The commonest complaint about women on probation was their inability/refusal to keep appointments. The following comment was typical:

I have difficulty getting them to report. The majority I have to visit at home—I'd never get them in.

But home visiting had its problems as well. One probation officer talked about a voluntary associate who called 'religiously' every week on one young woman and her cohabitee:

They know what time she's coming—and they go out!

But elusiveness consists of more than mere physical avoidance of contact. Many probation officers became frustrated by the women's failure to tell them things which the officers considered to be important to discuss. This inability/refusal to engage in what was seen to be appropriate self-disclosure (without which officers felt impotent to offer help) was one of the modes of behaviour which was categorized as 'not responding' to supervision. In these situations, the probation officers felt that the women went through the motions of adhering to the conditions of their probation orders but lacked commitment to changing their behaviour or attitudes. Ironically, such a state of affairs has become increasingly acceptable in relation to male offenders but continues to cause professional discomfort in relation to women.

The absence of 'self-identity' amongst the women was another feature of their 'rootedness'. The women appeared to be defined—and to define themselves—in relation to other people and how they believed that other people viewed them. Given this struggle for identity, it is perhaps not surprising that the women sometimes seemed indecisive.

The effect of this indecisiveness and lack of self-identity was that probation officers felt they could rarely do any preventive work with women. They rarely reached a stage where they felt that the women were able to *anticipate* problems or develop reliable coping strategies which might help to forestall crises. Having to respond constantly—and sometimes exclusively—at the point of crisis, without being able to help clients develop their own strategies for coping with and preventing future crises is very wearing and can actually create a state of crisis in the worker him/herself (O'Hagan, 1986).

But there was a further frustration in working with women which exacerbated both their elusiveness and their demands. That frustration arose from a feeling amongst probation officers that some women, far from being hapless victims, were sometimes rather stubborn and devious.

Probation officers frequently described themselves as 'being manipulated' by their women clients. The comparable term used in relation to male clients was 'being conned' and most officers prided themselves on their ability to detect men who are 'trying it on' or not telling the truth. It was apparently more difficult to detect such behaviour in women because it appeared to take the form of selective truth telling, rather than outright 'lying'. Women, one is given to understand, are particularly adept at representing the truth in ways which compel workers to act against their better judgement. Whilst all relationships are, to some degree, marked by manipulation, the particular frustration provoked in probation officers by these women was due to their ability, despite being 'chaotic' and 'inadequate', to exploit the contradictions of the gender contract. Probation officers know that official discourse obliges them to buttress any desire on the part of these women to undertake approbated feminine roles, however passively or apparently disingenuously that desire is expressed. Challenging such expressions would involve the officer in accepting the women's self-defined reality and openly acknowledging the inadequacies of existing definitions. The only alternative is to reconstruct such women as being forever manipulative—and therefore dismissable:

> Sandra is a manipulative lady who plays off one agency against another. Caution and discretion are needed in dealing with her.

But constructing women as essentially deceptive makes it impossible for officers either to define 'reality' in relation to these women or to accept their own definitions of reality. Thus, they remain forever unknowable.

Deviousness was seen as a mechanism requiring a greater degree of agency than either elusiveness or making demands. Manipulative women were viewed as being quite powerful and their behaviour provoked anger amongst officers rather than indulgence or understanding. Most would have preferred outright defiance but incidents of such refusal were rare. One probation officer, however, had undertaken the time-consuming job of finding a choice of no less than three alternatives which *he* saw as solutions to a client's accommodation problems, including a place in a probation hostel:

> I wanted her to go to the hostel but she refused all three alternatives. She said to the magistrates, 'Please send me to prison'.

Probation officers were frequently at a loss to understand such self-defeating behaviour yet, as O'Dwyer and Carlen (1985) have suggested, the line between surviving and failing to survive in situations of oppression is a very narrow one. These women were engaging in the emotional/social equivalent of 'cutting up'. Unable to 'hit back' at the system, they internalized their responses to its pains and tensions and self-mutilated in an attempt to remain independent of others' inroads upon them. Such behaviour may well be interpreted within the rhetoric of 'Alternatives to Custody' as demonstrating a lack of motivation or commitment to making 'constructive' use of the opportunity of a probation order. What is frequently misunderstood is that what is being avoided is not so much the probation contract as the 'gender contract' and the fear that the former is bound to involve the latter. What is also frequently overestimated is the degree of choice which women have about alternative strategies both for avoiding crime and for negotiating with courts about their treatment. Poverty, isolation and lack of self-esteem do not create conditions conducive to the negotiation of the rational, fair and acceptable contract implied by the 'non-treatment paradigm' of probation practice. However, even when account is taken of such structural inequalities there is, initially at least, no easy way of reconciling a feminist perspective with probation practice, as the next section demonstrates.

CONTRACT AVOIDANCE—WINNING MODES?

Elusiveness, demands, deviousness and refusal constitute what have been described elsewhere as 'losing modes' (O'Dwyer and Carlen, 1985). But there were some *rewards* for probation officers working with these women. Obvious progress might be hard to detect, but those officers who were content to set modest goals often found that they were offering a much-needed service, which was consistent with the Probation Service's traditional motto, 'Advise, Assist and Befriend'. Most of the women I spoke to impressed me as being reluctant converts to probation. They had been initially suspicious, or even downright fearful, of being on probation. They had, however, come to see that there were benefits to be gained either by paying lip-service to the idea of probation or by accepting what they perceived to be a genuine offer of friendship and help from another individual who was 'nice' and who had access to certain resources (and who was coincidentally designated 'probation officer'). As Kirwin (1985, p. 39) observes:

> Being treated in a normal humane manner is often a pleasant surprise for . . . clients . . .

Gwen was afraid that, in addition to the control exercised over her by her doctor, she would now be under surveillance by agents of the criminal justice system:

> I was very frightened of probation—I felt as though I was being owned by the police (*sic*). I felt as though my life wasn't my own.

She had feared that being on probation would mean that she would have to forego the right and the capacity to 'own' herself—that is, to define her own actions in the future. Such remarks also serve to explain why some women prefer to go to prison, despite the availability of apparently preferable alternatives.

But she, along with most of the others, appeared to have been won over by the 'helpfulness' of her particular probation officer. The process had started in court where, as

Powell (1985, p. 18) has stated, probation officers have traditionally been expected to 'offer immediate help—or at least a calm and clear explanation—to the distressed and uncomprehending' in court. Indeed, several of the women expressed appreciation of the presence of their probation officer in this bewildering setting:

> I could look at Mrs A and think there was a familiar face.

Later on in the relationship, 'helpfulness' was defined by the women in two ways: firstly, material help and secondly, non-intrusive listening and advice-giving. In other words, the kind of help which the women looked for and appreciated most from their probation officers consisted of money (or at least help in obtaining it) and befriending.

Kirwin (1985, p. 41) argues that probation officers frequently use their distrust of 'presenting problems' to justify refusing to undertake 'mundane' tasks for clients, such as 'phoning and writing to the DHSS, housing departments and fuel boards or arranging nursery places'. Such 'mundane' tasks, however, may be daunting for women who are already lacking in confidence and self-esteem. A willingness by probation officers to use their professional authority and credibility (not to mention their telephones and postage) to negotiate with officialdom on their clients' behalf was certainly appreciated by the women, especially if there were no therapeutic 'strings' attached.

Apart from giving, or helping to obtain, material assistance, the most important function served by probation officers—according to the women—was that of alleviating loneliness. Being available, having time to listen—this was the service women wanted from their probation officers.

For two women, Maureen and Ivy, who already saw themselves as burdens on their own families, a sympathetic and disinterested listener was invaluable in preserving the remnants of family support:

> I can tell her anything. . . . You can't tell your children—you've got to tell someone who's not involved. You don't want to foist your troubles on your family because they won't come and see me. They'll say, 'Oh, crikey—neurotic'—which perhaps I am.
>   (Ivy)

> I like to come and talk to Mrs C. It's somebody to talk to and it's better than going blabbering and shouting your head off in the house.
>   (Maureen)

It might be argued that, by befriending, probation officers are merely pandering to the ideology of the family, still allowing family members to channel all their problems on to 'mum', who then gets a probation officer to help her, instead of working with the whole family, 'helping them to understand the tremendous contradictory pressures placed upon them by the economic structures of capitalist society' (Corrigan and Leonard, 1976, p. 29). In response, many probation officers would no doubt reply, 'It's all right for you to talk' (Cohen, 1975, p. 76) and continue with the one aspect of their role which appears to be rewarding for worker and client.

The building up of this relationship of trust, however, takes time. Pauline was experiencing her third probation order and described her probation officer thus:

> She's like an old friend and I know what she's like, so that now I trust her.

Eileen had known her probation officer even longer:

> I've been involved with Miss D. since 1968 . . . when I was 14. She's been a great help—she's been involved 15 years—we've got an understanding.

In the efficiency-conscious Probation Service of the 1980s, such a lengthy nurturance could hardly be justified as the most cost-effective use of officer resources! And there is, of course, no guarantee that such hard-won trust and understanding will actually prevent further criminal activity. As far as Pauline was concerned, the opposite seemed to be the case. Soon after I interviewed her, she committed a further offence.

A third way in which probation officers might be said to be of help to women was through *empowering*. Empowering consisted of providing the women with the kind of environment in which they could actually *achieve* something for themselves. *What* they achieved was not within the control of the probation officer—and sometimes it was not what the officer had originally intended. Nevertheless, the crucial characteristic of such provision was that it created a space in which the women were enabled to make some genuine *choices,* albeit within heavily circumscribed limits. In a small way, it allowed the women to exploit the gender contract in ways which were not self-defeating. Examples of this typically involved the creation of, or facilitating access to, work opportunities, though frequently such work was of a voluntary nature and the extent to which this might serve to keep the women in poverty must not be overlooked.

One logical extension of this *empowering* process was to allow women to do 'voluntary' work in order to discharge their obligations to the court. The issue of the appropriateness of Community Service for women is a vexed one (Dominelli, 1984) but there was no doubt that the women I interviewed who had served such orders had not only thoroughly enjoyed their work, but had experienced a sense of achievement as well. Having admitted that she never paid fines, Carol said:

> The only thing I think they should give is Community Service, because then *you* don't have to fork any money out and *they* don't have to fork money out (for prison). And I like working . . . I don't mind cleaning—I'll clean the whole house for you as long as you appreciate it.

On the other hand, one probation officer responsible for placing women in Community Service schemes felt that women fared better when they were not asked to do 'women's work', although he did feel that women might feel 'more comfortable' if such teams had women supervisors.

There is, therefore, a dilemma for the probation officer who wants to resist the prescriptive description of her/his female clients within the discourse of femininity. As can be seen from these accounts, many women are not seeking to break out of the ideologies that confine them to domesticity, sexual passivity and sickness. Rather, they want to have the worst effects of those ideologies alleviated. The most appreciated probation officers were those who worked tactically to obtain material help, those who befriended in a one-to-one relationship and those who provided part-time work opportunities which were role-appropriate (so that the women could feel confident in doing them well), relatively private and anonymous (so that the women did not feel conspicuous or stigmatized) and above all, *appreciated!* Such findings appear to confirm those of Willis that:

> Probation is primarily concerned with bringing relief and service to clients whose circumstances might have otherwise appeared to them intolerable . . . and this so-cial work assistance is something clients both want and appreciate.
> (1986, p. 177)

But individual solutions do not provide the alternative material and ideological condi-tions within which the women can constitute themselves differently—only collective political and policy solutions can do that. Such is the trap in which probation officers are also caught.

AGENDA FOR CHANGE

It has been argued in this article that there is a need to examine the implications for work with female offenders of the gradual but possibly irreversible change in the philosophy of the Probation Service. Following the government's new proposals for punishment in the community (Home Office, 1988b), Probation Services are being ex-horted to monitor and evaluate their work to test its effectiveness in terms of (amongst other things) 'participation of ethnic minority and female offenders' (Home Office, 1988c). If such evaluation is genuinely to accommodate the increased awareness of gen-der inequalities and injustices in the criminal justice system then three areas require sys-tematic examination:

1. Defining the Needs of Female Offenders

Many probation officers would now acknowledge that the routine emphasis on the role expectations of 'normal' womanhood in social inquiry reports on female offenders dis-advantages many women who do not readily fit those stereotypes. (It has also been sug-gested recently [Mair and Brockington, 1988] that, since the very existence of a report may push any defendant 'up tariff' and since women are more likely than men to be re-ferred for a report, the preparation of reports may, of itself, indirectly discriminate against women). The problem posed for individual officers who lack policy support is to find ways of challenging those stereotypes without disadvantaging women even fur-ther. Social inquiry reports are inescapably individualized documents and any attempt to take account of the social and economic disadvantage of whole classes of defendants is fundamentally incongruous with the project. Nevertheless, when preparing reports, officers are challenged to find alternative ways of portraying women which cut across the stereotypes of domesticity, sexuality and pathology. One of the ways of doing this might be systematically to highlight the variety of motivation that exists for criminal activity by both men and women. Refusing to accept that women commit crimes for fundamentally different reasons from men is an obvious, though rarely acknowledged, starting point to the achievement of fairer treatment (by which is meant that offenders of either sex in the same material circumstances should receive similar sentences for similar offences). The fact that many female offenders are *not* in the same circumstances as their male counterparts will then become much clearer and will not be conflated with assumptions about the psychology of female offending.

2. Deciding the Moment of Intervention

The debate about the relative merits of earlier or later intervention by welfare agencies is one which both extends beyond considerations of gender and has tended to ignore gender. Much work has been done, for example, on the implications for recidivism amongst juveniles (for which read 'boys') of early formal intervention (Rutter and Giller, 1983; Rutherford, 1986), and it would be comforting to regard these insights as directly transferable to work with women. Undoubtedly many women *have* been placed on probation in the past for petty first offences because they are seen to be 'in need' and undoubtedly this has served to escalate them up the tariff if they do reoffend. But the ideology of radical nonintervention is dependent on the existence of apposite, though hitherto unrecognized, informal resources in the community which will, once recognized and mobilized, serve to support the delinquent through the 'bad patch' into responsible citizenship. As many critics of the decarceration movement have pointed out, however, the reality of 'community care' frequently means no more than the shunting of deviants from the case-load of one agency to another. If this is indeed the case with some female offenders, it may be necessary for the Probation Service to accept the unpalatable fact that those women who break the law as a result of material, social or emotional need are *not* likely to receive help from any other source. The challenge in relation to such women is whether early intervention can *empower* them to take more control over their lives or whether it inevitably restricts their choices and places them at greater risk of custody. As Mair and Brockington (1988) observe, there is an urgent need for research which will compare the subsequent conviction patterns of a carefully matched group of male and female offenders after they have received a probation order.

3. Deciding the Nature of Intervention

Provision for female offenders needs to be considered on two broad fronts—direct provision by the Probation Service and policy campaigns directed at the judiciary and the government. It is becoming apparent that the current paucity of direct provision by the Service for those women who, by virtue of the frequency of their lawbreaking or their failure to fit the stereotypes, are at risk of custody is resulting in their imprisonment by default. There is a need for the Service to give more attention to *separate* and appropriate provision for women in Day Centres, Community Service and accommodation schemes. There exists a fairly wide variety of provision of social (that is, 'survival') skills training, especially in day centres, but such groups are usually dominated by men.

Women are rarely expressly excluded but, understandably, few have the interest, confidence—or social skills—to participate. Although there have always been 'wives' groups' run by the Probation Service, the idea of regarding women as people 'in their own right' with their own survival needs requiring specialist separate provision, is a relatively new and controversial one. The fact that increasing numbers of young, poor women are persistently offending does, however, challenge probation officers to consider, for example, (as some Probation areas already have) the provision of separate offence-focused groups for women. The *content* of these might differ markedly from that of groups of men, including such things as coping with stress, assertiveness training and skills in working/campaigning with other women.

Direct provision by the Service for women who are not at risk of immediate imprisonment is more difficult to justify within the rhetoric of 'Alternatives to Custody'. Nevertheless, as this study has indicated, the efforts of probation officers, on a one-to-one basis, to obtain money for women clients, open doors to new opportunities for them and simply (though unfashionably) befriend them meets a need which is clearly expressed by the women themselves. Where these same women can be directed towards other, non-statutory sources of help and support, this is obviously preferable for their self-esteem, but, in the absence of alternative provision, such work by probation officers should not be undervalued. It does, however, have its limitations and can only be justified in the long-term if it is coupled with pressure from the Service for broader social, economic and judicial reforms.

CONCLUSION

Assumptions about femininity define the experiences of all women, but easier material circumstances enable some women to resist the consequences of those definitions more successfully than others. Ultimately, discussion of the issues outlined above will be sterile unless those engaged at all levels of policy-making and practice are prepared to examine the acquisition of their own gender identities and the impact of their own life experiences on their attitudes and professional practice. Only through such self-examination coupled with political will can we hope to empower female offenders as we struggle to make sense of the contradiction that exists between formal criminal justice and substantive social justice.

ACKNOWLEDGEMENTS

I am grateful to the staff and clients of the Staffordshire Probation Service who assisted in this research and to the University of Keele for funding its first year.

REFERENCES

Allen, H. (1987) *Justice Unbalanced*, Milton Keynes, Open University.
Bottoms, A. and McWilliams, W. (1979) 'A Non-Treatment Paradigm for Probation Practice', *British Journal of Social Work*, 9, pp. 159–202.

Carlen, P., Hicks, J., O'Dwyer, J., Christina, D. and Tchaikowsky, C. (1985) *Criminal Women*, Cambridge, Polity Press.

Carlen, P. and Worrall, A. (1987) *Gender, Crime and Justice*, Milton Keynes, Open University Press.

Cohen, S. (1975) 'It's All Right for You to Talk: Political and Sociological Manifesto for Social Work Action', in Bailey, R. and Brake, M. (eds.) *Radical Social Work*, London, Edward Arnold.

Corrigan, P. and Leonard, P. (1978) *Social Work Practice Under Capitalism: a Marxist Approach*, London, Macmillan.

Dominelli, L. (1984) 'Differential Justice: Domestic Labour, Community Service and Female Offenders', *Probation Journal*, 31, pp. 100–103.

Eaton, M. (1986) *Justice for Women?*, Milton Keynes, Open University Press.

Harris, R. J. (1980) 'A Changing Service: The Case for Separating Care and Control in Probation Practice', *British Journal of Social Work*, 10, pp. 163–84.

Home Office (annually), *Criminal Statistics, England and Wales*, London, HMSO.

Home Office (1986) *The Sentence of the Court*, London, HMSO.

Home Office (1987) *Probation Statistics England and Wales 1986*, London, Home Office.

Home Office (1988a) *Home Office Statistical Bulletin No. 8/88*, London, HMSO.

Home Office (1988b) *Punishment, Custody and The Community*, Cm 424, London, HMSO.

Home Office (1988c) 'Tackling Offending: An Action Plan', Letter to Chief Probation Officers.

Kirwin, K. (1985) 'Probation and Supervision', in Walker, H. and Beaumont, B. (eds.) *Working with Offenders*, London, Macmillan.

Mair, G. and Brockington, N. (1988) 'Female Offenders and the Probation Service', *Howard Journal*, 27, pp. 117–26.

Mathieson, T. (1972) *The Defences of the Weak*, London, Tavistock; first published in 1965.

O'Dwyer, J. and Carlen, P. (1985) 'Surviving Holloway and Other Women's Prisons', in Carlen, P. *et al. Criminal Women*, Cambridge, Polity Press.

O'Hagan, K. (1986) *Crisis Intervention in Social Services*, London, Macmillan.

Powell, M. (1985) 'Court Work', in Walker, H. and Beaumont, B. (eds.) *Working with Offenders*, London, Macmillan.

Pointing, J. (ed.) (1986) *Alternatives to Custody*, Oxford, Blackwell.

Raynor, P. (1978) 'Compulsory Persuasion: A Problem for Correctional Social Work', *British Journal of Social Work*, 8, pp. 411–24.

Raynor, P. (1985) *Social Work, Justice and Control*, Oxford, Blackwell.

Rutherford, A. (1986) *Growing Out of Crime*, Harmondsworth, Pelican.

Rutter, M. and Giller, H. (1983) *Juvenile Delinquency: Trends and Perspectives*, Harmondsworth, Pelican.

Seear, N. and Player, E. (1986) *Women in the Penal System*, London, Howard League.

Walker, H. and Beaumont, B. (eds.) (1985) *Working with Offenders*, London, Macmillan.

Willis, A. (1986) 'Help and Control in Probation: An Empirical Assessment of Probation Practice', in Pointing, J. (ed.) *Alternatives to Custody*, Oxford, Blackwell.

Worrall, A. (1987a) *Nondescript Women? A Study of the Judicial Construction of Female Lawbreakers as Abnormal Criminals and Abnormal Women,* Unpublished Ph.D thesis, available from the University of Keele Library.

Worrall, A. (1987b) 'Sisters in Law? Women Defendants and Women Magistrates' in Carlen, P. and Worrall, A. (eds.) *Gender, Crime and Justice,* Milton Keynes, Open University Press.

Worrall, A. (1989, in press) *Offending Women,* London, Routledge.

CHAPTER 116

CASTLES IN THE AIR

Welfare Services for Ex-prisoners

M. J. Cree, J. A. Hoffman, and D. N. Riley

Prison aftercare, as a sector of New Zealand's welfare industry, has yielded few positive returns to its taxpaying shareholders. A 1981 governmental review of the entire penal system of the nation depicted a welfare aftercare network notable for its bureaucratic requirements, fragmentation, and likely failures (Casey 1981).

Funding had been part of the problem. Over the years official prison aftercare services had received meagre support for their endeavours (Casey 1981, p. 144, Davey & Dwyer 1984, p. 62). Coupled with an emphasis on charity and religious affiliation, agencies' low levels of funding caused many ex-prisoners to seek assistance elsewhere.

Other avenues of help were not necessarily more productive for prospective consumers. Local experiences confirmed literature commentary suggesting that some alternative welfare agencies amounted to nothing more than administrative 'hollow shells' (Algie 1975; Salisbury Street Foundation 1980; Smith 1981). Voluntary welfare organisations were the targets of much of the criticism, usually based on personal case studies and anecdotes as the only supporting evidence. The problems were not peculiar to New Zealand. In Australia the voluntary sector has encountered similar mixed responses of criticism alongside support (Scott 1981; Zdenkowski and Brown 1982). In both countries the voluntary sector accounted for a sizeable portion of the social service network delivering practical aid.

On the surface, there appeared to be a classic market mismatch between available services and consumer demands. Among the various reasons put forward to explain the dislocation was the view that prison aftercare did not constitute an attractive line of business, least of all to some organisations who had turned in upon themselves.

Reprinted from *Australian Journal of Social Issues*, Vol. 21, No. 3 (August 1986), pp. 220–227, by permission of the publisher.

Situations arise in public, commercial and voluntary bureaucracies when people have vested interests in maintaining the organisation and their position in it. A reversal of ends and means may result and the stated goal of the service becomes a means to maintain the organisation (Scott 1981, p. 45–46).

National networks of criminal justice and penal policy had not provided adequate assistance or administrative models for localised prison aftercare services. The 1981 penal policy review committee had said of the nation's 128 year history of imprisonment that many changes were simply haphazard, piecemeal responses to urgent needs or popular theories derived from overseas.

There has been no sustained attempt to formulate a New Zealand policy which would establish criteria for the development and evaluation of our own penal measures (Casey 1981, p. 21).

Against this background there was an apparent need for information about aftercare and its relationship to the broader welfare service network. As outlined in the following sections, research at a local level has shown that prison aftercare services in the community suffer from a lack of effective planning and organisation. The overall picture is one of an aftercare system characterised by ignorance and a lack of cohesion, and one which cannot be relied upon to provide the assistance ex-prisoners require.

PRISON AFTERCARE RESEARCH

Beyond the general review of New Zealand's penal policy there is little local information available on prison aftercare. Most data are limited to that found in the annual reports of organisations commenting on their own performance during their past year of service.

Responding to this shortage of information a pilot research study was developed in the Canterbury region of New Zealand representing approximately ten per cent of the national population. Named the Prison Aftercare Project, the study attempted to develop an empirical picture of aftercare resources within its specific region. Emphasis was placed on what the nationwide policy report had termed 'the community', existing governmental services, and the interaction and organisational links between the two.

One of the research procedures used by the Prison Aftercare Project took the form of a self report survey questionnaire. The purpose of the instrument was to test the knowledge and experience of a range of organisations and individuals located in the community whom the general public could reasonably expect to be providing aftercare aid and services to ex-prisoners.

For the purposes of sampling and subsequent analysis, respondents were classified within five discrete subgroup clusters, determined by the researchers' perceptions of their social proximity to the demands of ex-prisoners seeking aftercare assistance. The subgroups were:

Justice (probation officers, psychologists, prison chaplains);

Health (social workers, counsellors, doctors and nurses likely to be in contact with offenders);

Other Government Services (Departments of Social Welfare, Education, Labour, Maori and Internal Affairs and Housing Corporation);

Professional/Semi-Professional Community Services (church-based welfare agencies, local authority community workers, marriage guidance, and Alcohol Counselling Centre);

Voluntary Community Services (Prisoners' Aid and Rehabilitation Society, Rotary and other service clubs, professional associations, and special interest groups).

The survey questionnaires were given to heads of welfare agencies to distribute to individuals, nominated by them, with a known interest or involvement with the criminal justice system. One trained interviewer liaised with all respondents. Questionnaires were sent to 171 respondents, of whom 109 replied, giving an overall response rate of 63.7 per cent of the total sample.

SURVEY QUESTIONS

The findings in this paper were taken from the responses to two of the 36 questions put to all respondents. These two questions focussed on the interrelationship between the problems facing ex-prisoners after their release from prison and community welfare services who might be expected to deal with these problems.

The first question asked respondents: 'If you were asked to assist a prison inmate with re-entry into the community, which organisation/services would you expect to deal proficiently with the difficulties in the following list?' A list of 29 possible issue-areas followed, covering common problems known to face released prisoners. Beside each answer a space was provided for respondents to write in the name or names of welfare agencies to whom they would make a referral. Next, respondents were asked to rate the helpfulness of any agency or organisation with which they had had contact in the previous 12 months on behalf of a released prisoner.

FINDINGS

For the purposes of this paper the responses were divided into five broad categories: non-responders to the referral question, the spread of problem areas leading to agency referrals, agency referrals for each problem area, the referral pathway, and the helpfulness of agencies with which respondents had established contact.

Non-responders

There were numerous instances in this part of the survey where a respondent did not list a welfare agency alongside one of the 29 particular problem areas facing ex-prisoners. Normally it would be incorrect to infer any significance from a non-response of this kind. However, in this particular research venture non-respondents can be treated differently given that agency staff were invited to present their best possible impression of welfare service provision. Accordingly, it is argued, the researcher can reasonably infer that where respondents, in spite of a request to present the best possible image, did not list any referral agency whatsoever next to a problem area, then they were not aware of a service to whom referral would be appropriate.

For some particular types of problems up to one third of the total number of respondents did not offer responses, which indicated uncertainty about referral avenues. These specific problem areas included making new friends (32 per cent), removing tattoos (32 per cent), obtaining insurance (30 per cent), learning life skills (28 per cent), and sexual deviance (28 per cent). To the ex-prisoner some, if not all of these problem areas present social relocation issues requiring urgent aftercare assistance.

Other problem areas fitted more comfortably with referral knowledge and the service resources available to respondents, as evidenced by the lower rate of non-responses. These problem areas included getting clothing (6 per cent), alcohol problems (9 per cent), getting a job (10 per cent), emergency finance (10 per cent), and getting furniture (10 per cent).

Justice subgroup respondents were distinctive, being the only subgroup where all respondents listed an agency for one or more problem areas. This total response phenomenon was evident in the following particular problem areas: obtaining furniture, obtaining clothing, drug problems, alcohol problems, budgeting advice and psychiatric problems.

Spread of Problem Areas Leading to Agency Referrals

It has been possible to determine the scope of services offered by particular welfare organisations (at least in the opinion of the respondents) by noting the number of different problem areas referred to those agencies. There were 29 possible problems for referral. Some organisations were referred to by numerous respondents for a wide variety of problems, while others were mentioned by a sole respondent to deal with a single problem.

Among the agencies or services considered significant in terms of the scope of their services to released prisoners were the Prisoners' Aid and Rehabilitation Society (29 problems); 'Help' information guide (29); Probation Service (26); Citizens' Advice Bureau (24); church groups (19); Department of Social Welfare (15); counsellors (13); psychologists (12); Campbell Counselling Centre (11); hospital services (11); doctors (9); Community Mental Health Team (8); and Anglican Social Services (7).

Agency Referrals for Each Problem Area

The spread of referrals shows that a large number of welfare agencies or organisations (up to 24) were referred to for handling a single problem area, rather than referrals being made to a small number of organisations with a specialised orientation towards that specific problem.

Overall, in only four of the twenty-nine problems posited were fewer than ten agencies referred to, and only three of these involved problems requiring specialised sets of skills or knowledge. Two salient inferences seem to emerge from this section of the data. The first indicates that among welfare aftercare services in the region studied, there is the perception of a wide spread of services available from different agencies and organisations. The second suggests that simultaneously there is little consensus between referring personnel as to which agencies are the most suitable sources for dealing with each problem area facing the released prisoner.

The Referral Pathway

A major aspect of the referral concept is the referral pathway, that is, referrals to each organisation or agency by the subgroups of respondents—Justice, Health, Other Government Departments, Professional/Semi-Professional and Voluntary/Public interest groups. This was an interesting finding as the responses made it possible to identify the source of the significant proportions of referrals.

It was also possible to identify cases where a single respondent consistently listed one agency for many problem areas; often constituting 100 per cent of the referrals in that case. This type of broad band referral response occurred with respect to three particular organisations who have common information dissemination roles with regard to ex-prisoner needs (Prisoners' Aid Society, Citizens Advice Bureau, Help—a locally popular service listing booklet). Out of a total of 109 respondents, four persons fell within this broad band category. Moreover, referring cases to either the Citizens' Advice Bureau or the 'Help' directory does not constitute a direct outcome. As referral sources, they are both only steps in the process.

Overall, thirteen agencies or organisations were referred to for seven or more problem areas, but in only a few cases were referrals to a particular agency or organisation dominated by one subgroup of respondents across most problem areas. Justice subgroup respondents tended to make up a large proportion of referrals to the Probation Service and Anglican Social Services. The voluntary subgroup tended to cite the Citizens' Advice Bureau, the Community Mental Health Team and doctors. For the remainder, there was a generally even spread of referrals from all subgroups.

In looking at those agencies and organisations referred to for seven or more problem areas, a search for common factors among them was made. Of the 13 involved, three were government departments or services, four were private or voluntary non-church-based agencies, three were health-related services and three were church-based agencies. This represents a wide spread of services over most types of organisations even though, to a certain extent, each of the four types mentioned cater for different problem areas.

Also, it is instructive to note the two organisations which probably have the most direct link with prison aftercare, the Probation Service and the Prisoners' Aid and Rehabilitation Society (PARS), and to observe their role in this referral area more closely. Referral to the Probation Service was made by several respondents for 26 of 29 problem areas, with the bulk of referrals coming from the Justice subgroup, and the fewest from the Voluntary subgroup. This finding seems to indicate that respondents from the Voluntary (and also to a certain extent the Professional/Semiprofessional) subgroup are either not aware of the sorts of assistance offered by the Probation Service or have had experiences which lead them to services elsewhere.

The Prisoners' Aid Society was referred to for all problem areas, but in only 13 cases was the Society cited twice or more. Problem areas referred most frequently to the Society were those associated with practical aid, liaison roles, and the more immediate needs of a released prisoner such as clothing, finance and housing. Conversely, in the many instances where only a small number of referrals were made to the Prisoners' Aid Society, the problems required specialised skills and knowledge which, in actuality, were not directly available from that organisation. Proportionately more referrals to the Prisoners' Aid Society came from the Voluntary subgroup of respondents, a significant number of whom seemed to prefer this organisation over the government-run Probation Service.

Helpfulness

As a further probe to test the depth of aftercare knowledge, respondents were asked to comment on their referral practices over the previous twelve months. The method asked respondents to identify the agency referred to, and then provide a five-item scale with which they could rate the degree of 'helpfulness' of the referral.

Fewer than 25 per cent of all survey respondents answered this question and the majority of those who did respond reported that they had found most agencies helpful. Speculation on the meaning of this low response seems warranted. While 75 per cent or more of the respondents were able to list agencies to which they would refer in a hypothetical situation, in practice they had not made any such referrals in the previous twelve months. One implication, for instance, is that a marked gap exists between notional referral pathways and actual referral pathways when it comes to solving the problems of ex-prisoners.

OVERALL PATTERNS

Several observations can be made concerning prison aftercare services in the Canterbury region from the referral patterns which emerged out of the questionnaire responses:

- Many people, presumed to be informed in the area of prison aftercare, did not know to which organisation or agency to refer released prisoners for basic and common problems. This result implies either ignorance on the part of the people involved, a lack of publicity by the organisations offering the services or a combination of the two.
- While some agencies and organisations were referred to for a number of different problem areas (for a particular type of problem or a general range), indicating a considerable depth of service offered, a large number were referred to for only one or a few problems. This pattern suggests that an ex-prisoner would need to be referred to a number of different organisations if he or she had multiple needs requiring immediate help.
- There was a multitude of agencies and organisations referred to for each problem area, indicating little consensus as to which were the most suitable for any particular problem but at the same time giving a wide range of different types of organisations from which to choose.
- In only a few cases were referrals to a particular agency or organisation dominated by one subgroup of respondents across most problem areas. Where this trend did occur it was usually marked. The implication is that either the agency or organisation referred to was particularly highly thought of among personnel from these subgroups, or they consistently referred to this organisation in ignorance of others available.
- The Probation Service and Prisoners' Aid and Rehabilitation Society (PARS)—the two organisations presumed to have strong links with the prison aftercare system—

were referred to for most problems. But while referrals to the Probation Service were dominated by government (Justice) personnel, conversely referrals to the Prisoners' Aid Society were predominantly from respondents in voluntary social service organisations.

CONCLUSION

Effective provision of welfare services extends far beyond the mere creation and maintenance of social service outlets. One of the disabling myths of welfare is that simply because of their existence as altruistic responses to welfare needs social service organisations should be presumed to be effective (Scott 1981). In New Zealand there is a marked paucity of research with regard to the needs of minority social groups like prisoners and ex-prisoners and their access to aid schemes.

By obtaining the views of a chosen range of specialist welfare service providers in the Canterbury region of New Zealand, the Prison Aftercare Project has identified significant data about prison aftercare referral pathways and their usage. National significance of the data can be obtained by treating the Canterbury region as roughly representative of ten per cent of the overall population of New Zealand and its social services.

Given the formal evidence that at the national level of policy New Zealand's penal system has been shaped by piecemeal responses and haphazard reforms, it is a concern to find similar trends at the local level. These patterns include lack of cohesion, co-ordination, planning and effective co-operation.

As for service consumers—prisoners and ex-prisoners—the Prison Aftercare Project's findings from this segment of its study afford grounds for considerable dismay. The results help to explain the many informal and widespread complaints that community based aftercare in Canterbury amounts to a 'waste of time'. There are obvious policy ramifications. Before extra resources are channelled into this field of welfare existing social services need to be evaluated and, where necessary, rationalised.

This is imperative if prison aftercare is to become linked with a broader social movement towards de-institutionalisation of offenders. Any steps towards more and better evaluation of services will require courage and commitment as some of the entrenched service providers do not seem troubled by the current state of uncertain and uneven provision and the resource allocation myths they may represent.

ACKNOWLEDGEMENTS

The Prison Aftercare Project was established in the Canterbury region of New Zealand in May, 1982 as a pilot research project in the field of prison aftercare. Funding has come from the Welfare Services Committee of the NZ Lottery Board.

REFERENCES

Algie, J. (1975), *Social Values, Objectives and Action,* London: Kogan Page Ltd.
Casey, M. E. (1981), *Report of the Penal Policy Review Committee 1981,* Wellington: Government Printer.

Davey, J. and Dwyer, M. (1984), *Meeting Needs in the Community: A Discussion Paper on Social Services,* New Zealand Planning Council, No. 19, Wellington.

Salisbury Street Foundation (1980), 'Submissions to the Penal Policy Review 1981', Salisbury Street Foundation, Christchurch.

Scott, D. (1981), *'Don't Mourn for Me, Organise . . .' The Social and Political Uses of Voluntary Organisations,* Sydney: George Allen and Unwin.

Smith, M. (1981), *Background Papers:* 29, 30, 42, Penal Policy Review, Justice Department, Wellington.

Wilkins, L. T. (1969), *Evaluation of Penal Measures,* New York: Random House.

Zdenkowski, G. and Brown D. (1982), *The Prison Struggle: Changing Australia's Penal System,* Melbourne: Penguin.

Accepted for publication March 1985.

PART VII

RESOURCE PROBLEMS

It is difficult to understand why this topic has not been addressed as a distinct category in the various previous editions of this book. Problems of inadequate resources and the concomitant difficulties that they cause have long been an exclusive professional focus of social work. Indeed for many, the image of Lady Bountiful with her food basket is the stereotype of the social worker. However, in spite of this, addressing such problems in clinical practice has frequently been perceived as being of second-class value, an activity that is not quite proper. In fact, at times in our history we have called this "indirect work," with the understanding that real practice, or "direct work," was our therapeutic relationships with our clients.

I suggest that one of the reasons we have not addressed our clients' lack of resources was the perception that this is not the stuff of real therapy. This was unfortunate. Over the decades there is much that we have learned about the debilitating results of a lack of basic resources and, equally important, of the ways that making resources available in a respectful, helpful, understanding manner can facilitate growth and development. Yet in spite of our accumulated knowledge in this area it is not a subject about which we have written much. This is reflected in the fact that, in spite of the importance of this material, this is the second smallest section of the book.

Of course, we have always known that poverty is a critical problem in society and as a profession we have had a special concern about this. But along with our concern there has been an element of shame that in an affluent country, where we daily waste tons of food and millions of dollars of resources, we have not found a way to feed, clothe, and house our fellow citizens. One of the things that has facilitated this ability to overlook the problem is the fact that much of societal poverty is hidden.

Fortunately, there is an increasing awareness and sensitivity to the problem in general and the manner in which it is manifested in individuals and families. In recent decades the reality of street people and homeless people has made us

1269

all much more conscious of many aspects of poverty. The fact that, within a very few years, virtually every city of any size in North America found itself establishing food banks and centers to provide meals to hungry people is an embarrassment to most and, thankfully, a challenge to many.

The phenomenon of deinstitutionalization has contributed to this higher visibility. But perhaps more importantly, it has forged an acceptable connection to the mental health field, and hence has made poverty a more respectable therapeutic challenge.

One of the reasons why we have not given sufficient therapeutic attention to these problems is that frequently there is little we can do about them. We usually handle this by blaming the victim. Thus, there is still a strong societal attitude that giving people money or food or clothing, except in dramatic circumstances, only contributes to dependency. Implied in this is a subtle, and often a not so subtle, perception that much of this type of problem is self-caused. Happily, the recent recession in North America, from which we are just emerging, has made us aware that many previously affluent persons who found themselves suddenly unemployed and in need were in this situation through no fault of their own, but because of complex, worldwide political-economic situations about which there was nothing they could do.

The idea that social workers should be able to prescribe money in the same way that our colleagues in medicine prescribe medication would have been unthinkable not long ago. Most of us have found that often it is easier to get a client very expensive medication and access to therapy for anxiety or depression than it is to get the $50.00 needed to pay the rent, the lack of which is the cause of much of the anxiety or depression in the first place. Interestingly, this is changing. In the last few weeks this author has heard of two public agencies where the social workers do have access to rather substantial amounts of money, upon which they can draw if they diagnose lack of funds as being critical to a particular presenting situation.

As we move from an attitudinal position in reference to this type of problem to a more diagnostic and therapeutic posture we are beginning to address this area of practice from a theoretical perspective. Hence in the articles in this section we see references to both "stress" and "coping" theory, two theoretical bodies to which, up to now, we have not devoted a great deal of attention.

The topic to which we have given the most attention in the general area of resource deficits is homelessness. In these we see again the stress on the differential understanding of situations. The articles on homelessness remind us of the complexities of this phenomenon and of the risk of using the term in an all-encompassing manner. There are several discrete groups of homeless persons and as always we need to accurately assess these in order to set realistic treatment and intervention strategies. For example, the articles remind us of the different housing needs when gender is considered and the growing awareness that life is frequently much harsher for homeless women than for men. The situation becomes even more complex when we look at situations involving homeless families.

Obviously, in addition to homelessness there are many other resource needs that need to be addressed from a clinical perspective to insure that as clinicians we understand the nature of the problem and its causes and develop strategies of intervention that accurately address the psychosocial reality of the client.

One of the interesting and highly important trends that appears to be emerging from this new focus on problems of resource deficit is an appreciation of the need to understand and include within our purview the micro and macro aspects of these issues. Unfortunately, social work still suffers from the heresy of dichotomization, or the tendency to separate various aspects of the profession into dyads.

Poverty in all its forms is of course a complex system issue that we need to fully understand from a macro perspective in order to sensitively understand it from a micro perspective. Thus, as a profession much of our effort needs to be directed to addressing root causes. This, of course, is not a new observation. What might be new is the need for an awareness that as practitioners sometimes all we have to offer our clients is understanding, compassion, and a resolute commitment to advocacy. We must not fall into the easy trap of offering therapy because we don't know what else to do and need to feel that we are doing something.

This is an exciting and critical area for social work, in which much more work needs to be done from a clinical perspective in conjunction with large systems strategies; it is an area where society expects us to lead the way!

BASIC RESOURCES

CHAPTER 117

ASSESSING FAMILY ACCESS TO BASIC RESOURCES

An Essential Component of Social Work Practice

Nancy R. Vosler

Social workers often have been the professionals of choice for work with families experiencing multiple crises. Much has been written regarding assessment and treatment of multiproblem families (Bernstein, Jeremy, & Marcus, 1986; Colon, 1980; Hutchinson & Nelson, 1985; Kaplan, 1986; Schlesinger, 1970; Wallace, 1967), families at risk (Buckley, 1985; Herzog, 1966), multideficit families (McKinney, 1970), dysfunctional families (Lindblad-Goldberg & Dukes, 1985; Weitzman, 1985), troubled families (Garbarino, Schellenbach, & Sebes, 1986; Hinckley, 1984; Hutchinson & Nelson, 1985), underorganized families (Aponte, 1986), difficult families (Schlosberg & Kagan, 1988), symptomatic families (Imber-Black, 1988), and families in perpetual crisis (Kagan & Schlosberg, 1989).

Much of this literature makes at least passing reference to issues of adverse economic conditions and the stress of poverty (McCubbin, 1979; Reid, 1985). However, assessment tools based on an integrative theoretical framework are needed for mapping the specific impacts of larger social systems on the family (Reid, 1985). The eco-map developed by Meyer (1976, 1983) and Hartman and Laird (1983) provides social workers with an overview of the family in the community (for further discussion of the ecological perspective, see DeHoyos & Jensen, 1985; Germain & Gitterman, 1987; Maluccio, 1981; Reid, 1985; Siporin, 1975, 1980). However, in light of rising poverty, related in part to cuts in social programs, specific tools are needed for social workers to assess families' access to adequate and stable basic resources (Hartman, 1989). These tools

Reprinted from *Social Work*, Vol. 35, No. 5 (September 1990), pp. 434–441, by permission of NASW Press. Copyright 1990, National Association of Social Workers, Inc., *Social Work*.

can help guide social work practice with overstressed families and their individual members.

After a brief review of stress and coping theory, including a multiple-level social systems perspective, this article presents an assessment tool, Family Access to Basic Resources (FABR), which social workers can use to accurately map specific family economic stressors. Two examples of the importance of this information are discussed, focusing on unemployed families and on families receiving Aid to Families with Dependent Children (AFDC).

THEORETICAL FRAMEWORK
Stress and Coping Theory

Stress and coping theory has emerged as an important theoretical framework for understanding both individuals and families (Figley & McCubbin, 1983; Hill, 1958; Lazarus & Folkman, 1984; McCubbin, 1979; McCubbin et al., 1980; McCubbin & Figley, 1983). In the family studies literature, stress and coping theory calls attention to different family responses to a particular event, focusing on the nature of the event itself, the resources on which the family can draw for assistance, the definition constructed by the family regarding the event (for example, is the event a normal occurrence, or is it a catastrophe?), and the nature of the crisis facing the family and its members. Stress for the family as a micro-social system and for individual family members can escalate or pile up, particularly when there are insufficient resources for dealing with the event. Inability of the family to deal with normal daily occurrences or major crisis events can result in dysfunctional behaviors, cognitions, and emotions for family members and in dysfunctional family organization and communication patterns.

Although a number of authors have recognized the importance of assessing the impact of the larger environment on family functioning (Bateman, 1983; Briar, 1988; De-Hoyos, 1989; Hartman & Laird, 1983; Imber-Black, 1988; Johnson, 1986; Maher, 1987; Meyer, 1976; Reid, 1985; Vondra, 1986; Zimmerman, 1985) the link between symptoms and chronic stress from lack of basic economic resources has not been explored sufficiently by these social work practitioners and researchers. It is critical for social workers to understand that, based on stress and coping theory, the absence of adequate and stable basic resources can result in chronic stress within the family system (Figley & McCubbin, 1983). Such chronic stress over time can lead to a variety of problems and symptoms. Just as stress from family system dysfunction can result in symptoms in individual family members (Aponte, 1976; Haley, 1976; Hartman & Laird, 1983; Minuchin, 1974), chronic stress from economic deprivation can result in symptomatic families, whom professionals have often labeled multiproblem families.

Multiple-Level Social Systems

Although resource deprivation is a major individual and family stressor, the structures within the national social system are fragmented, and families and individuals lack stable access to adequate basic resources (Anderson & Carter, 1984; Gilbert & Specht, 1986). At the national policy level, the United States has affirmed, albeit in a fairly fragmented way, that citizens of this nation have rights to adequate basic resources such as food, housing, health care, and education and training for work (Gilbert & Specht, 1986; Huttman 1981). Although the means for access to these resources have been argued over the years, most would agree that there are basic resources that must be available for individuals and families to function as healthy systems throughout the nation and the world.

Currently, many social welfare programs and many social work practice models are based on the assumption that basic resources are available in sufficient quality and quantity for all citizens and that the problem is connecting individuals and families to these resources (for a discussion of contrasting assumptions underlying two different welfare programs, see Vosler & Ozawa, 1988). Certainly, the U.S. national economic system generates enough food, clothing, and personal care items for all citizens of this nation; whether quality housing, health care, education, and family and developmental services currently are available might be subject to some debate, although most would agree that given commitment, resources, and time, these could be made available. Thus, a vague consensus exists within the United States that basic resources should be available to all citizens. These resources include food, housing and heating, clothing, personal care and recreation, health care (including physical and mental health care and drug abuse treatment), education, family and developmental services, and the ongoing means to procure these resources (such as transportation).

Recent research has demonstrated that many individuals and families in the United States do not have adequate and stable resources (Boulet, Debritto, & Ray, 1985; Danziger & Weinberg, 1986; Ellwood, 1988; Ford Foundation, 1989; Nichols-Casebolt, 1988; Ozawa, 1983; Schorr, A., 1986; Schorr, L., 1988; Wolock, Geismar, Lagay, & Raiffe, 1985–86; Wyers, 1988). This research demonstrates that because of the way in which work, wages, and resources for those not expected to compete for wages (including elderly people, disabled people, and children) are structured in the U.S. social system (including economic and social welfare policies and institutions), access to the basic necessities of life is, wittingly or unwittingly, withheld from increasing numbers of families and individuals, particularly children, minorities, and women.

Social structures that assure the availability of and access to adequate and stable resources for families in the United States currently include in-kind provision of some resources (for example, education); access to the market through employment and wages and money resources for special populations (for example, elderly people, disabled people, and some children); and other income and credit sources (Gilbert & Specht, 1986). In-kind provision of the resource itself, except for local organization of free public education, has not been a preferred means for structuring resources for at least a decade. However, some local communities and agencies still provide, to some people in some circumstances, public housing, public recreation facilities, free health and mental health clinics, food pantries, and used clothing. Such in-kind resources are often stigmatized ("for the poor only") and can be rather unstable because their provision depends increasingly on local taxes or on private goodwill and generosity.

An important issue for social workers to address is the way in which families' access to adequate and stable basic resources is ignored in the national social system. Some states or communities may provide almost nothing to some families, while others may do a reasonably good job of providing resources and access. If all U.S. citizens are members of one social system (including a national economic system), why do individuals and families have radically different access to the basic resources necessary for a healthy life? Some working parents have access to stable and adequate basic resources, but some do not; the same is true for children, elderly people, disabled people, minorities, and other special populations. Access to basic necessities seems to be a good idea espoused by most citizens however, there are currently no consistent organizational patterns for implementing these good ideas, except perhaps for picking up the pieces when a family system disintegrates under chronic stress (for example, when children are taken into foster care and perhaps eventually provided with access to a subsidized adoption). The system structures, as currently organized, are irrational and neglectful of many families. However, symptomatic families are easily blamed for their inability to provide for the basic needs of family members. The ability to discern and document ways in which current structures trap families in the chronic stress of inadequate and unstable basic resources can enable social workers to begin working in different ways with and on behalf of overstressed families and their members.

Family Access to Basic Resources

The multilevel stress and coping theoretical framework can provide social workers with perspectives for multivariate assessment and intervention at various system levels. The Family Access to Basic Resources (FABR) assessment tool can enable professionals, families, and individual family members to determine the extent of stress and stress pileup caused by inadequate or unstable basic family resources (Figure 117–1).

The FABR outlines assessment areas for exploration with the family so that both the social worker and the family can begin to understand potential sources of chronic stress from the larger social environment. Documentation of types of stress across families and within communities or agencies can be invaluable for social planning, advocacy, and lobbying within larger social systems, including work at neighborhood, local, state, and national levels.

Parts 1 and 2 of the FABR should ideally be filled out by the social worker before meeting with the family. Part 1 provides a rough estimation of monthly expenses for a family similar in size and composition to the family being assessed, based on local markets. If these figures are not already available, agencies or a local advocacy group could be called on to develop estimates based on adequate resources needed for a long-term decent standard of living for various household sizes and family configurations. The U.S. poverty line income standard is based on temporary emergency food rations; in contrast, the estimate in part 1 should meet the needs of a normal family. Each item should be filled in separately, and the total monthly dollar amount represents the amount of income needed per month for the family to have access to the basic necessities of life.

Part 2 lists resources that are available to some individuals and families. Assuming the professional has a working knowledge of how each of these programs is organized in the family's local community, maximum dollar amounts that should be available to the family being assessed can be filled in. Thus, using parts 1 and 2, the social worker can present the family with an overall picture of what their resource needs are and what assistance is available to them within the local system (based on resources provided at state and national system levels). This vital knowledge will enable the family and the

Figure 117–1
Family Access to Basic Resources (FABR)

PART 1—Monthly expenses for a family of this size and composition

Work expenses
   Transportation: $ _____
   Child care: $ _____
   Taxes: $ _____
Purchases for basic needs
   Decent housing: $ _____
   Utilities: $ _____
   Food: $ _____
   Clothing: $ _____
   Personal care: $ _____
   Recreation: $ _____

Health care
   Medical: $ _____
   Dental: $ _____
   Mental health: $ _____
   Special (e.g., substance abuse): $ _____
   Education: $ _____
   Family and developmental (counseling) services: $ _____
   Procurement of resources/services (e.g.,
     transportation): $ _____

   Monthly total: $ _____

PART 2—Potential monthly family resources

Money income
   Wages (If parents' occupations are
     known, what are average monthly wages
     for these types of jobs?): $ _____
   Child support (if applicable): $ _____
   Income transfers (for those unemployed
     or not expected to work)
     Unemployment insurance: $ _____
     Workmen's compensation: $ _____
     Social Security: $ _____
     Supplemental Security Income (SSI): $ _____
     Aid to Families with Dependent
       Children (AFDC): $ _____
     Other (e.g., general relief, emergency
       assistance): $ _____
Credits, goods, and services (free or
   sliding scale):
   Housing
     Section 8: $ _____
     Other housing assistance (e.g.,
       public housing, shelter,
       hotel/motel): $ _____
     Utilities assistance: $ _____
   Food
     Food stamps: $ _____
     Women's, Infants', and Children's
       Supplementary Food Program (WIC): $ _____
     Food bank, food pantry, and other food
       assistance: $ _____

Monthly total: $ _____

Clothing: Access to used clothing
     store?   Yes ☐   No ☐
Personal care and recreation:
   Access to free recreational
     facilities?   Yes ☐   No ☐
Health care
   Medicare?   Yes ☐   No ☐
   Medicaid?   Yes ☐   No ☐
   Health clinic?   Yes ☐   No ☐
   Dental clinic?   Yes ☐   No ☐
   Mental health services?   Yes ☐   No ☐
   Special services (e.g., drug abuse
     treatment)?   Yes ☐   No ☐
Education
   Public education?   Yes ☐   No ☐
   Special education?   Yes ☐   No ☐
   Tutoring?   Yes ☐   No ☐
   General Equivalency Diploma (GED)?   Yes ☐   No ☐
   Job training?   Yes ☐   No ☐
Family and developmental (counseling)
   services
   Family services?   Yes ☐   No ☐
   Support groups?   Yes ☐   No ☐
   Family life education?   Yes ☐   No ☐
Procurement
   Transportation?   Yes ☐   No ☐

PART 3—Current resources

A. Access to resources last month

Money income
   Wages (use net pay; then subtract other
     work expenses from Part 1 above,
     including child care, transportation,
     etc.): $ _____
   Child support: $ _____
   Income transfers: $ _____
Credits, goods, and services
   Housing: $ _____
   Food: $ _____

Clothing: $ _____
Personal care and recreation: $ _____
Health care: $ _____
Education: $ _____
Family and developmental
   services: $ _____
Procurement: $ _____

Monthly total: $ _____

Figure 117–1 (continued)

B. Resource stability

How stable was each resource over the past year (very stable, somewhat stable, somewhat unstable, very unstable)? Discuss for each type of resource.

Wages: Overall access to wages through employment? Types of jobs available? Part-time or full-time? Wage levels? Benefits? How would/do you deal with child care or supervision of youth? Quality of child care? Do you have choices? How would/do you deal with an ill child? How would/do you get to and from work? What education and training are needed for good jobs? What education and training opportunities are available? Have you been laid off or terminated or experienced a plant closing? Number of times unemployed? Length of time unemployed?

Child support: How is this received? How was the amount decided? Are checks regular? Are payments up to date? Other problems?

Income transfers: What experiences have you had in receiving benefits? What kinds of attitudes have you encountered? How adequate are benefits relative to your family's expenses? Has a check been cut? Has a check been delayed? Have you been dropped from benefits for reasons you didn't understand?

Housing: Rent or own? Choice? Maintenance a problem? Are utilities adequate? Have you been put on a waiting list or been dropped from Section 8 or other housing assistance? Have you had to move or been evicted because the landlord converted to higher rents, condominiums, etc.? Have you experienced homelessness?

Food: Quality? Variety? Have your Food Stamps or WIC been cut or delayed? If so, do you understand why? Has other food assistance been cut or changed?

Clothing: Variety for different roles?

Personal care and recreation: What kinds of recreation? Individual? Family?

Health care: High quality? Choice? Available in a crisis? Have you been dropped from health care coverage with an employer or from Medicaid? If so, why? Have you or another family member been put on a waiting list, for example, for medical or dental care, for counseling for a mental health problem, or for treatment for alcohol or drug abuse? If so, how long did the person have to wait for services?

Education: High quality? Available for all ages? For special needs? Choice? Have you participated in education or training paid for with loans? If so, how are you managing loan repayments?

Family and developmental services: High quality? Choice? Available in a crisis? Have you or another family member been put on a waiting list, for example, for family counseling? If so, how long did the person have to wait for services?

Procurement: Bus? Car? What's within walking distance? How reliable is transportation (e.g., bus and/or car)? How close are bus lines to home, work, child care, shopping, etc.?

Other comments and reflections:

social worker to understand specific stressors, because family members are likely to blame themselves or other family members when resources are not available. Few family members or professionals have been taught to look for stressors in the structured lack of access to adequate basic resources.

Sections A and B of part 3 can be filled out by the family during one or more assessment sessions. Section A reflects current income and resources. Section B asks how stable these resources have been over the past year. Questions include the following: Has the welfare check been cut or delayed? Has the family lost Section 8 housing assistance (perhaps because the landlord converted to condominiums)? Has the family lost Medicaid coverage (perhaps because a parent was mandated to take a job that did not provide health benefits)? Was a family member put on a long waiting list for drug treatment, for counseling for a mental health problem, or for family counseling? How reliable is the transportation system? Is bus service available? How expensive is it to maintain a reliable car? These questions provide qualitative probes for a fuller understanding of particular aspects of resource deficits and unstable access to resources.

Use of the FABR can facilitate discussion of specific external stressors experienced by the family. By understanding these stressors, the social worker may be able to identify specific organizational family patterns or individual behavioral responses that could be interpreted by family members or by the community as a problem but could be viewed in a systems context as symptoms of chronic external stress. Specific interventions, perhaps at multiple system levels, then can be devised.

The FABR alerts the social worker and the family that individual- or family-level change may not be enough. If stable access to adequate basic resources of good quality is not available within the current environment, the problem (that is, the symptom of stress) is very likely to reappear until adequate resources are consistently available to the family or family member. In the United States, an estimated 67 million to 100 million people, most of whom live within a family system of some kind, currently are economically insecure or are struggling to survive at a subsistence level (Wyers, 1988).

In earlier times it seemed easier, although not as effective in the long run, for some social workers to use only individual perspectives (whether psychodynamic or behavioral) rather than to learn and to use new family system paradigms to help solve family members' problems. Wills (1978) found that human services professionals tend to perceive and focus on aspects of clients' problems that are manageable and treatable. Changing the social structures that limit or deny some families access to basic resources is a major undertaking in the United States. Although this may seem to be an unmanageable and untreatable problem to some, and therefore one that is left unexplored, system realities cannot be denied for long without serious damage to the system as a whole. Macrosystem change, though often slow and painful, is the only clear means to healthy functioning for all family systems in this society.

FAMILIES UNDER STRESS FROM EXTERNAL SYSTEMS

Like individuals and family systems, larger social systems develop and change over time. It is now widely recognized that changes are occurring in national and global economic systems that are likely to affect many U.S. citizens and their families (Bluestone & Harrison, 1982; Briar, 1988; Halberstam, 1986; Reich, 1989). Jobs that previously have been unionized and have provided adequate wages and benefits (for example, manufacturing jobs in the steel and auto industries) have increasingly been transferred to non-unionized areas, particularly the Third World, and this trend is expected to continue. These jobs are being replaced in the U.S. economic system with low-wage, often part-time, nonbenefit jobs that do not provide adequate or stable access to basic resources for individuals and their families (Vosler, Wallace, Dubeck, Maume, & Dyehouse, 1989; Wallace & Rothschild, 1988).

The social contract for the AFDC welfare program is being changed from one that provides somewhat stable (though often very inadequate) access to basic resources for some mothers to one that demands participation by these women in the often unstable low-wage job market. Many of these jobs do not guarantee access to comprehensive, quality child and health care or provide assurance that the family's resource base will not be further eroded by layoffs, the need to care for a child who is temporarily ill, or any other event that, because of previously existing chronic economic stress, can become an instant family catastrophe (Vosler & Ozawa, 1988). Larger social system changes threaten to destabilize already shaky access to basic resources, and limited or unequally distributed resources threaten to become even more inadequate for many citizens and their families. The FABR may be particularly helpful in assessing families in which a parent has been or is currently unemployed and families in which parents or children have been or are receiving welfare.

Families Affected by Unemployment

Because of economic changes at the national level, a number of families in the United States have been affected by loss of employment in the past decade (Beckett, 1988; Briar, 1988; Vosler et al., 1989). When unemployment is temporary, when the transition to reemployment is buffered by family support and social resources (such as adequate unemployment benefits), and when reemployment wages and benefits are comparable to those of previous employment, there may be only minor temporary stress associated with the change for the worker and his or her family. However, if finding a satisfactory new job is difficult, perhaps because of high local unemployment, because of a mismatch between worker skills and local job market needs, or because of a glut of job openings for part-time jobs with low wages and few or no benefits, stress may pile up for both the worker and for other family members. Some research indicates that members of such families may be at risk for physical or emotional difficulties, alcohol and drug abuse, family conflict (including marital and parent-child difficulties), and child or spouse abuse (Briar, 1988; Vosler et al., 1989).

When such families ask for or are referred for help, they may blame each other for current problems. Family members may not see the connection between physical, behavioral, or interpersonal difficulties and the stress from inadequate resources (including the likely loss of health benefits and consequent delay of treatment until a problem comes to a crisis point). Using the FABR, the social worker can trace with the family the reduction of access to basic resources and the increasing instability of income and therefore the inability to secure needed goods and services. The social worker may then be able to help the family recognize some of the sources of current stress and help turn the family's attention from fighting each other to cooperating with each other in the struggle for essentials. In addition, efforts may need to focus on empowering family members to become involved with professionals and other citizens in demanding needed changes in the larger systems of which they are a part.

Families Receiving AFDC

Recent and ongoing changes in social welfare policies at the national level, particularly changes in the AFDC program, have affected and are likely to continue to affect families receiving welfare benefits. Although the AFDC program began with the purpose of aiding poor children, the recently passed welfare reform bill (the Family Support Act of 1988, Public Law 100-485) requires that states mandate parents whose youngest child is 3 years or older to participate in a Job Opportunities and Basic Skills (JOBS) program. Although some benefits, including transitional child care and medical coverage, initially are provided, there is no guarantee that jobs available to these parents (primarily women) will supply income sufficient for access to basic quality resources. Also, there is no guarantee that employment will be stable enough so that families can arrange their lives and create a new equilibrium of family patterns and relationships (including, for example, after-school care; ill-child backup care; time for doctors' appointments or teacher conferences; or time for doing laundry, going grocery shopping, and participating in family recreational activities). (For further discussion of welfare-to-work programs and family system transition, see Vosler & Ozawa, 1988.)

With major federal cuts in social programs over the past decade (Wolock et al., 1985–86), any family receiving welfare is likely to be experiencing unstable access to inadequate resources and is likely already to be under substantial stress. Using the FABR as an assessment tool, social workers can help these families understand the sources of their stress so that, for example, overburdened mothers are less likely to turn frustration and blame toward themselves, resulting in depression and hopelessness, or toward their children, potentially resulting in abuse. Work performed with these families must be based on empowerment and should include advocacy, public education, lobbying, and political involvement toward changing the social and economic structures that deny stable access to adequate quality basic resources for parents and their children.

CONCLUSION

The multilevel stress and coping framework and the FABR assessment tool provide social workers with an enlarged view for work with families and with individual family members. The conceptual framework broadens the assessment from focusing only on the person, the family, or the local neighborhood or community system to viewing stress as something generated by structural problems in the national economic and social welfare systems, which fail to provide stable access to adequate quality basic resources required by all citizens. Documentation of families' lack of access to adequate resources through the use of the FABR can enable social workers, agencies, professional organizations, and advocacy groups to understand the effects of resource deprivation. They can use this understanding as a basis for multilevel systems practice, including not only provision of services to individuals and families, but also public education, lobbying, and political involvement toward changes at the neighborhood, local, state, and national levels.

Based on documentation using the FABR, empirical studies can begin tracking the extent of resource deprivation for families. These studies can also determine the effects of stress from inadequate or unstable access to quality resources on family structures (for example, underorganization) as well as on the health and mental health of family members. Multivariate assessments at multiple systems levels gradually will provide knowledge regarding the effects of specific stressors (such as homelessness) and the effects of the pileup of multiple stressors. The effects of specific policy changes can also be delineated (for example, comparing various approaches to welfare reform). Longitudinal studies, including large-scale or networked projects, can provide understanding of particular stressors for particular kinds of families or understanding of particular stressors within a state or region.

The view that stress is generated by structural problems in the national economic and social welfare systems provides a unifying theoretical framework for social work educational curricula, bridging the gap between micro and macro practice. For some families, stress can be tracked increasingly from structural problems in larger systems (for example, unemployment or unstable employment, low wages, inadequate or deteriorating housing, lack of access to health care, lack of quality child care), from various family problems, or from depression in an overwhelmed single parent. In such situations, clinical work with the individual or family, although clearly important on an emergency basis, is not a solution to the symptom. Resolution of the problem will require additional work toward change in the structures of the larger systems either with or on behalf of the client and his or her family. Although connections among multiple systems are often complex and difficult to track completely, students might begin to understand such multi-level work within, for example, a settlement house setting, even though the focal system for a particular set of interventions might be the neighborhood or a particular family (Vosler, 1989).

Finally, the framework allows social workers who struggle in the public domain (for example, in child welfare or juvenile justice settings) or in jobs working with families in neighborhoods with high concentrations of welfare recipients or in areas of high unemployment to see that their own and their clients' pain, frustration, and sense of helplessness is not some kind of pathology, but rather a healthy response of outrage toward larger social system realities. Too often promises are explicitly or implicitly made that hard work will result in access to adequate resources, but the truth is that many families experience homelessness, poor schools, and inadequate health coverage and receive food stamps that last at most 3 weeks out of a month. If the truth is seen and energies are directed toward public education, activism, and political involvement, then perhaps democracy can be made to work and larger social systems will be forced to change.

REFERENCES

Anderson, R. E., & Carter, I. (1984). *Human behavior in the social environment: A social systems approach* (3rd ed.). New York: Aldine.

Aponte, H. (1976). Underorganization in the poor family. In P. J. Guerin, Jr. (Ed.), *Family therapy: Theory and practice* (pp. 249–283). New York: Gardner.

Aponte, H. J. (1986). If I don't get simple, I cry. *Family Process, 25,* 531–548.

Bateman, R. W. (1983). Strengthening families: Social policy and related issues. *Social Thought, 9*(1), 35–46.

Beckett, J. O. (1988). Plant closings: How older workers are affected. *Social Work, 33*(1), 29–33.

Bernstein, V. J., Jeremy, R. J., & Marcus, J. (1986). Mother-infant interaction in multi-problem families: Finding those at risk. *Journal of the American Academy of Child Psychiatry, 25*(5), 631–640.

Bluestone, B., & Harrison, B. (1982). *The deindustrialization of America.* New York: Basic Books.

Boulet, J., Debritto, A. M., & Ray, S. A. (Eds.). (1985). *Understanding the economic crisis: The impact of poverty and unemployment on children and families.* Ann Arbor, MI: University of Michigan, The Bush Program in Child Development and Social Policy.

Briar, K. H. (1988). *Social work and the unemployed.* Silver Spring, MD: National Association of Social Workers.

Buckley, S. (1985). Parent aides provide support to high risk families. *Children Today, 14*(5), 16–19.

Colon, F. (1980). The family life cycle of the multiproblem poor family. In E. A. Carter & M. McGoldrick (Eds.). *The family life cycle* (pp. 343–381). New York: Gardner.

Danziger, S. H., & Weinberg, D. H. (Eds.). (1986). *Fighting poverty: What works and what doesn't.* Cambridge, MA: Harvard University Press.

DeHoyos, G. (1989). Person-in-environment: A tri-level practice model. *Social Casework, 70*(3), 131–138.

DeHoyos, G., & Jensen, C. (1985). The systems approach in American social work. *Social Casework, 66*(8), 490–497.

Ellwood, D. T. (1988). *Poor support: Poverty in the American family.* New York: Basic Books.

Family Support Act of 1988, 42 U.S.C. §1305.

Figley, C. R., & McCubbin, H. I. (Eds.). (1983). *Stress and the family: Vol. II. Coping with catastrophe.* New York: Brunner/Mazel.

Ford Foundation. (1989). *The common good: Social welfare and the American future.* New York: Ford Foundation.

Garbarino, J., Schellenbach, C. J., & Sebes, J. M. (Eds.). (1986). *Troubled youth, troubled families.* New York: Aldine.

Germain, C. B., & Gitterman, A. (1987). Ecological perspective. In A. Minahan (Ed.-in-Chief), *Encyclopedia of social work* (18th ed., Vol. 1, pp. 488–496). Silver Spring, MD: National Association of Social Workers.

Gilbert, N., & Specht, H. (1986). *Dimensions of social welfare policy* (2nd ed.). Englewood Cliffs, NJ: Prentice-Hall.

Halberstam, D. (1986). *The reckoning.* New York: Morrow.

Haley, J. (1976). *Problem-solving therapy.* San Francisco: Jossey-Bass.

Hartman, A. (1989). Still between client and community. *Social Work, 34*(5), 387–388.

Hartman, A., & Laird, J. (1983). *Family-centered social work practice.* New York: Free Press.

Herzog, E. (1966). Social and economic characteristics of high-risk mothers. In F. Haselkorn (Ed.), *Mothers-at-risk* (pp. 26–47). New York: Adelphi University School of Social Work Publications.

Hill, R. (1958). Social stresses on the family: Generic features of families under stress. *Social Casework, 39,* 139–150.

Hinckley, E. C. (1984). Homebuilders: The Maine experience. *Children Today, 13*(5), 14–17, 37.

Hutchinson, J. R., & Nelson, K. E. (1985). How public agencies can provide family-centered services. *Social Casework, 66*(6), 367–371.

Huttman, E. D. (1981). *Introduction to social policy.* New York: McGraw-Hill.

Imber-Black, E. (1988). *Families and larger systems: A family therapist's guide through the labyrinth.* New York: Guilford.

Johnson, H. C. (1986). Emerging concerns in family therapy. *Social Work, 31,* 299–306.

Kagan, R., & Schlosberg, S. (1989). *Families in perpetual crisis.* New York: Norton.

Kaplan, L. (1986). *Working with multiproblem families.* Lexington, MA: Lexington Books.

Lazarus, R. S., & Folkman, S. (1984). *Stress, appraisal, and coping.* New York: Springer.

Lindblad-Goldberg, M., & Dukes, J. L. (1985). Social support in black, low-income, single-parent families: Normative and dysfunctional patterns. *American Journal of Orthopsychiatry, 55*(1), 42–58.

Maher, T. F. (1987). The loneliness of parenthood. *Social Service Review, 61*(1), 91–101.

Maluccio, A. N. (Ed.). (1981). *Promoting competence in clients: A new/old approach to social work practice.* New York: Free Press.

McCubbin, H. I. (1979). Integrating coping behavior in family stress theory. *Journal of Marriage and the Family, 41*(2), 237–244.

McCubbin, H. I., & Figley, C. R. (Eds.). (1983). *Stress and the family: Vol. I. Coping with normative transitions.* New York: Brunner/Mazel.

McCubbin, H. I., Joy, C. B., Cauble, A. E., Comeau, J. K., Patterson, J. M., & Needle, R. H. (1980). Family stress and coping: A decade review. *Journal of Marriage and the Family, 42,* 855–871.

McKinney, G. E. (1970). Adapting family therapy to multideficit families. *Social Casework, 51,* 327–333.

Meyer, C. H. (1976). *Social work practice* (2nd ed.). New York: Free Press.

Meyer, C. H. (Ed.). (1983). *Clinical social work in the eco-systems perspective.* New York: Columbia University Press.

Minuchin, S. (1974). *Families and family therapy.* Cambridge, MA: Harvard University Press.

Nichols-Casebolt, A. M. (1988). Black families headed by single mothers: Growing numbers and increasing poverty. *Social Work, 33*(4), 306–313.

Ozawa, M. N. (1983). The economic predicament of female-headed families. *New England Journal of Human Services, 3*(3), 32–37.

Reich, R. B. (1989, May 1). U.S. income inequality keeps on rising. *The New Republic,* pp. 23–26.

Reid, W. J. (1985). *Family problem solving.* New York: Columbia University Press.

Schlesinger, B. (1970). *The multi-problem family: A review and annotated bibliography* (3rd ed.). Toronto: University of Toronto Press.

Schlosberg, S. B., & Kagan, R. M. (1988). Practice strategies for engaging chronic multiproblem families. *Social Casework, 69*(1), 3–9.

Schorr, A. L. (1986). *Common decency: Domestic policies after Reagan.* New Haven, CT: Yale University Press.

Schorr, L. B. (1988). *Within our reach: Breaking the cycle of disadvantage.* New York: Anchor Press.

Siporin, M. (1975). *Introduction to social work practice.* New York: Macmillan.

Siporin, M. (1980). Ecological systems theory in social work. *Journal of Sociology and Social Welfare, 7,* 507–532.

Vondra, J. I. (1986). Socioeconomic stress and family functioning in adolescence. In J. Garbarino, C. J. Schellenbach, & J. M. Sebes (Eds.), *Troubled youth, troubled families* (pp. 191–234). New York: Aldine.

Vosler, N. R. (1989). A systems model for child protective services. *Journal of Social Work Education, 25*(1), 20–28.

Vosler, N. R., & Ozawa, M. N. (1988). An analysis of two approaches to welfare-to-work. *New England Journal of Human Services, 8*(4), 15–21.

Vosler, N. R., Wallace, M., Dubeck, P. J., Maume, D. J., & Dyehouse, J. M. (1989). *A model for understanding dislocated manufacturing workers and their families.* Manuscript submitted for publication.

Wallace, D. (1967). The Chemung County evaluation of casework service to dependent multiproblem families; Another problem outcome. *Social Service Review, 41,* 379–389.

Wallace, M., & Rothschild, J. (1988). Plant closings, capital flight, and worker dislocation: The long shadow of deindustrialization. In M. Wallace & J. Rothschild (Eds.), *Research in politics and society* (Vol. III, pp. 1–35). Greenwich, CT: JAI Press.

Weitzman, J. (1985). Engaging the severely dysfunctional family in treatment: Basic considerations. *Family Process, 24,* 473–485.

Wills, T. A. (1978). Perceptions of clients by professional helpers. *Psychological Bulletin, 85,* 968–1000.

Wolock, I., Geismar, L., Lagay, B., & Raiffe, P. (1985–1986). Forced exit from welfare: The impact of federal cutbacks on public assistance families. *Journal of Social Service Research, 9*(2/3), 71–96.

Wyers, N. L. (1988). Economic insecurity: Notes for social workers. *Social Work, 33*(1), 18–22.

Zimmerman, S. L. (1985). Families and economic policies: An instrumental perspective. *Social Casework, 66*(7), 424–431.

CHAPTER 118

THE PLIGHT OF HOMELESS WOMEN

Madeleine R. Stoner

L ast winter Rebecca Smith, age sixty-one, died in New York City. She froze to death in the home she had constructed for herself inside a cardboard box. She preferred it, she said, to any other home. Rebecca Smith had spent much of her life in a state psychiatric hospital under treatment for schizophrenia. Life in the box was preferable. In a sense, many people watched her die: her neighbors, the police, the Red Cross, and finally a city-dispatched social worker and psychiatrist. In a larger sense, the nation watched too, because her death made the front page of the *Washington Post*.[1]

The senseless tragedy of Rebecca Smith's death immediately prompted nationwide concern for the plight of the homeless. Those who have worked with the homeless find this new acknowledgment of the thousands of homeless people in our midst rather strange. They also find somewhat remarkable the morbid curiosity demonstrated about them and the quickness with which they are branded a bunch of smelly sociopaths, chronic "crazies," to be dealt with someplace, but not here. Yet people and organizations are beginning to pay thoughtful attention to the problems of the homeless, and programs and services are emerging to meet the needs of this long-neglected population. Concerned groups are organizing to provide an increasingly vocal advocacy network for coping with the needs of the homeless. Despite this activity, however, existing public and private welfare policies preclude adequate service delivery for the homeless population.

The intent of this article is to describe the homeless population and the special needs of women within it. In carrying out this intent, the article first reviews apparent causes of homelessness and the types of programs that currently exist for women. It then suggests a design for a comprehensive service system for homeless women and concludes with a proposal for political and social action that will be essential if the systemic causes of homelessness are to be eliminated.

Reprinted from *Social Service Review*, Vol. 57, No. 4 (December 1983), pp. 565–581, by permission of the publisher.

The rapidly increasing number of homeless people in America poses a new challenge to cities all over the nation. New York City has had to divert major resources to cope with an expanding street population because a court decree requires the city to provide public shelter for homeless men.[2] Throughout the country the capacity of agencies to make a place for everybody is being severely tested. Columbus, Ohio, a city badly hit by the declining economy, was forced to open the first public shelter accommodating 150 people a night.[3] The Traveler's Aid Society in affluent Houston has housed as many as 1,000 economically disabled people a month. This is nearly 40 percent more than the previous year.[4] In Denver, one church opened a shelter and within a week 400 people had applied.[5] In 1981 the Community Services Society of New York estimated that 36,000 people in that city were without homes.[6] More recently, Los Angeles County Department of Mental Health officials estimated that a minimum of 30,000 people are living on its streets.[7]

While these numbers are alarming, they also are misleading because there are so many methodological barriers to obtaining a sound census of the homeless. What is important is that public and private agencies, researchers, and the media are reporting readily visible evidence that the number of homeless people is rising and that radical changes in their circumstances and composition have taken place over the past fifteen years. These changes call into question the propriety of relief measures that traditionally have been applied to the contemporary homeless population.

Workers with the homeless report that more women, elderly, and young people—particularly black women and members of other minority groups—have slipped into a population once dominated by older alcoholic white men.[8] Any profile that attempts to develop an aggregate notion of the type of person in today's homeless population obscures the most distinctive features of this group: its variety and its heterogeneity. Surveys of these people are unreliable as they include only those who have been in public or private shelters. Yet, these clearly serve only a small proportion of street people.

Clarification of the picture of who the homeless are is possible by considering why people find themselves homeless. Summary evidence from those who have studied the homeless population indicates that the antecedents of homelessness are: (1) lack of housing, (2) unemployment and poverty, (3) deinstitutionalization, and (4) domestic violence and abuse.[9]

Research conducted by the Vera Institute of Justice on user characteristics of homeless people in a women's shelter demonstrated that there is a direct link between such factors as evictions and lockouts and the consequence of homelessness.[10] As economic pressures for the reclamation of land for renovation and upgrading mount, evictions will continue to increase. The City of New York's Human Resources Administration has reported that a fourth of the recent applicants to its men's shelters are there due to job loss.[11]

Census data on poverty reveal that from 1980 to 1981 an additional 2.2 million people entered the official poverty index as unemployment figures increased.[12] According to the Census Bureau figures, the burden of this poverty falls disproportionately on families headed by women, on children, on young adults, and on ethnic minority groups.[13] The "feminization of poverty" has particular significance in the growing and shifting homeless population. Many women have no place to turn but to the streets. Significantly related to both income and homelessness is another fact, namely, that public assistance is denied to people who have no address.[14] People lose their benefits when they become homeless and, in turn, the means of finding another home.

There is considerable documentation to indicate the presence of large numbers of severely disturbed individuals in streets and shelters, many with histories of psychiatric hospitalization. Ill-planned deinstitutionalization, such as that leading to the death of Rebecca Smith, often is cited as the most prominent cause of homelessness. Whether or not this is so, recent studies have attested to the growing number of psychiatrically disabled among the homeless poor. An informal census conducted in the Los Angeles skid row district indicated that 90 percent of the women there were mentally ill and had histories of psychiatric hospitalization.[15]

Many homeless women and adolescent females report that they left their homes after repeated incidents of abuse by their spouses, rape, incest, and desertion. Despite the strengths of the Domestic Violence Prevention Act, cutbacks in expenditures for welfare programs include severe slashes in provisions for battered and abused women and displaced homemakers.[16]

LIVING AND COPING PATTERNS OF HOMELESS WOMEN

Although there is a substantial body of literature concerning male vagrants and transients, until recently very little existed concerning unaffiliated women who are not alcoholic. Bahr and Garrett[17] conducted studies comparing dislocation factors among men and women in urban shelters and explained the differences by sex in the etiology of homelessness and the family backgrounds of this population. They also examined the drinking habits of men and women admitted to emergency shelters in New York City. Judith Strasser[18] provided a sensitive descriptive profile of the shopping bag lady population, exploring personal appearance, hygiene, daily routines, health conditions, and their use of services. Ambulatory schizophrenic women were described in a report by the New Orleans Traveler's Aid Society.[19] Most recently the media have exposed the box people—the Rebecca Smiths who have come to inhabit city streets or live underground in subway stations.

Because the little that has been written about homeless women has focused on the skid row environment and alcoholism, research is needed that does not treat women as derelicts but as homeless people with specific women's problems and needs. This is necessary because the apparent systematic avoidance of dealing with homeless women in research and literature suggests that women receive harsher judgment and less adequate services than men even at this marginal level of society. As women and their families continue to enter the ranks of the homeless—as victims of the economy, of landlords, of a depleted mental health system, and of spouses—society can no longer neglect them.

What may be a benchmark study of this problem was conducted by the Manhattan Bowery Corporation in 1979.[20] The strength of this report, which was not widely circulated, lies in the fact that it dispels many of the myths about shopping bag ladies. Several of its findings are particularly important: (1) Little is known about the homeless population, except that we are sure its numbers are growing. (2) The three municipal shelters for women in New York City are unable to meet the growing demands of the homeless population. It is the only city in the United States providing public shelter for women. (3) Homeless women are singularly vulnerable to crime, the elements, and other hazards of the streets. (4) Some characteristics, viewed as bizarre (e.g., foul odors), are conscious defense mechanisms. (5) Mental disability per se is not a pervasive reason for women's alleged refusal to use available services. (6) The primary causes of their disaffiliation are to be found in the socioeconomic circumstances of poor, middle-aged, and elderly women—in particular, their isolation. Homeless women do not choose their circumstances. They are victims of forces over which they have lost control.

One of the first studies that looked beyond the alcoholic woman was conducted by Baumohl and Miller in Berkeley, California, in 1974.[21] They observed that there was a substantial presence of women among the homeless in that city, larger than had been found in comparable studies of the homeless. Their report pointed out several differences between men and women of the street. The women are younger, less educated, away from home for shorter periods of time, and they more frequently obtain income from legitimate sources. Despite the fact that more women than men receive either public assistance or money from home in order to survive, many are forced to panhandle, deal drugs, shoplift, or become prostitutes. This homeless style of life, hazardous for anyone, holds acute dangers for women, rape being high among them. The study reported that most women trade sexual favors for food, shelter, and other necessities, and it described frustrated desires for conventional monogamous relationships and intense conflicts following coercive sexual encounters.

A 1982 study of vagrant and transient women in Columbia, South Carolina, reported that the study sample was predominantly Caucasian, forty years of age or younger, natives of South Carolina, and none having more than a high school education. The majority were not employed, and most had incomes of less than $3,000 per year.[22] An important distinction between this study and previously cited ones is that it encompassed a broader environment than skid row and did not specifically focus on alcoholism. In relation to problems perceived by the study sample, the majority were dissatisfied with their present lives and identified as their most serious problems lack of money, nowhere to live, unemployment, separation from family, lack of friends, and illness. The majority who were sick sought professional care in health clinics. Most respondents hoped to be employed and have a place to live within one year.

This study also produced findings that significantly differed from previous descriptions of disaffiliation. One was that although the study sample complained of loneliness and isolation, there was a greater sense of affiliation than in earlier studies. Another finding pertained to the use of services: the majority of the sample received meals from a women's shelter and had sought help from social service agencies, but a sizable minority had not sought such help. Most services used by the study sample were general or lay community oriented rather than specifically designed to meet the needs of women and, in particular, homeless women.[23] This suggests that homeless women may only turn to shelters when other social services are unavailable.

In a survey of 100 first-time applicants in 1979,[24] the Vera Institute of Justice has produced the most detailed study of user characteristics of the New York City Women's Shelter. The demographic data closely parallel the men's shelter population and disclose that: (1) half of the women were under forty, with 16 percent sixty years and older; (2) 40 percent were white, and 44 percent were black; and (3) 61 percent had lived in the city for at least one year.

The most useful data from the Vera Institute Study for application to the design of services and preventive measures are those citing reasons for selecting shelter. Of those women who gave information on prior residence, 13 percent had come directly from hospitals. Nearly half had lived in single rooms in hotels immediately prior to coming to the shelter. Over a fourth of the first-time applicants cited as their reason for seeking shelter illegal lockouts or evictions, or ejection from a household (by family or friend).

The question of who the homeless women are cannot be completely answered without considering how they are portrayed. Earlier research, reinforced by popular notions, supported views of homeless women as derelict eccentrics who choose their life-style. The persistent denial of women's existence on skid row only served to consolidate long-held beliefs that homeless women are even more derelict and eccentric than homeless men, and thus the most socially undesirable of all marginal people. Equating the term derelict with homelessness has contributed to a belief that this is a "less needy" population. Because women have been less visibly homeless and less troublesome or feared than men, society and social agencies have regarded them as even "less needy" than homeless men. As a consequence, these unacknowledged women have tended to fall between the threads of the safety net, into the streets.

A personal testament to this notion has come from Jill Halverson, director of the Downtown Women's Center in Los Angeles, who reports that she always perceived skid row as being only for men. During her ten years first as a public welfare caseworker and then as a caseworker in alcoholic rehabilitation programs, she saw women sleeping in parking lots, in X-rated movie houses, and in roach-infested cheap hotel rooms. She discovered that women were on skid row, but that all of the agencies on Los Angeles' skid row were geared to serve men, not women.[25]

Images portrayed in the popular press appear to be changing. The tendency to blame the victim and the notions of dereliction and eccentricity are fading. At a conference in Orange County, California, in August 1982, conferees attested to the fact that homelessness is not confined to large cities. It is a national problem that reaches the smallest communities as well. Estimates that there are 4,000 homeless women in Orange County bear this out.[26] As Orange County and other communities across the nation are witnessing the increasing numbers of homeless single women and homeless women with children, there is an increasing awareness that these women are the by-products of the "feminization of poverty," often the result of family breakdowns through divorce, desertion, and abuse that have led to mortgage foreclosures or evictions for nonpayment of rent.

IMPLICATIONS FOR SOCIAL WORK PRACTICE

The growing population of homeless women holds immediate and far-reaching implications for social work practice and for the design of effective social services. With the exception of a loosely organized system of emergency shelters, little exists among traditional and alternative service agencies to meet the special needs of this population. The prospect of starting from the beginning to tackle this social problem is especially daunting in an atmosphere of declining resources, but to do so is imperative. We need a system that goes beyond emergency shelter to provide food, services, and a range of living facilities to meet the varied but basic needs of the wide spectrum of women who are now homeless. And to meet this urgent need it is necessary that preventive activities include political and economic elements. However, the formulation of any systematic and comprehensive plan must take into account the strengths and weaknesses of the programs for homeless women that currently exist and assess their potential as effective answers to this serious problem.

The current programs for homeless women appear to have four characteristics: (1) they are predominantly under private auspices, (2) they are proportionately fewer than those available for homeless men, (3) there are fewer professional social workers or other professionally trained people directly involved in staffing women's shelters, and (4) existing shelters for women tend to operate with lower standards of care than those for men.

Until very recently, there were 800 beds in Los Angeles' skid row for homeless men, but only two for women. Now there are thirty-five beds for women.[27] Similar patterns prevail throughout the nation, suggesting a woeful failure to serve the population of women in need of shelter. It is likely that life for many women outside the shelters is worse, but it may also be possible that the prevailing substandard conditions in many women's shelters makes life on the street more attractive. Rebecca Smith believed this.

New York City now has four public shelters for women. Four years ago, it had one.[28] New York City is notable for operating public shelters because of the court decree requiring the city to provide meals, clothing, and beds; social and medical services are limited. The admissions procedures are more stringent then those for men in public shelters. At intake a delousing shower is required, just as it is in shelters for men, along with an inventory of all belongings and evidence of psychiatric clearance from Bellevue Hospital. Gynecological exams are required by two of the shelters.

Whatever their bed capacity, shelters are overcrowded, and they accommodate more women than there are beds by filling hallways, chairs, and even using table tops. Facilities are adequate according to certification standards, but these standards are low. In one such shelter, Bushwick Annex, investigators found substantial fire code and food handling violations, inadequate toilet facilities, overcrowding, and inadequate staffing and security. These shelters tend to be located in fringe areas of the city, surrounded by dangerous and isolated neighborhoods where the women seeking the shelter are constantly harassed. Two of the shelters provide meals, but not on their premises. The women are transported by bus to another shelter for breakfast; they remain in the second shelter until they are bused back at night to sleep.[29]

New York City is an exception: most cities are not legally required to provide shelter. More typically, cities operate programs like Sundown in Los Angeles County. Sundown provides a list of hotels that will put people up for the night or a weekend. The program sometimes provides food, but essentially arranges one night's support for which transients do not qualify. Sundown staff report a growing demand. Approximately 1,300 people called the program asking for food and shelter in 1981. During the first few months of 1982, the calls averaged 1,400 a month and are expected to increase.[30]

Throughout the nation, the main source of refuge for homeless women consists of private nonprofit shelters. Public shelters that operate outside of New York, as in Washington, D.C., are restricted to men. On the whole, the private shelters are sponsored by organizations such as the Volunteers of America, churches and missions, and groups of concerned individuals. The Traveler's Aid Society, Salvation Army, and the Young Women's Christian Association also provide services, but these tend to be confined to the provision of food, drop-in centers, and travel arrangements home.[31]

There are two types of private shelters—the smaller, more casually run operation, and the longer-established institutions deeply rooted in mission work. Shelter provisions in the missions are characterized by intake and admissions procedures similar to those of public shelters. Waiting lists are common and rates are not cheap. Monies are taken out of Supplemental Security Income checks, and psychiatric care is often required of residents. Conditions vary among the missions but closely resemble those of the public shelters.

The more casual programs that prevail in the private sector attract full occupancy, primarily because they are smaller and offer a more humane and dignified quality of care according to most shelter residents. Operating costs are met by donations, voluntary labor, and contributions of clothes, furniture, and food. Social workers, psychologists, and psychiatrists are involved only peripherally on a consulting or emergency basis in most of these programs. Generally, these shelters are informal and stress the dignity and privacy of residents, many of whom are known only by first names. Many of the volunteer staff are residents of the shelters. A Catholic church in Boston's Pine Street has turned its basement over to a group of volunteers who operate a shelter there and have moved from their homes to live in the shelter. Some of these people have donated the proceeds from the sales of their homes to operate the shelter.[32] Social life is encouraged in these shelters, and it is known that strong bonds often develop among shelter residents, particularly in the less formal facilities. Because of their religious auspices, religious relics are seen everywhere. Religious services are held, but attendance is generally not required. Many of the shelters will accept no public funding, even when offered, because of their distaste for regulations and bureaucracy.[33]

Physical conditions in these private shelters vary. Some provide only mattresses on the floor, but the emphasis on human dignity and patience appears to compensate for less than adequate standards. An added advantage of many of these shelters is their connection to other services, such as religion-affiliated hospitals. They also operate as a network in some cities so that homeless women can be found by their families. There is reason to believe that women tend to prefer these smaller, casual shelters to the public shelters because of their nonjudgmental ambience as well as their less restrictive policies and practices.

The Christian Housing Facility in Orange County, California, provides a unique service for families. It offers temporary shelter, food, and counseling. Priority of services goes to families or victims of family violence. In 1981 this facility had 1,536 residents, a 300 percent increase from the previous year. The main facility is a remodeled house, but motels are used in emergency cases. This shelter views its function as that of helping people return to permanent housing. Residents are required to submit to counseling and search for jobs. Once they are hired, residents pay 10 percent of their salary to the house. According to its 1980 annual report, 504 persons, 103 of these children, left with a home, a job, and an income after an average twenty-day stay.[34]

Christian Housing is an example of a shelter designed to help people in transition. Its model of service differs from that of the mission and informal church settings in that it works with those people who are most capable of independent functioning rather than the "down and out."

Most night shelters provide little in the way of day services, and so, even with a meal and a bed, street life remains a reality for most of the homeless people who turn to such facilities. Drop-in shelters providing other services are beginning to emerge.

The Downtown Women's Center, opened by Jill Halverson in Los Angeles' skid row four years ago, is a prototype of drop-in centers. It is a former sheet metal shop that is now a bright and cheerful daytime drop-in center for as many as fifty homeless women a day. At the center the women can shower, eat a hot meal, and nap on one of four daybeds. A sense of community is fostered. A senior consulting psychiatrist from the community services division of Los Angeles County's Department of Mental Health who has studied and cares about the plight of homeless women visits the center regularly. He provides a range of services for the women, from individual therapy to group sessions and informal rap groups. The type of care given at the center departs from most traditional notions of what constitutes good psychiatric care, and there is a sense that no rules apply to therapy with homeless women except that they will respond positively when they have a sense that they are in a supportive environment where staff are patient, caring, and respectful. The director of the center possesses no professional training or qualifications and will not accept public funding. She does, however, accept offers of help from private individuals and groups.

In New York City, the Antonio G. Olivieri Center for Homeless Women opened in February 1981 as a daytime drop-in center for homeless men and women. However, male applicants so far outnumbered female applicants that the services were redirected to women only.[35] This center offers meals, showers, delousing, assistance with income entitlements, and access to medical and social services. Women are not required to give their names, nor are they obliged to take part in any activities. The center is open twenty-four hours daily, every day, and offers a form of shelter without beds. Women sleep on chairs, the floor, and desk tops. Tolerant and caring staff make this overcrowded, understaffed, and chaotic center a secure environment for women. Because of the high demand on the center, it has established a time limit of two weeks of continuous care, after which women are assured of seven days' lodging in the public shelter. They may then return to the Olivieri Center for another two weeks.

In addition to night shelters and drop-in centers, outreach services are expanding to deal with homeless people. The Manhattan Bowery Project sends out mobile vans with workers to locate homeless people and offer them food, shelter, and clothing.[36] Responses to such outreach programs vary. Center workers made every possible attempt to bring Rebecca Smith into care, but she refused.

As the number of homeless women continues to increase and the reasons for their plight extend beyond mental illness and alcoholism, women are turning to shelters that in the past they might have turned away from, or not sought at all. Some women who are homeless because of mental illness or alcoholism have tended to avoid shelters and escape from the rigors of mental hospitals and detoxification centers. This was Rebecca Smith's case history. The new homeless women who are increasingly in this plight for reasons related to unemployment, poverty, eviction, and abuse appear to be more accepting of social services and shelters.

What is clear from this survey of shelters and services for homeless women is the fact that public shelters operate under restrictive and demeaning policies and practices. Women prefer the private shelters and, among these, choose to be in a small and informal setting, no matter its conditions, rather than the more institutional missions with characteristics of public shelters. The overcrowding in all shelters dispels the myth that women choose life in the streets. Most women want shelter, but given the scarcity of private shelters and the harsh conditions of public and mission facilities, it is understandable why many homeless women continue to find themselves without any place to sleep at night.

A COMPREHENSIVE SERVICE SYSTEM FOR HOMELESS PEOPLE

The evidence from drop-in centers, churches, missions, public shelters, and outreach efforts demonstrates the need for additional and better-quality shelter. Most programs presently operating are, at best, temporary and do not begin to approach the full dimensions of the problem.

Rational planning to meet the needs of homeless people in general, and homeless women in particular, must take into account the heterogeneity of the population and provide a range of housing and services. Some advocates for the homeless have proposed a three-tiered approach to the development of housing and services: (1) emergency shelter and crisis intervention, (2) transitional or community shelters, and (3) long-term residence.[37] Each would incorporate a cluster of elements, identified briefly below.

The *basic emergency shelter*, the first tier of shelter, should be made as accessible and undemanding as standards of hygiene and security allow. Clean bedding, wholesome food, adequate security and supervision, and social services should be available. Existing facilities such as school buildings, churches, armories, and converted houses could be adapted for such purposes. Each shelter should be community based as opposed to being in physically or geographically isolated locations.

Transitional housing would recognize that there are homeless people who, given the opportunity and supports, could eventually live independently. This type of shelter would make more demands on residents in terms of assuming self-responsibility and would provide longer-term social services and vocational rehabilitation. Staff would actively attempt to secure appropriate entitlements as well as necessary clinical care. Transitional housing settings could provide an address enabling residents to receive public assistance.

Long-term residence in effect would provide homes and offer services and aids necessary in the everyday lives of residents. The broad scope of such a program, incorporating aspects of low-income housing and a full complement of service personnel, does not make it a realistic prospect in today's political climate. Nonprofit sponsorship of such programming is more feasible than public funding and support.[38]

An outstanding example of such a three-tiered approach is the Skid Row Development Corporation in Los Angeles. Formed in 1978, the corporation is funded through private (the Los Angeles Central City Association) and public sources (the Los Angeles Community Redevelopment Agency), but its goal is to be independent from city and county funding. Starting with a first-year operating budget of $95,000, after two years it generated an operating budget of $300,000, and the figure is growing.[39]

The primary service objective of the corporation is to provide an alternative housing resource to emergency shelter on skid row by recycling apartments in south central Los Angeles. The corporation has designed transitional housing for indigent women and men. Its Women's Transitional Housing Program calls for a separate building apart from its men's facility. Plans are under way for the completion of long-term housing, and the corporation has planned a series of projects to relocate and rehabilitate apartment buildings slated for demolition in various parts of the city and county. Those who do well in transitional housing will be priority tenants, and the remaining units will be rented to individuals and families needing affordable housing.[40]

Ballington Plaza opened in July this year under the auspices of the Skid Row Development Corporation and is practical proof that long-term housing for the homeless population can be developed and filled where there is the interest and will to do so. This 270-unit housing complex located in Los Angeles' skid row is intended for low-income men and women who are elderly or handicapped and neither drug- nor alcohol-dependent. It offers the first real alternative to sleeping in the streets, transient hotels, or run-down missions. Rents range from $95 to $155 per month. It has full security, cooking facilities, and is an attractive three-story yellow stucco building with bay windows and a large central courtyard with grass, benches, and a parklike setting. This is a prime example of a suitable facility: it is the first in the nation to provide permanent housing for the homeless population. Most programs continue to be confined to the provision of temporary shelter, and many have time limits on the length of stay.

RECOMMENDATIONS FOR POLICY CHANGES AND SOCIAL ACTION

The underlying causes of homelessness show every sign of persisting, and the dimensions of the problem are increasing. Structural unemployment, inadequate and insufficient community-based psychiatric care, housing scarcity, domestic violence and abuse, and the recent cutbacks in income maintenance programs and social services are intensifying it. Given a confused and confusing political climate unsympathetic to the needs of the more vulnerable people in the country, it is difficult to gauge the prospects for a more enlightened public policy toward the homeless population in general and for bringing greater balance to providing for homeless men and women. There are hopeful signs, however, that the public is beginning to understand that the roots of mass homelessness lie in the pathology of society, not of individuals. There is increased public sympathy for the homeless and for their need for more adequate shelters. This is evidenced by the rapid rise of advocates for homeless people. Coalitions on behalf of the homeless are springing up throughout the nation: in Boston, Denver, Portland, Seattle, Los Angeles, New York, and Philadelphia. A National Coalition for the Homeless has begun to provide an active lobby and information resource for homeless people and their advocates.[41] The leverage that these advocacy groups can muster at local and national levels in the courts, legislatures, and social agencies is critical in improving the lot of the homeless as well as reducing their numbers.

An important event, already mentioned, occurred in New York in 1981 when the Consent Decree settling the *Callahan v. Carey* case was signed and forced New York City to open more shelters for men and, indirectly, women. A subsequent court action was initiated when, on February 24, 1982, a class action suit, *Eldredge v. Koch,* was filed in New York State Supreme Court on behalf of homeless women in an effort to upgrade and expand shelters. The suit contends that the conditions in the public facilities effectively deter many homeless women from applying for shelter.[42] Resorting to the courts is a powerful tool that other cities and states have not utilized enough with respect to homeless women. Even though public shelters do not adequately deal with the needs of the homeless population, with the courts' help, these may nevertheless be a powerful beginning to securing entitlement shelter.

Many of the existing coalitions are actively attempting to educate the public about the homeless population and to dispel the many negative stereotypes, attitudes, and myths about them. This is an important strategy, and there have been discernible changes in public views of the homeless. In addition to securing improved shelter, changing attitudes, and legal action, advocates of the homeless must direct their energies toward changing policies in several areas mentioned below:

1. Every effort must be made to ensure a quantitatively and qualitatively adequate supply of emergency shelter and to apply equal standards to shelters for women and men. New York Governor Mario Cuomo's budget of $50 million to build or remodel 6,000 units of housing for the homeless is an example for other states.

2. Shelters should be accessible to the target population, and their admissions procedures should be simple. Shelters should be community based, in contrast to policies operating in some cities that support physically isolated shelters.[43]

3. Community efforts to develop transitional and permanent housing and vocational rehabilitation modeled on the Skid Row Development Corporation in Los Angeles should be undertaken and supported.

4. The diminishing rate of single-room occupancy hotels, despite their problems, should be reviewed. Cities and counties should drop tax incentives for conversion of these hotels. Despite their adverse conditions, single-room occupancy beds are at a premium, and many people consider themselves fortunate to obtain and keep them. Departments of welfare should, however, implement programs that would guarantee that monthly checks go directly to beneficiaries, rather than the hotel owners.

5. Departments of mental health and mental retardation should expand their outreach programs so that their links with homeless people can precede—and possibly preclude—police intervention. Increasing the number of mobile vans, drop-in centers, and crisis-intervention provisions would be steps in this direction. Outreach efforts also need to provide clinical certifications necessary to obtain Supplemental Security Income and Disability benefits, for which some homeless men and women can only qualify once they obtain a residence. Staff of the Skid Row Project sponsored by the Los Angeles County Department of Mental Health have conducted training sessions for agencies that serve the homeless to inform their workers about the details and requirements for obtaining such benefits. Preliminary reports indicate that there was a 90 percent increase in the number of homeless people receiving such benefits in 1982 since these sessions took place.

6. Cities and states, along with private agencies, should be encouraged to build or convert facilities so that there are adequate supplies of transitional and permanent affordable housing.

7. Support for legislation to prevent further erosion of the single-room housing stock and illegal evictions or lockouts is needed. The Gottfried-Calandra anti-lockout and illegal eviction bill would allow city police in New York to intervene on the tenants behalf when they are illegally locked out or dispossessed from their homes.[44] This bill can serve as a model for other cities.

8. Mental health agencies and health settings can redirect some of their programs to meet the needs of homeless women in spite of reduced operating budgets. This would include revised practices and increased support services related to deinstitutionalization. Recent policies that direct mental health services toward chronic mental illness provide the legal framework for developing these services.

9. The public assistance allowance should be raised to account for inflation. Unless this happens, homeless people who become ready to assume independent households will not be able to afford the necessary rents and the tide of building abandonment will continue.

There is evidence that public curiosity, sympathy, and genuine concern for the plight of homeless men and women are increasing. Examples of well-run supportive services for this population are also on the rise in communities throughout the country. But the comprehensive programming based on the three-tiered approach that offers a range of housing and linkages to services and a sense of community is seldom seen.

As the ranks of the homeless increase, and the numbers of women within those ranks rises, concerted and planned action must be taken to develop policies and programs that will prevent another Rebecca Smith from dying in her cardboard home.

NOTES

1. *Washington Post* (February 4, 1982).
2. Callahan et al. v. Carey et al., Index No. 42582/79, Supreme Court of the State of New York.
3. These data were reported at a conference sponsored by the National Conference on Social Welfare (The Homeless: An Action Strategy, Boston, April 28–29, 1982).
4. Ibid.
5. Ibid.
6. Ellen Baxter and Kim Hopper, "Private Lives/Public Spaces: Homeless Adults on the Streets of New York City," mimeographed (New York: Community Service Society of New York, February 1981).
7. Rodger Farr, "The Skid Row Project," mimeographed (Los Angeles: Los Angeles County Department of Mental Health, June 1982).
8. *Los Angeles Times* (July 11, 1982).
9. Baxter and Hopper, pp. 30–48.
10. Vera Institute of Justice, "First Time Users of Women's Shelter Services: A Preliminary Analysis," mimeographed (New York: Vera Institute of Justice, 1981).
11. Jennifer R. Wolch, "Spatial Consequences of Social Policy: The Role of Service Facility Location in Urban Development Patterns," in *Causes and Effects of Inequality in Urban Services,* ed. R. Rich (Lexington, Mass.: Lexington Books,

1981).

12. U.S. Bureau of the Census, "U.S. Poverty Rate, 1966–1981."

13. Ibid.

14. Los Angeles County, Department of Public Social Services General Relief Regula-tions, Regulations 40–131, Determination of Eligibility. Section 3.31 requires the following identifying information: proof of identity, social security number, proof of residence, statement of intent to continue living in Los Angeles, and proof of U.S. citizenship. Regulation 40–119.2 states that general relief applicants are to be referred to the district office where they first appeared to request aid. Interim relief can be given if the applicant possesses an affidavit from a salaried employee of a board-and-care facility, alcoholism recovery home or detoxification center, or a recognized community agency within Los Angeles County. These regulations are prototypical of general relief regulations throughout the United States and serve as deterrents to homeless people who seek public assistance.

15. These data were first reported by Rodger Farr and Kevin Flynn, who directed the Skid Row Project of the Los Angeles County Department of Mental Health in June 1982.

16. Anne Minahan, "Social Workers and Oppressed People," *Social Work* 26 (May 1981): 183–84.

17. Gerald R. Garrett and Howard M. Bahr, "Women on Skid Row," *Quarterly Journal of the Studies of Alcohol* 34 (December 1973): 1228–43, and "The Fam-ily Backgrounds of Skid Row Women," *Signs* 2 (Winter 1976): 369–81.

18. Judith A. Strasser, "Urban Transient Women," *American Journal of Nursing* 78 (December 1978): 2076–79.

19. New Orleans Traveler's Aid Society, *Flight Chronic Clients* (New Orleans, 1980).

20. K. Schwam, "Shopping Bag Ladies: Homeless Women" (report to the Fund for the City of New York, Manhattan Bowery Corporation, April 1, 1979).

21. Jim Baumohl and Henry Miller, "Down and Out in Berkeley" (report prepared for the City of Berkeley, University of California Community Affairs Committee, May 1974).

22. John T. Gandy and Leonard Tartaglia, "Vagrant and Transient Women: A Social Welfare Issue," mimeographed (report prepared for the National Conference on Social Welfare, Columbia, South Carolina, May 1982), pp. 6–8.

23. Ibid., pp. 13–16.

24. Vera Institute of Justice (n. 10 above).

25. This was reported in personal interviews with J. Halverson during the spring and summer of 1982.

26. This estimate was reported at a conference on homeless women in Orange County, California, August 1982.

27. Rodger Farr, "The Skid Row Project" (n. 7 above), and Concerned Agencies of Metropolitan Los Angeles Directory of Services for the Homeless," mimeo-graphed (Los Angeles, December 1982).

28. Kim Hopper, Ellen Baxter, Stuart Cox, and Laurence Klein, "One Year Later: The Homeless Poor in New York City, 1982," mimeographed (New York: Com-munity Service Society Institute for Social Service Research, 1982).

29. Ibid.

30. *Los Angeles Times* (July 11, 1982).
31. This information is based on interviews with staff of the agencies, investigation of annual reports, and program descriptions on file with the United Way of America.
32. These data were reported at the conference in Boston, April 28–29, 1982 (see n. 3 above).
33. Reported at the Boston conference (see n. 3 above). The Downtown Women's Center is another example of such refusal to accept public funds.
34. Christian Temporary Housing Facility, *1980 Annual Report* (Orange, Calif.: Christian Temporary Housing Facility, 1980).
35. Hopper et al. (n. 28 above).
36. Reported at the Boston conference (see n. 3 above) by Marsha Martin, director of the Manhattan Bowery Project.
37. D. Sakano, "Homeless New Yorkers: The Forgotten among Us" (testimony given at the New York State Assembly hearings, November 19, 1981).
38. Hopper et al. (n. 28 above).
39. Skid Row Development Corporation, *Annual Report, 1979–1980* (Los Angeles: Skid Row Development Corporation, 1981).
40. Ibid.
41. The National Coalition for the Homeless is based at the Community Service Society of New York.
42. Eldred et al. v. Koch et al., in pretrial discovery process at the time of this writing, Supreme Court of the State of New York.
43. *New York Times* (February 11, 1983).
44. New York Senate, Illegal Eviction Law, 1982, Introduction 3538-B, Amendment to Multiple Dwelling Law of New York, Proposed Amendment Section 302-D.

CHAPTER 119

SOCIAL WORK WITH HOMELESS FAMILIES

Gill Stewart and John Stewart

Social work with homeless families dwelt on the margins of practice even before the assumption of homelessness into a housing policy context over a decade ago. We investigate how this specialism has persisted in a hostile environment. It is the singular combination of statutory child care and protection requirements with the awful circumstances of being made homeless and then living in temporary accommodation which generates the need for concern by social services management and practitioners. That situation is of long-standing, but the implementation of the 1989 Children Act provides an opportunity to refocus attention on the basis of knowledge and experience gained from practice.

Local authority welfare departments were responsible for accommodating homeless families, under a residual provision in Part III of the National Assistance Act 1948, until specific legislation made that a housing department responsibility in 1977. During that period, homelessness moved from being a welfare issue towards redefinition in terms of housing need, but with social work involvement increasingly coming under criticism (Harvey, 1969; Rose, 1971, pp. 8–12; Thomas, 1975; Bailey, 1980; Coventry Workshop, 1982). Academic critiques suggested that social services' continuing responsibility for homelessness contributed to families with housing problems being labelled inappropriately as 'deviants' (Minns, 1972; Means, 1977). There was little if any practice literature about what social workers with the homeless actually did under the old welfare departments, although some innovative practice was described in voluntary organizations (Moody, 1968). Seebohm had recommended that lead responsibility for dealing with homelessness should be transferred to housing departments and that

Reprinted from *British Journal of Social Work*, Vol. 22, No. 3 (1992), pp. 271–289, by permission of Oxford University Press.

where social work help was required it should be the same as for other families (Seebohm, 1968, para. 405).

Social workers had the unenviable task of responding to a problem whose solution
required a resource—housing—over which they had no control. It was unpopular work
and they were said to have 'breathed a sigh of relief' when legal responsibility was
transferred (May and Whitbread, 1975; Stevenson and Parsloe, 1978, pp. 36, 369–70;
Cooper, 1980, pp. 79–80; Kent County Council, 1981, para. 5.1; Satyamurti, 1981).
The Housing (Homeless Persons) Act, 1977, placed a corporate responsibility on local
authorities to make provision for homeless people in defined circumstances. Housing
departments had the main duties, but in the Codes of Guidance which accompany the
Act, social services departments were urged to co-operate in its implementation (Department of the Environment (D.o.E.) *et al.*, 1983, para. 3.2—now D.o.E. *et al.*, 1991,
chap. 15; more strongly expressed for Scottish social work departments in Scottish Development Department (SDD), 1980, paras. 7.5–7.6).

The 1977 Act has been described by Hudson (1987, p. 180) as an attempt by two
central government departments to impose collaboration upon the two local authority
departments concerned. That policy was by no means new. A Ministry circular urged
co-operation as early as 1959 (Ministry of Housing and Local Government and Ministry of Health, 1959, para. 6), and there were further exhortations in 1966 and 1974
(D.o.E. *et al.*, 1974, para. 13). As one-third of local housing authorities had not implemented the circular of 1974 asking for a transfer of homelessness responsibilities to
housing, intensive lobbying was followed by legislation in 1977 (Stewart and Stewart,
1978). Yet homelessness remained marginal to government policy. It was not even
mentioned in the last White Paper on housing (D.o.E., 1987); and there was a real possibility that the specific legislation (re-codified as Part III of the Housing Act 1985)
would be repealed following a review just ten years after its introduction.

Meanwhile, officially recorded levels of homelessness nearly tripled over twelve
years, rising from 53,110 to 145,800 in 1990. Although these figures are widely held to
be unreliable and an underestimate (for example, National Audit Office, 1990), analysis of the profile is of relevance as it is a demographic group with high 'client potential'.
Some 80 per cent of those accepted are families with dependent children or expecting
their first baby, half being lone parents (Evans and Duncan, 1988, pp. 3, 43). Two
major academic research projects into homelessness were conducted during the mid-
1980s: nationally and government funded by the Birmingham University Centre for
Urban and Regional Studies (CURS); and in London by John Greve of Leeds University
and the School for Advanced Urban Studies (SAUS) at Bristol University, funded by the
GLC. While they and other studies contain much valuable material, none of these
sources considers a social work perspective, nor pays significant attention to the contribution of social services departments.

There are similar views amongst administrators and professionals. Hence the Association of Metropolitan Authorities (AMA) (carrying both social services and housing responsibilities) mentioned social workers in its report on homelessness on a par with
health visitors who are, of course, employed by health authorities (AMA, 1990, p. 12).
In its Code of Practice on social services support for families in temporary accommodation, the London branch of the Association of Directors of Social Services (ADSS) and
the Association of London Authorities noted that: 'authorities must always bear in

mind that *homelessness is primarily a housing problem* and that anything done by so-cial services can only alleviate the symptoms of the problem' (ADSS, 1985, para. 3.1; original emphasis).

Questionnaire surveys of London social services departments conducted from the Social Services Inspectorate (SSI) and the Thomas Coram Foundation revealed only some of the specialist teams and individuals who were in post at the time (Howarth, 1987, p. 13; SSI, 1989, p. 12). The CURS researchers and the Audit Commission re-ported one or two social work teams among their sample authorities but apparently did not interview them (Audit Commission, 1989, para. 85; Niner, 1989, p. 58; also Asso-ciation of District Councils, 1987, paras. 5.1.5, 9.3). It appeared that a social services contribution to helping homeless families was scarcely recognized. In our research, none of the social work teams interviewed was aware of the others' existence. They wanted to be put in contact so a planning group was formed to organize a conference, which was attended by around eighty specialist practitioners (some of whom wrote background papers, edited by Stewart and Stewart, 1982). As an alternative there was some interest among national social work organizations (British Association of Social Workers (BASW), 1986; Central Council for Education and Training in Social Work (CCETSW), 1989; SSI, 1989, p. 5). However, this proved to be London-centric and dominated by voluntary organizations (Crane, 1990). So by the end of the decade the existence of specialist social work teams was still not generally known among policy makers and researchers.

RESEARCH INTO PRACTICE

The objectives of our research were: to identify the location, the nature, and if possible the extent, of continuing social services involvement with homeless families; to discover what social workers do in working with this client group; and to compare their atti-tudes and values with those of homeless persons unit (HPU) officers.

There was a quantitative and two qualitative stages to this research. Experience and other research had indicated that attempting to locate specialist homeless families teams within social services by administering a questionnaire was unproductive. In order to locate the teams, a three-year systematic analysis of job advertisements which had been placed in the national press and practitioner publications was carried out. The criterion for an advertisement being included in our analysis was that 'homelessness' was specifically mentioned as constituting at least part of the work in a statutory agency (reported in Stewart and Stewart, 1981; Stewart and Stewart, 1983). In addition at this stage all advertisements resulted in telephone approaches being made to the rele-vant social services/work departments to establish the existence of a post and/or a team.

The second stage of research was qualitative in nature, based on fixed-topic list in-terviews with social workers in specialist homeless families teams and the correspond-ing HPU officers. The selection of seven social work specialists reflected the known spread of homelessness specialists nationally, as derived from stage one of the research. Additional criteria in selection of this sample were regional location and urban charac-teristics. The composition of these teams was such that we were able to interview both practitioner and managerial grade officers

The third stage was a comprehensive literature review. The relevant policy context is clearly housing at national and local government level. However, there are additional social services and social work policy contexts where the literature is diverse, hence we have drawn upon a wide range of material in order to validate and contextualize our data.

In this paper we present an analysis of the qualitative stages of our research, looking at the practice of homeless families teams: first by examining the 'homelessness process' and second by examining inter-agency relations.

THE HOMELESSNESS PROCESS

Statutory homelessness is a three-stage process. First there is the application leading to acceptance as homeless by the HPU, with its investigations and possible rejection; next a period in temporary accommodation; finally rehousing (which we examine elsewhere; Stewart and Stewart, 1992 forthcoming). Although housing authorities have statutory responsibilities other agencies may become involved. Each will have a different agency setting, ethos, and statutory responsibilities which will shape the implementation of policy within the available resources. The presence of children is the linking theme in homeless families which more often than not leads to the involvement of social services, as well as health and education professionals. Those agencies often become involved because the process of homelessness potentiates problems with children for which they have statutory responsibilities. In this section we shall examine how and why social service specialists become involved and how agencies differ in their practices.

Prevention

Both the Scottish and the English and Welsh *Codes of Guidance* place most emphasis on social services co-operation in the area of 'prevention' (SDD, 1980, para. 7.7a; D.o.E. *et al.*, 1991, paras. 10.2 and 15.5). However, the different agencies' expectations of what 'preventing homelessness' might mean vary and are incompatible in practice.

There is an expectation in the *Code of Guidance* that social workers might assist in the recovery of rent arrears and give rent guarantees in order to avoid eviction, because financial and personal difficulties are associated (D.o.E. *et al.*, 1991, paras. 10.5, 10.6e, 10.14, and 15.4). The social workers who were interviewed generally rejected the role of rent collector, regarding it as the housing department's job. On the other hand, they thought it appropriate to help families with benefit and debt problems, and several teams had arrangements whereby they were notified of impending evictions (but not mortgage foreclosures) so that they could visit or attend the court.

Another area in which social services co-operation is expected concerns 'domestic disputes', which are the most common single official cause of homelessness. The D.o.E.'s survey of local authority policies found that social services were often called upon to make assessments of 'domestic disputes'; for example, only 17 per cent of housing authorities (fewer in the shires) would accept a woman's word that she had experienced violence at home, and social workers were most likely to be asked for verification (Evans and Duncan, 1988, pp. 18–19).

Disputes between partners is a sensitive issue for social workers, not least because reality makes observance of the *Code of Guidance* unlikely. To illustrate, some research has suggested that they are reluctant to intervene in violence between adults, or even to recognize it, unless children are at risk, because of an over-riding concern to maintain the family unit (reviewed by Smith, 1989, pp. 75–6). However, the social workers in our study felt strongly that women should be given the benefit of any doubt and that they should not be forced to remain in a violent relationship through the action, or in-action, of a helping agency. Their concern was to keep children safely with their mothers, not to persuade women to continue living with violent men as the *Code of Guidance* might suggest when stressing the need to keep families together (SDD, 1980, para. 3.11; D.o.E. *et al.*, 1991, paras. 6.5 and 10.23). Not taking such action, as the CURS researchers noted, means that 'prevention' in this context merely meant delay and that women who had been subject to violence and sent home again for reconciliation would reappear with 'depressing frequency . . . often several times' (Niner, 1989, p. 42).

The social services managers who were interviewed understood 'prevention' as meaning the duty to prevent reception into care under children's legislation. Lack of adequate housing is a recurring factor in the background of families who are referred to social services departments, as recent research has shown (for example, Packman *et al.*, 1986; Bebbington and Miles, 1989; Gibbons, 1990). 'Unsatisfactory home conditions' continued to be cited as a major reason for care admissions during the 1980s, although homelessness was recorded less frequently as the only reason in the course of the decade (*House of Commons Debates*, 5 May 1987, written answers col. 366; changes in reasons for admission to care are discussed in Timaeus, 1990). In support of management and good practice, a consortium of organizations lobbied for an amendment to the Children Bill which would have prevented social services departments from taking children into care solely because of the homelessness of the parents. The amendment failed, but the consortium believed that 'the relationship between homelessness and admission to local authority care *is a child care law and practice issue*, not only a feature of housing policy' (emphasis in original), hence making explicit the multiple policy contexts of family homelessness.[1]

The respective strengths of the social services' preventive duty and housing responsibilities towards homeless families were tested in two judicial reviews which went to the court of appeal, both involving decisions of 'intentional' homelessness (Wandsworth, *Times Law Review*, 5 February 1981; Tower Hamlets, *Times Law Review*, 28 April 1988). Investigation of 'intentionality' is discretionary but a family which is considered to have contrived homelessness deliberately or by default, loses any right to be housed and even to remain in temporary accommodation. Formal social services involvement in preventing 'intentional' homelessness, which was envisaged by the *Codes of Guidance* (particularly SDD, 1980, para. 2.15), has not happened to any great extent. This is partly because most housing authorities apparently use their power to investigate 'intentionality' as a threat to deter applicants rather than a routine procedure, so relatively few families are formally affected (Evans and Duncan, 1988, ch. 3). But it is also because specialist teams avoid involvement. One of the specialist social work teams which

[1] *Briefing on Amendment 7 to Clause 17 of the Children Bill.* On these points we are indebted to Jane Tunstill, social policy adviser of the National Council of Voluntary Child Care Organizations, which with BASW and Family Rights Group formed the lobby consortium.

we interviewed had been established primarily to deal with 'intentionally' homeless families, but it soon reached a working agreement whereby the housing department's Homeless Persons Unit (HPU) changed their practice and the team was able to concentrate on working with families living in temporary accommodation. In an inner London borough which was planning to appoint a specialist social work team, the housing liaison adviser (a principal officer in social services) had already rejected the suggestion of helping the HPU with the consequences of their 'intentional' homelessness decisions, which she regarded as a self-inflicted problem.

Families who are judged to be 'intentionally' homeless have few options left. One senior social worker said: 'When this happens, the family need a great deal of fortitude and social work support because they have to be able to withstand the stress of living in overcrowded conditions with relatives or the difficult conditions of a commercial hotel, indefinitely. It is the policy of the team to maintain support to these families until permanent accommodation has been secured, but the circumstances keep the social worker on tenterhooks for long periods of time.' Tyra Henry's mother was regarded as 'intentionally' homeless after 'abandoning' a tenancy and moving into her own mother's crowded flat, with social work approval. The housing department's refusal to rehouse the extended family together was identified by the inquiry panel as an important factor leading to renewed contact with the child's violent father and her subsequent death (Sedley, 1987).

Social workers and housing workers follow different interpretations of 'prevention' informed by their statutory responsibilities and practice aims. Social workers' idea of prevention would mean trying to get families accepted as statutorily homeless so that they remained safely together and did not become literally roofless. Housing officers, on the other hand, tended to see prevention in terms of minimizing the number of successful applications. This can amount to denial and using all manner of delaying tactics in the hope that applicants will 'disappear', as the CURS researchers reported (Niner, 1989, pp. 27, 37, 41).

Temporary Accommodation

Although the *Code of Guidance* (D.o.E. *et al.*, 1991, para. 13.4) makes only incidental reference to social workers' involvement with families living in temporary accommodation, that is how all of the specialist social workers whom we interviewed spent most of their time. Professional concern and research effort have been concentrated on the difficulties faced by families living in bed and breakfast accommodation, but the alternatives may be little better (for example, Bayswater Hotel Homelessness Project, 1987; Murie and Jeffers, 1987; Niner, 1989, ch. 3; Miller, 1990; and Storie, 1990, for a literature review). Bed and breakfast is reported to be the least popular type of temporary accommodation. On the other hand, both social workers and homelessness officers said that some families were reluctant to move because at least the rent and fuel bills were paid for them in hotels, whereas mounting debt was a likelihood after rehousing; friendships and communal support would be lost; the permanent tenancies on offer were in even worse condition or in 'bad' areas where lone mothers were afraid to take their children.

The main areas of difficulty for families in temporary accommodation have been identified as, first, access to mainstream services, particularly education, health services, and social security benefits; and secondly, personal health and safety. Educationists are concerned about children's interrupted or non-existent schooling and poor performance (ILEA, 1987*a,b*; HMI, 1990). Health concerns have centered on: the poor diet of children living in bed and breakfast accommodation with inadequate cooking facilities; increased risk of infection in such crowded conditions; and difficulty in registering with GPs or being contacted by a health visitor (Conway, 1988; Health Visitors Association (HVA) and BMA, 1988; Association of Community Health Councils for England and Wales (ACHCEW), 1989). Clients, homeless or not, complain to social workers about social security. Benefit delay commonly follows a change of address so homeless people are affected more than others (MORI, 1990, p. 15; Stewart and Stewart, 1991, ch. 3). Worries concerning personal safety were important to families, including the dangers of confining young children to crowded and badly maintained buildings where there was unprotected electrical equipment; and an undercurrent of sexual and racial harassment, sometimes inflicted by hotel staff or other residents.

A specialist team's internal report described the scope and purpose of what they did: 'The families tend to see their needs mainly in practical terms—housing, moving, money, and furniture. Their overwhelming need is for reassurance about their housing position—will they be given permanent housing, how long will they have to wait, where will it be? The social work team feels strongly that these issues should be dealt with by the housing department, but the need is not recognized. . . . Therefore the social workers spend a great deal of their time in temporary accommodation containing families' anxieties.' And one team leader explained: 'The reason I would say that we as social workers need to be involved is largely from the advocacy point of view. So many of them feel so dependent on the state systems whether it's for money or for housing, and just feel that they can't fight for that on their own. . . . It doesn't necessarily have to be social workers, but I mean it is one of the social work functions.'

Our teams had tried different ways of contacting families. Being notified of new arrivals by the HPU or by hostel/hotel managers was considered unsatisfactory for two reasons: it was unreliable and would be intrusive. Holding 'surgeries' at advertised times left the initiative with families, and meant non-statutory homeless families could also call. Management co-operation was rarely a problem because the availability of advice took pressure off their own staff and as a London boroughs working party commented: 'lack of information increases tension between homeless families and their Councils and is a source of considerable irritation' (ALA/LBA committee papers, 18 March 1987).

The use of information leaflets reduced bombardment but relied heavily on housing workers to give them out. Social workers were then able to concentrate on queries which required their negotiating skills: 'Complaints over the condition of the hotel itself are the most difficult to negotiate as it is more likely to bring workers into conflict with the hotel management.' While requests for transfer to better temporary accommodation were not welcomed by HPUs, social workers seemed to be able to achieve such transfers (Thomas and Niner, 1989, p. 16).

Some teams reacted to the dearth of facilities for families in temporary accommodation by setting up new ones. Day care and play space were priorities in a situation where, as one senior social worker pointed out, there were more under fives than in all of that authority's children's homes combined. The team in a northern city had managed to get EEC funding for adult literacy classes, because 'We have found that many of the parents lack basic education which limits their ability to sort out their own difficulties and frustrates their efforts to manage independently when they are rehoused.'

Although it is encouraging to note the support of drop-in centres for families living in temporary accommodation in the *Children Act 1989 Guidance and Regulations,* nothing new is being suggested (Department of Health (D.o.H.) 1991 Vol. 2, para. 3.16). A case could be made for providing family centres linked to temporary accommodation by defining the children of homeless families as 'in need' under S.17 of the Act, because their 'health or development is likely to be significantly impaired' (following the guidance, ibid. paras. 3.18–3.24; the options are discussed in a briefing paper from the London Homelessness Forum, 1990). But social services departments would have to impose this obligation on themselves, without the support of guidance from above and without extra funding. Nor can one look to the National Health Service and Community Care Act 1990. Homeless families are just the wrong client group. Only 'women suffering domestic violence' could be included in the community care plans which ought to identify services and arrange for 'intermittent . . . social care needs', presumably in a women's refuge (D.o.H., 1990, para. 2.25).

Counselling about relationships and child care difficulties was valued by many families and the need for it was stressed by interviewees: 'Once a housing department gets its hands on a family and puts it into temporary accommodation, that family is immediately put into a system which is essentially disruptive to family life. So if you've got a functioning family who does just need a roof over its head and they spend six months in the system and come out of that system at the end of it as a non-functioning non-viable family unit, to use jargon—possibly the presence of a specialist social work team like ours gets rid of some of the problem because of our specialism and the continuity. Many of the families are just constantly having to move around and area teams can't cope with that.'

Reactive counselling and support can shade into more pro-active child protection, described by an interviewee as 'the task of "social policing" which families do not request and may prove suspicious and openly hostile'. It is clear from their Code of Practice that London directors were worried about the possibility of a child abuse death in temporary accommodation (ADSS, 1985). An area team in an inner London borough warned: 'The stresses felt by well housed families that we work with are compounded by homelessness or impermanence and there is great concern for the integrity of these more vulnerable family groups. There is a higher risk of child abuse and the recognition and identification of abusing factors is an acutely felt responsibility' (internal agency report, 1986).

That area team had increasing numbers of children from homeless families on its 'at risk' register; but one year later another team covering the bed and breakfast district in a near-by borough made what it considered to be a positive decision not to register the children of homeless families unless there were compelling individual reasons. An interviewee from a northern city explained a similar decision which had been taken at a political level: 'We don't put families under surveillance on the outer estates where they're living in awful conditions, so why should we do it when they're homeless? The pressures are not necessarily any worse.'

So far, there has been no child abuse fatality resulting in an inquiry report, while a family was actually living in temporary accommodation. In reviewing nineteen inquiries into child abuse, Noyes (1991, p. 109) comments on the lack of analysis of the families' social contexts and the possibility of housing deprivation being a relevant issue, although he does not mention homelessness. Yet at least six deaths in the mid/late 1980s have been the children of formerly homeless families. In addition to the issues surrounding Tyra Henry, Stephanie Fox's parents were placed in a residential family centre before being housed under homelessness procedures in a high-rise flat as their first home. The mothers of Sukina Hammond and Liam Johnson took refuge in temporary accommodation from their partner's violence but returned because there seemed to be no alternative. The mothers of Kimberley Carlile and Doreen Mason met and moved in with violent partners while they were homeless (Blom Cooper, 1987; Sedley, 1987; Avon Social Services Department, 1989; Islington Social Services Department, 1989; Southwark Area Review Committee, 1989; Wandsworth Area Child Protection Committee, 1990).

While there appears to be more professional anxiety than actual risk of serious abuse in temporary accommodation, it is also clear that homeless mothers and their children are especially vulnerable to violent men. The absence of men and the likelihood of being overheard in converted buildings which have thin partition walls where residents are crowded together with other lone mothers are probably the main reasons for the relative lack of violence in these hotels. Commenting that 'The incidence of child abuse occurring while families are in temporary accommodation is negligible, despite the stress which the parents are under', a team leader explained: 'A more common problem is child neglect. The hotel staff, health visitor and other residents are concerned about parents who do not feed their children, leave them in wet and soiled clothes, do not supervise them adequately and leave them alone for hours.' The Department of Health's *Protecting Children* offers no guidance for social workers on how to assess 'reasonable parenting' in the highly abnormal environment of a bed and breakfast hotel. While recognizing the strains associated with 'poor housing'—homelessness is not mentioned— the guide warns: 'Nevertheless, parents have a responsibility to provide adequate shelter, clothing, warmth and food for their children' (D.o.H., 1988, p. 63).

The range of work which has been described monopolized social workers' attention as the 1980s wore on. As one senior social worker said: 'The social work team were bogged down in temporary accommodation—prevention of homelessness and resettlement had to be abandoned.' The records kept by that team showed their services were used by 75 per cent of families who passed through the hostels or hotel in the city, many more than in authorities without a specialist team (exact comparison is not possible with Randall *et al.*, 1982, pp. 26–7, and Thomas and Niner, 1989, p. 75).

INTER-AGENCY RELATIONS

Inter-agency relations are complicated by managers and policy makers responding to different agendas of 'need' and statutory obligations. Even in the same tier of local government this may be a site of discord. Social workers and HPU officers can simultaneously share common concerns and experience dislike for each other's practices. Hence conflicting expectations and stereotyped attitudes between housing officer and social workers are perhaps at their most marked over homelessness. These were exemplified, from the housing side, in their professional association's evidence to the Barclay Committee wherein social workers were characterized as: 'young and freshly qualified, . . . who will be entirely subjective and idealistic about clients and will seek all manner of handouts and special treatment for them, without ever expecting them to stand on their own feet. By contrast, the housing officer might see himself as objective and fair in ordering priorities . . . employ(ing) . . . techniques of management which he believes will develop independence and self-respect for the common good' (Institute of Housing, 1982; Fox, 1978, discusses these stereotypes).

These views were still in evidence in most of the housing departments in which we interviewed (in this our findings reflect those of the CURS case studies; Niner, 1989, p. 100), yet writing as chief examiner for the Institute, Spicker (1989, p. 23) maintained that such attitudes were outmoded. Any professional posturing tended to be concentrated among middle managers in both departments, while often a degree of solidarity was expressed between practitioner grade staff. One team leader explained the inter-agency conflict and practitioner camaraderie thus: 'We subscribe to the social services ethos. We don't have the same sort of values and rules . . . [Housing] have. . . . If we came under the auspices of the Housing Department, we would lose that alternative perspective. So when we argue with Aid Centre workers, not only do we argue in relation to the law . . . but we're able to demonstrate that there is a need to re-examine the decision that they've made and we have quite a large degree of success and an immense amount of conflict and argument . . . I think you have to learn how to deal with this conflict. I mean we do have disputes and arguments and sometimes I find myself having to go above the head of [a HPU officer]. Somebody went above my head only yesterday, but I don't hold it against them and we were talking today and it doesn't matter; it doesn't create a rift between us.'

This sympathy between two groups who were commonly opposed in negotiating positions, can be explained in terms of what Pawson (1987, pp. 39–41) has described as the cultural isolation of those working with homeless people. Association with a stigmatized client group encourages separation from the professional mainstream and alignment with others who are perceived to be doing similar work. Thus a team leader in London referred to a form of 'guerrilla social work' whereby workers in different boroughs helped each other out: 'we operate a kind of knock for knock consultation with other people around London'.

Communication between specialist social work teams and their HPUs was generally adequate for working purposes, although routine liaison meetings were gradually abandoned as work pressure increased. There was an exception in one authority where the existence of the social work team was barely tolerated by the HPU senior and some local politicians. That team changed its name to Central Family Support Team, which enabled it to survive. In the early 1980s certain other specialist social work teams were renamed to avoid mention of homelessness, until in the mid-decade publicity about bed and breakfast hotels made social work with homeless families politically acceptable again.

Discord at practitioner level centred on different ways of working. The methods used by social workers were negotiation, particularly with the HPU, and advocacy directed at getting clients accepted as homeless. Families often approached social work agencies themselves for this form of help. From the evidence available, between a quarter and a third of households accepted as homeless have had contact with a social worker before or at the time of leaving their last accommodation; they are most likely to be lone parents or pregnant single women. In addition, research has shown that up to three-quarters of women in refuges have contacted a social worker by the time of their last violent attack (Randall *et al.*, 1982, p. 26; Smith, 1989, p. 75; Thomas and Niner, 1989, p. 75).

In view of their opposing role, it is therefore not surprising when social workers are described by housing researchers as being a problem for housing officials, making unwelcome referrals and allegedly taking insufficient account of the pressures on HPU staff. The Audit Commission (1989, para. 84) reported that housing departments believed social services did not understand their difficulties. Typically these issues and tensions do not apply to our specialist teams, but to duty social work in area teams, or when crises arise in work with allocated child care cases.

To address the problem, the Audit Commission (1989, pp. 32, 52) called for improved liaison procedures between housing and social services departments and the Code of Guidance has emphasized this as 'vital' (D.o.E. et al., 1991, para. 15.5). Specialist homeless families social work teams and their housing counterparts have necessarily developed collaborative arrangements (as argued by senior social worker Owens (1988)). But co-operation with housing departments is not a priority for social services management. Curiously, given the evidence we have presented, social services receive no encouragement to liaise with housing over child protection (DHSS and Welsh Office, 1988). Housing departments tend to work independently of other services, seeking 'co-operation' only when they want something done. Social workers giving evidence to the Tyra Henry inquiry regarded their housing department 'like the weather', unpredictable and impervious to influence (Sedley, 1987, pp. 45). The former Central Policy Review Staff's observation still holds true: housing has priority and other local authority departments are expected to adapt (Central Policy Review Staff (CPRS), 1978, para. 28.1).

Our research suggests that agency setting is important in providing a balance between geographic propinquity and discrete sets of aims, structures, and practices. Sharing office premises was useful when the territory was neutral and independent of either department; for example, within a joint neighbourhood team of social workers and housing officers being administered by the chief executive's department. Seconding or outposting of social workers into the housing department's HPU was generally not effective although it is the Audit Commission's recommended solution (1989, para. 85; and the Association of District Councils, 1987). It tended to lead to either conflict and isolation or, more commonly, incorporation into the attitudes and working practices of the dominant host agency. The most reliable prospect for successful collaboration combined separate agency location, with negotiated liaison procedures, and a clear professional identity for both groups. That entailed specialist homeless families teams retaining a generic social work role, with responsibility for any child care or mental health statutory work.

Besides those inter-agency relations mentioned, there is an inter-authority dimension in conurbations where homeless families are commonly placed far from their local neighbourhood. Two-fifths of all authorities, including nearly three-quarters of London boroughs, regularly use temporary accommodation outside their own boundaries. Disruption to family life and difficulties for local services are both amplified in this situation.

CONCLUSIONS

The development of social work with homeless families during the 1980s showed practitioners and their managers trying to reconcile policy makers' expectations about what social workers should do, with the continuing needs of clients whose circumstances saw little or no improvement. Social work in this particularly pressured area is beset by a lingering stigma attached to the client group, and stereotyped interprofessional attitudes.

Academic analysis has also been coloured by differences in perception between housing problems and social need (for example, Niner, 1989, p.100). The housing researchers who have studied homelessness display ambivalent attitudes towards social work. Some add it to the list of services which are not available. Thus while recognizing that some of the families whom they interviewed had 'found real support from social workers,' the SAUS researchers concluded that 'in general services are not geared to their needs and there is remarkable inflexibility and lack of response' (Murie and Jeffers, 1987, pp. 149–50; also Murie, 1988). Others appear to doubt the value of what they understand by social work. The CURS researchers commented, in the context of social workers visiting temporary accommodation, that 'there is a difficult balance to be struck between providing contact and support, and appearing to imply that the family is inadequate in some way' (Niner, 1989, pp. 57–8). Less perceptively, the PSI researchers rejected any implication that homeless families had 'individual problems. . . . What these families need is not social workers or welfare workers going into the hotel rooms, but families being offered ways of getting out of them' (Bonnerjea and Lawton, 1987, pp. 57–8).

Such stereotypes of what constitutes social work, derived from a housing need and policy perspective, are not simply refuted by our interviewees, they are not to be found in their practice. Social welfare is also a policy context for homelessness because it engenders disruptions in relationships; lowers self-esteem and ability to cope; limits access to welfare services. In such circumstances social services departments have specific duties and powers concerning child care and protection. The reality is that we have legislation which gives rights to homeless people to be re-housed, in certain circumstances, but it puts them through a long and painful process. If a family did not have to go through that statutory process, perhaps it would not have to face the extra potential for destabilizing it, but it would also probably not enjoy valuable rights to re-housing. As homelessness has become institutionalized into a chronic British housing problem, social workers have to operate within the ambiguities and constraints of conflicting housing and welfare policies to discharge their statutory duties according to good practice. One accommodation has been specialist work.

Social work with homeless families is a specialism which survived genericism in the

1970s and managerialism in the 1980s. In the nineties, the practice of social work will be regulated by wide-ranging new legislation, but family homelessness is not mentioned in either the 1989 Children Act nor the NHS and Community Care Act 1990, nor in the voluminous guidance which accompanies both measures. Along with poverty, it forms a pattern on the wallpaper behind child protection work which is not officially discussed.

ACKNOWLEDGEMENTS

The authors express their gratitude to Dr Moira Peelo of Lancaster University Department of Applied Social Science and Graeme Brown of The Children's Society. Financial support from Lancaster University's Research Grants Committee is gratefully acknowledged.

REFERENCES

Association of Community Health Councils for England and Wales (1989) *Homelessness: the Effects on Health*, London, ACHCEW.

Association of Directors of Social Services, London branch (1985) *Social Services Support: A Code of Practice in the Use of Hotel/Hostel Accommodation for the Placement of Homeless Families*, London, Association of London Authorities.

Association of District Councils (1987) *Homelessness—Meeting the Tide, Initiatives in District Councils*, London, ADC.

Association of Metropolitan Authorities (1990) *Homelessness, Programme for Action*, London, AMA.

Audit Commission (1989) *Housing the Homeless: the Local Authority Role*, London HMSO.

Avon Social Services Department (1989) *Management Review of the Case of Sukina Hammond*, Bristol, Avon SSD.

Bailey, R. (1980) 'Social workers: pawns, police or agitators?', in Brake, M. and Bailey R. (eds.) *Radical Social Work and Practice*, London, Edward Arnold, pp. 215–27.

Bayswater Hotel Homelessness Project (1987) *Speaking For Ourselves: Families in Bayswater B&B*, London, Bayswater Hotel Homelessness Project.

Bebbington, A. and Miles, J. (1989) 'The background of children who enter local authority care', *British Journal of Social Work*, **19**(5), pp. 349–68.

Blom Cooper, L. (chair) (1987) *A Child in Mind: Protection of Children in a Responsible Society*, London, Greenwich Social Services Department.

Bonnerjea, L. and Lawton, J. (1987) *Homelessness in Brent*, London, Policy Studies Institute.

British Association of Social Workers (1986) *Housing—Its Effects on Child Care Policies and Practice*, Birmingham, BASW.

Central Council for Education and Training in Social Work (1989) *Welfare Rights in Social Work Education: Report by a Curriculum Development Group*, Paper 28.1, London, CCETSW.

Central Policy Review Staff (1978) *Housing and Social Policies: Some Interactions,* London, HMSO.

Conway, J. (ed.) (1988) *Prescription for Poor Health: The Crisis for Homeless Families,* London, Food Commission.

Cooper, D. M. (1980) 'Managing social workers', in Glastonbury, B. (ed.) *Social Work in Conflict: the Practitioner and the Bureaucrat,* London, Croom Helm.

Coventry Workshop (1982) 'The temporary tenants' campaign', in Craig, G., Derricourt, N. and Loney, M. (eds.) *Community Work and the State,* London, Routledge and Kegan Paul, pp. 107–14.

Crane, H. (1990) *Speaking From Experience: Working with Homeless Families,* London, Bayswater Hotel Homelessness Project.

Department of the Environment (1987) *Housing: the Government's Proposals* (Cm. 214), London, HMSO.

Department of the Environment, Department of Health and Social Security, and Welsh Office (1974) *Homelessness,* circular 18/74, London, HMSO.

Department of the Environment, Department of Health and Social Security, and Welsh Office (1983) *Housing (Homeless Persons) Act 1977 Code of Guidance (England and Wales),* 2nd edn., London, HMSO.

Department of the Environment, Department of Health and Welsh Office (1991) *Homeless Code of Guidance for Local Authorities,* 3rd edn., London, HMSO.

Department of Health (1988) *Protecting Children: A Guide For Social Workers Undertaking a Comprehensive Assessment,* London, HMSO.

Department of Health (1990) *Community Care in the Next Decade and Beyond,* London, HMSO.

Department of Health (1991), *The Children Act 1989, Guidance and Regulations, Volume 2: Family Support, Day Care and Educational Provision for Young Children,* London, HMSO.

Department of Health and Social Security (1985) *Review of Child Care Law,* London, HMSO.

Department of Health and Social Security and Welsh Office (1988) *Working Together: A Guide to Arrangements for Inter-Agency Co-operation for the Protection of Children From Abuse,* London, HMSO.

Evans, A. and Duncan, S. (1988) *Responding to Homelessness: Local Authority Policy and Practice,* London, HMSO.

Fox, D. (1978) 'The conflict between housing and social work', *Housing,* **14**(4), pp. 10–12.

Gibbons, J. (1990) *Family Support and Prevention: Studies in Local Areas,* London, HMSO.

Harvey, A. (1969) 'Homeless? You can't come here', *New Society,* 27 February, pp. 323–4.

Health Visitors' Association and BMA General Medical Services Committee (1988) *Homeless Families and Their Health,* London, British Medical Association.

Her Majesty's Inspectorate (1990) *A Survey of the Education of Children Living in Temporary Accommodation, April–December 1989,* Middlesex, Department of Education.

Howarth, V. (1987) *A Survey of Families in Bed and Breakfast Hotels*, London, Thomas Coram Foundation.

Hudson, B. (1986) 'In pursuit of coordination: housing and the personal social services', *Local Government Studies*, March/April, pp. 53–66.

Hudson, B. (1987) 'Collaboration in social welfare: a framework for analysis', *Policy and Politics*, 15(3), pp. 175–82.

Inner London Education Authority (1987a) *Homeless Families—Report to the Director of Education, Schools*, London, ILEA.

Inner London Education Authority (1987b) *Homeless Families: Implications for the Education Welfare Service*, London, ILEA.

Institute of Housing (1982) *Evidence to the National Institute of Social Work on the Role and Tasks of Social Workers*, mimeo, London, Institute of Housing.

Islington Social Services Department (1989) *Liam Johnson Review: Report of Panel of Inquiry*, London, London Borough of Islington.

Kent County Council, Officer Working Group (1981) *The Operation of the Housing (Homeless Persons) Act 1977 in Kent*, Maidstone, Kent Social Services Department.

London Boroughs Association (1989) *Giving Hope to London's Homeless—The Way Forward*, London, LBA.

London Homelessness Forum (1990) *The Children Act and Homeless Families—Some Implications*, London, The Children's Society.

May, J. S. and Whitbread, A. W. (1975) 'The downward spiral: a study of homeless families in Warwickshire', *Bulletin of the Clearing House for Local Authority Services Research*, 5, pp. 3–64.

Means, R. (1977) *Social Work and the 'Undeserving' Poor*, Birmingham, University of Birmingham, Centre for Urban and Regional Studies.

Miller, M. (1990) *Bed and Breakfast: Women and Homelessness Today*, London, Women's Press.

Ministry of Housing and Local Government and Ministry of Health (1959) *Homeless Families*, circular 17/59, London, HMSO.

Minns, R. (1972) 'Homeless families and some organisational determinants of deviancy', *Policy and Politics*, 1(1), pp. 1–21.

Moody, E. M. (1968) 'Working with the homeless', *Case Conference*, December, pp. 318–25.

MORI (1990) *Income Support: A Survey of Low Income Families*, London, National Audit Office.

Murie, A. (1988) 'Housing, homelessness and social work', in Becker, S. and MacPherson, S. (eds.) *Public Issues, Private Pain*, London, Social Services Insight.

Murie, A. and Jeffers, S. (eds.) (1987) *Living in Bed and Breakfast: The Experience of Homelessness in London*, Bristol, SAUS.

National Audit Office (1990) *Homelessness*, HCP 622, session 1989–90, London, HMSO.

Niner, P. (1989) *Homelessness in Nine Local Authorities: Case Studies of Policy and Practice*, London, HMSO.

Noyes, P. (1991) *Child Abuse: A Study of Inquiry Reports 1980–1989*, London, HMSO.

Owens, J. (1988) 'Housing and social work, pulling together', *Housing,* **24**(2), pp. 20–1.

Packman, J., Randall, J. and Jacques, N. (1986) *Who Needs Care? Social Work Decisions About Children,* Oxford, Blackwell.

Pawson, H. (1987) *Working With Homelessness: a Study of Organisational Issues in the Implementation of the Housing (Homeless Persons) Act by Inner London Authorities,* London, London Research Centre.

Randall, G., Francis, D. and Brougham, C. (1982) *A Place For the Family: Homeless Families in London,* London, SHAC.

Rose, H. (1971) *Rights, Participation and Conflict,* Poverty Pamphlet 5, London, Child Poverty Action Group.

Satyamurti, C. (1981) *Occupational Survival,* Oxford, Blackwell.

Scottish Development Department (1980) *Housing (Homeless Persons) Act 1977, Code of Guidance—Scotland,* Edinburgh, Scottish Development Department.

Sedley, S. (chair) (1987) *Whose Child! Report of the Public Inquiry Into the Death of Tyra Henry,* London, London Borough of Lambeth.

Seebohm, F. (chair) (1968) *Report of the Committee on Local Authority and Allied Personal Social Services* (Cmnd. 3703), London, HMSO.

Smith, L. J. F. (1989) *Domestic Violence: An Overview of the Literature,* Home Office Research Study 107, London, HMSO.

Social Services Inspectorate (Department of Health) London Region (1989) *Report of a Study Day on Family Homelessness, 1987,* London, Department of Health.

Southwark Area Review Committee (1989) *The Doreen Aston Report,* London, Lewisham Social Services Department.

Spicker, P. (1989) *Social Housing and the Social Services,* Harlow, Longman.

Stevenson, O. and Parsloe, P. (1978) *Social Service Teams: The Practitioner's View,* London, HMSO.

Stewart, G. and Stewart, J. (1978) 'The Housing (Homeless Persons) Act, 1977: a reassessment of social need', in Brown, M. and Baldwin, S. (eds.) *The Year Book of Social Policy in Britain 1977,* London, Routledge and Kegan Paul, pp. 22–48.

Stewart, G. and Stewart, J. (1981) 'Views of the homeless', *Social Work Today,* **13**(3), pp. 10–11.

Stewart, G. and Stewart, J. (1983) 'Collaboration over homelessness: challenging a consensus model of welfare services', in British Association of Social Workers, *Collaboration in Caring: Issues and Examples,* Birmingham, BASW, pp. 43–51.

Stewart, G. and Stewart, J. (1991) *Relieving Poverty? Use of the Social Fund by Social Work Clients and Other Agencies,* London, Association of Metropolitan Authorities.

Stewart, G. and Stewart, J. (1992, forthcoming) *Social Work and Housing,* Basinstoke, Macmillan.

Stewart, J. and Stewart, G. (eds.) (1982) *Social Work and Homelessness,* Lancaster, Lancaster University, Department of Social Administration.

Storie, J. (1990) *Bed, Breakfast and Social Work,* Social Work Monograph 86, Norwich, University of East Anglia.

Thomas, A. and Niner, P. (1989) *Living in Temporary Accommodation: A Survey of Homeless People,* London, HMSO.

Thomas, D. (1975) 'Chaucer House Tenants' Association: a case study', in Leonard, P. (ed.) *The Sociology of Community Action*, Keele, University of Keele, pp. 185–203.

Timaeus, I. (1990) 'The fall in the number of children in care: a demographic analysis', *Journal of Social Policy*, **19**(3), pp. 375–96.

Wandsworth Area Child Protection Committee (1990) *The Report of the Stephanie Fox Practice Review*, London, Wandsworth Social Services Department.

PART VIII

PUBLIC DISASTERS

This last section, "Public Disasters," is yet another new one. Although it only contains three articles it is important in that it draws attention to a critical new role that social workers are being called upon to play in many parts of the world.

Social workers have long been involved in assisting with the psychosocial sequellae of large public disasters. But this has usually been only on an emergency basis. That is, this function was not an expected one for the profession. Indeed, at one time there were serious questions raised as to whether social workers had a useful role in these situations. A cynical story in *The New Yorker* of many years ago described the imagined roles of various professions in a public emergency. All of the human service professionals were described as being busy carrying out their specific roles, except for the social workers, who were huddled in a corner planning to set up a committee to discuss what was to be done.

Several theoretical developments, to which social work has made important contributions, have emerged in recent years. These have led to an enriched understanding of how to assist persons who are in, or have recently experienced, this type of situation. These developments began with crisis theory and its expansion into the broader areas of "critical incident stress" and "post-traumatic stress," two areas in which social workers have played an important developmental role. These theories, which emerged from practice, have given a conceptual framework within which to understand, and thus to effectively address, the psychosocial upsets that are universally found in these situations. A particularly important component of our expanded knowledge of these high-stress situations is the awareness that unless their impact is dealt with immediately, there are frequently long-term and often misunderstood aftereffects that can greatly impede the return to the pre-event level of functioning.

This highly specific role of social workers in disasters has been quickly institutionalized in many areas. More and more it is taken for granted that practitioners will be available to move in quickly when a critical incident takes place that involves large numbers of people and high levels of danger, fear, anxiety, and stress.

Just as crisis theory emerged from the experience of practitioners in many disciplines in similar situations, so has this expanded understanding of the effects of critical incidents emerged from practice experience. Much of crisis theory emerged from efforts to understand the terrible impact of combat situations during times of war. Building on this knowledge our colleagues in military social work in the United States, England, and Canada have made major contributions to the development of a broader concept of critical incident stress reactions. However, this knowledge has not yet fully found its way into the general lexicon of practice.

We know that the very high-stress situations of military life have their direct counterparts in civilian life. It is useful to underscore the extent to which it is now common to see journalistic reports of the role that social workers play in such events as earthquakes, fires, plane crashes, schoolyard shootings, and in the immediate aftermath of suicides and violent deaths in close-knit social systems. This societal recognition of the important role of social work is a recent phenomenon. Of perhaps more importance is the fact that the crisis or disaster role of social workers is now reported matter of factly as a part of the disaster.

This critical role for the profession underscores two important structural challenges. The first is an educative one. As this ability to help in disasters becomes more and more expected of the profession, social workers should receive very pragmatic training in this role. With the very excellent training modules that have been developed by various groups, this should not present problems for faculties of social work.

The second challenge involves service delivery. Practice indicates that it is critical to effective intervention in these situations that help be available immediately. This is just as important as the availability of help immediately following the event. Of course, this requires both an ability and a willingness to move quickly to provide help wherever it is needed. Again, this is not what many agencies that function on a nine-to-five basis by appointment are accustomed to. However, in a very short time tremendous progress has been made. Increasingly, agencies and networks of agencies have embraced this role and developed disaster plans to insure readiness. More of this preparedness is needed, but it is happening. What is also needed are more contributions to the literature on the knowledge acquired both in the development of such plans and their utilization.

From a theoretical perspective, an important understanding of this component of practice emerges from a public health perspective. This perspective reminds us that in these situations we are for the most part dealing with healthy citizens in situations very much out of the ordinary. This has led to an understanding that, in addition to thinking of the immediate needs of those under stress, we need also to think about the needs of the helpers. Because of the nature of their experiences, or the nature of the work demanded of them, these people themselves experience levels of stress that have an impact. Thus, the terms "rescuing the rescuers" or "helping the helpers" have been useful in insuring that everyone involved in these situations has an opportunity to come to terms with their experiences. In a more philosophical vein, it has been an important recognition that, thankfully, our professional training does not remove our humanity and that we too can quickly find ourselves in a position of needing the knowledge and compassion of our colleagues.

An important spinoff of these developments is the understanding that these same impacts occur in situations where only an individual is involved. The same understanding is needed of the impact of private disasters on the helpee and the helper. Related to this is the need to take into account the political histories of our clients. As our cities become more and more multicultural we are finding among our clients many who have undergone horrible experiences of torture and suffering, events of which we may not be aware. Unless we understand these experiences we may miss essential areas where we can be critically helpful.

As this role becomes more and more incorporated into the armamentarium of the profession, contributions to the literature will expand, contributions that will help increase our growing knowledge in this field and thus enhance our skills in differential diagnosis and treatment in social work.

CHAPTER 120

THE MEXICO CITY EARTHQUAKE DISASTER

Corinne L. Dufka

O n the morning of September 19, 1985, the eighteen million inhabitants of Mexico City were struck by a devastating earthquake that measured 8.1 on the Richter scale. For longer than four minutes the city's inhabitants, one fourth of the nation's population, listened to the earth rumble, electric lines pop, glass shatter, and people scream. Thirty-six hours later another earthquake of almost equal magnitude struck and shook the city for longer than a minute. When the dust finally cleared, an estimated 20,000 were dead and 500,000 homeless.[1]

The city came to a screeching halt. Many of the city's and nation's social institutions were disrupted.[2] Those who lost their homes fled to the streets where they built shelters out of cardboard, wood, plastic, and aluminum. Families fled from the dwellings that they had inhabited for generations; many families were separated. According to the secretary of labor, approximately 100,000 people lost their jobs due to damage at work sites.[3] One study of 3,200 families—*damnificados*—who lost their homes in the earthquake reported that the majority of these families were headed by single women with small children, were near or below the poverty level, and worked out of their home (for example, preparing food to be sold on the street).[4] Damage to 761 schools, affecting more than 650,000 students, led many experts to speculate that one year of instruction would be lost.[5] Faced with unemployment, hundreds of people left the city in search of work, further fragmenting families and communities.

The author provided mental health services in an emergency clinic in one of the poorest and hardest-hit areas of Mexico City. The community was composed of working-class people, many of whom were near or below the poverty level. Prior to the

---

Reprinted from *Social Casework,* Vol. 31, No. 3 (1988), pp. 162–170, by permission of the publisher, Families International, Inc.

[1] George Russell, "Trouble after an Earlier Disaster," *Time Magazine,* 25 November 1985, p. 58.

[2] In 1985 the urban unemployment rate was 12 percent; 30 percent of Mexico City's families (average five people per family) resided in a single room. In 1984 the inflation rate was 60 percent. See Ed Magnuson, "A Noise Like Thunder," *Time Magazine,* 30 September 1985, pp. 34–43.

[3] *Uno Mas Uno,* 19 October 1985.

[4] *Uno Mas Uno,* 12 October 1985.

[5] *Ibid.*

earthquake, this community was seriously underserved medically and experienced many psychosocial stresses: alcoholism, family violence, depression, and so forth. During the first two weeks of operation the clinic provided emergency first aid and distributed needed supplies; after that time the medical staff treated non–disaster-related conditions. The clinic treated between 175 and 200 individuals daily. Those who manifested significant depression, anxiety, or somatization were referred for evaluation and counseling. Although the medical staff reported that approximately 75 percent of all patients who were seen experienced at least mild to moderate anxiety and depression, only those with the most serious symptomatology, approximately 10 percent, were referred.

During the second through the fifth weeks social work intervention reached 204 individuals, couples, and families. The majority of individuals were interviewed once, but those with more serious problems, 20 percent, were seen up to four times. Analysis of the information received from the respondents sheds light on (1) distinctions in crisis-response patterns with respect to the victim's age group and (2) the impact of past losses or traumas and current psychosocial stresses on the victim's response to the earthquake. Case histories are employed both to illustrate general observations about victims in crisis and to stress the importance of treating each client individually.

INTEGRATING CRISIS-INTERVENTION THEORY

Gerald Caplan described a crisis as a time-limited period of disequilibrium that follows the introduction of an external hazard; it is characterized by the ineffectiveness of one's customary means of coping.[6] The external situation is conceptualized as the hazard, whereas the inner, subjective experience is referred to as the crisis.[7] The hallmark of a crisis is the existence of tension that, left unresolved, results in the disorganization of the personality and solidification of dysfunctional behaviors and symptoms.

The existing literature substantiates that disasters precipitate both short- and long-term mental health problems. The short-term effects, measured in days or weeks, include anxiety, confusion, shock, a sense of isolation, and lack of responsiveness. The shock caused by disaster is thought to break through one's defenses and temporarily render the individual ineffective. Such long-term effects as a generalized heightened level of anxiety, depression, psychic numbness, and impairment of certain cognitive functions have been noted several years after a disaster. In general, however, although some individuals do develop serious symptoms and experience long-term sequelae, most disaster victims recover from the initial shock, disorganization, and emotional disturbance. The short-term effects of disaster are discussed in the present article.

From the reports of clients, co-workers, and others with whom the author spoke, disaster initially resulted in both shock and goal-oriented mobilization. A nineteen-year-old woman reported that on the day of the earthquake and for several days following it, "the streets were full of people, but nobody was talking. The only things you heard were sirens and people crying. The dust was so thick and it felt so eerie. There was just nothing to say." For the first two weeks following the disaster, people gener-

---

[6] Gerald Caplan, *Principles of Preventive Psychiatry* (New York: Basic Books, 1964).
[7] Margaret C. Bonnefil and Gerald F. Jacobson, "Family Crisis Intervention," *Clinical Social Work Journal* 7 (3, 1976: 200–13.

ally reported being preoccupied with gathering information on the whereabouts of family and friends; securing food, shelter, clothing, and blankets for their family and neighbors; and taking part in the rescue operation.

By the second week, anxiety was the most prevalent response. Rosemary Creed Lukton describes this transition: "Shock and disbelief seem to usher in the cycle of reactions, and are soon followed by a period of anxiety and disorganization as various coping mechanisms are found inadequate."[8] Anxiety in combination with difficulty in eating, sleeping, or both, and a sensation of dizziness, nausea, or both were either reported by the victims themselves or observed in approximately 75 percent of the patients who received social work intervention.

The fear or anticipation of another earthquake was most often identified as the primary source of anxiety. This fear of a subsequent earthquake was exacerbated by the numerous aftershocks that were reported in the succeeding weeks. A strong gust of wind or a large truck speeding through the street would bring on a resurgence of panic. The occurrence of two major earthquakes within a thirty-six-hour period significantly increased the intensity of the trauma. Many women who reported that they were able to control their anxiety after the first earthquake reported screaming, shaking, and crying without control after the second one.

The condition of one's home was the next most commonly reported source of anxiety. Those whose homes were damaged but had not collapsed reported shaking and hyperventilating upon entering their homes as well as lying awake at night staring at the ceiling. In many cases, their concern was well-founded; many homes had large cracks in the structure and would clearly not withstand another major earthquake.

The degree of depression accompanying this anxiety was associated with age, the extent of loss suffered, and recent loss or psychosocial problems that predated the earthquake. The most significant depressive symptomatology was manifested in adults older than forty-five years. Both anxiety and depression were intensified by disturbances in sleeping and eating habits, which were reported by approximately 40 percent of the individuals who were treated. Loss of homes and shortages of food and water made it impossible for victims to sleep and eat according to their normal patterns. Increased illness resulting from exposure to the elements and impurity of the water caused additional stress.

Nausea and dizziness, often to the point of stumbling, was the most commonly experienced symptom among all age groups; approximately 60 percent of those treated voiced this complaint. These symptoms were perhaps related to the victims' extreme sensitivity to the earth's movement—a sensitivity that was magnified by the hundreds of aftershocks that occurred in the weeks following the quake.

SEVERITY OF RESPONSE

The severity of symptoms varied considerably and was associated with both the extent of trauma experienced and the existence of current psychosocial problems. This relationship was clearly illustrated in L, a twenty-eight-year-old woman who worked as a nurse in one of the hospitals that suffered tremendous damage and loss of life. Having

[8] Rosemary Creed Lukton, "Myths and Realities of Crisis Intervention," *Social Casework* 63 (May 1982): 276–85.

been in the cafeteria when the earthquake struck, L survived, whereas many of her friends perished. Immediately following the disaster, she felt torn between returning to her home and two children and staying to help the patients and medical staff. She described dissociative episodes, which were often precipitated by arguments with her alcoholic and unemployed husband. During these episodes she would begin crying and screaming uncontrollably and then lapse into ten-minute periods of withdrawal after which she could not recall what had happened. She also complained of tremulousness, intrusive thoughts with morbid content, extreme restlessness, and an inability to display affection toward her children. The preexisting tension with her husband, the stress of losing her job, the loss of her support system, and survivor's guilt exacerbated the trauma.

Although the two individuals described in the following case example demonstrated good pre-morbid functioning and limited precrisis stress, the severity of their trauma precipitated transient psychotic symptoms. Seventeen-year-old F was first seen for treatment three weeks after the earthquake. He presented with complaints of fear, depression, sleeplessness, loss of appetite, and auditory hallucinations that consisted of hearing screams and rumbling sounds upon entering or exiting his home. He was distractible, disoriented regarding time and place, and had difficulty with concentration and short-term memory. He had been living next door to a twenty-five story apartment building that he had watched collapse during the earthquake. His home suffered extreme damage. For several days following the earthquake, he worked to free persons trapped beneath the rubble, several of whom were his close friends and had died during the earthquake. He described digging through the carnage and hearing the screams of the wounded for several days after the earthquake. The auditory hallucinations he described started approximately two weeks after the earthquake. Unsure whether the screams were real, F feared he was losing his mind and needed to be assured that auditory and sensory hallucinations commonly accompany severe stress reactions.

Twenty-year-old S could not locate her aunt and uncle in the days immediately following the disaster. After repeatedly returning to the neighborhood where they lived, she reluctantly went to the large stadium where the bodies of unidentified victims were placed. After several days of walking through rows of bodies and being shown photographs of scores of other victims, she was unable to locate them. During the third week following the earthquake, she complained of crying uncontrollably, of intrusive mental pictures of dead and mutilated bodies, and of extreme agitation. She reported that she was unable to complete household and child-care tasks, that she had lost ten pounds in three weeks, and that she experienced frequent nightmares. She had a disorganized and tangential thought process. Her trauma was complicated by the loss of her aunt and uncle, who had perished in the earthquake, and of the family home.

The disaster also precipitated decreased function in individuals with a previous history of psychiatric disturbance, as noted in the following two cases. Thirty-four-year-old G had been diagnosed as a chronic paranoid schizophrenic. When the earthquake struck, she ran from her home and watched it collapse. Shortly after the earthquake she became unresponsive to human contact, only occasionally becoming tearful and inquiring about the whereabouts of her daughter, who was often at her side. Although G appeared to respond to internal stimuli, the content of her delusions was difficult to elicit. Although she had not been hospitalized for approximately six months, the disaster precipitated a psychotic episode characterized by catatonic features.

Following her divorce six years previously, forty-three-year-old M suffered from major depression and had attempted suicide. Since then she described functioning marginally, with limited social support from her children, whom she described as "siding with their father." Following the loss of her home in the disaster, she became increasingly tearful and isolated and had suicidal ideation. Both M and G were referred to an appropriate psychiatric facility following their first interview.

DIVERSITY OF RESPONSE

Anxiety, depression, dizziness, and disturbances in eating and sleeping patterns were the most prevalent symptoms in the first several weeks after the disaster. There was considerable diversity in other symptoms and presenting complaints as well as in themes and feelings that accompanied these complaints. These symptoms followed specific patterns according to age group and developmental stage.

Children

Children's responses to the earthquake were characterized primarily by nightmares, behavioral problems, emotional upset, and increased dependency needs. Fear of loss of or separation from parents was the most common theme they expressed. In the following observations, early childhood (age two to five years) is distinguished from middle childhood (age six to eleven years).

When considering a child's response to disaster, it is imperative that workers consider the family dynamics and preexisting family problems. The mother of eleven-year-old T expressed concern about her son's agitation, loss of appetite, and withdrawn behavior. During treatment, the worker found that this behavior had occurred in a milder form for several months before the earthquake. T quickly refocused the discussion from the trauma of the earthquake to his father's alcoholism and its effect on his mother and him.

Nightmares or night terrors were the most common symptom in children from both young and middle childhood groups; 50 percent of children voiced this complaint. The nightmares of children in the two- to five-year-old group consisted mostly of imaginary creatures (witches, monsters), whereas the six- to eleven-year-old children, who had more concrete thought processes, dreamed about other disasters and the loss of loved ones, usually the father.

Regressive behaviors were the second most commonly noted symptom among those in early childhood; 25 percent manifested this behavior. For example, four-year-old R began to wet the bed, and two-and-a-half-year-old M, who had begun speaking short sentences before the earthquake, seldom spoke after the earthquake.

Almost half of those in middle childhood manifested tics and obsessive reactions. Nine-year-old C, who had been left alone on the morning of the quake, began grinding her teeth. Twitching, fingernail biting, squinting, and inability to swallow were noted by parents.

Increased dependency needs—fear of venturing forth and of being alone—were common in both age groups. The most extreme responses were observed in children who had lost a parent in the earthquake. For example, following the death of their mother, which had occurred at her workplace, five-year-old B and seven-year-old K stopped eating, became isolated, complained of nightmares, and cried for long periods. Children who were left alone during the earthquake also manifested symptoms. Six-year-old V's mother had just left the house to walk her other two children to school when the earthquake struck. V began screaming and crouched in a corner while she watched large pieces of plaster drop from the ceiling. In the weeks following, she could not tolerate being separated from her mother and refused to sleep or go to the bathroom alone. Her mother expressed considerable guilt at having left V alone, which may have contributed to V's symptomatology.

Adolescents

The adolescents (twelve to seventeen years) who were counseled were better able to identify and articulate their feelings. Fear regarding the collapse of their homes, loss of parents, and possibility of subsequent earthquakes was the most commonly expressed feeling. The disruption of peer relationships and school activities were consistent themes. Compared with older age groups, very little depression and somatic complaints were noted.

The dream content of adolescents was symbolic of the trauma they had experienced. For example, fourteen-year-old I dreamed repeatedly of a ground war being fought in Mexico City, and fifteen-year-old P dreamed that her entire family hovered above the crumbling city within the safe confines of a helicopter.

Younger Adults

Excessive anxiety was observed in more than 65 percent of adults between the ages of eighteen and forty-five years. Adults with symptoms of depression significantly outnumbered adolescents with similar complaints, although even among adults these symptoms occurred in only about 20 percent of the cases. Complaints of dizziness, headaches, extreme restlessness, periods of emotional numbness, insomnia, heart palpitations, startle reactions, and uncontrollable shaking were commonly reported. Women reported interruptions in their menstrual cycles, and lactating mothers reported losing their ability to breast-feed. Interpersonal tensions among family members, friends, and work associates; inability to make decisions; and decreases in the cognitive functions of concentration and short-term memory were also commonly reported.

Connection with, protection for, and responsibility to family members, especially children, were commonly noted themes. Many parents expressed considerable anxiety about the safety of their children, which they manifested in overprotective behaviors. This behavior was particularly noticeable in mothers who had left their children alone during the earthquake. For example, thirty-five-year-old W left four of her children alone while she walked her seven-year-old child to school. After the earthquake she refused to let them go out alone and described having attacks of extreme anxiety when she went out shopping. She experienced guilt feelings and often lay awake at night reliving the disaster and planning a safe escape. Several other women described being torn between caring for their families of creation and of origin.

Feelings of guilt, powerlessness, and loss of control were also commonly expressed.

Paradoxically, guilt was most often expressed by those persons who were most involved in the rescue efforts. Thirty-three-year-old E, whose family and home had been
unharmed, dug for bodies in the ruins of a large apartment building for several days
after the earthquake. After the fifth day, he could no longer tolerate the death around
him and tried to return to work as a mechanic. He complained that he was unable to
concentrate, that he had difficulty relating to his family, and that he felt an overwhelming sense of guilt for having left the rescue efforts and returned to work.

The feeling of powerlessness was expressed well by thirty-five-year-old A:

> Of all things I didn't expect the earth below us to fail. One minute I have my
> home, my table, my cups, my family . . . we didn't have much, but we had
> enough. There's nothing all the thinking and hoping and planning and working
> can do to stop it. If only we knew for sure that it wouldn't happen again, but in-
> stead we just wait and wait and wait. . . .

She felt that the livelihood and well-being of her family were beyond her control and in
the hands of God, the government, and relief agencies. The fear of a subsequent earthquake and the frustration and desperation of knowing that they could neither predict
nor prevent such an occurrence were commonly expressed by victims.

Older Adults

Depression was by far the most common complaint and observed symptom among
adults forty-six years of age and older (65 percent of cases). Religious and philosophical themes were noted in approximately 55 percent of cases within this age group.
Fifty-eight-year-old N lost his home in the earthquake. He complained of oversleeping,
decreased appetite, fatigue, and a "heavy weight" on his chest. He was tearful as he described the disappointment he felt at having worked all his life to provide his family
with a home that was destroyed in a matter of moments. A religious man, he interpreted the earthquake as a sign of the end of the world and felt truly hopeless as he
waited for its destruction: "God gives all and takes all away." He spoke with sadness
and confusion as he questioned why his life should end this way after having striven to
be a good and righteous person.

In addition to the loss of loved ones and possessions, the loss of community contributed to depression in many persons in this age group. Forty-six-year-old P was forced
to move from her partially destroyed home where she had lived for twenty-five years
and move in with one of her eight children. She spoke of feeling "alone, listless, and defeated" and described sitting around all day unable to mobilize enough energy to help
her daughter or make any attempt to reconstruct her life. She repeated painfully that
"nothing will ever be the same" and longed for her home, her usual daily activities, and
her neighbors, the majority of whom were now living elsewhere with extended family
members. Kai Erikson describes this loss of community and its effects as a "collective
trauma" in which "boundaries are drawn around whole groups of people, not sepa-

rate individuals."[9] The importance of this notion within Latin cultures should be noted.

Victims used the existence of God both to explain the tragedy and to provide a sense of control and predictability. Through the earthquake, God was believed to be punishing humanity for diverse and sometimes specific reasons—for having wars, performing abortions, using drugs, and abandoning religion. One woman believed God chose Mexico City because criminals from throughout the country migrated there. Although punitive, God was also perceived as benevolent because one's life, home, or family was spared. Many individuals who began the counseling session by expressing considerable fear and anxiety about another earthquake found solace in the idea that God alone could protect them and decide their fate. They acknowledged a renewed respect for God's power and a renewed religious commitment arising from this experience. In their desperation and terror before the possibility of another earthquake, faith seemed essential.

The themes of responsibility to family noted in persons who were in early adulthood were commonly replaced by fears of having to be dependent on their children among the older patients. The fear that was commonly expressed by children and adolescents resurfaced in patients in this age group (more than 50 percent of those counseled). Their fears were generalized and vague, surfacing primarily when they were alone and in the dark.

EFFECTS OF PREVIOUS LOSS, TRAUMA, AND PSYCHOSOCIAL PROBLEMS

Past experiences of loss, trauma, or both contributed to a disaster victim's symptomatology; this was observed in approximately 17 percent of adolescent and adult cases. This phenomenon often co-existed with depressive symptomatology. For example, twenty-six-year-old N worked as a clerk in one of the hospitals that collapsed during the quake. Although she was not at work during the earthquake, she worked in the rescue operation for several days following it. Many of her work associates died. Several days after she stopped working with the rescue effort, she began crying uncontrollably and complained that she was unable to concentrate. She also described being preoccupied with her father, who had died seven years before in a bus accident several hours away from Mexico City. She described dreams in which she would walk through a desert to find him lying dead and reported intrusive memories about their relationship. The eldest of eight children, she had quickly assumed responsibility for the family following his death. She described taking care of the funeral arrangements, caring for the emotional needs of her mother, and how she obtained employment to help support the family. She described her relationship with her father as very close, although she appeared not to have mourned his death. The current crisis restimulated her latent grief.

Seventeen-year-old D complained of extreme anxiety, inability to concentrate, insomnia, and loss of appetite. He was quite tearful during the interview. He was afraid to leave his home and, when he did leave, worried constantly about his elderly mother being alone. He appeared agitated and distracted. The family lived very close to an oil refinery where one year previously a disastrous explosion had resulted in significant

---

[9] Kai Erikson, *Everything in Its Path: Destruction of a Community in the Buffalo Creek Flood* (New York: Simon and Schuster, 1976), pp. 190–94.

loss of life. According to his father, D manifested increased anxiety and withdrawal for several months following this explosion but had slowly been returning to his previous level of functioning. Although D's home and family had not been affected by the earthquake, the cumulative effects of both disasters complicated his response significantly. The incomplete resolution of the first trauma and preexisting family dysfunction, including marital problems between his parents, were considered during treatment.

The significance of past loss was also observed in a mother whose son had been murdered eight months before, in a young mother whose infant had recently died, and in a middle-aged woman whose husband had left her a year ago. The earthquake exacerbated preexisting depression in all three cases.

In some instances the trauma of the earthquake stimulated a willingness to explore current psychosocial and family problems for which professional help had not previously been sought (15 percent of the adolescent and adult cases). Whether this willingness was due to the sudden availability of mental health workers or because the earthquake had tipped a precarious emotional balance is unclear. Forty-eight-year-old G complained of sadness, loss of appetite, and loss of motivation since the earthquake, which had left her home partially destroyed. After describing the effects and disruption caused by the earthquake, she quickly began describing her twenty-six-year-old alcoholic son, who had recently lost his job, broken up with his wife, and moved back in with her. She expressed feelings of disappointment, frustration, and guilt and reported a history of significant family problems, including physical abuse from her alcoholic spouse. What appeared to be a long-standing depression had clearly been exacerbated by the stress of the disaster.

The same relationship between preexisting psychosocial problems and current trauma was illustrated by a young woman who had been unable to conceive a baby, several individuals who complained of marital discord, and a young woman who had had a seven-year incestuous relationship with her stepfather.

Although the symptomatology and anxiety responses of these individuals were generally moderate to serious, their disaster experiences generally were relatively mild. It was interesting to note how quickly those clients with an unresolved trauma or current psychosocial problems would refocus the content of the session away from the earthquake and onto the underlying issue. Thus the earthquake provided an important opportunity for therapeutic intervention.

CRISIS-INTERVENTION TREATMENT STRATEGIES

"Any event," Mardi Horowitz has noted, "is appraised and assimilated in relation to the past history and current cognitive and emotional set of the person who experiences it."[10] The level of stress that triggers disorder and leads to dysfunction is different for each individual.[11] For this reason, crisis-intervention strategies have recently been defined as either generic or individual. The generic approach identifies a set of responses common to a particular hazard (for example, rape or death). The responses are orga-

---

[10] Mardi J. Horowitz, *Stress Response Syndromes* (New York: Jason Aronson, 1976), pp. 22–23.
[11] A. C. McFarlane, "Life Events, Disasters and Psychological Distress," *Mental Health in Australia* 1 (December 1984): 4–6.

nized into predictable stages through which the client is supported and directed by a counselor whose goal is to enhance coping and foster adaptive behaviors. The individual approach emphasizes the preexisting conflicts and underlying psychodynamics that complicate responses to crises. These complicated responses often result in more troubling symptoms that, if untreated, can result in decreased functioning. Thus the more individual approach is more psychodynamically oriented; it addresses issues in the person's history.

The first intervention task for assisting the Mexico City earthquake victims was to determine which approach—the generic or individual—would be more appropriate. This determination was made by evaluating the person-in-situation, the presenting complaint, the victim's experience at the time of the earthquake, the extent of loss suffered, the socioeconomic situation, current social supports, recent stressors, history of losses, psychiatric history, present state of physical health, and usual coping methods. If the worker determined that the stress reaction was severe enough, or the potential for long-term sequelae great enough, the person was referred to a psychiatric facility or mental health center. Such referrals were made for children who lost a parent as well as for individuals who manifested transient psychotic symptoms, had a history of psychiatric disturbance, and whose underlying psychodynamics seemed to significantly complicate their response to the disaster.

For those patients who were better able to benefit from the generic approach, three treatment tasks were established:

1. *Help the client identify and express his or her feelings.* Many individuals had not discussed their feelings associated with the disaster because they were afraid that they would burden their family or prolong the trauma. Thirty-one-year-old G's assertion was typical: "I don't want to talk about it. It will only make me more frightened. I just want to forget about it." Some parents discouraged their children from talking about the earthquake because they thought that was the "healthy" thing to do. Many clients who did not suffer so great a loss in the disaster as did some of their friends or relatives felt ashamed when discussing their own trauma. Others felt embarrassed by not being able to control their grief and fear. Clients were encouraged to explore and communicate their feelings not only within the counseling sessions but also on a continuing basis with family and friends.

The existence of nightmares and intrusions often indicated a fear of remembering the event. Those who suffered from this symptom were encouraged to discuss the content and associated feelings of their dreams with significant others. As children were less able to articulate their feelings, parents were urged to listen for themes of fear in their children's play and to help their children articulate these feelings.

2. *Communicating a sense of hope.* As clients attempted to reorder their lives as parents, students, or workers, they were confronted with a sense of desperation and fear that life would never again be joyful or normal. Twenty-year-old R described her disappointment in returning to her classes at the university to find them completely irrelevant. Forty-year-old Y described the emptiness he felt both at home and at work and his fear it would never dissipate. Amid the destruction, the media coverage, and the constant reminders of the tragedy, it was essential that workers convey hope and assurance that all crises eventually end.

3. *Educating the client on aspects of human response to crisis.* Clients commonly expressed concern that their response or the response of their children was abnormal. This concern was particularly prevalent among those who had experienced delayed symptoms. Lack of communication among friends and family members exacerbated this belief. Even if this fear of "going crazy," as so many clients described it, was not verbalized, the worker explained that symptoms such as anxiety, memory loss, inability to concentrate, intrusive thoughts, dizziness, depression, disturbances in sleeping and eating patterns, and startle reactions were normal. This assurance was almost always met with expressions of relief.

Parents were counseled that the regressive behaviors, tics, and increased dependency noted in their children were generally limited in time and symptomatic of their emotional upset and need for safety. Ways to increase their children's sense of security—maintaining closer physical contact with them and not leaving them alone—were discussed. The importance of monitoring children's symptoms over the subsequent months and seeking professional help if improvement did not occur was also stressed.

Clients received a brief explanation of why they were in a state of crisis and how the process of integrating the crisis into their life was often a lengthy one. Mention of the repetitive, involuntary swings between acute stress and emotional numbness, as described by Horowitz, was included in this explanation.[12] Many victims reported that these issues were relevant to their experience. They were advised that they and their children might experience an unexpected resurgence of panic following thunder and windstorms, and they were alerted to the possibility of anniversary reactions.

Through these educational measures, many clients reestablished a sense of control. If the victim could anticipate and therefore prepare for a resurgence of anxiety, the intensity of the stress reactions might be reduced. The medical staff were advised of these three tasks of generic interventions so they could both reinforce the work of the social worker and reach those clients with symptoms not severe enough to warrant referral for mental health services.

Evaluative tools for assessing the efficacy of the social work intervention were unavailable; consequently, the impact of the intervention was difficult to assess. The majority of clients described feeling mild to moderate symptom relief following the therapeutic contacts. The 20 percent of clients who were seen more than once generally displayed decreasing symptomatology. However, whether this would have occurred without social work intervention could not be evaluated.

The importance of commemorative and community events in providing an outlet for grief, providing meaning to suffering, and restoring a sense of community integrity should not be overlooked. On October 23, 1985, which was declared Day of the Medical Worker, the hundreds of medical personnel who perished in the earthquake were commemorated, and on November 2, 1985, the traditional Day of the Dead holiday more than 5,000 people gathered to mourn the dead with poetry, music, and dance. In addition, several protest marches condemned governmental corruption and demanded property reforms, thus creating a sense of community solidarity.

---

[12] Horowitz, *Stress Response Syndromes.*

CONCLUSION

Continued descriptive and empirical studies on the human responses to disaster are needed to further the development of crisis intervention theory and, more important, to develop appropriate programs to meet the acute and long-term needs of disaster victims. This descriptive study contributes to the body of knowledge on both the short-term response to crisis and the variability of response with respect to age group and developmental stage and considers how past loss or trauma and current psychosocial problems complicate responses to crisis. Finding these complicated responses also in individuals whose disaster experiences were relatively mild supports the notion of personal vulnerability.

The large number of individuals who presented with anxiety reactions and related symptoms clearly substantiates the need for social work services following a disaster. The social worker's role included evaluation, treatment, and referral of clients as well as education of medical staff.

Prevention and education were the primary objectives of client intervention. Those individuals identified through a complete psychosocial assessment to be at high risk for psychological decompensation, complicated bereavement, or long-term dysfunction were referred for ongoing treatment. The treatment aim was to reduce tension by facilitating the expression of feelings. It was hoped that by educating clients on the parameters and manifestations of appropriate response, tension would be reduced, self-understanding fostered, and a sense of control reinstilled. The broad aim of treatment was to convey a sense of hope and to remind clients that all crises are limited in time.

Clearly, thousands will date their lives from the disastrous earthquake that struck Mexico City on that September morning. Through comprehensive and continuous crisis intervention services, one hopes that this tragedy might be accompanied by an increase in self-understanding, family support, and community cohesion and not by individual, family, and community dysfunction.

CHAPTER 121

GROWING UP UNDER THE MUSHROOM CLOUD

Burt Shachter

I learned that Bob, a 15-year-old adolescent in therapy with me, had threatened to commit suicide after a quarrel with his girlfriend. Specifically, his mother told me that she had overheard Bob threatening to turn on the oven and put his head in. After some exploration of the issue with Bob, I determined that this threat had not been a serious one. When I subsequently asked him if there were ever circumstances in which he might actually kill himself, Bob responded with little hesitation: "Only if I knew the bomb was going to come in 15 minutes—then I'd probably do it."

One might wonder if such fear of nuclear catastrophe is an idiosyncratic concern of a single emotionally troubled teenager, or may it, at least in part, reflect a more pervasive preoccupation among youths? If the latter is the case, what effect does such preoccupation have on the development of children and youths? And, further, if we assume that the threat has a deleterious effect, what do we adults—parents, mental health professionals, politicians, or whoever—do about it? What can be done, and what should be done?

PAST FINDINGS

Until recent years, studies of the effects on children and youths of the threat of nuclear weapons have been scarce. Although social work journals have dealt at length with the effects of family violence on parents and children, they have generally been silent on the influence of threatened nuclear violence in the larger world. A few studies have been reported in journals outside of social work. In 1964, Schwebel conducted one of the earliest studies, in which questionnaires dealing with the views of 3,000 junior high and high school students on war and civil defense were evaluated.[1] Schwebel's survey showed that children know and care about the threat of nuclear war and that they know and fear the dangers of nuclear disaster. However, the study could offer no clarity on how mental anguish gets converted to pathology. At about the same time,

Escalona and her colleagues conducted a questionnaire survey of children, from ages 4 through adolescence.[2] The young people were asked what they thought the world would be like by the time they grew up. More than 70 percent spontaneously mentioned nuclear weapons and destructive war as a likely possibility. A relatively high proportion expressed pessimism about the future. Escalona concluded that there was an adverse influence on the developmental process in normal children because of the threat of nuclear disaster.

Apart from the contributions of Schwebel and Escalona, little systematic study of this issue existed until the mid-1970s. Yet, the advent of nuclear weaponry has long been with us. Hiroshima and Nagasaki take us back more than 40 years to 1945. Atomic weapons were subsequently developed by the Soviet Union in 1949, Great Britain in 1952, and France in 1960. To gain perspective, I checked my intensive exploratory study of 13 emotionally disturbed male adolescents, age 17 through 20, conducted 20 years ago.[3] Although this study dealt with "Identity Crisis Resolution and Occupational Processes" and not specifically with the nuclear experience, a question used in a structured interview as part of the study dealt with perceptions of the future. Each of the 13 subjects was asked: *How do you see the future? Do you feel that the world is a safe place in which to grow older? Tell me how you feel about it.*

Of the 13 subjects, 12 (or 92 percent) saw their futures in pessimistic terms, as fraught with danger, violence, or forbidding uncertainty. Seven of the subjects (or 54 percent) made reference to some kind of cataclysmic war, with six of these spontaneously envisioning either an atomic or nuclear war. The sample, of course, was small, and one has to allow for projections flowing from intrapsychic factors or experiences with family violence. Yet, the content of such fears would seem to have been shaped in part by the external advent of nuclear technology. Perhaps even more illuminating are some verbatim responses of those who referred to nuclear bombs, without solicitation from the interviewer:

Fine (age 19): I don't want to get older. There's little meaning in life. . . . When I die I want to come back. It's not a safe world. People are too much for themselves. You can't trust people. The A-bomb scares me. It's like dying and not coming back. Someone might drop the bomb. I don't know if it will happen.

Short (age 17): That's a silly question. We're fed propagandist ideas in this country. I couldn't care less about the A-bomb. If people get angry enough at each other, they'll push the button. I can't say for sure. What happens will happen. . . . Science can kill more people with less effort than before. They're working on neutron rays. They draw out neutrons from human cells. They can kill you by filling you up with too many neutrons or they can kill you by withdrawing neutrons.

Shapiro (age 18): The street is not even safe. My future is a big question. As for the world, if I'm lucky, they won't blow it up before I die. We'll be here til some maniac pushes a button by mistake. Someone will survive. It'll start up all over again. That'll be a mistake. It's screwed up so far. Why start all over again?

Hart (age 20): Will the bomb be dropped at any minute? Well, it's an age of reason. There's more talking than acting. We'll know more about ourselves. We'll be less active. Why be a hero? I don't know what goes on elsewhere. America is a better place to be brought up in. Maybe, there's a better place, like Norway or Sweden.

Hall (age 17): No, I don't think I have a chance of growing older—especially if Goldwater [1964 Presidential candidate] gets in power. The Chinese will get atomic weapons and conquer the world. I don't know what will be left to take over. It will be one big mess. If I didn't need such high requirements to be an astronaut, that's what I'd be. I'd take a woman and escape.[4]

As we consider such responses, I must again emphasize that the population I interviewed was a skewed, and not a random sample of all youths. Certainly, from their statements, an inner life reflecting aggression and fear is projected onto the world. Yet, emotionally disturbed adolescents such as these do not censor painful external stimuli as easily as others do. They often possess a special sensitivity to dangers implied and real. They may experience more acutely what others sense in more subterranean ways. Their spontaneous reference to and clear awareness of "the bomb," even 20 years ago, suggests an interplay between internal pathology and the toxic effect of a nuclear age in which the future and human continuity are in doubt. The specifics of whether and how such nuclear threat in and of itself translates into developmental pathology requires much more extensive study.

RECENT FINDINGS

An awareness of the lack of systematic study of the effects of the nuclear threat on children and adolescents prompted the American Psychiatric Association's Task Force on the Psychosocial Impacts of Nuclear Developments, in 1977, to invite child psychiatrists Beardslee and Mack to address the matter. Reviewing studies, including Schwebel's and Escalona's studies cited earlier, of the effects on children and adolescents of the threat of nuclear war, Beardslee and Mack concluded:

Our fundamental experience has been that when children and adolescents are specifically questioned about nuclear threat, a substantial number do indicate they are worried and afraid. It is not possible from the available evidence to know what percentage of youngsters are deeply concerned about the threat of nuclear annihilation, but all studies agree that some children and adolescents are. The problem of understanding what impact this worry and fear have on personality development and daily lives of young people is complex. More research is much needed.[5]

Backman conducted one study—broader and more rigorously designed than earlier ones—that suggested troublesome awareness was escalating.[6] His findings on the impact of the threat of nuclear war were derived from an examination of adolescent attitudes toward the military and the draft. Backman surveyed students in seven consecutive graduating classes—1976 through 1982—in 130 public and private high schools in 48 states. The total yearly sample size ranged from 16,662 to 18,924. There was a steady rise in the percentage of those worried about nuclear threat. In 1976, 19.9 percent of male seniors never worried about it. By 1982, 4.6 percent of the male seniors never worried. Similarly, in 1976, 7.2 percent of the male seniors said that they worried about it often, whereas in 1982, 31.2 percent did. Female high school students demonstrated a similar strong increase in alarm.

Probably most revealing is a study of the responses of Russian children to the nuclear threat.[7] In the summer of 1983, a team of three U.S. psychiatrists, Chivian, Mack, and Waletzky, was granted an unprecedented opportunity to travel to the Soviet Union and study the psychological effects of the threat of nuclear war on Soviet children.[8] The psychiatrists accompanied by their own translator, visited two Pioneer camps—the Soviet equivalent of summer camps in the United States, except that they are under governmental auspices—Gargarin and Orlyonok. There they conducted videotaped interviews with approximately 50 children, age 11 to 15 years. The young people, interviewed singly and in groups without the presence of adult staff, were questioned to find out the following:

- At what age did they learn about the effects of nuclear war?
- What did they know about the consequences of nuclear war?
- Did they believe that there would be a nuclear war in their lifetimes?
- Did they believe they would survive a nuclear war?
- How did they feel when they thought about nuclear war?
- Did their feelings about nuclear war affect their plans for the future?

The team also administered a questionnaire study to approximately 300 children—the first ever to be administered to Soviet children on the subject of nuclear war. The data obtained were compared with the responses to a similar 1983 study of 900 children in California, conducted by Goldenring and Doctor, on perceptions of nuclear war.[9] (Comparative responses by the Soviet children and by the U.S. children to three key questions reported in the project summary, are summed up in Table 121–1.)

The following were a few illustrative verbatim comments by Russian children to Mack's question, "If there were a nuclear war, what would happen?"

Oskana (age 11), Moscow: The atomic bombs were dropped a fairly long time ago, but children are still being born with the effects of radiation.

Sergei (age 13), Moscow: Many casualties, many, many casualties. And they will principally be people who want peace, children, old people.

Elena (age 13), Moscow: And if a war like that starts, it will be absolutely terrible. Nobody will be needed, not teachers, doctors. Everything around will die.[10]

To Chivian's question, "Do any of you ever think that there might be a nuclear war in your lifetimes?" illustrative comments were as follows:

Boris (age 13), Minsk: We hope that never happens. The consequences are terrible.

Table 121–1

Comparison of Responses of Soviet and U.S. Children to Questions about Nuclear War
(percentage)

Question	Responses of Soviet Children (N = 300)		Responses of U.S. Children (N = 900)	
1. Do you think a nuclear war	Yes	11.8	Yes	38.5
between the U.S. and USSR will	No	54.5	No	16.0
happen in your lifetime?	Uncertain	33.7	Uncertain	44.5
2. If there were a nuclear war,	Yes	2.9	Yes	16.5
do you think you and your family	No	80.7	No	41.5
would survive?	Uncertain	16.4	Uncertain	41.1
3. Do you think nuclear war	Yes	93.3	Yes	65.0
between the U.S. and the USSR	No	2.8	No	14.5
can be prevented?	Uncertain	3.9	Uncertain	20.0

Source: Excerpted from data presented in E. S. Chivian, J. E. Mack, and J. P. Waletzky, *What Soviet Children Are Saying about Nuclear War,* Project Summary (Boston: International Physicians for the Prevention of Nuclear War, 1983), p. 10; and J. Goldenring and R. Doctor, "California Adolescents' Concerns about the Threat of Nuclear War," in J. Solantaus et al., eds., *Impact of the Threat of Nuclear War on Children and Adolescents: Proceedings of an International Research Symposium* (Helsinki, Finland: International Physicians for the Prevention of Nuclear War, 1985).

Irina (age 13), Estonio: We don't believe things like that. The Soviet Union struggles for peace.

Sveta (age 13), Riazan: War will never happen because the Soviet Union and America will, will, will come to terms.

Valery (age 14), Moscow: Technology has reached a high level at the rocket installation stage. It seems to me that one person could do it all. Could push the button and that would be it. Rockets would be launched at us and we would launch rockets back.[11]

In its simplest terms, Chivian, Mack, and Waletsky's study affirms that both Soviet and U.S. children in varying degrees are aware of and frightened by the prospects of nuclear holocaust. Soviet children seem more hopeful than U.S. children that nuclear war can be prevented (93.3 percent as compared to 65 percent). U.S. children are more prone than Soviet children to expect a nuclear war in their lifetimes (38.5 percent to 11.8 percent). If there were a nuclear war, hardly any of the Soviet children contemplate survival (2.9 percent). A somewhat higher percentage of U.S. children (16.5 percent) believe that they would survive a nuclear war. The whys and wherefores of these differences are worth speculation. One wonders, for example, how the strong emphasis on nuclear matters in the Soviet school curriculum, described by Chivian and his colleagues, influences the findings? Suffice it to say that, at this point in our understanding, substantial numbers of children from *both* of the nuclear superpowers are painfully aware of and uneasy about the consequences of the nuclear arms race.

In a talk at New York University, Mack described the attitudes—stereotypic, fearful, angry, distrustful, and anti-Communistic—toward Russian people held by a group of primarily black inner-city youths, in a Boston high school.[12] After viewing the video-taped responses of Russian children, who seemed similarly fearful and desirous of peace, the youths expressed a change of attitudes, reflecting a wish to communicate with Russian children in a way that might foster friendlier co-existence.[13]

Consciousness was also raised by the fictionalized drama on television of the impact of a nuclear attack on a Middle-Western town. The drama, *The Day After,* was seen by over one hundred million Americans, the second largest audience ever for a TV movie.[14] Although a debate raged then and continues in somewhat muted form about the advisability of such showings, especially to family audiences, *The Day After* cut through the defensive denial and selective inattention to nuclear dangers and awakened concern about potential nuclear war and how we might experience it.

U.S. News and World Report conducted a survey of 825 students from colleges and universities across the country on the nuclear threat.[15] It found that these students showed "a deep concern about the mounting arms race."[16] The survey asked: "Do you expect a nuclear war in your lifetime?" In response, 29.1 percent of the students said yes; 36.3 percent said no; and 34.6 percent were unsure. One might note that the 29.1 percent who expected nuclear war is a figure close to the 31.2 percent of male high school seniors who reported "worrying often" about the nuclear threat in the 1982 Backman study.[17] Despite the confirmation of concern among a substantial number of youths about the possibility of nuclear war, *U.S. News and World Report* stressed that the majority of such youths are "reluctant to panic, either in changing their own plans, or in recommending bold new initiatives by the U.S. Government."[18]

EFFECT ON DEVELOPMENT

A pervasive and escalating anxiety-ridden awareness of nuclear danger among children and adolescents is becoming clear. The effect of such awareness on the developmental process is suggestive but less clear. Until further research affirms or disavows these effects, there is a suggestion that the nuclear threat has a deleterious effect on development in children and adolescents, (1) of faith in the future and identity formation, (2) of confidence in the adults who must assure that future, (3) of the inner resources for coping with death, and (4) of the willingness to invest in family relationships and enduring, intimate commitments.

Although identity formation is a lifelong process, its roots in childhood experience and its consolidation in adolescence are pivotal to growth. What Erikson referred to as ego identity includes a vision of the future that is promising and a sense of viable adult role that can be played in that future.[19] One is compelled to ask how the threat of nuclear annihilation and the possibility of no future at all influence that identity.

Erikson, furthermore, saw *fidelity* as a key component in the identity-forming process:

> As to youth and the question of what is in the center of its most passionate and most erratic striving, I have concluded that *fidelity* is the vital strength which it needs to have an opportunity to develop, to employ, to evoke—and to die for.[20]

Webster's defines fidelity as "faithfulness; careful and exact observation of duty, or performance of obligations or vows: good faith."[21] What happens to fidelity or good faith when, as Mack pointed out, "an important part of this sense of things being out of control is the perception that authority for nuclear war has slipped out of human control and has been taken over by technology"?[22] Faith and its accompanying passionate striving implies a world that is in control, that is changeable and perfectable. When adults as model problem-solvers seem impotent and when the rhetoric of confrontation and the promise of a Star Wars technology supplant efforts at arms control and conflict resolution, what happens to fidelity and the identity-forming process?

With the future murky and human continuity itself in jeopardy, we must consider the effect of the nuclear war threat on the willingness of young people to invest in durable, intimate relationships, in the generativity of young adulthood, in seeing their personal continuity reflected in contributing to the growth of new generations. Although the high divorce rate of recent years and the diminution of the birthrate obviously have multifaceted explanations, it is plausible that the nuclear situation is one contributing factor.

> What happens to the child's concept of death and capacity to cope with death in a rational way when death ceases becoming an end stage of the growth process, or an incidental accidental happening, but rather becomes a catastrophic threat for all humans by our own doing?[23]

In recent years, object relations theorists such as Mahler and Kernberg have determined, through research and clinical experience, that the process by which we develop as separate and individuated humans depends on our ability to integrate the positive and negative representations of ourselves and others.[24] Such development is facilitated when we learn how to tolerate ambivalence and accept both the good and bad parts of ourselves and others. Failure at such integration contributes to the skewing of developmental processes, the lack of empathy, and the seeing of others as either all good or all bad. One wonders how rhetoric by national leaders about "the God-fearing" versus "evil empires" influences this process. As child psychiatrist Rogers wrote:

> The splitting of mankind into good and bad is a luxury in which politicians can indulge, not psychiatrists. We have the responsibility simultaneously to see the good and the bad and to integrate them in our empathic understanding. This is an exercise in empathy far beyond our usual horizon. From it, we can learn the limitations of our abilities for tolerance and understanding.[25]

I contend that the splitting that prevails on a global level among many peoples (Russians versus Americans, Jews versus Arabs, Protestant Irish versus Catholic Irish, Iranians versus Iraqis)—exacerbated by confrontational politics and powerful technology—provides a context that may not be conducive to ego integration and empathy in particular individuals. We must, at least, understand far better the interplay between the particularities of development in individuals and families on the one hand and behavior among large national groups on the other.

IMPLICATIONS FOR MENTAL HEALTH PROFESSIONALS

While we, as social workers and other mental health professionals are addressing in research and clinical investigations the effects of the nuclear threat on childhood and adolescent development, what can we do in the meantime? Perhaps we can most usefully begin with ourselves. Those of us in the business of healing others and enabling others to grow are not immune from defending ourselves against the despair of the nuclear threat. The relative paucity of research and clinical investigation suggests the tendency toward "denial" and "numbing" referred to by Lifton.[26] Those who have chosen the effect of the nuclear threat on development as an area of clinical inquiry and research have been discouraged by others who claim this area is too politicized and stressful for the generation of "hard data."[27]

Some have even accused those who have been trying to deal forthrightly with the subject matter of resorting to scare tactics. *The New York Times* published a letter from Ernest W. Lefever, President of the Ethics and Public Policy Center in Washington, D.C., commenting on a 30-second TV spot announcement by the Massachusetts Department of Mental Health. The advertisement showed a little girl, saying: "When I grow up, I want to be alive."

According to Lefever, "The ad is a profound disservice to both children and adults because it distorts reality, sponsors unreasoning fear and encourages utopian illusions."[28] In another letter in the same issue of *The New York Times,* Richard E. Sincere, Jr., a member of the Board of Directors of the American Civil Defense Association, commented: "The . . . ad may be counterproductive by perpetuating certain falsehoods about the war's consequences."[29]

Although there are those who counsel against open debate and dialogue on the effects of nuclear matters on human development, I see great risk in continued silence and avoidance. When children are fearful (as they increasingly are, as affirmed by the studies cited earlier), isolation and secrecy can exacerbate the children's state of fearfulness and can contribute to distorted perceptions and ineffectual repression. Defensive reactions may lead both children and adults into "magical" thinking that entertains scenarios of "limited" nuclear war or nuclear conflagration that may harm others but not "us." Or, silence can encourage a despairing fatalism that feeds a destructive sense of powerlessness. As Kennan wrote:

> We have gone on piling weapon upon weapon, missile upon missile, new levels of destructiveness upon old ones. We have done this helplessly, almost involuntarily—like the victims of some sort of hypnotism, like men in a dream, like lemmings heading for the sea.[30]

We cannot wait for our research to be definitive. There is too much at stake, and we must act on the best information available until greater certainty arises. We must deal with our own anxieties and the anxieties of the young people we profess to help. As Mack suggested, "Little can be done to help our young people unless adults address the apathy and helplessness that we experience in relation to the arms race and the threat of nuclear war."[31]

Human psychology has certainly shown us that we can look at painful truths and sources of anxiety if we do not do it alone and if there is some degree of reassurance that is feasible and not false. Schwebel has emphasized the importance of adult role modeling and *empowerment* associated with action to alter current despairing circumstances.[32]

A note of caution must be sounded here. Beardslee and Mack reminded us that in our work with parents and in our direct work with their children, we should be aware of the developmental stage of the child and his or her capacity for thinking about the future.[33] Very young children (for example, 8 years or younger) may lack the cognitive ability to think about the future as adolescents or adults might. Younger children think more concretely, and what will be reassuring to them may be quite different from what will reassure adolescents. Simpler, more direct modes of reassurance are indicated for younger children.

Other practice ramifications will become clearer as research and clinical experience yield findings that can guide our interventions with children, adolescents, and parents. However, we can safely say that the matter of the nuclear arms race—and its effects on the perceptions, hopes, aspirations, identities, and relationships between human beings— can no longer be ignored. As mental health clinicians, we will need to become attuned to clues from our clients related to nuclear anxieties and despair. We will need to understand better the interplay between developmental experience, intrapsychic life, and family processes on the one hand and a potentially catastrophic nuclear confrontation that threatens human existence on the other. We will need to translate our understandings into relevant interventive strategies and techniques. Along with Educators for Social Responsibility (New York City) and other such groups, we will also have a stake in generating new educational programs that can address nuclear matters in a preventive context.

Finally, those of us who might help calm the fears of the younger generation and demonstrate some measure of empowerment and realistic reassurance must become more aware of how our own perceptions of nuclear matters influence our clinical work. We need hope for ourselves. Perhaps that hope is best expressed in these words of Erikson, writing of the United States and Russia:

> If their competition can be halted before it leads to mutual annihilation, it is just possible that a new mankind seeing that it can now both build and destroy on a gigantic scale will focus its intelligence . . . on the ethical question concerning the workings of human generations—beyond products, powers and ideas. . . . A new ethics must eventually transcend the alliance of ideology and technology for the great question will be how man, on ethical and generational grounds, will limit the use of technological expansion even where it might for a while enhance prestige and profit.[34]

NOTES AND REFERENCES

1. M. Schwebel, "Nuclear Cold War: Student Opinion and Professional Responsibility," in Schwebel, ed., *Behavioral Science and Human Survival* (Palo Alto, Calif.: Science & Behavior Books, 1965).

2. S. Escalona, "Children and the Threat of Nuclear War," in Schwebel, ed., *Behavioral Science and Human Survival.*

3. B. Shachter, "Identity Crisis and Occupational Processes: An Intensive Exploratory Study of Emotionally Disturbed Male Adolescents," *Child Welfare,* 47 (January 1968), pp. 26–37.

4. Culled from structured interview protocols used in my research in preparing the article, "Identity Crisis and Occupational Processes."

5. W. A. Beardslee and J. E. Mack, "Adolescents and the Threat of Nuclear War: The Evolution of a Perspective," *Yale Journal of Biology and Medicine,* 56 (1983), p. 90.

6. J. Backman, "American High School Seniors View the Military: 1976–1982," *Armed Forces and Society,* 10, No. 1 (1983), pp. 86–94.

7. E. S. Chivian, J. E. Mack, and J. P. Waletzky, *What Soviet Children Are Saying about Nuclear War,* Project Summary (Boston: International Physicians for the Prevention of Nuclear War, 1984). (Photocopy.) Subsequently, the results of the project were published in E. Chivian et al., "Soviet Children and the Threat of Nuclear War: A Preliminary Study," *American Journal of Orthopsychiatry,* 55 (October 1985), pp. 590–599.

8. The project was jointly sponsored by the International Physicians for the Prevention of Nuclear War (Boston, Mass.) and the Research Program for the Study of Human Continuity, Department of Psychiatry, Harvard Medical School (Cambridge, Mass.)

9. J. Goldenring and R. Doctor, "California Adolescents' Concerns about Threat of Nuclear War," in J. Solantaus et al., eds., Impact of the Threat of Nuclear War on Children and Adolescents: Proceedings of an International Research Symposium (Helsinki, Finland: International Physicians for the Prevention of Nuclear War, 1985).

10. Chivian, Mack, and Waletzky, *What Soviet Children Are Saying about Nuclear War,* p. 3.

11. Ibid., pp. 3–6.

12. J. E. Mack, "Security Reconsidered: The Impact of the Nuclear Threat on Children and Adolescents," presentation at Symposium: Nuclear Threat Builds Anxiety in World's Children, as reported in *News Brief for Friends of the School* (New York: New York University, School of Social Work, June 1984), p. 2.

13. Ibid.

14. "'Day After' Fades, but Debate Lingers," *The New York Times,* June 19, 1984, p. A12.

15. "Nuclear Threat Through Eyes of College Students," *U.S. News and World Report,* April 16, 1984, pp. 33–37.

16. Ibid., p. 37.

17. Backman, "American High School Seniors View the Military."

18. "Nuclear Threat Through Eyes of College Students," p. 37.

19. E. H. Erikson, *Childhood and Society* (2nd ed.: New York: W. W. Norton, 1963).

20. E. H. Erikson, *Identity: Youth and Crisis* (New York: W. W. Nortin, 1968), p. 233.

21. *Webster's Deluxe Unabridged Dictionary* (2nd ed.: New York: Simon & Schuster, 1979), p. 681.

22. J. E. Mack, "The Psychological Impact of Nuclear Arms Competition on Children and Adolescents," *Testimony to Select Committee on Children, Youth and Families, United States House of Representatives*, Washington, D.C., September 20, 1983, p. 12.

23. Comments from M. Frank, presentation at Symposium: Nuclear Threat Builds Anxiety in World's Children, as reported in *News Briefs for Friends of the School* (New York: New York University, School of Social Work, June 1984), p. 2.

24. M. Mahler, F. Pine, and A. Bergman, *The Psychological Birth of the Human Infant* (New York: Basic Books, 1975); and O. Kernberg, *Object Relations Theory and Clinical Psychoanalysis* (New York: Jason Aronson, 1975).

25. R. Rogers et al., "Soviet-American Relationships under the Nuclear Umbrella," *Psychosocial Aspects of Nuclear Developments*, Task Force Report No. 20 (Washington, D.C.: American Psychiatric Association, 1982), cited in J. E. Mack, "But What About the Russians?" *Harvard Magazine* (March–April 1982), p. 53.

26. R. Lifton, *The Broken Connection* (New York: Simon & Schuster, 1979).

27. In a personal communication, J. E. Mack (Harvard University) and M. Schwebel (Rutgers University) related experiences of such discouragement from colleagues and others, April 13, 1984.

28. E. W. Lefever, "Ill-Conceived Doomsday Message for Children." Letter to Editor, *The New York Times*, May 10, 1984.

29. R. E. Sincere, Jr., "Prepare We Must." Letter to Editor, *The New York Times*, May 10, 1984.

30. G. Kennan, communication cited in Mack, "But What About the Russians?" p. 23.

31. J. E. Mack, "Psychosocial Effects of the Nuclear Arms Race," *The Bulletin of the Atomic Scientists*, 37 (April 1981), p. 21. See also J. E. Mack, "The Perceptions of U.S.–Soviet Intentions and Other Psychological Dimensions of the Nuclear Arms Race," *American Journal of Orthopsychiatry*, 52 (October 1982), pp. 590–599, as well as other articles in the same issue on nuclear war and the arms race.

32. M. Schwebel, "Children's Reactions to the Nuclear War Threat: Trends and Implications," address delivered at Growing Up Under the Mushroom Cloud: Impact of the Nuclear Threat on the Mental Health of Children and Parents. Eleventh Annual Symposium, School of Social Work, New York University, April 13, 1984.

33. Beardslee and Mack, "Adolescents and the Threat of Nuclear War," pp. 89–90.

34. Erikson, *Identity: Youth and Crisis*, p. 259.

Accepted January 22, 1985

CHAPTER 122

TRAIN CRASH

Social Work and Disaster Services

Leona Grossman

In a fast-moving, technological society it is to be expected that the unpredictabilities in nature as well as human fallibility will continue to result in periodic catastrophes. What science may have accomplished in mastery over the natural environment seems to be balanced out by what its sophisticated technology has confounded.

However horrendous it may seem, the possibility of danger and disaster is indigenous to today's world. Two emerging issues are involved in all such happenings: how to cope and how to prevent. The focus on prevention has received by far the greater emphasis in its concern with such matters of technological safety as prevention of mine casualties, safety devices in factories, railroads, airplanes, and so forth. Investigations into responsibility and the possibility of legal reprisal act as powerful control agents. A fair amount of research has been conducted on natural disasters that have claimed large numbers of lives. It is only recently, however, that serious attention has been given to the human perspective: the intricate processes people use to cope with disasters, which have now been identified as "disaster behavior."

Several case studies and theoretical analyses of disasters have appeared in the literature of disciplines other than social work.[1] In the past ten years, however, the subject has been dealt with only rarely in social work journals.[2] Although written accounts of such incidents usually contain some skew, they still have pragmatic value. Since disasters evoke strong, instantaneous emotional responses, research of the "hard-fact" variety is a bit more difficult.

Reprinted from *Social Work,* Vol. 18, No. 5 (1973), pp. 38–44, by permission of the publisher.

[1] *See,* for example, A. F. C. Wallace, *Tornado in Worcester: An Exploratory Study of Individuals and Community Behavior in an Extreme Situation,* "Disaster Study No. 3" (Washington, D.C.: National Academy of Sciences–National Research Council, 1965); George H. Grosser, Henry Wechsler, and Milton Greenblatt, eds., *The Threat of Impending Disaster: Contributions to the Psychology of Stress* (Cambridge, Mass.: The M.I.T. Press, 1964); R. R. Dynes, *Organized Behavior in Disaster* (Lexington, Mass.: D. C. Heath & Co., 1970); R. I. Leopold and H. Dillon, "Psycho-Anatomy of Disaster: Long-Term Study of Post-Traumatic Neuroses in Survivors of a Marine Explosion," *American Journal of Psychiatry,* 119 (April 1963), pp. 913–921.

[2] Herbert Blaufarb and Jules Levine, "Crisis Intervention in an Earthquake," *Social Work,* 17 (July 1972), pp. 16–19; Richard I. Shader and Alice J. Schwartz, "Management of Reactions to Disaster," *Social Work,* 11 (April 1966), pp. 99–104.

THE STUDY OF DISASTERS

The literature on behavior in extreme situations can be divided into three general categories: popular and journalistic accounts, official reports, and scientific or professional studies. Popular accounts generally reach a wide audience and convey their message with dramatic impact and strong human appeal, though their scientific usefulness may be limited.[3] Official reports constitute more technical accounts that are frequently found in organizational journals, annual reports, or trade magazines. These are usually pragmatic. Scientific literature is varied and can be subdivided into scholarly studies and professional studies. Thus far, the scholarly studies have been descriptive and usually noninterpretive.[4] Professional studies "employ the concepts, categories of observation, and research techniques of the disciplines they represent," and are usually specific studies dealing with specific variables.[5]

Several scientific studies of behavior in extreme situations are of value in developing generalizations. Those that deal with situations of specific stress offer some possibilities for constructing a "disaster theory."[6]

Behavioral scientists have not been drawn to research on disasters. This may be because they tend to view such extreme events as isolated incidents, without observing the patterns they follow, or because these events do not lend themselves to control by scientific procedures.[7]

Only within the last decade have a few efforts been made to institute systematically controlled studies of disasters. Many of the larger universities have developed research projects with funding from the National Academy of Sciences–National Research Council. These studies have been essentially sociological, initially stimulated, perhaps, by the possibility of nuclear attack.

In 1963 the Disaster Research Center at Ohio State University was instituted and has since conducted field work at approximately seventy-three disaster sites. These studies have concentrated on various aspects of community organization in disaster situations.[8]

THEORY

All definitions of disaster include the idea of a destructive force, nonhumanly or humanly induced, that strikes without warning and has a widely disruptive impact on normal functioning. Disasters harbor the potential for widespread public upset. In organizing one's thinking about disasters, it is possible to draw upon concepts from several areas of knowledge. There is a large body of material on psychological responses to

---

[3] John R. Hersey, *Hiroshima* (New York: Alfred A. Knopf, 1964).

[4] J. E. Thompson, *The Rise and Fall of the Maya Civilization,* (Norman, Okla.: University of Oklahoma Press, 1954).

[5] Wallace, op. cit.

[6] *See,* for example, Irving L. Janis, *Air War and Emotional Stress* (New York: McGraw Hill Book Co., 1951); A. H. Leighton, "Psychological Factors in Major Disasters," *Medical Projects Reports* (Rochester, N.Y.: University of Rochester, 1951); Bruno Bettelheim, "Individual and Mass Behavior in Extreme Situations," *Journal of Abnormal and Social Psychology,* 38 (October 1943), pp. 417–452; R. A. Lucas, *Men in Crisis* (New York: Basic Books, 1969).

[7] Wallace, op. cit., pp. 14–17.

[8] Dynes, op. cit., pp. 10–14.

situations of severe stress.[9] Such studies have revolved around specific situations that attempt to formalize the range of individual responses and evaluate the adaptive and nonadaptive aspects. Related to this are the many and varied analyses of panic behavior that focus on the instinct to flee in critical situations.[10]

Wallace formulated the concept of a "disaster syndrome" that is usually manifested by aimless wandering, stunned or dazed responses, extreme passivity or suggestibility, sleep disturbance, irritability, somatic distresses, restlessness, and isolation.[11] Recently this concept has been refined and elaborated into a "post-stress syndrome."[12] In his well-known studies of reactions to the Coconut Grove fire in a Boston nightclub in 1942, Lindemann has connected many of these reactions to the more fundamental processes of bereavement, mourning, and grief.[13]

All these pieces of theory or sets of generalizations fit, at least in part, into reactions to disasters and offer possible explanations for the range of observable behavior. They are drawn from psychological and social psychological theory and are usually based on empirical evidence taken from a number of incidents.

A particularly interesting structural and more sociological framework for understanding the natural history of a disaster has been developed by Powell and Rayner.[14] They divide a disaster into seven sequential phases: warning, threat, impact, inventory, rescue, remedy, and recovery, and attribute specific variables to each phase. All seven of these phases need not occur in each disaster. Some, like the Chicago transit crash to be described, start with impact, omitting the phases of warning and threat.

More important, continued study must be made of treatment following a disaster. The reality of a threat to survival and the urgency of immediate rescue have naturally tended to overshadow the covert psychological wounds. These might not immediately express themselves in behavior, but might become embedded in mental functioning and have disturbing residual effects. Some of the recent professional literature on death and mourning has an important relevance.[15] Studies have emphasized the effectiveness of encouraging survivors to talk about their experiences and emotions.[16]

ANALYSIS

The intent of this paper is to discuss and analyze only one part of the total event, that concerning the participation of social workers and their interactions with the victims' friends and relatives. It is not often that one witnesses in such dramatic form the basic

[9] *See* Grosser et al., op. cit.; Irving L. Janis, *Psychological Stress* (New York: John Wiley & Sons, 1958); Henry Krystal, ed., *Massive Psychic Trauma* (New York: International Universities Press, 1969).

[10] Duane P. Schultz, *Panic Behavior: Discussion and Readings* (New York: Random House, 1964).

[11] Wallace, op. cit.

[12] H. C. Archibald and R. D. Tuddenham, "Persistent Stress Reactions after Combat," *AMA Archives of General Psychiatry,* 12 (May 1965), pp. 475–481.

[13] Erich Lindemann, "Symptomatology and Management of Acute Grief," *American Journal of Psychiatry,* 101 (September 1944), pp. 141–148.

[14] J. W. Powell and J. Rayner, *Progress Notes: Disaster Investigations, July 1, 1951–June 30, 1952.* (Washington, D.C.: Chemical Corps Medical Laboratories, Army Chemical Center, 1952).

[15] Elisabeth Kübler-Ross, *On Death and Dying* (New York: Macmillan Co., 1970).

[16] S. E. Perry, E. Silber, and D. A. Block, *The Child and His Family in Disaster: A Study of the 1953 Vicksburg Tornado,* "Disaster Study No. 5" (Washington, D.C.: National Academy of Sciences–National Research Council, 1956); Archibald and Tuddenham, op. cit.

application of professional values and skills. Unusual as well is the opportunity to observe collective behavior at this level of emotional intensity and stress.

The article will deal with the participation of a social work staff, some of whom were personally involved while others were more removed and could observe the processes unfold with more perspective. This can be considered a natural history of a disaster, with attempts to analyze selected aspects, speculate on meanings, and hopefully, arrive at a few generalizations. It is particularly valuable, because it offers an unsimulated field experience. Through collective input and corrections by members of the staff and people of other disciplines, the usual pitfalls of bias have been kept to a minimum. The analysis was undertaken immediately following the events in order to reduce the distortion of retrospect.[17]

This undoubtedly would have been a more valid analysis had a team of uninvolved researchers been able to study the situation with complete objectivity. Several disaster rescue centers that are now studying the problems seriously have made this recommendation. Perhaps this is something that the field of social work should consider in relation to its own professional interests and range of experiences.

TRAIN CRASH

On October 30, 1972, a crash on a local Chicago railroad claimed the lives of forty-five passengers and left more than three hundred persons injured. The catastrophe occurred at 7:27 A.M. on a Monday, when passengers were on their way to work. These were able-bodied, young to middle-aged workers, going about their beginning-of-the-week routine. Disaster struck with no warning.

The impact was immediate and critical. Certainly on the part of the victims there was no thought that such an event could conceivably take place. Most of these commuters had been using this transit system for some time. Although the possibility of casualties in daily living exists, the majority of people are not normally preoccupied with such a likelihood. In this era of escalating stress, the only plausible attitude is to maintain a realistic vigilance for the possibility of crisis. This has some implications for mental health in our present society. It makes added demands on the adaptive capacities of individuals, organizations, and communities.

In this situation, the time of the accident and the fact that it occurred at a train depot situated between two hospitals were among the more fortunate factors in the tragedy. In fact, one of the hospitals, the Michael Reese Hospital and Medical Center, had just completed and rehearsed its disaster plan so that it could immediately mobilize and institute a significant rescue operation. The fire and police departments were also prepared to join the hospital in meeting the immediate challenge. Without these factors the list of deceased might have been significantly longer.

---

[17] The staff met as a group several times immediately following this event. They talked among themselves, checking out their reactions and feelings. After a little while, when they were somewhat removed from the emotional impact of that particular day, they were able to evaluate and conceptualize their experiences.

IMPACT

Although the literature on disasters discusses impact in terms of those who are direct victims of the disaster, the definition needs to be enlarged to include other people also acutely involved. Extreme events such as this one have multiple impact points. One was the impact on family members and friends who, on hearing of the incident, rushed to the scene. This group of people under severe stress remained in communication with the social work staff throughout that eventful day. They came in droves and were directed to the lobby and lounge of the nurses' residence. The initial effect was total chaos.

A second point of impact was on the staff of social workers at Michael Reese Hospital, most of whom did not know of the accident until their arrival that morning. Faced with this challenge, the staff quickly recovered from the initial shock and confusion and, joining the throngs in the nurses' residence, organized themselves into a functioning subsystem.

Morale was high and the staff reacted instantaneously to each task, accepting requests from whoever issued them and attempting to suppress any uncontrollable anxiety. The initial mobilization of forces rapidly assumed a structure in which roles were covertly defined and rational leadership emerged. It was this spirit of cohesiveness that provided the stability required by the fragmented subsystem of relatives and friends. This supports the generalization that "high group morale and cohesiveness will generally minimize the disaster effects of impact."[18] At the termination of the impact phase, the two subsystems (professional and lay) were moving in complementary fashion, each gaining strength from the other. Urgent needs for comfort and help demanded the support and total involvement of the social work staff and in the end neutralized the mechanisms that usually separate professionals from clients.

The staff had to deal with its own set of interpersonal reactions before it could function as an organic whole. Following the initial shock and immediate immersion, there was some recoil, some jockeying for power or status. There was competition for social credits, measured by the number of relatives and friends who looked to them for help. Staff members later reported having been pushed aside by their colleagues and experiencing momentary anger. But such feelings were not reinforced because of the urgency of other needs. The situation itself determined the structure that finally emerged. Each staff member discovered some satisfying level of usefulness, accepted the leadership of others, and developed effective modes of nonverbal communication through symbols and cues. These were important, since time did not always permit speech.

INVENTORY AND RESCUE

For the purposes of this analysis these two phases, which Powell and Rayner's model separates, can be combined. One phase flowed into the other. In the inventory phase, survivors began to feel concern for others and to reach out helpfully. At the point of rescue, outside professionals, other hospital staff, nearby service departments, members of the clergy, and volunteer workers moved in to offer further support. As family and

---

[18] Shader and Schwartz, op. cit., p. 101.

relatives engaged in their desperate search for survivors, the professionals were there to inform, guide, and offer hope and comfort.

Great reliance was put on the steady dissemination of information. Lists of the injured and dead were relayed continuously to the social work staff from the hospital's public relations department. Social workers, supported by members of the clergy, acted as the major informers.

The waiting population proved to be admirably controlled. Family members clung together and comforted one another. Strangers sat side by side, locked in their personal thoughts, not speaking but observant of others' reactions. A few people attached themselves to members of the staff, returning periodically for news. They seemed patient when reassured that someone was personally concerned about them. Volunteers stayed with people who seemed lost and confused, or who wanted to talk or cry. Some needed physical comfort such as someone to hold their hand or pat their shoulder. Even staff needed this from each other. The function of touching is frequently underestimated and even frowned upon in a professional relationship, but in this case the taboo was lifted. In essence, the staff responded in a totally human way and the overall effects were appropriate. Food played an important part in the role of comforting. The hospital had supplied generous amounts of coffee and sandwiches for all staff and visitors.

As the day wore on, the tension mounted and families began to search for information with increased anxiety. Their relentless questioning might easily have overtaxed an already fatigued staff who remained, nonetheless, remarkably patient. As it became clear that the remaining groups might have to face the news of a death, the level of staff empathy increased. Relatives and friends were encouraged to express their fears, to cry, and to talk endlessly. Efforts to sustain hope continued; other hospitals were contacted in a further search for more complete information. The increased activity was again used to suppress the mounting anxiety and concern.

A final handful of families had to be directed to the morgue to identify relatives. This tragic episode was handled by one of the priests. Emotional responses were extreme—one Mexican woman experienced an "ataque," others wept or screamed. Families turned to one another in their sorrow; professionals seemed locked out, or chose to remove themselves.

AFTERMATH

"An experience of extreme danger is not over once the danger is past, even for those who survive it intact. Something has intruded into their emotional life which requires some time to assimilate."[19] This was relevant to all who experienced the Chicago disaster.

Despite the exhaustion of most staff members after this experience there was, nevertheless, a feeling of having accomplished something and of having extended oneself fully to others. But there were also the disquieting feelings of having observed and empathized with severe loss and grief. In practically each staff member, this aroused repressed memories of past personal loss, and responses ranged from emotional outbursts to attempts at denial. Staff meetings, informal discussions, and group meetings with pa-

---

[19] Martha Wolfenstein, *Disaster: A Psychological Essay* (Glencoe, Ill.: Free Press, 1957), p. 135.

tients held over a period of several weeks eventually helped to reconcile the arduous events of that day.

A joint decision was made to help those survivors interested in working out their mourning and grief. All those with whom staff members had worked and those who had been treated in the emergency room were notified. Although attendance was small, these follow-up meetings proved meaningful for those who came. Several persons attended a few times, others just once. The groups were composed of survivors, relatives, and staff members.

Analysis of the process in these groups revealed some similarities to ordinary reactions of shock or mourning. To begin with, survivors tended to ruminate over the precise details of the crash in an attempt to work through their own preoccupations. The less verbal members appeared to be listening intently, as if vicariously going through the experience. Most persons seemed to recall minutely what had been happening just before the crash. Many had superstitious reasons for why they survived while others were killed. Some wondered about their decision that day not to ride in their usual car, which was subsequently demolished.

Several who came away shaken but not badly injured struggled with reactions of moral censorship in the belief that they should have done more to help others. They were disappointed in themselves, because their immediate response had been to flee from danger rather than turn back to help. One young woman had not even allowed herself to face this truth until well into the meeting. Then, after listening to others, she was able to say what was truly troubling her and evidently had motivated her to attend. Her belief in herself as a helpful person had been shattered by her flight reaction. She prefaced this disclosure by unconsciously citing what appeared to be an irrelevant account of how she had offered shelter and food to a stranger the night before the accident. The comparison between this incident and her behavior at the accident indicated how confused she felt about herself as a "good" person. Some discussion about the range of panic reactions helped to put her feeling of self-worth together again, although she will probably be haunted with this for some time.

The somatic effects of the accident were fairly consistent: headaches, sleep disturbances, startle reactions, and gastric distresses. One survivor experienced immediate amnesia and could not recall how he had escaped without injury from the car that had been demolished and had claimed the highest number of casualties. The method in which he might have escaped worried him and he strained to put together the pieces of his memory. Another survivor had developed a tremor in one hand. Others were grappling with phobias of one kind or another, and practically all the victims were afraid to board the train again.

Survivors discovered that talking to each other had a cathartic effect and as such was a vital part of recovery. They uniformly felt that not even close family members could fully understand and empathize with their experience. Those few relatives who did accompany survivors to the sessions gained a better understanding. In some situations we could almost see the walls that separated relatives and survivors break down and could sense the change of attitude. In one situation the mother of a daughter who had been injured in the crash accompanied the young woman to some of the sessions. She expressed irritation and guilt for not having "been with my daughter in time of need." Through this irrational reaction the staff gained insight into the relationship of overdependency that existed between the two. This experience underscored the importance of working through feelings with close relatives as well as survivors, since guilt reactions are prevalent in both groups. In this case the group discussion helped the participants recognize and accept these emotions while pointing out their irrationality.

In several instances, the emotional reactions to this event were linked to past experiences either real or vicarious. A few of the men had had army experiences and this disaster touched off feelings of horror, fear, shame, disgust, or guilt. Having mutually shared these past experiences, certain of them were able to form bonds and to support each other's feelings. On the other hand, there was the occasional tendency to deprecate and embarrass others for not being "more courageous." These reactions came from persons who used them to hide their own feelings of inadequacy. Depression and sudden outbursts of anger of the "why me" variety were constantly present.

The social work staff were totally involved in these group sessions. Because they themselves had experienced a wide range of emotions they were able to relate with empathy and reflect more openly upon their reactions. This made each group session an existential "experience." Growth in insight, and closer relationships with one another were some of the positive gains from this intense involvement.

Efforts were made to reach out to the families of the deceased. Although each overture seemed to be appreciated, the bereaved families were not interested in talking with each other. They sought the intimacy of family or the comfort of religion, but they seemed to have no immediate wish for contact with strangers.

There remained one more group of survivors—patients who had been seriously enough injured to require hospitalization. This coincided with the traditional role of hospital social work. These patients had the same urgent need to talk of the accident in detail and compare impressions. The feelings of grief and anger felt by those close to them needed attention as well. In one extreme situation there seemed to be a pathological denial of the severity of the survivor's condition, but this was attributed to a preexisting disturbed relationship.

CONCLUSIONS

This experience provided verification of some assumptions concerning the behavior of people in stressful situations. Under serious threat, most adults are oriented toward mutual helpfulness rather than toward destructiveness or panic, especially if consolidated leadership is provided to create models for positive action. Even under extreme conditions, behavior can be fundamentally adaptive and orderly. For this to happen, a social structure that permits mutual caring and helpful involvement must exist. In its commitment to the survivors, the social work staff offered such a model. Because of the pressures of daily routine, it is frequently possible to lose sight of these cardinal professional values.

Personal experience, especially of a highly emotional kind, provides significant opportunities for growth through self-reflection and feedback. In this situation members of the staff revealed qualities that had never before surfaced. This produced increased mutual respect. The total experience reconfirmed the effectiveness of the social work role in crisis intervention, in which action as well as a high level of empathy and respect for human dignity are major priorities.

INDEX